TINA

P9-DFA-605

THE NEW AMERICAN
ROGET'S
COLLEGE
THESAURUS

in Dictionary Form

Revised Edition Prepared by

PHILIP D. MOREHEAD

A SIGNET BOOK

NEW AMERICAN LIBRARY

TIMES MIRROR

HOW TO USE THIS THESAURUS

PETER MARK ROGET WAS AN ENGLISH PHYSICIAN who was born in 1779 and died in 1869. As a hobby he liked to make lists of words and group them together when they were related to one another. Some were related because they were synonyms, such as *illegal* and *unlawful;* some because they were antonyms, such as *peaceful* and *warlike;* some because they were reminders of one another, such as *father* and *mother.* Altogether Mr. Roget made a thousand different groups, or *categories,* of related words. Every word he knew or could find in the dictionaries that he had was classified in one or more of these categories.

In 1852 Mr. Roget's list of words was published. He called the book a *thesaurus,* or treasury, of words. There were not many words in the first ROGET'S THESAURUS, compared to the number in a volume like this, but his book was the first collection of synonyms, antonyms, and other related words. Not only writers but many others found it invaluable. Dozens of editors, beginning with Mr. Roget's son, have revised the original Thesaurus, added to it, and brought it up to date (for many of the words in the original Roget list are now obsolete and many common words of today were unknown in his time); but every edition is still called ROGET'S THESAURUS in honor of the man who first had the idea.

This edition of ROGET'S THESAURUS is both a dictionary of synonyms and antonyms and a thesaurus or "treasury" of related words. To use it, simply look up the word for which you wish to have a synonym, an antonym, or a word related in some other way.

When a word is printed in SMALL CAPITALS, it means that if you look up that word, in its proper alphabetical order, you will find additional synonyms or other related words applying to the word you were looking up. Often you will also find other words of related meaning but different parts of speech: for example, when you are looking up a noun you will be referred to related verbs, adjectives, etc.

Frequently only one form of a word is entered in the alphabetical word list. You will find synonyms for the other forms by referring to the entries printed in SMALL CAPITALS under the listed word. For example, to find synonyms for *optimistic,* look under *optimism* in the alphabetical word list and refer to HOPE or CHEERFULNESS.

A word or phrase in parentheses shows how the preceding word is to be used in a sentence. A word or phrase in brackets is explanatory in some cases, and in other cases indicates that the bracketed word or phrase may or may not be used with the adjoining word, depending on the preference of the writer.

This is not a dictionary. It does not define words, except to the extent that they are defined in their synonyms. A word that has no natural synonyms is not entered merely to define it. The publishers of this Thesaurus also publish a companion volume, THE NEW AMERICAN WEBSTER DICTIONARY, in which may be found definitions of the words in this book.

Antonyms formed by simply adding *un-, in-, dis-,* etc., are not given, nor are words listed when they are simple negatives of other words. For example, such a word as *unloved* is not entered, since one may merely look up the positive term, but *unbearable* is entered because the positive term has various dissimilar meanings.

Synonyms are often labeled *colloq.* (colloquial, informal, conversational); *slang, dial.* (dialectal), etc. This is a warning that either the entry word or the synonym in this sense is substandard. The reader may consult the dictionary for further information.

Familiar dictionary abbreviations are used for parts of speech: *n.*, noun; *v.*, verb; *v.i.*, intransitive verb; *v.t.*, transitive verb; *adj.*, adjective; *adv.*, adverb; *pron.*, pronoun; *prep.*, preposition; *conj.*, conjunction; *interj.*, interjection.

FOREIGN PHRASES. This Thesaurus includes foreign words and phrases related to English words and phrases; but foreign words and phrases that are not wholly anglicized are not listed in regular alphabetical order. They are collected on the final pages of this book, with definitions and with reference to the entries or categories in which their synonyms and related English phrases may be found.

Preface to the Revised Edition

THIS NEW REVISED EDITION contains thousands of new entries and categories to help the user find even more quickly exactly the right word for which he is searching. Up-to-date colloquial and slang terms and phrases have been added, making this indispensable reference tool uniquely valuable for today's world.

Philip D. Morehead
Boston, 1977

A

abaft, *adv.* aft, astern, behind. See REAR, NAVIGATION. *Ant.,* FRONT.

abandon, *v.t.* relinquish, resign, give up, forgo, surrender, discontinue, waive, abdicate; leave, quit, evacuate, withdraw (from); desert, forsake, maroon, discard, drop. *Colloq.,* let go, throw up, pull out of, have done with, turn one's back on, wash one's hands of. *Slang,* pull out on; rat on. See RELINQUISHMENT. *Ant.,* see PURSUIT.

abandon, *n.* RASHNESS, recklessness, imprudence, impetuosity, impulsiveness, audacity. *Ant.,* CARE.

abandoned, *adj.* dissipated, immoral, shameless, corrupt, unprincipled, depraved; lost, incorrigible, reprobate, unbridled. See IMPURITY. *Ant.,* see VIRTUE. (See also ABANDON, *v.*)

abase, *v.t.* humble (see ABASH); demean, degrade; dishonor; cast down. See HUMILITY, DESCENT.

abash, *v.t.* humiliate, humble, shame; embarrass, disconcert, discountenance, awe. *Colloq.,* mortify, crush, take down a peg, put one's nose out of joint. See MODESTY. *Ant.,* see VANITY.

abate, *v.* DECREASE, lessen, moderate, diminish, subside; allay, slake, slacken, subdue; curtail, remit. *Colloq.,* let down (on), take off the edge (of). *Ant.,* INCREASE.

abbey, *n.* convent, monastery, nunnery, priory, cloister(s). See TEMPLE.

abbreviate, *v.* abridge, condense, contract, shorten, curtail, digest, clip, truncate, prune. See SHORTNESS, CONTRACTION. *Ant.,* see LENGTH.

abdicate, *v.* relinquish, resign, renounce, abandon, quit, surrender. See RELINQUISHMENT.

abdomen, *n.* belly, paunch, epigastrium, venter; midriff (*inexact*). *Colloq.,* corporation (*jocular*), solar plexus, guts (*now vulgar*). See INTERIOR.

abduct, *v.t.* kidnap, carry off, steal, transport, spirit away. *Colloq.,* shanghai. *Slang,* snatch. See STEALING.

aberration, *n.* DEVIATION, variation, distortion, disorientation; aberrance, INSANITY; ERROR. *Colloq.,* brainstorm. *Ant.,* TRUTH, SANITY.

abet, *v.t.* AID, assist, support; encourage, incite, instigate. *Ant.,* see HINDRANCE.

abeyance, *n.* suspension, suppression. See END.

abhor, *v.t.* HATE, dislike, detest, loathe, despise; abominate, execrate. *Colloq.,* can't stand. *Slang,* get a pain [in the neck] from. *Ant.,* LOVE.

abide, *v.* dwell, reside, live, stay; accept, endure, submit (to). See ABODE.

ability, *n.* POWER, SKILL, competency, capacity, efficiency, capability, aptitude, faculty, talent. *Colloq.,* knowhow. *Slang,* what it takes. *Ant.,* UNSKILLFULNESS, IMPOTENCE.

abject, *adj.* servile, degraded, contemptible; miserable, wretched; base. *Colloq.,* hangdog. See SERVILITY. *Ant.,* see INSOLENCE.

abjure, *v.* forswear, recant, renounce. See RELINQUISHMENT.

able, *adj.* capable, competent, skillful, efficient. See POWER, SKILL. *Ant.,* see IMPOTENCE, UNSKILLFULNESS.

able-bodied, *adj.* healthy, fit, robust. See STRENGTH, HEALTH.

abnormal, *adj.* aberrant, eccentric, irregular, anomalous; INSANE; monstrous. See UNCONFORMITY. *Ant.,* see SANITY, CONFORMITY.

aboard, *adv. & prep.* on, on board; astride; alongside. See PRESENCE.

ABODE

Nouns—**1,** abode, dwelling, residence, domicile, address, habitation, berth, seat, lodging *or* lodgings, lodging place, quarters, headquarters, housing, place. *Colloq.,* diggings. *Slang,* dump, joint.

3

2, home, homeplace, homestead, hearth, hearthstone, fireside, inglenook, ingleside, household, ménage, housing, roof; ancestral halls, fatherland, native land, native soil, country.

3, retreat, asylum, cloister, hermitage, hideaway, hiding-place, sanctuary, *sanctum sanctorum*, cave, nest, den, cell, hive, hole, lair, haunt. *Slang*, hangout, hideout, stamping ground.

4, camp, barrack *or* barracks, bivouac, encampment, quarters, tent, case-mate, motel, tourist camp, trailer camp.

5, house, dwelling, building, place, hall; casa, mansion, palace, villa, lodge, hermitage, castle, cottage, chalet, bungalow, manor-house; brown-stone [house], flat, apartment [house], two-(*etc.*) family house, farm-house, ranch house, split-level, town house, penthouse, tenement, hotel, ark, temple, skyscraper, trailer. *Slang*, diggings, digs, pad.

6, hut, adobe, booth, bunkhouse, hogan, cabin, cottage, dugout, hutch, hovel, igloo, tupek, lean-to, log cabin, Quonset hut, rancho, shack, shanty, tepee, wickiup, wigwam, kiosk. *Slang*, dump, flophouse, [hobo] jungle.

7, inn, caravansary, club, hospice, hostel, hostelry, hotel, motel, rooming house, tavern; public house, barroom, alehouse, saloon; coffee house, canteen, café, restaurant. *Slang*, dive, dump, flophouse, gin mill, pub, honkytonk, greasy spoon.

8, barn, cow barn, cowshed, doghouse, kennel, pound, henhouse, hutch, warren, pen, pigsty, shed, stable, stall, storehouse, booth, coop, dove-cote, aviary, birdcage, birdhouse, perch, roost.

9, auditorium, armory, assembly hall, assembly room, study hall, audi-ence hall, concert hall, theater, gymnasium; meeting house, chapel, church, TEMPLE. *Slang*, gym.

10, estate, hacienda, ranch, farm.

11, village, hamlet, town, pueblo, township, municipality, metropolis, city, capital, county seat, suburb, county, parish, state, province, coun-try; ghetto, quarter; provinces, hinterlands. *Colloq.*, burg, one-horse town, Main Street. *Slang*, jerkwater [town], hick town, jumping-off place, sticks.

12, street, place, terrace, road, avenue, boulevard, row, alley, court, quadrangle, close, yard, passage, mews; square, mall, piazza, arcade, gardens, marketplace, block, commons.

13, anchorage, dock, basin, wharf, quay, port, harbor.

14, sanatorium, sanitarium, hospital, asylum, health resort, rest home, spa, watering place.

Verbs—see LOCATION, PRESENCE.

Adjectives—urban, suburban, rural, rustic, provincial; metropolitan, cos-mopolitan; domestic, foreign.

---

abolish, *v.t.* annul, cancel, nullify, abrogate; exterminate. *Colloq.*, wipe out. See DESTRUCTION. *Ant.*, see PRODUCTION.

abominable, *adj.* odious, detestable, execrable, accursed, loathsome. See HATE. *Ant.*, see LOVE.

abortion, *n.* miscarriage, premature delivery [birth]; illegal operation; failure, fiasco; monstrosity, freak. See FAILURE.

abound, *v.i.* teem, swarm, be plentiful. See SUFFICIENCY. *Ant.*, see ABSENCE.

about, *adv. & prep.* —*adv.* around, round, on all sides; approximately; nearly, almost. See RELATION, NEARNESS. *Ant.*, see DIFFERENCE, DIS-TANCE. —*prep.* concerning, regarding, anent, respecting.

above, *adv. & prep.* —*adv.* aloft, overhead, up; earlier, before. See HEIGHT. *Ant.*, see LOWNESS. —*prep.* over, beyond; surpassing; more than, exceeding.

aboveboard, *adj.* open, straightforward, candid. See PROBITY.

abrade, *v.t.* rub, wear (away), grind, grate. See FRICTION. *Ant.*, see SMOOTHNESS.

abridge, v. abbreviate, shorten, condense, reduce, compress, contract, summarize, epitomize. See SHORTNESS. *Ant.,* see LENGTH.

abroad, adv. overseas, away, outside; roaming, wandering, at large. See ABSENCE. *Ant.,* see PRESENCE.

abrogate, v.t. discard, abandon; cast out; repeal, annul, retract. See REJECTION, NULLIFICATION.

abrupt, adj. sudden, hasty, precipitate, short, curt; steep, precipitous, sheer, sudden *or* sharp [turn, *etc.*]. *Colloq.,* jerky. See SHARPNESS, INSTANTANEITY. *Ant.,* see BLUNT.

abscond, v.i. decamp, bolt, run away, flee, fly, depart. *Colloq.,* take off, take French leave. *Slang,* breeze, blow, scram, take a powder. See AVOIDANCE. *Ant.,* see PURSUIT.

ABSENCE

Nouns—**1,** absence, withdrawal; nonexistence; nonresidence, noninhabitance, nonpresence, nonattendance, absenteeism, truancy; DISAPPEARANCE, DISPERSION. *Colloq.,* hooky, cut, French leave.

2, emptiness, void, vacuum, vacuity, vacancy; depletion, exhaustion; exemption; blank, clean slate.

3, absentee, truant; missing person; MIA.

4, nobody, nobody present, nobody on earth, not a soul, nary a soul, nobody under the sun, nary one, no one, no man, never a one.

Verbs—be absent, absent oneself, go away, stay away, keep away, keep out of the way, play truant, play hooky, take French leave, absent oneself without leave, slip away, slip off, slip out, keep aloof, hold aloof, withdraw, vacate. *Colloq.,* not show up, make oneself scarce, take French leave, cut. *Slang,* go A.W.O.L., jump, skip.

Adjectives—**1,** absent, non-attendant, not present, away, non-resident, missing, missing in action, lost, wanting, omitted, nowhere to be found, out of sight, gone, lacking, away from home, truant, absent without [official] leave, A.W.O.L., abroad, oversea, on vacation. *Colloq.,* minus.

2, empty, vacant, void, vacuous, untenanted, unoccupied, uninhabited, tenantless, deserted, abandoned, devoid, forsaken, bare, hollow, blank, clear, dry, free from, drained. *Colloq.,* Godforsaken.

Adverbs—nowhere; elsewhere; neither here nor there; somewhere else, not here. *Dial.,* nowheres.

Prepositions—without, wanting, lacking, less, minus, *sans*.

Antonym, see PRESENCE.

---

absent-mindedness, n. See INATTENTION.

absolute, adj. complete, perfect, thorough, entire, total, essential, sheer, positive; unrestricted, unbounded, full, plenary; despotic, autocratic, supreme. See COMPLETION, GREATNESS. *Ant.,* see INSUFFIENCY, LITTLENESS.

absolution, n. cleansing, exoneration, FORGIVENESS, shrift, dispensation, discharge. *Ant.,* RETALIATION.

absolve, v.t. forgive, cleanse, shrive, discharge, pardon. See FORGIVENESS. *Ant.,* see RETALIATION.

absorb, v. assimilate, take in, suck up; incorporate, integrate; engross, preoccupy, obsess. See THOUGHT, RECEIVING. *Ant.,* see REJECTION.

abstain, v.i. forbear, refrain, desist, withhold. See AVOIDANCE, MODERATION. *Ant.,* see PURSUIT.

abstemious, adj. abstaining, abstinent, temperate, sober. See MODERATION. *Ant.,* see DRUNKENNESS.

abstract, adj. theoretical, metaphysical; abstruse, recondite. See IMAGINATION. *Ant.,* concrete.

abstract, v. & n. —v. withdraw, excerpt (from), remove. See STEALING. —n. compendium, summary, epitome, précis, abridgment.

abstruse, adj. profound, recondite, esoteric, subtle, deep, obscure, enigmatical. See UNINTELLIGIBILITY. *Ant.,* see SIMPLENESS.

ABSURDITY

Nouns—**1,** absurdity, absurdness, imbecility, nonsense; paradox, inconsistency; inanity, fatuity, stupidity, asininity; ludicrousness, ridiculousness, ridiculosity, comicality.

2, blunder, muddle, bull, Irish bull; sophism, bathos; anticlimax, letdown; travesty, parody, caricature, lampoonery; foolery, buffoonery, mummery. *Colloq.,* monkey trick, monkey shine, moonshine.

3, jargon, doubletalk, twaddle, gibberish, fustian, empty talk. *Colloq.,* poppycock, stuff and nonsense. *Slang,* bull. See UNMEANINGNESS.

4, FOLLY; nonsense; RASHNESS; irrationality; paradox (see CONCEALMENT).

Verbs—**1,** play the fool, talk nonsense, talk through one's hat, absurd, go from the sublime to the ridiculous.

2, make a fool of, make absurd, burlesque, caricature, lampoon, ridicule.

Adjectives—**1,** absurd, nonsensical, preposterous, senseless, inconsistent, incongruous, ridiculous, extravagant, quibbling, foolish, fantastic, silly, unmeaning, without rhyme or reason, farcical, ludicrous, asinine, inane, stupid. *Slang,* screwy.

2, unintelligible, confused, MEANINGLESS, senseless.

Antonym, see MEANING.

---

abundance, *n.* plenty, copiousness, SUFFICIENCY, profusion, luxuriance, fullness; affluence, opulence, wealth. *Ant.,* see INSUFFICIENCY.

abuse, *v. & n.* —*v.t.* mistreat, injure, damage; malign, scold, berate, vilify, curse; flay. —*n.* injury, desecration; insult. See DISAPPROBATION. *Ant.,* see APPROBATION.

abut, *v.* join, touch, border (on). See NEARNESS.

abyss, *n.* abysm, deep, DEPTH(S), gulf, chasm, pit, bottomless pit, chaos.

academic, *adj.* scholastic, collegiate; educational; scholarly, erudite; theoretical. See TEACHING.

academy, *n.* SCHOOL, college, preparatory school, finishing school; society, learned society. See TEACHING.

accede, *v.i.* agree, ASSENT, CONSENT, acquiesce, concede, concur, yield, comply. *Ant.,* see DISSENT.

accelerate, *v.* hasten, expedite, anticipate, speed (up), quicken. See EARLINESS, HASTE. *Ant.,* see LATENESS, SLOWNESS.

accent, *v. & n.* —*v.* accentuate, emphasize, stress; pronounce. —*n.* emphasis, stress, tone; diacritical mark; pronunciation. See LANGUAGE, SPEECH, SOUND.

accept, *v.* ASSENT; take; adopt, believe, honor, admit, approve. See RECEIVING. *Ant.,* see DISSENT, GIVING.

access, *n.* APPROACH, avenue, way; admittance, entrée. *Colloq.,* [an] in; a line (to). *Ant.,* see REGRESSION.

accession, *n.* acceding, consent, ASSENT; increase, ADDITION, ACQUISITION; attainment. *Ant.,* DISSENT, LOSS.

accessory, *adj. & n.* —*adj.* contributory, helping; AUXILIARY, incident (to). —*n.* accomplice, assistant, confederate. See ADDITION.

accident, *n.* mishap, injury, casualty; CHANCE, contingency, fortuity. See ADVERSITY. *Ant.,* design, INTENTION.

acclaim, *v. & n.* —*v.t.* applaud, PRAISE, hail, salute, greet, pay respects to. —*n.* See PRAISE.

acclimate, acclimatize, *v.t.* accustom, inure, habituate. See HABIT.

acclivity, *n.* ASCENT, rise, incline, pitch, slope, grade. *Ant.,* see DESCENT.

accolade, *n.* honors, laurels, tribute, REWARD; decoration, embrace, kiss. See APPROBATION.

accommodate, *v.* adapt, adjust, conform, fit, suit; oblige, help out; lend money (to); put up (give lodging to). See AID, AGREEMENT. *Ant.,* see HINDRANCE, DISAGREEMENT.

ACCOMPANIMENT

Nouns—**1,** accompaniment, adjunct, attribute; concomitance, company, association, companionship, partnership, copartnership, fellowship, coefficiency.

2, concomitant, accessory, coefficient; companion, attendant, fellow, associate, consort, spouse, colleague, comrade; accompanist; partner, copartner; satellite, hanger-on, shadow; escort, bodyguard, chaperon, retainer, duenna, convoy; cavalier, squire. *Colloq.*, chum, flunky, pal. *Slang*, pard.

Verbs—accompany, attend, hang on, wait on, go hand in hand with, keep company, row in the same boat, associate with, consort with, take up with; escort, chaperon, convoy. *Colloq.*, tote, squire. *Slang*, drag.

Adjectives—accompanying, attendant, concomitant, fellow, associated with, coupled with, accessory.

Adverbs—with, together with, along with, in company with, hand-in-hand, arm-in-arm, side-by-side, cheek-to-cheek, together.

Antonym, see DISJUNCTION.

---

accomplice, *n.* accessory, abettor, confederate, crony; partner, colleague. *Slang*, sidekick. See AUXILIARY.

accomplish, *v.t.* do, complete, fulfill, perform, effect, execute, achieve, consummate. See COMPLETION. *Ant.*, see FAILURE.

accomplished, *adj.* proficient, versed; talented. See SKILL. *Ant.*, see UNSKILLFULNESS.

accord, *v. & n.* —*v.i.* harmonize, conform, agree, accede. See AGREEMENT, ASSENT. —*v.t.* grant, bestow: see GIVING. —*n.* AGREEMENT, harmony, correspondence, conformity.

accordingly, *adv.* hence, so, therefore, thus; correspondingly, consistently, agreeably. See CIRCUMSTANCE, AGREEMENT.

accost, *v.t.* greet, hail, address. See SPEECH. *Ant.*, ignore.

account, *v. & n.* —*v.i.* report, relate, narrate. See DESCRIPTION. —*v.t.* attribute. See CAUSE. —*n.* report, recital, narrative, DESCRIPTION, story, tale, history, chronicle, statement.

ACCOUNTING

Nouns—**1,** accounting, accountancy, bookkeeping, audit, calculation, reckoning, [commercial, business] arithmetic.

2, accountant, bookkeeper, calculator, actuary, Certified Public Accountant, C.P.A., chartered accountant (*Brit.*), auditor, [bank] examiner, clerk.

3, accounts, statistics, finance, budget, money matters.

4, ledger, journal, day book, cash book, petty cash book, bank book, pass book, balance sheet, profit and loss statement, accounts payable ledger, accounts receivable ledger, sales ledger.

5, asset, liability, expenditure, bill, invoice, balance, account, credit, debit.

Verbs—**1,** keep accounts, enter, post, book, credit, debit, carry over, balance, balance accounts, balance the books; bill, invoice, compute, settle accounts; take stock, take inventory; audit, examine the books.

2, falsify accounts, doctor accounts.

---

accredit, *v.* authorize, license, certificate, sanction. See REPUTE. *Ant.*, See DISREPUTE.

accretion, *n.* see INCREASE.

accrue, *v.* accumulate, grow, inure. See ACQUISITION. *Ant.*, see LOSS.

accumulate, *v.* amass, gather; aggregate, collect, hoard. *Colloq.*, bank, rake in. See ACQUISITION. *Ant.*, see LOSS.

accurate, *adj.* correct, exact, precise, truthful. *Colloq.*, on the button or nose. See TRUTH. *Ant.*, see DEVIATION, ERROR.

ACCUSATION

Nouns—**1,** accusation, charge, indictment, incrimination, inculpation; condemnation, denunciation, censure, invective, jeremiad; implication, imputation, slur; complaint, blame, reproach, recrimination, reproof; retort, reply in kind. See DISAPPROBATION.

2, LAWSUIT, litigation; plaint, complaint, citation, allegation; indictment, arraignment, impeachment, true bill; libel, slander.

3, accuser, critic, ENEMY; plaintiff, complainant; prosecutor, district attorney, attorney general. *Colloq.*, D.A.

4, accused, defendant, respondent, co-respondent, libelee.

Verbs—**1,** accuse, charge, tax (with), incriminate; inculpate, blame, complain against *or* of, reproach, reprove; indict, arraign, impeach, implicate, cite, summon. *Colloq.*, throw the book at.

2, denounce, inform (against), challenge, take to task, call to account. *Colloq.*, tell on, tattle (on), pin (something) on. *Slang*, put the finger on, point the finger (at), rat (on); frame, trump up a charge.

Adjectives—accusing, accusatory; incriminatory, recriminatory, reproachful; imputative.

Antonyms, see APPROBATION, VINDICATION.

---

accustom, *v.* habituate, familiarize, inure, addict. See HABIT.

ache, *n. & v.* —*n.* PAIN. —*v.i.* hurt, smart, throb, PAIN. *Ant.*, see PLEASURE.

achieve, *v.t.* accomplish, attain, reach. See COMPLETION. *Ant.*, see FAILURE, NEGLECT.

acid, *adj.* sour, bitter, tart, vinegary; acrimonious, cutting, caustic. See SOURNESS, DISCOURTESY. *Ant.*, see SWEETNESS, COURTESY.

acknowledge, *v.* admit, confess, own; ANSWER, receipt. See ASSENT, DISCLOSURE. *Ant.*, see DISSENT, CONCEALMENT.

acquaint, *v.t.* inform, notify, tell; familiarize, teach. See INFORMATION.

acquaintance, *n.* familiarity, experience, KNOWLEDGE, ken; fellowship, association; FRIEND. *Ant.*, see IGNORANCE.

acquiesce, *v.i.* agree, accede, ASSENT, concur, CONSENT. *Ant.*, see DISSENT.

ACQUISITION

Nouns—**1,** acquisition, acquirement, obtainment, procurement; collection, accumulation, amassing, gathering, reaping, gleaning, picking (up).

2, receipt, profit, proceeds, produce, benefit; earning, pay, wages, emolument, salary, income, remuneration, REWARD; inheritance, legacy, bequest, patrimony, birthright, heritage. See RECEIVING.

3, seizure, confiscation, commandeering, expropriation; conquest, annexation; patronage, unearned increment; snatching, STEALING, theft, robbery, fraud, graft, bribery; spoils, plunder, loot, BOOTY, pay-off. *Colloq.*, the take, gravy, split, pickings, velvet.

4, acquirer, obtainer, *etc.*; buyer, purchaser, vendee; inheritor, legatee; good bargainer *or* trader; winner, captor, thief. *Colloq.*, horse-trader.

5, acquisitiveness, desire to acquire; ambition, hunger, avidity (for possessions); covetousness, avarice; greed, voracity.

Verbs—**1,** acquire, get, gain, obtain, secure, derive; win, earn, realize, receive, take; collect, amass, reap, scrape together; inherit; PURCHASE. *Colloq.*, come in for, step into; get hold of, rake in. *Slang*, clean up, line one's pockets.

2, profit, benefit, gain; make money by, turn to advantage, gain an advantage.

3, accrue (to), benefit, be profitable (to), fall to.

Adjectives—**1,** acquisitive; avaricious, greedy, grasping, covetous. *Slang*, on the make.

2, profitable, remunerative, gainful, paying, advantageous, productive. See MONEY.

Antonym, see LOSS.

---

acquit oneself, behave, perform, conduct oneself. See CONDUCT.

ACQUITTAL

Nouns—acquittal, exculpation, exoneration, VINDICATION; discharge, release; reprieve, respite; absolution. See FORGIVENESS, LIBERATION.

Verbs—acquit, exculpate, exonerate, clear, absolve; pardon, grant amnesty to, reprieve, discharge, release. *Colloq.,* whitewash; let off. *Slang,* spring.

Adjectives—acquitted, vindicated, *etc.;* quit, free, clear; in the clear.

Antonym, see CONDEMNATION.

---

acrobat, *n.* gymnast, tumbler, contortionist. See DRAMA, STRENGTH.
acting, *adj.* substitute, representative, DEPUTY. See ACTION, DRAMA.
acrid, *adj.* pungent, biting, acid; corrosive, caustic. See TASTE.
acrimony, *n.* bitterness, rancor, acerbity, asperity, RESENTMENT.
across, *adv. & prep.* —*adv.* crosswise, athwart. —*prep.* on, over, athwart. See CROSSING.
act, *n. & v.* See ACTION, DRAMA, CONDUCT.

ACTION

Nouns—**1,** action, performance, operation, execution, PRODUCTION; process, procedure, transaction; affair, effort, job, deed, business, work, handiwork; CONDUCT, COMPLETION, EXERTION.
2, proceeding, LAWSUIT; battle, WARFARE.
3, doer; see AGENCY.

Verbs—**1,** act, do, perform, function, officiate, serve; operate, work, practice, exercise, commit; progress, advance, accomplish, cover ground; labor, toil, drudge, ply.
2, see DRAMA, AGENCY.

Adjectives—active, operative, in operation, in action, at work, on duty; functional, effective, efficient. See ACTIVITY.

Adverbs—in the act, conspicuously, flagrantly, *in flagrante delicto,* redhanded.

Antonym, see INACTIVITY, NEGLECT.

ACTIVITY

Nouns—**1,** activity, action, activeness, ENERGY, animation; briskness, quickness, alertness, sharpness; readiness, alacrity, zeal, eagerness, vivacity, vigor, spirit; EXERTION.
2, movement, bustle, stir, fuss, ado; restlessness, wakefulness, sleeplessness, insomnia.
3, industry, diligence, assiduity, assiduousness, vigilance, sedulity; perseverance, persistence, patience.
4, interference, intrigue, tampering, meddling, dabbling, supererogation.
5, zealot, fanatic, enthusiast, devotee. *Colloq.,* busybody; hustler, gogetter. *Slang,* live wire.

Verbs—**1,** act, do, accomplish, bestir oneself; be active, busy, *etc.*
2, haste, make haste, bustle, fuss, push. *Colloq.,* pitch in, look sharp, be sharp, make the dust fly, get on the stick; put one's best foot forward; spread oneself thin, bite off more than one can chew.
3, plod, drudge, persist; buckle down, stick to, take pains.
4, meddle, interfere, tamper, intrude, obtrude. *Colloq.,* butt in, horn in, put in one's oar, poke one's nose in, be nosy.

Adjectives—**1,** active, brisk, alert, spry, sharp, smart, quick, enterprising; ENERGETIC, eager, sedulous; lively, alive, vivacious, wideawake, keen, eager; frisky, forward, spirited; strenuous, zealous. *Colloq.*, up and doing, quick on the trigger, on the jump, on the go, on the job, on one's toes, in high gear. *Slang*, on the beam, snappy.

2, working, on duty, at work; industrious, diligent, sedulous, painstaking, businesslike. *Colloq.*, in harness.

Adverbs—actively, *etc.* See HASTE.

Antonyms, see INACTIVITY, REPOSE.

---

actor, actress, *n.* performer, player; tragedian, comedian, Thespian; play-actor; doer, worker. See AGENT, DRAMA.

actual, *adj.* real, veritable, true, genuine; concrete, factual. See EXISTENCE. *Ant.*, see NONEXISTENCE.

actuate, *v.* move, induce, compel, persuade; start, get under way. See CAUSE, BEGINNING.

acumen, *n.* acuteness, discernment, shrewdness, penetration; INTELLIGENCE.

acute, *adj.* shrewd, discerning, quick, astute; sharp, poignant, keen, pointed, severe. *Colloq.*, smart. See INTELLIGENCE.

adage, *n.* proverb, saw, saying, aphorism, motto. See KNOWLEDGE.

adamant, *adj.* adamantine, hard; inflexible, immovable, firm. See HARDNESS, OBSTINACY, RESOLUTION. *Ant.*, see SOFTNESS, DOUBT.

adapt, *v.* suit, conform, regulate, fit; ADJUST, convert, reconcile, harmonize, make suitable. See AGREEMENT, CONFORMITY.

add, *v.* increase; reckon, sum up, total; join. See ADDITION.

addict, *n.* devotee, fan, enthusiast; habitual user, slave (to). *Slang*, head, junkie, freak, mainliner. See HABIT.

ADDITION

Nouns—**1,** addition, increase, expansion, introduction, annexation, accession; corollary, concomitant, ACCOMPANIMENT.

2, adjunct; affix, prefix, suffix; appendix, insertion, interpolation, postscript, subscript, addendum, supplement, appendage; extension, annex, wing; rider, codicil, tab.

Verbs—**1,** add, affix, annex, superimpose, append, join, subjoin; tack on to, saddle with; amplify, enlarge. *Colloq.*, hitch on.

2, enumerate, total, compute, figure, calculate, reckon.

Adjectives—added, *etc.;* additive, accessory, supplementary, additional.

Adverbs—in addition, more, plus, extra, besides, also. *Colloq.*, to boot, into the bargain, over and above, and so forth, and so on.

Antonym, see DECREASE.

---

address, *v. & n.* —*v.t.* direct; court, woo; accost, greet, approach, speak to. —*n.* street and number; residence, home; speech, discourse, oration; cleverness, dexterity. See DIRECTION, SPEECH.

adduce, *v.t.* present, bring forward, cite, mention. See EVIDENCE.

adept, *adj. & n.* —*adj.* skillful, dexterous, apt; practiced, expert, proficient. —*n.* expert, master, connoisseur. See EXPERT. *Ant.*, see UNSKILLFULNESS.

adequate, *adj.* enough, sufficient, serviceable, satisfactory, ample. See SUFFICIENCY.

adherent, *n.* follower, believer; partisan, disciple. See ACCOMPANIMENT, LEARNING.

adhesive, *adj.* sticky, gummy, gluey. See COHERENCE.

adjacent, *adj.* near, close by, next to; touching, bordering, contiguous, neighboring. See NEARNESS.

adjoin, *v.* touch, abut, border, meet, neighbor. See NEARNESS.

adjourn, *v.* defer, postpone; discontinue; END.

adjunct, *n.* ADDITION, appendix, appendage, annex; augmentation, part, accessory, reinforcement, extension; complement, postscript, insertion.

adjure, *v.t.* charge, bind *or* command (by oath), appeal to, entreat. See REQUEST.

adjust, *v.t.* fix, ADAPT, true, regulate, straighten; settle, compensate, harmonize; equalize, rate. See ARRANGEMENT.

ad-lib, *v., colloq.,* extemporize, improvise. See IMPULSE.

administer, *v.t.* govern, rule, control; give, dose, treat with, dispense. See AUTHORITY, GIVING.

admire, *v.t.* love, esteem, idolize, venerate, RESPECT; regard; WONDER, marvel. *Ant.,* HATE.

admission, *n.* concession, confession; DISCLOSURE; entry, admittance, ingress; [cover] charge, minimum; CONSENT.

admit, *v.t.* let in; induct, matriculate; concede, acknowledge; receive, allow. *Colloq.,* come clean. See DISCLOSURE, RECEIVING.

admonition, *n.* caution, WARNING.

adolescence, *n.* YOUTH, minority, juvenility; teens, teen-age, nonage; puberty. *Ant.,* see AGE.

adopt, *v.t.* embrace, take to oneself, borrow, assume; foster, give a home to, accept as one's own. See CHOICE. *Ant.,* see REJECT.

adore, *v.t.* LOVE, worship, admire, idolize. *Ant.,* HATE.

adorn, *v.t.* decorate, ORNAMENT, embellish, deck, garnish, beautify.

adrift, *adj.* afloat; drifting, loose. See DISJUNCTION, DISPERSION.

adroit, *adj.* dexterous, deft, handy, skillful. See SKILL. *Ant.,* maladroit.

adult, *adj. & n.* —*adj.* grown, grown-up, full-grown, mature, ripe. —*n.* grown-up; major, senior. *Colloq.,* old-timer. See AGE, MALE, FEMALE.

adulterate, *v.t.* mix, water down, weaken, dilute; corrupt. See DETERIORATION.

adultery, *n.* infidelity, fornication, licentiousness. See IMPURITY.

advance, *v. & n.* —*v.* progress, go forward, proceed; further, abet, second. —*n.* progress, rise; success, gain; prepayment. See PROGRESSION.

advantage, *n.* SUPERIORITY, upper hand, leverage, the better (of); gain, odds, profit, advancement, favor. *Colloq.,* pull, ace in the hole. See INCREASE. *Ant.,* disadvantage.

adventure, *n.* enterprise, undertaking; happening, EVENT; risk, hazard, venture.

adventurer, *n.* voyager, traveler, wanderer, roamer; gambler, fortune-hunter; free-lance, soldier of fortune. See TRAVEL, CHANCE.

adversary, *n.* opponent, enemy, rival, OPPOSITION. See COMBATANT.

ADVERSITY

Nouns—**1,** adversity, affliction; bad, ill, adverse *or* hard luck *or* fortune; evil lot; frowns of fortune; evil star *or* genius; ups and downs of life; hard case *or* lines; peck of troubles, hell upon earth; slough of despond. See EVIL, FAILURE, PAIN.

2, trouble, hardship, curse, blight, blast, load, pressure, POVERTY, tough sledding.

3, evil day; time out of joint; hard times; rainy day; gathering clouds, ill wind; visitation, infliction, affliction; bitter pill; care, trial, ordeal.

4, mishap, mischance, misadventure, misfortune; disaster, calamity, catastrophe; accident, casualty, cross, reverse, check, *contretemps,* rub; losing game; fall, downfall, ruination, undoing; DESTRUCTION.

Verbs—be badly off; go hard *or* ill with; fall on evil days; go downhill; go to rack and ruin; go to the dogs; fall from high estate; decay, sink, decline, go down in the world; have seen better days; come to grief; be all over *or* up with; bring a hornet's nest about one's ears. *Slang,* draw a blank; lose one's shirt.

Adjectives—**1,** unfortunate, unblest, unhappy, unlucky; unprosperous;

luckless, hapless; out of luck; in trouble, in a bad way; in an evil plight; under a cloud; clouded; ill *or* badly off; in adverse circumstances; poor, down in the world, down at heel, down and out, undone; on the road to ruin, on one's last legs, on the rocks; born under an evil star; ill-fated, ill-starred, ill-omened. *Slang*, on the ropes, in a jam, out on a limb.

2, adverse, untoward; disastrous, calamitous, ruinous, dire. *Slang*, up the spout, down the tube(s).

Adverbs—if the worst come to the worst; from bad to worse; out of the frying pan into the fire.

Antonym, see PROSPERITY.

---

advertisement, *n.* announcement, public notice, notice, bill; commercial, ad, want ad; publicity. *Colloq.*, plug, blurb. See PUBLICATION.

ADVICE

Nouns—**1,** advice, counsel, suggestion, recommendation; advocacy, exhortation, PERSUASION, expostulation, DISSUASION, admonition, WARNING; guidance, DIRECTION, instruction; charge, injunction.

2, adviser, prompter, counselor; monitor, mentor, Nestor, teacher (see TEACHING).

3, guide, manual, chart, reference, consultation, conference, INFORMATION.

Verbs—**1,** advise, counsel, suggest, prompt, admonish, recommend, prescribe, advocate, exhort, persuade; enjoin, charge, instruct, dictate; expostulate, dissuade, warn.

2, advise with; consult together; compare notes; hold a council, deliberate, be closeted with, confer, consult.

Adjectives—**1,** advisory, consultative, consultant; recommendatory, hortative, persuasive, dissuasive, admonitory, WARNING.

2, advisable, expedient, desirable, commendable; fitting, proper, suitable, meet.

---

advocate, *v. & n.* —*v.* favor, plead; recommend, suggest. See SUPPORT. —*n.* patron, supporter, scholar; lawyer. *Ant.*, OPPONENT.

aerial, *adj.* airy, atmospheric; lofty, soaring; graceful, ethereal; visionary. See AIR, HEIGHT, INSUBSTANTIALITY, IMAGINATION.

aeronaut, aeronautics, *n.* See AVIATION.

aesthetic, esthetic, *adj.* artistic, tasteful, beautiful. See BEAUTY.

affable, *adj.* friendly, sociable, gracious, approachable. See COURTESY.

affair, *n.* occasion, occurrence, EVENT, happening; business; party, festivity; amour, love affair, liaison. *Colloq.*, to-do, fuss, shindig, blowout.

affect, *v.t.* influence, touch; concern, relate to; move, stir. See RELATION.

AFFECTATION

Nouns—**1,** affectation, affectedness, artificiality, insincerity, histrionics, OSTENTATION; charlatanism, quackery; pose, pretension, airs; pedantry, euphuism; preciosity, preciousness; mannerism, conceit, foppery, dandyism, coxcombry. *Slang*, side. See ORNAMENT.

2, stiffness, formality; prudery, demureness, coquetry.

3, fop, faker, sham, pedant, bluestocking, prig; charlatan, DECEIVER.

Verbs—affect, act, put on *or* give oneself airs, feign, sham, simper, mince, attitudinize, pose, strike an attitude.

Adjectives—affected, pretentious, artificial, insincere, pedantic, stilted, stagy, theatrical, sham, mock, histrionic; unnatural, self-conscious, stiff, starchy, formal, prim, smug, demure, prudish, priggish, conceited, foppish, dandified; finical, finicky; mincing, simpering, namby-pamby.

Antonym, see SIMPLENESS, MODESTY.

---

affection, *n.* LOVE, regard, esteem, liking. *Ant.*, indifference.

AFFECTIONS

Nouns—**1,** affections, character, qualities, disposition, nature, spirit, tone; temper, temperament; idiosyncrasy; frame of mind; predilection, turn of mind, bent, bias, predisposition, penchant, proneness, proclivity, propensity; vein, humor, mood, grain, mettle; sympathy, LOVE.

2, soul, heart, breast, bosom, heartstrings, heart of hearts, cockles of one's heart; passion, fervor, ardor, verve, zeal.

Verbs—LOVE, HATE.

Adjectives—**1,** touched, affected, characterized; disposed, prone, inclined, having a bias; tinctured, imbued, eaten up with.

2, inborn, inbred, innate, ingrained; deep-rooted, ineffaceable, ineradicable.

Adverbs—at heart; heart and soul. See FEELING.

---

affidavit, *n.* deposition, attestation. See EVIDENCE.

affiliate, *v. & n.* —*v.i.* join, unite. —*n.* subsidiary, partner. See COÖPERATION, COMPACT.

AFFIRMATION

Nouns—**1,** affirmation, statement, allegation, assertion, predication, declaration, averment.

2, asseveration, adjuration, swearing, oath, affidavit, deposition; avouchment, avowal, assurance; protestation, profession, word; acknowledgment, ASSENT. See RECORD, CHOICE.

3, remark, observation, expression, position, proposition; saying, dictum, sentence. See CERTAINTY.

4, PROMISE, pledge, vow; AGREEMENT.

Verbs—**1,** assert, say, affirm, predicate, declare, state; protest, profess; have one's say, declare oneself, speak up, give voice *or* utterance (to).

2, put forth, put forward; advance, allege, propose, propound, enunciate, broach, set forth, hold out, maintain, contend, claim; announce, pronounce, pretend.

3, depose, depone, aver, avow, avouch, asseverate, swear, attest (to); take one's oath; make an affidavit; kiss the book, vow, swear till one is black in the face; cross one's heart; be sworn, call Heaven to witness; vouch, warrant, certify, assure; swear by bell, book and candle.

4, insist, take one's stand upon; emphasize, lay stress on; lay down the law; raise one's voice; dogmatize, have the last word; rap out; repeat. See BELIEF.

5, PROMISE, commit oneself, assure, warrant, covenant.

Adjectives—declaratory, predicatory, pronunciative, affirmative; positive, CERTAIN; express, explicit, PATENT; absolute, emphatic, flat, broad, round, pointed, marked, distinct, decided, confident, trenchant, dogmatic, definitive, formal, solemn, categorical, peremptory; unretracted; predicable.

Adverbs—affirmatively, in the affirmative, *etc.*; with emphasis, *ex cathedra*, without fear of contradiction.

Antonym, see NEGATION.

---

afflict, *v.t.* beset, trouble, grieve, hurt, burden (with). See PAIN.

affluent, *adj.* flowing; abundant, plentiful; rich, wealthy. See WEALTH, PROSPERITY. *Ant.,* see POVERTY.

afford, *v.t.* manage, bear (expense); supply, yield, produce; make available, furnish. See GIVING.

affront, *v. & n.* insult, slight, snob. See DISRESPECT.

afraid, *adj.* scared, frightened, alarmed, panicky, terror-stricken, fearful, apprehensive, cowardly, timorous, mousy. See FEAR. *Ant.,* see COURAGE.

aft, *adv.* abaft, astern, rearward. See REAR. *Ant.,* see FRONT.

after, *prep., adj. & adv.* —*prep.* past, beyond, behind. —*adj.* later, subsequent, following. —*adv.* subsequently, afterward, not now, later. *Ant.,* before.

again, *adv.* once more, afresh, anew, repeatedly, twice; encore. See REPETITION.

against, *prep.* in OPPOSITION to, counter *or* contrary to, facing, vis-à-vis; dead against, at cross purposes. See CONTACT.

AGE

Nouns—1, age, OLDNESS; old age, advanced age; senility, senescence; years, anility, gray hairs, climacteric, menopause; declining years, decrepitude, superannuation; second childhood, dotage; vale of years, decline of life, three-score years and ten; ripe age; longevity; gerontology, geriatrics; era, period (see CHRONOMETRY).

2, adulthood, manhood, virility, maturity; prime of life; years of discretion, majority; adult. *Colloq.,* no [spring] chicken.

3, seniority, eldership; elder; VETERAN; primogeniture; firstling; *doyen*, father; senior citizen.

Verbs—1, be aged, grow old; age; decline, wane.

2, come of age, come to man's estate, attain majority, have cut one's eyeteeth, have sown one's wild oats.

Adjectives—1, aged, old, elderly, senile; matronly, anile; in years; ripe, mellow, run to seed, declining, waning, past one's prime; grayheaded, hoary, venerable, timeworn, antiquated, *passé*, effete, decrepit, superannuated; advanced in life *or* years; past one's prime, stricken in years; wrinkled; having one foot in the grave.

2, of full age; out of one's teens, grown up, mature, full grown, in one's prime, middle-aged, manly, virile, adult; womanly, matronly; marriageable, nubile; of a certain age, no [spring] chicken, old as Methuselah; patriarchal, ANCIENT.

Antonym, see YOUTH.

AGENCY

Nouns—agency, operation; force, working, power, function; office, maintenance, exercise, work, play; interworking, interaction; causality, causation (see CAUSE); INSTRUMENTALITY, INFLUENCE, ACTION; METHOD, *modus operandi.* See AGENT, SUBSTITUTION.

Verbs—1, operate, work; act, act upon; perform, play, support, sustain, maintain; take effect, quicken, strike.

2, come *or* bring into operation *or* play; have free play *or* rein; bring to bear upon.

Adjectives—operative, efficient, efficacious, practical, effectual; at work, on foot; acting, doing; in operation, in force, in action, in play; acted upon.

agenda, *n.* schedule, calendar, docket, program, PLAN.

AGENT

Nouns—1, doer, agent, performer, perpetrator, operator; executor, executrix, administrator, administratrix; practitioner, worker, stager.

2, representative, commissioner, DEPUTY, proxy, broker, factor, attorney; salesman, traveler, drummer; legate, minister, apostle, messenger; advertising agent, book agent, press agent, publicity agent, theatrical agent.

3, factotum, SERVANT: workman, artisan; craftsman, mechanic, operative; working *or* laboring man; hewers of wood and drawers of water, laborer, navvy; hand, man, hired man, handyman, journeyman, hack; tool, beast of burden, drudge.

4, maker, artificer, artist, wright, manufacturer, architect, builder, mason, smith, mechanic, engineer.

5, co-worker, party to, participator in, *particeps criminis, dramatis personae;* personnel. See AGENCY.

aggravate, *v.* worsen, heighten, intensify, INCREASE; provoke, irritate, annoy, exasperate, exacerbate. See IRASCIBILITY. *Ant.,* see PACIFICATION, DECREASE.

aggregate, *n.* total, amount, sum; combination, whole, all. See ASSEMBLAGE.

aggression, *n.* offense, ATTACK, war, invasion; belligerence. *Ant.,* see DEFENSE.

agile, *adj.* nimble, active, spry, limber, lithe; brisk, quick, acrobatic, athletic. See ACTIVITY. *Ant.,* see INACTIVITY.

AGITATION

Nouns—**1,** agitation, stir, tremor, shake, ripple, jog, jolt, jar, jerk, shock; trepidation, quiver, quaver, dance; twitter, flicker, flutter.
2, perturbation, commotion, turmoil, turbulence, tumult, hubbub, rout, bustle, fuss, racket, EXCITEMENT, flurry; DEMONSTRATION.
3, spasm, throe, throb, twinge, pang, palpitation, convulsion, paroxysm, disturbance, DISORDER, restlessness, CHANGEABLENESS; frenzy. *Slang,* heebie-jeebies.
4, ferment, fermentation; ebullition, effervescence, hurly-burly; tempest, storm, ground swell, heavy sea, whirlpool, vortex; maelstrom, whirlwind (see WIND).
Verbs—**1,** shake, tremble, quiver, quaver, quake, shiver, twitter, writhe, toss, shuffle, tumble, stagger, bob, reel, sway; wag, wiggle, waggle; wriggle [like an eel]; dance, stumble, shamble, flounder, totter, flounce, flop, prance; throb, pulsate, beat, palpitate, go pit-a-pat; flutter, flitter, flicker, bustle.
2, ferment, effervesce, foam; seethe, boil (over); bubble (up); toss about; shake like an aspen leaf; shake to its foundations; reel to and fro [like a drunken man].
3, agitate, shake, convulse, toss, tumble, bandy, wield, brandish, flap, flourish, whisk, jerk, hitch, jolt; jog, jiggle, joggle, jostle, buffet, hustle; disturb, stir, shake up, churn, jounce, wallop, whip, vellicate.
Adjectives—shaking, agitated, tremulous; giddy; convulsive, unquiet, restless, all atwitter. *Colloq.,* nervous. *Slang,* jittery, jumpy, strung out, uptight.
Adverbs—by fits and starts; hop, skip and jump; in convulsions *or* fits.
                  Antonym, see REPOSE.

agnostic, *n.* unbeliever, skeptic, doubter. See DOUBT.

agony, *n.* PAIN, torture, excruciation; anxiety, anguish.

agree, *v.* yield, coincide, harmonize; conform, confirm, match, jibe (with); suit, please, satisfy. See AGREEMENT.

agreeable, *adj.* pleasant, congenial, compatible, harmonious. See AGREEMENT, SOCIALITY.

AGREEMENT

Nouns—**1,** agreement, accord, accordance; unison, harmony, CONCORD, concordance, concert; CONFORMITY, conformance; UNIFORMITY, consonance; consistency, congruity, keeping; congeniality; correspondence, parallelism, apposition, union.
2, fitness, aptness, appropriateness, relevancy, pertinency; case in point; aptitude, coaptation, propriety, applicability, admissibility, commensurability, compatibility; cognation, RELATION; right man in the right place; very thing; just the thing.
3, adaptation, adjustment, accommodation, reconciliation, assimilation; consent, ASSENT, concurrence, coÖPERATION.
4, COMPACT, contract, pact, meeting of minds.
5, negotiation, bargaining, diplomacy, mediation; ratification.
Verbs—**1,** agree, accord, harmonize, get along, get on; consent, ASSENT,

acquiesce; correspond, tally, respond; meet, suit, fit, befit, do, adapt (to); fall in with, chime in with, square with, comport with; dovetail, assimilate; fit like a glove; match, become one; see eye to eye. See SIMILARITY.

2, fit, suit, adapt, accommodate, adjust; dress, regulate, readjust; accord, harmonize, reconcile; dovetail, square. See EQUALITY.

3, contract, covenant, engage, promise; stipulate; make *or* come to terms; close, close with, conclude, settle, compromise; strike a bargain, come to an understanding; confirm, ratify; sign, seal.

Adjectives—**1,** agreeing, suiting, in accord, accordant, concordant, consonant, congruous, correspondent, congenial; becoming; harmonious, reconcilable, conformable; in accordance, in harmony *or* keeping with; at one with, of one mind, of a piece; consistent, compatible, proportionate; commensurate; in phase. *Slang,* in whack.

2, apt, apposite, pertinent, pat; to the point *or* purpose; happy, felicitous, germane, applicable, relevant, admissible; fit, adapted, apropos, appropriate, seasonable, suitable, deft; meet, EXPEDIENT; at home, in one's proper element.

3, confirmed, ratified; signed, sealed and delivered.

Antonym, see DISAGREEMENT.

AGRICULTURE

Nouns—**1,** agriculture, cultivation, husbandry, farming, tillage, agronomy, gardening; horticulture, arboriculture, floriculture, vintage; landscape gardening; georgics, geoponics.

2, husbandman, horticulturist, gardener, florist; agriculturist; gentleman farmer, country squire; yeoman, farmer, granger, cultivator, tiller of the soil; sharecropper; plowman, reaper, sower; rustic. *Colloq.,* hayseed, hick, rube, peasant, [country] bumpkin, clod(hopper).

3, farm, field, meadow, garden; nursery, greenhouse, hothouse, conservatory; bed, border, seed-plot; lawn, park, *parterre;* plantation, ranch, homestead; arboretum, orchard, vineyard, vinery. See ABODE.

Verbs—cultivate, till the soil, farm, garden; sow, plant, reap, mow, cut, dress the ground; dig, delve, dibble, hoe, plow, harrow, rake, weed.

Adjectives—agricultural; arable; praedial, rural, rustic, country, georgic; horticultural.

ahead, adv. before, in advance (of), leading, winning. See TIME, SUPERIORITY.

AID

Nouns—**1,** aid, assistance, help, succor, relief, rescue; support, lift, advance, furtherance, promotion, operation; patronage, championship, countenance, favor, interest, advocacy; ministration; subministration; accommodation.

2, supplies, reinforcements; SUPPORT, ADJUNCT, AUXILIARY.

3, helper, assistant, aid, aide; accessory, confederate; AGENT; ally, colleague.

Verbs—**1,** aid, assist, help, succor, lend one's aid; come to the aid of; contribute, subscribe to; give *or* lend a hand, give one a lift, take in tow.

2, relieve, rescue, set on one's legs; pull through; give new life to, be the making of; reinforce; push forward; give a lift to; give a leg up; promote, further, forward, advance; speed, expedite, quicken, hasten; support, sustain, uphold, prop, hold up; bolster.

3, cradle, nourish, nurture, nurse, suckle, foster, cherish, foment; feed *or* fan the flames; serve; do service to, tender to, pander to, administer to; care for, tend, attend, wait on, take care of, squire.

4, oblige, accommodate, humor, encourage.

5, second, stand by, stick by, stick up for; back up; abet, take up the cudgels for; espouse (the cause of), advocate, give moral support to, keep in countenance, patronize; smile upon, favor, befriend, take in hand, side with; be of use to, benefit.

Adjectives—aiding, auxiliary, adjuvant, helpful, coadjuvant; ministrant, ancillary, accessory, subsidiary; at one's beck; friendly, amicable, favorable, propitious, well-disposed, neighborly, obliging.

Adverbs—with *or* by the aid of; on *or* in behalf of; on account of; for the sake of; on the part of.

Antonym, see HINDRANCE.

---

ail, *v.i.* fall ill, be sick, suffer, fail (in health). See DISEASE.

aim, *n. & v.* —*n.* purpose, goal, end, course. —*v.* point, direct, aspire to, try for. See DIRECTION.

aimless, *adj.* random, undirected, haphazard, CHANCE: driftless, idle, wanton. See DISORDER, DEVIATION. *Ant.*, see DIRECTION.

AIR

Nouns—**1,** air, atmosphere, ether, ozone; ventilation, fresh *or* open air; sky, welkin; blue sky. See VAPOR.

2, troposphere, tropopause, layer, ozone layer, stratosphere, [Kennelly-] Heaviside layer, ionosphere, exosphere.

3, weather, climate, rise and fall of the barometer, isobar, weather map; aerology, meteorology, climatology; aneroid barometer, baroscope.

4, aeronautics, AVIATION.

5, aria, tune; see MUSIC.

6, APPEARANCE.

Verbs—**1,** air, ventilate, fan; aerate. See WIND.

2, publicize; see PUBLICATION.

Adjectives—**1,** containing air, flatulent, effervescent; windy.

2, atmospheric, airy, aerial, aeriform; meteorological.

Adverbs—outdoors, al fresco.

Antonym, see SUFFOCATE.

---

air-pipe, *n.* air shaft, airway; funnel, vent, tube, flue, chimney, ventilator; nostril, nozzle, blowhole; windpipe, spiracle, larynx, throat; pipe.

airplane, airship, *n.* See AVIATION.

aisle, *n.* passageway, path, corridor, PASSAGE.

akin, *adj.* related, allied, kindred, like. See RELATION.

alacrity, *n.* promptness, responsiveness, speed, quickness. See ACTIVITY.

alarm, *n. & v.* —*n.* alarum, WARNING; tocsin; S.O.S., siren, danger signal, red light, red flag; condition red; bugbear, bogey, bugaboo. —*v.* frighten, panic, scare; shock, horrify; make uneasy; sound the alarm, bell *or* tocsin; alert, warn; cry wolf. See FEAR. *Ant.*, see SAFETY.

album, *n.* scrapbook, RECORD; loose-leaf BOOK; collection, ASSEMBLAGE, set.

alcoholic, *adj.* beery, winy, spirituous; convivial. See DRUNKENNESS.

alert, *adj.* watchful, on guard, wary; quick, ready, prepared, careful. See CARE.

alien, *adj. & n.* —*adj.* foreign, strange. —*n.* foreigner, stranger, immigrant.

alienate, *v.t.* estrange, make hostile. *Colloq.*, turn off. See HATE.

alienist, *n.* psychiatrist. *Slang*, headshrinker. See INSANITY.

alight, *v. & adj.* —*v.i.* descend, get off, land; dismount; arrive, disembark. See ARRIVAL, DESCENT. *Ant.*, DEPARTURE, ASCENT. —*adj.* glowing, lighted; on fire; burning. See LIGHT. *Ant.*, see DARKNESS.

align, *v.* line up, true, range, straighten; regulate; array, take sides. See ARRANGEMENT, STRAIGHTNESS.

alike, *adj.* analogous, resembling, like; akin; same, identical. See SIMILARITY. *Ant.*, see DIFFERENCE.

alimony, *n.* maintenance; child support. See PAYMENT.

alive, *adj.* living, animate, quick, breathing; quick-witted, alert, brisk, spry. See LIFE, INTELLIGENCE, ACTIVITY. *Ant.,* see DEATH.

all, *n.* sum, total, aggregate, entirety. See WHOLE. *Ant.,* PART.

allay, *v.t.* lessen; soothe, mitigate, ease; calm. See MODERATION. *Ant.,* see VIOLENCE, INCREASE

allege, *v.* state, assert, affirm (see AFFIRMATION); assume, imply; accuse. See ACCUSATION.

allegiance, *n.* loyalty, DUTY, devotion, homage. See OBEDIENCE. *Ant.,* see DISOBEDIENCE.

alleviation, *n.* lessening, mitigation; relief. See MODERATION. *Ant.,* VIOLENCE, INCREASE.

alley, *n.* passage, narrow street, lane, walk. See OPENING. *Ant.,* CLOSURE.

alliance, *n.* association, federation, league; treaty, accord; connection. See COÖPERATION, RELATION. *Ant.,* OPPOSITION.

allied, *adj.* combined, joined, leagued, connected, related. See COMBINATION.

allot, *v.* grant, assign, share, distribute. See APPORTIONMENT.

allow, *v.* grant, permit, concede; tolerate, suffer, let. See DISCLOSURE, PERMISSION. *Ant.,* see RESTRAINT.

allowance, *n.* stipend, salary, remittance; concession; permission. See GIVING, DISCOUNT.

alloy, *n. & v.* —*n.* compound, MIXTURE; admixture. See COMPOSITION. —*v.* adulterate, mix, combine. See MIXTURE.

allude, *v.* suggest, imply, connote. See CAUSE, INTERPRETATION.

allure, *n. & v.* —*n.* attraction, charm. —*v.* tempt, ATTRACT, CHARM, entice. See DESIRE.

allusion, *n.* reference, suggestion, hint, quotation, ATTRIBUTION.

ally, *n.* friend, co-worker, helper, supporter. See AID. *Ant.,* ENEMY.

almanac, *n.* calendar, ephemeris. See CHRONOMETRY.

almighty, *adj.* great, all-powerful, omnipotent. *Colloq.,* extreme. See DEITY.

almost, *adv.* nearly, not quite, all but, approximately. See NEARNESS. *Ant.,* see DISTANCE.

alms, *n.* charity, dole, gratuity. See GIVING.

aloft, *adv.* on high, overhead, above, up; in the air. See HEIGHT. *Ant.,* see LOWNESS.

alone, *adj. & adv.* —*adj.* apart, solitary. —*adv.* individually. See UNITY. *Ant.,* see ACCOMPANIMENT.

alongside, *adv.* beside, neck-and-neck, abreast, side by side. See PARALLELISM, SIDE. *Ant.,* see OBLIQUITY, OPPOSITION.

aloof, *adj.* distant, unneighborly, reserved, remote. See SECLUSION, DISTANCE. *Ant.,* see SOCIALITY, NEARNESS.

aloud, *adv.* audibly, vociferously, loudly. See LOUDNESS. *Ant.,* see SILENCE.

alphabet, *n.* letters; ABC's, crisscross row; rudiments, basics. See BEGINNING, LANGUAGE.

already, *adv.* by now, previously. See TIME, INSTANTANEITY.

also, *adv.* too, furthermore, besides, likewise. See ADDITION.

alter, *v.* CHANGE, modify, rearrange, vary, qualify. *Ant.,* see STABILITY.

alternate, *n. & v.* —*n.* substitute. —*v.* take turns, change, vacillate. See DISJUNCTION, OSCILLATION. *Ant.,* see CONTINUITY.

alternative, *n.* preference, choice of two, option. See CHOICE. *Ant.,* see REFUSAL.

although, *conj.* albeit, nothwithstanding, though. See COMPENSATION. *Ant.,* see AGREEMENT.

altitude, *n.* HEIGHT, loftiness, tallness; elevation, perpendicular distance. *Ant.,* LOWNESS.

altogether, *adv.* entirely, all, collectively, totally. *Colloq.,* nude. See WHOLE. *Ant.,* PART.

altruism, *n.* BENEVOLENCE; selflessness; generosity, liberality, philanthropy. *Ant.,* MALEVOLENCE.

always, *adv.* at all times, invariably, continually, ever. See UNIFORMITY. *Ant.,* never.

amalgamation, *n.* MIXTURE, blend, COMBINATION: unification, merger, federation.

amass, *v.t.* collect, accumulate; STORE, pile *or* heap up. See ASSEMBLAGE.

amateur, *n.* nonprofessional, beginner, novice, tyro; dilettante; volunteer. See BEGINNING, TASTE.

amative, amatory, *adj.* loving, affectionate; amorous, ardent; erotic. See LOVE. *Ant.,* see HATE.

amaze, *v.t.* astonish, astound, SURPRISE. See WONDER.

ambassador, *n.* envoy, emissary; consul. See DEPUTY.

ambiguous, *adj.* vague, undecided, uncertain; not specific; obscure, undefined. See DOUBT. *Ant.,* see CERTAINTY.

ambition, *n.* purpose, wish, hope, desire, INTENTION; aspiration, goal, end; resolve; zeal. See DESIRE, OSTENTATION. *Ant.,* see INDIFFERENCE.

ambush, *n. & v.* —*n.* ambuscade; hiding-place, cover, threat; disguise, camouflage; pitfall, trap, blind; bushwhacking. —*v.t.* lie in wait for; attack unexpectedly; bushwhack. See CONCEALMENT.

ameliorate, *v.* get better, make progress *or* headway, improve. See IMPROVEMENT.

amenable, *adj.* agreeable; pliant, yielding, submissive. See DUTY, ASSENT. *Ant.,* see REFUSAL, NEGLECT.

amend, *v.* change; correct, rectify; improve; enlarge. See IMPROVEMENT. *Ant.,* see DETERIORATION.

amiable, *adj.* friendly, agreeable, kindly, pleasant; likeable. See COURTESY. *Ant.,* see DISCOURTESY.

amidst, *prep.* amid, AMONG, midst, mid (*poetic*). See MIXTURE.

amiss, *adv.* wrong, ill, badly, improperly. See EVIL. *Ant.,* see GOOD.

ammunition, *n.* bullets, shot, powder, bombs. *Colloq.,* ammo. See ARMS.

amnesia, *n.* forgetfulness, loss of MEMORY.

amnesty, *n.* pardon, remission, moratorium. See OBLIVION.

among, *prep.* midst, in the middle, included in, with. See MIXTURE.

amorous, *adj.* loving, passionate, AMATIVE. See LOVE. *Ant.,* see HATE.

amorphous, *adj.* shapeless, formless; indefinite, vague. See FORMLESSNESS, DISORDER.

amount, *n.* QUANTITY, sum, total, aggregate.

ample, *adj.* adequate, sufficient, plenty; large, expansive, roomy, spacious. See GREATNESS, SPACE. *Ant.,* see LITTLENESS.

amplify, *v.t.* enlarge, swell, magnify. See INCREASE, EXPANSION.

amputate, *v.* sever, cut off. See DECREASE.

amulet, *n.* charm, token, talisman, good-luck piece. See PREDICTION.

AMUSEMENT

Nouns—**1,** amusement, entertainment; diversion, divertisement, *divertissement,* distraction; recreation, hobby, avocation, relaxation, pastime, sport; labor of love, PLEASURE.

2, fun, frolic, merriment, jollity, joviality, laughter, REJOICING, jocosity, drollery, tomfoolery, mummery; pleasantry, WIT, quip, quirk.

3, play, game, gambol, romp, prank, antic, lark, escapade, spree, skylarking; vagary, monkeyshine, monkey trick, practical joke, RIDICULE.

4, dance, hop, ball, masquerade; reel, rigadoon, saraband, hornpipe, bolero, fandango, cancan, minuet, waltz, polka, galop, jig, fling, *allemande,* gavotte, mazurka, kozotzky, morisco, morris dance, quadrille, country dance, cotillion, *cotillon;* one-step, two-step, fox trot, turkey trot, Charleston, jitterbugging, bunnyhop, black bottom, cakewalk, tango, cha-cha, mambo, samba; tap dance, soft shoe. *Colloq.*, drag, hop, prom.

5, festivity, merrymaking, party (see SOCIALITY); fete, festival, gala, revel, revelry, carnival, Mardi Gras, brawl, saturnalia, high jinks; feast, banquet, wassail, carouse, carousal; jollification, junket, wake, picnic, field-day; treat; round of pleasures, dissipation, a short life and a merry one; jubilee, CELEBRATION, holiday; red letter day; May Day.

6, place of amusement, theater, ballroom, music hall; park, arbor, bowling green *or* alley, rink, casino, fun fair, amusement park, resort, watering place; midway, boardwalk.

7, game, sports, gymnastics, athletics, Olympic games, rodeo, racing; billiards, bowls; cards, chess, checkers, draughts, backgammon, dominoes, solitaire; gambling, CHANCE; fishing, hunting, safari; aquatics, swimming, water sports.

8, toy, plaything, bauble; doll, PUPPET, teetotum, knickknack.

Verbs—**1,** amuse, entertain, divert, enliven; tickle the fancy, titillate, raise a smile, put in good humor; convulse with laughter; bring down the house, be the death of one; recreate, solace, cheer, please, interest, treat, regale.

2, amuse oneself; play (a game, pranks, tricks, *etc.*); sport, disport, toy, wanton, revel, junket, feast, carouse, make merry; drown care; drive dull care away; frolic, gambol, frisk, romp, caper; sow one's wild oats, have one's fling, take one's pleasure; make holiday; go a-Maying; while away the time; kill time; dally. *Colloq.*, step out, have fun, cut a caper, carry on. *Slang*, cut loose, whoop it up, make a night of it, go to town, let one's hair down.

Adjectives—**1,** amusing, entertaining, diverting, recreative, pleasant, pleasing; laughable, ludicrous, witty; festive, jovial, jolly, jocund, roguish, rompish, playful (as a kitten), sportive.

2, amused, pleased, tickled.

Antonym, see WEARINESS, PAIN.

---

anachronism, *n.* misdate, prolepsis, anticipation; metachronism, parachronism, prochronism.

anemia, *n.* bloodlessness, lack of blood. See DISEASE, IMPOTENCE. *Ant.*, see POWER.

analogous, *adj.* like, parallel; related; corresponding, similar, resembling. See SIMILARITY. *Ant.*, see OBLIQUITY, DIFFERENCE.

analysis, *n.* breakdown, separation, disintegration; investigation, study. See INQUIRY, DECOMPOSITION. *Ant.*, synthesis, COMBINATION.

anarchy, *n.* lawlessness, terrorism, chaos, confusion, disorganization; nihilism. See DISORDER. *Ant.*, see AUTHORITY.

anatomy, *n.* body structure, framework; zoötomy; analysis. See REMEDY, INQUIRY.

ANCESTRY

Nouns—**1,** ancestry, paternity, maternity, parentage, RELATION; house, stem, trunk, branch, tree, stock, stirps, pedigree, lineage, blood, kin, line, family, tribe, sept, race, clan; family tree, genealogy, descent, extraction, birth; forefathers, patriarchs.

2, parent, father, sire, dad, papa; paterfamilias; genitor, progenitor, procreator; ancestor; grandsire, grandfather, forebears; motherhood, maternity; mother, dam, ma, mama, materfamilias, grandmother, granddam.

Adjectives—parental, paternal, maternal; family, ancestral, linear, patriarchal; direct, lineal, collateral.

Antonym, see DESCENT.

---

anchor, *n. & v.* —*n.* grapnel, kedge; mainstay, safeguard. —*v.* fasten, bind, attach; hold fast. See STABILITY.

anchorage, *n.* REFUGE, SECURITY, LOCATION, mooring, road(stead), harbor.

ancient, *adj.* aged, venerable; antique, antiquated; archaic, hoary. See OLDNESS. *Ant.,* see NEWNESS.

and, *conj.* moreover, also, in addition; plus, to boot, besides. See ADDITION, ACCOMPANIMENT.

anecdote, *n.* sketch, story, tale, joke, narrative. See DESCRIPTION.

ANGEL

Nouns—1, angel, archangel; celestial being, choir invisible, heavenly host; seraph, cherub; ministering spirit, guardian angel.

2, angelology; seraphim, cherubim, thrones, dominations *or* dominions, virtues, powers, principalities, archangels, angels.

Adjectives—angelic, seraphic, cherubic, celestial, divine, supernatural.

Antonym, see DEMON.

anger, *n. & v.* —*n.* RESENTMENT, irritation; rage, choler, fury; annoyance. —*v.* inflame, irritate, annoy, provoke, pique, incense; enrage, infuriate.

angle, *n.* peak, corner, point; fork; OBLIQUITY; aspect, guise. *Slang,* approach. See ANGULARITY.

anguish, *n.* agony, anxiety, PAIN.

ANGULARITY

Nouns—1, angularity, obliquity; angle, cusp, bend, FOLD, NOTCH, fork, bifurcation; elbow, knee, knuckle, ankle, groin, crotch, crutch, crane, fluke; scythe, sickle; zigzag; corner, coign, quoin, nook, recess, niche, oriel; salient, projection.

2, right, acute, obtuse *or* oblique angle.

3, angulation; angular measurement, elevation, distance, velocity; trigonometry, trig; goniometry, altimeter, clinometer, graphometer, goniometer; theodolite; sextant, quadrant.

4, triangle, trigon, wedge; rectangle, square, lozenge, diamond; rhomb, rhombus; quadrangle, quadrilateral; parallelogram; quadrature; polygon, pentagon, hexagon, heptagon, octagon, decagon; cube, rhomboid; tetrahedron, octahedron, dodecahedron, icosahedron; prism, pyramid; parallelepiped.

5, lankiness, boniness, ungainliness.

Verbs—bend, fork, bifurcate, crinkle.

Adjectives—angular, bent, crooked; aquiline, sharp; jagged, serrated; falciform, furcated, forked, bifurcate, zigzag; dovetailed; knockkneed, crinkled, akimbo, geniculated; oblique (see OBLIQUITY).

Antonyms, see DIRECTION, CIRCULARITY.

anile, *adj.* childish, foolish, simple; senile. See AGE, OLDNESS.

ANIMAL

Nouns—1, animal kingdom, animal life, fauna; beast, brute, creature, living thing, creeping thing, dumb animal; domestic animal, wild animal, game; flesh, flesh and blood, corporeality, carnality; animation, animality.

2, biology, zoölogy, mammalogy, ornithology, herpetology, ichthyology, entomology; biologist, *etc.*

3, vertebrate, invertebrate; quadruped, biped; mammal, marsupial, cetacean; reptile, snake, amphibian; fish, crustacean, shellfish, mollusk, worm; insect, zoöphyte, arachnid, protozoan, animalcule.

4, livestock; cattle, kine, bird, poultry, fowl, swine; beasts of the field.

5, yearling, youngling, colt, filly, whelp, cub. See YOUTH.

Adjectives—1, animal, zoölogical; bestial, carnal, corporal, corporeal, physical, fleshly; sensual; human.

2, mammalian, cetaceous, avian, reptilian, vermicular, piscatory; piscine, molluscous; aquatic, terrestrial; domestic, wild; carnivorous, herbivorous, insectivorous, omnivorous; equine, bovine, canine, feline, *etc.*

animate, *v. & adj.* —*v.* liven, impel; cheer, enliven, enspirit, encourage, inspire. —*adj.* moving; living. See CHEERFULNESS, EXCITEMENT, ANIMAL. *Ant.,* see DEJECTION, INACTIVITY.

animosity, *n.* antipathy, enmity, hatred, ill will. See HATE, RESENTMENT.

annalis, *n.* recorder, historian, compiler, chronicler. See RECORD.

annex, *v.* add, acquire, join, attach, affix. See ADDITION.

annihilate, *v.* demolish, destroy; eliminate, exterminate, end; wreck. See DESTRUCTION, NONEXISTENCE.

anniversary, *n.* CELEBRATION.

annotate, *v.* make notes on, gloss, explain. See INTERPRETATION.

announce, *v.* tell, proclaim, publish, make known; broadcast, report. See INFORMATION, PREDICTION.

annoy, *v.* vex, tease, harass, disturb, molest, trouble, bother, irritate, PAIN. *Colloq.,* peeve. *Ant.,* see PLEASURE.

annual, *adj. & n.* —*adj.* yearly, seasonal, anniversary. See REGULARITY. —*n.* yearbook, RECORD, [annual] report.

annul, *v.t.* cancel, repeal, rescind, recall, retract, revoke, nullify, quash; dissolve (a marriage); set aside, invalidate. See NULLIFICATION.

anoint, *v.* oil, salve; crown.

anonymous, *adj.* unknown, unnamed, nameless, incognito. See NOMENCLATURE.

another, *adj.* different, one more. See DIFFERENCE. *Ant.,* see IDENTITY.

ANSWER

Nouns—**1,** answer, response, reply; acknowledgment; riposte, rejoinder, return, retort; repartee; antiphon; password; echo, oracle. *Colloq.,* comeback.

2, discovery, DISCLOSURE, solution, explanation, clue, INDICATION.

Verbs—**1,** answer, respond, reply; rebut, retort, rejoin; give answer; acknowledge, echo; CONFUTE.

2, satisfy, set at rest; determine, solve.

Adjectives—answering, responsive, conclusive.

Antonym, see INQUIRY.

antagonism, *n.* animosity, ill-will, antipathy; ENMITY, hostility, opposition. *Ant.,* AGREEMENT.

antecede, *v.t.* go before, precede. See PRIORITY.

anteroom, *n.* waiting room, entrance; lobby, vestibule, foyer. See RECEPTACLE.

anthem, *n.* song, hymn, chorale; national anthem. See MUSIC, WORSHIP.

ANTIBIOSIS

Nouns—**1,** antibiosis (see REMEDY); antibody, antibiotic, counteragent.

2, antibiotics, wonder drugs, miracle drugs; toxin, antitoxin, penicillin, gramicidin; bacitracin, chloromycetin, dihydrostreptomycin, erythromycin, gumagillin, magnamycin, neomycin, polymycin, streptomycin, terramycin.

3, sulfa, sulfonamide, sulfadiazine, sulfanilamide, sulfapyridine, sulfathiazole.

Adjectives—antibiotic, bactericidal, bacteriostatic.

antic, *n.* caper, escapade, prank, gambol, FOLLY. See AMUSEMENT.

anticipate, *v.* await, expect, hope for; precede; foresee. See PREPARATION.

anticipation, *n.* hope, outlook, expectation, enjoyment (beforehand); prematurity. See FUTURE, EARLINESS.

antidote, *n.* emetic, counterirritant. See REMEDY.

antipathy, *n.* repugnance, hate, aversion, abhorrence; incompatibility. See HATE. *Ant.,* liking.

antiquary, *n.* archaeologist, historian, student of the PAST. See OLD-NESS.

antiquated, *adj.* outdated, ancient, old, behind-the-times, outmoded. See OLDNESS. *Ant.,* see NEWNESS.

antiquities, *n.* relics, ruins, remnants. See OLDNESS.

antiquity, *n.* old times; the past, ancient history; yesterday. See PAST.

anxiety, *n.* concern; fear, mental anguish, apprehensiveness, worry. See CARE, FEAR, PAIN.

anyhow, *adv.* anyway; at any rate; nevertheless. See NEGATION.

apart, *adv.* separately, alone, independently; away. See DISTANCE, DISJUNCTION.

apartment, *n.* flat, suite, rooms, maisonette, tenement, walk-up. See ABODE.

apathy, *n.* coldness, INSENSIBILITY, unconcern. *Ant.,* FEELING, INTEREST.

ape, *n. & v.* —*n.* monkey, gorilla, anthropoid, simian. —*v.* IMITATE, copy, mimic. *Ant.,* originate.

aphorism, *n.* MAXIM, adage, proverb.

apiece, *adv.* for each, for one, respectively, individually. See SPECIALITY.

apology, *n.* excuse, regret, amends, pardon. See ATONEMENT.

apostate, *n.* backslider, renegade, turncoat, deserter, recreant; double dealer, opportunist. See CHANGEABLENESS, IMPIETY. *Ant.,* see STABILITY, PIETY.

appall, appal, *v.i.* horrify, shock; disgust, revolt. See FEAR, PAIN. *Ant.,* GRATIFY, PLEASE.

apparatus, *n.* machine, machinery; equipment, instruments. See INSTRUMENTALITY.

apparent, *adj.* plain, obvious, visible; EVIDENT, manifest, perceptible. See APPEARANCE, VISIBILITY. *Ant.,* HIDDEN, MYSTERIOUS.

apparition, *n.* phantom, ghost, specter; dream. See VISION.

appeal, *n.* entreaty, plea, begging, petition; ATTRACTION. See REQUEST.

APPEARANCE

Nouns—**1,** appearance, phenomenon, sight, show, scene, view; outlook, prospect, vista, perspective, bird's-eye view, scenery, landscape, picture, tableau; display, exposure, setting, *mise en scène.*

2, pageant, spectacle; peep show; magic lantern, phantasmagoria, panorama, diorama; pageantry, OSTENTATION, INDICATION.

3, aspect phase, seeming; shape, FORM, guise, look, complexion, color, image, mien, air, cast, carriage, port, demeanor; presence, expression, first blush; point of view, light.

4, lineament, feature; contour, face, countenance, physiognomy, visage, phiz, cast of countenance, profile, cut of one's jib.

Verbs—appear, become visible; seem, look, show; have, take on *or* assume the appearance *or* semblance of; look like; cut a figure, figure; present to the view. See VISION.

Adjectives—apparent, seeming, ostensible; on view; evident, manifest.

Adverbs—apparently, ostensibly, seemingly, as it seems, on the face of it, *prima facie;* at first blush, at first sight; in the eyes of; to the eye.

Antonyms, see ABSENCE, VISIBILITY.

appease, *v.t.* mollify, pacify, moderate, soothe; satisfy, slake. See PLEASURE.

append, *v.t.* add, attach (to), affix. See ADDITION.

appendage, *n.* ADDITION; tag, attachment; tail. See ADJUNCT.

appetite, *n.* hunger, DESIRE; relish, gusto; craving.

appetizer, *n.* relish; hors d'œuvre, antipasto; dainty, delicacy. See FOOD, TASTE.

applause, *n.* praise; cheers, acclaim, plaudits, clapping. See APPROBATION.

appliance, *n.* device, machine, implement; attachment, accessory, medical appliance. See MEANS, REMEDY.

applicable, *adj.* fitting, suitable, appropriate, relevant, pertinent. See UTILITY.

application, *n.* diligence, assiduity; suitability, relevancy; form (to fill out). See REQUEST, RELATION, ATTENTION.

apply, *v.* put on, USE; ask, solicit; work, persevere. See REQUEST.

appoint, *v.* prescribe, assign, ordain; place (in a job), nominate; equip. See COMMISSION, APPORTIONMENT.

appointment, *n.* meeting, interview, engagement; office. *Colloq.,* date, rendezvous, tryst. See BUSINESS, SOCIALITY.

APPORTIONMENT

Nouns—**1,** apportionment, allotment, consignment, assignment, appointment; appropriation; dispensation, distribution, division, partition, deal. **2,** dividend, portion, contingent, share, allotment, lot, measure, dose, dole, meed, pittance; quantum, ration; ratio, proportion, quota, modicum, allowance.

Verbs—apportion, divide; distribute, dispense; billet, allot, detail, cast, share, mete; portion, parcel *or* dole out; deal, carve, administer; partition, assign, appropriate, appoint. *Slang,* divvy (up). See COÖPERATION.

Adjectives—apportioning; respective; proportional, proportionate, commensurate; divisible.

Adverbs—respectively, *pro rata,* each to each, severally, individually.

appraise, *v.* estimate, JUDGE, evaluate, assess.

appreciate, *v.* prize, esteem, value; INCREASE (in value); comprehend, understand; realize worth. See APPROBATION, KNOWLEDGE. *Ant.,* see DECREASE.

apprehend, *v.* seize, arrest; grasp, see, understand, perceive. See KNOWLEDGE, LAWSUIT.

apprehension, *n.* FEAR, anxiety, distrust; arrest, seizure; understanding. See LAWSUIT, KNOWLEDGE. *Ant.,* HOPE, trust.

apprenticeship, *n.* training, probation. See LEARNING.

APPROACH

Nouns—**1,** approach, drawing near, nearing, approximation; convergence; access, accessibility, admittance, advent. See PURSUIT, NEARNESS. **2,** procedure, address, METHOD; advance(s), overture(s), initiative. *Colloq.,* pass, proposition. See OFFER, SOCIALITY.

Verbs—**1,** approach, approximate; near, draw near; come to close quarters; move toward; drift; make up to; gain upon; pursue; tread on the heels of; hug the shore; loom ahead, impend (see DESTINY). **2,** address, broach (a subject); undertake, tackle; begin; make overtures *or* advances to, accost, waylay. *Colloq.,* make a pass at, proposition.

Adjectives—approaching, near, approximate; impending, imminent, destined; on the horizon, on the brink *or* verge of, in the wind; approachable, accessible, *etc.*

Antonym, see REGRESSION, DISTANCE, AVOIDANCE.

APPROBATION

Nouns—**1,** approbation, approval, sanction, advocacy; esteem, estimation, good opinion, favor, admiration; appreciation, regard, account, popularity, kudos, credit; REPUTE.

2, commendation, praise, laudation; good word; meed, tribute, encomium; eulogy, panegyric; homage, hero worship; benediction, blessing, benison.

3, applause, plaudit, clapping (of hands); acclaim, acclamation, cheer; paean, hosanna; thumbs up.

Verbs—**1,** approve; think good, much, well *or* highly of; esteem; value, prize; set great store by; do justice to, appreciate; honor, hold in esteem, look up to, admire; like, favor, wish God speed; hail. *Colloq.*, hand it to.

2, stand *or* stick up for; clap *or* pat on the back; endorse, give credit, recommend; commend, praise, laud, compliment, pay a tribute, applaud, cheer, encore; panegyrize, eulogize, cry up, puff, extol, magnify, glorify, exalt, swell, make much of, FLATTER; bless, give a blessing to; have *or* say a good word for; speak well *or* highly of; sing, sound *or* resound the praises of. *Slang,* give a big hand.

3, redound to the honor *or* credit of; do credit to; recommend itself; pass muster.

4, be praised; receive honorable mention; be in favor *or* high favor with; ring with the praises of, gain credit, stand well in the opinion of; bring down the house; stop the show.

Adjectives—**1,** approving, commendatory, complimentary, benedictory, laudatory, panegyrical, eulogistic, lavish of praise.

2, approved, praised, popular; in good odor; in high esteem; RESPECTED.

3, deserving, worthy, praiseworthy, commendable, meritorious, estimable, creditable, unimpeachable; beyond all praise. *Colloq.*, in one's good books.

Adverbs—with credit, well. See GOOD.

Interjections—hear, hear! bravo! bravissimo! olé! nice going, so far so good; viva! encore!

Antonym, see DISAPPROBATION.

---

appropriate, *adj.* proper, fit, timely, suitable. See AGREEMENT. *Ant.*, inappropriate; see DISAGREEMENT.

appropriate, *v.t.* take, seize, confiscate; allot, assign. See BORROW. *Ant.*, see RELINQUISHMENT.

approve, *v.t.* accept, like, support, recognize, ratify, endorse. *Colloq.*, O.K. See APPROBATION.

approximate, *adj.* near, close, roughly correct. See NEARNESS, SIMILARITY, RELATION.

apt, *adj.* suitable, appropriate, fitting; quick, clever, skillful. *Colloq.*, likely. See AGREEMENT, SKILL.

aquatic, *adj.* watery; oceanic, marine, fresh-water, salt-water. See NAVIGATION.

aquiline, *adj.* Roman-nosed, beaked, curved, hooked. See ANGULARITY.

arable, *adj.* tillable, farmable; fertile. See AGRICULTURE.

arbitrary, *adj.* despotic, dictatorial; unreasonable; discretionary, willful. See RESOLUTION.

arbitration, *n.* intervention, MEDIATION, settlement (of dispute).

arbitrator, *n.* JUDGE, referee, umpire, mediator. See JUDGMENT.

arbor, *n.* bower, pergola. See ABODE, RECEPTACLE.

arch, *n.* curve, arc, vault. See CONVEXITY.

arch, *adj.* CUNNING, sly, roguish.

archaic, *adj.* old, ancient; historic; obsolete, outdated. See AGE, OLD-NESS. *Ant.,* modern, up-to-date.

archer, *n.* bowman. See COMBATANT, ARMS.

archetype, *n.* model, ideal type. See PREPARATION.

architect, *n.* builder, planner, designer, creator. See AGENT, ARTIST.

architecture, *n.* building, construction. See PRODUCTION, FORM.

archive, *n.* chronicle, annal, RECORD.

ardent, *adj.* warm, passionate, zealous; fervent, eager. See ACTIVITY, LOVE. *Ant.,* apathetic, cool.

ardor, *n.* fervor, passion, enthusiasm, elan, zeal, WARMTH. See FEELING, LOVE, VIGOR.

area, *n.* space, tract, territory, expanse. See REGION.

ARENA

Nouns—**1,** arena, field, theater; platform, hustings; stage, boards, playhouse; amphitheater, coliseum, Colosseum, stadium, bowl; hippodrome, circus, race course *or* track, turf, cockpit; playground, gymnasium, ring, lists, tilting ground. See AMUSEMENT, CONTENTION.

2, theater [of war]; battlefield, battleground, front, field of combat, target; camp, encampment. See WARFARE, CONTENTION.

---

argument, *n.* debate, dispute; evidence, case. See REASONING, CONTENTION.

arid, *adj.* dry, parched; jejune, barren; insipid, dull, uninteresting See DRYNESS, DULLNESS. *Ant.,* see MOISTURE, WIT.

arise, *v.i.* get up, awake; originate, begin. See BEGINNING, ASCENT.

aristocracy, *n.* patricians, NOBILITY, upper classes. *Ant.,* see POPULACE

arm, *n.* limb, member; branch, wing; weapon, strength. See ARMS, PART, POWER.

armistice, *n.* truce, respite, lull (in fighting), peace. See PACIFICATION

armor, armour, *n.* steel plate, mail, shielding. See DEFENSE.

ARMS

Nouns—**1,** arms, weapon(s), firearms, armament, matériel; panoply, stand of arms, military establishment; armory, arsenal, STORE: armor (see DEFENSE).

2, ammunition, munitions, explosive, charge; ball, bolt, shot, grape [shot], chain shot, bullet, dumdum bullet, cartridge, shell, fragmentation shell, shrapnel; missile, projectile, grenade, bomb, depth charge, ashcan, atomic bomb, A-bomb, fission bomb, hydrogen bomb, H-bomb, thermonuclear bomb, blockbuster, torpedo, bombsight, guided missile, Nike, I.C.B.M. (intercontinental ballistic missile), V1, V2; cap and ball, powder and shot, cap, fuse, proximity fuse, detonator; powder, gunpowder, smokeless powder, cordite, melinite, lyddite, guncotton, nitroglycerine, TNT (trinitrotoluene), nuclear *or* thermonuclear warhead, neutron bomb.

3, artillery, gun(s), gunnery, cannon, battery, ordnance, ballistics; piece, fieldpiece, rifle, howitzer, mortar, siege artillery, coast artillery, field artillery, Big Bertha, French 75, two-pounder, ten-pounder, 8-inch, 16-inch, *etc.;* carronade, culverin, basilisk, falconet, jingle, swivel, petard; antiaircraft, AA, ack-ack. See PROPULSION.

4, machine gun, submachine gun, pompom, Gatling gun, Maxim gun, Bren gun, Thompson *or* Tommy gun. *Slang,* chopper.

5, small arms; musket, musketry, carbine, rifle, shotgun, fowling piece, breachloader, muzzle-loader, chassepot, blunderbuss, harquebus, arquebus, matchlock, flint-and-steel; .22, .25, .32, .38, .44, .45, 30-30, 30-'06, *etc.;* 8-gauge, 12-gauge, 16-gauge, *etc.;* Kentucky long rifle, Springfield, Enfield, Winchester, Lee-Enfield, Garand, *etc.;* pistol, automatic, semiautomatic, derringer, repeater, revolver, hammerless (revolver), six-shooter, six-gun; Colt, Smith & Wesson, Luger, Beretta, *etc. Slang,* gat, rod, heater, zip gun.

6, armor, armored vehicle, tank, panzer division.

7, sword, saber, broadsword, cutlass, falchion, scimitar, bilbo, rapier, skean, claymore, creese, kris; dagger, dirk, hanger, poniard, stiletto, stylet, dudgeon, bayonet; foil, epée, blade, steel; ax, poleax, battleax, halberd, tomahawk; bowie knife, bolo, kukri, pigsticker, switchblade knife, yataghan; cold steel.

8, pike, lance, spear, spontoon, javelin, dart, djerrid, arrow, reed, shaft, bolt, boomerang, harpoon, gaff; fishing spear.

9, club, mace, truncheon, staff, bludgeon, cudgel, life-preserver, shil-lelah; quarterstaff; battering ram (see IMPULSE); bat, cane, stick, knuckle-duster, brass knuckles *or* knucks; blackjack, sap, billy, night-stick.

10, bow, crossbow, arbalest, catapult, sling; archery, archer, bowman.

11, warship; see SHIP.

12, gas, poison gas; see KILLING.

---

army, *n.* troops, soldiers, military force; host, crowd, throng. See COMBATANT, MULTITUDE.

aroma, *n.* FRAGRANCE, smell; quality, characteristic. See SPECIALITY.

around, *adv. & prep.* surrounding, about; near, neighboring. See NEAR-NESS.

arouse, *v.* rouse, awaken; stir, excite, stimulate, whet. See EXCITEMENT.

arraignment, *n.* indictment, charge, accusation; censure. See ACCUSA-TION, LAWSUIT.

ARRANGEMENT

Nouns—**1,** arrangement; PLAN, PREPARATION, disposition, allocation, dis-tribution, sorting; grouping; assortment, allotment, apportionment; taxonomy, organization, analysis, classification.

2, digest, synopsis, compendium; table, register, RECORD, resumé; file, index, card index.

3, ORDER, array, system; regularity, uniformity, symmetry.

4, standard, form, formula, principle, RULE.

Verbs—**1,** arrange, dispose, place, form; put, set *or* place in order; set out, collate, pack, marshal, range, size, rank, group, parcel out, allot, distribute, deal; dispose of, assign places to; assort, sort; put *or* set to rights, put in shape *or* in array, reduce to order. *Colloq.,* pigeonhole.

2, classify, divide, segregate, alphabetize, file, string together, register, RECORD, catalog, tabulate, index, graduate, digest; harmonize, metho-dize, regulate, systematize, coördinate, organize.

3, unravel, disentangle, disembroil.

Adjectives—arranged, methodical, orderly, tidy, neat, regular, systematic. *Colloq.,* to rights, cut and dried.

Adverbs—methodically, systematically, like clockwork, in apple-pie or-der.

Antonym, see DISORDER.

---

array, *n.* CLOTHING, apparel; army, host, MULTITUDE; ARRANGEMENT, system.

arrears, *n. pl.* DEBT, bill (overdue).

arrest, *v.* seize, apprehend, capture, stop, halt, retard, suspend. *Colloq.,* nab, pinch, bust. See END, RESTRAINT, LAWSUIT.

ARRIVAL

Nouns—**1,** arrival, advent, landing; debarkation, disembarkation; home-coming, return, rencounter; reception, welcome.

2, home, goal, landing-place, destination; harbor, haven, port; terminus; anchorage, REFUGE; attainment (see COMPLETION).
3, newcomer, visitor. *Colloq.*, newborn child.
4, introduction, entrance, admittance, admission, RECEPTION.
Verbs—1, arrive, get to, come to, reach, attain; come up with *or* to; overtake; join, rejoin.
2, light, alight, dismount; land, go ashore, debark, disembark; detrain, deplane; put in *or* into; visit, cast anchor, pitch one's tent; get to one's journey's end; come *or* get back *or* home; return; appear, put in an appearance, come in, drop in. *Slang*, check in, blow in, hit town.
Antonym, see DEPARTURE.

---

arrogance, *n.* pride, haughtiness, self-importance; INSOLENCE, presumptuousness. *Ant.*, HUMILITY; see MODESTY.
arrogate, *v.* usurp, claim, seize; assume, appropriate, TAKE.
arrow, *n.* shaft, bolt; missile; pointer. See ARMS, DIRECTION.
arsenal, *n.* armory, storehouse, supply (of weapons); resources. See ARMS.
art, *n.* craft, skill, cunning; science, technics; fine arts; PAINTING, SCULPTURE. See REPRESENTATION.
artful, *adj.* deceptive, wily, shrewd, CUNNING: clever, skillful, adept, adroit. See SKILL. *Ant.*, naïve, clumsy.
article, *n.* object, thing; story, piece, essay, report. See SUBSTANCE, PUBLICATION.
articulate, *adj. & v.* —*adj.* jointed, segmented (see JUNCTION); distinct, intelligible; literate, lucid. —*v.* pronounce, enunciate, utter, put in words, verbalize. See SPEECH, INTELLIGIBILITY.
artifice, *n.* trick, stratagem, ruse; device; cunning. See DECEPTION.
artificial, *adj.* manmade, handcrafted; false, substitute, synthetic; sham, fake, deceptive; affected, unnatural. See AFFECTATION, DECEPTION.
artillery, *n.* guns, cannon, ordnance. See ARMS.
artisan, *n.* mechanic, craftsman, workman. See EXERTION, SKILL.

ARTIST

Nouns—1, artist, virtuoso, master, maestro, academician, craftsman.
2, painter, limner, drawer, sketcher; illustrator, protraitist, water-colorist, miniaturist, pointillist, surrealist, genre painter, landscapist, seascapist; engraver, designer, etcher; reëtcher, retoucher; cartoonist, caricaturist; copyist, draftsman.
3, sculptor, sculptress, carver, chaser, modelist.
4, author, writer, poet, dramatist, novelist; actor, actress, Thespian, performer, dancer, ballerina; musician, composer, arranger, orchestrator, soloist, pianist, *etc.*; architect, builder; photographer, cameraman, cinematographer; commercial artist, advertising artist, layout man.
Antonym, see UNSKILLFULNESS.

---

artistic, *adj.* talented, accomplished, cultural; beautiful, esthetic; skillful, masterly. See BEAUTY, TASTE.
artless, *adj.* simple; ingenuous, unsophisticated, naïve; guileless, innocent.
artlessness, *n.* SIMPLENESS, simplicity, naïveté, INNOCENCE, unsophistication; straightforwardness, bluntness. *Ant.*, see DECEPTION.

ASCENT

Nouns—ascent, ascension, ELEVATION, mounting, rising, rise, LEAP; upswing, upsurge; acclivity, hill; flight of steps *or* stairs, stairway, staircase; ladder, accommodation ladder, gangway, fire escape; elevator, lift, escalator. See OBLIQUITY.
Verbs—ascend, rise, mount; arise, uprise; spring *or* shoot up; aspire, climb, clamber, surmount; scale the heights; tower, soar, hover; LEAP.

Adjectives—rising, scandent, buoyant; in the ascendant.
Adverbs—up, uphill.

Antonym, see DESCENT.

---

ascertain, *v.t.* find, discover, make sure of, LEARN. See KNOWLEDGE.

ASCETICISM

Nouns—**1**, asceticism, puritanism, austerity; abstinence, abstemiousness; mortification, maceration, sackcloth and ashes, flagellation; penance, fasting. See ATONEMENT.
2, ascetic, anchoret, anchorite, hermit, RECLUSE; puritan, sabbatarian.
Adjectives—ascetic, austere, puritanical, anchoritic; abstinent, abstemious.

Antonym, see PLEASURE, GLUTTONY.

---

ascribe, *v.t.* refer, impute, accredit; assign.
ashamed, *adv.* abashed, mortified, embarrassed. See REGRET, MODESTY.
ashen, *adj.* pale, waxen, gray, bloodless, wan. See COLORLESSNESS.
ashore, *adv.* on land, on shore. See LAND.
aside, *adv. & n.* —*adv.* apart, aloof, away. See DISTANCE. —*n.* digression, parenthesis; byplay, (stage) whisper, INSERTION. See CONCEALMENT, DEVIATION.
asinine, *adj.* mulish, donkeyish; stupid, silly. See IGNORANCE, ABSURDITY.
ask, *v.* interrogate, question, inquire; REQUEST, demand; plead, beg, entreat, beseech, implore. See INQUIRY.
askew, *adj.* crooked, awry, lopsided, oblique. See DISTORTION. *Ant.*, straight.
asleep, *adj.* in bed, dozing, napping, sleeping; quiescent, dormant; numb, dead (see DEATH). *Colloq.*, dead to the world, out like a light. See REPOSE, INACTIVITY, INATTENTION.
aspect, *n.* look, APPEARANCE, side, view; expression, mien, bearing; phase, stage.
aspirant, *n.* candidate, seeker, entrant, applicant. See REQUEST.
aspire, *v.i.* seek, desire, aim, strive (for). See HOPE.
ass, *n.* donkey, jackass, burro; fool, simpleton. See CARRIER, FOOL.
assail, *v.t.* ATTACK, set upon, assault; criticize. See OPPOSITION.
assassin, *n.* killer, slayer, murderer, thug. See KILLING.
assault, *v. & n.* See ATTACK.

ASSEMBLAGE

Nouns—**1**, assemblage, assembly, gathering, forgathering, convocation, congregation, council, caucus, conclave, congress, convention, concourse, conflux, convergence; muster, levy, mobilization, posse, *posse comitatus*, roundup; caravan, convoy. See SOCIALITY.
2, compilation, collection, miscellany, store, compendium; symposium, panel; library, museum, menagerie; treasury, anthology.
3, crowd, throng; flood, rush, deluge; rabble, mob, press, crush, horde, body, tribe; crew, gang, knot, squad, band, party; swarm, shoal, school, covey, flock, herd, drove; array, bevy, galaxy; clique, coterie, faction, set, fraternity, sorority; corps, company, troop, army, host, MULTITUDE; clan, brotherhood, fellowship, association, PARTY.
4, volley, shower, storm cloud; group, cluster, clump, set, batch, lot, pack; budget, assortment, bunch, bundle, fascine, bale; shock, rick, fardel, stack, sheaf, haycock.
5, accumulation, congeries, heap, lump, pile, agglomeration, conglomeration, aggregation, concentration, congestion, quantity.
Verbs—**1**, be *or* come together, assemble, collect, muster; meet, unite, join, rejoin; cluster, flock, swarm, surge, stream, herd, crowd, throng,

associate; congregate, conglomerate, concentrate; rendezvous, resort, come, flock *or* get together; forgather, huddle.

2, get *or* bring together, assemble, muster, collect, collocate, call up, gather, convene, convoke, convocate; rake up, dredge; heap, mass, pile, pack, put up, cram; agglomerate, aggregate; compile; group, concentrate, unite, amass, accumulate; scare up.

Adjectives—assembled, closely packed, massed, dense, serried, crowded, teeming, swarming, populous; cumulative.

Antonym, see DISJUNCTION.

ASSENT

Nouns—**1,** assent, acquiescence, admission; nod; accord, accordance, concord, concordance; AGREEMENT, AFFIRMATION; recognition, acknowledgment, avowal; confession (of faith).

2, unanimity, common consent, acclamation, chorus; *vox populi*, public opinion; CONCURRENCE, COÖPERATION, consensus.

3, ratification, confirmation, corroboration, substantiation; approval, acceptance, indorsement, CONSENT; compliance, willingness.

4, alacrity, readiness, eagerness, DESIRE; docility, pliability.

Verbs—**1,** assent, nod, acquiesce, agree; receive, accept, accede, accord, concur, lend oneself to, CONSENT: coincide, reciprocate, go with, be at one with, go along (with), chime in, echo, be in tune with, recognize; subscribe (to), conform (to), defer to; say yes, ditto, amen *or* aye (to), O.K.

2, acknowledge, own, admit, allow, avow, confess, concede, come (a)round to, abide by; confirm, affirm; ratify, approve, indorse, O.K., countersign; corroborate.

3, come to an understanding, come to terms; swim with the stream; be in the fashion, join in the chorus; be in every mouth; catch on (become fashionable).

Adjectives—**1,** assenting; of one accord *or* mind; of the same mind, at one with; agreed, acquiescent, content, willing.

2, uncontradicted, unchallenged, unquestioned, uncontroverted; carried, agreed; unanimous, agreed on all hands, carried by acclamation, affirmative.

Adverbs—**1,** yes, yea, ay, aye; true, good, well, very well, well and good; granted; even so, just so, to be sure; truly, exactly, precisely, that's just it, indeed, certainly, of course, indubitably, unquestionably, surely, sure, assuredly, no doubt, doubtless, and no mistake!; be it so, so be it, amen; willingly. *Slang*, yes sirree, yes sirree Bob!, you said a mouthful, you said it!

2, affirmatively, in the affirmative; with one voice, with one accord, unanimously, by common consent, in chorus, to a man, without a dissentient voice; as one man, one and all, on all hands.

3, willingly, fain, freely; heart and soul; with pleasure, nothing loath, graciously, without reluctance, of one's own accord.

Antonym, see DISSENT.

assert, *v.t.* avow, declare, say, claim, affirm, state. See AFFIRMATION. *Ant.*, see NEGATION.

assess, *v.t.* value, price, appraise, estimate; charge, tax. See JUDGE.

assets, *n. pl.* possessions, PROPERTY, goods, capital. *Ant.*, see LIABILITY.

assign, *v.* give to, hand over; allot, distribute; delegate, commission. See APPORTIONMENT, GIVING.

assimilate, *v.t.* digest, absorb; incorporate, merge (with). See JUNCTION, CHANGE.

assist, *v.t.* AID, help, second, support.

associate, *v. & n.* —*v.* join, fraternize, ally, combine (with), unite, connect, relate, link. See JUNCTION, RELATION. —*n.* friend, comrade; colleague, co-worker, partner.

association, *n.* club, organization; fraternity; partnership, COMBINATION, league; SIMILARITY, analogy.

assort, *v.t.* arrange, classify; mix. See ARRANGEMENT.

assume, *v.t.* suppose, take for granted; put on, affect, appropriate. See SUPPOSITION, ACQUISITION.

assumed, *adj.* false, fictitious; pseudonymous, adopted; taken, given, granted. See DECEPTION, GIVING.

assurance, *n.* sureness, confidence, CERTAINTY; insolence, boldness; pledge, safety, guarantee, PROMISE, EXPECTATION.

assured, *adj.* confident, bold; guaranteed, certain, sure, settled. See CERTAINTY, VANITY. *Ant.,* timid; see FEAR.

assure, *v.t.* certify, make sure; insure, pledge, PROMISE. See CERTAINTY.

astern, *adv.* aft, to the rear, abaft. See REAR.

astir, *adv.* afoot; moving; up and about. See ACTIVITY.

astonish, *v.t.* surprise, amaze, astound. See WONDER.

astray, *adv.* lost, wandering; wrong, amiss, in error. See DOUBT.

astringent, *adj.* sour, tart; binding, styptic. See CONTRACTION.

astrology, *n.* stargazing, soothsaying, forecasting. See PREDICTION.

ASTRONAUTICS

Nouns—**1,** astronautics, space travel; space *or* celestial navigation, astrogation, astronavigation; outer- *or* interplanetary space; aerospace. See SPACE, AVIATION.

2, rocket, space ship; space station; [communication, weather, observation, *etc.*] satellite; probe; [ascent *or* descent] stage, drop-off, capsule; free fall, weightlessness; docking; injection *or* insertion [into orbit]; launch site, Cape Canaveral; escape velocity, launch window, reentry corridor; countdown, [number for] go; launch]; payload.

3, astronaut, cosmonaut, spaceman.

Verbs—launch; inject *or* insert into orbit. *Colloq.,* blast off.

astronomy, *n.* cosmology, cosmogony, astrochemistry, astrophysics. See UNIVERSE.

astute, *adj.* clever, shrewd, quick, acute. See INTELLIGENCE. *Ant.,* STUPID.

asylum, *n.* retreat, REFUGE, sanctuary, shelter; home, orphanage, sanitarium, sanatorium; mental hospital, psychopathic ward.

asymmetric, asymmetrical, *adj.* uneven, irregular; formless. See DISTORTION, FORMLESSNESS. *Ant.,* regular, symmetrical.

atheist, *n.* heretic, unbeliever. See IRRELIGION. *Ant.,* see BELIEF.

athletic, *adj.* sporting, gymnastic, acrobatic; agile, powerful, strong. See STRENGTH, AMUSEMENT.

atmosphere, *n.* AIR, sky, ether, ozone; mood, aura, ambience, FEELING, ENVIRONMENT.

atom, *n.* particle, iota, speck. See LITTLENESS, POWER.

atomize, *v.t.* spray, vaporize, pulverize. See VAPOR.

ATONEMENT

Nouns—**1,** atonement, reparation; COMPENSATION, quittance, quits; expiation, redemption, reclamation, conciliation, propitiation. See PENITENCE.

2, amends, apology, *amende honorable,* satisfaction, COMPENSATION; peace offering, burnt offering; scapegoat, sacrifice, sacrificial lamb.

3, penance, fasting, maceration, sackcloth and ashes, white sheet, shrift, flagellation, lustration; purgation, purgatory.

Verbs—**1,** atone (for); expiate; propitiate; make amends, pay for, make good; reclaim, redeem, redress, repair; ransom, absolve, purge, shrive; do penance, repent (in sackcloth and ashes); set one's house in order; wipe off old scores; make matters up; pay the penalty; recant. *Colloq.,* take back, eat one's words, eat humble pie, eat crow.

2, apologize, beg pardon, ask forgiveness, give satisfaction; fall on one's knees.

Adjectives—propitiatory, conciliatory, expiatory; sacrificial, piacular; apologetic.

Antonyms, see RESOLUTION, IMPIETY.

---

atrocity, *n.* outrage, enormity, brutality; barbarism. See MALEVOLENCE.
attach, *v.t.* connect, fasten; join, add on, affix. See ADDITION, JUNCTION.
attachment, *n.* ADDITION, ADJUNCT, appendage; legal seizure (see LAWSUIT); affection; LOVE, loyalty, devotion.

ATTACK

Nouns—**1,** attack; assault (and battery); onset, onslaught, charge; aggression, offense; WARFARE; incursion, inroad, invasion; irruption, outbreak; sally, sortie, raid, foray; boarding, *escalade;* siege, investment, besiegement, beleaguerment; storming, bombing, air attack, air raid, blitz, blitzkrieg, bombardment, cannonade.
2, fire, volley, fusillade, broadside; raking, crossfire; cut, thrust, lunge, pass; kick, punch; devastation, DESTRUCTION. See IMPULSE.
3, assailant, aggressor, offender, invader; pusher, go-getter.

Verbs—**1,** attack, assault, assail; set *or* fall upon; make *or* go to war (on *or* against); charge, impugn; break a lance with, enter the lists; aggress; assume *or* take the offensive; strike the first blow; throw the first stone; lift a hand *or* draw the sword (against); take up the cudgels; march (against); march upon, invade, harry; show fight.
2, strike (at), thrust at, hit, kick, slap, cut, shy (a stone), pelt; deal a blow (at); fetch one a blow, fling oneself at *or* upon, lunge at, pounce upon; lace into, light into, tear into, pitch into, launch out against; bait, slap on the face; make a pass at; bear down upon; close with, come to grips with, come to close quarters, bring to bay; ride full tilt against; let fly at, rush at, run at, fly at, have at; attack tooth and nail; press one hard; run down, strike at the root of; lay about one, run amuck. *Slang,* lay into; gang up on. See PUNISHMENT, IMPULSE.
3, fire at, shoot at; open fire, pepper, bombard, shell, pour a broadside into, fire a volley; beset, besiege, beleaguer; lay siege to, invest; sap, mine; storm, board, scale the walls; cut and thrust, bayonet, butt, batter; bomb, strafe, dive-bomb, blitz.

Adjectives—attacking; aggressive, offensive; up in arms, on the warpath; forceful, belligerent, combative, warlike; competitive, pushing.

Adverb—on the offensive.

Antonym, see DEFENSE.

---

attain, *v.t.* win, gain, achieve; reach, succeed. See ARRIVAL, SUCCESS.
attempt, *n.* trial, effort, try, endeavor, ESSAY.
attend, *v.* accompany, escort; be present; heed, listen. See ACCOMPANIMENT, ATTENTION, PRESENCE.

ATTENTION

Nouns—**1,** attention, mindfulness, intentness, intentiveness, THOUGHT, thoughtfulness, advertence; observance, observation, consideration, reflection, heed, notice, note, regard; circumspection, study, scrutiny, inspection.
2, diligence, application, minuteness, attention to detail, absorption (of mind), preoccupation (with).
3, indication, calling *or* drawing attention to.

Verbs—**1,** attend (to), observe, look, see, view, remark, notice, regard, take notice, mark; give *or* pay attention, heed, be attentive, listen, hear, lend an ear to; trouble one's head about; give a thought to; occupy oneself with; contemplate; look into; see to; turn the mind to, apply oneself to, have an eye to; bear in mind, take into account *or* consideration; keep in sight *or* view; have regard to; take cognizance of, entertain, recognize; make *or* take note of; note.

2, glance at *or* over; cast the eye over; run over, dip into, scan, skim (through), examine cursorily. *Slang*, give the once-over.

3, examine closely *or* intently; scan, scrutinize, consider; pore over, inspect, review, take stock of; fix, rivet *or* devote the mind *or* thoughts on *or* to; go over with a fine-toothed comb.

4, watch, hearken, listen (to); prick up the ears; keep the eyes open *or* peeled; be all ears, hang on one's words; have an ear to the ground.

5, catch *or* strike the eye; attract attention *or* notice; awaken *or* invite interest; be arresting *or* absorbing; intrigue; be uppermost in one's mind.

6, indicate; bring under one's notice; point out; lay the finger on, direct, call *or* draw attention to; show.

Adjectives—**1**, attentive, mindful, observant, regardful; alive *or* awake to; observing; occupied with; engrossed, wrapped up in; absorbed, rapt; breathless; intent on, open-eyed, on the watch.

2, absorbing, engrossing, eye-catching.

Interjections—see! look! mark! lo! behold! hark! mind! observe! lo and behold! attention! *nota bene;* N.B.; this is to give notice.

Antonym, see NEGLECT.

---

attenuate, *v.* weaken; thin out, rarefy. See DECREASE, NARROWNESS.

attest, *v.* testify, bear witness, depose, certify, swear, vouch. See EVIDENCE, INDICATION, SUPPORT.

attic, *n.* upper room, loft, garret. See RECEPTACLE, HEIGHT.

attire, *n.* dress, CLOTHING, garb, array.

attitude, *n.* stand, pose, posture, position. See LOCATION.

attorney, *n.* LAWYER, solicitor, advocate, barrister, AGENT.

attract, *v.* allure, interest, CHARM, captivate, fascinate; draw (see ATTRACTION). See DESIRE, ATTRACTIVE.

ATTRACTION

Nouns—attraction, attractiveness; drawing to, pulling towards, adduction, magnetism, gravity, gravitation; lodestone, lodestar; magnet, siderite.

Verbs—attract; draw *or* pull towards; adduce.

Adjectives—attracting, attrahent, attractive, adducent, adductive; magnetic.

Antonym, see REFUSAL.

---

attractive, *adj.* charming, alluring; engaging, interesting, winning, prepossessing; captivating, fascinating; seductive. *Colloq.*, cute.

ATTRIBUTION

Nouns—**1**, attribution, ascription, assignment, reference to; accounting for; imputation, derivation from, credit; explanation, reason, CAUSE, motive; etiology; INTERPRETATION. See ANCESTRY.

2, attribute, trait, characteristic, quality, property; adjunct, symbol.

Verbs—attribute, ascribe, assign, impute; refer, lay, point *or* trace to; set down to; charge with *or* to; credit with *or* to; blame on *or* to; ground on; lay at the door of; account for, derive from, read into; fix responsibility *or* blame.

Adjectives—attributed, attributable, referable, assignable, ascribable; due to, derivable from, owing to. See EFFECT.

Adverbs—**1**, hence, thence, therefore, for, since, on account of, because, owing to; on that account; thanks to, forasmuch as; whence, *propter hoc.*

2, why? wherefore? whence? *Colloq.*, how come?

attrition, *n.* See PENITENCE, DETERIORATION.

auction, *n.* bidding, vendue, SALE: offering, offer.

audacity, *n.* boldness, COURAGE, nerve, temerity, daring, brass, gall; impudence; confidence, RASHNESS, insolence.

audience, *n.* hearing, interview; onlookers, hearers; assembly. See DRAMA, SPEECH.

auditorium, *n.* hall, meeting place; theater. See DRAMA, ARENA.

augment, *v.* See INCREASE.

augur, *v.* foretell, prophesy, predict, signify, presage. See PREDICTION.

august, *adj.* grand, noble, exalted, majestic, venerable. See GREATNESS.

auspice, *n.* omen, token; (*pl.*) patronage, protection, protectorship. See PREDICTION, AID.

auspicious, *adj.* favorable, promising, propitious; fortunate. See HOPE, PREDICTION, PROSPERITY. *Ant.,* UNFORTUNATE, UNTIMELY.

austere, *adj.* harsh, stern, severe, rigorous; ascetic, abstemious. See SEVERITY, ASCETICISM. *Ant.,* LUXURIOUS.

authentic, *adj.* genuine, real, authoritative, trustworthy. See TRUTH, CERTAINTY. *Ant.,* sham, false; see FALSEHOOD.

authentication, *n.* verification, confirmation. See SECURITY.

author, *n.* creator, originator; writer, inventor. See BOOK, WRITING, PRODUCTION.

authoritative, *adj.* official, decisive; imperative, peremptory; truthful, reliable; scholarly. See AUTHORITY, CERTAINTY.

AUTHORITY

Nouns—**1,** authority, power, right, jurisdiction, title, prerogative; influence, prestige, patronage; command, control, rule, sway; dominion, sovereignty, empire, supremacy; suzerainty, seigniory; the crown, the sovereign; the state, realm, administration, people, body politic, polity; divine right, dynasticism, dynasty, régime.

2, government, administration; autocracy, aristocracy, oligarchy, hierarchy, theocracy, patriarchy, plutocracy, democracy; monarchy, absolute monarchy, kingdom, chiefdom; caliphate, pashalik; proconsulship, consulship; prefecture, magistracy; directory, triumvirate, *etc.;* absolutism, despotism, tyranny, imperialism, czarism, dictatorship, authoritarianism, Fascism, Nazism, monolithic government, *Führer prinzip,* boss rule; communism, Marxism, socialism, syndicalism, collectivism, People's Republic; anarchism, nihilism; bureaucracy, red tape, officialdom; feudalism, feodality; gynarchy, gynocracy, matriarchy, petticoat government; autonomy, home rule, representative government; constitutional government, constitutional *or* limited monarchy. *Colloq.,* brass, the man.

3, mastery, hold, grasp, grip; octopus, fangs, clutches, talons; rod of empire, scepter.

4, usurpation, assumption *or* arrogation of authority.

5, sovereign, ruler, emperor, empress, king, queen, prince, princess; czar, tsar, Kaiser; boss, dictator, Duce, Führer, despot, tyrant, Pharaoh, judge, autocrat; president, chairman, the chair, premier, prime *or* first minister; potentate, chief, caliph, sultan, pasha, emir, sheik; master, captain, skipper, commanding officer, person in authority.

6, accession, succession, installation, coronation.

7, MASTER, lord, *padrone;* superior, director, head, leader, foreman; mayor, *major domo,* prefect, chancellor, provost, magistrate, alcalde, burgomaster, seneschal, warden. *Slang,* top banana, top dog, honcho.

Verbs—**1,** have *or* wield authority; head, lead, command; dominate, control, boss; dictate, dispose, command, rule, govern, administer; preside; wear the crown, ascend the throne; have the upper *or* whip hand; rule the roost; lord it over, bend to one's will, give the law to, lay down the law; have under one's thumb, hold in the hollow of one's hand.

2, be under, subject to, *or* in the power of.
Adjectives—**1,** ruling, regnant, at the head, dominant, paramount, supreme, predominant, preponderant, in the ascendant, influential; gubernatorial; imperious; authoritative, executive, administrative, clothed with authority, official, *ex officio;* imperative, peremptory, overruling, absolute; arbitrary.
2, regal, sovereign, royal, monarchical, kingly, imperial, princely.
3, at one's command; in one's power; under control.
Adverbs—at one's pleasure; by a stroke of the pen; *ex cathedra;* with a high hand.

Antonym, see SUBJECTION, OBEDIENCE.

---

authorization, *n.* authority, sanction, warrant; PERMISSION. *Colloq.*, O.K.
autocrat, *n.* dictator, czar, despot, monarch. See AUTHORITY.
autograph, *n.* signature. See WRITING, EVIDENCE.
automatic, *adj.* mechanical; self-operating; instinctive. See NECESSITY.
automobile, *adj. & n.* —*adj.* self-propelling. See POWER. —*n.* car, VEHICLE.
autonomy, *n.* independence; self-government. See FREEDOM.
autopsy, *n.* post-mortem, examination (of cadaver). See INTERMENT.
autumn, *n.* fall, harvest time. See TIME.

AUXILIARY

Nouns—auxiliary, assistant; adjuvant, adjutant, ADJUNCT, help, helper, helpmate, helpmeet, helping hand; colleague, partner, mate, confrère; coöperator, coadjutor, collaborator; ally, friend, confidant, *fidus Achates*, pal, alter ego; confederate; accomplice, accessory, *particeps criminis;* aid, aide, aide-de-camp; secretary, amanuensis, clerk, associate, right hand, man Friday; handmaid, servant; puppet, cat's-paw, tool, Trilby, satellite, adherent; disciple, devotee, votary; seconder, backer, upholder, abettor, advocate, partisan, champion, patron, friend at court; friend in need, guardian angel.
Verbs—help, AID, assist, second.
Adjectives—helping, helpful, accessory; subsidiary, subservient; supplementary, reserve, extra.

Antonym, see HINDRANCE, OPPOSITION.

---

avail, *v.* serve, do, suffice; help, benefit; use. See SUCCESS, UTILITY.
available, *adj.* handy, ready, convenient; usable. *Colloq.*, on tap. See PREPARATION, UTILITY. *Ant.,* unavailable; see ABSENCE.
avalanche, *n.* landslide, snowslide; overwhelming victory. See DESCENT, SUCCESS.
avenge, *n.* retaliate, REVENGE.
avenue, *n.* thoroughfare, boulevard, artery; MEANS, access. See PASSAGE.
average, *n. & adj.* —*n.* normal, mean, rule, standard. —*adj.* mean, normal, ordinary, passable, fair. See MIDDLE, UNIMPORTANCE.
averse, *adj.* loath, reluctant, against, opposed, unwilling. See OPPOSITION, DISAPPROBATION. *Ant.,* willing.
avert, *v.t.* keep off, turn aside, ward off; turn away; prevent. See HINDRANCE.

AVIATION

Nouns—**1,** aviation, flight, flying; avigation, aerial navigation; aeronautics, aerodynamics, aerostatics; air power, air transportation, airline (scheduled *and* nonscheduled), air coach; airways, airport, airfield, airdrome, landing field, flying field, runway, control tower, windsock; ballooning, balloonery; skydiving, soaring; gliding.
2, air warfare; Air Force, RAF, Luftwaffe; formation flying, echelon;

bombing, dive-bombing, pursuit, dogfight; group, wing, flight, squadron.
3, aircraft, heavier-than-air, lighter-than-air; balloon, captive balloon, observation balloon, barrage balloon; airship, dirigible, Zeppelin, blimp; airplane, aeroplane, plane, monoplane, biplane, wedgewing, seaplane, amphibian, hydroplane, flying boat; airliner, transport, pursuit plane, interceptor, fighter, bomber; jet plane, turbojet, propjet, JATO; Caravelle, Concorde; autogiro, helicopter, whirlybird, Sikorsky; kite, boxkite; glider, crate, box, ship, jenny; parachute; airbus.
4, fuselage, tail, rudder, fin, stabilizer; cockpit, gondola, nacelle; propeller, prop; reciprocating engine, radial engine, jet engine, rocket; airfoil, wing, aileron, elevator; stick, Joyce *or* joy stick; landing gear, pontoon, altimeter, artificial horizon, artificial pilot, tachometer, airspeed indicator, rate-of-climb indicator, turn and bank indicator, inclinometer; bomb bay.
5, takeoff, landing, three-point landing, pancake; zoom, loop, loop-the loop, soar, climb, glide; Immelmann turn, barrel roll; dive, nose dive, spiral, spin, tailspin; buzz, hedgehopping; thrust, lift, drag; airstream, slipstream, backwash, sideslip, drift; flying circus, barnstorming, stunt flying; skywriting; point of no return; visibility, ceiling, ceiling zero; air pocket, headwind, tailwind.
6, aviator, aeronaut, airman, balloonist, pilot, co-pilot, navigator, bombardier; Daedalus, Icarus, Darius Green; air marshal, flying officer; airborne troops, paratroops.
7, space travel; see ASTRONAUTICS.
Verbs—fly, aviate, pilot, go by air; zoom, climb, stall, yaw, pitch, roll, bank, dive, glide, taxi, take off, land; stunt, buzz, hedgehop; strafe, divebomb; crash, crack up, prang, conk out, bail out. *Slang,* skyjack.
Adjectives—aeronautic; airworthy; air-minded; airsick; airborne.

avidity, *n.* eagerness, longing; avarice, greed, DESIRE.
avocation, *n.* hobby. See AMUSEMENT, BUSINESS.

AVOIDANCE

Nouns—**1,** avoidance, evasion, elusion; abstention, abstinence, forbearance, refraining, INACTIVITY; neutrality, nonbelligerency; retreat, REGRESSION, DEPARTURE, ESCAPE; truancy, hooky, French leave (see ABSENCE); subterfuge, quibble, equivocation; circuit, DEVIATION. *Colloq.,* sidestep, dodge. *Slang,* the slip, the go-by, the runaround, the brush-off.
2, shirker, slacker, malingerer, deserter, absentee, dodger, quitter; truant, fugitive, runaway, absconder, refugee; abstainer, teetotaler, nonparticipant. *Slang,* welsher, goldbrick.
Verbs—**1,** avoid, shun, eschew, refrain (from), not do, let alone, steer clear of, fight shy of; abstain, keep aloof, keep one's distance; evade, elude, dodge; give a wide berth to, set one's face against; shy away from; make way for, give place to; take no part in, have no hand in. *Colloq.,* give the runaround. *Slang,* lay off.
2, decamp, fly, bolt, elope, abscond; depart, go away; show *or* take to one's heels, beat a retreat, make oneself scarce, run for it, cut and run, steal away, slip off, take off; walk out on, go back on. *Colloq.,* shake off. *Slang,* skedaddle, shove off, skiddoo, take it on the lam, vamoose.

Antonym, see PURSUIT.

avowal, *n.* declaration, admission, confession; assertion, AFFIRMATION. See DISCLOSURE.
await, *v.* expect, wait for, anticipate, look forward to; impend, approach. See EXPECTATION, FUTURITY, LATENESS.
awake, *adj.* alert, heedful, observant, attentive. See ATTENTION.

award, *n.* prize, medal; compensation; decision, adjudication. See GIVING, JUDGMENT.

aware, *adj.* knowing, cognizant, informed; alert (to). See KNOWLEDGE.

away, *adv.* absent, elsewhere, far-off, gone. See DISTANCE.

awe, *n.* reverence, respect; FEAR, dread.

awkward, *adj.* clumsy, ungraceful, ungainly; gauche; embarrassing. See UNSKILLFULNESS.

awry, *adj.* askance, crooked, askew; out of order, dislocated; mistaken, amiss, wrong. *Slang,* cockeyed, screwy. See OBLIQUITY, DISORDER, ERROR.

ax, axe, *n.* chopper, hatchet. See ARMS, SHARPNESS. *Slang,* instrument.

axiom, *n.* rule, proposition; aphorism, maxim, truism. See TEACHING.

axis, *n.* shaft, pivot; combination, league. See ROTATION.

axle, *n.* axis, spindle, pivot. See MIDDLE.

azure, *adj.* BLUE, sky-blue, cerulean. See COLOR.

B

babble, *v.i.* chatter, prattle, gossip; rave, gibber; gurgle. See LOQUACITY, ABSURDITY.

baby, *n.* INFANT, babe, child, tot; nursling, suckling; offspring. *Colloq.,* kid. *Ant.,* VETERAN.

bachelor, *n.* unmarried man, Coelebs, celibate. See CELIBACY. *Ant.,* see MARRIAGE.

back, *n. & v.* —*n.* REAR; behind, posterior, reverse; stern, aft; derrière. *Ant.,* FRONT. —*v.t.* SUPPORT, AID, assist; promote, finance; stand behind, encourage. —*v.i.* move backward, reverse. *Ant.,* see HINDRANCE.

backbone, *n.* spine, spinal column; COURAGE, determination, fortitude, pluck. *Colloq.,* grit, guts. *Ant.,* see COWARDICE.

backfire, *v.i.* boomerang, go awry, return to haunt one. See FAILURE, RECOIL.

background, *n.* setting, surroundings; experience, training; family, ancestors; social position. See ANCESTRY, ENVIRONMENT.

backsliding, *n.* REVERSION, recidivism, lapse; heterodoxy, apostasy; REGRESSION, RELAPSE.

backward, *adj.* retarded, slow, underdeveloped; delayed, tardy; unwilling, loath. See DULL, REAR.

badge, *n.* emblem, identification, label, sign. See INDICATION.

BADNESS

Nouns—**1,** badness, hurtfulness, virulence, perniciousness, malignancy, malignity; ill-treatment, annoyance, molestation, abuse, oppression, persecution, outrage, tyranny; atrocity, torture, brutality, cruelty; injury, damage; ill turn, bad turn; peccancy, abomination; painfulness, pestilence, DISEASE; guilt, depravity, vice, IMPURITY, wickedness. See MALEVOLENCE.

2, bane, plague-spot, insalubrity; evil star, ill wind; skeleton in the closet, thorn in the side, thorn in the flesh.

3, bad influence, evil genius; imprecation, malediction, anathema. *Colloq.,* hoodoo. *Slang,* Jonah, jinx. See EVIL, EVILDOER.

4, imperfection, defectiveness, poorness, inferiority, mediocrity, indifference, ERROR, wrong.

5, IMPROBITY, knavery, immorality, turpitude, depravity, corruption; debasement, degradation, pollution; profligacy; atrocity.

Verbs—**1,** hurt, harm, injure, PAIN, wound; maltreat, abuse, ill-treat; molest; buffet, bruise, scratch, maul; smite, SCOURGE, crucify, break on the wheel *or* rack; do violence, do harm, do a mischief (to); stab, pierce, outrage, violate. *Colloq.*, kick around.

2, wrong, aggrieve, oppress, persecute; trample upon, tread upon, put upon; overburden, weigh down, victimize.

3, be vicious, sin, err, transgress, go astray; misdo, misbehave; fall, lapse, slip; trespass, deviate, sow one's wild oats. *Colloq.*, cut up, hack off *or* around.

Adjectives—**1,** bad, ill, untoward, arrant, as bad as can be, dreadful; horrid, horrible; dire; rank, peccant, foul, fulsome; rotten, rotten at the core, decayed, decomposed, putrid, tainted. *Slang*, cheesy, punk, lousy.

2, hurtful, harmful, baneful, baleful; injurious, deleterious, UNHEALTHY, detrimental, pernicious, mischievous, full of mischief, mischief-making, malefic, malignant, noxious, nocuous, noisome; prejudicial; disserviceable, disadvantageous; unlucky, sinister; obnoxious; disastrous; inauspicious; oppressive, burdensome, onerous; malign, MALEVOLENT; corrupt, virulent, venomous, envenomed, corrosive; poisonous, toxic, septic, deadly, KILLING, pestilent; destructive.

3, mean, paltry, injured, deteriorated, unsatisfactory, exceptionable, indifferent; below par, INFERIOR, imperfect; ill-contrived, ill-conditioned; wretched, pathetic, sad, grievous, deplorable, lamentable; pitiable; woeful, painful, unfortunate.

4, evil, wrong; depraved, vile, base, villainous; shocking, flagrant, scandalous, nefarious; reprehensible, wicked, sinful; hateful; abominable, repugnant, abhorrent, revolting, repulsive, repellent, disgusting, odious, detestable, execrable, cursed, accursed, confounded; damned, damnable; infernal, diabolic, malevolent, devilish; vicious. *Colloq.*, beastly, ungodly.

Adverbs—badly, amiss, awry, wrong, ill; to one's cost; where the shoe pinches.

Antonym, see GOODNESS.

---

badger, *v.t.* nag, pester, tease, torment. See PAIN.

baffle, *v.* foil, frustrate, balk, block; puzzle, nonplus, bewilder. See HINDRANCE.

bag, *n. & v.* —*n.* RECEPTACLE, case, container, pouch, sack. —*v.* trap, capture, take, catch; sag, droop, hang; bulge, protrude, swell. See TAKING.

baggage, *n.* luggage, impedimenta; trunks, suitcases, valises. See PROPERTY.

bail, *n.* SECURITY, bond, pledge; guarantee, surety.

bailiff, *n.* constable, beagle, bailie; sheriff, marshal, officer. See SAFETY.

bait, *n. & v.* —*n.* lure, temptation. —*v.t.* decoy, lure, tempt; plague, worry, badger, ruffle. See ATTRACTION, PAIN.

bake, *v.* roast, cook; harden, dry; fire. See HARDNESS, HEAT.

balance, *n. & v.* —*n.* equilibrium, steadiness, stability; surplus, excess, rest, remainder; scales. See EQUALITY. —*v.* offset, even, square; equalize, level, adjust; equal, match. See NUMBER, RELATION.

balcony, *n.* gallery, loggia, porch, portico; tier, loge, mezzanine, dress circle. *Slang*, peanut gallery, paradise. See DRAMA, SUPPORT.

bald, *adj.* bare, unadorned; hairless; treeless; undisguised. See DIVESTMENT.

baleful, *adj.* hostile; malignant; hurtful, injurious. See BADNESS.

balk, *v.* rebel; stop, shy; disappoint, hinder, thwart, foil, frustrate. See HINDRANCE, FAILURE.

ball, *n.* dance, reception, party; shot, projectile; sphere, globe. See AMUSEMENT, ARMS, CIRCULARITY.

ballad, *n.* song; poem, folklore; chantey, spiritual; calypso; balladry. See MUSIC.

balloon, *n.* airship, aerostat, dirigible; free, sounding, kite, pilot *or* dirigible balloon; fire balloon, montgolfier. *Colloq.,* blimp. See AVIATION.

ballot, *n. & v.* —*n.* vote, CHOICE, poll; franchise, VOICE. —*v.* poll, vote.

balm, *n.* ointment, salve, analgesic; sedative, anodyne. See MODERATION, REMEDY.

ban, *n.* PROHIBITION, restriction, proscription, interdict. See RESTRAINT.

banal, *adj.* mediocre, common; trivial, TRITE. See WEARINESS, MEDIOCRITY.

band, *n.* strip, tape; belt, strap; FILAMENT; group, crowd; orchestra, brass band, military band. See ASSEMBLAGE, MUSICAL INSTRUMENTS, COLOR.

bandage, *n.* tourniquet, dressing; Band-Aid. See REMEDY.

bandit, *n.* THIEF, robber, highwayman; brigand; outlaw.

bane, *n.* curse, mischief; thorn in the side, scourge, PAIN, nuisance, pest; harm, injury, DESTRUCTION; trouble; bale; poison, venom. See PUNISHMENT, EVIL, MALEVOLENCE. *Ant.,* see REMEDY, BENEVOLENCE, GOODNESS.

bang, *n. & v.* —*n.* IMPULSE, snap, clap, crash. —*v.* beat, slam, pound, batter.

banish, *v.t.* exile, dismiss, expel. See EJECTION, PUNISHMENT. *Ant.,* repatriate; see RECEIVING.

bank, *n. & v.* —*n.* slope, hillside; mound, heap, ridge; beach, shore. See OBLIQUITY, LAND. —*v.* tilt, angle, slope. See ANGULARITY, AVIATION.

bankrupt, *adj. & v.* —*adj.* insolvent, ruined; indigent, penniless, destitute. *Slang,* broke. —*v.* impoverish; pauperize. See DEBT, FAILURE, POVERTY. *Ant.,* see MONEY, SUCCESS.

banner, *n.* flag, pennant; symbol, badge. See INDICATION.

banter, *n.* jest, chaff, badinage. *Colloq.,* kid. See WIT.

baptize, *v.* sprinkle, immerse, dip; name, christen; cleanse. *Colloq.,* dunk. See NOMENCLATURE, RITE.

banquet, *n.* feast, regale, junket. *Colloq.,* big feed. *Slang,* shindig. See FOOD, AMUSEMENT.

bar, *n. & v.* —*n.* barrier, obstacle; hurdle; legal profession, court, bench; rod, bolt, rail. See PRISON, LAWYER, LAWSUIT. —*v.* forbid; restrict, reject; lock, bolt, fasten. See RESTRAINT. *Ant.,* see PERMISSION.

barbarian, *n.* foreigner, outsider, alien, savage, ruffian; EVILDOER.

barbarism, *n.* solecism; savagery, brutality, inhumanity, violence; ignorance, rudeness, vulgarity. See DISCOURTESY, MALEVOLENCE. *Ant.,* see COURTESY.

barbecue, *n.* cookout; rotisserie, spit. See FOOD.

bare, *adj.* unclothed, nude; uncovered; empty, unfurnished; mere, simple. See DIVESTMENT, INSUFFICIENCY. *Ant.,* see CLOTHING, SUFFICIENCY.

barefaced, *adj.* brazen, shameless, impudent. See MANIFESTATION.

bargain, *n. & v.* —*n.* deal, agreement, transaction; inexpensiveness. See CHEAPNESS, AGREEMENT. *Ant.,* see DEARNESS. —*v.* contract, negotiate, haggle, BARTER.

barge, *n.* boat, scow, freighter. See SHIP.

barge in, *colloq.,* burst in, crash, bust in. See INGRESS, HINDRANCE.

bark, *n. & v.* —*n.* COVERING, rind, skin, shell; yelp, yap, bay. —*v.* howl, yelp. See CRY.

barrage, *n.* ATTACK, bombardment. *Ant.,* see DEFENSE.

barrel, *n.* keg, tun, cask, vat; cylinder. See RECEPTACLE.

barren, *adj.* unfertile, unprofitable; sterile; stark, bare; UNPRODUCTIVE.

barricade, *n.* blockade, stockade; fence, barrier. See DEFENSE, INCLOSURE.

barrier, *n.* obstacle, impediment, HINDRANCE. See INCLOSURE, PRISON.

BARTER

Nouns—**1,** barter, exchange, truck, INTERCHANGE; marketing; trade, commerce, buying and selling; traffic, business, custom, shopping; commercial enterprise, speculation, jobbing, stock-jobbing, brokerage, stockbroking, agiotage; reciprocation; trading, dealing, transaction, negotiation; free trade. *Colloq.*, swap, pig in a poke, black market. See SALE.

2, dealer, trader, MERCHANT, businessman, AGENT.

Verbs—**1,** barter, exchange, truck; INTERCHANGE; trade, traffic, buy and sell, give and take, carry on, ply *or* drive a trade; be in business, be in the city; keep a shop, deal in, employ one's capital in. *Colloq.*, swap.

2, speculate, give a sprat to catch a herring; buy in the cheapest and sell in the dearest market; rig the market.

3, trade, deal *or* have dealings with; transact *or* do business with, open *or* keep an account with; patronize; bargain; drive *or* make a bargain; negotiate, bid for; haggle, dicker, cheapen, beat down; outbid, underbid; ask, charge; strike a bargain; contract, compact. See AGREEMENT.

Adjectives—commercial, mercantile, trading; interchangeable, marketable, staple, in the market, for sale; wholesale, retail.

Adverbs—across the counter; in *or* on the market.

---

base, *n. & v.* —*n.* basis, foundation, groundwork, SUPPORT; basement, substructure; ground; root; footing, floor; pavement; bottom; bedrock. —*v.* found, establish; predicate; ground, rest upon, build upon. *Ant.*, see HEIGHT.

base, *adj.* debased, impure; counterfeit, spurious; low, vile, despicable. See DISREPUTE, IMPURITY. *Ant.*, see REPUTE, VIRTUE.

basement, *n.* CELLAR, vault; see LOWNESS. *Ant.*, see HEIGHT.

bashful, *adj.* shy, diffident, self-effacing, timid. See MODESTY. *Ant.*, see VANITY.

basic, *adj.* fundamental, essential; alkaline. See INTRINSIC, IMPORTANCE.

basin, *n.* bowl, vessel, sink; hollow, valley. See CONCAVITY, RECEPTACLE. *Ant.*, see CONVEXITY.

basis, *n.* base, groundwork, foundation. See SUPPORT. *Ant.*, see HEIGHT.

bask, *v.i.* luxuriate, revel, [take] delight *or* PLEASURE in; prosper, flourish; sunbathe, sun. See PROSPERITY, HEAT.

basket, *n.* hamper, crate, pannier. See RECEPTACLE.

bass, *adj.* low, deep-toned, deep. See SOUND.

bastard, *n. & adj.* —*n.* illegitimate [child], love child, foundling, bantling; sham, counterfeit, fraud. See POSTERITY, FALSENESS. —*adj.* illegitimate, natural, misgotten; false, spurious; mongrel, hybrid. See MIXTURE, FALSENESS.

bat, *n.* cudgel, club, stick, nightstick; brickbat. See ARMS.

batch, *n.* baking; set, series, run, lot, QUANTITY.

bath, *n.* washing, wash; dip, plunge; shower, Turkish bath, sauna, whirlpool. See CLEANNESS, WATER.

batter, *v.* smash, dent, destroy; beat, bruise. See DESTRUCTION, IMPULSE. *Ant.*, see SAFETY.

battery, *n.* assault, ATTACK; guns, artillery; array, ASSEMBLAGE; Leyden jar, voltaic cell, accumulator, [wet *or* dry] cell, solar *or* storage battery. See ENERGY, VIOLENCE, ARMS.

battle, *n.* fight, struggle, engagement, combat; contest. See WARFARE.

battleship, *n.* man of war, SHIP of the line, dreadnought, battle wagon.

bawdy, *adj.* coarse, ribald, gross, broad. See IMPURITY.

bawl, *v.*, *colloq.*, yell, bellow; CRY, sob. See LOUDNESS.

bay, *n.* estuary, bayou, fiord, sound. See WATER.

be, *v.* exist, breathe; occur, take place. See EXISTENCE. *Ant.*, see NON-EXISTENCE.

beach, *n. & v.* —*n.* shore, coast(line); strand, sands, shingle. —*v.*

ground, run aground *or* ashore, strand. *Colloq.*, hit the beach. See
NAVIGATION, LAND.

beacon, *n.* lighthouse, lightship, watchtower; beam; signal fire; signal,
guide, WARNING. See INDICATION, LIGHT.

beak, *n.* nose, bill, neb. *Slang,* magistrate. See CONVEXITY.

beam, *v. & n.* —*v.* shine, glow. —*n.* ray, gleam; joist, timber. See
LIGHT, MATERIALS, SUPPORT.

bear, *v.* endure, tolerate; suffer; render, yield, hold, sustain; carry, transport, convey. See FEELING, PRODUCTION, SUPPORT.

bearded, *adj.* hairy, whiskered, awned, hirsute. See ROUGHNESS.

beardless, *adj.* (clean-)shaven, hairless, smoothfaced; youthful. See
DIVESTMENT.

bearing, *n.* course, trend; carriage, manner; MEANING, significance, import; RELATION, connection, association. See DIRECTION, FRONT, PRES-
ENCE.

beast, *n.* brute, quadruped; horse; blackguard. See ANIMAL, CARRIER,
DISCOURTESY.

beat, *n. & v.* —*n.* accent, rhythm; pulse; track, course. See POETRY,
REGULARITY, WAY. —*v.* throb, pulsate; strike, batter, bruise; conquer,
defeat. See OSCILLATION, IMPULSE, PUNISHMENT, SUPERIORITY.

beatify, *v.* sanctify, hallow, consecrate, bless. See PIETY.

beatnik, *n., slang,* hipster, hippie, yippie, Bohemian. See UNCON-
FORMITY.

BEAUTY

Nouns—**1,** beauty, the beautiful, loveliness, attractiveness; form, elegance, grace, charm, beauty unadorned; symmetry; comeliness, fairness,
pulchritude; polish, style, gloss; good looks.
2, bloom, brilliancy, radiance, splendor, gorgeousness, magnificence;
grandeur, glory; delicacy, refinement, elegance.
3, Venus, Hebe, the Graces, peri, houri, goddess; witch, enchantress;
charmer, reigning beauty, belle; Adonis, Narcissus. *Colloq.*, eyeful,
picture, dream, stunner, peach, knockout, raving beauty, good-looker.
4, beautifying; make-up, cosmetics; decoration, adornment, embellishment, ORNAMENTATION.

Adjectives—**1,** beautiful, beauteous; handsome; pretty, lovely, graceful,
elegant; delicate, dainty, refined; fair, personable, comely, seemly;
bonny, good-looking; well-favored, well-made, well-formed, well-proportioned; proper, shapely; symmetrical, regular, harmonious, sightly.
Colloq., easy on the eyes, nifty, stunning, devastating, long on looks,
(well-)built.
2, brilliant, shining; splendid, resplendent, dazzling, glowing; glossy,
sleek; rich, gorgeous, superb, magnificent, grand, fine, sublime.
3, artistic, aesthetic; picturesque, well-composed, well-grouped; enchanting, attractive, becoming, ornamental; undeformed, undefaced, unspotted; spotless, immaculate; PERFECT, flawless.

Antonym, see UGLINESS.

---

because, *adv. & conj.* —*adv.* by reason of, owing to. —*conj.* since, for,
for the reason that, as. See CAUSE.

beckon, *v.* signal, summon, call. See INDICATION.

become, *v.t.* befit, accord with, behoove; turn into, change to. See
DUTY, CHANGE.

becoming, *adj.* ornamental, decorative; fit, proper, seemly. See BEAUTY,
RIGHT. *Ant.,* unbecoming; see UGLINESS, WRONG.

bed, *n.* couch, cot, resting place; BASE, foundation; garden. See SUP-
PORT.

bedlam, *n.* asylum, madhouse; confusion, uproar, turmoil. See IN-
SANITY, DISORDER.

befit, *v.t.* suit, harmonize with, fit; become, behoove. *See* AGREEMENT, DUTY. *Ant.*, see NEGLECT, DISAGREEMENT.
before, *adv.* foremost, ahead; forward; sooner, previously, heretofore. See FRONT, PRIORITY. *Ant.*, see REAR, SEQUENCE.
beg, *v.* implore, beseech, petition, ask; ask alms. See POVERTY, REQUEST.
beget, *v.t.* engender, procreate, reproduce, generate. See PRODUCTION.
beggar, *n.* suppliant, pauper, mendicant. See POVERTY.
beginner, *n.* tyro, novice, recruit. See LEARNER. *Ant.*, VETERAN.

BEGINNING

Nouns—1, beginning, commencement, opening, outset, incipience, inception; introduction; alpha, initial; installation, inauguration, debut; embarkation, rising of the curtain, curtain raiser; outbreak, onset; initiative, move, first move; thin end of the wedge; fresh start, new departure. *Colloq.*, kickoff, take-off; coming-out.
2, origin, CAUSE; source, rise; bud, germ, egg, embryo, rudiment; genesis, birth, nativity, cradle, infancy; start, starting point; dawn, morning.
3, title page; head, heading, caption, title; introduction, prelude, prologue, preamble, preface, foreword; front, forefront, van, vanguard.
4, entrance, entry, INGRESS; inlet, orifice, mouth, lips; porch, portal, portico, door; gate, gateway; postern, wicket, threshold, vestibule; outskirts, border, EDGE, frontier.
5, rudiments, elements, outlines, grammar, primer, alphabet, ABC, first principles. See PREPARATION.
Verbs—1, begin, commence, rise, arise, originate, conceive, initiate, introduce, inaugurate; open, dawn, set in, enter upon; set out, DEPART; embark in; make one's debut; set about, get under way, set to work, make a beginning *or* start; take the first step; break ground, break the ice, break cover; cross the Rubicon; open fire; undertake. *Colloq.*, get going.
3, usher in; lead off, lead the way, take the lead, start from scratch, take the initiative; inaugurate, head; lay the foundations, prepare, found, CAUSE, set up, set on foot, start the ball rolling; launch, broach; open the door to.
Adjectives—1, initial, initiatory, initiative; primary, pristine; inceptive, introductory, incipient; inaugural; embryonic, rudimentary; primeval, primordial, primitive, aboriginal; natal.
2, first, foremost, leading; maiden.
Adverbs—at the beginning, in the beginning; first, in the first place, *imprimis*, first and foremost; in the bud, in its infancy; from the beginning, from its birth; *ab initio*; formerly, heretofore. *Colloq.*, from the word go, at the drop of a hat.
Antonym, see END.

behalf, *n.* interest, benefit, advantage. See SUBSTITUTION.
behave, *v.i.* act, bear oneself, conduct oneself. See ACTION, CONDUCT.
behead, *v.t.* decapitate, decollate. See KILLING, PUNISHMENT.
behind, *adv. & prep.* —*adv.* rearward, aft, backward; after, subsequently. —*prep.* in back of, following. See REAR.
behold, *v. & interj.* —*v.* see, espy; look at, watch, observe. —*interj.* lo and behold! *ecce*! lo! look! *voilà*! See VISION, ATTENTION.
being, *n.* life, EXISTENCE, subsistence; person, creature. See SUBSTANCE. *Ant.*, see NONEXISTENCE.

BELIEF

Nouns—1, belief; credence; credit; assurance; faith, trust, troth, confidence, presumption, dependence on, reliance on. *Colloq.*, store. *Slang*, stock.

2, persuasion, conviction, CERTAINTY; opinion, mind, view; conception, thinking; impression, IDEA; surmise, conclusion, JUDGMENT.

3, tenet, dogma, principle, precept, article of faith; ASSENT; system of opinions, school, doctrine, articles, canons; declaration or profession of faith; tenets, creed, orthodoxy; catechism, TEACHING, cult, ism; PROPAGANDA.

4, credibility, believability, plausibility; PROBABILITY.

Verbs—**1,** believe, credit; give credence to; see, realize; assume, receive; take for; take it; consider, esteem, presume; count on, depend on, pin one's faith on, rely on, swear by; take on trust or credit; take for granted or gospel. *Colloq.*, set store by, bet on, bank on, bet one's bottom dollar on, buy. *Slang*, take stock in.

2, know, know for certain; have no doubt; rest assured; persuade or satisfy oneself; make up one's mind.

3, confide in, believe in, put one's trust in; take one's word for, take at one's word.

4, think, hold; opine, be of opinion, conceive, fancy, apprehend; have, hold, entertain, hazard or cherish a belief or an opinion.

5, satisfy, persuade, assure; convince, convict, convert; wean, bring round; bring or win over; indoctrinate, TEACH; carry conviction; bring home to.

Adjectives—certain, sure, assured, positive, cocksure, satisfied, confident, unhesitating, convinced, secure; indubitable, undeniable, indisputable, incontrovertible; credible, reliable, trustworthy, infallible, to be depended on; satisfactory; probable; persuasive, impressive. See CREDULITY.

Antonym, see DOUBT.

---

belittle, *v.t.* run down, disparage, depreciate, dwarf, slight. See DETRACTION. *Ant.*, see APPROBATION.

bell, *n.* alarm, signal, call; chime; ring. See INDICATION.

belligerent, *adj.* warlike, pugnacious, quarrelsome. See CONTENTION. *Ant.*, see PACIFICATION.

bellow, *v.i.* roar, shout, bawl. See CRY.

belly, *n. & v.* —*n.* stomach, paunch, (pot)belly, maw; underside. *Colloq.*, tummy, breadbasket; pod, bay window, corporation, beer belly, pot, gut, swagbelly. See SIZE. —*v.* swell, billow, puff. See CONVEXITY.

belong, *v.i.* merge, form part of; be someone's; relate to. See JUNCTION, POSSESSION, RELATION.

below, *adv. & prep.* —*adv.* subordinate, lower, underneath. —*prep.* under, beneath. See INFERIORITY, LOWNESS. *Ant.*, ABOVE.

belt, *n. & v.* —*n.* girdle, band; strip; zone; circuit. —*v.t.* bind, encircle. *Colloq.*, whip. See CIRCULARITY.

bench, *n.* seat, settee; court, bar; board. See SUPPORT, LAWSUIT.

bend, *n. & v.* —*n.* curve, turn; angle, fork. See ANGULARITY, CURVATURE. *Ant.*, see DIRECTION. —*v.i.* give, yield; curve, bend. —*v.t.* control; shape. See SOFTNESS.

beneath, *adv. & prep.* —*adv.* underfoot, under, below. —*prep.* under; unworthy of. See LOWNESS. *Ant.*, ABOVE.

benefactor, *n.* good or guardian angel; friend, helper, patron; altruist, philanthropist, good Samaritan, savior, sponsor, friend-in-need. See AID, GIVING, BENEVOLENCE. *Ant.*, see EVILDOER.

beneficial, *adj.* useful, helpful, salutary, advantageous. See GOODNESS, USE. *Ant.*, see EVIL, WASTE.

beneficiary, *n.* legatee, pensioner, donee. See RECEIVING. *Ant.*, see GIVING.

benefit, *n. & v.* —*n.* profit, advantage, gain, GOOD, avail. See USE. —*v.* help, serve, assist; improve. See BENEVOLENCE, UTILITY. *Ant.*, MALEVOLENCE, EVIL.

BENEVOLENCE

Nouns—1, benevolence, Christian charity; God's grace; good will; altruism, PHILANTHROPY, unselfishness; good nature, kindness, kindliness, loving-kindness, benignity, brotherly love, charity, humanity, fellow-feeling, sympathy; goodness of heart; *bonhomie;* kindheartedness; amiability, milk of human kindness, tenderness; LOVE; FRIENDSHIP; tolerance, consideration, generosity; mercy, PITY.

2, charitableness, bounty, almsgiving; good works, beneficence, act of kindness, good turn; good offices, labor of love; public service, social science, sociology.

3, philanthropist, good Samaritan, sympathizer, altruist, humanitarian. See BENEFACTOR, GIVING, GOODNESS.

Verbs—bear good will; mean well by; wish well; take an interest in, sympathize with, feel for; have one's heart in the right place; do as you would be done by; meet halfway; treat well; give comfort, do a good turn; benefit, render a service, be of use; AID, philanthropize; heap coals of fire on [a person's] head.

Adjectives—1, benevolent, benign; kindly, well-meaning; amiable, cordial, obliging, accommodating, indulgent, gracious, complacent, good-humored; unselfish, magnanimous; warmhearted, kindhearted; merciful, charitable, beneficent, altruistic, humane, bounteous, bountiful; public-spirited.

2, good-natured; sympathetic; complaisant, courteous; well-meant, well-intentioned; LIBERAL, generous, gracious.

3, fatherly, motherly, brotherly, sisterly; paternal, maternal, fraternal.

Adverbs—benevolently, charitably, with good intentions, with the best intentions; with all one's heart; liberally, generously.

Antonym, see MALEVOLENCE.

---

bent, *n.* liking, fondness; inclination, trend, nature, propensity. See DESIRE, TENDENCY, WILLINGNESS. *Ant.,* see UNWILLINGNESS.

bequest, *n.* legacy, inheritance; patrimony; heritage. See GIVING.

bereft, *adj.* bereaved, deprived of, denuded. See LOSS. *Ant.,* see ACQUISITION.

berth, *n.* bunk, compartment; position, office; lodging. See BUSINESS, SUPPORT.

beset, *v.t.* besiege, surround, ATTACK, invest; stud. See ORNAMENT.

beseech, *v.t.* beg, implore. See REQUEST.

beside, *prep.* by, near, alongside, abreast. See NEARNESS. *Ant.,* see DISTANCE.

besides, *adv.* also, further, moreover. See ADDITION.

besiege, *v.t.* surround, beleaguer, storm, beset; plague, pester. See ATTACK. *Ant.,* see DEFENSE.

best, *adj.* choice, precious, unequalled, unparalleled. See GOODNESS, PERFECTION. *Ant.,* see EVIL, IMPERFECTION.

bestial, *adj.* beastlike, brutal, brutish, ANIMAL. See MALEVOLENCE, VIOLENCE.

bestow, *v.t.* donate, present, confer, give, bequeath. See GIVING. *Ant.,* see RECEIVING.

bet, *v.* wager, stake, gamble, play, lay odds. See CHANCE.

betray, *v.* play false, trick; divulge, reveal. See DECEPTION, DISCLOSURE.

betrothal, *n.* engagement, espousal. See MARRIAGE.

better, *v.t.* mend, correct, relieve; defeat. See IMPROVEMENT, SUPERIORITY. *Ant.,* see DETERIORATION.

BETWEEN

Nouns—1, interjacence, intervenience, interlocation, interpenetration; permeation; interjection, interpolation, interlineation, interspersion, intercalation; interlocution, aside; parenthesis; episode; fly-leaf; embolism; intervention, interference, interposition, intrusion, obtrusion; insinuation; INSERTION, dovetailing; infiltration; partition, septum, diaphragm, midriff; party-wall, panel; half-way house.

2, intermediary; go-between, middleman, medium; intruder, interloper, trespasser, meddler. *Slang,* buttinsky, chiseler, gate-crasher.

Verbs—**1,** intervene, slide in, interpenetrate, permeate; pervade.

2, put between, introduce, import; interpose, interject, intercalate, interpolate, interline, interleave, intersperse, interweave, interlard; INSERT; sandwich, let in, wedge in, worm in, run in, work in, dovetail, splice, mortise; insinuate, smuggle; infiltrate, ingrain; interfere, put an oar in, thrust one's nose in; intrude, obtrude; have a finger in the pie. *Slang,* butt in, horn in, barge in, muscle in.

Adjectives—interjacent, intervenient, intervening, intermediate, intermediary, intercalary, interstitial; embolismal; parenthetical; episodic, mediterranean; intrusive; interfering; merged.

Adverbs & Prepositions—between, betwixt; among, amongst; amid, amidst; in the thick of; betwixt and between; parenthetically, *obiter dictum.*

Antonym, see EXTERIOR.

---

beverage, *n.* liquor, drink, potable. See FOOD.

beware, *v.* take care, be on guard; avoid, shun. See WARNING.

bewilder, *v.t.* puzzle, confuse, perplex; daze, stagger. See DOUBT, SECRET, WONDER.

bewitch, *v.t.* fascinate, charm; enchant, hypnotize. See SORCERY.

beyond, *adv. & prep.* —*adv.* farther, yonder. —*prep.* over; past. See DISTANCE, SUPERIORITY. *Ant.,* see NEARNESS, INFERIORITY.

bias, *n. & v.* —*n.* prejudice, unfairness, partiality; bent, inclination; slope, diagonal. —*v.t.* influence, sway, prejudice. See DISTORTION, OBLIQUITY, TENDENCY. *Ant.,* see JUSTICE, DIRECTION.

Bible, *n.* Gospel, scripture, the Good Book, the Book. See SACRED WRITINGS.

bicker, *v.i.* quarrel, wrangle, dispute; flicker, flutter; gurgle, ripple. See DISCORD, AGITATION.

bicycle, *n.* velocipede; tandem, two-wheeler. *Colloq.,* bike. See VEHICLE.

bid, *n. & v.* —*n.* OFFER; invitation. —*v.* COMMAND, REQUEST; invite, enjoin. *Ant.,* see REFUSAL.

bier, *n.* litter, catafalque. See INTERMENT.

big, *adj.* large, bulky, huge; mountainous, enormous; massive, impressive; important, weighty. See GREATNESS, SIZE. *Ant.,* see LITTLENESS.

bigot, *n.* fanatic, dogmatist, zealot, formalist. See CERTAINTY.

bill, *n.* score, reckoning; invoice, statement, dun; account, charges; note, banknote, greenback; BEAK. See ACCOUNTING, MONEY.

billow, *v. & n.* —*v.i.* surge, swell. —*n.* undulation, wave. See WATER.

bin, *n.* compartment, container, crib, bunker, box, RECEPTACLE.

bind, *v.t.* restrain, secure, fasten; obligate. See COMPULSION, RESTRAINT, JUNCTION. *Ant.,* see DISJUNCTION.

biography, *n.* life story, history, memoirs. See DESCRIPTION.

bird, *n.* fowl, songbird, warbler; cock, hen; nestling, fledgling. See ANIMAL.

birth, *n.* origin, creation; genesis, inception; childbirth, parturition, delivery. See BEGINNING, PRODUCTION. *Ant.,* see END, DESTRUCTION.

biscuit, *n.* cracker, hardtack, cookie; roll, bun; cake. See FOOD.

bisect, *v.* divide, bifurcate, halve, split, cleave, separate.

bishop, *n.* prelate, primate, lawn sleeves; overseer; episcopacy. See CLERGY.

bit, *n.* scrap, mite; slice, piece; tool, drill; curb. See PART, LITTLENESS. *Ant.,* WHOLE.

bite, *n. & v.* —*n.* morsel, scrap; wound; itch. —*v.* cut; SNAP, nip. See FOOD.

biting, *adj.* sharp, piercing, keen; PUNGENT, ACRID: forceful, telling. See VIGOR. *Ant.,* see WEAKNESS.

bitter, *adj.* stinging, cutting; malignant, spiteful; rigorous; acrid, unpalatable. See MALEVOLENCE, SEVERITY. *Ant.,* see BENEVOLENCE, MODERATION.

blab, blabber, *v.i.* babble, chatter, tattle, gossip. See LOQUACITY, DISCLOSURE.

black, *n. & v.* —*n.* darkness, midnight, Stygian hue; Negro. See COLOR. —*v.t.* shine, polish (shoes).

blackball, *v.* exclude, ostracize, reject, boycott. See EXCLUSION, AVOIDANCE.

blacken, *v.t.* besmirch; smudge; malign, slander. See COLOR, DETRACTION.

blackguard, *n.* rascal, villain; scoundrel. See EVILDOER.

blackmail, *n.* extortion, exaction. *Colloq.,* protection. *Slang,* hush money; shakedown. See STEALING.

bladder, *n.* sac, vesicle, blister. See RECEPTACLE.

blade, *n.* cutter, edge; sword; knife; leaf (of grass); dandy, sport. See SHARPNESS, VEGETABLE.

blame, *n. & v.* —*n.* criticism, censure; culpability, GUILT. —*v.t.* charge, reproach, condemn. See ATTRIBUTION, DISAPPROBATION. *Ant.,* see APPROBATION.

bland, *adj.* affable, gracious; mild, unflavored. See COURTESY. *Ant.,* see DISCOURTESY, PUNGENCY.

blank, *adj.* empty, unfilled; vacant, vacuous, expressionless; unloaded. See NONEXISTENCE, INSUBSTANTIALITY.

blanket, *n. & v.* —*n.* COVERING. —*v.t.* cover; conceal.

blare, *n.* blast, peal, fanfare. See LOUDNESS.

blasphemy, *n.* irreverence, profanity; heresy. See IMPIETY. *Ant.,* see PIETY.

blast, *n. & v.* —*n.* explosion; discharge; gust; invective, ATTACK. —*v.t.* destroy, shatter, ruin; explode. See VIOLENCE, DESTRUCTION. *Ant.,* see PRODUCTION.

blaze, *n.* fire, flame; mark, spot. See HEAT, INDICATION.

blazon, *v.* proclaim, advertise; embellish, decorate. See PUBLICATION, ORNAMENT.

bleach, *v.t.* whiten, blanch, lighten, dye. See COLORLESSNESS.

bleak, *adj.* raw, desolate, unsheltered; discouraging, unauspicious. See COLD, ADVERSITY.

blear, *adj.* blurred, dim; indistinct; bloodshot. See DIMNESS, DIMSIGHTEDNESS.

bleed, *v.* flow, hemorrhage; let blood; overcharge, fleece; suffer. *Colloq.,* soak, skin. See PAIN, PAYMENT.

blemish, *n. & v.* —*v.* flaw, defect, disfigurement, IMPERFECTION; spot, taint, mark, stain, blot; wen, mole, pimple, scar; smear, smudge. —*v.* disfigure, mar, flaw, spoil; bruise, rot; stain; discolor, smear, spot, smudge; injure, harm, hurt; sully, disgrace, tarnish. *Ant.,* see CLEANNESS, PERFECTION.

blend, *n. & v.* —*n.* combination, MIXTURE, cross-breed. —*v.* merge, amalgamate; shade.

bless, *v.t.* hallow, glorify, consecrate; praise; thank. See DEITY.

blessing, *n.* benediction, commendation; godsend, boon. See APPROBATION, GOOD. *Ant.,* see DISAPPROBATION, EVIL.

blight, *n. & v.* —*n.* DETERIORATION, decay, rot; rust, smut. —*v.t.* stunt, rot, impair, corrupt; thwart, foil. See PAIN.

blind, *n. & adj.* —*n.* AMBUSH, DECEPTION; screen, shade, shutter; ruse, subterfuge. —*adj.* sightless, unseeing; undiscerning. See BLINDNESS, INATTENTION.

BLINDNESS

Nouns—**1,** blindness, sightlessness, anopsia; blind spot; amaurosis; cataract; DIMSIGHTEDNESS, benightedness; darkness.

2, Braille, Moon's type, New York point, American Braille; seeing-eye dog.

Verbs—be blind, not see; lose sight; grope in the dark; blind, darken, benight, obscure, eclipse, hide; put one's eyes out, gouge; blindfold, hoodwink, throw dust into one's eyes; screen, hide, dazzle. See CONCEALMENT.

Adjectives—blind; eyeless, sightless, unseeing; dark, stone-blind; undiscerning; unperceiving; dimsighted; blind as a bat, a mole *or* an owl.

Adverbs—blindly, sightlessly, gropingly; blindfold; darkly.

Antonym, see VISION.

blink, *v.* wink; flash, twinkle; disregard, ignore. See VISION, NEGLECT.

bliss, *n.* happiness, ecstasy, rapture, PLEASURE. *Ant.,* see PAIN.

blister, *n.* vesicle; bubble, sac. See RECEPTACLE.

blithe, *adj.* gay, lighthearted, merry. See CHEERFULNESS. *Ant.,* see DEJECTION.

blitz, blitzkrieg, *n.* ATTACK, bombing, raid; victory. See WARFARE.

blizzard, *n.* gale, storm, snowstorm, windstorm. See WIND.

bloat, *v.* distend, swell, puff up. See INCREASE. *Ant.,* see CONTRACTION.

blob, *n.* drop, mass; splash, blemish. See CONVEXITY.

bloc, *n.* party, faction, ring; union, alliance, coalition. See COÖPERATION, ASSEMBLAGE.

block, *n. & v.* —*n.* HINDRANCE, obstruction; row, street; square (see ABODE); mass, lump; cube. —*v.t.* impede, check, stop, bar; thwart, foil.

blockade, *n. & v.* —*n.* barrier, stoppage, embargo, siege. —*v.t.* obstruct, bar, barricade. See CLOSURE, EXCLUSION. *Ant.,* see OPENING.

blond, *adj.* light-colored, fair-skinned; light-haired, golden, yellow, flaxen, platinum. See COLORLESSNESS.

blood, *n.* serum, essence; gore; kindred, relationship, kinship; sap. See RELATION, FLUIDITY.

bloodless, *adj.* anemic; pale; unfeeling, cold; peaceful, unwarlike. See COLORLESSNESS, PEACE.

bloodletting, *n.* phlebotomy, venesection. See REMEDY.

bloodshed, *n.* KILLING; slaughter, shambles. See WARFARE.

bloodthirsty, *adj.* murderous, savage, inhuman. See KILLING, MALEVOLENCE. *Ant.,* see BENEVOLENCE.

bloody, *adj.* gory, sanguinary, bleeding; red; bloodthirsty. See KILLING.

bloom, *n. & v.* —*n.* blossom, flower; flowering. —*v.i.* blossom; mature; glow, flourish, thrive. See HEALTH, PROSPERITY, VEGETABLE.

blossom, *n.* flower, bud, bloom; develop, flourish. See VEGETABLE.

blot, *v. & n.* —*v.* stain, blemish, spot; sully. —*n.* spot, smear, blemish. See DISREPUTE, DESTRUCTION.

blow, *n. & v.* —*n.* knock, stroke, hit; DISAPPOINTMENT; blast, WIND, breeze, gale. See IMPULSE. —*v.* brag; gasp, pant, puff; sound; storm, breeze, whiff, waft. See SOUND, WIND. *Slang,* miss; squander. See FAILURE, WASTE.

blowup, *n.* EXPLOSION. *Colloq.,* outburst; enlargement. See EXPANSION.

blue, *adj.* azure, indigo; sapphire, turquoise, aquamarine, cobalt; Delft; (of laws) severe, Puritanical. *Colloq.,* sad, dejected, depressed, dispirited, downhearted. See COLOR, KNOWLEDGE, DEJECTION. *Ant.,* see CHEERFULNESS.

bluff, *n., adj. & v.* —*n.* cliff, bank, headland. —*adj.* mislead, brag, intimidate, hoax. See BOASTING, DECEPTION.

blunder, *n. & v.* —*n.* ERROR, mistake, slip; botch; mess; solecism.

—*v.i.* botch, fail, err; mismanage, bungle, flounder. See FAILURE, UN-SKILLFULNESS. *Ant.*, see SUCCESS.

blunt, *v. & adj.* —*v.t.* DULL, deaden, numb; callous, make insensitive; moderate. *Ant.*, see SHARPNESS. —*adj.* DULL; direct; brusque; un-diplomatic, forthright. See DISCOURTESY.

blur, *v.* blot, smear; swim, be indistinct. See IMPERFECTION, VISION.

blush, *v.i.* COLOR, flush, glow, redden; embarrassment, MODESTY.

bluster, *n. & v.* —*n.* bravado; braggadocio, bullying, BOASTING, hector-ing; FRONT. —*v.i.* swagger, play the bully, hector, vapor, gasconade; make a fuss, disturbance *or* uproar. *Ant., see* MODESTY.

board, *n. & v.* —*n.* COUNCIL, cabinet, panel, committee, directorate; plank; cardboard; provisions, fare. —*v.* lodge, feed. See FOOD, LAYER.

BOASTING

Nouns—**1,** boasting, boast, vaunting, vaunt; pretense, pretensions; puff; flourish, *fanfaronnade;* gasconade; braggadocio, bravado, flourish, swag-ger, bunkum; bounce; rodomontade, bombast, *or* tall talk, magnilo-quence, grandiloquence; heroics; chauvinism; EXAGGERATION; VANITY, much cry and little wool, highfalutin(g). *Slang*, dog, side, bunk, hot air, front.

2, boaster; braggart, Gascon, pretender, *soi-disant;* blusterer, bully, hectorer. *Slang*, blowhard, windbag, loudmouth.

Verbs—boast, make a boast of, brag; vaunt, puff, flourish, strut, swag-ger; preen *or* plume oneself; bluster, bluff; exult, crow over, neigh, chuckle, triumph; throw up one's cap. *Colloq.*, talk big, show off, blow one's own horn. *Slang*, give oneself airs, put on side *or* dog, put up a big front.

Adjectives—boastful, magniloquent, pretentious, *soi-disant;* vainglorious, conceited; bombastic, pompous, extravagant, high-flown, ostentatious, heroic, grandiose; jubilant, triumphant, exultant; in high feather; flushed with victory; cock-a-hoop; on stilts.

Adverbs—boastfully, bombastically, *etc.*

Antonym, see MODESTY.

---

boat, *n.* vessel, SHIP, craft; skiff, dory, dinghy, launch; liner, steamer; gondola, rowboat, canoe, outrigger; sailboat; bark. See NAVIGATION, CONCAVITY.

bob, *v. & n.* —*v.t.* dock, cut, curtail. —*v.i.* nod, bow, curtsy; jerk, LEAP, float. —*n.* haircut; shilling. See AGITATION, OSCILLATION, RE-SPECT.

bodily, *adj. & adv.* —*adj.* corporeal, physical, material. See INSUB-STANTIALITY. —*adv.* wholly, entire, completely. see WHOLE.

body, *n.* anatomy; torso; structure, FORM; substance, SUBSTANTIALITY; ASSEMBLAGE, throng, aggregate; lump; person, figure, thing; WHOLE.

bog, *n.* swamp, morass, quagmire, MARSH, fen.

bogus, *adj.* false, fake; counterfeit, spurious. *Slang*, phony. See DE-CEPTION.

bogy, bogey, *n.* specter, spook, bugaboo; DEMON, hobgoblin, gremlin.

boil, *n. & v.* —*n.* sore, suppuration. —*v.* bubble, seethe; scald; cook; storm, fume, rage. See DISEASE, HEAT, VIOLENCE.

boisterous, *adj.* noisy, vociferous; unrestrained, rambunctious, riotous, stormy, uproarious; rough. See EXCITEMENT. *Ant.*, inexcitable.

bold, *adj.* daring, audacious, forward; intrepid, brave; impudent. See COURAGE, INSOLENCE. *Ant.*, see COWARDICE, SERVILITY.

bolt, *n. & v.* —*n.* lock, latch, bar; stroke, flash. See CLOSURE, LIGHT-NING. —*v.* run, dash, run away; winnow, sift; gobble, gulp. See ESCAPE, GLUTTONY.

bomb, *n.* (bomb)shell, explosive. *Colloq.*, Molotov cocktail. See ARMS.

bombast, *n.* BOASTING, exaggeration, bluster, braggadocio, grandiloquence.

bond, *n.* union, connection, tie; accord, sympathy; guaranty, pledge; shackle. See JUNCTION, RELATION, SECURITY. *Ant.,* see DISJUNCTION.

bondage, *n.* slavery, serfdom, SUBJECTION; helotry, peonage. *Ant.,* FREEDOM.

bonus, *n.* reward, gift, premium, extra, dividend. See GIVING.

bony, *adj.* skeletal, stiff; osseous; lank, lean. See HARDNESS.

BOOK

Nouns—**1,** book, writing, work, volume, folio, tome, opus; manuscript; treatise, dissertation; novel; tract, brochure; libretto; handbook, codex, manual, textbook, pamphlet, broadside, booklet, circular; PUBLICATION, edition, pocket edition, production; encyclopedia; dictionary, lexicon, glossary, thesaurus; concordance, anthology, gazetteer, almanac, digest, compilation; part, issue, number, album, portfolio; periodical, review, serial, magazine; annual, journal.

2, writer, author, publisher, littérateur, essayist, novelist, short-story writer, playwright, dramatist, poet; editor; lexicographer, annotator, commentator; journalist, newspaperman, critic, reviewer, correspondent; hack, hackwriter, ghostwriter; librettist. *Colloq.,* potboiler, penny-a-liner, free lance, inkslinger.

3, ledger, account book (see ACCOUNTING); betting book (bookmaking).

bookkeeping, *n.* auditing, reckoning, ACCOUNTING.

bookworm, *n.* SCHOLAR, pedant; bibliophile. *Colloq.,* grind, longhair.

boom, *v. & n.* —*v.* push, boost, plug; flourish; thunder, drum, rumble (see LOUDNESS). —*n.* beam, spar, jib; prosperousness, SUCCESS. See IMPULSE, NAVIGATION, PROSPERITY.

boorish, *adj.* ill-mannered, vulgar, rude; rustic, clownish. See VULGARITY.

boost, *n. & v.* —*n.* AID, help, indorse; lift, hoist. —*v.i.* assist, promote, recommend; lift, hoist. See APPROBATION, ELEVATION. *Ant.,* see HINDRANCE, DISAPPROBATION.

boot, *n. & v.* —*n.* footwear, shoe; Hessian boot; blucher, hip *or* jack boot; seven-league boots. See CLOTHING. —*v.t.,* *slang,* kick out, dismiss, give the boot.

booty, *n.* spoil, plunder, prize, loot, graft, swag, boodle, pork barrel, pickings, pillage, blackmail; prey. See ACQUISITION.

border, *n.* EDGE, LIMIT, margin, rim; frontier, boundary; trim (see ORNAMENT).

bore, *n. & v.* —*n.* diameter, caliber; nuisance, pest. See BREADTH, WEARINESS. *Ant.,* see NARROWNESS, AMUSEMENT. —*v.* drill, pierce; tire, weary, annoy. See OPENING.

borrow, *v.* take, receive (as a loan); appropriate, adopt, adapt, imitate, make use of; plagiarize, copy; pawn, pledge; pirate, steal, filch, pilfer. See DEBT.

bosh, *n.* nothing; nonsense. *Slang,* bunk. See SPEECH, ABSURDITY.

bosom, *n. & adj.* —*n.* breast, bust; heart, FEELING. See CONVEXITY. —*adj.* intimate, close, confidential. See FRIEND.

boss, *n.* knob, stud; manager, supervisor. See CONVEXITY, AUTHORITY.

botany, *n.* vegetable physiology, science of plant life, phytology; horticulture; vegetation, flora. See VEGETABLE.

botch, *v.* bungle, blunder; mar, spoil; mismanage. *Colloq.,* butcher. See UNSKILLFULNESS. *Ant.,* see SKILL.

both, *pron. & adj.* —*pron.* the two, twain, pair. —*adj.* dually, equally, as well as, together. See COPY, EQUALITY, UNIFORMITY.

bother, *n. & v.* —*n.* nuisance, annoyance; trouble; perplexity, worry. —*v.t.* irritate, pester, worry. See PAIN. *Ant.,* see PLEASURE.

bottle, *n.* flask, jug, carafe, decanter; flacon, phial; canteen. See RE-CEPTACLE.

bottom, *n.* BASE, foot, sole; foundation, support. *Ant.,* see HEIGHT.

bottomless, *adj.* abysmal, unfathomable; profound. See DEPTH.

bough, *n.* limb, branch, offshoot, arm. See PART, VEGETABLE.

boulder, *n.* See ROCK.

boulevard, *n.* avenue, thoroughfare; promenade. See PASSAGE.

bounce, *n.* rebound, spring; LEAP. *Slang,* eject.

bound, *v. & adj.* —*v.* LIMIT, confine, delimit, demarcate; LEAP, spring, VAULT. See CIRCUMSCRIPTION. —*adj.* see BIND.

boundary, *n.* LIMIT, border, confines. See CIRCUMSCRIPTION.

boundless, *adj.* infinite, endless, vast, limitless, illimitable. See INFINITY.

bounty, *n.* grant, subsidy; premium; generosity, munificence. See AID, BENEVOLENCE.

bouquet, *n.* FRAGRANCE, perfume, aroma; corsage, boutonniere, nosegay, garland. See ORNAMENT.

bourgeois, *adj.* middle-class; conservative. See MIDDLE.

bout, *n.* contest, match; prizefight. See CONTENTION.

bow, *n. & v.* —*n.* obeisance, curtsy, kowtow, salaam; FRONT, prow. —*v.i.* nod, incline, bend; yield, concede. See COURTESY, OBEDIENCE.

bow, *n.* curve, arc, crescent; bowknot; crossbow. See CURVATURE, ARMS.

bowels, *n., pl.* intestines, guts, viscera, innards; depths, recesses. See INTERIOR, DEPTH.

bower, *n.* nook, arbor, grotto. See RECEPTACLE.

bowl, *n.* basin, vessel, dish, pan; cup, beaker; ARENA. See RECEPTACLE.

bowling, *n.* tenpins, duckpins, candlepins; ninepins, skittles; lawn bowling, bowls. See AMUSEMENT.

box, *n.* chest, case, carton, container; coffin. See RECEPTACLE.

boy, *n.* lad, YOUTH; servant (*now offensive*). See INFANT. *Ant.,* see AGE.

boycott, *v.t.* shun, blackball, ostracize. See REFUSAL.

brace, *v.t. & n.* —*v.t.* invigorate, refresh; SUPPORT, prop, strengthen. —*n.* bracket, stay, girder; pair. See NUMERATION, POWER. *Ant.,* see IMPOTENCE.

bracelet, *n.* armlet, wristlet, bangle; handcuffs, manacles, shackles. See ORNAMENT, RESTRAINT.

bracket, *n.* SUPPORT, shoulder; brace, group, class; parenthesis. See CONNECTION.

brag, *v.i.* boast, vaunt; swagger, bluster; bluff. See BOASTING.

braid, *n. & v.* —*n.* trim, ribbon. —*v.t.* intertwine, interweave, plait. See CROSSING, ORNAMENT.

brain, *n.* cerebrum, cerebellum; mentality, intelligence, mind; gray matter; INTELLECT.

brainwash, *v.t.* commit menticide, counterindoctrinate, misinform, twist, pervert. See TEACHING, DECEPTION, DISTORTION.

brake, *v.* retard, check, curb; slow down, stop. See SLOWNESS.

branch, *n. & v.* —*n.* member, arm, bough, limb, ramification; descendant, shoot, offshoot; PART. See ANCESTRY, VEGETABLE. *Ant.,* see WHOLE. —*v.i.* fork, divide, bifurcate; radiate. See DEVIATION.

brand, *n.* kind, sort, stamp; stigma, stain; mark, identification, trademark; branding iron; torch. See DISREPUTE, HEAT.

brandish, *v.t.* flourish, wave, make a show of, flaunt, display. See AGITATION, DEMONSTRATION, THREAT.

brat, *n.* imp, pest, *enfant terrible,* monster. See DISOBEDIENCE, YOUTH.

bravado, *n.* bluster, braggadocio, BOASTING.

brave, *adj. & v.* —*adj.* courageous, fearless, valiant, bold. —*v.t.* defy, dare. See COURAGE. *Ant.,* see COWARDICE.

brawl, *n.* quarrel, fight, free-for-all, hubbub. See CONTENTION.

breach, *n.* split, rift, schism; dissension, DISCORD; hole, chasm, OPENING; violation, infringement. See ILLEGALITY, DISCOURTESY.

BREADTH

Nouns—1, breadth, width, broadness, scope, extent, span; latitude, amplitude, spaciousness, expanse; diameter, bore, caliber, radius; thickness, bulk, corpulence, SIZE. See EXPANSION.
Verbs—broaden, widen, amplify, extend, enlarge, expand; thicken.
Adjectives—broad, wide, ample, extended; thick; outspread, outstretched; vast, spacious, immense, extensive, comprehensive.
Antonym, see NARROWNESS.

break, *n. & v.* —*n.* breach, interruption, disconnection, fracture, fissure, crack; boon, advantage. See DISJUNCTION. —*v.* crack, fracture, shatter; tame, subdue; violate, infringe. See BRITTLENESS, NEGLECT, DOMESTICATION.
breakdown, *n.* FAILURE; [nervous] prostration, crack-up. See INSANITY.
breakwater, *n.* mole, sea wall, jetty. See REFUGE.
breast, *n.* bosom, bust, mamma; spirit, affections. See CONVEXITY.
breath, *n.* respiration, inhalation, exhalation; breeze. See LIFE, WIND.
breathless, *adj.* puffing, panting, short-winded, out of breath *or* wind; excited, overcome. See EXCITEMENT, FATIGUE, WONDER.
breeches, *n.* knickers, knickerbockers; small clothes; trousers, pantaloons. See CLOTHING.
breed, *v. & n.* —*v.* create, multiply, generate, produce. —*n.* strain, race, stock. See RELATION, PRODUCTION.
breeding, *n.* background; culture, gentility, lineage. See COURTESY.
breeze, *n.* zephyr, gust, breath (of air). See WIND.
brevity, *n.* CONCISENESS, succinctness, briefness, SHORTNESS. *Ant.*, see LOQUACITY.
brew, *v. & n.* —*v.* stew, cook, steep, simmer; ferment, distill; scheme, foment, PLAN. —*n.* beer, ale; soup, stew; MIXTURE, melange, *etc.* See FOOD.
bribe, *n. & v.* —*n.* tribute, tip, perquisite, graft, bait. *Colloq.,* hush-money, grease, payola; fix. —*v.t.* tip, overtip, suborn, tempt, corrupt. *Colloq.,* grease. See BOOTY, GIVING.
bric-a-brac, *n.* knickknacks, curios. See ORNAMENT.
brick, *n.* block; adobe, clay; loaf, lump, bar, briquet(te). See MATERIALS, PRODUCTION.
bridal, *adj.* nuptial, connubial. See MARRIAGE.
bridge, *n. & v.* —*n.* span, trestle, viaduct, causeway; auction, contract. —*v.t.* connect, span, link, cross. See JUNCTION.
bridle, *v.* curb, check; harness; bristle. See RESTRAINT.
brief, *adj. & n. & v.* —*adj.* short, succinct, terse; quick, fleeting. —*n.* summary, argument. —*v.t.* instruct. See CONTRACTION, INFORMATION, LAWSUIT. *Ant.,* see LOQUACITY.
brigand, *n.* bandit, thug, highwayman, robber, pirate. See THIEF.
bright, *adj.* brilliant, shining, glistening; luminous; clever, intelligent; gay, flashing, sparkling. See COLOR, INTELLIGENCE, LIGHT. *Ant.,* see IGNORANCE, DARKNESS.
brilliant, *adj.* resplendent, radiant; luminous, sprakling, bright; (conspicuously) intelligent, clever, quick-witted. See BEAUTY, INTELLIGENCE, LIGHT. *Ant.,* DULL; see DARKNESS.
brim, *n.* EDGE, margin, border, rim, brink, bluff.
brindled, *adj.* particolored, banded, brindle, tabby. See VARIEGATION.
bring, *v.t.* fetch, carry, convey; command (a price); occasion. See CAUSE, TRANSFER. *Ant.,* SEND.
brink, *n.* EDGE, margin, brim, rim, bluff; verge, turning point.

brisk, *adj.* alert, quick, lively, animated, sprightly; cool, sharp. See ACTIVITY, COLD. *Ant.,* see INACTIVITY.

bristle, *n. & v.* —*n.* hair, stubble, brush. See ROUGHNESS. *Ant.,* see SMOOTHNESS. —*v.i.* stand (erect), stick up; stiffen (as with anger). See SHARPNESS, RESENTMENT.

BRITTLENESS

Nouns—brittleness, fragility, friability, frangibility, frailty; crispness, delicacy, crumbliness.

Verbs—break, crack, snap, split, shiver, splinter, crumble, shatter, fracture; bust, fly, give way; fall to pieces, break up, disintegrate, fragment, crumble into dust.

Adjectives—brittle, frangible, friable, fragile, breakable, frail, gimcrack, shivery, splintery; splitting; eggshell; crisp, crumbly, short, brittle as glass.

Antonym, see COHERENCE.

---

broach, *v.t.* launch, introduce; tap, open. See BEGINNING, OPENING.

broad, *adj.* wide; extensive; marked (as an accent); sweeping, comprehensive; liberal, tolerant. See BREADTH, MODERATION. *Ant.,* NARROW.

broadcast, *v. & n.* —*v.* scatter, distribute, disseminate; spread, transmit, publish. —*n.* program, show, telecast, hook-up. See PUBLICATION.

brochure, *n.* pamphlet, booklet, leaflet, circular, broadside; tract, treatise. *Colloq.,* literature. See WRITING, BOOK.

broil, *v. & n.* —*v.* cook, grill, roast, HEAT. —*n.* brawl, riot, disturbance, fracas. See CONTENTION.

broker, *n.* AGENT, jobber, middleman, factor, pawnbroker, stockbroker.

brood, *n. & v.* —*n.* hatch, progeny, breed. See DESCENT. —*v.i.* ponder, mope, meditate, ruminate. See THOUGHT.

brook, *n.* stream, creek, rivulet, run. See RIVER.

broom, *n.* brush, mop, besom, whisk. See CLEANNESS.

broth, *n.* stock, bouillon, consommé (see SOUP); decoction, potion, elixir. See FOOD, FLUIDITY.

brother, *n.* friar; cadet, *frère, Frater;* kinsman, sibling; fellow, colleague, associate; soul brother. See CLERGY, RELATION, FRIEND, SIMILARITY.

brotherhood, *n.* kinship, family; association, fraternity, fellowship. See RELATION, ASSEMBLAGE, FRIEND. *Ant.,* see ENMITY.

brow, *n.* forehead; SUMMIT, crest. See FRONT.

browbeat, *v.t.* See BULLY.

brown, *v.t.* burn, toast, sear, scorch, braise, singe; sunburn, tan, bronze. See COLOR, HEAT.

browse, *v.* graze, feed, ruminate, nibble, pasture; glance at, contemplate, examine. See FOOD, INQUIRY.

bruise, *n. & v.* —*n.* contusion, injury, black-and-blue spot, mouse, black eye. —*v.t.* batter, contuse, injure, crush. See PAIN, IMPULSE.

brunet, *adj.* dark, dark-haired, dark-complexioned; brown, swarthy. See COLOR.

brush, *n. & v.* —*n.* bristle; thicket, shrubbery; broom. —*v.* sweep; graze. See CLEANNESS, NEARNESS.

brusque, *adj.* gruff, curt, abrupt. See DISCOURTESY. *Ant.,* see COURTESY, SMOOTHNESS.

brute, *n.* beast, ANIMAL; ruffian, scoundrel. *Colloq.,* bull. See EVILDOER, MALEVOLENCE.

bubble, *n. & v.* —*n.* globule, blob. See CONVEXITY. —*v.i.* effervesce, boil, gurgle. See AGITATION.

bucket, *n.* pail, tub. *Slang,* growler. See RECEPTACLE.

buckle, *n. & v.* —*n.* clasp, fastening. —*v.* bend, twist; collapse. See CONNECTION, DISTORTION.

bud, *v.i.* sprout, shoot; germinate; burgeon; mature. See EXPANSION.

buddy, *n.* comrade, pal, chum. See FRIEND. *Ant.*, see ENEMY.

budge, *v.* move, stir, shift; alter, change, EFFECT, INFLUENCE. See MOTION.

budget, *n.* funds, MONEY, expenses; APPORTIONMENT, allowance; ACCOUNTING.

buff, *adj. & v.* —*adj.* orange, yellow, tan. See COLOR. —*v.t.* polish, SMOOTH.

buffer, *n.* fender, bumper, polisher. See DEFENSE, SMOOTHNESS.

buffet, *v. & n.* —*v.t.* strike, slap, punch. —*n.* stroke, blow. See IMPULSE.

buffet, *n.* sideboard, cupboard, cabinet; refreshments; counter. See RECEPTACLE, FOOD.

buffoon, *n.* FOOL, clown, jester; comedian, mountebank. See DRAMA, WIT.

bug, *n. & v.* —*n.* insect, arthropod, mite, nit, bedbug; vermin. *Slang*, tap, wiretap; flaw, defect, fault; enthusiast (see ACTIVITY). See ANIMAL, LITTLENESS, DIFFICULTY. —*v.*, *slang*, (wire)tap; pester, annoy, bother. see PAIN, ACTIVITY.

bugbear, *n.* bogy, goblin, bugaboo. See SPECTER.

build, *v.t.* construct, make, fashion; erect. See FORM, PRODUCTION.

bulb, *n.* knob, globe; tuber, corm; lamp. See CONVEXITY, VEGETABLE, LIGHT.

bulge, *v.* swell, protrude, project, bag. See CONVEXITY. *Ant.*, see CONCAVITY.

bulk, *n.* SIZE, QUANTITY, measure, amount, volume; mass, expanse; body; generality, majority.

bullet, *n.* missile, shot, ball, lead, slug, shell; buckshot, BB shot. See ARMS.

bulletin, *n.* report, statement, INFORMATION. *Colloq.*, flash.

bullfighter, *n.* matador; picador, banderillo; toreador. See AMUSEMENT.

bully, *n. & v.* —*n.* BLUSTERER, swaggerer, brawler; plug-ugly; tyrant. —*v.t.* intimidate, browbeat, hector, bulldoze. See BOASTING, EVILDOER.

bulwark, *n.* fortification, rampart; safeguard; barrier, parapet. See DEFENSE.

bump, *v.* collide, knock, strike, hit. See IMPULSE.

bun, *n.* roll, sweet roll, Danish [pastry], hot-cross bun; knot, chignon. See FOOD, ROUGHNESS.

bunch, *n.* crowd, group; cluster, bundle. See CONVEXITY.

bundle, *n.* package, parcel, packet; bunch, bale. *Slang*, riches, WEALTH. See ASSEMBLAGE.

bung, *n.* stopper, cork, plug, CLOSURE.

bungle, *v.* spoil; botch; blunder. *Slang*, goof. See UNSKILLFULNESS.

bunk, *n.* bed, berth, cot. *Colloq.*, applesauce. *Slang*, nonsense, buncombe, claptrap, humbug, bosh. See BOASTING.

buoy, *n.* float; marker; bellbuoy, lifebuoy. See NAVIGATION.

buoyant, *adj.* light, floating; resilient, springy; confident, sanguine. See ASCENT, HOPE.

burden, *n.* HINDRANCE, load, weight, encumbrance; charge. *Ant.*, see AID.

bureau, *n.* department, office; chest, dresser; secretary, desk; division, branch, section, AGENCY, COMMISSION. See RECEPTACLE.

bureaucracy, *n.* officialism; officiousness; red tape. See AUTHORITY.

burglar, *n.* thief, housebreaker, robber, yegg, second-story man, cracksman. See STEALING.

burlesque, *n. & v.* —*n.* farce, parody; comedy, buffoonery. —*v.t.* satirize, parody, mimic, caricature. See IMITATION, RIDICULE.

burn, *v.* oxidize, consume; blaze, flame; fire; sear, char, scorch; destroy. See HEAT. *Ant.*, see COLD.

burrow, *n. & v.* —*n.* hole, tunnel, excavation, tube, foxhole. —*v.* dig, mine, penetrate. See CONCAVITY.

burst, *v.* rupture, break, rend; explode, shatter. *Slang,* bust. See VIOLENCE.

bury, *v.t.* inter, inhume, immure; cover, sink; relegate. See CIRCUM-SCRIPTION, INTERMENT. *Ant.,* disinter.

bus, *n.* omnibus, motorbus, coach, jitney, trolley [bus]. See VEHICLE.

bush, *n.* shrub, clump, thicket, hedge. See VEGETABLE.

bushy, *adj.* hairy, shaggy, dense, bushlike. See ROUGHNESS.

BUSINESS

Nouns—**1,** business, occupation, employment; PURSUIT; UNDERTAKING, venture; affair, concern, matter, case; task, work, job, chore, errand, commission, mission, charge, care, assignment. *Slang,* racket.

2, province, function, bailiwick, lookout, department, station, capacity, sphere, orb, field, line; walk, walk of life; beat, round, range, routine; race, career; vocation, calling, profession, cloth, faculty; art; craft, handicraft; trade, commerce, industry.

3, office, place, post, position, incumbency, living; situation, berth, employ; service; appointment, engagement; avocation. See ACTIVITY.

4, market, marketplace, mart, agora, fair, bazaar; STORE, shop, stall, booth, workshop; exchange, stock exchange, curb, bourse, rialto, pit, Wall Street, the street, bank.

5, businessman, MERCHANT, banker, broker, buyer, seller, bear, bull; financier, speculator; firm, concern, house, company, limited company, corporation, partnership.

Verbs—**1,** busy *or* occupy oneself with; undertake; contract, attempt; turn one's hand to; do business, keep a shop; ply one's trade.

2, officiate, preside, control; serve, act; do duty; discharge the duties of; hold office; hold a situation; be engaged in, have in hand; have on one's hands, bear the burden; have one's hands full. *Colloq.,* hold down a job, be into (something).

Adjectives—businesslike, orderly, thorough, methodical, efficient, systematic; workaday; professional; vocational; official, functional; authoritative; busy, in hand, afoot; on foot, on the fire; going on; acting.

Antonyms, see INACTIVITY, REPOSE.

---

bustle, *n.* stir, rustle, fluster, flurry, ado. See ACTIVITY, AGITATION. *Ant.,* see INACTIVITY.

busy, *adj.* occupied, engaged, engrossed; employed; diligent; meddlesome. See ACTIVITY, BUSINESS. *Ant.,* idle; see INACTIVITY.

busybody, *n.* gossip, meddler, talebearer, snooper. *Colloq.,* kibitzer. See CURIOSITY, ACTIVITY.

but, *conj. & prep.* —*conj.* still, yet, however. —*prep.* except, save, saving, excepting. See COMPENSATION.

butcher, *v.t.* slaughter, kill; bungle, spoils. See KILLING, UNSKILLFULNESS.

butt, *n.* target, goat, LAUGHINGSTOCK.

buttocks, *n.* rump, seat, hindquarters, breech. *Colloq.,* fanny, bottom. See REAR.

button, *n. & v.* —*n.* fastener; disk, boss; badge, emblem. —*v.* fasten, loop, close. See CLOSURE, JUNCTION, ORNAMENT. *Ant.,* see DISJUNCTION.

buttress, *n.* SUPPORT, abutment; prop, brace.

buy, *v. & n.* —*v.* PURCHASE, procure; draw, obtain; shop, market. —*n.* bargain (see CHEAPNESS). *Ant.,* see SALE.

buzz, *v. & n.* —*v.* drone, hum, whirr; bustle, fuss, hurry; whisper, gossip. —*n.* hum, whirr, *etc. Colloq.,* [telephone] call, ring. See SOUND, EXCITEMENT.

by, *adv. & prep.* beside, alongside. See AGENCY, CAUSE, SIDE. *Ant.,* see OPPOSITION.

bygone, *adj.* former, PAST; antiquated, obsolete. *Ant.,* see FUTURITY.

bystander, *n.* witness, observer; SPECTATOR, onlooker. See PRESENCE.

byway, *n.* lane, short cut, byroad. See DEVIATION, WAY.

byword, *n.* saying, proverb; shibboleth, password. See MAXIM.

C

cab, *n.* taxi, taxicab, hack, hackney, hansom. See VEHICLE.

cabal, *n.* junto, clique, conspiracy, plot; coterie. See ASSEMBLAGE.

cabin, *n.* shack, shed, shanty, lodge, hut, cottage; stateroom, cockpit. See RECEPTACLE, ABODE.

cabinet, *n.* room, boudoir, chamber, closet; étagère, case; repository; ministry, board, COUNCIL. See RECEPTACLE.

cable, *n.* rope, line, cord; cablegram. See FILAMENT, COMMUNICATION.

cad, *n.* scoundrel, bounder, churl. See EVILDOER, DISCOURTESY.

café, *n.* coffeehouse, coffee shop; saloon, bar; cabaret, bistro. See FOOD.

cage, *n. & v.* —*n.* prison, enclosure, bars; aviary, pen. —*v.t.* RESTRAIN, confine, imprison, incarcerate, pen. See RESTRAINT. *Ant.,* LIBERATE.

cajole, *v.t.* flatter, wheedle, inveigle; beguile, blandish; coax. *Colloq.,* jolly. See DECEPTION. *Ant.,* see SEVERITY.

cake, *v. & n.* —*v.i.* bake, harden; consolidate; thicken, congeal, condense. See COHERENCE. —*n.* mass, brick, block, floe. See DENSITY.

calamity, *n.* trouble, distress, misfortune, catastrophe, misery, affliction, disaster. See ADVERSITY. *Ant.,* see PROSPERITY.

calculate, *v.* compute, reckon; count, appraise; estimate. *Colloq.,* consider, deem, figure. See NUMERATION.

calculating, *adj.* scheming, crafty, shrewd, designing, CUNNING. See PLAN.

calefaction, *n.* See HEAT.

calendar, *n.* almanac; diary, journal; register, schedule; docket. See TIME.

calf, *n.* offspring, young. *Colloq.,* dogie. See ANIMAL.

caliber, *n.* gauge, bore; quality; ability, capability, capacity. See BREADTH, SIZE, SKILL.

calibrate, *v.t.* measure, graduate.

call, *v. & n.* —*v.* CRY, shout, yell; summon, bid; convoke, muster; choose, appoint, elect; name, designate; visit, interview. See CHOICE, ASSEMBLAGE, COMMAND, NOMENCLATURE, SOCIALITY. —*n.* summons, demand; shout, yell; signal; impulse, urge; visit.

calling, *n.* vocation, profession; occupation, trade, BUSINESS.

callous, *adj.* horny, tough; unfeeling, insensitive, insensible, hardened. See HARDNESS, INSENSIBILITY. *Ant.,* see SOFTNESS, SENSIBILITY.

calm, *adj. & v.* —*adj.* placid, serene, unruffled, cool, composed, undisturbed, unperturbed; phlegmatic, sedate; tranquil, still, motionless, halcyon; peaceful, pacific. —*v.t.* still, pacify. See REPOSE, SILENCE. *Ant.,* see EXCITEMENT.

camera, *n.* See OPTICAL INSTRUMENTS.

camouflage, *v. & n.* —*v.t.* disguise, conceal, fake. —*n.* disguise, mask, simulation. See CONCEALMENT.

camp, *n.* encampment, bivouac, cantonment, shelter. See ABODE.

campaign, *n. & v.* —*n.* operations; plan. —*v.i.* canvass, electioneer; fight, war. See WARFARE, CHOICE. *Ant.,* see PACIFICATION.

campus, *n.* grounds, quadrangle. *Colloq.,* quad. See SCHOOL.

can, *n. & v.* —*n.* tin, container. *Slang,* jail; toilet. See RECEPTACLE. —*v.t.* preserve, put up.

canal, *n.* PASSAGE, CHANNEL, waterway; ditch, culvert, conduit.

cancel, *v.t.* .obliterate, efface, delete; postmark. See NULLIFICATION, DESTRUCTION. *Ant.*, see AFFIRMATION.

cancer, *n.* carcinoma, sarcoma, malignancy, growth, tumor. See DISEASE.

candid, *adj.* frank, straightforward; outspoken, blunt; impartial. See SIMPLENESS. *Ant.*, see DECEPTION.

candidate, *n.* nominee, office-seeker; applicant, aspirant; probationer. See REQUEST.

candle, *n.* taper, wax, wax candle, dip, cierge. See LIGHT.

candor, *n.* honesty, impartiality; simplicity, naïveté, INNOCENCE. See TRUTH.

candy, *n.* confection, confectionery, sweet, bonbon, kiss. See SWEETNESS.

cane, *n. & v.* —*n.* switch, stick, rod, birch, walking *or* swagger stick; canebrake. See SUPPORT. —*v.* thrash, flog, switch, beat. See PUNISHMENT.

cannibal, *n.* man-eater, savage, anthropophagus. See EVILDOER.

cannon, *n.* gun, field gun *or* piece; artillery, ordnance, battery. See ARMS.

canoe, *n.* dugout, kayak, bungo, pirogue. See SHIP.

canon, *n.* decree, code, law; principle; criterion; round, catch. See ORTHODOXY, ADVICE, MUSIC.

canopy, *n.* covering, awning; tester; vault, sky; pavilion, cope; howdah. See COVERING.

cant, *n.* pretense, hypocrisy, insincerity; argot, lingo, SLANG, jargon.

canteen, *n.* flask, waterbag; commissary. See RECEPTACLE, STORE.

canvas, *n.* sail, tarpaulin, tent; circus; PAINTING. See COVERING, NAVIGATION.

canvass, *v.t.* examine, sift, discuss; solicit, campaign, poll, survey, seek; peddle, sell. See INQUIRY, REQUEST, SALE.

canyon, *n.* ravine, defile, gorge, gulch, chasm. See INTERVAL, DEPRESSION.

cap, *n. & v.* —*n.* headdress; skullcap; tam-o'-shanter, beret, beanie; kepi. —*v.* cover; match, outdo, excel. See CLOTHING, COVERING.

capable, *adj.* able, competent, proficient; susceptible. See SKILL. *Ant.*, see UNSKILLFULNESS.

capacity, *n.* content, volume, SIZE; aptitude, faculty; talent, skill, capability. See INTELLECT, POWER. *Ant.*, see LITTLENESS, IMPOTENCE.

cape, *n.* mantle, cloak, tippet, fichu, pelerine, bertha; SHAWL; headland, promontory, point, tongue, peninsula. See CLOTHING, CONVEXITY.

caper, *v. & n.* —*v.i.* LEAP, jump, gambol, frisk, prance, skip, caracole, hop, spring. —*n.* LEAP; prank, antic, trick, practical joke. See WIT.

capital, *adj. & n.* —*adj.* excellent, paramount, first-rate, first-class, unequaled, GOOD; IMPORTANT, primary, major, preëminent, principal; metropolitan. *Ant.*, see EVIL, UNIMPORTANCE. —*n.* metropolis, seat; funds, stock, assets, resources; opulence, riches, MONEY, WEALTH. See ABODE.

caprice, *n.* fancy, humor, idiosyncrasy, whim, crotchet, quirk; fad, vagary; whims(e)y, prank; escapade; vacillation, CHANGEABLENESS, eccentricity, capriciousness, fickleness, inconstancy. *Ant.*, see STABILITY.

capsize, *v.* overturn, upset, turn turtle, turn *or* tip over. See INVERSION.

captain, *n.* commander, MASTER, skipper; leader; chief, headman. See AUTHORITY. *Ant.*, see SERVANT.

caption, *n.* title, subtitle, headline, heading, subhead, legend. See WRITING.

captious, *adj.* caviling, carping, hairsplitting, faultfinding, hypercritical. See IRASCIBILITY.

captivate, *v.t.* CHARM, fascinate, infatuate, enchant, enamor; enthrall, enslave, bewitch. See DESIRE, PLEASURE. *Ant.*, see PAIN.

capture, *v.t.* seize, apprehend, arrest, TAKE; grab, nab, collar; bag, snare, trap. *Ant.,* see FREEDOM.

car, *n.* automobile, VEHICLE; bus, omnibus, trolley, coach, Pullman; cage; sedan, coupé, limousine, convertible. *Colloq.,* sleeper; jalopy.

carcass, *n.* corpse; remains, shell, hull (see REMAINDER).

CARE

Nouns—**1,** care, solicitude, heed, heedfulness; scruple, conscientiousness, PROBITY; watchfulness, vigilance, surveillance, eyes of Argus, watch, vigil, lookout, watch and ward. See SAFETY.

2, alertness; ACTIVITY, ATTENTION; prudence, circumspection, CAUTION; forethought, precaution, FORESIGHT, PREPARATION.

3, tidiness, ORDER, CLEANNESS; accuracy, exactness; minuteness, attention to detail, meticulousness.

Verbs—**1,** be careful, take care, take pains, be cautious; take precautions; pay attention to; take care of; look *or* see to; look after; keep an eye on; keep watch, mount guard, watch; keep in sight *or* view; mind; mind one's business; keep tabs on.

2, look sharp; keep a sharp lookout; have all one's wits about one; watch for, expect; keep one's eyes open *or* peeled; sleep with one eye open; mind one's Ps and Qs; speak by the card; pick one's steps.

3, observe; do one's duty; make good; keep one's word *or* promise.

4, stop, look and listen; *timeo Danaos, festina lente, caveat emptor.*

Adjectives—**1,** careful, regardful, heedful; particular, painstaking, prudent, cautious; considerate, thoughtful; deliberative, provident, prepared; alert, guarded, on one's guard, on the *qui vive,* on the alert, on watch, on the lookout; awake, broad awake, vigilant; watchful, wakeful, Argus-eyed, wide-awake, expectant.

2, tidy, orderly, shipshape, clean; accurate, exact; scrupulous, conscientious.

Adverbs—carefully, *etc.;* with care, gingerly.

Antonym, see NEGLECT.

---

career, *n.* profession, calling, lifework; progress, success; history. See CONDUCT, BUSINESS.

careless, *adj.* carefree, nonchalant, unconcerned, free, casual, offhand; negligent, thoughtless, inconsiderate, inattentive, unobservant, unthinking; slack, slovenly; reckless, rash, indiscreet. See NEGLECT, INDIFFERENCE.

caress, *v.t.* hug, kiss, clasp, embrace; fondle, pet, stroke, dandle. See ENDEARMENT.

cargo, *n.* freight, lading, shipment, load. See PASSAGE.

caricature, *n. & v.* —*n.* burlesque, parody, travesty. —*v.* satirize, exaggerate, take off, distort, MISREPRESENT. *Ant.,* see REPRESENTATION.

carnage, *n.* KILLING, massacre, bloodshed, slaughter; shambles, butchery.

carnal, *adj.* bodily, fleshly; worldly, sensual. See ANIMAL, IRRELIGION.

carnival, *n.* festival, fête, gala; masquerade, bacchanal. *Colloq.,* jamboree. See AMUSEMENT, REJOICING.

carnivorous, *adj.* cannibal, flesh-eating; predatory, predaceous. See FOOD.

carol, *n.* song, lay, madrigal, noël. See MUSIC.

carom, *n.* cannon, rebound; shot. See RECOIL, IMPULSE.

carouse, *v.i.* feast, revel; debauch, drink. *Colloq.,* booze, go on a toot. See AMUSEMENT, DRUNKENNESS. *Ant.,* see WEARINESS, MODERATION.

carpenter, *n.* cabinetmaker, woodworker, joiner. See PRODUCTION.

carpet, *n.* rug, mat, drugget; wall-to-wall, oriental, *etc.* See COVERING.

carriage, *n.* bearing, presence, mien, behavior, conduct, front; wagon, cart, stage, stagecoach, coach, equipage. See APPEARANCE, VEHICLE.

CARRIER

Nouns—**1,** carrier, porter, bearer; redcap, skycap; stevedore; conveyer, transporter; freighter, shipper; courier, messenger, runner; coolie; postman, mailman, letter carrier; engineer, conductor, motorman; teamster, trucker, truck driver, helper, expressman; chauffeur, driver, cabbie, hackie; coachman.
2, common carrier; railroad, railway, train; local, express, limited, freight (train); airline, airliner, transport; street car, trolley (car), tram, subway, tube, el, elevated line, interurban, rapid transit; omnibus, bus, coach, jitney, stage(coach), charabanc, taxi(cab), cab, hack; sledge, cart, dray, truck, trailer, semitrailer, VEHICLE.
3, beast of burden; horse, draft horse, packhorse, carthorse; ass, burro, jackass, hinny, jennet, donkey, mule; camel, dromedary, ox, llama, elephant; reindeer, dog, husky; carrier pigeon, passenger pigeon, homing pigeon.
4, basket, box, carton, tray, *etc.* See RECEPTACLE.
Antonym, see PASSAGE.

---

carrion, *n.* flesh; corpse, carcass, remains; offal, scavengers. See UNCLEANNESS, DECOMPOSITION.
carry, *v.t.* uphold, SUPPORT; transport, bear, TRANSFER. *Colloq.*, lug, tote.
cart, *n.* wagon, carriage, tumbrel, tumbril; pushcart. See VEHICLE.
cartel, *n.* See SYNDICATE.
cartoon, *n.* sketch, drawing; lampoon, caricature; comic strip. *Colloq.*, comics, funnies, funny papers. See REPRESENTATION, UNIMPORTANCE.
carve, *v.i.* cut, slice; mold, shape, fashion; chisel, engrave, sculpture. See DISJUNCTION, FORM.
case, *n.* instance, situation, plight; sheath, scabbard, holster; portfolio; suit, action, litigation; argument, proposition; box, container, carton, casket, cabinet; bag, suitcase, handbag, grip, valise. See BUSINESS, COVERING, LAWSUIT, RECEPTACLE, CIRCUMSTANCE.
cash, *n.* MONEY, coin, silver, paper; specie, ready money. *Slang*, brass, dust.
cask, *n.* barrel, hogshead, keg, butt. See RECEPTACLE.
casket, *n.* coffin, reliquary; chest, box. See RECEPTACLE.
cast, *v. & n.* —*v.t.* throw, toss, heave, hurl, sling, fling; mold. See FORM, PROPULSION. —*n.* APPEARANCE, aspect, air; company, actors; casting, copy, mold, sculpture. See DRAMA, FORM.
caste, *n.* CLASS, rank, degree.
castle, *n.* tower, fort, fortress, stronghold; donjon, keep. See DEFENSE.
castrate, *v.t.* emasculate, unman; geld, spay. See IMPOTENCE.
casual, *adj.* accidental, adventitious, random, haphazard, cursory, happy-go-lucky; incidental, CHANCE, fortuitous, contingent, conditional.
casualty, *n.* chance, accident; disaster, calamity, misfortune. See ADVERSITY. *Ant.*, see PROSPERITY.
cat, *n.* feline, puss, pussy, tomcat, tabby, grimalkin, alley cat, mouser, kitten; lion, tiger, leopard. See ANIMAL.
catacombs, *n.* charnel house; vaults, tombs, caves. See INTERMENT.
catalogue, *n.* list, index, RECORD.
catastrophe, *n.* calamity, convulsion, débâcle, disaster, upheaval, cataclysm, paroxysm; END. See ADVERSITY.
catch, *v.t.* take, seize; overtake; trawl, land, net, hook; surprise, detect; snare, trap; capture, arrest, apprehend; snatch. *Slang*, nab. See ACQUISITION. *Ant.*, see FREEDOM.
catching, *adj.*, *colloq.*, see CONTAGIOUS.
category, *n.* CLASS, group; bracket, rank, kind; status, place; pigeonhole.

cater, *v.i.* purvey, sell, PROVISION, serve; indulge, humor. See SALE, CARE.

cathartic, *adj.* laxative, physic, purgative, aperient, purifying. See REMEDY.

catholic, *adj.* tolerant, liberal; universal, GENERAL. See BREADTH. *Ant.,* see NARROWNESS.

cattle, *n.* livestock; kine, cows, bulls, steers. See ANIMAL.

CAUSE

Nouns—1, cause, origin, source, principle, element; leaven; groundwork, base, basis, foundation, SUPPORT; spring, fountain, fountainhead, headspring, head; genesis; descent, paternity, ANCESTRY; pivot, hinge, turning-point, lever; key; straw that breaks the camel's back.

2, causality, causation, origination; PRODUCTION; ground; reason (why); why and wherefore, *rationale*, occasion, derivation; undercurrents.

3, rudiment, fundamentals, egg, germ, embryo, bud, root, radix, radical, etymon, nucleus, seed, stem, stock, stirps, trunk, taproot; nest, cradle, nursery, womb, nidus, birthplace, hot-bed.

4, INFLUENCE, weight, sway, leverage; MOTIVE, impulse, consideration, motivation; temptation, enticement, inducement, allurement; inspiration, exhortation, persuasion, solicitation.

5, occasioner, prime mover, author, creator, producer, progenitor; mainspring, agent.

Verbs—1, be the cause of; originate; give rise to; cause, occasion, sow the seeds of, kindle; bring to pass, bring about; produce, create; give birth to, generate; set up, set afloat, set on foot; found, broach, institute, lay the foundation of; lie at the root of.

2, procure, induce; draw down, open the door to; evoke, entail, operate; elicit, provoke; conduce to, contribute; have a hand in, have a finger in the pie; determine, decide, turn the scale; have a common origin; derive from. See EFFECT.

3, move, prompt, motivate; weigh, tell, carry weight; sway, persuade, bear upon; inspire, inspirit, stimulate, rouse, arouse, animate, incite, instigate; impel, propel, enforce; hound, press, urge, exhort, spur, egg on.

Adjectives—caused, causal, original; primary, primitive, primordial; ab-original; radical; embryonic, in embryo, *in ovo;* seminal, germinal; at the bottom of; connate, having a common origin.

Adverbs—because, by reason of, on account of; therefore.

Antonym, see EFFECT.

caustic, *adj.* corrosive, burning, mordant; sarcastic, satirical, biting, acrimonious; severe. See DISCOURTESY, RESENTMENT, DETRACTION. *Ant.,* see COURTESY, SERVILITY.

CAUTION

Nouns—1, caution, cautiousness, discretion, prudence, heed, circumspection, calculation; deliberation, forethought, FORESIGHT; vigilance, CARE; WARNING. See SAFETY.

2, coolness, self-possession, presence of mind, *sang-froid;* worldly wisdom, Fabian policy. See FEAR.

Verbs—1, be cautious, take care, take heed, have a care; mind, be on one's guard, keep watch; watch one's step; make assurance doubly sure; think twice; look before one leaps; count the cost; look to the main chance; feel one's way; see how the land lies; wait to see how the cat jumps; bridle one's tongue; let well enough alone, keep out of harm's way; keep at a respectful distance; be on the same side.

2, *timeo Danaos; festina lente; cave canem; caveat emptor;* stop, look, and listen.

Antonym, see RASHNESS.

cavalry, *n.* horse soldiers, horsemen, dragoons. See COMBATANT.
cave, *n.* recess, grotto, cavern; lair, burrow; den. See CONCAVITY, ABODE.
cavil, *v.i.* carp, find fault, DISSENT, take exception; be captious, quibble, split hairs. See IRASCIBILITY. *Ant.,* see ASSENT.
cavity, *n.* hole, excavation, hollow, pit; opening, depression, pocket, dent. See CONCAVITY. *Ant.,* CONVEXITY.
cease, *v.i.* stop, desist, discontinue; END, terminate; halt, pause. *Ant.,* see CONTINUITY.
ceaseless, *adj.* continual, incessant (see CONSTANT).
cede, *v.t.* yield, grant, relinquish; assign, transfer; surrender, hand over. See RELINQUISHMENT. *Ant.,* see POSSESSION.
ceiling, *n.* roof, cupola, vault, canopy; maximum, LIMIT. See COVERING.

CELEBRATION

Nouns—**1,** celebration, solemnization, jubilee, commemoration; ovation, pæan; triumph, jubilation; inauguration, installation, presentation; coronation ceremony, RITE.
2, bonfire, salute, salvo; flourish of trumpets, fanfare, colors flying, illuminations, fireworks; TROPHY, triumphal arch.
3, fête, festival, festivity, gala, gala occasion, holiday; harvest home; red-letter day; thanksgiving.
4, REJOICING, jubilation, jubilee, merrymaking.
Verbs—**1,** celebrate, keep, signalize, do honor to, commemorate, solemnize, hallow; inaugurate, install, crown.
2, pledge, drink to, toast; rejoice, make merry, kill the fatted calf, hold jubilee, jubilate. See REJOICING.
Adjectives—celebrated; famous; see REPUTE.
Antonym, see INDIFFERENCE.

celebrity, *n.* star, notable, name; eminence, fame, renown. See REPUTE.
celestial, *adj.* heavenly, angelic, divine, holy; unearthly, supernal, beatific; solar, astral, empyreal. See DEITY, HEAVEN. *Ant.,* see HELL.

CELIBACY

Nouns—**1,** celibacy, singleness, single blessedness; bachelorhood, bachelorship, spinsterhood; misogamy, misogyny; virginity, *pucelage*; maidenhood; chastity.
2, unmarried man, bachelor, Cœlebs, agamist, misogamist, misogynist; monk; unmarried woman, spinster; maid, maiden, virgin; *femme sole*, old maid.
Adjectives—celibate, unmarried, unwedded, wifeless, spouseless; single; maiden, virgin, chaste.
Antonym, see MARRIAGE.

cell, *n.* protoplasm; cage, jail; compartment, room, vault. See RECEPTACLE, PRISON.
cellar, *n.* basement, boiler room; storeroom; subcellar; vault, shelter; wine, cyclone, *etc.* cellar. See RECEPTACLE, LOWNESS.
cement, *n.* mortar, plaster, concrete, putty, tar, solder; adhesive, glue, mucilage, paste. See CONNECTION.
cemetery, *n.* graveyard, churchyard, burial ground. *Slang,* Boot Hill. See INTERMENT.
censor, *n. & v.* —*n.* reviewer, critic; watchdog. —*v.t.* expurgate, delete, cut, edit; suppress, muzzle, SILENCE. See RESTRAINT, DEDUCTION.
censorious, *adj.* severe, critical, fault-finding, condemnatory. See SEVERITY.
censure, *v. & n.* —*v.t.* upbraid, chide, reprove, criticize, blame. *Slang,* hit, knock, pan. —*n.* blame, criticism, disapproval. See DISAPPROBATION. *Ant.,* see APPROBATION.

census, *n.* poll, enumeration, count. See NUMERATION.
center, *n.* core, heart, MIDDLE, hub, nave; midpoint; focus, focal point, dead center; nucleus, pole, axis; spine.
centralization, *n.* centrality, centralness, focalization; concentration, convergence, convergency; cynosure; magnetism; center of attraction; focus; combination, merging, unity, oneness, federation. See MIDDLE.
ceramics, *n.* pottery, clayworking; SCULPTURE; crockery, earthenware, china, porcelain, ironstone, stoneware; enamel, cloisonné; brick, terracotta, adobe, glass. See HEAT, MATERIALS.
cereal, *n.* grain, seed; gruel, porridge, pabulum. See FOOD.
ceremony, *n.* ritual, formality, punctilio, protocol; form, observance, RITE, sacrament, function. See OSTENTATION.

CERTAINTY

Nouns—**1,** certainty; certitude, sureness, surety, assurance; dead *or* moral certainty; infallibility, reliability; NECESSITY.
2, positiveness, assuredness; dogmatism, dogmatist; doctrinaire, bigot, opinionist, Sir Oracle; *ipse dixit.*
3, fact, matter of fact; *fait accompli*; guarantee.
Verbs—**1,** be certain; stand to reason; admit of no doubt; render certain, insure, assure; clinch, make sure; determine, decide, settle, fix; set at rest, make assurance doubly sure.
2, dogmatize; lay down the law; bet one's bottom dollar; know like a book.
Adjectives—**1,** certain, sure, assured; solid, well-founded; unqualified, absolute, positive, determinate, definite, clear, unequivocal, categorical, unmistakable, decisive, decided, ascertained, known, proven.
2, inevitable, unavoidable; sure as fate, sure as death and taxes; unerring, infallible; unchangeable; to be depended on; trustworthy, reliable; bound.
3, unimpeachable, undeniable, unquestionable; indisputable, incontestable, incontrovertible, indubitable; irrefutable, conclusive, without power of appeal; beyond a doubt, without a shadow of doubt; past dispute; beyond all question; undoubted, doubtless; clear as day.
4, authoritative, authentic, official, *ex cathedra.*
Adverbs—certainly, for certain, certes (Arch.), sure, no doubt, doubtless; and no mistake; sure enough; to be sure; of course, as a matter of course, at any rate, at all events; without fail; come what may *or* will; sink or swim; rain or shine; sight unseen; truly; no question; not a shadow of doubt.

Antonym, see DOUBT.

---

certificate, *n.* certification, warrant, diploma; policy, debenture, stock. See EVIDENCE, SECURITY.
cessation, *n.* stop, stoppage, ceasing; halt, arrestment; END, conclusion; desistance, discontinuance; pause, rest, lull, respite; period. See DEATH. *Ant.,* see CONTINUITY.
chafe, *v.t.* HEAT, WARM; wear, rub; vex, anger, annoy, gall, eat. See RESENTMENT, PAIN. *Ant.,* see PLEASURE.
chaff, *n.* husks, WASTE; banter, jesting, WIT, raillery.
chagrin, *n.* mortification, vexation. See PAIN. *Ant.,* see PLEASURE.
chain, *n.* series, progression, course, row, string; bond, fetter; concatenation. See CONTINUITY, CONNECTION.
chair, *n.* chairman, moderator, speaker, master of ceremonies, toastmaster; seat, stool, rocker, throne; professorship, judgeship, fellowship. *Colloq.,* M.C., emcee. See DIRECTOR, SUPPORT, TEACHING.
challenge, *v. & n.* —*v.* query, controvert, question, dispute; dare, defy. *Colloq.,* stump. See DOUBT. *Ant.,* see BELIEF, OBEDIENCE. —*n.* exception; invitation [to fight]. See CONTENTION.

chamber, *n.* room, apartment, salon; bedroom, cell; hall, exchange, bourse; legislature, assembly. See RECEPTACLE, LEGALITY.

chameleon, *n.* reptile, lizard; turncoat, renegade, Proteus. See ANIMAL, CHANGEABLENESS. *Ant.,* see STABILITY.

champion, *v. & n.* —*n.* defender, protector, squire, knight; backer, supporter; conqueror, victor, winner. See AID, SUCCESS. *Ant.,* see FAILURE. —*v.t.* defend, protect.

CHANCE

Nouns—**1,** chance, accident, lot; fate, kismet, karma, DESTINY, luck, fortune; hap, hazard; casualty, contingency, adventure, fortuity; indetermination. See NECESSITY.

2, speculation, venture, UNCERTAINTY; random shot, guessing game, blind bargain, shot *or* leap in the dark, pig in a poke; fluke; potluck.

3, gambling, risk, gaming, lottery; betting, bet, stake, wager, dicing, game; wheel of Fortune, tossup, toss of the dice, roulette, Russian roulette, heads or tails, turn of the card(s) *or* wheel, raffle; casino, lottery, gambling house, policy *or* numbers racket, gambling hell, gaming table(s), bucket shop; race track, the turf, bookmaking, parimutuel [window(s)], Totalizator, handbook, bookmaker, bookie; gambler, gamester, dicer, adventurer, speculator, horseplayer, bettor, crapshooter, pokerface, *etc.*

4, probability, POSSIBILITY, contingency, expectancy; odds, odds-on, edge, advantage; theory of probabilities, law of averages.

Verbs—**1,** chance, befall, hap, turn up; fall to one's lot, be one's fate; happen upon, light upon, run into *or* across, stumble on.

2, chance (it), gamble, risk, venture, speculate; try one's luck, tempt fortune, take a chance, trust to chance; draw lots, toss a coin; shoot the works, go for broke; game, hazard, stake, bet, wager, play (for); go out on a limb.

3, be possible or probable; have *or* stand a chance; bid fair; seem likely; expect, think likely, dare say, flatter oneself.

Adjectives—**1,** chance, random, accidental, adventitious, casual, fortuitous, contingent, causeless, indeterminate, uncontrollable; hit-or-miss, catch-as-catch-can; aleatric.

2, unintentional, undirected, purposeless, undirected, haphazard, unpremeditated, unwitting.

3, PROBABLE, possible, likely, potential, conceivable, in the cards.

Adverbs—**1,** by chance, casually, at random, haphazard; incidentally, *en passant*, by the way; adrift.

2, possibly, probably, likely; perhaps, perchance, peradventure; maybe, mayhap, haply; God willing, *Deo volente, D.V.,* wind and weather permitting. *Colloq.,* like as not, dollars to doughnuts, on the off chance.

Antonym, see NECESSITY.

chandelier, *n.* candelabra, candlestick. See PENDENCY.

CHANGE

Nouns—**1,** change, alteration, mutation, permutation, diversification, VARIATION, modification, SUBSTITUTION, modulation, mood, QUALIFICATION, innovation, metastasis, DEVIATION, turn; diversion; break.

2, transformation, transfiguration; metamorphosis; transmutation; transubstantiation; metagenesis, transanimation, transmigration, metempsychosis; avatar; alterative.

3, CONVERSION; REVOLUTION, overthrow; inversion, eversion, reversal; displacement; transposition; transference, TRANSFER; CHANGEABLENESS, tergiversation. See DIFFERENCE.

Verbs—**1,** change, alter, vary, wax and wane; temper, modulate, diversify, qualify, tamper with; turn, shift, veer, tack, chop, shuffle, swerve, warp, deviate, turn aside, avert, evert, intervert; pass to, take a turn, turn the corner; work a change, modify, vamp, superinduce.

2, transform, translate, transfigure, transmute, transume; metamorphose; ring the changes; convert, reduce, resolve; innovate, introduce new blood, shuffle the cards; influence, turn the scale; shift the scene, turn over a new leaf; resume; recast, remodel, revamp; reverse, overturn, upset; invert, transpose; reform, reorganize; disturb.

3, be converted (into), turn into, become, come to; grow, mature, mellow, ripen; resolve (self) into; assume the form, *etc.*, of.

Adjectives—changed, altered; new-fangled, novel; CHANGEABLE, variable; transitional; modifiable; alternative.

Antonym, see STABILITY.

CHANGEABLENESS

Nouns—**1**, changeableness, alterability; mutability; inconstancy, fickleness; versatility; mobility; instability, vacillation, indecision, IRRESOLUTION; fluctuation, fluidity, vicissitude; alternation, OSCILLATION; restlessness, fidgets, disquiet, disquietude, inquietude; unrest; AGITATION; iridescence.

2, moon, Proteus, Cheshire cat, chameleon, quicksilver, shifting sands, weathervane, kaleidoscope, harlequin, Cynthia of the minute, April showers; wheel of fortune; TRANSIENTNESS.

3, CAPRICE, whimsy, vagary, coquetry, fad; capriciousness.

Verbs—fluctuate, vary, waver, flounder, flicker, flitter, flit, flutter, shift, shuffle, shake, totter, tremble, vacillate, turn and turn about, ring the changes; sway or shift to and fro; change one's mind; oscillate; vibrate; alternate; have as many phases as the moon. See CHANGE.

Adjectives—changeable, changeful; alterable; changing; mutable, variable, checkered; kaleidoscopic, ever-changing; protean; versatile; inconstant, unsteady, unstable, unfixed, unsettled; fluctuating; restless; agitated; erratic, fickle; irresolute, capricious; volatile, mercurial; touch-and-go; fitful, spasmodic; vibratory; vagrant, wayward; desultory; afloat; alternating; plastic, mobile; transient; iridescent; convertible, modifiable.

Adverbs—see-saw; off and on.

Antonym, see STABILITY.

changeless, *adj.* immutable, unchanging. See PERMANENCE, STABILITY.

changeling, *n.* child; Proteus; waverer, turncoat, renegade. See MYTHICAL DEITIES, CHANGEABLENESS. *Ant.,* see STABILITY.

channel, *n.* duct, conduit, PASSAGE; waterway, canal; pipe, tube, tunnel; aqueduct; wavelength, broadcasting channel; means of communication; way, road, route; artery, vein, blood vessel.

chant, *n.* song; plainsong or chant, Gregorian or Anglican chant; intonation, incantation; psalm, canticle, requiem. See MUSIC, HYMN.

chaos, *n.* DISORDER, shambles, confusion, jumble, disorganization; abyss, void. *Ant.,* see ORDER.

chaperon, *n.* attendant, guide, escort; matron, monitor. See SAFETY.

chaplain, *n.* clergyman, *etc.* *Slang,* padre, sky pilot. See CLERGY.

chapter, *n.* division, section; verse, canto, passage; branch, lodge, post, corps. See BOOK.

char, *v.t.* burn, singe, scorch, sear, carbonize. See HEAT.

character, *n.* type, manner, kind, CLASS; nature, disposition, temperament, personality; sign, brand, stamp; figure, LETTER, hieroglyphic, ideograph, pictograph. *Colloq.,* personage, eccentric, crank, original.

characteristic, *adj. & n.* —*adj.* distinctive, typical, peculiar. —*n.* quality, trait, mark, lineament, feature, peculiarity, attribute, distinction. See INDICATION, IDENTITY.

charge, *v. & n.* —*v.* command, exhort, instruct; assess, value, tax, burden; set a price; debit; strike, attack; fill, load, prepare; accuse, score. —*n.* ACCUSATION, allegation, impeachment, indictment; command, order, mandate, requirement; onset, onslaught, ATTACK; price, expense, tax, burden, liability, encumbrance, assessment, rate, debit; supervision, custody, ward, trust, CARE; load, blast. See ADVICE, COMPLETION, PAYMENT. *Ant.,* see DEFENSE.

charitable, *adj.* kind, generous, liberal, kindly, Christian, forgiving, bighearted; altruistic, eleemosynary. See BENEVOLENCE, GIVING. *Ant.,* see MALEVOLENCE, RECEIVING.

charlatan, *n.* quack, pretender, fraud, mountebank, cheat. See DECEPTION.

charm, *v. & n.* —*v.t.* fascinate, hypnotize, enamor, bewitch, enchant, disarm, captivate, ATTRACT; soothe, calm, allay. —*n.* attractiveness, personality, captivation, fascination; amulet, talisman, good-luck piece, incantation, spell, magic. See DESIRE, LOVE, PLEASURE, SORCERY. *Ant.,* see HATE, PAIN.

chart, *n.* map, plan, graph. See INFORMATION.

charter, *n. & v.* —*n.* grant, sanction, license, franchise, AUTHORITY: compact, AGREEMENT. —*v.* establish, license; rent, lease, hire, let, book. See PERMISSION, COMMISSION.

chase, *v.t.* pursue, follow, hunt; dispel, put to flight, rout, repel. See PURSUIT. *Ant.,* see AVOIDANCE.

chasm, *n.* canyon, crevasse, rift, fissure, cleft; abyss. See GULF.

chaste, *adj.* virtuous, pure, undefiled, clean, innocent; SIMPLE, classic, severe. See INNOCENCE, SIMPLENESS. *Ant.,* see IMPURITY.

chastise, *v.t.* chasten, castigate, discipline. See PUNISHMENT, RESTRAINT.

chatter, *n.* prattle, talk, gabble, gibberish. *Colloq.,* patter. See LOQUACITY. *Ant.,* see SILENCE.

chauvinist, *n.* jingo, warmonger, nationalist, patriot; boaster, blusterer, swashbuckler. *Slang,* [male] chauvinist pig. See WARFARE, BOASTING.

CHEAPNESS

Nouns—**1,** cheapness, inexpensiveness, cut rates, low price; good buy, loss leader, markdown, bargain; sale, discount, depreciation, drug on the market; irregulars, seconds; bargain basement, cutthroat competition. *Slang,* steal.

2, triviality, paltriness, insignificance; trashiness, worthlessness. See LOWNESS.

3, gratuity; gift (see GIVING); free *or* complimentary seats, Annie Oakley, pass, free admission; nominal price; labor of love. *Colloq.,* comp, freebie.

Verbs—be cheap, cost little; come down in price, be marked down; buy for a song; buy at a bargain, buy dirt cheap; get one's money's worth; beat down; depreciate, undervalue; cut (competitor's) throat. *Colloq.,* paper the house. See ECONOMY, LOWNESS.

Adjectives—**1,** cheap; underpriced, low-priced; moderate, reasonable, inexpensive; worth the money; economical; cheap at the price; dirt-cheap; reduced, cutrate, half-price, marked down; depreciated, unsalable, a drug on the market.

2, gratuitous, gratis, free, for nothing; without charge, untaxed; scot-free; free of cost, complimentary; honorary. *Colloq.,* on the house, dime a dozen; five-and-ten.

3, trivial, paltry, insignificant; trashy, worthless.

Adverbs—cheaply, inexpensively; for a song; at cost [price], at a reduction.

Antonym, see PAYMENT, IMPORTANCE.

---

cheat, *v.i.* deceive, defraud, swindle, hoodwink, gull, dupe, delude, hoax, victimize. *Colloq.,* bilk, gouge, gyp, skin, take, fleece. See DECEPTION.

check, *v. & n.* —*v.t.* control, test, verify, tally, count; RESTRAIN, repress, halt, stop, arrest, impede, interrupt, curb; stunt. —*n.* draft, money order; interruption, rebuff; setback, reverse, stop, RESTRAINT; supervision, control, tab; drag, block, brake; pattern, design, plaid, tartan; ticket, token, bill, stub. See ADVERSITY, HINDRANCE, MONEY.

checkered, *adj.* varied, irregular; colorful; checked, plaid. See VARIEGATION.

cheek, *n.* INSOLENCE, impertinence, sauce, impudence, effrontery; jowl. *Slang*, nerve, brass, gall, face, sass. See SIDE. *Ant.*, see COURTESY.

CHEERFULNESS

Nouns—**1,** cheerfulness; geniality, gaiety, sunniness; cheer, good humor, spirits, high spirits, animal spirits; glee, high glee, light heart; optimism (see HOPE). See LIGHTNESS, PLEASURE.

2, liveliness, life, alacrity, vivacity, animation.

3, mirth, merriment, hilarity, exhilaration; joviality, jollity; levity, jocularity, WIT; playfulness, fun, glee; laughter, merrymaking, AMUSEMENT.

4, contentment, contentedness; happiness, complacency, satisfaction, serenity, comfort, peace of mind, CONTENT.

Verbs—**1,** be cheerful, have the mind at ease, smile, put a good face upon, keep up one's spirits; see the bright side; cheer up, brighten up, light up, bear up; chirp, take heart, cast away care, drive dull care away, perk up; rejoice, carol, chirrup; frisk, lilt. *Slang*, feel one's oats, kick up one's heels; keep a stiff upper lip.

2, cheer, enliven, elate, exhilarate, gladden, inspirit, animate, raise the spirits, inspire; invigorate, encourage, heaven, refresh; applaud. *Slang*, jazz up, give a shot in the arm.

Adjectives—**1,** cheerful; genial, happy, cheery, of good cheer, smiling, sunny, blithe; in good spirits; high-spirited; happy as the day is long; gay as a lark; light, lightsome, lighthearted; buoyant, debonair, bright, free and easy, airy; saucy, jaunty.

2, lively, spry, sprightly, spirited, animated, vivacious; brisk, sparkling; sportive; full of play, full of spirit; all alive.

3, merry as a cricket *or* grig; joyful, joyous, jocund, jovial; jolly, blithesome, gleeful, hilarious, rattling; playful, playful as a kitten, tricksy, frisky, frolicsome; jocose, jocular, waggish; mirthloving, laughter-loving, mirthful, rollicking; elated, exultant, jubilant, flushed; rejoicing; cock-a-hoop; cheering, inspiriting, exhilarating; pleasing.

Adverbs—cheerfully, cheerily, with relish, with zest; in fine fettle, in high spirits *or* feather. *Slang*, sitting on top of the world, riding high.

Antonym, see DISCONTENT.

---

cherish, *v.t.* nurture, nourish, foster, protect, nurse; entertain, harbor, cling to; prize, treasure, hold dear, revere. See CARE, LOVE. *Ant.*, see NEGLECT, HATE.

cherub, *n.* ANGEL; cupid, amor; child, moppet, urchin; infant.

chest, *n.* case, box, casket; coffer; cabinet, commode, locker, bureau; thorax, breast. See CONVEXITY, RECEPTACLE.

chew, *v.t. & i.* masticate, eat, gnaw, grind, champ. See FOOD.

chic, *n. & adj.* See STYLE, STYLISH.

chicanery, *n.* See DECEPTION.

chicken, *n.* fowl, cock, hen, pullet; fryer, broiler, capon. See ANIMAL, FOOD.

chide, *v.* scold, lecture, chastise; taunt, RIDICULE. See DISAPPROBATION.

chief, *n.* leader, chieftain, president; captain, commander, general; superior, foreman, overseer; elder. See AUTHORITY. *Ant.*, see SERVANT.

child, *n.* tot, offspring, bairn, son, daughter. *Slang*, kid, brat. See YOUTH. *Ant.*, see OLDNESS, ANCESTRY.

childbirth, *n.* delivery, parturition, labor pains. See PRODUCTION.

childish, *adj.* infantile, puerile, juvenile, youthful, babyish; brattish; senile, simpleminded, weak, foolish, silly; credulous, naïve, trustful. *Slang,* kiddish. See CREDULITY, SIMPLENESS. *Ant.,* see DOUBT, INTELLIGENCE.

chill, *n.* shivering, shakes, ague; COLDNESS, chilliness; frost. *Ant.,* see HEAT.

chimera, *n.* fancy, fantasy; monster. See IMAGINATION, MYTHICAL DEITIES.

chimney, *n.* fissure, cleft; smokestack, spout, flue, pipe. See OPENING, GULF. *Ant.,* see CLOSURE.

china, *n.* chinaware, CERAMICS. *Colloq.,* dishes. See RECEPTACLE.

chip, *n.* piece, splinter, fragment, flake. See PART. *Ant.,* see WHOLE.

chisel, *v.* trim, pare, sculpt, carve. *Colloq.,* swindle, cheat. See DECEPTION, DEDUCTION, FORM.

chivalrous, *adj.* knightly, gallant, noble, courteous, brave. See COURTESY.

CHOICE

Nouns—**1,** choice, option, selection, determination, discrimination, pick, preference; volition, predilection, DESIRE; adoption, decision, JUDGMENT; alternative; dilemma.

2, election, poll, ballot, vote, voice, suffrage; plebiscite; *vox populi;* electioneering; voting. *Colloq.,* ticket.

3, voter, balloter, elector; suffragist; electorate, constituency.

Verbs—**1,** choose, elect; fix upon, settle, decide; determine, make up one's mind (see RESOLUTION); exercise one's option; adopt, take up, embrace, espouse.

2, vote, poll, ballot; hold up one's hand; divide.

3, select; pick, pick and choose; pick over, pick out, single out; cull, glean, winnow; pick up, pitch upon; pick one's way; indulge one's fancy; set apart, mark out for; prefer; have rather, have as lief; fancy, DESIRE; take a decisive step; commit oneself to a course; cross the Rubicon; cast in one's lot with; take for better or for worse.

Adjectives—optional, elective; discretionary, voluntary, selective, preferential; chosen; CHOICE; GOOD; on approval; on the bandwagon.

Adverbs—optionally, at pleasure, at will, at one's discretion; at the option of; whether or not; once for all; for one's money; by choice, by preference; rather, before, sooner.

Antonym, see REFUSAL.

---

choke, *v.t. & i.* strangle, SUFFOCATE, garrotte, throttle; stifle; obstruct, clog, jam, plug. See CLOSURE, KILLING. *Ant.,* see OPENING.

choose, *v.* See CHOICE.

chop, *v.t. & i.* cut, mince, chip; cleave, lop, hack, hew; strike; lop. See DISJUNCTION.

chord, *n.* harmony, accompaniment; triad, arpeggio. See CONCORD, MUSIC.

chore, *n.* job, task, assignment, DUTY; (*pl.*) housework, rounds. See EXERTION.

chorus, *n.* choir, singers, choristers, dancers; refrain. See MUSICIAN, MUSIC.

christen, *v.t.* baptize, sponsor, name; initiate. See NOMENCLATURE, RITE.

Christian, *n.* believer, gentile, churchman. See RELIGION, PIETY.

Christmas, *n.* yule, Noël. See RITE.

chronic, *adj.* continuing, persistent, constant; confirmed, settled, inveterate, rooted. See CONTINUITY.

chronicle, *n.* account, history, annals, RECORD.

chronological, *adj.* measured, dated; sequential, in SEQUENCE. See TIME.

CHRONOMETRY

Nouns—**1,** chronometry, horometry, chronology, horology; date, epoch; style, era, times.
2, almanac, calendar, ephemeris; register, registry; chronicle, annals, journal, diary.
3, clock, watch, stopwatch, digital watch, chronometer, chronoscope, chronograph; repeater; timekeeper, timepiece; dial, sundial, gnomon, pendulum, hourglass, water glass, clepsydra; time signal. See TIME.
Verbs—fix *or* mark the time; date, register, chronicle; measure, beat *or* mark time; bear date.
Adjectives—chronological, chronometrical, chronoscopic, chronographical.

chubby, *adj.* plump, heavy, stout; obese, overweight. See SIZE.
chuckle, *v. & n.* laugh, chortle, cluck, snicker, cackle. See REJOICING.
chum, *n., colloq.,* pal, buddy (see FRIEND).
chunk, *n., colloq.,* lump, hunk, wad, gob, scrap. See PART, SIZE.
church, *n.* worship, service; ministry, clergy; denomination; Christendom, Holy Church; chapel, cathedral, synagogue, shrine, altar, TEMPLE.
churchdom, *n.* priesthood; RELIGION, CLERGY; church. *Ant.,* see IRRELIGION.
churl, *n.* villein, ceorl; peasant, rustic, yokel; boor, varlet, knave. See EVILDOER, DISCOURTESY.
churn, *v.* mix, cream, blend; agitate, whip, seethe, boil. See AGITATION.
chute, *n.* rapids; fall, DESCENT; white water; ramp, incline, shoot, slide, hopper. See WATER, PASSAGE, OBLIQUITY.
cigar, *n.* cheroot, stogie; panatela, perfecto, corona, belvedere; cigarillo; Havana. See PUNGENCY.
cigarette, *n.* smoke; regular, king-size, long(-size), plain, oval, corktip, filter tip, 100's. *Slang,* coffin nail, cig, fag, butt, gasper, tube, weed, reefer. See PUNGENCY.
cinch, *n., slang,* certitude, sure thing, child's play, snap, breeze, picnic, pushover, lead-pipe cinch; sinecure. See FACILITY.
cinder, *n.* slag, ash(es); brand, ember, coal; lava. See REMAINDER, HEAT.
cipher, *n.* naught, zero; nonentity; cryptogram, codes, cryptology; monogram, device. See CONCEALMENT.
circle, *v. & n.* —*n.* encircle, ring, girdle; circumnavigate; circumscribe, compass. —*n.* circumference; ring, circlet; sphere, orb, disk; set, clique. See PARTY, CIRCULARITY, CIRCUMSCRIPTION.

CIRCUIT

Nouns—circuit, circumference, circle, compass; itinerary (of circuit judge); contour, OUTLINE; route, bypass, roundabout way, detour, loop, winding, zigzag, DEVIATION; orbit.
Verbs—circuit, circle, girdle, loop; go roundabout, bypass, go out of one's way; detour, meander.
Adjectives—circuitous, indirect, roundabout; zigzag, deviating, wandering; circumlocutory.

CIRCUITY

Nouns—circuity, circuition, circulation, CIRCULARITY; turn, curvet; excursion; circumvention; circumnavigation, circumambulation; CIRCUIT; turning, evolution; coil, corkscrew, spiral; cycle.
Verbs—circuit, circumnavigate, circumambulate, circumvent; veer, tack, go the round, make the rounds of; put a girdle around the earth; turn, bend, wheel; go about, put about; wheel, heel; go round, turn round, twine, embrace, describe a circle; come full circle; wind, circulate, meander; whisk, twirl; twist. See CONVOLUTION.

CIRCULARITY

Nouns—**1,** circularity, sphericity, roundness; rotundity.

2, circle, circlet, circumference, ring, areola, hoop, annulus, annulet, bracelet, armlet; ringlet; eye, grommet, loop; wheel, round, trolley, hub, nave; cycle, orb, ball, sphere, globe, orbit, zone, belt, cordon, band; sash, girdle, cestus, cincture, baldric, fillet, wreath, garland; crown, corona, halo; coronet, chaplet, snood, necklace, collar; noose, lasso; meridian, equator, parallel, tropic.

3, ellipse, oval, ovoid, ellipsoid, spheroid, cycloid; epicycloid, epicycle; hemisphere, semicircle; quadrant, sextant, sector, segment.

Verbs—circle, surround; enclose, encompass; rotate, revolve.

Adjectives—circular, round, rounded, annular, ball-shaped, orbed, spherical, spheroidal, globular, cylindrical; oval, ovate; elliptical, egg-shaped; ROTUND.

Antonym, see ANGULARITY.

circulate, *v.t. & i.* pass, go about, change hands, mix, move; spread, publish, diffuse, disseminate, report, propagate; revolve, turn, circle. See MONEY, PASSAGE, PUBLICATION, ROTATION.

circumference, *n.* perimeter, boundary, compass. See OUTLINE.

circumlocution, *n.* periphrasis, verbiage, prolixity, garrulity, wordiness, indirection. See LOQUACITY. *Ant.,* see CONTRACTION.

CIRCUMSCRIPTION

Nouns—circumscription, limitation, INCLOSURE; confinement, RESTRAINT; bound, LIMIT, boundary; envelope.

Verbs—circumscribe, LIMIT, bound, confine, enclose; surround, compass about; imprison, immure, incarcerate, restrict, restrain; wall in, fence in, hem in, hedge round; picket, pen, corral, enkraal; enfold, enclose, envelop, embrace, incase, wrap up; invest, clothe.

Adjectives—circumscribed, begirt, lapped; buried *or* immersed in; embosomed, in the bosom of, imbedded; hemmed in, pent in *or* up, mewed up; immured, imprisoned, encaged; landlocked; seagirt.

Antonym, see FREEDOM.

CIRCUMSTANCE

Nouns—**1,** circumstance, situation, phase, position, posture, attitude, place, environment, point; terms; régime; footing, standing, status, STATE; OCCASION, eventuality, juncture, conjunction; contingency, event; quandary, dilemma, predicament; emergency, exigency, crisis, pinch, pass, impasse, push; turning point; bearings, how the land lies. *Colloq.,* pickle, fix, kettle of fish, hole.

2, OCCURRENCE, incident, fact, happening, phenomenon.

Verbs—OCCUR; meet with, encounter, undergo; fall to the lot of, be one's lot; suffer, endure; pass *or* go through.

Adjectives—circumstantial; given; conditional, provisional; critical, crucial; modal; contingent, incidental; adventitious, EXTRINSIC; occasional.

Adverbs—**1,** in the circumstances, under the circumstances; thus, in such wise; accordingly; therefore, consequently, that being the case, such being the case; that being so, since, seeing that; so, then; conditionally, provided, if, in case; if so, in the event of; in such a contingency *or* case; occasionally; provisionally, unless, except, without; according to circumstances, as the case may be, as the wind blows. *Colloq.,* thusly.

2, eventually; in the (natural) course (of things); as things go.

Antonym, see NONEXISTENCE.

circumvent, *v.t.* surround, entrap; frustrate, thwart, forestall, balk, foil. See DECEPTION, HINDRANCE. *Ant.,* see AID.

circus, *n.* ring, ARENA; carnival, menagerie; sideshow, midway; travesty, FOLLY. *Colloq.*, the big top, greatest show on earth. See AMUSEMENT.

cistern, *n.* tank, reservoir; rain barrel. See STORE, RECEPTACLE.

cite, *v.t.* illustrate, mention, bring forward, quote; arraign, summon; commend, reward. See EVIDENCE.

citizen, *n.* INHABITANT, resident, denizen; urbanite, cosmopolite; native.

city, *n.* town, municipality; capital, metropolis. *Colloq.*, burg, big town. See ABODE.

civil, *adj.* courteous, mannerly, polite, well-bred; civic, secular, lay. See COURTESY. *Ant.*, see DISCOURTESY, CLERGY.

civilize, *v.t.* educate, cultivate, refine; reclaim, enlighten. See IMPROVEMENT. *Ant.*, see DETERIORATION.

claim, *v. & n.* —*v.t.* ask, demand, requisition, require; lay claim to; contend, allege, assert. See AFFIRMATION, COMMAND, RIGHT. *Ant.*, see NEGATION. —*n.* demand, requisition, requirement, prerogative; lien, hold; plea, counterclaim; title. See COMMAND, LAWSUIT, PROPERTY.

claimant, *n.* pretender, pleader, claimer, heir. See RIGHT.

clairvoyance, *n.* second sight, foreknowledge, PREDICTION, extrasensory perception, ESP, psi; fortune-telling, divination; insight. See SUPERNATURALISM, INTUITION.

clamber, *v.i.* scramble, crawl, shin up. See ASCENT.

clammy, *adj.* moist, damp, COLD, sweaty. See MOISTURE.

clamor, *n.* outcry, noise, hullabaloo, uproar, racket, tumult, din. See CRY, LOUDNESS. *Ant.*, see SILENCE.

clamp, *n.* grip, vise; fastener, clasp. See CONNECTION.

clan, *n.* family, blood, tribe, sept; brotherhood, association; breed, caste. See ASSEMBLAGE, RELATION.

clandestine, *adj.* SECRET, stealthy, furtive, sly, undercover; veiled; on the sly; illicit, fraudulent. See CONCEALMENT.

clang, *v.i.* resound, peal, toll, ring. See LOUDNESS.

clap, *v.t. & i.* applaud, acclaim; strike, slap, bang, slam; impose, put. See APPROBATION, IMPULSE. *Ant.*, see DISAPPROBATION.

clarify, *v.t.* cleanse, filter, refine, purify; render, melt; explain, elucidate, throw light on, clear up. See PURITY, LIQUEFACTION, INTERPRETATION.

clash, *v. & n.* —*v.t.* collide, conflict; disagree, dispute, differ, contend. —*n.* collision, impact, concussion, brunt, noise, conflict, DISAGREEMENT. See IMPULSE, CONTENTION. *Ant.*, see AGREEMENT.

clasp, *v.t.* hug, embrace, enfold; fasten, hook, buckle; clutch, hold. See COHERENCE, ENDEARMENT, JUNCTION. *Ant.*, see DISJUNCTION.

CLASS

Nouns—**1,** class, classification, division, category, head, section; department, province, domain; order, family, genus, species, variety; race, tribe, caste, sept, clean; breed; type, sect, set, coterie, clique; rank, station, estate; assortment; feather, stripe, blood, ilk, kidney; suit; range; gender, sex, kin; kind, sort, manner, description, denomination, designation; character, stamp. See SIMILARITY.
2, rank, standing, status, station, [social] level, caste; rating, worth, quality; class warfare *or* struggle. See SOCIOLOGY, DEGREE.
3, students, pupils; seminar, lecture; classroom. See SCHOOL, LEARNING.
4, *slang,* chic, vogue, style, ELEGANCE; carriage, mien, bearing, APPEARANCE.

Verbs—class, classify, sort, screen; rank, rate, organize, arrange, catalogue, categorize; characterize, type.

Adjectives—**1,** classified, distinct, specified; systematic, ordered, organized.
2, *slang,* classy, stylish, chic, elegant.

classic, *adj.* standard; chaste, simple. See SIMPLENESS.

classification, *n.* grouping, category, allocation; ARRANGEMENT, systematization, taxonomy, ORDER. See CLASS.

clatter, *n.* rattle, noise, racket, din. See LOUDNESS.

clause, *n.* article, paragraph, proviso, condition, stipulation, PART, section.

claw, *n.* talon, nail; pincer, nipper. *Slang,* hook.

clay, *n.* earth, potter's clay, kaolin; mud, loam; flesh. See LAND, MANKIND.

CLEANNESS

Nouns—**1,** cleanness, cleanliness, PURITY, spotlessness; purification, circumcision; purgation, lustration, ablution; bath, shower, cleansing, wash, washing, lavation; dry-cleaning; sanitation, disinfection; fumigation; irrigation, lavage; drainage, sewerage, plumbing. See WATER.

2, bath, shower bath, lavatory, lavabo, bathhouse, public bath, swimming pool, Turkish *or* steam bath; laundry, washhouse.

3, brush, broom, besom; mop, hose, sponge, swab; carpet sweeper, dustpan, dust mop, vacuum cleaner; washing machine; duster; washcloth, washrag; towel, napkin; soap, detergent, scouring powder, cleanser, disinfectant.

4, washerwoman, laundress; charwoman, maid, day-worker; houseman; cleaning man *or* woman, street-sweeper *or* cleaner. *Colloq.,* whitening.

Verbs—**1,** clean, cleanse; rinse, wring, flush, wipe, mop, sponge, scour, rub, swab, scrub; dust, brush up; vacuum; wash, lave, launder; purify; expurgate; clarify, refine, filter, filtrate; drain, strain.

2, disinfect, purge, sterilize, fumigate, ventilate, deodorize; whitewash; sandblast.

3, sift, winnow, pick, weed, comb, rake, brush, sweep.

Adjectives—clean, cleanly; pure, chaste, immaculate; spotless, stainless; without a stain, unstained, unspotted, unsoiled, unsullied, untainted, unadulterated, uninfected; sweet; neat, spruce, tidy, trim; bright as a new penny; snowy, snow-white, white; spic and span, clean as a whistle.

Antonym, see UNCLEANNESS.

clear, *adj.* clear-cut, plain, sharp, understandable, vivid; fair, unclouded, cloudless, fine; open, evident; lucid, pellucid, transparent, limpid; liquid, pure, silvery. See KNOWLEDGE, VISION. Ant., see CONCEALMENT, DARKNESS.

cleave, *v.t. & i.* stick, hold fast, adhere, cling; sever, shear, split, rive, rend, divide. See COHERENCE, DISJUNCTION.

cleft, *n.* split, rift, gap, fissure, opening, crack, orifice, crevice; interstice, chasm, chink. See INTERVAL, GULF.

CLERGY

Nouns—**1,** clergy, ministry, priesthood, presbytery, rabbinate, ulema, imamate; the cloth. See RELIGION.

2, clergyman, divine, ecclesiastic, churchman, priest, minister, preacher, pastor, leader of the flock, shepherd; father, father in Christ; padre, abbé, curé; patriarch; reverend; confessor.

3, Pope, pontiff, cardinal, eminence, reverence, primate, metropolitan, archbishop, bishop, prelate, diocesan, suffragan, priest, confessor; rabbi; caliph, imam, muezzin; dean, subdean, archdeacon, prebendary, canon, rector, parson, vicar, chaplain, curate; deacon, preacher, reader, lecturer; missionary, propagandist, Salvationist, revivalist, gospel singer *or* preacher, evangelist; churchwarden, sidesman; almoner, verger, beadle, sexton, sacristan; acolyte, altar boy; chorister. *Slang,* sky pilot.

4, cenobite, conventual, abbot, prior, monk, friar, lay brother, pilgrim; Jesuits, Franciscans, Gray Friars, Friars minor, Minorites; Capuchins, Dominicans, Black Friars; Carmelites; Augustinians, Austin Friars;

Carthusians, Benedictines, Cistercians, Trappists, Cluniacs, Maturines; Templars, Hospitallers; abbess, prioress, canoness; mother superior, nun, sister, novice, postulant.

5, holy orders, ordination, consecration, induction; clericalism, theocracy, hierarchy, ecclesiology; monasticism, monkhood, asceticism, cloistered life; papacy, pontificate; prelacy; consistory, synod, council, Sanhedrin.

Verbs—call, ordain, consecrate, induct; take orders, take the veil, take vows; beatify, canonize.

Adjectives—ordained, in holy orders, called to the ministry; clerical, priestly, ecclesiastical, pastoral, ministerial; episcopal, hierarchical; pontifical, papal.

Antonym, see LAITY, LAY.

---

clerk, *n.* salesman, -woman *or* -person; registrar, scribe, secretary; copyist, writer. See CLERGY, SALE, WRITING.

clever, *adj.* adroit, skillful; talented, adept, gifted. *Colloq.*, smart, cute. See SKILL. *Ant.*, see UNSKILLFULNESS.

cliché, *n.* stereotype, plate, cut (see PRINTING); truism, commonplace, platitude; banality, triviality, chitchat. *Colloq.*, bromide. See MAXIM.

click, *v.*, *slang*, fall into place, jibe; go over, succeed, make the grade. See SUCCESS.

client, *n.* customer, buyer, patron. See SALE.

cliff, *n.* precipice, palisade, crag, bluff, steep.

climate, *n.* weather; temperature, rainfall, precipitation, *etc.*; region. See AIR.

climax, *n.* acme, zenith, SUMMIT, pinnacle; turning point, culmination.

climb, *v.t.* mount, scale, ascend, rise, go up; succeed; clamber, scramble. *Colloq.*, swarm, shinny, shin. See ASCENT. *Ant.*, see DESCENT.

clinch, *v.t.* confirm, conclude successfully; fasten, secure, rivet, clamp; clench, grapple; seize, grasp. See COMPLETION, JUNCTION, POSSESSION.

cling, *v.i.* stick, hold, cleave, adhere; grasp, hold on to, hug; persist. See COHERENCE, LOVE, RESOLUTION. *Ant.*, see RELINQUISHMENT.

clinic, *n.* dispensary, hospital, polyclinic, ward. See REMEDY.

clip, *v.t.* cut, snip, scissor, trim, shorten; prune, mow; dock. *Slang*, gyp, fleece. See SHORTNESS, STEALING.

clique, *n.* set, circle, group, coterie. *Colloq.*, crowd, bunch. See COMBINATION, PARTY.

cloak, *n.* cape, wrap, mantle, robe, domino; shield, cover, disguise. See CLOTHING, DECEPTION.

clock, *n.* timepiece, chronometer (see CHRONOMETRY); Big Ben; electric clock, clock radio; [taxi] meter.

clog, *v.t.* obstruct, block, congest, choke; hamper, encumber, jam, impede, restrain. See HINDRANCE. *Ant.*, see AID, OPENING.

cloister, *n.* abbey, priory, convent, hermitage, monastery; quiet retreat, sanctuary. See ABODE, SECLUSION.

close, *adj.* compact, dense, firm; stifling, oppressive, muggy, stale, stuffy; stingy, tightfisted, frugal, niggardly; taut; confining, constrictive; near, intimate; secretive, reticent, reserved; approximate. See DENSITY, HEAT, JUNCTION, NEARNESS, PARSIMONY, SILENCE. *Ant.*, see RARITY, COLD, DISJUNCTION, DISTANCE, WASTE, LOQUACITY.

close, *v. & n.* See CLOSURE.

closet, *n.* cupboard, cabinet; locker, wardrobe, clothespress; room, cubbyhole. See RECEPTACLE, SPACE.

CLOSURE

Nouns—closure, occlusion; blockade, obstruction, HINDRANCE; shutting up, CONTRACTION; constipation; embolism; blind alley, dead end, stone wall, *cul de sac*; imperforation, imperviousness, impermeability; STOPPER; cloture.

Verbs—close, occlude, plug; stop, shut *or* dam up; block, blockade; obstruct, hinder; fasten, bar, bolt, barricade, latch, lock, stop, seal, fence in, plumb; choke, strangle, throttle; ram down, tamp, dam, cram; trap, cage, hood, clinch; shut the door; confine, restrain (see RESTRAINT).

Adjectives—closed, shut, unopened; unpierced, imporous, imperforate, impervious, impermeable; impenetrable; impassable; untrodden; unventilated; airtight, watertight, waterproof; vacuum-packed, hermetically sealed; tight, snug, close.

Antonym, see OPENING.

clot, *n. & v.* —*n.* lump, clump, blob, dollop. —*v.* coagulate, thicken; clabber, curdle, sour. See DENSITY, DISEASE.

cloth, *n.* material, stuff, fabric, textile; fiber, synthetic; goods, dry, bolt *or* piece goods, remnant; napkin, dust cloth, *etc.* See MATERIALS, CLOTHING.

CLOTHING

Nouns—**1,** clothing, clothes, apparel, wear, dress, attire, array, raiment, garments, garb, costume, trousseau; millinery, footwear, underwear, outerwear; vestments.

2, suit, dress suit, evening clothes, tuxedo; coat, dinner coat *or* jacket, jacket, blazer; cutaway, frock coat, Prince Albert, overcoat, Mackinaw, mackintosh, lumberjack, lumberjacket, raincoat, slicker, Inverness, ulster, pea-jacket; sweater, cardigan, pullover, vest, blouse, tunic, waistcoat; trousers, pants, breeches, slacks, Levi's, overalls, dungarees, jeans; shirt, sportshirt; linen, undershirt, underpants, shorts, drawers, union suit, B.V.D.s; supporter, jockstrap, codpiece, dressing gown, smoking jacket, pajamas, pyjamas, nightshirt; shoe, boot, riding boot, Oxford, brogan, loafer, sneakers, moccasin; overshoes, galoshes, rubbers; spats, garters, chaps, leggings, puttees; hat, headgear, tophat, silk hat, opera hat, gibus, derby, Homburg, fedora, porkpie, felt hat, straw, panama, beaver, cap, nightcap, sailor, beret, beanie, skullcap, sombrero, shako, helmet, busby, kepi, overseas cap; tie necktie, cravat, Ascot, bow tie, four-in-hand. *Colloq.,* tux. *Slang,* togs, duds, glad rags, soup and fish, tails; P.J.s; topper, stovepipe, kelly; cut-offs; threads.

3, dress, gown, frock; suit, tailormade; blouse, bodice, middy blouse, sweater, shirtwaist, tunic; skirt, jumper, hoopskirt, crinoline; housedress, housecoat, smock, apron, negligée, robe, tea gown, kimono; coat, jacket, shortie; underwear, lingerie, slip, half-slip, petticoat, camisole, chemise, shift; corset, girdle, foundation, garter belt, stepins, brassière, bandeau; nightgown, pajamas; shoe, pump, Oxford, wedgie, casuals, sandal, slipper, mules, walking shoe; hat, bonnet, cloche, chapeau, hood, cowl, snood; hose, hosiery, stockings, nylons. *Colloq.,* woolies, undies, panties; bra. See ORNAMENT, OSTENTATION.

4, equipment, accouterments, trappings; harness, gear; uniform, dress uniform, fatigues; civilian clothes; cassock, robe, vestments. *Slang,* mufti, civvies.

Verbs—clothe, dress, attire, garb, costume, gown; invest; don, put on, wear; accouter, equip, rig out, fit out, harness.

Adjectives—clothed, costumed, attired, dressed, clad.

Antonym, see DIVESTMENT.

cloudburst, *n.* downpour, deluge, spate, squall, thundershower. See WATER.

CLOUDINESS

Nouns—cloudiness, cloud, overcast; cumulus, altocumulus, cirrus, cirrocumulus, stratus, cirro-stratus, nimbus; scud, raincloud, thunderhead; fog, mist, vapor, steam, haze, haziness, murk, murkiness. *Slang,* smog, soup, pea soup. See DARKNESS, DIMNESS.

Verbs—cloud, cloud over, shadow, obscure, overcast, threaten; SHADE.
Adjectives—cloudy, overcast, murky, misty, foggy, hazy, lowering, dirty, muggy; threatening; shady, umbrageous; obfuscated; opaque.
Antonym, see LIGHT.

---

clout, *n. & v.* belt, swat, whack. See IMPULSE. *Slang*, INFLUENCE, impact, pull.
clown, *n.* buffoon, comic, comedian, jester; boor; rustic, simpleton, clodhopper, oaf, bumpkin. *Colloq.*, duffer, lout, booby, nincompoop. See DRAMA, ABSURDITY. *Ant.*, see INTELLIGENCE.
cloy, *v.i.* glut, satiate, surfeit, sate; pall, bore. See SUFFICIENCY.
club, *n.* cudgel, stick, bat, bludgeon; society, fraternity, sorority, association; nightclub, resort, rendezvous. See ARMS, ASSEMBLAGE.
clubfooted, *adj.* splayfooted, deformed, Dutch-footed. See DISTORTION.
clue, *n.* solution, suggestion, intimation, hint, key; guide. See ANSWER, INDICATION.
clump, *n.* cluster, bunch, patch, thicket, grove. See ASSEMBLAGE.
clumsy, *adj.* awkward, heavy, lumbering; bungling, stupid, bumbling, left-handed, incompetent; cumbersome, unwieldy. See UNSKILLFULNESS. *Ant.*, see SKILL.
cluster, *n.* bunch, clump, group. See ASSEMBLAGE, CONVEXITY.
clutch, *v.t.* hold fast, grip, keep, cling to, clench; snatch, seize, grasp, grab, collar; grip, clasp, squeeze, embrace. See ACQUISITION, POSSESSION. *Ant.*, see RELINQUISHMENT.
clutter, *n.* DISORDER, mess, jumble; litter, trash, rubbish, debris.
coach, *v. & n.* —*v.t.* teach, help, tutor. —*n.* trainer, director, teacher; stage, stagecoach, bus, omnibus, car, carriage, Pullman. See TEACHING, VEHICLE.
coagulate, *v.i.* clot, clabber, thicken, curdle; set, congeal. See DENSITY.
coal, *n.* ember, cinder; anthracite, bituminous *or* soft coal, charcoal, lignite, coke. See FUEL, HEAT.
coalition, *n.* union, alliance, league, axis; merger, bloc. See PARTY.
coarse, *adj.* rough, harsh-textured, coarse-grained; uncouth, rude, crude, crass, low, vulgar, gross, common, unrefined; broad, bawdy, ribald. See ROUGHNESS, UGLINESS. *Ant.*, see BEAUTY, TASTE, SMOOTHNESS.
coast, *n.* shore, tideland, shoreline, waterfront, seacoast, beach. See LAND.
coat, *v. & n.* —*v.t.* cover, crust; plaster, paint, varnish, glaze; plate; protect. —*n.* jacket, overcoat, ulster, sack, cutaway, tunic; tegument, shell, envelope, skin, peel, rind, surface, cover. See CLOTHING, COVERING.
coax, *v.t.* cajole, inveigle, wheedle, persuade, urge. See CAUSE.
cocktail, *n.* mixed drink, aperitif; martini, old-fashioned, daiquiri, *etc.*; salad, appetizer. See FOOD, DRUNKENNESS.
cockeyed, *adj.* cross-eyed, strabismic. *Slang*, drunk. See VISION, DISTORTION.
code, *n.* cipher, secret writing, cryptogram; law, canon, principle, codex, constitution, system, standard, rule. See LEGALITY, CONCEALMENT.
coerce, *v.t.* compel, drive, force, make. See COMPULSION.
coexist, *v.i.* coincide, accompany; live and let live, tolerate. See SYNCHRONISM.
coffee, *n.* mocha, espresso, cappuccino. *Slang*, java, mud. See FOOD.
coffer, *n.* chest, strong box, vault; (*pl.*) treasury. See RECEPTACLE.
coffin, *n.* casket, bier, pine box, sarcophagus. See INTERMENT.
cogent, *adj.* potent, forceful, convincing, persuasive, weighty, strong, compelling, trenchant. See POWER. *Ant.*, see IMPOTENCE.
cogitate, *v.i.* reflect, think, muse, ponder, mull, consider, meditate. See THOUGHT.
cognizant, *adj.* sensible (of), aware, knowing, conscious, observant. See SENSIBILITY. *Ant.*, see INSENSIBILITY.

cohabit, *v.i.* live *or* sleep together; live in sin. *Slang*, shack up. See MARRIAGE.

COHERENCE

Nouns—**1,** coherence, adherence, adhesion, adhesiveness; concretion, accretion; conglutination, coagulation, agglutination, agglomeration; aggregation; consolidation, set, gel, jell, jelly, cementation; sticking, soldering; tenacity, toughness; stickiness, viscosity; inseparability; conglomerate, concrete. See DENSITY.

2, gum, glue, lute, mucilage, size; jelly, gelatine, starch, gluten, albumen; mire, mud, slush, ooze; syrup, molasses. See CONNECTION.

Verbs—**1,** cohere, adhere, stick, cling, cleave; hold, take hold of, hold fast, close with, clasp, hug; grow together, hang together; twine around; stick like a leech; stick close; cling like ivy, cling like a burr.

2, glue; agglutinate, conglutinate; cement, lute, paste, gum; solder, weld; cake, consolidate, solidify, agglomerate; gel, jell, jelly.

Adjectives—**1,** cohesive, adhesive, adhering, tenacious, tough; sticky; united, unseparated, sessile, inseparable, indivisible, inextricable, unbreakable, shatterproof, infrangible; compact, dense, solid.

2, mucilaginous, gelatinous, glutinous; viscid, viscous, semiliquid; mucid, mucous, tacky; deliquescent, emulsive; thick.

Antonym, see DISJUNCTION.

---

coil, *n.* spiral, curl, roll, winding, circle, CONVOLUTION.

coin, *v. & n.* —*v.t.* mint, strike, stamp; invent, originate, make. See FORM, PRODUCTION. —*n.* MONEY, specie, currency, change, piece; gold, silver, copper, nickel, dime, cent, *etc. Colloq.*, tin, brass.

coincidence, *n.* CONCURRENCE, conjunction, concomitance, correspondence, AGREEMENT.

COLD

Nouns—**1,** cold, coldness, frigidity, severity, inclemency; iciness, winter, cold wave, cold snap; Siberia, Arctic, Antarctic; polar regions.

2, ice, snow, snowflake, snow flurry, snowfall, snowstorm, blizzard, snowdrift; sleet; hail, hailstone; rime, frost, hoarfrost; icicle, iceberg, ice floe, ice field, glacier.

3, chilliness, chill, coolness, shivering, goose flesh, rigor, horripilation, chattering of teeth, frostbite, chilblains.

4, refrigeration; refrigerator, icebox, cooler; ice tray, ice cube, dry ice; refrigerant, ammonia, freon; freezer, deepfreeze, cold storage, locker.

Verbs—be cold, shiver, quake, shake, tremble, shudder, quiver; perish with cold; chill, ice, freeze, quickfreeze. See REFRIGERATE.

Adjectives—cold, cool; chill, chilly; gelid, frigid, frozen, algid; fresh, keen, bleak, raw, inclement; bitter, biting, cutting, nipping, piercing; pinching; icy, glacial, frosty, freezing, wintry, boreal, arctic, Siberian, icebound, snowbound; shivering, frostbitten, frost-nipped; stone cold, cold as marble, cold as charity; cool as a cucumber; blue with cold; quickfrozen.

Adverbs—under refrigeration, on ice.

Antonym, see HEAT.

---

colander, *n.* strainer, sieve, screen, sifter, riddle. See OPENING.

cold-blooded, *adj.* merciless, unfeeling, ruthless, heartless, nerveless, cool. See MALEVOLENCE. *Ant.*, see BENEVOLENCE.

colic, *n.* bellyache, stomachache; indigestion; gripe. See PAIN, DISEASE.

collaborate, *v.i.* coöperate, pull together, pitch in. See COÖPERATION.

collapse, *v. & n.* —*v.i.* break down, fail; cave in. —*n.* prostration, dejection, exhaustion; downfall, ruin; cave-in. See FAILURE, IMPOTENCE. *Ant.*, see SUCCESS, POWER.

collar, *n. & v.* —*n.* neckband, neckwear; necklace; gorget, bertha, dicky. See CLOTHING, ORNAMENT. —*v.t.* nab, arrest, catch. See RESTRAINT.

collate, *v.t.* assemble, gather, compile, edit. See COMPOSITION.

colleague, *n.* associate, aide, partner, companion; co-worker, confrère. See FRIEND. *Ant.*, see ENEMY.

collect, *v.t.* gather, collate, assemble, amass, compile; demand, ask payment, exact; throng, congregate, flock; scrape up, round up, garner, accumulate, save. See ASSEMBLAGE.

college, *n.* SCHOOL, academy, university, seminary, institute, institution; junior college; finishing school; association, guild.

collide, *v.i.* bump, bunk, crash, clash, meet violently; interfere, impinge. See IMPULSE.

collision, *n.* impact, concussion; smashup, crash; clash, opposition, interference; conflict, engagement, discord. *Colloq.*, fender-bender. See CONTENTION.

colloquial, *adj.* chatty, idiomatic, informal, conversational, vernacular. See CONVERSATION.

collusion, *n.* conspiracy, scheme, intrigue, cabal; DECEPTION; logrolling, price-fixing. *Colloq.*, hookup. *Slang*, cahoots. See PLAN, COÖPERATION.

colonize, *v.t.* settle, pioneer, establish, found, populate; transport. See LOCATION. *Ant.*, see DISPLACE.

COLOR

Nouns—1, color, hue, tint, tinge, shade, dye, complexion, tincture, cast, livery, coloration, glow, flush; tone, key; pure, primary, positive *or* complementary color; three primaries; spectrum, chromatic dispersion; secondary color, tertiary color; coloring, pigmentation, perspective, value; brilliance, saturation; light, dark, medium.

2, chromatics; spectrum analysis; prism, spectroscope; VIBGYOR (the spectrum: violet, indigo, blue, green, yellow, orange, red); rainbow, kaleidoscope.

3, pigment, coloring matter, paint, dye, wash, distemper, stain; medium; mordant; oils, oil paint, watercolor, crayon, pastel, tempera, wash. See PAINTING.

4, black, jet, ink, ebony, coal, pitch, soot, crow, lampblack, blueblack, India ink.

5, blue, ultramarine, cobalt, Prussian blue, indigo, lapis lazuli, sapphire, turquoise.

6, brown, ocher, umber, sienna, sepia.

7, gray, neutral, silver, dun.

8, green, Paris green, emerald green, vert, celadon, verdancy.

9, orange, ocher, cadmium.

10, purple, amethyst, lilac, heliotrope.

11, red, scarlet, cinnabar, lake, cochineal, vermilion, red lead, madder, rouge.

12, white, milkiness, snow, COLORLESSNESS.

13, yellow, gold, gamboge, yellow ocher, chrome yellow, banana, lemon.

14, VARIEGATION, iridescence, play of colors; chameleon.

Verbs—color, dye, tinge, stain, varnish, tint, paint, wash, ingrain, grain, illuminate, emblazon, bedizen, imbue; paint.

Adjectives—1, colored, colorific, chromatic, prismatic; full-colored, high-colored; double-dyed; polychromatic; bright, brilliant, vivid, intense, deep; fresh, unfaded; rich, gorgeous, gay; gaudy, florid; garish; showy, flaunting, flamboyant, flashy; raw, crude; glaring, flaring; discordant, harsh, clashing, inharmonious; mellow, harmonious, pearly, sweet, delicate, tender, refined.

2, black, sable, sloe-black, inky, coal-black, charcoal, jet-black, pitchy, sooty.

3, blue, azure, cerulean, sky-blue, sea-blue, royal blue, copen.

4, brown, bay, tan, sorrel, auburn, chestnut, bronze, coppery, cinnamon, russet, chocolate, walnut, mahogany, khaki, cocoa, coffee, drab.
5, gray, steel-gray, French-gray, ashen, silvery, dove-gray, slaty.
6, green, emerald-green, pea-green, sea-green, bottle-green; olive.
7, orange, apricot, flame-colored, tangerine.
8, purple, violet, plum-colored, magenta, puce.
9. red, scarlet, crimson, pink, carmine, vermilion, cardinal, cerise, maroon, carnation, ruby-red, blood-red, beet-red, brick-red, Chinese red.
10, white, snowy, milky, chalky, creamy, pearly, ivory, off-white, oyster-white.
11, yellow, gold, saffron, lemon, cream-colored, amber, écru, buff, beige.
12, variegated, parti-colored, many-hued; iridescent, kaleidoscopic, opalescent; pied, paint, pinto, piebald, motley, mottled, marbled, dappled, pepper-and-salt, plaid, calico, brindled, tabby, grizzled, tortoiseshell, patchwork, crazy quilt.

Antonym, see COLORLESSNESS.

COLORLESSNESS

Nouns—colorlessness, acromatism; decoloration, discoloration; pallor, pallidity; paleness, etiolation; neutral tint, monochrome, black-and-white.

Verbs—lose color, fade, become colorless, turn pale, pale; deprive of color, decolorize, bleach; tarnish, achromatize, blanch, etiolate, wash out, tone down.

Adjectives—uncolored, colorless, achromatic, aplanatic, hueless, pale, pallid; pale-faced; faint, dull, cold, muddy, leaden, dun, wan, sallow, dead, dingy, ashy, lurid, ghastly, deathly, ghostly, cadaverous, glassy, lackluster; blond, ash-blond, platinum-blond, fair; white; pale as death, pale as a ghost; white as a sheet.

Antonym, see COLOR.

colossus, *n.* giant, titan, monster, prodigy. See SIZE. *Ant.,* see LITTLENESS.

column, *n.* pillar, shaft; formation (of troops, figures, *etc.*) See HEIGHT.

coma, *n.* stupor, unconsciousness; torpor. See INSENSIBILITY, INACTIVITY.

comb, *v.t.* scrape, cleanse; dress, tease, back-comb. See CLEANNESS.

combat, *n.* conflict, WARFARE; battle, close combat. See CONTENTION.

COMBATANT

Nouns—**1,** combatant; disputant, litigant, belligerent; fighter, assailant; swashbuckler, fire-eater, duel(l)ist, bully; fighting-man, prizefighter, pugilist, boxer, bruiser, gladiator, wrestler; swordsman.

2, warrior, soldier, man-at-arms; campaigner, VETERAN; military man, G.I., doughboy, Tommy Atkins, *poilu*; armed force, troops, soldiery, forces, the army, standing army, regulars, militia, volunteers, auxiliaries, reserves, national guard, beefeater; guards, guardsman.

3, janizary; myrmidon; spahi, Cossack; irregular, mercenary; levy, draft; conscript, recruit, cadet, draftee, selectee, enlistee; guerrilla, partisan; commando.

4, private, rank and file, trooper, legionnaire, legionary, cannon fodder; officer, commander, subaltern, ensign, standard bearer; spearman, pikeman; halberdier, lancer; musketeer, rifleman, sharpshooter, sniper, skirmisher; grenadier, fusileer; archer, bowman.

5, horse *or* foot-soldier; infantry, infantryman, artillery, artilleryman, cavalry, cavalryman, horse; tanks, panzer, armor; paratrooper, paramarine; Uhlan, dragoon, hussar; cuirassier; gunner, cannoneer, bombardier; sapper, miner, engineer; light infantry, rifles, *chasseur,* zouave, camel corps, cameleers.

6, army, host; division, column, wing, detachment, parrison, brigade, regiment, corps, battalion, squadron, company, platoon, battery, squad; guard, legion, phalanx, cohort.
7, marine, navy, naval forces, fleet, flotilla, armada, squadron; man-of-war, ship of the line, ironclad, ship, warship, frigate, gunboat, flagship, cruiser; privateer; troopship, transport, corvette, torpedo boat, submarine, battleship, scout, dreadnaught, aircraft carrier, destroyer. *Slang,* gob, gyrene.
8, aviator, airman, pilot, bombardier, gun crew, tail gunner, belly gunner, navigator; dogfighter, ace; fighter, flying fortress, bomber, pursuit plane, transport, jet, dive bomber; wing, flight, formation, escadrille, squadron, echelon; air force, air arm, Luftwaffe. *Slang,* fly boy, birdman.

---

combat fatigue, shell shock, war neurosis, trauma. See DISEASE.

COMBINATION

Nouns—combination, composite; MIXTURE; JUNCTION, union, unification; synthesis; incorporation, merger, amalgamation, embodiment, coalescence, crasis, fusion, blending, absorption, centralization; compound, amalgam, composition, alloy; resultant; impregnation; union, alliance, syndicate, federation, affiliation, association. *Slang,* combo. See COÖPERATION.
Verbs—combine, unite, incorporate, amalgamate, affiliate, compound, embody, absorb, reembody, blend, merge, fuse, melt into one, (inter)-mix, (inter)mingle, consolidate, coalesce, centralize, impregnate; put together, lump together; cement a union, marry; federate, associate, syndicate, fraternize. *Colloq.,* gang up, throw *or* go in with, join up with.
Adjectives—combined, affiliated, allied, united; impregnated with, ingrained. *Slang,* in cahoots.
    Antonyms, see DECOMPOSITION, DISJUNCTION.

---

combustible, *adj.* inflammable, burnable, flammable. See FUEL.
come, *v.i.* arrive, reach; APPROACH, move toward, near; befall, happen, OCCUR. See ARRIVAL. *Ant.,* see DEPARTURE.
comeback, *n., colloq.,* recovery, revival, RESTORATION, return. *Slang,* retort, rejoinder. See ANSWER.
comedown, *n.* DESCENT, decline; setback, reverse; DISAPPOINTMENT, letdown.
comedy, *n.* play, stage play, show; satire, parody, burlesque, travesty; comedy of errors; tragicomedy; humor, WIT, AMUSEMENT. See DRAMA.
comely, *adj.* attractive, good-looking, handsome, fair, pleasing. See BEAUTY. *Ant.,* see UGLINESS.
comfort, *n.* luxury; ease, coziness; enjoyment, satisfaction; solace, consolation; cheer, aid. See PLEASURE, RELIEF. *Ant.,* see PAIN, DISCONTENT.
comic, *adj.* funny, hilarious, laughable, sidesplitting, clownish, ludicrous, comical, droll, slapstick, farcical. See ABSURDITY.

COMMAND

Nouns—**1,** command, commandment, order, ordinance, act, law, fiat, bidding, dictum, behest, call, beck, nod; despatch, dispatch, message; direction, injunction, charge, instructions; appointment, fixture. *Colloq.,* say-so. See AUTHORITY.
2, demand, exaction, imposition, requisition, claim, ultimatum, terms, REQUEST, REQUIREMENT.
3, dictation, dictate, mandate; caveat, decree, precept; writ, ordination, bull, edict, dispensation, prescription, brevet, ukase, warrant, passport, *mittimus, mandamus,* summons, subpoena, *nisi prius,* citation; word of

command; bugle call, trumpet call; beat of drum, tattoo; order of the day.

Verbs—command, order, decree, enact, ordain, dictate, direct, give orders; prescribe, set, appoint, mark out; set *or* impose a task; set to work; bid, enjoin, charge, call upon, instruct; require, exact, impose, tax, task; demand, insist on, compel (see COMPULSION); claim, lay claim to, reclaim; cite, summon; call for, send for; subpoena; beckon; issue a command; make a requisition, decree, *or* order; give the word, give the signal; call to order; lay down the law; assume command (see AUTHORITY); remand.

Antonym, see OBEDIENCE.

---

commandeer, *v.t.* confiscate, usurp, appropriate, seize. See TAKING.

commander, *n.* captain, commanding officer, skipper, commodore; chief, headman, chieftain, leader. See MASTER.

commando, *n.* ranger, raider, guerrilla, saboteur. See COMBATANT.

commemorate, *v.t.* CELEBRATE, solemnize, observe, keep, memorialize. See RECORD. *Ant.*, see OBLIVION.

commence, *v.t.* See BEGINNING.

commend, *v.t.* praise, applaud, cite, acclaim, approve, compliment, recommend. See APPROBATION. *Ant.*, see DISAPPROBATION.

comment, *n.* observation, remark, note, reflection, criticism, annotation; aside, opinion. See INTERPRETATION.

commentator, *n.* reviewer, critic, editor, news analyst, newscaster. See INTERPRETATION.

commerce, *n.* BUSINESS, merchandising, trade, trading, BARTER.

commissary, *n.* commissar; STORE, canteen, Post Exchange, PX. See PROVISION.

COMMISSION

Nouns—**1**, commission, delegation; consignment, assignment; procuration; deputation, legation, mission, embassy; COMMITTEE; agency, power of attorney; DEPUTY; proxy; task errand, charge, warrant, brevet, diploma; permit, PERMISSION, mandate, AUTHORITY.

2, appointment, nomination, charter; ordination; installation, inauguration, investiture; accession, coronation, enthronement.

3, fee, percentage, PAYMENT. *Colloq.*, rake-off.

Verbs—commission, delegate, depute; consign, assign; charge; intrust, entrust; commit; authorize, empower, permit; put in commission, accredit; engage, hire, employ, bespeak, appoint, name, nominate, ordain; install, induct, inaugurate, invest, crown; enroll, enlist.

Adjectives—commissioned, delegated, assigned, *etc.*; sent to committee.

Adverbs—for, instead of, in place of, in lieu of, as proxy for.

Antonym, see NULLIFICATION.

---

commit, *v.t.* perpetrate, perform, do; consign, entrust, deliver; confide, commend; take in custody, remand, condemn, imprison. See ACTION, COMMISSION, LAWSUIT.

committee, *n.* COMMISSION, sub-committee, delegation, panel, board; COUNCIL, junta; committee of the whole. See COMMISSION, PART.

commitment, *n.* COMMISSION; PROMISE, pledge, DUTY, AGREEMENT, involvement.

commodious, *adj.* spacious, capacious, ample, roomy; serviceable, adaptable. See SPACE, USE.

commodity, *n.* goods, article, wares, product. See MERCHANDISE.

common, *adj.* ordinary, standard, usual, conventional; prevalent, general, universal, current, popular, customary, regular; vulgar, illbred, inferior, trivial, plebeian, coarse. See CONFORMITY, HABIT. *Ant.*, see UNCONFORMITY.

commoner, *n.* gentleman, freeman, yeoman, tradesman, bourgeois; plebeian; citizen, subject. See POPULACE, COUNCIL.

commonplace, *adj.* ordinary, usual, everyday; prosy, monotonous, stale, tedious, hackneyed, threadbare, trite, banal. See HABIT. *Ant.,* see WIT.

commonwealth, *n.* state, community, body politic, government. See AUTHORITY.

commotion, *n.* stir, fuss, ferment, hurlyburly, ado; turmoil, AGITATION, tumult, DISORDER, disturbance, EXCITEMENT, turbulence. *Ant.,* see ORDER.

commune, *v. & n.* —*v.i.* communicate, converse; share *or* exchange thoughts *or* feelings. See CONVERSATION, COMMUNICATION. —*n.* community, municipality, township, REGION; collective, mir, kolk(h)oz, kibbutz.

COMMUNICATION

Nouns—**1,** communication; messages, tidings, news (see INFORMATION). **2,** communicator; messenger, envoy, emissary, legate; nuncio, ambassador; marshal, herald, crier, trumpeter, bellman, courier, runner; Mercury, Iris, Ariel; commissionaire; errand-boy; operator (radio, telephone, switchboard, *etc.*).

3, radio, television, cable, wireless, telephone, radiotelephony, telegraphy, *etc.*; newspapers, press, fourth estate; magazines, reviews, journals; switchboard.

4, bulletins; wire service, press service, syndicate service; mail, post, post office; letter-bag; telegram, cable, wire; carrier-pigeon; heliograph, wigwag, semaphore, signal; news flash, press release.

5, telepathy, thought transference, telekinesis, extrasensory perception. **6,** intercourse; conversation, exchange of talk *or* ideas. See SPEECH, SOCIALITY.

7, newsman, reporter, newscaster, broadcaster, publisher, *etc.* See PUBLICATION, INFORMATION.

Verbs—communicate, send messages, inform, tell, apprise, make aware; broadcast, newscast, publish, print, write, preach, disseminate news *or* information; radio, telegraph, wire, call, phone, telephone, cable; signal. See PUBLICATION.

Antonym, see CONCEALMENT.

---

communion, *n.* talk, conversation, intercourse, communication; concord, agreement, unity; sympathy; MASS, Lord's Supper, Sacrament, Eucharist. See RITE, SOCIALITY.

communist, *n.* socialist, anticapitalist, Marxist, communalist, leftist. *Colloq.,* Red; fellow-traveler, pink, parlor pink.

community, *n.* neighborhood, district, commonwealth; body, society, group; partnership, society. See PARTY, SOCIALITY.

compact, *n.* contract, covenant, AGREEMENT, bargain, bond, indenture; stipulation, COMPROMISE; pact, treaty; league, alliance; negotiation, bargaining, diplomacy, mediation; promise. *Colloq.,* deal.

compact, *adj.* CONCISE, succinct, terse, pithy, condensed; dense, thick, solid snug, tight. See DENSITY, CONTRACTION. *Ant.,* see RARITY, INCREASE.

companion, *n.* FRIEND, associate, colleague; pal, chum, comrade; shadow; escort; accomplice. See ACCOMPANIMENT. *Ant.,* see ENEMY.

company, *n.* companionship, fellowship; association, corporation, partnership; caste, troupe; group, assembly; troop, platoon, squad; society. *Colloq.,* crowd, gang, party. See ACCOMPANIMENT, ASSEMBLAGE, COMBATANT, DRAMA, BUSINESS, SOCIALITY.

compare, *v.* contrast; place side by side; collate, confront, parallel, relate, test. See RELATION, SIMILARITY.

compartment, *n.* division, partition, section, part; chamber, bin, cell. See SPACE, RECEPTACLE.

compass, *v. & n.* —*v.* bound, surround, define, encircle; beset, besiege; reach, accomplish, effect. —*n.* bounds, extent, scope, area, circumference, range; guide; gamut; needle (Naut.). See DIRECTION, LIMIT.

compassion, *n.* sympathy, tenderness, kindness, mercy, condolence; PITY, ruth, commiseration, heart. *Ant.,* see MALEVOLENCE.

compatible, *adj.* harmonious, well-matched, suitable, congruous. See AGREEMENT. *Ant.,* see DISAGREEMENT.

compatriot, *n.* countryman. See FRIEND. *Ant.,* see ENEMY.

compel, *v.t.* See COMPULSION.

compendium, *n.* abstract, précis, epitome, summary, digest, synopsis, abridgment, condensation; compilation, anthology. See CONTRACTION, ASSEMBLAGE, SHORTNESS.

COMPENSATION

Nouns—compensation, equation; commutation; satisfaction, indemnification, indemnity; COMPROMISE; neutralization; NULLIFICATION; counteraction, reaction; measure for measure; retaliation, equalization (see EQUALITY); robbing Peter to pay Paul; offset; counterpoise, counterbalance, ballast; equivalent, *quid pro quo*; bribe, hush money; recompense, PAYMENT; amends, ATONEMENT, redress, damages, balm.

Verbs—make compensation, compensate, indemnify; counteract, countervail, counterpoise; balance; outbalance, overbalance, counterbalance; set off; hedge, square, give and take; make up for, cover, fill up, neutralize, nullify; equalize; make good; recoup, square oneself, redeem, atone. *Colloq.,* lean over backwards.

Adjectives—compensating, compensatory; counteracting, countervailing, *etc.*; equivalent, equal.

Adverbs—in return, in consideration; but, however, yet, still, notwithstanding; nevertheless; although, though; albeit; at all events, at any rate; be that as it may, for all that, even so, on the other hand, at the same time, however that may be; after all, after all is said and done; taking one thing with another.

Antonym, see LOSS.

---

compete, *v.i.* vie, contend, strive, rival, cope with. See CONTENTION, OPPOSITION. *Ant.,* see PACIFICATION, COÖPERATION.

competence, *n.* capability, capacity, ability, efficiency, proficiency; means, resources, income, sufficiency. See SKILL, WEALTH. *Ant.,* see UNSKILLFULNESS, POVERTY.

compile, *v.t.* edit, write, make, compose; collect, arrange. See COMPENDIUM, COMPOSITION.

complacent, *adj.* CONTENT, pleased; self-satisfied, smug; apathetic, blasé, indifferent, unruffled. See INDIFFERENCE, AFFECTATION.

complaint, *n.* ACCUSATION, charge; DISEASE, ailment, sickness, indisposition, disorder; lament; grievance. See LAMENTATION. *Ant.,* see VINDICATION, HEALTH, REJOICING.

complement, *n. & v.* —*n.* ADDITION, rest, REMAINDER, extra, surplus; counterpart, opposite; personnel, staff. —*v.t.* complete, realize, fulfill, fill *or* round out; balance, offset, neutralize. See COMPLETION, PART.

COMPLETION

Nouns—1, completion; accomplishment, achievement, fulfillment; execution, performance; despatch, dispatch; consummation, culmination; finish, conclusion; close, END, terminus, ARRIVAL; wind-up; finale, dénouement; catastrophe, issue, outcome, upshot, result; final touch, crowning touch, finishing touch; *coup de grâce; ne plus ultra, fait accompli;* missing link; PERFECTION; elaboration; finality.

2, completeness, totality, wholeness, entirety; unity; all; solidity, solidarity; ideal, limit; SUFFICIENCY.

3, impletion; repletion, saturation, high water; fill, load, bumper, brimmer; bellyful. *Colloq.,* full house, the works.

*Verbs—***1,** complete, effect, effectuate; accomplish, achieve, compass, consummate; bring to maturity, bring to perfection; perfect, elaborate.

2, do, execute, make; go through, get through; work out, enact; bring about, bring to pass, bring to a head; despatch, dispatch; polish off; make short work of; dispose of, set at rest; perform, discharge, fulfill, realize; put in practice, carry out, make good, be as good as one's word; drive home; do thoroughly, not do by halves, go the whole hog; see out *or* through; round out, be in at the death, persevere, carry through, play out, exhaust. *Colloq.,* mop up, fill the bill, turn the trick, knock off, pull off, make a go of it, put through. *Slang,* do up brown, do to a turn, go all out.

3, finish, close, bring to a close, END, wind up, stamp, clinch, seal, set the seal on, put the seal to; give the final touch to; put the last hand to; crown, cap, cap the climax.

4, ripen, mature, culminate; come to a head, come to a crisis; come to its end; die a natural death, die of old age; run its course, run one's race; reach the goal; reach, arrive; get in the harvest.

5, fill, charge, load; replenish, piece out, eke out; fulfill, fill up, saturate. *Colloq.,* go the whole hog, go the limit.

*Adjectives—*complete, entire; WHOLE, perfect; full, good, absolute, thorough, plenary; solid, undivided; with all its parts; exhaustive, concluding, conclusive, final; radical, sweeping, thoroughgoing; dead; consummate, unmitigated, sheer, unqualified; unconditional, free; abundant, sufficient (see SUFFICIENCY); brimming, brimful, chock-full; saturated, crammed; replete, redundant, fraught, laden, heavy-laden; completing, supplemental, supplementary, complementary.

*Adverbs—*completely, altogether, outright, wholly, totally, *in toto,* quite; thoroughly, conclusively, finally; effectually, for good and all, nicely, fully, in all respects, in every respect; out and out, leaving no stone unturned, to all intents and purposes; utterly, to the utmost, all out, all hollow, stark; heart and soul, root and branch; down to the ground; lock, stock and barrel; bag and baggage; to the top of one's bent, to the limit, as far as possible; throughout; from first to last, from beginning to end, from end to end, from one end to the other, from head to foot, from top to toe, from top to bottom; fore and aft; every whit, every inch; *cap-à-pie,* up to the brim, up to the ears; with a vengeance. *Colloq.,* to the nines, to a fare-you-well; from the word go. *Slang,* for fair, from hell to breakfast, from soup to nuts; till Hell freezes over.

Antonym, see INSUFFICIENCY, NEGLECT.

---

complex, *adj.* intricate, manifold, complicated, involved, knotty. See DISORDER. *Ant.,* see SIMPLENESS.

complexion, *n.* hue, color, tinge, tint; skin texture; aspect, APPEARANCE. See COLOR.

complicate, *v.t.* involve, embarrass, confuse; perplex; compound. See AGITATION. *Ant.,* see ARRANGEMENT.

complicity, *n.* guilt, association; collusion, participation, connivance, conspiracy. See COÖPERATION. *Ant.,* see OPPOSITION.

compliment, *v.t.* praise, flatter, commend, congratulate. See APPROBATION. *Ant.,* see DISAPPROBATION.

complimentary, *adj.* commendatory; courteous, polite; (con)gratulatory, laudatory, favorable; free, gratis, on the house. See APPROBATION, FLATTERY, NONPAYMENT.

comply, *v.t.* CONSENT, conform, yield, submit, obey. See OBEDIENCE. *Ant.,* see REFUSAL, DISOBEDIENCE.

component, *n.* integral part; part, element, factor, constituent, ingredient; link, feature, member. *Colloq.*, makings, fixings.

composed, *adj.* cool, unruffled, collected, self-possessed; calm, tranquil. See INEXCITABILITY. *Ant.*, see EXCITABILITY.

COMPOSITION

Nouns—**1,** composition, constitution, formation; COMBINATION, INCLUSION, admission, comprehension, reception. *Colloq.*, getup, setup.
2, composition, typography, make-up, typesetting. See PRINTING.
3, composition, musical work, authorship. See MUSIC, WRITING.
Verbs—be composed of, be made of, be formed of; consist of, be resolved into; include, hold, comprehend, take in, admit, embrace, embody; involve; implicate, drag into; compose, COMPOUND, constitute, form, make, put together, make up; enter into the composition of, be a component.
Adjectives—composing, containing, constituting, *etc.*
   Antonym, see DECOMPOSITION, INSUBSTANTIALITY.

---

composure, *n.* placidity, serenity, self-possession, calmness. See MODERATION, REPOSE. *Ant.*, see EXCITEMENT.

compound, *v.t.* combine, compose, concoct, amalgamate, mix; join, unite. See MIXTURE.

comprehend, *v.t.* comprise, embrace, INCLUDE; grasp, apprehend, conceive, understand, see, know. See KNOWLEDGE. *Ant.*, see EXCLUDE, IGNORANCE.

comprehensive, *adj.* full, extensive, inclusive, all-embracing, catholic, sweeping; wholesale, wide, broad, general, expansive. See COMPONENT, GENERALITY. *Ant.*, see SPECIALITY.

compress, *v.t.* reduce, digest, abridge, consolidate, condense; crowd, squeeze, contract. See DENSITY. *Ant.*, see INCREASE, RARITY.

comprise, *v.t.* consist, involve, embrace, cover, embody; INCLUDE, comprehend, contain. See NUMBER.

COMPROMISE

Nouns—compromise, commutation, MEDIATION; settlement, concession, middle term, COMPENSATION.
Verbs—**1,** compromise, commute, compound; take the mean, split the difference, strike a balance, meet one halfway, give and take; come to terms, CONTRACT; submit to arbitration; patch up, bridge over, arrange; adjust differences; agree; make the best of, make a virtue of necessity; take the will for the deed. *Slang*, go fifty-fifty.
2, mediate, arbitrate, reconcile, intercede, intervene.
Adjectives—conciliatory, diplomatic, give-and-take; mediatory, mediating, intermediary, intercessory.
   Antonym, see OBSTINACY, RESOLUTION.

COMPULSION

Nouns—compulsion, coercion, coaction, constraint, duress, obligation; enforcement, pressure, conscription; force, brute force, main force, physical force; the sword, martial law; draft, conscription; RESTRAINT, NECESSITY, *force majeure*; Hobson's choice. *Colloq.*, strong arm.
Verbs—compel, force, make, drive, coerce, constrain, enforce, necessitate, oblige; force upon, press; cram, thrust *or* force down the throat; make a point of, insist upon, take no denial; put down, dragoon; extort, wring from; drag into; bind over; pin *or* tie down; require, tax, put in force, put teeth in; restrain; hold down; commandeer, draft, conscript, impress.
Adjectives—compulsory, compelling; coercive, coactive; inexorable; obligatory, stringent, contingent, peremptory; forcible, not to be trifled with; irresistible.

Adverbs—compulsorily, by force, by force of arms; on *or* under compulsion, perforce; at sword's point, forcibly; under protest, in spite of; against one's will; under press of; *de rigueur*, willy-nilly.

Antonym, see FREEDOM.

---

compunction, *n.* See REMORSE.

compute, *v.t. & i.* figure, calculate, reckon; count, enumerate, number, tally. See NUMERATION.

computer, *n.* calculator; cybernetic machine, robot, automaton. See NUMERATION.

comrade, *n.* FRIEND, companion, mate, fellow, chum, playmate, roommate, associate. *Colloq.*, buddy. *Ant.*, see ENEMY.

con, *v.t.*, *slang*, see SWINDLE.

CONCAVITY

Nouns—**1**, concavity, depression, dip; hollow, hollowness; indentation, intaglio, cavity, hole, dent, dint, dimple, follicle, pit, *sinus alveolus*, lacuna; excavation, crater; trough, furrow; honeycomb; cup, basin, bowl; cell, RECEPTACLE; socket.

2, valley, vale, dale, dell, dingle, bottom, blade, grove, glen, gully, cave, cavern, cove; grot, grotto; alcove, *cul-de-sac*; arch, arcade, curve; bay, gulf.

3, excavator, sapper, miner, digger, steam shovel, spade, *etc.*

Verbs—be concave; cave in; render concave, depress, hollow; scoop, scoop out; gouge, dent, dint; dig, delve, excavate, mine, sap, undermine, burrow, tunnel; stave in.

Adjectives—concave, depressed, hollow, stove in; retiring; retreating, cavernous; cellular, porous; spongy, honeycombed, alveolar; infundibular, funnel-shaped, cupular, bell-shaped; campaniform, capsular, vaulted, arched.

Antonym, see CONVEXITY.

CONCEALMENT

Nouns—**1**, concealment; hiding; screen, smoke screen, AMBUSH, camouflage, trench, foxhole; disguise, masquerade, cloak, veil; incognito; cryptography, steganography, code.

2, stealth, stealthiness; slyness, CUNNING; SECLUSION, privacy, secrecy, secretness.

3, reticence; reserve; mental reservation; silence, taciturnity; *arrière pensée*, suppression, circumlocution, evasion, white lie, fib, misprision; underhand dealing; closeness, secretiveness, mystery; latency; stowaway; jargon, cant, officialese, shop talk. *Slang*, gobbledygook, doubletalk.

4, detective, operative, sleuth, private investigator, federal agent; secret agent, spy. *Colloq.*, plainclothesman, G-man. *Slang*, dick, flatfoot, bull; gumshoe.

Verbs—**1**, conceal, hide, secrete, put out of sight; lock up, bottle up; cover, screen, cloak, veil, shroud; draw the veil *or* curtain; curtain, shade, eclipse, becloud, mask, camouflage, disguise; ensconce, muffle, smother; whisper. *Slang*, stash, plant, launder.

2, keep from, keep to oneself; keep dark, bury; sink, suppress; keep out of sight; keep in the background; stifle, hush up, smother, withhold, reserve; keep a secret, keep one's own counsel; hold one's tongue; not let the right hand know what the left is doing; hide one's light under a bushel.

3, keep *or* leave in the dark, blind, blindfold, hoodwink, mystify; puzzle, bamboozle, deceive (see DECEPTION), nonplus.

4, be concealed, hide oneself; lie in ambush, lie low, lurk, sneak, skulk, slink, prowl; play hide and seek; hide in holes and corners.

Adjectives—**1**, concealed, hidden; secret, recondite, arcane, esoteric,

Masonic, mystic, cabalistic, occult, dark; cryptic, private, privy, clandestine, close, inviolate.

2, under cover, in ambush, in hiding, in disguise; in the dark; clouded, invisible; buried, underground, *perdu*; secluded (see SECLUSION); undisclosed, untold; covert, mysterious, unintelligible; inviolable; confidential, classified, top *or* most secret; unsuspected, LATENT.

3, furtive, stealthy, feline; skulking, surreptitious, underhand, hole and corner; sly, CUNNING; secretive, evasive; reserved, reticent, uncommunicative, buttoned up, taciturn.

Adverbs—secretly, in secret, privately, in private; in the dark; behind closed doors, in closed session, hugger-mugger, under the rose, under the counter, under the table; *sub rosa*, in the background, aside, on the sly, with bated breath, *sotto voce*, in a whisper; in confidence, in strict confidence; confidentially; off the record, between ourselves, between you and me; *entre nous, in camera*; underhand, by stealth, like a thief in the night; stealthily, behind the scenes, behind one's back; incognito.

Antonym, see DISCLOSURE.

---

concede, *v.t.* CONSENT, yield, give in, assent, allow; accede; grant, admit, acknowledge, confess; RELINQUISH, cede, give up, surrender. See DISCLOSURE, GIVING. *Ant.*, see REFUSAL.

conceit, *n.* VANITY, pride, egotism, superciliousness, self-esteem; epigram, *bon mot*, quip; whim, IMAGINATION, fantasy, fancy, caprice, notion, quirk. See WIT. *Ant.*, see MODESTY.

conceive, *v.t.* devise, frame, imagine, visualize, fancy; grasp, realize, take in, understand; form, become pregnant. *Colloq.*, get in a family way. See IMAGINATION, KNOWLEDGE, PRODUCTION. *Ant.*, see IGNORANCE.

concentrate, *v.t.* strengthen, distill, intensify, condense, consolidate; fix, aim, focus; converge, center, localize; collect, assemble, gather. See ASSEMBLAGE, MIDDLE, DENSITY. *Ant.*, DISPERSE; see RARITY.

concentration camp, detention camp, prison camp *or* farm, POW camp, compound, stalag; gas chamber, extermination center; death camp; Auschwitz, Bergen-Belsen, Buchenwald, Dachau, Treblinka. See PRISON.

concept, *n.* conception, conceit, THOUGHT, idea, abstraction, INTERPRETATION.

concern, *v. & n.* —*v.t.* regard, affect, relate, refer to, pertain to, have to do with, bear upon, belong to; treat of; interest. —*n.* matter, affair; CARE, anxiety, worry, solicitude, regard; significance, IMPORT, interest. See RELATION. *Ant.*, see NEGLECT, UNIMPORTANCE.

concert, *n.* recital, program, serenade, musicale; COÖPERATION, AGREEMENT, harmony, accord; conspiracy. See MUSIC. *Ant.*, see DISAGREEMENT, OPPOSITION.

conciliate, *v.t.* reconcile; PACIFY, appease, placate, mollify, propitiate; win, curry favor. *Slang*, square. See CONTENT, FORGIVENESS.

concise, *adj.* succinct, short, brief, pithy, pointed, terse, laconic, epigrammatic, summary, compact. See SHORTNESS. *Ant.*, see LOQUACITY.

conclude, *v.t.* end, close, finish, windup, terminate; infer, deduce; arrange, settle; resolve, judge, determine. See COMPLETION, RESOLUTION.

concoct, *v.t.* prepare, invent, devise, contrive; brew; mix, cook; plan, make up, hatch. See PREPARATION.

concord, *n.* accord, harmony; AGREEMENT; sympathy, rapport, congruousness, congruence; concurrence; union, unity; PEACE, ASSENT; alliance, league, compact; entente; understanding. *Ant.*, see DISAGREEMENT, CONTENTION.

concrete, *adj.* actual, real, tangible solid, hard; specific, definite, exact, particular. See SUBSTANCE, DENSITY. *Ant.*, see INSUBSTANTIALITY.

concubine, *n.* hetaera; mistress, paramour, kept woman; white slave, slave girl, wench, harem girl, odalisque; demimondaine, courtesan, PROSTITUTE.

concur, *v.i.* agree, ASSENT, CONSENT, harmonize; see eye to eye with, pull together, parallel; unite; acquiesce. *Colloq.,* jibe. *Ant.,* see DIS-AGREEMENT.

concurrence, *n.* See COÖPERATION, AGREEMENT, CONVERGENCE.

concussion, *n.* shock, blow, collision, impact; injury. See IMPULSE, PAIN.

CONDEMNATION

Nouns—condemnation, conviction, proscription, damnation; death warrant; attainder, attainture, attaintment; DISAPPROBATION, disapproval, censure. *Slang,* rap, frame-up.

Verbs—condemn, convict, find guilty, damn, doom, sign the death warrant, sentence, pass sentence on; attaint, confiscate, proscribe, sequestrate; disapprove, censure, denounce, blame.

Adjectives—condemnatory, damnatory; denunciatory; condemned, damned, convicted; self-convicted.

Antonym, see ACQUITTAL.

---

condense, *v.t. & i.* abridge, digest, curtail, abbreviate, shorten, cut, epitomize; thicken, concentrate, distill, solidify. See DENSITY, SHORT-NESS. *Ant.,* see RARITY, LENGTH.

condescend, *v.i.* stoop, deign, descend, vouchsafe. See MODESTY, VANITY.

condiment, *n.* seasoning, sauce, spice, relish, herb; salt, pepper, cayenne, mustard, curry, onion, garlic, pickle, catsup, vinegar, mayonnaise, olive oil, salad dressing. See TASTE.

condition, *n.* fitness; STATE, birth, rank, place, estate, station, class; demand, QUALIFICATION, proviso; plight, situation, status, position, pass, case, circumstances. See REPUTE. *Ant.,* see DISREPUTE.

condolence, *n.* LAMENTATION, sympathy, PITY, consolement, consolation, compassion, commiseration.

condominium, *n.* coöperative [apartment house], coöp. See ABODE.

conduce, *v.i.* lead, tend, contribute, redound, advance. See TENDENCY.

CONDUCT

Nouns—1, conduct, dealing, transaction, ACTION, BUSINESS; tactics, game, expedient, policy, polity; generalship, statesmanship, seamanship; strategy, strategics; PLAN, program, execution, manipulation, treatment, campaign, career, life, course, walk, race; husbandry; housekeeping, housewifery; stewardship; *ménage*; régime; economy, economics; political economy; management; government, DIRECTION.

2, conduct, behavior, deportment, comportment; carriage, demeanor, guise, mien, bearing, manner, OBSERVANCE; course of conduct, line of conduct, course of action; rôle, process, ways, practice, procedure, *modus operandi*; method.

Verbs—1, conduct, transact, execute, administer; deal with, have to do with; treat, handle, take steps, take measures; despatch, dispatch; proceed with, discharge; carry on, carry through, carry out, carry into effect; work out; go through, get through; enact; put into practice; officiate.

2, conduct oneself, behave oneself, comport oneself, demean oneself, carry oneself, acquit oneself; act one's age, give a good account of oneself; run a race, lead a life, play a game; take *or* adopt a course; steer *or* shape one's course; play one's part *or* cards; shift for oneself; paddle one's own canoe.

Adjectives—conducting, *etc.,* strategical, tactical, businesslike, practical, executive.

conductor, *n.* guide, escort, director; manager, operator, supervisor; guard; drum major, leader, maestro, choirmaster; transmitter, conveyor. *Colloq.,* time beater. See CARRIER, DIRECTOR, MUSICIAN.

cone-shaped, *adj.* conic(al), conoid(al); coniferous, pyramidal. See SHARPNESS.

confederacy, *n.* league, federation, union, alliance; compact, combine. See COMBINATION, PARTY.

confederate, *n.* AID, ally; accomplice; companion, associate.

confer, *v.i.* converse, discuss; consult, debate, deliberate; talk, parley, palaver; GIVE, grant, bestow. See ADVICE, CONVERSATION.

confess, *v.t.* acknowledge, avow, own, admit; disclose, tell, reveal, unbosom, unburden, divulge. See DISCLOSURE, PENITENCE.

confidant, *n.* confidante *(fem.),* FRIEND, intimate. *Ant.,* see ENEMY.

confide, *v.t. & i.* trust, believe in, rely on; entrust; commit; tell, divulge, unbosom, unburden. See BELIEF, DISCLOSURE. *Ant.,* see CONCEALMENT.

confidence, *n.* assurance, certainty, positiveness; spirit, boldness, self-reliance; communication, privacy, secret; faith, trust. See BELIEF, COURAGE, HOPE. *Ant.,* see DOUBT.

confidential, *adj.* See PRIVATE.

configuration, *n.* FORM, figure, shape, contour; grouping, ARRANGEMENT.

confine, *v.t.* imprison, incarcerate, immure, jail, detain; cage, pen; restrict, bound, limit. See CIRCUMSCRIPTION. *Ant.,* see FREEDOM.

confinement, *n.* childbirth, childbed; RESTRAINT, imprisonment, incarceration, captivity, custody, detention; CIRCUMSCRIPTION, limitation, restriction. See PRISON. *Ant.,* see FREEDOM.

confirm, *v.t.* establish, fix, strengthen; ratify, sanction, validate, approve, indorse; verify, substantiate, prove, uphold, corroborate. See ASSENT, EVIDENCE, STABILITY. *Ant.,* see DISSENT, REFUSAL.

confiscate, *v.t.* take, seize, commandeer, appropriate; CONDEMN, sequester. See ACQUISITION. *Ant.,* see RESTITUTION.

conflict, *n.* battle, combat, strife, fight, encounter, clash, collision, struggle; discord, antagonism, dissension, hostility. See CONTENTION, DISAGREEMENT, OPPOSITION, WARFARE. *Ant.,* see PACIFICATION, COÖPERATION.

CONFORMITY

Nouns—1, conformity, conformance; OBSERVANCE, symmetry; adaptation, adjustment; conventionality, custom; AGREEMENT, compliance; UNIFORMITY, orthodoxy.

2, object lesson, example, instance, specimen, sample, quotation; exemplification, illustration, case in point; pattern, PROTOTYPE.

3, conformist, conventionalist, formalist; stickler. *Colloq.,* bookman.

Verbs—1, conform, accommodate, adapt, adapt oneself to; be regular; follow, go by *or* observe the rules; comply with, tally with, chime in with, fall in with; be guided by; follow the fashion *or* crowd; lend oneself to; pass muster, do as others do; in Rome do as the Romans do; go *or* swim with the stream *or* current. *Colloq.,* keep in step, toe the mark, come up to scratch; go by the book.

2, exemplify, illustrate, cite, quote, give a case; produce an instance.

Adjectives—conformable, conforming, adaptable; regular (see REGULARITY), according to rule, well regulated, orderly; conventional, customary, ordinary, common, habitual, usual; typical, normal, formal; canonical, orthodox, sound, strict, rigid, positive, uncompromising; shipshape; exemplary, illustrative, in point.

Adverbs—conformably, by rule; agreeably to; in conformity with, in accordance with, in keeping with; according to; consistent with; as usual; in order; of course, as a matter of course; *pro forma,* for form's sake, by the book, according to Hoyle; invariably, uniformly; for example, for instance; *exempli gratia; e.g.*

Antonym, see UNCONFORMITY.

confound, *v.t.* confuse, bewilder, perplex, nonplus, dum(b)found, dismay, mix up, puzzle; rout, overcome, overthrow. See DISORDER, DOUBT. *Ant.*, see CERTAINTY.

confrère, *n.* See ASSOCIATE.

confront, *v.t.* face, oppose; resist, brave. See OPPOSITION.

confuse, *v.t.* perplex, confound, distract, disconcert, flurry, addle, fluster, bewilder; disorder, mix, embroil, muddle, disarrange, misplace; abash; embarrass. See DISORDER. *Ant.*, see ARRANGEMENT.

CONFUTATION

Nouns—confutation, refutation; answer, complete answer; disproof, conviction, rebuttal; invalidation; exposure, exposition; retort; *reductio ad absurdum*; knockdown argument. *Colloq.*, squelcher, crusher, clincher.

Verbs—confute, refute; parry, negative, disprove, expose, show up, show the fallacy of, rebut, defeat; demolish, destroy (see DESTRUCTION); overwhelm, overthrow, overturn; scatter to the winds, explode, invalidate; silence; put to silence, reduce to silence; clinch an argument; shut up; not leave a leg to stand on, cut the ground from under one's feet. *Colloq.*, squash, squelch, tear down, blow skyhigh.

Adjectives—confuting, confuted, confutative; refuted, refutable; condemned on one's own showing, condemned out of one's own mouth.

Antonym, see DEMONSTRATION.

---

congeal, *v.t. & i.* solidify, harden, fix, gel, jell, set, coagulate, stiffen, thicken; freeze; condense. See DENSITY, COLD. *Ant.*, see RARITY.

congenial, *adj.* compatible, agreeable, sympathetic, kindred, harmonious. See AGREEMENT. *Ant.*, see DISAGREEMENT.

congest, *v.i.* overfill, clog, block; plug, stop *or* stuff up; crowd, jam, choke, cram, throng; constipate, clot. See CLOSURE, OVERRUNNING, DISEASE.

CONGRATULATION

Nouns—congratulation, gratulation; felicitation; salute; compliments, compliments of the season.

Verbs—congratulate; gratulate; felicitate; wish one joy; compliment, tender *or* offer one's congratulations; wish many happy returns of the day; congratulate oneself, pat oneself on the back (see REJOICING).

Adjective—congratulatory.

---

congregation, *n.* ASSEMBLAGE, assembly, gathering, collection, meeting, aggregation; church, parish, flock, fold, brethren.

congress, *n.* COUNCIL, assembly, legislature, parliament; meeting, convention; intercourse. See ASSEMBLAGE.

conjecture, *n.* SUPPOSITION, hypothesis, extrapolation, speculation, guess; inference, surmise. See THOUGHT.

conjugate, *adj.* yoked, united, mated; related, paronymous, coderived. See JUNCTION, WORD. *Ant.*, see DISJUNCTION.

conjure, *v.* cast spells, enchant; invoke, summon up; beseech, implore, beg. See SORCERY, REQUEST, WARNING.

CONNECTION

Nouns—**1,** connection, bond, tie, link; connective, interconnection; nexus; neck, isthmus; bridge, tunnel, causeway.

2, ligature, ligament; sinew, tendon, umbilical cord; cable, wire, strap, bridle, halter, lines, reins; thong, lasso, lariat; rope, cord, twine, string.

3, fastening, clamp, clasp, buckle, button, snap, hook, hook and eye, zipper, Velcro fastener; lace, lacing, latch, bolt, lock, padlock; anchor, buoy, moorings, guy rope, hawser, grappling iron, cable, painter; leash; belt, suspenders, braces, girdle, sash, cummerbund.

4, knot, slipknot, running knot, bowknot, surgeon's knot, square knot, *etc.*, noose.

5, nail, brad, finishing nail, spike, screw, toggle bolt, staple, tack, thumbtack, rivet.

6, cement, glue, paste, mucilage, gum; mortar, stucco, putty, lime, plaster, solder.

Verbs—connect, link, join (see JUNCTION), combine, attach, fasten; associate, relate (see RELATION).

Antonym, see DISJUNCTION.

---

connivance, *n.* COÖPERATION, collusion, CONSENT, complicity; PERMISSION, toleration, allowance, sufferance. *Ant.*, see OPPOSITION.

connoisseur, *n.* EXPERT, virtuoso; critic, JUDGE, epicure, adept. See TASTE. *Ant.*, see VULGARITY, IGNORANCE.

connotation, *n.* implication, suggestion, association; MEANING, FEELING.

conquer, *v.t.* prevail, overcome, overthrow, vanquish, subdue, subjugate; win, triumph. See SUCCESS. *Ant.*, see FAILURE.

consanguinity, *n.* kin, kinship, kinfolk, kinsman, kinswoman, relation(s); relationship, blood, blood tie, family, ilk, breed; stock, strain; lineage, line; kidney; root, branch, tree; brotherhood, sisterhood; parentage, paternity, maternity; tribe, clan; generation; offspring, children, progeny; house, household; kith and kin; cousins, *etc.* See RELATION.

conscientious, *adj.* faithful, honorable, incorruptible, upright, trusty; scrupulous, just; religious; strict, thorough, particular, careful, painstaking. See CARE, PROBITY. *Ant.*, see NEGLECT, IMPROBITY.

conscious, *adj.* sensible, cognizant, percipient, understanding, keen; awake, aware, sentient. See INTELLIGENCE, KNOWLEDGE. *Ant.*, see IGNORANCE.

conscription, *n.* enlistment, draft, impressment. See COMPULSION.

consecrate, *v.t.* bless, sanctify, hallow; seal, dedicate, devote. See PIETY. *Ant.*, see IMPIETY.

consecutive, *adj.* See CONTINUITY.

consensus, *n.* CONCORD, AGREEMENT; general *or* popular opinion, common BELIEF; poll, polling, sampling; silent majority.

CONSENT

Nouns—consent, ASSENT, acquiescence; approval, compliance, AGREEMENT, concession; yielding, yieldingness; accession, acknowledgment, acceptance; settlement, ratification, confirmation; permit, PERMISSION, PROMISE.

Verbs—consent; ASSENT, yield, admit, allow, concede, grant; come over, come (a)round; give in, acknowledge; give consent, comply with, acquiesce, agree to, fall in with, accede, accept, embrace an offer, close with, take at one's word, have no objection; satisfy, meet one's wishes, settle, come to terms; not refuse, turn a willing ear (see WILLINGNESS); jump at; deign, vouchsafe; PROMISE.

Adjectives—consenting, acquiescent, compliant, willing; permissive; agreed, agreeable; unconditional.

Adverbs—yes, by all means, willingly, if you please, as you please; be it so, so be it, well and good, of course.

Antonym, see REFUSAL, DISSENT, DISAGREEMENT.

---

consequence, *n.* EFFECT, END, result, sequel, outcome, product, fruit; IMPORT, account, concern, interest, significance, matter, moment; notability, esteem, greatness, value, prominence; self-importance, arrogance, pomposity. See IMPORTANCE. *Ant.*, see UNIMPORTANCE.

consequential, *adj.* necessary, consequent, sequential; inferable, deducible; indirect, resultant; supercilious, pompous, arrogant, vainglorious, self-important. See EFFECT, VANITY. *Ant.*, see MODESTY.

conservation, *n.* maintenance, protection, keeping, preservation. See STORE. *Ant.*, see DESTRUCTION, WASTE.

conservative, *adj.* unprogressive; unchanging, stable; reactionary, die-hard, Tory. *Slang,* mossback. See STABILITY. *Ant.,* see CHANGE.

conserve, *v.t.* See STORE.

consider, *v.t.* deliberate, ponder, brood, contemplate, meditate, ruminate, reflect; speculate, turn, revolve, weigh, muse; believe, JUDGE, deem; regard, heed, mark, notice, mind; entertain; review, esteem. See ATTENTION, THOUGHT. *Ant.,* see RASHNESS.

considerable, *adj.* large, sizable, substantial, important, big; tolerable, fair, respectable; material, noteworthy, weighty; intense, extraordinary. See GREATNESS, IMPORTANCE, SIZE. *Ant.,* see UNIMPORTANCE, LITTLENESS.

considerate, *adj.* THOUGHTFUL, kind, solicitous, humane, sympathetic. See FEELING. *Ant.,* see NEGLECT, DISRESPECT.

consideration, *n.* THOUGHT, deliberation; contemplation, reflection, rumination; CARE, regard; esteem, deference; ATTENTION, notice; IMPORTANCE, consequence; MOTIVE, reason, ground, basis; gratuity, fee. See BENEVOLENCE, RESPECT, REWARD. *Ant.,* see MALEVOLENCE, INATTENTION, NEGLECT.

consign, *v.t.* deliver, commit, assign, delegate; remit, remand; send, dispatch, ship; condemn, devote. See TRANSFER, PASSAGE.

consignee, *n.* trustee, nominee, committee; delegate; commissary, commissioner; emissary, envoy, messenger; diplomatist, ambassador (see DEPUTY); functionary, curator, treasurer (see TREASURY); AGENT, factor, bailiff, clerk, secretary, attorney, solicitor, proctor, broker, underwriter, commission agent, auctioneer, one's man of business; factotum, DIRECTOR; negotiator, go-between; middleman; employe(e); SERVANT, caretaker; traveler, salesman, traveling salesman, drummer.

consignment, *n.* goods, shipment; delivery, consignation, commitment; allotment, assignment; task, charge. See APPORTIONMENT, COMMISSION, TRANSFER.

consist, *v.i.* lie, reside, inhere; include, comprise. See EXISTENCE, COMPOSITION. *Ant.,* see NONEXISTENCE, DECOMPOSITION.

consistent, *adj.* accordant, coherent, uniform, congruous, conformable, compatible, consonant, harmonious; reconcilable; homogeneous, regular. See AGREEMENT. *Ant.,* see DISAGREEMENT.

consolation, *n.* CONDOLENCE, solace, sympathy; assuagement, sop; encouragement. See RELIEF.

console, *v. & n.* —*v.t.* See COMFORT. —*n.* SUPPORT, bracket; cabinet.

consolidate, *v.t.* unite, join, combine, affiliate, federate, syndicate, merge, pool, fuse, incorporate; compress; solidify. See JUNCTION, DENSITY. *Ant.,* see RARITY.

consonance, *n.* AGREEMENT, HARMONY; SIMILARITY; accordance, concord. *Ant.,* see DISAGREEMENT, DISCORD.

conspicuous, *adj.* prominent, notable, eminent, outstanding; signal, striking, salient, noticeable, obvious, marked; glaring, obtrusive, notorious, flagrant. See REPUTE, VISION. *Ant.,* see DISREPUTE, CONCEALMENT.

conspire, *v.i.* plot, intrigue, collude, scheme; concur, combine. See PLAN.

constant, *adj.* sta(u)nch, loyal, steadfast; fast, firm, unwavering, unchanging, unswerving, unflagging; PERMANENT, abiding, enduring; steady, stable; regular, even; continual, incessant. See PROBITY, STABILITY. *Ant.,* see CHANGE.

constellation, *n.* star group, cluster, asterism; sign of the zodiac; ASSEMBLAGE, confluence, gathering. See UNIVERSE.

constituency, *n.* constituents, following, clientele; electorate, voters; district, ward. See CHOICE.

constituent, *adj. & n.* —*adj.* integral, formative; elective, appointive, electoral. —*n.* COMPONENT; voter, supporter, elector. See CHOICE.

constitute, *v.i.* form, be, make, frame, compose; total; set up, establish, found; appoint, EFFECT. See CAUSE, COMPOSITION.

constitution, *n.* nature, make-up, temperament, physique, disposition; structure, construction; state, condition; law, edict, code, charter; designation, settlement; creation, foundation. See COMPOSITION, HABIT, LEGALITY.

constraint, *n.* pressure, force, stress; RESTRAINT, confinement, repression; reserve, embarrassment, stiffness; COMPULSION, obligation, coercion, necessity, duress. *Ant.*, see FREEDOM, WILL.

constrict, *v.t.* contract, limit, CONTRACT, bind, cramp, squeeze, compress; choke, strangle, strangulate. *Ant.*, see EXPAND.

construction, *n.* building, fabrication, composition; formation, structure, erection; conformation; creation; translation, explanation. See FORM, INTERPRETATION, PRODUCTION. *Ant.*, see DESTRUCTION.

consult, *v.i.* advise, confer, counsel, discuss, consider. See ADVICE, THOUGHT.

consume, *v.t.* destroy, demolish, annihilate; burn, decompose, corrode; devour, swallow, eat, drink; exhaust, drain, use up, expend. See DESTRUCTION, USE, WASTE. *Ant.*, see PRESERVATION.

consumer, *n.* customer, purchaser, client. See PURCHASE.

consummate, *adj. & v.* —*adj.* COMPLETE, perfect, finished, absolute; sheer, unmitigated; profound, intense. —*v.t.* COMPLETE, achieve, accomplish; PERFECT. See COMPLETION.

consumption, *n.* destruction; use; burning; tuberculosis. See DISEASE, WASTE. *Ant.*, see ECONOMY, STORE.

CONTACT

Nouns—contact, contiguity, proximity, NEARNESS; apposition, juxtaposition, abutment, TOUCH, CONNECTION, osculation, meeting, encounter, syzygy, coincidence, coexistence; adhesion; border(land), frontier, LIMIT; tangent.

Verbs—be in contact, be contiguous, join, adjoin, abut; grace, touch, meet, osculate, come in contact, coincide; coexist; adhere; march with, rub elbows *or* shoulders, keep in touch, hobnob. See COHERENCE.

Adjectives—in contact, contiguous, contingent, adjacent, touching; conterminous, end to end, osculatory; tangent, tangential; hand to hand; close to, in touch with, shoulder to shoulder, cheek by jowl.

Antonym, see INTERVAL.

contagion, *n.* communicability, infection, epidemic, pestilence, virus; DISEASE, transmission; poison, toxicity. See PASSAGE.

contagious, *adj.* catching, infectious, epidemic, communicable, transmittable, pestilential, noxious, contaminative. *Colloq.*, catching. See TRANSFER, DISEASE.

contain, *v.t.* receive, carry, accommodate; INCLUDE, comprise, involve, incorporate, embrace, embody, comprehend, hold; restrain, check. See COMPOSITION.

container, *n.* RECEPTACLE, utensil, jar, bottle, vase, vessel; box, carton, package, crate, bag, sack, can, case.

contaminate, *v.t.* corrupt, infect, taint, pollute, soil; defile, sully, befoul, stain, dirty; debauch, deprave, degrade. See DETERIORATION, UNCLEANNESS. *Ant.*, see IMPROVEMENT, CLEANNESS.

contemplate, *v.t.* consider, meditate, ponder, muse, reflect; propose, purpose, PLAN, mean, aim, intend, design; view, behold. See THOUGHT, VISION. *Ant.*, see CHANCE, BLINDNESS.

contemporary, *adj.* simultaneous; coexistent, contemporaneous, coeval, synchronous, coincident, concomitant. See TIME.

CONTEMPT

Nouns—contempt, contemptuousness, disdain, scorn, despisal, contumely; slight, sneer, disparagement, DETRACTION, DISAPPROBATION; derision, DIS-

RESPECT; arrogance, insolence; ridicule, mockery; hoot, catcall. *Colloq.*, slam, dig, cut, cold shoulder.

Verbs—**1,** be contemptuous of, despise, contemn, scorn, disdain, feel contempt for, disregard, slight, not mind; pass by, NEGLECT; look down upon, hold cheap, hold in contempt; think nothing of, think small beer of; UNDERESTIMATE; take no account of, care nothing for; set no store by; not care a straw (see UNIMPORTANCE); set at naught.

2, laugh up one's sleeve, snap one's fingers at, shrug one's shoulders, snub, turn up one's nose at, pooh-pooh, damn with faint praise; sneeze at, sneer at; curl one's lip, toss one's head, look down one's nose at; draw oneself up; laugh at *or* off; be disrespectful; point the finger of scorn, hold up to scorn, laugh to scorn; scout, hoot, flout, hiss, scoff at, jeer, mock, revile, taunt; turn one's back, turn a cold shoulder; trample upon, trample underfoot; spurn, kick; fling to the winds. *Colloq.*, cut, leave in the lurch *or* out in the cold, steer clear of, have no truck with, draw the color line. *Slang*, cut dead, pass up, give the go-by, brush off.

Adjectives—**1,** contemptuous; disdainful, scornful; withering, contumelious, supercilious, cynical, haughty, bumptious, cavalier; derisive.

2, contemptible, despicable; pitiable, pitiful; unimportant, despised, downtrodden; unenvied.

Adverbs—contemptuously, arrogantly, insolently, *etc.*

Interjections—bah! pooh! pshaw! tut! fiddle-de-dee! away with! *Slang*, in your hat! come off it!

Antonym, see APPROBATION, RESPECT.

---

contend, *v.i.* engage, contest, battle, struggle, strive, vie, compete; maintain, assert, argue, hold, allege; dispute, debate. See AFFIRMATION, CONTENTION, REASONING.

CONTENT

Nouns—content, contentment, contentedness; complacency, satisfaction, ease, peace of mind; serenity; CHEERFULNESS; comfort, well-being; reconciliation, conciliation; RESIGNATION, patience, SUBMISSION. See PLEASURE.

Verbs—**1,** be content; rest satisfied, let well enough alone, feel oneself at home, hug oneself; take in good part; ASSENT, be reconciled to, make one's peace with; get over it; take heart, take comfort; put up with, bear.

2, render content, tranquilize; set at rest *or* ease; comfort; set one's heart *or* mind at ease *or* rest; speak peace; conciliate, reconcile, win over, propitiate, disarm, beguile; content, satisfy; gratify, please; soothe, assuage, mollify.

Adjectives—**1,** content, contented, satisfied, at ease, at home; with the mind at ease, *sans souci*, easygoing, not particular; imperturbable, conciliatory; unrepining; resigned, patient, cheerful; unafflicted, unvexed, unmolested, unplagued; serene; at rest; snug, comfortable; in one's element.

2, satisfactory, tolerable, adequate, bearable, acceptable, desirable.

Adverbs—contentedly, to one's heart's content; all for the best.

Interjections—very well, so much the better, well and good; that will do.

Antonym, see DISCONTENT.

CONTENTION

Nouns—**1,** contention, strife, contest, contestation, altercation; struggle; belligerency, pugnacity, combativeness; competition, rivalry; litigation (see LAWSUIT); OPPOSITION.

2, controversy, polemics; debate; argument, discussion, war of words; logomachy; paper war; high words, quarrel; bone of contention; discord, friction, incompatibility, misunderstanding, wrangling; dispute, squabble, tiff; disunion, breach; *casus belli*; WARFARE.

3, conflict, skirmish, dogfight; encounter; *rencontre*, rencounter; collision, affair, brush, fight; battle royal, pitched battle; combat, action, engagement, joust, tournament; tilt, tilting, tourney, list; death struggle, Armageddon; shindy; fracas, clash of arms; tussle, scuffle, brawl, fray; mêlée, scrimmage, bush-fighting; naval engagement, sea fight. *Colloq.*, set-to, mix-up, free-for-all. *Slang*, scrap, run-in, hassle, rhubarb.

4, duel, single combat, monomachy; feud, vendetta; satisfaction, passage of arms, affair of honor.

5, wrestling, pugilism, boxing, fisticuffs; spar, mill, round, bout, game, event; prize-fighting; jujitsu, gymnastics; athletics; sports, games of skill, gymkhana.

6, match, race, relay race, foot race, dash, hurdles, automobile race, bicycle race, boat race, regatta; horse-racing, heat, steeplechase, handicap, claiming race, stake race, sweepstakes, trot, pace, Derby, sport of kings; field day; turf, sporting, bull-fight.

7, contender, contestant (see COMBATANT, OPPOSITION).

Verbs—**1,** contend, contest, oppose, strive, struggle, fight, combat, battle, engage, skirmish; contend with, grapple with, close with; try conclusions with, have a brush with, join issue, come to blows, be at loggerheads, set to, come to scratch, meet hand to hand; wrangle, quarrel.

2, scramble, wrestle, spar, exchange blows, exchange fisticuffs, tussle, tilt, box, stave, fence, encounter, fall foul of, measure swords; take up the cudgels *or* glove *or* gauntlet; enter the lists, couch one's lance; give satisfaction; lay about one, break the peace, lift one's hand against. *Colloq.*, square off, pitch into. *Slang*, scrap, put up a scrap, take on, lay into, light into; pull a gun.

3, compete with, cope with, vie with, race with; emulate; contend for, run a race.

Adjectives—contending; at loggerheads, at war, at issue; competitive, rival; belligerent; contentious, combative, bellicose, unpeaceful; warlike (see WARFARE); quarrelsome, pugnacious; pugilistic.

Antonym, see PACIFICATION.

---

contents, *n.* dimensions (of a container); capacity, volume; cargo, freight, load, loading; burden; cupful, basketful, bottleful, *etc.*; stuffing, packing, filling, wadding. See RECEPTACLE, COMPOSITION.

contest, *v.t.* See CONTENTION.

contestant, *n.* contender, competitor, competer, *etc.* See CONTENTION.

context, *n.* setting, background, ENVIRONMENT, surroundings; position, situation; relationship, connections. See ACCOMPANIMENT, MEANING.

contiguity, *n.* juxtaposition, abutment, NEARNESS, proximity, adjacency, union, meeting. See CONTACT. *Ant.*, see DISTANCE, INTERVAL.

continental, *adj.* mainland (see LAND); cosmopolitan, formal, sophisticated, worldly, urbane, suave; charming. See FASHION, CONDUCT.

contingency, *n.* CHANCE, POSSIBILITY, likelihood, accident, casualty, prospect; situation, predicament, case. See CIRCUMSTANCE.

contingent, *adj.* possible; provisional, conditional, provisory, dependent; incidental, accidental, casual. See CHANCE, LIABILITY. *Ant.*, see INTENTION.

continual, *adj.* invariable, steady, regular, persistent, repeated, incessant; constant, unceasing. See FREQUENCY, CONTINUITY.

continuance, *n.* continuation, CONTINUITY, SEQUENCE, succession; persistence, perseverance, endurance; extension; prolongation; maintenance, perpetuation, permanence, unceasingness, ceaselessness; run, series, REPETITION. See FREQUENCY. *Ant.*, see END, SHORTNESS.

continue, *v.* persist; keep, go, carry, run *or* hold on; maintain, keep up; sustain, uphold; prolong, remain, last, endure, withstand; protract, prolong, persevere; be permanent; stay, stick. See CONTINUITY, SEQUENCE. *Ant.*, see END, SHORTNESS.

CONTINUITY

Nouns—continuity; consecutiveness; succession, round, suite, progression, series, train, chain; CONTINUANCE, continuation, perpetuity; concatenation, scale; gradation, course; procession, column; retinue, caravan, cortège, cavalcade, rank and file, line of battle, array; running fire; pedigree, genealogy, lineage, race; rank, file, line, row, range, tier, string, thread, team; suit; colonnade.

Verbs—follow in a series, form a series; fall in; arrange in a series, string together, thread, graduate; tabulate, list, file.

Adjectives—continuous, continued; consecutive; progressive, gradual; serial, successive; immediate, unbroken, entire; linear; in a line, in a row; uninterrupted, unintermitting, unremitting; ceaseless; perennial, evergreen; constant, chronic, continual, repeated, persistent, repeating, persisting.

Adverbs—continuously, *etc.; seriatim;* in a line, in succession, in series, in turn; running, gradually, step by step, at a stretch; in file, in column, in single file, in Indian file.

Antonym, see DISJUNCTION.

---

contortion, *n.* DISTORTION, twist, dislocation, deformity; grimace.
contour, *n.* outline, profile, shape, form, conformation, figure. See APPEARANCE.
contraband, *adj.* forbidden, illegal, illicit, prohibited, smuggled. See RESTRAINT.
contraception, *n.* birth control, planned parenthood; rhythm method; zero population growth. See UNPRODUCTIVENESS.
contraceptive, *n.* prophylactic, sheath, condom, pessary, diaphragm, coil, loop, IUD, oral contraceptive, jelly, suppository. *Slang,* rubber. See UNPRODUCTIVENESS.
contract, *n.* compact, AGREEMENT, promise, bargain, covenant, stipulation, convention. *Ant.,* see DISAGREEMENT.

CONTRACTION

Nouns—**1,** contraction, reduction, diminution; DECREASE; defalcation, decrement; lessening, shrinking, astringency; emaciation, attenuation, tabefaction, consumption; atrophy.
2, condensation, compression, compactness; COMPENDIUM, squeezing; strangulation; corrugation; contractility, compressibility; coarctation.

Verbs—**1,** contract, become small, become smaller; lessen, decrease, dwindle, shrink, narrow, shrivel, collapse, wither, lose flesh, reduce, wizen, fall away, waste, wane, ebb; decay, deteriorate (see DETERIORATION).
2, contract, render smaller, lessen, diminish, draw in, narrow, coarctate; constrict, constringe; condense, compress, squeeze, cramp, corrugate, crush, crumple up, warp, purse up, pack, stow; pinch, tighten, strangle; cramp; stunt, dwarf; pare, reduce, attenuate, rub down, scrape, file, grind, chip, shave, shear; shorten; circumscribe; restrain. See SHORTNESS, CIRCUMSCRIPTION, RESTRAINT.

Adjectives—contracting, contractive; astringent; shrunk, strangulated, wizened, stunted; waning, neap; compact.

Antonym, see INCREASE.

---

contractor, *n.* builder, architect, PADRONE; entrepreneur. See AGENT.
contradict, *v.t.* gainsay, deny, belie, controvert, refute, disprove, overthrow; dispute, dissent. See CONTENTION. *Ant.,* see IDENTITY, EVIDENCE.
contraption, *n., colloq.* See CONTRIVANCE.
contrariness, *n.* contrariety, OPPOSITION, obstinacy; antagonism, DISAGREEMENT, DISOBEDIENCE. *Ant.,* see AGREEMENT, OBEDIENCE.

contrary, *adj.* opposed, opposite, counter, contradictory; unfavorable, adverse; captious, willful, perverse; hostile, antagonistic. See OPPOSITION. *Ant.,* see AGREEMENT, COÖPERATION.

contrast, *n.* DIFFERENCE, opposition, antithesis, foil, dissimilarity, unlikeness, disparity; converse, counterpoint, obverse, contrary. See OPPOSITION. *Ant.,* see IDENTITY, SIMILARITY.

contravene, *v.t.* violate, infringe upon; oppose, contradict, defy; thwart, hinder, block, stop, impede. See OPPOSITION, NEGATION, HINDRANCE.

contretemps, *n.* embarrassment; mischance, mishap. See FAILURE, DIFFICULTY.

contribute, *v.t. & i.* give, subscribe, donate; help, aid, assist; conduce, advance, tend, serve, redound, go. See GIVING, CAUSE. *Ant.,* see RECEIVING.

contributor, *n.* giver, subscriber, donor; author, correspondent, editor, columnist, reviewer; helper. See BOOK, GIVING.

contrivance, *n.* device, invention, construction, machine, apparatus, gear; PLAN, scheme, trick, stratagem. *Colloq.,* contraption. See INSTRUMENT.

control, *v. & n.* —*v.t.* command, dominate, govern, rule, regulate, direct, master; restrain, subdue, modify, check; test, verify. *Ant.,* see FREEDOM. —*n.* COMMAND, mastery, domination, sway, upper hand, power, regimentation, government, DIRECTION, management, dominion; RESTRAINT, ceiling, regulation. *Ant.,* see FREEDOM.

controversy, *n.* CONTENTION, dispute, argument, discussion, debate, quarrel, wrangle, altercation. *Ant.,* see AGREEMENT.

controvert, *v.t.* deny, contradict, contravene, traverse (*Legal*), impugn, refute, confute, oppose, dispute, counter. See DEFENSE, NEGATION. *Ant.,* see AFFIRMATION.

contusion, *n.* bruise, abrasion, black-and-blue mark. See DISEASE.

conundrum, *n.* riddle, question, problem, enigma; puzzle. See SECRET.

convalesce, *v.i.* recover, recuperate, rally, revive, improve. See HEALTH.

convene, *v.i.* ASSEMBLE, gather, collect, congregate, meet; convoke. *Ant.,* DISPERSE.

convenience, *n.* accessibility, handiness, availability, suitability; advantage, accommodation, comfort, opportunity, ease. See USE. *Ant.,* see USELESSNESS.

convent, *n.* cloister, nunnery, abbey, priory. See TEMPLE.

convention, *n.* ASSEMBLAGE, gathering, congregation, congress, meeting, caucus, council; convocation; RULE, custom, usage, formality, practice; propriety, conventionality. See FASHION.

conventional, *adj.* customary, accepted, orthodox, approved, habitual, usual; formal. See CONFORMITY. *Ant.,* see UNCONFORMITY.

CONVERGENCE

Nouns—convergence, confluence, concourse, conflux, congress, concurrence, concentration; appulse, meeting; ASSEMBLAGE, resort; FOCUS; asymptote.

Verbs—converge, concur; come together, unite; meet, fall in with; close with, close in upon; centralize, center round, center in; enter in; pour in; gather together, unite, concentrate, bring into focus.

Adjectives—convergent, confluent, concurrent; centripetal; asymptotic.

Antonym, see DIVERGENCE.

CONVERSATION

Nouns—**1,** conversation, interlocution; collocution, colloquy, converse; confabulation; talk, discourse; oral communication, communion, commerce; dialogue, duologue. *Colloq.,* confab. *Slang,* talkfest, bull session.

2, chat, chit-chat, *causerie*; small talk, table talk, idle talk, tattle, gossip, tittle-tattle; prattle; *on dit*; talk of the town.

3, conference, parley, palaver, interview, audience, audition, *pour-parler; tête-à-tête;* RECEPTION, *conversazione;* congress, COUNCIL; debate, logomachy, war of words. *Colloq.,* powwow, gab. *Slang,* huddle, confab.

4, interlocutor, conversationalist, dialogist, talker, spokesman, interpreter; gossip, tattler; Paul Pry; chatterer (see LOQUACITY).

Verbs—**1,** converse, talk together; confabulate; hold a conversation, carry on *or* engage in a conversation; put in a word; shine in conversation; bandy words; parley; palaver; chat, gossip, tattle; prate. *Slang,* chin, chew the rag, go into a huddle, shoot the breeze. See SOCIALITY.

2, discourse, confer, consult, advise, confer *or* commune with; hold converse, hold a conference; talk it over; be closeted with; talk in private.

Adjectives—conversing, talking; interlocutory; conversational, conversationable, discursive, discoursive; chatty, sociable, colloquial.

---

converse, *adj., n. & v.* —*adj.* transposed, reversed, turned about; reciprocal; other, opposite, contrary. —*n.* reverse, contrary, opposite; counterpart, reciprocal; vice versa. See OPPOSITION. —*v.* See CONVERSATION.

conversion, *n.* reduction, transformation; CHANGE, retooling, changeover, adaption; transmutation, transmogrification; alchemy; RESOLUTION, assimilation; change of religion; reformation, metamorphosis, metempsychosis; sex change. See DIFFERENCE, REVOLUTION.

convert, *v. & n.* —*v.t.* CHANGE, change *or* make over; retool, adapt; reorganize, remodel, regenerate; change (the religion of); reduce; transmute, transform, transmogrify; render; apply. See CHANGEABLENESS. —*n.* neophyte, disciple; renegade, apostate; transsexual.

CONVEXITY

Nouns—**1,** convexity, prominence, projection, swelling, bulge, protuberance, protrusion, growth.

2, excrescence, intumescence, outgrowth, tumor, tubercle, tuberosity; hump, hunch, bunch; tooth, knob, elbow; bulb, node, nodule; tongue; pimple, wen, weal, pustule, growth, sarcoma, carbuncle, corn, wart, furuncle, polyp, fungus, blister, boil (see DISEASE); papilla; breast, bosom, nipple, teat, mammilla; nose, proboscis, beak, snout; belly; withers, back, shoulder, lip. *Colloq.,* corporation, pot.

3, hill, HEIGHT, cape, promontory, headland; peninsula, neck, isthmus, point of land; reef; mole, jetty, ledge, spur.

4, cupola, dome, arch, balcony, eaves; pilaster; relief, bas relief, cameo.

Verbs—be convex, project, bulge, protrude, pout, bunch; jut out, stand out, stick out, poke out; stick up, bristle, start up, shoot up; swell, hand over, bend over; beetle; render prominent; raise, emboss, chase.

Adjectives—convex, prominent, protuberant; projecting; bossed; nodular, bunchy; clavate; mammiform; papulous; hemispheric, bulbous; bowed, arched; bold; bellied; tuberous, tuberculous; tumorous; cornute, odontoid; lentiform, lenticular; salient, in relief, raised, repoussé; bloated.

Antonym, see CONCAVITY.

---

convey, *v.t.* bear, carry, transport, transmit; impart, communicate; TRANSFER, grant, cede, will. See INFORMATION.

conveyance, *n.* VEHICLE, wagon, van, bus, car; TRANSFER, assignment, sale, legacy, disposal; transmission, communication. See PASSAGE.

convict, *v. & n.* —*v.t.* condemn, find guilty, doom, sentence. See JUSTICE, LAWSUIT, DISAPPROBATION. *Ant.,* see VINDICATION. —*n.* criminal, felon, jailbird, prisoner, captive. See EVILDOER, PRISON.

conviction, *n.* BELIEF, persuasion, faith, opinion, view; CONDEMNATION, sentence, penalty. *Ant.,* doubt, ACQUITTAL.

convince, *v.t.* persuade, satisfy, assure. See BELIEF. *Ant.,* see DOUBT.
conviviality, *n.* SOCIALITY, sociability, festivity, gaiety, joviality.
convoke, *v.t.* convene, assemble, summon, call, collect, gather. See ASSEMBLAGE. *Ant.,* DISPERSE.

CONVOLUTION

Nouns—**1,** convolution, winding; involution, circumvolution; wave, undulation, tortuosity, anfractuosity; sinuosity, sinuation; meandering, circuit; twist, twirl, windings and turnings; ambages; torsion; inosculation; reticulation, CROSSING.
2, coil, roll, curl, curlicue, buckle, spiral, helix, cockscrew, worm, volute, rundle; tendril; scallop, escalop; serpent, eel, maze, labyrinth.
Verbs—convolve, be convoluted, wind, twine, turn and twist, twirl; wave, undulate, meander; inosculate; entwine, intwine; twist, coil, roll; wrinkle, curl, crisp, twill; frizz, frizzle; crimp, crape, indent, scallop; wring, intort; contort; wreathe.
Adjectives—convoluted; winding, twisting, tortile, tortuous; wavy; undulatory; circling, snaky, snakelike, serpentine; anguilliform, vermiform; vermicular; mazy, sinuous, flexuous, sigmoidal; spiral, coiled, helical, turbinated; involved, intricate, complicated, perplexed; labyrinthine; peristaltic.
Adverbs—convolutely, in and out, round and round.
Antonym, see DIRECTION.

---

convoy, *v.t.* accompany, escort, conduct; watch, protect, guard, support. See ACCOMPANIMENT.
convulse, *v.t.* agitate, shake, disturb, trouble, excite, stir; rend, wring, hurt. See AGITATION, PAIN.
cook, *v.t.* prepare, concoct, fix, make; roast, broil, boil, fry, *etc. Colloq.* doctor. *Slang.* ruin, spoil. See HEAT.
cookery, *n.* cooking, cuisine; culinary art. See FOOD, PREPARATION.
cookie, *n.* wafer, biscuit; shortbread, sugar cookie, gingersnap, *etc.* (see FOOD).
cool, *v. & adj.* —*v.t.* chill, REFRIGERATE, ice, freeze, harden; calm, allay. See COLD, MODERATION. *Ant.,* see HEAT. —*adj.* COLD, chilly, frigid; bold, impudent; INEXCITABLE, self-controlled, calm, deliberate, composed, indifferent, unemotional, self-possessed; easygoing, placid; unfriendly, distant, lukewarm. *Ant.,* warm; see FRIEND, EXCITEMENT, HEAT.

COÖPERATION

Nouns—**1,** coöperation; coadjuvancy, coadjutancy; coagency, coefficiency; concert, concurrence, participation, collaboration; union, UNITY, combination, collusion, complicity, conspiracy.
2, association, alliance, colleagueship, copartnership; confederation, coalition, fusion; coöperative, coöp; union; logrolling; fraternity, fellowship, freemasonry; unanimity, ASSENT; esprit de corps, party *or* team spirit; clanship, partisanship; concord, AGREEMENT. See PARTY.
Verbs—**1,** coöperate, concur; conduce, combine; fraternize; conspire, collude, connive, concert, lay heads together; confederate, be in league with; unite one's efforts; keep together, pull together, club together, hang together, hold together, league together, band together; be banded together; stand shoulder to shoulder; act in concert, join forces; understand one another, play into the hands of, hunt in couples. *Colloq.,* play ball.
2, side with, go along with, go hand in hand with, join hands with, make common cause with, unite with, join with, mix oneself up with, take part with, cast in one's lot with; join with, enter into partnership with; rally round, follow the lead of; come to, pass over to, come into

the views of; be in the same boat. *Colloq.*, throw in with, line up with.

3, be a party to, lend oneself to; participate; have a hand in, have a finger in the pie; take part in; second, AID, take the part of, play the game of; espouse a cause, espouse a quarrel. *Colloq.*, sit in, chip in. *Adjectives*—coöperating, in coöperation *or* league; coadjuvant, coadjutant; participatory, partaking; favorable to; unopposed. *Slang*, in cahoots with.

Adverbs—coöperatively; as one man; together; unanimously; shoulder to shoulder; side by side; hand in hand; in common; share and share alike; pro rata.

Antonym, see OPPOSITION.

coördinate, *v.t.* equalize, adapt, harmonize, synchronize, adjust; organize. See ARRANGEMENT. *Ant.*, see DISORDER.

cop, *v. & n.* —*v.* seize, grab, take; steal, filch, pilfer; win, capture. See ACQUISITION. —*n.*, slang, see POLICEMAN.

cope, *v.i.* contend, strive, deal with, oppose; face, stand up (to); manage, handle; keep under control; be up to. See CONTENTION.

copious, *adj.* adequate, abundant, plentiful, ample, rich, full, overflowing; wordy, profuse, diffuse, prolix. See SUFFICIENCY. *Ant.*, see INSUFFICIENCY.

copulate, *v.i.* unite, join, couple; mate; have coitus; cohabit, breed, fornicate, make love, live together, have relations. See MARRIAGE, DESIRE.

COPY

Nouns—**1,** copy, facsimile, counterpart, effigy, FORM, likeness, similitude, semblance, cast, ecotype; IMITATION; model, adumbration, study; portrait, REPRESENTATION; tracing; duplicate; Xerox, photocopy, instant copy; transcript, transcription; reflex, reflection; replica, facsimile; shadow, echo; chip off the old block; reprint, REPRODUCTION; second edition; REPETITION; apograph, fair copy, revise, revision; close. *Slang*, fake, dupe, ditto; spittin' image, dead ringer. See SIMILARITY.

2, parody, caricature, burlesque, travesty, paraphrase; counterfeit (see DECEPTION). *Slang*, take-off.

Verbs—copy, duplicate, imitate, reproduce, trace, transcribe; Xerox, photocopy; parody, burlesque, mimic, travesty; forge, counterfeit; echo; reprint. *Colloq.*, fake.

Adjectives—faithful; lifelike, similar (see SIMILARITY).

cord, *n.* string, rope, band, bond, twine, tie. See FILAMENT, CONNECTION.

cordial, *adj.* sincere, heartfelt; hearty, genial, friendly, amicable, kindly, warm. See COURTESY. *Ant.*, see DISCOURTESY.

core, *n.* center, interim, heart, nucleus, kernel; pith, nut, nub, substance, gist. See MIDDLE, IMPORTANCE. *Ant.*, see EDGE.

cork, *n. & v.* —*n.* stopper, plug, bung; float, bob. —*v.t.* stop, plug, calk, bung, seal. See CLOSURE, MATERIALS.

corner, *n.* angle; nook, niche; control, monopoly; predicament. See ANGULARITY, POSSESSION, DIFFICULTY. *Ant.*, see CURVATURE.

corny, *adj., slang,* sentimental, mushy, sticky; old-fashioned, stale, musty, banal, clichéd. See OLDNESS, DULLNESS.

coronary, *adj. & n.* —*adj.* coronal, crownlike, ringlike, round, circular. —*n.* [coronary] thrombosis, heart attack, apoplexy, paralysis, stroke. See CIRCULARITY, DISEASE.

corporation, *n.* association, syndicate, company, society, partnership, merger, trust. See PARTY, BUSINESS.

corps, *n.* body, company, outfit, AGENCY, branch, service. See ASSEMBLAGE.

corpse, *n.* body, cadaver, carcass; remains, mortal remains; bones, skeleton, dry bones; relics; dust, ashes, earth, clay; mummy, fossil; carrion, food for worms *or* fishes; tenement of clay, this mortal coil; the deceased, the decedent, the departed; shade, ghost. *Slang,* stiff. See DEATH.

corpulence, *n.* fatness, fleshiness, obesity, plumpness, portliness, bulk. See SIZE. *Ant.,* see NARROWNESS, LITTLENESS.

correct, *v. & adj.* —*v.t.* improve, rectify, right, repair, remedy, amend, set right, reform, better; reprove, punish, chastise, discipline; counteract, neutralize. See IMPROVEMENT, DISAPPROBATION. —*adj.* RIGHT, regular, true, strict, accurate, exact, precise, perfect. *Slang,* right on. *Ant.,* see WRONG.

correlation, *n.* correlativity; reciprocalness, reciprocation, reciprocity; mutuality, mutualness; interrelation, correspondence; analogy; likeness, SIMILARITY, INTERCHANGE. See RELATION.

CORRESPONDENCE

Nouns—**1,** correspondence, letter, epistle, COMMUNICATION, message, note, billet, billet doux, love letter; postcard; missive, favor; despatch, dispatch; bulletin, these presents; rescript, rescription; form letter, circular; chain letter; post, mail, airmail, special delivery *or* handling, priority mail.

2, correlation, likeness, SIMILARITY; analogy; homology; concurrence, AGREEMENT; congruity, CONFORMITY; relation, concordance, harmony.

3, correspondent, writer, reporter, contributor. See WRITING.

Verbs—**1,** correspond, correspond with; write to, send a letter to; keep up a correspondence, acknowledge, ANSWER, reply; intercommunicate, communicate.

2, match, tally, suit, correlate, agree, fit, harmonize; be analogous, homologous, like *or* similar; confirm, accord, complement.

Adjectives—correspondent, corresponding; epistolary; postal.

corridor, *n.* hall, hallway, gallery, arcade, PASSAGE; skyway, airway, route.

corrigible, *adj.* amendable, rectifiable; amenable, tractable, docile. See IMPROVEMENT, WILL. *Ant.,* see DETERIORATION, REFUSAL.

corroborate, *v.t.* See CONFIRM.

corrode, *v.t.* consume, gnaw, bite, rust, decay, wear; eat, etch. See DETERIORATION. *Ant.,* see IMPROVEMENT.

corrugate, *v.t.* FURROW, wrinkle, groove. See ROUGHNESS. *Ant.,* see SMOOTHNESS.

corrupt, *v. & adj.* —*v.t.* demoralize, vitiate, deprave, defile, degrade, debase, debauch; bribe, pervert; contaminate, spoil, taint. —*adj.* wicked, demoralized, immoral, impure, dissolute, depraved, profligate, base; vicious; rotten, infected, tainted, spoiled. See IMPROBITY, UNCLEANNESS, EVIL. *Ant.,* see PROBITY, INNOCENCE.

cosmetic, *adj. & n.* —*adj.* beautifying, adorning, decorative. —*n.* cosmetics, preparation, makeup. *Slang,* war paint, face, mask. See BEAUTY, ORNAMENT.

cosmic, *adj.* universal, galactic, heavenly; vast, grandiose; harmonious, orderly. See UNIVERSE.

cosmopolitan, *adj.* sophisticated, urbane, polished; informed, tolerant. See KNOWLEDGE.

cost, *n.* price, charge, expense, expenditure, outlay, disbursement, PAYMENT.

costly, *adj.* expensive, high-priced, dear, precious, valuable; extravagant; gorgeous, sumptuous. See EXPENDITURE.

costume, *n.* CLOTHING, clothes, dress, garb, attire, apparel; uniform. *Colloq.,* outfit, rig.

cot, *n.* bed, pallet, couch; cottage, hut, cabin. See SUPPORT, ABODE.

couch, *n.* bed, cot, pallet; lounge, divan, settee, convertible, davenport, chaise longue. See SUPPORT.

cough, *n.* hack, racking cough; expectoration. See DISEASE, EJECTION.

COUNCIL

Nouns—**1,** council, committee, subcommittee, comitia, chamber, board, bench, staff, directory, chapter, syndicate, junta, hearing; cabinet, privy council; senate, upper house, house of representatives, lower house; parliament, chamber of deputies, legislature, congress, diet; county council, city council; court, chamber, tribunal, court of appeal(s); consistory, convocation, synod, congregation; diocesan, plenary, or ecumenical council; vestry.

2, convention, assembly, gathering, ASSEMBLAGE, conclave, caucus, meeting, sitting, seance, conference, session, quorum.

3, statesman, senator, congressman, representative, member of parliament, M.P., councilor, assemblyman, legislator; jurist, judge, justice.

Verbs—sit, convoke, meet, assemble; deliberate, debate; serve, attend, hold court.

Adjectives—consultative, consultatory, consultory; bicameral, unicameral.

Adverbs—in council, committee, session, executive session, conference, etc.

count, *v.t.* compute, enumerate, tell, score, figure, account, matter, reckon; esteem, call, make, consider, estimate. See JUDGE, NUMERATION.

countenance, *n.* face, features, visage, physiognomy; approval, sanction, acceptance, favor, patronage; expression, complexion, aspect. *Slang*, mug. See APPEARANCE, APPROBATION, FRONT.

counter, *adj.* opposing, opposite, contrary, counterclockwise, cross, against. See OPPOSITION. *Ant.*, see IDENTITY.

counteract, *v.* check, defeat, fight; thwart, nullify, negate, frustrate; counterbalance; overthrow; neutralize, render harmless. See OPPOSITION, NULLIFICATION. *Ant.*, see AID.

counterevidence, *n.* rebuttal, disproof, refutation, NULLIFICATION, VINDICATION, CONFUTATION, contradiction. *Ant.*, see EVIDENCE.

counterfeit, *adj. & n.* —*adj.* IMITATION, false, sham, forged, bogus, bastard, spurious. *Slang*, fake, phony. —*n.* forgery, slug, sham, brummagem, dummy, pretense. *Slang*, fake, phony. See DECEPTION, FALSEHOOD. *Ant.*, see TRUTH.

counterpart, *n.* COPY, duplicate, double, facsimile, replica; likeness, image, similitude, match, parallel, twin, mate; complement. See IDENTITY, SIMILARITY. *Ant.*, see DIFFERENCE.

counterpoise, *n.* balance, counterweight, equilibrium, equipoise. See COMPENSATION.

countersign, *n.* signal, sign, seal; password, shibboleth, watchword, identification. See INDICATION.

countless, *adj.* innumerable, myriad, infinite, numberless, uncountable, incalculable, illimitable. See MULTITUDE. *Ant.*, see RARITY.

country, *n.* LAND, REGION, tract, district, territory; countryside, plain, fields; state, people, fatherland, home, nation, power. *Slang*, the sticks. See AUTHORITY, SPACE.

countryman, *n.* national, citizen, compatriot; rustic, farmer. *Slang*, rube, hick, hayseed. See FRIEND, PEOPLE. *Ant.*, see ENEMY.

coup, *n.* act, ACTION, stroke; master stroke; ATTACK, *coup de main; coup de grâce*, death blow, quietus, END; *coup d'état*, REVOLUTION, counterrevolution, takeover, *Putsch*, purge, subversion. See PLAN.

couple, *v.t.* join, tie, link; yoke, unite, pair; marry. See JUNCTION, DUPLICATION, MARRIAGE. *Ant.*, see DISJUNCTION.

coupon, *n.* certificate, ticket, slip; premium *or* trading stamp; ration. See INDICATION, RECORD.

COURAGE

Nouns—1, courage, bravery, valor; resoluteness, boldness; spirit, daring, gallantry, heroism, intrepidity; contempt of danger, defiance of danger; audacity; RASHNESS, dash; DEFIANCE; confidence, self-reliance; chivalry, prowess, derring-do; resolution, determination.

2, manliness, manhood; nerve, pluck, mettle, game; heart, heart of grace; face, virtue, hardihood, fortitude; firmness, STABILITY; heart of oak; perseverance. *Colloq.*, backbone, spunk, what it takes. *Slang*, sand, guts.

3, exploit, feat, enterprise, achievement; deed, heroic deed, heroic act; bold stroke.

4, man of courage, man of mettle; hero, heroine, demigod, demigoddess; lion, tiger, panther, bulldog; gamecock, fighting-cock; bully, fire-eater.

Verbs—1, be courageous; dare, venture, make bold; brave, beard, defy; face, confront, brave, defy, despise *or* mock danger; not turn a hair; look in the face; face up to; face; meet; put a bold face upon, show fight; go through fire and water, run the gantlet; bell the cat, take the bull by the horns, beard the lion in his den.

2, take, muster, summon up *or* pluck up courage; nerve oneself, take heart; hold up one's head; screw one's courage to the sticking place; come up to scratch; stand to one's guns; stand against; bear up, bear up against; hold out; persevere. *Colloq.*, keep a stiff upper lip. *Slang*, stand the gaff.

3, give courage, inspire courage; reassure, encourage, embolden, inspirit, cheer, nerve, put upon one's mettle, rally, raise a rallying cry; pat on the back, make a man of, keep in countenance.

Adjectives—1, courageous, brave; valiant, valorous; gallant, intrepid; spirited, spiritful; high-spirited, high-mettled; mettlesome, plucky; manly, manful; resolute; stout, stouthearted; iron-hearted, lion-hearted; enterprising; adventurous; venturous, venturesome; dashing, chivalrous; soldierly, warlike, heroic; strong-minded, hardy, doughty; firm, determined, dogged, indomitable, persevering. *Colloq.*, gritty, bold as brass, gutsy.

2, bold, bold-spirited; daring, audacious; fearless, dauntless, undaunted, unappalled, undismayed, unawed, unabashed, unalarmed, unflinching, unshrinking, unblenching, unapprehensive; confident, self-reliant; bold as a lion; fierce, savage; pugnacious, bellicose.

Antonym, see COWARDICE.

COURSE

Nouns—1, course, progress, passage, process, succession, lapse, flow, flux, stream, current, tide, march, step *or* flight of time; due course; duration.

2, age, eon; aorist. *Colloq.*, blue moon; dog's *or* coon's age.

3, race, career, CIRCUIT; way, path, route, road; DIRECTION, progress; orbit, itinerary; order, succession, bearing, comportment, CONDUCT; series, system, ARRANGEMENT. See PASSAGE.

Verbs—1, elapse, lapse, flow, run, proceed, advance, pass; roll on, wear on, press on; flit, fly, slip, slide, glide; run its course, run out; expire; go by, pass by; be past.

2, hunt, pursue, chase; run; TRAVEL; race. See PURSUIT.

Adjectives—elapsing, passing; aoristic; progressive.

Adverbs—in time, in due time, in season; in [due] course, in the fullness of time, in process.

Antonym, see PERIOD.

---

court, *v. & n.* —*v.t.* solicit, invite; curry favor, cultivate, cajole, praise; woo, sue, make love. *Colloq.*, spark. —*n.* inclosure, yard, courtyard, quadrangle, patio; tribunal, bench, bar, jurisdiction, session; addresses, attention; palace, hall; retinue, following, train. See ENDEARMENT, COURTESY, REQUEST, LAWSUIT, SERVANT.

COURTESY

Nouns—**1**, courtesy; courteousness; RESPECT, good manners, good behavior, good breeding; manners; politeness, urbanity, comity, gentility, breeding, cultivation, polish, presence; civility, civilization; amenity, suavity; good temper, good humor, amiability, easy temper, complacency, soft tongue, condescension, HUMILITY, affability, complaisance, amiability, gallantry.

2, compliment; fair words, soft words, sweet words; honeyed phrases; ceremonial; salutation, reception, presentation, introduction, mark of recognition, nod, recognition; welcome, respects, devoir; valediction, farewell, goodbye; regards, remembrances; kind regards, kind remembrances; love, best love, duty; CONDOLENCE.

3, obeisance, reverence, bow, courtesy, curtsy, scrape, salaam, kowtow, bowing and scraping; kneeling; genuflection (see WORSHIP); obsequiousness; salute, hand-shake, grid of the hand, embrace, hug, squeeze; accolade; loving cup; love token, kiss, buss (see ENDEARMENT).

Verbs—**1**, be courteous, show courtesy; receive, do the honors, usher, greet, hail, bid welcome; welcome, welcome with open arms; shake hands; hold out, press *or* squeeze the hand; bid Godspeed; speed the parting guest; cheer; serenade.

2, salute; embrace, kiss (see ENDEARMENT); kiss hands; drink to, pledge, hob and nob; move to, nod to; smile upon; uncover, cap; touch *or* take off the hat; doff the cap; present arms; make way for; bow; make one's bow; scrape, curtsy, courtesy; bob a curtsy, kneel; bow, bend the knee, prostrate oneself (see WORSHIP).

3, visit, wait upon, present oneself, pay one's respects, pay a visit (see SOCIALITY); dance attendance on (see SERVILITY); pay attentions to; do homage to (see RESPECT).

4, mind one's Ps and Qs, behave oneself, be all things to all men, conciliate, speak one fair, take in good part; look as if butter would not melt in one's mouth; mend one's manners.

5, render polite; polish, cultivate, civilize, humanize.

Adjectives—courteous, polite, civil, mannerly, urbane; well-behaved, well-mannered, well-bred, well brought up; good-mannered, polished, civilized, cultivated; refined (see TASTE); gentlemanly; gallant; fine-spoken, fair-spoken, soft-spoken; honey-mouthed, honey-tongued; oily, bland; obliging, conciliatory, complaisant, complacent; obsequious; on one's good behavior; ingratiating, winning; gentle, mild; good-humored, cordial, gracious, affable, familiar; neighborly.

Adverbs—courteously; with a good grace; with open *or* outstretched arms; in good humor.

Antonym, see DISCOURTESY.

---

courtship, *n.* suit, flirtation, affair, wooing. See ENDEARMENT, CHOICE.
cove, *n.* inlet, creek, bay, lagoon; nook.
covenant, *v. & n.* —*v.i.* contract, agree, undertake, stipulate, engage, bargain. —*n.* agreement contract, bargain, pact. See AGREEMENT.

COVERING

Nouns—**1**, covering, cover; superposition, superimposition; canopy, awning, tent, pavilion, marquee; umbrella, parasol, sunshade; veil, SHADE; shield, DEFENSE; CLOTHING. See CONCEALMENT.

2, roof, ceiling, thatch, tile; tiling, slates, slating, leads; shed, ABODE.

3, coverlet, counterpane, sheet, quilt, blanket, bedclothes, bedding; rug, carpet, linoleum; tapestry, drugget; tarpaulin; housing.

4, peel, crust, bark, rind, cortex, husk, shell, coat; capsule; sheath, sheathing; pod; casing, case; wrapper, wrapping; envelope, vesicle.

5, veneer, facing; pavement; scale, LAYER; coating, paint; varnish; incrustation, ground, enamel; whitewash, plaster, stucco, compo; lining; cerement; ointment, grease.
6, integument; skin, pellicle, fleece, fell, fur, leather, hide; pelt, peltry; cuticle; epidermis.
Verbs—cover; superpose, superimpose; overlay, overspread; wrap, incase; face, case, veneer, pave, paper; tip, cap, bind; coat, paint, varnish, pay, incrust, stucco, dab, plaster, tar; wash; besmear, smear; bedaub, daub; anoint, do over; gild, plate, japan, lacquer, enamel, whitewash; overlie, overarch, overlap, overhang; CONCEAL.
Adjectives—covering, cutaneous, dermal, epidermal, cortical, cuticular, tegumentary, skinlike, skinny, scaly, squamous; covered, imbricated, armor-plated, ironclad; under cover.
Antonym, see DIVESTMENT.

---

covet, *v.t.* DESIRE, long for, crave, grudge, want, envy, wish.
cow, *n.* bovine, calf, heifer; kine, cattle. See ANIMAL.

COWARDICE

Nouns—cowardice, cowardliness, pusillanimity; timidity, effeminacy; poltroonery, baseness; dastardness, dastardy; abject fear, funk; Dutch courage; FEAR, white feather, faint heart, cold feet.
2, coward, poltroon, dastard, sneak, craven, recreant; milksop, white-liver, sissy; alarmist, terrorist, pessimist; runagate, runaway, fugitive. *Colloq.*, rabbit, baby chicken(-liver). *Slang*, scaredy- or fraidy-cat.
Verbs—be cowardly, be a coward; cower, skulk, sneak; quail, flinch, shy, fight shy, slink, turn tail; run away (see AVOID); show the white feather.
Adjectives—coward, cowardly; fearful, shy; timid, timorous; skittish; poor-spirited, spiritless, soft, effeminate; weak-minded, weak-hearted, faint-hearted, chicken-hearted, lily-hearted, pigeon-hearted; lily-livered, white-livered; milksop; unable to say "Boo" to a goose, afraid of one's shadow; dastard, dastardly; base, craven, sneaking, recreant; unwarlike, unsoldierlike, shy, shrinking, unmanned; frightened, afraid (see FEAR).
Antonym, see COURAGE.

---

cowboy, *n.* cowherd, cowman, cattleman, cowpuncher, rancher, cow-hand, buckaroo; wrangler, trail boss, top hand; vaquero, gaucho, ranchero. *Colloq.*, cowpoke, waddy; pard(ner); broncobuster. See DOMESTICATION.
cower, *v.i.* stoop, cringe, shrink, crouch, quail; fawn, grovel. See COWARDICE, SERVILITY. *Ant.*, see COURAGE.
coworker, *n.* associate, confrere, colleague. See AGENT.
coy, *adj.* bashful, reserved; chary; shrinking, shy, demure, retiring; coquettish. See MODESTY. *Ant.*, see VANITY.
cozy, *adj.* snug, comfortable, homey, *gemütlich*; warm, plush. See PLEASURE.
crabbed, *adj.* ill-tempered, irascible, surly, growly, cross, peevish; difficult, complex; illegible, squeezed, irregular. See IRASCIBILITY, DISTORTION.
crack, *v. & n.* —*v.t.* SNAP, pop, rend, explode, bang; crackle; break, split, burst, cleave, fracture, crush. *Slang*, fail, bust, break down. See DISJUNCTION. *Ant.*, see JUNCTION. —*n.* SNAP, break, fracture; crevice, crackle, craze, chink, flaw, cleft, rift, rent, fissure; slit, rut, groove, seam; pop, crash, clap. *Ant.*, see COHERENCE.
craft, *n.* SKILL, expertness; art, handicraft; trade; vessel, SHIP, boat, CUNNING, artifice, artfulness, deceit, trickery. See BUSINESS. *Ant.*, see SIMPLENESS, NAVIGATION, UNSKILLFULNESS.
cram, *v.t.* crowd, stuff, press, force, drive, jam, pack, choke; satiate,

surfeit, gormandize, gorge, guzzle; teach, study. See CLOSURE, GLUTTONY, TEACHING.

cramp, *v.t.* restrict, restrain, compress, hamper, handicap; fasten; cripple, paralyze, incapacitate. See HINDRANCE, IMPOTENCE. *Ant.,* AID, POWER.

crank, *n. & v.* —*n.* handle, winder, key; quirk; eccentric, fanatic. *Colloq.,* crackpot, grouch, crab. *Slang,* oddball, screwball, nut. See UNCONFORMITY. —*v.* crank up, start; wind, turn, twist. See ROTATION.

crash, *n.* collision, shock, smash, shattering; failure, collapse, downfall; burst, blast. See DESTRUCTION, IMPULSE, LOUDNESS.

crass, *adv.* coarse, crude, gross, unrefined, raw; dense, stupid. See DENSITY, VULGARITY. *Ant.,* see RARITY, TASTE.

crate, *v. & n.* —*v.* pack, box, encase. —*n.* box, shipping case. See RECEPTACLE.

crater, *n.* volcano; hole, OPENING, DEPRESSION, pit, mouth.

crave, *v.t.* DESIRE, long for, yearn for; ask, beg, seek, solicit, REQUEST, supplicate, beseech, pray, petition; need, require. See NECESSITY.

crawl, *v.i.* creep, lag, drag; cringe, fawn, cower, grovel. See SERVILITY, SLOWNESS. *Ant.,* see INSOLENCE, VELOCITY.

crayon, *n.* grease *or* wax pencil, pastel, chalk. See PAINTING.

craze, *v.t.* derange, unbalance, madden, unsettle. See INSANITY.

crazy, *adj.* insane (see INSANITY).

creak, *v.i.* squeak, grind, grate, rasp, stridulate. See LOUDNESS, SOUND.

cream, *n.* crème, top milk, rich milk; best, flower, pick, élite; gist, kernel; cosmetic. See GOODNESS, FOOD, IMPORTANCE. *Ant.,* see POPULACE, UNIMPORTANCE.

crease, *n. & v.* —*n.* FOLD, pleat; bend; mark, wrinkle, FURROW; bullet, scrape, wound, cut. —*v.* mark, FOLD, pleat, FURROW, wrinkle, wound.

create, *v.t.* CAUSE, make, form, bring into being, fashion, originate, occasion, constitute; PRODUCE, procreate, raise, rear, propagate, breed; devise, design, conceive, invent, construct, build; bring to pass; IMAGINE, visualize, envisage. See PRODUCTION. *Ant.,* see DESTRUCTION.

creator, *n.* DEITY, God, Supreme Being; author, maker, fashioner, originator, producer, inventor, designer. See CAUSE, PRODUCTION.

creature, *n.* ANIMAL, BEAST; creation, being, thing; human being, individual, mortal; SERVANT, instrument, slave, tool, dependent.

credence, *n.* BELIEF, assurance, reliance, credit, trust; recognition, acceptance, acknowledgment. *Ant.,* see DOUBT.

credentials, *n.* papers, documents, dossier, RECORD; voucher, pass, passport, license, diploma. See EVIDENCE, INDICATION.

credible, *adj.* probable, likely; believable, trustworthy, reliable; conceivable, thinkable. See BELIEF. *Ant.,* see DOUBT.

CREDIT

Nouns—**1,** credit, trust, score, tally, account; loan (see LENDING); letter of credit; draft; mortgage, lien, debenture, paper credit, floating capital. *Colloq.,* tick, tab.

2, creditor, lender, lessor, mortgagee; dun; usurer.

3, BELIEF, trust; recognition, acknowledgment; faith, reliance, confidence; honor, merit; asset; reputation, financial standing.

Verbs—**1,** charge; keep an account with; run up an account with; entrust, credit, accredit; place to one's credit *or* one's account; give credit, take credit. *Slang,* fly a kite.

2, believe, accept; trust; have *or* put faith in; enter *or* apply (on the credit side); honor.

Adjectives—crediting, credited; accredited.

Adverbs—on credit, to the account *or* credit of. *Slang,* on tick, on the cuff.

Antonym, see DEBT.

CREDULITY

Nouns—**1,** credulity, credulousness, gullibility; infatuation; self-delusion, self-deception; superstition; one's blind side; blind faith; bigotry, obstinacy. See BELIEF.

2, credulous person, DUPE.

Verbs—**1,** be credulous; swallow, gulp down; take on trust *or* faith; take for granted, take for gospel; run away with a notion *or* idea; jump to a conclusion, rush to a conclusion; take the shadow for the substance; catch at straws. *Colloq.*, swallow whole. *Slang*, swallow hook, line and sinker; bite; take the bait; fall for.

2, impose upon, deceive (see DECEPTION), dupe, delude, gull.

Adjectives—credulous, gullible; easily deceived, unsuspecting, simple, green, soft, childish, silly, stupid; overcredulous, overconfident; infatuated; superstitious.

Antonym, see DOUBT.

---

creed, *n.* BELIEF, tenet, doctrine, persuasion, credo, dogma, faith, formula.

creep, *v.i.* crawl, worm, swarm; grovel. See SLOWNESS. *Ant.*, see VELOCITY.

cremation, *n.* burning, incineration, suttee. See HEAT, INTERMENT.

crescent-shaped, *adj.* crescent, lunate, moon-shaped, luniform. See CURVATURE.

crest, *n.* crown, tuft, topknot, comb, plume; summit, peak, ridge, tip, height, top; seal, device; culmination, climax. See CONVEXITY, HEIGHT. *Ant.*, see SUPPORT.

crevice, *n.* cleft, split, fissure, break, breach, OPENING, DISJUNCTION, hole, slit, chink; nook, cranny, SPACE, INTERVAL, cavity; crevasse.

crew, *n.* force, gang, band, set, throng, mob, squad; ASSEMBLAGE, company; sailors. See NAVIGATION.

crib, *n.* manger, trough, box, stall, bin; cot, bed, cradle; hut, hovel; translation, key; plagiarism. *Slang*, pony, trot. See ABODE, RECEPTACLE, SUPPORT.

crime, *n.* offense, misdemeanor, felony, outrage; transgression, sin, evil, wrongdoing; illegality, lawbreaking. See GUILT. *Ant.*, see INNOCENCE.

criminal, *n.* offender, malefactor, felon, sinner, culprit, convict, EVILDOER.

crimp, *v. & n.* —*v.t.* wave, curl, crinkle, wrinkle, ripple; gather, bunch, pinch, tighten, FOLD, pleat, plait. —*n.* curl, NOTCH. See CONVOLUTION.

cringe, *v.i.* cower, stoop, flinch, wince, crouch, shrink; fawn, truckle, crawl, grovel; sneak. See AVOIDANCE, SERVILITY. *Ant.*, see INSOLENCE.

crinkle, *v. & n.* —*v.* wrinkle, roughen, crease, crumple, rumple, ripple, FOLD, crimp, corrugate. —*n.* wrinkle, crease. See CONVOLUTION, ROUGHNESS.

cripple, *v.t.* disable, incapacitate, unfit; lame, paralyze, maim; hurt, enfeeble, cramp. See IMPOTENCE, HINDRANCE, DISTORTION. *Ant.*, see POWER.

crisis, *n.* turning point; juncture; exigency, emergency, extremity, pinch, trial, crux. See CIRCUMSTANCE, DIFFICULTY.

crisp, *adj.* brittle, curly, blunt, friable; sharp, definite, lively, clean-cut, clear; cold, stiff; SHORT, crunchy, crumbly; firm, fresh; bracing. See FEELING, FOOD. *Ant.*, see SOFTNESS.

criterion, *n.* standard, model, rule, test, measure, norm, touchstone. See MEASUREMENT.

critic, *n.* judge, connoisseur, expert, reviewer, commentator; censor, censurer. See DETRACTION, TASTE.

critical, *adj.* exacting, captious, censorious, fault-finding, disparaging; judicious, accurate, analytical; decisive; urgent, crucial; dangerous,

risky. See DISAPPROBATION, IMPORTANCE. *Ant.*, see APPROBATION, UN-
IMPORTANCE.

criticize, *v.t.* JUDGE, censure, excoriate, blame, reprove, flay; examine,
dissect, analyze, review. *Slang*, roast, pan; bad-mouth, nit-pick. See
DISAPPROBATION. *Ant.*, PRAISE.

crockery, *n.* pottery, earthenware, CERAMICS. See RECEPTACLE.

crook, *n., colloq.*, see CRIMINAL, EVILDOER.

crooked, *adj.* bent, curved, angular, sinuous, winding, askew, zigzag,
twisted, warped; false, dishonest, fraudulent, deceptive, sneaking;
oblique, aslant, distorted, awry. See IMPROBITY, DISTORTION. *Ant.*, see
FORM.

crop, *n.* craw, gorge; whip; harvest, yield, fruit, product. See PRODUC-
TION.

cross, *n., v. & adj.* —*n.* rood, crucifix; (*Cap.*) Christianity, the Church,
Gospel; crosspiece, cross mark, X, ex; gibbet; burden, trial, trouble,
affliction; hybrid, MIXTURE, crossbreed; half-caste, halfbreed. —*v.*
crossbreed, cross-pollinate, mix; traverse, go across, ford; mark out,
cancel, strike out; pass over; lie across *or* athwart; bar, line, crosshatch; circumvent, thwart, frustrate, foil, oppose, hinder, obstruct. See
CROSSING, CONTENTION, NULLIFICATION, OPPOSITION, TRAVEL, DIRECTION.
—*adj.* opposite, converse; peevish, touchy, snappish, testy, perverse;
out of sorts *or* humor; sulky, sullen; ill-tempered. *Colloq.*, grouchy,
crabby, cranky. See IRASCIBILITY. *Ant.*, see AGREEMENT, PLEASURE.

cross-examine, *v.t.* See INTERROGATE.

CROSSING

Nouns—**1,** crossing, intersection, crossroad(s), grade crossing; underpass, bridge, tunnel; textile, fabric; interdigitation; decussation, trans-
version; inosculation, anastomosis, intertexture, mortise; CONVOLUTION;
reticulation, network, net, plexus, web, mesh, twill, skein, sleeve, felt,
lace; wicker; mat, matting; plait, trellis, wattle, lattice, grating, grille,
gridiron, tracery, fretwork, filigree, reticle; tissue; cross, chain, wreath,
braid, cat's cradle, know; entanglement (see DISORDER).

2, thwarting, circumvention, frustration (see CONTENTION, OPPOSITION).

Verbs—cross, intersect, interlace, intertwine, intertwist, interweave, inter-
digitate; interlink; decussate; twine, entwine, weave, inweave, twist,
wreathe; anastomose, inosculate, dovetail, splice, link; mat, plait,
braid, felt, twill; tangle, entangle, ravel; net, know; dishevel, raddle.

Adjectives—crossing, crossed; matted, transverse; cross, cruciform, crucial; retiform, reticular, reticulated; areolar, cancellated, grated, barred,
streaked; textile.

Adverbs—across, athwart, transversely; crosswise, obliquely, sidewise.

---

cross-shaped, *adj.* decussate, cruciform, cruciate. See CROSSING.

crotch, *n.* fork, divergence, branch, EDGE, corner; groin, inguinal region,
inguen; genitals, genitalia. See ANGULARITY.

crouch, *v.i.* bend, squat, stoop, bow; cower, cringe, fawn. See DEPRES-
SION, SERVILITY. *Ant.*, see ELEVATION, INSOLENCE.

crowd, *n.* ASSEMBLAGE, gathering, concourse, horde, press, mass, gang,
mob, multitude; host, herd, swarm, rout, crush, throng; set, coterie,
clique; populace, rabble, *hoi polloi*. See POPULACE.

crown, *v. & n.* —*v.t.* coronate, wreathe, enthrone, adorn, invest, install;
top, cap, head, crest; COMPLETE, perfect, round out, finish. —*n.* chaplet, circlet, diadem, coronet, aureole; laurel, wreath, garland, reward,
prize; pate, crest, top.

crucial, *adj.* decisive, determining, final; urgent, critical, supreme; trying, severe; cruciform. See IMPORTANCE. *Ant.*, see UNIMPORTANCE.

crude, *adj.* ROUGH, raw, unfinished, unwrought, unrefined, incomplete;
unprepared, sketchy; coarse, crass, imperfect, plain, rude, tasteless,

gross, immature, vulgar, uncouth. See IMPERFECTION, VULGARITY. *Ant.*, see COMPLETION, ELEGANCE.

cruel, *adj.* acute, painful (see PAIN); coldblooded, harsh (see MALEVO-LENCE).

cruelty, *n.* cold-bloodedness, harshness, barbarity, savagery, brutality, persecution, sadism, torture. See MALEVOLENCE. *Ant.*, see BENEVO-LENCE.

cruise, *n. & v.* —*n.* voyage, trip, journey, tour, course, sail; ride, flight. *Colloq.*, shakedown. —*v.i.* voyage, sail, yacht, steam; soar, coast; wander, rove, roam, meander, range; hunt. See TRAVEL.

crumb, *n.* bit, fragment, scrap, mite, flake, speck, morsel, jot, ort; leav-ing, leftover. See PART, LITTLENESS.

crumble, *v.i.* disintegrate, break up, fall to pieces; decay, degenerate. See DESTRUCTION, DETERIORATION.

crush, *v.t.* press, mash, squash, squeeze, bruise; overcome, conquer, vanquish, subdue, quell, overwhelm, suppress, blot out; shame, discon-cert. See CONTRACTION, DESTRUCTION. *Ant.*, see PRODUCTION, EXPAN-SION.

crust, *n.* cake, coating, rind, shell, hull, incrustation. See COVERING. *Ant.*, see INTERIOR.

cryptography, *n.* cipher, cryptogram, code, steganography. See WRIT-ING.

CRY

Nouns—cry, shout, call; vociferation, exclamation, outcry, hullaballoo, chorus, clamor, hue and cry; plaint; lungs; stentor (see LOUDNESS); bark, ululation.

Verbs—cry, roar, shout, bawl, bellow, halloo, halloa, whoop, yell, howl, scream, screech, shriek, squeak, squeal, squall, whine, pule, pipe; call, bark, bray, mew, ululate; weep (see LAMENTATION); cheer; hoot; grum-ble, moan, groan, shrill; snore, snort; grunt; vociferate; raise *or* lift up the voice; call out, sing out, cry out; exclaim; rend the air thunder; shout at the top of one's voice *or* lungs; strain the throat *or* voice *or* lungs; give a cry.

Adjectives—crying, clamant, clamorous; vociferous; stentorian (see LOUD-NESS); open-mouthed, loudmouthed.

Antonym, see SILENCE.

---

crystal, *adj.* TRANSPARENT, lucid, pellucid, crystalline, clear.

cub, *n.* offspring, whelp, youngster, pup, puppy; novice. See ANIMAL, YOUTH. *Ant.*, see OLDNESS.

cube, *n. & v.* —*n.* solid, square, die, dice; hexahedron. See ANGU-LARITY, NUMERATION. —*v.t.* dice, chop, cut. See DISJUNCTION.

cuddle, *v.* snuggle, nestle, curl up, huddle; clasp, fondle. See ENDEAR-MENT.

cudgel, *n.* club, bludgeon, staff, shillelagh, stick. See ARMS.

cue, *n.* hint, clue, intimation; catchword, signal, password. See INDI-CATION, INFORMATION.

culminate, *v.* conclude, finish, END; crown; come to a head. See COM-PLETION, HEIGHT, PERFECTION.

culprit, *n.* offender, malefactor, wrongdoer, criminal, felon, convict. See EVILDOER. *Ant.*, see GOODNESS, INNOCENCE.

cult, *n.* cultus, sect, RELIGION, denomination; WORSHIP, devotion, RITE; school (of thought), BELIEF; mystique, fad, craze, vogue. See SEC-TARIANISM.

cultivate, *v.t.* farm, till, work, grow, develop; civilize, refine; pursue, court; foster, advance, cherish. See AGRICULTURE, IMPROVEMENT.

cultivation, *n.* farming, tillage, husbandry, AGRICULTURE; elevation, civilization, refinement, breeding; learning, education; pursuit. See IMPROVEMENT, PRODUCTIVENESS. *Ant.*, see UNPRODUCTIVENESS.

culture, *n.* cultivation, tillage; development, education, learning; enlightenment; refinement, breeding, polish; civilization. See AGRICULTURE, COURTESY, IMPROVEMENT, KNOWLEDGE. *Ant.*, see IGNORANCE.

cumbersome, *adj.* unwieldy, clumsy, burdensome, ponderous, cumbrous, oppressive. See HINDRANCE, UNSKILLFULNESS. *Ant.*, see CONVENIENT, SKILL.

CUNNING

Nouns—**1,** cunning, cunningness, craft, craftiness; slyness; finesse, intrigue; subtlety, artificiality; maneuvering; temporization; circumvention.

2, chicane, chicanery; sharp practice, fraud, knavery, jugglery; CONCEALMENT, guile, duplicity; FALSEHOOD. See DECEPTION.

3, diplomacy, politics; Machiavellianism; jobbery, backstairs influence. *Colloq.*, graft, wire-pulling.

4, art, artifice; device, machination; plot, PLAN, maneuver, stratagem, dodge, artful dodge, wile; trick, trickery, DECEPTION, ruse, side-blow, shift, go by, subterfuge, evasion; white lie, UNTRUTH; *tour de force*; tricks of the trade, net, trap.

5, schemer, intriguer, strategist; diplomat, politician; Machiavelli; sly boots, fox, Reynard. *Colloq.*, Philadelphia lawyer, grafter, Indian giver. *Slang*, slicker.

Verbs—be cunning, contrive, PLAN, live by one's wits; play both ends against the middle; maneuver, scheme, conspire, intrigue, finesse, double, temporize; circumvent, steal a march upon; throw off one's guard; surprise; waylay, undermine, play a deep game, play tricks with; be too much for, get the better of; flatter, make things pleasant; gerrymander.

Adjectives—cunning, crafty, artful; SKILLFUL, subtle, feline, vulpine; cunning as a fox, cunning as the serpent; deep, deep-laid; profound; designing, scheming, contriving; intriguing, strategic, diplomatic, politic, Machiavellian, time-serving; artificial, tricky, wily, sly, insidious, stealthy; underhand, deceitful (see DECEPTION); crooked, shrewd, acute; sharp, sharp as a needle; canny, astute, leery, knowing, up to snuff, too clever by half.

Adverbs—cunningly, slyly, on the sly.

Antonym, see ARTLESSNESS.

cup, *n.* mug, tankard, chalice, glass, goblet; [Holy] Grail; excavation, hollow, crater. See CONCAVITY, RECEPTACLE.

cupboard, *n.* closet, storeroom; buffet, locker, press; pantry. See RECEPTACLE.

curb, *v. & n.* —*v.t.* RESTRAIN, subdue, control, check, repress; guide, manage; slacken, retard. See SLOWNESS. *Ant.*, VELOCITY. —*n.* restraint, check, control; curb market; brim, margin. See HINDRANCE, EDGE, SALE.

curdle, *v.* clabber; curd, clot, thicken, coagulate, congeal, lump, clot, cake; separate; spoil, turn, sour. See DENSITY, DETERIORATION.

cure, *v.t.* heal, restore, relieve; preserve, dry, smoke, tan, pickle. See REMEDY, PRESERVATION.

curfew, *n.* bedtime, vespers; LIMIT; siren, tocsin, whistle. See TIME, INDICATION.

curio, *n.* bric-a-brac, knickknack, objet d'art, ORNAMENT, whatnot, antique, gewgaw, gimcrack. See UNIMPORTANCE.

CURIOSITY

Nouns—**1,** curiosity, curiousness; interest, thirst for knowledge; inquiring mind; inquisitiveness; meddling; voyeurism. *Colloq.*, nosiness.

2, curious person; sightseer; questioner; newsmonger, gossip, busybody, peeping Tom, voyeur, Paul Pry; eavesdropper. *Slang*, nosy Parker, snooper, rubberneck.

Verbs—be curious, take an interest in, stare, gape; prick up the ears, see sights; pry, peep; meddle. *Slang*, snoop, rubberneck.
Adjectives—curious, inquisitive, burning with curiosity, overcurious, curious as a cat; inquiring (see INQUIRY); prying; inquisitorial.
Antonym, see INDIFFERENCE.

---

curl, *v.t.* roll, wave, ripple, spiral, twist, coil. See CONVOLUTION.

currency, *n.* MONEY, coin, bill, cash, specie; publicity, circulation; topicality, timeliness. See PUBLICATION.

current, *adj. & n.* —*adj.* common, prevalent, PRESENT, in vogue, prevailing; accepted, abroad, rife; existing, circulating, rumored, published. See GENERALITY, NEWS. —*n.* stream, flow; movement, tendency; draft, circulate. See RIVER, WIND.

curse, *v. & n.* —*v.t.* execrate, damn, swear, denounce; blaspheme. —*n.* malediction, IMPRECATION, execration, anathema; bane, plague. *Ant.*, see APPROBATION.

curt, *adj.* SHORT, CONCISE, brief, succinct; snappish, tart, brusque, rude, bluff, BLUNT, abrupt. *Ant.*, see LOQUACITY, LENGTH.

curtail, *v.t.* shorten, clip, cut, abbreviate; abate, diminish, reduce, lessen, abridge; deprive. See SHORTNESS, DECREASE. *Ant.*, see LENGTH, INCREASE.

curtain, *n.* screen, veil, valance, drapery, portière, hanging, blind, SHADE. See AMBUSH, CONCEALMENT. .*Ant.*, see DISCLOSURE.

CURVATURE

Nouns—**1,** curvature, curving, curvity, curvation; incurvity, incurvation; bend; flexure, flexion; conflexure; crook, hook, bending; deflexion, inflexion; arcuation, devexity, turn; deviation, detour, sweep; curl, curling; bough; recurvity, recurvation; rotundity; sinuosity (see CONVOLUTION). See CIRCULARITY, ROTUNDITY.

2, curve, arc, arch, arcade, vault, bow, crescent, halfmoon, horseshoe, loop, crane-neck, parabola, hyperbola; catenary, festoon; conchoid, cardioid; caustic; tracery.

Verbs—**1,** be curved, sweep, swag, sag; deviate (see DEVIATION); turn; reenter.

2, render curved, curve, bend, incurvate; deflect, inflect; crook; turn, round, arch, arcuate, arch over, concamerate; bow, curl, recurve, frizzle.

Adjectives—curved, curviform, curvilineal, curvilinear; devious; recurved, recurvous; bowed, vaulted, hooked; falciform, falcated; semicircular, crescentic; luniform, lunilar; semilunar; conchoidal; cordiform, cordated; cardioid; heart-shaped, bell-shaped, pear-shaped, fig-shaped; hook-shaped; kidney-shaped, reniform; lens-shaped, lentiform, lenticular; bowlegged (see DISTORTION); oblique (see OBLIQUITY); annular, circular (see CIRCULARITY).

Antonym, see STRAIGHTNESS.

---

cushion, *n. & v.* —*n.* pillow, bolster; ottoman, hassock; fender, bumper, *etc.*; buffer. See SOFTNESS. —*v.t.* pad, soften, ease, absorb; protect, buffer, come BETWEEN. *Colloq.*, soften the blow, let down easy. See SUPPORT.

custody, *n.* CARE, safekeeping, charge, protection, keeping; imprisonment, bondage. See RESTRAINT, SAFETY. *Ant.*, see FREEDOM.

custom, *n.* practice, use, usage, wont, fashion, precedent, rule; HABIT, *mores*, convention; patronage, support, trade.

customary, *adj.* accustomed, wonted, usual, ordinary, regular, natural, normal, traditional; conventional; habitual. See RULE, HABIT.

customer, *n.* buyer, purchaser, shopper, patron, client, consumer; prospect, contact. See BUSINESS, PURCHASE.

cut, *v.t.* incise, carve, dissect, slice, shave, trim, shape; separate, divide, split, sever; abridge, shorten, diminish, reduce, curtail; hurt, sting, wound, snub, ignore; reap, gather. See DISJUNCTION, SHORTNESS. *Ant.*, see INCREASE, JUNCTION, LENGTH.

cute, *adj.*, *colloq.*, see PRETTY, FACETIOUS.

cutting, *adj.* SHARP, incisive, keen-edged; biting, stinging, acrimonious, sarcastic, caustic, tart; bitter, raw, nippy. See DISAPPROBATION.

cycle, *n.* period, age, epoch; circle, round; bicycle, velocipede, tricycle. *Slang,* bike. See TIME, VEHICLE, CIRCULARITY.

cyclone, *n.* tornado, twister, gale, hurricane; vortex. See VIOLENCE.

cylinder, *n.* barrel, tube, roller. See CIRCULARITY.

cynic, *n.* MISANTHROPE, pessimist; philosopher. See THOUGHT. *Ant.*, see SIMPLENESS.

cynical, *adj.* misanthropic, sneering, satirical, pessimistic, distrustful, sarcastic, cutting, disdainful, contemptuous, censorious; surly, snarling, captious. See CONTEMPT, DISAPPROBATION. *Ant.*, see APPROBATION.

czar, *n.* tsar, emperor, Caesar, king, Czar of all the Russias. See MASTER.

D

dab, *n. & v.* —*n.* spot, pinch, small quantity. See LITTLENESS. —*v.t.* hit lightly. See IMPULSE.

dabble, *v.* splash, spatter; patter, trifle, fritter away. See INACTIVITY, WATER.

dagger, *n.* dirk, stiletto, poniard, knife, bodkin. See ARMS.

daily, *adj.* everyday, diurnal, quotidien; once a day. See REGULARITY.

dainty, *adj.* delicate, exquisite, pretty; fastidious; delicious. See BEAUTY, TASTE. *Ant.*, see UGLINESS.

dally, *v.i.* trifle, delay, prolong, idle; flirt, philander. See AMUSEMENT, LATENESS. *Ant.*, see ACTIVITY.

dam, *n. & v.* —*n.* dike, seawall, levee, breakwater, embankment, floodgate. See INCLOSURE. —*v.t.* embank, sandbag; clog, plug, stop up, jam. See RESTRAINT, HINDRANCE.

damage, *v. & n.* —*v.t.* harm, injure, mar, impair. —*n.* DETERIORATION; injury. *Ant.*, see IMPROVEMENT.

damn, *v.t.* See CONDEMNATION.

damp, *adj. & v.* —*adj.* dank, humid. See MOISTURE, WATER. —*v.t.* dampen, muffle, subdue.

dance, *n. & v.* —*n.* party, ball. *Colloq.*, hop, prom. See AMUSEMENT, —*v.i.* glide, jig, flutter. *Colloq.*, trip the light fantastic. See AGITATION.

dandy, *n.* beau, coxcomb, dude, FOP, macaroni.

DANGER

Nouns—**1,** danger, peril, jeopardy, risk, hazard, insecurity, precariousness, slipperiness; instability; defenselessness.

2, exposure, LIABILITY; vulnerability; vulnerable point, heel of Achilles; forlorn hope.

3, dangerous course, leap in the dark, RASHNESS; road to ruin; hairbreadth escape; cause for alarm; source of danger; breakers ahead; storm brewing; clouds gathering; apprehension, WARNING.

4, trap, snare, pitfall, lure, whirlpool, maelstrom, ambush.

Verbs—**1,** be in danger; be exposed to danger, run into danger, encounter danger; run a risk; lay oneself open to (see LIABILITY); lean on a broken reed; feel the ground sliding from under one; have to run for it; have the odds against one; hang by a thread; totter; sleep *or* stand on a volcano; sit on a barrel of gunpowder, sit on a powderkeg, live in a glass house.

2, endanger, bring in danger, place in danger, put in danger; expose to danger, imperil; jeopardize; compromise.

3, adventure, venture, risk, hazard, stake, set at hazard; beard the lion in his den, play with fire, skate on thin ice, risk one's neck; run the gantlet; dare (see COURAGE); engage in a forlorn hope; sail too near the wind (see RASHNESS).

Adjectives—**1,** dangerous, hazardous, perilous, parlous; at stake, in question; precarious, ticklish; slippery; fraught with danger; untrustworthy; built upon sand, tottering, unstable, unsteady; shaky, topheavy, tumble-down, ramshackle, crumbling; hanging *or* trembling in the balance; threatening (see WARNING), ominous, ill-omened; alarming (see FEAR); explosive.

2, in danger, endangered; unsafe, unprotected, insecure; defenseless, unshielded, vulnerable, exposed; open (to), LIABLE (to); at bay, on the rocks; hanging by a thread, between Scylla and Charybdis, between two fires; on the edge, brink *or* verge of a precipice, in the lion's den, on slippery ground, under fire, not out of the woods; with one's back to the wall; unprepared, off one's guard; helpless, in a bad way, in the last extremity. *Colloq.*, out on a limb; on thin ice. *Slang*, on the spot.
Antonym, see SAFETY.

---

dangle, *v.i.* hang, suspended; swing. See PENDENCY, OSCILLATION.
dare, *v.t.* face, defy, challenge, brave; venture upon *or* into. See DEFIANCE, COURAGE. *Ant.*, see COWARDICE.

DARKNESS

Nouns—**1,** darkness, dark; blackness (see COLOR); obscurity, gloom, murk; dusk, DIMNESS; SHADE, shadow, umbra, penumbra; skiagraphy; shading; distribution of shade; chiaroscuro.

2, Cimmerian darkness, Stygian darkness; night; midnight; dead of night; witching hour.

3, obscuration; adumbration; obfuscation; extinction, extinguishment, eclipse, total eclipse; gathering of the clouds; blackout, dim-out.

Verbs—be dark; darken, obscure, shade; dim; tone down, lower; overcast, overshadow; eclipse; obfuscate; adumbrate; cast into the shade; cloud, becloud; dim, bedim; darken, bedarken; cast, throw *or* spread a shadow; extinguish; put, blow *or* snuff out; doubt.

Adjectives—dark, darksome, darkling, darkened; obscure, tenebrous, somber, pitch dark, pitchy; black (see COLOR); sunless, moonless, lightless (see LIGHT); dusky; unilluminated; nocturnal; dingy, lurid, gloomy; murky; shady, umbrageous; overcast, dim (see DIMNESS); cloudy, opaque; dark as pitch, dark as a pit.

Adverbs—darkly, in the dark, in the shade.
Antonym, see LIGHT.

---

darling, *n. & adj.* —*n.* sweetheart, dearest, dear one, angel, treasure; hero, pet, idol, fair-haired boy. —*adj.* beloved, FAVORITE; charming, winsome, adorable. *Colloq.*, cute. See ENDEARMENT.
dart, *v. & n.* —*v.* hurl, cast, throw; spring, rush. See VELOCITY, PROPULSION. —*n.* javelin, spear, arrow. See ARMS.
dash, *v. & n.* —*v.t.* shatter, smash; frustrate, dishearten; hurl, cast. See DEPRESSION, DEJECTION, PROPULSION. —*n.* élan, spirit; spurt, *soupçon*, trace, slight addition. See ACTIVITY, VELOCITY, LITTLENESS.
date, *n. & v.* —*n.* day, TIME, moment; age, era, epoch; DURATION. *Colloq.*, rendezvous, tryst; escort, suitor, steady; blind date. —*v.* place (in time), begin, start; outmode, age. *Colloq.*, court, escort, take out, show the town *or* a good time, go [out] with, go steady. See SOCIALITY.
daunt, *v.t.* intimidate, cow, dismay. See FEAR.
dawdle, *v.i.* idle, loaf, kill time. *Slang*, goldbrick, goof off. See INACTION, SLOWNESS.
dawn, *n.* BEGINNING, origin, inception; early stage. *Ant.*, see END.

day, *n.* daytime, LIGHT; dawn, daybreak; around the clock; era, period. See TIME.

daydream, *n.* reverie, castle in the air, fancy. See HOPE, IMAGINATION.

daze, *v.t.* confuse, dazzle, bewilder, awe; stun, shock, stupefy. See WONDER, SURPRISE, RESPECT, LIGHT.

dazzle, *v.t.* blind; impress, overpower; dum(b)found, bewilder. See RESPECT, WONDER.

dead, *adj.* deceased, perished, defunct; lifeless, inanimate; obsolete, extinct. See DEATH, NONEXISTENCE. *Ant.,* see LIFE, EXISTENCE.

deaden, *v.t.* benumb; muffle; damp. See INSENSIBILITY, IMPOTENCE, SILENCE. *Ant.,* see SENSIBILITY.

deadlock, *n.* impasse, bottleneck, stalemate; standstill, standoff, tie, draw, even match; hung jury. See EQUALITY.

DEAFNESS

Nouns—**1,** deafness, hardness of hearing; surdity; deafmutism; INATTENTION.

2, lip-reading; deaf-and-dumb alphabet, dactylology, manual alphabet.

Verbs—be deaf, have no ear; shut *or* close one's ears; turn a deaf ear to; render deaf, deafen; stun.

Adjectives—deaf, earless, surd; hard or dull of hearing; unhearing; deafmute; stone-deaf, tone deaf, deaf as a post; inattentive, oblivious of; deafened.

Antonym, see HEARING.

deal, *v.t.* apportion, allocate, allot, distribute; BARTER; inflict; give, bestow, dole. See APPORTIONMENT, GIVING.

dear, *adj. & n.* —*adj.* expensive (see DEARNESS); precious, beloved, cherished, darling. —*n.* darling, beloved, love. *Colloq.,* honey, dearie, sweetheart. *Slang,* baby, babe, toots, tootsie, sugar. See LOVE, ENDEARMENT.

DEARNESS

Nouns—dearness, costliness; high price; famine price; overcharge; extravagance, exorbitance; extortion; heavy pull upon the purse; pretty penny; inflation. *Slang,* highway robbery.

Verbs—be dear, cost much, cost a pretty penny; rise in price, look up; overcharge, bleed [white], fleece, extort; pay too much; pay through the nose, pay dear. *Colloq.,* hold up, soak, gyp, skin; jack up.

Adjectives—dear, high, high priced; of great price, expensive, costly, precious, dear bought; unreasonable, extravagant, exorbitant, extortionate; at a premium; not to be had for love or money; beyond *or* above price; priceless, of priceless value; worth its weight in gold; more precious than rubies.

Adverbs—dear, dearly; at great cost.

Antonym, see CHEAPNESS.

DEATH

Nouns—**1,** death; expiration; decease, demise; END, cessation; loss of life, extinction of life, ebb of life; dissolution, departure, passing away, obit, release, eternal rest, rest, quietus, fall; loss, bereavement.

2, death warrant, death watch, death rattle, deathbed; stroke of death, agonies of death, shades of death, valley of the shadow of death, jaws of death, hand of death; last breath, last gasp, last agonies; dying day, dying breath; swan song; *rigor mortis*; Stygian shore. *Slang,* curtains, last roundup.

3, Death, King of terrors, King of Death; Grim Reaper, angel of death, Azrael; mortality; doom.

4, natural death, sudden death, violent death, untimely end, drowning, watery grave; suffocation, asphyxia; fatal disease (see DISEASE); death blow (see KILLING); euthanasia; genocide, extermination, mass murder; suicide.

5, necrology, bills of mortality, obituary; death-song (see LAMENTATION).
6, see CORPSE.

Verbs—**1,** die, expire, perish; drown, smother, suffocate; meet one's death, meet one's end; pass away, be taken; yield *or* resign one's breath; resign one's being *or* life; end one's days *or* life; breathe one's last; cease to live *or* breathe; depart this life; be no more; lose one's life, lay down one's life, relinquish *or* surrender one's life; sink into the grave; close one's eyes; fall dead, drop dead, drop down dead; break one's neck, give up the ghost, yield up the ghost; die in harness; die a violent death (see KILLING). *Slang*, kick off, kick the bucket, cash in, cash in one's chips; check out, croak, pop off; take a ride, be put on the spot, sign off.

2, pay the debt to nature, shuffle off this mortal coil, take one's last sleep; go the way of all flesh; come, turn *or* return to dust; cross the Styx; go to one's long account, go to one's last home, go west, go to Davy Jones' locker; cross the bar; receive one's death warrant, make one's will, die a natural death, go out like a candle; come to an untimely end; catch one's death.

Adjectives—**1,** dead, lifeless; deceased, demised, departed, defunct; late, gone, no more; exanimate, inanimate; out of the world, taken off, released; departed this life; dead and gone; launched into eternity, gathered to one's fathers; numbered with the dead; stillborn, extinct; lethal, fatal, deadly; dying, moribund. *Colloq.*, dead as a doornail; stiff; stone dead.

2, dying, moribund, *in extremis*; in the jaws of death; going, going off; on one's deathbed; at the point of death, at death's door, at the last gasp; with one foot in the grave. *Colloq.*, done for, on one's last legs; on the spot.

Antonym, see LIFE.

---

debasement, *n.* abasement, debauchery, corruption, degradation, DISREPUTE; adulteration, impairment, IMPURITY, MIXTURE. *Ant.*, see REPUTE, PROBITY.

debate, *n. & v.* —*n.* argument, dispute, controversy; forum, panel discussion. See DIFFERENCE, DISAGREEMENT, CONTENTION. —*v.* argue, discuss, dispute; bandy words, take sides, lock horns, contend. See DISSENT, REASONING.

debris, *n.* rubbish, rubble, detritus, wreckage, trash. See DESTRUCTION, REMAINDER.

DEBT

Nouns—**1,** debt, indebtedness, obligation, LIABILITY, indebtment, debit, score; charge, charge account; arrears, deferred payment, deficit, default; insolvency, nonpayment, bankruptcy, bad debt; interest, premium, usury; floating debt, floating capital.

2, debtor, debitor; mortgagor; defaulter; borrower. *Slang*, deadbeat.

3, lending, loan, advance, accommodation; financing, mortgage; borrowing, raising money, pledging, hypothecation, pawning.

4, lender, banker, mortgagee, pawnbroker, pawnshop.

Verbs—**1,** be in debt, owe; incur *or* contract a debt; run up a bill, run up a score, run up an account; borrow; run into debt, get into debt; outrun the constable; answer for, go bail for. *Slang*, run a tab, go on tick.

2, lend, advance, finance, accommodate (with), loan; mortgage, hypothecate, pledge, pawn, hock; borrow from Peter to pay Paul. *Slang*, touch.

3, repudiate, stop payment, dishonor. *Slang*, go broke.

Adjectives—indebted; liable, chargeable, answerable for, in debt, in embarrassed circumstances; in difficulties; encumbered, involved; involved in debt, plunged in debt; deep in debt; deeply involved; up against it; in the red; fast tied up; insolvent; minus, out of pocket; unpaid; unrequited, unrewarded; owing, due, in arrears, outstanding. *Slang*, in hock, on the cuff, short, broke.

Antonym, see PAYMENT.

decadent, *adj.* ruined, fallen; depraved, EVIL; debauched, dissolute; sentimental, nostalgic; blase, cynical. See DETERIORATION, KNOWLEDGE.

decay, *n. & v.* —*n.* DECOMPOSITION, DETERIORATION, disintegration, dilapidation, putrefaction, rot, caries. —*v.i.* rot, putrefy, mortify; disintegrate. *Ant.*, see IMPROVEMENT.

decease, *n. & v.* See DEATH.

deceive, *v.* See DECEPTION.

deceiver, *n.* trickster, sharper, swindler, liar; humbug, charlatan, quack, mountebank; impostor, fraud, faker, sham, hoaxer, hoax, cheat; pretender, hypocrite; Judas. *Slang*, con man, four-flusher, ringer. See DECEPTION.

decent, *adj.* decorous, chaste, pure in heart; acceptable, reasonable, tolerable. See PROBITY, GOODNESS. *Ant.*, see IMPURITY, BADNESS.

DECEPTION

Nouns—**1,** deception, deceptiveness; falseness, untruth; imposition, imposture; fraud, fraudulence, deceit, deceitfulness, guile, bluff; knavery; CUNNING; FALSEHOOD.

2, delusion, illusion, gullery; juggling, jugglery; sleight of hand, legerdemain; prestidigitation; magic (see SORCERY); conjuring, conjuration; hocus pocus; trickery, chicanery; cozenage, circumvention, connivance, collusion; treachery, dishonesty (see IMPROBITY); practical joke; trick, cheat, wile, blind, feint, plant, bubble, fetch, catch, juggle, reach, hocus, thimble-rig, card-sharping, artful dodge, swindle; tricks upon travelers; stratagem, artifice; theft. *Colloq.*, hokey-pokey, sell, fake, hanky-panky. *Slang*, con game, racket, shell game, gyp; blarney, spoof.

3, snare, trap, pitfall, springe, decoy, gin; noose, hook; bait, decoy duck, baited trap; mousetrap, beartrap, steel trap, mantrap; cobweb, net, meshes, toils; AMBUSH; trapdoor, sliding panel, false bottom; spring-net, spring-gun, masked battery; mine, booby trap.

4, mockery, IMITATION, copy; counterfeit, sham, make-believe, forgery, fraud; lie; hollow mockery; whited sepulcher; tinsel, paste, false jewelry; man of straw; ormolu; jerrybuilding; illusion (see ERROR); mirage; German silver; Britannia metal; gerrymander. *Colloq.*, gold brick. *Slang*, phony.

5, DECEIVER; wolf in sheep's clothing, cheat, fraud; magician, conjuror; dodger, swindler, *etc.*

Verbs—**1,** deceive, take in; defraud, cheat, jockey, cozen, nab, play one false, bilk, bite, pluck, swindle, victimize, gull, hoax, dupe; abuse; mystify, blind one's eyes; blindfold, hoodwink; throw dust into the eyes; impose upon, practice upon, play upon, put upon, palm upon, foist upon; snatch a verdict; palm off; circumvent, overreach; outreach, outwit, outmaneuver; get around; steal a march upon, give the go-by, leave in the lurch. *Colloq.*, gouge, slip one over on. *Slang*, give the runaround, diddle, do, take for, get away with.

2, set a trap, lay a trap, lay a snare for; bait the hook, spread the toils, decoy, waylay, lure, beguile, delude, inveigle; hook, trick, entrap, ensnare; nick, springe; catch in a trap; entangle, hocus, practice on one's credulity, fool, befool, pull the wool over one's eyes; humbug; stuff up, sell; play a trick upon; play a practical joke upon; balk, trip up, send on a fool's errand; make game of, make a fool of, make an April fool of, make an ass of; trifle with, cajole, flatter; come over; dissemble, lie (see FALSEHOOD); misinform; mislead (see ERROR); betray (see IMPROBITY). *Colloq.*, bamboozle, fourflush, flimflam, bilk, put over.

3, load the dice, stack the cards *or* deck; live by one's wits, play at hide and seek; obtain money under false pretenses (see STEALING); conjure, juggle, practice chicanery; brace, touch, soak; swipe, pinch, lift (see STEALING); pass off, palm off, foist off, fob off.

Adjectives—deceived, deceiving guileful, CUNNING, deceptive, deceitful; delusive, delusory; illusive, illusory; elusive, insidious; untrue (see FALSEHOOD); mock, sham, make-believe, counterfeit, pseudo, spurious, so-called, pretended, feigned, trumped up, bogus, fraudulent, tricky, factitious, artificial, bastard; surreptitious, illegitimate, contraband, adulterated, sophisticated; unsound, rotten at the core; disguised; meretricious; tinsel, pinchbeck; catchpenny; brummagem; simulated, plated. *Colloq.*, fake, doctored. *Slang*, phony.

Adverbs—deceptively, *etc.*; under false colors, under cover of; behind one's back, cunningly; slyly; on the sly.

decide, *v.t.* determine, elect; settle, fix; arbitrate. See RESOLUTION, CHOICE, CERTAINTY.

decipher, *v.t.* make out, decode; translate, interpret. See DISCLOSURE.

decision, *n.* firmness, RESOLUTION, JUDGMENT, determination; verdict, finding. See LAWSUIT.

deck, *n. & v.* —*n.* floor, platform; flooring; quarterdeck, forecastle, fo'c's'le; after, boat, flight, *etc.* deck; pack [of cards]. —*v.t.* deck out, bedeck, attire, garb, apparel; ORNAMENT, decorate. See CLOTHING, COVERING.

declaim, *v.i.* recite, harangue, rant. See SPEECH.

declaration, *n.* AFFIRMATION, proclamation, statement, avowal. See PUBLICATION, SPEECH, EVIDENCE. *Ant.*, SILENCE.

decline, *n. & v.* —*n.* retrogression, decadence, wasting, DISEASE, AGE, DETERIORATION. *Ant.*, see HEALTH, YOUTH, IMPROVEMENT. —*v.* worsen, slump; refuse, turn down (an offer). See DETERIORATION, OLDNESS, AGE, REFUSAL. *Ant.*, see IMPROVEMENT, NEWNESS, YOUTH.

DECOMPOSITION

Nouns—decomposition, disintegration, decay, corruption, UNCLEANNESS; analysis, dissection, RESOLUTION, catalysis, dissolution; dispersion; DISJUNCTION.

Verbs—decompose, decompound; disintegrate; corrupt; analyze, disembody, dissolve; resolve into its elements, separate into its elements; catalyze, electrolyze; dissect, decentralize, break up; disperse; unravel, unroll; crumble into dust.

Adjectives—decomposed, corrupt, decayed; catalytic, analytical.

Antonym, see COMPOSITION.

---

decoration, *n.* ORNAMENT, garnishment, trimming; trophy.

decorum, *n.* comportment, deportment, decency; protocol; RELATION. See CONFORMITY.

decoy, *v.t.* entice, lure, entrap. See ATTRACTION, DECEPTION.

DECREASE

Nouns—**1,** decrease, diminution; lessening, subtraction, reduction, abatement, declension; shrinking, CONTRACTION, coarctation; abridgment, shortening, extenuation; DEDUCTION, DISCOUNT.

2, subsidence, wane, ebb, decline; DESCENT, decrement, reflux, depreciation; DETERIORATION, mitigation, MODERATION.

Verbs—**1,** decrease, diminish, lessen; abridge, shorten, shrink, contract, drop, fall *or* tail off; fall away, waste, wear; wane, ebb, decline; descend, subside; melt, die *or* fade away; retire into the shade, fall to a low ebb; run low, out, dry *or* short; dwindle, slacken, peter out.

2, bate, abate, discount; depreciate; lower, weaken, attenuate, fritter away; mitigate, moderate, dwarf, throw into the shade; reduce, subtract.

Adjectives—unincreased, decreased, decreasing, short, diminishing, waning, wasting away, wearing out, reduced, lessening, ebbing, dwindling, petering out, fading, disappearing, vanishing, falling off; dwarfish.

Adverbs—on the wane, on the decrease, smaller and smaller, less and less.

Antonym, see INCREASE.

---

decree, *n.* COMMAND, JUDGMENT, edict, ordinance, law, fiat. See LEGAL-ITY. *Ant.*, see MISJUDGMENT, ILLEGALITY.

decrepit, *adj.* delapidated, broken-down; shaky; doddering, senile. *Colloq.*, on one's last legs, ready for the scrap heap. *Slang*, kaput. See DETERIORATION, DISEASE, OLDNESS, WEAKNESS, USELESSNESS.

dedicate, *v.t.* give, devote, consecrate. See USE, REPUTE.

deduce, *v.* infer, conclude, gather, derive; reason, reckon, suppose, assume, presume, deem, opine, think, believe. See THOUGHT, REASONING.

DEDUCTION

Nouns—**1,** deduction; removal; excision; subtraction, subtrahend, minuend; minus, minus sign; abstraction, abbreviation, curtailment (see SHORTNESS); reduction (see DECREASE); retrenchment; amputation, truncation.

2, inference; see PROBABILITY, JUDGMENT.

3, decrement; DISCOUNT, rebate; LOSS; WASTE.

Verbs—deduct, subduct, subtract, take away; remove, excise, cut out; abstract, abbreviate, curtail; reduce; retrench; amputate, truncate; deduce, discount; abate, rebate; pare, shave, prune.

Adjectives—deducted, deductive, deducible, subtractive.

Prepositions—minus, diminished by, less; without, except, barring, excluding.

Antonym, see ADDITION.

---

deed, *n.* act, ACTION, feat, achievement; exploit; legal document, transfer. *Ant.*, see INACTIVITY.

deem, *v.* consider, judge, regard; assess. *Colloq.*, calculate, reckon. See JUDGMENT, BELIEF, SUPPOSITION.

deep, *adj. & n.* See DEPTH.

deface, *v.t.* mar, disfigure, tarnish, mutilate, blemish; maim, mangle, scar. See DISTORTION, DETERIORATION, IMPERFECTION. *Ant.*, see IMPROVEMENT.

defame, *v.t.* traduce, vilify, revile, calumniate, asperse, abuse, malign. See DISREPUTE, DETRACTION. *Ant.*, see REPUTE.

default, *n. & v.* —*n.* FAILURE, omission, breach, NEGLECT; NONPAYMENT, delinquency, arrears; AVOIDANCE, nonappearance. —*v.* fail, back out; NEGLECT, disregard; defalcate, not pay; absent oneself, be missing. *Colloq.*, no show, renege; welch, welsh.

defeat, *v.t. & n.* —*v.t.* thwart, frustrate, foil, outwit; rout, conquer, overcome, vanquish, subdue. *Slang*, lick. See HINDRANCE, FAILURE. *Ant.*, see AID, SUCCESS. —*n.* frustration, rout, vanquishment.

defect, *n. & v.* —*n.* decrement, BLEMISH, fault, flaw; IMPERFECTION; deficiency, lack, incompleteness. *Ant.*, see WHOLE, PERFECTION. —*v.i.* desert, flee, abandon. See RELINQUISHMENT, ESCAPE.

DEFENSE

Nouns—**1,** defense, protection, guard, ward; shielding, PRESERVATION, guardianship; self-defense, self-preservation; RESISTANCE; safeguard (see SAFETY).

2, shelter, CONCEALMENT; fortification; munition, munitionment; bulwark, foss(e), moat, ditch, intrenchment; dike, parapet, embankment, mound, mole, bank; earthwork; fieldwork; fence, wall, dead wall; paling, sunk fence, haha, palisade, INCLOSURE; barrier, barricade; boom; portcullis, *chevaux de frise*; abatis; battlement, rampart, scarp; glacis, casemate, buttress, abutment; breastwork, curtain, bastion, redan, ravelin; redoubt; lines, loophole, machicolation; barrage balloon, radar screen, DEW line (Distant Early Warning line).

3, hold, stronghold, fastness; asylum, sanctuary, REFUGE; keep, dungeon, fortress, citadel, capitol, castle; tower, tower of strength; fort, blockhouse; shelter, air-raid shelter.

4, armor, shield, buckler, aegis, breastplate, cuirass, habergeon, mail, coat of mail, hauberk, lorication, helmet, steel helmet, siege cap, casque, cask, shako, bearskin; weapon, ARMS; antiaircraft battery.

5, defender, protector, guardian, guard, bodyguard, champion, knight-errant; garrison, patrol, national guard (see COMBATANT); sentinel, sentry, lookout; KEEPER, watchman; watchdog.

Verbs—defend, forfend, fend; shield, screen, shroud; fence round (see CIRCUMSCRIPTION); fence, intrench; guard (see SAFETY); guard against; take care of; bear harmless; keep off, ward off, fight off, beat off; parry, repel, repulse, put to flight; hold at bay, keep at bay, keep at arm's length; stand on the defensive, act on the defensive; man the barricades, hold the fort; show fight; maintain *or* stand one's ground; stand by; hold one's own; bear the brunt; fall back upon, hold. *Colloq.*, dig in, stonewall; go to bat for, stick up for.

Adjectives—defending, defensive; protective, preservative; mural, fortified, armored, armed, armed at all points, armed to the teeth; panoplied; ironplated, ironclad; loopholed, castellated, machicolated, casemated; defended, invulnerable, proof against.

Adverbs—defensively; on the defense, on the defensive; in defense; at bay.

Antonym, see ATTACK.

defenseless, *adj.* exposed, unprotected, open, bare, vulnerable. See WEAKNESS.

defer, *v.* delay, suspend, postpone, stay, procrastinate; submit, yield, give in, abide by, RESPECT. See ASSENT, LATENESS, OBEDIENCE. *Ant.,* see INSOLENCE.

DEFIANCE

Nouns—defiance, dare, challenge, THREAT; provocation; warcry, war-whoop; rebellion (see DISOBEDIENCE); INSOLENCE; contempt; daring.

Verbs—defy, dare, double-dare, beard, brave (see COURAGE); bid defiance to, set at naught, set at defiance; hurl defiance at; face down, fly in the face of; dance the war dance; snap the fingers at, bite the thumb, thumb one's nose at; laugh to scorn; disobey; show fight, show one's teeth, show a bold front; bluster, look big, stand akimbo; double the fist; shake the fist; threaten; throw in the teeth; challenge, call out; throw down the gauntlet, gage *or* glove. *Colloq.*, toss one's hat in the ring, call a bluff.

Adjectives—defiant; defying, daring; with arms akimbo; insolent, contemptuous, bold; rebellious.

Adverbs—defiantly, in defiance, in the teeth of; under one's very nose.

Antonym, see OBEDIENCE, FEAR.

deficient, *adj.* lacking, wanting, inadequate, insufficient, imperfect, incomplete. See INFERIORITY, FAILURE, IMPERFECTION.

deficit, *n.* See DEFICIENCY, DEBT.

defile, *v. & n.* —*v.t.* DIRTY, (be)foul, tarnish, blacken; corrupt, debauch, contaminate; DISHONOR, debase, sully, drag in the dust, give a bad name. See UNCLEANNESS, IMPURITY, EVIL, DISREPUTE. *n.* ravine, gorge, PASSAGE.

define, *v.t.* explain, interpret; circumscribe, LIMIT, demarcate. See INTERPRETATION, NOMENCLATURE, CIRCUMSCRIPTION.

definite, *adj.* exact, explicit, plain, limited, precise, unequivocal. See SPECIALITY, LIMIT, CERTAINTY, TRUTH, EVIDENCE.

deflate, *v.t.* exhaust, empty; reduce, humble. See CONTRACTION.

deflect, *v.* bend, curve, twist; deviate, avert, swing, sidetrack. See DEVIATION.

deformity, *n.* malformation, disfigurement, monstrosity, DISTORTION, UGLINESS, IMPERFECTION.

defraud, *v.t.* swindle, cheat, dupe, fleece. *Slang,* gyp. See STEALING, DECEPTION.

defy, *v.t.* See DEFIANCE.

degeneracy, *n.* DETERIORATION, demoralization; viciousness, depravity, turpitude, VICE.

degradation, *n.* DETERIORATION, DISREPUTE, humiliation, shame, abasement; degeneracy, VICE.

DEGREE

Nouns—degree, grade, extent, measure, amount, ratio, standard, HEIGHT; pitch; reach, amplitude, range, scope, caliber; gradation, graduation, shade; tenor, compass, LIMIT; sphere, station, status, rank, standing, CLASSIFICATION, rate, way, sort; point, mark, INDICATION; stage, intensity, STRENGTH. *Colloq.,* notch, hole.
Adjectives—comparative, relative; gradual, shading off.
Adverbs—by degrees, gradually, inasmuch, however, howsoever; step by step, bit by bit, little by little, inch by inch, drop by drop; by inches, by slow degrees; in some degree, in some measure; to some extent.
Antonym, see DISORDER.

dehydrate, *v.t.* dry (out), desiccate, evaporate. See DRYNESS, PRESERVATION.

DEITY

Nouns—**1,** Deity, Divinity; Godhead, Godship; Omnipotence, Providence.
2, God, Lord; Jehovah, Yahweh, Jah, JHVH, Tetragrammaton; Supreme Being, First Cause; Author *or* Creator of all things; the Infinite, Eternal; the All-powerful, -wise, -merciful, *or* -holy.
3, [*attributes, perfections and functions*] infinite power, infinite wisdom, goodness, justice, truth, mercy; omnipotence, omniscience, omnipresence; unity, immutability, holiness, glory, majesty, sovereignty, infinity, eternity; the Trinity, Holy Trinity, Trinity in Unity; God the Father, Maker, Creator, *or* Preserver; creation, preservation, divine government; theocracy, thearchy; Providence, ways *or* dispensation of Providence; God the Son, Jesus, Christ, the Messiah, Anointed, Saviour, Redeemer; the Son of God, Man, *or* David; the Lamb of God, the Word; Emmanuel, Immanuel; the King of Kings and King of Glory, Prince of Peace, Good Shepherd, Light of the World, the Incarnation; salvation, redemption, atonement, propitiation, mediation, intercession, judgment, God the Holy Ghost, the Holy Spirit, Paraclete; inspiration, unction, regeneration, sanctification, consolation; special providence, *Deus ex machina*; avatar.
4, Allah; God of Abraham, *etc.*; Lord of Hosts, the Lord God.
Verbs—create, uphold, preserve, govern, atone, redeem, save, propitiate, predestinate, elect, call, ordain, bless, justify, sanctify, glorify.
Adjectives—almighty, holy, hallowed, sacred, divine, heavenly, celestial, sacrosanct, superhuman, supernatural; ghostly, spiritual, hyperphysical, unearthly; theistic, theocratic; anointed.
Adverbs—divinely, by divine right; with the help of God.
Antonym, see MANKIND.

DEJECTION

Nouns—**1,** dejection, dejectedness; depression; lowness *or* depression of spirits; weight on the spirits, damp on the spirits; low spirits, bad spirits, drooping spirits, depressed spirits; heart sinking; heaviness of heart; heaviness, gloom; WEARINESS, disgust of life; homesickness; DISCONTENT; melancholy; sadness, melancholia, doldrums, vapors, megrims, spleen, horrors, hypochondria, pessimism; despondency, slough of despond; disconsolateness, discontent; hope deferred, blank despondency.

2, grief, sorrow, heartache, prostration; broken heart; despair; gravity, solemnity; long face, grave face, death's-head at the feast. *Colloq.*, blues, dumps, blue devils.

3, hypochondriac, pessimist; mope. *Colloq.*, wet blanket. *Slang*, sourpuss, killjoy.

Verbs—1, be dejected, grieve; mourn, lament; take on, give way, lose heart, despond, droop, sink; lower, look downcast, frown, pout; hang down the head; pull *or* make a long face; laugh on the wrong side of the mouth; grin a ghastly smile; look blue; lay *or* take to heart; mope, brood over; fret, sulk; pine, yearn, repine, REGRET; despair.

2, refrain from laughter, keep one's countenance, keep a straight face; be grave, look grave; repress a smile.

3, depress, discourage, dishearten; dispirit; damp, dull, lower, sink, dash, knock down, unman, prostrate, break one's heart; frown upon; cast a gloom *or* shade on; sadden; damp one's hopes, dash one's hopes, wither one's hopes; weigh on the mind, lie heavy on the mind; prey on the mind; depress the spirits.

Adjectives—dejected, cheerless, joyless, spiritless; uncheerful, unlively; unhappy, sad, triste, melancholy, dismal, somber, dark, gloomy, clouded, murky, lowering, frowning, lugubrious, funereal, mournful, lamentable, dreadful; dreary, flat, dull, dull as ditchwater *or* dishwater; depressing; oppressed with, *or* a prey to melancholy; downcast, downhearted; down in the mouth, down on one's luck; heavyhearted; in the dumps, in the sulks, in the doldrums; in bad humor, sullen, mumpish, dumpish; mopish, moping; moody, glum; sulky, discontented, out of sorts, out of humor, out of spirits; ill at ease, low-spirited, in low spirits; weary, discouraged, disheartened; desponding; chopfallen, crestfallen.

2, sad, pensive, tristful; doleful, woebegone, tearful, lachrymose, in tears, melancholic, hypochondriacal, bilious, jaundiced, atrabilious, saturnine, splenetic; lackadaisical; serious, sedate, staid; grave, grave as a judge, sober, solemn, demure; grim, grimfaced, grim-visaged, rueful, wan, long-faced.

3, disconsolate; unconsolable, inconsolable; forlorn, comfortless, desolate, sick at heart; soul-sick, heart-sick; in despair, lost; overcome, broken down, borne down, bowed down; heart-stricken; cut up, dashed, sunk; unnerved, unmanned; downfallen, downtrodden; brokenhearted; careworn.

Adjectives—dejectedly, with a long face, with tears in one's eyes; sadly, etc.

Antonym, see CHEERFULNESS.

---

delay, *v. & n.* —*v.* put off, retard, postpone; linger, daily, loiter, procrastinate. See LATENESS, SLOWNESS, HINDRANCE. —*n.* postponement, procrastination. See DURABILITY.

delectable, *adj.* delightful, delicious, exquisite. See PLEASURE, TASTE, BEAUTY.

delegate, *n. & v.t.* —*n.* DEPUTY, envoy, agent. —*v.t.* COMMISSION, entrust, depute, empower. See SUBSTITUTION.

delete, *v.t.* erase, cancel, expunge, take out, cross out, excise.

deliberate, *adj. & v.* —*adj.* intentional, studied; cool, careful, thoughtful, unhurried. See MEASUREMENT, SLOWNESS. —*v.i.* ponder, consider, think, weight. See THOUGHT, ADVICE.

delicacy, *n.* sensitiveness, tact, nicety; frailty, daintiness, exactness; tidbit, luxury; discrimination, TASTE, fastidiousness. See PURITY, IMPOTENCE, BEAUTY, FOOD.

delicious, *adj.* delectable, luscious, toothsome, palatable, savory. See TASTE.

delightful, *adj.* pleasing, enjoyable, charming, attractive, alluring. See PLEASURE.

delineate, *v.t.* outline, draw, sketch, limn, portray, depict. See PLAN, REPRESENTATION.

delinquent, *adj. & n.* —*adj.* neglectful, defaulting, undutiful; culpable; negligent. —*n.* defaulter; transgressor, troublemaker, lawbreaker; juvenile delinquent, J.D. See DEBT, EVILDOER. *Ant.*, see GOODNESS.

delirious, *adj.* mad, raving, wandering, unbalanced, frenzied. See INSANITY, FEELING, EXCITEMENT. *Ant.*, see SANITY.

deliver, *v.* discharge, give forth, emit, deal; free, liberate, release, emancipate; convey, carry to; save, rescue, redeem; rid; grant, cede, surrender; pronounce, speak, utter. *Colloq.*, make good (deliver the goods); bring home the bacon. See GIVING, FREEDOM, SPEECH.

delivery, *n.* surrender; conveyance; RELINQUISHMENT; childbirth, parturition; rescue, ESCAPE, salvation, *redemption* (see LIBERATION); address (see SPEECH). *Ant.*, see DANGER, RESTRAINT.

deluge, *n.* stream, flood, inundation; downpour, spate; plethora. See SUFFICIENCY, WATER.

delusion, *n.* DECEPTION, SORCERY; illusion, fantasy, misconception, hallucination. See VISION, ERROR, INSANITY.

demand, *v. & n.* —*v.t.* require, charge; levy, exact, order, requisition. See COMMAND, PAYMENT. —*n.* REQUIREMENT, requisition; ultimatum; market, PRICE; COMMAND, SALE.

demented, *adj.* deranged, crazed, insane. See INSANITY.

demerit, *n.* black mark, minus, fault; defect, failing. See IMPERFECTION, FAILURE.

demobilize, *v.* discharge, muster out, send home; disarm, demilitarize; disband, scatter. See DISPERSION, LIBERATION.

democratic, *adj.* unassuming, nonsnobbish; popular. See MODESTY, CHOICE.

demolish, *v.t.* raze, level, ruin, wreck, destroy, wipe out. See DESTRUCTION. *Ant.*, see PRODUCTION.

DEMON

Nouns—1, demon, demonry, demonology; evil genius, fiend, familiar, devil; bad spirit, unclean spirit; cacodemon, incubus, succubus; Frankenstein's monster; SATAN; Mephistopheles, Asmodeus, Belial, Ahriman; fury, harpy.

2, vampire, ghoul, ogre, ogress; gnome, affreet, genie, imp, bogie, kobold, fairy, brownie, pixy, elf, gremlin, dwarf, urchin, Puck, leprechaun, troll, sprite, bad fairy, nix, will-o'-the-wisp, poltergeist.

3, ghost, specter, apparition, spirit, shade, shadow, vision, hobgoblin; bugaboo, bogey; wraith, spook, banshee; evil eye. See EVIL, HELL.

4, merman, mermaid, merfolk; siren; satyr, faun; changeling, elf-child.

Adjectives—demonic, demoniacal; supernatural, weird, uncanny, unearthly, spectral; ghostly, ghostlike; elfin, elflike; fiendish, fiendlike; impish, haunted; satanic, diabolic(al), devilish; infernal, hellish, Plutonic.

Antonym, see ANGEL.

DEMONSTRATION

Nouns—demonstration, substantiation, proof, verification, authentication, confirmation, corroboration; conclusiveness, probation; EVIDENCE; test (see EXPERIMENT); argument (see REASONING).

Verbs—demonstrate, prove, confirm, substantiate, corroborate, establish; make good, show; evince, verify; settle the question; make out, make out a case; prove one's point, have the best of the argument; draw a conclusion (see JUDGMENT); follow, stand to reason; hold good, hold water.

Adjectives—demonstrating, demonstrative, demonstrable; probative, unanswerable, convincing, conclusive; apodictic, irresistible, irrefutable, irrefragable; categorical, decisive, crucial; demonstrated, proven; unanswered, unrefuted; evident; deducible, consequential, inferential, following.

Adverbs—of course, in consequence, consequently, as a matter of course; *quod erat demonstrandum*, Q.E.D.

Antonym, see CONFUTATION.

demoralize, *v.t.* disconcert, disorganize, confuse; corrupt, deprave. See IMPOTENCE, EVIL.

demote, *v.t.* downgrade, reduce, degrade. *Slang*, bust. See PUNISHMENT, DECREASE.

demur, *v.i. & n.* —*v.i.* hesitate, object, scruple. See DOUBT, DISSENT. —*n.* objection, irresolution, delay. See DISSENT, LATENESS.

demure, *adj.* modest, sedate, staid; diffident; prim, coy. See MODESTY.

den, *n.* lair, haunt, cavern; sanctum, study; dive, hangout. See ABODE, RECEPTACLE.

denial, *n.* NEGATION, repudiation, REFUSAL, contradiction; COUNTER-EVIDENCE, DISSENT, abnegation, TEMPERANCE. *Ant.*, see BELIEF, AGREEMENT.

denomination, *n.* NOMENCLATURE, name, title; CLASS, SCHOOL, PARTY, kind, sect, persuasion. See HETERODOXY.

denote, *v.t.* signify, indicate, express, mean, specify. See EVIDENCE, MEANING, INDICATION.

denouement, *n.* RESOLUTION, solution, END, outcome. See DISCLOSURE.

denounce, *v.t.* decry, censure, arraign, charge, accuse; curse, rail at. See DISAPPROBATION, ACCUSATION.

DENSITY

Nouns—**1**, density, denseness, solidity; solidness; impenetrability, impermeability; incompressibility; imporosity; cohesion (see COHERENCE); constipation, consistence, spissitude; specific gravity.

2, condensation; solidification; consolidation; concretion, coagulation; petrifaction, HARDNESS; crystallization, precipitation; deposit, thickening; indivisibility, indissolubility, infrangibility.

3, solid body, mass, block, knot, lump; concretion, concrete, conglomerate; precipitate; cake, clot, stone, curd; bone, gristle, cartilage.

Verbs—be dense, become solid, render solid; solidify, concrete, set, take a set, consolidate, congeal, coagulate; curd, curdle; fix, clot, cake, precipitate, deposit; cohere, crystallize; petrify, harden; condense, thicken, inspissate; compress, squeeze, ram down, constipate. *Colloq.*, jell.

Adjectives—dense, solid; solidified; coherent, cohesive (see COHERENCE); compact, close, serried, thickset; substantial, massive, lumpish; impenetrable, impermeable, imporous; incompressible; constipated; concrete, knotted, knotty; gnarled; crystalline; thick, stuffy; undissolved, unmelted, unliquefied, unthawed; indivisible, infrangible, indissolvable, indissoluble, infusible.

Antonyms, see RARITY, VAPOR.

dent, *n. & v.* —*n.* indentation, DEPRESSION, hollow, dimple, IMPERFECTION. —*v.t.* indent, buckle, mar. *Colloq.*, EFFECT, make an impression, register.

denunciation, *n.* ACCUSATION; DISAPPROBATION, censure, condemnation, arraignment; MALEDICTION, diatribe, anathema; THREAT.

deny, *v.t.* contradict, negate; refuse, withhold; doubt, reject; oppose, protest. See NEGATION, REFUSAL, RESTRAINT. *Ant.*, see BELIEF, AGREEMENT.

deodorant, *n.* antiperspirant; cream, spray, roll-on; [air] freshener. See ODOR.

department, *n.* PART, section, division; service, AGENCY, bureau; sphere, domain, JURISDICTION, BUSINESS, concern; REGION.

DEPARTURE

Nouns—**1**, departure, leaving, decampment; retreat, embarkation; outset, start; removal; exit, EGRESS, exodus, hejira, evacuation, flight.

2, leave-taking, valediction, adieu, farewell, goodbye; stirrup-cup. *Colloq.*, send-off.

3, starting point, starting post; point *or* place of departure *or* embarkation; port of embarkation.

Verbs—**1,** depart; go, go away; take one's departure, set out; set off, march off, put off, start off, be off, move off, get off, pack off, go off, take oneself off; start, issue, march out, debouch; go forth, sally forth; sally, set forward; be gone, shake the dust off one's feet.

2, leave a place, quit, vacate, evacuate, abandon; go off the stage, make one's exit; retire, withdraw, remove; go one's way, go along, go from home; take flight, take wing; spring, fly, flit, wing one's way; fly away; embark; go on board, go aboard, set sail; put to sea, go to sea; sail, take ship; get under way, weigh anchor, strike tents, decamp; take leave; see off, say goodbye, bid goodbye; DISAPPEAR, take French leave; abscond, avoid, (see AVOIDANCE). *Colloq.*, clear out, push off. *Slang*, toddle along, mosey along, check out, beat it, blow, lam, take the air, light out.

Adjectives—departing, leaving; valedictory; outward bound.

Adverbs—whence, hence, thence; with a foot in the stirrup; on the wing, on the move.

Interjections—farewell! adieu! GOODBYE! goodday! au revoir! fare you well! God bless you! God speed! *Colloq.*, byebye! *Slang*, so long! *Antonym*, see ARRIVAL.

---

depend, *v.i.* rely, trust; dangle, be pendent; be contingent, rest. See BELIEF, CERTAINTY, PENDENCY.

depict, *v.t.* delineate, picture, limn, portray. See REPRESENTATION.

depletion, *n.* emptiness, exhaustion, ABSENCE, INSUFFICIENCY. *Ant.*, see RESTORATION.

deplorable, *adj.* lamentable, sad, regrettable, disastrous. See BADNESS, PAIN, ADVERSITY, DISREPUTE. *Ant.*, see APPROBATION.

deploy, *v.* send, spread *or* fan out; distribute, locate. See EXPANSION, LOCATION.

deport, *v.t.* conduct (oneself), behave; expel. See CONDUCT, DEPARTURE.

deport, *v.t.* send away, banish, exile, expatriate. See EJECTION.

depose, *v.* swear, affirm, testify; dethrone, uncrown, unseat, oust, disbar. See NULLIFICATION.

deposit, *n.* precipitate, sediment, dregs, lees; pledge, PAYMENT, SECURITY. See REMAINDER.

deposition, *n.* affidavit, testimony, AFFIRMATION, dethronement, deposal. See EVIDENCE, NULLIFICATION.

depository, *n.* storehouse, warehouse, vault, TREASURY. See STORE.

depravity, *n.* degeneracy, corruption, turpitude, degradation, vileness. See BADNESS, EVIL, DETERIORATION.

deprecate, *v.t.* protest; regret; disfavor, disapprove; expostulate, inveigh *or* remonstrate (against). See DISAPPROBATION. *Ant.*, see APPROBATION.

depreciate, *v.* disparage, derogate, discredit, belittle. *Colloq.*, run down. *Slang*, knock; cheapen, slump, fall. See DETRACTION, CHEAPNESS. *Ant.*, APPROBATION.

DEPRESSION

Nouns—**1,** depression, lowering; dip (see CONCAVITY); abasement, debasement; reduction.

2, overthrow, overset, overturn; upset; prostration, subversion, precipitation; bow; curtsy; genuflection, kowtow, obeisance. See RESPECT.

Verbs—**1,** depress, lower, let down, take down, take down a peg; cast; let drop, let fall; sink, debase, bring low, abase, reduce, pitch, precipitate; dent (see CONCAVITY).

2, overthrow, overturn, overset; upset, subvert, prostrate, level, fell; cast down, take down, throw down, fling down, dash down, pull down, cut

down, knock down; raze, raze to the ground; trample in the dust; pull about one's ears.
3, sit, sit down; couch, crouch, squat, stoop, bend, bow; courtesy, curtsey; bob, duck, dip, kneel; bend, bow the head, bend the knee; bow down; cower.
Adjectives—depressed; at a low ebb; prostrate, overthrown; downcast.
Antonym, see ELEVATION.

deprive, *v.t.* dispossess, divest, despoil, usurp. See LOSS, ACQUISITION. *Ant.*, see GIVING.

DEPTH

Nouns—depth; deepness, profundity, depression, CONCAVITY; hollow, hole, shaft, well, crater; GULF, bowels of the earth, bottomless pit; HELL; abyss, chasm; deep sea, deeps, depths, ocean bottom; soundings, depth of water, draught, submersion; plummet, plumbline, sound, probe; sounding rod, sounding line; lead. *Colloq.*, Davy Jones' locker. See LOWNESS.
Verbs—be deep, render deep, deepen; PLUNGE; sound, have the lead, take soundings; dig, excavate.
Adjectives—deep, deep-seated; profound, sunk, buried; submerged, subaqueous, submarine, subterranean, underground; bottomless, soundless, fathomless; unfathomed, unfathomable; abysmal; deep as a well; yawning; knee-deep, ankle-deep.
Adverbs—beyond one's depth, out of one's depth; over head and ears.
Antonym, see SHALLOWNESS, HEIGHT.

deputy, *n.* AGENT, representative, delegate; substitute, proxy; envoy; factor; deputy sheriff. See SUBSTITUTION.
derangement, *n.* craziness, madness, lunacy, mania, aberration, dementia; disturbance, upset, imbalance; confusion, turmoil, DISORDER; disconcertment, discomfiture, discomposure. See AGITATION, INSANITY. *Ant.*, see ARRANGEMENT, SANITY.
derelict, *n. & adj.* —*n.* wreck, hull; abandoned property *or* person; drifter, beachcomber, castaway. —*adj.* castaway, wrecked, stranded, abandoned, deserted, forsaken; delinquent, negligent, neglectful, remiss. See NEGLECT, RELINQUISHMENT. *Ant.*, see DUTY.
dereliction, *n.* abandonment; NEGLECT; RELINQUISHMENT, desertion; negligence, failure in duty, delinquency. *Ant.*, see DUTY.
derisive, *adj.* mocking, sarcastic, contemptuous, supercilious, disdainful. See RIDICULE, DISRESPECT, CONTEMPT, DETRACTION.
derive, *v.* get, obtain, deduce; originate, arise. See ACQUISITION, RECEIVING, CAUSE.
derogatory, *adj.* discreditable, depreciative, disparaging, defamatory, humiliating. See DISREPUTE, DETRACTION. *Ant.*, see APPROBATION.

DESCENT

Nouns—descent, descension, declension, declination, inclination, fall; falling, drop, cadence; subsidence, lapse; comedown, downfall, tumble, slip, tilt, trip, lurch; cropper, stumble; declivity, dip, hill; avalanche, debacle, landslip, landslide.
Verbs—**1,** descend; go down, drop down, come down; fall, gravitate, drop, slip, slide, settle; decline, set, sink, droop, come down a peg.
2, dismount, alight, light, get down; swoop; stoop; fall prostrate, precipitate oneself; let fall (see DEPRESSION); tumble, trip, stumble, lurch, pitch, topple; topple down, tumble down, tumble over; tilt, sprawl, plump down. *Colloq.*, come a cropper, take a spill *or* header.
Adjectives—descending, descendent; decurrent, decursive; deciduous; nodding to its fall.
Adverbs—down, downhill, downward, downstream, downstairs.
Antonym, see ASCENT.

DESCRIPTION

Nouns—**1,** description, account, statement, report; exposé, DISCLOSURE; specification, particulars; summary, brief, abstract, *précis*, resumé; return, RECORD, catalogue, list; guidebook, INFORMATION; delineation, REPRESENTATION, sketch; monograph; minute account, detailed account, circumstantial account, graphic account; narration, recital, rehearsal, relation.

2, history; biography, autobiography; necrology, obituary; narrative, memoir, memorials; annals, chronicle, tradition, legend, story, tale, historiette; personal narrative, journal, life, adventures, fortunes, experiences, confessions; work of fiction, novel, novella, romance, love story, detective story; fairy tale, nursery tale; fable, parable, apologue. *Slang*, thriller, whodunit.

3, narrator, relator, historian, recorder, biographer, fabulist, novelist; raconteur, anecdotist, story-teller.

Verbs—describe, narrate, relate, recite, recount; set forth, draw a picture, limn, picture; portray, represent, characterize, particularize; sum up, run over, recapitulate, rehearse, fight one's battles over again; unfold, tell; give an account of, render an account of; report, make a report, draw up a statement; enter into details *or* particulars.

Adjectives—descriptive, graphic, narrative, well-drawn; historical, epic, suggestive, traditional; legendary; anecdotal, expository, storied; biographical, autobiographical.

Antonym, see DISTORTION.

---

desert, *n.* waste, barren, wilderness, solitude; reward, due, merit. See USELESSNESS, SPACE; GOODNESS, JUSTICE.

desert, *v.* leave, forsake, abandon; secede, run away; leave in the lurch, be faithless. *Colloq.*, ditch. See AVOIDANCE.

deserve, *v.t.* merit, be worthy of. See JUSTICE.

design, *n. & v.* —*n.* PLAN, INTENTION, scheme, project; REPRESENTATION, drawing, diagram, pattern; decoration. See MEANING. —*v.t.* PLAN, intend; draw, sketch.

designate, *v.t.* name, specify, indicate; appoint. See NOMENCLATURE, ATTENTION, CHOICE.

DESIRE

Nouns—**1,** desire, wish, fancy, fantasy; want, need, exigency.

2, mind, inclination, leaning, bent, animus, partiality, penchant, predilection; propensity, weakness, proclivity, WILLINGNESS; liking, LOVE, fondness, relish. *Slang*, yen.

3, longing, hankering, longing eye, wistful eye; solicitude, anxiety; yearning, coveting; aspiration, ambition, vaulting ambition; eagerness; zeal, ardor; impatience, overanxiety; impetuosity.

4, appetite, sharp appetite, keenness, hunger, torment of Tantalus, ravenousness, voracity, GLUTTONY; thirst, thirstiness; drought, mouth-watering; itch, itching. *Colloq.*, sweet tooth.

5, avidity; avarice, greed, greediness, itching palm, covetousness, grasping, craving, rapacity, passion, rage, furor, mania, dipsomania, kleptomania; prurience, cacoëthes, cupidity, lust, concupiscence (see GLUTTONY).

6, desirer, lover (see LOVE), amateur, enthusiast, votary, devotee, aspirant, solicitant, candidate. *Slang*, fan.

7, desideratum; want, REQUIREMENT; consummation devoutly to be wished; attraction, magnet, allurement, fancy, temptation, seduction, fascination, prestige, height of one's ambition, idol; whim, whimsy; hobby, hobbyhorse.

Verbs—**1,** desire, wish, wish for; be desirous, have a longing; HOPE; care for, affect, like, list; take to, take kindly to, cling to, take a fancy to; fancy; prefer, choose (see CHOICE); have an eye to, have a mind to; find it in one's heart, be willing, have a fancy for, set one's eyes upon; take into one's head, have at heart, be bent upon; set one's cap for, set one's heart upon, set one's mind upon; covet; want, miss, need, feel the want of; would fain have, would fain do; would be glad of.

2, be hungry, have a good appetite; hunger after, thirst after, crave after, lust after, itch after, hanker after; die for; burn to; fingers itch to; desiderate; sigh for, cry for, gasp for, pine for, pant for, languish for, yearn for, long for, be on thorns for hope for; aspire after; catch at, grasp at, jump at; woo, court, solicit; fish for, whistle for; ogle. *Colloq.*, make a play for.

3, cause desire, create desire, excite desire, provoke desire; whet the appetite; appetize, titillate, allure, attract, take one's fancy, tempt; hold out temptation, tantalize, make one's mouth water.

Adjectives—**1,** desirous, desiring, inclined, willing; partial (to), fain, wishful, optative; anxious, wistful, curious; at a loss for, sedulous, solicitous.

2, craving, hungry, sharp-set, peckish, ravening, with an empty stomach, thirsty, athirst, parched with thirst, dry, pinched with hunger, famished, hungry as a hunter, horse, *or* churchmouse; greedy, greedy as a hog, piggish; overeager; voracious, omnivorous, ravenous, open-mouthed, covetous, avaricious, rapacious, grasping, extortionate, exacting, sordid, insatiable, insatiate; unquenchable, quenchless; unsatisfied, unsated, unslaked.

3, eager, avid, keen; burning, fervent, ardent; agog; all agog; breathless, impatient, impetuous, bent on, intent on, set on, mad after, rabid, dying for, bad off for, devoured by desire; aspiring, ambitious, vaulting, skyaspiring.

4, desirable; desired, in demand; pleasing (see PLEASURE); appetizing, tantalizing.

Adverbs—desirously, wistfully, fain; solicitously, yearningly, fondly, ambitiously, *etc.*

Antonym, see HATE, SUFFICIENCY.

---

desist, *v.i.* stop, cease, abstain, quit, forbear. See END. *Ant.*, see CONTINUITY.

desk, *n.* escritoire, secretary, lectern; bureau. See RECEPTACLE, AGENCY.

desolate, *adj. & v.* —*adj.* bleak, barren, inhospitable, unpeopled; lonely, abandoned, forlorn; comfortless, miserable. See ABSENCE, SECLUSION, DEJECTION. *Ant.*, see ABODE, SOCIALITY. —*v.t.* waste, depopulate, devastate. See DESTRUCTION, DETERIORATION.

despair, *n.* hopelessness, sadness, DEJECTION, despondency, discouragement. *Ant.*, see HOPE, CHEERFULNESS.

desperado, *n.* bravo, outlaw, cutthroat, ruffian, thug. See RASHNESS, EVILDOER.

desperate, *adj.* hopeless, incurable; reckless, rash, foolhardy; furious, heroic. See DEJECTION, RASHNESS.

despicable, *adj.* detestable, hateful, contemptible. See HATE, REPULSION.

despise, *v.t.* scorn, disdain, hold in contempt, DISLIKE. *Ant.*, see RESPECT.

despite, *prep.* in spite of, regardless of, notwithstanding; contrary to [expectations], in the teeth *or* face of. See OPPOSITION, IRRELATION, NEGLECT.

despondent, *adj.* downcast, melancholy, depressed, dejected, disconsolate, wretched; discouraged, dispirited, prostrate. *Colloq.*, down in the mouth. See DEJECTION, DISAPPOINTMENT, HOPELESSNESS.

despotism, *n.* dictatorship, autocracy, tyranny, oppression. See SEVERITY, AUTHORITY.

dessert, *n.* sweet, savory, confection, treat, trifle. See SWEETNESS, FOOD.

destination, *n.* goal, terminus, port; DESTINY, END, objective. *Ant.*, see BEGINNING, DEPARTURE.

DESTINY

Nouns—**1,** destiny, future existence; imminence, future state, next world, world to come, afterlife; futurity.

2, destiny, fate, kismet, God's will, act of God, the will of God *or* Allah; Karma; doom, determinism, fatalism, predestination, predetermination, NECESSITY, inevitability; luck, star, lot, fortune, destination; a cross to bear, a row to hoe; wheel of fortune, spin *or* turn of the wheel, fall of the dice *or* cards; the mills of the gods; hour of destiny.

Verbs—impend; hang *or* lie over; threaten, loom, await, come on, approach, stare one in the face; ordain, foreordain, preordain; predestine, doom, have in store for.

Adjectives—destined, impending, about to be, about to happen, coming, in store, to come, instant, at hand, near; near *or* close at hand; overhanging, hanging over one's head, imminent; brewing, preparing, forthcoming; in the wind, in the cards, in the offing, in reserve; in prospect, expected (see EXPECTATION), looming in the distance *or* future *or* on the horizon.

Adverbs—**1,** in time, in the long run; all in good time; eventually, whatever may happen, as chance *or* luck would have it.

2, fatally, fatalistically, imminently, *etc.*; in the hands of fate, in the lap of the gods, in God's hands; out of luck, in luck; by chance.

Antonym, see CHANCE, NECESSITY.

---

destitute, *adj.* wanting, lacking; stripped, bereft, penniless, poverty-stricken. *Slang,* down and out. See INSUFFICIENCY, POVERTY.

DESTRUCTION

Nouns—**1,** destruction; waste, dissolution, breaking up; disruption; consumption; disorganization.

2, fall, downfall, ruin, perdition, crash, smash, havoc, debacle; breakdown, breakup; prostration; desolation, bouleversement, wreck, shipwreck, catastrophe, cataclysm; extinction, annihilation; destruction of life (see KILLING); OBLITERATION; knock-down blow; doom, crack of doom.

3, destroying, demolition, demolishment; overthrow, subversion, REVOLUTION, sabotage; suppression; abolition, abrogation (see NULLIFICATION); sacrifice, ravage, devastation, incendiarism, extirpation, extermination, eradication; EXTRACTION; road to ruin; dilapidation, DETERIORATION.

4, destroyer, exterminator; nihilist; blight, moth; executioner.

Verbs—**1,** be destroyed, perish, fall, fall to the ground; tumble, topple; go *or* fall to pieces; break up; crumble to dust; go to the dogs, go to the wall, go to smash, go to wreck, go to pot, go to wrack and ruin; go by the board, go all to smash; be all over with, be all up with; totter to its fall.

2, destroy, do *or* make away with; exterminate; nullify, annul, OBLITERATE, wipe out; sacrifice, demolish, dismantle (see USELESSNESS); tear up; overturn, overthrow, overwhelm; upset, subvert, put an end to; seal the doom of; break up, cut up; break down, cut down, pull down, mow down, beat down; suppress, quash, put down; cut short, take off, blot out; dispel, dissipate, dissolve; consume; disorganize. *Colloq.,* do for, wipe out, cook one's goose. *Slang,* cook, lay out, K.O., knock into a cocked hat; total.

3, smash, quell, squash, squelch, crumple up, shatter, shiver; batter; tear to pieces, crush to pieces, cut to pieces, pull to pieces, pick to pieces; nip; ruin; strike out; throw down, knock down; fell, sink, swamp, scuttle, wreck, shipwreck, engulf, submerge; lay in ashes, lay in ruins; sweep away, eradicate, erase, expunge; raze, level.

4, deal destruction, lay waste, ravage, gut; swallow up, devour, desolate, devastate, sap, mine, blast, confound; exterminate, extinguish, quench, annihilate; snuff out, put out, stamp out; prostrate; trample under foot; make short work of, make a clean sweep of, make mincemeat of; cut up root and branch; fling *or* scatter to the winds; throw overboard; strike at the root of, sap the foundations of; spring a mine, blow up.

Adjectives—destroyed, disrupted, perishing, trembling, nodding *or* tottering to its fall; in course of destruction; extinct; destructive, subversive, ruinous, incendiary, deletory; destroying; suicidal; deadly (see KILLING).
Antonym, see PRODUCTION.

desultory, *adj.* aimless, fitful, rambling unmethodical, erratic. See DISORDER, IRREGULARITY, DEVIATION, DIFFUSENESS.

detach, *v.t.* separate, disconnect, remove, sever, unfix, unfasten. See DISJUNCTION. *Ant.*, see JUNCTION.

detachment, *n.* separation, isolation, DISJUNCTION; preoccupation, aloofness, abstraction; PART; detail. See INATTENTION, COMBATANT.

detail, *n. & v.* —*n.* PART, unite, item; minute, particular, trifle. See SPECIALITY, UNIMPORTANCE. —*v.t.* particularize, itemize; appoint, assign. See SPECIALITY, CHOICE, APPORTIONMENT.

detain, *v.t.* delay, check, hold back; keep, retain. See LATENESS, HINDRANCE.

detect, *v.t.* discover, find out, perceive, espy, ferret out. See DISCLOSURE. *Ant.*, see CONCEALMENT.

detective, *n.* investigator, AGENT; policeman, plainclothesman, operative, undercover man; Sherlock Holmes. *Colloq.*, sleuth(hound), shadow. *Slang*, private eye, gumshoe, shamus, house dick, Fed. See INQUIRY, JUSTICE.

deter, *v.t.* restrain, hinder, discourage, give pause, disincline. See RESTRAINT, HINDRANCE, FEAR. *Ant.*, see HOPE.

detergent, *adj. & n.* —*adj.* detersive, clean(s)ing, washing; solvent, saponaceous. —*n.* soap; wetting agent; solvent; clean(s)er. See CLEANNESS.

DETERIORATION

Nouns—**1,** deterioration, debasement; wane, ebb; decline, declension; relapse, backsliding (see REGRESSION); recession, retrogradation, DECREASE.
2, degeneracy, degeneration, degenerateness, degradation; depravation, depravement; depravity, perversion, prostitution; demoralization, retrogression; decadence.
3, impairment, injury, damage, loss, detriment, outrage, havoc, inroad, ravage; scathe; vitiation; discoloration, oxidation; poisoning, leaven; pollution, contamination; canker; adulteration, alloy.
4, decay, DECOMPOSITION, disintegration, dilapidation, ravages of time, wear and tear; corrosion, erosion; mouldiness, rottenness; moth and rust, dry rot, blight; atrophy, collapse; attrition, disorganization, devastation, DESTRUCTION.

Verbs—**1,** deteriorate, be deteriorated, become deteriorated, degenerate; have seen better days, fall off; wane (see DECREASE); ebb; retrograde (see REGRESSION); decline, droop; go down, sink, go downhill, go from bad to worse; jump out of the frying pan into the fire; run to seed, lapse, be the worse for; break down, break; spring a leak, crack, start; shrivel (see CONTRACTION); fade, go off, wither, molder, rot, decay, go bad; rust, crumble, shake; totter, totter to its fall; perish (see DEATH). *Colloq.*, go to pot.
2, deteriorate; weaken (see IMPOTENCE); put back; taint, infect, contaminate, poison, envenom, canker, corrupt, exulcerate, pollute, vitiate, debase; denaturalize, leaven; deflower, debauch, defile, deprave, degrade; pervert, prostitute, demoralize, brutalize; render vicious; stain; discolor, alloy, adulterate, tamper with, prejudice; blight, rot, corrode, erode; wear away, wear out; gnaw, gnaw at the root of; sap, mine, undermine,

shake, sap the foundations of, break up, disorganize, dismantle, dismast; destroy (see DESTRUCTION).

3, injure, impair, damage, harm, hurt, scathe, spoil, mar, despoil, dilapidate, waste; overrun; ravage; pillage (see STEALING); wound, stab, pierce, maim, lame, cripple, hamstring, mangle, mutilate, disfigure, blemish, deface, warp. *Colloq.*, play the devil with, play hell with, crack up.

Adjectives—**1**, deteriorated, altered, altered for the worse; injured, sprung; withering, spoiling, on the wane, on the decline; degenerate, effete; depraved; worse; the worse for; out of repair *or* tune; imperfect (see IMPERFECTION); the worse for wear; battered: weathered, weatherbeaten; stale, passé, shaken, dilapidated, frayed, faded, wilted, shabby, secondhand, threadbare; worn, worn to a thread, worn to a shadow, worn to rags; reduced to a skeleton; at a low ebb, in a bad way, on one's last legs; undermined; deciduous; tottering; past cure, hopeless; deleterious (see BADNESS). *Colloq.*, seedy, tacky; done for, out of commission. *Slang*, out of whack.

2, decayed, motheaten, wormeaten; mildewed, rusty, mouldy, spotted, time-worn, moss-grown; discolored; wasted, crumbling, mouldering, rotten, cankered, blighted, tainted; decrepit; broken down; done for, done up; worn out, used up.

Antonym, see IMPROVEMENT.

---

determination, *n.* RESOLUTION, WILL, firmness; JUDGMENT.

determine, *v.t.* decide, resolve; END, settle; delimit, define, bound; specify, find out, restrict, differentiate; INFLUENCE, affect. See RESOLUTION, CIRCUMSCRIPTION, CAUSE. *Ant.*, see DOUBT.

deterrent, *adj. & n.* —*adj.* preventive, retardative, prohibitive, defensive. —*n.* prevention, RESTRAINT; DEFENSE, obstacle, HINDRANCE, stumbling block.

detest, *v.t.* HATE, abhor, despise, abominate, DISLIKE. *Ant.*, see APPROBATION.

dethrone, *v.t.* depose; oust. See LAXITY, ABROGATION.

detonate, *v.* set, touch, *or* let off; discharge, explode, blow up, shoot (off), fire; go off. See IMPULSE, LOUDNESS, VIOLENCE.

detonator, *n.* fuse cap, squib, powder, primer, match See VIOLENCE, IMPULSE.

detour, *n.* DEVIATION, digression, excursion; byway, bypass. See AVOIDANCE.

DETRACTION

Nouns—**1**, detraction, derogation, disparagement, depreciation, vilification, obloquy, scurrility, scandal, defamation, aspersion, traducement, slander, calumny, evil-speaking, backbiting; underestimation; libel, lampoon, skit; sarcasm, cynicism, derision, RIDICULE; criticism, invective (see DISAPPROBATION).

2, detractor, derogator, defamer, backbiter, slanderer; lampooner, satirist, traducer, libeler, calumniator, reviler, vituperator, castigator; shrew; reprover, censurer; cynic, critic, caviler, carper. *Colloq.*, knocker.

Verbs—detract, derogate, decry, depreciate, disparage; run down, cry down, sneer at (see CONTEMPT); deride, RIDICULE; criticize, pull to pieces, asperse, cast aspersions, blow upon, bespatter, blacken; vilify, revile, give a dog a bad name, brand, malign, backbite, libel, lampoon, traduce, slander, defame, calumniate, bear false witness against; speak ill of; anathematize, dip the pen in gall, view in a bad light. *Colloq.*, run down, take down a peg, bad-mouth.

Adjectives—detracting, detractory, derogatory, defamatory, disparaging, libelous; scurrilous; abusive; slanderous, calumnious, calumniatory; sarcastic, sardonic, satirical, cynical.

Antonym, see APPROBATION.

detriment, *n.* harm, injury, DANGER, DETERIORATION; LOSS, LIABILITY; discredit, prejudice, disgrace; obstacle, HINDRANCE, impediment. See DISREPUTE.

devaluate, *v.* See DEPRECIATE.

devastate, *v.t.* waste, ravage, desolate, pillage; ruin, raze, destroy, demolish. See DESTRUCTION, DETERIORATION. *Ant.*, PRODUCTION.

develop, *v.* evolve, unfold, mature, grow; CAUSE, bring about, cultivate, produce, amplify. See INCREASE, TEACHING, IMPROVEMENT.

DEVIATION

Nouns—deviation; swerving, obliquation, warp, refraction; flection, sweep; deflection, deflexure; declination; diversion, divergence, digression, departure from, aberration; zigzag; detour, bypass, byroad, circuit; wandering, vagrancy; evagation; oblique motion, sidling, knight's move. See CIRCUITY.

Verbs—**1**, deviate, alter one's course, depart from, turn, trend; bend, curve (see CURVATURE); swerve, heel, bear off; deflect; divert, divert from its course; put on a new scent, shift, shunt, wear, draw aside, crook, warp.

2, stray, straggle; sidle, diverge, part, separate; digress, wander, wind, twist, meander, veer, tack; turn aside, turn a corner, turn away from; wheel, steer clear of; ramble, rove, drift; go astray, go adrift; yaw, dodge; step aside, ease off, make way for, shy; fly off at a tangent; glance off; wheel about, face about; turn to the right about; go out of one's way, lose one's way *or* bearings.

Adjectives—deviating, deviative, aberrant, errant; excursive, discursive; devious, desultory, loose; rambling; stray, erratic, vagrant, undirected; divergent, radial, forked, centrifugal; circuitous, indirect, zigzag; crablike; off one's beat, off the beaten track.

Adverbs—astray from, round about, wide of the mark; to the right about, all manner of ways; circuitously; obliquely, sidling.
Antonym, see DIRECTION.

---

device, *n.* scheme, trick, stratagem, ruse, expedient; badge, emblem, motto; mechanism, contrivance, INSTRUMENT, invention, gadget. See DECEPTION.

devil, *n.* satan, DEMON, fiend; wretch, unfortunate.

devious, *adj.* See DEVIATION, CIRCUITY, DECEPTION.

devise, *v.t.* bequeath, will; produce, invent, fashion, concoct. See GIVING, PRODUCTION, IMAGINATION.

devoid, *adj.* lacking, without, destitute, empty. See ABSENCE, INSUFFICIENCY. *Ant.*, see SUFFICIENCY, COMPLETION.

devote, *v.t.* give (oneself) to, employ (oneself) at; destine, dedicate, consecrate; attend, study. See UNDERTAKING, BUSINESS, NECESSITY, ATTENTION. *Ant.*, see AVOIDANCE.

devotee, *n.* enthusiast, zealot, fanatic, votary, follower, disciple. See AMUSEMENT, DESIRE, PIETY. *Slang*, fan, addict.

devour, *v.t.* eat; wolf; consume, destroy. See FOOD, GLUTTONY, DESTRUCTION, USE.

devout, *adj.* pious, reverent, religious, godly, worshiping, fervent, sincere. See PIETY, FEELING. *Ant.*, see IRRELIGION.

dexterous, *adj.* skillful, adroit, deft, clever. See SKILL. *Ant.*, see UNSKILLFULNESS.

diabolic, *adj.* devilish, demoniac, wicked, impious, malevolent. See DEMON, BADNESS, MALEVOLENCE.

diagnosis, *n.* diagnostics; analysis, examination, explanation; symptomatology, sem(e)iology; conclusion, finding, JUDGMENT. See INTERPRETATION.

diagonal, *adj.* crosswise, slantwise, aslant, oblique; cattycorner; inclined; tilted, pitched, zigzag. See OBLIQUITY.

diagram, *n. & v.* —*n.* PLAN, sketch, chart, blueprint, map. —*v.t.* draw, OUTLINE, layout.

dial, *n.* face, indicator, gauge; disk. See INDICATION.

dialect, *n.* language, diction, tongue; vernacular, idiom, argot, patois, jargon, cant; barbarism, colloquialism. See SPEECH.

dialogue, dialog, *n.* CONVERSATION; speeches, part, lines, script. See DRAMA.

diameter, *n.* BREADTH, THICKNESS, width, caliber, bore. See SIZE.

diamond, *n.* gem(stone), jewel; engagement ring; parallelogram, lozenge, rhomb(oid), rhombus, check. *Slang,* sparkler, ice. See ORNAMENT, ANGULARITY.

diary, *n.* journal, log, chronicle; memoirs. See BOOK, RECORD.

dicker, *n.* bargain, negotiate, haggle; trade, BARTER. See BUSINESS, SALE.

dictate, *v.t.* enjoin, COMMAND, draw up, say for transcription; domineer, browbeat. See ADVICE, ARROGANCE.

dictatorial, *adj.* dogmatic, opinionated, despotic, arbitrary. See CERTAINTY, SEVERITY, ARROGANCE.

dictionary, *n.* wordbook, lexicon, vocabulary. See BOOK.

dictum (*pl.* **dicta**), *n.* saying, MAXIM; decision, judgment; pronouncement. See AFFIRMATION.

die, *v.i.* expire, perish, pass away; demise, cease; fade out. *Slang,* go west, croak, kick the bucket. See DEATH, END.

die, *n.* mold, matrix, punch, thread-cutter, prototype, perforator.

diehard, *adj. & n.* —*adj.* stubborn, obstinate; inflexible, dogmatic. —*n.* reactionary, conservative; fanatic, bigot. See TENACITY, STABILITY.

diet, *n.* parliament, congress; food, aliment, edibles, intake, victuals; regimen. *Slang,* grub, chow. See FOOD, REMEDY, ASSEMBLAGE.

DIFFERENCE

Nouns—difference; variance, variation, variety; diversity, dissimilarity; DISAGREEMENT, odds, incompatibility; DEVIATION; disparity, inequality, distinction, contradistinction; nice distinction, fine distinction, delicate distinction, subtle distinction, subtlety; incongruence, shade of difference, nuance; discordance, dissonance; discrimination; antithesis, contrariness; modification; moods and tenses; different thing, horse of another color. *Colloq.,* different story, something else again; no such thing.

Verbs—be different, differ, vary, mismatch, contrast; divaricate, diverge, deviate, disagree with; differentiate, specialize; vary, modify, CHANGE; discriminate, distinguish.

Adjectives—differing, different, diverse, heterogeneous; distinguishable, varied, modified; diversified, various, divers, all manner of; variform, daedal; incongruous, incompatible; distinctive, characteristic; discriminative; other, another, not the same; unequal, unmatched; widely apart, DISSIMILAR.

Adverbs—differently; otherwise.

Antonym, see IDENTITY.

---

differentiate, *v.t.* discriminate, distinguish, compare, contrast, isolate, particularize. See DIFFERENCE. *Ant.,* see SIMILARITY.

DIFFICULTY

Nouns—**1,** difficulty, difficultness; hardness; impracticability, impossibility; hard work, uphill work; hard task, Herculean task; task of Sisyphus, Sisyphean labor; tough job. *Colloq.,* large order, hard row to hoe.

2, dilemma, horns of a dilemma; embarrassment; perplexity, uncertainty; intricacy; entanglement; crossfire; awkwardness, delicacy, Gordian knot, net, mesh, maze; coil (see CONVOLUTION); nice point, delicate point; vexed question, poser, puzzle, riddle, paradox; hard nut to crack; bone to pick.

3, quandary, strait, pass, pinch, pretty pass, stress, plight, brunt; critical situation, crisis; trial, rub, crux, emergency, exigency; scramble; quagmire, hot water, hornet's nest; sea of troubles; pretty kettle of fish; pickle, stew, imbroglio, mess, ado, impasse, deadlock; fix, *cul de sac*; hitch; stumbling block, HINDRANCE. *Colloq.*, scrape, jam, hole.

Verbs—**1,** be difficult, go against the grain, try one's patience, put one out; put to one's wit's end; go hard with; try one; pose, perplex; bother, nonplus, bring to a deadlock; be impossible.

2, meet with difficulties, labor under difficulties, get into difficulties; labor under a disadvantage; be in difficulty; fish in troubled waters, buffet the waves, swim against the stream *or* tide; have much ado with, have a hard time of it; bear the brunt; grope in the dark, lose one's way.

3, get into difficulties, get into a scrape; bring a hornet's next about one's ears; flounder, boggle, struggle; not know which way to turn (see DOUBT); stick at, stick in the mud, stick fast; come to a standstill. *Colloq.*, put one's foot in it, get all balled up. *Slang*, take it on the chin.

4, render difficult; encumber, embarrass, nonplus, ravel, entangle, involve; put a spoke in the wheel, hinder (see HINDRANCE). *Colloq.*, stump, tree.

Adjectives—**1,** difficult, not easy, hard, tough; troublesome, toilsome, irksome; laborious, onerous, arduous, Herculean, formidable; sooner *or* more easily said than done; difficult *or* hard to deal with; ill-conditioned.

2, awkward, unwieldy, unmanageable; intractable, stubborn, obstinate (see RESOLUTION); perverse, refractory, plaguy, trying, thorny, rugged; knotted, knotty; pathless, trackless, labyrinthine, convoluted (see CONVOLUTION); intricate, complicated, tangled; impracticable, impossible, not feasible; desperate, hopeless; embarrassing, perplexing, uncertain (see DOUBT); at the end of one's rope *or* tether, at one's wits' end, at a standstill; nonplused; stranded, aground, stuck fast; up a tree, at bay, driven into a corner, driven from pillar to post, driven to extremity, driven to the wall; out of one's depth, thrown out. *Colloq.*, in a pickle, floored. *Slang*, behind the eightball, in the soup, in a spot, in Dutch, up the creek.

Adverbs—with difficulty, with much ado; hardly, uphill; against the stream, against the grain; in the teeth of, in a pinch; at long odds.
Antonym, see FACILITY.

DIFFUSENESS

Nouns—diffuseness; amplification, expatiation, enlargement, expansion, inflation; superfluity; dilation, dilating; verbosity, verbiage, cloud *or* flow of words, LOQUACITY; peroration, harangue, REPETITION; tautology, battology; pleonasm, exuberance, redundance; thrice-told tale; prolixity; circumlocution; periphrase, periphrasis; roundabout phrases; episode; expletive; penny-a-lining; richness.

Verbs—be diffuse, be superfluous, be loquacious; run on, descant, expatiate, enlarge, dilate, amplify, expand, inflate; protract; spin, draw, launch *or* branch out; rant; maunder, harp upon; repeat, iterate; dwell upon, insist upon; digress, ramble, beat about the bush, perorate.

Adjectives—diffuse, profuse; wordy, verbose; copious, exuberant, pleonastic, lengthy; longwinded, long-drawn-out; spun out, protracted; prolix; maundering; circumlocutory, periphrastic, roundabout; digressive; discursive; rambling, episodic; flatulent frothy.

Adverbs—diffusely, redundantly, *etc.*, at large, *in extenso*.
Antonym, see CONCISENESS.

dig, *v.* shovel, spade, excavate, grub, delve; labor, speed. See CONCAVITY.

digest, *v. & n.* —*v.t.* prepare, transform; absorb, assimilate; ruminate, ponder, weigh; shorten, abridge, condense. See THOUGHT, CHANGE, ARRANGEMENT, IMPROVEMENT. —*n.* list, catalog; abstract, condensation, compendium. *Ant.,* see WHOLE.

digit, *n.* member, finger, toe; dewclaw; figure, numeral, cipher. See NUMERATION.

dignity, *n.* REPUTE; nobility, eminence; PRIDE, stateliness, decorum; GREATNESS, station, honor.

digress, *v.i.* diverge, ramble, deviate. See DEVIATION, LOQUACITY.

dike, *n.* embankment, levee; ditch. See INCLOSURE.

dilapidated, *adj.* decayed, disintegrating, crumbling, tumbledown, ramshackle. See DETERIORATION. *Ant.,* see NEWNESS.

dilate, *v.* expatiate, descant; stretch, distend, enlarge. See INCREASE. *Ant.,* see LITTLENESS, CONTRACTION.

dilemma, *n.* predicament, perplexity, quandary. See DOUBT, DIFFICULTY.

dilettante, *n.* amateur, enthusiast; dabbler, poetaster; lightweight, poseur, pretender, faker. See TASTE, IGNORANCE.

diligence, *n.* application, industry, assiduity, ACTIVITY.

diluted, *adj.* thin, weak, watery. See IMPOTENCE, WATER.

dimension, *n.* amplitude, area, extent, measurement, SIZE.

diminish, *v.* lessen, reduce, shrink, abridge; wane, dwindle, peter out. See LITTLENESS, CONTRACTION. *Ant.,* see EXPAND, INCREASE.

diminutive, *adj.* small, little, tiny, wee. See LITTLENESS. *Ant.,* see GREATNESS, HEIGHT, SIZE.

DIMNESS

Nouns—dimness, obscurity, shadow, shade, gloom; DARKNESS, OPACITY, partial darkness, partial shadow, eclipse; partial eclipse; dusk, gloaming, twilight, evening, shades of evening; moonlight, moonbeam, moonshine, starlight, candlelight, firelight; paleness, half-light, faintness, nebulosity, glimmer, glimmering, aurora, daybreak, dawn.

Verbs—be dim, grow dim; flicker, twinkle, glimmer; loom, lower; fade, pale, gutter (out), dim, bedim, obscure, blur, cloud, mist; fog, befog; shadow, overshadow.

Adjectives—dim, dull, lackluster, dingy, darkish, dark; obscure, indistinct, faint, shadowed, glassy; cloudy, misty, opaque; muggy, nebulous, nebular; overcast, muddy, lurid, leaden, dun, dirty; looming; pale, colorless.

Antonym, see LIGHT.

---

dimsighted, *adj.* nearsighted, short-sighted, myopic, astigmatic; purblind; night-blind; bleary, red-eyed, peering, squinting; strabismic, blurry; cross-eyed. *Colloq.,* cockeyed, blind as a bat. See OBSCURITY, DARKNESS. *Ant.,* see VISION.

din, *n.* noise, LOUDNESS, SOUND, reverberation, racket; DISCORD, cacophony.

diner, *n.* dining car, luncheonette, lunchroom. *Slang,* eatery. See FOOD.

dingy, *adj.* discolored, grimy, dirty. See DIMNESS. *Ant.,* see LIGHT, COLOR.

dip, *n. & v.* —*n.* plunge, dive; declivity, slope; swim. See OBLIQUITY. —*v.t.* immerse, plunge.

diploma, *n.* certification, COMMISSION, franchise; degree. *Colloq.,* sheepskin. See QUALIFICATION.

diplomacy, *n.* statesmanship, statecraft, negotiation; shuttle diplomacy; finesse, tact, *savoir-faire*; SKILL, CUNNING, shrewdness, strategy.

diplomat, *n.* envoy, ambassador; statesman; foreign-service officer. See CUNNING, COMPROMISE, FLATTERY.

dire, *adj.* appalling, calamitous, fateful, dreadful, ominous; deplorable. See FEAR, ADVERSITY.

direct, *v. & adj.* —*v.t.* guide, lead; regulate, govern, CONDUCT, head, manage, supervise, boss, rule; aim, point; order, COMMAND, prescribe, bid, instruct, teach, coach, prompt; show, lead the way; address. —*adj.* straight, undeviating (see DIRECTION); BLUNT.

DIRECTION

Nouns—**1,** direction, bearing, course, set, drift, tenor, orientation, TENDENCY; incidence; bending, trending, dip, tack, aim; collimation; steering, steerage.

2, point of the compass, cardinal points; north, east, south, west; orient, sunrise; occident, sunset; rhumb, azimuth, line of collimation.

3, line, path, road, range, quarter, line of march; alignment.

4, direction, management, government, CONDUCT, legislation, regulation, guidance; reins, reins of government; supervision, superintendence; surveillance, oversight; control, charge; COUNCIL, command, AUTHORITY; helm, rudder, needle, compass; guiding star, loadstar, lodestar, polestar; cynosure. *Colloq.,* joystick.

5, directorship, presidency, premiership, senatorship, director; chair, portfolio; statesmanship, statecraft, kingcraft; ministry, ministration; administration; stewardship, proctorship; jurisdiction, AGENCY, regime.

Verbs—**1,** direct, bend, trend, tend, verge, incline, dip, determine; point toward; aim at, level at; go toward, steer toward; keep *or* hold a course; be bound for; bend one's steps toward; direct, steer, bend *or* shape one's course; go straight, go straight to the point.

2, ascertain one's direction, orient, get one's bearings, see which way the wind blows; box the compass; follow one's nose.

3, direct, manage, govern, CONDUCT; ORDER, prescribe, cut out work for; head, lead, lead *or* show the way; take the lead, lead on; regulate, guide, steer, pilot; take the helm; have the reins, handle the reins, hold the reins, take the reins; drive; tackle. *Colloq.,* run.

4, superintend, supervise; overlook, control, keep in order, look after, see to, legislate for; administer, ministrate; have care of, have charge of; have *or* take the direction; take over; pull the strings *or* wires; RULE, COMMAND; hold office; preside, take, occupy *or* be in the chair; pull the stroke oar. *Colloq.,* boss.

Adjectives—**1,** direct, straight, undeviating, unswerving, straightforward; directed toward; pointing toward; bound for.

2, directing, managing, governing, *etc.*; hegemonic, dictatorial; governmental, presidential, gubernatorial, mayoral, *etc.*

Adverbs—**1,** directly, directionally, straight, northward, northerly, *etc.*; hither, thither, whither; straight as an arrow; pointblank; in a line with; full tilt at; as the crow flies; before the wind; windward, leeward, in all directions, in all manner of ways. *Colloq.,* every which way.

2, in charge, at the helm of, at the head of; on the throne, in the hands of. *Colloq.,* in the saddle, on top, in the driver's seat, behind the wheel.

Prepositions—through, via, by the way of; toward.

Antonym, see DEVIATION.

directly, *adv.* straightway, immediately, instantly, promptly; bluntly, flatly, unequivocally; expressly; straight. See INSTANTANEITY, DIRECTION.

DIRECTOR

Nouns—**1,** director, manager, governor, rector, comptroller, controller; superintendent, supervisor; overseer, foreman, overlooker; inspector, visitor, ranger, surveyor, ædile, moderator, monitor, taskmaster; MASTER, leader, ringleader, demagogue, conductor, precentor, bellwether, agitator. *Colloq.,* boss, strawboss.

2, head, president; speaker, chair, chairman, -woman, *or* -person; captain, MASTER; superior; mayor; vice president, prime minister, premier;

officer, functionary, minister, official, bureaucrat; officeholder; statesman, strategist, legislator, lawgiver, politician; Minos, Draco; arbiter, JUDGE, board, COUNCIL; secretary of state.

3, vicar, DEPUTY, steward, factor; AGENT, bailiff, middleman; factotum, majordomo, seneschal, housekeeper; shepherd; croupier; proctor, procurator.

4, director, guide, conductor, cicerone, pilot, helmsman, steersman; guiding star, North Star, Polaris, lodestar; driver, Jehu, charioteer.

---

dirge, *n.* requiem, threnody, funeral hymn, elegy. See LAMENTATION.

dirty, *adj.* unclean, filthy, soiled, foul; murky, miry, stormy; vile, sordid, mean; dishonest. See UNCLEANNESS, DIMNESS, IMPROBITY. *Ant.*, see CLEANNESS.

disable, *v.t.* incapacitate, cripple, damage, unfit, maim. See IMPOTENCE.

disadvantage, *n.* drawback, check, HINDRANCE. See EVIL.

DISAGREEMENT

Nouns—**1,** disagreement; discord, discordance; dissonance, dissidence, discrepancy; UNCONFORMITY, incongruity, incongruence; discongruity, misalliance; jarring; DISSENT, dissension, conflict, OPPOSITION; intrusion, interference; disunity.

2, disparity, mismatch, misjoining, disproportion, disproportionateness, variance, DIVERGENCE; repugnance.

3, unfitness, inaptitude, impropriety; inapplicability; inconsistency, irrelevancy, irrelation.

Verbs—disagree; clash, jar, dispute, quarrel, contend (see CONTENTION); interfere, intrude, come amiss; not concern, mismatch.

Adjectives—**1,** disagreeing, discordant, discrepant, incongruous; hostile, repugnant, incompatible, irreconcilable, inconsistent with; unconformable, exceptional; intrusive; disproportionate, unharmonious; unconsonant; divergent.

2, inapt, unapt, inappropriate, improper; unsuited, unsuitable; inapplicable; unfit, unfitting, unbefitting; unbecoming; ill-timed, unseasonable, *mal à propos*, inadmissible; inapposite, irrelevant; uncongenial; ill-assorted, mismatched, misjoined, misplaced; unaccommodating, irreducible, uncommensurable; out of character, out of keeping, out of proportion, out of joint, out of tune, out of place, out of season, out of its element; at odds with, at variance with.

Adverbs—in disagreement, in defiance, in contempt, in spite of; discordantly.

Antonym, see AGREEMENT.

DISAPPEARANCE

Nouns—disappearance; evanescence; eclipse; occultation; DEPARTURE, exit; EGRESS; vanishing point; dissolving views.

Verbs—disappear, vanish, dissolve, fade, melt away, pass, go, avaunt; be gone; leave no trace, evaporate; undergo an eclipse; retire from sight; lose sight of; depart (see DEPARTURE); go up in smoke, fade into thin air.

Adjectives—disappearing, vanishing, evanescent; missing, lost; lost to sight, lost to view; gone.

Antonym, see APPEARANCE.

DISAPPOINTMENT

Nouns—disappointment, sad disappointment, bitter disappointment, frustration; blighted hope, balk; blow; slip 'twixt cup and lip; nonfulfillment of one's hopes; trick of fortune; false *or* vain expectation; forlorn hope; miscalculation; mirage, fool's paradise; disillusion(ment); MISJUDGMENT. See FAILURE, DISCONTENT, REGRET, HOPELESSNESS.

Verbs—be disappointed; not realize one's hopes; look blue; look aghast (see WONDER); find to one's cost; laugh on the wrong side of one's mouth; balk, jilt, bilk; play one false, play one a trick; dash the cup from the lips; tantalize; dum(b)found, DISILLUSION, disgruntle, dissatisfy (see DISCONTENT).

Adjectives—disappointed, disconcerted, aghast; out of one's reckoning; crushed, dashed, *etc.*

Adverbs—disappointing, disappointingly, not up to par.

Antonym, see EXPECTATION, SUCCESS.

DISAPPROBATION

Nouns—**1**, disapprobation, disapproval; improbation; disesteem, disvaluation; odium, DISLIKE.

2, dispraise, discommendation; blame, obloquy; DETRACTION, disparagement, depreciation; denunciation; CONDEMNATION; ostracism, boycott. *Colloq.*, blacklist, blackball.

3, animadversion, reflection, stricture, objection, exception, criticism; hypercriticism, picking, quibbling; sardonic grin, sardonic laugh; sarcasm, insinuation, innuendo; lefthanded compliment; satire; sneer, derision, CONTEMPT; taunt, DISRESPECT. *Colloq.*, knock, slam.

4, cavil, carping, censure, censoriousness; reprehension, remonstrance, expostulation, reproof, reprobation, admonition, reproach; chiding, upbraiding, rebuke, reprimand, castigation, lecture, scolding, trimming; correction, setdown, rap on the knuckles, rebuff; slap, home thrust, hit; frown, scowl, black look; diatribe; jeremiad, tirade, philippic. *Colloq.*, tongue-lashing, blowup, dressing down, rating, talking to. *Slang*, bawling out, what-for, calling down.

5, abuse, vituperation, invective, objurgation, contumely; hard words, cutting words, bitter words; clamor, outcry, hue and cry; hiss, hissing; sibilation, cat-call; execration.

Verbs—**1**, disapprove; DISLIKE; lament (see LAMENTATION); object to, take exception at, be scandalized at, think ill of; view with disfavor, view with jaundiced eyes; disvalue, improbate.

2, frown upon, look grave; knit the brows; shake the head at, shrug the shoulders; turn up the nose (see CONTEMPT); look askance, make a wry face at; set one's face against.

3, dispraise, discommend, disparage; deprecate, speak ill of, not speak well of; condemn; blame; lay blame upon; censure, reproach, pass censure on, reprobate; impugn; remonstrate, expostulate, recriminate; reprehend, chide, admonish; bring to account, call to account, call to order; take to task, reprove, lecture, bring to book; rebuke, correct; reprimand, chastise, castigate, lash, trounce, trim. *Colloq.*, knock, tonguelash, lace into, pick at, jump on, dress down, rip into, jump down one's throat, tell off, roast, haul over the coals, score, lay out. *Slang*, rap, call down, give what-for, jaw, lay into, light into.

4, accuse (see ACCUSATION); impeach, denounce; expose, brand, stigmatize; show up; raise a hue and cry against.

5, execrate, exprobate, look daggers, vituperate; abuse, scold, rate, objurgate, upbraid, fall foul of; jaw; rail, rail at; bark at; anathematize, call names; revile, vilify, vilipend; bespatter; backbite; rave against, fulminate against, exclaim against, protest against, inveigh against, declaim against, cry out against, raise one's voice against; decry; run down; clamor, hiss, hoot, mob, boycott, ostracize; draw up *or* sign a round robin; animadvert upon, reflect upon; look askance at; cast reflection upon, cast a slur upon; insinuate, damn with faint praise.

6, scoff at, point at; twit, taunt (see DISRESPECT); sneer at (see CONTEMPT); satirize, lampoon; defame (see DETRACTION); depreciate, find fault with, criticize, cut up; pull *or* pick to pieces; take exception; cavil, carp at; be censorious, pick holes, make a fuss about, kick against.

7, take down, set down; snub, snap one up, snap a person's head off; give a rap on the knuckles; throw a stone at; have words with.

8, incur disapprobation, incur blame, scandalize, shock, revolt; get a bad name, forfeit one's good name, be under a cloud, bring a hornet's nest about one's ears; be in one's bad books; take blame, stand corrected; have to answer for.

Adjectives—disapprobatory, disapproving, scandalized; disparaging, condemnatory, damnatory, denunciatory, reproachful, abusive, objurgatory, clamorous, vituperative; defamatory (see DETRACTION); satirical, sarcastic, sardonic, cynical, dry, sharp, cutting, biting, severe, withering, trenchant, hard upon; censorious, critical, captious, carping, hypercritical; sparing of praise, grudging of praise; disapproved, in bad odor, unapproved; unblest; at a discount, exploded; weighed in the balance and found wanting; blame-worthy, reprehensible, to blame, worthy of blame; answerable, uncommendable, exceptionable, not to be thought of; bad, vicious (see IMPROBITY). *Colloq.*, in bad, in the doghouse.

Adverbs—with a wry face; reproachfully, *etc.*

Interjections—thumbs down! it won't do! it will never do! God forbid! Heaven forbid! away with! shame! for shame!

Antonym, see APPROBATION.

---

disarm, *v.* lay down weapons, demilitarize, turn swords into plowshares; pull one's teeth; pacify, appease, charm. See PACIFICATION, IMPOTENCE, SOCIALITY.

disaster, *n.* calamity, cataclysm, misfortune, catastrophe, tragedy. See ADVERSITY, EVIL.

disbelief, *n.,* **disbelieve,** *v.t.* See DOUBT.

disburse, *v.t.* pay out, spend, lay out; allot, apportion. See PAYMENT, APPORTIONMENT.

discard, *v.t.* reject, abandon, eliminate, repudiate, throw aside. See REFUSAL, NEGLECT, NULLIFICATION.

discern, *v.t.* espy; discover, perceive, distinguish, detect. See VISION.

discernment, *n.* acumen, sagacity, shrewdness, insight, astuteness; DISCRIMINATION; INTELLIGENCE. *Ant.,* see VACUITY, INSENSIBILITY.

discharge, *v.t.* dismiss, retire; expel, shoot, fire; perform, do; settle, pay; free, acquit. See FREEDOM, VIOLENCE, CONDUCT, PAYMENT, ACQUITTAL.

disciple, *n.* follower, devotee, adherent, pupil. See LEARNING.

discipline, *n.* training, drill, practice; RESTRAINT, control, repression; PUNISHMENT, correction. See TEACHING.

disclaim, *v.t.* disavow, deny, repudiate; disown, renounce. See NULLIFICATION, NEGATION.

DISCLOSURE

Nouns—1, disclosure, divulgence, unveiling, revealing, revealment, revelation; exposition, exposure, exposé; whole truth; telling (see INFORMATION); acknowledgment, admission, concession; avowal; confession, confessional, shrift; dénouement, manifestation, PUBLICATION; clue, hint.

2, DISCOVERY, detection, realization, ascertainment, find, finding, unearthing; explanation, answer; first sight *or* glimpse; new method, *etc.*

Verbs—1, disclose, uncover, discover, unmask, dismask, draw, draw aside, lift *or* raise the veil *or* curtain; unveil, unfold, unseal, break the seal; lay open, lay bare; bring to light; let into the secret; tell, inform (see INFORMATION); breathe, utter, blab, let out, let fall, let drop, let slip; betray; bruit abroad, broadcast; tell tales, tell tales out of school; come out with; give vent to, give utterance to; open the lips, blurt out, vent, hint, intimate, whisper about; speak out, make manifest, make public; disabuse, set right, correct, open the eyes of. *Colloq.*, let on, let the cat out of the bag. *Slang*, spill the beans, peach.

2, acknowledge, allow, concede, grant, admit, own, confess, avow; turn inside out, make a clean breast; declare oneself, show one's hand *or* cards; unburden oneself *or* one's mind; open one's mind, lay bare one's mind; unbosom oneself; say *or* speak the truth; turn King's, Queen's *or* state's evidence. *Colloq.,* let one's hair down, get off one's chest. *Slang,* shoot off one's mouth, come clean, sing.

3, be disclosed, transpire, come to light; come in sight (see APPEAR-ANCE); become known, escape the lips; come, leak *or* crop out; show its face *or* colors; break through the clouds, flash on the mind. *Slang,* come out in the wash.

4, DISCOVER; solve, unravel, smell out. *Colloq.,* spot, dope out.
Adjectives—disclosed, expository, revelatory, *etc.*

Antonym, see CONCEALMENT.

---

discomfort, *n.* uneasiness, distress, annoyance, embarrassment; PAIN, soreness. *Ant.,* see RELIEF.

disconcert, *v.t.* upset, discompose, embarrass; perplex, confuse; frustrate, thwart. See AGITATION, HINDRANCE.

disconnection, *n.* interruption, cessation, break, DISCONTINUANCE, separation, detachment, uncoupling, DISJUNCTION; disengagement, IRRELATION.

disconsolate, *adj.* inconsolable, comfortless, hopeless; melancholy, forlorn, sad. See DEJECTION. *Ant.,* see HOPE, PLEASURE.

DISCONTENT

Nouns—**1,** discontent, discontentment; dissatisfaction; inquietude, vexation, soreness, mortification, heartburning; querulousness, LAMENTATION; hypercriticism. *Slang,* gripe, the blahs.

2, malcontent, grumbler, growler, croaker. *Colloq.,* grouch. *Slang,* griper, grouser, fussbudget, crab.

3, disappointment, frustration; blighted hope; blow; nonfulfillment; vain expectation, disillusionment; mirage, fool's paradise; REGRET.

Verbs—**1,** be discontented, be dissatisfied; quarrel with one's bread and butter; repine; REGRET; take on, take to heart; shrug the shoulders; make a wry face, pull a long face; knit one's brows; look blue, look black, look blank, look glum, cut off one's nose to spite one's face; take in bad part, take ill; fret, chafe, grumble, croak; lament (see LAMENTATION). *Colloq.,* put out, cut up. *Slang,* grouse, gripe.

2, cause discontent, dissatisfy, vex, disappoint, mortify, disconcert, dishearten.

Adjectives—discontented, dissatisfied, unsatisfied, ungratified; dissident; dissenting, malcontent, exigent, exacting, hypercritical; repining, regretful; down in the mouth, morose, dejected (see DEJECTION); in high dudgeon, in the dumps, in bad humor; glum, sulky, sullen; sour, soured, out of humor, out of temper; disappointing; unsatisfactory. *Colloq.,* grumpy, grouchy, sore.

Antonyms, see CHEERFULNESS, PLEASURE.

DISCONTINUANCE

Nouns—discontinuance, discontinuity; DISJUNCTION, disconnection, interruption, break, fracture, flaw, fault, crack, cut; gap, INTERVAL; *cæsura;* broken thread; parenthesis, episode; rhapsody, patchwork; intermission; recurrence, alternation (see REGULARITY). *Colloq.,* letup.

Verbs—be discontinuous, alternate, intermit; discontinue, pause, interrupt; stop, cease; intervene; break in upon; interpose (see BETWEEN); break the thread; disconnect, disjoin; cut off, curtail, suspend, quit, lay off, desist, END.

Adjectives—discontinuous, unsuccessive, broken, interrupted, disconnected, unconnected; parenthetical, episodic; fitful, irregular (see IRREGULARITY); spasmodic, desultory, intermitting, intermittent; alternate, recurrent, periodic; few and far between.

Adverbs—discontinuously, sporadically, at intervals; by snatches, by fits and starts; fitfully.

Antonym, see CONTINUITY.

DISCORD

Nouns—**1,** discord, discordance, disaccord, dissidence, DISAGREEMENT, dissonance; friction; variance, difference, DISSENSION, dissent, schism, feud, fraction; misunderstanding, cross purposes, odds; division, split, rupture, disruption, house divided against itself; disunion, breach; ENMITY, HATE.

2, quarrel, dispute, tiff, controversy, squabble, altercation, words, high words, wrangling, cross questions and crooked answers; polemics, litigation.

3, strife, CONTENTION, WARFARE, outbreak, open rupture, declaration of war; jar, jarring, clash, shock, jostling, broul, brawl, row, racket, hubbub, embroilment, imbroglio, fracas, breach of the peace, scrimmage, rumpus; breeze, squall; riot, disturbance, DISORDER, commotion, AGITATION, donnybrook.

4, subject of dispute, ground of quarrel, battleground, disputed point; bone of contention, bone to pick; apple of discord, *casus belli*; question at issue, vexed question; troublous times; cat-and-dog life.

5, dissonance, cacophony, caterwauling; harshness, STRIDENCY; babel.

Verbs—**1,** be discordant, disagree; clash, far, jostle, pull different ways, conflict, misunderstand, differ, DISSENT; have a bone to pick with.

2, fall out, quarrel, dispute, litigate; controvert (see NEGATION); squabble, wrangle, bicker, nag; spar, have words with, fall foul of; split; break, part company with; declare war; try conclusions, join an issue; pick a quarrel, sow dissension; embroil, entangle, widen the breach; set at odds, pit against.

Adjectives—**1,** discordant; disagreeing, out of tune, ajar, on bad terms; dissenting, unreconciled, unpacified; quarrelsome, unpacific; controversial, polemic, disputatious; factious; litigious, litigant; pettifogging; at odds, at loggerheads, at variance, at issue, at cross purposes, at sixes and sevens, up in arms, in hot water, embroiled; torn, disunited, divisive, disruptive.

2, discordant, dissonant, out of tune, tuneless, unmusical, unmelodious, unharmonious, harsh, cacophonous.

Antonym, see CONCORD.

---

discount, *v. & n.* —*v.t.* rebate, allow, reduce; deduct, lessen, diminish; mark down, lower (the price); disregard, ignore; belittle. —*n.* allowance, qualification; markdown, rebate, refund, deduction; percentage. *Colloq.*, rakeoff, kickback. See DECREASE, CHEAPNESS. *Ant.*, see INCREASE.

discourage, *v.t.* depress, dishearten, dismay; dissuade, deter. See DEJECTION, DISSUASION, FEAR.

discourse, *v.i.* talk, discuss; declaim, hold forth, dissertate. See CONVERSATION, SPEECH.

DISCOURTESY

Nouns—**1,** discourtesy, discourteousness; ill-breeding; rudeness, ill manners, bad manners; uncourteousness, inurbanity; illiberality, incivility; DISRESPECT, insult, INSOLENCE, impudence; barbarism, barbarity, brutality, misbehavior, blackguardism, conduct unbecoming a gentleman, VULGARITY; churlishness, perversity; moroseness, sullenness; sternness, austerity; moodiness, captiousness, IRASCIBILITY; cynicism, tartness, acrimony, acerbity, virulence, asperity.

2, scowl, black look, frown; short answer, rebuff; hard words, contumely; unparliamentary language.

3, bear, brute, boor, churl, blackguard, beast; frump. *Colloq.*, crosspatch, saucebox.

Verbs—be discourteous, be rude; insult (see INSOLENCE); treat with discourtesy; take a name in vain; make bold with, make free with; take a liberty; stare out of countenance, ogle, point at, put to the

blush; cut; turn one's back upon, turn on one's heel; give the cold
shoulder; keep at a distance, keep at arm's length; look coldly upon;
show the door to; answer back, send away with a flea in the ear, add
insult to injury; lose one's temper; sulk; frown, scowl, glower, pout;
snap, snarl, growl.

Adjectives—**1**, discourteous, uncourteous; uncourtly; ill-bred, ill-mannered, disrespectful, ill-behaved, unmannerly, impolite; unpolished, uncivilized, ungentlemanly; unladylike; blackguard; vulgar (see VULGARITY);
indecorous; foul-mouthed, abusive; uncivil, ungracious, unceremonious;
cool; pert, forward, obtrusive, impudent, rude, saucy, precocious.
Colloq., fresh, sassy.

2, repulsive, unaccommodating, unneighborly, ungentle, ungainly; rough,
ragged, bluff, blunt, gruff, churlish, boorish, bearish; brutal, brusque,
stern, harsh, austere, cavalier, tart, sour, crabbed, sharp, short, trenchant, sarcastic, biting, caustic, virulent, bitter, acrimonious, venomous,
contumelious; snarling; curly; perverse; sullen, peevish, irascible (see
IRASCIBILITY).

Antonym, see COURTESY.

---

discover, *v.t.* uncover, reveal, disclose, manifest; find, discern, espy,
descry; see detect, unearth; realize. See DISCLOSURE, LOCATION, INTER-
PRETATION.

discovery, *n.* revelation, DISCLOSURE; detection, first sight *or* glimpse;
unearthing; find, finding; invention, innovation. See LOCATION, NEW-
NESS. *Ant.*, see CONCEALMENT.

discredit, *v.t.* disparage, stigmatize, shame; doubt, disbelieve, impeach.
See DISREPUTE, DOUBT. *Ant.*, see APPROBATION, BELIEF.

discreditable, *adj.* disreputable, disgraceful, reprehensible, shameful,
inglorious. See VICE.

discreet, *adj.* prudent, judicious, careful, wary, cautious. See CAUTION,
CARE. *Ant.*, see RASHNESS.

discretion, *n.* JUDGMENT; tact, taste, finesse. See SENSIBILITY, INTELLI-
GENCE, TASTE.

discrimination, *n.* differentation, DIFFERENCE, distinction; TASTE, judgment, insight, critical perception, discernment; bias, prejudice, EXCLU-
SION. *Ant.*, see INDIFFERENCE.

discursive, *adj.* wandering, rambling, desultory, digressive. See DEVIA-
TION. *Ant.*, see CONCISENESS.

discuss, *v.t.* talk over, debate, canvass, argue, analyze. See AGITATION,
REASONING.

disdain, *n.* scorn, CONTEMPT, ARROGANCE, INSOLENCE, hauteur. *Ant.*,
see RESPECT.

DISEASE

Nouns—**1**, disease, illness, sickness; ailing; morbidity, infirmity, ailment,
indisposition; complaint, DISORDER, malady; distemper; breakdown,
debility, INSANITY; visitation, attack, seizure, stroke, fit, convulsion;
decay, DETERIORATION; motion sickness; jet lag.

2, delicacy, loss of health, invalidation, invalidism, cachexia, atrophy,
marasmus; indigestion, dyspepsia; autointoxication; tuberculosis, consumption, palsy, epilepsy, paralysis, infantile paralysis, poliomyelitis,
muscular dystrophy; paresis; prostration; fever, malaria, typhoid, typhus,
scarlet fever. *Colloq.*, galloping consumption, T.B.

3, sore, ulcer, abscess, boil; pimple, swelling, carbuncle, rot, canker,
cancer, carcinoma, caries, mortification, corruption, gangrene, leprosy,
eruption, rash, breaking out; inflammation.

4, invalid, patient, case; cripple, leper, consumptive, paralytic.

5, pathology, etiology, therapeutics, diagnosis.

6, insalubrity, insalubriousness, unhealthiness; taint, pollution, infection,
contagion, septicity, toxicity, epidemic, endemic; plague, pestilence,
virus, pox.

Verbs—be ill, ail, suffer, labor under, be affected with, be afflicted with; complain of; droop, flag, languish, halt; sicken, peak, pine; gasp; keep one's bed; feign sickness, malinger (see FALSEHOOD); disease, derange, affect, attack; take sick, fall ill, catch, pick up *or* come down with (a disease).

Adjectives—**1,** diseased; ailing, ill, ill of, taken ill, seized with; indisposed, unwell, sick, squeamish, poorly, seedy; laid up, confined, bedridden, invalided, in the hospital, on the sick list, in sick bay (Naut.); out of health, out of sorts; valetudinary. *Slang,* off one's feed, under the weather.

2, unsound, unhealthy; sickly, morose, infirm, drooping, flagging, lame, crippled, halting; withered; palsied, paralytic, dyspeptic, weak (see IMPOTENCE); decrepit; decayed, deteriorated; incurable, hopeless; in declining health; cranky; in a bad way, in danger, prostrate; moribund (see DEATH).

3, insalubrious, unhealthful, morbid, tainted, vitiated, contaminated, poisoned, poisonous; noxious, toxic, septic, virulent; harmful, insanitary. *Antonym,* see HEALTH.

---

disenchant, *v.,* **disenchantment,** *n.* See DISILLUSION.

disengage, *v.t.* cut loose, [set] free, release. See LIBERATION, DISJUNCTION.

disentangle, *n.* extricate, [set] free; untangle, unsnarl; organize, ORDER; comb, card. See DISJUNCTION, LIBERATION.

disfigure, *v.t.* deface, mar, mutilate, deform, BLEMISH.

disgrace, *v.t.* degrade, abase, dishonor, humiliate. See DISREPUTE. *Ant.,* see REPUTE.

disguise, *n.* camouflage, make-up, dissimulation, CONCEALMENT, mask, pretense. See DECEPTION.

disgust, *v. & n.* —*v.t.* nauseate, sicken, revolt, repel. —*n.* aversion, nausea, loathing, abhorrence. See HATE, PAIN.

dish, *n.* tableware, plate, saucer, *etc.*; serving; specific food, recipe. See RECEPTACLE.

dishonest, *adj.* untrue, untrustworthy, deceitful, false, cheating, fraudulent, crooked. See FALSEHOOD, IMPROBITY. *Ant.,* PROBITY.

dishonor, *n. & v.* —*n.* treachery, infamy, perfidy; infidelity, adultery; DISRESPECT, DISREPUTE, disgrace. See IMPROBITY, WRONG. —*v.t.* See DISGRACE.

disillusion, *n. & v.* —*n.* disillusionment, disenchantment, revelation; DISAPPOINTMENT, cynicism, REGRET. *Colloq.,* comedown. —*v.t.* disenchant, disabuse, remove the scales from one's eyes, enlighten; disappoint, puncture one's balloon, pour cold water on, deflate, bring down to earth. *Colloq.,* debunk. See DISCLOSURE, TRUTH, ADVICE.

disincline, *v.t.* dissuade, indispose, discourage. See DISLIKE, DISSUASION.

disinfect, *v.t.* sterilize, sanitize, purify, fumigate, cleanse. See CLEANNESS.

disinherit, *v.t.* disown, deprive, cut off. See TAKING.

disintegrate, *v.* break up, separate, decompose; decay, decompose, crumble, dissolve, fall apart. See DISJUNCTION, DECOMPOSITION. *Ant.,* see WHOLE, PROBITY.

DISINTERESTEDNESS

Nouns—disinterestedness; generosity; unselfishness, liberality, liberalism; BENEVOLENCE; elevation, loftiness of purpose, exaltation, magnanimity; chivalry, heroism, sublimity, altruism devotion; self-denial, -abnegation, -sacrifice *or* -immolation; stoicism, martyrdom, suttee; labor of love.

Verbs—be disinterested, be generous, devote oneself, make a sacrifice, put oneself in the place of others; do as one would be done by.

Adjectives—disinterested; unselfish; self-denying, self-sacrificing, devoted; generous; handsome, liberal, noble; noble-minded, high-minded; high, elevated, lofty, exalted, spirited, stoical, magnanimous, large-hearted, chivalrous, heroic, altruistic, sublime.

Antonym, see SELFISHNESS.

DISJUNCTION

Nouns—1, disjunction, disconnection, disunity, disunion, disassociation, disengagement; abstraction, abstractedness; isolation; insularity, insulation; oasis; separateness, severalty; DISPERSION, APPORTIONMENT.

2, separation; parting, detachment, segregation; DIVORCE; elision; *cæsura*, division, subdivision, break, fracture, rupture; compartition; dismemberment, disintegration, dislocation; luxation; severance, disseverance; scission, rescission, abscission; laceration; disruption; avulsion, divulsion; section, resection, cleavage; dissection; DECOMPOSITION.

3, fissure, breach, rent, split, rift, crack, slit, incision, fission.

4, discontinuity; interruption, break, gap, interval, fracture; parenthesis, intermission, cesura; alternation. See DISCONTINUANCE.

5, displacement, dislocation, transposition, dislodgement, removal, EJECTION; displaced person, D.P., refugee, exile; fish out of water.

Verbs—1, be disjoined, come off, fall off, fall to pieces; peel off; get loose.

2, disjoin, disconnect, disengage, disunite, dissociate, DIVORCE, part, detach, separate, cut off, rescind, segregate; set apart, keep apart; insulate, isolate; cut adrift; loose(n), unloose, undo, unbind, unchain, unlock, unpack, unravel; disentangle; set free, liberate.

3, sunder, divide, subdivide, sever, dissever, abscind; cut; incise; saw, chop, cleave, rive, rend, split, splinter, chip, crack, snap, break, tear, burst; rend asunder, wrench, rupture, shatter, shiver; hack, hew, slash; whittle. *Colloq.*, smash to smithereens.

4, cut up, carve, dissect, anatomize; take to pieces, pull to pieces, pick to pieces; disintegrate, dismember, disbranch, disband, disperse, displace, dislocate, disjoint; break up; mince; comminute, pulverize; apportion (see APPORTIONMENT).

Adjectives—disjoined, discontinuous, multipartite, abstract; disjunctive; isolated, insular, separate, disparate, discrete, apart, asunder, far between, loose, free; unattached, unannexed, unassociated; distinct; adrift; straggling; unconnected; scissile, divisible.

Adverbs—disjunctively, separately; one by one, severally, apart; adrift, asunder, in twain; in the abstract, abstractedly.

Antonym, see JUNCTION.

DISLIKE

Nouns—dislike, distaste, disinclination; reluctance; backwardness, UNWILLINGNESS; repugnance, disgust, queasiness, turn, nausea, loathing; averseness, abomination, antipathy, abhorrence, horror; ENMITY, HATE, hatred, detestation, animosity, RESENTMENT; phobia (see FEAR).

Verbs—1, dislike, mislike, mind, object to; not care for; have, conceive *or* entertain *or* take a dislike to; have no taste for, have no use for, have no stomach for; shun, avoid (see AVOIDANCE); eschew; shrink from, recoil from; shrug shoulders at, shudder at, turn up the nose at, look askance at; abhor; HATE; have enough of, be satiated (see SATIETY).

2, cause *or* excite dislike; disincline, repel, sicken; make sick; turn one's stomach, nauseate, disgust, shock, go against the grain; stick in the throat; make one's blood run cold; pall.

Adjectives—disliking, averse, loath, adverse; shy of, sick of, disinclined; queasy; disliked, uncared for, unpopular; out of favor; repulsive, repugnant, repellent; abhorrent, insufferable, fulsome, nauseous, sickening, abominable, detectable; loathsome, offensive; disgusting, disagreeable.

Antonym, see APPROBATION, LOVE.

dislocate, *v.t.* displace, disarrange; disjoin, disarticulate. See DISJUNC-
TION. *Ant.*, see ARRANGEMENT, LOCATION.
dislodge, *v.t.* displace, topple; expel, evict, drive out. See EJECTION.
Ant., see LOCATION, RECEIVING.
disloyal, *adj.* unfaithful, false; untrue, inconstant. See IMPROBITY.
Ant., see PROBITY.
dismal, *adj.* cheerless, depressing, gloomy; somber, funereal. See DARK-
NESS, DEJECTION. *Ant.*, see LIGHT, HOPE.
dismantle, *v.t.* take apart; raze, demolish; disrobe, undress. See DE-
STRUCTION, DIVESTMENT. *Ant.*, see PRODUCTION.
dismay, *n. & v.t.* —*n.* consternation, terror; discouragement. See FEAR,
DEJECTION. —*v.t.* appall; discourage. *Ant.*, see HOPE, CHEERFULNESS.
dismember, *v.t.* disjoint, disarticulate, dissect, tear limb from limb, cut
to pieces, mangle. See DECOMPOSITION, DISJUNCTION.
dismiss, *v.t.* send away; discharge, liberate, disband; cancel (*Law*).
See NULLIFICATION, EJECTION, FREEDOM. *Ant.*, see RECEIVING.

DISOBEDIENCE

Nouns—**1,** disobedience, insubordination, contumacy; infraction, infringement; naughtiness; violation, noncompliance; nonobservance.
2, revolt, rebellion, outbreak, rising, uprising, insurrection, riot, tumult,
DISORDER; strike, resistance; barring out; defiance; mutiny, mutinousness,
mutineering; sedition, treason; *lèse majesté*; violation of law (see ILLE-
GALITY); defection; secession.
3, insurgent, mutineer, rebel, revolter, rioter, traitor, communist, anarchist, demagogue; seceder, runagate, brawler.
Verbs—disobey, violate, infringe; shirk (see NEGLECT); defy; riot, run
riot, run amuck, fly in the face of; take the law into one's own hands;
kick over the traces; strike, resist (see OPPOSITION); secede; mutiny,
rebel; turn restive; champ at the bit, strain at the leash.
Adjectives—disobedient; uncomplying, uncompliant; unsubmissive,
naughty, unruly, ungovernable; insubordinate, refractory, contumacious;
recalcitrant; resisting (see OPPOSITION); lawless, mutinous, seditious,
insurgent, riotous, rebellious, defiant.
Antonym, see OBEDIENCE.

DISORDER

Nouns—**1,** disorder, DERANGEMENT; irregularity; anomaly, UNCONFORM-
ITY, anarchy, anarchism; untidiness, disunion; DISCORD; confusion, con-
fusedness; disarray, jumble, huddle, litter, lumber; mess, mash, mishmash, muddle, hash, hodgepodge; dishevelment; laxity; imbroglio,
chaos, medley.
2, complexity; complexness, complication, implication; intricacy, intrica-
tion; perplexity; network, maze, labyrinth; wilderness, jungle, involution, entanglement; coil, CONVOLUTION, tangled skein, knot, Gordian
knot, wheels within wheels.
3, turmoil, ferment, AGITATION, to-do, trouble, row, disturbance, convulsion, tumult, uproar, riot, rumpus, scramble, fracas, embroilment,
mêlée, rough and tumble; whirlwind; Babel, Saturnalia, Donnybrook
Fair; confusion twice confounded.
Verbs—be disorderly; put out of order; derange; ravel, ruffle, rumple,
mess, muss, dishevel.
Adjectives—**1,** disorderly, orderless; out of order, out of place, irregular,
desultory; anomalous, straggling; unmethodical; unsymmetric, unsys-
tematic; untidy, slovenly; dislocated; promiscuous, indiscriminate;
chaotic, anarchical; unarranged, disarranged; confused; deranged; topsy-
turvy, shapeless; disjointed, out of joint; all over the place.
2, complex, confused, intricate, complicated, perplexed, involved, labyrinthine, entangled, knotted, tangled, inextricable; tumultuous, riotous,

violent (see VIOLENCE). *Colloq.*, out of kilter *or* whack; helter-skelter, mussy, messy, sloppy. *Slang*, balled *or* fouled up.

Adverbs—irregularly, *etc.*, by fits and starts; pell-mell; in a ferment; at sixes and sevens, at cross purposes; upside down. *Colloq.*, higgledy-piggledy; harum-scarum, willy-nilly, every which way.

Antonym, see ORDER.

disorganize, *v.t.* upset, disrupt, disorder, derange, discourage. See DIS-ORDER. *Ant.*, see ARRANGEMENT.

disown, *v.t.* disinherit; disclaim, repudiate, deny, disavow. See NEGA-TION.

disparage, *v.t.* depreciate, belittle, decry, run down; asperse, traduce. See DISAPPROBATION, DISRESPECT. *Ant.*, see APPROBATION.

dispatch, *v. & n.* —*v.t.* send; expedite; kill, accomplish. See VELOCITY, KILLING. —*n.* message, telegram; promptness, expedition; haste, speed; consummation, killing. See INFORMATION, ACTIVITY, HASTE, COMPLE-TION. *Ant.*, see SLOWNESS.

dispel, *v.t.* scatter, dissipate, disperse, dissolve. See DESTRUCTION, DIS-JUNCTION. *Ant.*, see ASSEMBLAGE.

dispense, *v.t.* distribute, apportion, sell, administer. See GIVING, APPOR-TIONMENT. *Ant.*, see ASSEMBLAGE.

DISPERSION

Nouns—dispersion, DISJUNCTION, DIVERGENCE; scattering, dissemination, diffusion, dissipation, distribution, APPORTIONMENT, spread, disbanding.

Verbs—disperse, scatter, sow, distribute, disseminate, diffuse, shed, spread, overspread, dispense, disband, disembody, dismember, appor-tion; blow off, let out, dispel, cast forth, strew, cast, sprinkle; issue, deal out, retail, intersperse; cast adrift; scatter to the winds; sow, broadcast; spread like wildfire.

Adjectives—dispersed, disseminated, broadcast, sporadic, widespread; epidemic (see GENERALITY); adrift, stray; disheveled, streaming.

Adverb—here and there; to the four winds.

Antonym, see ASSEMBLAGE.

DISPLACEMENT

Nouns—**1,** displacement, misplacement, dislocation (see DISPLACEMENT); transposition; EJECTION, dislodgment, exile (see SECLUSION); removal (see TRANSPORTATION); fish out of water; dispossession, disestablish-ment.

2, displaced person, D.P.; refugee, evacuee; Ishmael, outcast; exile, émigré. See EXCLUSION.

Verbs—displace, dislocate, displant, dislodge, disestablish; exile, seclude, transpose; set aside, move, remove; take away, take off; unload, empty (see EJECTION); TRANSFER, dispel; disarrange, DISORDER; vacate, depart (see DEPARTURE); dispossess, disestablish.

Adjectives—displaced, misplaced, dislocated, unplaced, unhoused, un-harbored, unestablished, unsettled; dispossessed, homeless; out of place; out of its element.

Antonym, see LOCATION.

display, *n. & v.* —*n.* show, exhibition, pomp, OSTENTATION. —*v.t.* show, manifest, exhibit, disclose; flaunt, show off. See EVIDENCE. *Ant.*, see CONCEALMENT.

displease, *v.t.* offend, vex, annoy, irritate, disturb. See PAIN. *Ant.*, please.

disposed, *adj.* tending, inclined, prone, bent (upon), fain. See WILL.

disposition, *n.* ARRANGEMENT, classification, disposal, distribution, state; temperament, temper, nature, spirit; inclination, TENDENCY, propensity.

dispossess, *v.t.* evict; confiscate, usurp. See TAKING.

disprove, *v.t.* refute, confute, explode, defeat, negative. See NEGATION. *Ant.,* see EVIDENCE.

dispute, *v. & n.* —*v.t.* contradict, controvert, DOUBT, contest, question; argue, debate, quarrel, bicker. See NEGATION, REASONING, DISAGREEMENT, CONTENTION. —*n.* debate, argument, DISAGREEMENT. *Ant.,* see AGREEMENT.

disqualify, *v.t.* disable, unfit, incapacitate, disfranchise. See IMPOTENCE.

disquiet, *n.* disquietude, AGITATION, uneasiness, anxiety, unrest; commotion.

disregard, *v.t.* ignore, neglect, overlook; disobey, defy; underestimate. See DISRESPECT, NEGLECT. *Ant.,* see RESPECT, ATTENTION.

DISREPUTE

Nouns—**1,** disrepute, disreputableness, discredit, ill repute, bad name, bad odor, ill favor; DISAPPROBATION; ingloriousness, derogation, abasement, debasement; abjectness; degradation, odium, obloquy, opprobrium, ignominy; dishonor, disgrace; shame, humiliation; scandal, baseness, vileness, turpitude, IMPROBITY, infamy.

2, tarnish, taint, defilement, pollution, stigma, stain, blot, spot, brand, reproach, imputation, slur; badge of infamy, blot on one's escutcheon; bend *or* bar sinister.

Verbs—**1,** be in disrepute, be discredited, incur disgrace, have a bad name; disgrace oneself; stoop, foul one's own nest; look foolish, cut a sorry figure; slink away.

2, shame, disgrace, put to shame, dishonor, reflect dishonor upon; be a reproach to, derogate from; stigmatize, tarnish, stain, blot, sully, taint; discredit; degrade, debase, defile; expel (see PUNISHMENT); impute shame to, brand, post, vilify, defame, slur, give a bad name; disbar, unfrock, excommunicate.

Adjectives—**1,** disreputable, shameful; disgraceful, discreditable, despicable, heinous, questionable; unbecoming, unworthy; derogatory, degrading, humiliating, ignoble, *infra dignitatem*, undecorous; scandalous, infamous, too bad, deplorable, unmentionable; ribald, opprobrious; arrant, shocking, outrageous, notorious; odious, execrable; ignominious, scrubby, dirty, abject, vile, beggarly, pitiful, low, mean, knavish, shabby, base, dishonorable (see IMPROBITY).

2, in disrepute, at a discount, under a cloud, out of favor, down in the world, down at heel; stigmatized, discredited, disgraced; inglorious, nameless, obscure, unnoticed, unhonored, unglorified.

Antonym, see REPUTE.

DISRESPECT

Nouns—**1,** disrespect, disesteem, disestimation, disfavor, DISREPUTE, disparagement, DISAPPROBATION; DETRACTION; irreverence; slight, NEGLECT; superciliousness, CONTEMPT, contumely; affront, dishonor, insult, indignity, outrage, DISCOURTESY; practical joking, left-handed compliment, scurrility, scoffing, derision; mockery, irony, RIDICULE, sarcasm.

2, hiss, hoot, gibe, flout, jeer, taunt, sneer, quip, slap in the face. *Slang,* razzberry.

Verbs—**1,** hold in disrespect, despise (see CONTEMPT); disregard, slight, trifle with, set at naught, pass by, push aside, overlook, turn one's back upon, laugh up one's sleeve; spurn, scorn.

2, be disrespectful, be discourteous, treat with disrespect, set down, browbeat; dishonor, desecrate; insult, affront, outrage; speak slightingly of; disparage (see DISAPPROBATION); call names, drag through the mud, point at, indulge in personalities; bite the thumb.

3, deride, scoff, sneer, laugh at, snigger, RIDICULE, gibe, mock, jeer, taunt, twit, roast, burlesque, laugh to scorn (see CONTEMPT); make game of, make a fool of; play a practical joke; lead one a dance; scout, hiss, hoot, mob. *Slang,* razz, give the razz(berry).

Adjectives—disrespectful; irreverent; disparaging (see DISAPPROBATION); insulting, supercilious (see CONTEMPT); rude, derisive, sarcastic; scurrilous, contumelious; unrespected, unenvied, unsaluted, unregarded, disregarded.

Antonym, see RESPECT.

---

disrobe, *n.* undress (see DIVESTMENT).

disrupt, *v.* disorganize; disturb, upset; turn inside-out *or* upside-down; mess up, play havoc with. See DESTRUCTION, DISJUNCTION, DISCONTINUITY.

dissatisfy, *v.t.* DISCONTENT, displease, disappoint; vex, annoy, anger. *Ant.*, see PLEASURE.

dissect, *v.t.* cut up, anatomize; examine, analyze. See DISJUNCTION, INQUIRY.

dissemble, *v.* pretend, feign, dissimulate; camouflage, conceal. See CONCEALMENT, FALSEHOOD. *Ant.*, see TRUTH.

disseminate, *v.* distribute; see DISPERSION.

DISSENT

Nouns—**1,** dissent, dissension, dissidence, DISCORD, discordance, DISAGREEMENT, nonagreement; difference *or* diversity of opinion; UNCONFORMITY; protestantism, recusancy, schism; disaffection; secession (see RELINQUISHMENT), apostasy, recantation (see CHANGEABLENESS); DISCONTENT, caviling; protest, objection, expostulation, demur, exception, drawback; contradiction (see NEGATION); noncompliance (see REFUSAL).

2, dissentient, dissenter; recusant, schismatic, nonconformist; protestant, sectarian.

Verbs—dissent, demur; call in question, DOUBT; differ, beg to differ, disagree, contradict (see NEGATION); say no, refuse assent, refuse to admit; cavil, object, quibble, protest, raise one's voice against, take issue; repudiate; scruple; shake the head, shrug the shoulders; look askance; secede (see RELINQUISHMENT); recant (see CHANGEABLENESS). *Colloq.*, kick.

Adjectives—dissenting, dissident, dissentient; discordant, negative (see NEGATION), unconsenting, refusing (see REFUSAL); noncontent; protestant, recusant; unconvinced, unconverted; sectarian, denominational, schismatic; unavowed, unacknowledged; out of the question; discontented (see DISCONTENT); unwilling.

Adverbs—dissentingly, at variance, at issue with; under protest.

Interjections—God forbid! not for the world! by no means! pardon me! *Colloq.*, not on your life! no sir(r)ee! not by a long shot!

Antonym, see ASSENT.

---

dissertation, *n.* lecture, sermon, tract; discussion, disquisition; treatise, discourse; exposition, study; critique, criticism; essay, theme, thesis; comment, commentary; explanation. See REASONING, INTERPRETATION, INQUIRY.

disservice, *n.* disfavor, WRONG, INJUSTICE; detriment, DETRACTION.

dissimilarity, *n.* DIFFERENCE, differentness; unlikeness, unequality, variance, divergence, dissimilitude; uniqueness, novelty, originality; no comparison. *Ant.*, see SIMILARITY, COMPARISON.

dissipate, *v.t.* scatter, dispel, diffuse; WASTE, squander. *Ant.*, see PRESERVATION.

dissipated, *adj.* profligate, debauched, dissolute, licentious. See INTEMPERANCE, IMPURITY. *Ant.*, see PURITY.

dissolute, *adj.* vicious, dissipated. *Ant.*, see PROBITY, GOODNESS.

dissolve, *v.* destroy, liquefy, break up, end; melt, vanish, evaporate, fade, disintegrate. See DECOMPOSITION.

dissonance, *n.* DISCORD, cacophony, inharmoniousness; DISAGREEMENT, dissension. *Ant.*, see AGREEMENT, CONCORD.

DISSUASION

Nouns—dissuasion, determent, deterrent, dehortation, expostulation, remonstrance, admonition, warning; DEPRECATION; discouragement, damper, cold water, wet blanket; RESTRAINT; curb (see PRISON); check, HINDRANCE; ADVICE.

Verbs—dissuade, dehort, cry out against, remonstrate, expostulate, warn; advise; disincline, indispose, discourage, dispirit, dishearten, disenchant; deter; hold back, keep back, restrain; repel; turn aside (see DEVIATION); wean from; act as a drag, hinder; throw cold water on, damp, cool, chill, blunt, calm, quiet, quench; deprecate.

Adjectives—dissuading, dissuasive; dehortatory, expostulatory; monitory.

Antonym, see BELIEF, CAUSE.

DISTANCE

Nouns—distance; SPACE, remoteness, farness; elongation; offing, background; removedness; perspective; parallax; reach, span, stride; MEASUREMENT; outpost, outskirt; horizon; aphelion; foreign parts, *ultima Thule*, *ne plus ultra*, antipodes, interstellar space; long range, giant's stride. *Colloq.*, jumping-off place.

Verbs—be distant; extend to, stretch to, reach to, spread to; range; remain at a distance; keep away, stand away, keep off, stand aloof, stand clear of.

Adjectives—distant, remote, telescopic; far off, faraway; wide of; stretching to; yon, yonder; ulterior, transmarine, transpontine, transatlantic, transpacific, transalpine; tramontane; ultramontane, ultramundane; hyperborean, antipodean; inaccessible, out of the way; unapproached, unapproachable; incontiguous. *Colloq.*, God-forsaken; to hell and gone; back of beyond.

Adverbs—far off, far away; afar, off, away, a long way off; aloof; wide of, clear of; out of the way, out of reach; abroad, yonder, farther, further, beyond; far and wide, over the hills and far away; from pole to pole, to the ends of the earth, out of this world; out of hearing, nobody knows where; wide of the mark, a far cry to; apart, asunder; wide apart, wide asunder; at arm's length.

Antonym, see NEARNESS.

---

distasteful, *adj.* unpalatable, unappetizing, unattractive, unpleasant, uninviting, disagreeable, offensive. See PAIN, SOURNESS. *Ant.*, see PLEASURE.

distend, *v.t.* stretch, expand, dilate, inflate, swell. See INCREASE. *Ant.*, see CONTRACTION.

distill, *v.* extract, express, concentrate; drip, trickle, evaporate.

distinct, *adj.* separate, unattached, discrete; definite, explicit; sharp, clear, well defined. See DISJUNCTION, VISION. *Ant.*, see DIMNESS.

distinction, *n.* DIFFERENCE, separateness, variation; DISCRIMINATION; dignity, refinement, ELEGANCE; eminence, importance, REPUTE. *Ant.*, see SIMILARITY.

distinguish, *v.t.* differentiate, characterize; separate, discriminate; discern, pick out. See DIFFERENCE, TASTE, VISION.

distinguished, *adj.* notable, renowned, celebrated, famous, eminent. See REPUTE. *Ant.*, see MEDIOCRITY.

DISTORTION

Nouns—**1,** distortion, detortion, contortion; twist, torque, torsion; crookedness, OBLIQUITY; grimace; deformity, malformation, malconformation; monstrosity, misproportion, asymmetry (see FORM), anamorphosis; UGLINESS; mutilation, disfigurement; talipes, clubfoot.
2, perversion, misinterpretation, misconstruction.
3, misinterpretation, misrepresentation, FALSEHOOD, EXAGGERATION, perversion.

Verbs—1, distort, contort, twist, warp, wrest, writhe, deform, misshape, mutilate, disfigure.

2, pervert, misinterpret, misconstrue.

Adjectives—distorted, contorted, out of shape, irregular, unsymmetrical, awry, wry, askew, crooked; not true, not straight; on one side, deformed, misshapen, misbegotten, misproportioned, ill-proportioned; ill-made; monstrous, grotesque; humpbacked, hunchbacked; bandy, bandylegged, bowlegged; knockneed; taliped, splay-footed, clubfooted; round-shouldered; snub-nosed; stumpy, short (see SHORTNESS); gaunt, thin; bloated.

Adverbs—distortedly, crookedly, *etc.*; all manner of ways.

Antonym, see FORM.

---

distract, *v.t.* divert, turn aside; confuse, madden; entertain, amuse. See DEVIATION, AMUSEMENT.

distracted, *adj.* agitated, frenzied, frantic; distraught, bewildered. See EXCITEMENT, UNCERTAINTY.

distress, *n. & v.* —*n.* discomfort, trouble, DANGER, PAIN, affliction, trial, privation, harassment, grief, anxiety. See POVERTY, ADVERSITY. *Ant.*, see COMFORT, SAFETY. —*v.t.* trouble, harrow, PAIN, worry, grieve; hurt.

distribute, *v.t.* allot, parcel, apportion; disperse, scatter; divide, classify. See APPORTIONMENT, ARRANGEMENT. *Ant.*, see ASSEMBLAGE.

district, *n.* REGION, province, ward, quarter, section, tract, bailiwick.

distrust, *n. & v.* —*n.* DOUBT, suspicion, disbelief. —*v.t.* suspect, disbelieve, mistrust. See DOUBT, FEAR.

disturb, *v.t.* worry, agitate, trouble; disarrange, confuse; interrupt, unsettle. See AGITATION, DISJUNCTION.

DISUSE

Nouns—1, disuse, forbearance, abstinence; obsoleteness, obsolescence; RELINQUISHMENT, discontinuance, cessation.

2, desuetude, disusage, want of habit, want of practice, unaccustomed-ness, newness to; nonprevalence.

Verbs—1, not use; do without, dispense with, let alone, not touch, for-bear, abstain, spare, waive, neglect; keep back, reserve.

2, lay up, lay by, lay on the shelf; shelve; set aside, put aside, lay aside; obsolesce, supersede.

3, discard (see EJECTION); abandon, dismiss, give warning; throw aside, relinquish; make away with, destroy (see DESTRUCTION); cast overboard; cast to the winds; jettison, dismantle (see USELESSNESS).

4, be unaccustomed to, break a habit, wean oneself of a habit.

Adjectives—1, disused, not used, unemployed, unapplied, undisposed of, unspent, unexercised, untouched, untrodden, unessayed, ungathered, un-culled; uncalled for, not required; run down, obsolete, obsolescent.

2, unaccustomed, unused, unwonted, unseasoned, unhabituated, un-trained, new, green, unskilled (see UNSKILLFULNESS); unhackneyed; un-usual (see UNCONFORMITY); nonobservant.

Antonym, see USE.

---

ditch, *n.* channel, trench, gully, canal, moat, watercourse. See FURROW.

dither, *n.* fluster, twitter, flurry, confusion. See AGITATION, EXCITEMENT.

ditto, *adv.* as before, again, likewise; in the same way. See COPY.

dive, *n.* plunge, dip, swoop; nose dive, power dive. See DESCENT.

diverge, *v.i.* separate, branch off, fork; sunder; divaricate, deviate; differ, vary, disagree; veer, swerve; detach; go off at a tangent; radiate. See DIFFERENCE, DEVIATION. *Ant.*, see AGREEMENT.

divergence, *n.* DIFFERENCE; DEVIATION; dispersion; fork, forking, branch-ing off; ramification, variation; DISAGREEMENT; divergency. *Ant.*, see AGREEMENT.

diversion, *n.* AMUSEMENT, entertainment, divertisement, pastime, recrea-tion, sport; variation, CHANGE.

diversity, *n.* DIFFERENCE, dissimilarity. VARIATION, variety. *Ant.*, see CONFORMITY.

divert, *v.t.* amuse, beguile, entertain; distract, turn aside. See AMUSEMENT, DEVIATION.

DIVESTMENT

Nouns—divestment, divestiture; taking off, undressing; nudity; bareness, undress, dishabille; nudation, denudation; decortication, depilation, excoriation, desquamation; mo(u)lting; exfoliation; ecdysis. *Colloq.*, the altogether, the buff, the raw.

Verbs—**1,** divest; uncover, denude, bare, strip; undress, disrobe (see CLOTHING); uncoif; dismantle; put off, take off, cast off; doff; slough off. **2,** peel, pare, decorticate, excoriate, skin, scalp, flay; expose, lay open; exfoliate, mo(u)lt; cast the skin.

Adjectives—divested, denuded, bare, naked, shorn, nude; undressed, undraped; exposed, ecdysiastic, in dishabille; threadbare, ragged; in a state of nature, in one's birthday suit, with nothing on, stark naked; bald, bald-headed, bald as an egg; bare as the back of one's hand; out at elbows; barefoot; leafless, napless, hairless, beardless, cleanshaven. *Colloq.*, in the buff, in the altogether. *Slang*, raw, in the raw.

Antonym, see CLOTHING.

divide, *v.* separate; partition, allot, assign; separate, split, part. *Colloq.*, split up. See APPORTIONMENT, DISJUNCTION.

dividend, *n.* share, PART, portion; interest, bonus. *Slang*, plum. See APPORTIONMENT, ADDITION.

divination, *n.* PREDICTION, prophecy, augury, guess; SORCERY.

divine, *adj.* godlike, superhuman, celestial, holy, spiritual; religious. See DEITY, RELIGION.

division, *n.* severance, separation, DISCORD, DISJUNCTION, schism; apportionment, partitionment; PART, section; unit, group. *Ant.*, see UNITY.

DIVORCE

Nouns—**1,** divorce, divorcement, separation, annulment, parting of the ways. *Colloq.*, split-up.
2, divorcé, divorcée, grass widow, grass widower.

Verbs—divorce, get a divorce; separate, break up. *Colloq.*, split up; go to Reno.

Antonym, see MARRIAGE.

divulge, *v.t.* disclose, reveal, let slip, tell. *Slang*, spill the beans, let the cat out of the bag. See DISCLOSURE. *Ant.*, see SECRET.

dizzy, *adj.* giddy, lightheaded. *Slang*, silly, mixed-up, flighty. See INSANITY.

do, *v.t.* perform, achieve, contrive, manage; solve, finish, work out; serve, render. See ACTION, COMPLETION, PRODUCTION. *Colloq.*, swindle, defraud.

docile, *adj.* gentle, tractable, teachable, submissive. See ASSENT. *Ant.*, see UNCONFORMITY.

dock, *n. & v.* —*n.* dockage, mooring; berth, wharf, pier, slip, quay; anchorage, marina, boat *or* ship's basin; drydock, jetty; harbor, haven, prisoner's dock, witness stand. See SUPPORT. —*v.* cut, trim, curtail, reduce, deduct; fine, penalize. See SHORTNESS, PUNISHMENT.

docket, *n.* calendar, agenda, register. See RECORD, INDICATION.

doctor, *n.* physician, surgeon; learned man, sage. See REMEDY.

doctrine, *n.* creed, theory, dogma, tenet, principle. See BELIEF.

document, *n.* INSTRUMENT, writing, record, manuscript.

dodge, *v.* elude, evade, escape, avoid; duck, serve. See DEVIATION, AVOIDANCE.

dog, *n.* canine, cur, whelp; puppy, pup, tyke, bitch, slut. See ANIMAL. *Slang,* pooch, mutt.

dogma, *n.* doctrine, tenet, BELIEF.

dogmatic, *adj.* dictatorial, imperious, arrogant, peremptory, positive, opinionated. See CERTAINTY, MISJUDGMENT.

doldrums, *n.pl.* lull, calm; depression, despondency, DEJECTION. *Colloq.,* blues.

dole, *n.* alms, pittance. *Slang,* handout. See INSUFFICIENCY.

doll, *n.* dolly, plaything; kewpie doll, Barbie doll; puppet, Muppet, marionette, figurine; voodoo. *Slang,* babe, baby[doll], sweetheart. See AMUSEMENT, BEAUTY.

dollar, *n.* *Slang,* buck, bean, iron man, simoleon, cartwheel. See MONEY.

dolphin, *n.* porpoise, see hog *or* pig, cetacean. See MAMMAL.

domain, *n.* REGION, realm, dominion, territory, LAND, sphere of action; estate.

dome, *n.* vault, cupola. See COVERING.

domestic, *adj.* household, homely; family, home, internal; native, home-grown, home-bred; tame. See ABODE, SECLUSION, DOMESTICATION.

DOMESTICATION

Nouns—**1,** domestication, taming; animal husbandry; cattle-raising, dairy farming, ranching, stock breeding, horse training; veterinarianism, veterinary medicine.

2, menagerie, zoo, aquarium; stable, barn, sty, kennel, corral, ranch, henhouse, fishpond, hatchery; aviary, apiary.

3, husbandman, breeder, keeper, dairy farmer, groom, stableman; cowboy, cowpuncher, herdsman, shepherd, sheepherder, rancher, swineherd; apiarist, beekeeper; veterinary. *Colloq.,* vet, cowpoke.

Verbs—domesticate, tame, breed, train, break; groom, feed, water, milk, shear; round up, corral, housebreak.

Adjectives—domesticated, domestic, tame, broken; housebroken.

---

domicile, *n.* See ABODE.

dominate, *v.t.* govern, control; domineer, overbear, tyrannize; predominate, stand out. See AUTHORITY, POSSESSION.

domineer, *v.i.* tyrannize, overbear, bully. See INSOLENCE, SEVERITY.

dominion, *n.* POWER, AUTHORITY; domain, state, territory. See REGION, PROPERTY.

don, *v.t.* assume, put on. See CLOTHING.

donation, *n.* contribution, gift, present, benefaction, grant. See GIVING. *Ant.,* see ACQUISITION.

donkey, *n.* ass, jackass, burro; blockhead, FOOL.

do-nothing, *n.* fence-sitter, (time-)waster, drone, idler. See INACTION.

doom, *n.* DESTINY, lot, fate, fortune; judgment, damnation, CONDEMNATION, DESTRUCTION, death.

door, *n.* gate, portal, entrance; barrier; inlet, outlet, path. See OPENING, INGRESS, EGRESS.

doorkeeper, *n.* porter, tiler, gatekeeper, *concierge,* sentry. See DEFENSE.

dormitory, *n.* quarters, lodging, hostel, bunks. *Colloq.,* dorm. See ABODE.

dose, *n.* dosage, measure, portion; mouthful, *etc.* See REMEDY, APPORTIONMENT.

dossier, *n.* file, folder, papers, documents, RECORD. See INFORMATION.

dot, *n.* spot, speck, point; jot, whit, jota. See LITTLENESS.

dote, *v.i.* like, be fond of; worship, adore, be infatuated (with). See LOVE.

double, *adj., v.t. & n.* —*adj.* twofold, duplicate, duplex, dual. See DUPLICATION. —*v.t.* duplicate, increase, twofold. —*n.* twin, counterpart; understudy, stand-in.

double-cross, *v. & n., colloq.,* BETRAY, betrayal; see IMPROBITY.
double-dealing, *adj. & n.* See DUPLICITY.
double-talk, *n., slang,* gibberish, jargon, nonsense, cant. See ABSURDITY.

DOUBT

Nouns—**1,** doubt, dubiousness, dubiety; unbelief, skepticism, disbelief; agnosticism, IRRELIGION; incredulity, discredit; credibility gap.
2, jealousy, suspicion, distrust, anxiety, concern; green-eyed monster.
3, uncertainty, hesitation, hesitancy, perplexity; irresolution, indecision; demur, scruple, qualm, misgiving; dilemma, quandary; bewilderment, vacillation, CHANGEABLENESS.
4, doubter; unbeliever, doubting Thomas, man from Missouri; waverer, chameleon, flibbertygibbet.
Verbs—**1,** doubt, be doubtful, disbelieve, discredit; misbelieve; refuse to admit, DISSENT; refuse to believe; doubt the truth of; be skeptical *or* sceptical, distrust, mistrust; suspect, have doubts, harbor suspicions; have one's doubts; take with a grain of salt.
2, demur, stick at, pause, hesitate, falter, object, cavil, scruple. *Colloq.,* smell a rat.
3, cast doubt upon, raise a question; bring *or* call in question; question, challenge; dispute, deny (see NEGATION); cavil; cause *or* raise a doubt *or* suspicion.
4, be unbelievable, fill with doubt, startle, stagger; shake *or* stagger one's faith *or* belief.
5, be uncertain; wonder whether; shilly-shally, compromise; vacillate, waver, see-saw; hem and haw, sit on the fence.
Adjectives—**1,** doubting, unbelieving; incredulous, skeptical, sceptical; distrustful of, shy of, suspicious of; heretical, faithless; dubious, scrupulous.
2, doubtful, uncertain, irresolute; disputable, debatable, controversial, dubious; questionable; suspect, suspicious; open to suspicion, open to doubt; staggering, hard to believe, incredible, not to be believed, inconceivable; fallible; undemonstrable; controvertible.
Adverbs—with a grain of salt, with reservations.
Antonym, see BELIEF.

---

doughnut, *n.* cruller, *beignet,* friedcake. *Slang,* dunker, tire. See FOOD.
doughty, *adj.* redoubtable, brave, bold, gallant, daring, spunky. See COURAGE.
douse, *v.* soak, drench, souse; put out, extinguish. See WATER, DARKNESS.
dowager, *n.* widow; matron, *grande dame,* beldam. *Slang,* battle-ax. See FEMALE.
dowdy, *adj.* frumpy, frowsy, down-at-heels; inelegant, old-fashioned. See INELEGANCE.
dower, *n.* dowry, dot; inheritance. See PROPERTY.
down, *adv.* downward; under, beneath, below. See LOWNESS. *Ant.,* see HEIGHT.
down-and-out, *adj.* needy, destitute, poor, on the skids. See POVERTY.
downcast, *adj.* down-hearted; modest, bashful. See HUMILITY, MODESTY.
downfall, *n.* drop, comedown, disgrace, demotion; overthrow; collapse, crash. See DESCENT, FAILURE, DESTRUCTION. *Ant.,* see SUCCESS.
downhearted, *adj.* dejected, discouraged, downcast, sad. See DEJECTION.
downright, *adv. & adj.* —*adv.* plainly, bluntly; extremely. See ARTLESSNESS, GREATNESS. —*adj.* unqualified, frank, absolute.
downtrodden, *adj.* oppressed, subjugated; spurned, scorned; in the dust *or* mire, treated like dirt; underprivileged. See SUBJECTION, POVERTY.
downy, *adj.* fluffy, feathery, fleecy, flocculent, soft. See SMOOTHNESS. *Ant.,* see ROUGHNESS.

doze

doze, *n.* drowse, snooze, nap; take forty winks. See REPOSE, INATTEN-
TION.

drab, *adj.* grayish, brownish, dun; monotonous, DULL, humdrum, uninteresting. *Ant.,* see COLOR.

draft, *n. & v.t.* —*n.* sketch, OUTLINE; breeze, air current, WIND; drink,
dram; conscription, levy, load, pull, displacement; bill of exchange,
demand note. See FOOD, COMPULSION, MONEY. —*v.t.* outline; draw,
sketch, formulate; conscript, enlist, impress. See COMPULSION.

draftee, *n.* recruit, inductee, conscript. *Slang,* rookie. See COMBATANT.

draftsman, *n.* delineator; artist. See REPRESENTATION.

drag, *v.* draw, pull, tow, tug, haul; protract, draw out; lag, dawdle, inch
along. See SLOWNESS.

drain, *v. & n.* —*v.* draw off, empty, exhaust, deprive; leak, drip, dry up.
See EGRESS, WASTE. —*n.* outlet, spout, sewer, ditch, gutter.

dram, *n.* draft, drink. See FOOD, MEASUREMENT.

DRAMA

Nouns—**1,** drama, the drama, the stage, the theater, play; showbusiness,
theatricals, theatrics; dramaturgy, stagecraft; histrionics; sock and
buskin; Muse of Tragedy, Melpomene; Muse of Comedy, Thalia;
Thespis; puppetry, Punch and Judy.

2, play, drama, stage play, piece, vehicle; tragedy, comedy, tragicomedy;
opera, operetta, musical comedy, review, vaudeville, burlesque, farce, divertissement, extravaganza, harlequinade, pantomime, burlesque, *opéra
bouffe*, ballet, spectacle, masque, melodrama; monolog(ue), duolog(ue),
dialog(ue); trilogy; charade, mystery, morality play, miracle play; puppet show. *Slang,* legit.

3, act, scene, tableau; introduction; prologue, epilogue; turn, number;
entr'acte, intermission, intermezzo, interlude, afterpiece; curtain; curtain
call, encore.

4, performance, REPRESENTATION, *mise en scène*, stagery, stagecraft, acting; impersonation; stage business, slapstick, buffoonery; part, role,
character, cast, *dramatis personae*, road company, repertory, repertoire,
summer theatre, amateur theatricals, [summer] stock. *Slang,* ham acting; gag.

5, motion picture, moving picture, film, cinema, talking picture. *Colloq.,*
movie, movie show, talkie, the films, flickers, silverscreen.

6, theater, legitimate theater, playhouse, opera house; house; music hall;
amphitheater, circus, hippodrome; puppet *or* marionette show. *Colloq.,*
movie theater, off- *or* off-off-Broadway theater.

7, auditorium, front of the house, stalls, boxes, pit, orchestra, balcony,
loges, gallery; greenroom; stage, proscenium; scene, the boards; trap;
mezzanine floor; flies; floats, lights, spotlight, footlights; orchestra;
dressing rooms; flat, drop, wing, screen, side-scene; transformation
scene, curtain; theatrical costume; make-up, greasepaint; properties.
Colloq., props, follow spot. *Slang,* peanut gallery.

8, actor, player; stage player; performer; trouper, protagonist, leading
man *or* woman; supporting cast; comedian, tragedian, villain, ingenue,
understudy, foil, vaudevillian, Thespian, star; pantomimist, clown, harlequin, buffo, buffoon, farceur, Pantaloon, Columbine; Punch, Punchin-
ello; super, supernumerary, spear carrier, mummer, masker; mountebank; tumbler, juggler, acrobat; contortionist; librettist, scenario-writer,
dramatic author; playwriter, playwright; dramatist. *Slang,* ham, ham
actor, heavy, matinee idol, stooge, straight man, bit player.

Verbs—act, play, perform; put on the stage; personate (see REPRESENTA-
TION); mimic, IMITATE, enact; play a part, act a part; rehearse; rant;
tread the boards; star.

Adjectives—dramatic, theatrical, scenic, histrionic, comic, tragic, farcical,
tragicomic, melodramatic, operatic; stagy.

Adverbs—on the stage, on the boards; before the footlights.

drape, *n. & v.* —*n.* drapery, curtain, tapestry; ARRANGEMENT, hang, fall, look. See COVERING, PENDENCY, CLOTHING. —*v.t.* hang curtains, *etc.*; shape, cut; dress, clothe, caparison; swathe, shroud, veil. See ORNAMENT.

drastic, *adj.* extreme, stringent, severe; strong, decisive, vigorous; rash, impulsive. See SEVERITY, STRENGTH, RASHNESS.

draw, *v.t.* haul, drag, pull, tug, extract; attract, allure; depict, sketch; draft; win, receive; displace; inhale; elicit, get; eviscerate. See ATTRACTION, COMPOSITION, PAINTING.

drawback, *n.* HINDRANCE, handicap, clog, encumbrance, restraint; objection, disadvantage. *Ant.*, see SUPERIORITY.

drawing, *n.* picture, sketch, plan; delineation; selection; hauling, pull. See PAINTING, TRACTION, CHOICE.

dreadful, *adj.* fearful, dire, frightful, shocking, horrible, awful. See FEAR.

dream, *n.* vision, fantasy, reverie, fancy; daydream, chimera, nightmare; delusion, hallucination. See IMAGINATION, INSUBSTANTIALITY.

dreary, *adj.* cheerless, gloomy, somber; depressing, lonely, wearisome. See DEJECTION, WEARINESS. *Ant.*, see CHEERFULNESS, HOPE.

dregs, *n.* refuse, sediment, silt, lees, grounds, heeltaps; scum, riffraff, off-scourings. See REMAINDER, POPULACE.

drench, *v.t.* douse, souse, soak, wet, saturate. See WATER. *Ant.*, see DRYNESS.

dress, *v.t. & n.* —*v.t.* clothe, attire, array; scold, reprove, berate, whip; adorn, garnish, decorate; align, equalize; prepare, bandage. See CLOTHING, DISAPPROBATION, ORNAMENT, REMEDY. *Ant.*, see DIVESTMENT. —*n.* CLOTHING, costume, vesture, garb, raiment, apparel, habit; frock, gown.

dresser, *n.* chest of drawers, vanity [table], dressingtable. See RECEPTACLE.

dressing, *n.* decoration, ORNAMENT; sauce, seasoning, CONDIMENT; garnish; bandage, application, gauze pad. See FOOD, REMEDY.

dressmaker, *n.* seamstress; stylist, fashion designer, *modiste, couturier, couturière.* See CLOTHING.

dressy, *adj.* stylish, fashionable, smart, chic; fancy, showy. See OSTENTATION.

drift, *n. & v.i.* —*n.* pile, heap, deposit; movement, DEVIATION; tendency, meaning; mine passage. See ASSEMBLAGE, DIRECTION, MEANING. —*v.i.* procede aimlessly; pile up; approach, MOTION. *Ant.*, see STABILITY.

drill, *v.t. & i.* pierce, bore; train, exercise, practice. See OPENING, TEACHING.

drink, *v. & n.* —*v.* consume, swallow, imbibe; toss off, drain, guzzle; toast. *Slang*, lap up, swig, sop up; consume, swallow, tipple. —*n.* draft, potation; beverage, liquor. *Slang*, booze, hooch, moonshine. See FOOD, DRUNKENNESS. *Ant.*, see MODERATION.

drip, *v.i.* drop, dribble, trickle; leak, percolate. See WATER.

drive, *v.t.* propel, impel; urge forward, pursue; steer, control; conduct, carry out; ram, hammer, thrust; urge, force, compel, coerce. See COMPULSION, DIRECTION, TRAVEL, PROPULSION.

drivel, *n. & v.i.* —*n.* drool, slaver, slobber; nonsense, babble. —*v.i.* drool, slobber, babble, talk nonsense, dote. See ABSURDITY.

driver, *n.* chauffeur, teamster, wagoner, cabman, hack, cabby. See TRAVEL.

drizzle, *n. & v.* sprinkle, mist, rain, spray. See MOISTURE, WATER.

droop, *v.i.* bend, loll, slouch, sag; sink, languish, waste; wilt. See DEJECTION, DISEASE.

drop, *v. & n.* —*v.* let fall; give up, abandon; fall, plunge; faint, collapse; cease, terminate, END; drip. See DESCENT, RELINQUISHMENT, IMPOTENCE. —*n.* globule, bead; minim; bit, mite. See LITTLENESS.

dross, *n.* refuse; slag; waste, trash, rubbish. See HEATING, USELESSNESS.

drought, *n.* aridity, DRYNESS, thirst; lack, want, need, scarcity. See IN-SUFFICIENCY.

drown, *v.* suffocate (in liquid); submerge, inundate; muffle, overpower. See WATER, KILLING, SILENCE, DEATH.

drowsy, *adj.* sleepy, tired, somnolent; lazy, languid. See WEARINESS.

drudge, *v.i.* toil, slave, grub, plod, hack, grind, plug. See EXERTION.

drug, *n. & v.* —*n.* medicine, physic, elixir, preparation, prescription, REMEDY; narcotic, dope; white elephant, a drug on the market. —*v.* narcotize, dope; medicate, dose; knock out, put to sleep. See INSENSI-BILITY.

druggist, *n.* apothecary, pharmacist, chemist. See REMEDY.

DRUNKENNESS

Nouns—**1,** drunkenness, intoxication; intemperance; drinking, inebriety, inebriation; ebriety, ebriosity; insobriety; wine-bibbing; bacchanals, bacchanalia, libations; alcoholism, dipsomania, oenomania; delirium tremens. *Colloq.,* D.T.s. *Slang,* hangover, pink elephants, binge, tear, bust, bat, bender, toot, jag.

2, liquor, hard liquor, drink, alcoholic drink, spirits, grog, the bottle, little brown jug; brandy, cognac, applejack, hard cider, gin, rum, whiskey, liqueur, cordial; the grape, wine, white wine, red wine, cocktail, mixed drink, toddy. *Colloq.,* moonshine, nightcap, pick-me-up, hair of the dog; booze, hooch.

3, drunkard, alcoholic, dipsomaniac, sot, toper, tippler, bibber, wine-bibber; hard drinker; soaker, sponge, tosspot; thirsty soul, revel(l)er, carouser; Bacchanal, Bacchanalian; Bacchante; devotee of Bacchus. *Colloq.,* boozer, guzzler, souse, drunk. *Slang,* lush, tank, rumhound, barfly, wino, dipso.

4, drug scene; overdose; trip, high.

Verbs—**1,** get drunk, be drunk; see double; take a drop, take a drop too much; imbibe, drink, tipple, guzzle, swizzle, soak, sot, carouse; take to drink; drink up, drink hard, drink like a fish; drain the cup, take a hair of the dog that bit one; wet one's whistle, crack a bottle, pass the bottle; toss off. *Colloq.,* tope, booze, swig, swill. *Slang,* liquor up, lush, get high, hit the bottle, paint the town red, have a jag on, pass out.

2, make one drunk, inebriate, fuddle, befuddle, besot, go to one's head. *Slang,* pollute, plaster.

3, take drugs, smoke. *Slang,* turn on, get stoned *or* high, [take a] trip, smoke [pot], shoot up.

Adjectives—drunk, tipsy; intoxicated; inebrious, inebriate, inebriated; in one's cups; in a state of intoxication; mellow, cut, fresh, high, merry, elevated; flush, flushed; flustered, disguised; topheavy; overcome; maudlin, crapulous, dead *or* roaring drunk. *Colloq.,* drunk as a lord, drunk as an owl; boozy, out. *Slang,* boiled, soused, shellacked, fried, polluted, tanked, cockeyed, spifflicated, squiffed, stinko, tight, three sheets to the wind, out cold, stiff, blotto, high as a kite, feeling no pain, cut of it; freaked out, turned on, hyped up, stoned, zonked.

Antonym, see MODERATION.

DRYNESS

Nouns—**1,** dryness, aridity, aridness, drought, ebb tide, low water; desiccation; thirst; siccation; dehydration, anhydration; drainage; mummification.

2, dullness; see SLOWNESS.

Verbs—be dry, render dry, dry, dry up, soak up, sponge, swab, sipe; evaporate, desiccate; drain, parch, sear, wither; dehydrate.

Adjectives—dry, anhydrous, dehydrated, arid; dried, undamped; juiceless, sapless; sear; thirsty, husky; rainless, without rain; *sec, brut,* fine; dry as a bone, bone-dry, dry-as-dust, dry as a stick, dry as a mummy, dry as a biscuit; waterproof, watertight; desertlike, unirrigated, waterless, parched.

Antonym, see MOISTURE.

---

dual, *adj.* duplex, twofold, double, duplicate, twin, binary. See NUMERATION.

dubious, *adj.* doubtful, uncertain; questionable, unreliable. See DOUBT. *Ant.*, see CERTAINTY.

duck, *v.* nod, bob, dodge, RECOIL; dodge, avoid, elude; dip, immerse, PLUNGE. See AVOIDANCE.

duct, *n.* channel, canal, tube, pipe, flue. See PASSAGE.

ductile, *adj.* tractile, malleable; yielding, pliant; compliant, docile, obedient. See SOFTNESS, OBEDIENCE.

due, *adj., adv. & n.* —*adj.* owed, owing, payable, outstanding, unpaid; rightful, proper, fit, appropriate, apropos; lawful, licit. See JUSTICE, RIGHT, CAUSE, PAYMENT. —*adv.* duly, properly; in due course *or* time, in the course of events. See TIME, DIRECTION. —*n.* reward, deserts; PAYMENT, fee, toll, dues.

dues, *n.pl.* assessment, fee; deserts. See JUSTICE, PAYMENT.

duel, *n.* single combat, contest, competition, rivalry; affair of honor. See CONTENTION.

dull, *adj. & v.* —*adj.* unsharp, BLUNT; deadened, numb; spiritless, vapid, vacuous; dead, lifeless; sluggish, listless, lethargic; lackluster, dim, cloudy, obscure, stale, jaded. —*v.t.* blunt. See SLOWNESS, DULLNESS. *Ant.*, see LIGHT, SHARPNESS, DULLNESS.

DULLNESS

Nouns—dullness, heaviness, flatness; infestivity, DEJECTION; stupidity (see IMBECILITY); want of originality, monotony (see WEARINESS); prose, matter of fact; banality, triteness; platitude; boredom.

Verbs—be dull, prose, be caught napping; render dull, damp, depress, throw cold water on, lay a wet blanket on; fall flat; bore.

Adjectives—dull, unentertaining, uninteresting, boring, unlively, unimaginative; dry(-as-dust); prosy, prosaic; matter-of-fact, commonplace, pointless; insipid, vapid, heavy; banal, trite, hackneyed; stupid, dense, obtuse, thick, slow; flat, humdrum, platitudinous, monotonous, tedious, wearisome, melancholic; stolid, plodding, pedestrian; deadened, numb; dead, lifeless.

Antonym, see WIT, INTELLIGENCE.

---

dum(b)found, *v.t.* confound, flabbergast, disconcert; astonish. See WONDER.

dumbness, *n.* aphonia, MUTENESS, aphony, mutism; deaf-mutism, voicelessness; silence, taciturnity, inarticulateness. *Colloq.*, stupidity.

dummy, *n.* (deaf)mute; puppet, manikin; proxy, agent, stand-in. *Colloq.*, stooge. See MUTENESS, REPRESENTATION, SUBSTITUTION.

dump, *v. & n.* —*v.* drop, let fall; discharge, unload; abandon, jettison, scrap, junk, discard; flood the market. *Slang*, ditch. See WASTE, REJECTION. —*n.* trashheap, junkpile, midden; STORE, depot, depository. *Slang*, den, dive, joint, greasy spoon, flophouse, flea trap. See ABODE, WASTE, UNCLEANNESS.

dunce, *n.* dullard, moron, fool, simpleton, simple Simon, nitwit; dolt, oaf, clod. *Slang*, bonehead, meathead, boob, dope. See IGNORANCE, FOLLY.

dungarees, *n.pl.* jeans, overalls, Levis, chinos. See CLOTHING.

dungeon, *n.* pit, cell; jail, PRISON; black hole of Calcutta. See RESTRAINT.

dupe, *n. & v.* —*n.* gull, victim, cully, cat's-paw; fool; puppet, tool; butt, laughingstock, April fool. *Slang*, easy mark, sucker, chump, soft touch, pushover, pigeon. —*v.t.* cheat, defraud, swindle; hoodwink, deceive, delude. See CREDULITY, DECEPTION.

duplicate, *n., adj. & v.* —*n.* duplication, double, reproduction, replica, COPY, reduplication; iteration, REPETITION; renewal; counterpart; gemination, twin. —*adj.* double(d), bifold, biform, bilateral, two-fold, two-sided, duplex; double-faced; twin, ingeminate; second. —*v.* (re)double, reduplicate; geminate, COPY, repeat; renew (see RESTORATION). *Ant.,* see DIFFERENCE, UNCONFORMITY.

duplicity, *n.* duality; double dealing, two-facedness, treachery, deceitfulness, fraud, guile. See NUMERATION, FALSEHOOD, IMPROBITY. *Ant.,* see TRUTH.

DURABILITY

Nouns—**1,** durability, durableness, persistence, lastingness, CONTINUANCE, standing; permanence, STABILITY, survival, survivance; longevity, AGE; distance of time; protraction of time, prolongation of time; delay (see LATENESS).

2, diuturnity; AGE, century, eternity; SLOWNESS, perpetuity, PERMANENCE. *Colloq.,* blue moon, dog's age, month of Sundays, coon's age.

Verbs—**1,** endure, last, stand, remain, abide, continue; tarry, be late, drag on, protract, prolong; spin out, eke out, draw out; temporize, gain time, make time, talk against time; outlast, outlive, survive; live to fight again.

2, perpetuate, immortalize; maintain.

Adjectives—durable, lasting; of long duration, of long standing; permanent, chronic, long-standing; intransient, intransitive; intransmutable, persistent, lifelong, livelong; everlasting, immortal; longeval, long-lived; diuturnal, evergreen, perennial; never-ending, unremitting; perpetual, interminable, eternal; unfailing; lingering, protracted, prolonged, spun out, long-pending, long-winded; slow.

Adverbs—**1,** durably, long; for a long time, for an age, for ages, for ever so long; for many a long day; long ago; all day long, all year round, the live-long day, as the day is long; morning, noon and night; hour after hour, day after day; for good; permanently.

2, always, ever, evermore, forever, for aye, world without end, perpetually. *Colloq.,* for keeps, for good, till Hell freezes over, till the cows come home.

Antonym, see TRANSIENTNESS.

---

duration, *n.* continuance, persistence; term, time, period. See TIME, LENGTH.

duress, *n.* See PRISON, COMPULSION.

during, *prep.* pending, through, in the time of, until. See TIME.

dusk, *n.* twilight, gloaming; semidarkness; gloom, half-light. See DIMNESS.

dust, *n.* powder; earth, soil, pounce; dirt, lint, ash, soot, flue. See POWDERINESS, UNCLEANNESS.

DUTY

Nouns—**1,** duty, moral obligation, accountableness, accountability, liability, onus, responsibility; bounden duty; call of duty; allegiance, fealty, tie; engagement, PROMISE; part; function, calling, BUSINESS.

2, morality, morals, ethics; Ten Commandments; conscientiousness, PROBITY; conscience, inward monitor, still small voice; sense of duty.

3, propriety, fitness, seemliness, decorum, the thing, the proper thing.

4, OBSERVANCE, fulfillment, discharge, performance, acquittal, satisfaction, redemption; good behavior.

Verbs—**1,** be the duty of, be incumbent on, be responsible, behoove, become, befit, beseem; belong to, pertain to; fall to one's lot; devolve on; lie upon, lie on one's head, lie at one's door; rest with, rest on the shoulders of.

2, take upon oneself, PROMISE, be bound to, be sponsor for; incur a responsibility; be under obligation, stand under obligation; have to answer for, owe it to oneself.

3, impose a duty, enjoin, require, exact; bind, bind over; saddle with, prescribe, assign, call upon, look to, oblige.

4, enter upon, perform, observe, fulfill, discharge, satisfy or acquit oneself of a duty or an obligation; act one's part, redeem one's pledge, do justice to, be at one's post; do one's duty (see VIRTUE); be on good behavior, mind one's Ps and Qs.

Adjectives—obligatory, binding, imperative, peremptory; stringent, severe, behooving, incumbent on; obligated, under obligation, obliged by, bound by, tied by; saddled with; due to, beholden to, bound to, indebted to; tied down; compromised; duty bound; amenable, liable, accountable, responsible, answerable; right, meet, due, moral, ethical, casuistical, conscientious, etiological.

Adverbs—dutifully, in duty bound, on one's own responsibility, at one's own risk.

Antonym, see NEGLECT.

---

dwarf, *n.* midget, pygmy, Lilliputian. *Colloq.,* runt. *Slang,* shrimp. See LITTLENESS. *Ant.,* see SIZE.

dwell, *v.i.* live, reside, abide. *Slang,* hang out; harp, iterate. See PRESENCE, REPETITION, ABODE.

dwelling, *n.* ABODE, residence, lodging, home, habitation, domicile.

dwindle, *v.i.* diminish, shrink, lessen, run low, wash away. See DECREASE. *Ant.,* see INCREASE.

dye, *v.t.* COLOR, tint, stain. *Ant.,* see COLORLESSNESS.

dynamic, *adj.* forceful, vigorous, impelling; propulsive. See POWER, IMPULSE. *Ant.,* see IMPOTENCE.

dynasty, *n.* royal line or succession, family, house. See MASTER, RELATION.

dysentery, *n.* flux; diarrhea; cramps. *Slang,* the grips, trots or runs. See DISEASE.

E

each, *adv.* every, apiece, severally, seriatim, respectively.

eager, *adj.* desirous, keen, fervent, fervid, hot-headed, earnest, intent; zealous, ardent, agog; avid, anxious, athirst. See ACTIVITY. *Ant.,* see INACTIVITY.

eagle, *n.* erne, ringtail, eaglet, bald eagle, golden eagle, harpy, sea eagle. See ANIMAL.

ear, *n.* head, spike; auricle, concha; handle, knob; heed, observance. See EFFECT, ATTENTION, HEARING.

earful, *n.,* colloq., harangue, tirade; gossip, info, tip, the lowdown; a piece of one's mind, bawling out. See NEWS, SPEECH, INFORMATION.

EARLINESS

Nouns—**1,** earliness, punctuality, promptitude, despatch, dispatch, expedition, readiness. See UNPREPAREDNESS.

2, HASTE, speed, celerity, swiftness, rapidity, acceleration; suddenness, abruptness.

3, prematurity, precocity, precipitation, anticipation; a stitch in time.

Verbs—**1,** be early, be beforehand, take time by the forelock, anticipate, forestall; have the start; steal a march upon; gain time, preëmpt, bespeak. *Slang,* jump the gun, get or have the jump on.

2, accelerate, expedite, hasten, quicken; make haste, hurry, speed, scamper, run, race, rush.

Adjectives—**1,** early, prime, timely, seasonal, punctual, forward; prompt, instant, ready; summary.

2, premature, precipitate, precocious; prevenient, anticipatory, ahead of time; forward, advanced.

3, sudden, instantaneous, instant, abrupt; unexpected; near, near at hand, immediate.

Adverbs—**1,** early, soon, anon, betimes, ere long, before long, punctually, promptly, to the minute, in time, in good time, in good season, in due time, time enough.

2, beforehand, prematurely, precipitately, hastily, too soon, before its time; in anticipation; unexpectedly.

3, suddenly, instantaneously, at short notice, *extempore*, on the spur of the moment, in short order, right away *or* off, at once, on the spot, on the instant, at sight, offhand, out of hand, straightway; forthwith, incontinently, summarily, immediately, briefly, shortly, quickly, speedily, apace, presently, at the first opportunity, by and by, in a while, directly.

Antonym, see LATENESS.

---

earn, *v.t.* work for, gain, win; deserve, merit, rate; make a living, be gainfully employed. See ACQUISITION, REWARD, EXERTION.

earnest, *adj.* intent, intense, serious, grave, solemn, sober, weighty, purposeful, determined; eager, impassioned, animated, cordial, zealous, fervent, ardent. See FEELING, IMPORTANCE, RESOLUTION.

earnings, *n.pl.* pay, PAYMENT, salary, wages, fees, paycheck, remuneration; [net *or* gross] income, revenue, gain, proceeds, receipts, yield, gross, net; dividends, interest; commissions. *Colloq.,* take, haul. *Slang,* gravy, payoff, bread, gate, cut, split.

earth, *n.* planet, globe, world; ground, LAND, dirt, soil, mold. See UNIVERSE.

earthenware, *n.* crockery, china, pottery, CERAMICS, stoneware. See HEAT.

earthling, *n.* earthdweller, mortal, terrestrian; flesh and blood. See MANKIND.

earthly, *adj.* terrestrial; material, worldly, sensual, temporal, mundane, secular; conceivable, possible. See IRRELIGION, LAND, POSSIBILITY.

earthquake, *n.* tremor, seism, quake, shock. See VIOLENCE, AGITATION.

earthy, *adj.* EARTHLY; popular, vulgar, crude, unrefined; elemental, simple, primitive, down-to-earth; robust, vigorous, Rabelaisian; lewd, racy, bawdy, gutsy. See LAND, INELEGANCE, SIMPLENESS, IMPURITY.

ease, *n.* comfort, luxury; rest, repose; CONTENT, enjoyment, complacency; FREEDOM, relief; leisure, convenience; FACILITY, readiness, expertness; unconstraint, naturalness. See PLEASURE. *Ant.,* see DISCONTENT, DIFFICULTY, PAIN.

eastern, *adj.* east, oriental. See DIRECTION.

easy, *adj.* comfortable, restful, indolent, unconcerned, untroubled; free, unembarrassed, careless, smooth, unconstrained, natural, graceful; effortless, ready, facile, simple; moderate, MILD, gentle, indulgent; tractable, compliant; light, unexacting. See FACILITY. *Ant.,* see DIFFICULTY, SEVERITY.

easygoing, *adj.* happy-go-lucky, cheerful; unconcerned, untroubled, careless; effortless, FACILE; tractable, compliant. See CONTENT, ELEGANCE, WILLINGNESS.

eat, *v.t. & i.* consume, devour, feed, fare; erode, corrode, wear, rust. See FOOD, DETERIORATION. *Ant.,* see IMPROVEMENT.

eavesdrop, *v.i.* listen in, spy, snoop, overhear; bug, tap. See HEARING, CURIOSITY.

ebb, *v.i.* recede, fall back, outflow, withdraw; decline; waste, decay. See DECREASE, REGRESSION. *Ant.,* see INCREASE.

eccentric, *adj.* elliptic, parabolic, hyperbolic; irregular, deviating; peculiar, queer, odd, strange, bizarre, singular; erratic, cranky, abnormal. See INSANITY, UNCONFORMITY. *Ant.,* see SANITY, CONFORMITY.

ecclesiastical, *adj.* churchly, sacerdotal, priestly, clerical. See RELIGION,

echo, *v. & n.* —*v.i.* reverberate, resound, reply, ring; repeat, reproduce. See IMITATION, REPETITION. —*n.* reverberation, REPETITION, response, repercussion.

eclipse, *v.t.* obscure, darken, cloud, hide, conceal; outshine, surpass, overshadow. See DARKNESS, REPUTE. *Ant.*, see LIGHT, DISREPUTE.

ecology, *n.* conservation; ecosystem; autecology, *etc.* See ENVIRONMENT.

ECONOMY

Nouns—1, economy, thriftiness, frugality, thrift, CARE, husbandry, good housewifery, good management *or* administration, retrenchment.

2, savings, reserves; parsimony, cheeseparing, stinginess, scrimping.

Verbs—be economical, frugal, thrifty, saving, *or* sparing; economize, save; retrench; cut corners, skimp, make both ends meet, meet one's expenses, pay one's way; husband, save money, lay by *or* away, put by, lay aside, store up; hoard, accumulate, amass, salt away; provide for a rainy day; feather one's nest.

Adjectives—economical, frugal, careful, thrifty, saving, chary, sparing, parsimonious, miserly, stingy, scrimping.

Adverbs—sparingly, frugally, thriftily, economically, carefully, parsimoniously.

Antonym, see WASTE.

ecstasy, *n.* rapture, joy, transport, bliss, exaltation; gladness, intoxication, enthusiasm; trance, frenzy, inspiration. See PLEASURE. *Ant.*, see PAIN.

eddy, *n.* countercurrent, whirlpool. See WATER, ROTATION.

EDGE

Nouns—1, edge, verge, brink, brow, brim, margin, confine, LIMIT, boundary, border, skirt, rim, flange, SIDE; mouth, jaws, lip.

2, threshold, door; portal, entrance, gate, gateway; coast, shore.

3, frame, fringe, flounce, frill, trimming, edging, skirting, hem, welt, furbelow, valance, selvage.

Verbs—edge, verge, border, bound, skirt, rim, fringe; sidle *or* inch along.

Adjectives—border, bordering, rimming, fringing, marginal, skirting; labial, labiated, marginated.

Adverbs—edgewise, edgeways, sidewise, sideways.

Antonym, see INTERIOR.

edict, *n.* decree, bull, law, rule, order, fiat, proclamation. See COMMAND.

edification, *n.* instruction, enlightenment, education. See TEACHING.

edifice, *n.* building, structure; palace, church. See PRODUCTION.

edit, *v.t.* redact, revise, arrange, digest, correct, prepare; select, adapt, compose, compile; issue, publish. See IMPROVEMENT, PUBLICATION. *Ant.*, see DETERIORATION.

edition, *n.* redaction; issue, impression, printing. See PUBLICATION.

editorialize, *v.* expatiate, expound; use the editorial "we." *Colloq.*, spout, sound off, put in one's two cents. See WRITING, CONTENTION.

educate, *v.t.* teach, train, instruct, enlighten, edify, school; develop, cultivate; discipline, form. See TEACHING.

educated, *adj.* lettered, literate. See KNOWLEDGE. *Ant.*, see IGNORANCE.

educe, *v.t.* draw forth, bring out, develop, elicit, evolve; deduce, infer, evoke. See EXTRACTION, DEDUCTION.

efface, *v.t.* OBLITERATE, erase, expunge, excise, delete, dele, strike, cancel, wipe out, blot. *Ant.*, see RECORD.

EFFECT

Nouns—1, effect, consequence, result, upshot, issue, outcome, consummation, SEQUEL, END, conclusion, dénouement; outgrowth, aftermath, aftereffect. *Slang,* payoff.

2, PRODUCTION, produce, product, output, work, handiwork, performance; creature, creation; offspring, offshoot, fruit, first-fruits, crop, harvest; effectiveness.

Verbs—**1,** effect, CAUSE, produce, bring about, give rise to.

2, be the effect of; be due *or* owing to; originate in *or* from; rise, arise, spring, proceed, emanate, come, grow, issue, *or* result from; come out of; depend, hang, *or* hinge upon.

Adjectives—**1,** owing to, resulting from, due to, attributable to, caused by, dependent upon, derived from, evolved from; derivative, hereditary.

2, consequent, resultant, contingent, eventual.

Adverbs—of course, it follows that, therefore, naturally, consequently, as a consequence, in consequence, through, necessarily, eventually.

Antonym, see CAUSE.

---

effective, *adj.* efficacious, effectual, adequate, telling, potent, active, operative, dynamic; causative; efficient, capable. See POWER, USE.

effeminate, *adj.* womanish, unmanly, WEAK, SOFT.

effervesce, *v.i.* bubble, hiss, foam, fizz, ferment. See AGITATION.

effete, *adj.* exhausted, spent, depleted; barren, sterile, fruitless; weak, corrupt, decadent. See UNPRODUCTIVENESS, WEAKNESS, IMPURITY.

efficient, *n.* effective, effectual, efficacious, operative; skillful, capable, productive, competent. See POWER, SKILL. *Ant.,* see IMPOTENCE, UN-SKILLFULNESS.

effigy, *n.* dummy, icon, puppet, caricature, doll; COPY, counterpart, replica, simulacrum; representative, substitute; Guy Fawkes. See REPRESENTATION.

effort, *n.* EXERTION, endeavor; strain, stress, attempt, venture, struggle, trial, labor, work, achievement, production. *Colloq.,* push. *Ant.,* see REPOSE.

effortless, *adj.* EASY, facile; natural, simple; glib, fluent. *Colloq.,* easy as pie, easy as falling off a log *or* taking candy from a baby. See FACILITY.

effrontery, *n.* shamelessness, brazenness, INSOLENCE, DISCOURTESY, audacity.

egg-shaped, *adj.* oval, oviform, ovate, ovoid, elliptical. See ROTUNDITY.

ego, *n.* self, personality, I. See INSUBSTANTIALITY, INTELLECT.

egoism, *n.* individualism, selfishness, self-seeking, conceit. See VANITY.

egotism, *n.* VANITY, self-exaltation, self-conceit. See EXAGGERATION, VANITY.

EGRESS

Nouns—**1,** egress, exit, issue, emergence, outbreak, outburst, eruption, emanation, evacuation, exudation, leakage, oozing, gush, outpouring, effluence, effusion, drain, drainage, outflow, outcome, output, discharge, EXCRETION.

2, export, expatriation, deportation, emigration, exodus, DEPARTURE; emigrant, migrant, colonist, outcast.

3, outlet, vent, spout, tap, sluice, floodgate; exit, way out, mouth, window, gate, gateway, porthole, door, OPENING, path, conduit.

Verbs—**1,** emerge, emanate, issue, pass off, evacuate, exit, exeunt, depart, escape.

2, leak, run out, percolate, exude, strain, drain, ooze, filter, filtrate, dribble, gush, spout, flow, well out, poor, trickle; effuse, debouch, come forth, break *or* burst out.

Adjectives—emergent, emerging, outgoing, emanative, effluent, eruptive, leaky.

Antonym, see INGRESS.

---

ejaculate, *v.t.* eject, discharge, spew *or* shoot out; blurt out. See EJECTION.

EJECTION

Nouns—**1,** ejection, emission, effusion, rejection, expulsion, eviction, extrusion, trajection, discharge.
2, egestion, evacuation, vomiting, eructation, bloodletting, removal, phlebotomy, tapping, drainage, clearance, EXCRETION.
3, deportation, banishment, exile, ostracism, coventry; excommunication, interdict; deposition, relegation, extradition, dislodgment, DISPLACEMENT; discharge, dismissal, ouster. *Slang*, the gate, the sack, the air, the bum's rush.
Verbs—**1,** give vent to, let out, send out, exhale, excrete, shed, void, evacuate, emit, extrude, effuse, spend, expand, pour forth; squirt, spurt, spill, slop, perspire, exude, tap, draw off, bail out, broach.
2, eject, reject, expel, discard; throw *or* push out, off, away, *or* aside; shovel *or* sweep out; brush off, cast adrift, turn *or* bundle out; throw overboard, send packing, turn out, pack off; bow out, show the door to; boycott; discharge, read out of, send flying, kick upstairs. *Slang*, give the gate, the sack, *or* the bum's rush to; fire; give *or* get the air.
3, evict, oust, dislodge, relegate, deport, banish, exile, empty; drain, clear off *or* out, suck, draw off, clean out, make a clean sweep of, purge; displace.
4, unpack, unlade, unload, unship.
Adjectives—emitting, emissive, ejective, expulsive, eliminative.
Interjections—begone! get you done! get away! go away! off with you! go about your business! be off! avaunt! *Slang*, take off! get lost! beat it! scram!

Antonym, see RECEIVING.

---

eke out, *v.t.* manage, just *or* barely make, squeeze out. See SUFFICIENCY.
elaborate, *v. & adj.* —*v.t.* work out, develop, devise, labor, perfect, embellish, execute, refine. See COMPLETION, IMPROVEMENT. —*adj.* labored, studied, complicated, detailed, painstaking, finished, perfected. See COMPLETION, PREPARATION.
elapse, *v.i.* slip away, pass, expire, intervene, glide. See PASSAGE.

ELASTICITY

Nouns—**1,** elasticity, springiness, spring, resilience, buoyance, extensibility, ductility, stretch, rebound, RECOIL, adaptability.
2, rubber, India rubber, caoutchouc, whalebone, baleen, gum elastic.
Verbs—be elastic, spring back, RECOIL, rebound, stretch, expand.
Adjectives—elastic, tensile, springy, resilient, buoyant, extensible, ductile, stretchable, adaptable.

Antonym, see INELASTICITY.

---

elate, *v.t.* EXCITE, enliven, exhilarate, exalt, animate, lift up, flush, elevate; please, gladden, delight. See CHEERFULNESS. *Ant.*, see DEJECTION, DEPRESSION.
elbow, *n. & v.* —*n.* bend, angle, dogleg (see ANGULARITY). —*v.* jab, poke; push, prod, shove; make one's way through. See IMPULSE, MOTION.
elder, *adj. & n.* —*adj.* older, earlier, superior, senior. See AGE. —*n.* ancestor, senior. See AGE.
elect, *v.t.* choose, select, decide on, fix upon; call, ordain. See CHOICE. *Ant.*, see REFUSAL.
electric, *adj.* voltaic, magnetic, galvanic; thrilling, exciting, stimulating. See FEELING, POWER. *Ant.*, see INSENSIBILITY, IMPOTENCE.
electrify, *v.t.* galvanize, magnetize, charge; EXCITE, thrill, stimulate, animate; stun, bewilder, startle. See POWER, WONDER.
electrode, *n.* terminal; anode, cathode, conductor. See END.

ELEGANCE

Nouns—1, elegance, refinement, clarity, PURITY, ease, grace, gracefulness, polish, finish, propriety, appropriateness, good taste, harmonious simplicity, rhythm, harmony, symmetry.

2, (good) style, euphony, classicism, purism; purist, classicist, stylist.

Verbs—show elegance *or* refinement; discriminate; round a period.

Adjectives—1, elegant, polished, classical, correct, artistic, chaste, pure, appropriate, refined, in good taste, harmonious.

2, easy, fluent, mellifluous, balanced, euphonious; neatly put, well expressed.

Antonym, see VULGARITY.

---

elegy, *n.* dirge, lament, requiem, threnody. See LAMENTATION, POETRY.

element, *n.* COMPONENT, part, substance, constituent, ingredient; factor, principle, germ, rudiment, fundamental, origin. See CAUSE.

elementary, *adj.* rudimentary, incipient, primary, fundamental, basic; introductory; SIMPLE, uncompounded.

elephantine, *adj.* huge, clumsy; mammoth. See SIZE. *Ant.*, see LITTLENESS.

ELEVATION

Nouns—1, elevation; raising, lifting, erection; sublimation, exaltation; prominence, eminence; advancement, promotion, preferment; uplift, IMPROVEMENT; HEIGHT, hill, mount, mountain.

2, lever, crane, derrick, windlass, capstan, winch, crowbar, jimmy, pulley, crank, jack, dredge, elevator, lift, dumbwaiter, hoist, Escalator, moving stairway.

Verbs—1, heighten, elevate, raise, lift, erect, set up, stick up, heave, buoy, weigh.

2, exalt, sublimate, place on a pedestal, promote, advance, improve.

3, take up, fish up; dredge.

4, stand up, spring to one's feet; hold one's head up, rise up, get up, jump up.

Adjectives—1, elevated, raised, lifted up; erect; eminent, lofty; stilted.

2, ennobled, exalted, uplifted.

Antonym, see DEPRESSION.

---

elf, *n.* sprite, fairy, imp, puck, pixy; gnome, goblin. See MYTHICAL DEITIES.

elicit, *v.t.* draw forth, extract, evoke, educe, extort. See EXTRACTION. *Ant.*, instill.

eligible, *adj.* qualified, fitted, suitable, desirable. See EXPEDIENCE.

eliminate, *v.t.* expel, excrete, remove, get rid of, exclude, set aside, drop, cast out, eradicate; omit, ignore, leave out, neglect, pass over; suppress, extract; (see EXTRACTION); refine, simplify, clarify.

elite, *adj. & n.* —*adj.* select, CHOICE, prime. —*n.* [the] elect, CHOICE, cream, flower; chosen people; inner circle, aristocracy, *beau* or *haut monde*; the four hundred; cream of the crop, *crème de la crème*. See SUPERIORITY.

elixir, *n.* potion, essence, quintessence; philosopher's stone. See REMEDY.

elliptical, *adj.* EGG-SHAPED; condensed, cut, lacunal. See CONCISENESS.

elongate, *v.* lengthen, extend, string out. See INCREASE, LENGTH, EXPANSION.

elope, *v.i.* run away, decamp, abscond. See MARRIAGE, SECRET, ESCAPE.

eloquence, *n.* oratory, rhetoric, power; fluency, persuasiveness, volubility. See LOQUACITY, SPEECH, POWER. *Ant.*, see SILENCE, IMPOTENCE.

elucidate, *v.t.* clarify, illuminate, illustrate; explain, interpret, expound, demonstrate. See INTERPRETATION.

elude, *v.t.* ESCAPE, evade, avoid; dodge, foil, baffle.

elusive, *adj.* evasive, slippery, subtle, shifty, tricky, baffling; deceptive, illusory, intangible, fugitive. See AVOIDANCE, TRANSIENTNESS.

emaciated, *adj.* starveling, thin, haggard, wasted, gaunt, drawn, scrawny. *Colloq.,* skin and bones. See DETERIORATION, NARROWNESS.

emanate, *v.t. & i.* emit, effuse, exhale, radiate; flow, proceed, issue, come, spring, arise. See EGRESS. *Ant.,* see INGRESS.

emancipate, *v.t.* LIBERATE, free, release, deliver, manumit, set free, enfranchise. See FREEDOM. *Ant.,* see RESTRAINT.

emasculate, *v.t.* unman, castrate, geld, alter, effeminize; devitalize, debilitate; dispirit, demoralize. See WEAKNESS, DETERIORATION.

embalm, *v.t.* preserve, mummify. See INTERMENT, PRESERVATION, MEMORY.

embankment, *n.* dike, mole, bulwark, bank, wall, levee; barrier, rampart. See DEFENSE.

embark, *v.t.* ship, board, set sail, sail; begin, engage, elist, invest. See DEPARTURE, UNDERTAKING. *Ant.,* ARRIVAL.

embarrass, *v.t.* discomfort, demoralize, disconcert, discomfit, nonplus, bother, abash, encumber, trouble, hamper, complicate, perplex. See DIFFICULTY. *Ant., see* FACILITY.

embassy, *n.* mission, ministry, legation, consulate. See COMMUNICATION, AGENCY.

embellish, *v.t.* ORNAMENT, decorate, adorn, beautify, deck, bedeck, enrich.

embezzle, *v.t. & i.* steal, misappropriate, misapply, peculate, defalcate. See STEALING.

embitter, *v.t.* SOUR, envenom, poison, exasperate, anger, irritate. See AGGRAVATION, DETERIORATION. *Ant.,* see RELIEF, IMPROVEMENT, SWEETNESS.

emblem, *n.* symbol, token, sign, mark, device. See INDICATION.

embody, *v.t.* incorporate, join, organize, impersonate, personify, incarnate; comprise, contain, include; express, voice.

emboss, *v.* knob, stud, engrave, chase. See CONVEXITY, ORNAMENT.

embrace, *v.t.* clasp, clutch, hold, fold, hug, cherish, love, caress; include, comprehend, take in, comprise, involve, embody; encircle, enclose, surround; receive, welcome; take up, adopt, espouse. See CHOICE, COMPOSITION, ENDEARMENT. *Ant.,* see REFUSAL.

embroidery, *n.* needlework, crewelwork, gros *or* petit point. See ORNAMENT, JUNCTION.

embryo, *n.* fetus, egg, germ, bud; incipience, conception. See BEGINNING.

emerge, *v.i.* issue, appear; arise, come forth. See EGRESS. *Ant.,* see INGRESS.

emergency, *n.* juncture, crisis; exigency, necessity, pinch, extremity. See CIRCUMSTANCE.

emigration, *n.* migration, departure, exodus. See EGRESS. *Ant.,* see INGRESS.

eminence, *n.* height, altitude, elevation; distinction, rank, importance. See GREATNESS, REPUTE. *Ant.,* see DISREPUTE, LOWNESS.

emissary, *n.* diplomat, messenger (see AGENCY, COMMUNICATION).

emit, *v.t.* discharge, emanate, radiate, breathe, exhale, send forth, throw off, issue; deliver; voice. See EJECTION, SPEECH. *Ant.,* see RECEIVING.

emotion, *n.* FEELING, sentiment, passion, sensibility, sensation.

empathy, *n.* understanding, comprehension, transfer. See FEELING, SENSIBILITY.

emperor, *n.* sovereign, Caesar, Kaiser, monarch; empress. See MASTER, RULE.

emphasize, *v.t.* accentuate, stress, mark, underline, underscore. See AFFIRMATION, IMPORTANCE. *Ant.,* see NEGATION, UNIMPORTANCE.

empire, *n.* realm, domain, imperium; sovereignty, sway. See AUTHORITY, REGION.

empirical, *adj.* experiential, perceptual, practical, firsthand; commonsense, pragmatic; by trial and error, by feel. See EXPERIMENT, KNOWLEDGE.

employ, *v.t.* USE, occupy, make use of, devote, utilize; hire, engage.

employee, *n.* SERVANT, helper, hand; clerk, assistant. *Ant.*, see MASTER.

empower, *v.t.* enable, make able, endow, invest; authorize, commission. See PERMISSION, POWER. *Ant.*, see RESTRAINT, IMPOTENCE.

empty, *v. & adj.* —*v.t.* void, deplete, exhaust, evacuate, drain, deflate, discharge, unload. See CONTRACTION, EJECTION. *Ant.*, see INCREASE. —*adj.* hollow, vacant, exhausted, depleted, untenanted, devoid; prolix, verbose, long-winded, garrulous; hungry; vain, unsubstantial, useless, foolish, trivial, unfeeling, fruitless, inane. See ABSENCE, FOLLY. *Ant.*, see PRESENCE, SUBSTANCE.

empyrean, *adj.* heavenly, empyreal, celestial, sublime; fiery. See UNIVERSE.

emulate, *v.t.* rival, vie, compete, strive, contend. See OPPOSITION, REPUTE. *Ant.*, see COÖPERATION, DISREPUTE.

enable, *v.t.* empower, invest, endow; authorize. See POWER. *Ant.*, see IMPOTENCE.

enact, *v.t.* decree, make, pass, order, ordain; play; execute, perform, do. See ACTION, COMMAND, PASSAGE. *Ant.*, see INACTIVITY.

enchant, *v.t.* bewitch, conjure; captivate, please, charm, delight, fascinate. See PLEASURE, SORCERY. *Ant.*, see PAIN.

encircle, *v.t.* ENVIRON, surround, embrace, encompass, inclose; span, ring, loop, girdle.

enclosure, *n.* See INCLOSURE.

encounter, *v. & n.* —*v.t.* meet, come across; engage, struggle, contend. See ARRIVAL, OPPOSITION, CONTENTION. *Ant.*, see DEPARTURE, COÖPERATION. —*n.* meeting, interview; collision; combat, battle, skirmish, brush, engagement. See CONTENTION, IMPULSE. *Ant.*, see PACIFICATION.

encourage, *v.t.* animate, strengthen, hearten, fortify, inspirit, cheer, inspire, reassure, rally, comfort; abet, embolden, incite, urge, instigate; help, foster, promote, advance, advocate. See HOPE, CAUSE. *Ant.*, see DEJECTION.

encroach, *v.i.* advance, infringe, usurp, invade, trespass, intrude, overstep, violate. See INJUSTICE. *Ant.*, see JUSTICE.

encumber, *v.t.* burden, hamper, load, clog, oppress; obstruct, hinder, impede, embarrass, retard, check, handicap. See HINDRANCE. *Ant.*, see AID.

encyclopedic, *adj.* extensive, exhaustive, comprehensive. See INCLUSION.

END

Nouns—**1,** end, close, termination, conclusion, finis, finish, finale, period, terminus, stopping (point); CESSATION, stop, expiration, halt.

2, extreme, extremity; acme, peak; tip, nib, point; tail, tail end, fag end, bitter end, verge, peroration.

3, consummation, dénouement, finish, COMPLETION, doomsday, crack of doom, day of Judgment, final curtain, last stages, expiration, DEATH, end of all things, quietus, finality. *Slang,* payoff, curtains.

4, finishing stroke, death blow, knockout, K.O., *coup de grâce.*

5, goal, destination, object, purpose.

Verbs—**1,** end, close, finish, terminate, conclude, be all over, expire, die (see DEATH); come to a close, run its course, run out, pass away, be through.

2, bring to an end, put an end to, make an end of, determine; complete; stop, shut up shop, ring down the curtain; call a halt.

3, CEASE, halt, expire, lapse, stop; curtail, cut short; abort.

Adjectives—**1,** ending, final, terminal, definitive, crowning, completing, last, ultimate, conclusive.

2, end, at an end, settled, decided, over, played out.

Adverbs—finally, definitely, conclusively; at the last; once and for all, to the bitter end.

Antonym, see BEGINNING.

---

endanger, *v.t.* imperil, jeopardize, COMPROMISE, expose. See DANGER.

ENDEARMENT

Nouns—1, endearment, caress; blandishment; fondling, billing and coo-ing, dalliance, embrace, salute, kiss, buss, smack, osculation.
2, courtship, affections, wooing, suit, addresses, *amour*, lovemaking, LOVE, flirting, flirtation, gallantry; coquetry. *Slang*, necking, spooning, petting, smooching.
3, lover's knot, love token, love letter; *billet-doux*, valentine.
4, engagement, betrothal, marriage, honeymoon.
5, flirt, coquette; philanderer; lover; paramour. *Slang*, vamp, gold digger, *femme fatale*; wolf, Don Juan, Casanova, loverboy, sheik.
6, dear, darling, sweetheart, precious, LOVE, honey, honeybunch.
Verbs—1, caress, fondle, pet; coax, wheedle, cosset, coddle, make much of; cherish, foster; clasp, hug, cuddle, fold in one's arms, nestle; em-brace, kiss, buss, smack, salute.
2, make love, bill and coo; toy, dally, flirt, coquet, philander; court, woo, pay addresses; set one's cap for, be sweet on; ogle, cast sheep's eyes on. *Slang*, spoon, pet, neck; make a pass at, pitch woo, smooch, spark.
3, fall in love with; propose, pop the question; plight one's troth.
Adjectives—1, endearing, winsome, lovable, kissable, affectionate, caress-ing.
2, lovesick, lovelorn. *Slang*, spoony.
Antonyms, see DETRACTION, HATE.

---

endeavor, *v. & n.* —*v.i.* try, attempt, seek, struggle, strive, ESSAY, labor, aim, OFFER. *Ant.*, see REFUSAL. —*n.* trial, try, attempt, effort, struggle, exertion, OFFER. *Ant.*, see REFUSAL.
endless, *adj.* interminable, incessant, uninterrupted, unceasing, continu-ous, PERPETUAL; never-ending, unending, everlasting, continual, undying, eternal, imperishable; boundless, indefinite, illimitable, unlimited, im-measurable. See CONTINUITY. *Ant.*, see DISCONTINUITY, INSTANTANEITY.
endow, *v.t.* dower, settle upon, bequeath, bestow, enrich, endue; furnish, invest, clothe. See GIVING. *Ant.*, see RECEIVING.
endowment, *n.* PROPERTY, fund, foundation; gift, bestowal, dower, dowry; power; ability, faculty, aptitude, capacity; talent, bent. See GIVING, SKILL.
endue, *v.t.* clothe, furnish. See POWER. *Ant.*, see IMPOTENCE.
endure, *v.t. & i.* continue, remain, wear, last; abide, bear, suffer, bear up, sustain, undergo; tolerate, put up with, stand, brook, permit. See FEELING, DURABILITY, SUPPORT. *Ant.*, see CHANGE.
enemy, *n.* foe, OPPONENT, adversary, antagonist, foeman; Fate, Fury, *bête noir*, archenemy, Nemesis, evil *or* malignant spirit; antipathy, aver-sion; inimical person *or* power. See HATE, OPPOSITION. *Ant.*, FRIEND.

ENERGY

Nouns—1, energy, force, POWER, potency, might, STRENGTH; VIGOR, vim, intensity, ELASTICITY, go dash, drive, high pressure; RESOLUTION, mettle, backbone, exertion, excitation. *Slang*, pep, punch, ginger.
2, ACTIVITY, AGITATION, effervescence, fermentation, ebullition, splutter, perturbation, stir, bustle; radioactivity, kinetic *or* dynamic energy, driving force; erg, dyne.
3, dynamo, generator; motor, engine, FUEL, electricity, atomic power.
Verbs—energize, stimulate, kindle, excite, sharpen, intensify, inflame, fire, arouse, stir up, key up. *Slang*, pep up, give a shot in the arm.

Adjectives—strong, energetic, forcible, forceful, active, intense, potent, powerful, keen, vivid, incisive, trenchant, brisk, rousing, electrifying. *Adverbs*—energetically, strongly. *Colloq.*, like mad.
Antonym, see INERTNESS.

enervate, *v.t.* weaken, devitalize, unnerve, paralyze, soften, emasculate, unman, debilitate, enfeeble, effeminate. See IMPOTENCE, SOFTNESS.
enfold, *v.t.* envelop, enclose, encompass; embrace. See INCLOSURE, ENDEARMENT.
enforce, *v.t.* compel, force, oblige; urge, lash, goad; strengthen; execute, sanction, put in force. See COMPULSION, CAUSE.
enfranchise, *v.t.* LIBERATE, set free, release; naturalize; empower, license, qualify. See PERMISSION. *Ant.*, see RESTRAINT.
engage, *v.t.* bind, obligate, pledge, PROMISE, betroth; hire, enlist, employ, book, retain, brief; reserve, secure; occupy, interest, engross, attract, entangle, involve, interlock; set about, take up; fight, contend. See COMMISSION, UNDERTAKING, USE, WARFARE. *Ant.*, see NULLIFICATION, WASTE.
engagement, *n.* betrothal, obligation, PROMISE, agreement, pledge; appointment, interview; occupation, employment; battle, action, skirmish, brush, encounter. See BUSINESS, CONTENTION, SOCIALITY. *Ant.*, see PACIFICATION.
engine, *n.* motor, machine; MEANS, device; engine of war. See ARMS, METHOD.

ENGRAVING

Nouns—1, engraving, chalcography; line, mezzotint, stipple engraving; drypoint, etching, copperplate, steel, wood engraving; xylography, glyptography, cerography, lithography, photolithography, glyphography; gravure, photogravure, rotogravure; photoengraving.
2, impression, print, engraving, plate, etching, lithotint, cut, linoleum cut, woodcut; mezzotint, aquatint. See PRINTING.
3, graver, burin, etching-point, style; plate, stone, wood-block, negative, die, punch, stamp.
Verbs—engrave, grave, stipple, etch, bute, lithograph.
Adjectives—sculptured, engraved, graven; carved, carven, chiseled.

---

engross, *v.t.* copy, write, transcribe; absorb; monopolize, control; occupy, engage, fill. See DEPTH, ATTENTION.
engulf, *v.t.* swamp, flood, immerse, engorge, swallow up; encircle, envelop, encompass. See CIRCUMSCRIPTION, DESTRUCTION, INCLUSION.
enhance, *v.t.* intensify; exaggerate; advance, augment, INCREASE, elevate. *Ant.*, see DECREASE.
enigma, *n.* question, riddle, mystery, puzzle, problem, conundrum, SECRET.
enigmatical, *adj.* mysterious, occult, hidden, secret; inexplicable, obscure, puzzling, intricate, abstruse, incomprehensible; inscrutable. See DARKNESS, UNINTELLIGIBILITY. *Ant.*, see LIGHT, SIMPLENESS.
enjoin, *v.t.* COMMAND, bid, direct, order, instruct, charge; counsel, admonish; PROHIBIT, forbid, restrain; exact, require. See ADVICE, DUTY. *Ant.*, see NEGLECT, PERMISSION.
enjoy, *v.t.* like, relish, love, gloat over, delight in; experience; hold, possess. See PLEASURE, POSSESSION. *Ant.*, see PAIN.
enlarge, *v.t.* increase, extend, widen, broaden; aggrandize, amplify, magnify, augment, expand, elaborate, expatiate; dilate, distend, swell. See INCREASE, GREATNESS. *Ant.*, see CONTRACTION, LITTLENESS.
enlighten, *v.t.* brighten, illuminate; educate, civilize, instruct, INFORM, teach, edify. See LIGHT, KNOWLEDGE.
enlist, *v.* volunteer, sign up; recruit, draft, muster, press [into service], impress. See COMBATANT, WILL.

enliven, *v.t.* animate, exhilarate, inspirit, quicken, fire, brighten, stimulate, rouse, invigorate; cheer, elate, encourage. See CHEERFULNESS. *Ant.,* see DEJECTION.

enmity, *n.* hostility, unfriendliness, antagonism, HATE, ill-will; grudge rancor, anger, spite, animus, animosity, dislike, antipathy; feud, vendetta. *Ant.,* see FRIEND.

ennoble, *v.t.* dignify, exalt, raise, ELEVATE, glorify, uplift. See REPUTE.

enormity, *n.* wickedness, offense, atrocity, outrage; immensity, enormousness, GREATNESS. See GUILT. *Ant.,* see LITTLENESS, INNOCENCE.

enormous, *adj.* monstrous, excessive; large, titanic, tremendous, huge, immense, colossal, gigantic, vast, prodigious, stupendous. See SIZE.

enough, *adj.* adequate, sufficient, equal; ample, abundant, plenteous. See SUFFICIENCY.

enrage, *v.t.* anger, exasperate, provoke, incense, irritate; madden, inflame, infuriate. See RESENTMENT.

enrapture, *v.t.* transport, enravish, entrance, enchant; please, delight, charm, captivate, bewitch. See PLEASURE.

enrich, *v.t.* endow, aggrandize, make wealthy; embellish, ORNAMENT, adorn, beautify; fertilize; cultivate, develop. See IMPROVEMENT, MONEY. *Ant.,* see DETERIORATION, POVERTY.

enroll, *v.t.* LIST, record, enter, register; enlist, serve. *Ant.,* see EJECTION.

en route, on *or* along the way; in transit, on the road. See TRAVEL.

enshrine, *v.t.* consecrate, hallow; commemorate. See MEMORY, WORSHIP.

ensign, *n.* FLAG; badge, emblem, insignia; standard-bearer. See INDICATION.

enslave, *v.t.* subjugate, enthrall; suppress, dominate, hold dominion over; oppress, tyrannize; addict. See SUBJECTION, SEVERITY, HABIT.

ensnare, *v.t.* (en)trap, catch, net, bag; seduce, entice. See DECEPTION, TAKING.

ensue, *v.t. & i.* follow, succeed, supervene, happen, result; pursue, seek after. See EFFECT. *Ant.,* see CAUSE.

entail, *v.t.* restrict, LIMIT; involve, imply, call for, require. See INCLUSION, RESTRAINT, RELATION.

entangle, *v.t.* tangle, ravel, mesh, entrap, mat, ensnare, inveigle, twist, snarl; perplex, involve, embroil, embarrass. See DECEPTION, DIFFICULTY, DISORDER. *Ant.,* see FACILITY, ARRANGEMENT.

enter, *v.t.* penetrate, pierce; go in, come in; trespass, invade, board; begin, start, take up; LIST, record, inscribe, enroll, register, file; join. See COMPOSITION, INGRESS. *Ant.,* see EGRESS.

enterprise, *n.* project, scheme, venture, adventure, attempt, UNDERTAKING, essay; business; energy. *Colloq.,* push, go-ahead. See ACTIVITY. *Ant.,* see INACTIVITY.

enterprising, *adj.* energetic, venturesome, adventurous; eager, ambitious. *Colloq.,* pushing. See ACTIVITY, COURAGE.

entertain, *v.t. & i.* receive, welcome; amuse, divert, regale; harbor, shelter, cherish; maintain, keep up; consider, dwell upon, heed. See ATTENTION, SOCIALITY, THOUGHT. *Ant.,* see NEGLECT, SECLUSION.

enthrall, *v.t.* enslave, subjugate; captivate, fascinate, charm. See PLEASURE, SUBJECTION. *Ant.,* see PAIN, FREEDOM.

enthusiasm, *n.* ecstasy, frenzy, fanaticism; fire, spirit, force; ardor, zeal, fervor, vehemence, eagerness; optimism, assurance. See ACTIVITY, FEELING, HOPE, POWER. *Ant.,* see INACTIVITY, DEJECTION, IMPOTENCE.

entice, *v.* (al)lure, tempt, attract; induce, coax, cajole, woo; bewitch, enchant, seduce; deceive, hoodwink. See DECEPTION, MOTIVE, ATTRACTION.

entire, *adj.* COMPLETE, absolute, unqualified; total, gross, all; WHOLE, intact, undiminished, unimpaired, perfect, unbroken; undivided, unalloyed.

entitle, *v.t.* qualify, fit, capacitate, authorize; name, call, designate, dub, style. See NOMENCLATURE, JUSTICE. *Ant.,* see INJUSTICE.

entity, *n.* thing, being; WHOLE, UNITY; abstration, EXISTENCE. See MANKIND.

entourage, *n.* retinue, train. See ASSEMBLAGE, SERVANT.

entrails, *n.* viscera, intestines, bowels, *Colloq.*, insides, guts. See INTERIOR.

entrance, *n.* entry, INGRESS, entree, incoming, ingoing; debut, induction; admission, access, admittance, approach; entry, aperture, door, lobby, gate, portal, way; BEGINNING, start, commencement, introduction; invasion, penetration. See RECEIVING. *Ant.*, see END, EGRESS, EJECTION.

entrap, *v.t.* See ENSNARE.

entreat, *v.t.* REQUEST, ask, beg, crave, pray, beseech, implore, supplicate, plead, solicit, coax.

entrepreneur, *n.* producer, angel, impresario; investor. See BEGINNING, CHANCE.

entrust, *v.t.* COMMISSION, charge, delegate; consign, commit. See AUTHORITY.

entry, *n.* INGRESS; memorandum, posting, listing; entrant, contestant, contender, competitor. See RECORD, ENTRANCE, CONTENTION.

entwine, *v.t. & i.* twine, interlace, twist, wreathe, weave. See CROSSING.

enumerate, *v.t.* compute, count, tell off, number, name over; mention, recount, rehearse, recapitulate, detail, specify. See NUMERATION.

enunciate, *v.t.* announce, state, proclaim, declare; pronounce, articulate. See AFFIRMATION, VOICE. *Ant.*, see NEGATION.

envelop, *v.t.* COVER, wrap, enshroud, enfold, surround, inclose, hide.

envelope, *n.* COVERING, wrapper, casing, capsule; film, skin, integument, shell, sheath; receptacle. See ENCLOSURE. *Ant.*, see LINING.

ENVIRONMENT

Nouns—environment, encompassment, circumjacence, circumference, atmosphere, medium, surroundings; environs, outposts, outskirts, suburbs, purlieus, precincts, vicinity, background, setting, *milieu*; INFLUENCE. *Colloq.*, stamping ground, hangout. See NEARNESS. . . .

Verbs—lie around *or* about, environ, surround, compass, encompass, inclose, enclose, encircle, embrace, lap, gird, hem in, circumscribe.

Adjectives—circumjacent, circumambient, ambient, surrounding, encompassing, enclosing, suburban, neighboring, vicinal.

Adverbs—around, about; on every side, on all sides, all around, round about.

---

envoy, *n.* See DIPLOMAT.

envy, *n. & v.* —*n.* enviousness, jealousy; covetousness, cupidity, spite; ill-will, malice; greenness. —*v.* begrudge; DESIRE, crave, covet, hanker, turn green. *Ant.*, see BENEVOLENCE.

eon, *n.* aeon; AGE, [long] TIME, epoch. *Colloq.*, dog's *or* coon's age.

ephemeral, *adj.* short-lived, fugitive, TRANSIENT, transitory, fleeting, evanescent, momentary, diurnal. *Ant.*, see DURABILITY.

epic, *adj. & n.* —*adj.* heroic, majestic, elevated, noble; Homeric, Virgilian; larger than life, on a grand scale. See GREATNESS. —*n.* heroic poem, saga, edda; epos, tale; rhapsody, eulogy. See POETRY.

epicure, *n.* epicurean, *bon vivant, gourmet.* See TASTE.

epidemic, *n. & adj.* —*n.* DISEASE, pestilence, plague, contamination. —*adj.* pestilential, infectious, contagious; raging, rife, pandemic, ubiquitous. See EXPANSION, INCLUSION.

epigram, *n.* aphorism, bon mot, saying, MAXIM, well-turned phrase. See WIT.

epilogue, *n.* afterward, postscript, postlude; summation; valedictory, last word, END. See SEQUENCE, SPEECH.

episode, *n.* digression, excursus; OCCURRENCE, incident, happening, action.

epistle, *n.* LETTER, communication, missive.

epitome, *n.* compendium, abridgment, abstract, synopsis, summary, brief.

epoch, *n.* date; period, era, age. See TIME.

EQUALITY

Nouns—**1,** equality, parity, coextension; symmetry, balance, poise, evenness, monotony, level, equivalence; equipoise, equilibrium, ponderance; par, quits; IDENTITY, likeness, SIMILARITY, equalizer, equalization, equation, coördination, adjustment.

2, tie, draw, dead heat. *Colloq.*, photo finish.

3, match, peer, compeer, equal, mate, fellow, brother, equivalent, parallel; tit for tat; a Roland for an Oliver, an eye for an eye.

Verbs—**1,** be equal, equal, match, keep pace with, come up to, be on a level with, balance; measure up to.

2, make equal, equalize, level, balance, equate, trim, adjust, poise, fit, strike a balance, restore equilibrium, readjust; handicap; share and share alike.

Adjectives—**1,** equal, even, level, monotonous, coequal, symmetrical, coördinate; on a par with; up to the mark.

2, equivalent, tantamount; quits; homologous; synonymous, analogous, similar, as broad as it is long, much the same, the same; equalized, drawn, neck-and-neck; half-and-half. *Slang*, fifty-fifty.

Adverbs—equally, to all intents and purposes, nip and tuck; on even footing. *Colloq.*, from scratch.

Antonym, see DIFFERENCE.

equanimity, *n.* evenness, composure, repose, poise; calmness, serenity, tranquillity, self-possession, self-control, INEXCITABILITY. *Ant.*, see EXCITEMENT.

equilibrium, *n.* balance, equipoise, STABILITY; MEAN, MODERATION, neutrality; EQUALITY, parity, symmetry; composure, self-possession, RESTRAINT.

equip, *v.t.* furnish, outfit, provide; accouter, appoint, dress, accommodate, array, attire; arm, gird. See CLOTHING, PREPARATION.

equipment, *n.* furniture, furnishings, gear, harness, supplies, apparatus, accouterment, appointment, outfit, apparel. See CLOTHING, INSTRUMENT.

equitable, *adj.* fair, just, ethical, RIGHT, honest; unbiased, dispassionate, evenhanded; deserved, merited, condign, due. *Colloq.*, fair-and-square, on the up-and-up. See JUSTICE, PROBITY, DISINTERESTEDNESS.

equivalent, *adj. & n.* —*adj.* EQUAL, alike, identical, same, tantamount, synonymous; analogous, correspondent, interchangeable; convertible, reciprocal. See RELATION, INTERPRETATION. —*n.* equal; price, worth; analogue. See COMPENSATION, SUBSTITUTION.

equivocation, *n.* equivocalness; quibble, quibbling; evasion, shiftiness; ambiguity, double meaning, *double-entendre*; DECEPTION, prevarication, white lie; DISTORTION, half-truth, sophistry, casuistry; dodge, subterfuge. *Colloq.*, smoke screen, red herring. See CONCEALMENT, FALSEHOOD. *Ant.*, see TRUTH, DISCLOSURE.

era, *n.* See TIME.

eradicate, *v.t.* abolish; blot out, erase, extirpate, exterminate, weed out, eliminate, uproot. See DESTRUCTION, EJECTION. *Ant.*, see PRODUCTION.

erase, *v.t.* efface, rub out, expunge, cancel, obliterate, blot out. See DESTRUCTION. *Ant.*, see PRODUCTION.

erect, *v. & adj.* —*v.t.* raise, exalt; rear; build, construct; establish, set up, institute; create. See ELEVATION, PRODUCTION. *Ant.*, see DEPRESSION, DESTRUCTION. —*adj.* upright, straight, vertical, perpendicular; uplifted. See DIRECTION. *Ant.*, see CURVATURE.

erosion, *n.* eating away, wearing away, disintegration. See DETERIORATION. *Ant.*, see IMPROVEMENT.

erotic, *adj.* sexual, sensual; carnal, lascivious; obscene, pornographic; hot, spicy. *Slang*, sexy, raunchy, X-rated. See DESIRE, IMPURITY, LOVE.

err, *v.i.* mistake, misjudge; nod, slip, trip, blunder; sin, transgress; fall, wander, stray. See ERROR, BADNESS. *Ant.*, see TRUTH, VIRTUE.

errand, *n.* business, COMMISSION, mission, charge, task, trip, message.

erratic, *adj.* abnormal, IRREGULAR, eccentric, odd, CAPRICIOUS, queer, peculiar; wandering, uncertain, changeable. See CHANGEABLENESS.

ERROR

Nouns—**1,** error, fallacy; falsity (see FALSEHOOD), untruth; misconception, misapprehension, misunderstanding; inexactness, inaccuracy; LAXITY, misconstruction, misinterpretation, miscomputation, MISJUDGMENT, misstatement.

2, mistake, miss, fault, blunder; oversight; misprint, erratum; slip, blot, flaw, trip, stumble; slip of the tongue, *lapsus linguae,* slip of the pen, lapse; solecism; typographical *or* clerical error; malapropism; bull, break. *Slang,* boner, howler, typo, blooper.

3, delusion, illusion, false impression, self-deception; bias; heresy; hallucination, optical illusion, dream, fancy, fable, fantasy, phantom, mirage.

Verbs—**1,** mislead, misguide, lead astray, lead into error, beguile, misinform, delude, give a false impression, falsify, misstate; deceive, lie; dupe.

2, err, be in error, be mistaken; mistake, receive a false impression, be in the wrong; take for; blunder, misapprehend, misconceive, misinterpret, misunderstand, miscalculate, midjudge; be at cross purposes, slip up, slip a cog.

3, trip, stumble, lose oneself, go astray.

Adjectives—**1,** erroneous, untrue, false, fallacious; apocryphal, unreal, ungrounded; groundless, unsubstantial; heretical, unsound, illogical, untrustworthy, unauthenticated; exploded, refuted.

2, inexact, inaccurate, incorrect, ungrammatical, faulty.

3, illusive, illusory, delusive; mock, imaginary, spurious, fancied, deceptive, deceitful, perverted.

4, in error, mistaken, aberrant, wide of the mark, astray, at fault, on a false scent, at cross purposes.

Antonym, see TRUTH.

---

erudite, *adj.* learned, literate, wise; authoritative. See LEARNING.

eruption, *n.* efflorescence, rash; outbreak, commotion; discharge, expulsion. See DISEASE, EJECTION, VIOLENCE. *Ant.*, see HEALTH, RECEIVING, MODERATION.

escalate, *v.* intensify, worsen, INCREASE.

escapade, *n.* jaunt, adventure, prank; frolic, caper, spree. See AMUSEMENT.

ESCAPE

Nouns—**1,** escape, elopement, flight; evasion, avoidance, retreat; narrow escape *or* squeak, close call, hairbreadth escape; impunity, reprieve, deliverance, liberation, manumission, rescue; jailbreak, freedom. *Slang,* close shave, getaway, lam.

2, outlet, loophole, OPENING, EGRESS; puncture, aperture; safety-valve, fire escape, ladder, life net, lifeboat, parachute; refuge, sanctuary, asylum; ACQUITTAL.

3, refugee, fugitive, escapee, runaway, runagate, deserter.

Verbs—escape, get off, get well out of, save one's bacon, weather the storm; elude, make off, give one the slip, slip through the fingers, wriggle out of; break out *or* loose, make a getaway, find a loophole. *Slang,* get away with murder, fly the coop, take it on the lam, lam out.

Adjectives—escaping, escaped, fled, free, scotfree, at large, well out of.

Adverbs—on the run. *Slang,* on the lam, over the hill.

Antonym, see RESTRAINT.

escort, *v. & n.* —*v.t.* accompany, conduct, convoy, guard, walk, attend, usher. See SAFETY. *Ant.*, see DANGER. —*n.* attendant, companion, conductor, convoy, bodyguard.

ESSAY

Nouns—1, essay, trial, endeavor, attempt, try; venture, adventure, speculation, EXPERIMENT, trial, random shot. *Colloq.*, go. *Slang*, shot, crack, whack.

2, COMPOSITION, article, DISSERTATION, discourse, paper, monograph.

Verbs—try, essay, EXPERIMENT, endeavor, strive, attempt; venture, adventure, speculate, take a chance, tempt fortune; try one's luck, try one's hand, feel one's way, have a go at, shoot at, make a go of it, give it a whirl.

Adjectives—essaying, experimental, tentative, empirical, probationary.

Adverbs—experimentally, tentatively, on trial, by rule of thumb.

---

espionage, *n.* intelligence, counterespionage, counterintelligence; reconnaisance, investigation. *Colloq.*, cloak-and-dagger work, undercover work. See SECRET, INQUIRY.

esplanade, *n.* promenade, boardwalk; parkway, quadrangle, mall. See PASSAGE.

essence, *n.* being, substance, element, entity, reality, nature, life; extract, distillation; perfume; principle, inwardness; sense, gist, core, kernel, pith, quintessence, heart, purport. See BELIEF, FORM, REQUIREMENT, SUBSTANCE.

essential, *adj.* SUBSTANTIAL, material, constitutional, fundamental, elementary, absolute; necessary, needful, requisite, cardinal, indispensable, vital; inherent, INTRINSIC, basic. See FORM, REQUIREMENT. *Ant.*, see EXTRINSIC.

establish, *v.t.* confirm, fix, settle, secure, set, stabilize; sustain, install, root, ensconce; appoint, enact, ordain; found, institute, constitute, create, organize, build, set up; verify, prove, substantiate; determine, decide. See EVIDENCE, PRODUCTION, STABILITY. *Ant.*, see DESTRUCTION, CHANGEABLENESS.

estate, *n.* state, rank, condition, station, DEGREE; PROPERTY, fortune, possessions, effects, interest, land, holdings.

esteem, *n.* RESPECT, regard, favor, admiration, estimation, honor; reverence, worship. See APPROBATION. *Ant.*, see DISAPPROBATION, DISRESPECT.

estimate, *v. & n.* —*v.t.* consider, gauge, JUDGE; value, appraise, evaluate, rate, assess, measure; compute, reckon, calculate. See NUMERATION. —*n.* JUDGMENT, opinion, appraisal, report, criticism; calculation. See NUMERATION. *Ant.*, see MISJUDGMENT.

estrange, *v.t.* alienate, separate, withdraw; fall out, be unfriendly; disunite, part, wean; transfer. See DISJUNCTION. *Ant.*, see JUNCTION, FRIEND.

estuary, *n.* arm, inlet, firth, fjord; mouth, delta. See WATER, INGRESS.

etch, *v.* engrave, incise, scratch, carve, corrode. See REPRESENTATION, FURROW.

eternal, *adj.* perpetual, endless, everlasting, continual, ceaseless; timeless, infinite, unending; constant; immortal, imperishable, deathless. See DURABILITY. *Ant.*, see INSTANTANEITY.

ethereal, *adj.* airy, delicate, light, tenuous, fragile, fairy; HEAVENLY, celestial, empyreal. See INSUBSTANTIALITY. *Ant.*, see HELL, SUBSTANCE.

ethics, *n.* morals, morality, rules of conduct. See DUTY. *Ant.*, see NEGLECT.

etiquette, *n.* manners, decorum, custom, formality, good form. See FASHION.

Eucharist, *n.* Communion, Mass, viaticum, sacrament. See RITE.

eulogize, *v.t.* praise, compliment, celebrate, glorify, laud, panegyrize, extol. See CELEBRATION. *Ant.*, see DETRACTION.

euphoria, *n.* elation, joy, high spirits, CHEERFULNESS, PLEASURE, well-being, buoyance; eupepsia; the pink of condition. *Slang,* high. See CONTENT.

evacuate, *v.t.* empty, clear, eject, expel, purge, scour; discharge, defecate, void, emit; leave, quit, vacate, abandon. See DEPARTURE.

evade, *v.t.* avoid, elude; dodge, shun; baffle, foil, parry; escape, slip away; ignore, violate, neglect; equivocate, prevaricate, quibble. See AVOIDANCE.

evaluate, *v.t.* value, appraise, estimate, assess, PRICE. See MEASUREMENT.

evangelical, *adj.* proselytizing, apostolic, missionary. See PIETY, RELIGION.

evaporate, *v.t. & i.* emanate, pass off, escape; vaporize, distill; condense, solidify, dehydrate; dessicate; vanish, disappear. See DRYNESS, INSUBSTANTIALITY. *Ant.,* see MOISTURE, SUBSTANCE.

evasion, *n.* elusion, AVOIDANCE, ESCAPE; subterfuge. See DECEPTION, EQUIVOCATION.

even, *adj.* level, EQUAL, smooth, flat, flush, UNIFORM, regular, unvaried, PARALLEL; equable, even-tempered, unruffled, placid; equitable, fair, impartial, just; straightforward, plain, direct; abreast, alongside; true, plumb, STRAIGHT. See HORIZONTAL. *Ant.,* see INJUSTICE, OBLIQUITY, CURVATURE, UNCONFORMITY.

evening, *n.* dusk, nightfall, eventide, close of day; gloaming, twilight; sundown, sunset; curfew; eve, even (*Poetic*); decline, old age, sunset years.

event, *n.* occasion, occurrence, happening; affair, episode, incident; gala affair *or* occasion, holiday; experience; CIRCUMSTANCE, issue, outcome, result.

eventual, *adj.* final, ultimate, coming; contingent. See FUTURITY, CHANCE. *Ant.,* see PAST.

ever, *adv.* always, eternally, perpetually, incessantly, continually, constantly, forever; once, at any time; in any case, at all. See DURABILITY. *Ant.,* see INSTANTANEITY.

everlasting, *adj.* unending, neverending, without end; ageless, sempiternal; constant, ceaseless, continual, incessant. See INFINITY, CONTINUITY.

every, *adj.* each, all; complete, entire.

everyday, *adj.* habitual, usual, routine, workaday. See HABIT.

everyone, *n.* everybody, *tout le monde.*

evict, *v.t.* eject, oust, remove, expel, put out, dispossess. See EJECTION.

EVIDENCE

Nouns—1, evidence, facts, premises, data, grounds, INDICATION, DEMONSTRATION, confirmation, corroboration, SUPPORT, ratification, proof; state's, king's, queen's, oral, documentary, hearsay, external, extrinsic, internal, intrinsic, circumstantial, *ex parte*, presumptive, collateral *or* constructive evidence.

2, testimony, attestation, deposition, affirmation; examination; exhibit.

3, citation, reference, AUTHORITY, warrant, credential, testimonial; diploma, voucher, certificate, docket, RECORD, document, deed, warranty; signature, seal, identification.

4, witness, indicator, eyewitness, deponent, sponsor, [innocent] bystander, testifier, attestor, onlooker.

Verbs—1, be evidence, evince, evidence, manifest, show; betoken, tell of, indicate, denote, imply, involve, argue, bespeak; have *or* carry weight, tell, speak volumes, speak for itself.

2, rest *or* depend upon; bear witness, give evidence, testify, depose, witness, vouch for; sign, seal, set one's hand and seal, certify, attest, acknowledge.

3, confirm, ratify, support, bear out, uphold, warrant, establish, authenticate, substantiate, verify, DEMONSTRATE.

4, adduce, attest, cite, quote, refer, bring into court; allege, plead; produce witnesses; collect evidence, make out a case. *Colloq.*, have *or* get the goods on one.

Adjectives—evidential, documentary; indicative, indicatory, deducible; grounded on, founded on, based on, corroborative, confirmatory; supportive, authentic, conclusive; circumstantial, by inference, according to, *a fortiori.*

Antonym, see NEGATION.

evident, *adj.* apparent, plain, obvious, distinct; broad, unmistakable, palpable, patent, open, MANIFEST, clear; downright, overt, indubitable. See APPEARANCE, CERTAINTY. *Ant.,* see DOUBT.

EVIL

Nouns—**1,** evil, ill, harm, hurt; mischief, nuisance; disadvantage, drawback; disaster, accident, casualty, mishap, misfortune, calamity, catastrophe, tragedy, ruin, DESTRUCTION, ADVERSITY, mental anguish *or* suffering; BANE, curse, SCOURGE. *Slang,* jinx, Jonah, hoodoo, hex.

2, blow, buffet, stroke, scratch, bruise, wound, gash, mutilation; damage, LOSS, DETERIORATION.

3, BADNESS, wickedness, sin, depravity, VICE, iniquity, IMPIETY, immorality, corruption.

4, outrage, WRONG, injury, foul play; bad *or* ill turn; disservice, spoliation, grievance, crying evil.

Verbs—harm, hurt, injury, wrong, wound, ruin, outrage, dishonor, victimize.

Adjectives—**1,** evil, bad, ill, sinful, wicked, wrong, depraved, vicious, immoral, corrupt.

2, harmful, hurtful, injurious, malignant, malevolent, prejudicial, virulent, disastrous, ruinous.

Adverbs—badly, amiss, wrong, ill, to one's cost.

Antonym, see GOODNESS.

EVILDOER

Nouns—**1,** evildoer; sinner, transgressor, profligate, LIBERTINE; oppressor, despot, tyrant; incendiary, anarchist, destroyer, vandal, iconoclast, terrorist.

2, savage, brute, ruffian, barbarian, caitiff, desperado; bully, rough, hooligan, hoodlum, tough, plugugly, hellion; fraud, swindler, confidence man, THIEF; murderer, killer (see KILLING); cutthroat, butcher, villain; rascal, knave, scalawag, rogue, badman, scapegrace, rowdy, scamp, Apache; pimp, procurer, whoremaster, white slaver; criminal, felon, convict, jailbird, delinquent, troublemaker, forger; black sheep, blackguard, prodigal son, fallen angel, ne'er-do-well. *Slang,* torpedo, trigger man, gorilla, hood.

3, hag, beldam(e), Jezebel, jade, nag, shrew, fishwife; murderess; ogress, harpy, Fury, maenad; adulteress, paramour, mistress; prostitute, whore, harlot, strumpet, trull, trollop, wanton, loose woman, courtesan; madam(e), procuress, bawd, hussy, streetwalker, drag, white slave; dragon, harridan, vixen, virago; witch, siren, Circe, Delilah, Medusa, Gorgon; enchantress, sorceress. *Slang,* roundheels.

4, monster, fiend, DEMON, devil, devil incarnate, fiend in human shape; Frankenstein's monster; cannibal, bloodsucker, vampire, ghoul, vulture, ogre.

5, culprit, offender, malefactor; recidivist; traitor, betrayer, Judas (Iscariot), Benedict Arnold, Quisling; conspirator, snake in the grass; turncoat, renegade, apostate; informer. *Slang,* rat, squealer. See IMPROBITY.

Antonym, see GOODNESS.

evince, *v.t.* exhibit, display, show, manifest, EVIDENCE, demonstrate, disclose, indicate, prove. *Ant.,* see NEGATION.

evoke, *v.t.* draw forth, summon, invoke; envision, imagine; suggest, bring to mind, cause one to feel; produce, CAUSE. See IMAGINATION, EXTRACTION.

evolution, *n.* evolvement, unfolding, growth, expansion, development, elaboration; Darwinism, natural selection; mutation. See PRODUCTION, PROGRESSION, CHANGE. *Ant.*, see REGRESSION.

exacerbate, *v.* aggravate, intensify, worsen; enrage, embitter, irritate, vex. *Colloq.*, make one's blood boil. See INCREASE, IRASCIBILITY.

exact, *v.* & *adj.* —*v.t.* ask, require, claim, demand; extort, take, wring, wrest, force, impose. See COMMAND. —*adj.* strict, rigorous; accurate, precise, delicate, nice, fine, correct, literal, verbatim; faithful, lifelike, close; definite, absolute, direct. See MEANING, SIMILARITY, TRUTH. *Ant.*, see DIFFERENCE, ERROR.

EXAGGERATION

Nouns—exaggeration, EXPANSION, magnification, overstatement, hyperbole, stretch, strain, coloring, high coloring, false coloring, caricature, extravagance; Baron Munchausen; fringe, embroidery, traveler's tale, yarn, tall story *or* tale, overestimation, tempest in a teapot; much ado about nothing; puffery, boasting, rant; figure of speech, stretch of the imagination; flight of fancy.

Verbs—exaggerate, magnify, pile up, aggravate; amplify, expand, OVERESTIMATE, hyperbolize; overstate, overdraw, overpraise, overshoot the mark, strain, stretch, strain *or* stretch a point, spin a long yarn; draw the longbow, run riot, heighten, overcolor, embroider, misrepresent, puff, boast.

Adjectives—exaggerated, overwrought; bombastic, florid, flowery, magniloquent, high-flown, hyperbolical; fabulous, extravagant, preposterous; egregious, outré; high-flying, tall, steep.

Antonym, see TRUTH.

---

exalt, *v.t.* elevate, raise, advance, lift up, dignify, promote, honor; praise, glorify, magnify, extol, aggrandize, elate, uplift; intensify, heighten. See APPROBATION, ELEVATION, INCREASE. *Ant.*, see DISAPPROBATION, DEPRESSION, DECREASE.

examine, *v.t.* investigate, inspect, survey, probe, canvas, search; scrutinize, peruse, dissect, scan; test, interrogate, try, question; audit, review. See ATTENTION, INQUIRY. *Ant.*, see NEGLECT, ANSWER.

example, *n.* sample, specimen, piece; instance, case, illustration; pattern, type, standard, copy, model, idea; precedent; warning; problem, exercise. See CONFORMITY, TEACHING. *Ant.*, see UNCONFORMITY.

exasperate, *v.t.* anger, enrage, infuriate; irritate, vex, nettle, provoke, roil, peeve, annoy. See RESENTMENT.

excavation, *n.* cavity, hole, pit, mine, shaft, quarry, opening. See CONCAVITY. *Ant.*, see CONVEXITY.

exceed, *v.t.* transcend, surpass, excel, outdo, outstrip, beat; overstep, pass, overdo, go beyond. See SUPERIORITY. *Ant.*, see INFERIORITY.

excel, *v.t.* exceed, surpass, eclipse, outdo, outstrip. See SUPERIORITY. *Ant.*, see INFERIORITY.

except, *prep.* unless, saving, save, but, excepting, barring. See UNCONFORMITY. *Ant.*, see CONFORMITY.

exception, *n.* EXCLUSION, omission, rejection, reservation, limitation; objection, cavil, complaint; irregularity. See DISAPPROBATION, UNCONFORMITY.

exceptional, *adj.* abnormal; unusual, uncommon, extraordinary, rare; special, superior. See UNCONFORMITY. *Ant.*, see IMITATION.

excerpt, *n.* extract, quote, citation, selection; sentence, verse, section, PASSAGE.

excess, *n.* immoderation, INTEMPERANCE, dissipation, indulgence; superabundance, superfluity, extravagance, exorbitance; REDUNDANCE, remainder. *Ant.*, see MODERATION.

excessive, *adj.* immoderate, inordinate, extravagant, exorbitant, unreasonable, outrageous, superfluous, extreme, vast. See DEPTH, GREATNESS.

exchange, *n.* reciprocity, substitution; trade, BARTER, commence; conversion, INTERCHANGE; market.

EXCITABILITY

Nouns—**1,** excitability, impetuosity, vehemence, impatience, intolerance; irritability, IRASCIBILITY; disquiet(ude), AGITATION. *Slang,* jitters.

2, VIOLENCE, fierceness, rage, anger, fury, furor(e); desperation; mania, madness (see INSANITY), distraction, raving, delirium, frenzy, hysterics.

3, fascination, infatuation, fanaticism; quixotism, quixotry.

Verbs—**1,** be excitable *or* impatient, chafe, champ at the bit, be in a stew, fidget, fuss, toss; jump, twitch, jerk, jitter.

2, lose one's temper, burst out; fly off [at a tangent]; explode, flare up, burn; boil (over), foam, fume, seethe, rage, rave, rant, tear; run wild, go mad; go into hysterics; run riot, run amuck, go off half-cocked. *Slang,* get one's goat, fly off the handle, blow one's top.

Adjectives—**1,** excitable, irritable, irascible; seething, hot, boiling, burning; impatient, intolerant; feverish, febrile, hysterical; mettlesome, skittish; delirious, mad, moody, unquiet; mercurial, electric, galvanic; impulsive, impetuous, passionate, uncontrolled, ungovernable, irrepressible.

2, vehement, demonstrative, violent, wild, furious, fierce, fiery, hotheaded.

3, overzealous, enthusiastic, impassioned, fanatical, rabid.

        Antonym, see INSENSIBILITY.

EXCITEMENT

Nouns—**1,** excitement, excitation; stimulation, piquancy, provocation; animation, AGITATION, perturbation; fascination, intoxication, enravishment, entrancement, high pressure; passion, thrill.

2, disturbance, tumult, turmoil, commotion, hubbub, fluster, fuss, bustle, hurly-burly, hullabaloo, pandemonium, furor(e).

3, excitability, impetuosity, turbulence; impatience, IRASCIBILITY; effervescence, ebullition; fanaticism.

Verbs—**1,** excite, affect, TOUCH, move; impress, strike, interest, animate, inspire, impassion, stir *or* warm the blood; awaken, evoke, provoke; raise, arouse, stir; fire, kindle, enkindle, set on fire, inflame, fan the flames, foster, heat, warm, foment, raise to fever heat. *Colloq.,* rev up.

2, stimulate, inspirit, stir up, work up, sharpen, whet, incite, give a fillip, put on one's mettle; stir *or* play on the feelings; touch a chord, go to one's heart, touch to the quick.

3, absorb, rivet the attention, prey on the mind, intoxicate; overwhelm, overpower, upset; turn one's head, carry *or* sweep off one's feet, fascinate, enrapture.

4, agitate, perturb, ruffle, fluster, shake, disturb, startle, shock, stagger; give one a turn; stun, irritate, sting; cut to the quick, try one's temper, pique, infuriate, madden, make one's blood boil, lash into fury, get on one's nerves.

5, be excited, flare up; work oneself up; seethe, boil, simmer, foam, fume, rage, rave; run amuck *or* mad, lose one's head. *Colloq.,* burst a blood vessel, have a fit.

Adjectives—**1,** excited, wrought up, on the *qui vive,* in a quiver, in a fever, in hysterics; black in the face, overwrought; hot, flushed, feverish; all atwitter; flaming, boiling, boiling over, seething, foaming (at the mouth), fuming, raging; wild, frantic, mad, distracted, beside oneself, out of one's mind *or* wits, ready to burst, stung to the quick.

2, exciting, warm, glowing, fervid, swelling, heart-stirring, thrilling; soul-stirring, agonizing, sensational, hysterical; overpowering, overwhelming, piquant, spicy, provocative, tantalizing. *Colloq.,* mind-blowing.

3, excitable, irritable, irascible, impatient; feverish, hysterical; mettlesome, skittish; jumpy, nervous, jittery; tempestuous, impulsive, impetuous, ungovernable; demonstrative, fiery, hotheaded, enthusiastic, impassioned, fanatical, rabid.

Adverbs—excitedly, excitingly; with bated breath. *Colloq.*, in a dither, all agog.

Antonym, see INDIFFERENCE.

exclaim, *v.i.* cry out, shout, ejaculate, clamor, vociferate. See CRY.

EXCLUSION

Nouns—exclusion, omission, exception, REJECTION, repudiation, relegation; preclusion, elimination, dismissal, DISPLACEMENT; separation, segregation, isolation, ostracism; PROHIBITION; exile, banishment, EJECTION; silent treatment.

Verbs—exclude, bar; prohibit, preclude; leave out, rule *or* count out, reject, repudiate, blackball; lay, put *or* set aside; relegate, pass over, omit, eliminate, weed out, throw over, thrown overboard; strike out; separate, disjoin, segregate, isolate, ostracize; displace; keep *or* shut out, except; restrain, hinder, prevent; withhold; exile, banish, eject.

Adjectives—exclusive, cliquish, clannish; closed; sole, unique; one and only, barring all others; exclusory, prohibitive; select, restrictive; excluded, left out, isolated, solitary, banished, inadmissible, unacceptable.

Prepositions—exclusive of, barring, except; with the exception of; save.

Antonym, see INCLUSION.

excommunicate, *v.t.* expel, curse, unchurch. See EXCLUSION.
excrescence, *n.* outgrowth, protuberance, appendage. See CONVEXITY.

EXCRETION

Nouns—1, excretion, discharge, emanation, exhalation, exudation, extrusion, secretion, effusion, extravasation, evacuation, dejection, defecation, EJECTION.

2, perspiration, sweat, saliva, spittle, rheum, sputum, spit, salivation, catarrh, diarrhea, *ejecta, excreta,* urine, feces, excrement; hemorrhage, bleeding, flux.

Verbs—excrete, eject, discharge, emit, evacuate, defecate; emanate, exhale, exude, perspire, sweat; cast off, shed.

Adjectives—excretive, excretory, ejective, eliminative; fecal, urinary; sweaty.

excruciating, *adj.* torturing, painful, agonizing, racking, acute. See PAIN. *Ant.,* see PLEASURE.
excursion, *n.* expedition, trip, sally, tour, outing, JOURNEY, jaunt; digression. See DEVIATION.
excuse, *v.t.* pardon, remit, overlook, condone, forgive, extenuate, justify; exonerate, absolve, acquit, exempt, free, apologize. See VINDICATION. *Ant.,* see RETALIATION, ACCUSATION.
execrable, *adj.* abominable, bad, detestable; poor, inferior, wretched. *Ant.,* see GOODNESS.
execute, *v.t.* perform, do, accomplish, make, administer, enforce, effect; finish, complete, fulfill; kill, put to death, behead, lynch, hang, gas, electrocute; seal, sign. See COMPLETION, PUNISHMENT.
executive, *n.* director, manager, official, administrator. *Colloq.,* boss. *Slang,* brass.
exemplify, *v.t.* typify; illustrate, explain, quote. See CONFORMITY. *Ant.,* see UNCONFORMITY.

EXEMPTION

Nouns—exemption, FREEDOM, irresponsibility, immunity, liberty, license, release, exoneration, excuse, dispensation, exception, absolution, discharge, exculpation; RELEASE.

Verbs—exempt, release, acquit, discharge, remit; liberate, free, set at liberty, let off, pass over, spare, excuse, dispense with, give dispensation, license; stretch a point, absolve, forgive, exonerate.

Adjectives—**1,** exempt, free, at liberty, scot-free, released, unbound, unencumbered, irresponsible, unaccountable, not answerable, immune, privileged, excusable, allowance.

2, not having, devoid of, destitute of, without, unpossessed of, unblest with, exempt from, off one's hands; tax-free, untaxed, untaxable.

Antonym, see LIABILITY, DUTY.

EXERTION

Nouns—**1,** exertion, ENERGY, effort, strain, tug, pull, stretch, struggle, bout, spurt, trouble, pains, endeavor.

2, gymnastics, exercise, workout, athletics, calisthenics, acrobatics; training, sport, play, drill; ado.

3, labor, work, toil, task, travail, manual labor, sweat of one's brow, elbow grease, wear and tear, toil and trouble, yeoman work, uphill work, drudgery, slavery, heavy duty.

4, laborer, worker, toiler, drudge, slave; workhorse, packhorse, galley slave, Trojan. *Slang,* workaholic.

Verbs—**1,** exert oneself, strive, strain, pull, tug, ply, struggle, try.

2, labor, work; toil, moil, sweat, plug, plod, drudge, slave; buckle down, dig in, bear down, wade into, come to grips; set one's shoulder to the wheel; work like a horse; burn the candle at both ends; keep one's nose to the grindstone; persevere, take pains, do one's best, strain every nerve, spare no pains, move heaven and earth, burn oneself out. *Slang,* sweat blood.

Adjectives—laboring; laborious; strained, toilsome, troublesome, wearisome, uphill, Herculean; hardworking, painstaking, strenuous, energetic.

Adverbs—laboriously, lustily; with might and main, with all one's might, tooth and nail, hammer and tongs, heart and soul; by the sweat of one's brow; energetically. *Colloq.,* like mad.

Antonym, see REPOSE.

---

exhale, *v.t.* breathe, expel, emanate, emit, expire, transpire, respire, blow. See EXCRETION, WIND.

exhaust, *v.t.* drain, empty, let out, deflate; weaken, deplete, overtire, prostrate, fag, FATIGUE; spend, impoverish, consume, use, expend; develop, finish, end. See COMPLETION, EJECTION. *Ant.,* see RECEIVING, RESTORATION.

exhibit, *v.t.* show, present, display, produce, demonstrate, stage, expose, evince; reveal; flaunt. See EVIDENCE, OSTENTATION, PRODUCTION. *Ant.,* see DESTRUCTION.

exhilarate, *v.t.* elate, exalt, inspirit; enliven, animate, cheer, make merry, invigorate, gladden. *Ant.,* see DEJECTION.

exhort, *v.* urge, prompt, admonish. *Colloq.,* egg on. See ADVICE, WARNING.

exhume, *v.t.* dig up, disinter, excavate; discover, locate; call up, recall. See MEMORY, EXTRACTION, DISCOVERY.

exigency, *n.* demand, need, necessity, distress, DIFFICULTY, extremity, urgency, pressure, pinch, crisis, emergency, juncture. See CIRCUMSTANCE, DESIRE.

exile, *v.t.* expel, remove, banish, expatriate. See DISPLACEMENT.

EXISTENCE

Nouns—**1,** existence, LIFE, being, entity, *ens, esse,* subsistence, coëxistence, PRESENCE.

2, reality, actuality; positiveness, fact, matter of fact, stubborn fact, not a dream, no joke, sober reality, TRUTH, verity, actual existence.

Verbs—exist, be; have being, subsist, live, breathe; stand, obtain, be the case; occur, consist in, lie in, have place, prevail, endure, find oneself, vegetate, come *or* bring into existence; arise, begin; come forth, appear, become, be converted.

Adjectives—1, existing, existent, extant; in existence, current, prevalent. 2, real, actual, positive, absolute, authentic, true; substantial, substantive, enduring, well-founded.

Adverbs—actually, really, truly, positively, in fact, in point of fact, in reality, indeed, *de facto, ipso facto.*

Antonym, see NONEXISTENCE.

---

exit, *n.* departure; withdrawal; DEATH. See EGRESS. *Ant.,* see LIFE, INGRESS.

exodus, *n.* departure, flight, migration, EGRESS, issue.

exonerate, *v.t.* exculpate, free, clear, absolve, acquit. See VINDICATION.

exorbitant, *adj.* excessive, immoderate, unreasonable; extravagant, expensive, DEAR. See GREATNESS. *Ant.,* see CHEAPNESS, LITTLENESS.

exorcise, *v.t.* expel, drive *or* cast out; adjure, conjure. See SORCERY.

exotic, *adj.* foreign, alien; strange, outlandish, *outré,* bizarre, rare; vivid, colorful, extravagant. See UNCONFORMITY, ATTRACTION, EXCITEMENT.

expanse, *n.* area, stretch, spread, reach, extent, breadth. See SPACE.

EXPANSION

Nouns—expansion, INCREASE, enlargement, extension, augmentation, amplification, dilation, aggrandizement, spread, increment, growth, development, swell, turgescence, turgidity, turgidity; obesity, dropsy, tumefaction, tumescence, swelling, tumor, tumidity; diastole, distension; puffiness, inflation; germination, upgrowth; development; overgrowth, hypertrophy.

Verbs—1, expand, widen, enlarge, extend, grow, increase, swell, fill out; dilate; stretch, spread; spring up, bud, burgeon, sprout, germinate, put forth, open, burst forth, gain flesh, outgrow, overrun, be larger than. 2, extend, aggrandize, distend, develop, amplify, widen, magnify, inflate, stuff, pad, cram, exaggerate; fatten. *Colloq.,* blow up.

Adjectives—expanded, larger, swollen, expansive, widespread, overgrown, exaggerated, bloated, fat, turgid, tumid, hypertrophied, pot-bellied; obese, puffy, distended, bulbous, full-blown, full-grown, big.

Antonym, see CONTRACTION.

---

expatiate, *v.i.* enlarge, descant, dilate, expand; rant. See LOQUACITY. *Ant.,* see CONTRACTION.

expatriate, *n.* exile, displaced person; exurbanite. See DISPLACEMENT, SECLUSION.

EXPECTATION

Nouns—1, expectation, expectancy, anticipation, reckoning, calculation, foresight, PREDICTION, imminence, contingency; contemplation, lookout, prospect, perspective, horizon. 2, suspense, waiting, anxiety, apprehension, curiosity; HOPE, BELIEF, faith.

Verbs—expect, look for, look out for, look forward to; hope for, anticipate; have in prospect, keep in view, wait *or* watch for, keep a sharp lookout for, await; bide one's time; foresee, prepare for, predict, forestall, count upon, believe in, think likely.

Adjectives—1, expectant, expecting; open-mouthed, agape, all agog, on tenterhooks; ready, curious, eager, anxious, apprehensive. 2, expected, foreseen, in prospect, prospective, in view, impending, imminent. *Colloq.,* on deck.

Adverbs—expectantly, on the watch, with bated breath, with ears pricked up, on edge.

Interjections—no wonder! of course!

Antonym, see DOUBT.

EXPEDIENCE

Nouns—expedience, expediency, desirableness, desirability, advisability, eligibility, seemliness, fitness, UTILITY, propriety, opportunism, opportunity.

Verbs—be expedient *or* suitable, suit *or* befit the occasion, strike the right note.

Adjectives—expedient, acceptable, convenient, worthwhile, meet, fitting, due, proper, eligible, seemly, becoming, opportune, in season, suitable.

Adverbs—expediently, conveniently; in the right place, at the right moment.

Antonym, see INEXPEDIENCE.

---

expedition, *n.* haste, dispatch, promptness, speed, alacrity; JOURNEY, quest, tour, trip, jaunt, excursion; crusade, campaign. See ACTIVITY, WARFARE. *Ant.*, see INACTIVITY.

expel, *v.t.* eject, extrude, excrete, discharge, dispel, eliminate; exclude, remove, evict, dislodge, dispossess, oust; excommunicate; banish, exile, deport, expatriate. *Slang*, bounce. *Ant.*, see RECEIVING.

expend, *v.t.* spend, lay out, pay, pay out, disburse; USE, consume; exhaust; give; WASTE, use up. See PAYMENT. *Ant.*, see RECEIVING.

expenditure, *n.* expense(s), outlay, spending, PAYMENT, cost(s); disbursement, outgo, overhead; price; purchase(s). See USE, WASTE. *Ant.*, see RECEIVING.

expensive, *adj.* costly, dear, high, exorbitant. See DEARNESS.

experience, *v.t.* have, know, see, meet, encounter; undergo, suffer, brave, sustain; enjoy, realize, apprehend, understand. See OCCASION, FEELING, KNOWLEDGE, TASTE. *Ant.*, see IGNORANCE.

EXPERIMENT

Nouns—**1,** experiment, experimentation, ESSAY; analysis, investigation, trial; verification, probation, proof; criterion, test, check, assay, ordeal; empiricism, rule of thumb, trial and error.

2, feeler; trial balloon, test flight, scout, straw in the wind, speculation, random shot, leap *or* shot in the dark.

Verbs—**1,** experiment, ESSAY, try; put on trial, put to the *test* or proof; test, practice upon; try one's strength.

2, grope, feel *or* grope one's way; throw out a feeler, send up a trial balloon, see how the land lies, see how the wind blows, feel the pulse, beat the bushes, try one's fortune; explore, inquire. *Colloq.*, see how the ball bounces.

Adjectives—experimental, probative, probationary, analytic, tentative, empirical, under probation, on trial.

---

expert, *n. & adj.* —*n.* adept, connoisseur, virtuoso, master; master hand, top sawyer, prima donna, first fiddle, old hand; practiced eye, marksman, crack; conjuror; veteran, champion, ace; old stager *or* campaigner; genius, mastermind, tactician, strategist. *Slang*, sharp, shark, wizard, whiz. —*adj.* proficient, adept, apt, skilled, crack. *Ant.*, see UNSKILLFULNESS.

expertise, *n.* SKILL, skillfulness, KNOWLEDGE, LEARNING, facility, proficiency, mastery; professionalism, *savoir-faire*. *Colloq.*, know-how. See PERFECTION.

expire, *v.i.* exhale, breathe out, emit; die, perish; END, cease, terminate, stop. See DEATH, WIND. *Ant.*, see LIFE, BEGINNING.

explain, *v.t.* expound, solve, elucidate, resolve, fathom, account for; demonstrate, construe, interpret, define, describe, develop, detail, criticize, comment. See ANSWER, MEANING, INTERPRETATION. *Ant.*, see INQUIRY.

explicit, *adj.* express, written, unreserved, outspoken, plain, positive, clear, unambiguous, open, definite. See INFORMATION, EVIDENCE.

explode, *v.t.* destroy; burst, detonate, fire, discharge; reject; refute, expose, disprove. See NEGATION, VIOLENCE. *Ant.,* see EVIDENCE, MODERATION.

exploit, *v. & n.* —*v.t.* utilize, profit by; abuse, misapply. *Colloq.,* milk, work. See USE. —*n.* deed, act, feat, achievement. See COURAGE.

explore, *v.t.* seek, search, fathom, prospect, penetrate, range, examine, investigate, inquire into. See INQUIRY. *Ant.,* see ANSWER.

exponent, *n.* expounder, representative; backer, defender; power, superscript. See TEACHING, REPRESENTATION, SUPPORT.

export, *n.* commodity, exportation. See EGRESS. *Ant.,* see INGRESS.

expose, *v.t.* disclose, reveal, divulge; unearth; unmask, denude, bare, uncover; exhibit, display; offer, submit; subject to, risk, weather, lay open, endanger, imperil; turn out, cast out, abandon; denounce, brand. See DANGER, DISAPPROBATION, DISCLOSURE, DIVESTMENT, EVIDENCE. *Ant.,* see SAFETY, APPROBATION, CONCEALMENT, CLOTHING.

exposition, *n.* explanation, exegesis, elucidation, commentary; show, exhibition; fair; statement, discourse; exposure, abandonment. See DISCLOSURE, INTERPRETATION, EVIDENCE, BUSINESS. *Ant.,* see CONCEALMENT.

expostulate, *v.i.* remonstrate, reason, dissuade; object, protest, rebuke. See ADVICE, DISAPPROBATION.

expound, *v.t.* state, express, set forth; explain, interpret, elucidate. See TEACHING.

express, *v.t.* squeeze, press out; extort; exude; represent, symbolize, show, demonstrate, reveal, denote, signify, delineate, exhibit, depict; state, tell, frame, enunciate, broach, expound, couch, utter, voice, communicate, speak; ship. See EVIDENCE, MEANING, SPEECH.

expression, *n.* representation, symbolization, INDICATION; statement, utterance, wording, COMMUNICATION; modulation, shading, INTERPRETATION; idiom, PHRASE, term; aspect, look, pose; token; saying. See AFFIRMATION, APPEARANCE, MANIFESTATION.

expulsion, *n.* ejection, eviction, ousting, dislodgement, dismissal; EXCLUSION, excommunication; banishment, exile, deportation, expatriation, ostracism; excretion, discharge. *Ant.,* see INCLUSION.

expurgate, *v.t.* bowdlerize; purge, purify, cleanse; emasculate, castrate. See CLEANNESS. *Ant.,* see UNCLEANNESS.

exquisite, *adj.* accurate, exact; fastidious, appreciative, discriminating; choice, selected, refined, rare; accomplished, perfected; intense, keen, SHARP, excellent, delicate, beautiful, matchless, dainty, charming, delightful. See BEAUTY, TASTE, GOODNESS, PLEASURE. *Ant.,* see UGLINESS, EVIL, PAIN.

extant, *adj.* surviving, existent. See EXISTENCE. *Ant.,* see NONEXISTENCE.

extemporaneous, *adj.* unpremeditated, spontaneous, extempore, improvised, impromptu, offhand, unprepared. See IMPULSE. *Ant.,* see PREPARATION.

extemporize, *v.t. & i.* compose, improvise, make up. *Colloq.,* fake, wing it. See UNPREPAREDNESS.

extend, *v.t.* continue, lengthen, elongate, widen, enlarge, stretch, draw out, prolong, protract, expand, spread, broaden; increase; hold out, proffer. See INCREASE, LENGTH. *Ant.,* see CONTRACTION, SHORTNESS.

extension, *n.* widening, enlargement, stretching, EXPANSION, amplification, distension, ADDITION, continuance, continuation, lengthening, protraction, prolongation, protrusion, projection, ramification; comprehension; expanse, sweep, stretch. See INCREASE, PRODUCTION, SPACE.

extenuate, *v.t.* excuse, forgive, pardon, mitigate, palliate; attenuate; diminish, weaken. See VINDICATION. *Ant.,* see RETALIATION, ACCUSATION, POWER.

EXTERIOR

Nouns—**1,** exterior, exteriority, outwardness, externality, extraneousness, eccentricity, circumjacence.

2, outside, surface, superficies; skin (see COVERING), superstratum, facet, SIDE.

Verbs—be exterior, be outside, lie around, surround, encompass, environ, enclose, encircle, loop, gird, hem in.

Adjectives—exterior, external, outer, outmost, outermost, outward, round about, superficial, skin deep, eccentric, EXTRINSIC.

Adverbs—externally, outwardly, out, outer, without, outward(s); out-of-doors, in the open air, *al fresco.*

Antonym, see INTERIOR.

---

exterminate, *v.t.* abolish, destroy, annihilate; extirpate, eradicate, root out. See DESTRUCTION. *Ant.*, see PRODUCTION.

external, *adj.* EXTERIOR, outward, outer, outside, extraneous; foreign; perceptible, visible, physical, extraneous, superficial. *Ant.*, see INTERIOR.

extinct, *adj.* extinguished, quenched; exterminated, nonexistent, obsolete; died out, passed away, dead, gone. *Ant.*, see EXISTENCE.

extinguish, *v.t.* destroy, annihilate, eradicate, suppress, end; quench, choke, put *or* blow out, douse, snuff; smother, suffocate; quell, subdue. See DARKNESS, DESTRUCTION, REFRIGERATION.

extol, *v.t.* praise, applaud, commend, glorify; celebrate, exalt. See APPROBATION. *Ant.*, see DISAPPROBATION.

extort, *v.t.* elicit, extract, draw, exact; wring, wrench, force; squeeze. See ACQUISITION, STEALING. *Ant.*, see RESTORATION.

extra, *adj.* additional, accessory, spare, supplementary, redundant. See ADDITION, AUXILIARY.

EXTRACTION

Nouns—**1,** extraction, removal; elimination, extrication, eradication, evulsion; wrench, expression, squeezing; extirpation, extermination, EJECTION, suction.

2, EVOLUTION, derivation, origin, ANCESTRY, DESCENT.

3, extractor, corkscrew, forceps, pliers; pump, pulmotor, vacuum cleaner.

Verbs—**1,** extract; draw, pull, tear *or* pluck out; wring from, wrench, extort, root out, rout out, dig out; grub up, rake out, uproot, pull up; extirpate, eradicate, eliminate, remove; express, squeeze out.

2, educe, elicit, evolve, extract, derive, bring forth. *Colloq.*, milk, pump.

Antonym, see ADDITION, INSERTION.

---

extradite, *v.t.* deliver, deport, expel; turn *or* hand over. See EJECTION, PUNISHMENT, TRANSPORTATION.

extraneous, *adj.* foreign, alien; ulterior, exterior, external, outlandish; excluded, inadmissible, exceptional. *Ant.*, see RELATION.

extraordinary, *adj.* unusual, singular, uncommon, remarkable, phenomenal, abnormal; eminent, rare, notable. See GREATNESS, UNCONFORMITY. *Ant.*, see LITTLENESS, CONFORMITY.

extravagant, *adj.* profuse, PRODIGAL, lavish, excessive, extreme; wasteful, profligate, rampant, wild; bombastic, fantastic; high, exorbitant, unreasonable; unreal, flighty, visionary; absurd, fanciful, grotesque. See GREATNESS, IMAGINATION, ABSURDITY. *Ant.*, see CHEAPNESS, LITTLENESS.

extreme, *adj.* remote, utmost, farthest, last, final, ultra, radical, drastic; excessive, inordinate, deep, intense, desperate, outrageous, immoderate, greatest. See END, GREATNESS, REVOLUTION. *Ant.*, see BEGINNING, LITTLENESS.

extremity, *n.* utmost, limit, edge, boundary, tip; limb (of the body); destitution, need, distress. See ADVERSITY, END.

extricate, *v.t.* free, disentangle, loose, liberate, relieve, disengage. See FREEDOM. *Ant.,* see RESTRAINT.

extrinsic, *adj.* extrinsical, objective, extraneous, foreign, adventitious, incidental, accidental, nonessential, subsidiary, contingent, outward, external. *Ant.,* INTRINSIC.

exuberance, *n.* zest, enthusiasm, VIGOR, ebullience, ENERGY, EXCITEMENT; high spirits, CHEERFULNESS; abundance, bounty, effusion. See SUFFICIENCY.

exude, *v.t. & i.* emit, discharge, ooze, leak, trickle, drain. See EGRESS. *Ant.,* see INGRESS.

exult, *v.i.* rejoice, vaunt, jubilate, gloat, triumph, glory. *Colloq.,* crow. See BOASTING, REJOICING. *Ant.,* see LAMENTATION.

eye, *n. & v.* —*v.t.* watch, ogle, stare, view, observe, scrutinize, inspect. See VISION. *Ant.,* see BLINDNESS. —*n.* orb, visual, organ; optic; eyesight, perception; VISION. *Ant.,* see BLINDNESS.

eyesight, *n.* See VISION.

eyesore, *n.* UGLINESS, offense, blemish. *Ant.,* see BEAUTY.

F

fable, *n.* parable, allegory, moral tale, apologue; myth, fiction, story. See DESCRIPTION, FALSEHOOD. *Ant.,* TRUTH.

fabric, *n.* cloth, textile, material, tissue; structure, framework. See PRODUCTION, FORM.

fabricate, *v.t.* build, construct, manufacture; invent, make up, trump up, concoct. See PRODUCTION, IMAGINATION, FALSEHOOD, DECEPTION.

fabulous, *adj.* legendary, mythical; extravagant, incredible, stupendous, prodigious. See DESCRIPTION, EXAGGERATION, GREATNESS.

façade, *n.* FRONT; APPEARANCE, aspect, style; pretense, false front, mask, persona; simulation, AFFECTATION. See FALSENESS.

face, *n. & v.* —*n.* countenance, visage, physiognomy, lineaments, features; FRONT, façade, facet, obverse; van, first line. *Slang,* mug, map, phiz, puss. See APPEARANCE. —*v.t.* encounter, confront, veneer, plate, sheathe. See OPPOSITION, COVERING.

facet, *n.* face, surface, plane, bezel, culet; aspect, phase. See ATTRIBUTION.

facetious, *adj.* whimsical, joking, tongue-in-cheek; ironic(al), sarcastic, satirical, derisive. *Slang,* wise, smart. See WIT, LEVITY, AFFECTATION.

FACILITY

Nouns—facility, ease; easiness; capability; feasibility, practicability (see CHANCE); flexibility, pliancy (see SOFTNESS); SMOOTHNESS; dexterity, SKILL; plain sailing, smooth sailing; smooth water, fair wind; clear coast, clear stage; sinecure, child's play; full *or* free play (see FREEDOM); disencumbrance, disentanglement; LUBRICATION; PERMISSION. *Slang,* snap, soft snap, cinch, breeze, picnic.

Verbs—1, be easy, be feasible; go smoothly, run smoothly; have full *or* free play (see FREEDOM); work well; flow *or* swim with the stream; drift *or* go with the tide; see one's way; have it all one's own way; have the game in one's own hands; walk over the course; win in a walk, win hands down; take in one's stride; make light of, make nothing of; be at home in.

2, render easy, facilitate, smooth, ease; popularize; lighten, lighten the labor; free, clear; disencumber, disembarrass, disentangle, disengage; disobstruct, unclog, extricate, unravel; untie *or* cut the knot; disburden, unload, exonerate, emancipate, free from; humor; lubricate; relieve (see

RELIEF); leave the matter open; give the reins to; make way for; open the door to; prepare the ground *or* way; smooth *or* clear the ground, way, path *or* road; pave the way, bridge over; permit (see PERMISSION); leave a loophole. *Colloq.*, grease the ways.

Adjectives—**1,** facile, simple, easy; feasible, practicable; easily managed *or* accomplished; within reach, accessible, easy of access, open to.

2, manageable, wieldy; tractable; submissive; yielding, ductile; pliant, soft; glib, slippery; smooth (see SMOOTHNESS); unburdened, disburdened, disencumbered, unembarrassed; exonerated; unloaded, unobstructed, in the clear, untrammeled; unrestrained; free; at ease, light; at home; in one's element. *Colloq.*, soft, nothing to it, easy as falling off a log, like water off a duck's back. *Slang*, easy as pie.

Adverbs—facilely, easily; readily, smoothly, swimmingly, on easy terms, without a hitch; single-handed; without striking a blow.

Antonym, see DIFFICULTY.

---

facsimile, *n.* duplicate, counterpart, reproduction, COPY, replica. See IDENTITY, DUPLICATION.

fact, *n.* reality, actuality, certainty; OCCURRENCE, event, phenomenon. See EXISTENCE. *Ant.*, FALSEHOOD.

faction, *n.* clique, combination, cabal, splinter party; sect, denomination; DISCORD, dissidence, dissension. See PARTY.

factor, *n.* COMPONENT, element, part, constituent, condition; AGENT.

factory, *n.* manufactory, mill, shop, works, WORKSHOP.

faculty, *n.* ability, aptitude, power, talent, knack; professorate, teaching staff. See SKILL, LEARNING.

fad, *n.* craze, rage, vogue; fancy, hobby. See CHANGEABLENESS.

fade, *v.i.* pale, dim, bleach, whiten; vanish, disappear; languish, wither, shrivel. See DIMNESS, COLORLESSNESS, NONEXISTENCE, DETERIORATION.

failing, *n.* fault, frailty, shortcoming; foible. See VICE, WEAKNESS.

FAILURE

Nouns—**1,** failure, unsuccessfulness, nonsuccess, nonfulfillment; dead failure, abortion, miscarriage; labor in vain; no go; inefficacy; vain attempt, abortive attempt, slip 'twixt cup and lip.

2, blunder, mistake, ERROR; fault, omission, miss, oversight, slip, trip, stumble, false *or* wrong step; *faux pas*; botch (see UNSKILLFULNESS); scrape, mess, fiasco, breakdown; mishap, misfortune, ADVERSITY; collapse, smash, blow, explosion; fall, downfall, ruin, perdition; wreck (see DESTRUCTION); deathblow; bankruptcy (see DEBT); wild-goose chase; losing game. *Slang*, flop, bomb, dud, washout, has-been.

3, repulse, rebuff, defeat, rout, overthrow, discomfiture; beating, drubbing; quietus; nonsuit; subjugation; checkmate, stalemate.

4, failure, also-ran, flash in the pan; victim; bankrupt. *Slang*, flop, goner, lemon, dud, bust.

Verbs—**1,** fail, be unsuccessful, not succeed; labor *or* toil in vain; lose one's labor; bring to naught, make nothing of; roll the stone of Sisyphus (see USELESSNESS); do by halves; lose ground (see REGRESSION); fall short of. *Slang*, flop, peter out, not get to first base.

2, miss, miss one's aim, miss the boat *or* bus, miss the mark; make a slip, blunder (see ERROR); make a mess of; miscarry; abort; go up like a rocket and come down like the stick; reckon without one's host, back the wrong horse.

3, limp, halt, hobble, slip, trip, stumble, miss one's footing; fall, tumble; lose one's balance; overreach oneself; flounder, falter, stick in the mud, run aground; tilt at windmills; come up against a stone wall; burn one's fingers; break one's back; break down, sink, drown, founder, have the ground cut from under one; get into trouble, get into a mess *or* scrape; come to grief (see ADVERSITY): go to the wall, go under, go to the dogs, go to pot; bite the dust; be defeated; have the worst of it, lose the day; come off second best, throw in the sponge *or* towel; lose; succumb; not have a leg to stand on. *Colloq.*, flunk, flunk out, go to smash; cut one another's throats, have two strikes against one. *Slang*, fall down on, lay an egg, fold up.

4, come to nothing, end in smoke; fall through, fall flat; slip through one's fingers; hang *or* miss fire; collapse; topple down (see DESCENT); go to wrack and ruin (see DESTRUCTION); go amiss, go wrong, go hard with, go on a wrong tack; take a wrong turn; explode; dash one's hopes (see FAILURE); sow the wind and reap the whirlwind; jump out of the frying pan into the fire. *Slang*, the jig is up.

Adjectives—**1,** unsuccessful, failing; tripping, at fault; unfortunate (see ADVERSITY); abortive, stillborn; fruitless, bootless; ineffectual, ineffective; inefficient, impotent (see IMPOTENCE); inefficacious; lame, hobbling, insufficient (see INSUFFICIENCY); unavailing, useless (see USELESSNESS).

2, aground, grounded, swamped, stranded, cast away, wrecked, foundered, capsized, shipwrecked; nonsuited; foiled; defeated, vanquished, conquered; struck down, borne down, broken down; downtrodden; overborne, overwhelmed; all up with; lost, undone, ruined, broken, bankrupt (see DEBT); played out; done up, done for; dead beat, knocked on the head; destroyed (see DESTRUCTION); frustrated, crossed, unhinged, disconcerted, dashed; thrown off one's balance; unhorsed; in a sorry plight; hard hit; left in the lurch; stultified, befooled, dished, hoist by one's own petard; victimized, sacrificed; wide of the mark (see ERROR); thrown away (see WASTE); unattained; uncompleted. *Colloq.*, whipped, licked, out of the running. *Slang*, washed out.

Adverbs—unsuccessfully; to little or no purpose, in vain.

Antonym, see SUCCESS.

---

faint, *v. & adj.* —*v.i.* swoon; lose heart *or* courage; fail, fade, weaken. *Colloq.*, pass out. —*adj.* see WEARINESS, COLORLESSNESS, IMPOTENCE.

faintness, *n.* WEAKNESS; giddiness, dizziness; shakiness; DIMNESS (of color *or* light); LOWNESS (of sound), inaudibility; feebleness. *Ant.*, see LOUDNESS, POWER.

fair, *adj.* beautiful, handsome, goodlooking, pretty, comely; blond, light; unsullied, unblemished; pleasant, fine; impartial, equitable, just; moderate, passable; sunny, cloudless. See BEAUTY, COLORLESSNESS, DRYNESS, JUSTICE. *Ant.*, DARKNESS, UGLINESS, INJUSTICE.

fairy, *n.* fay, sprite, pixy, elf, brownie, gnome, leprechaun. See MYTHICAL DEITIES.

faith, *n.* trust, reliance, confidence, EXPECTATION; BELIEF, creed.

faithful, *adj.* loyal, devoted; conscientious, trustworthy; exact, lifelike. See PROBITY, OBEDIENCE. *Ant.*, FALSEHOOD, IMPROBITY.

faithless, *adj.* unfaithful, disloyal, untrue, inconstant, treacherous. See IMPROBITY. *Ant.*, see PROBITY.

fake, *n.* counterfeit, imposture, make-believe; impostor. See DECEPTION.

fakir, *n.* ascetic, dervish; yogi(n). See ASCETICISM, CLERGY.

fall, *v. & n.* —*v.i.* plunge, drop, sink, tumble, topple; perish, be deposed, come to grief; happen, occur, take place; sin, misbehave, lapse. See DESCENT, DESTRUCTION, DETERIORATION. *Ant.*, SUCCESS. —*n.* slope, declivity; downfall, defeat, comedown; drop, slump; plunge, tumble, header; autumn.

fallacy, *n.* ERROR, untruth, misconception; false meaning. *Ant.*, TRUTH.

fallible, *adj.* unreliable, untrustworthy, dubious. See DOUBT.

fallout, *n.* radioactive dust, contamination. See ARMS, WARFARE.

fallow, *adj.* uncultivated, untilled, unsown. See NEGLECT.

false alarm, crying "wolf," FAILURE; hoax, bugbear. See ALARM.

FALSEHOOD

Nouns—**1,** falsehood, falseness; falsity, falsification; DECEPTION, untruth; guile; lying, misrepresentation; mendacity, perjury, forgery, invention, fabrication.

2, perversion of truth, suppression of truth; perversion, distortion, false coloring; EXAGGERATION, prevarication, equivocation, shuffling, fencing, evasion, fraud; mystification, CONCEALMENT, simulation, IMITATION, dissimulation, dissembling; DECEPTION, deceit; sham, pretense, pretending, malingering. *Colloq.,* make-believe, play-acting, bunk; whitewash.

3, lip service; hollowness; duplicity, double-dealing, insincerity, hypocrisy, cant, humbug; pharisaism; Machiavellianism; crocodile tears, mealy-mouthedness, quackery; charlatanism, charlatanry; cajolery, flattery; Judas kiss; perfidy, bad faith, unfairness (see IMPROBITY); artfulness (see SKILL); misstatement (see ERROR). *Colloq.,* front. *Slang,* four-flushing.

4, half-truth, white lie, pious fraud; irony.

5, liar, fibber, prevaricator, falsifier, perjurer; Ananias, Baron Munchausen.

Verbs—**1,** be false, speak falsely, tell a lie, lie, fib; lie like a trooper; forswear, perjure oneself, bear false witness; misstate, misquote, miscite, misreport, misrepresent; belie, falsify, pervert, distort; put a false construction upon, misinterpret; misinform, mislead; prevaricate, equivocate, quibble; fence, mince the truth, beat about the bush, blow hot and cold, play fast and loose; garble, gloss over, disguise, color, varnish, dress up, embroider; exaggerate. *Slang,* throw the bull.

2, invent, fabricate; trump up, get up; forge, hatch, concoct; romance, imagine (see IMAGINATION); cry "wolf!"; dissemble, dissimulate; feign, assume, put on, pretend, make believe; play false, play a double game; act a part; play a part; affect; simulate; palm off, pass off for; counterfeit, sham, make a show of; malinger; cant, play the hypocrite, deceive (see DECEPTION). *Colloq.,* let on, play-act, play possum, put on a front. *Slang,* four-flush, go through the motions.

Adjectives—false, deceitful, mendacious, unveracious, fraudulent, dishonest; faithless, truthless, trothless; unfair, uncandid, evasive; uningenuous, disingenuous; hollow, insincere, forsworn; canting; hypocritical, pharisaical; Machiavellian, two-faced, double-dealing; Janus-faced; smooth-faced, smooth-spoken, smooth-tongued, tongue in cheek; plausible; mealy-mouthed; affected; collusive, collusory, artful, CUNNING; perfidious (see IMPROBITY); spurious, deceptive (see DECEPTION); untrue, falsified.

Adverbs—falsely; slily, slyly, crookedly, *etc.*

Antonym, see TRUTH.

---

falter, *v.i.* hesitate, waver, hang back, vacillate; shuffle, stumble, totter; stammer. See DOUBT, SLOWNESS, SPEECH.

fame, *n.* REPUTE, renown, prestige, celebrity; honor, distinction, glory, eminence; notoriety. See IMPORTANCE. *Ant.,* DISREPUTE.

familiar spirit, genius, dæmon, familiar, supernatural attendant. See MYTHICAL DEITIES.

familiarity, *n.* intimacy, acquaintance, fellowship; KNOWLEDGE; informality, unconstraint; forwardness, impudence. See FRIEND, SOCIALITY, FREEDOM.

family, *n.* household; forefathers, children, descendants, lineage; clan, tribe, kindred; group, association, classification. See RELATION, ANCESTRY.

famine, *n.* starvation, hunger, scarcity. See INSUFFICIENCY. *Ant.,* SUFFICIENCY.

famish, *v.* starve, die of hunger; be HUNGRY; pinch, exhaust. See INSUFFICIENCY, KILLING.

famous, *adj.* noted, famed, renowed, celebrated, well-known, distinguished. See REPUTE. *Ant.,* see DISREPUTE.

fan, *n. & v.* —*n.* fanner, blower, winnower, flabellum; ventilator. See WIND. —*v.t.* blow, winnow, cool, refresh, ventilate, stir up. *Slang,* strike out. See AIR, COLD.

fan, *n.* devotee, follower, enthusiast, supporter. *Slang,* rooter, addict, groupie. See ACTIVITY.

fanatic, *n.* ZEALOT, enthusiast, dogmatist.

fanciful, *adj.* whimsical, capricious, fantastic, quaint, bizarre; quixotic, imaginary. See UNCONFORMITY, IMAGINATION, CAPRICE.

fancy, *n.,* *v.* & *adj.* —*n.* IMAGINATION; idea, CAPRICE, whim, preference; reverie, daydream. See DESIRE. —*v.t.* imagine; believe; like, DESIRE, take to. See BELIEF, SUPPOSITION, IMAGINATION. —*adj.* ornate, showy; superior, extravagant. See ORNAMENT, OSTENTATION.

fanfare, *n.* flourish, tantara; CELEBRATION, OSTENTATION. *Colloq.,* to-do.

fang, *n.* tooth, eyetooth, tusk. See SHARPNESS.

fantastic, *adj.* bizarre, grotesque; imaginative, fanciful; extravagant, irrational, absurd. See IMAGINATION, ABSURDITY.

far, *adv.* & *adj.* —*adv.* remotely, distantly, widely, afar. —*adj.* remote, distant. See DISTANCE. *Ant.,* NEARNESS.

farce, *n.* buffoonery, ABSURDITY, burlesque; broad comedy, travesty.

fare, *v.* & *n..* —*v.i.* get on, make out, get along; prosper, thrive; eat, dine, regale onself. See CIRCUMSTANCE, FOOD. — *n.* passage, carfare, token; luck, outcome; FOOD, diet, table, board, provisions. See TRAVEL, PRICE.

farewell, *interj.* & *n.* —*interj.* good-by(e)! *vale! aloha! auf Wiedersehen! a rivederci! adieu! au revoir!. Slang,* so long. —*n.* parting, leave-taking, DEPARTURE, Godspeed, valedictory. *Ant.,* ARRIVAL.

farm, *n.* & *v.* —*n.* ranch, rancho, plantation, farmstead, grange. —*v.t.* cultivate, till. See AGRICULTURE.

farsighted, *adj.* hypermetropic, eagle-eyed; foresighted, longheaded, prudent, provident. See PREDICTION, VISION, PREPARATION.

farther, *adj.* & *adv.* —*adj.* more distant, further, additional. —*adv.* beyond, in addition, moreover.

fascination, *n.* charm, ATTRACTION, allurement, captivation, enamorment; bewilderment; enchantment, SPELL; obsession. See LOVE.

fascism, *n.* totalitarianism, authoritarianism; dictatorship; reactionism, nationalism; national socialism, red fascism, Falangism, Nazism; neo-fascism. See PARTY, AUTHORITY, SEVERITY.

FASHION

Nouns—**1,** fashion, style, *ton, bon ton,* society; good society, polite society; drawing room, civilized life, civilization; town; *haut monde, beau monde,* high life, court; world; *haute couture;* fashionable world; Vanity Fair; show, OSTENTATION.

2, manners, breeding, politeness, COURTESY; AIR, demeanor, APPEARANCE; *savoir faire;* gentlemanliness, gentility; decorum, propriety, convention, conventionality, punctilio; form, formality; etiquette, social usage, custom, HABIT; mode, vogue, go, rage, TASTE, distinction; dress (see CLOTHING). *Slang,* the last word, *le dernier cri.*

3, man *or* woman of fashion, man *or* woman of the world; height of fashion, leader of fashion; arbiter; upper ten thousand (see NOBILITY); élite. *Colloq.,* upper crust, the four hundred; socialite. *Slang,* café society.

4, See METHOD, PRODUCTION.

Verbs—be fashionable, be the rage; follow the fashion, conform to the fashion; go with the stream (see CONFORMITY); keep up appearances, behave oneself; set the style *or* fashion; bring into style *or* fashion. *Colloq.,* be in the swim.

Adjectives—fashionable, in fashion, modish, stylish, recherché; new-fangled, *à la mode, comme il faut;* presentable; conventional, customary, genteel; well-bred, well-mannered, well-behaved, well-spoken; gentlemanly, lady-like; civil, polite, courteous (see COURTESY); polished, refined, thoroughbred, courtly; *distingué; dégagé,* suave, jaunty; dashing, fast.

Antonym, see VULGARITY.

fast, *v.i. & adj.* —*v.i.* starve, diet, abstain. —*adj.* swift, speedy, fleet, quick, rapid; secure, firm, permanent, profound; wild, rakish. See VELOCITY, JUNCTION, CLOSURE, IMPURITY. *Ant.*, SLOWNESS.

fasten, *v.t.* secure, make fast, attach, fix, bind, lock up. See JUNCTION, CLOSURE, RESTRAINT.

fastening, *n.* fastener, lock, catch, clasp, latch, hook, CONNECTION, link; button, zipper, hook [and eye], buckle; nail, tack, staple, screw, bolt, rivet, peg; thread; glue, cement. See JUNCTION, COHERENCE.

fastidious, *adj.* finicky, finical, per(s)nickety, squeamish; nice, overnice; particular, fussy, crotchety; delicate, meticulous, precise, exact, precious; clean, dainty, well-groomed; punctilious; thin-skinned, queasy; prudish; straitlaced; effeminate; namby-pamby; critical, discriminating, choosy; astute, keen. *Colloq.*, picky. See CLEANNESS, CARE. *Ant.*, see UN-CLEANNESS, NEGLECT, DISORDER.

fasting, *n.* fast, abstention from food; voluntary hunger; rigid dieting; starvation, hunger, famishment; hunger strike; total abstinence (from food). *Ant.*, see FOOD, GLUTTONY.

fat, *adj.* plump, stout, corpulent, obese, portly, chubby; fertile, profitable, rich; greasy, unctuous. See SIZE. *Ant.*, LITTLENESS.

fatal, *adj.* deadly, lethal, mortal; fateful, critical. See KILLING.

fatalism, *n.* determinism, predestination; SUBMISSION, apathy, nonresistance; passivity, stoicism. See DESTINY, INDIFFERENCE.

fatality, *n.* FATALISM; mortality, deadliness; casualty, accident, DEATH.

fate, *n.* DESTINY, lot, fortune, doom, predestination, chance. See NECESSITY.

fateful, *adj.* ominous, prophetic, portentous, foreboding; momentous, critical, crucial, decisive. See DESTINY, IMPORTANCE, DANGER.

fates, *n.pl.* Moirai, Parcae, Norns. See NECESSITY, DESTINY.

father, *n.* sire, forefather, male parent; founder, patriarch; priest, pastor. See ANCESTRY, CLERGY. *Eccl.* The Father, God.

fatherland, *n.* homeland, native country, home. See ABODE.

fathom, *v.t.* measure, take a sounding; plunge, reach the bottom of; investigate, probe, study, delve into. See MEASUREMENT, INTELLECT.

fathomless, *adj.* bottomless, abyssal; cryptic, mystifying, obscure, insoluble, puzzling, enigmatic. See DEPTH, SECRET, CONCEALMENT.

fatigue, *v. & n.* —*v.* weary, tire, exhaust; jade, fag; bore, irk, wear; weaken, debilitate, overstrain, overtax, overwork. —*n.* tiredness, WEARINESS, exhaustion, lassitude, feebleness; exertion, strain; faintness, labor, work, toil, drudgery; jadedness, ennui, boredom. *Ant.*, see RESTORATION.

fatuous, *adj.* vain, foolish, inept. *Slang*, dumb, sappy. See FOLLY, ABSURDITY.

faucet, *n.* tap, spigot, cock, spout, valve; spile, bung. See CLOSURE, OPENING.

fault, *n.* failing, shortcoming, peccadillo; flaw, blemish, defect, imperfection; ERROR, slip, inadvertency; sin, venial sin, vice, minor vice. See GUILT, IMPERFECTION. *Ant.*, TRUTH.

faultfinding, *adj.* captious, carping, caviling, critical, censorious. See DISAPPROBATION. *Ant.*, see APPROBATION.

faultless, *adj.* flawless, perfect, correct, impeccable; *sans peur et sans reproche*. See PERFECTION, INNOCENCE, PURITY.

favor, *n.* good will, esteem, APPROBATION, approval; partiality, bias, interest; patronage, backing; concession, dispensation; kindness, service, good turn; token, badge. See AID, PERMISSION, GIVING.

favorable, *adj.* auspicious, propitious, advantageous, opportune, commendatory, favorable, well-inclined. See OCCASION, OMEN, AID.

favorite, *n. & adj.* —*n.* darling, pet; idol, hero, jewel, apple of one's eye; CHOICE, preference; spoiled child *or* darling; sweetheart, darling, dear one. *Colloq.*, teacher's pet, white-haired boy. —*adj.* dearest; beloved, preferred, CHOICE. See LOVE. *Ant.*, see HATE, REFUSAL.

fawn, *v.i.* cringe, grovel, toady, truckle, cower, ingratiate, curry favor, flatter. See SERVILITY.

fay, *adj.* elfin, impish, pixie, pixilated; coy, arch. See LEVITY.

faze, *v.t., colloq.,* deter, daunt, ruffle; disconcert, bother, rattle, hold back, interfere with. See HINDRANCE, HOPELESSNESS.

FEAR

Nouns—**1,** fear, fearfulness, timidity, timorousness, diffidence, want of confidence; solicitude, anxiety, worry, care, apprehension, apprehensiveness, misgiving; mistrust, DOUBT, suspicion, qualm; hesitation, irresolution; fright, alarm, dread, awe, terror, dismay, consternation, panic, scare, stampede.

2, nervousness, restlessness, inquietude, disquietude; flutter, trepidation, fear and trembling, perturbation, tremor, quivering, shaking, trembling, palpitation, cold sweat; abject fear (see COWARDICE); funk, heartsinking, despondency, DESPAIR. *Colloq.,* buck fever, creeps, shivers, gooseflesh. *Slang,* jitters, heebie-jeebies.

3, intimidation, terrorism, reign of terror, THREAT, menace.

4, bugbear, bugaboo; scarecrow; hobgoblin, DEMON; nightmare, Gorgon, ogre; *bête noire.*

Verbs—**1,** fear, stand in awe of; be afraid; have qualms; be apprehensive, distrust, DOUBT; hesitate; falter, funk, cower, crouch; skulk (see COWARDICE); take fright, take alarm, panic, stampede.

2, start, wince, flinch, shy, shrink; fly, flee (see AVOIDANCE); tremble, shake; shiver, shiver in one's boots *or* shoes; shudder, flutter; tremble like a leaf *or* an aspen leaf, quake, quaver, quail; grow *or* turn pale; blench, stand aghast.

3, inspire *or* excite fear *or* awe; raise apprehensions; alarm, startle, scare, cry "wolf," disquiet, dismay; fright, frighten; affright, terrify; astound; frighten out of one's wits; awe; strike terror; appal(l), unman, petrify, horrify; make one's flesh creep, make one's hair stand on end, make one's blood run cold, make one's teeth chatter; take away one's breath; make one tremble; haunt; prey *or* weigh on the mind.

4, put in fear, terrorize, intimidate, cow, daunt, overawe, abash, deter, discourage; browbeat, bully; threaten (see WARNING), menace.

Adjectives—**1,** fearing, frightened, in fear, in a fright, afraid, fearful; timid, timorous, chicken-hearted; nervous, diffident, coy, faint-hearted, tremulous, shaky, afraid of one's shadow, apprehensive, restless, fidgety.

2, aghast; awestricken, horror-stricken, terror-stricken, panic-stricken; frightened to death, white as a sheet; pale as death, pale as ashes, pale as a ghost; breathless, in hysterics. *Colloq.,* yellow. *Slang,* chicken.

3, inspiring fear, alarming, formidable, redoubtable; perilous (see DANGER); portentous, ominous; fearful, dreadful, fell; dire, direful; shocking, terrible, terrifying, terrific; tremendous; horrid, horrible, horrific; ghastly; awful, awe-inspiring.

Adverbs—in fear, fearfully, with fear and trembling, with the tail between the legs.

Antonyms, see HOPE, COURAGE.

fearless, *adj.* bold, brave, courageous, dauntless, gallant, daring, valorous, valiant, intrepid. See COURAGE. *Ant.,* CARE, COWARDICE.

feasible, *adj.* practicable, possible, workable. See CHANGE. *Ant.,* see DIFFICULTY.

feast, *n.* banquet, spread, repast; holiday, holyday, festival. See FOOD, RITE, SUFFICIENCY. *Ant.,* INSUFFICIENCY.

feat, *n.* deed, gest, accomplishment, exploit; stunt. See ACTIVITY, COURAGE, DIFFICULTY.

feather, *n.* plume, plumage, down, aigrette; kind, sort, variety. See COVERING.

feature, *n.* lineament, aspect; trait, peculiarity, property; something

noteworthy, outstanding characteristic; presentation, film, story. See
FORM, INDICATION, IMPORTANCE.

fecund, *adj.* fertile, inventive, creative. See IMAGINATION, PRODUCTION.

federation, *n.* league, union, confederacy, association, alliance. See
COÖPERATION, PARTY.

fee, *n.* PAYMENT, pay; COMPENSATION, emolument; assessment, dues, tax;
gratuity, tip.

feeble, *adj.* See WEAKNESS, IMPOTENCE, DIMNESS.

feed, *v.* eat, dine, consume; graze, devour; nourish, nurture, bait, graze;
supply, provide, furnish. See FOOD.

feedback, *n.* RESTORATION, renewal, recovery; response. See ANSWER.

feeler, *n.* antenna, tentacle; palp(us), vibrissa; whisker; test, tentative
offer, probe, trial balloon. See FEELING, TOUCH, INQUIRY.

FEELING

Nouns—**1,** feeling, sensation, sentience, emotion, SENSIBILITY, sensitivity;
endurance, tolerance, sufferance, experience, response; PITY, pathos,
sympathy, LOVE; impression, inspiration, affection, tenderness; warmth,
glow, unction, gusto, vehemence; fervor, fervency; heartiness, cordiality;
earnestness, eagerness; ardor, élan, zeal, passion, enthusiasm, verve,
furor(e), fanaticism; EXCITEMENT; excitability, ecstasy; PLEASURE.

2, blush, suffusion, flush; tingling, thrill; turn, shock; AGITATION; quiver,
heaving, flutter, flurry, fluster, twitter, tremor; throb, throbbing; lump in
the throat; pulsation, palpitation, panting; trepidation, perturbation;
pother, stew, ferment.

3, TOUCH, tangibility, contact, manipulation.

Verbs—**1,** feel, receive an impression; be impressed with; entertain, harbor *or* cherish feeling; respond; catch fire, catch infection; enter the
spirit of.

2, bear, suffer, support, sustain, endure, abide, experience, TASTE, prove;
labor *or* smart under; bear the brunt of, brave, stand.

3, swell, glow, warm, flush, blush, change color, mantle; turn color, turn
pale, turn black in the face; tingle, thrill, heave, pant, throb, palpitate,
go pit-a-pat, tremble, quiver, flutter, twitter; shake, be agitated, be
excited, look blue, look black; wince, draw a deep breath. *Colloq.*, blow
off steam.

4, TOUCH; handle, finger, paw; fumble, grope.

Adjectives—**1,** feeling, sentient, sensuous; sensorial, sensory; emotive,
emotional; tactile, tactual, tangible, palpable.

2, warm, quick, lively, smart, strong, sharp, acute, cutting, piercing, incisive; keen, razor-sharp; trenchant, pungent, racy, piquant, poignant,
caustic.

3, impressive, deep, profound, indelible; pervading, penetrating, absorbing; deep-felt; heartfelt; swelling, soul-stirring, electric, thrilling, rapturous, ecstatic.

4, earnest, wistful, eager, breathless; fervent, fervid; gushing, passionate,
warmhearted, hearty, cordial, sincere, zealous, enthusiastic, flowing,
ardent, burning, consumed with, red-hot, fiery, flaming; seething, boiling; rabid, raving, feverish, fanatical, hysterical; impetuous, excitable;
gung-ho.

5, impressed by, moved by, touched, affected, seized by, imbued with;
devoured by; wrought up, excited, struck all of a heap; rapt, in a quiver,
enraptured.

Adverbs—feelingly, with feeling, heart and soul, from the bottom of one's
heart, at heart, *con amore, con brio,* heartily, devoutly, head over heels.
Antonym, see INSENSIBILITY.

feign, *v.t.* simulate, pretend, counterfeit, sham. See FALSEHOOD, AFFEC-
TATION.

feint, *n.* diversion, trick; pretense, artifice, evasion; sleight-of-hand, legerdemain; bobbing and weaving; red herring. See CUNNING, DECEPTION.

felicitous, *adj.* happy, well-chosen, pertinent, apt, pat, neat. See AGREEMENT, ELEGANCE.

feline, *adj.* catlike; cattish, *etc.*; stealthy, CUNNING; catty.

fell, *v.t.* bring down, cut down, chop down, drop. See DISJUNCTION.

fellow, *n.* person, man, boy; comrade, associate, colleague; compeer, equal; SCHOLAR. *Colloq.,* chap, guy. See MANKIND, FRIEND, EQUALITY, SOCIALITY.

fellowship, *n.* companionship, camaraderie, comradeship; neighborliness, amity; sodality, sorority, fraternity; scholarship. See SOCIALITY, FRIENDSHIP, COÖPERATION, REPUTE.

FEMALE

Nouns—1, female, womankind, womanhood, femininity, muliebrity; fair sex, weaker sex. *Slang*, femme, frail, dame, skirt, broad, sister, tomato.
2, madam, madame, mistress, Mrs., Ms., lady, donna, belle, matron, dowager, goody, gammer; good woman, goodwife; squaw; wife (see MARRIAGE); matronhood; miss, mademoiselle; girl (see YOUTH).
3, hen, bitch, sow, doe, roe, mare, she-goat, nanny-goat, ewe, cow; lioness, tigress; vixen.
Adjectives—female, feminine, womanly, ladylike, matronly, maidenly; womanish, effeminate, unmanly.
Antonym, see MALE.

---

feminist, *n.* suffragist, suffragette. See FEMALE.

fence, *n.* barrier, barricade, wall, stockade, paling, hedge, railing. *Slang*, receiver (of stolen goods). See INCLOSURE, EVILDOER.

fend, *v.* defend, protect, take care of; ward, hold or stave off; avert; shift [for oneself], be on one's own. See CARE, DEFENSE, REPULSION.

ferment, *n. & v.* —*n.* yeast, leaven; uproar, turmoil, agitation. See ACTIVITY. —*v.i.* effervesce, work, raise, seethe.

ferocity, *adj.* fierceness, savagery, brutality, cruelty. See MALEVOLENCE, VIOLENCE, IRASCIBILITY. *Ant.,* see MODERATION.

ferret out, spy, search *or* hunt out. *Colloq.,* fish out. See INQUIRY.

ferry, *n. & v.* —*n.* ferryboat, scow, lighter, barge, raft, launch, tender; shuttle, air lift, airdrop. —*v.* convey, transport, shuttle. See TRANSFERENCE, TRANSPORTATION, PASSAGE.

fertile, *adj.* prolific, productive, fruitful, rich; creative, inventive. See PRODUCTION, IMAGINATION.

fertilization, *n.* impregnation, procreation, pollination; soil enrichment. See PRODUCTION.

fertilizer, *n.* manure, compost, guano; soil enricher. See AGRICULTURE.

fervent, *adj.* earnest, fervid, ardent, eager; vehement, impassioned, intense. See DESIRE, FEELING.

fervor, *n.* intenseness, enthusiasm, ardor, passion, zeal. See ACTIVITY, FEELING.

fester, *n.* suppurate, ulcerate, rankle; infect. See DISEASE, DECOMPOSITION.

festivity, *n.* CELEBRATION, merrymaking; gaiety, jollity. See AMUSEMENT.

fetch, *v.t.* retrieve, bring, carry; heave, deal, yield.

fetid, *adj.* stinking, malodorous, foul, smelly, noisome. See MALODOROUSNESS. *Ant.,* see FRAGRANCE.

fetish, *n.* charm, amulet, talisman; obsession, mania. See DESIRE, IDOLATRY.

fetter, *v.t.* shackle, manacle, handcuff, (en)chain, put in irons; tie up, tie hand and foot, hobble, hog-tie, strap down. See RESTRAINT, PRISON.

feud, *n. & v.* —*n.* CONTENTION, quarrel, strife, conflict; rancor, grudge, rivalry, revenge, vendetta. —*v.i.* quarrel, struggle. See ENMITY, WARFARE.

feudalism, *n.* vassalage, serfdom, feudal system. See AUTHORITY, SERVANT.

fever, *n.* pyrexia, frenzy, delirium. See DISEASE, INSANITY.

feverish, *adj.* febrile, hectic, hot; restless, agitated. See HEAT, EXCITEMENT.

few, *adj.* not many, little; scant, scanty, meager, scarce, rare; INFREQUENT; several, two or three, hardly any. See LITTLENESS, RARITY.

fiancé, fiancée, *n.* affianced, betrothed, engaged *or* pledged (one); husband- *or* bride-elect. *Colloq.,* intended. See MARRIAGE, PROMISE.

fiasco, *n.* FAILURE, miscarriage, slip, misfire; defeat, LOSS, botch, mess. *Colloq.,* flop, fizzle. *Slang,* dud, bust, washout, turkey.

fiat, *n.* decree, COMMAND, edict, mandate, RULE. See AUTHORITY.

fiber, *n.* filament, thread, strand; shred; TEXTURE, structure.

fickleness, *n.* capriciousness, instability, inconstancy. See CHANGEABLENESS. *Ant.,* see PROBITY, DURABILITY.

fiction, *n.* fabrication, falsehood; romance, myth, hypothesis. See FALSEHOOD, DESCRIPTION. *Ant.,* see TRUTH.

fidelity, *n.* faithfulness, reliability, loyalty; exactness. See TRUTH, PROBITY. *Ant.,* see IMPROBITY.

fidget, *v.i.* be restless, be impatient, toss, twitch, twiddle. See AGITATION.

field, *n.* clearing, grassland; expanse, range, plot; playground, links, court, airport, aerodrome, ARENA; scope, sphere, realm. See REGION, AMUSEMENT, BUSINESS.

fiend, *n.* DEMON, evil spirit, imp. *Colloq.,* addict, buff, fan, fanatic, enthusiast, nut. See EVIL, DESIRE, INSANITY, FEELING.

fierce, *adj.* ferocious, truculent; tigerish, savage; intense, violent; aggressive, bellicose; vehement. See VIOLENCE, WARFARE, EXCITEMENT. *Ant.,* see MODERATION.

fiery, *adj.* impetuous, hot-tempered, fervid; irritable; blazing, glowing; inflamed. See HEAT, EXCITEMENT, IRASCIBILITY.

fiesta, *n.* CELEBRATION, holiday, fête, FESTIVAL.

fight, *n.* battle, affray, brawl, quarrel; contest, struggle; pugnacity. *Slang,* scrap, mill. See CONTENTION.

fighter, *n.* COMBATANT; boxer, prize fighter, pugilist. *Slang,* pug, bruiser.

figment, *n.* invention, fantasy, pipe dream, chimera. See IMAGINATION.

FIGURATIVE

Nouns—figurativeness, figure of speech; metaphor; way of speaking, colloquialism; phrase; figure, trope, metonymy, enallage, catachresis, synecdoche, autonomasia; irony; image, imagery; metalepsis, type, anagoge, simile, personification, allegory, apologue, parable, fable; allusion, adumbration; application; hyperbole, EXAGGERATION.

Verbs—speak figuratively, employ figures of speech, employ metaphor; personify, allegorize, adumbrate; apply, allude to.

Adjectives—figurative, metaphorical, catachrestic, typical, parabolic, symbolic, allegorical, allusive, anagogical; ironical; colloquial.

Adverbs—figuratively, metaphorically; so to speak, so to say; as it were; in a manner of speaking.

Antonym, see MEANING, LITERAL.

figure, *n. & v.* —*n.* FORM, shape, configuration, outline; body; REPRESENTATION, image, effigy; APPEARANCE; pattern, diagram; figure of speech (see FIGURATIVE); emblem, symbol, NUMBER, digit; figurehead; cast, bust, statue. —*v.* ornament, decorate; symbolize, represent, signify, delineate, embody; imagine, conceive, picture; draw, outline; compute, calculate, do sums; appear, perform, act; cut a figure, matter; stand out.

FILAMENT

Nouns—1, filament, line; fiber, fibril; funicle, vein, hair, capillament, capillary, cilium, tendril, gossamer; hairline.

2, string, thread, cotton, sewing silk, twine, twist; whipcord, tape, ribbon, cord, rope, yarn, hemp, oakum, jute.

3, strip, shred, slip, spill, list, band, fillet, ribbon; roll, lath, splinter, shiver, shaving; cable, wire, cord, line.

Adjectives—filamentous, filaceous, filar, filiform; fibrous, fibrilous; threadlike, wiry, stringy, ropy; capillary, capilliform; funicular, wire-drawn; anguilliform; flagelliform; hairy, ciliate.

---

file, *n. & v.t.* —*n.* ARRANGEMENT, classification; LIST, dossier, record, catalogue, inventory. —*v.t.* classify, arrange, store; catalogue, record; submit, deliver. See STORE.

filial, *adj.* dutiful; sonlike, daughterly. See DESCENT.

filigree, *n.* ornamentation, tracery, scrollwork, arabesque. See ORNAMENT.

fill, *v.t.* make complete, load, pervade, permeate; plug, cork; occupy, serve well, satisfy. See COMPLETION, SUFFICIENCY, PRESENCE, CLOSURE, BUSINESS.

film, *n.* coating, membrane; haze, blur, scum. See COVERING.

filter, *v. & n.* —*v.* filtrate, strain, sieve; percolate, pass through; purify, refine, leach. See CLEANNESS, EGRESS. —*n.* strainer, sifter, sieve, percolator; cheesecloth; optical filter. See OPENING.

filth, *n.* dirt, ordure; obscenity. See UNCLEANNESS, IMPURITY. *Ant.*, see CLEANNESS.

fin, *n.* flipper, process, lobe, pinna; propellor, rudder; lug, ear, blade. See NAVIGATION, PART.

final, *adj.* last, terminal, ultimate; decisive. See END, COMMAND.

finance, *v. & n.* —*v.t.* capitalize, back, fund, subsidize; put up money for; underwrite, guarantee. —*n.* banking, BUSINESS; budget, purse, treasury. See MONEY.

find, *v.t.* discover, detect, espy; acquire, get, gain, obtain; learn, ascertain, perceive; provide; decide. See ACQUISITION, DISCLOSURE. *Ant.*, see LOSS.

finding, *n.* find, DISCOVERY, ACQUISITION, windfall; JUDGMENT, verdict.

fine, *n., v.t. & adj.* —*n.* PENALTY, forfeit, amercement. —*v.t.* amerce, mulct, penalize. —*adj.* pure, superior; admirable, excellent; small, tiny, slender; flimsy, delicate; worthy, estimable; skilled, accomplished; refined, polished; subtle, nice; keen, sharp; fair, pleasant. See GOODNESS, BEAUTY, LITTLENESS, NARROWNESS.

finery, *n.* frippery, frills, tinsel. See ORNAMENTATION.

finger, *n. & v.t.* —*n.* digit; pointer, pinky. See FEELING, DIRECTION. —*v.t.* TOUCH, toy with; thumb, feel.

finish, *v.t. & n.* —*v.t.* END, terminate, complete, conclude; perfect, polish. See COMPLETION. —*n.* COMPLETION, conclusion; SKILL, polish, surface, patina.

fire, *n. & v.t.* —*n.* flame, blaze, conflagration, holocaust; enthusiasm, verve. See HEAT, FEELING. —*v.t.* kindle, ignite; shoot, detonate; inspire, arouse. *Slang,* dismiss, discharge. See HEAT, PROPULSION, POWER.

fireplace, *n.* hearth, ingle, inglenook, chimney. See HEATING, FURNACE.

firewood, *n.* faggots, logs, kindling. See FUEL.

firm, *adj. & n.* —*adj.* immovable, secure; unalterable, steadfast; solid, hard; steady, vigorous; resolute, determined. See STABILITY, PROBITY, DENSITY, RESOLUTION. *Ant.*, see CHANGEABLENESS, SOFTNESS. —*n.* partnership, company, business house. See PARTY.

firmament, *n.* sky, HEAVEN; vault of heaven; welkin, empyrean; starry cope.

first, *adj. & adv.* —*adj.* earliest, original, prime; leading, chief, fundamental. See BEGINNING, FRONT. *Ant.*, END. —*adv.* firstly, originally, at first; before, ahead; sooner, rather. See BEGINNING, PRIORITY, CHOICE.

first-class, first-rate, *adj.* choice, excellent, first-water; best, outstanding, palmary; de luxe, luxurious. *Colloq.*, top-drawer. *Slang*, A-one, four-star, swanky, ritzy. See SUPERIORITY.

fish, *v. & n.* —*v.* angle; pull out, dredge, seek, solicit. See PURSUIT, DESIRE. —*n.* See ANIMAL.

fisherman, *n.* fisher, angler, piscator; whaler, clam digger, *etc.* See TAKING.

fission, *n.* cleavage, scission, DISJUNCTION; nuclear fission, splitting the atom, atom-smashing.

fissure, *n.* cleft, chink, OPENING, crack, rift, breach.

fit, *n., v. & adj.* —*n.* CAPRICE, whim, fancy, notion; paroxysm, convulsion, seizure. See AGITATION. —*v.* equip, furnish, outfit; adapt; grace, beautify; accommodate; clothe; suit, meet, conform. See AGREEMENT, EQUALITY, PREPARATION, BEAUTY, CLOTHING. —*adj.* appropriate, suitable, fitting, proper; expedient, advantageous; vigorous, well, sound. See AGREEMENT, OCCASION, HEALTH. *Ant.,* see DISAGREEMENT.

fix, *v.t.* stabilize, establish; repair, adjust, mend; settle, decide; place. See STABILITY, RESTORATION, AGREEMENT, LOCATION. *Ant.,* see DISJUNCTION.

fixation, *n.* focus, ATTENTION, *idée fixe*, obsession, compulsion, mania. *Colloq.,* bee in one's bonnet. *Slang,* hang-up. See OBSTINACY, INSANITY.

fixture, *n.* attachment, fitting, appendage. See PERMANENCE, SUPPORT.

fizzle, *v.i.* effervesce, bubble, ferment, foam; sizzle, hiss. *Colloq.,* collapse, disintegrate; fade *or* die out; fail, flop. *Slang,* conk out. See FAILURE.

flabby, *adj.* limp, soft, flaccid. See SOFTNESS. *Ant.,* see HARDNESS.

flaccid, *adj.* flabby, soft, weak. See SOFTNESS, WEAKNESS. *Ant.,* see HARDNESS.

flag, *n. & v.i.* —*n.* banner, pennant, ensign, standard; iris; flagstone. See INDICATION. —*v.i.* droop, pine, languish. See INACTIVITY, DISCONTINUITY.

flagon, *n.* flask, bottle, carafe, mug. See RECEPTACLE.

flagrant, *adj.* glaring; notorious; outrageous, shocking. See EVIDENCE, EVIL.

flair, *n.* JUDGMENT, discernment, TASTE; talent, gift, TENDENCY, SKILL; verve, style, bravura, flourish.

flake, *n.* fleck, floccule, scale, chip, shaving; snowflake. See LAYER, COLD.

flamboyant, *adj.* extravagant, ostentatious; pompous, strutting; high-flown, grandiloquent. *Colloq.,* splendiferous. See ORNAMENT, OSTENTATION, VANITY, SPEECH.

flame, *n.* blaze, fire; excitement, passion, zeal. See HEAT, EXCITEMENT. *Ant.,* see COLD.

flank, *n. & v.t.* —*n.* SIDE, wing (of an army). —*v.t.* be beside, go around a side. *Ant.,* see OPPOSITION.

flap, *n. & v.i.* —*n.* tab, fly, lap, tag. —*v.i.* swing, sway, flop, beat; wave. See MOTION.

flare, *v. & n.* —*v.* blaze (up), burst into flame; shine, glow; spread out, swell, splay. —*n.* torch, flambeau, signal [light]; CURVATURE, swelling, burst. See LIGHT, EXPANSION, HEAT.

flash, *v.i.* flare, blaze; burst, streak; gleam, scintillate; retort. See LIGHT, WIT.

flashy, *adj.* gaudy, showy, garish. See OSTENTATION. *Ant.,* see MODERATION.

flask, *n.* bottle, vial, flacon, ampul(e), RECEPTACLE.

FLATNESS

Nouns—**1,** flatness, horizontality, levelness; level; SMOOTHNESS, evenness; plane surface, plane, PLAIN, level (see HORIZONTAL); plate, platter, table, tablet, slab.

2, DULLNESS, SLOWNESS, lifelessness, tameness, tastelessness; monotony, staleness, vapidity, deadness; absoluteness, bluntness, forthrightness, positiveness, directness.

Verbs—render flat, flatten; level, smooth; steam-roll(er); iron, press, smooth.

Adjectives—flat, plane, even, flush; discoid; level, HORIZONTAL; flat as a pancake, flat as a flounder, flat as a board.

Antonyms, see CONCAVITY, CONVEXITY.

FLATTERY

Nouns—**1**, flattery, adulation, blandishment, cajolery; fawning, wheedling, coquetry, sycophancy, flunkeyism, SERVILITY, toadying, snobbishness; incense, honeyed words, flummery; placebo, butter; lip service, euphemism, unctuousness. *Colloq.*, soft soap, blarney.

2, flatterer, adulator; eulogist, euphemist; optimist, encomiast, white-washer; toady, sycophant, courtier; puffer, touter, *claqueur*; parasite, hanger-on (see SERVILITY).

Verbs—flatter, adulate, praise to the skies, puff; wheedle, cajole, coax; fawn (upon); humor, soothe, pet; overpraise; collogue; truckle, pander to; pay court to; court; curry favor with; overestimate, exaggerate. *Colloq.*, soft soap, butter up, lay it on thick, pull one's leg.

Adjectives—flattering, adulatory; mealy-mouthed, honey-mouthed; honeyed, fawning, smooth, smooth-tongued; soapy, oily, unctuous, specious; fine-spoken, plausible, servile, sycophantic, fulsome, courtly.

Adverbs—flatteringly, fulsomely, fawningly, *etc.*

Antonym, see DETRACTION.

---

flatulence, *n.* windiness, belching, eructation, gassiness; conceit, pompousness. See GASEOUSNESS, ORNAMENT.

flaunt, *v.t.* parade, display; brandish. See OSTENTATION.

flavor, *n.* TASTE, seasoning, savor. *Ant.*, FLATNESS.

flavorless, *adj.* See TASTELESS.

flaw, *n.* IMPERFECTION, defect, fault, mar, crack; ERROR, mistake; gust, squall, flurry. See WIND. *Ant.*, see PERFECTION.

fleck, *n.* speck, speckle, flyspeck; blotch, spot, stain. See IMPERFECTION.

flee, *v.i.* decamp, run away, fly, abscond. See AVOIDANCE.

fleece, *v.t.* swindle, despoil, rob, strip. See STEALING, DECEPTION.

fleet, *n. & adj.* —*n.* navy; flotilla, squadron, argosy, armada. See SHIP, COMBATANT. —*adj.* swift, speedy, nimble; transient, brief. See VELOCITY, TRANSIENTNESS. *Ant.*, see SLOWNESS.

flesh, *n.* animal tissue, meat, pulp; MANKIND, materiality, carnality; blood relative. See FOOD, RELATION.

flexible, *adj.* pliant, limber, lithe, supple, adaptable. See SOFTNESS. *Ant.*, see HARDNESS.

flicker, *v.i.* waver, flutter, quiver, blink. See CHANGEABLENESS, LIGHT.

flier, *n.* aviator, aeronaut, airman, astronaut, pilot, co-pilot; leaflet, handbill, circular. *Slang*, birdman, flyboy. See AVIATION, PUBLICATION.

flight, *n.* decampment, hegira, ESCAPE, elopement; course, onrush; covey, flock, shower, volley; wing, squadron. See AVOIDANCE, MOTION, ASSEMBLAGE.

flighty, *adj.* lightheaded; scatterbrained, frivolous. See INATTENTION, INSANITY. *Ant.*, see STABILITY.

flimsy, *adj.* sleazy, gossamer, fragile; tenuous, unsubstantial; feeble, weak. See IMPOTENCE, RARITY. *Ant.*, see DENSITY, POWER.

flinch, *v.i.* wince, shrink, RECOIL. See AVOIDANCE, COWARDICE.

fling, *v.t.* throw, cast, hurl, sling. See PROPULSION.

flippant, *adj.* pert, impertinent, disrespectful; thoughtless, frivolous. *Slang*, fresh. *Colloq.*, flip.

flirt, *n. & v.i.* —*n.* coquette, philanderer. *Slang*, vamp. See INSOLENCE, ENDEARMENT. —*v.i.* coquet, philander, dally; jerk, fling, throw, toss.

flit, *v.i.* fly, dart, decamp, dash off, take wing, hurry away. See DEPARTURE, MOTION.

float, *v.* glide, drift, be wafted, hover, soar, be buoyed up; ferry, ship, raft; launch. See TRAVEL, STABILITY.

flock, *n.* drove, herd; covey, flight, bevy; congregation. See MULTITUDE.

flood, *n.* deluge, inundation; torrent, freshet; cloudburst, spate; superabundance. See SUFFICIENCY, WATER.

floodgate, *n.* dam, spillway, weir, lock; sluice(-gate), CONDUIT; flume, penstock; RESTRAINT, control, inhibition. See CLOSURE.

floor, *n.* flooring, deck, pavement; story, level; rostrum. See SUPPORT, RECEPTACLE.

flop, *v. & n.* —*v.i.* fall, drop, thud, plump down; loll, idle; flutter, flap. *Colloq.*, fail, lay an egg, bust. *Slang*, sleep, bed down. See DESCENT, FAILURE, REPOSE. —*n., colloq.*, FAILURE, dud, fiasco. *Slang*, bust, clinker, turkey, lemon, bomb, egg.

florid, *adj.* ruddy, flushed; showy, rococo, flowery. See COLOR, OSTENTATION.

flounder, *v.i.* wallow, welter, struggle, stagger, fumble, grope. See DOUBT, UNSKILLFULNESS.

flourish, *v. & n.* —*v.* wave, wield, flaunt, brandish; grow, prosper, thrive. See VEGETABLE, PROSPERITY, AGITATION. —*n.* ornamental stroke; fanfare; bold gesture. See MUSIC, OSTENTATION.

flow, *v.i.* run, glide, trickle, stream, sweep along; issue. See MOTION, WATER.

flower, *n.* bloom, blossom, posy; élite, elect, best, pick; ORNAMENT. See VEGETABLE, GOODNESS.

flowery, *adj.* florid, high-flown, flamboyant; blossomy. See ORNAMENT, OSTENTATION.

flowing, *adj.* running, gliding; fluent, graceful, smooth; loose, billowy. See WATER, ELEGANCE.

fluctuate, *v.i.* alternate, wave, vacillate, vary, shift. See CHANGEABLENESS. *Ant.*, see STABILITY.

fluent, *adj.* flowing, graceful, voluble. See ELEGANCE, LOQUACITY.

fluffy, *adj.* downy, flocculent, cottony. See SOFTNESS. *Ant.*, see HARDNESS.

fluid, *n. & adj.* liquid; gas, vapor; juice, sap, lymph; plasma, blood, gore; ichor; solution, decoction, brew. —*adj.* See FLUIDITY.

FLUIDITY

Nouns—**1,** fluidity, liquidity; liquidness, GASEOUSNESS; fluid, liquid, liquor; lymph, juice, sap, serum, plasma, blood, serosity, ichor; solubility, solubleness, LIQUEFACTION; hydrology, hydrostatics, hydrodynamics; STREAM. See MOTION.
2, see CHANGEABLENESS.
Verbs—be fluid, flow (see RIVER); liquefy, melt.
Adjectives—liquid, fluid, serous, juicy, watery (see WATER); succulent, sappy; plastic; fluent, flowing; liquefied, uncongealed; soluble.

---

flurry, *n. & v.t.* —*n.* squall, gust, scud, blast; hubbub, ferment. See WIND, ACTIVITY. —*v.t.* ruffle, excite, fluster. See AGITATION.

flush, *v. & n.* —*v.* blush, redden; rinse; start, rouse. See COLOR, CLEANNESS. —*n.* blush, redness; elation, thrill; gush, rush. See HEAT, FEELING, WATER.

flute, *n.* groove, channel; pipe, piccolo, fife. See FURROW, MUSICAL INSTRUMENTS.

flutter, *v.* flicker, tremble, flap, shake, whip; bustle, fidget, twitter, quiver; agitate, ruffle. See AGITATION, HASTE, EXCITEMENT.

flux, *n.* flow, current, COURSE; MOTION, CHANGE, transition; continuum; solvent, metal fusion; EXCRETION.

fly, *v.i.* soar, wing, aviate; float, wave; speed, bolt, dart; flee, decamp, vamoose, disperse, scatter. See AVIATION, VELOCITY, AVOIDANCE, ESCAPE.

foam, *n. & v.i.* —*n.* froth, suds, lather, spume. —*v.i.* froth, spume. See CLOUDINESS.

focus, *n. & v.* —*n.* point; focal *or* central point; concentration, convergence; center, hub; core, heart, nucleus; sharpness (*Photog.*). See MIDDLE, VISION. —*v.* concentrate, converge; centralize, contract; rally, gather, meet.

foe, *n.* ENEMY, adversary, antagonist, opponent. *Ant.*, see FRIEND.

fog, *n.* mist, smog, vapor, haze, cloud; uncertainty, obscurity. See CLOUDINESS.

foil, *v.t. & n.* —*v.t.* frustrate, baffle, balk, circumvent. See DISAPPOINTMENT. *Ant.*, see AID. —*n.* contrast, setoff; leaf, sheet (of metal); dueling sword. See OPPOSITION, LAYER, ARMS.

fold, *n. & v.* —*n.* crease; bend, lapping, plait; wrapping, wrap; wrinkle, corrugation; flap, lapel, turnover; gather, pleat, ruffle, flounce; crow's-feet; furrow; pen, kraal, corral (see INCLOSURE). —*v.* double (over); crease, bend; swathe, swaddle, wrap; wrinkle, furrow; gather, pleat; hug, clasp, embrace; envelop; enfold. See ROUGHNESS. *Ant.*, see SMOOTHNESS.

foliage, *n.* leafage, verdue. See VEGETABLE.

folk, *n.* people, commonalty, race; kin. See MANKIND, POPULACE.

folklore, *n.* mythology, legends, old wives' tales. See BELIEF, INFORMATION.

follow, *v.* go *or* come after; succeed; tread on the heels of; come *or* be next; pursue (see PURSUIT); attend, associate with, go with, accompany; adhere to, SUPPORT; obey, heed; copy, imitate, use as a model; practice; ensue, result, be the outcome of. See SEQUENCE. *Ant.*, see PRIORITY.

following, *n.* followers, supporters, adherents; attendance, train, retinue. See ACCOMPANIMENT, AID. *Ant.*, see OPPOSITION.

FOLLY

Nouns—**1,** folly, shallowness, silliness, foolishness; nonsense; frivolity, trifling, ineptitude, inconsistency; giddiness; INATTENTION; irrationality, eccentricity (see INSANITY); extravagance, ABSURDITY; RASHNESS.

2, fool, dunce, idiot, tomfool, wiseacre, simpleton, imbecile, donkey, ass, goose, ninny, dolt; trifler, babbler; oaf, lout, loon, dullard, dunderhead, blockhead, loggerhead; halfwit, lackwit, harebrain; clod, clodhopper. *Colloq.*, nincompoop, chump, booby, duffer, bonehead, num(b)skull, chucklehead, fathead. *Slang*, jerk, sap, loony, boob, ass, dumbbell, square, rube, dimwit.

3, child, baby, INFANT, innocent, milksop, sop; dotard, driveler; old fogy, old woman; crone, grandmother.

4, greenhorn, DUPE; IGNORAMUS; lubber, bungler, blunderer; MADMAN.

5, jester; see HUMORIST.

Verbs—**1,** be a fool, fool, trifle, drivel; play the fool, talk nonsense. *Slang*, horse around.

2, dupe, cheat, delude, gull, deceive. See DECEPTION.

Adjectives—**1,** foolish, silly, senseless, irrational, nonsensical, inept.

2, unwise, injudicious, improper, unreasonable, without reason, ridiculous, silly, stupid, asinine, ill-advised, ill-judged, inconsistent, irrational, extravagant, nonsensical; idle, useless (see USELESSNESS); inexpedient, frivolous, trivial (see UNIMPORTANCE).

Antonyms, see WISDOM, SAGE.

---

fond, *adj.* affectionate, loving tender; foolish, doting. See LOVE.

fondle, *v.t.* pet, caress, cuddle, cosset, snuggle, embrace, make love to. *Slang*, neck, smooch, make out, spoon; feel (up). See ENDEARMENT.

font, *n.* fount(ain); basin, baptistery; spring, source; reservoir; type, case, face. See WATER, RECEPTACLE, STORE, PRINTING.

FOOD

Nouns—**1,** food, aliment, nourishment, nutriment; sustenance, nurture, subsistence, provender, fodder, provision, ration, keep, commons, board; fare, cheer; diet, regimen; bread, staff of life; prey; forage, pasture, pasturage; comestibles, eatables, victuals, edibles; meat, viands; delicacy, dainty; fleshpots; festive board; ambrosia; good cheer; hearty meal; soul food. *Slang*, grub, chow; junk food.

2, meal, repast, feed, spread; mess; dish, plate, course; refreshment, entertainment; refection, collation, picnic; feast, banquet; breakfast; *déjeuner*, lunch, luncheon; dinner, supper, snack, dessert; potluck, *table d'hôte*; table, cuisine, bill of fare, menu. *Colloq.*, brunch; square meal.

3, meat, joint, roast; *pièce de résistance*, *entrée*, *hors d'œuvre*; hash, stew, ragout, fricassee; pottage, potage, broth, soup, consommé, purée; pie, pasty, *vol-au-vent*; pudding, omelet; pastry; sweets; CONDIMENT.

4, drink, beverage, liquor, nectar, broth, soup; potion, dram, draught; nip, sip, sup, gulp. *Colloq.*, swig, pull, soft drink. *Slang*, swill.

5, wine, spirits, liquor, liqueur, cocktail, beer, ale; grog, toddy, flip, punch, negus, cup, wassail; gin, whisk(e)y (see DRUNKENNESS); coffee, chocolate, cocoa, tea. *Slang*, hair of the dog [that bit one].

6, eating, ingestion, mastication, manducation, rumination; GLUTTONY; mouth, jaws, mandible, chops; drinking, potation, draught, libation; carousal (see AMUSEMENT); DRUNKENNESS.

Verbs—**1,** eat, feed, fare, devour, swallow, take; gulp, bolt, snap; fall to; despatch, dispatch; take down, get down, gulp down; lay in, tuck in; lick, pick, peck; gormandize (see GLUTTONY); bite, champ, munch, crunch, chew, masticate, nibble, gnaw; live on; feed on, batten on, fatten on, feast upon; browse, graze, crop; regale, carouse; eat heartily, do justice to; banquet; break bread, break one's fast; breakfast, lunch, dine, take tea, sup. *Colloq.*, put away; drink like a fish; come and get it! soup's on!

2, drink, drink in, drink up, drink one's fill; quaff, sip, sup; lap; wash down; tipple (see DRUNKENNESS).

Adjectives—eatable, edible, esculent, comestible, alimentary; cereal; dietetic; culinary; nutritive, nutritious; succulent; potable, bibulous; omnivorous, carnivorous, herbivorous, graminivorous; macrobiotic, organic.

---

fool, *n. & v.* See FOLLY.

foolhardy, *adj.* daring, brash, reckless, venturesome. See RASHNESS. *Ant.*, see CARE.

foolish, *adj.* silly, fatuous; unwise, ill-considered; ridiculous, nonsensical, absurd. See ABSURDITY.

foot, *n.* BASE, bottom, footing; hoof, paw; foot soldiers, infantry. See SUPPORT, COMBATANT.

foothold, *n.* (toe)hold, footing, grip, SUPPORT; BEGINNING, start, access, CHANCE, opportunity. *Colloq.*, a foot in the door, first rung on the ladder.

footing, *n.* foothold; basis, BASE, foundation, status, rank, CONNECTION.

fop, *n.* dandy, dude, swell, buck, blade, gay blade, coxcomb, macaroni; exquisite. *Slang*, toff, snappy dresser, Dapper Dan, Beau Brummell, clotheshorse. See AFFECTATION, OSTENTATION. *Ant.*, see DISORDER.

forage, *n. & v.* —*n.* fodder, feed, FOOD; pasturage, herbage. —*v.* seek food, pasture, graze, feed; hunt, search, beat the bushes; raid, maraud, pillage, plunder, loot, ravage. *Slang*, scrounge around. See STEALING, INQUIRY, PURSUIT.

forbearance, *n.* INACTION, RESTRAINT; patience, long-suffering; TEMPERANCE, clemency, BENEVOLENCE, mercy; pardon, FORGIVENESS.

forbid, *v.t.* prohibit, inhibit, interdict, ban, taboo. See RESTRAINT.

forbidding, *adj.* prohibitive; repellent, fearsome (see FEAR); unpleasant, abhorrent; stern, menacing; unfriendly, distant. See THREAT, COLD, UGLINESS.

force, *n.* COMPULSION, coercion; STRENGTH, brawn, might; MEANING, effect; troops, soldiery, army. See COMBATANT.

ford, *n. & v.* —*n.* wading place; shoal. —*v.* wade, cross. See PASSAGE, WATER.

fore, *adj.* foremost; former, prior, previous. See FRONT, PRIORITY.

foreboding, *n.* portent; presentiment, premonition, apprehension. See PREDICTION.

forecast, *v.t.* predict, divine, prognosticate; foretell, presage, portend. See PREDICTION.

forefathers, *n.* ancestors, forebears, sires, progenitors. See ANCESTRY.

foregoing, *adj.* preceding, previous, former, aforesaid. See PRIORITY. *Ant.,* see SEQUENCE.

forehead, *n.* brow, sinciput; head, temples. *Slang,* dome. See FRONT.

foreign, *adj.* alien, strange, exotic; extraneous, unrelated. *Ant.,* see INHABITANT.

foreman, *n.* superintendent, overseer. *Colloq.,* (straw)boss. See DIRECTOR.

foremost, *adj.* leading, first, precedent; chief, best, principal. See BEGINNING.

forensic, *adj.* legal, juridical; controversial. See LAWSUIT, REASONING.

forerunner, *n.* precursor, predecessor; harbinger; herald, announcer, John the Baptist; leader, vanguard, scout, picket. See PRIORITY.

foresight, *n.* providence, forethought, prudence, PREPARATION; foreknowledge, prescience; anticipation; clairvoyance, second sight; prevision; foreboding, premonition, presentiment; foretaste, preview; foreshadowing, foretelling, forecasting, prophecy, prophetic vision. See EXPECTATION, FUTURITY.

forest, *n.* wood, woods, tall timber, timberland, woodland; grove, copse, thicket, coppice. See VEGETABLE.

forestry, *n.* woodcraft, silviculture; dendrology, forestage; conservation; reforestation. See AGRICULTURE.

foretell, *v.t.* presage, portend; forecast, prognosticate, predict. See PREDICTION.

forethought, *n.* prudence, providence; premeditation, anticipation. See PREPARATION.

forever, *adv.* always, ever, eternally; incessantly, unceasingly. See DURABILITY.

foreword, *n.* PREFACE, prologue, introduction, *avant-propos,* preamble; [address] to the reader. See PRECEDENCE, BOOK.

forfeit, *n.* PENALTY, fine. See LOSS.

forge, *v.t.* make, fabricate; invent, counterfeit. See PRODUCTION, FALSEHOOD.

forgery, *n.* IMITATION, counterfeit; kited *or* bad check. *Slang,* snide; phony *or* bum check. See FALSENESS, ILLEGALITY.

forget, *v.t.* disregard, overlook, dismiss, omit; disremember. See NEGLECT, OBLIVION. *Ant.,* see MEMORY.

FORGIVENESS

Nouns—forgiveness, pardon, condonation, grace, remission, absolution, amnesty, oblivion; indulgence; reprieve; excuse, exoneration, quittance, release, indemnity; bill, act, covenant *or* deed of indemnity; exculpation, ACQUITTAL; conciliation; reconciliation, PACIFICATION; propitiation; longanimity, placability.

Verbs—**1,** forgive, pardon, condone, think no more of, let bygones be bygones, shake hands, forget an injury, forgive and forget; excuse, pass over, overlook; wink at (see NEGLECT); bear with; allow for, make allowances for; let one down easily, not be too hard upon, bury the hatchet; let off, remit, absolve, give absolution, reprieve; acquit (see ACQUITTAL).

2, beg, ask *or* implore pardon; conciliate, propitiate, placate; make one's peace with, make up a quarrel (see PACIFICATION).

Adjectives—forgiving, placable, conciliatory, indulgent; forgiven, unresented, unavenged, unrevenged.

Antonym, see RETALIATION.

forgo, *v.t.* relinquish, abandon; deny oneself, give up, do without, pass up. *Colloq.,* cut out, swear off. See RELINQUISHMENT.

fork, *v.i.* bifurcate, diverge, separate, branch off. See DISJUNCTION.

forlorn, *adj.* abandoned, deserted, forsaken; hopeless, wretched, miserable. See SECLUSION, HOPELESSNESS. *Ant.,* see SOCIALITY, CHEERFULNESS.

FORM

Nouns—**1,** form, formation, forming, figure, shape; conformation, configuration; make, frame, construction, cut, set, build, trim, cut of one's jib; stamp, type, cast, mo(u)ld; FASHION; contour, OUTLINE; architecture, structure; sculpture.

2, feature, lineament, anatomy, profile; turn; phase, aspect, APPEARANCE; posture, attitude, pose.

3, morphology, histology, structural botany; isomorphism.

Verbs—form, shape, figure, FASHION, carve, cut, chisel, hew, cast; roughhew; rough-cast; sketch; block out, hammer out; trim; lick into shape, put into shape; model, knead, work up into, set, mo(u)ld, sculpture; cast, stamp; build, construct.

Adjectives—formed, formative; plastic, fictile; isomorphous.

Antonym, see DISORDER.

formal, *adj.* structural, INTRINSIC; external, superficial, outward; formulated, stylized, conventionalized, ceremonial, ritual(istic), conventional, traditional; solemn, dignified; stuffy, strict, prim, perfunctory; correct, proper, RIGHT, through channels. *Colloq.,* according to Hoyle; black tie; white tie [and tails]. See CONFORMITY, FASHION, ELEGANCE, AFFECTATION.

formality, *n.* formalness (see FORMAL); punctilio, convention, etiquette; due course, process *or* form, red tape; mere formality, lip service. See RULE, AUTHORITY, UNMEANINGNESS.

format, *n.* FORM, ARRANGEMENT, PLAN, make-up, layout, design; style.

former, *adj.* erstwhile, whilom, sometime, quondam; foregoing, preceding. See PAST, PRIORITY.

formidable, *adj.* appalling, tremendous; arduous, Herculean. See FEAR, DIFFICULTY.

FORMLESSNESS

Nouns—formlessness, shapelessness, amorphism, informity; deformity, disfigurement, defacement, derangement, mutilation; DISORDER, chaos, DISTORTION.

Verbs—deface, disfigure, deform, mutilate, truncate, misshape; derange, DISORDER, distort.

Adjectives—formless, shapeless, amorphous; unformed, unhewn, uncut, unfashioned, unshapen; rough, rude, rugged, barbarous; chaotic; blank, vague, nebulous; misshapen, disordered, distorted.

Antonym, see FORM.

formulate, *v.t.* frame, devise, concoct, formularize. See PRODUCTION.

forsake, *v.t.* desert, abandon; quit, forswear. See RELINQUISHMENT.

fort, *n.* stronghold, fortress, fortification. See DEFENSE.

forth, *adj.* forward, onward; out (of), from; away (from). See DIRECTION.

forthright, *adj.* downright, straightforward, frank, candid, outspoken; unequivocal, explicit, honest. *Colloq.,* straight from the shoulder, man-to-man. See PROBITY, SIMPLENESS.

fortify, *v.t.* strength, buttress, barricade; uphold, sustain. See POWER, EVIDENCE.

fortitude, *n.* COURAGE, patience, endurance.

fortunate, *adj.* lucky, blest, to be congratulated; auspicious, propitious, opportune. *Colloq.,* born under a lucky star *or* with a silver spoon in one's mouth. See PROSPERITY, CHANCE, SUCCESS.

fortune, *n.* fate, lot; CHANCE, luck; WEALTH, possessions, property. See NECESSITY, DESTINY. *Ant.,* see POVERTY.

fortuneteller, *n.* clairvoyant, crystal gazer, astrologer, numerologist, phrenologist, palmist, palm-reader. See PREDICTION, SORCERY.

forum, *n.* market place, agora; court, tribunal, COUNCIL; colloquium, symposium, panel, town meeting. *Slang,* bull session. See COMMUNICATION.

forward, *adj. & v.t.* —*adj.* FRONT, anterior, foremost; precocious; ready; prompt; enterprising, aggressive; intrusive, officious; pert, saucy, flip; future, coming. See EARLINESS, ACTIVITY, INSOLENCE. —*v.t.* advance, impel, dispatch, deliver.

fossil, *n.* relic, petrification; fogy. See OLDNESS, VETERAN.

foster, *v.t.* nourish, nurture, cherish; encourage, support. See AID. *Ant.,* see NEGLECT.

foul, *adj.* dirty, soiled, disgusting; stormy, unpleasant; obscene, indecent; unfair, underhand. See UNCLEANNESS, IMPURITY, IMPROBITY. *Ant.,* see CLEANNESS.

found, *v.t.* establish, institute, originate. See PRODUCTION.

foundation, *n.* base; basis; endowment; institution. See LOCATION, SUPPORT.

founder, *n. & v.i.* —*n.* producer, establisher, originator. —*v.i.* sink, be swamped; collapse, crash; go lame. See NAVIGATION, FAILURE.

foundling, *n.* waif, orphan, bastard. See YOUTH, REJECTION.

foundry, *n.* works, iron- *or* steelworks, smelter; smithy. See WORKSHOP.

fountain, *n.* spring, well, jet, spray; source. See CAUSE, WATER, STORE.

fowl, *n.* bird; hen, stewing chicken. See ANIMAL, FOOD.

fox, *n.* reynard; slyboots, crafty person. *Slang,* slicker. See ANIMAL, DECEPTION.

foyer, *n.* lobby, vestibule, anteroom, entry, entrance hall. See INGRESS.

fraction, *n.* part; half, quarter, eighth, *etc.*; portion, piece, bit; section, segment; scrap, fragment; very small part. *Ant.,* see WHOLE.

fracture, *n.* break, split, crack, cleft. See DISJUNCTION.

fragile, *adj.* delicate, frail, breakable; tenuous, gossamer. See IMPOTENCE, BRITTLENESS. *Ant.,* see POWER, COHERENCE.

fragment, *n.* bit, part, portion, scrap. See PART. *Ant.,* see WHOLE.

FRAGRANCE

Nouns—**1,** fragrance, aroma, redolence, spice, spiciness, perfume, perfumery, bouquet; ODOR, essence.

2, incense; frankincense, myrrh; pastil, pastille; perfumes of Arabia; attar; bergamot, balm, civet, musk, potpourri; nosegay; scent, scentbag; sachet, smelling salts, vinaigrette; cologne, eau de Cologne.

Verbs—be fragrant, have a perfume; smell sweet; scent, perfume, embalm.

Adjectives—fragrant, aromatic, redolent, spicy, balmy, scented; sweetsmelling, sweet-scented; perfumed; fragrant as a rose; muscadine, ambrosial.

Antonym, see MALODOROUSNESS.

frail, *adj.* fragile, brittle, delicate; weak, infirm, weak-willed. See IMPOTENCE, DOUBT. *Ant.,* see POWER.

frame, *v.t. & n.* —*v.t.* construct, fashion, fabricate, formulate, enclose; incriminate falsely, trump up. See PRODUCTION, ARRANGEMENT, ACCUSATION. —*n.* framework, skeleton; EDGE, boundary, confines; temper; humor; form; shape; plot, conspiracy. See SUPPORT.

franchise, *n.* privilege, right, prerogative. See FREEDOM.

frank, *adj.* ingenuous, candid, straightforward, forthright, sincere, open. See TRUTH, SIMPLENESS. *Ant.,* see DECEPTION, CONCEALMENT.

frankfurter, *n.* frankfurt, sausage, wiener. *Colloq.,* frank, wienie, hot dog, red-hot. See FOOD.

frantic, *adj.* distraught, distracted, frenzied, wild. See INSANITY, EXCITEMENT.

fraternity, *n.* brotherhood; fellowship; secret society. See CONSANGUIN-
ITY, PARTY.

fraternize, *v.i.* associate, band together; consort with, mingle with. See
SOCIALITY.

fraud, *n.* deception, swindle; imposture, artifice; imposter, humbug.
Slang, confidence game, bunco. See DECEPTION. *Ant.,* see TRUTH.

fraught, *adj.* filled with, loaded, laden, beset. See CONTENTS, FEELING.

fray, *n.* fracas, fight, skirmish; brawl, melee, free-for-all. See CONTEN-
TION.

frazzle, *v.t., colloq.,* fray, abrade, wear out; vex, exasperate, get on one's
nerves. See DETERIORATION, RESENTMENT.

freak, *n.* abnormality, fluke, monstrosity; CAPRICE, sport, whim. See
UNCONFORMITY.

FREEDOM

Nouns—**1,** freedom, liberty, independence; license, PERMISSION; FACILITY;
immunity, EXEMPTION; release, parole, probation, discharge.

2, scope, range, latitude, play; free play, full play, full scope; swing, full
swing, elbow room, margin, rope, wide berth, liberty hall.

3, franchise, emancipation, liberation, enfranchisement; autonomy, self-
government, self-determination; liberalism, free trade; nonintervention,
noninterference, Monroe Doctrine; free speech, freedom of speech *or*
of the press.

4, freeman, freedman, citizen.

5, free land, freehold; allodium; mortmain.

Verbs—**1,** be free, have scope, have the run of, have one's own way, have
a will of one's own, have one's fling; do what one likes, wishes, pleases
or chooses; go at large, feel at home; fend for oneself; paddle one's
own canoe; stand on one's rights; be one's own man; shift for oneself;
take a liberty; make free with, make oneself at home; take leave, take
French leave.

2, set free, LIBERATE, release, let go; permit (see PERMISSION); allow *or*
give scope to; give a horse his head; make free of; give the freedom of;
give the franchise; enfranchise; *laisser faire;* live and let live; leave to
oneself, leave alone, let alone. *Colloq.,* give one leeway, give one
enough rope.

3, unfetter, untie, loose, unchain, unshackle, unbind; disengage, disentangle, clear, extricate, unloose.

Adjectives—**1,** free, free as air; independent, at large, loose, scot free;
left alone, left to oneself; free and easy; at one's ease; *dégagé,* quite at
home; wanton, rampant, irrepressible, unvanquished; freed, liberated;
freeborn; autonomous, freehold, allodial. *Colloq.,* on one's own.

2, in full swing, uncaught, unconstrained, unbuttoned, unconfined, unrestrained, unchecked, unprevented, unhindered, unobstructed, unbound,
uncontrolled, untrammeled, unsubject, ungoverned, unenslaved, un-
enthralled, unchained, unshackled, unfettered, unreined, unbridled, uncurbed, unmuzzled; unrestricted, unlimited, unconditional; absolute;
discretionary, optional (see CHOICE); exempt; unassailed, unforced,
uncompelled; impartial, unbiased, spontaneous.

Adverbs—*ad libitum,* at will, freely, *etc.*

Antonym, see SUBJECTION.

---

free-for-all, *n.* fight, mêlée, brawl, fracas; knock-down-drag-out [affair].
See CONTENTION.

freethinker, *n.* skeptic, agnostic, doubter; iconoclast. See IRRELIGION.

freeway, *n.* highway, parkway, boulevard, expressway. See PASSAGE.

freeze, *v.* congeal, turn to ice, make ice; harden; die; immobilize; chill,
ice, frost, refrigerate; kill. See COLD, INACTIVITY.

freight, *n.* cargo, load, shipment; burden. See TRAVEL.

freighter, *n.* cargo ship, lighter, trader, [tramp] steamer, transport,
tanker. See SHIP.

frenetic, *adj.* frantic, hectic, distraught. *Colloq.,* jittery. See EXCITABILITY.

frenzy, *n.* fury, agitation; excitement, enthusiasm; delirium, furor. See VIOLENCE, EXCITEMENT.

FREQUENCY

Nouns—frequency, oftenness; REPETITION, RECURRENCE, persistence; PERSEVERANCE; prevalence; CONTINUANCE.

Verbs—do frequently; do nothing but, keep on, continue (see CONTINUITY); persist; recur.

Adjectives—frequent, many times, not rare, incessant, perpetual, continual, constant, steadfast, unceasing; everyday, repeated (see REPETITION); habitual (see HABIT).

Adverbs—often, oft, ofttimes, oftentimes; frequently; repeatedly (see REPETITION); not unfrequently; in rapid succession; many at time, daily, hourly, every day; perpetually, continually, constantly, incessantly, without ceasing, at all times, night and day, day after day; morning, noon and night; ever and anon; most often; commonly, habitually (see HABIT); sometimes, occasionally, between times, at times, now and then, once in a while, from time to time, often enough, again and again. *Colloq.,* every so often.

Antonym, see RARITY.

---

fresh, *adj.* novel, recent; new, unfaded, unjaded, unhackneyed, unused; healthy, vigorous, unfatigued; unsalted; cool, refreshing, keen; inexperienced. *Slang,* impertinent. See ADDITION, NEWNESS, COLD, HEALTH. *Ant.,* see OLDNESS, WEARINESS.

freshen, *v.t.* refresh, revive, brace up; renovate, spruce up; ventilate, air out, cool off; deodorize, sweeten. See RESTORATION, CLEANNESS.

freshman, *n.* plebe, underclassman; novice, greenhorn, tenderfoot. *Colloq.,* frosh. See LEARNING, BEGINNING.

fret, *v.* agitate, irritate, vex; worry, chafe, fume, complain. See PAIN, AGITATION.

friar, *n.* monk, brother; fra. See CLERGY.

FRICTION

Nouns—friction, attrition, rubbing; frication, confrication, abrasion, sanding, sandpapering, erosion, limation, rub; massage.

Verbs—rub, scratch, abrade, file, rasp, scrape, scrub, fray, graze, curry, buff, scour, polish, rub up; gnaw; file, sand, sandpaper, grind (see POWDERINESS); massage, knead.

Adjectives—frictional, abrasive, attritive.

Antonym, see SMOOTHNESS.

FRIEND

Nouns—**1,** friend, acquaintance, neighbor, well-wisher; alter ego; bosom friend, fast friend; partner; fidus Achates; *persona grata*; associate, compeer, comrade, mate, companion, confrère, intimate, confidant(e). **2,** patron, Maecenas; tutelary saint, good genius, advocate, partisan, sympathizer; ally; friend in need; associate. **3,** crony, chum, pal; playfellow, playmate; schoolfellow, schoolmate; shopmate, shipmate, messmate; fellow, boon companion. *Slang,* sidekick. **4,** Pylades and Orestes, Castor and Pollux, Nisus and Euryalus, Damon and Pythias, David and Jonathan, Three Musketeers. **5,** friendship, friendliness, amity, brotherhood; harmony, concord, peace; cordiality, fraternization; fellowship, familiarity, intimacy, comradeship. See SOCIALITY.

Verbs—be friendly; make friends with, receive with open arms; fraternize; befriend. *Colloq.,* hit it off, take to, stand in with.

Adjectives—friendly, amicable, cordial; hospitable, neighborly, brotherly, sisterly; hearty, warmhearted, familiar; on good terms, friends with.

Antonym, ENEMY.

---

fright, *n.* dread, dismay, terror, panic, alarm, consternation. See FEAR.

frigid, *adj.* COLD, icy, freezing; passionless, cold-blooded, formal. See INSENSIBILITY. *Ant.,* see HEAT.

frill, *n.* trimming, decoration, ORNAMENT; ruffle, flounce, furbelow; extra. *Colloq.,* icing, topping.

fringe, *n.* EDGE, border, outskirts; edging; perimeter.

frisk, *v.t.* caper, cavort, FROLIC. *Colloq.,* cut up, carry on. *Slang,* horse around; search, shakedown, fan. See AMUSEMENT, INQUIRY.

frisky, *adj.* playful, pert, peppy. *Colloq.,* full of beans. See VIGOR.

fritter, *v.t.* squander, WASTE, dissipate.

frivolity, *n.* LEVITY, flightiness, giddiness, FOLLY. See UNIMPORTANCE.

frolic, *v.i.* play, gambol, caper, romp, disport. See AMUSEMENT.

FRONT

Nouns—**1,** front, forefront, fore, forepart; foreground; face, disk, frontage, façade, proscenium, frontispiece; anteriority; priority; obverse; pioneer, forerunner; BEGINNING.

2, front rank, front lines; van, vanguard; advanced guard; outpost.

3, face, brow, forehead, visage, physiognomy, countenance, features; rostrum; beak; bow, stem, prow, jib. *Slang,* mug, puss, kisser.

Verbs—be in front, stand in front; front, face, confront, brave, defy; bend forward; come to the front, come to the fore.

Adjectives—front, fore, frontal, anterior.

Adverbs—frontward, in front; before, in the van, ahead, right ahead; foremost, headmost; in the foreground, in the lee; before one's face, before one's eyes; face to face, vis-à-vis.

Antonym, see REAR.

---

frontier, *n.* borderland, outskirts; wilderness; new land. See EDGE, LIMIT.

frost, *n.* rime, hoarfrost, cranreuch; icing, coldness, COLD.

froth, *n. & v.* —*n.* foam, suds, lather, spume; head, cream, collar; scum; LEVITY, triviality, frivolity. —*v.i.* foam, spume, effervesce, ferment, bubble, fizz. See AGITATION, AIR.

frown, *v.i. & n.* —*v.i.* scowl, lower, glower; look with disfavor (upon). See IRASCIBILITY, DISAPPROBATION. —*n.* scowl, disapproving look. *Ant.,* see APPROBATION.

frowsy, *adj.* unkempt, slovenly, frumpy. See DISORDER, UNCLEANNESS.

frozen, *adj.* glacial, gelid; frostbitten, COLD; motionless, paralyzed, petrified; coldhearted, frigid, insensitive. See INSENSIBILITY, INACTION.

frugal, *adj.* prudent, saving, provident, thrifty; sparing, stinting. See ECONOMY, MODERATION. *Ant.,* see WASTE.

fruit, *n.* product, yield, harvest; offspring, result, outgrowth. See PRODUCTION, EFFECT.

fruitful, *adj.* productive, fertile; prolific; profitable. See PRODUCTIVENESS.

fruitless, *adj.* unavailing, unprofitable, vain; barren. See USELESSNESS, UNPRODUCTIVENESS.

frustrate, *v.t.* defeat, thwart, circumvent, cross, baffle, nullify. See HINDRANCE. *Ant.,* see AID, SUCCESS.

fry, *v.* sauté, panfry, deep-fry, frizzle, griddle, skillet-cook. See HEAT, FOOD.

FUEL

Nouns—**1,** fuel, firing, combustible; inflammable, burnable; fossil fuel, peat, turf; lignite; bituminous, anthracite, glance *or* cannel coal; coal dust, culm, coke, charcoal; OIL, kerosene, petroleum, gasoline, petrol;

gas (see GASEOUSNESS); firewood, kindling, fag(g)ot, log; cinder, embers; atomic *or* nuclear fuel, plutonium, uranium. See HEAT.
2, tinder, punk, amadou, touchwood; brand, torch; fuse, detonator, cap; spill, wick, match, flint, lighter; candle.
Verbs—fuel, furnish with fuel; feed, fire, stoke.
Adjectives—combustible, inflammable, burnable; fiery.

---

fugitive, *adj. & n.* —*adj.* transient, ephemeral, evanescent, fleeting. —*n.* runaway, eloper, absconder; refugee, escapee. See AVOIDANCE, ESCAPE.
fulfill, *v.t.* satisfy, realize, gratify; execute, discharge; effect, carry out. See COMPLETION. *Ant.,* see FAILURE.
full, *adj.* filled, sated, satiated, glutted, gorged; replete; whole, complete, entire; loose, baggy; sonorous; plump, rounded; brimming. See COMPLETION, SUFFICIENCY. *Ant.,* see INSUFFICIENCY.
full-blooded, *adj.* thoroughbred, pure bred, whole-blooded. See PURITY.
fullness, *n.* repletion; COMPLETION, copiousness; looseness; sonorousness. See SUFFICIENCY. *Ant.,* see NONCOMPLETION.
fulminate, *v.* boom, thunder, roar; detonate, explode; rail, berate, castigate, excoriate. See VIOLENCE, DETRACTION, IMPRECATION.
fulsome, *adj.* obnoxious, vile, foul, noisome; unctuous, obsequious, fawning; cloying, excessive; tasteless, offensive. See REPULSION, SERVILITY, VULGARITY.
fumble, *v.* grope, search; paw; fluff, flubb, muff, bungle. See UNSKILLFULNESS.
fume, *v.i.* chafe, fret, rage; smoke, reek. See PAIN, RESENTMENT, HEAT.
fun, *n.* sport, diversion, amusement, jollity. See AMUSEMENT.
function, *n. & v.* —*n.* faculty, office, duty, role, province; observance, economy. See AGENCY, BUSINESS, RITE. —*v.i.* operate, act, serve. See ACTIVITY.
functionary, *n.* official, administrator, bureaucrat. See AGENCY.
fund, *n. & v.* —*n.* resources, STORE, cache, reserve, accumulation; (*pl.*) assets, wealth, MONEY, capital. *Colloq.,* slush fund, kitty. —*v.t.* set aside, lay away, STORE; invest in, FINANCE.
fundamental, *adj.* basic, essential, underlying, original, clemency, intrinsic; rudimentary.
funeral, *n.* obsequies; burial, INTERMENT, entombment.
funereal, *adj.* mournful, sad, solemn, somber, lugubrious; black, dark. See DARKNESS, DEJECTION. *Ant.,* see CHEERFULNESS.
funnel, *n.* cone, bottleneck, CHANNEL, flue, chimney, shaft.
funny, *adj.* amusing, droll, comic; absurd, laughable, mirth-provoking, ludicrous. See WIT, ABSURDITY.
fur, *n.* hide, pelt, coat, peltry, skin, pelage; hair, down; fur coat. See COVERING.
furies, *n.* avengers, Erinyes, Eumenides, Dirae. See DEMON.
furious, *adj.* raging, violent, fierce, storming, turbulent, unrestrained. *Colloq.,* mad, angry. See RESENTMENT, VIOLENCE.
furlough, *n.* leave [of absence], pass, shore leave, liberty. See INACTIVITY.
furnace, *n.* See HEAT.
furnish, *v.t.* equip, outfit; provide, yield, supply. See SUBSTITUTION, PRODUCTION. *Ant.,* see DIVESTMENT.
furniture, *n.* chattel, furnishings, appurtenances. See SUPPORT.
furor, *n.* VIOLENCE, frenzy, fury; commotion, disturbance; EXCITEMENT, hubbub, hullaballoo, AGITATION; craze, mania, fad. See IRASCIBILITY.

FURROW

Nouns—furrow, groove, rut, scratch, streak, stria, crack, score, incision, slit; chamfer, fluting; CHANNEL, gutter, trench, ditch, dike, moat, foss(e), trough, kennel; ravine (see INTERVAL); seam, line, thread. See FOLD.

Verbs—furrow, plow, plough; incise, score, cut, seam, channel; engrave (see ENGRAVING), etch, bite in; flute, chamfer; pucker, wrinkle, knit; corrugate.
Adjectives—furrowed, ribbed, striated, flute; corduroy.

---

further, *adj. & v.* —*adj.* farther, more remote, more, additional. See ADDITION. —*v.t.* AID, advance, promote, expedite.
furtive, *adj.* stealthy, sly, surreptitous, sneaking, skulking, covert. See CONCEALMENT. *Ant.*, see DISCLOSURE.
fury, *n.* rage, frenzy; VIOLENCE, turbulence. See INSANITY.
fuse, *v.* merge, unite, combine, amalgamate; melt, dissolve. See JUNCTION, MIXTURE, HEAT.
fuss, *n.* ado, bustle, hubbub, confusion, AGITATION; fret, fidget.
futile, *adj.* ineffectual, vain, idle, useless. See IMPOTENCE, USELESSNESS. *Ant.*, see UTILITY.

FUTURITY

Nouns—futurity, future, hereafter, time to come; approaching *or* coming years *or* ages; millenium, doomsday, day of judgment, crack of doom; remote future; approach of time, advent, time drawing on, womb of time; DESTINY, POSTERITY, eventuality; prospect (see EXPECTATION); foresight.
Verbs—look forward, anticipate, expect (see EXPECTATION), foresight; forestall (see EARLINESS); come on, draw on; draw near; approach, await; threaten, impend (see DESTINY).
Adjectives—future, to come, coming, impending (see DESTINY); next, near; near at hand, close at hand; eventual, ulterior, in prospect (see EXPECTATION).
Adverbs—in (the) future, prospectively, hereafter, tomorrow, the day after tomorrow; in course of time, in process of time, in the fullness of time; eventually, ultimately, sooner or later, in the long run; one of these days; after a while, after a time; from this time, henceforth, thence; thenceforth, whereupon, upon which; soon, on the eve of, on the point of, on the brink of; about to; close upon.
Antonym, see PRIORITY.

G

gabble, *v.* chatter, prattle; gibber. *Colloq.*, gab, blab, chin, jaw. See LOQUACITY, ABSURDITY, SPEECH.
gadfly, *n.* horsefly; goad, spur; irritant. See CAUSE.
gadget, *n.* contrivance, device, invention, machine; MEANS. *Colloq.*, thingamajig, what-you-may-call-it, whatchumacallit, contraption, doodad. See PLAN.
gaff, *n. & v.* spear, hook. *Colloq.*, punishing ordeal, rough going; pace. See ARMS.
gag, *v.* muffle, silence; choke, strangle. See SILENCE. *Ant.*, see SPEECH.
gaiety, *n.* gayness, merriment, frivolity, merrymaking, CHEERFULNESS.
gain, *n. & v.* —*n.* ACQUISITION, INCREASE, profit; amplification. —*v.* earn, win; reach, attain; persuade. See ADDITION. *Ant.*, see LOSS, DECREASE.
gait, *n.* step, pace, stride; trot, gallop, walk; shuffle, saunter. See MOTION.
gaiter, *n.* legging, overshoe, spat(s). See CLOTHING.

galaxy, *n.* ASSEMBLAGE, MULTITUDE, group, gathering.

gale, *n.* WIND, storm, tempest.

gall, *n. & v.* —*n.* bitterness. —*v.* irritate, chafe; annoy, exasperate; vex. See PAIN. *Ant.*, see PLEASURE.

gallant, *n. & adj.* —*n.* gigolo; squire of dames, escort. —*adj.* chivalrous, polite; brave, courageous. See COURAGE, COURTESY. *Ant.*, see COWARDICE, DISCOURTESY.

gallery, *n.* balcony, corridor; loft; salon. See DRAMA, PAINTING, SCULPTURE.

gallop, *n. & v.* run, canter. See MOTION. *Ant.*, see INACTIVITY.

gallows, *n.* gibbet, scaffold, crosstree, hanging tree, yardarm. See PUNISHMENT, KILLING.

gambit, *n.* ATTACK; stratagem, ruse, artifice. *Slang,* ploy. See DECEPTION, CUNNING, BEGINNING.

gamble, *n. & v.* —*n.* CHANCE, wager, risk. —*v.* speculate, risk, bet.

gambler, *n.* speculator, gamester. *Slang,* bookie, piker, tinhorn. See CHANCE.

gambol, *v.* leap, frolic, cavort, romp; play. See AMUSEMENT.

game, *n. & adj.* —*n.* AMUSEMENT, diversion, sport, play; contest, match; plan, purpose; CHANCE. —*adj.* sporting; gritty, plucky. See COURAGE, RESOLUTION.

gamut, *n.* scale; scope, extent, compass, SEQUENCE. See CONTINUITY, COMPLETION.

gang, *n.* group, band; set, clique; association; mob, horde. See MULTITUDE, PARTY.

gangling, *adj.* lanky, gawky, spindly; ungainly, awkward. See NARROWNESS.

gangrenous, *adj.* mortified, necrose. See DISEASE. *Ant.*, see HEALTH.

gangster, *n.* hoodlum, hooligan, thug, racketeer, tough; syndicate man. *Colloq.,* mobster. *Slang,* goon, hood. See THIEF, ILLEGALITY, EVIL.

gap, *n.* DISCONTINUITY; INTERVAL; OPENING; vacancy; break, lacuna, hiatus. *Ant.*, see CONTINUITY, NEARNESS, CLOSURE.

gape, *v.* open, spread, yawn; stare, gaze. See OPENING, WONDER. *Ant.*, see CLOSURE.

garbage, *n.* WASTE, refuse, trash, rubbish, junk, scraps. See USELESSNESS.

garble, *v.* deface, distort, misreport. See DISTORTION. *Ant.*, see TRUTH.

garden, *n.* herbary, nursery; flowerbeds. See AGRICULTURE.

garish, *adj.* bright, showy, gaudy. See VULGARITY. *Ant.*, see TASTE.

garland, *n.* ORNAMENT, festoon, wreath, lei.

garment, *n.* CLOTHING, robe, dress, vestment(s), habiliment.

garner, *v.* harvest, collect, accumulate. See STORE.

garnish, *v.* ORNAMENT, trim, decorate, embellish; season, flavor.

garret, *n.* crawl space, loft, attic. See RECEPTACLE, HEIGHT.

garrison, *n. & v.* —*n.* fortress, fort, outpost, stronghold; camp, bivouac; billet, barracks, soldiery. —*v.* occupy, encamp, billet; defend, secure, protect, fortify. See DEFENSE.

garrulity, *n.* LOQUACITY, wordiness, prolixity, verbosity, talkativeness.

gas, *n.* aëriform *or* elastic fluid; VAPOR, fume, reek; AIR, ether; fuel; helium, neon, hydrogen, nitrogen, oxygen, *etc.* (*chemical gases*); firedamp, chokedamp, methane, ethane, marsh gas; carbonation (soda water, *etc.*); flatulence; illuminating gas, natural gas, laughing gas (nitrous oxide), tear gas, poison gas (lewisite, carbon monoxide, mustard gas, chlorine, phosgene, *etc.*); gas attack. *Colloq.,* gasoline, petrol. *Slang,* hot air, bombast, empty talk. *Ant.*, see DENSITY.

gaseous, *adj.* gassy, gaslike; flatulent; volatile, evaporable; gasiform, aëriform; carbonated; reeky, reeking, fumy, smelly. See GAS, ODOR, VAPOR.

gash, *n. & v.* slash, gouge, slit; cut; scratch, score. See DISJUNCTION. *Ant.*, see JUNCTION.

gasp, *v.i.* pant, labor, choke; puff; exclaim. See WEARINESS.

gate, *n.* OPENING, gateway, entry, portal; sluice, floodgate. See IN-CLOSURE.

gather, *v.* infer, conclude; congregate, group, amass; shirr, pucker; collect, harvest, glean; cluster, huddle, herd; fester, suppurate. See IN-CREASE, DISEASE, ASSEMBLAGE. *Ant.,* see DECREASE, DISJUNCTION.

gauche, *adj.* awkward, clumsy; uncultured. See UNSKILLFULNESS, ROUGHNESS. *Ant.,* see SMOOTHNESS, SKILL.

gaudy, *adj.* garish; showy; cheap, blatant, tawdry; flashy. See CHEAP-NESS, COLOR. *Ant.,* see SIMPLENESS, COLORLESSNESS.

gauge, *n.* & *v.* —*n.* measure, templet, template; caliber, SIZE. —*v.* measure, estimate, JUDGE, evaluate. See MEASUREMENT.

gaunt, *adj.* haggard, bony, lean, emaciated; repellant. See NARROW-NESS. *Ant.,* see BREADTH.

gauze, *n.* net, tulle, malines, scrim, marquisette, gossamer, cheesecloth, bandage. See MATERIALS, TRANSPARENCY, INSUBSTANTIALITY.

gay, *adj.* lively, vivacious, blithe; convivial, festive. See CHEERFULNESS, COLOR. *Ant.,* see DEJECTION, COLORLESSNESS.

gaze, *v.* stare, ogle, pore, look, watch. See VISION.

gazette, *n.* newspaper, tabloid, bulletin. See PUBLICATION, NEWS.

gear, *n.* CLOTHING, dress; cogwheel; equipment, tools, apparatus. See INSTRUMENT.

gelatin, *n.* jelly, aspic, gelée; gluten, pectin, agar-agar. See COHERENCE.

gelid, *adj.* frozen, COLD; icy, frosty, ice-cold.

gem, *n.* jewel, stone; prize; work of art. See ORNAMENT, GOODNESS.

genealogy, *n.* pedigree, DESCENT, ancestry, lineage, stock; POSTERITY.

GENERALITY

Nouns—**1,** generality, generalization; universality, broadness, collectivity; average; catholicity, catholicism; miscellany, miscellaneousness; prevalence; DISPERSION.
2, everyone, everybody [and his brother]; all hands, all the world and his wife; anybody. *Colloq.,* whole kit and caboodle. *Slang,* the works.
Verbs—be general, prevail, be going about; generalize, render general.
Adjectives—general, generic, collective; broad, comprehensive, sweeping; encyclopedic, widespread, dispersed; universal, catholic, common, all-inclusive, worldwide; ecumenical; transcendental; prevalent, prevailing, rife, epidemic, besetting; all over, covered with; every, all; unspecified, impersonal; customary (see HABIT).
Adverbs—generally, in general, generally speaking; always, for better or worse; for the most part, in the long run; whatever, whatsoever; to a man, one and all, all told.

Antonym, see SPECIALITY.

generate, *v.* make, produce; proliferate, procreate, breed, impregnate; engender. See POWER, PRODUCTION. *Ant.,* see IMPOTENCE, DESTRUCTION.

generation, *n.* AGE, descent, lifetime; procreating, breeding, begetting. See RELATION, PRODUCTION. *Ant.,* see DESTRUCTION.

generosity, *n.* BENEVOLENCE, philanthropy, liberality, munificence, prodigality; altruism, magnanimity. See GIVING. *Ant.,* see ECONOMY.

genesis, *n.* creation, origin, formation, BEGINNING, birth. See PRODUC-TION.

genetic, *adj.* genic, inherited, hereditary, innate. See ANCESTRY, REPRO-DUCTION, CAUSE, ATTRIBUTION.

genial, *adj.* affable, cordial, jovial, friendly, hearty, pleasant. See CHEER-FULNESS. *Ant.,* see DEJECTION.

genius, *n.* spirit, pixy; brilliance, INTELLIGENCE; talent, bent, gift, ability. See SKILL, INTELLECT.

genre, *n.* kind, category, species, type, CLASS. See WRITING.

gentle, *adj.* mild, calm; soothing, kindly, tolerant; considerate, courteous;

well-bred, high-born; tame, docile. See COURTESY, MODERATION, NO-BILITY, DOMESTICATION. *Ant.*, see DISCOURTESY, VIOLENCE.

gentleman, *n.* aristocrat, cavalier, esquire. See MALE, PROBITY, NO-BILITY.

gentleness, *n.* MODERATION, mildness; kindness, amenity, lenience. *Ant.*, see VIOLENCE.

gentry, *n.* See NOBILITY.

genuine, *adj.* true, right, real, authentic; sincere, unaffected; honest, valid. See GOODNESS, PURITY. *Ant.*, see BADNESS, IMPURITY.

geometrical, *adj.* geometric, planimetric; patterned, designed, symmetric; formal, stylized. See ORDER, ORNAMENT.

germ, *n.* microörganism; seed, embryo; microbe, bacterium; BEGINNING, rudiment. See CAUSE. *Ant.*, see END, EFFECT.

germane, *adj.* relevant, pertinent, apropos, to the point. See RELATION.

germicide, *n.* germ-killer; bactericide, insecticide, antiseptic. See REMEDY.

germinate, *v.* impregnate; sprout; begin. See CAUSE.

gesticulate, *v.* gesture, motion, wave, pantomime, mime. See INDICATION.

gesture, *n. & v.* —*n.* motion, signal, gesticulation. —*v.i.* wave, signal, nod, beckon. See INDICATION.

get, *v.* secure, obtain, procure, take, acquire; win, earn, attain; understand, comprehend. See ACQUISITION. *Ant.*, see LOSS.

getaway, *n.* ESCAPE, breakout, flight; head start. See DISAPPEARANCE.

getup, *n., colloq.*, rig, outfit, garb, dress, CLOTHING.

gewgaw, *n.* trinket, knickknack, bauble. See ORNAMENT.

geyser, *n.* hot spring, spout, gusher; Old Faithful. See WATER, EJECTION.

ghastly, *adj.* pale, deathly, ashen, livid; horrible, terrible, fearsome, hideous. See UGLINESS, COLORLESSNESS. *Ant.*, see BEAUTY, COLOR.

ghost, *n.* apparition, phantom, spirit, SHADE, specter.

ghostly, *adj.* ghostlike, spectral, phantasmal. See DEATH.

ghoul, *n.* graverobber, body snatcher; DEMON, vampire; blackmailer. See EVIL.

giant, *n.* jumbo, monster, titan, colossus. See SIZE. *Ant.*, see LITTLENESS.

gibe, *n.* sneer, taunt, jeer, ridicule. See DISRESPECT. *Ant.*, see RESPECT.

giddy, *adj.* frivolous, irresponsible; dizzy, flighty, capricious. See INSANITY, CHANGEABLENESS.

gift, *n.* present, donation, favor, bounty; contribution, gratuity, tip; largess(e); talent, aptitude, ability. See GIVING, POWER. *Ant.*, see RECEIVING, IMPOTENCE.

gigantic, *adj.* monstrous, elephantine, titanic, huge, enormous, colossal, immense. See SIZE. *Ant.*, see LITTLENESS.

giggle, *v.* laugh, chuckle, titter. See AMUSEMENT.

gimmick, *n., slang*, artifice, trick, MEANS, technique; GADGET. *Colloq.*, angle.

gingerly, *adv.* carefully, prudently, timidly, charily, hesitantly. See CAUTION, FEAR.

gird, *v.* bind, strap, secure; encircle, surround; support, fortify. See POWER, CIRCULARITY.

girdle, *n.* band, belt, girth; corset, cummerbund. See CLOTHING, CIRCULARITY.

girl, *n.* lass, maid, damsel; SERVANT, clerk. See FEMALE.

girl friend, *n., colloq.*, sweetheart, girl, LOVE, date. *Slang*, steady, flame, moll.

girth, *n.* OUTLINE; circumference, belt, girdle, band.

gist, *n.* MEANING, essence, significance, point.

giveaway, *n., colloq.*, DISCLOSURE, dead giveaway; premium, bonus, door prize, handout, come-on, something for nothing. See SALE.

GIVING

Nouns—**1,** giving, bestowal, donation; presentation, presentment; accordance; cession, concession; delivery, consignment; dispensation; communication; endowment; investment, investiture; award; almsgiving, charity, liberality, generosity, philanthropy (see BENEVOLENCE).
2, gift, donation, present, *cadeau*, boon, favor; benefaction, grant; offering, oblation, sacrifice, immolation; bonus, bonanza.
3, allowance, contribution, subscription, subsidy, tribute; alimony, pension; fee, recompense (see PAYMENT); consideration; bribe, bait; peace-offering.
4, bequest, legacy, devise, will; dot, appanage; voluntary settlement, voluntary conveyance, transfer; amortization.
5, alms, charity, largess(e), bounty, dole; oblation, offertory; honorarium, gratuity, Christmas box, Easter offering; tip, drink money, *pourboire*, lagniappe, premium. *Slang*, handout.
6, giver, grantor; donor, testator, testatrix; feoffer, settlor.
7, godsend, manna, windfall, blessing.
8, liberality, generosity, munificence, lavishness, magnanimity, bountifulness.
Verbs—**1,** give, donate, bestow, confer, grant, accord, award, assign; present, give away, dispense, dispose of, deal out, dole out, mete out, pay out, squeeze out; make a present, allow, contribute, subscribe; invest, endow, settle upon, bequeath, will, leave, devise; deliver, hand, pass, make over, turn over; entrust, consign, vest in; concede, cede, yield, part with, spend; pay (see PAYMENT).
2, furnish, supply, make available, help; administer to, minister to; afford, spare; accommodate with, favor with; shower down upon; lavish, pour on, thrust upon; bribe; cross, tickle *or* grease the palm; offer, sacrifice, immolate. *Colloq.,* chip in. *Slang,* kick in, tip, fork over, cough up.
Adjectives—giving, given; allowed, allowable; donative, concessional; communicable; charitable, eleemosynary; LIBERAL.
Antonyms, see RECEIVING, ACQUISITION.

---

glad, *adj.* happy, content, joyful; blithe, beatific; pleased; blissful. See PLEASURE. *Ant.,* see PAIN.
glade, *n.* clearing, glen, cañada. See LAND.
glamour, *n.* charm, romance, enchantment, bewitchment, captivation, allure; sex appeal. See SORCERY.
glance, *n. & v.* —*n.* glimpse, *coup d'œil*; ray, beam, look; ricochet, skim, stroke. —*v.i.* peek, glimpse, look; graze, brush, strike. See VISION.
glare, *n. & v.* —*n.* scowl, frown, glower; stare. —*v.i.* flare, shine, glitter; blinding light. See LIGHT, VISION. *Ant.,* see DARKNESS, BLINDNESS.
glaring, *adj.* fierce; bright, dazzling, showy; conspicuous, flagrant. See COLOR, MANIFESTATION.
glass, *n.* crystal; mirror, lens, slide; beaker, tumbler, goblet, snifter; pane; (*pl.*) spectacles, eyeglasses. See OPTICAL INSTRUMENTS, RECEPTACLE.
glassy, *adj.* glazed, vitreous, crystalline; mirrory, smooth, polished; clear, bright, transparent; fragile, brittle. See TRANSPARENT, HARDNESS, SMOOTHNESS, BRITTLENESS.
glaze, *n.* luster, shine; coating; ice; glass, glassiness. See SMOOTHNESS, COVERING.
gleam, *n. & v.* —*n.* light, beam, flash, glimmer, ray. —*v.i.* shine, glow, glitter, glimmer. See LIGHT. *Ant.,* see DARKNESS.
glee, *n.* CHEERFULNESS, delight, joy, merriment, gaiety, mirth. *Ant.,* see DEJECTION.
glib, *adj.* smooth, facile, fluent, voluble, ready. See LOQUACITY. *Ant.,* see CONTRACTION, SILENCE.

glide, *v.i.* float, flow, skim; slip, slide, coast; pass, elapse; skate, swim, ski. See MOTION, AVIATION.

glimmer, *n. & v.* —*n.* glance, appearance, view, flash, slight. —*v.i.* peep, glance, see, peek. See VISION.

glimpse, *v. & n.* GLANCE; see VISION.

glint, *n. & v.* —*n.* luster, brightness, gleam; stare, gaze, steely look. —*v.* flash, gleam, glisten, scintillate; glance, glimpse. See LIGHT, VISION.

glisten, *v.* glister, shine, gleam, glint, glitter, coruscate. See LIGHT.

glitter, *v.i. & n.* shine, flash, gleam, twinkle, glow, glisten, glint, sparkle, beam. See LIGHT. *Ant.,* see DARKNESS.

gloat, *v.i.* boast, exult, rejoice; stare, gape; revel, glory, delight. See BOASTING, PLEASURE. *Ant.,* see PAIN.

globe, *n.* ball, sphere; earth; orb. See ROTUNDITY, UNIVERSE.

globule, *n.* drop, bead, droplet, blob; spherule. See ROTUNDITY, LITTLENESS.

gloom, *n.* DEJECTION, sadness, dolefulness, melancholy; shadow, shade, dimness, obscurity; pessimism. See DARKNESS. *Ant.,* see LIGHT, CHEERFULNESS.

glorify, *v.* exalt, magnify, revere; exaggerate; praise, honor; transform; flatter. See ELEVATION, REPUTE. *Ant.,* see DEPRESSION, DISREPUTE.

glory, *n.* aureole, halo, nimbus; radiance, brilliance; fame, dignity; effulgence; honor, kudos, renown. See BEAUTY, LIGHT, REPUTE. *Ant.,* see UGLINESS, DARKNESS, DISREPUTE.

gloss, *n.* luster, sheen, shine, finish, polish; glaze, veneer; DECEPTION, speciousness. See LIGHT, SMOOTHNESS. *Ant.,* see DARKNESS, ROUGHNESS.

glove, *n.* mitten, gauntlet. See CLOTHING.

glow, *n. & v.* —*n.* flush, sheen, light, radiance, warmth. —*v.* shine, gleam, flush, burn, blaze, flame. See HEAT, LIGHT, FEELING.

glower, *v.* scowl, frown, glare. See RESENTMENT.

glue, *n. & v.* —*n.* mucilage, paste, cement, adhesive. —*v.* stick, attach; adhere, cement.

glum, *adj.* morose, dismal, sullen, moody, gloomy, surly, low, unhappy. See DEJECTION. *Ant.,* see CHEERFULNESS.

glut, *v. & n.* —*v.* stuff, cram, choke, pack, jam. —*n.* surplus, surfeit, plethora, saturation, SATIETY, REDUNDANCE.

GLUTTONY

Nouns—**1,** gluttony, gluttonousness, hoggishness; greed, greediness; voracity, rapacity, edacity, crapulence; epicurism; good living, high living; guzzling; good cheer, blow out; feast; gastronomy.

2, epicure, bon vivant, gourmand, gourmandizer, gourmet; glutton, cormorant; gastronome. *Colloq.,* pig, hog.

Verbs—be gluttonous, gormandize, gorge; overgorge, overeat; engorge, eat one's fill, indulge one's appetite; cram, stuff; guzzle; bolt, raven, wolf, devour, gobble up; gulp; eat out of house and home; have a tapeworm inside. *Colloq.,* eat like a horse.

Adjectives—gluttonous, greedy, hungry, voracious, rapacious, edacious, omnivorous, crapulent, swinish; gorged, overfed; insatiable.

Antonym, see ASCETICISM.

---

gnarled, *adj.* knotty, burred, cross-grained; misshapen, deformed; rough, wiry, rugged. See DISTORTION, ROUGHNESS.

gnash, *v.t.* grind, champ, crunch, gnaw, bite. See RESENTMENT, LAMENTATION.

gnaw, *v.* chew, masticate, crunch; rankle, irritate, distress. See FOOD, PAIN. *Ant.,* see PLEASURE.

gnome, *n.* dwarf, goblin, elf, kobold, gremlin. See DEMON, MYTHICAL DEITIES.

go, *v.i.* leave, depart, withdraw, retire, exit; vanish, disappear, evaporate, evanesce; operate, work, run, function, succeed; proceed, pass; wend, stir; extend, reach; elapse, pass; wither, fade, die; burst, explode. See DEPARTURE, PASSAGE.

goad, v. prick, stab, prod, poke, spur; urge, egg (on), incite, impel, drive, motivate, CAUSE. *Slang*, needle. See IMPULSE, MOTIVE, HASTE.

goal, n. object, end, aim, ambition; (*in games*) finish line, home, cage, goalposts, end zone, basket, field goal, foul; point, tally, marker. See DESIRE.

gob, n., *colloq.*, lump, dab, dollop (see PART); (*pl.*) piles, lots, heaps. *Slang*, oodles. See QUANTITY, MULTITUDE.

gobble, v. eat, devour, bolt, wolf, gulp. *Colloq.*, engulf, swallow up, consume, exhaust, take over. See INCLUSION, SUPERIORITY, GLUTTONY.

go-between, n. AGENT, intermediary, broker, middleman, dealer; pander. See INSTRUMENTALITY, REPRESENTATION.

god, n. deity, idol, divinity; Olympian; goddess. See MYTHICAL DEITIES.

godless, adj. unbelieving, faithless; atheistic, agnostic, skeptic(al); heathenish, pagan, infidel; impious, irreligious. See IMPIETY, IRRELIGION.

godly, adj. divine; pious, reverent, religious, devout, righteous. See PIETY. *Ant.*, see IMPIETY.

godsend, n. miracle, blessing, manna [from heaven], WINDFALL, boon. *Slang*, [lucky] break. See PROSPERITY, CHANCE.

go-getter, n., *colloq.*, doer, intrepreneur; zealot, enthusiast. *Slang*, drumbeater, hustler, operator, wheeler-dealer. See ACTIVITY, VIGOR.

gold, n. MONEY, wealth; bullion, *aurum*; gilding, gilt, goldplate. See COLOR. *Ant.*, see POVERTY.

golden, adj. gilded, aureate, yellow; gold; precious, valuable, priceless; unequaled. See GOOD, COLOR. *Ant.*, see EVIL, COLORLESSNESS.

gong, n. cymbal, tocsin, tam-tam. See MUSICAL INSTRUMENTS, WARNING.

GOOD, GOODNESS

Nouns—**1,** goodness, good; excellence, merit; VIRTUE, value, worth, price; welfare, benefit; BENEVOLENCE. See PROBITY.

2, SUPERIORITY, PERFECTION, masterpiece, *chef d'œuvre*, prime, flower, cream, pride, élite, pick, nonesuch, nonpareil, *crême de la crême*, flower of the flock, salt of the earth; champion; all wool and a yard wide.

3, gem, gem of the first water; bijou, precious stone, jewel, pearl, diamond, ruby, brilliant, treasure; good thing; *rara avis*, one in a million.

4, good man, model, prince, paragon, angel, saint; BENEFACTOR, philanthropist, altruist.

Verbs—**1,** produce *or* do good, be beneficial, profit (see UTILITY); serve, help, avail, benefit; confer a benefit; be the making of, do a world of good, make a man of; produce a good effect; do a good turn, improve (see IMPROVEMENT).

2, be good, excel, transcend, be superior (see SUPERIORITY); stand the test; pass muster; challenge comparison, vie, emulate, rival.

Adjectives—**1,** good, beneficial, valuable, of value, excellent, superior (see SUPERIORITY); serviceable, useful (see UTILITY); advantageous, profitable, edifying, salutary, healthful (see HEALTH); genuine (see TRUTH); moderately good, tolerable (see IMPERFECTION); best, first-class, first-rate, capital, prime; harmless, unobnoxious, innocuous, innocent, inoffensive. *Colloq.*, above par, tiptop, topnotch, top-drawer, A-1, gilt-edge(d). *Slang*, bang-up, grand, great, swell.

2, VIRTUOUS, moral, creditable, laudable, exemplary.

Adverbs—to the good, beneficially, in one's favor *or* interests. *Colloq.*, out of this world; not half bad.

Antonym, see BADNESS.

---

good-bye, good-by, *interj. & n. —interj.* farewell, till we meet again, God be with you, Godspeed, fare thee well; *adieu, adios, au revoir,* *arrivederci, auf wiedersehn, aloha, ave, shalom, sayonara, pax vobiscum.* *Colloq.,* so long, see you [later], *ciao;* cheerio. —*n.* farewell, leave-taking, word of parting. See DEPARTURE.

good-for-nothing, *n. & adj.* —*n.* knave, rogue, ne'er-do-well, do-nothing, nobody; lazybones, loafer, sloth, wastrel, fainéant. *Colloq.,* bum. —*adj.* no-account, useless, worthless, futile. See IMPROBITY, WASTE.

good-looking, *adj.* handsome, pretty, comely, *etc.* See BEAUTY.

good-natured, *adj.* kind-hearted, kindly, easygoing, even-tempered, pleasant, agreeable, amiable, sociable. See CHEERFULNESS, BENEVOLENCE.

goods, *n.pl.* belongings, wares, merchandise, stock, effects; commodities. See PROPERTY.

goof, *n. & v.* See ERROR.

gorge, *n. & v.* —*n.* gully, ravine, canyon, pass. See INTERVAL, DEPRESSION. —*v.* overeat, gormandize, stuff, bolt, gulp. See GLUTTONY.

gorgeous, *adj.* beautiful, superb, breathtaking, magnificent, splendid. See BEAUTY. *Ant.,* see UGLINESS.

gory, *adj.* bloody; bloodthirsty, sanguinary, gruesome. See KILLING.

gospel, *n.* good news, glad tidings; synoptic; dogma, CERTAINTY, TRUTH. See SACRED WRITINGS.

gossip, *n. & v.* —*n.* busybody, talebearer, chatterer; reports, rumors. —*v.i.* talk, speculate, report, tattle, whisper. See CURIOSITY, INFORMATION, SPEECH.

gouge, *v.* scoop, channel, dig, cut grooves, rout out. *Colloq.,* defraud, overcharge, cheat, swindle. *Slang,* skin, fleece, scalp. See DECEPTION, STEALING.

gourmet, *n.* epicure, *bon vivant;* gastronome, gastrophile. See FOOD, PLEASURE, TASTE.

govern, *v.t.* RULE, reign, administrate, preside, CONDUCT, COMMAND; hold power, sway *or* the reigns; INFLUENCE, sway; restrain, moderate, temper, LIMIT, curb, bridle, check. See MODERATION, RESTRAINT, AUTHORITY, DIRECTION.

governess, *n.* nurse, nanny; preceptress, gouvernante; matron. See TEACHING, DEFENSE.

government, *n.* régime, administration; control, rule, regulation; state, economy; kingship, regency; protectorate, democracy, republic, autocracy, dictatorship, totalitarian state. See AUTHORITY, DIRECTION.

gown, *n.* peignoir, negligée, nightgown; dress, garment, evening gown, robe; vestment(s), cassock; frock, smock; slip. See CLOTHING.

grab, *v.* take, snatch, seize, capture; clutch; annex. See ACQUISITION. *Ant.,* see RESTORATION.

grace, *n. & v.* —*n.* delicacy, tact, culture; graciousness, courtesy; attractiveness, charm; compassion, mercy; saintliness, PIETY, sinlessness. —*v.* honor, decorate; improve. See BEAUTY, TASTE.

graceful, *adj.* lithesome, lissom(e), svelte, sylphlike, gainly; easy, fluent; willowy; pleasing, elegant, attractive. See FORM, BEAUTY.

graceless, *adj.* ungracious, tactless; inept, awkward, clumsy; inelegant; sinful, corrupt. See UGLINESS, EVIL. *Ant.,* see BEAUTY, VIRTUE.

gracious, *adj.* gentle, courteous, tactful; kind, thoughtful, benign; affable, obliging. See BENEVOLENCE, COURTESY. *Ant.,* see DISCOURTESY.

grade, *n.* level, quality, class; rank, standing; gradation, slope, tilt, slant. See OBLIQUITY.

gradual, *adj.* gentle, slow, progressive, moderate, lingering, leisurely. See DEGREE, SLOWNESS.

graduate, *n. & v.* —*n.* measure, beaker. —*v.* raise, adjust, modify; measure, classify, grade. See AGREEMENT, ARRANGEMENT.

graft, *v. & n.* —*v.* inoculate, bud, transplant, implant, join. See VEGETABLE. —*n.* transplanted shoot *or* part; corruption, porkbarrel politics, political swindling. See IMPROBITY.

grain, *n.* fruit, cereal, seed, grist, kernel; TEXTURE, temper, TENDENCY, DIRECTION; mite, speck, bit. See LITTLENESS.

GRAMMAR

Nouns—**1**, grammar; accidence, syntax, analysis, synopsis, praxis, punctuation, syllabication, syllabification; parts of speech; participle; noun, substantive, pronoun, verb, adjective, adverb, preposition, interjection, conjunction; inflection, inflexion, case, declension, conjugation.

2, tense; present, past, preterit(e), future; imperfect, perfect, past perfect, pluperfect; progressive, *etc.*

3, mood, mode; infinitive, indicative, subjunctive, imperative.

4, STYLE; philology, LANGUAGE; PHRASE, phraseology.

Verbs—parse, analyze; punctuate; conjugate, decline, inflect.

Antonym, see ERROR.

---

grand, *adj.* large, impressive, magnificent, stately, majestic; pretentious, ostentatious. See GREATNESS, NOBILITY, OSTENTATION.

grandeur, *n.* GREATNESS, magnificence; show, ostentation; splendor, majesty; eminence, stateliness, loftiness. See REPUTE. *Ant.*, see LITTLENESS.

grandfather, *n.* grandpa, grandsire; gaffer, old man. See ANCESTRY.

grandmother, *n.* granny, grandma, nana, nanny; old woman. See ANCESTRY.

grant, *n. & v.* —*n.* gift, allotment, contribution. —*v.* bestow, give, yield; agree, concede; permit; contribute, consent. See GIVING, PERMISSION.

granular, *adj.* grainy, mealy, gritty, granulated, sandy. See POWDERINESS.

grapevine, *n.* rumor; pipeline, a little bird. See COMMUNICATION.

graph, *n.* diagram, chart, plot; bar, circle, *etc.* graph. See REPRESENTATION.

graphic, *adj.* pictorial, descriptive; vivid; diagrammatic; delineative; picturesque; forcible, powerful. See PAINTING, SCULPTURE, MEANING, POWER.

grapple, *v.* seize, grasp, clutch, struggle, contend. See OPPOSITION, CONTENTION.

grasp, *v.* hold, clasp, seize; comprehend, understand. See MEANING, ACQUISITION, TAKING.

grass, *n.* lawn, greenery, turf, sod, verdure. See VEGETABLE.

grassland, *n.* pasturage, grazing, pasture, prairie, meadowland, PLAIN.

grate, *v.* scrape, grind, rasp, abrade, scratch, rasp. See FRICTION.

grateful, *adj.* appreciative, thankful; welcome, agreeable, refreshing. See GRATITUDE, PLEASURE. *Ant.*, see INGRATITUDE.

gratification, *n.* satisfaction; entertainment; fulfillment; diversion, feast; ease, comfort; indulgence, consummation. See PLEASURE. *Ant.*, see PAIN.

grating, *n.* lattice, openwork, grillwork, grid. See CROSSING.

GRATITUDE

Nouns—gratitude, gratefulness, thankfulness; indebtedness; acknowledgment, recognition, thanksgiving; thanks, praise, benediction; paean; *Te Deum*, WORSHIP, grace; thank-offering; requital.

Verbs—be grateful, thank; give, render, return, offer *or* tender thanks; acknowledge, requite; thank *or* bless one's [lucky] stars.

Adjectives—grateful, thankful, appreciative, obliged, beholden, indebted to, under obligation.

Interjections—thanks! much obliged! thank you! thank Heaven! Heaven be praised! thanks a million! *gracias! merci!*.

Antonym, see INGRATITUDE.

---

gratuitous, *adj.* baseless, uncalled for, unwarranted; free, gratis. See CHEAPNESS, FREEDOM, SOPHISTRY.

gratuity, *n.* tip, largesse; present, gift; fee. See CHEAPNESS, GIVING.

grave, *n. & adj.* —*n.* burial place, sepulcher, tomb, mausoleum. See INTERMENT. —*adj.* important, weighty, serious; sedate, dignified; momentous, solemn; dull, somber. See COLOR, DEJECTION, IMPORTANCE. *Ant.,* see UNIMPORTANCE.

gravel, *n.* stones, pebbles, calculi; rubble, scree; alluvium, detritus, attritus, ballast, shingle, beach. See POWDERINESS, HARDNESS.

GRAVITY

Nouns—**1,** gravity, gravitation; weight, weighing; heaviness; ponderosity, pressure, burden; ballast, counterpoise; lump, mass, load, lading, freight; lead, millstone. *Colloq.,* heft.

2, weight; avoirdupois, troy, apothecaries' weight; grain, scruple, dram, ounce, pound, load, stone, hundredweight, ton, carat, pennyweight.

3, balance, scales, steelyard, beam, weighbridge, spring balance.

4, gravity, seriousness, solemnity, SOBRIETY; IMPORTANCE, weight, moment, momentousness.

Verbs—be heavy; gravitate, weigh, press, cumber, load; weight, weigh down; outweigh, overbalance.

Adjectives—**1,** gravitational, weighty; weighing; heavy, ponderous, ponderable; lumpish, lumpy; cumbersome, burdensome; cumbrous, unwieldy, massive. *Colloq.,* hefty.

2, grave, sober, solemn, serious; important, critical; momentous.

Antonym, see LEVITY.

---

gray, *adj.* dun, mousy, slaty, *etc.*; clouded, overcast, drab, dingy, dull, depressing, bleak; aged, old, venerable. See COLOR, COLORLESSNESS, CLOUDINESS, DULLNESS, DEJECTION, OLDNESS.

graze, *v.* TOUCH, brush; scratch, abrade, rub; pasture, browse, feed, crop. See FOOD, FRICTION.

grease, *n. & v.* —*n.* OIL, fat; graphite; suet, lard, tallow. —*v.* lubricate; anoint. See SMOOTHNESS.

GREATNESS

Nouns—**1,** greatness, magnitude; amount, SIZE, dimensions; MULTITUDE, number; immensity, enormity; INFINITE; might, strength, POWER, intensity, fullness.

2, IMPORTANCE, eminence, prominence, grandeur, distinction, fame, REPUTE, notability.

3, great quantity, quantity, deal, volume, world; bulk, mass (see WHOLE); stock (see STORE); bushel, load, cargo; cartload, vanload, truckload, shipload; flood, spring tide; abundance, SUFFICIENCY; majority, plurality, predominance. *Colloq.,* plenty, sight, pot, scads, oodles, slew, heap.

Verbs—run high, soar, tower, transcend; rise to a great height; know no bounds; enlarge, INCREASE; expand.

Adjectives—**1,** great; greater (see SUPERIORITY); large, considerable, fair, above par; big, huge (see SIZE); ample; abundant, enough (see SUFFICIENCY); full, intense, strong; passing (*archaic*), heavy, plenary, deep, high; signal, at its height, in the zenith; worldwide, widespread, extensive; wholesale; many (see MULTITUDE).

2, goodly, noble; mighty; arch; profound, intense, consummate; extraordinary; important (see IMPORTANCE); unsurpassed (see SUPERIORITY); complete (see COMPLETION).

3, vast, immense, enormous, extreme; exaggerated (see EXAGGERATION); marvelous (see WONDER); unlimited, infinite. *Colloq.,* whopping, fearful, terrific.

4, absolute, positive, stark; perfect, finished; remarkable, noteworthy.

Adverbs—**1,** great; absolutely, completely, entirely (see COMPLETION); abundantly (see SUFFICIENCY); greatly, much, in a great measure, richly; to a large *or* great extent; on a large scale; wholesale; mightily, powerfully; intensely. *Colloq.,* no end, plenty, real, mighty.

2, supremely, preëminently, superlatively (see SUPERIORITY); immeasurably, infinitely; immoderately, monstrously (see EXAGGERATION); remarkably, notably, exceptionally, marvelously (see WONDER). *Colloq.,* terribly, awfully.

Antonym, see LITTLENESS.

---

greed, *n.* DESIRE; cupidity, avidity, avarice; covetousness, rapacity; greediness.

greenhouse, *n.* hothouse, solarium, herbarium, conservatory, nursery. See AGRICULTURE.

greet, *v.* address, hail, salute; welcome, receive, entertain, admit. See COURTESY, RECEIVING. *Ant.,* see DISCOURTESY, GIVING.

grenade, *n.* bomb, shell, explosive. *Slang,* pineapple, egg. See ARMS.

grief, *n.* distress, bereavement, sorrow, dolor; affliction, trouble, tribulation. See PAIN. *Ant.,* see PLEASURE.

grievance, *n.* complaint, annoyance, irritation; injustice, wrong; tribulation, injury. *Slang,* gripe. See EVIL, PAIN. *Ant.,* see GOODNESS.

grieve, *v.* distress, pain, hurt, sadden, injure; mourn, sorrow, deplore. See LAMENTATION, PAIN.

grievous, *adj.* depressing, intense, sad; severe, flagrant; appalling, troublesome; atrocious. See PAIN.

grill, *n. & v.* —*n.* grating, grid. —*v.* broil, roast, toast, sear, pan-fry, barbecue. See FOOD.

grim, *adj.* fearful, stern, fierce, forbidding; inflexible; ruthless; grisly, horrible. See RESOLUTION, UGLINESS. *Ant.,* see DOUBT, BEAUTY.

grimace, *n.* face, scowl, leer, expression, *moue.* See DISTORTION, AFFECTATION.

grimy, *adj.* soiled, dirty, foul, filthy. See UNCLEANNESS. *Ant.,* see CLEANNESS.

grin, *n. & v.* —*n.* smile, smirk, sneer, leer. —*v.* bare the teeth; smile, sneer, grimace, smirk; grin from ear to ear. See REJOICING.

grind, *v.* pulverize, crush; sharpen, whet, file, polish; masticate, crunch; rasp, grate; oppress, harass. See FRICTION, SEVERITY, POWDERINESS.

grip, *n. & v.* —*n.* handle; handclasp; hold, control; suitcase, bag, satchel. —*v.* seize, grasp, clutch, hold. See ACQUISITION, RECEPTACLE.

gripe, *v., colloq.,* complain, grumble, mutter. See IRASCIBILITY.

grit, *n.* sand, roughage, gravel; COURAGE, pluck, stamina, endurance. See RESOLUTION, POWDERINESS.

groan, *n. & v.* —*n.* CRY, LAMENTATION, moan. —*v.i.* grumble, lament, moan, whine, whimper.

grocery, *n.* grocery store, greengrocery, purveyor's; supermarket, market; (*pl.*) provisions, victuals, FOOD, supplies. See STORE.

grog, *n.* [hot] buttered rum; hot toddy; potion. See FOOD.

groggy, *adj.* dizzy, stupefied, incoherent, sleepy, half-asleep. *Slang,* punchy, out of it. See WEARINESS, UNINTELLIGIBILITY.

groom, *n. & v.* —*n.* bridegroom, benedict. —*v.* dress, tend, polish, curry. See DOMESTICATION, CLOTHING.

groove, *n.* FURROW; HABIT, routine, rut; trench, channel, indentation.

grope, *v.i.* feel, essay, fumble; attempt; hunt, search. See FEELING.

gross, *adj.* bulky, large, fat, obese; coarse, crass; brutish, callous, unrefined, insensitive; vulgar, crude, sensual; obscene. See GREATNESS, VULGARITY. *Ant.,* see LITTLENESS, TASTE.

grotesque, *adj.* strange, unnatural, abnormal; bizarre, fantastic, odd; misshapen, startling. See ABSURDITY, UNCONFORMITY.

grotto, *n.* cave, cavern; crypt, vault; spelunk. See CONCAVITY.

grouchy, *adj., colloq.,* cross, sharp, sulky, testy, grumpy, gruff, sullen, ill-tempered, sour, out of sorts. See IRASCIBILITY, DISCONTENT.

ground, *n., v. & adj.* —*n.* earth, terra firma, soil; foundation, basis; cause, reason; viewpoint. —*v.* base, establish; settle, fix; instruct. —*adj.* pulverized, grated; whittled, sharpened, abraded. See LAND, SUPPORT, CAUSE.

groundless, *adj.* unsubstantiated, foundationless, imaginary, baseless, unauthorized, unfounded. See INSUBSTANTIALITY.

grounds, *n.pl.* dregs, lees; property, land, estate, yard; MOTIVE, reason, CAUSE. See UNCLEANNESS, REMAINDER, PROPERTY, ARENA.

groundwork, *n.* foundation, framework; inception, beginning; basis. See BASE, SUPPORT.

group, *n. & v.* —*n.* ASSEMBLAGE, company, association; clique, set; collection, cluster, company. —*v.* collect, gather, classify, sort, combine; cluster. See ARRANGEMENT.

grove, *n.* thicket, coppice, copse, woodland. See VEGETABLE.

grovel, *v.* fawn, creep, cringe; wallow, humble (oneself). See SERVILITY.

grow, *v.* mature, become, develop; increase, extend, expand, enlarge; nurture, raise, cultivate; germinate, breed, sprout; flourish, thrive. See AGRICULTURE, INCREASE, VEGETABLE.

growth, *n.* development, EVOLUTION, INCREASE; adulthood, maturity; harvest, crop, produce, yield; flora, VEGETABLE; tumor, cancer, node, polyp, mole, tubercule, cyst, excrescence, swelling, protuberance, wen. See EXPANSION, PROSPERITY, DISEASE, CONVEXITY.

growl, *v.* mutter, grumble; snarl; complain, howl. See LAMENTATION.

grubby, *adj.*, *colloq.*, dingy, poor, shabby, scurvy; ignoble, base, mean. See INFERIORITY, MALEVOLENCE.

grudge, *v.* stint, dole; begrudge, withhold. See PARSIMONY.

gruel, *n.* porridge, oatmeal, cereal, grout. See FOOD.

grueling, *adj.* severe, exhausting, strenuous. See DIFFICULTY, SEVERITY.

gruesome, *adj.* ghastly, fearful, grisly, hideous. See UGLINESS. *Ant.*, see BEAUTY.

gruff, *adj.* bluff, surly, rough, harsh, coarse. See DISCOURTESY, ROUGHNESS.

grumble, *v.* rumble, growl, complain, mutter. See LAMENTATION.

grunt, *v.* snort, rasp; oink; complain, lament. See VOICE, LAMENTATION.

guarantee, *v.* vouch, undertake, warrant; pledge; promise, insure, secure. See SECURITY.

guard, *n. & v.* —*n.* safeguard, shield, baffle; cover, protection; pad, hood; catch; protector, sentinel, watchman, sentry; escort, patrol, convoy; warder, warden. —*v.t.* protect, defend, shield, watch, patrol. See DEFENSE, SAFETY, COVERING. *Ant.*, see ATTACK.

guerrilla, *n.* irregular, partisan, rebel; *franc-tireur*, sniper, terrorist, bush fighter. See WARFARE, COMBATANT.

guess, *n. & v.* —*n.* surmise, supposition, assumption, conjecture, theory. —*v.* suppose, divine, predict, surmise, conjecture. See SUPPOSITION.

guest, *n.* visitor, company, caller, FRIEND. See TRANSIENTNESS.

guide, *n. & v.* —*n.* tracker, leader, instructor, pilot; map, instructions; guidebook, chart, manual. —*v.* lead, direct; regulate; train. See CONDUCT, DIRECTION, INFORMATION, TEACHING.

guidebook, *n.* guide, manual; Baedeker, Michelin, atlas, *vade mecum*; gazetteer, directory; instructions, operating manual. See DIRECTION, TEACHING.

guild, *n.* COMBINATION, union, association, club, society.

guile, *n.* DECEPTION, deceitfulness; trickery, cunning, craftiness.

guileless, *adj.* artless, innocent, naïve, unsuspecting, ingenuous, honest. See INNOCENCE. *Ant.*, see DUPLICITY.

GUILT

Nouns—guilt, guiltiness, culpability, chargeability, criminality, IMPROBITY, sinfulness (see BADNESS); misconduct, misbehavior, misdoing, misdeed; malpractice, fault, sin, ERROR, transgression, dereliction, delinquency; lapse, slip, trip, *faux pas*, peccadillo; flaw, blot, omission; failing, FAILURE; offense, trespass; misdemeanor, misfeasance, misprision; malefaction, malfeasance, crime, felony; enormity, atrocity, outrage; deadly sin; mortal sin.

Adjectives—guilty, to blame, culpable, sinful, criminal; derelict, at fault, censurable, reprehensible, blameworthy; exceptionable.
Adverbs—guiltily; *in flagrante delicto*; red-handed, in the act.
Antonym, INNOCENCE.

guiltless, *adj.* inculpable, innocent, blameless, faultless. See INNOCENCE.
guise, *n.* APPEARANCE, aspect, pretense, semblance; costume, mien.
gulch, *n.* gully, ravine, canyon, arroyo, gorge; riverbed. See PASSAGE.
gulf, *n.* arm (of the sea), bay; chasm, canyon, abyss; OPENING; rift, gap, separation; void, crevasse, pit, abysm, deep.
gullible, *adj.* confiding, unsuspicious, believing, trustful. See CREDULITY.
gully, *n.* arroyo, gulch, trench, ditch, wadi, gorge, ravine. See INTERVAL.
gun, *n.* pistol, firearm, revolver, cannon, musket, rifle. See ARMS.
gunfire, *n.* gunplay, shooting, burst, volley, salvo. See WARFARE, PROPULSION.
gunman, *n.* thug, ruffian, gangster. *Slang,* hood. See EVILDOER.
gunner, *n.* carabineer, cannoneer; artilleryman; hunter; marksman. See COMBATANT, PROPULSION.
gush, *v.* pour, flow, jet, spurt; effuse, issue, emit, spout. See EGRESS, FEELING.
gust, *n.* puff, burst, flurry, blow, breeze, blast. See EXCITEMENT, WIND.
gusto, *n.* PLEASURE, enthusiasm, enjoyment, relish, zest, delight.
gut, *v.* eviscerate, disembowel; rip, rend, slash, strip; burn out, lay waste, demolish. See DESTRUCTION.
guts, *n.pl.* bowels, entrails, innards, viscera; SUBSTANCE, gist, essence. *Colloq.,* determination, endurance, intestinal fortitude, COURAGE; audacity, impudence. See INTERIOR, INSOLENCE.
gutter, *n.* curb, ditch, spillway, trough. See PASSAGE.
guttural, *adj.* throaty, rasping, husky, hoarse. See ROUGHNESS.
guzzle, *n.* drink, swallow, slurp, swig. See DRUNKENNESS.
gymnasium, *n.* athletic club, gameroom; ARENA.
gymnastics, *n.pl.* athletics, acrobatics, exercises, calisthenics. See CONTENTION.
gypsy, *n.* nomad, vagrant, idler; flirt, coquette. See TRAVEL, ENDEARMENT.
gyrate, *v.* turn, whirl, twirl, spin, revolve, rotate. See ROTATION.

H

HABIT

Nouns—**1,** habit, habitude, wont, way; prescription, custom, use, usage; practice; matter of course, prevalence, OBSERVANCE; conventionalism, conventionality; mode, FASHION, vogue; etiquette; CONFORMITY; rule, standing order, precedent, routine, red tape; rut, groove, beaten path; bad habit; addiction, quirk, trick; training, EDUCATION; seasoning, hardening, inurement; second nature, acclimatization.
2, habitué, addict, frequenter, drunkard (see DRUNKENNESS). *Colloq.,* dope fiend.
Verbs—**1,** be wont, fall into a custom, conform to (see CONFORMITY); follow the beaten path.
2, be habitual, prevail; come into use, take root; become second nature.
3, habituate, inure, harden, season, caseharden; accustom, familiarize; naturalize, acclimatize; keep one's hand in; train, educate; domesticate; take to, get the knack of; learn; cling to, adhere to; repeat (see REPETITION).
Adjectives—**1,** habitual, customary; accustomed; of everyday occurrence;

wonted, usual, general, ordinary, common, frequent, everyday; well-trodden, well known; familiar, hackneyed, trite, commonplace, conventional, regular, set, stock, established, routine, stereotyped; prevailing, prevalent; current; fashionable (see FASHION); deep-rooted, inveterate, besetting; ingrained.

2, wont; used to, given to, addicted to, habituated to; in the habit of; seasoned, imbued with; devoted to, wedded to.

Adverbs—habitually; always (see CONFORMITY); as usual, as is one's wont, as a rule, for the most part; generally, of course, most often, frequently.

Antonyms, see DISUSE, IRREGULARITY.

---

habitat, *n.* habitation; environment, native heath; quarters. See ABODE.

hack, *v.* chop, hew, slash, cut. See DISJUNCTION.

hackneyed, *adj.* dull, trite, stale, used, banal, commonplace. See HABIT. *Ant.,* see IMAGINATION.

hag, *n.* harridan, vixen, termagant, shrew, witch, crone. See EVILDOER.

haggard, *adj.* thin, worn, drawn, gaunt; emaciated, cadaverous, skeletal. See WEARINESS, UGLINESS.

haggle, *v.* cavil; bargain, chaffer, dicker. See SALE.

hail, *n. & v.* —*n.* pellet, hailstone. —*v.* hail; salute, greet; call, summon; accost, address. See COURTESY, SPEECH. *Ant.,* see DISCOURTESY, SILENCE.

hair, *n.* filament, hirsuteness; thatch; crowning glory, tresses; beard, whisker(s); mop, locks, bristles; pile, nap. See ROUGHNESS.

haircut, *n.* barbering, trim, hairdo; crew cut, butch, flattop, fuzz-cut; razor cut; hair styling. See FASHION.

hairdo, *n.* coiffure, hair style; set, cut, shape; permanent [wave]; bob, pigtail, ponytail, bangs, braids, ringlets; pageboy, chignon, gamin cut, *etc.* See FASHION.

hairdresser, *n.* coiffeur, coiffeuse, hair stylist; barber, tonsor; wigmaker, *perruquier.* See BEAUTY.

hairless, *adj.* beardless; bald, bare; clean-shaven, smooth-faced. See DIVESTMENT, SMOOTHNESS.

halcyon, *adj.* calm, tranquil, peaceful, quiet, pleasant. See MODERATION.

hale, *adj.* healthy, robust, hearty, vigorous, sound. See HEALTH. *Ant.,* see DISEASE.

half, *n.* hemisphere; bisection; moiety. See NUMERATION.

half–breed, *n.* mestizo, *métis(se)*, mulatto; half-blood, half-caste; mule; hybrid, mongrel. See MIXTURE.

halfhearted, *adj.* INDIFFERENT, apathetic, listless, unenthusiastic; insincere; timid. *Ant.,* see DESIRE.

halfway, *adj. & adv.* —*adj.* midway, equidistant, MIDDLE. —*adv.* half, part(ly), BETWEEN, en route. *Colloq.,* so-so, more or less. See INCOMPLETENESS.

half–witted, *adj.* unintelligent, foolish, moronic; mentally retarded. See INSANITY. *Ant.,* see INTELLIGENCE.

hall, *n.* PASSAGE, corridor; auditorium, building; college; dormitory; edifice. See ABODE.

hallelujah! *interj.* praise the Lord!, alleluia, hosanna. See RELIGION.

hallmark, *n.* imprint, badge, mark, cachet, stamp; guarantee, AUTHORITY; characteristic, feature, attribute, trait, SPECIALITY.

hallow, *v.* bless, sanctify, consecrate, enshrine. See PIETY.

hallucination, *n.* phantasm, phantom, mirage; fancy, delusion, chimera, illusion; DECEPTION. See NONEXISTENCE, ERROR.

hallway, *n.* vestibule, lobby, foyer, gallery; PASSAGE, corridor.

halo, *n.* corona, aura, nimbus, glory, aureole. See LIGHT.

halt, *v., n. & adj.* —*v.* stop, check, arrest, pause, cease. —*n.* stop, interruption, immobility. —*adj.* crippled, disabled. See END. *Ant.,* see CONTINUITY.

halter, *n.* harness, bridle, tether, hackamore; noose; shoulder strap, brassiere. *Colloq.,* bra. See CLOTHING.

ham, *n. & v., slang.* —*n.* hambone, ham actor, show-off, grandstand player. —*v.* ham it up; overact, emote, chew the scenery, pull out all the stops. See DRAMA.

hamburger, *n.* chopped *or* ground meat, forcemeat, meatball, meat patty; meat loaf, Salisbury steak, steak tartar; beef- *or* cheeseburger. see FOOD.

hamlet, *n.* village, town. *Slang,* whistle stop. See ABODE.

hammer, *v. & n.* —*v.* strike, beat, drum, pound, ram. —*n.* mallet, gavel, sledge. See IMPULSE, REPETITION.

hamper, *v.* encumber, hinder, impede, trammel, obstruct, fetter, restrict. See HINDRANCE. *Ant.,* see AID.

hand, *n. & v.* —*n.* fist, extremity; helper, workman, employee, laborer; playing cards held; handwriting. *Colloq.,* applause; greeting. See AGENCY, INDICATION, WRITING. —*v.* pass, deliver, convey, give, transmit. See GIVING. *Ant.,* see RECEIVING.

handbag, *n.* pocketbook, purse; valise, grip, portmanteau. See RECEPTACLE.

handbook, *n.* guide, instructions, manual. See INFORMATION.

handcuff, *n. & v.* —*n.* manacle(s). *Slang,* bracelet(s). —*v.* shackle, manacle, fetter. See RESTRAINT. *Ant.,* see FREEDOM.

handful, *n.* fistful, grip; QUANTITY, few, some. *Colloq.,* trouble, problem, nuisance, DIFFICULTY. *Slang,* pain in the neck. See BADNESS.

handicap, *v.* penalize, encumber, inconvenience, burden, hamper. See HINDRANCE. *Ant.,* see AID.

handicraft, *n.* craftwork, handiwork; woodcraft, stonecraft, *etc.*; SKILL, workmanship, dexterity, artisanship, artistry, craftsmanship. See PRODUCTION.

handily, *adv.* neatly, effortlessly, easily, with dispatch. See FACILITY.

handkerchief, *n.* nose cloth, sudarium; neckerchief, bandanna, foulard; scarf, headcloth, headkerchief. See COVERING, ORNAMENT.

handle, *n. & v.* —*n.* shaft, hilt, grip, knob. —*v.* manipulate, USE, wield; direct, control, manage; feel, paw, TOUCH; operate, direct, conduct. See DIRECTION, SERVANT.

handler, *n.* trainer, coach; masseur; dealer, jobber, AGENT. See SALE, AGENCY.

handmade, *adj.* handcrafted, -wrought, -carved, *etc.*; individualized; crude, imperfect, makeshift. See PRODUCTION.

hand-me-down, *adj.* secondhand, castoff, discarded. See CLOTHING, OLDNESS.

handout, *n.* alms, offering, charity; handbill. See GIVING, PUBLICATION.

handsome, *adj.* attractive, comely, good-looking, personable; fine; generous, ample; striking. See BEAUTY, BENEVOLENCE. *Ant.,* see UGLINESS, ECONOMY.

handwriting, *n.* calligraphy, penmanship, script, graphology, chirography. See WRITING.

handy, *adj.* convenient, near, available, ready; adept, dexterous, apt; competent, capable; expert. See SKILL, UTILITY. *Ant.,* see UNSKILLFULNESS, USELESSNESS.

handyman, *n.* Jack-of-all-trades, odd-job man, factotum; janitor. See SKILL.

hang, *v.* dangle, trail, drop, drape; pend; execute; lynch; suspend; put up (picture, *etc.*), fasten, place. See COHERENCE, PUNISHMENT.

hangout, *n., colloq.,* resort, haunt, rendezvous, stamping ground, clubhouse; saloon, dive, den. See REFUGE.

hangover, *n., colloq.,* crapulence, nausea, PAIN; katzenjammer, *gueule de bois,* the morning after [the night before]; holdover, atavism, survival, vestige, relic, remnant. See DRUNKENNESS, REMAINDER.

hang-up, *n., slang,* thing, obsession, preoccupation. See INSANITY.

hanker, *v.* DESIRE, covet, crave, long for, yearn for.

haphazard, *adj.* CHANCE, casual, aimless, random; hit-or-miss.

happen, *v.* befall, eventuate, occur. See CHANCE.

happy, *adj.* fortunate, lucky; gay, contented, joyous, ecstatic; felicitous, apt; glad. See AGREEMENT, CHEERFULNESS, PLEASURE. *Ant.,* see DIS-AGREEMENT, DEJECTION, PAIN.

harangue, *n.* SPEECH; discourse; tirade, scolding, diatribe; address, declamation.

harass, *v.* distress, badger, trouble, vex, plague, torment, irritate, heckle, beset; worry; afflict, depress; sadden. *Slang,* needle. See PAIN. *Ant.,* see PLEASURE.

harbinger, *n.* OMEN, sign, forerunner, token, precursor.

harbor, *n. & v.* —*n.* REFUGE; port, retreat; haven, shelter; mole. —*v.* protect, shield, shelter; cherish, keep.

hard, *adj.* firm, rigid, strong; unsympathetic, unloving, unfriendly; callous; solid, impermeable; strenuous, difficult, puzzling; severe, serious, short, intensive. See HARDNESS, INSENSIBILITY. *Ant.,* see SOFTNESS.

hard-core, *adj.* dedicated, faithful; severe, intense. See SEVERITY, PROBITY.

harden, *v.* anneal, fire; steel; congeal, thicken; accustom, inure, blunt. See HABIT, HARDNESS, INSENSIBILITY. *Ant.,* see SOFTNESS, SENSIBILITY.

hard-hearted, *adj.* cruel, pitiless, ruthless, merciless, uncompassionate, callous, unsympathetic, tough. *Colloq.,* hard as nails. See INSENSI-BILITY.

hardly, *adv.* scarcely, barely; improbably; rarely. See RARITY. *Ant.,* see FREQUENCY.

HARDNESS

Nouns—**1,** hardness, rigidity, inflexibility, temper, callosity; SEVERITY; toughness; petrifaction; lapidification, lapidescence; vitrification, ossification; crystallization.

2, Mohs scale; flint, marble, rock, crystal, quartz, granite, adamant, diamond; iron, steel; nails; brick; concrete.

Verbs—harden, stiffen, petrify, temper, ossify, vitrify; callous; set, congeal.

Adjectives—hard, rigid, stubborn, stiff, firm; starch, starched; stark, unbending, unlimber, unyielding; inflexible, tense; proof; diamondlike, diamantine, adamantine, adamant; concrete, stony, granitic, vitreous; horny, calloused, corneous; bony, osseous.

Antonym, see SOFTNESS.

---

hardship, *n.* ADVERSITY, difficulties, trouble; calamity, affliction. *Ant.,* see PROSPERITY.

hard up, *adj., colloq.,* poor, needy (see POVERTY); frustrated, at one's wit's end. *Slang,* up against it; hungry; sex-starved, horny. See DESIRE.

hardware, *n.* housewares, tools, utensils; ironmongery, plumbing supplies, *etc. Slang,* guns, weaponry, ARMS. See INSTRUMENTALITY, MEANS.

hardy, *adj.* sturdy, tough, vigorous; resolute, daring; durable. See COURAGE, DURABILITY. *Ant.,* see COWARDICE, IMPOTENCE, TRANSIENT-NESS.

harem, *n.* seraglio; bridal suite. *Slang,* love nest. See ABODE.

hark, *v.* listen, harken; hear. See HEARING, ATTENTION.

harlot, *n.* bad woman, libertine, strumpet, PROSTITUTE; paramour, courtesan.

harm, *n. & v.* —*n.* DETERIORATION, EVIL, dishonor, injury. —*v.* TOUCH, damage, injure; desecrate, abuse, break; DETERIORATION; EVIL. *Ant.,* see IMPROVEMENT, GOODNESS.

harmless, *adj.* GOOD, INNOCENT, innocuous, inoffensive. See SAFETY.

harmony, *n.* AGREEMENT, concurrence, concord; (musical) accompaniment; order, symmetry; tunefulness, euphony; congruity; proportion;

unison; peace, amity, friendship. See PACIFICATION, MUSIC, CONFORMITY. *Ant.*, see CONTENTION.

harness, *n. & v.* —*n.* bridle, traces, hackamore; gear. —*v.* control, utilize; curb, yoke. See DOMESTICATION, RESTRAINT.

harp, *n. & v.* —*n.* lyre, psaltery. See MUSICAL INSTRUMENTS. —*v.* dwell (on), repeat, din, iterate, nag, pester. See REPETITION.

harrowing, *adj.* distressing, wrenching, tragic, nerve-racking. See PAIN.

harry, *v.* plunder, pillage; distress, plague, ATTACK, harass, hound. See TAKING, MALEVOLENCE:

harsh, *adj.* acrimonious, ungenial, severe, rough, ungracious; sharp, sour; discordant, hoarse, grating; brutal, heartless, cruel; austere, stern; rigorous, hard. See DISCOURTESY, ROUGHNESS, SEVERITY. *Ant.*, see COURTESY, SMOOTHNESS.

harvest, *n.* crop, yield, product, issue, outcome. See EFFECT, STORE, PRODUCTION.

hash, *n. & v.* —*n.* MIXTURE, medley, mix. *Colloq.*, jumble, mishmash, confusion, botch. *Slang*, rehash, review; hashish, marijuana. See OLDNESS. —*v.t.* mince, chop, dice. *Colloq.*, hash over, discuss (see INQUIRY).

HASTE

Nouns—haste, urgency; despatch, dispatch; acceleration, spurt, forced march, rush, dash; VELOCITY; precipitancy, precipitation, precipitousness; impatience, impetuosity; brusquerie; hurry, drive, scramble, bustle.

Verbs—**1,** haste, hasten; make haste, hurry, rush, dart, dash, whip on, push on, press; scurry, scuttle along, bustle, scramble, plunge, bestir oneself (see ACTIVITY); lose no time, make short work of; work against time. *Colloq.*, hurry up, hustle, make tracks, step on it. *Slang*, shake a leg, make it snappy, get a move on.

2, speed, speed up, expedite; quicken, accelerate. *Slang*, step on the gas, give 'er the gun.

Adjectives—hasty, hurried, brusque; abrupt, cursory, precipitate, headlong, furious, boisterous, impulsive, impetuous, eager, impatient, hot-headed; feverish, breathless, pressed for time, hard-pressed, urgent.

Adverbs—hastily, precipitately, helter-skelter, slapdash, full-tilt, headlong; apace, amain; all at once (see INSTANTANEITY); at short notice, immediately (see EARLINESS); express, posthaste; on the double, in a jiff(y).

Antonym, see SLOWNESS.

hat, *n.* cap, headgear, bonnet; headdress; derby, bowler; turban, cloche. See CLOTHING.

hatch, *v.* invent, originate; incubate; concoct, devise. See DOMESTICATION, FALSEHOOD, IMAGINATION.

HATE

Nouns—**1,** hate, hatred, abhorrence, loathing; disaffection, disfavor; alienation, estrangement, coolness; enmity, hostility, animosity, RESENTMENT; umbrage, pique, irritation, grudge; dudgeon, spleen, spite, despite, venom, venomousness, bitterness, bad blood; acrimony; malice, MALEVOLENCE, implacability, REVENGE; repugnance, DISLIKE, odium, unpopularity; detestation, antipathy, revulsion. *Colloq.*, chip on one's shoulder.

2, object of hatred, abomination, aversion, *bête noire*; enemy.

Verbs—**1,** hate, detest, despise, abominate, abhor, loathe; shrink from, view with horror, hold in abomination, revolt against, execrate; DISLIKE. *Colloq.*, have it in for.

2, excite *or* provoke hatred, be hateful; repel, envenom, incense, irritate, rile; horrify.

3, be unfriendly, on bad terms, estranged, *etc.*

Adjectives—**1,** averse, set against, hostile; bitter, acrimonious (see DIS-COURTESY); implacable, revengeful (see RETALIATION); invidious, spite-ful, malicious (see MALEVOLENCE).

2, hated, despised, unloved, unbeloved, unlamented, unmourned, dis-liked; forsaken, rejected, lovelorn, jilted.

3, obnoxious, hateful, abhorrent, despicable, odious, abominable, re-pulsive, loathsome, offensive, shocking; disgusting, disagreeable.

Antonym, see LOVE.

---

haughty, *adj.* overbearing, arrogant, supercilious, proud, lordly, superior. See HEIGHT, INSOLENCE. *Ant.*, see LOWNESS, SERVILITY.

haul, *v.* drag, pull, draw; transport, deliver; lug.

haunt, *n. & v.* —*n.* SHADE, ghost, spirit, spook; resort, rendezvous, re-treat, den. *Slang,* hangout. —*v.* frequent, attend; obsess; visit. See FEAR, DEATH, ABODE.

have, *v.* own, hold; retain, possess; keep, maintain. See POSSESSION.

haven, *n.* REFUGE, sanctuary, asylum, shelter; harbor, port; snuggery; protection. See SAFETY.

havoc, *n.* devastation, DESTRUCTION, wreckage; DISORDER, chaos, con-fusion; ravagement, vandalism; WARFARE; KILLING; disaster, catastrophe.

hawker, *n.* street salesman, vivandière, street crier (see MERCHANT).

haywire, *adj., slang,* confused, mixed-up, berserk, screwy, insane; out of control, out of commission; balled *or* bollixed up. See DISORDER, INSANITY.

hazard, *n. & v.* —*n.* DANGER, CHANCE, risk, gamble; accident, adventure, contingency. —*v.* risk, venture, gamble.

haze, *n.* film, opacity; mist, fog; dimness, obscurity. See CLOUDINESS.

head, *n. & v.* —*n.* pate, poll; (*slang*) noggin, bean; chief, DIRECTOR, manager, leader; title, heading, caption; talent, ability, JUDGMENT; CLASS, category, type, grouping. See BEGINNING, INTELLECT, HEIGHT. *Slang,* acidhead, addict. —*v.* lead, direct, precede; guide, RULE, control, manage. See DIRECTION, PRIORITY.

headache, *n.* migraine, megrim, splitting headache; hangover; problem, burden, DIFFICULTY, nuisance. *Colloq.,* the misery. See PAIN.

headdress, *n.* headgear, millinery; coiffure; plumage, warbonnet. See COVERING, ORNAMENT.

headland, *n.* promontory, spit, cape, spur, cliff, bluff, escarpment. See CONVEXITY, HEIGHT.

headlong, *adj.* hasty, hurried; rash, precipitate; heedless, reckless.

headquarters, *n.pl.* main office; base of operations; government, general staff, chief (see MASTER). *Colloq.,* HQ. See AUTHORITY, CENTRALITY, ABODE.

headstone, *n.* GRAVESTONE; foundation stone, cornerstone; cairn, dol-men, cromlech; shaft, pillar, column. See INTERMENT, INDICATION.

headstrong, *adj.* obstinate, perverse, stubborn. See OBSTINACY.

headway, *n.* PROGRESSION, advance; gain, accomplishment, achievement.

heal, *v.* mend, cure; repair, restore; ease. See REMEDY, RESTORATION.

HEALTH

Nouns—**1,** health, healthiness; sanity; soundness; vim, vigor and vitality; strength, robustness; bloom, prime; *mens sana in corpore sano*; hygeia; clean bill of health; convalescence, recovery, cure.

2, salubrity, healthfulness; hygiene, sanitation. See CLEANNESS.

Verbs—**1,** be healthy; bloom, flourish; be in *or* enjoy good health; conva-lesce, recuperate, recover (see RESTORATION); get better, improve (see IMPROVEMENT); take a new lease on life; cure, restore.

2, be salubrious, be healthful, agree with.

Adjectives—**1,** healthy, well, sound, hearty, hale, fresh, green, whole; florid, flush, hardy, stanch, brave, robust, vigorous; unscathed, unin-jured, untainted; in the pink of condition; sound as a bell; fresh as a

daisy, fresh as a rose, in one's prime. *Colloq.*, fine, in the pink, in fine feather *or* fettle, chipper, fit as a fiddle, peppy.
2, salubrious, healthful, wholesome, sanitary, prophylactic, benign, bracing, tonic, invigorating; good for; hygienic; innocuous, innocent, harmless, uninjurious, uninfectious, sanitary.
Antonym, see DISEASE.

heap, *n.* pile, load, stack, mound, ASSEMBLAGE. *Colloq.*, great deal, heaps, scads, oodles, piles (see QUANTITY).

HEARING

Nouns—**1,** hearing, sense of hearing; audition; auscultation; eavesdropping; audibility; acute ear, *etc.*; ear for music.
2, ear, auricle, acoustic organ, auditory apparatus, eardrum, tympanum; hearing aid, ear trumpet, speaking trumpet; amplifier, amplification, bone conduction; otology; acoustics (see SOUND).
3, hearer, auditor, listener, eavesdropper; audience.
4, hearing, interview, audience; trial (see INQUIRY). *Colloq.*, audition.
Verbs—**1,** hear, overhear; hark, harken; listen, give an ear, lend an ear, bend an ear, heed, attend, prick up one's ears.
2, become audible, fall upon the ear, catch *or* reach the ear, be heard; ring, resound. *Colloq.*, be all ears, listen in, drink in.
Antonym, see DEAF.

hearsay, *n.* NEWS, gossip, rumor, talk, report.
hearse, *n.* bier; funeral wagon. *Slang*, dead *or* meat wagon. See INTERMENT.
heart, *n.* center, substance; kernel, pith, gist, core; breast; spirit, COURAGE; sympathy, affection, understanding; nature, soul. See TENDENCY, MIDDLE, CENTRALITY.
heartbroken, *adj.* miserable, unhappy, wretched, hurt, forlorn, disheartened, disconsolate, anguished. See PAIN, DEJECTION. *Ant.*, see PLEASURE.
heartburn, *n.* cardialgia, pyrosis; rue, remorse, resentment, PAIN, ENVY.
hearten, *v.* cheer, encourage, brighten, reassure, comfort, rally. See COURAGE, CHEERFULNESS.
heartfelt, *adj.* sincere, earnest; profound; meaningful, cordial; emphatic, enthusiastic. See DEPTH, DEARNESS, FEELING.
hearth, *n.* fireside, fireplace; ingle(nook); family [circle]. See HEAT.
heartless, *adj.* unmerciful, cruel, cold, unfeeling, uncaring, unsympathetic, callous; unkind, inconsiderate, insensitive. *Ant.*, see BENEVOLENCE.
heart-to-heart, *adj.* intimate, confidential; frank, candid. *Colloq.*, off the record, *entre nous*, private. See DISCLOSURE, SECRET.
hearty, *n. & adj.* —*n.* comrade, sailor. —*adj.* sturdy, robust, strong, well, vigorous, healthy. See FEELING, HEALTH.

HEAT

Nouns—**1,** heat, caloric; temperature, warmth, ardor, fervor, fervency; incalescence, incandescence; flush, glow; temperature, fever; white heat, blood heat, body heat, fever heat.
2, fire, spark, scintillation, flash, combustion, flame, blaze; bonfire; campfire, forest fire, wildfire, sheet of fire, lambent flame; devouring element; sun; fireworks, pyrotechnics.
3, torridity, hot weather, summer, midsummer, dogdays; heat wave, hot spell, sirocco, simoom; broiling sun; pyrology; thermology, thermotics, thermodynamics, THERMOMETER.
4, heater, stove, range, microwave [oven]; furnace; hot air, steam heat, hot water, radiator, register; blast furnace, electric furnace; kiln, oven; forge, crucible, alembic; Bunsen burner; torch, acetylene torch, electric

welder; crematory, pyre; incinerator; fireplace, hearth, grate; brazier; bed warmer, electric blanket, heating pad; heat pump; heliostat.
5, see FUEL.
Verbs—heat, warm; be hot, glow, flush, sweat, swelter, bask, smoke, reek, stew, simmer, seethe, boil, burn, broil, blaze, flame; smo(u)lder; parch, fume, pant; thaw.
Adjectives—**1,** hot, warm; mild, genial; tepid, lukewarm, unfrozen; thermal, thermic, calorific; fervent, fervid; ardent, aglow; red-hot, white-hot, piping-hot; like a furnace, like an oven; hot as fire, like the fires of Hell.
2, sunny, torrid, tropical, estival, canicular; close, sultry, stifling, stuffy, sweltering, suffocating, oppressive; reeking; baking.
3, fiery, incandescent, incalescent; candent, glowing, smoking; on fire; blazing, in flames, alight, afire, ablaze; smo(u)ldering, in a glow, feverish, in a sweat; blood-hot, warm as toast; volcanic, plutonic, igneous; isothermal, isothermic.

Antonym, see COLD.

heathen, *n. & adj.* —*n.* pagan, infidel, unbeliever. —*adj.* irreligious, idolatrous, pagan; unconverted; atheistic. See IRRELIGION. *Ant.,* see RELIGION, BELIEF.
heave, *v.* lift, hoist, raise; throw, pitch, toss; swell, expand; undulate. See ELEVATION.

HEAVEN

Nouns—**1,** heaven, kingdom of heaven, kingdom of God, of God; future state, eternal blessedness, eternity; Paradise, Eden, abode *or* isle of the blessed; celestial bliss, glory. *Slang,* Kingdom come.
2, Olympus; Elysium, Elysian fields, garden of the Hesperides, Valhalla, Nirvana, the happy hunting grounds, seventh heaven.
3, sky, firmament, welkin, blue empyrean, the ether, heavens.
4, Golden Age, Utopia, never-never land, millennium, land of Canaan, promised land.
Adjectives—heavenly, celestial, supernal, unearthly, from on high, paradisiac(al), paradisaic(al), beatific, elysian, ethereal, Olympian.

Antonym, see HELL.

heavenly, *adj.* celestial (see HEAVEN); blessed, angelic, saintly, holy. *Colloq.,* delectable, delightful, wonderful, marvelous. See GOOD.
heavy, *adj.* weighty, weighted, ponderous; unwieldy; massive; grave; burdensome; oppressive, cumbersome; tedious, tiresome; dull, gloomy, overcast; strong, pressing, large; loaded, sagging; somber, dismal, dejected, sad, melancholy; slow, inert, sluggish; grievous, serious. See WEIGHT, DEJECTION. *Ant.,* see LIGHTNESS.
heavy-duty, *adj.* durable, sturdy; tough, rugged, well-built. See DURABILITY.
heckle, *v.t.* plague, taunt; challenge; interrupt; dispute. See DISAGREEMENT. *Ant.,* see AGREEMENT.
hectic, *adj.* feverish, febrile; excited, agitated; frenetic, wild, turbulent. *Colloq.,* difficult, arduous. See DIFFICULTY, EXERTION.
hector, *v.* bully, torment, plague, domineer, bluster. See INSOLENCE.
hedge, *n. & v.* —*n.* shrubbery, hedgerow. —*v.* evade; protect, shelter; temporize; trim. See COMPROMISE.
heed, *n. & v.* —*n.* ATTENTION, notice, regard, consideration. —*v.* observe, CARE, notice, attend, regard; consider. See OBEDIENCE, COURTESY.
heedless, *adj.* disregardful, remiss, careless, negligent, thoughtless; unobservant, unnoticing, undiscerning; reckless. See INATTENTION.
heel, *n. & v.* —*n., slang,* cad, bounder, scoundrel, rat, louse, s.o.b. See EVIL. —*v.t.* turn around, pivot, swivel. *Slang,* shadow, tail; supply, furnish, outfit, PROVISION. —*v.i.* follow, pursue, go after. See PURSUIT, DEVIATION, DISCOURTESY.

hefty, *adj., colloq.,* weighty; bulky, burly, brawny; beefy, corpulent. see SIZE, GRAVITY.

HEIGHT

Nouns—**1,** height, altitude, elevation; eminence, pitch; loftiness, sublimity; tallness, stature, prominence (see CONVEXITY).
2, mount, mountain; hell, cape; headland, foreland; promontory, ridge, hogback; dune; vantage ground; down; moor, moorland; Alp; uplands, highlands; heights, SUMMIT; knoll, hummock, hill, hillock, barrow, mound, mole; steeps, bluff, cliff, crag, tor, peak, pike, escarpment, edge, ledge, brae, height.
3, tower, pillar, column, obelisk, monument, steeple, spire, minaret, campanile, turret, dome, cupola, pole, pikestaff, maypole, flagstaff; topmast, topgallantmast, moonraker; skyscraper, high-rise; ceiling, COVERING.
4, colossus, giant (see SIZE).
Verbs—be high, tower, soar, command; hover, cap, culminate; mount, perch, surmount; cover (see COVERING); overtop (see SUPERIORITY); stand on tiptoe; grow, upgrow, rise (see ASCENT); heighten, elevate (see ELEVATION).
Adjectives—high, elevated, eminent, exalted, lofty; tall; gigantic, towering, soaring, elevated, upper; highest, top, topmost, uppermost; capital; paramount; upland, hilly, mountainous, alpine, aerial; sky-high, tall as a steeple. *Colloq.,* high as a kite.
Adverbs—on high, high up, aloft, up, above, aloof, overhead; upstairs, abovestairs; in the clouds; on tiptoe, on stilts.
Antonym, see LOWNESS.

heinous, *adj.* dreadful, abominable; terrible, awful; atrocious, hateful, monstrous. See BADNESS, EVIL.
heir, heiress, *n.* legatee, inheritor, beneficiary. See POSSESSION.
heirloom, *n.* POSSESSION, keepsake, memento, souvenir, antique. See PROPERTY.

HELL

Nouns—**1,** hell, Hades, bottomless pit, place of torment; Pandemonium, Tophet; hellfire, everlasting fire, fire and brimstone; underworld; purgatory, limbo, gehenna, abyss, bottomless pit; hell on earth.
2, Tartarus, Hades, Avernus, Styx, Stygian creek, pit of Acheron, Cocytus; infernal regions, inferno, realms of Pluto; Pluto, Rhadamanthus, Erebus; Charon; Satan (see DEMON).
Adjectives—hellish, infernal, Stygian, Plutonian.
Antonym, see HEAVEN.

hello, *n. & interj.* —*n.* greeting, salutation, welcome; reception. —*interj.* good day, good morning, good afternoon, good evening; how are you? how do you do? *bonjour, buon giorno, guten Tag, aloha. Colloq.,* hi, hi there, howdy, how's tricks? ahoy! *ciao.* See ATTENTION, COURTESY.
helm, *n.* tiller, wheel (*Naut.*); AUTHORITY, COMMAND, scepter. See DIRECTION.
helmet, *n.* headgear, skullcap, casque, headpiece; crest, morion. See CLOTHING.
help, *n. & v.* —*n.* servants, staff, employees; aid, assistance, succor; relief, REMEDY. —*v.* assist, serve, befriend; relieve, ameliorate, better. See AID, IMPROVEMENT. *Ant.,* see DETERIORATION, HINDRANCE.
helper, *n.* AUXILIARY, co-worker; benefactor. See AID. *Ant.,* see HINDRANCE.
helpful, *adj.* beneficial, contributory, favorable; useful, worthwhile, furthering, improving; serviceable, salutary; remedial. See IMPROVEMENT.
helpless, *adj.* impotent, powerless; defenseless, vulnerable, resourceless; prostrate, crippled; dependent. See IMPOTENCE. *Ant.,* see POWER.

hen, *n.* fowl, chicken, bird, pullet. *Slang*, woman. See ANIMAL.

hence, *adv.* herefrom, away; so, therefore. See CAUSE, DEPARTURE.

henchman, *n.* hireling, underling; flunky, lackey; tool, puppet; accomplice. *Slang*, stooge, yesman, ward heeler, errand boy. See SERVANT.

henpecked, *adj.* hagridden; browbeaten, nagged, hounded; led by the nose, jumping through hoops. See OBEDIENCE, SUBJECTION.

hep, *adj., slang,* hip, in the know, wise (to), up on, cool. See KNOWLEDGE.

herald, *n. & v.* —*n.* forerunner, precursor, announcer, messenger, harbinger. —*v.* proclaim, announce, declare; introduce; precede, warn, inform. See PREDICTION, PRIORITY.

heraldry, *n.* blazonry, emblazonment. See ARMS, INDICATION.

herb, *n.* potherb, SPICE, seasoning, CONDIMENT. See VEGETATION, REMEDY.

herd, *n. & v.* —*n.* group, flock, drove; gathering; troop, pack, crowd. See MULTITUDE. —*v.* drive, tend, collect; gather, assemble; corral, group. See ASSEMBLAGE. *Ant.,* see DISJUNCTION.

herder, herdsman, *n.* shepherd, cowherd, pasturer, shepherdess, herdboy, cowboy. See DOMESTICATION.

here, *adv.* hereabouts, hither, hitherward. See ARRIVAL, LOCATION.

hereafter, *adv.* subsequently, henceforth, henceforward, eventually, ultimately. See FUTURITY. *Ant.,* see PAST.

hereditary, *adj.* inheritable, transmissible, heritable, ancestral, patrimonial. See ANCESTRY, DESCENT.

heresy, *n.* unbelief, dissent, HETERODOXY. See IRRELIGION.

heritage, *n.* bequest, inheritance, legacy, hereditament, patrimony. See POSSESSION, PROPERTY.

hermetic, *adj.* mystic, magic, alchemic; airtight, vacuum-packed, airproof. See SORCERY, SUPERNATURALISM, CLOSURE.

hermit, *n.* anchorite, recluse, ascetic, solitary. See ASCETICISM.

hero, *n.* victor, defender, champion, redeemer; inspiration, ideal, model, paragon; knight in [shining] armor; main character, protagonist, lead; darling, favorite, idol. *Slang*, big shot, hot shot. See COURAGE, IMPORTANCE, DRAMA, SUPERIORITY.

heroic, *adj.* courageous, intrepid, valiant, brave, mighty, fearless, gallant; great, huge, large. See COURAGE, SIZE. *Ant.,* see COWARDICE, LITTLENESS.

heroin, *n.* diamorphine. *Slang,* (big) H, horse, snow. See NARCOTIC.

hesitate, *v.i.* falter, waiver, shrink, demur. See DOUBT. *Ant.,* see RESOLUTION, CERTAINTY.

HETERODOXY

Nouns—**1,** heterodoxy, syncretism; sectarianism, nonconformity, secularism, denominationalism, cultism; heresy, schism, ERROR, false doctrine; schismaticism, recusancy; backsliding, apostasy, atheism, IRRELIGION.

2, bigotry (see OBSTINACY); fanaticism, zealotry, iconoclasm; hyperorthodoxy, precisianism, bibliolatry, sabbatarianism, puritanism, idolatry; DISSENT, superstition.

3, sectarian, seceder, separatist, recusant, dissenter, dissident, nonconformist, nonjuror.

4, sect, denomination, faction, division, schism, organization, group, school, church, following, fellowship, ism, faith.

Adjectives—heterodox, sectarian, heretical, denominational, nonconformist, unorthodox, unscriptural, uncanonical, apocryphal; schismatic, recusant, iconoclastic, dissenting, dissident, secular; pantheistic, polytheistic; bigoted, prejudiced, exclusive, narrow, intolerant, fanatical, dogmatical; superstitious, ideological, visionary; idolatrous.

---

heterogeneous, *adj.* diverse, mixed, conglomerate; unlike, dissimilar. See DIFFERENCE. *Ant.,* see SIMILARITY.

hew, *v.t.* fell; chop, cut, hack; chip. See DISJUNCTION.

heyday, *n.* prime, HEIGHT, peak, zenith; glory, full bloom, top of one's form; halcyon, golden *or* palmy days; golden age, YOUTH. See VIGOR.

hiatus, *n.* INTERVAL, gap, interruption, lacuna, void. See INCOMPLETION.

hibernate, *v.i.* winter; become dormant. *Colloq.,* hole up. See REPOSE, INACTION.

hidden, *adj.* concealed, secreted; covered, screened, obscured; suppressed; veiled, disguised, camouflaged; latent, unmanifested. See CONCEALMENT. *Ant.,* see DISCLOSURE, INFORMATION.

hide, *n. & v.* —*n.* skin, pelt, coat; leather. See COVERING. —*v.* cover, secrete, cloak, veil; dissemble, falsify; disguise, camouflage. See CONCEALMENT. *Ant.,* see DISCLOSURE, INFORMATION.

hidebound, *adj.* bigoted, prejudiced, narrow; illiberal; unyielding. See IMPIETY. *Ant.,* see PIETY.

hideous, *adj.* abominable, frightful, odious, dreadful, detestable, horrible, repulsive, unsightly, revolting. See UGLINESS. *Ant.,* see BEAUTY.

hierarchy, *n.* rank, officialdom; ORDER, ranking, succession. See DIRECTOR.

high, *adj.* elevated, lofty, tall; towering, eminent; acute, sharp, shrill; prominent, important, directorial; costly, dear, expensive; overripe, gamy. *Colloq.,* elated. *Slang,* drunk; advanced. See HEIGHT. *Ant.,* see LOWNESS.

highborn, *adj.* patrician, noble, royal, aristocratic. See NOBILITY.

highbrow, *n. & adj.* —*n.* intellectual. *Slang,* egghead, longhair, brain. —*adj.* intellectual, intelligent, brainy, cultured. See INTELLECT.

highest, *adj.* ultimate; supreme, topmost, loftiest, utmost, uppermost; greatest, head; maximum; superlative; crowning. See SUMMIT.

high-handed, *adj.* arrogant, authoritarian. *Colloq.,* pushy. See INSOLENCE.

high-strung, *n.* taut, tense, temperamental, excitable, touchy, testy, on edge; volatile. *Colloq.,* edgy, jumpy. See EXCITABILITY, SENSIBILITY.

highway, *n.* road, turnpike, highroad, thoroughfare. See TRAVEL.

highwayman, *n.* THIEF, robber, footpad, thug, bandit.

hijack, *v.t., slang,* highjack, steal, commit highway robbery. See STEALING.

hike, *n. & v.* —*n.* walk, tramp, jaunt, march; hitchhike. *Colloq.,* raise, increase. —*v.* walk, march; raise, inflate, boost, hitch up, adjust higher. *Colloq.,* thumb a ride. See INCREASE.

hilarity, *n.* CHEERFULNESS, mirth, amusement, enjoyment, gaiety, laughter, glee.

hill, *n.* grade, slope; rise, ascent; elevation, mound. See HEIGHT. *Ant.,* see LOWNESS.

HINDRANCE

Nouns—**1,** hindrance, prevention, preclusion, obstruction, stoppage; interruption, interception, impedition; retardment, retardation; embarrassment, coarctation, stricture, restriction; RESTRAINT; inhibition, PROHIBITION; blockade, CLOSURE, DIFFICULTY.

2, interference, interposition; obtrusion; discouragement, DISSUASION.

3, impediment, let, obstacle, obstruction, knot, check, hitch, contretemps; drawback, objection; stumbling block, ill wind; head wind, OPPOSITION; trammel, hobble, tether; counterpoise; bar, stile, turnstile, barrier; gate, portcullis; barricade (see DEFENSE); wall, breakwater; bulkhead, block, buffer, stopper, boom, dam, weir.

4, encumbrance; clog, drag, stay, stop; preventive, prophylactic; load, burden, onus, millstone, *impedimenta*; dead weight; lumber, pack; incubus, old man of the sea; remora; red herring, false trail.

5, damper, wet blanket, hinderer, marplot, killjoy, interloper; opponent (see OPPOSITION).

Verbs—**1,** hinder, impede, delay; embarrass; interpose, interfere, meddle;

keep, fend, stave *or* ward off; obviate; avert, turn aside, draw off, prevent, forfend, nip in the bud; retard, slacken, check, let; counteract, countercheck; preclude, debar, foreclose, estop, inhibit (see PROHIBITION); shackle, restrain (see RESTRAINT); restrict. *Colloq.,* drag one's feet, stonewall.

2, obstruct, stop, stay, bar, block, block up; barricade; dam up, close (see CLOSURE); put on the brake, put a spoke in the wheel; put a stop to (see END); interrupt, intercept; oppose (see OPPOSITION); hedge in, cut off; cramp, hamper; clog, cumber, encumber; choke; saddle *or* load with; overload, trammel, tie one's hands; inconvenience, incommode, discommode. *Slang,* gum up, throw a monkey wrench in the works.

3, fall foul of; handicap; thwart, foil, frustrate, disconcert, balk, baffle, override, circumvent; spoil, mar, clip the wings of, cripple (see DETERIORATION); dishearten, DISSUADE, deter, discourage; discountenance, throw cold water on, throw a wet blanket on; cut the ground from under one, take the wind out of one's sails, undermine; be *or* stand in the way of; act as a drag; be a millstone around one's neck. *Colloq.,* cook one's goose, spike one's guns. *Slang,* cramp one's style.

Adjectives—hindering, preventive, deterrent; obstructive, impeditive, interceptive; in the way of, unfavorable; onerous, burdensome, cumbersome, cumbrous; binding, blocking, obtrusive; hindered, waterlogged, heavy-laden; hard-pressed; inhibitory, preclusive; prophylactic; prohibitive.

Antonym, see AID.

---

hinge, *n.* joint, pivot, center, axis; basis, crisis; hook. See CAUSE, JUNCTION.

hint, *n. & v.* —*n.* intimation, suggestion, allusion, reference, implication; tip; trace; reminder; insinuation. See INFORMATION, MEMORY. —*v.i.* suggest, allude, imply, intimate. See INFORMATION.

hinterland, *n.* country; inland, backwoods. *Colloq.,* the sticks. See INTERIOR.

hip, *adj., slang,* wise, in, on to; cool, gone, beat; swinging, jazzy, with it, making the scene; bohemian. See UNCONFORMITY.

hippie, *n., slang,* hipster, beat, beatnik, yippie; bohemian, nonconformist; [cool] cat, swinger; hepcat; hip chick. See UNCONFORMITY.

hire, *n. & v.* —*n.* rental, employment; fee, remuneration. —*v.* rent, lease; employ, engage. See USE, DEBT.

hireling, *n.* mercenary, henchman, underling, minion, SERVANT.

hiss, *n. & v.* —*n.* sibilation, fizz, sizzle; spit. —*v.* sibilate, fizz, sizzle; CONDEMN.

history, *n.* RECORD, chronicle, annals, biography; story, narrative; memoirs, autobiography; tale, anecdote. See DESCRIPTION.

histrionic, *adj.* theatrical; affected, exaggerated, dramatic. See DRAMA.

hit, *n. & v.* —*n. Colloq.,* success, smash; favorite; popularity. —*v.* strike, club, batter; touch, contact, reach, find; knock, smite. See ARRIVAL, CHANCE, IMPULSE.

hitch, *n. & v.* —*n.* HINDRANCE, knot; obstruction, obstacle, inconvenience, impediment; interruption, pause, stop; tug, jerk, pull; limp, hobble; accident, mischance. See AGITATION, SLOWNESS, END. —*v.* hobble, shuffle, limp; tie, knot, fasten, yoke; attach. See JUNCTION, SLOWNESS. *Ant.,* see DISJUNCTION.

hitchhike, *v., slang,* hitch, thumb [a ride], bum a ride. See TRAVEL.

hit-or-miss, *adj.* random, haphazard, CHANCE; experimental. See EXPERIMENT.

hoard, *n. & v.* —*n.* collection, store, reserve, stock, supply, savings. —*v.* save, preserve, retain, store, amass; treasure; hide; accumulate, collect.

hoarse, *adj.* threaty, raucous, harsh, husky, thick, grating, rasping; croaking, STRIDENT.

hoary, *adj.* old, aged, venerable, ancient; frosty, white; gray, grayed. See AGE. *Ant.,* see YOUTH.

hoax, *n. & v.t.* —*n.* DECEPTION, trick; deceit, fraud, fakery, humbug, canard. —*v.t.* dupe, deceive, trick, fool, swindle; (*slang*) sell. See SALE.

hobble, *n. & v.* —*n.* shackle, bond, binding. —*v.* limp, stagger; halt, bind, shackle, handicap, limit. See RESTRAINT, SLOWNESS.

hobby, *n.* avocation, AMUSEMENT, fad, recreation, relaxation, whim. See BUSINESS.

hobnob, *v.i.* consort, associate, socialize, mix. *Colloq.,* pal around, chum, hang out with. See SOCIALITY.

hobo, *n.* tramp, drifter, vagabond, vagrant; beggar, freight-hopper, rod-rider; knight of the road, rolling stone. *Colloq.,* bum, deadbeat. *Slang,* bo(e), bummer, vag. See INACTIVITY, TRAVEL.

hocus-pocus, *n.* MAGIC, sleight-of-hand; trickery, deceit, DECEPTION.

hodgepodge, *n.* MIXTURE, medley, conglomeration; stew, hash, jumble.

hog, *n.* pig, swine, boar, sow; beast, glutton. See ANIMAL.

hoist, *n. & v.t.* —*n.* elevator, lift, derrick, crane. —*v.t.* lift, raise, jack, rear. See ELEVATION.

hold, *n. & v.* —*n.* grasp, clutch, grip; tenure, POSSESSION; control, IN-FLUENCE, domination; ownership, keeping; anchor, rein. —*v.* have, occupy, retain, own, possess; restrain, repress, control, pinion, curb; check, stop, interrupt, pause; clutch, grasp, grip, seize; pin, clip, fasten; believe, declare, opine, state, think; insist, persist; last, endure, continue; cling, cleave, stick, adhere; keep, defend, protect, guard. See BELIEF, COHERENCE, DEFENSE, DURABILITY, RECEIVING, RESTRAINT, RETENTION, STORE, SUPPORT, RESOLUTION.

holding, *n.* PROPERTY, POSSESSION, tenure; claim, interest.

holdup, *n., colloq.,* robbery, theft, hijack(ing), armed robbery. *Slang,* stickup, heist. See STEALING.

hole, *n.* OPENING, aperture, gap, cavity; excavation, hollow; slot, puncture; cave; space. See CONCAVITY.

holiday, *n.* vacation; festival, celebration, recreation. See AMUSEMENT.

hollow, *n. & adj.* —*n.* CONCAVITY, depression, dent; cavity, hole; valley, gully, basin; channel, groove; FURROW. *Ant.,* see CONVEXITY. —*adj.* thin, unresonant; sepulchral, deep, empty, void, unfilled, vacant; unsound, weak, uncertain, unconvincing; specious, false, unsubstantiated, inadequate.

holy, *adj.* consecrated, saintly; blessed, sacred, godly. See PIETY, DEITY. *Ant.,* see IMPIETY.

homage, *n.* RESPECT, tribute, honor; deference, allegiance, devotion; veneration; submission; reverence. See OBEDIENCE.

home, *n.* domicile, residence, ABODE, dwelling; shelter, refuge, asylum, sanctuary; habitat, habitation, environment; native land, fatherland, country, homeland. *Colloq.,* stateside.

homecoming, *n.* return, ARRIVAL, journey's end.

homeless, *adj.* unhoused; nomadic; outcast, desolate. See EXCLUSION.

homely, *adj.* plain, simple; unbeautiful; homelike; homespun; rustic; unpretentious, down-to-earth. See SIMPLENESS, UGLINESS. *Ant.,* see BEAUTY, ORNAMENT.

homesick, *adj.* nostalgic; pining (for home); melancholy. See REGRET.

homicide, *n.* KILLING, murder, manslaughter, assassination.

homogeneity, *n.* UNIFORMITY, AGREEMENT, SIMILARITY, likeness.

homosexual, *n. & adj.* —*n.* gay [man *or* woman]; man-woman, woman-man, androgyne, epicene, transvestite, bisexual; lesbian; pervert, deviate. *Slang,* homo, queer, pansy, fairy, fruit, fag(got), swish, queen; lesbo, dyke. —*adj.* gay, lesbian, homophile, homoerotic. See UNCONFORMITY, DEVIATION.

honesty, *n.* candor, frankness; sincerity; trustworthiness, uprightness; truthfulness, veracity, PROBITY. *Ant.,* see IMPROBITY, DECEPTION.

honor, *n. & v.t.* —*n.* PROBITY, integrity; REPUTE, glory, title, distinction, award; WORSHIP, RESPECT, deference. —*v.t.* revere, reward; elevate; recognize; respect; accept (as payable). *Ant.*, see DISREPUTE.

honorary, *adj.* nominal, in name only; titular; gratuitous; emeritus. See CHEAPNESS, NOMENCLATURE.

hood, *n. & v.t.* —*n.* COVERING; cape, cowl, coif. *Slang,* gangster, hoodlum. See CLOTHING, EVILDOER. —*v.t.* shield, cover, protect; camouflage; blindfold. See CONCEALMENT.

hoodoo, *n.* Jonah, bad luck, jinx; witchcraft, voodoo, obeah; SORCERY, SPELL.

hoodwink, *v.t.* delude, deceive, fool, hoax; blind. See DECEPTION, BLINDNESS, CONCEALMENT.

hoof, *n.* foot, ungula; dewclaw. See SUPPORT, TRAVEL.

hook, *n. & v.t.* —*n.* CURVATURE, crook, bend; gaff. —*v.t.* catch, fasten; curve, bend; link, join. See JUNCTION. *Ant.,* see DISJUNCTION.

hookup, *n., colloq.,* CONNECTION, JUNCTION; circuit, rigging; tie-up, union, alliance, COMBINATION, RELATION; merger, COÖPERATION, partnership; pact, treaty, AGREEMENT. See COMMUNICATION.

hooligan, *n.* loafer; thug, strong-arm man, tough, ruffian. See EVILDOER.

hop, *n. & v.i.* —*n., colloq.,* dance; LEAP, spring. —*v.i.* jump, LEAP, bounce, spring, bound, dance.

HOPE

Nouns—**1,** hope, hopes, DESIRE; trust, confidence, reliance, faith, BELIEF; assurance, secureness, security; reassurance.

2, good omen, good auspices, promise; good, fair, *or* bright prospect; clear sky; ray of hope, cheer; silver lining; Pandora's box, balm in Gilead. *Slang,* pie in the sky.

3, assumption, presumption; anticipation, EXPECTATION; hopefulness, buoyancy, optimism, enthusiasm, aspiration.

4, castles in the air *or* in Spain, pot of gold at the end of the rainbow; Utopia, millennium, hope of Heaven (see HEAVEN); daydream, airy hopes, fool's paradise; mirage.

Verbs—**1,** hope, trust, confide, rely on, lean upon; pin one's hopes upon (see BELIEF); feel *or* rest assured, feel confident.

2, DESIRE, wish, anticipate; look on the bright side of, see the sunny side, make the best of it, hope for the best; put a good face upon; keep one's spirits up; take heart, be of good cheer; flatter oneself.

3, hope against hope, clutch at straws, count one's chickens before they are hatched, knock on wood.

4, encourage, cheer, assure, reassure, buoy up, embolden; promise, bid fair, augur well, look up.

Adjectives—**1,** hoping, in hopes, hopeful, confident; secure, certain (see BELIEF); sanguine, in good heart, buoyed up, buoyant, elated, flushed, exultant, enthusiastic; fearless, undespairing, self-reliant.

2, within sight of; promising, propitious; of good omen; auspicious, encouraging, cheering, bright, roseate, rose-colored.

Antonym, see DEJECTION.

HOPELESSNESS

Nouns—**1,** hopelessness, futility, IMPOSSIBILITY; despair, desperation; despondency, DEJECTION; pessimism; hope deferred, dashed hopes; vain expectation, DISAPPOINTMENT. *Slang,* fat chance.

2, forlorn hope; bad job; slough of despond, cave of despair; jam tomorrow, and jam yesterday—but never jam today.

3, pessimist, Job's comforter; bird of ill omen; cynic, killjoy.

Verbs—lose hope, despair, give up, give over; falter; despond, throw up one's hands. *Colloq.,* throw in the towel *or* sponge.

Adjectives—**1,** hopeless, desperate, despairing, in despair, forlorn, inconsolable, dejected, brokenhearted.

2, out of the question, not to be thought of, futile, impracticable, impossible (see IMPOSSIBILITY); beyond hope, past mending, past recall; at the end of one's rope *or* tether; given up, incurable, beyond remedy; ruined, undone.

Antonym, see HOPE.

---

horde, *n.* mass, group, throng, mob, gang, crowd, pack. See MULTI-TUDE, ASSEMBLAGE.

horizon, *n.* skyline, sea line; azimuth; edge of the world; LIMIT, CIRCUMSCRIPTION, scope, range, sphere; INFLUENCE, reach; prospect, outlook. See FUTURITY.

HORIZONTAL

Nouns—1, horizontality, horizontalness, FLATNESS; level, plane; stratum, LAYER; horizon, azimuth; recumbency, lying down, reclination, proneness, supination, prostration.

2, floor, platform, billiard table; terrace, esplanade, parterre, tableland, plateau, prairie, ledge; sea level.

Verbs—1, be horizontal, lie, recline, couch; lie down, lie flat; sprawl, loll.

2, lay (down *or* out); level, flatten, even, equalize, align; prostrate, knock down, floor, fell, bowl over.

Adjectives—horizontal, level, even, plane; flat [as a pancake], on an even keel; alluvial; calm; smooth as glass; recumbent; lying, prone, supine, couchant, prostrate.

Adverbs—horizontally, on a level, on one's back, on all fours.

Antonym, see VERTICAL.

---

horn, *n.* antler, cornu, callus, nail; saddle horn, pummel, pommel; wind instrument, blower, tooter, tin horn; ram's horn, shofar; French horn, trumpet, *etc.* (see MUSICAL INSTRUMENTS); horn of plenty, cornucopia; powder horn. See HARDNESS, SHARPNESS, RECEPTACLE.

horny, *adj.* tough, callous(ed), sclerotic. See HARDNESS. *Slang*, hard-up, oversexed; lecherous, lascivious. See DESIRE.

horrible, *adj.* alarming, dreadful, horrifying, appalling, frightful, horrendous, hideous, abominable, revolting, execrable, dire. See FEAR, PAIN.

horrid, *adj.* HORRIBLE. *Colloq.*, foul, shocking; troublesome, vexatious; nasty, bratty. See UGLINESS, PAIN, BADNESS.

horror, *n.* terror; loathing, disgust, revulsion; detestation, abhorrence; dread, aversion. See HATE, FEAR.

hors d'oeuvres, appetizers, canapés, antipasto, smorgasbord. See FOOD.

horse, *n.* equine; stallion, mare, colt, filly, foal, gelding; steed, mount; trotter, pacer, hackney; nag, hack, pony, charger; cavalry; sawhorse; broncho, mustang, cayuse; Arab. See ANIMAL, CARRIER, COMBATANT.

horseman, *n.* equestrian, rider; cavalryman, chevalier, jockey. See TRAVEL.

hose, *n. & v.* —*n.* hosing, tubing; stockings, socks; tights, leotard. See CLOTHING. —*v.t.* spray, sprinkle, water; extinguish, put out. See WATER.

hospital, *n.* sanitarium, sanatorium; clinic; pesthouse; infirmary. See REMEDY.

hospitality, *n.* SOCIALITY, cordiality; welcome, entertainment.

host, *n.* MULTITUDE, throng, mass, horde, army, legion, array; element; entertainer, innkeeper, hostess. See COMBATANT, FRIEND.

hostage, *n.* SECURITY, pledge, guarantee, bond.

hostel, *n.* shelter, lodgings; hotel, hostelry; hospice. See ABODE.

hostile, *adj.* antagonistic, opposed, warlike, unfriendly, belligerent. See HATE. *Ant.*, see FRIEND.

hot, *adj.* heated, roasted, burning, torrid, fervid, incandescent, flaming, fiery, ardent, boiling; peppery, biting. See HEAT, SHARPNESS.

hotbed, *n.* source, CAUSE, generator, inciter; trouble spot, powder keg, ferment, brew, yeast. See DANGER.

hotel, *n.* inn, hostelry, tavern. See ABODE.

hotheaded, *adj.* hot, passionate; quick-tempered, peppery, irascible; willful, headstrong, rash, impetuous. See RASHNESS, VIOLENCE, IRASCIBILITY.

hound, *n. & v.t.* —*n.* dog; beagle, basset, bloodhound, dachshund, greyhound, foxhound, *etc.*; cur, wretch. See ANIMAL, EVILDOER. *Ant.*, see GOODNESS. —*v.t.* plague, worry, pursue, harass, bait, persecute; hunt; drive, incite. See MALEVOLENCE. *Ant.*, see BENEVOLENCE.

house, *n. & v.t.* —*n.* ABODE, residence, dwelling, habitation; cottage, bungalow, mansion; shanty, hut, shack; legislature; firm, organization, company; family, ancestry, lineage. —*v.t.* shelter, protect; cover, contain, harbor. See CONTINUITY, ABODE, PARTY, SAFETY.

housebroken, *adj.* tamed, domesticated, trained, disciplined. See DOMESTICATION.

household, *n.* establishment; domicile, family. See RELATION.

hovel, *n.* shanty, hut, cabin, shack, den, shed. See ABODE.

hover, *v.i.* fly; poise, hang, linger; waver, vacillate. See AIR, DOUBT, NEARNESS.

how, *adv.* whereby, wherewith, why, however.

howl, *n. & v.i.* —*n.* bellow, shriek, yowl, bay, keen. —*v.i.* wail, complain, ululate, bawl, yowl. See CRY, LAMENTATION, WIND.

hub, *n.* center, midpoint, axis, focus, MIDDLE. See IMPORTANCE.

hubbub, *n.* tumult, noise, uproar, racket, disturbance, din. See LOUDNESS.

huddle, *v.i.* crowd, group, gather, bunch, lump, collect. See ASSEMBLAGE.

hue, *n.* COLOR, tint, shade; tone, complexion, tinge.

huff, *n.* pique, nettle, tiff; RESENTMENT, offense, umbrage, petulance, tantrum, the sulks. See IRASCIBILITY.

hug, *v.t.* caress, embrace, enfold, clasp; cherish; press, fit. See LOVE, NEARNESS.

huge, *adj.* tremendous, gargantuan, enormous, gigantic, vast, immense. See SIZE.

hullaballoo, *n.* uproar, EXCITEMENT; ATTENTION, publicity, ballyhoo.

hum, *n. & v.i.* —*n.* buzz, murmur, drone, bumble. —*v.i.* thrum, drone, buzz, murmur, croon, burr; sing. See SOUND.

human, *adj. & n.* —*adj.* mortal; earthly; humane, civilized. —*n.* man, woman, child, girl, boy; earthling. See MANKIND.

humane, *adj.* kind, merciful, tender, sympathetic; civilized. See BENEVOLENCE. *Ant.*, see MALEVOLENCE.

humble, *adj. & v.t.* —*adj.* lowly, unassuming, modest; meek, submissive; poor, obscure, paltry, mean. —*v.t.* abase, shame, humiliate. See MODESTY, INFERIORITY, LOWNESS, OBSCURITY, SIMPLENESS.

humbug, *n.* DECEIVER, imposter, pretender; deception, hoax, fraud; charlatanry.

humdrum, *adj.* DULL, routine, monotonous, prosaic, tiresome; ordinary, unremarkable, unexciting.

humid, *adj.* moist, damp, wet, dank. See MOISTURE. *Ant.*, see DRYNESS.

humiliate, *v.* shame, degrade, debase, demean, humble, degrade, cause to eat humble pie *or* crow; cause to lose face. *Colloq.*, squelch. *Ant.*, see VANITY.

HUMILITY

Nouns—humility, humbleness; meekness, lowliness, LOWNESS; (self-) abasement; SUBMISSION, resignation; MODESTY, blush, suffusion, confusion; humiliation, degradation, mortification; letdown, comedown, setdown; condescension, affability, COURTESY. *Colloq.*, comeuppance, humble pie.

Verbs—**1**, be humble, deign, vouchsafe, condescend; humble *or* demean oneself, stoop, submit; yield the palm; lower one's tone, sober down;

not dare to show one's face, hide one's face, not have a word to say
for oneself; feel shame, eat humble pie; blush, redden, change color;
hang one's head, look foolish, feel small. *Colloq.*, sing small, draw
in one's horns, eat crow.

2, humble, humiliate; let down, set down, take down; put in one's
place, bring to one's knees, put into the shade (see DISREPUTE); stare
out of countenance; confuse, mortify, disgrace, crush. *Colloq.*, take
down a peg.

Adjectives—humble, lowly, meek; modest, soberminded; unoffended; submissive, servile (see SERVILITY); humbled, bowed down, resigned,
abashed, ashamed, dashed; out of countenance; down in the mouth;
on one's knees, browbeaten; democratic, affable.

Adverbs—humbly, meekly, with downcast eyes, on bended knee; on all
fours.

Antonym, see PRIDE.

---

humor, *n. & v.t.* —*n.* disposition, mood, temper; CAPRICE, drollery, WIT;
fun; jest; choler, melancholy, depression, anger; facetiousness. —*v.t.* indulge, favor, grant, oblige, gratify. See PERMISSION.

humorist, *n.* joker, jester, wag, wit; comedian, comic, clown, buffoon;
funmaker; merry-andrew, fool; practical joker; punster. *Colloq.*, gagman, wisecracker. See WIT.

hump, *n.* hunch, lump, bulge, knob, excrescence; humpback; pile,
heap; ridge, hill. See ELEVATION, HEIGHT.

hunch, *n., colloq.*, intimation, sense, FEELING; inkling, notion, SUPPOSI-
TION, hint, INTUITION, guess.

hunger, *n. & v.i.* —*n.* DESIRE, craving; famine, hungriness, emptiness;
GLUTTONY, appetite, voracity, greed. —*v.i.* desire, crave, yearn; famish,
starve.

hunk, *n.* piece, PART, chunk, clab, lump, mass. *Colloq.*, chaw.

hunt, *n. & v.* —*n.* chase, drag; PURSUIT, search. —*v.t.* chase, stalk,
follow, trace, pursue, run, trail, hound. —*v.i.* shoot, poach, trap, snare,
hawk, ferret. See INQUIRY.

hurdle, *n.* DIFFICULTY, HINDRANCE, snag, impediment; problem, obstacle,
challenge.

hurl, *v.t.* throw, project, pitch, toss, fling, cast; dart. See PROPULSION.

hurricane, *n.* storm, tempest; VIOLENCE, furor(e); cyclone, typhoon,
whirlwind. See WIND.

hurry, *v.* press, rush, drive, force; hasten, speed, accelerate, quicken,
facilitate, scurry. See HASTE.

hurt, *n. & v.* —*n.* damage, PAIN, ache, injury, wound, bruise, offense;
loss, harm; distress, grief. —*v.* ache, PAIN, throb; injure, wound; damage, harm; offend, distress; grieve; bruise. See BADNESS, DETERIORATION,
EVIL. *Ant.*, see GOODNESS, IMPROVEMENT, PLEASURE.

husband, *n.* mate, spouse; benedict, bridegroom; man. See MARRIAGE.

husbandry, *n.* See AGRICULTURE.

hush, *n. & v.t.* —*n.* silence, quiet, stillness, calm. —*v.t.* calm, stifle,
muffle; soothe, allay, still; hide, suppress. See CONCEALMENT, MODERA-
TION, SILENCE.

husk, *n.* shell, integument, rind, skin. See COVERING.

husky, *adj.* strong, sturdy, powerful, robust, healthy; harsh, throaty,
hoarse. See STRENGTH, SOUND.

hussy, *n.* wanton, trollop, wench, tramp, slut, baggage. See FEMALE,
INSOLENCE.

hustle, *v.* jostle, jolt, poke, prod. *Colloq.*, rush, bustle, hasten. See
EXERTION, ACTIVITY. *Slang*, push, promote, advertise; con, swindle;
fleece, deceive, inveigle; lead on, take, hoodwink, sucker; sell a bill
of goods; solicit, walk the streets. See DECEPTION, IMPURITY.

hustler, *n., colloq.*, go-getter, live wire, dynamo. See EXERTION, ACTIVITY.
Slang, gambler, swindler, sharp(er); PROSTITUTE. See DECEPTION, IM-
PURITY.

hut, *n.* shack, shanty, hovel, shelter, cabin. See ABODE.

hybrid, *n. & adj.* —*n.* MIXTURE, crossbreed, cross, mongrel; mestizo, mulatto, quadroon, octroon, half-caste, half-breed, Creole. —*adj.* mixed, crossbred; mongrel; graded, half-blooded. See UNCONFORMITY.

hygienic, *adj.* cleanly, sanitary, uncontaminated; wholesome, salutary; clean. See HEALTH, CLEANNESS.

hymn, *n.* song of praise; hallelujah, hosanna; canticle, sacred song, spiritual; psalm, paean, song of devotion; psalmody; chant, plainsong; anthem; response; evensong, vespers, matins; noël, nowell, Christmas carol. See RELIGION, MUSIC.

hypnotic, *adj.* mesmeric, fascinating, magnetic; soporific, narcotic, quieting, lethargic; irresistible.

hypochondriac, *n.* worrier, self-tormenter, pessimist; morbid person. See DEJECTION. *Ant.*, see CHEERFULNESS.

hypocrisy, *n.* deceit, dissembling, pretense, falsity, DECEPTION, insincerity; sanctimony, cant, Phariseeism. See FALSEHOOD, IMPIETY. *Ant.*, see TRUTH, PIETY.

hypothesis, *n.* condition; SUPPOSITION, theory, postulate, assumption.

hysterical, *adj.* uncontrolled, wild, emotional; convulsive; frenzied, frenetic. See FEELING.

I

ice, *n. & v.* —*n.* frost, rime, frozen water; glacier, iceberg, floe; icicle. *Slang*, diamonds. —*v.* freeze, chill. See COLD.

iceberg, *n.* berg, floe, ice pack, ice sheet, glacier. See COLD.

icebox, *n.* See COLD.

icy, *adj.* freezing, COLD, frosty, frigid, gelid, rimed, frozen; Arctic, polar. *Ant.*, see HEAT.

idea, *n.* THOUGHT, concept, notion; opinion, conceit, BELIEF, impression; principle; invention, IMAGINATION. See SUPPOSITION, APPEARANCE, PREPARATION.

ideal, *n. & adj.* —*n.* model, paragon; idol, hero; perfect example. See PERFECTION. —*adj.* visionary; unattainable, Platonic, abstract, Utopian, perfect; impracticable. See IMAGINATION. *Ant.*, see IMPERFECTION.

idealist, *n.* visionary, dreamer; perfectionist, Utopian. See PERFECTION.

IDENTITY

Nouns—identity, identicalness, oneness, sameness; coincidence, coalescence; convertibility; EQUALITY; selfness, self, oneself, individuality; identification; monotony, synonymity; tautology (see REPETITION); facsimile, COPY; *alter ego* (see SIMILARITY); same; selfsame, very same, one and the same; very thing, actual thing; no other. See UNITY.

2, selfness, self, individuality, SPECIALITY; very thing; no other; personality; I, ego, myself, himself, *etc.*

Verbs—be identical, coincide, coalesce; diagnose; treat as the same, treat as identical; render the same, render identical; identify; recognize the identity of.

Adjectives—identical; the same, selfsame; coincident, coalescent, coalescing; indistinguishable; one; synonymous, analogous, equivalent (see EQUALITY); much the same, much of a muchness; unaltered; tantamount.

Adverbs—specially, in particular; each, apiece, one by one, in detail; identically.

Adverbs—identically, *etc.*

Antonym, see DIFFERENCE.

idiocy, *n.* imbecility, vacuity, cretinism, feeblemindedness; foolishness, vapidity, senselessness. See FOLLY. *Ant.,* see INTELLECT.

idle, *adj. & v.i.* —*adj.* vain, useless, futile, fruitless, pointless, aimless; out of work, unemployed, inactive; at rest; vacant, empty. See USELESSNESS, INACTIVITY, VANITY. *Ant.,* see ACTIVITY, USE, UTILITY. —*v.i.* rest; loaf, dawdle, trifle, dillydally. *Ant.,* see USE, ACTIVITY.

IDOLATRY

Nouns—**1,** idolatry, idolism; demonism, demonolatry; idol worship, demon worship, devil worship, fire worship, sun worship; zoölatry, fetishism; bibliolatry; deification, apotheosis, canonization; hero worship; animism.

2, sacrifice, hecatomb, holocaust; human sacrifice, immolation, infanticide, self-immolation, suttee.

3, idolater, idol worshiper, devil worshiper, *etc.*

4, idol, golden calf, graven image, fetish, avatar, *lares et penates,* household gods.

Verbs—idolatrize, idolize, worship (idols, pictures, relics); deify; canonize, make sacrifice.

Adjectives—idolatrous, pagan; hero-worshiping.

Antonym, see RELIGION.

---

if, *conj.* supposing, in case that, provided; whether. See SUPPOSITION.

ignition, *n.* firing, kindling; combustion; electronic ignition. See HEATING.

ignoble, *adj.* vile, base; knavish; detestable; low, common. See VULGARITY, POPULACE. *Ant.,* see NOBILITY.

ignominious, *adj.* shameful, disgraceful; degrading, humiliating. See DISREPUTE. *Ant.,* see REPUTE.

ignoramus, *n.* dunce, dolt, know-nothing; greenhorn; novice. *Slang,* lowbrow, dumbell, dope, stupe, stupid. See FOOL, IGNORANCE. *Ant.,* see KNOWLEDGE.

IGNORANCE

Nouns—**1,** ignorance, nescience; illiteracy; DARKNESS, blindness; incomprehension, inexperience, simplicity, SIMPLENESS; unawareness.

2, unknown quantities, sealed book, *terra incognita,* virgin soil, unexplored ground; dark ages.

3, smattering, glimmering; dilettantism, superficiality; bewilderment (see DOUBT); incapacity; blind spot.

Verbs—be ignorant, not know, have no idea, have no notion, have no conception; not have the remotest idea; not know from Adam; ignore, be blind to; keep in the dark *or* in ignorance (see CONCEALMENT); see through a glass darkly; not know what to make of.

Adjectives—**1,** ignorant; unknowing, unaware, unacquainted, unapprised, unwitting, witless; a stranger to; unconversant; uninformed, uncultivated, unversed, uninstructed, untaught, uninitiated, untutored, unschooled, unguided, unenlightened; behind the times; in the dark, benighted; hoodwinked, misinformed; at sea (see DOUBT). *Colloq.,* out of it.

2, shallow, superficial, green, rude, empty, half-learned, illiterate.

Adverbs—ignorantly, unawares; for anything one knows; not that one knows.

Antonym, see KNOWLEDGE.

---

ignore, *v.t.* overlook, pass by, disregard; slight, omit, NEGLECT; snub. See IGNORANCE.

ill, *adj. & adv.* —*adj.* unwell, sick, indisposed; nauseous. See DISEASE. *Ant.,* see HEALTH. —*adv.* poorly, badly; wrongly, improperly; clumsily. See UNSKILLFULNESS, BADNESS.

ill-bred, *adj.* unmannerly, boorish, rude, coarse; ignoble, base. See DISCOURTESY, POPULACE. *Ant.,* see COURTESY, NOBILITY.

ILLEGALITY

Nouns—**1,** illegality, lawlessness, unlawfulness, unconstitutionality; illegitimacy, bar sinister, bastardy; criminality; outlawry; extralegality; DISOBEDIENCE, UNCONFORMITY.

2, violence, brute force; tyranny, despotism; mob law, lynch law, martial law, drumhead law, law of the streets, kangaroo court; rebellion, *coup d'état, Putsch,* usurpation.

3, offense, crime, transgression, infringement, felony, violation *or* breach (of law), delinquency. See EVILDOER.

4, racketeering, confidence *or* bunco game, swindling, *etc.*

5, undueness, invalidity, impropriety, absence of right, usurpation, encroachment.

Verbs—offend against *or* violate the law; break *or* flout the law; take the law into one's own hands; smuggle, run, poach.

Adjectives—illegal, prohibited, UNDUE, unsanctioned, not allowed, unlawful; outlaw(ed), illegitimate, illicit, contraband, actionable, criminal; unchartered, unconstitutional; unwarranted, unwarrantable; unauthorized; informal, unofficial, injudicial, extrajudicial; lawless, arbitrary, licentious; despotic, summary, irresponsible; unanswerable, unaccountable; null and void. *Colloq.*, hot.

Adverbs—illegally; with a high hand; in violation; outside *or* beyond the law.

Antonym, see LEGALITY.

Illegible, *adj.* unreadable, indecipherable; unintelligible, indistinct; illwritten, scrawled; jumbled, pied. See UNINTELLIGIBILITY, OBSCURITY.

Illegitimate, *adj.* bastard; unlawful, illicit, crooked; illogical. See ILLEGALITY. *Ant.,* see RIGHT, LEGALITY.

Illicit, *adj.* illegal, unlawful, unsanctioned. See ILLEGALITY. *Ant.,* see LEGALITY, RIGHT.

Illiterate, *adj.* unlettered, unlearned, uneducated. See IGNORANCE.

Ill-mannered, *adj.* ill-bred, rude, coarse, boorish. See DISCOURTESY.

Illness, *n.* malady, malaise, ailment; sickness, DISEASE. *Ant.,* see HEALTH.

Illogical, *adj.* unreasoned, faulty, fallacious, specious, implausible, absurd; ridiculous. *Ant.,* see REASONING.

Ill-treatment, *n.* abuse, cruelty, mistreatment, maltreatment; manhandling; carelessness. See NEGLECT, BADNESS.

Illuminate, *v.t.* LIGHT, illumine; clarify, elucidate, explain; decorate (with gold). *Ant.,* see DARKNESS.

Illusion, *n.* delusion, hallucination, VISION, apparition; chimera, mirage, bubble, figment [of the mind *or* imagination]; dream, fool's paradise; misconception, self-delusion, ERROR; optical illusion, legerdemain. See IMAGINATION, FALSENESS, INSUBSTANTIALITY, SKILL.

Illustrate, *v.t.* design pictures for, decorate (with pictures); give as an example, exemplify; explain, clarify. See ORNAMENT, INTERPRETATION.

Illustrious, *adj.* renowned, eminent, distinguished, famous, celebrated. See REPUTE. *Ant.,* see DISREPUTE.

Image, *n.* picture; reflection; double, counterpart, likeness; portrait, statue, figure; IDEA, concept. See SIMILARITY, APPEARANCE, REPRESENTATION.

Imagery, *n.* invention, fancy, figments; figures of speech, tropes, metaphors, similes, analogies. See DESCRIPTION, IMAGINATION, WRITING.

IMAGINATION

Nouns—**1,** imagination, imaginativeness; originality; invention; fancy; creativeness, inspiration; verve, improvisation.

2, ideality, idealism; romanticism, utopianism, castle-building; dreaming; ecstasy; reverie, trance; somnambulism.

3, conception, concept, excogitation; cloudland, wonderland, dreamland; flight of fancy; brain child; imagery; conceit, figment, figment of the imagination; myth, dream, VISION, shadow, chimera; phantasm, unreality, illusion, hallucination, mirage, fantasy; whim, whims(e)y; vagary, rhapsody, romance, extravaganza; bugbear, nightmare; castles in the air, castles in Spain; Utopia, Atlantis, happy valley, millennium; fairyland; fabrication, creation; FICTION; stretch of the imagination (see EXAGGERATION). *Colloq.*, pipedream.

4, imaginer, idealist, romanticist, visionary; romancer, dreamer; enthusiast; rainbow-chaser; tilter at windmills.

Verbs—imagine, fancy, conceive; idealize, realize; dream, dream of; create, originate, devise, invent, coin, fabricate; improvise; set one's wits to work; strain one's imagination; rack, ransack *or* cudgel one's brains; excogitate; give play to the imagination; indulge in reverie; conjure up a vision; suggest itself (see THOUGHT).

Adjectives—imagined, imaginary; imagining, imaginative; original, inventive, creative, fertile; fabulous, legendary, mythological; chimerical, visionary; notional; fancy, fanciful, fantastic(al); whimsical; fairy, fairylike; romantic, high-flown, flighty, extravagant, fanatic, enthusiastic, Utopian, quixotic; ideal, unreal; in the clouds, unsubstantial (see INSUBSTANTIALITY); illusory (see ERROR).

Antonym, see SIMPLENESS.

---

imbalance, *n.* INEQUALITY, asymmetry, instability; DIFFERENCE, disparity.
imbecility, *n.* See INSANITY. *Ant.*, see SANITY, KNOWLEDGE.
imbue, *v.t.* saturate; tinge, COLOR, suffuse; instill, inspire, INFLUENCE. See MIXTURE.

IMITATION

Nouns—**1,** imitation; copying, transcription; REPETITION, DUPLICATION, reduplication, quotation; paraphrase, takeoff, parody, travesty, burlesque; COPY, plagiarism, counterfeiting, forgery (see FALSEHOOD); reflection; REPRODUCTION; mockery, mimicry; simulation, pretense, sham, impersonation, imposture; facsimile, REPRESENTATION; semblance; assimilation.

2, imitator, mimic, echo, cuckoo, parrot, ape, monkey, mockingbird; forger, plagiarist, counterfeiter. *Colloq.*, copycat.

Verbs—imitate, copy, mirror, reflect, reproduce, repeat; echo, reëcho, catch; transcribe; match, parallel; mock, take off, mimic, ape, simulate, personate, impersonate; act (see DRAMA); represent (see REPRESENTATION); counterfeit, parody, travesty, caricature, burlesque; feign, dissemble (see FALSEHOOD); follow, pattern after; follow suit; take after, model after; emulate.

Adjectives—imitated, imitating; mock; mimic; modeled after, molded on; quasi, pseudo; paraphrastic; literal; imitative; secondhand; imitable; unoriginal.

Adverbs—imitatively; literally, to the letter, *verbatim, literatim; sic*; word for word.

Antonyms, see IDENTITY, TRUTH.

---

immaculate, *adj.* clean, spotless, unsullied; chaste, pure, virgin, untouched. See CLEANNESS, PURITY. *Ant.*, see GUILT, UNCLEANNESS.
immanent, *adj.* INTRINSIC, innate, inherent; universal (as God).
immaterial, *adj.* unsubstantial, incorporeal, disembodied; irrelevant, impertinent; impalpable, intangible; trivial, unimportant, inconsequential. See INSUBSTANTIALITY, UNIMPORTANCE. *Ant.*, see SUBSTANCE, RELATION, IMPORTANCE.
immature, *adj.* half-grown; unripe, green; undeveloped; raw, callow, young; enready. See UNPREPAREDNESS, YOUTH.
immediate, *adj.* prompt, instant, present; next; first. See EARLINESS.
immemorial, *adj.* prehistoric, ancient; beyond recollection. See OLDNESS.

immense, *adj.* vast, great, tremendous, huge, infinite; overwhelming. See SIZE.

immerse, *v.* bathe, dip, baptize; duck, plunge; submerge. See OBLIQUITY, WATER.

immigrant, *n.* newcomer, settler, colonist. *Colloq.,* greenhorn. See INGRESS. *Ant.,* see EGRESS.

imminent, *adj.* impending, close at hand, about to occur; near, threatening. See EARLINESS.

immoderate, *adj.* excessive, overdone; extreme; unreasonable, extravagant. See GREATNESS. *Ant.,* see MODERATION.

immodest, *adj.* forward, bold, vain, conceited, egotistic(al), arrogant; ostentatious, blatant, flagrant, extravagant; suggestive, risqué, revealing, low-cut; unseemly, indecorous, indecent. *Slang,* sexy. See IMPURITY, INSOLENCE.

immoral, *adj.* WRONG, EVIL; corrupt, lewd, bawdy; dissolute, licentious, loose, indecent, adulterous; vicious, dishonest. See BADNESS, EVIL. *Ant.,* see RIGHT, VIRTUE.

immortal, *adj. & n.* —*adj.* everlasting; divine, godlike; deathless, imperishable; famous, glorious. *Ant.,* see INSTANTANEITY, DEATH. —*n.* god, demigod; great man. See DEITY, GREATNESS.

immovable, *adj.* immobile, fixed, unbudging; firm, steadfast, rocklike; stubborn, obdurate. See RESOLUTION, STABILITY. *Ant.,* see MOTION.

immunity, *n.* EXEMPTION, freedom (from); privilege. *Ant.,* see SENSIBILITY, TENDENCY.

impact, *n.* brunt, shock; percussion; collision; contact, TOUCH, bump, slam. See IMPULSE. *Ant.,* see RECOIL, AVOIDANCE.

impair, *v.t.* damage, weaken, wear (out), spoil, mar; vitiate, reduce. See DETERIORATION. *Ant.,* see IMPROVEMENT, RESTORATION.

impart, *v.t.* share, give, lend; tell, disclose, divulge, reveal, communicate. See GIVING, INFORMATION. *Ant.,* see SECRET.

impartial, *adj.* nonpartisan; unprejudiced, unbiased, fair; dispassionate, disinterested, equitable. See PROBITY, EQUALITY. *Ant.,* see MISJUDGMENT.

impasse, *n.* deadlock; blind alley, stone wall, dead end; standstill. See END.

impassioned, *adj.* ardent, fervent; heated; passionate, hot; frenzied, frantic; stirred, excited. See EXCITEMENT. *Ant.,* see COLD.

impassive, *adj.* stolid, phlegmatic; stoical, calm; undemonstrative, unimpressible, immobile, immovable; unsusceptible. See INSENSIBILITY. *Ant.,* see EXCITEMENT, SENSIBILITY.

impatient, *adj.* eager, hurried, restless. *Colloq.,* anxious, uneasy, intolerant, peevish, vexed. See EXCITABILITY. *Ant.,* see INEXCITABILITY.

impeach, *v.t.* accuse, charge, indict, arraign; censure, cite, impute; try, court-martial. See ACCUSATION, LAWSUIT.

impediment, *n.* HINDRANCE, obstacle, block, obstruction.

impel, *v.t.* drive, push, urge, move forward; force, constrain; incite, compel, induce. See IMPULSE, MOTION.

impend, *v.i.* threaten, be about to occur, hang over; loom. See DESTINY.

impenetrable, *adj.* solid, dense; impermeable, impassable; -proof; abstruse, mysterious, esoteric; unintelligible; incomprehensible, unfathomable. See DENSITY.

IMPENITENCE

Nouns—impenitence, irrepentance, recusance, remorselessness, gracelessness, incorrigibility; hardness of heart, induration, obduracy. See VICE.

Adjectives—impenitent, uncontrite, obdurate; hard, hardened; seared, recusant; unrepentant; relentless, remorseless, graceless, shriftless; lost, incorrigible, irreclaimable; unreclaimed, unreformed; unrepented, unatoned.

Antonym, see PENITENCE, ATONEMENT, PITY.

---

imperative, *adj. & n.* —*adj.* urgent, essential, necessary, compulsory; unavoidable. See COMMAND, REQUIREMENT. *Ant.,* see USELESSNESS. —*n.* COMMAND; (*Gram.*) word of command; imperative mood. *Colloq.,* a must.

imperceptible, *adj.* unnoticeable, indistinguishable; hard to see, slight, minute, indiscernible. See SMALLNESS, INVISIBILITY. *Ant.,* see VISIBILITY.

IMPERFECTION

Nouns—**1,** imperfection; imperfectness, incompleteness, faultiness; deficiency; inadequacy, INSUFFICIENCY, peccancy, BADNESS; immaturity, mediocrity, shortcoming.

2, fault, defect, weak point; mar, blemish; flaw, snag, DISTORTION; taint, attainder; bar sinister; WEAKNESS; half-blood; drawback. *Colloq.,* no great shakes; not much to boast of; catch; screw loose; a fly in the ointment.

3, BLEMISH, deformity, disfigurement, mar, injury; eyesore.

Verbs—be imperfect, not pass muster, fall short. *Colloq.,* get by.

Adjectives—**1,** imperfect, deficient, defective; faulty, unsound, tainted; out of order, out of tune; cracked, leaky; sprung; warped (see DISTORTION); lame; injured (see DETERIORATION); peccant, bad (see BADNESS); frail, WEAK, lame, infirm; inadequate, insufficient; found wanting; below par; shorthanded; below *or* under its full strength *or* complement. *Colloq.,* not up to scratch. *Slang,* on the blink; fouled (up), snafu.

2, indifferent, middling, ordinary, mediocre; average, MEAN; so-so; tolerable, fair, passable; pretty well, pretty good; good enough, well enough; decent; not bad, not amiss; bearable, better than nothing; secondary, inferior, run of the mine *or* mill, secondrate, second-best. *Colloq.,* fair to middling.

3, blemished, pitted, discolored, impaired, marred, deformed.

Adverbs—imperfectly, almost; to a limited extent, rather (see LITTLENESS); pretty, moderately; only; considering, all things considered, enough.

Antonym, see PERFECTION.

imperialism, *n.* colonialism, empire, expansionism; exploitation, "the White man's burden"; communism, capitalism. See AUTHORITY.

imperil, *v.t.* endanger, jeopardize, risk. See DANGER. *Ant.,* see SAFETY, ESCAPE.

imperishable, *adj.* everlasting, indestructible, permanent, undying, immortal. See PERPETUITY. *Ant.,* see DEATH, TRANSIENTNESS.

impersonal, *adj.* removed, distant; impartial, fair; businesslike; general, abstract, unemotional. See DISINTERESTEDNESS, COLD.

impersonate, *v.t.* pose (as); imitate, take off (*Colloq.*), mimic; personify; play the impostor. See REPRESENTATION.

impertinent, *adj.* insolent, saucy, fresh (*Colloq.*), cheeky, impudent; irrelevant, inapt, inapposite. See INSOLENCE. *Ant.,* see COURTESY, RELATION.

impervious, *adj.* impenetrable, impermeable; safe, proof; invulnerable, immune; oblivious, indifferent, unaware. See DEFENSE, INSENSIBILITY, INDIFFERENCE.

impetuous, *adj.* impulsive, rash, headlong; rushing, unrestrainable. See IMPULSE, VIOLENCE. *Ant.,* see RESTRAINT.

impetus, *n.* IMPULSE, ENERGY, force; stimulus, CAUSE, INFLUENCE, MOTIVE.

IMPIETY

Nouns—**1,** impiety, impiousness; sin; irreverence; profaneness, profanity, profanation; blasphemy, desecration, sacrilege; scoffing; hardening, fall from grace; backsliding, declension, perversion, reprobation, IRRELIGION.

2, assumed piety, hypocrisy (see FALSEHOOD); pietism, cant, pious fraud;

lip service; misdevotion, formalism, austerity; sanctimony, sanctimoniousness; pharisaism, precisianism; sabbatism, sabbatarianism; sacerdotalism; bigotry (see NARROWNESS).

3, sinner, EVILDOER; scoffer, blasphemer, profaner, sacrilegist; worldling; hypocrite; backslider; bigot; Pharisee, ranter, fanatic; sons of Belial, children of darkness.

Verbs—profane, desecrate, blaspheme, revile, scoff; swear (see IMPRECATION); commit sacrilege; fall from grace, backslide.

Adjectives—impious; irreligious; desecrating, profane, irreverent, sacrilegious, blasphemous; unhallowed, unsanctified, unregenerate; hardened, perverted, reprobate; hypocritical, canting, sanctimonious, unctuous, pharisaical, overrighteous; bigoted, fanatical.

Adverbs—impiously; under the mask, cloak, pretence, form or guise of religion.

Antonym, see PIETY.

implant, *v.t.* plant, embed, fix, set in; inculcate, instill; graft, engraft.

implement, *n. & v.* —*n.* tool, utensil, INSTRUMENT. —*v.* equip; affect; fulfill. See POWER, USE. *Ant.*, see HINDRANCE, NULLIFICATION.

implicate, *v.t.* involve, entangle, embroil; incriminate; connect, associate. See ACCUSATION. *Ant.*, see DISJUNCTION.

implication, *n.* involvement; allusion, inference; innuendo, suggestion. See MEANING.

implicit, *adj.* unspoken, tacit, understood, implied, inferred. See MEANING.

implore, *v.t.* beg, beseech, entreat, plead. See REQUEST.

imply, *v.t.* hint, suggest, infer, intimate; involve. See EVIDENCE, INFORMATION.

impolite, *adj.* rude, inconsiderate, uncivil, ill-mannered, ill-bred. See DISCOURTESY. *Ant.*, see COURTESY.

import, *n. & v.* —*n.* MEANING, significance, IMPORTANCE; trend, drift, purport. See INGRESS. —*v.* bring in; introduce; imply, indicate. See MEANING.

IMPORTANCE

Nouns—1, importance, import, consequence, moment, prominence, consideration, mark, materialness, primacy; significance, concern; emphasis, interest; distinction, prestige, grandeur, majesty; GREATNESS, SUPERIORITY, notability, REPUTE; weight, value, GOODNESS; usefulness (see UTILITY).

2, GRAVITY, seriousness, solemnity; no joke, no laughing matter; pressure, urgency, stress; matter of life and death; exigency.

3, memorabilia, notabilia, great doings; red-letter day, milestone, turning point.

4, substance, gist, essence; main chance, be all and end all, cardinal point; sum and substance, *sine qua non*; breath of life; cream, salt, core, kernel, heart, nucleus; key, keynote, keystone; cornerstone; trump card; salient points; essentials, fundamentals. *Colloq.*, where its at.

5, personage, notable, figure, prima donna, chief. *Slang*, big gun, VIP.

Verbs—1, import, signify, matter, boot, be somebody, carry weight; cut a figure (see REPUTE); overshadow; count for; lie at the root of.

2, attach importance to, value, care for; set store by; mark (see INDICATION); underline; put in italics or capitals, capitalize, italicize; accentuate, emphasize, stress, lay stress on; make a fuss or stir about, make much of.

Adjectives—1, important; of importance, momentous, material; not to be overlooked, not to be despised, not to be sneezed at; egregious; weighty, influential; of note (see REPUTE); notable, prominent, salient, signal; memorable, remarkable; worthy of remark, worthy of notice; never to be forgotten; stirring, eventful, significant, telling, trenchant, emphatic, pregnant.

2, grave, serious; urgent, pressing, critical, instant.

3, paramount, essential, vital, all-absorbing; cardinal, chief, main, prime, primary, principal, leading, capital, foremost, overriding; in the front rank, first-rate; superior (see SUPERIORITY); considerable (see GREAT-NESS); marked; rare (see RARITY).

Adverbs—importantly, materially, in the main; above all, *par excellence.*

Antonym, see UNIMPORTANCE.

---

impose, *v.t.* burden (with), inflict; force (upon); levy, tax; delude, take advantage (of), palm off, foist; obtrude. See DECEPTION.

imposing, *adj.* dignified, awe-inspiring; impressive; grand, stately, commanding. See REPUTE.

imposition, *n.* nuisance, bother, inconvenience; INSOLENCE, intrusion; infringement, invasion of privacy; unfairness, INJUSTICE; HINDRANCE.

IMPOSSIBILITY

Nouns—impossibility, what can never be; HOPELESSNESS; impracticability, infeasibility, insuperability. *Colloq.*, no go.

Verbs—have no chance; square the circle; skin a flint; make a silk purse out of a sow's ear; make bricks without straw; build castles in the air; bite off more than one can chew; be in two places at once; give the moon.

Adjectives—impossible; absurd, contrary to reason; unreasonable, incredible (see DOUBT); visionary; inconceivable (see IMPROBABILITY); unimaginable; impracticable, unachievable; infeasible; insuperable, insurmountable; unattainable, unobtainable, out of reach; out of the question; desperate, hopeless; inaccessible, impassable; impervious, unnavigable; inextricable, ineluctable.

Antonym, see POSSIBILITY.

---

impostor, *n.* fake, faker; pretender, masquerader, fraud. See DECEIVER.

imposture, *n.* masquerade, pretense; fraud, DECEPTION; impersonation.

IMPOTENCE

Nouns—**1,** impotence; inability; disability; disablement, impuissance, incapacity, incapability; inaptness, ineptitude, inefficiency, incompetence; disqualification. See WEAKNESS.

2, inefficacy (see USELESSNESS); FAILURE; helplessness, prostration, exhaustion, enervation; emasculation, castration.

3, eunuch; cripple; blank cartridge, flash in the pan, dummy. *Slang,* washout, dud.

Verbs—**1,** be impotent; collapse, faint, swoon, drop.

2, render powerless; unman, unnerve, enervate; emasculate, castrate, geld; disable, disarm, incapacitate, disqualify, unfit, invalidate, deaden, cramp, exhaust, weaken, debilitate; muzzle, cripple, maim, lame, hamstring, draw the teeth of; throttle, strangle, garrote, silence; break the back; unhinge, unfit. *Colloq.*, hog-tie.

Adjectives—**1,** impotent, powerless, unable, incapable, incompetent; inefficient, ineffective; inept; unfit, unfitted; unqualified, disqualified; unendowed; crippled, disabled; paralytic, paralyzed; emasculate(d); waterlogged, rudderless; on one's back; done up, dead beat, exhausted, shattered, demoralized; without a leg to stand on, *hors de combat,* out of commission.

2, harmless, unarmed; defenseless, unfortified, indefensible, vincible, pregnable, untenable; null and void, nugatory, inoperative, good for nothing; ineffectual (see FAILURE); inadequate (see INSUFFICIENCY); inefficacious (see USELESSNESS).

Antonym, see POWER.

---

impound, *v.t.* jail, restrain; confine, corral, encage; seize, take, confiscate, expropriate, appropriate. See INCLOSURE, TAKING.

impoverish, *v.t.* pauperize, make poor; exhaust, drain; reduce, deplete;

rob; weaken. See POVERTY, INSUFFICIENCY. *Ant.*, see IMPROVEMENT, MONEY.

impracticable, *adj.* unworkable, inexpedient, not feasible; idealistic, visionary; unrealistic. See DIFFICULTY, IMPOSSIBILITY.

impractical, *adj.* impracticable; unwise, imprudent, unrealistic; unsound, illogical; harebrained, foolish. See DIFFICULTY, IMPOSSIBILITY, FOLLY.

IMPRECATION

Nouns—imprecation, malediction, malison, curse, denunciation, execration; anathema, ban, proscription, excommunication, commination, fulmination; calumny, calumniation, contumely, invective, diatribe, jeremiad, tirade, vituperation, disparagement, obloquy; abuse, billingsgate, sauce; cursing, profanity, swearing, oath; THREAT.

Verbs—imprecate, curse, damn, swear (at); execrate, beshrew, scold; anathematize (see DISAPPROBATION); vilify, denounce, proscribe, excommunicate, fulminate, thunder against; threaten; defame (see DETRACTION).

Adjectives—imprecatory, denunciatory, proscribed, abusive, cursing, cursed, accursed.

Interjections—woe to! woe betide! damn! confound! blast! curse! devil take! hang! out with! a plague upon! out upon!

Antonym, see APPROBATION.

impregnate, *v.t.* fertilize, fecundate, pollinate, inseminate; infuse, soak, permeate, saturate. *Colloq.*, get in trouble. *Slang*, knock up. See REPRODUCTION.

impress, *v.t.* stamp, mark, print, imprint, engrave; dint, dent; inspire, affect strongly, overawe; interest; strike; draft, compel (service). *Colloq.*, crimp, shanghai. See EXCITEMENT, PRINTING, RESTRAINT, INDICATION.

impression, *n.* PRINTING, ENGRAVING, mark, stamp; dent, opinion, feeling; inkling, suspicion. See BELIEF, SENSIBILITY.

impressive, *adj.* imposing, effective; awesome, majestic, stately, moving, stirring, weighty, large, considerable. See FEELING, GREATNESS, EFFECT. *Ant.*, see UNIMPORTANCE.

imprint, *n. & v.* —*n.* impress, stamp, impression; cachet, trademark, colophon, seal, symbol, device; result, INFLUENCE, EFFECT. See INDICATION. —*v.t.* impress, stamp, fix; inscribe, seal; make one's mark on. See INDICATION.

imprison, *v.t.* lock up, detain; hold, jail, incarcerate. See RESTRAINT.

IMPROBABILITY

Nouns—improbability, unlikelihood, unlikeliness; small *or* long chance, Chinaman's chance, ghost of a chance; long odds; incredibility (see DOUBT). See HOPELESSNESS, IMPOSSIBILITY.

Verbs—be improbable, be unlikely, be a strain on the imagination.

Adjectives—improbable, unlikely, contrary to all reasonable expectation, doubtful; rare, infrequent (see INFREQUENCY); unheard-of, implausible.

Antonym, see PROBABILITY.

IMPROBITY

Nouns—**1,** improbity; dishonesty, dishonor; disgrace, DISREPUTE; fraud, DECEPTION; lying, FALSEHOOD; bad faith; infidelity; inconstancy, faithlessness, Judas kiss, betrayal; breach of promise, trust *or* faith; renegation, renegadism, disloyalty, treason, high treason; apostasy (see CHANGEABLENESS, GUILT); IMPURITY. See EVILDOER.

2, villainy, baseness, abjection, debasement, turpitude, moral turpitude, laxity; perfidy, perfidiousness, treachery, duplicity, double-dealing; unfairness, knavery, roguery, rascality, foul play; trickery, venality, nepotism; corruption; simony, barratry, graft, malfeasance.

3, VICE, depravity, infamy, looseness, profligacy. See LIBERTINE.

Verbs—**1,** be dishonest, play false; forswear, break one's word, faith *or* promise; jilt, betray; sell out; lie (see FALSEHOOD); live by one's wits; misrepresent; steal (see STEALING); hit below the belt. *Colloq.*, go back on.

2, be vicious, sin, fall, lapse, slip, trip, offend, trespass, deviate, misdo, misbehave; go to the devil, go wrong.

Adjectives—**1,** dishonest, dishonorable, unscrupulous; fraudulent (see DECEPTION); knavish, disgraceful, disreputable (see DISREPUTE); wicked, sinful, VICIOUS, criminal.

2, false-hearted, unfair; two-faced; crooked, insidious, Machiavellian, dark, slippery; perfidious, treacherous, perjured; infamous, arrant, foul, base, vile, ignominious, blackguard; corrupt, venal; recreant, inglorious, discreditable, improper; faithless, false, unfaithful, disloyal; treacherous, renegade; untrustworthy, unreliable, undependable, trustless; lost to shame, dead to honor.

Adverbs—dishonestly, like a thief in the night, underhandedly, by fair means or foul.

Antonym, see PROBITY.

improper, *adj.* indecent, bawdy, lewd, *risqué*, indelicate, immodest, WRONG, inapt, unsuitable, mistaken, unfitting, incorrect, inexcusable, erroneous, out of place, misplaced. See DISCOURTESY, IMPURITY. *Ant.*, see RIGHT, PURITY.

impropriety, *n.* misbehavior, vulgarity, immodesty; bad manners, indecorum; unfitness, unsuitability. See INEXPEDIENCE, DISAGREEMENT.

IMPROVEMENT

Nouns—**1,** improvement, uplift; melioration, amelioration, betterment; mend, amendment, emendation; advancement, advance, progress, PROGRESSION; ASCENT; promotion, preferment; ELEVATION, INCREASE; cultivation, civilization; culture. *Colloq.*, crusade, crusading.

2, reform, reformation, revision; correction, refinement, enhancement, elaboration, PERFECTION, purification (see CLEANNESS); repair, RESTORATION; recovery.

3, reformer, radical, progressive. *Colloq.*, do-gooder, crusader.

Verbs—**1,** improve; better, mend, amend; turn to good account, profit by, reap the benefit of; make good use of, make capital of; advance (see PROGRESSION); ascend (see ASCENT); INCREASE; fructify, ripen, mature; pick up, come about, rally, take a turn for the better; turn over a new leaf, turn the corner; recover (see RESTORATION). *Colloq.*, look up, snap out of it.

2, meliorate, ameliorate; palliate, mitigate; turn the tide; correct, rectify; enrich, mellow, elaborate, fatten; promote, cultivate, advance, forward, enhance; bring forward, bring on; foster (see AID); invigorate, strengthen.

3, touch up, brush up, refurbish, renovate, polish, make the most of, set off to advantage; prune; repair, restore (see RESTORATION); put in order.

4, revise, edit, correct; doctor, REMEDY; purify; relieve, refresh, infuse new blood *or* life into; reform, remodel, reorganize.

Adjectives—improving, improved;; progressive; better, better off, better for; reformatory, emendatory; reparatory, restorative, remedial; corrigible, improvable.

Adverbs—*Colloq.*, over the hump, out of the woods.

Antonym, see DETERIORATION.

improvise, *v.* invent, devise (at the moment), extemporize. *Colloq.*, ad lib. See IMPULSE. *Ant.*, see REPARATION.

imprudent, *adj.* careless, incautious, rash; unwise, injudicious, ill-advised; senseless, foolish. See RASHNESS, INEXPEDIENCE, FOLLY.

impudence, *n.* INSOLENCE; gall, cheek, effrontery, boldness. *Colloq.*, nerve, freshness. See DISCOURTESY. *Ant.*, see COURTESY, FEAR, CARE.

IMPULSE

Nouns—**1**, impulse, impulsion, impetus; momentum; push, thrust, shove, jog, jolt, brunt, throw; explosion (see VIOLENCE); PROPULSION; percussion, concussion, collision, clash, encounter, cannon, shock, crash, bump; impact; charge, ATTACK; beating, PUNISHMENT; dynamics, mechanics.

2, blow, dint, stroke, knock, tap, rap, slap, smack, pat, dab; fillip; slam, bang; hit, whack, cuff, swap, punch, thump, pelt, kick; cut, thrust, lunge. *Colloq.*, bat, clout, lick, clip. *Slang*, belt, sock, wallop, the old one-two.

3, hammer, sledgehammer, maul, mallet, flail; ram, battering ram, piledriver, punch, bat; cudgel, weapon; ax(e) (see SHARPNESS).

4, sudden thought; impromptu, improvisation; inspiration, flash, spurt; jam session.

Verbs—**1**, give impetus; impel, push; start, set going; drive, urge; thrust, prod; elbow, shoulder, jostle, hustle, shove, job, jolt, bump; impinge.

2, strike, knock, hit, tap, rap, slap, pat, thump, beat, bang, slam, dash; punch, whack; hit hard, strike hard; batter; pelt, buffet, belabor; fetch one a blow; poke at, pink, lunge; kick, butt; make a pass at, strike at, ATTACK; whip (see PUNISHMENT). *Colloq.*, belt, lambaste, clip, swat, larrup, wallop. *Slang*, knock galley-west, waste.

3, collide; fall *or* run foul of; throw (see PROPULSION).

4, improvise, extemporize, ad-lib, invent, devise. *Colloq.*, fake, wing it.

Adjectives—**1**, impelling, impellent; dynamic, impelled.

2, impulsive, extemporaneous, impromptu, offhand, improvised, unmeditated, unpremeditated; natural, unguarded; spontaneous, voluntary (see WILL).

Adverbs—**1**, impulsively, explosively, *etc.*

2, impulsively, extempore, extemporaneously; offhand, impromptu, improviso; on the spur of the moment.

Antonym, see THOUGHT, RECEIVING.

---

impunity, *n.* freedom (from reprisal), EXEMPTION, immunity (to laws). See ACQUITTAL.

IMPURITY

Nouns—**1**, impurity; UNCLEANNESS; immodesty; grossness, indelicacy, indecency; pornography, obscenity, ribaldry, smut, bawdy, *double entendre*.

2, concupiscence, lust, carnality, flesh, salacity; pruriency, lechery, lasciviousness, lewdness, lubricity; incontinence, unchastity; debauchery, license, immorality, libertinism, fornication, liaison; wenching, venery, dissipation; incest; perversion, sodomy, pederasty, homosexuality, Lesbianism; sadism, masochism; seduction, defloration, defilement, abuse, violation, rape, (criminal) assault (*euphemisms*); harlotry, whoredom, concubinage; cuckoldry, adultery, infidelity.

3, immorality, laxity, looseness of morals, iniquity, turpitude, depravity, pollution, profligacy, shame, vice.

4, brothel, bagnio, bawdyhouse, whorehouse, house of ill fame, bordello; red-light district, combat zone.

Verbs—debauch; defile; deflower, rape, ravish, seduce; prostitute; abuse, violate; commit adultery.

Adjectives—**1**, impure; unclean; immodest, shameless; indecorous, indelicate, indecent; loose, coarse, gross, broad, promiscuous; smutty, ribald, obscene, bawdy, pornographic, risqué; concupiscent, prurient, lustful; lewd, lascivious, lecherous, libidinous, ruttish, salacious; unfaithful, adulterous; incestuous; unchaste, incontinent; light, wanton, licentious, rakish, debauched, dissipated, dissolute; loose, meretricious, of easy virtue, on the streets; gay.

2, VICIOUS, immoral, dissolute, profligate, sinful, iniquitous.

Antonym, see PURITY.

inability, *n.* IMPOTENCE, incapacity, powerlessness, UNSKILLFULNESS, incompetence, inefficiency. *Ant.,* see POWER, SKILL.

inaccessible, *adj.* unapproachable, incommunicado; sheltered, guarded; restricted, taboo, sacrosanct; aloof, cold, cool, distant, withdrawn. See DISTANCE, CONCEALMENT, SECLUSION, TACITURNITY, INSENSIBILITY.

inaccurate, *adj.* erroneous, fallacious, incorrect, WRONG; mistaken; inexact, unprecise; misleading. See ERROR. *Ant.,* see TRUTH, CARE.

INACTIVITY

Nouns—**1,** inactivity; inaction; inertness; obstinacy; lull, cessation, REPOSE, rest, quiescence; rustiness; idleness, sloth, NEGLECT, laziness, indolence; unemployment, dilatoriness, dawdling; malingering; passiveness, passivity, dormancy; stagnation; procrastination; time on one's hands; *laissez faire*, noninterference; *dolce far niente*, lotusland.

2, dullness, languor; sluggishness, SLOWNESS, delay (see LATENESS); torpor, torpidity, torpescence; stupor, stupefaction, INSENSIBILITY; drowsiness, nodding; mesmerism, hypnotism, lethargy; heaviness, FATIGUE, weariness.

3, sleep, slumber, somnolence, sound *or* heavy sleep; Morpheus; coma, swoon, trance; catalepsy; dream; hibernation, estivation; nap, catnap, doze, siesta. *Colloq.,* forty winks, snooze. *Slang,* shuteye.

4, sedative, tranquil(l)izer, sleeping draft *or* pill, soporific, opiate (see REMEDY). *Slang,* knockout drops.

5, idler, drone, do-little, dummy, silent partner; fifth wheel; truant (see AVOIDANCE); lounger, loafer; lubber, slowpoke (see SLOWNESS); opium eater, lotus-eater; slug; laggard, sluggard; clock-watcher, good-for-nothing; slumberer, sleepyhead, dormouse.

6, halt, standstill, full stop; stalemate, impasse, block, check, checkmate; red light.

Verbs—**1,** be inactive, let the grass grow under one's feet; take one's time, dawdle, lag, hang back, slouch, loll, lounge, loaf, laze, loiter; sleep at one's post *or* at the switch, flag, languish.

2, relax, take it easy; vegetate, lie fallow; waste, consume, kill *or* lose time; twiddle one's thumbs; not lift a finger *or* hand; idle, trifle, fritter *or* fool away time; piddle, potter, putter, dabble, fiddle-faddle, dally, shilly-shally, dilly-dally; ride at anchor, rest on one's oars, rest on one's laurels; hang fire, postpone. *Colloq.,* cool one's heels.

3, sleep, slumber; hibernate; oversleep; sleep like a top *or* log; doze, drowse, snooze, nap; dream; snore; nod, yawn; go to bed, turn in; REPOSE. *Colloq.,* drop off. *Slang,* hit the hay, hit the sack, pound the ear.

Adjectives—**1,** inactive; motionless, quiescent, stationary; unoccupied, idle; indolent, lazy, slothful, idle, remiss, slack, torpid, sluggish, languid, supine, heavy, dull, leaden, lumpish; inert, inanimate; listless, dilatory, laggard; lagging slow; rusty, flagging, lackadaisical, pottering, irresolute.

2, sleeping, asleep; dormant, comatose, dead to the world, in the arms of Morpheus; sleepy, drowsy, somnolent; torpid, lethargic, heavy; napping; tranquil(l)izing, soporific, hypnotic; balmy, dreamy; sedative. *Slang,* dop(e)y; out of this world.

Antonym, see ACTIVITY.

---

inadequate, *adj.* scanty, wanting, short, below par; incomplete, partial, deficient, lacking. See INSUFFICIENCY. *Ant.,* see SUFFICIENCY.

inadvertent, *adj.* unintentional, adventitious, accidental, CHANCE; heedless, inattentive, careless, regardless, thoughtless. See INATTENTION. *Ant.,* see ATTENTION.

inadvisable, *adj.* inexpedient, not recommended; impracticable; ill-advised, unwise, imprudent; risky. See INEXPEDIENCE.

inane, *adj.* pointless, senseless; empty, vacuous; idiotic, foolish. See ABSURDITY. *Ant.,* see MEANING, KNOWLEDGE.

inanimate, *adj.* inorganic; lifeless, insentient, unconscious, dead; listless, inactive, inert, supine, dormant, comatose. See DEATH, INACTIVITY, INSENSIBILITY.

inappropriate, *adj.* unbecoming, unsuitable, WRONG, improper; inapt, unfitting, inadvisable. See DISAGREEMENT. *Ant.*, see AGREEMENT.

inarticulate, *adj.* voiceless, speechless, mute, stammering; unexpressed, unspoken, indistinct; unjointed. See SILENCE, DISJUNCTION. *Ant.*, see VOICE, JUNCTION.

INATTENTION

Nouns—inattention, inattentiveness; abstraction, absence of mind, preoccupation, distraction; reverie, woolgathering, daydreaming, brown study, detachment; inconsiderateness, oversight; inadvertence, inadvertency; nonobservance, disregard; thoughtlessness, heedlessness (see NEGLECT); insouciance, indifference, coldness, neutrality, apathy; INSENSIBILITY; RASHNESS, carelessness, nonchalance, unconcern.

Verbs—1, be inattentive, pay no attention, disregard, overlook; pass by, NEGLECT; ignore, think little of; close *or* shut one's eyes to; spurn, disdain, not care a fig *or* straw, dismiss from one's thoughts *or* mind; think no more of; set *or* put aside; turn a deaf ear to, turn one's back upon; take no notice of. *Dial.*, pay no mind. *Slang*, don't give *or* care a hang, a rap *or* a damn.

2, abstract oneself, dream, daydream, woolgather. *Colloq.*, moon.

3, escape notice; escape attention; go in one ear and out the other; forget (see OBLIVION); fall on deaf ears.

4, divert, distract; disconcert, discompose; confuse, perplex, bewilder, fluster, muddle, dazzle. *Colloq.*, fuddle, rattle, faze. *Slang*, ball up.

Adjectives—1, inattentive; unobservant, unmindful, unheeding, undiscerning; inadvertent, regardless, listless, indifferent; blind, deaf; cursory, percursory; inconsiderate, offhand, thoughtless; unconcerned, insouciant, devil-may-care; lukewarm, cool, cold, indifferent, apathetic; heedless, careless.

2, absent, abstracted, distraught, distrait; lost in thought; rapt, in the clouds, in a fog; bemused; preoccupied; engrossed; off one's guard; napping, dreamy, woolgathering, sleeping, asleep, dead to the world.

Antonym, see ATTENTION.

inaudible, *adj.* unhearable; faint, muffled. See SILENCE, WEAKNESS.

inaugurate, *v.t.* install (in office), induct, invest; start, launch, initiate, institute, open. See BEGINNING. *Ant.*, see END.

inauspicious, *adj.* unpropitious, ill-omened, unfavorable, unlucky. See PREDICTION, ADVERSITY. *Ant.*, see PROSPERITY.

inborn, *adj.* natural, native, innate, inherent. See DISPOSITION.

incalculable, *adj.* inestimable, immeasurable; vast. See GREATNESS, ADVERSITY.

incapable, *adj.* powerless, unable; inefficient, incompetent; unqualified, unfitted, untrained. See INSUFFICIENCY. *Ant.*, see SUFFICIENCY.

incapacity, *n.* DISABILITY, IMPOTENCE, incompetence; inability, lack, deficiency. *Ant.*, see POWER.

incarnate, *v.t.* shape, form, embody; animate, quicken (with life). See SUBSTANCE. *Ant.*, see INSUBSTANTIALITY.

incendiary, *n.* pyromaniac, firebug; arsonist. See HEAT.

incense, *v. & n.* —*v.t.* inflame, HEAT; infuriate, anger, ire; perfume, scent, thurify. See RESENTMENT, SMELL. —*n.* perfume, FRAGRANCE, scent, ODOR, bouquet; frankincense, musk, myrrh, sandalwood; honor, glory, ATTENTION.

incentive, *n.* stimulus, goad, spur; MOTIVE, reason; provocation.

incessant, *adj.* endless, continual, unceasing; uninterrupted. See FREQUENCY, CONTINUITY. *Ant.*, see END, DISJUNCTION.

inch, *v.* advance slowly, creep, crawl; EDGE, worm. See TRAVEL, SLOWNESS.

incident, *n.* occasion; EVENT, episode, happening; minor adventure.

incidental, *adj.* secondary, minor, subordinate; casual, CHANCE, accidental; current.

incite, *v.t.* stir, urge, impel; actuate, provoke, instigate; encourage, stimulate; spur, goad. *Colloq.,* fan the flowers. See IMPULSE, CAUSE.

inclement, *adj.* unlenient, harsh, severe, merciless; foul (of weather), cold, windy, bitter. See SEVERITY. *Ant.,* see PITY.

incline, *v. & n.* —*v.* stoop, slant, tilt, slope; pitch, lurch; tend, INFLUENCE, bias. See TENDENCY. —*n.* OBLIQUITY, grade; gradient, slant, bias, slope (see *v.*); ramp, ASCENT, upgrade; downgrade, DESCENT.

inclination, *n.* propensity, leaning, bent, predisposition; slope, slant, ramp; fondness, liking; predilection. See TENDENCY, OBLIQUITY, DESIRE.

INCLOSURE

Nouns—**1,** inclosure, enclosure, envelope, case, RECEPTACLE, wrapper, girdle.

2, pen, fold; sheepfold, paddock, pound, coop, sty, pigsty, stall, kennel, corral, net, kraal, compound.

3, wall; hedge, fence, pale, paling, balustrade, rail, railing, dike, ditch, fosse, moat, levee.

4, barrier, barricade, parapet, rampart, stockade; jail (see PRISON).

Verbs—enclose, inclose, confine, surround, circumscribe, envelope, pen in, hem in, impen.

Antonym, see EXTERIOR.

INCLUSION

Nouns—inclusion, admission, acceptance, RECEPTION; comprehension, incorporation; COMPOSITION, CONTENTS.

Verbs—include, comprise, comprehend, contain, admit, embrace, receive; enclose, circumscribe (see CIRCUMSCRIPTION); compose, incorporate, encompass; reckon or number among; count in; refer to, place under, take into account; pertain *or* relate to.

Adjectives—included, including, inclusive; compendious, comprehensive; of the same class.

Adverbs—inclusively, comprehensively, *etc.*

Antonym, see EXCLUSION.

incoherence, *n.* unintelligibility, irrationality, inconsistency; incongruity; maundering, raving; nonadhesion; immiscibility; looseness, FREEDOM. See DISJUNCTION. *Ant.,* see COHERENCE.

incombustible, *adj.* noninflammable, flameproof, fireproof, unburnable. See COLD. *Ant.,* see HEAT.

income, *n.* revenue; dividends, interest; receipt(s), emoluments, fees, earnings. See ACQUISITION. *Ant.,* see PAYMENT.

incomparable, *adj.* peerless, matchless, nonpareil, inimitable. See SUPERIORITY.

incompatible, *adj.* inharmonious, inconsistent, antipathetic, incongruous, uncongenial; clashing, discordant, disagreeing. See DISAGREEMENT. *Ant.,* see AGREEMENT.

incompetence, *n.* disqualification; inability, inefficiency; IMPOTENCE; unfitness, incapability, incapacity, UNSKILLFULNESS. See INSANITY.

INCOMPLETENESS

Nouns—**1,** incompleteness, scantiness, short measure, half measures, shortcoming; INSUFFICIENCY, deficiency, IMPERFECTION, inadequacy, DISCONTINUANCE; immaturity (see UNPREPAREDNESS).

2, noncompletion, nonfulfillment, nonperformance, nonexecution, NEGLECT.

3, deficit, want, lack, defalcation, omission, caret; INTERVAL, break, gap, missing link; defect, flaw, fault, weak point, WEAKNESS.

Verbs—**1,** be incomplete; fall short, lack, want, need (see INSUFFICIENCY).

2, leave unfinished, leave undone, let alone, let slide, let slip, NEGLECT; lose sight of, hang fire, collapse, be slow to, do things by halves, lie down on the job.

Adjectives—**1,** incomplete, uncompleted, unfinished, left undone; imperfect, defective, deficient, partial, wanting, failing; in default, in arrears, short (of); hollow, meager, poor, lame, half-and-half, perfunctory, sketchy, crude; mutilated, garbled, mangled, docked, lopped, truncated, catalectic. *Colloq.,* skimpy, half-baked.

2, unaccomplished, unperformed, unexecuted; in progress, going on, in hand, proceeding, under way, under construction.

Adverbs—incompletely; by halves, partly, partially; on paper, on the drawing board, in the blueprint *or* planning stage.

Antonym, see COMPLETION.

incomprehensible, *adj.* unintelligible; unfathomable, abstruse, inscrutable. *Ant.,* see MEANING.

inconceivable, *adj.* unimaginable; unthinkable; incredible. See IMPOSSIBILITY, DOUBT, UNINTELLIGIBILITY.

inconclusive, *adj.* indecisive, uncertain. See INCOMPLETENESS, UNCERTAINTY.

incongruity, *n.* disharmony; inconsistency, incompatibility, ABSURDITY. *Ant.,* see AGREEMENT, COHERENCE.

inconsiderate, *adj.* careless, heedless, thoughtless; tactless; neglectful. See NEGLECT. *Ant.,* see THOUGHT, CARE.

inconsistency, *n.* CHANGEABLENESS, fickleness; incompatibility; CONTRARINESS, contradiction. *Ant.,* see AGREEMENT.

inconspicuous, *adj.* unnoticeable, unobtrusive; not prominent. See INVISIBILITY. *Ant.,* see VISIBILITY.

inconstant, *adj.* unstable, irregular; fickle, changeable, faithless. See CHANGEABLENESS. *Ant.,* see STABILITY.

inconvenient, *adj.* awkward, embarrassing, troublesome; inopportune, untimely, unseasonable; unsuitable.

incorporate, *v.* embody; federate, merge, consolidate; unite, blend, join. See JUNCTION.

incorrect, *adj.* WRONG, erroneous, fallacious; mistaken, false, untrue, inaccurate, unprecise. See ERROR, FALSEHOOD. *Ant.,* see TRUTH, RIGHT.

incorrigible, *adj.* irreclaimable, abandoned, beyond redemption; intractable, hopelessly delinquent. See EVILDOER. *Ant.,* see VIRTUE.

INCREASE

Nouns—increase, augmentation, enlargement, extension; dilation, EXPANSION; advance, appreciation; gain, profit, increment, accretion; accession, ADDITION; development, growth; aggrandizement, AGGRAVATION; intensification, magnification, multiplication; rise, ASCENT; EXAGGERATION, exacerbation; bonus; spread, dispersion; flood tide.

Verbs—**1,** increase, augment, add to, enlarge, extend; dilate, sprout, EXPAND, swell, burgeon, bud; grow, wax, get ahead, gain strength; advance; develop, grow, run up, shoot up; rise; ascend (see ASCENT); enhance, amplify; raise, give a bonus. *Slang,* step up, jack up, hike.

2, aggrandize; raise, exalt; deepen; heighten; strengthen; intensify, enhance, magnify, redouble; aggravate, exaggerate; exasperate, exacerbate; add fuel to the flames, spread, disperse; escalate.

Adjectives—increased, increasing, multiplying, enlarged, on the increase, undiminished; additional, extra, added (see ADDITION); swollen, turgid, bloated, distended; larger, bigger, exaggerated.

Adverbs—increasingly, *etc.; crescendo.*

Antonym, see DECREASE.

incredibility, *n.* unbelievableness, inconceivableness; absurdity, preposterousness. See DOUBT. *Ant.,* see BELIEF.

INCREDULITY

Nouns—**1,** incredulity, incredulousness, skepticism; want of faith (see IRRELIGION); DOUBT, distrust, suspicion, suspiciousness, scrupulosity, unbelief, disbelief; sophistication, ungullibility.

2, unbeliever, disbeliever, skeptic; infidel, heretic (see HETERODOXY).

Verbs—be incredulous, distrust, DOUBT, disbelieve, refuse to believe, reject (see REJECTION); shut one's ears *or* eyes to, turn a deaf ear to; hold aloof; ignore, dispute, question. *Colloq.*, not swallow.

Adjectives—incredulous, skeptical; sophisticated, ungullible; unbelieving, unconvinced; doubtful, dubious, distrustful, questioning, quizzical, disputing; hesitant, uncertain, suspicious, scrupulous, apprehensive, wary, chary, qualmish; faithless, heretical. *Slang,* leery, not born yesterday.

Antonym, see CREDULITY.

---

incriminate, *v.t.* blame, indict, inculpate; impeach, put under suspicion; implicate, entangle. *Slang,* put the finger on, frame, pin the rap on. See ACCUSATION, INCLUSION.

incur, *v.t.* acquire; become liable to risk; bring about. See LIABILITY.

incurable, *adj.* hopeless, doomed; irremediable, irreparable; unhealable. See DISEASE. *Ant.,* see REMEDY.

incursion, *n.* encroachment; inroad, invasion; attack, foray, raid. See DESCENT.

indebted, *adj.* obligated, beholden. See LIABILITY, DEBT, GRATITUDE.

indecent, *adj.* immoral, obscene, improper; salacious, lewd, lascivious, bawdy; immodest. See IMPURITY, UNCLEANNESS. *Ant.,* see PURITY, CLEANNESS.

indecision, *n.* irresolution, hesitation, uncertainty, vacillation, shilly-shally. See DOUBT. *Ant.,* see RESOLUTION, CERTAINTY.

indefinite, *adj.* unclear, undefined, blurred; vague, uncertain, unspecified; indeterminate; equivocal. See DOUBT. *Ant.,* see CERTAINTY.

indent, *v.t.* impress, hollow, dent, dint; NOTCH; knock in; set in; incise, cut; pit, dimple. See CONCAVITY.

independence, *n.* FREEDOM, liberty; self-reliance; self-government, autonomy; self-sufficiency; (enough) money. See FREEDOM, MONEY.

independent, *adj. & n.* —*adj.* absolute; free; self-governing, self-reliant; unconnected, separate (from), exclusive (of); well off, comfortable, well-to-do. See FREEDOM, WEALTH. —*n.* nonpartisan; free lance, lone wolf.

indestructible, *adj.* unbreakable, invulnerable. See STRENGTH, DURABILITY.

index, *n. & v.* —*n.* measure, scale, table, LIST; pointer, INDICATION. —*v.t.* tabulate, categorize, post; catalogue, register, ORDER.

INDICATION

Nouns—**1,** indication; symbolism, symbolization; denotation, connotation, signification; specification, designation; sign, symbol; index, indicator; point, pointer; exponent, note, token, symptom; MANIFESTATION; type, figure, emblem, cipher, device; REPRESENTATION; epigraph, motto; lineament, feature, trait, characteristic, earmark, peculiarity, PROPERTY; diagnosis; footprint, fingerprint; means of recognition.

2, gesture, gesticulation; pantomime; wink, glance, leer; nod, shrug, beck; touch, nudge; dactylology, sign language; cue, implication, suggestion, hint (see INFORMATION), clue, key; scent, track, spoor.

3, signal, rocket, blue light, watchfire, watchtower; telegraph, semaphore, flagstaff; cresset, fiery cross; calumet, white flag.

4, mark, line, stroke, dash, score, stripe, scratch, tick, dot, point, NOTCH, nick; asterisk, star, dagger; punctuation; period, comma, colon, semi-colon, interrogation point, question mark, exclamation point, quotation marks, dash, parentheses, brace, brackets; red letter, italics, sublineation, underlining, underscoring; accent, diacritical mark, acute, grave, circumflex, macron, dieresis, tilde.

5, identification, badge, caste mark; criterion; countercheck, countermark, countersign, counterfoil; tally, label, ticket, billet, letter, counter, card, bill; stamp; trademark, service mark, brand, hallmark; signature; autograph; credentials (see EVIDENCE); attestation; cipher; seal, signet; superscription, endorsement; title, heading, docket; shibboleth, watchword, catchword, password; open sesame; cachet; insignia, ensign; banner, flag, colors, streamer, standard, eagle, oriflamme, tricolor, Stars and Stripes; pennon, pennant, jack, ancient, gonfalon, union jack; bunting; heraldry; crest; arms, coat of arms; armorial bearings, hatchment, scutcheon, escutcheon; shield, supporters.

6, beacon, cairn, post, staff, flagstaff, hand, pointer, vane, cock, weathervane, guidepost, signpost; landmark, lighthouse; polestar, lodestar; address, direction, name; sign, signboard, milestone; traffic signal, traffic light, stoplight.

7, call, bugle, trumpet, bell, alarum, cry.

Verbs—**1,** indicate, denote, betoken, imply, argue, testify (see EVIDENCE); connote, designate, specify, manifest, reveal, disclose, exhibit; represent, stand for; typify, symbolize.

2, signal; warn, wigwag, semaphore, flag; beck, beckon; nod; wink, glance, leer, nudge, shrug, gesticulate.

3, wave; unfurl, hoist *or* hang out a banner; wave the hand; give a cue, show one's colors; give *or* sound an alarm; sound the tocsin, beat the drum; raise a (hue and) cry; siren, *etc.*

4, note, mark, stamp, earmark; label, ticket, docket; dot, spot, score, dash, trace, chalk; print.

Adjectives—indicating, indicative, indicatory; denotative; connotative; diacritical, representative, representational, significant, suggestive; typical, symbolic, symptomatic, characteristic, demonstrative, diagnostic, exponential, emblematic.

Adverbs—indicatively; in token of; symbolically.

Antonym, see CONCEALMENT.

---

indict, *v.i.* accuse *or* charge formally; arraign. See ACCUSATION.

INDIFFERENCE

Nouns—**1,** indifference, neutrality; coldness, frigidity; unconcern, insouciance, nonchalance; inattention, lack of interest, anorexia, apathy, INSENSIBILITY; supineness (see INACTIVITY); disdain (see CONTEMPT); recklessness, RASHNESS; carelessness, NEGLECT.

2, sameness, equivalence, EQUALITY.

Verbs—be indifferent, be neutral; take no interest in, have no desire for, have no taste for, have no relish for; not care for; care nothing for, care nothing about; not care a straw (see UNIMPORTANCE); not mind; set at naught, make light of; spurn, disdain (see CONTEMPT).

Adjectives—indifferent, neutral, cold, frigid, lukewarm; cool, cool as a cucumber; unconcerned, insouciant, phlegmatic, dispassionate, easygoing, devil-may-care, careless, listless, lackadaisical; half-hearted; unambitious, unaspiring, undesirous, unsolicitous, unattracted; unattractive, unalluring, undesired, undesirable, uncared for, unwished, unvalued; all one (to); insipid; vain.

Adverbs—indifferently; for aught one cares.

Interjections—never mind! who cares!

Antonym, see ATTENTION, DESIRE.

---

indigenous, *adj.* native; innate, inborn; inherent, natural (to). See INTRINSIC INHABITANT.

indigestion, *n.* dyspepsia, nausea; gastritis, heartburn, stomach ache, sour stomach, acidosis; flatulence; colic. See DISEASE.

indignation, *n.* RESENTMENT, ire, wrath, anger; displeasure, vexation.

indirect, *adj.* oblique; roundabout, circuitous; not straight; underhand, crooked, furtive; hinted, implied, inferential. See DEVIATION. *Ant.,* see DIRECTION.

indiscretion, *n.* carelessness, recklessness; blunder, *faux pas*, lapse, slip. See GUILT. *Ant.,* see CARE.

indiscriminate, *adj.* random, CHANCE; uncritical, injudicious. See IN-DIFFERENCE.

indispensable, *adj.* vital, needful, necessary; essential, required. See NECESSITY. *Ant.,* see USELESSNESS.

indistinct, *adj.* inaudible; imperceptible, unclear, foggy, blurry, shadowy; vague, obscure, dim; faint. See DIMNESS. *Ant.,* see VISION.

individual, *adj. & n.* —*adj.* particular, peculiar, special; specific; personal, proper. —*n.* person; personality; entity; somebody, anybody. See SPECIALITY.

individuality, *n.* UNCONFORMITY, differentness; distinctness; oneness; uniqueness; personality; peculiarity, originality; character. *Ant.,* see CONFORMITY.

indivisible, *adj.* one; inseparable, indissoluble. See UNITY, WHOLE.

indoctrinate, *v.t.* instruct, inculcate. *Colloq.,* brainwash. See TEACH-ING.

indolence, *n.* ease; sloth, idleness, sluggishness, laziness; INACTIVITY. *Ant.,* see ACTIVITY.

indomitable, *adj.* invincible, unconquerable, unbeatable. See STRENGTH.

indorse, *v.t.* approve, support, second; recommend; subscribe (to); sign. See APPROBATION, AGREEMENT. *Ant.,* see DISAPPROBATION.

induce, *v.t.* CAUSE, bring about; urge, persuade, impel influence; EFFECT. See MOTIVE. *Ant.,* see RESTRAINT.

induction, *n.* inauguration, installation (in office); inference, REASONING, conclusion; generalization.

indulge, *v.t.* pamper, spoil, favor, humor; gratify; take pleasure (in); revel. See PLEASURE. *Ant.,* see SEVERITY.

industrious, *adj.* active, busy, hard-working; diligent, assiduous, sedulous. See ACTIVITY.

industry, *n.* labor, work; occupation, trade, BUSINESS, ACTIVITY; diligence.

ineffective, *adj.* useless, vain, unavailing; impotent, impracticable, worthless; weak, inefficient. See WEAKNESS. *Ant.,* see POWER, USE.

ineffectual, *adj.* futile, unproductive, barren; INEFFECTIVE. See WEAK-NESS.

INELASTICITY

Nouns—inelasticity; flabbiness, limpness, flaccidity, laxity, SOFTNESS; inductibility, inflexibility, HARDNESS; inextensibility.

Adjectives—inelastic, unstretchable, inextensible; flabby, flaccid, limp, lax, soft; inductile, inflexible, irresilient, rigid, unyielding, unpliant.

antonym, see ELASTICITY.

INELEGANCE

Nouns—inelegance, gracelessness, harshness, tastelessness, VULGARITY; stiffness; barbarism. *Slang,* SOLECISM; mannerism, artificiality, AFFEC-TATION. See WORD.

Adjectives—inelegant, graceless, ungraceful; harsh, abrupt; dry, stiff, cramped, formal, forced, labored; artificial, mannered, ponderous; turgid, affected, euphuistic; barbarous, barbaric, uncouth, vulgar, gross, grotesque, rude, crude, halting.

Antonym, see ELEGANCE.

---

inept, *adj.* incompetent, unskilled, clumsy, all thumbs. See UNSKILL-FULNESS.

INEQUALITY

Nouns—inequality, disparity, odds, DIFFERENCE; unevenness; imbalance, partiality; SHORTCOMING; makeweight; SUPERIORITY; INFERIORITY.

Verbs—be unequal, countervail; tip the scale; kick the beam; topple (over); overmatch; not come up to; trim, trim ship.

Adjectives—unequal, uneven, disparate, partial; unbalanced, overbalanced; topheavy, lopsided; unequaled, matchless, peerless, unique, inimitable.

Antonym, see EQUALITY.

---

inertness, *n*. inertia, INACTIVITY, stillness, movelessness; laziness, sluggishness, torpor, lethargy, sloth, indolence; dullness, lifelessness, dispiritedness; passiveness, passivity. *Ant.*, see ACTIVITY.

inevitable, *adj*. inescapable, unavoidable, sure. See CERTAINTY. *Ant.*, see DOUBT.

inexact, *adj*. unprecise, incorrect, WRONG, erroneous; vague, loose, undefined, indefinite, unspecified. See ERROR, UNINTELLIGIBILITY.

INEXCITABILITY

Nouns—1, inexcitability, imperturbability (see *Adjectives*); even temper, tranquillity, dispassion; tolerance, patience; hebetude, hebetation; INSENSIBILITY; stupefaction.

2, coolness, calmness, composure, placidity, indisturbance, imperturbation, sangfroid, serenity; quiet, quietude; peace of mind.

3, staidness, GRAVITY, SOBRIETY, Quakerism; fortitude, stoicism; self-possession, self-control, self-command, self-restraint; presence of mind.

4, SUBMISSION, resignation; sufferance, endurance, long-sufferance, forbearance, tolerance, longanimity; fortitude; patience of Job, MODERATION; repression *or* subjugation of feeling; RESTRAINT; tranquilization.

Verbs—1, be composed, *laissez faire*, take things as they come; take it easy, live and let live; take in good part.

2, bear up; endure, brave, disregard, tolerate, suffer, stand, stand for, bide; bear with, put up with, abide with; acquiesce; submit, yield (see SUBMISSION); resign *or* reconcile oneself to; brook, swallow, pocket, stomach; make light of, make the best of, make a virtue of necessity; put a good face on, keep one's countenance. *Colloq.*, take lying down.

3, compose, appease, moderate; repress, restrain; master one's feelings; bite one's lips *or* tongue; calm *or* cool down. *Slang*, hold one's horses, keep one's shirt on.

Adjectives—1, inexcitable, unexcitable; imperturbable; unsusceptible, insensible; dispassionate, coldblooded, enduring, stoical, Platonic, philosophical, staid, sober-minded; nonchalant, coolheaded.

2, easygoing, peaceful, placid, calm; quiet, tranquil, serene; cool [as a cucumber], undemonstrative, temperate; composed, collected.

3, meek, tolerant; patient [as Job]; submissive (see SUBMISSION); tame; content, resigned, chastened, subdued, lamblike; gentle [as a lamb]; mild [as milk]; armed with patience, long-suffering.

Adverbs—inexcitably, *etc.*; in cold blood.

Antonym, see EXCITABILITY.

---

inexcusable, *adj*. unpardonable, unforgivable, unjustifiable. See ACCUSATION.

inexhaustible, *adj*. limitless, endless; unfailing. See SUFFICIENCY. *Ant.*, see INSUFFICIENCY.

INEXPEDIENCE

Nouns—inexpedience, inexpediency; undesirableness, undesirability; discommodity, impropriety, ineligibility, inaptitude; unfitness (see DISAGREEMENT); USELESSNESS, inconvenience; disadvantage, UNTIMELINESS.

Verbs—be inexpedient, come amiss; embarrass, hinder (see HINDRANCE); inconvenience.

Adjectives—inexpedient, undesirable; inadvisable, unappropriate; improper, objectionable; unapt, inconvenient, embarrassing, disadvantageous; unfit, inconstant; incommodious, discommodious; ill-contrived *or* -occasioned, unsatisfactory; inopportune, untimely, unseasonable; out of place, improper, unseemly, injudicious; clumsy, awkward; cumbrous, cumbersome; limbering, unwieldy, hulky; unmanageable, impracticable.

Antonym, see EXPEDIENCE.

---

inexperienced, *adj.* green, raw, untrained, fresh; naïve. See UNSKILL-FULNESS. *Ant.*, see SKILL.

inexpressible, *adj.* unutterable, ineffable, beyond words, indescribable. See GREATNESS.

infallible, *adj.* reliable, dependable, RIGHT; unfailing, unerring, unerrable, certain. See CERTAINTY. *Ant.*, see DOUBT, ERROR.

infamous, *adj.* shameful, abominable, disgraceful, unspeakable, contemptible; heinous, atrocious, base, discreditable. See IMPROBITY. *Ant.*, see PROBITY.

infancy, *n.* babyhood, childhood; BEGINNING, cradle, genesis. See YOUTH. *Ant.*, see AGE, OLDNESS.

infant, *n.* baby, babe, suckling, nursling, child; boy, girl; bairn, *enfant*, papoose; offspring, young; brat, tot, toddler. *Colloq.*, kid, kiddy, chick, *bambino*; pup, whelp, kitten, cub, foal, colt, lamb; big baby, thumbsucker, crybaby. *Slang*, mama's boy. See YOUTH. *Ant.*, see AGE.

infantry, *n.* soldiery, troops; foot soldiers. See COMBATANT.

infatuation, *n.* enamorment, fascination (by); passion; folly; gullibility; dotingness. See LOVE, CREDULITY.

infection, *n.* epidemic, contagion, plague, contamination; ILLNESS; taint, toxicity, gangrene, poisoning. See DISEASE.

infectious, *adj.* See CONTAGIOUS.

infer, *v.t.* gather, reason, deduce, conclude; presume; construe. See REASONING.

INFERIORITY

Nouns—**1,** inferiority, minority, subordinacy; SHORTCOMING, inadequacy, deficiency; minimum; smallness; IMPERFECTION; poorness, meanness; subservience.

2, inferior, subordinate, junior, underling; second fiddle. *Slang*, second-stringer; long shot.

Verbs—fall short of, not pass, not measure up to. *Colloq.*, take a back seat. See DECREASE.

Adjectives—inferior, smaller (see LITTLENESS); minor, junior, less, lesser, deficient, minus, lower, subordinate, secondary; second-rate, imperfect; short, inadequate, out of depth; subaltern; weighted in the balance and found wanting; not fit to hold a candle to. *Colloq.*, out of the picture.

Adverbs—below par; at the bottom of the scale; at a low ebb. *Colloq.*, not up to snuff.

Antonym, see SUPERIORITY.

---

infernal, *adj.* hellish, Plutonian, Stygian; fiendish, diabolical, demoniac(al). See EVIL. *Ant.*, see VIRTUE.

infest, *v.t.* overrun, invade; molest, torment. See PRESENCE, DISEASE.

infidelity, *n.* betrayal, treachery; faithlessness, fickleness; adultery; skepticism, unbelief. See IMPROBITY, IRRELIGION.

infiltrate, *v.* penetrate, pervade, permeate; enter, worm in, mix with, assimilate into. See INGRESS.

INFINITY

Nouns—infinity, infinitude, infiniteness; immensity, limitlessness, inexhaustibility, immeasurability, incalculability, illimitability, interminability; eternity, PERPETUITY, endlessness.

Verbs—be infinite, boundless, *etc.*; go on *or* endure forever; immortalize; have no bounds, limit *or* end.

Adjectives—infinite, immense; numberless, countless, sumless, measureless; innumerable, immeasurable, incalculable, illimitable, interminable, endless, unfathomable, bottomless, inexhaustible; indefinite; without number, without measure, limit *or* end; incomprehensible; limitless, boundless; untold, unnumbered, unmeasured, unbounded; perpetual, eternal.

Adverbs—infinitely, *etc.*; *ad infinitum*; perpetually.
Antonym, see LIMIT.

infirmity, *n.* fault; feebleness; illness. See IMPOTENCE, WEAKNESS, DISEASE.

inflame, *v.* anger, excite, arouse; incite, animate, kindle; HEAT, blaze up; provoke, irritate; redden, flush. See VIOLENCE.

inflammable, *adj.* burnable, combustible. See HEAT.

inflate, *v.t.* puff *or* blow up, aerate; expand, dilate, distend; exaggerate. See WIND, INCREASE, VANITY. *Ant.*, see CONTRACTION.

inflect, *v.* bend, turn, curve; modulate, vary; (*Gram.*) conjugate, decline. See CURVATURE, CHANGE, GRAMMAR. *Ant.*, see DIRECTION.

inflexible, *adj.* unbending, rigid, unyielding; firm, rocklike, steadfast; grim, stern. See HARDNESS, RESOLUTION. *Ant.*, see SOFTNESS, DOUBT.

inflict, *v.t.* burden *or* trouble with; impose, put upon; do (to); give (punishment, *etc.*). See SEVERITY.

infliction, *n.* SCOURGE, affliction; trouble; adversity; curse, disgrace; imposition; administering (to).

INFLUENCE

Nouns—**1,** influence; IMPORTANCE; weight, pressure, preponderance, prevalence, sway; predominance, predominancy; POWER, sway; ascendancy; dominance, hegemony, reign, control, AUTHORITY; capability; interest, bias, protection, patronage, auspices (see AID); footing; PURCHASE, SUPPORT; play, leverage, fulcrum, vantage point; intrigue. *Slang*, pull, drag.

2, influential person, patron, friend at court, power behind the throne.

Verbs—have influence, be influential; carry weight, weigh, tell; have a hold upon, sway, bias, pull the strings; bear upon, work upon; move, prompt, persuade, motivate (see MOTIVE); prevail, dominate, predominate; outweigh, overweigh; override, overbear; gain headway, rage, be rife; spread like wildfire; have, get *or* gain the upper hand; bring into line. *Colloq.*, have the inside track, have it all over. *Slang*, have an in, have in one's pocket.

Adjectives—influential; important (see IMPORTANCE); weighty; prevailing, prevalent, rife, rampant; dominant, regnant, predominant, ascendant.

Adverbs—influentially, with telling effect.

influx, *n.* inflow, INGRESS, infiltration; inroad, invasion, ARRIVAL; immigration. See FLUIDITY.

informal, *adj.* casual, free, easy, irregular; unofficial; unconventional, unceremonious. See UNCONFORMITY. *Ant.*, see CONFORMITY.

INFORMATION

Nouns—**1,** information, enlightenment, acquaintance, KNOWLEDGE; publicity (see PUBLICATION); COMMUNICATION, intimation; notice, notification; enunciation, annunciation; WORD, advice(s), announcement; REPRE-

SENTATION, presentment; case, estimate, specification, report, advice, monition; release, communiqué, dispatch; tidings, bulletin, news, intelligence; (news) flash, spot news; scoop, beat, exclusive (story), inside story *or* information; returns, RECORD; account, DESCRIPTION; statement, AFFIRMATION. *Slang*, info, dope, lowdown, inside story.

2, mention, acquainting; instruction, TEACHING; outpouring; intercommunication, communicativeness; hint, suggestion, innuendo, implication, allusion, inkling, whisper, passing word, word in the ear, subaudition, cue, byplay; gesture (see INDICATION); gentle *or* broad hint; word to the wise; insinuation. *Slang*, hot tip.

3, informant, authority, teller, spokesman, intelligencer, publisher, broadcaster, newscaster, reporter, exponent, mouthpiece; informer, talebearer, scandalmonger, eavesdropper, detective; spy, newsmonger, messenger (see COMMUNICATION); *amicus curiæ*; Sherlock Holmes; pilot, guide. *Colloq.*, squealer, stool pigeon, tipster, tattletale. *Slang*, snitcher, tout.

4, guidebook, handbook; manual; map, plan, chart, gazetteer; itinerary (see TRAVEL).

5, rumor, gossip, hearsay; scandal, titbit, canard; item, topic, talk of the town, common currency, byword, household word.

Verbs—**1,** inform, tell, acquaint, impart, make acquainted with, apprize, advise, enlighten, awaken; give a piece of one's mind, tell one plainly, speak volumes, open up; let fall, mention, express, intimate, represent, communicate, make known; publish (see PUBLICATION); notify, signify, specify, disclose (see DISCLOSURE); explain (see INTERPRETATION); undeceive, correct, disabuse, open the eyes of; let one know; give one to understand; give notice; point out; instruct, teach; direct the attention to (see ATTENTION). *Colloq.*, fill one in on, put wise.

2, announce, annunciate, report; bring, send, leave *or* give word; retail, render *or* give an account (see DESCRIPTION); state, affirm (see AFFIRMATION).

3, hint, give an inkling of, imply, insinuate, intimate; allude to, suggest, prompt, give the cue, breathe; get to; whisper; inform on, betray, turn state's evidence. *Colloq.*, tip off; put a flea in one's ear; tell on, squeal, tattle, rat, doublecross; let in on, spill, spill the beans, let the cat out of the bag.

4, be informed, know (see KNOWLEDGE); learn, receive news, get wind *or* scent of; gather (from); awaken to, open one's eyes to; become alive *or* awake to; hear, overhear, find out, understand; come to one's ears, come to one's knowledge, reach one's ears. *Colloq.*, catch on. *Slang*, get wise to, wise up.

Adjectives—informative, informed, informational, reported, published; expressive, explicit, open, clear, plainspoken; declaratory, expository; enunciative, communicative, communicatory; knowledgeable.

Antonym, see CONCEALMENT.

---

infrequency, *n.* rareness, rarity; fewness; seldomness, uncommonness, unusualness; scarceness, oddness. *Ant.*, see FREQUENCY.

infringement, *n.* trespass, encroachment; infraction, breach; plagiarism, violation (of copyright, patent, *etc.*). See ILLEGALITY. *Ant.*, see LEGALITY.

infuriate, *v.t.* enrage, anger, madden, incense; incite, provoke, nettle, peeve, rankle. *Colloq.*, rile, make one's blood boil. See RESENTMENT.

infuse, *v.t.* steep, soak; introduce, implant, instill; tinge, imbue; pour into, mix in. See MIXTURE.

ingenuity, *n.* SKILL; cleverness; inventiveness; originality. See IMAGINATION.

ingenuous, *adj.* artless, naïve, simple; candid, frank, open; trusting, unsuspecting. See SIMPLENESS.

ingratiating, *adj.* charming, winsome, winning, captivating; pleasing, attractive. See COURTESY.

INGRATITUDE

Nouns—1, ingratitude, ungratefulness, thanklessness.
2, ingrate, a serpent in one's bosom.
Verbs—look a gift horse in the mouth; bite the hand that feeds one.
Adjectives—ungrateful, unmindful, unthankful; thankless, ingrate, wanting in gratitude; forgotten, unacknowledged, unthanked, unrequited, unrewarded; ill-requited.
Antonym, see GRATITUDE.

ingredient, *n.* COMPONENT, PART, element, constituent.

INGRESS

Nouns—1, ingress; entrance, entry, entrée; introgression; influx; intrusion, inroad, incursion, invasion; irruption; penetration, interpenetration; import, infiltration; immigration; access, admission, admittance, reception; insinuation (see BETWEEN); INSERTION; inlet; way in; mouth, door, OPENING, path, way; conduit, channel; immigration.
2, incomer, immigrant, colonist; entrant; newcomer; fifth column.
Verbs—enter; go in, come in, pour in, flow in, creep in, slip in, pop in, break in, burst in; gain entrée; set foot on; burst *or* break in upon; invade, intrude; insinuate itself; penetrate, interpenetrate; infiltrate; find one's way into, wriggle into, worm oneself into; trespass; give entrance to, receive, insert; bore from within.
Adjectives—ingressive; incoming, ingoing, inward; entrant.
Antonym, see EGRESS.

INHABITANT

Nouns—1, inhabitant, habitant; resident, dweller, indweller; occupier, occupant; householder, boarder, renter, lodger, tenant; inmate; incumbent, sojourner, *locum tenens*, settler, colonist, squatter, nester; backwoodsman, islander; denizen, citizen; burgher, townsman, burgess; villager, cottager; aborigine; compatriot, fellow citizen. *Slang*, city slicker, sooner; hick, hayseed, rube.
2, native, indigene, aborigine; newcomer.
3, population, POPULACE, public, people (see MANKIND); colony, settlement, household; garrison, crew.
Verbs—inhabit, be present (see PRESENCE); dwell, reside, sojourn, occupy, lodge; settle; squat; colonize; billet.
Adjectives—indigenous; native, natal; aboriginal, primitive; domestic, domiciled, naturalized, vernacular, domesticated; domiciliary.
Antonym, see RELATION.

inhale, *v.* breathe; breathe in. See WIND.
inherent, *adj.* native, innate; INTRINSIC, essential.
inherit, *v.t.* succeed (to); get, acquire, receive; possess. See ACQUISITION.
inhibit, *v.* circumscribe, restrain; hamper, check, cramp; repress, suppress. See RESTRAINT. *Ant.*, see FREEDOM.
inhuman, *adj.* cruel, barbarous, bestial, brutal, sadistic, savage. See MALEVOLENCE, EVIL. *Ant.*, see BENEVOLENCE.
iniquity, *n.* vice, immorality; sin, wickedness, transgression, crime, wrongdoing; INJUSTICE.
initial, *adj. & n.* —*adj.* first, BEGINNING, introductory, primary. *Ant.*, see END. —*n.* letter, monogram.
initiate, *v.t.* admit, introduce, take in (a member); start, commence, inaugurate, institute. See BEGINNING. *Ant.*, see END.
inject, *v.t.* insert, introduce; wedge in, force in; inoculate; intersperse, interject. See BETWEEN.
injunction, *n.* COMMAND, order, admonition; direction; REQUIREMENT.
injure, *v.t.* wound, hurt; damage, abuse, deface, mar, impair; WRONG,

disgrace, dishonor; insult; mistreat; maltreat. See DETERIORATION, EVIL, MALEVOLENCE. *Ant.*, see IMPROVEMENT.

INJUSTICE

Nouns—injustice, unjustness, unfairness, bias, partiality, prejudice, inequity, inequitableness; favoritism, nepotism, partisanship. See IMPROBITY, ILLEGALITY, WRONG.

Verbs—**1,** be unjust, do injustice to, be unfair, be inequitable, favor, show partiality.

2, lynch, railroad, frame.

Adjectives—unjust, unfair, partial, prejudiced, inequitable, partisan, nepotistic, biased, one-sided.

Antonym, see JUSTICE.

---

inkling, *n.* clue, suggestion, hint; whisper; surmise. See INFORMATION.

inlet, *n.* creek, cove; entrance, INGRESS; channel. *Ant.*, see EGRESS.

inmate, *n.* prisoner, détenu; tenant, occupant. See INHABITANT, PRISON.

inn, *n.* hotel, hostelry; tavern, bar and grill. See ABODE.

innate, *adj.* natural, inborn; inherent; congenital. See INTRINSIC.

inner, *adj.* inward, internal, INTERIOR, inside. *Ant.*, see EXTERIOR.

innkeeper, *n.* host, hostess; taverner, tavernkeeper; landlord; hotelier, Boniface. See PROVISION.

INNOCENCE

Nouns—**1,** innocence, guiltlessness, blamelessness, incorruption, impeccability; PURITY, VIRTUE, virginity, chastity; artlessness, naïveté, SIMPLENESS; immaculacy, CLEANNESS.

2, innocent, child, lamb, dove, saint, newborn babe; virgin, maid.

Verbs—be innocent, have a clear conscience; exonerate, acquit (see ACQUITTAL); exculpate (see VINDICATION.) *Colloq.*, whitewash.

Adjectives—innocent, not guilty; unguilty; guiltless, faultless, sinless, stainless, bloodless, spotless, *sans peur et sans reproche*; clean, immaculate; unspotted, unblemished, unerring; unsullied, undefiled (see PROBITY); unravished, virginal, pure, white as snow, virtuous; unhardened, Saturnian; Arcadian, artless, naïve, simple, unsophisticated; inculpable, unculpable; unblamed, unblamable, blameless, above suspicion; irreproachable, irreprovable, irreprehensible; unexceptionable, unobjectionable, unimpeachable; salvable; venial; harmless, inoffensive, innocuous; dovelike, lamblike; innocent as a lamb, saint, child, babe unborn, *etc.*; more sinned against than sinning, unreproved, unimpeached. *Colloq.*, in the clear.

Adverbs—innocently, *etc.*; with clean hands; with a clear conscience.

Antonym, see GUILT.

---

innocuous, *adj.* harmless, mild, inoffensive; innocent. See HEALTH. *Ant.*, see DETERIORATION.

innovation, *n.* CHANGE, alteration; NEWNESS, novelty; variation; departure.

innuendo, *n.* hint, implication, intimation, allusion. See SUPPOSITION.

innumerable, *adj.* countless, uncountable; myriad, numberless. See INFINITE. *Ant.*, see LIMIT.

inoculate, *v.t.* vaccinate; variolate; immunize; infect. See REMEDY.

inoffensive, *adj.* innocuous, harmless, unaggressive; blameless. See INNOCENCE.

inopportune, *adj.* unseasonable, untimely, ill-timed; inconvenient, awkward. See UNTIMELINESS. *Ant.*, see OCCASION.

input, *n.* INFORMATION, KNOWLEDGE; contribution. *Colloq.*, two cents.

INQUIRY

Nouns—**1,** inquiry, enquiry; question, REQUEST; search, research, quest; PURSUIT; examination, test, intelligence test; review, scrutiny, investigation, inspection, probe; trial, hearing; inquest, inquisition; exploration, exploitation, ventilation; sifting, calculation, analysis, dissection; resolution; induction; Baconian method; autopsy, *post mortem*; strict inquiry, close inquiry, searching inquiry, exhaustive inquiry; narrow search, strict search; study, CONSIDERATION. *Colloq.*, exam.

2, questioning, interrogation, interrogatory; interpellation; challenge, examination, cross-examination, catechism; feeler, Socratic method, leading question; discussion (see REASONING); reconnoitering, reconnaissance; prying, espionage. *Colloq.*, grilling, third degree.

3, question, query, problem, proposition, *desideratum*, point to be solved, subject of inquiry, field of inquiry, subject of controversy; point *or* matter in dispute; moot point; issue, question at issue; bone of contention (see DISCORD); fair question, open question; questionnaire; enigma (see SECRET); knotty point (see DIFFICULTY).

4, inquirer, investigator, inquisitor, inspector, querist, examiner, prober, cross-examiner; spy; detective, operative; catechist; analyst; quidnunc (see CURIOSITY). *Colloq.*, private eye, op. *Slang*, shamus.

Verbs—**1,** inquire, seek, search; look for, look about for, look out for; scan, reconnoiter, explore, sound, rummage, ransack, pry, peer, look round; look *or* go through *or* over; spy; peer *or* pry into every hole and corner; trace; ferret out; unearth; leave no stone unturned; seek a clue, hunt, track, trail, hound; follow the trail *or* scent; pursue (see PURSUIT); thresh out; fish for; feel *or* grope for.

2, investigate; follow up; look at, look into; preexamine; discuss, canvass, agitate; examine, study, consider, calculate; delve into, probe, sound, fathom; scrutinize, analyze, anatomize, dissect, sift, winnow; audit, review; take into consideration (see THOUGHT); take counsel (see ADVICE). *Colloq.*, kick around.

3, ask, question, demand; ventilate; grapple with *or* go into a question; interrogate, catechize, pump, cross-question, cross-examine; pick the brains of; feel out. *Colloq.*, give the third degree.

Adjectives—inquiring, inquisitive, curious; catechetical, inquisitorial, analytic; in search of, in quest of; on the lookout for, interrogative; in question, in dispute, in issue, under discussion, under consideration, under investigation; *sub judice*, moot, proposed; doubtful (see DOUBT).

Adverbs—what? why? wherefore? whence? whither? where? how goes it? how is it? what is the reason? what's the matter? what's in the wind? what on earth? when? who? *Colloq.*, how come? what's up? what's new?

Antonym, see ANSWER.

---

inquisition, *n.* examination, questioning; tribunal (Spanish Inquisition); cross-examination; probe, investigation; INQUIRY. *Colloq.*, third degree, brainwashing. See SEVERITY, MALEVOLENCE.

inquisitive, *adj.* questioning; curious, prying, meddlesome, busybodyish. See CURIOSITY.

INSANITY

Nouns—**1,** insanity, lunacy, derangement, craziness, feeblemindedness; psychosis, psychopathy, schizophrenia, split personality, paranoia, *dementia praecox*, neurosis; madness, mental illness, abnormality, aberration; dementia, frenzy, raving, delirium, hallucination; lycanthropy; rabies, hydrophobia; disordered reason *or* intellect; diseased, unsound *or* abnormal mind; anility, senility, dotage.

2, vertigo, dizziness, swimming; sunstroke, moon-madness.

3, fanaticism, infatuation, craze; oddity, idiosyncrasy; eccentricity, twist, quirk.

4, mania; monomania, megalomania, nymphomania, bibliomania, pyromania, logomania, Theomania, kleptomania, dipsomania, Anglomania; delirium tremens; hypochondriasis (see DEJECTION); melancholia, hysteria; phobia (see FEAR).

5, MADMAN, idiot, imbecile, cretin, moron, lunatic. *Slang*, nut, loon.

6, insane asylum, sanitarium, sanatorium, mental hospital *or* institution, bedlam, madhouse. *Slang*, nuthouse, booby hatch, bughouse, loony bin.

7, psychiatrist, alienist (see INTELLECT). *Colloq.*, shrink, head doctor.

Verbs—**1,** be insane, be out of one's mind; lose one's senses *or* reason; lose one's faculties *or* wits; go mad, run mad *or* amuck, rave, rant, dote, ramble, wander; drivel; take leave of one's senses; lose one's head. *Slang*, have a screw loose, have bats in the belfry, not have all one's marbles *or* buttons; go off one's nut *or* rocker; see things; flip (one's lid), flip *or* freak out.

2, render insane, drive mad *or* crazy, madden, dement, addle the wits of, derange; infatuate, obsess, turn the brain, turn one's head.

Adjectives—**1,** insane, mad, lunatic; crazy, crazed, *non compos mentis*; unhinged, unbalanced, psychopathic, psychotic, psychoneurotic, manic-depressive; not right, cracked, touched; bereft of reason; unhinged, unsettled in one's mind; insensate, reasonless, beside oneself, demented, daft; frenzied, frenetic; possessed, possessed of a devil; far gone, maddened, moonstruck; scatterbrained, crackbrained, off one's head; maniacal; delirious, irrational, lightheaded, incoherent, rambling, doting, wandering; amuck, frantic, raving, stark mad, staring mad. *Slang*, crazy as a bedbug, loco, dotty, psycho, nutty, screwy, wacky, bananas, off the wall, freaky, bonkers; tetched, pixilated, bughouse; mental (*Brit.*).

2, rabid, giddy, vertiginous, wild; mazed, flighty; distracted, distraught; mad as a hatter *or* March hare; of unsound mind; touched (in one's head), not in one's right mind; out of one's mind, senses *or* wits; on the ragged edge. *Slang*, off one's nut.

3, fanatical, obsessed, infatuated, odd, eccentric; hipped; hypochondriac; imbecile, silly.

4, monomaniacal, kleptomaniacal, *etc.*

Adverbs—insanely; like one possessed; maniacally, *etc.*

Antonym, see SANITY.

---

insatiable, *adj.* greedy, voracious; unappeasable, quenchless, unquenchable. See DESIRE. *Ant.*, see SUFFICIENCY.

inscribe, *v.t.* write; mark, engrave; enter, enroll, LIST. See WRITING.

insect, *n.* bug; fly, moth, butterfly, beetle, ant, *etc.* See ANIMAL.

insecurity, *n.* DANGER, UNCERTAINTY, risk, hazard, jeopardy.

INSENSIBILITY

Nouns—**1,** insensibility, insensibleness; moral insensibility; inertness, inertia, impassibility, impassibleness, impassivity; inappetency, apathy, phlegm, dullness, hebetude, supineness, lukewarmness.

2, coldness, cold fit, cold blood, cold heart; frigidity, *sangfroid*; stoicism, imperturbability, inexcitability; nonchalance, unconcern, dry eyes; insouciance, indifference; recklessness, RASHNESS, callousness; heart of stone, marble, deadness; thickness of skin.

3, torpor, torpidity, lethargy, coma, trance; SLEEP, vegetation, suspended animation; stupor, stupefaction; paralysis, palsy.

4, numbness; unfeeling, anesthesia, analgesia, narcosis.

5, anesthetic, ether, chloroform, nitrous oxide, opium; refrigeration.

Verbs—**1,** be insensible, become insensible, black out, draw a blank; have a rhinocerous hide; show insensibility, not mind, not care, not be affected by; have no desire for, have, feel, *or* take no interest in; not care a straw (see INDIFFERENCE); disregard (see NEGLECT); set at naught; turn a deaf ear to; vegetate.

2, render insensible *or* callous; blunt, obtund, numb, benumb, paralyze, chloroform, deaden, hebetate, stun, stupefy; inure, harden, harden the heart; steel, caseharden, sear.

Adjectives—**1,** insensible, unconscious; impassive, impassible; dispassionate; blind to, deaf to, dead to; unsusceptible, insusceptible; unimpressionable, passionless, spiritless, heartless, soulless; unfeeling, indifferent, lukewarm, careless, regardless; inattentive, neglectful.

2, callous, thickskinned, pachydermatous, impervious; hard, hardened, inured, casehardened; steeled against; proof against; imperturbable, inexcitable, unfelt; unconcerned, nonchalant, insouciant, *sans souci.*

3, unambitious; unaffected, unruffled, unimpressed, uninspired, unexcited, unmoved, unstirred, untouched, unshocked, unstruck; unblushing, shameless; unanimated, vegetative; apathetic, phlegmatic; dull, frigid; cold, coldblooded, coldhearted; cold as charity; flat, obtuse, inert, supine, languid, half-hearted; numb, numbed; comatose; anesthetic, stupefied, chloroformed; dead, deadened; narcotic.

Adverbs—insensibly, *etc.*; in cold blood; with dry eyes.

Antonym, see SENSIBILITY.

INSERTION

Nouns—insertion, inset, inlay; injection, inoculation (see *Verbs*); ADDITION; INTERMENT; entering wedge (see INGRESS); penetration.

Verbs—insert, inset, inlay; put, press, pack *or* stuff in; inject, inoculate; introduce, insinuate, impregnate, implant, graft, bud; intervene (see BETWEEN); infuse, instill; add; bury, inter; immerse, submerge; pierce (see OPENING).

Antonym, see EXTRACTION.

insight, *n.* discernment, perceptiveness, perception; INTUITION; penetration, understanding. See KNOWLEDGE.

insignia, *n.pl.* badges (of office), emblems. See INDICATION.

insignificance, *n.* meaninglessness; inconsequentiality, UNIMPORTANCE, triviality, smallness, worthlessness. See CHEAPNESS. *Ant.*, see IMPORTANCE, MEANING.

insincere, *adj.* false, deceptive; hypocritical, two-faced; half-hearted; untrue; affected. See DECEPTION, AFFECTATION. *Ant.*, see TRUTH, FEELING.

insinuate, *v.t.* hint, suggest, intimate; ingratiate (oneself), curry favor; insert, instill, introduce (stealthily). See INFORMATION, STEALING.

INSIPIDITY

Nouns—insipidity, vapidity; tastelessness, WEAKNESS (see *Adjectives*); DULLNESS, MEDIOCRITY, INDIFFERENCE.

Adjectives—**1,** insipid, tasteless, flavorless, savorless, gustless, unseasoned, zestless; weak, stale, flat, mild, bland; mild-and-water, watery. **2,** uninteresting, unentertaining, prosaic, prosy, monotonous, jejune, boring, stupid, insulse, tame, dull, dry; vapid, flat, banal; mawkish, wishy-washy; spiritless, lacklustrous, pointless, lifeless, amort, dead.

Antonym, see TASTE.

insist, *v.i.* state (firmly, repeatedly), maintain, hold to; persist; urge, press; demand (strongly). See AFFIRMATION, COMPULSION.

insnare, ensnare, *v.t.* trap, entrap; capture, catch; entangle, ensnarl, entoil; bait, decoy. See DECEPTION.

INSOLENCE

Nouns—**1,** insolence, arrogance; haughtiness, airs; overbearance; presumption, pomposity, snobbery; domineering, tyranny, terrorism (see SEVERITY); DEFIANCE.

2, impertinence, sauciness, flippancy, petulance, bluster; swagger, swaggering, bounce; impudence, assurance, audacity; hardihood, front, shamelessness, effrontery, PRIDE, VANITY. *Colloq.*, brass, cheek, face, nerve, sauce, sass; smart aleck. *Slang*, gall, crust, lip; wise guy.

Verbs—**1,** be insolent, bluster, vapor, swagger, swell, give oneself airs, snap one's fingers; swear (see AFFIRMATION); roister; arrogate; assume, presume; make bold, make free; take a liberty, patronize. *Slang*, have a nerve.

2, domineer, bully, dictate, hector; lord it over; exact; snub, huff, beard, fly in the face of; bear down, beat down; browbeat, intimidate; trample down *or* under foot; dragoon, ride roughshod over. *Slang,* upstage.

3, outface, outlook, outstare, outbrazen, outbrave; stare out of countenance; brazen out; lay down the law; talk big, act big; talk back, get on a high horse; toss the head, carry with a high hand; overreach.

Adjectives—**1,** insolent, haughty, arrogant, imperious, dictatorial, arbitrary; highhanded, high and mighty; contumelious, supercilious, snobbish, overbearing, intolerant, domineering, overweening, high-flown. *Colloq.,* stuck-up; cocky, uppity. *Slang,* high-hat, fresh, nervy, flip.

2, flippant, pert, cavalier, saucy, sassy, forward, impertinent, malapert; precocious, assuming, would-be, bumptious; bluff; brazen, shameless, aweless, unblushing, unabashed; boldfaced, barefaced, brazenfaced; impudent, audacious, presumptuous, free and easy; roistering, blustering, hectoring, swaggering, vaporing.

Adverbs—insolently, *etc.*; with a high hand; where angels fear to tread.
Antonym, see SERVILITY.

---

insolvency, *n.* FAILURE, bankruptcy; lack of funds. See DEBT. *Ant.,* see PAYMENT, MONEY.

insomnia, *n.* sleeplessness; chronic wakefulness. See ACTIVITY. *Ant.,* see REPOSE.

inspect, *v.t.* examine, scrutinize; check, check up; oversee; investigate, look into. See ATTENTION, VISION.

inspire, *v.* breathe, breathe in; stimulate, animate, liven, enliven; spur, give an incentive. See EXCITEMENT.

inspiration, *n.* breathing; inhalation; happy thought. *Colloq.,* brainstorm; creative impulse. See REVELATION, TRUTH.

instability, *n.* CHANGEABLENESS, unsteadiness; unsoundness; inconstancy, undependableness. *Ant.,* see STABILITY, PROBITY, FREQUENCY.

install, *v.t.* put in, set up; induct, inaugurate, invest. See LOCATION, CELEBRATION.

installment, *n.* down payment, time payment; episode, PART (of a series); installation, setting up *or* putting in. See LOCATION.

instance, *n.* example, illustration, demonstration. See CONFORMITY.

instant, *adj. & n.* —*adj.* prepared instantly; sudden, immediate, direct, instantaneous; lightninglike. See INSTANTANEITY. —*n.* second, moment; minute; twinkling, jiffy.

INSTANTANEITY

Nouns—**1,** instantaneity, instantaneousness, immediacy, precipitancy, suddenness, abruptness; moment, instant, second, minute; twinkling, trice, flash, breath, crack, burst, flash of lightning.

2, epoch, time; time of day *or* night; hour, minute; very minute, very time, very hour; present time, right, true, exact *or* correct time. *Colloq.,* jiffy. *Slang,* half a shake, sec.

Adjectives—instantaneous, momentary, sudden, instant, abrupt; extemporaneous; precipitate, immediate, hasty; quick as thought, quick as lightning.

Adverbs—instantaneously, instantly, immediately, now, right now, in less than no time; presto, *subito,* instanter, suddenly, at a stroke, at a word, at the drop of a hat; in a moment, in the twinkling of an eye, at one jump, in the same breath, at once, all at once; plump, slap; at one fell swoop; at the same instant; immediately, *ex tempore,* on the spot, on the spur of the moment; just then; slapdash. *Colloq.,* in a jiffy, like a shot, yesterday, in nothing flat, in two shakes. *Slang,* like a bat out of hell.
Antonym, see LATENESS.

---

instead, *adv.* in place, in lieu (of); substituting for. See SUBSTITUTION.

instigate, *v.t.* incite, provoke; initiate; stimulate, urge, promote. See CAUSE.

instill, *v.t.* inculcate; implant, impart; pour in, mix in, infuse. See MIXTURE, TEACHING.

instinct, *n.* TENDENCY; knack, IMPULSE, prompting, discernment; INTUITION.

institute, *v.t. & n.* —*v.t.* found, inaugurate; organize, start, begin, commence; originate, organize. See BEGINNING. —*n.* institution; SCHOOL, college; foundation; society; museum; hospital, *etc.*

instruction, *n.* TEACHING, tutelage, education; training, coaching; COMMAND, ORDER, direction, directive; ADVICE.

instrument, *n.* utensil, implement, tool, device, contrivance; hammer, saw, lever, key, knife, *etc.*; MEANS, AGENCY; appliance, apparatus; representative; MUSICAL INSTRUMENT; machine, mechanism, motor, engine; document, deed, paper, RECORD, charter; speedometer, thermometer; controls, gauges (of a plane *or* vehicle), *etc.*

instrumentalist, *n.* player, MUSICIAN; pianist, violinist, cellist, *etc.*

INSTRUMENTALITY

Nouns—**1,** instrumentality; instrument, AID; subservience, subserviency; MEDIATION, intervention, medium, intermedium, vehicle, hand; AGENCY; expedient (see PLAN); MEANS. See MUSICAL INSTRUMENT.

2, AGENT, minister, handmaiden, servant, slave; midwife, *accoucheur,* obstetrician; go-between; robot, cat's-paw; stepping-stone; key, master key, skeleton key, passkey, latchkey; open sesame; passport, *passepartout,* safeconduct, pass. *Slang,* Annie Oakley.

3, instrument, tool, device, implement, appliance, apparatus, contrivance, machine; hammer, chisel, plane, saw, screw, nail, screwdriver, knife, rasp, file; lever, crowbar, pry, prize, jimmy, jack; motor, engine, treadle, pedal; gear, paraphernalia, machinery; pulley, block and tackle, crane, derrick; belt, conveyor belt; wheels, gears, cam, clockwork, cog flywheel; can opener, scissors, shears, lawnmower, *etc.*

Verbs—be instrumental; subserve, minister, mediate, intervene; officiate.

Adjectives—instrumental; useful (see UTILITY); ministerial, subservient, mediatorial; intermediate, intervening.

Adverbs—instrumentally; through, by, per; whereby, thereby, hereby; by the agency of; by dint *or* means of; by virtue of; through the medium of; along with; by *or* with the aid of, by fair means or foul; somehow or other, anyhow, somehow; by hook or crook. *Colloq.,* come Hell or high water.

---

insubordinate, *adj.* disobedient, intractable; mutinous, insurgent; stubborn, obstinate. *Colloq.,* too big for one's britches. See DISOBEDIENCE, DISRESPECT.

INSUBSTANTIALITY

Nouns—**1,** insubstantiality, unsubstantiality; nothingness, nihility; nothing, naught, nil, nullity, zero, cipher, no one, nobody; never a one; no such thing, none in the world; nothing whatever, nothing at all, nothing on earth; not a particle (see LITTLENESS); all talk, moonshine, stuff and nonsense; shadow; phantom; dream (see IMAGINATION); *ignis fatuus;* air, thin air; bubble; mockery; hollowness, blank; void (see ABSENCE); inanity, fool's paradise.

2, nobody, puppet, dummy, man of straw, John Doe and Richard Roe; cipher, nonentity; flash in the pan.

3, immateriality, immaterialness; incorporeality, disembodiment; spirit, soul, ego; spiritualism, spirituality.

Verbs—be insubstantial; vanish, evaporate, fade, dissolve, melt away; disappear, vanish; immaterialize, dematerialize; disembody, spiritualize.

Adjectives—insubstantial, unsubstantial; baseless, groundless; unfounded, ungrounded; bodiless, incorporeal, spiritual, immaterial, unearthly;

psychical, supernatural; visionary, imaginary (see IMAGINATION);
dreamy; shadowy, ethereal, airy, spectral; vacant, vacuous; empty (see
ABSENCE); blank, hollow; nominal; null; inane.
Antonym, see SUBSTANCE.

insufferable, *adj.* abominable, unspeakable, incorrigible; unendurable,
unbearable, insupportable; agonizing, excruciating. See PAIN.

INSUFFICIENCY

Nouns—**1,** insufficiency; inadequacy, inadequateness; incompetence, IM-
POTENCE; deficiency, incompleteness, IMPERFECTION, SHORTCOMING,
emptiness, poorness, depletion, vacancy, flaccidity; ebb tide; low water;
bankruptcy, insolvency (see DEBT).
2, paucity; stint; scantiness, smallness; none to spare; bare necessities;
scarcity, dearth; want, need, deprivation, lack, POVERTY, destitution, indigence, exigency; inanition, starvation, famine, drought; dole, pittance;
short allowance *or* rations, half-rations.
Verbs—**1,** be insufficient, not suffice, fall short of (see FAILURE); run dry;
want, lack, need, require; be in want, live from hand to mouth.
2, render insufficient, exhaust, deplete, drain of resources; impoverish
(see WASTE); stint, begrudge (see PARSIMONY); cut back, retrench;
bleed white.
Adjectives—**1,** insufficient, inadequate; too little (see LITTLENESS); not
enough; unequal to; incompetent, impotent (see IMPOTENCE); weighed
in the balance and found wanting; perfunctory (see NEGLECT); deficient;
wanting, imperfect; ill-furnished, ill-provided, ill-stored, badly off.
2, slack, at a low ebb; empty, vacant, bare; short (of), out of, destitute
(of), devoid (of), denuded (of); dry, drained; not to be had for love
or money, not to be had at any price; empty-handed.
3, meager, poor, thin, sparing, spare, stinted; starved, half-starved,
famine-stricken, famished; jejune; scant, small, scarce; scurvy, stingy;
at the end of one's tether; without resources (see MEANS); in want,
poor (see POVERTY); in debt (see DEBT). *Colloq.*, skimpy. *Slang*, shy
of, fresh out of.
Adverbs—insufficiently, *etc.*; in default, for want of; failing.
Antonym, see SUFFICIENCY.

insular, *adj.* isolated; islanded, insulated; aloof; narrow, limited, illiberal;
isolationist. See NARROWNESS.
insulate, *v.t.* cover, protect, shield; set apart, isolate, detach. See
COVERING, DISJUNCTION. *Ant.*, see JUNCTION.
insult, *n. & v.* —*v.* slap, abuse, affront, offend. See DISCOURTESY. *Ant.*,
see COURTESY. —*n.* outrage; slap, affront, sauce, cheek, impudence.
insurance, *n.* guarantee, guaranty, warranty, coverage, protection; insurance policy (fire, life, auto, burglary, *etc.*); assurance, SECURITY.
insurgent, *adj. & n.* —*adj.* rebellious, insubordinate, mutinous, in revolt,
uprising. See DISOBEDIENCE. *Ant.*, see OBEDIENCE. —*n.* rebel, insubordinate, mutineer, revolutionist, insurrectionist. See OPPOSITION.
insurrection, *n.* uprising, riot, eruption; mutiny, REVOLUTION, insurgence.
intact, *adj.* whole, unimpaired, uninjured; untouched. See COMPLETION.
Ant., see DETERIORATION.
intake, *n.* consumption, ingestion, assimilation. See RECEIVING.
intangible, *adj.* immaterial, vague, impalpable; untouchable; unspecific;
not concrete, abstract. See INSUBSTANTIALITY.
integrate, *v.t.* unite, fuse; synthesize, blend; complete. See COMBINA-
TION.
integrity, *n.* honor, PROBITY, uprightness; wholeness, completeness, oneness. See WHOLE. *Ant.*, see IMPROBITY.

INTELLECT

Nouns—**1,** intellect, intellectuality, mentality, brain, brains, mind, understanding, reason (see REASONING), rationality; faculties, senses, consciousness, observation, percipience, perception, apperception, perspicuity, grasp, intelligence, INTUITION, association of ideas, instinct, conception, JUDGMENT, wits, mental capacity, genius; WIT, ability, SKILL, WISDOM; logic, THOUGHT, meditation.
2, soul, spirit, ghost, inner man, heart, breast, bosom; seat of thought; sensory, brain; head, cerebrum, cranium; gray matter. *Slang,* upper story, noodle.
3, psychology, psychopathology, psychotherapy, psychiatry, psychoanalysis, psychometry; ideology; philosophy; phrenology, craniology, cranioscopy; ideality, idealism; transcendentalism, spiritualism, immateriality; THOUGHT.
4, psychologist, psychopathologist, alienist, psychiatrist, psychometrist, psychotherapist, psychoanalyst, analyst.
Verbs—intellectualize (see THOUGHT); note, notice, mark; take notice, take cognizance; be aware, be conscious; realize; appreciate; ruminate (see THOUGHT); fancy, imagine (see IMAGINATION).
Adjectives—intellectual, mental, rational, subjective, metaphysical, spiritual, ghostly; psychical, psychological; cerebral; percipient, aware, conscious; subconscious; immaterial; logical, reasoning, reasonable; thoughtful, thinking, meditative, contemplative.
Antonym, see INSANITY.

INTELLIGENCE

Nouns—intelligence, capacity, comprehension, apprehension, understanding; INTELLECT; parts, sagacity, mother wit, wit, *esprit,* intelligence quotient, I.Q., acuteness, shrewdness; acumen, subtlety, penetration; perspicacy, perspicuity, perspicacity, percipience; discernment, good judgment; levelheadedness, DISCRIMINATION; CUNNING; refinement (see TASTE); KNOWLEDGE; head, brains, mind; eagle eye; genius, inspiration, soul; talent, aptitude (see SKILL).
Verbs—be intelligent; have all one's wits about one; understand; grasp an idea; comprehend; take a hint; see through, see at a glance, see with half an eye; penetrate; discern (see VISION); foresee.
Adjectives—intelligent, quick, keen, acute, alive, awake, bright, sharp; nimble- *or* quick-witted; wide awake; canny, shrewd, astute; clear-headed; far-sighted; discerning, perspicacious, penetrating, piercing; alive to, aware of (see KNOWLEDGE); clever (see SKILL); arch (see DECEPTION). *Colloq.,* brainy, not so dumb. *Slang,* have all one's marbles, not born yesterday.
Antonyms, see IGNORANCE, INSANITY.

intelligibility, *n.* clearness, clarity, explicitness; comprehensibility; lucidity, perspicuity; legibility, plain speaking, precision; obviousness; realization, recognition. See MEANING, INTERPRETATION. *Ant.,* see UNINTELLIGIBILITY.

INTEMPERANCE

Nouns—**1,** intemperance, indulgence, overindulgence, high living, self-indulgence; voluptuousness; epicurism, epicureanism; sybaritism; DRUNKENNESS, PRODIGALITY; dissipation, licentiousness, debauchery; crapulence, incontinence; revel(s), revelry; debauch, carousal, jollification, drinking bout, wassail, Saturnalia, orgies; excess, too much; sensuality, animalism, carnality; pleasure; luxury, luxuriousness; lap of pleasure, lap of luxury; GLUTTONY.
2, drunkard, addict, voluptuary, sybarite, glutton, gourmand, sensualist.
Verbs—be intemperate, indulge, overindulge, exceed; live well, live high, live on the fat of the land; wallow, plunge into dissipation; revel, rake,

live hard, run riot, sow one's wild oats; slake one's appetite *or* thirst; swill; pamper; burn the candle at both ends.

Adjectives—intemperate, inabstinent; sensual, self-indulgent; voluptuous, luxurious, licentious, wild, dissolute, rakish, fast, debauched; brutish; carplous, crapulent, swinish, piggish; epicurean, sybaritical; bred in the lap of luxury; indulged, pampered, full-fed, prodigal.

Antonym, see TEMPERANCE.

intend, *v.* MEAN, purpose, plan; have in mind; aim, contemplate.

intense, *adj.* violent, sharp, strong; passionate, vivid; deep, dark; poignant, keen, acute; extreme. See FEELING, DEPTH, HEIGHT, POWER.

intensify, *v.* deepen, strengthen, heighten, sharpen; concentrate; aggravate (see INCREASE). See HEIGHT.

intensity, *n.* DEPTH; FEELING; POWER, force, STRENGTH, vigor; darkness (shade), brilliance; extremity.

INTENTION

Nouns—**1,** intent, intentionality; purpose; project, PLAN, UNDERTAKING; predetermination; design, ambition; contemplation, mind, animus, view, purview, proposal; study; lookout; decision, determination, resolve, RESOLUTION; set *or* settled purpose, ultimatum; wish, DESIRE, MOTIVE. **2,** final cause, *raison d'être*; object, aim, END; drift, tenor, TENDENCY; goal, target, prey, quarry, game; destination, mark.

Verbs—intend, purpose, design, mean; have to; propose to oneself, harbor a design; have in view *or* mind; have an eye to; bit for, labor for; be after, aspire after, endeavor; aim at, drive at; take aim; set before oneself; study to; hitch one's wagon to a star; take upon oneself, undertake, take into one's head; meditate, contemplate; think, dream *or* talk of; premeditate (see PREDETERMINE); compass, calculate; destine, propose; project, PLAN, have a mind to (see WILLINGNESS); DESIRE, pursue (see PURSUIT).

Adjectives—intended, intentional, advised, express, determinate, prepense, bound for; intending, minded; bent upon, earnest, resolute; at stake; on the fire, in view, in prospect.

Adverbs—intentionally, *etc.*; advisedly, wittingly, knowingly, designedly, purposely, on purpose, by design, studiously, pointedly; with intent; deliberately, with premeditation; with one's eyes open, in cold blood; to all intents and purposes; with a view to, with an eye to; in order to, in order that; to the end that, with the intent that; for the purpose of, with the view of, in contemplation of, on account of; in pursuance of, pursuant to.

Antonym, see CHANCE.

inter, *v.t.* bury, entomb, inearth. See INTERMENT.

intercede, *v.i.* mediate, arbitrate; intervene, interpose. See COMPROMISE.

intercept, *v.t.* stop, interrupt, check, hinder; catch, nab, seize; cut off. See HINDRANCE.

INTERCHANGE

Nouns—interchange, EXCHANGE, interchangeableness, interchangeability; commutation, permutation, intermutation; reciprocation, reciprocity, transposition, shuffling; alternation; hocus-pocus; barter; a Roland for an Oliver, tit for tat, an eye for an eye, RETALIATION; crossfire, battledore and shuttlecock; *quid pro quo*, musical chairs. See TRANSFER.

Verbs—interchange, exchange, counterchange, transpose, bandy, shuffle, change hands, change partners, swap, permute, reciprocate, commute; give and take, put and take, pay back, requite, return the compliment; play at puss in the corner, retaliate.

Adjectives—interchanged, interchanging, interchangeable, reciprocal, mutual, communicative, intercurrent.

Adverbs—in exchange, *vice versa*, backward(s) and forward(s), by turns, turn and turn about.

Antonym, see SUBSTITUTION.

---

intercourse, *n.* communication; CONVERSATION, converse, communion; coitus, congress; SOCIALITY; fellowship, association; commerce, dealings, BUSINESS, trade.

interest, *v. & n.* —*v.* concern; TOUCH, affect; fascinate, engross, intrigue; hold (the attention), engage, absorb. See EXCITEMENT. —*n.* concern; welfare, benefit; PAYMENT (of a percentage), sum, advantage, profit; PART, share, holding; claim, title. See DEBT, IMPORTANCE, RIGHT, PROPERTY.

interfere, *v.i.* butt in, meddle, interpose; hinder, hamper; clash, obstruct, collide, oppose. See HINDRANCE, BETWEEN.

interference, *n.* HINDRANCE; OPPOSITION, conflict; static, jamming.

INTERIOR

Nouns—interior, interiority; intrinsicality; inside, insides, subsoil, substratum; CONTENTS; substance, pity, marrow; backbone; heart, bosom, breast; vitals, viscera, entrails, bowels, belly, intestines, guts; womb; lap; recesses, innermost recesses; cave (see CONCAVITY).

Verbs—be inside, be within; place within, keep within; enclose, circumscribe (see CIRCUMSCRIPTION); intern(e); imbed, insert; imprison (see RESTRAINT).

Adjectives—interior, internal; inner, inside, inward, inmost, innermost; deep-seated; intestinal; inland; subcutaneous; interstitial (see BETWEEN); inwrought; enclosed; intramural; domestic, indoor, vernacular; endemic.

Adverbs—internally, inwardly, inward(s), inly; herein, therein, wherein; indoors, within doors; at home, in the bosom of one's family.

Prepositions—in, inside, within.

Antonym, see EXTERIOR.

---

interloper, *n.* intruder, trespasser; uninvited guest; meddler, interferer, intermeddler. See BETWEEN.

interlude, *n.* intermission, intermezzo, *entr'acte*; pause, interval; episode; gap, space. See TIME.

intermediary, *n.* go-between, mediator; arbiter, arbitrator, umpire, referee; middleman. See BETWEEN, COMPROMISE.

intermediate, *adj.* BETWEEN; MIDDLE, intervening; half-way. See MEAN.

INTERMENT

Nouns—**1,** interment, burial, sepulture; inhumation.

2, obsequies, funeral (rites), last rites, extreme unction; wake; pyre, funeral pile, cremation, immolation; knell, passing bell, tolling; dirge (see LAMENTATION); dead march, muffled drum; elegy, panegyric, funeral oration; epitaph; obit, obituary, death notice.

3, grave clothes, shroud, winding sheet, cerement; coffin, casket, shell, sacrophagus, urn, pall, bier, hearse, catafalque, cinerary urn.

4, grave, pit, sepulcher, tomb, vault, crypt, catacomb, mausoleum, golgotha, house of death, narrow house; cemetery, necropolis; burial place, burial ground; graveyard, churchyard; God's acre; cromlech, barrow, cairn; bonehouse, charnel house, morgue, mortuary; monument, marker, cenotaph, shrine; stele, gravestone, slab, tombstone; memorial. *Slang,* boneyard.

5, undertaker, embalmer, mortician, sexton, gravedigger.

Verbs—inter, bury; lay in the grave, consign to the grave *or* tomb; entomb, intomb, inhume; lay out; perform a funeral; cremate, immolate; embalm, mummify.

Adjectives—funereal, funebrial; mortuary, sepulchral, cinerary; elegiac; necroscopic.

Adverbs—in memoriam; post-obit, *post-mortem*; beneath the sod.
Interjections—rest in peace! *requiescat in pace*; R.I.P.

---

intermission, *n.* pause, INTERVAL, break; entr'acte. See REPOSE, DRAMA.
intermittent, *adj.* fitful, off-and-on, recurrent; periodic, discontinuous, interrupted, broken; flickering. *Ant.*, see REGULARITY.
intern, interne, *v.t. & n.* —*v.t.* detain, hold; shut up *or* in, confine. See INTERIOR. —*n.* internee; prisoner; student doctor, resident doctor.
internal, *adj.* inner, inside, INTERIOR; innate, inherent; domestic (not foreign), inland.
international, *adj.* worldwide, global, universal. See UNIVERSE, AUTHORITY.
interpose, *v.i.* step in *or* between; interfere, meddle; mediate, arbitrate; intervene, interrupt. See HINDRANCE, COMPROMISE, BETWEEN.

INTERPRETATION

Nouns—**1,** interpretation, definition; explanation, explication; solution, ANSWER; *rationale*; strict interpretation; DEMONSTRATION; MEANING; acception, acceptation, acceptance; LIGHT, reading, lection, construction, version; semantics.
2, translation, rendering, rendition; literal translation, free translation; secret; clue (see INDICATION); DISSERTATION; ATTRIBUTION. *Colloq.*, trot, pony, bicycle.
3, exegesis; expounding, exposition; comment, commentary; inference, deduction (see REASONING); illustration, exemplification; glossary, annotation, scholium, note; elucidation; symptomatology; reading of signs, semeiology; diagnosis, prognosis; metoposcopy; paleography, philology (see WORD); equivalent, synonym; polyglot.
4, decipherment, decodement; cryptography, cryptanalysis; key, solution, ANSWER, light.
5, interpreter, explainer, translator; expositor, exponent, expounder; demonstrator, definer, simplifier, popularizer; oracle, teacher; commentator, annotator; decoder, cryptographer, cryptanalyst.
Verbs—interpret, explain, define, construe, translate, render; do into, turn into; paraphrase, restate; read; spell out, make out; decipher, unravel, disentangle; find the key of, enucleate, resolve, solve; read between the lines; account for; find *or* tell the cause of; throw *or* shed light; clear up, elucidate; illustrate, exemplify; unfold, expound, comment upon, annotate; key; popularize; understand by, put a construction on, be given to understand. *Colloq.*, get across; psych out.
Adjectives—interpretive, interpretative; definitive; inferential, deductive, explanatory, expository; explicative, explicatory; exegetical, illustrative; polyglot; literal; paraphrastic, metaphrastic; cosignificative, synonymous; equivalent (see EQUALITY).
Adverbs—interpretively, interpretatively, in explanation; that is to say, *id est, videlicet*, to wit, namely, in short, in other words; literally, strictly speaking, in plain words *or* English; more simply.
Antonym, see ABSURDITY.

---

interrogation, *n.* INQUIRY, inquisition, questioning; probe, investigation, examination; cross-examination.
interrupt, *v.* stop, check; suspend, cut short, hinder, obstruct; butt in, interpose, break in. See END, HINDRANCE.
intersect, *v.i.* cut; bisect; interrupt; meet, cross.

INTERVAL

Nouns—interval, interspace; separation, DISJUNCTION; break, fracture, gap, hole, OPENING; chasm, hiatus, caesura; interruption, interregnum; interstice, lacuna, cleft, mesh, crevice, chink, rime, creek, cranny, crack, chap, slit, fissure, scissure, rift, flaw, breach, rent, gash, cut, incision,

leak, dike, haha; gorge, defile, ravine, canon, crevasse, abyss, abysm; gulf; inlet, firth, frith, strait, gulch, gully; pass; FURROW; parenthesis (see BETWEEN); void (see ABSENCE); incompleteness, DISCONTINUITY.
Verbs—set at intervals, separate, space, gape, open.
Adjectives—with an interval, far between; intervaled, spaced.
Adverbs—at intervals, discontinuously.
Antonym, see CONTACT.

intervene, *v.i.* interfere, interrupt, interpose; come between; mediate, arbitrate; intercede; occur, happen, take place. See BETWEEN, COMPROMISE, OCCASION.

interview, *v.t. & n.* —*v.t.* converse with; question (for information or opinion). —*n.* questioning; consultation; meeting. See SPEECH.

intimate, *adj., v.t. & n.* —*adj.* close, friendly, familiar; private, personal. —*v.t.* hint, suggest; announce, impart. —*n.* FRIEND, crony, boon *or* bosom companion. See NEARNESS, DISCLOSURE.

intimidate, *v.t.* bully, cow, scare, subdue, frighten; overawe, terrify. See FEAR.

intolerable, *adj.* beyond endurance, unbearable, insupportable, insufferable. See PAIN. *Ant.*, see PLEASURE.

intolerance, *n.* bigotry, bias, prejudice; dogmatism, NARROWNESS.

intoxicate, *v.* make drunk, inebriate; fuddle, befuddle; excite, exalt, elate, overjoy. See DRUNKENNESS, EXCITEMENT. *Ant.*, see MODERATION.

intractable, *adj.* unmanageable, ungovernable; obstinate, perverse; refractory, rebellious. See UNCONFORMITY. *Ant.*, see CONFORMITY.

intricate, *adj.* complicated, complex; involved, devious, CUNNING. See DISORDER.

intrigue, *n. & v.* —*n.* plot, conspiracy, skullduggery; spying, espionage, scheming; love affair, amour. See LOVE. —*v.* fascinate, interest; plot, plan, scheme; spy.

INTRINSIC

Nouns—**1,** intrinsicality, inbeing, inherence, inhesion; subjectiveness; ego; essence; essentialness, essentiality, essential part, quintessence, incarnation, quiddity, gist, pith, core (see MIDDLE); marrow, sap, lifeblood, backbone, heart, soul; important part (see IMPORTANCE); principle.
2, nature, constitution, character, type, quality, PROPERTY, crasis, diathesis; ring [of truth, *etc.*].
3, HABIT, temper, temperament; spirit, humor, grain; moods, features, aspects; peculiarities (see SPECIALITY); idiosyncrasy; idiocrasy (see TENDENCY); diagnostics; endowment, capacity; capability (see POWER).
Verbs—be intrinsic *or* innate, inhere; be *or* run in the blood; be born to.
Adjectives—intrinsic(al); subjective; fundamental, normal; implanted, inherent, essential, natural; innate, inborn, inbred, ingrained, inwrought; radical; incarnate; thoroughbred, hereditary, inherited, immanent; congenital, connate, running in the blood; ingenerate, indigenous; in the grain, bred in the bone, instinctive; inward, internal, INTERIOR; to the manner born; virtual; characteristic; invariable, incurable, ineradicable, fixed.
Adverbs—intrinsically, at bottom, in the main, in effect, practically, virtually, substantially, fairly.
Antonym, see EXTRINSIC.

introduce, *v.t.* usher, bring in; present, acquaint (with); insert, interpolate; initiate, institute. See BEGINNING, PRECEDENCE, BETWEEN.

introduction, *n.* preface, foreword, prelude; presentation; (new) acquaintanceship; INSERTION, BEGINNING. See COURTESY, RECEIVING.

intrude, *v.i.* interlope, intervene, interfere; butt in, trespass, encroach; overstep, obtrude.

intrust, entrust, *v.t.* confide, trust, consign; charge; show faith *or* reliance in. See COMMISSION.

INTUITION

Nouns—intuition, intuitiveness, insight, perceptivity, instinct, association; apprehension, presentiment; rule of thumb; clairvoyance, sixth sense, extrasensory perception, second sight. See INTELLECT, INTELLIGENCE.
Verbs—sense, feel; guess, hazard a guess, talk at random; intuit.
Adjectives—intuitive, instinctive, impulsive; independent of reason, natural, innate, gratuitous, hazarded; unconnected.
Adverbs—intuitively, instinctively, by intuition; illogically; without rhyme or reason.

Antonym, see REASONING.

inure, *v.t.* toughen, accustom, familiarize, harden, habituate. See HARDNESS.
invade, *v.t.* enter, encroach, violate, trespass; ATTACK, assail, harry; encroach. See INGRESS.
invalid, *adj.* void, null, worthless, useless; valueless, unusable; sickly, ill, unhealthy, unwell, weak. See IMPOTENCE. *Ant.,* see POWER.
invalidate, *v.t.* nullify, cancel, annul, void, undo, unmake. See NULLIFICATION.
invaluable, *adj.* inestimable, priceless, pressing, invaluable, impayable. See GOODNESS, USE. *Ant.,* see EVIL, USELESSNESS.
invariable, *adj.* unvarying, constant, steady; predictable; fixed, uniform; monotonous; permanent. See PERMANENCE, STABILITY.
invasion, *n.* encroachment, infringement, violation; ATTACK. See WARFARE, ILLEGALITY.
inveigle, *v.i.* lure, attract, ensnare, cajole, entangle, persuade, decoy, allure. See DECEPTION.
invent, *v.t.* devise, conceive, contrive, originate; imagine, fabricate, improvise; create; spin; forge, design; feign. See IMAGINATION.
inventory, *n.* tally, count; ACCOUNTING, LIST; stock, goods, merchandise. See STORE.

INVERSION

Nouns—inversion, eversion, subversion, reversion, retroversion, introversion; contraposition, OPPOSITION; contrariety, contrariness; reversal; turn of the tide; overturn; somersault, somerset; revulsion; transposition, anastrophy, metastasis, anastrophe, tmesis, parenthesis; metathesis; palindrome; pronation and supination.
Verbs—be inverted; turn, go *or* wheel around *or* about; turn *or* topple over; capsize; invert, subvert, retrovert; introvert; reverse; overturn, upset, turn topsy-turvy; transpose, put the cart before the horse; turn the tables, turn turtle, keel over.
Adjectives—inverted, wrong side out; inside out, upside down; bottom upwards; supine, on one's head, topsy-turvy; inverse; reverse, opposite (see OPPOSITION); topheavy.
Adverbs—inversely, heels over head, head over heels, *vice versa.*

Antonym, see DIRECTION.

invest, *v.i.* endue, endow, clothe, array; surround, besiege, beleaguer; install, induct; dress, adorn; confer. See CELEBRATION, CLOTHING, POWER.
investigate, *v.t.* inquire, examine, question; search, probe. See INQUIRY.
invigorate, *v.i.* strengthen, liven, refresh, enliven, restore, energize, animate. See POWER. *Ant.,* see IMPOTENCE.
invincible, *adj.* inconquerable, powerful, indefatigable, unyielding, indomitable, uncompromising. See OPPOSITION, POWER. *Ant.,* see IMPOTENCE.

INVISIBILITY

Nouns—invisibility; nonappearance, imperceptibility; indistinctness, mystery, delitescence; CONCEALMENT; LATENCY; TRANSPARENCY.

Verbs—1, be invisible; lurk; escape notice.

2, render invisible, conceal, put out of sight; not see, lose sight of.

Adjectives—invisible, imperceptible; undiscernible; unapparent, nonapparent; out of sight, not in sight; behind the scenes *or* curtain; inconspicuous; unseen, covert, latent; eclipsed, under an eclipse; dim, faint (see DIMNESS); mysterious, dark, obscure, confused; indistinct, indistinguishable; shadowy, indefinite; undefined; ill-defined *or* -marked; blurred, out of focus, misty (see OPACITY); clouded (see CLOUDINESS), veiled.

Antonym, see VISIBILITY.

---

invite, *v.t.* summon, ask; tempt, attract, lure; bid; solicit; challenge; court. See REQUEST.

invoice, *n.* LIST, bill, summation.

invoke, *v.i.* beseech, plead, beg; call, summon; wish, conjure; attest. See REQUEST.

involuntary, *adj.* spontaneous, instinctive, automatic, reflex. See NECESSITY.

involve, *v.t.* imply, include; complicate, entangle, inculpate, incriminate, commit; mean. See COMPOSITION.

involved, *adj.* complicated, complex; incomprehensible, tangled, conglomerate, intricate, mazy; incriminated, embarrassed, inculpated. See CONVOLUTION.

invulnerable, *adj.* impregnable, invincible; unassailable, impenetrable; immune, proof; perfect, flawless, unimpeachable. See DEFENSE, SAFETY, PERFECTION.

inward, *adj.* inside, private; in, interior, incoming; mental, spiritual, hidden. See INTERIOR.

iota, *n.* bit, jot, particle, tittle, mite, morsel. See LITTLENESS.

IRASCIBILITY

Nouns—**1,** irascibility, temper; crossness; susceptibility; petulance, irritability, tartness, acerbity, pugnacity, contentiousness (see CONTENTION); excitability; bad, hot, fiery *or* quick temper; hot blood; ill humor, surliness, SULLENNESS; asperity, acrimony, churlishness, DISCOURTESY; fury, huff, miff, anger, RESENTMENT; MALEVOLENCE. *Colloq.*, crankiness.

2, hothead, blusterer; shrew, vixen, virago, termagant, scold, Xant(h)ippe; spitfire. *Colloq.*, fire-eater, crank, grouch, crosspatch. *Slang*, ugly customer, sourpuss, sorehead.

Verbs—be irascible, have a temper, have a devil in one; fire up, be angry (see RESENTMENT); sulk, mope, fret, frown, glower. *Colloq.*, be *or* get sore.

Adjectives—irascible; bad-tempered, ill-tempered; irritable, susceptible; excitable (see EXCITEMENT); thin-skinned, sensitive (see SENSIBILITY); fretful, fidgety; hasty, overhasty, quick, warm, hot, testy, touchy, huffy; pettish, petulant; waspish, snappish, peppery, fiery, passionate, choleric, shrewish; querulous, captious, moody, moodish; quarrelsome, contentious, disputatious; pugnacious, bellicose (see CONTENTION); cantankerous, churlish, discourteous (see DISCOURTESY); fractious, peevish; in a bad temper; sulky; angry (see RESENTMENT); resentful, vindictive (see RETALLIATION). *Colloq.*, grouchy, ugly, sore, cranky, cross as two sticks, cross as a bear.

Antonym, see COURTESY.

---

iridescent, *adj.* opalescent, prismatic; colorful, glowing. See COLOR.

irksome, *adj.* troublesome, irritating, tiresome, tedious, wearisome. See DIFFICULTY.

irony, *n.* RIDICULE, satire, sarcasm.
irrational, *adj.* unreasonable, insensible; brainless, brutish, reasonless, absurd. See ABSURDITY.

IRREGULARITY

Nouns—irregularity, variability, deviation, CAPRICE, UNCERTAINTY; tardiness, unpunctuality; intermittence, fitfulness, inconstancy.
Adjectives—irregular, uncertain, unpunctual, capricious, inconstant, desultory, fitful, intermittent, flickering; rambling, erratic, eccentric, spasmodic, variable, unstable, changeable, unpredictable, undependable.
Adverbs—irregularly, by fits and starts.
Antonym, see REGULARITY.

irrelevant, *adj.* inappropriate, unfitting, unrelated, inconsistent, in applicable. See DIFFERENCE.

IRRELIGION

Nouns—**1,** irreligion, irreligiousness, ungodliness, IMPIETY.
2, scepticism, DOUBT; unbelief, disbelief; incredulity, incredulousness; want of faith; pyrrhonism; agnosticism, iconoclasm, atheism; materialism; positivism; nihilism, infidelity, freethinking, antichristianity, rationalism, heathenism, paganism.
3, atheist, skeptic, sceptic, doubting Thomas; apostate, renegade; unbeliever, infidel, pyrrhonist; heathen, alien, gentile; freethinker, iconoclast, latitudinarian, rationalist; materialist, positivist, nihilist, agnostic; heretic; heathen, pagan.
Verbs—disbelieve, lack faith; DOUBT, question; scoff.
Adjectives—irreligious, undevout; godless, godforsaken, graceless, ungodly, unholy, unsanctified, unhallowed; atheistic, agnostic; sceptical, free-thinking; unbelieving, unconverted; incredulous, doubting, faithless, unchristian, gentile, antichristian; worldly, mundane, earthly, carnal.
Antonym, see RELIGION.

irreparable, *adj.* irremediable, hopeless. See HOPELESSNESS, DESTRUCTION.
irresistible, *adj.* overpowering, killing, overwhelming, stunning, puissant. See POWER. *Ant.,* see IMPOTENCE.
irresolute, *adj.* infirm of purpose, of two minds, half-hearted; dubious, undecided, unresolved, undetermined; hesitating, on the fence; at a loss; vacillating, unsteady, changeable, unsteadfast, fickle, capricious, volatile; weak, timid, cowardly. See DOUBT, FEAR, COWARDICE. *Ant.,* see COURAGE, RESOLUTION.
irresponsible, *adj.* negligent, remiss; reckless; unburdened. See RASHNESS, LEVITY.
irrevocable, *adj.* irreversible, past recall, done, absolute. See NECESSITY.
irrigate, *v.t.* water, moisten, flood, flush. See WATER, AGRICULTURE.
irritable, *adj.* fretful, petulant, peevish, touchy, sensitive. See IRASCIBILITY.
irritate, *v.t.* annoy, provoke, bother, trouble; irk, exasperate, nettle, ruffle. See EXCITEMENT, VIOLENCE, RESENTMENT.
island, *n.* isle, ait; cay, key; atoll, (coral) reef, ledge. See WATER, DISJUNCTION.
isolate, *v.t.* segregate; insulate, separate, quarantine. See DISJUNCTION.
isolation, *n.* separation, quarantine; loneliness, solitude, segregation. See SECLUSION. *Ant.,* see SOCIALITY.
issue, *n. & v.* —*n.* product; offspring; progeny; result; discharge; outcome, result; question, dispute. See EFFECT, EGRESS, INQUIRY, POSTERITY. —*v.i.* leave, depart, debouch, emerge; circulate, despatch, send, publish; emit, discharge, exude, eliminate; spout, spurt; flow, spring. See DEPARTURE, EFFECT, ESCAPE, MONEY, PUBLICATION.

itch, *n. & v.* —*n.* itching; desire to scratch; tickling; prickly sensation; mange, manginess; DESIRE, craving, hankering; cacoethes, cacoethes scribendi (writer's itch); the itch, scabies, psora; itchiness; burning, tingling. —*v.i.* tingle, prickle, burn; crave, long for, yearn, hanker.

item, *n.* piece, detail, particular; entry, article; term, paragraph.

itinerant, *adj.* wandering, nomadic, wayfaring; peripatetic; traveling. See TRAVEL.

itinerary, *n.* JOURNEY, route, circuit, course; guidebook.

J

jab, *n. & v.* punch, blow; poke. See IMPULSE.

jabber, *n. & v.i.* —*n.* gibberish, babble, blather, nonsense, jabberwocky; prattle, talk, gossip, chatter. —*v.i.* talk, rattle on, prattle, chatter, gibber, gabble. See SPEECH, ABSURDITY.

jack, *n. & v.t.* —*n.* MAN, fellow; KNAVE, bower; lifting device, lever; sailor, hand; jack-of-all-trades; ass, mule, donkey, rabbit; connection (electrical). *Slang,* money; applejack. See AGENCY. —*v.t.* lift, raise.

jackal, *n.* henchman, hireling. *Slang,* dogrobber. See ANIMAL.

jacket, *n.* coat, sack *or* suit coat, dinner *or* smoking jacket, tuxedo, sport coat; windbreaker, pea jacket *or* coat; COVERING; peel, rind, skin. See CLOTHING.

jackknife, *n.* pocket knife, penknife, switch-blade. *Slang,* shiv. See SHARPNESS.

jackpot, *n.* prize, bonanza, highest *or* all stakes. See CHANCE.

jaded, *adj.* weary; surfeited; blasé, dulled. See WEARINESS.

jagged, *adj.* sharp, rough, snaggy, notched, pointed, zigzag. See ROUGHNESS. *Ant.,* see SMOOTHNESS, FLATNESS.

jail, *n.* See PRISON.

jangle, *n. & v.* —*n.* harsh noise, DISCORD, clangor; ringing, jingle; bickering, dispute. —*v.* clash, clang, rattle, ring, jingle; upset (nerves). See SOUND.

janitor, *n.* caretaker, superintendent, custodian; concierge. See DEFENSE, CARE.

jam, *n. & v.* —*n.* crowd, press, crush; blockage, impasse; jelly, fruit preserve. See FOOD. —*v.* crowd, press, crush; wedge, shove, push, cram; block.

jar, *n. & v.* —*n.* vessel, Mason jar, container, jug. —*v.* shock, jolt; jounce, shake, rattle; clash. See DISAGREEMENT, IMPULSE, RECEPTACLE.

jargon, *n.* lingo, shoptalk, patois, cant, argot. *Slang,* jive, doubletalk; gibberish. See SPEECH, ABSURDITY.

jaundice, *n. & v.* —*n.* JEALOUSY, jaundiced eye; bitterness, rancor, HATE; prejudice, bias, bigotry, NARROWNESS. —*v.t.* predispose, prejudice, bias, color, distort. See DISTORTION.

jaunt, *n.* excursion, ride, cruise, escapade, lark; stroll. See TRAVEL.

jaunty, *adj.* stylish, smart, dapper; gay, breezy, brisk, debonair(e); jolly, ebullient; vivacious; cavalier. *Colloq.,* sporty; cocky. See FASHION, LEVITY.

jaw, *n. & v.i.* —*n.* mandible, jawbone. —*v.i.* chatter, talk, jabber. See SPEECH, LOQUACITY.

jazz, *n.* ragtime, blues, hot jazz, *le jazz hot*, Dixieland, swing, bop, bebop, rock 'n' roll; cool, progressive *or* modern jazz. See MUSIC.

JEALOUSY

Nouns—jealousy, ENVY, heartburn, jaundice, jaundiced eye; green- *or* yellow-eyed monster; distrust, mistrust, umbrage, RESENTMENT; suspicion, DOUBT, grudging; anxiety, concern, solicitude, watchfulness, vigilance.

Verbs—be jealous, ENVY, distrust, resent; suspect, DOUBT, grudge, covet.
Adjectives—jealous, jaundiced, green [with ENVY], covetous, envious; distrustful, resentful; doubtful, suspicious; anxious, concerned, solicitous; apprehensive, watchful, vigilant; intolerant, zealous, umbrageous.
Antonym, see BELIEF.

jeer, *v. & n.* —*v.* sneer, scoff, taunt, gibe, mock; RIDICULE, make fun of, belittle. —*n.* taunt, gibe, mockery; hoot, catcall, hissing. *Ant.*, see APPROBATION.
jelly, *n.* jam, preserve; gelatin; mush. See FOOD.
jeopardy, *n.* DANGER, risk, peril, hazard. *Ant.*, see SAFETY.
jerk, *v. & n.* —*v.* twist, tweak, pull, SNAP; start, twitch, jitter, jump. —*n.* start, jump, twitch; spasm; pull, SNAP. *Slang*, nitwit, FOOL; nobody. See IMPULSE.
jest, *n. & v.i.* —*n.* joke, jape; WIT, humor, clowning; practical joke; jocularity, pun, gag, wisecrack, witticism, *bon mot*; sport, fun; make-believe, fooling. —*v.i.* FOOL, joke; crack wise, gag; play the fool.
jester, *n.* WIT, HUMORIST, joker, gagman, comedian; FOOL, clown, buffoon.
jet, *v., n. & adj.* —*v.* STREAM, spurt, gush, shoot, spout, pour, rush, squirt. —*n.* STREAM, fountain; outgush, spurt; jet plane. See WATER, AVIATION. —*adj.* black, pitch, pitchy, ebony, ebon; dark, raven. See COLOR.
jewel, *n.* stone, gem; diamond, ruby, sapphire, *etc.* See ORNAMENT.
jewelry, *n.* gems, beads, trinkets, stones; bracelets, bangles, necklaces, *etc.* See ORNAMENT.
jilt, *v.t.* reject *or* cast off (a lover); leave in the lurch. See REFUSAL.
jingle, *n. & v.* —*n.* clink, tinkle, ring; jangle. See SOUND.
jingo, *n.* See CHAUVINIST.
jinx, *n. & v.* —*n.*, *colloq.*, curse, evil eye, bad luck, plague. *Slang*, [double] whammy. —*v.* curse, hex; bewitch, bedevil. See ADVERSITY, SORCERY.
jitter, *v.i. & n.* —*v.i.* twitch, fidget, jerk, jump, vibrate. See IMPULSE. —*n.* vibration. —*n.pl.* heebie-jeebies, shakes, nervousness. *Ant.*, see STABILITY.
job, *n.* work, occupation, calling; piece of work, stint; position, situation, duty. See BUSINESS.
jocularity, *n.* humor; mirth, laughter; sportiveness, jesting, joshing, kidding, facetiousness; WIT.
jog, *v.* jiggle, push, shake, jostle. See IMPULSE.
join, *v.* unite, link, connect, tie, bind; federate, associate, affiliate; become a member; marry. See JUNCTION, PARTY.
joint, *n. & adj.* —*n.* connection, link, juncture; articulation (of bones). *Slang*, dive, den, haunt, hangout. See JUNCTION, ABODE. —*adj.* combined, shared, common to both parties. See JUNCTION, PARTY.
joke, *n. & v.i.* —*n.* funny story, jest, gag, pun; wisecrack, witticism, WIT, *bon mot*; fooling, kidding, joshing, lack of earnestness. —*v.i.* josh, jest, gag. *Slang*, horse around.
jolly, *adj.* joyous, frolicsome, mirthful; buoyant, elated. See CHEERFULNESS.
jolt, *v.* shake (up), shock, stun; lurch, pitch; bump, collide, crash. *Slang*, give a kick in the pants. See IMPULSE.
jostle, *v.t.* push, bump; elbow, shoulder; collide with. See IMPULSE.
journal, *n.* diary, daybook, record; newspaper, magazine, periodical. See PUBLICATION, CHRONOMETRY.
journalist, *n.* newsman, newspaperman, reporter; writer, editor, copyreader. See RECORD, BOOK.
journey, *n. & v.* —*n.* trip, tour; voyage, cruise, crossing; expedition; tramp, hike; pilgrimage, hadj; caravan; trek. —*v.* travel; voyage, sail, cross; tour, roam, range, venture, explore; ride, drive, motor. See TRAVEL.

jovial, *adj.* genial, cordial; gay, merry; jolly, convivial. See CHEERFUL-NESS. *Ant.,* see DEJECTION.

joy, *n.* REJOICING; PLEASURE, happiness, delight, mirth, gayety; *joie de vivre. Colloq.,* fun. *Ant.,* see DEJECTION.

jubilant, *adj.* joyful; triumphant, exultant; elated, REJOICING, in high spirits. *Ant.,* see DEJECTION.

jubilee, *n.* CELEBRATION; anniversary; REJOICING.

judge, *n. & v.* —*n.* jurist, justice, (the) court; chancellor; judge of assize, recorder, justice of the peace, j.p., magistrate; his worship, his honor, his Lordship, Lord Chancellor, Chief Justice; archon, tribune, praetor; mufti, cadi, mullah; judge advocate; arbiter, arbitrator, mediator, umpire, referee; censor; connoisseur; tribunal. *Slang,* beak. —*v.* adjudge, adjudicate; arbitrate, try, try a case, sit in judgment, sentence, condemn; deem, conclude, consider, appraise. See JUSTICE, TASTE.

JUDGMENT

Nouns—**1,** judgment, adjudication, arbitration; result, conclusion, upshot; DEDUCTION, inference, corollary; decision, determination, rendition; finding, opinion, verdict, award, decree, sentence; CONDEMNATION, doom, day of judgment, Judgment Day; *res judicata.* See LAWSUIT.

2, JUDGE; jury, grand *or* petty jury; tribunal, court, forum, bench; circuit court, court of appeals, appellate court, Supreme Court; courtroom, chambers, dock, jury-box, witness-box, witness stand. *Slang,* kangaroo court.

3, estimation, valuation, assessment, appraisal, appreciation, consideration, deliberation, judication; opinion, notion, THOUGHT, viewpoint, BELIEF; estimate, commentary; CHOICE, VOICE, vote, plebiscite; discernment, discretion, TASTE; SENSIBILITY, INTELLIGENCE, reason, sagacity; sense.

4, arbiter, umpire, referee; master, moderator, mediator, conciliator; censor, critic, commentator, connoisseur, AUTHORITY, expert.

Verbs—**1,** judge, conclude; come to, arrive at *or* draw a conclusion; make up one's mind; ascertain, determine, deduce; settle, give an opinion; decide, try *or* hear a case *or* cause; pronounce, rule, pass judgment, sentence, condemn, doom (see CONDEMNATION); adjudge, adjudicate, arbitrate, sit in judgment; bring in a verdict; confirm, decree, award; pass under review.

2, estimate, appraise, value, assess; review, consider, believe; form an opinion about; comment, criticize, examine, inquire. *Colloq.,* size up.

Adjectives—**1,** judicial, judiciary, forensic, legal; determinate, conclusive; censorious, condemnatory; tribunal.

2, discerning, discriminating, sensible, astute, judicious, circumspect; intelligent, rational, reasonable, sagacious, wise.

Adverbs—therefore, wherefore, this being so *or* the case; all things considered, all things being equal, on the whole; in my opinion.

Antonym, see ERROR.

jug, *n.* bottle, urn, pitcher, flagon, tankard. See RECEPTACLE.

juggle, *v.* manipulate; conjure; trick, cheat. See DECEPTION.

juicy, *adj.* moist, sappy, not dry, succulent; rich, tasty, tempting. See TASTE. *Ant.,* see DRYNESS.

jumble, *n. & v.* —*n.* mixup, confusion, DISORDER; pi. —*v.* mix up, disarrange, muddle, mess. *Ant.,* see ARRANGEMENT.

jump, *n. & v.* hop, LEAP, bound, spring, vault; start, twitch, jerk.

JUNCTION

Nouns—**1,** junction, connection, conjunction, COHERENCE; joining, joinder, union, annex, annexation, attachment; ligation, accouplement; MARRIAGE, knot, wedlock; confluence; hookup, network, communication, concatenation; fusion, blend, merger; meeting, reunion, ASSEMBLAGE.

2, joint, joining, juncture, pivot, hinge, articulation, seam, suture, stitch; chain, link; miter, mortise, tenon, dovetail; interface.

3, combination, unification, incorporation, merger, amalgamation, coalescence, MIXTURE.

Verbs—**1,** join, unite, knot, knit, conjoin, connect, associate, put together, hold together, piece together, roll into one, combine, compound, incorporate.

2, attach, affix, fasten, bind, secure; blend, merge, fuse; tie, sew, stitch, tack, knit, button, hitch, knot, lash, truss, bandage, braid, splice, gird, tether, moor, picket, harness, chain; fetter, lock, latch, leash, couple, link, yoke, bracket, span, marry, wed.

3, pin, nail, bolt, clasp, clamp, screw, rivet, solder, weld, mortise, miter, dovetail, graft, entwine; interlace, entangle, intertwine.

Adjectives—**1,** joined, joint; conjoint, conjunct, conjunctive, corporate, compact, hand in hand.

2, firm, fast, tight, taut, secure, set, inseparable, indissoluble.

3, blent, blended, wedded, married, merged, fused. See MIXTURE.

Adverbs—jointly, in conjunction with, fast, firmly, intimately.

Antonym, see DISJUNCTION.

---

juncture, *n.* joint, point, connection; contingency, emergency. See JUNCTION.

junior, *n. & adj.* younger, lesser, subordinate. See INFERIORITY, AGE.

junk, *n. & v.* —*n.* rubbish, WASTE, refuse, trash, discard, castoffs; scrap, salvage, wreck, wreckage; stuff, miscellany, claptrap. See SHIP. —*v.t.* scrap, wreck, tear down, dismember; salvage; discard, cast off, jettison. See DESTRUCTION. *Ant.,* see PRESERVATION.

jurisdiction, *n.* judicature; administration; province, dominion, control; magistracy, AUTHORITY; municipality, corporation, bailiwick. See LEGALITY.

jurist, *n.* JUDGE; legal expert.

jury, *n.* trial jury, grand jury; panel; board of judges. See LAWSUIT.

just, *adj. & adv.* —*adj.* fair, RIGHT; impartial, nonpartisan; lawful, legal; exact, accurate, precise. See PROBITY. —*adv.* precisely, exactly; almost, nearly, within an ace of.

JUSTICE

Nouns—**1,** justice, justness, fairness, fair treatment, impartiality, equity, equitableness; poetic justice, rough justice; nemesis; scales of justice; fair trial, trial by jury. *Colloq.,* square deal, straight shooting, a square shake. See LAWSUIT, LEGALITY, PROBITY.

2, due, dueness, rightfulness, RIGHT, VINDICATION. See JUDGMENT.

Verbs—**1,** do justice to, be fair, treat fairly, deal fairly, be impartial, see justice done, play fair, give the devil his due. *Colloq.,* give a square deal, play the game, give a sporting chance.

2, be just, right *or* due; have right, title *or* claim to; be entitled to; have a claim upon, belong to, deserve, merit, be worthy of. *Colloq.,* rate.

3, demand, claim, call upon for, reclaim, exact, insist on, take one's stand, make a point of, require, lay claim to; substantiate, vindicate (see VINDICATION).

Adjectives—**1,** just, fair, impartial, equal, equable, fair and square, dispassionate, disinterested, unbiased, evenhanded.

2, just, RIGHT, equitable, due, square, fit, fitting, correct, proper, meet, becoming, seemly; decorous, creditable; allowable, lawful, legal, legitimate, licit.

3, having a right to, entitled to, deserving, meriting, worthy of; deserved, merited.

Adverbs—justly, rightfully, duly, by right, by divine right, fairly, in justice, as is just *or* fitting. *Colloq.,* on the level, aboveboard, on the square.

Antonym, see INJUSTICE.

justify, *v.* exonerate, excuse, warrant, vindicate, acquit, absolve; prove right, free from blame; make to fit, set properly. See VINDICATION, ARRANGEMENT.

jut, *v.i.* protrude, project, beetle, stand out, overhang. See CONVEXITY.

juvenile, *n. & adj.* —*n.* youngster, minor, adolescent; boy, girl. *Colloq.,* kin. —*adj.* puerile, young, undeveloped, immature; childish. See YOUTH. *Ant.,* see AGE.

K

kaleidoscopic, *adj.* variegated, varying; forming many patterns; colorful. See COLOR.

kaput, *adj.* ruined, done for, destroyed. See FAILURE, DESTRUCTION.

keel, *v. & n.* —*v.* provide with a keel; turn (over); keel over, fall down, drop like a log. See DESCENT. —*n.* bar *or* false keel, centerboard.

keen, *adj.* piercing, stinging, nippy; sharp, edged, cutting, razorlike; eager, enthusiastic, ardent; acute, clever, shrewd, quick. See DESIRE, SHARPNESS, FEELING, INTELLIGENCE.

keep, *v. & n.* —*v.* retain; hold; have, possess; receive, preserve; celebrate (holidays), maintain; sustain, continue; hold back, save, cling to, detain. See POSSESSION, PRESERVATION. *Ant.,* see RELINQUISHMENT. —*n.* donjon, dungeon; PRISON, prison tower, cell, jail.

keeper, *n.* custodian; jailer, warden, watchman, watchdog; gamekeeper; ranger; doorman, tiler; curator; protector, guardian; observer (of rites); celebrator; preserver; supporter, maintainer. See SAFETY, PRISON.

keepsake, *n.* memento, souvenir, reminder, token. See MEMORY.

keg, *n.* barrel, cask. See RECEPTACLE.

ken, *n.* KNOWLEDGE; scope.

kennel, *n.* doghouse, stall; hovel, hut, hutch. *Slang,* dump, dive. See ABODE.

kernel, *n.* nub, gist, core, pith, point, center, essence; grain, nut, seed, nucleus. See CENTRALITY, MEANING, IMPORTANCE.

kettle, *n.* pot, ca(u)ldron, boiler, teakettle. See RECEPTACLE.

key, *n.* answer, solution, code book, decipherment; pitch, tonality, register. See INTERPRETATION, MUSIC.

keynote, *n.* tonic (note of scale); basic principle.

kibitz, *v., colloq.,* advise, comment; butt in, interfere, meddle. See ADVICE.

kick, *v. & n.* —*v.* strike with the shoe, punt; spurn; stamp. *Colloq.,* complain, gripe, bellyache, grumble. —*n.* RECOIL; thrill, excitement, fun. *Colloq.,* complaint, grievance; gripe. See IMPULSE, OPPOSITION.

kickback, *n., colloq.,* backfire, RECOIL; refund, DISCOUNT, rebate; rakeoff; cut, commission; bribe, payoff, payola. See PAYMENT.

kid, *n. & v.* —*n.* young goat, kidling; kidskin. *Colloq.,* child, YOUTH. —*v., slang,* RIDICULE, tease, make fun of; deceive, fool. See DECEPTION.

kidnap, *v.* carry away (a person), abduct. See STEALING.

KILLING

Nouns—**1,** killing, homicide, manslaughter, murder, assassination; bloodshed, slaughter, carnage, butchery, decimation, pogrom, massacre, war, WARFARE.

2, death blow, finishing stroke, *coup de grâce,* quietus, gassing, electrocution, defenestration, execution; martyrdom; suffocation, poisoning, strangulation, garrot(t)e, hanging, decapitation, guillotine, violent death; traffic death, fatal accident, casualty, fatality.

3, butcher, slayer, murderer, Cain, assassin, cutthroat, garrotter, bravo, thug; executioner, hangman, headsman; regicide, matricide, parricide, fratricide, infanticide; suicide, suttee, hara-kiri, immolation; germicide, insecticide. *Slang,* hatchet *or* finger man.

4, hunting, coursing, shooting; sportsman, huntsman, fisherman, hunter, Nimrod; slaughterhouse, shambles, abattoir; charnel house.

Verbs—**1,** kill, put to death, slay, shed blood; murder, assassinate, butcher, slaughter, immolate, massacre, do away with, put an end to; run over; dispatch, do for. *Colloq.,* liquidate. *Slang,* bump off, take for a ride, knock off, wipe out, zap.

2, strangle, garrot(t)e, hang, throttle, poison, choke, stifle, gas, electrocute, suffocate, smother, asphyxiate, drown, execute, behead; put to the sword, stone, deal a death blow, wade knee-deep in blood; blow out one's brains, commit suicide; snuff out.

Adjectives—**1,** killing, murderous, sanguinary, bloodstained, bloodthirsty, homicidal, redhanded; bloody, ensanguined, gory.

2, mortal, fatal, lethal, deadly, internecine, suicidal.

Antonym, see LIFE.

---

kin, *n.* kin(s)folk, kinsman, kinswoman; blood relative *or* RELATION, family, clan; siblings, cousins. *Colloq.,* folks.

kind, *n. & adj.* —*n.* sort, species, CLASS, type, ilk, breed character, nature. —*adj.* gentle, tender; sympathetic; mild; friendly, obliging, benign; solicitous; lenient; helpful. See BENEVOLENCE.

kindergarten, *n.* nursery school, playschool; BEGINNING, start. See YOUTH.

kindle, *v.* ignite, start (fire), fire, set ablaze; stir, excite, rouse, provoke. See HEAT, EXCITEMENT.

kindling, *n.* tinder, FUEL, firewood, combustibles.

kindness, *n.* GOOD, friendliness, sympathy, mildness, BENEVOLENCE; favor, AID, SERVICE; graciousness, tenderness, gentleness; leniency, mercy. *Ant.,* see MALEVOLENCE.

kindred, *n.* relatives, kinfolk(s), kinsmen; clan, tribe; brothers, sisters, cousins, parents, *etc.*; kindred spirits, congenial people; SIMILARITY. See RELATION.

king, *n.* ruler, monarch, emperor, sovereign; royalty; MASTER.

kingdom, *n.* domain, empire, realm; LAND; country. See REGION.

kingly, *adj.* royal, majestic, regal, imperial; noble, magnificent. See AUTHORITY.

kinsman, *n.* relative, blood relation; clansman. See RELATION.

kiss, *n. & v.* —*n.* smack, osculation, caress, merest touch. See ENDEARMENT. —*v.* caress, osculate; brush lightly, TOUCH, graze.

kit, *n.* pack, sack, bag, knapsack; Dop kit; collection, ASSEMBLAGE, gear, outfit, supplies; do-it-yourself kit. See RECEPTACLE.

kitchen, *n.* scullery, galley, cookhouse, kitchenette. See RECEPTACLE.

knack, *n.* adeptness, ability, dexterity, handiness, trick, SKILL. *Ant.,* see UNSKILLFULNESS.

knapsack, *n.* haversack, pack; mochila, rucksack, kit [bag], bag, case. *Slang,* poke, turkey, bindle. See RECEPTACLE.

knave, *n.* rogue, rascal, villain, scamp, scapegrace, blackguard, reprobate, miscreant; jack, bower (*cards*); churl, menial, SERVANT. See EVILDOER. *Ant.,* see GOODNESS.

knead, *v.t.* press, squeeze, massage, manipulate, work. See MIXTURE, CONTRACTION.

kneel, *v.* bend (to pray), genuflect. See DEPRESSION.

knickknack, *n.* bric-à-brac, trifle, trinket, gewgaw. See ORNAMENT, UNIMPORTANCE.

knife, *n. & v.* —*n.* blade, EDGE, point, steel; carving, knife, *etc.*; snickersnee; dagger, poniard, dirk, bodkin, stiletto; scalpel, lancet. *Slang,* shiv, toothpick. See ARMS, SHARPNESS. —*v.t.* stab, sut, slice, slash; wound. *Colloq.,* knife in the back, betray. See DISJUNCTION.

knight, *n.* cavalier; chevalier; paladin, champion, Galahad; Templar; noble. See LOVE, DEFENSE, NOBILITY, CLERGY.

knit, *v.* weave, work with wool, interlace (yarn); draw together, contract. FURROW, wrinkle. See JUNCTION.

knob, *n.* knot, lump, node, protuberance, boss; door handle. See CONVEXITY.

knock, *v. & n.* —*v.* pound, strike, hit, rap, tap; tamp; bump, collide. *Colloq.*, belittle, depreciate. See IMPULSE, DISAPPROBATION. —*n.* stroke, bump; rap, rapping, noise. *Colloq.*, slur, aspersion.

knoll, *n.* hill, hillock, rise (of ground), mound, hummock. See HEIGHT.

knot, *n. & v.* —*n.* snarl, tangle; puzzle, problem; cluster, group; lump node; measure (*Naut.*). —*v.* tangle, snarl; tie, bind, fasten. See ASSEMBLAGE, CONVEXITY, DIFFICULTY.

KNOWLEDGE

Nouns—**1,** knowledge, cognizance, cognition, acquaintance, ken, privity, familiarity, comprehension, apprehension, recognition, appreciation; INTUITION, conscience, consciousness, awareness, perception, precognition; light, enlightenment; glimpse, insight, inkling, glimmer, suspicion, impression.

2, science, philosophy, theory, doctrine, encyclopedia; erudition, learning, lore, scholarship, reading, letters, literature, book-learning, bookishness, INFORMATION, store of knowledge, education, culture; attainments, accomplishments, proficiency, SKILL, wisdom, omniscience. *Colloq.*, knowhow.

3, study, instruction; reading, inquiry; apprenticeship. See SCHOOL, TEACHING.

4, SCHOLAR, SAGE, savant, pundit, academician.

Verbs—**1,** know, ken, wot; be aware of; ween, trow; possess; apprehend, conceive, comprehend, realize, understand, appreciate, fathom, make out; recognize, discern, perceive, see, experience.

2, know full well; have in one's head, have at one's fingertips, know by heart, be master of, know what's what; see one's way, discover, LEARN, study, ascertain.

Adjectives—**1,** knowing, cognitive, conscious, cognizant, aware, perceptive.

2, aware of, cognizant of, conscious of, apprised of, told, acquainted with, privy to, no stranger to, up to, alive to; proficient in, versed in, at home in; conversant with, familiar with. *Slang,* hip, hep, wise, wised up, with it.

3, erudite, scholarly, instructed, learned, lettered, educated, well-informed, well-read, well-grounded, well-educated, enlightened, shrewd, bookish, scholastic, solid, profound, accomplished, omniscient; sage, wise, intellectual; emeritus.

4, known, ascertained, well-known, recognized, noted, proverbial, familiar, hackneyed, trite, commonplace.

5, knowable, cognizable, ascertainable, perceptible, discernible, comprehensible.

Antonym, see IGNORANCE.

L

label, *n. & v.* —*n.* tag, tab, mark, sticker; slip, ticket; price tag; epithet, title; RECORD, INDICATION. *Colloq., handle.* —*v.t.* identify, tag, name; distinguish, describe. See NOMENCLATURE.

labor, *n.* work, toil; effort; task; travial, proletariat. See EXERTION. *Ant.*, idleness, leisure; capital; see INACTIVITY.

laboratory, *n.* workplace; research center. *Colloq.*, lab. See WORKSHOP.

laborious, *adj.* hard, arduous, tiresome, irksome. See EXERTION. *Ant.*, easy; see FACILITY.

labyrinth, *n.* maze, tangle, meander; complexity, intricacy. See DIS-ORDER.

lace, *n. & v.* —*n.* cord, lacing; braid; openwork, network. See CONNECTION, ORNAMENT. —*v.t.* weave, twine; interlace; bind, tie; flavor, mix, spike. See JUNCTION, MIXTURE. *Colloq.,* whip, lash.

lacerate, *v.t.* tear, mangle; harrow, distress. See PAIN.

lack, *n. & v.* —*n.* want, deficiency, shortage, need. —*v.t.* need, require. See INSUFFICIENCY. *Ant.,* see SUFFICIENCY.

lad, *n.* boy, youth, stripling. See YOUTH.

ladle, *n.* spoon, dipper; metal pot. See RECEPTACLE.

lady, *n.* gentlewoman, madam, dowager; noblewoman. See ARISTOCRACY, FEMALE.

ladylike, *adj.* womanly, feminine; genteel, well-bred. See COURTESY, FEMALE.

lag, *v.i.* linger, drag, fall behind, hang back. See SLOWNESS.

lagoon, *n.* laguna; pool, pond, inlet, cove; estuary, sound. See WATER.

lair, *n.* den, covert, burrow, form, cave. See ABODE.

laity, *n.* flock, fold, congregation; assembly; churchgoers; parishioners; parish, brethren, people; laymen, laywomen, laic; secular. See LAY. *Ant.,* see CLERGY.

lake, *n.* loch, lough; pond, pool, tarn, lakelet, mere. See WATER.

lame, *adj.* crippled, halt; weak, ineffectual. See DISEASE, FAILURE.

LAMENTATION

Nouns—**1,** lamentation, lament, wail, complaint, plaint, murmur, mutter, grumble, groan, moan, whine, whimper, sob, sigh, cry, outcry, scream, howl, frown, scowl. *Slang,* gripe, beef, bellyaching.

2, tears, weeping, lachrymation, languishment; condolence, sympathy, compassion, pity, consolation, commiseration.

3, mourning weeds, crape, sackcloth and ashes; knell, dirge, coronach, keen, requiem, elegy, monody, threnody, jeremiad.

4, lamenter, mourner, grumbler, Niobe, Jeremiah, Rachel.

Verbs—**1,** lament, mourn, deplore, grieve, weep over, bewail; REGRET; condole with, commiserate; fret, wear mourning, wear sackcloth and ashes.

2, sigh, heave a sigh; wail, cry, weep, sob, greet, blubber, snivel, whimper, pule, shed tears; burst into tears, cry one's eyes out; scream, mew, growl, groan, moan, roar, bellow; frown, scowl, make a wry face, gnash one's teeth, wring one's hands, tear one's hair, beat one's breast.

3, complain, murmur, mutter, whine, grumble, clamor, make a fuss about. *Slang,* gripe, bellyache.

Adjectives—lamenting, in mourning, in sackcloth and ashes, sorrowful, sorrowing, unhappy, mournful, tearful, lachrymose, plaintive, querulous, in tears, with tears in one's eyes; elegiac(al).

Interjections—alas! alack! O dear! too bad! sorry! woe is me! alas the day! alackaday! waly waly! what a pity! *O tempora, O mores!*

Antonym, see CELEBRATION.

---

lamina, *n.* LAYER, stratum, sheet, plate, scale. See COVERING.

laminate, *v.t.* stratify, plate, veneer, overlay. See LAYER.

lamp, *n.* LIGHT, lantern, floor *or* table lamp; light bulb; headlamp.

lance, *n. & v.* —*n.* dart, spear, pike, javelin, shaft. See ARMS, COMBATANT. —*v.* spear; pierce, prick, puncture; hurl, throw, fling, propel, send flying. See OPENING, DISJUNCTION, PROPULSION.

LAND

Nouns—**1,** land, earth, ground, dry land, *terra firma.*

2, continent, mainland, peninsula, delta; neck of land, isthmus, ISLAND; oasis, desert; promontory, highland; real estate, property, acres.

3, coast, shore, strand, beach, bank, lea, seaside, seacoast, rock-bound coast, alluvium.

4, soil, glebe, clay, loam, marl, mold, topsoil, subsoil, clod, rock, shale, chalk, gavel, dust, sand.
Verbs—land, light, alight, ground; disembark, come *or* go ashore.
Adjectives—earthly, terrestrial; continental, midland, littoral, riparian, alluvial, landed, territorial; earthy.
Adverbs—ashore, on shore, land, *etc.*; aground, on solid ground.
Antonym, see WATER.

---

landholder, *n.* landowner, occupant; landlord. See POSSESSION.

landing, *n.* docking, alighting, landfall, disembarkation; wharf, dock, levee, pier; runway, airstrip; three-point landing. See ARRIVAL, DESCENT, SUPPORT.

landlord, *n.* proprietor, owner; host, innkeeper, boniface; landlady. See POSSESSION, FRIEND. *Ant.,* tenant, guest.

landlubber, *n.* landsman, raw seaman. See NAVIGATION.

landmark, *n.* milestone, marker, INDICATION; cairn, menhir, monolith; turning point, highlight. See OCCURRENCE, IMPORTANT.

landscape, *n.* countryside; vista, view; landscaping, park. See VEGETABLE, ART.

landslide, *n.* avalanche, landslip; sweep, runaway, no contest. *Colloq.,* walkover, shoo-in. See DESCENT, SUCCESS.

lane, *n.* path, byway, passageway; route, corridor, track. See PASSAGE.

language, *n.* SPEECH, tongue, lingo, vernacular, mother tongue; idiom, parlance, phraseology; dialect, patois, cant, jargon, slang, argot; pig *or* dog Latin, pidgin English, *bêche de mer*; Esperanto, Ito, Basic English, lingua franca; dactylology, sign language; ancient *or* dead language. *Slang,* jive, doubletalk, gobbledygook; academese, journalese; body language. See MEANING, COMMUNICATION, WRITING.

languid, *adj.* weak, feeble, weary; listless, apathetic. See IMPOTENCE, INSENSIBILITY. *Ant.,* vigorous, energetic.

languish, *v.i.* weaken, fail, fade, decline; pine, droop. See IMPOTENCE, DISEASE, DEJECTION. *Ant.,* flourish.

languor, *n.* WEARINESS, lassitude, listlessness; indolence, inertia. See INACTIVITY.

lank, *adj.* lean, spare, gaunt, bony. See NARROWNESS. *Ant.,* stocky.

lantern, *n.* lamp, searchlight, torch, LIGHT; jack-o'-lantern. *Slang,* glim.

lapse, *n. & v.* —*n.* passage, interval; oversight, peccadillo. See END, CONVERSION, GUILT. —*v.i.* pass, glide away; err.

large, *adj.* big, great, huge, colossal, enormous, immense. See SIZE. *Ant.,* small, tiny, minute; see LITTLENESS.

lariat, *n.* rope, lasso(o), line. *Slang,* rawhide, cable, catgut. See FILAMENT.

lark, *n.* frolic, romp, gambol, caper, spree; prank, joke; caprice, whim, fancy, adventure, jaunt. See PLEASURE, FREEDOM, IMPULSE.

lascivious, *adj.* lustful, lewd, salacious, unchaste, wanton. See IMPURITY. *Ant.,* chaste, pure; see PURITY.

lash, *v.t.* beat, whip, flog, scourge; berate, rebuke, satirize. See PUNISHMENT, DISAPPROBATION.

lass, *n.* lassie; colleen; miss, maid, maiden (see GIRL).

latch, *n.* catch, latchet, hasp, clasp, lock; bolt, bar; coupling. See CLOSURE.

last, *v.i.* endure, persist, continue, abide. See TIME, DURABILITY.

late, *adj.* tardy; belated, delayed; dilatory; new, recent; former, sometime. See LATENESS, NEWNESS, PAST. *Ant.,* see EARLINESS.

LATENCY

Nouns—latency, passivity, inertia, dormancy, abeyance; ambiguity, mystery, secrecy, SECRET; invisibility, imperceptibility; cabala, SILENCE, TACITURNITY, CONCEALMENT; more than meets the eye *or* ear.
Verbs—be latent, lurk, smolder, underlie; lie hidden; keep back, conceal, veil, hide; laugh up one's sleeve;

Adjectives—latent, lurking, smoldering, occult, SECRET, hidden, delitescent, concealed; implied, unapparent, in the background, invisible, unseen; dark, unknown, unsuspected, undiscovered; unsaid, untold, unwritten, unpublished, unexposed, undisclosed; undeveloped, potential; dormant, quiescent; suspended, in abeyance, inactive, inert; veiled, covert, obscure.

Adverbs—in secret, under cover, in the background, behind the scenes, behind one's back, between the lines, on the tip of one's tongue.

Antonym, see APPEARANCE, DISCLOSURE.

LATENESS

Nouns—lateness, tardiness, SLOWNESS, unpunctuality; delay, procrastination, deferring, deferment, postponement, adjournment, prorogation, retardation, respite; protraction, prolongation; stop, stay, reprieve, moratorium.

Verbs—**1**, be late, tarry, wait, stay, bide, take time; dawdle, dilly-dally, linger, loiter, take one's time, gain time, bide one's time; hang fire, stand over, lie over.

2, put off, defer, delay, lay over, suspend, stave off, waive, retard, remand, postpone, adjourn, procrastinate, spin out, draw out, prorogue, hold *or* keep back, tide over, temporize, play for time, get under the wire, sleep on it.

3, lose an opportunity, be kept waiting, dance attendance; cool one's heels, wait, await. *Slang*, sweat it out.

Adjectives—late, tardy, slow, behindhand, belated, backward, unpunctual, dilatory, delayed, delaying, procrastinating, in abeyance; UNTIMELY.

Adverbs—late, backward; late in the day, at the eleventh hour, at length, at last, ultimately, behind time, too late, after hours, ex post facto; slowly, leisurely, deliberately, at one's leisure; in the nick of time, about time.

Interjections—too late! now or never!

Antonym, see EARLINESS.

---

latent, *adj.* See LATENCY.

lateral, *adj.* sidelong. See SIDE.

latest, *adj.* last, freshest, newest; in fashion, *le dernier cri.* *Slang*, hottest, just off the press, in. See LATENESS, NEWNESS.

lather, *n.* foam, froth, suds, spume, bubbles; head; shaving cream. *Colloq.*, EXCITEMENT, AGITATION, frenzy, stew. *Slang*, tizzy. See LEVITY.

latitude, *n.* range, extent, scope, FREEDOM.

latter, *adj.* later, last mentioned. See PAST. *Ant.*, former; see PRIORITY.

laud, *v.t.* praise, extol, eulogize. See APPROBATION. *Ant.*, belittle, disparage; see DISAPPROBATION.

laugh, *v.i.* guffaw, snicker, giggle, titter, chuckle. See REJOICING.

laughable, *adj.* ludicrous, amusing, comical; absurd; facetious, humorous. See ABSURDITY.

laughingstock, *n.* fool; target, butt, game, fair game, April fool; queer fish, odd fish; mockery; monkey, buffoon. *Slang*, fall guy. See RIDICULE. *Ant.*, see RESPECT.

laughter, *n.* laughing, guffaw, snicker, giggle, titter, chuckle. See REJOICING.

launch, *v.t.* float, start, get going; throw, cast, hurl. See BEGINNING, PROPULSION.

lavish, *adj. & v.* —*adj.* prodigal, profuse, bountiful, LIBERAL. *Ant.*, parsimonious. —*v.t.* give liberally; squander.

law, *n.* statute, ordinance, regulation, mandate; precept, axiom, jurisprudence. See RULE, MAXIM, PRECEPT, LEGALITY.

law-abiding, *adj.* obedient, upright. See OBEDIENCE, PROBITY. *Ant.*, lawness.

lawbreaker, *n.* felon, miscreant, criminal, wrongdoer. See ILLEGALITY, EVIL.

lawful, *adj.* legal, legitimate; permissible; valid. See LEGALITY, PERMISSION.

lawless, *adj.* disorderly, unruly, insubordinate, mutinous. See ILLEGALITY, DISOBEDIENCE. *Ant.,* law-abiding.

lawn, *n.* grass plot, green, greenyard. See AGRICULTURE, VEGETABLE.

LAWSUIT

Nouns—**1,** lawsuit, suit, action, CAUSE, litigation, proceedings, dispute; hearing, trial; jurisdiction (see LEGALITY); verdict, JUDGMENT, award; recovery, damages.

2, citation, arraignment, prosecution, impeachment; accusation, true bill, indictment; apprehension, arrest; committal; imprisonment; writ, summons, subpoena, habeas corpus, pleadings, declaration, bill, claim, bill of right, affidavit, answer, replication, PLEA, demurrer, rejoinder, rebuttal, summation; appeal, motion, writ of error, case, decision, precedent, reports.

3, JUDGE, justice, magistrate, surrogate, referee, chancellor; judiciary, the bench; coroner, sheriff, constable, bailiff, officer, policeman, gendarme, suitor, litigant, plaintiff, defendant, appellant, claimant; LAWYER, bar; juror, juryman.

4, court, tribunal, judicatory; court of law, equity, chancery, appeals; Supreme Court, woolsack, drumhead; court-martial. *Slang,* kangaroo court.

5, courtroom, chambers, dock, jury-box, witness-box *or* -stand.

Verbs—sue, litigate; bring to trial, put on trial, accuse, hale to court; prefer a claim, file; serve (with a writ), cite, apprehend, arraign, prosecute, bring an action against, indict, impeach, attach, distrain, commit, arrest, summon(s), give in charge; empanel a jury, implead, join issue, try; sit in judgment, judge, adjudicate; rule, award, affirm, deny.

Adjectives—litigious, litigant, contentious; judicial, legal, appellate.

lawyer, *n.* jurist; legal adviser; district *or* prosecuting attorney, attorney general, prosecutor; advocate, barrister, solicitor, counsel, counselor (-at-law); King's *or* Queen's counsel; attorney(-at-law); bencher; bar; pleader; Portia; a Daniel come to judgment; judge advocate; devil's advocate; pettifogger, shyster. *Colloq.,* D.A.; ambulance chaser; sea lawyer. *Slang,* mouthpiece, lip. See LAWSUIT.

lax, *adj.* loose, flaccid, limp, slack; remiss, careless, weak; relaxed, lawless, chaotic, disorderly; unbridled; anarchical, unauthorized. See SOFTNESS, MODERATION. *Ant.,* see AUTHORITY, HARDNESS.

laxative, *n. & adj.* —*n.* physic, cathartic, purgative, eliminant; enema, irrigation, cleansing. —*adj.* cathartic, relaxative, purgative, cleansing, eliminative. See REMEDY, CLEANNESS.

laxity, *n.* laxness, looseness, slackness, flaccidity, limpness; toleration, lenity, FREEDOM, relaxation, remission, loosening, DISORDER, disorganization, chaos. *Ant.,* see AUTHORITY, HARDNESS.

lay, *adj. & v.* —*adj.* secular, noncleric, nonprofessional. —*v.t.* put, place, deposit; allay, suppress; impose; ascribe; present. See LOCATION, RELIEF, JUSTICE, CAUSE.

LAYER

Nouns—**1,** layer, stratum, couch, bed, zone, substratum, floor, stage, story, tier, slab, fold, flap, ply, veneer, lap, table, tablet, board, plank, platter, course.

2, plate, lamina, sheet, flake, foil, wafer, scale, coat, peel, membrane, film, leaf, slice, rasher, shaving, integument.

3, stratification, shale, scaliness, squamosity, damination.

Verbs—slice, shave, pare, peel, plate, coat, veneer, cover, laminate, stratify.

Adjectives—lamellar, lamellate, laminated, micaceous; schistous, scaly, squamous, filmy, membranous, flaky, foliated, foliaceous, stratified, stratiform, tabular, discoid.

---

layman, *n.* laic, secular (see LAITY).

lazy, *adj.* indolent, slothful; slow, sluggish. See INACTIVITY. *Ant.,* industrious; see ACTIVITY.

lead, *v.t.* conduct, direct; precede; open, start; bring; spend, pass. See AUTHORITY, DIRECTION, PRIORITY, BEGINNING.

leaden, *adj.* gray, somber; slow, heavy, gloomy, cheerless. See DIMNESS, INACTIVITY.

leader, *n.* guide, bellwether; DIRECTOR, conductor; head, commander, chief. See AUTHORITY, MUSICIAN.

leadership, *n.* superintendence, chieftainship, stewardship, guidance. See DIRECTION, AUTHORITY.

leaf, *n.* frond, blade; lamina, sheet, flake. See VEGETABLE, LAYER.

leafage, *n.* foliage, leaves, verdure. See VEGETABLE.

league, *n. & v.* —*n.* ASSEMBLAGE, band, coalition, covenant, (con)federation, confederacy, junta, cabal. —*v.i.* confederate, unite, join. See JUNCTION.

leak, *v.i.* seep, ooze, escape; become known. See EGRESS, DISCLOSURE.

lean, *v. & adj.* —*v.i.* slant, incline; depend, rely; tend. See SUPPORT, BELIEF, TENDENCY. —*adj.* spare, meager, lank, gaunt. See NARROWNESS.

LEAP

Nouns—**1,** leap, jump, hop, spring, bound, vault; bounce (see RECOIL).

2, dance, caper; curvet, prance, skip, gambol, frolic, romp, buck.

3, leaper, jumper, kangaroo, jerboa, chamois, goat, frog, grasshopper, flea, hoptoad; jumping bean, jumping jack, pogo stick; spring.

4, high jump, broad jump, pole vault; lover's leap; springboard; leap frog, hopscotch; hop, skip and jump.

Verbs—leap, jump, hop, spring, bound, vault, cut capers, trip, skip, dance, prance, gambol, frolic, romp, cavort, caper, curvet, foot it, bob, bounce, flounce, frisk.

Adjectives—leaping, bounding, springy, saltatory, frisky, lively, bouncy, frolicsome, skittish.

Phrases—a hop, skip, and a jump; leap in the dark; look before you leap; leap year; which way the cat jumps. *Colloq.,* get the jump on, jump the gun; jump in the lake.

LEARNING

Nouns—**1,** learning, assimilation, absorption; erudition, KNOWLEDGE, scholarship, lore, enlightenment, culture; humanity, wisdom, breeding; study, education; reading, INQUIRY, contemplation; apprenticeship, pupilage, tutelage, novitiate, matriculation.

2, learner, beginner; student, scholar, pupil, schoolboy or -girl; apprentice, plebe, abecedarian; disciple, follower, apostle; self-taught man.

3, scientist, savant, SCHOLAR, pundit, SAGE; learned man, man of learning *or* letters; intelligentsia, literati, clerisy. *Colloq.,* bookworm, egghead, longhair.

Verbs—**1,** learn, acquire knowledge; MASTER; learn by rote *or* heart, commit to MEMORY, memorize; sit at the feet of; learn by experience, learn the hard way (see DIFFICULTY); learn a lesson; serve one's apprenticeship. *Colloq.,* learn the ropes; get the hang *or* knack of, catch on.

2, study, lucubrate, be studious, burn the midnight oil. *Colloq.,* cram, grind.

3, ascertain, hear (of), discover; come to one's knowledge.

Adjectives—learned, cultured, knowledgeable, erudite, literate; schooled, well-read, well-informed, wise; bookish; studious, scholastic, scholarly, academic, industrious.

Antonym, see TEACHING, IGNORANCE.

lease, *n. & v.* —*n.* leasehold; contract. See PROPERTY. —*v.t.* rent, let, demise; hire. See DEBT.

leash, *n.* leader, thong; hunting, trio. See RESTRAINT, NUMERATION.

least, *adj.* smallest, minimum, minutest. See INFERIORITY, LITTLENESS.

leathery, *adj.* tough, tanned, coriaceous. See TENACITY.

leave, *v.* —*v.t.* abandon, surrender; quit, forsake; deliver; cease, desist, forego; bequeath; relinquish. See DEPARTURE, RELINQUISHMENT, GIVING, END. —*v.i.* go away, depart. See DEPARTURE. *Ant.*, see ARRIVAL.

leaven, *n.* yeast, ferment; CAUSE, generator.

leave-taking, *n.* withdrawal, valediction; adieu, Godspeed. See DEPARTURE.

lecher, *n.* roué, rake, profligate, satyr. *Slang,* le(t)ch. See DESIRE, IMPURITY.

lecture, *v.t.* address, discourse, expound; reprove, rebuke, scold. See TEACHING, DISAPPROBATION.

ledge, *n.* shelf, bench, berm, reek, lode. See HEIGHT, SUPPORT.

leech, *n.* bloodsucker, parasite, bleeder; sycophant, toady. See SERVILITY.

leer, *n. & v.* —*n.* smirk, wink, oblique look. —*v.* ogle, make eyes, grimace, eye askance. See DESIRE, VISION.

LEFT

Nouns—1, left, sinistrality, sinistration; left hand, left side, near side; port(side), larboard; verso. *Slang,* (*Baseball*) lefty, southpaw, portsider.

2, left wing, radical, radicalism, Communist, Communism; red, pink; Socialist, Socialism.

Adjectives—left, sinister, sinistral, sinistrous, left-hand(ed), awkward, near, port(side), larboard(ed); radical, unconservative, leftish, Communistic, Communist, pink, socialistic, pinkish, red. *Slang,* Commie, pinko.

Adverbs—port, left-handedly, leftward(s). *Colloq.,* from left field (unexpectedly *or* unfairly).

Antonym, see RIGHT.

leftover, *adj. & n.* —*adj.* remaining, spare, surplus, extra, superfluous. —*n.* (*pl.*) REMAINDER, remains, leavings, scraps, odds and ends, WASTE. See FOOD.

leg, *n.* limb, SUPPORT; course, tack, lap; side. See TRAVEL.

LEGALITY

Nouns—1, legality, legitimacy, legitimateness, legalization, constitutionalism, constitutionality, lawfulness, legal process, due process of law.

2, legislation, legislature, law, code, codex, constitution, charter, enactment, statute, canon, precept, ordinance, regulation; bylaw; decree, order; sanction, AUTHORITY.

3, jurisprudence, codification, equity; common, civil, statute *or* constitutional law; ecclesiastical law; divine law, law of Moses, unwritten law; military law, maritime law; Uniform Code of Military Justice.

4, jurisdiction, administration, province, dominion, domain, bailiwick, magistracy, AUTHORITY, police power, eminent domain.

Verbs—1, legalize, legitimatize, legitimize, authorize, sanction; enact, ordain, decree order, pass a law, legislate; codify, formulate, regulate.

2, administer, govern, rule; preside, judge, arbitrate.

Adjectives—1, legal, legitimate, according to law, vested, constitutional, chartered, legalized, lawful, permitted, statutory; official, *ex officio*; legislative. *Slang,* legit; kosher.

2, jurisdictional, judicatory, judiciary, judicial, juridical; judging, judicious.
Adverbs—legally, legitimately, by law, in the eye of the law. *Slang*, on the square, on the up and up, on the level.
Antonym, see ILLEGALITY.

legend, *n.* tradition, tale, saga; myth, edda; inscription, motto. See DESCRIPTION, RECORD.
legendary, *adj.* fabled, storied; mythological; traditional, historical; unreal, illusory; famous, celebrated, of REPUTE. See IMAGINATION, DESCRIPTION.
leggings, *n.* gaiters, spats, puttees, chaps. See CLOTHING.
legible, *adj.* readable, decipherable, clear, plain. *Ant.*, illegible.
legion, *n.* horde, MULTITUDE, ASSEMBLAGE; army, corps. See COMBATANT.
legislator, *n.* lawmaker, congressman, senator, parliamentarian. See AUTHORITY, ASSEMBLAGE.
legislature, *n.* lawmaking body, congress, parliament. See ASSEMBLAGE.
legitimate, *adj.* lawful, legal; genuine, logical, justifiable. See LEGALITY, TRUTH, VINDICATION.
leisure, *n.* spare time; idle hours; time on one's hands; holiday, vacation; SLOWNESS, deliberation; rest, ease, idleness, REPOSE. *Ant.*, see HASTE, ACTIVITY.
lemon, *n., colloq.*, dud, FAILURE, bomb.
lend, *v.* advance, accommodate with, finance; loan; entrust, intrust; pawn; lend-lease; let, demise, lease, sublet. See DEBT. *Ant.*, BORROW.

LENGTH

Nouns—**1,** length, lengthiness, longitude, span, extent, distance, range; footage, yardage, mileage.
2, line, bar, stripe, string, row, streak, spoke, radius, diameter.
3, lengthening, prolongation, production, protraction, tension, extension, elongation.
4, line, nail, inch, hand, palm, foot, cubit, yard, ell, fathom, pole, rod, furlong, mile, league, chain; meter; centimeter, *etc.*; kilometer.
Verbs—**1,** stretch out, extend, sprawl, reach to, stretch to.
2, lengthen, render long, extend, elongate, stretch, prolong, produce, protract, let out, draw out, spin out.
3, enfilade, rake; look along; view in perspective.
Adjectives—**1,** long, lengthy, outstretched, lengthened, elongated, protracted, interminable, no end of, unshortened, over all.
2, linear, longitudinal, oblong, lineal.
Adverbs—lengthwise, at length, longitudinally, endwise, along, tandem, in a line, in perspective; from end to end, from stem to stern, from head to foot, from top to bottom, from head to toe; cap-a-pie; from dawn to dusk; fore and aft.
Antonym, see SHORTNESS.

LENIENCY

Nouns—lenity, leniency, lenience, MODERATION, tolerance, toleration, mildness, gentleness, favor; indulgence, clemency, mercy, forbearance, quarter, compassion, ruth, PITY.
Verbs—be lenient, tolerate, bear with, give quarter; spare, spare the rod [and spoil the child], PITY; indulge, spoil. *Slang*, pull one's punches; let one down easy.
Adjectives—lenient, mild, gentle, soft, tolerant, indulgent; moderate, easy-going; clement, compassionate, FORBEARING.
Antonym, see SEVERITY.

lens, *n.* refractor, eyeglass, magnifying glass, reading glass. See OPTICAL INSTRUMENTS.

less, *adj. & adv.* —*adj.* inferior, not so much, minor. —*adv.* under, short of. See INFERIORITY.

lessen, *v.t.* reduce, diminish, mitigate, abate, shorten. See DECREASE, MODERATION. *Ant.*, see INCREASE, EXAGGERATION.

lesson, *n.* instruction, task, exercise, example; admonition, reprimand. See TEACHING.

let, *v.t.* allow, permit, lease, rent. See PERMISSION.

letdown, *n.* DECREASE, letup, abatement, fall. *Colloq.*, comedown, setback, drawback; DISAPPOINTMENT, disillusion; blow, anticlimax. See FAILURE.

lethal, *adj.* deadly, fatal, mortal, KILLING, toxic, poisonous; virulent, pernicious, noxious, hurtful, malignant, injurious. See DANGER, DETERIORATION.

lethargy, *n.* lassitude, indifference, apathy, stupor. See INACTIVITY, INSENSIBILITY. *Ant.*, alertness, energy; see ACTIVITY.

letter, *n.* character, symbol; cuneiform, hieroglyphic; capital, majuscule; small letter, minuscule; alphabet, ABC; consonant, vowel, digraph, diphthong. See WRITING.

letup, *n.* lessening, slowup, slowdown, abatement, DECREASE; mitigation, alleviation; pause, lull, truce, cease-fire; interim, INTERVAL, interlude, respite, RELIEF; slack season, breathing spell. *Colloq.*, breather. See INACTION.

level, *adj. & v.* —*adj.* horizontal; flat; even; aligned; cool, well-balanced. See HORIZONTAL, SMOOTHNESS, EQUALITY. —*v.t.* raze; flatten; equalize. See DESTRUCTION, SMOOTHNESS. *Ant.*, build, restore.

lever, *n.* crowbar, pry, prize, jimmy. See ELEVATION.

leverage, *n.* advantage; purchase, hold. See INFLUENCE.

levity, *n.* lightness; imponderability, buoyancy, weightlessness; volatility; frivolity, flippancy, jocularity; flightiness, giddiness; triviality, want of seriousness. See LIGHT, CHANGEABLENESS, UNIMPORTANCE. *Ant.*, see GRAVITY, IMPORTANCE, WEIGHT.

levy, *n.* assessment; tax; draft, conscription. See ASSEMBLAGE, PRICE.

lewd, *adj.* obscene, salacious, indecent, unchaste. See IMPURITY. *Ant.*, pure, chaste; see PURITY.

LIABILITY

Nouns—liability, liableness, responsibility, possibility, probability, contingency, susceptibility; liabilites, debts (see DEBT); drawback, HINDRANCE. See TENDENCY.

Verbs—be liable, incur, lay oneself open to, risk, run the risk, stand a chance, lie under, expose oneself to, open a door to; be responsible for, answer for.

Adjectives—liable, subject, in danger, open to, exposed to, apt to, dependent on, responsible, ACCOUNTABLE, incurring; contingent, incidental, possible, on or in the cards, within range of, at the mercy of.

Adverbs—responsibly, *etc.*; at the risk of. *Colloq.*, likely.

Conjunctions—lest, for fear that.

Antonym, see EXEMPTION.

---

liar, *n.* prevaricator, equivocator, falsifier, fibber, deceiver. See DECEPTION, FALSEHOOD.

libel, *n.* defamation, calumniation, slander, aspersion. See DETRACTION.

LIBERALITY

Nouns—1, liberality, generosity, unselfishness, munificence, largess(e), bounty; charity, hospitality, beneficence, philanthropy; fullness, BROADNESS.

2, tolerance, catholicity, bigness, broad-mindedness, impartiality, lack of or freedom from bigotry, magnanimity. See DISINTERESTEDNESS.

3, gift, donation, present, gratuity, benefaction; giver, benefactor, philanthropist. *Colloq.*, big tipper. See GIVING.

Verbs—be liberal, spend freely, shower down upon, open one's purse strings, spare no expense, give *carte blanche*, lavish; liberalize, broaden.
Adjectives—**1,** liberal, free, generous, charitable, beneficent, philanthropic; bounteous, bountiful, unsparing, ungrudging, unstinting, lavish, profuse; open- *or* free-handed, open- *or* large-hearted; hospitable, unselfish, princely, prodigal, munificent.
2, tolerant, catholic, progressive, broad- *or* large-minded, magnanimous, impartial, unbigoted.
Adverbs—liberally, generously, *etc.*; with both hands.
Interjections—keep the change!
Antonym, see ECONOMY, STABILITY.

LIBERATION

Nouns—**1,** liberation, emancipation, enfranchisement, manumission, freeing; Emancipation Proclamation; ESCAPE, FREEDOM, liberty; deliverance, extrication, release, riddance; rescue, reprieve, respite, succor, ransom; redemption, salvation, saving, absolution; ACQUITTAL; discharge, dismissal, demobilization. See BENEVOLENCE.
2, liberator, emancipator, freer, deliverer, rescuer; redeemer, savior.
Verbs—**1,** liberate, free [from bondage], set free, set at liberty, give one's freedom; disenthral(l); emancipate, enfranchise, manumit; deliver, extricate, release, enlarge, ransom, reclaim; snatch from the jaws of death; redeem, absolve, save; acquit. *Slang,* spring.
2, discharge, dismiss, disband, demobilize; parole; let go, let loose, let out, let slip; turn *or* cast adrift; rid, be *or* get rid of; unfetter, untie, unloose(n), relax, unlock, unbolt, unbar, uncork, unbind, unhand, unchain, unshackle; disengage, separate, disentangle, disencumber; clear.
3, gain one's liberty, get clear *or* free of. See ESCAPE.
4, be liberated, go [scot] free, get off, get out.
Adjectives—liberated, freed, saved, *etc.*; free, out of harness, at liberty, at large; out of bondage, on parole, free as a bird; liberative, liberatory.
Antonym, see RESTRAINT.

libertine, *n.* voluptuary, rake, roué, debauchee, rip, profligate; lecher, satyr; pimp, pander, Don Juan, Casanova; courtesan, doxy, prostitute, strumpet, harlot, bawd, procuress, whore, wanton, *fille de joie*, streetwalker, tart, chippy, wench, trollop, light o' love; nymphomaniac. See IMPURITY, EVILDOER. *Ant.*, see GOODNESS.
liberty, *n.* freedom, independence, emancipation; right, license, privilege. See FREEDOM, PERMISSION. *Ant.*, slavery, dependence, suppression.
library, *n.* athenaeum, bookroom. See BOOK.
libretto, *n.* script; scenario, BOOK, dialogue, text, words; plot, story, synopsis, promptbook. See WRITING, MUSIC, DRAMA.
license, *n.* PERMISSION, authority; FREEDOM; licentiousness.
lick, *v. & n.* —*v.* lap (up), tongue, dart across; see TOUCH. *Colloq.,* beat, thrash, flog; overcome DEFEAT, rout. See IMPULSE, SUPERIORITY. —*n.* lap, licking, sip, taste, sup; bit, jot, modicum. See TOUCH, LITTLENESS. *Slang,* try, ESSAY, CHANCE; hot lick, blue note, vamp, improvisation, riff. See MUSIC.
lid, *n.* top, cover, COVERING, cap, crown, CLOSURE; RESTRAINT, censorship.
lie, *v.i.* prevaricate, falsify, deceive. See FALSEHOOD.
lie, *v.i.* recline; rest, be situated; extend. See LOCATION, PRESENCE.

LIFE

Nouns—**1,** life, vitality, existence, being, living, animation, vital spark, vital flame, respiration, breath, breath of life, lifeblood, life force, vital force, vivification, revivification, resurgence.
2, physiology, biology, embryology, biochemistry.
Verbs—**1,** live, be alive, be, breathe, respire, subsist, exist, walk the earth.

2, see the light, be born, come into the world, draw breath, quicken, revive, come to, come to life.

3, give birth to, bring to life, put life into, vitalize, vivify, reanimate, animate, keep alive, keep body and soul together, keep the wolf from the door, support life.

Adjectives—living, alive, vital, existing, extant, in the flesh, in the land of the living, breathing, quick, animated, lively, alive and kicking, tenacious of life.

Antonym, see DEATH.

---

life-giving, *adj.* generative, fecund, seminal, germinal; vivifying, invigorating, exhilarating. See LIFE, REPRODUCTION, ENERGY, VIGOR.

lifeless, *adj.* inanimate, inert, sluggish, spiritless. See DEATH. *Ant.*, living, lively; see LIFE.

lifelike, *adj.* realistic, natural, accurate. See SIMILARITY, DESCRIPTION.

life-preserver, *n.* lifesaver, left belt *or* jacket, Mae West, water wings. See SAFETY, SUPPORT.

lift, *v.t.* raise, elevate, exalt; uplift. See ELEVATION, IMPROVEMENT. *Ant.*, see DEPRESSION.

ligature, *n.* bond, tie, slur, surgical thread. See PRINTING, CONNECTION.

light, *adj.* airy, feathery, fluffy, puffy, vapory, zephyry; foamy, yeasty; subtle; weightless, ethereal, sublimated, volatile; buoyant, floating; portable; frivolous, jesting, jocular, lightsome; giddy, dizzy, flighty; flippant, pert, insouciant; humorous; trivial. See LIGHTNESS. *Ant.*, HEAVY.

LIGHT

Nouns—**1,** light, ray, beam, stream, gleam, streak, pencil; sunbeam, moonbeam, aurora, day, sunshine, light of day, sun, sunlight, moonlight, starlight, daylight, daybreak, noonday.

2, glow, glimmering, glimmer; glitter, shimmer, flicker, glint; spark, scintilla, sparkle, scintillation, flash, blaze, coruscation, flame, fire, lightning bolt.

3, luster, sheen, shimmer, gloss; tinsel, spangle; brightness, brilliancy, splendor, effulgence, dazzle, resplendence, dazzlement, phosphorescence, incandescence, luminousness, luminosity, lucidity, radiation, irradiation, radiance, illumination, reflection, refraction.

4, photology, photometry, photics, optics, catoptrics, photography, heliography, radioscopy.

5, luminary, illuminant; electric, fluorescent, neon, gas, *etc.* light; candlelight, lamplight, firelight; candle, taper, lamp, torch, brand, flambeau, lantern, searchlight, flashlight; bulb, globe, mantle, jet; chandelier, candelabrum, sconce, candlestick; limelight, footlights, spotlight; rocket, flare, beacon; fireworks, pyrotechnics; halo, aureole, nimbus, gloriole, aura, glory.

Verbs—**1,** shine, glow, glitter, glister, glisten, flicker, twinkle, gleam, flare, glare, beam, shimmer, glimmer, flicker, sparkle, scintillate, coruscate, flash, blaze, be bright, reflect light, dazzle, radiate, shoot out beams.

2, lighten, enlighten; light, light up, clear up, brighten, irradiate, shine, give *or* shed light, throw light upon, illume, illumine, illuminate, strike a light, kindle.

Adjectives—**1,** shining, luminous, luminescent, lucid, lucent, luciferous, light, lightsome, bright, vivid, resplendent, lustrous, shiny, beamy, scintillant, radiant, lambent; glossy, sunny, cloudless, clear, unclouded; glinting, gleaming, beaming, effulgent, splendid, resplendent, glorious, blazing, ablaze, meteoric, phosphorescent, glowing; lighted, lit, ablaze, on.

2, actinic, photographic, heliographic, optic, optical.

Antonym, see DARKNESS.

---

lightness, *n.* buoyancy; LEVITY, flightiness; gaiety, volatility; nimbleness, grace; paleness. See ACTIVITY. *Ant.*, heaviness, somberness, clumsiness.

lightning, *n.* thunderbolt, levin, firebolt, fulmination. See LIGHT.

like, *adj. & v.* —*adj.* similar, resembling, characteristic. See SIMILARITY. *Ant.,* unlike, dissimilar. —*v.t.* enjoy, desire, fancy. See PLEASURE, LOVE.

likeness, *n.* portrait, effigy, counterpart; similarity, resemblance. See SIMILARITY, REPRESENTATION.

liking, *n.* fondness, inclination, preference. See DESIRE, LOVE.

limb, *n.* branch; arm, leg, member. See PART, VEGETABLE.

limber, *adj.* flexible, pliable; LITHE. See ELASTICITY, EXERTION.

limbo, *n.* land of the lost, no man's land, neither here nor there, nowhere, borderland; OBLIVION, NEGLECT; PRISON. See HELL, UNCERTAINTY.

limelight, *n.* spotlight, footlights; publicity, notoriety, fame. See REPUTE.

LIMIT

Nouns—limit, boundary, bounds, confines; enclave; curbstone; term; bourn(e), verge, pale; termination, terminus, END, terminal, stint, frontier, precinct, border, marches, boundary line, landmark, line of demarcation, point of no return, Rubicon, turning point. See RESTRAINT.

Verbs—limit, restrict, bound, confine, define, circumscribe, restrain, qualify.

Adjectives—definite, determinate, terminal, frontier, limited, circumscribed, restricted, confined.

Adverbs—thus far, so far and no further, just so far; within bounds.

Antonyms, see FREEDOM, INFINITY.

limitless, *adj.* endless, inexhaustible, unbounded. See SUFFICIENCY.

limp, *adj. & v.* —*adj.* limber, flabby, soft. See SOFTNESS. —*v.t.* hobble, hitch; drag. See TRAVEL.

line, *v. & n.* —*v.t.* interline, face. —*n.* mark; cord, string; crease, wrinkle; verse, note; route, system; vocation, calling; lineage; row, file. See INDICATION, FILAMENT, POETRY, BUSINESS, ANCESTRY, CONTINUITY.

lineage, *n.* ANCESTRY, family, pedigree.

lineament, *n.* feature, characteristic, singularity. See APPEARANCE.

linear, *adj.* aligned, straight; lineal. See CONTINUITY, DIRECTION.

lineup, *n.* program, calendar; batting order. See LIST, ORDER, ARRANGEMENT.

linger, *v.i.* delay, dally, loiter, poke; remain, persist. See LATENESS, DURABILITY.

lingo, *n.* language, SPEECH, tongue; argot, cant, *etc.*; shop talk. *Slang,* jive.

lingerie, *n.* underthings, underwear. *Colloq.,* undies, unmentionables. See CLOTHING.

linguist, *n.* polyglot, philologist, etymologist. See SPEECH.

lining, *n.* inner coating, inner covering; interlining; filling, stuffing; wainscot, wainscoting; gasket, washer; facing, sheathing, bushing; ceiling. See COVERING, INTERIOR.

link, *n. & v.* —*n.* tie, BOND; component, liaison. See BETWEEN. —*v.t.* join, unite, couple. See JUNCTION.

lint, *n.* fluff, fuzz; threads; gauze, dressing. See MATERIALS, REMEDY.

lion, *n.* cat; hero, celebrity. See ANIMAL, REPUTE.

lip, *n.* EDGE, verge; labium, flange. *Slang,* impertinence.

LIQUEFACTION

Nouns—liquefaction, liquescence, liquidization, fluidization, melting, thaw; condensation, colliquation, dissolution, fusion; solution, infusion, lixivium, flux, decoction, MIXTURE; solvent, menstrum, dissolvent, resolvent; liquefacient; liquefier.

Verbs—liquefy, liquesce, render liquid; become liquid, run, melt, thaw, dissolve, resolve; deliquesce; liquidize, liquate, fluidize, condense; hold in solution, fuse, percolate, milk.

Adjectives—liquefied, fusil(e), condensed; melted, molten, thawed, *etc.*; in solution *or* suspension; liquefactive, liquescent, colliquative; liquifiable, soluble, dissoluble, dissolvable; solvent, melting.

Antonym, see DENSITY, VAPOR.

---

liqueur, *n.* cordial, *digestif, pousse-café.* See FOOD, DRUNKENNESS.
liquid, *adj.* fluid, smooth, flowing. See SOUND. *Ant.*, solid.
liquidate, *v.t.* pay, settle, wind up. See PAYMENT. *Slang,* kill.
liquor, *n.* liquid, fluid, broth, stock, juice, essence; spirits, whiskey, *Schnapps,* vodka, aquavit, rum, gin, brandy, applejack; corn, rye, Scotch, Irish, Bourbon, Canadian, *etc.*; alcohol, John Barleycorn; draft, dram, shot, snort. *Slang,* booze, moonshine, white mule. See FOOD, DRUNKENNESS.

LIST

Nouns—**1,** list, catalog(ue), beadroll, RECORD, register, cadastre, registry, directory; tabulation, tally [sheet], file; tariff, schedule; docket, calendar; roll, muster [roll]; enrollment, roster, slate, checklist; census, statistics, poll, ballot; bill [of lading], invoice, ledger, inventory; table, index; *catalogue raisonné*; glossary, vocabulary; lexicon, dictionary, thesaurus; syllabus; portfolio, prospectus, canon, synopsis; Domesday Book, Blue Book, Social Register, Who's Who; Yellow *or* White Pages; active, black, retired, sick, *etc.* list; registration, registry; matriculation. **2,** registrar, cataloguer, indexer, tabulator; actuary, statistician; computer.
Verbs—**1,** list, catalog(ue), RECORD, register, inventory; tally, file, tabulate; index, post, enter, set *or* jot down, inscribe; enroll, matriculate; itemize, schedule, chronicle; enumerate; blacklist.
2, list, incline, careen (see OBLIQUITY).
Adjectives—fair-trade, fixed, retail; inventrial; cadastral.

---

listen, *v.i.* harken, attend; hear; grant; heed. See HEARING, ATTENTION.
listless, *adj.* languid, spiritless, apathetic, lethargic. See INACTIVITY. *Ant.*, spirited, keen; see ACTIVITY.
literal, *adj.* verbatim, word-for-word, exact, prosaic. See MEANING.
literary, *adj.* bookish, scholarly. *Slang,* long-haired. See KNOWLEDGE.
literate, *adj.* lettered, educated. See KNOWLEDGE. *Ant.*, illiterate.
literature, *n.* books, belles-lettres, letters. See BOOK, SPEECH.
lithe, *adj.* lissome, supple, limber, flexible; spry, slender, svelte, willowy, sylphic. See ELASTICITY, NARROWNESS, ELEGANCE.
litigate, *v.t.* contest, dispute, sue, prosecute. See LAWSUIT.
litigious, *adj.* actionable; contentious, disputatious. See LAWSUIT.
litter, *n.* disorder, scraps; bedding; stretcher, palanquin; offspring. See VEHICLE, DESCENT. *Ant.*, order, neatness; see ARRANGEMENT.

LITTLENESS

Nouns—**1,** littleness, smallness, minuteness, diminutiveness, thinness, shortness, NARROWNESS, exiguity; epitome, abstract, brief; microcosm; rudiment; vanishing point.
2, dwarf, pygmy, pigmy, Lilliputian, chit, midget, peanut, urchin, elf, doll, puppet, Tom Thumb, manikin; homunculus.
3, animalcule, monad, mite, insect, fly, midge, gnat, shrimp, peewee, minnow, worm, maggot, entozoön, am(o)eba, microbe, germ, bacterium, grub, tomtit, runt, mouse, small fry, mustardseed, peppercorn, pebble, grain of sand, molehill.
4, point; atom, molecule, ion, electron, neutron; fragment, particle, crumb, powder; pinpoint, dot, speck, mote, jot; decimal, fraction; modicum, minimum; *minutiæ*; trifle; *coupçon*, shade, scintilla; grain, scruple, granule, minim; sip, dab, drop, droplet, dash, driblet, sprink-

ling, tinge; scrap, tag, splinter, chip, sliver, morsel, crumb; snick, snack; thimbleful; nutshell. *Colloq.*, smidgen.

5, micrography, microscopy, micrology, microphotography; microscope, micrometer, vernier.

Verbs—belittle, become small, decrease, contract.

Adjectives—**1,** little, SMALL, minute, diminutive, microscopic, inconsiderable, exiguous, puny, wee, tiny, petty; minikin, knee-high, miniature, pygmy, pigmy, undersized, dwarf, dwarfed, dwarfish, stunted, limited, cramped, Lilliputian; pocket(-size), portable, short; thin, weazened, scant, scrubby, granular, powdery, shrunken.

2, impalpable, intangible, evanescent, imperceptible, invisible, inappreciable, infinitesimal, atomic, molecular, rudimentary, embryonic.

Adverbs—little, slightly, in a small compass, on a shoestring, in a nutshell, on a small scale; partly, partially; some, rather, somewhat; scarcely, hardly, barely; merely.

Antonym, see SIZE.

---

liturgy, *n.* ritual, RITE, ceremony, service, WORSHIP; prayer book.

live, *v.i.* exist, be alive; abide; subsist; survive. See LIFE, DURABILITY, PRESENCE. *Ant.,* die, perish; see DEATH.

livelihood, *n.* living, living wage, salary, COMPENSATION; MEANS, wherewithal, resources, SUPPORT, (up)keep, subsistence, sustenance, daily bread, JOB.

liveliness, *n.* animation, vivacity, sprightliness. *Slang*, pep. See ACTIVITY. *Ant.,* see INACTIVITY.

living, *adj.* alive, quick, existing. See LIFE. *Ant.,* dead; see DEATH.

lizard, *n.* lacerta; gecko, chameleon.

load, *n.* burden; cargo, lading, shipment; charge. See GRAVITY, TRAVEL.

loadstone, *n.* magnet; allurement. See ATTRACTION.

loafer, *n.* idler, lounger, dawdler, vagrant. *Slang*, bum. See INACTIVITY.

loan, *n. & v.* —*n.* lending, borrowing; advance, credit; sinking fund; mortgage. *Slang*, touch. —*v.* give *or* extend credit; underwrite, finance. See LENDING.

loathe, *v.t.* detest, abhor, abominate. See HATE.

lobby, *n. & v.* —*n.* foyer, hall, vestibule, waiting room, lounge, entrance hall; lobbyism; pressure group; bloc, PARTY; lobbyists, advocates. See INFLUENCE, RECEPTACLE. —*v.* solicit, ask favors; promote, bring pressure; plump for, root for, pull strings. See INFLUENCE.

local, *adj.* restricted, narrow, provincial; native, endemic. See REGION.

locale, *n.* See LOCATION.

LOCATION

Nouns—**1,** location, localization, lodgment, stowage, collocation, packing, establishment, settlement, installation, fixation, placement, insertion. See ABODE.

2, place, situation, locality, locale, site, position, post, stand, neighborhood, environment, whereabouts; bearings, orientation; spot.

3, anchorage, mooring, encampment; plantation, colony, settlement, cantonment.

4, colonization, domestication, habitation, naturalization, acclimatization.

Verbs—**1,** place, situate, locate, localize, make a place for, put, lay, set, seat, station, lodge, quarter, post, park, install, house, stow, establish; fix, pin, root, graft, plant, lay down, deposit; cradle; moor, anchor, tether, picket; pack, tuck in; vest, replace, put back; billet on, quarter upon, saddle with, load, freight, put up.

2, inhabit, domesticate, colonize, naturalize, take root, sit down, settle down, settle, take up one's abode, establish oneself, squat, perch, bivouac, encamp, pitch one's tent, put up at, keep house.

Adjectives—located, placed, situate(d), ensconced, embedded, rooted, domesticated, vested in, moored, at anchor.

Adverbs—here, there, here and there; hereabout(s), thereabout(s), whereabout(s); in place.

Antonym, see DISJUNCTION.

---

lock, *v.t.* fasten, secure, make fast. See CLOSURE, JUNCTION.

locker, *n.* chest, compartment, cabinet, safe; lockbox, foot locker. See RECEPTACLE.

lodestone, *n.* See LOADSTONE.

lodge, *v.i.* dwell, sojourn; settle; file, be flattened. See LOCATION, PRESENCE.

lodger, *n.* guest, roomer, boarder, transient; lessee, tenant. See INHABITANT.

lodging, *n.* lodgings, accommodations (see HOME, APARTMENT). See ABODE.

loft, *n.* attic, garret; hayloft; studio. See ABODE, STORE.

lofty, *adj.* towering, high; haughty, patronizing; distinguished, noble; sublime. See HEIGHT, REPUTE, INSOLENCE.

log, *n.* timber, firewood; logbook, RECORD, diary, journal. See FUEL, NAVIGATION.

logical, *adj.* rational, reasonable, sane. See REASONING.

loincloth, *n.* breechclout, breechcloth. See CLOTHING.

loiter, *v.i.* linger, poke, dawdle. See SLOWNESS. *Ant.*, hasten, bustle.

loll, *v.i.* lounge, lie down, sprawl; loaf, idle. See REPOSE, INACTIVITY.

lone, *adj.* solitary, lonely; single. See SECLUSION.

lonely, *adj.* solitary, lone, lonesome, desolate, alone.

long, *adj. & adv.* —*adj.* lengthy, elongated; tedious; extended, protracted. See LENGTH. —*adv.* in great degree, for a time, during. See DURABILITY.

longing, *n.* yearning, craving, hankering, hunger. See DESIRE.

longshoreman, *n.* stevedore, roustabout; lader, stower, docker. See CARRIER.

long shot, *n.*, *colloq.*, long odds, outside CHANCE, gamble, IMPROBABILITY.

long-suffering, *adj.* forbearing, stoic, submissive, patient. See DURABILITY.

look, *v. & n.* —*v.i.* behold; perceive, discern; inspect, scan; stare; seem, appear. See VISION, APPEARANCE, ATTENTION. —*n.* glance, view; APPEARANCE, aspect. See VISION.

lookout, *n.* vigilance; observatory; watch, sentinel; prospect, vista. *Colloq.*, concern. See VISION, APPEARANCE, WARNING.

loop, *n.* ring, circle, noose, eyelet, ambit. See CIRCULARITY.

loophole, *n.* peephole, OPENING; alternative, way out, escape hatch. See ESCAPE.

loose, *adj. & v.* —*adj.* free, detached; flowing, unbound; vague, incoherent; unrestrained; dissipated. See DISJUNCTION, DIRECTION, BADNESS. —*v.t.* free; unbind, undo; relax. See FREEDOM.

loot, *n.* booty, spoil, plunder. See STEALING, MONEY.

lop, *v.* chop, snip, clip, dock, nip; shorten, cut off. See DEDUCTION, SHORTNESS.

lopsided, *adj.* asymmetrical, askew, aslant; unbalanced, unequal; one-sided, off-center. *Slang*, cockeyed, gimpy. See OBLIQUITY, INEQUALITY, DISTORTION.

LOQUACITY

Nouns—**1**, loquacity, loquaciousness, talkativeness, volubility, verbosity, garrulity, multiloquence, prolixity, flow of words, gift of gab, eloquence, fluency.

2, DIFFUSENESS, expatiation, dilation; REPETITION, prolixity.

3, jabber, gab, jabber, chatter, prattle, gossip, cackle, twaddle, blabber, blather, blarney, small talk. *Slang*, gas, hot air.

4, talker, chatterer, chatterbox, babbler, ranter, driveler, gossip, windbag, magpie, jay, parrot.

Verbs—be loquacious, run on, descant, expatiate, dilate; protract, spin out, dwell on, harp on; talk glibly, patter, prate, palaver, chatter, prattle, jabber, jaw, babble, gabble, talk oneself hoarse; digress, perorate, maunder, ramble; gossip. *Slang*, shoot the breeze, shoot off one's mouth, run off at the mouth.

Adjectives—loquacious, talkative, wordy, garrulous, prolix, verbose; profuse, copious, voluble, fluent, gossipy; diffuse, pleonastic, maundering, periphrastic, roundabout, digressive, rambling; glib, effusive, gushy, eloquent, chattering, chatty, open-mouthed; long-winded, long-drawn-out, discursive.

Adverbs—at length; *in extenso*; *ad nauseam*.

Antonym, see SILENCE.

---

lordly, *adj.* noble, imposing; imperious, arrogant, dictatorial. See REPUTE, INSOLENCE.

lore, *n.* erudition, scholarship, learning. See KNOWLEDGE.

LOSS

Nouns—loss; perdition; forfeiture, lapse, privation, bereavement, deprivation, dispossession, riddance, WASTE, dissipation, expenditure, leakage; DESTRUCTION.

Verbs—lose, incur *or* meet with a loss; miss, mislay, let slip, allow to slip through the fingers; forfeit, get rid of, WASTE, dissipate, squander.

Adjectives—**1,** losing, not having, shorn of, deprived of, denuded, bereaved, bereft, minus, cut off, dispossessed, rid of, quit of, out of pocket. **2,** lost, long-lost; dissipated, wasted, forfeited, missing, gone, irretrievable, destroyed, off one's hands.

Antonym, see ACQUISITION.

---

lot, *n.* fate, DESTINY, fortune; batch, sum.

lotion, *n.* wash, liniment; tonic, skin bracer. See CLEANNESS, REMEDY.

lottery, *n.* raffle, draw, lotto; allotment; fortune, CHANCE.

LOUDNESS

Nouns—**1,** loudness, noisiness, vociference, sonorousness, vehemence, intensity, power; stridency, raucousness, cacophony. **2,** resonance, reverberation, echo, ringing, tintinnabulation; roll, rumble, drumming, tattoo, rat-a-tat, rub-a-dub. **3,** din, clamor, clang, clangor, rattle, clatter, noise, roar, uproar, racket, pandemonium, hubbub, shrillness, hullaballoo; charivari; trumpet blast; fanfare, ring, peal, toll, alarum, blast, boom, thunder, thunderclap; boiler factory. **4,** flashiness (see OSTENTATION).

Verbs—be loud, peal, ring, swell, clang, boom, thunder, fulminate, roar, resound, reverberate; shout, vociferate, bellow, rend the air, fill the air, ring in the ear, pierce the ears, deafen, stun, make the rafters ring. *Slang*, raise the roof.

Adjectives—loud; sonorous; highsounding, big-sounding, deep, full, powerful, noisy, clangorous, thunderous, thundering, dinning, deafening, earsplitting, obstreperous, rackety, uproarious, shrill, clamorous, vociferous, stentorian, enough to wake the dead; flashy (see OSTENTATION).

Adverbs—loudly, noisily, aloud, at the top of one's voice, lustily, in full cry.

Antonym, see SILENCE.

---

lounge, *n. & v.* —*n.* sofa, settee, chaise longue, davenport, divan, daybed; lobby, bar. See SUPPORT, RECEPTACLE. —*v.* relax, REPOSE, loll, slouch, sprawl, make oneself comfortable. See INACTIVITY.

louse, *n.* vermin, bug, parasite. See INSECT. *Slang,* lout, scoundrel, cad, rascal, bounder, dog, stinker, bastard, s.o.b., rat. See IMPROBITY.

lousy, *adj., colloq.,* see BADNESS.

lout, *n.* bumpkin, clod, oaf, boor. *Slang,* hick, rube. See POPULACE.

louver, *n.* turret, dome, cupola; air vent; shutter, blind, jalousie. See OPENING.

LOVE

Nouns—**1,** love, fondness, liking; inclination, DESIRE; regard, admiration, affection, tenderness, heart, attachment, yearning; gallantry; PASSION, flame, devotion, infatuation, adoration, idolatry.

2, benevolence, sympathy, fellowship, friendship, humanity, brotherly love, mother or maternal love, parental affection.

3, Cupid, Venus, Eros; true lover's knot, engagement ring, love token; love affair, *amour, liaison,* romance, love story, plighted troth, courtship.

4, attractiveness, popularity, charm, fascination.

5, lover, suitor, follower, admirer, adorer, wooer, beau, honey, sweetheart, inamorato, swain, young man, boyfriend, flame, love, truelove; Lothario, Romeo, Casanova, Don Juan, gallant, paramour, *amoroso,* fiancé. *Slang,* wolf, lover boy.

6, inamorata, ladylove; idol, darling, duck, angel, goddess, true love, girl, sweetheart, beloved; betrothed, affianced, fiancée. *Colloq.,* steady, girl friend, honeybunch, date, sweetie.

Verbs—**1,** love, like, fancy, care for, favor, become enamored, fall *or* be in love with; revere, take to, make much of, hold dear, prize, hug, cling to, cherish, pet; adore, idolize, love to distraction, dote on, desire; throw oneself at, lose *or* give one's heart. *Slang,* go for, fall for, shine up to, be sweet on, be nuts about, carry a torch for; go steady; pitch woo, spoon, spark.

2, excite, love; win, gain *or* engage the love, affections *or* heart; take the fancy of; attract, endear, charm, fascinate, captivate, bewitch, seduce, enamor, enrapture, turn the head.

3, get into favor; ingratiate oneself, pay court to, set one's cap for; flirt; keep company.

Adjectives—**1,** loving, fond of; taken with, smitten, attached to, enamored, charmed, in love, lovesick, affectionate, tender, sweet on, amorous, amatory, amative, erotic, uxorious, ardent, passionate, romantic, rapturous, devoted. *Slang,* going steady.

2, loved, beloved, well beloved, dearly beloved, dear, dear one, precious, darling, pet, favorite.

3, lovable, adorable, lovely, sweet, attractive, seductive, winning, charming, engaging, enchanting, captivating, fascinating, bewitching.

Antonym, see HATE.

---

lovelorn, *adj.* lovesick; jilted. See LOVE, HATE.

lovely, *adj.* beautiful, comely, exquisite, captivating. See PLEASURE, BEAUTY.

lover, *n.* suitor, wooer, sweetheart. *Colloq.,* beau. *Slang,* boyfriend. See LOVE.

lovesick, *adj.* languishing, lovelorn. See LOVE.

lowborn, *adj.* humble, plebeian, common. See POPULACE.

lowbrow, *adj. & n., colloq.* —*adj.* uncultured, uneducated; popular, lower-class, plebeian. —*n.* vulgarian, illiterate, idiot. See IGNORANCE, POPULACE.

lower, *v.i.* lour, glower, scowl; be imminent, impend, APPROACH. See DANGER.

lowland, *n.* bottom(land), marshland, downs; dale, dell. See LAND, DEPRESSION.

low-priced, *adj.* See CHEAPNESS.

LOWNESS

Nouns—**1,** lowness, shortness, FLATNESS, deepness, depth; debasement, depression, prostration, HUMILITY, degradation.
2, lowlands; basement, cellar, dungeon, ground floor, hold; low water; low tide, ebb tide, neap tide, bottom floor, bedrock.
Verbs—**1,** below, lie low, lie flat, underlie, crouch, slouch, flatten, wallow, grovel, crawl.
2, lower, depress, let *or* take down, debase, reduce, drop, sink, humble, humiliate. See HUMILITY.
Adjectives—low, neap, debased, nether, nethermost, sunken, fallen, flat, level with the ground, lying low, crouched, squat, prostrate, depressed, deep.
Adverbs—under, beneath, underneath, below, down, downward(s), at the foot of, underfoot, underground, downstairs, belowstairs, at a low ebb, below par.

Antonym, see HEIGHT.

---

loyal, *adj.* faithful, true, devoted. See PROBITY. *Ant.,* disloyal, treacherous.
lubrication, *n.* greasing, oiling; oiliness; anointing, anointment, unction, unctuousness. See SMOOTHNESS, OIL. *Ant.,* see FRICTION.
lucid, *adj.* clear, limpid, transparent, understandable, rational. See TRANSPARENCY, REASONING. *Ant.,* cloudy, confused.
luck, *n.* CHANCE, fortune; good fortune. See PROSPERITY.
lucky, *adj.* fortunate, opportune, auspicious. See OCCASION.
lucrative, *adj.* profitable, well-paying, gainful, moneymaking, productive. See MONEY, COMPENSATION, PRODUCTION.
ludicrous, *adj.* ridiculous, absurd (see ABSURDITY).
lug, *v.* tote, transport, TRANSFER, convey, carry; draw, drag. See TRACTION.
luggage, *n.* BAGGAGE, impedimenta, bag and baggage. See PROPERTY.
lukewarm, *adj.* tepid; moderate, temperate, insipid, so-so, neither here nor there; indifferent (see INDIFFERENCE). See MODERATION, INSIPIDITY.
lull, *n.* calm, intermission. See END.
lumber, *n. & v.* —*n.* wood, logs, timber; planks, boards, paneling, *etc.* See MATERIALS. —*v.* trudge, plod, hobble, bumble. See SLOWNESS.
luminary, *n.* See LIGHT. *Ant.,* see DARKNESS.
luminous, *adj.* luminary, lighted, glowing; incandescent, radiant, lit, alight, self-luminous; phosphorescent, luminescent. See LIGHT. *Ant.,* see DARKNESS.
lump, *n.* PROTUBERANCE, swelling, chunk, mass; consolidation, aggregation. See SIZE, CONVEXITY, ASSEMBLAGE.
lunatic, *n.* MADMAN, bedlamite, maniac, psychopath.
lunch, *n.* luncheon, snack, collation. *Colloq.,* spread, bite. See FOOD.
lung, *n.* lights, bellow. See WIND.
lunge, *v. & n.* —*v.* surge, thrust, jab; lurch, LEAP, PLUNGE. —*n.* thrust, surge, onslaught. See IMPULSE.
lurch, *v.i.* sway, pitch, stagger, stumble. See NAVIGATION, DESCENT.
lure, *v.t.* entice, decoy, tempt, coax, reduce. See REQUEST, ATTRACTION.
lurid, *adj.* pallid, ghastly; glaring, eerie; sinister, sensational. See DARKNESS.
lurk, *v.i.* skulk, sneak, prowl. See CONCEALMENT.
luscious, *adj.* sweet, delicious, ambrosial. See TASTE, SWEETNESS.
lush, *adj. & n.* —*adj.* luscious, juicy, succulent; tender, ripe; LUXURIOUS. See TASTE, MOISTURE. —*n., colloq.,* drunkard, sot, barfly. See DRUNKENNESS.
lust, *n. & v.* —*n.* DESIRE, carnality, sex, sensuality, lasciviousness; satyriasis, nymphomania; voracity, avarice, greed, drive, itch. *Slang,*

sex mania, the hots; yen. —*v.i.* covet, crave, hunger, DESIRE, yearn, *etc.*

luster, *n.* gloss, sheen, brightness, splendor; brilliance, fame. See LIGHT, BEAUTY, REPUTE.

lusty, *adj.* robust, vigorous, hearty, sturdy. See HEALTH, SIZE.

luxuriant, *adj.* lush, abundant, profuse; fertile, rich. See PRODUCTION, VEGETABLE.

luxurious, *adj.* sumptuous, elegant; voluptuous, self-indulgent. See PLEASURE. *Ant.,* simple; see SIMPLENESS.

luxury, *n.* self-indulgence, prodigality; dainty; elegance, sumptuousness, extravagance. See PLEASURE. *Ant.,* simplicity; see SIMPLENESS.

lynching, *n.* hanging, murder; tar and feathering; mob rule. *Slang,* necktie party; kangaroo court. See PUNISHMENT, KILLING, INJUSTICE.

lyric, *n.* poem, song. See POETRY.

M

macabre, *adj.* ghastly, grisly; eerie, weird; morbid, hideous, grotesque, fantastic. See DEATH, UGLINESS.

machine, *n.* apparatus, contrivance, mechanism, device; motor, engine; airplane, car, bicycle; organization, cabal. See VEHICLE, PARTY, MEANS.

mad, *adj.* crazy, insane; rabid; frantic, foolish, turbulent. *Colloq.,* angry. See INSANITY, VIOLENCE. *Ant.,* see SANITY.

madden, *v.* infuriate, enrage, incense, craze; drive mad, derange; make one's blood boil. *Colloq.,* foam at the mouth. See RESENTMENT, IRASCIBILITY.

made-up, *adj.* fabricated, imagined, fanciful, make-believe, fictitious, false, made of whole cloth. See IMAGINATION, UNTRUTH, FALSENESS.

madhouse, *n.* See ASYLUM.

madman, madwoman, *n.* maniac, bedlamite, lunatic; demoniac, dipsomaniac, megalomaniac; neurotic, psychotic, psychopath, schizophrenic, catatonic, paranoiac; fury, madcap, corybant, fiend, monster, sex fiend; eccentric, fanatic, zealot. *Slang,* nut, crank, loony, bat, bug, screwball, oddball, case, crackpot. See INSANITY, FOLLY.

magazine, *n.* storehouse, arsenal, reservoir; periodical. See STORE, BOOK.

magic, *n. & adj.* —*n.* SORCERY; witchery, glamour, spell; legerdemain. —*adj.* mystic, occult; enchanting.

magician, *n.* witch, wizard, sorcerer; prestidigitator. See SORCERY.

magisterial, *adj.* arbitrary, dictatorial; arrogant, pompous. See INSOLENCE, CERTAINTY.

magistrate, *n.* See JUDGE.

magnanimous, *adj.* generous, high-minded, great-souled. See PROBITY.

magnet, *n.* loadstone, lodestone. See ATTRACTION.

magnetism, *n.* ATTRACTION, magnetic force. See POWER.

magnificent, *adj.* grand, splendid; awe-inspiring; noble, superb. See REPUTE.

magnify, *v.t.* enlarge, augment; laud, glorify. See INCREASE, APPROBATION. *Ant.,* see CONTRACTION.

magnitude, *n.* SIZE, bulk; extent; hugeness, immensity. See GREATNESS.

maid, *n.* girl, lass, maiden, miss; virgin, spinster; SERVANT, domestic. See YOUTH, CELIBACY.

maidenly, *adj.* modest; gentle; girlish. See YOUTH.

mail, *n. & v.t.* —*n.* post, letters, CORRESPONDENCE. —*v.t.* post, send, forward. See COMMUNICATION.

maim, *v.t.* cripple, disfigure, mutilate, lame. See DETERIORATION.

main, *n. & adj.* —*n.* conduit, pipe; strength, power; sea, OCEAN. —*adj.* chief, principal; sheer. See SUPERIORITY, PASSAGE.

mainly, *adv.* principally, primarily; mostly, largely, on the whole; above all, more than anything. See GENERALITY, IMPORTANCE.

mainstay, *n.* SUPPORT, supporter, dependence.

maintain, *v.t.* SUPPORT, carry; preserve, keep; possess, have; uphold; allege, affirm. See PRESERVATION, VINDICATION.

majestic, *adj.* noble, august, stately, imposing. See GREATNESS.

major, *adj.* principal, chief; greater. See SUPERIORITY. *Ant.,* see INFERIORITY.

majority, *n.* adulthood; preponderance, excess, SUPERIORITY. See YOUTH. *Ant.,* see INFERIORITY.

make, *v.t.* create, produce; prepare; obtain, get; cause, compel; amount to. See PRODUCTION, ACTION, COMPULSION.

make-believe, *n. & adj.* —*n.* fantasy, unreality, fiction, IMAGINATION; pretense, feigning, IMITATION, fakery, DECEPTION. —*adj.* MADE-UP; feigned, sham, whimsical, IMITATION. *Colloq.,* fake, phony. See FALSENESS.

makeshift, *n.* expedient, substitute, stopgap. See SUBSTITUTION.

make-up, *n.* COMPOSITION, personality; placement; cosmetics, beautification.

maladroit, *adj.* CLUMSY, awkward, inept. See UNSKILLFULNESS, INELEGANCE.

malady, *n.* DISEASE, sickness, illness, infirmity.

malcontent, *n.* grumbler, faultfinder; insurgent, rebel. *Colloq.,* griper. See DISCONTENT, OPPOSITION.

MALE

Nouns—**1,** male, man, he, *homo,* gentleman, sir, MASTER, yeoman, wight, swain, fellow, blade, chap, gaffer, husband, bachelor, Mr., mister, boy, stripling, youth, lad; *homme; hombre;* macho. *Slang,* guy, bloke, bimbo, bozo, geezer, *etc.*

2, cock, drake, gander, dog, boar, stag, hart, buck, horse, stallion, tomcat, ram, billygoat, bull, rooster, cob, capon, ox, gelding, steer.

3, mankind, human beings, human race, man; manhood, male sex, virility, manliness, maleness, masculinity.

Adjectives—male, masculine, manly, virile, gentlemanly, boyish; adult; manlike; macho; android, anthropoid.

Antonym, see FEMALE.

---

malediction, *n.* IMPRECATION, curse, anathema, execration. *Ant.,* see APPROBATION.

malefactor, *n.* EVILDOER, wrongdoer, criminal, felon. *Ant.,* see GOODNESS.

MALEVOLENCE

Nouns—**1,** malevolence; evil *or* bad intent; misanthropy, ill-nature; ENMITY, HATE; malignity, malice, malice aforethought, maliciousness, spite, resentment, venom, rancor; virulence, mordacity, acerbity, churlishness, hardness of heart, obduracy; cruelty, cruelness, brutality, savagery, ferocity, barbarity, inhumanity; truculence, ruffianism; heart of stone, evil eye, cloven foot *or* hoof, poison pen.

2, ill turn, bad turn, affront, insult, indignity, outrage, abuse, atrocity, ill usage, intolerance, persecution.

3, misanthrope, man-hater, misogynist, woman-hater, cynic.

Verbs—**1,** be malevolent, bear *or* harbor a grudge, bear malice.

2, hurt, injure, harm, wrong, do harm, outrage, disoblige, malign, molest, worry, harass, annoy, harry, bait, tease, play the devil with, wreak havoc, do mischief, hunt down, hound, persecute, oppress, grind, maltreat, bedevil, ill-treat, ill use, do one's worst, show *or* have no mercy. *Colloq.,* have it in for. *Slang,* do one dirt, rub it in.

Adjectives—**1,** malevolent, ill-disposed, ill-intentioned, evilminded, misanthropic, malicious, malign, malignant, rancorous, spiteful, caustic, bitter, acrimonious, virulent, malefic, maleficent, venomous, invidious.
2, harsh, disobliging, unkind, unfriendly, antisocial; churlish, surly, sullen; coldblooded, coldhearted, hardhearted, stony-hearted, selfish, unnatural, ruthless, relentless.
3, cruel, brutal, savage, ferocious, inhuman, barbarous, fell, truculent, bloodthirsty, murderous, atrocious, fiendish, demoniacal, diabolical, devilish, infernal, hellish, Satanic.
Antonym, see BENEVOLENCE.

---

malformation, *n.* DISTORTION, deformity. *Ant.,* see FORM.
malfunction, *v. & n.* —*v.i.* go amiss *or* wrong, fail. *Slang,* go haywire. —*n.* FAILURE, defect, misfire, miscarriage.
malice, *n.* MALEVOLENCE, spite, ill will, animosity. *Ant.,* see GOODNESS, BENEVOLENCE.
malign, *v.t.* libel, slander; calumniate, asperse, traduce, besmirch, MISREPRESENT; backbite. See DETRACTION.
malignant, *adj.* malign, vicious, criminal; harmful, virulent, pernicious; severe, fatal, incurable. See DISEASE, SEVERITY.
malinger, *v.i.* soldier, feign, shirk, slack. *Colloq.,* goldbrick. See AVOIDANCE.
mall, *n.* promenade, allée, avenue, parkway; shopping center. See PASSAGE.
mallet, *n.* hammer, club, maul. See ARMS.
malnutrition, *n.* deficiency; emaciation, anemia, marasmus; cachexia, gout, scurvy, pellagra, hookworm; obesity. See DISEASE.

MALODOROUSNESS

Nouns—**1,** malodorousness, malodor, fetor, fetidness, bad smell, smelliness, bad odor, stench, stink, foul odor, rankness, goatishness, goatiness, mephitis, mustiness, rancidness, rancidity, foulness; opprobrium; bad breath, halitosis.
2, polecat, skunk, stoat, rotten egg, asafoetida, skunk cabbage, stinkpot, stinker, stink bomb; stinkweed.
Verbs—be malodourous, have a bad smell, stink, stink in the nostrils, stink like a polecat, smell offensively.
Adjectives—malodorous, fetid, smelling, stinking, stinky, smelly, high, bad, foul, strong, offensive, noisome, gassy, rank, rancid, gamy, tainted, fusty, musty, putrid, suffocating, mephitic, goaty, goatish.
Antonym, see FRAGRANCE.

---

malpractice, *n.* wrongdoing, misdemeanor, malfeasance, misconduct. See BADNESS.
maltreat, *v.t.* abuse, ill-treat, misuse. See BADNESS.
mammoth, *adj. & n.* —*adj.* huge, giant, gigantic, tremendous, prodigious, colossal, enormous. See GREATNESS, SIZE. *Ant.,* see LITTLENESS. —*n.* elephant, behemoth.
man, *n. & v.* —*n.* See MALE, MANKIND. *Ant.,* see FEMALE. —*v.* run, operate; supply a crew *or* men for; staff. See DEFENSE.
manage, *v.t.* administer, conduct; control; contrive; manipulate. See DIRECTION.
manageable, *adj.* tractable, docile, obedient; wieldy, governable. See FACILITY. *Ant.,* see UNCONFORMITY.
management, *n.* DIRECTION, control, administration; directorate, administrating body.
manager, *n.* executive, superintendent, supervisor, director. *Colloq.,* boss.
mandate, *n.* COMMAND, edict, statute, ordinance; COMMISSION.
mandatory, *adj.* required, compulsory, binding, obligatory. See NECESSITY, COMMAND, COMPULSION.

maneuver, *n.* artifice, stratagem, tactic. See DECEPTION.

manger, *n.* trough, bin, crib, feed box. See RECEPTACLE.

mangle, *v.t.* break, crush, mutilate; press, iron. See DETERIORATION, SMOOTHNESS.

mangy, *adj.* itchy, scurvy, scaly, scrofulous; shabby, seedy, shoddy, ragged; sordid, squalid, wretched. See BADNESS, UNCLEANNESS, DETERIORATION, DISEASE.

manhandle, *v.t.* maul, batter, paw, maltreat, push around. See PAIN, AGITATION.

manhood, *n.* adulthood, maturity; VIRILITY, COURAGE, manliness.

mania, *n.* madness, frenzy, lunacy; obsession, craze; INSANITY.

maniac, *n.* See MADMAN.

manic, *adj.* maniacal, insane, frenzied. See EXCITABILITY, INSANITY.

manicure, *v.t.* trim, clip, cut, pare, file; polish, buff, lacquer.

manifest, *v. & adj.* —*v.t.* bring forward, show, display, evidence, trot out, bring to light; demonstrate; proclaim, publish, disclose. —*adj.* apparent, obvious, evident; salient, striking, prominent; flagrant; pronounced; definite, distinct; conspicuous, unmistakable, plain, clear; open, overt; patent. See EVIDENCE. *Ant.,* see CONCEALMENT.

manifestation, *n.* plainness, visibility; demonstration; exhibition; display, show, showing, showing off; indication, publicity, DISCLOSURE, revelation, openness, prominence, conspicuousness. See EVIDENCE. *Ant.,* see CONCEALMENT.

manifesto, *n.* proclamation, statement, pronouncement; credo, theory, BELIEF.

manifold, *adj. & v.* —*adj.* multiple, diverse, multiform; copied, repeated. See MULTITUDE, VARIEGATION, DIFFERENCE. —*v.* reproduce, COPY, multiply.

manipulate, *v.t.* operate, control, manage; juggle, falsify. See USE, DECEPTION.

MANKIND

Nouns—**1,** mankind, man, humanity, human race, human species, *homo sapiens,* humankind; human nature, mortality, flesh, generation.

2, anthropology, anthropography, ethnography, ethnology, sociology.

3, human being; person, individual, creature, fellow creature; mortal; somebody, one; soul, living soul; earthling; party; MALE, man, FEMALE, woman.

4, people; persons, folk; public, society, world, community, general public, nation, nationality, STATE, realm, commonweal, commonwealth, republic, body politic, population, POPULACE.

Adjectives—human; anthropoid; ethnic, racial; mortal, personal, individual; national, civil, public, social; cosmopolitan, universal.

---

manly, *adj.* masculine; straightforward, courageous, honorable. See COURAGE. *Ant.,* see FEMALE.

mannequin, *n.* dummy, DOLL; FASHION model. *Colloq.,* cover girl. See BEAUTY.

manner, *n.* kind, sort; style, mode; CONDUCT, behavior; way, method.

mannerism, *n.* eccentricity, peculiarity, idiosyncrasy; AFFECTATION.

manners, *n.* CONDUCT, behavior, deportment; COURTESY, politeness.

manor, *n.* mansion, hall, hacienda; estate, territory, demesne. See ABODE.

manpower, *n.* working force, staff; STRENGTH, capacity, potential; warpower, army, fighting force; womanpower.

mansion, *n.* house, manor, hall, villa. See ABODE.

mantle, *n.* COVERING; cloak, cape, robe. See CLOTHING.

manual, *adj. & n.* —*adj.* nonautomatic, by hand. —*n.* guide, handbook, text; keyboard, control, dial; system, exercise, regimen. See INFORMATION, MUSICAL INSTRUMENTS.

manufacture, *v.t.* make, produce, fabricate. See PRODUCTION.

manure, *n.* fertilizer, compost, dung. See AGRICULTURE.

manuscript, *n.* script, handwriting, author's original. See WRITING.

many, *adj.* numerous, multitudinous, manifold. See MULTITUDE.

many-colored, *adj.* polychrome, polychromatic, varicolored, pied, motley, variegated, colorful; mottled, brindled; kaleidoscopic. See VARIEGATION, COLOR.

many-sided, *adj.* versatile; multilateral, polyhedral. See CHANGEABLENESS, SIDE.

map, *n.* PLAN, chart, projection; diagram. *Slang,* face.

mar, *v.t.* disfigure, deface, blemish, scratch, impair. See DETERIORATION.

marathon, *adj.* nonstop, continuous, arduous; long, endless. See CONTINUITY.

marauder, *n.* raider, plunderer, freebooter, pillager. See STEALING.

marble, *adj.* hard, vitreous, unyielding; lifeless, insensible, cold; white, pale, colorless; variegated, particolored, pied, striated, mottled. See COLOR, HARDNESS, INSENSIBILITY.

march, *v.i.* tramp, pace, parade, file, advance. See TRAVEL.

margin, *n.* EDGE, border, rim, brink, verge, limit; leeway. See SPACE.

marijuana, *n.* marihuana; hemp, cannabis, hashish, bhang, ganja(h). *Slang,* tea, pot, hay, grass, smoke, reefer, Mary Jane. See HABIT.

marine, *adj.* nautical, naval; pelagic, maritime. See NAVIGATION.

mariner, *n.* sailor, seaman, crewman. *Colloq.,* tar, salt. See NAVIGATION.

marital, *adj.* hymeneal, spousal (see MATRIMONIAL).

maritime, *adj.* pelagic, oceanic; coastal, littoral, seaside; seafaring, nautical. See WATER, NAVIGATION, EDGE.

mark, *n. & v.t.* —*n.* goal; imprint, stain; label, badge; token, symptom; symbol; standard, demarcation. See INDICATION. —*v.t.* inscribe, stain; note; check, indicate; delimit. See ATTENTION.

marked, *adj.* noticeable, conspicuous; watched, followed. See INDICATION, SUPERIORITY.

marker, *n.* indicator, INDICATION, sign; counter, chip. *Slang,* I.O.U., chit.

market, *n.* marketplace, mart; agora; fair, bazaar; STORE, shop, stall, booth, counter; farmers' market, flea market, supermarket; chain store; exchange, stock exchange, change, curb, bourse, rialto, pit, Wall Street, the street; black market. See BUSINESS, SALE.

marksman, *n.* sharpshooter, dead shot, crackshot. See PROPULSION.

MARRIAGE

Nouns—**1,** marriage, matrimony, wedlock, union; intermarriage, nuptial tie, married state, bed and board, cohabitation, wedded bliss; engagement (see PREDICTION).

2, wedding, nuptials, Hymen, espousal; leading to the altar; epithalamium; temple of Hymen; honeymoon; sea of matrimony.

3, engagement, betrothal, understanding, proposal; fiancé(e), betrothed.

4, bride, bridegroom, groom; bridesmaid, maid of honor, matron of honor, best man, usher.

5, married man, Benedict, partner, spouse, mate, husband, man, good provider, consort, old man, squaw-man; married woman, bride, wife, partner, concubine, old woman, frau, goodwife, spouse, mate, helpmate, helpmeet, rib, better half, squaw, lady, matron. *Slang,* ball and chain.

6, (married) couple, pair, man and wife, bride and groom, newlyweds; Darby and Joan, Mr. and Mrs., lovebirds, loving couple.

7, monogamy, bigamy, polygamy, polygyny, polyandry, Mormonism; morganatic marriage, common-law marriage, concubinage.

Verbs—**1,** marry, wive, take a wife; be married, be spliced; wed, espouse. *Slang,* get hitched, walk down the aisle, tie the knot.

2, marry, join, couple, unite, make one, tie the nuptial knot; give in marriage.

3, propose; betroth, affiance, plight troth; bespeak; pin; publish banns.

Adjectives—matrimonial, marital, conjugal, connubial; wedded, nuptial, hymeneal, spousal, bridal; engaged, betrothed, affianced; marriageable, nubile.

Antonym, see CELIBACY, DIVORCE.

---

marsh, *n.* marshland, swamp, swampland, morass, moss, fen, bog, peat bog; mire, quagmire, quicksand; slough; sump; wash, bottoms, mud, slush. See WATER, MOISTURE.

marshal, *v. & n.* —*v.t.* array, dispose, order, arrange; mobilize, activate, assemble, collect, utilize. See ARRANGEMENT. —*n.* officer, authority, sheriff. See AUTHORITY.

mart, *n.* See MARKET.

martial, *adj.* military, warlike, soldierly. See WARFARE. *Ant.*, see PACIFICATION.

martyr, *n.* victim, sacrifice, scapegoat; symbol, example; sufferer; saint. See RELIGION.

martyrdom, *n.* martyrship; sacrifice, suffering, PAIN, DEATH, torture, agony; heroism, ASCETICISM; saintliness; long-suffering. See KILLING, PUNISHMENT.

marvel, *n.* WONDER, PRODIGY.

marvelous, *adj.* wonderful, prodigious, surprising, extraordinary. See WONDER.

mascot, *n.* pet, FAVORITE, ANIMAL, synonym. See REPRESENTATION.

masculine, *adj.* manly, strong, virile. See STRENGTH, MALE.

mash, *v.t.* crush, smash, squeeze, compress, bruise, batter. See IMPULSE.

mask, *n. & v.t.* —*n.* false face, disguise, CONCEALMENT; effigy; shield, COVERING. —*v.t.* screen, conceal, hide.

masquerader, *n.* masker, domino, mummer; impostor. See CONCEALMENT, DECEPTION.

Mass, *n.* Divine Service, Eucharist, Communion. See RITE.

mass, *n.* bulk, SIZE; lump, wad, accumulation. See ASSEMBLAGE.

massacre, *n.* KILLING, slaughter, butchery, carnage.

massage, *v.t.* rub, rub down; knead, stroke; manipulate. See FRICTION.

massive, *adj.* bulky, ponderous, solid, imposing. See SIZE. *Ant.*, see LITTLENESS.

mast, *n.* pole, timber, upright, column, spar. See SHIP.

master, *n.* padrone; lord; commandant, commander, captain; chief, chieftan, sachem, ataman, hetman; head, headman; governor, leader, superior, director, foreman, boss; potentate, liege, suzerain, sovereign, ruler, monarch; autocrat, dictator, despot, tyrant, oligarch; crowned head, emperor, czar, king, *etc.*; expert, ARTIST, adept. See AUTHORITY, SKILL, RULE. *Ant.*, see SERVANT, UNSKILLFULNESS.

masterpiece, *n.* masterwork, *chef d'œuvre*. See SKILL.

mastery, *n.* rule, victory; ascendency, supremacy; SKILL. See AUTHORITY.

mat, *n. & v.* —*n.* pad, rug, runner, doormat, doily. See COVERING. —*v.* tangle, snarl; plait, braid, weaven, entwine. See JUNCTION. *Ant.*, disentangle, unweave.

match, *n.* lucifer, vesta; linstock, fuse; complement, peer; contest, bout; union, matrimony. See EQUALITY, CONTENTION, MARRIAGE.

matchless, *adj.* unequaled, peerless, unrivaled. See SUPERIORITY.

matchmaker, *n.* marriage broker, *shadchen*, go-between. See MARRIAGE, AGENCY.

mate, *n.* companion, chum, comrade; consort, spouse; husband, wife. See ACCOMPANIMENT, FRIEND, MARRIAGE.

material, *adj. & n.* —*adj.* bodily, corporeal, corporal, physical; somatic, sensible, tangible, ponderable, palpable, substantial; embodied, real; venal, mercenary; materialistic. —*n.* cloth, fabric; matter, SUBSTANCE; written matter. See MATERIALS. *Ant.*, see INSUBSTANTIALITY.

materialistic, *adj.* material, WORLDLY; pleasure-seeking, hedonistic, sybaritic, epicurean; greedy, avaricious, mercenary. See IRRELIGION.

materiality, *n.* See SUBSTANCE.

materialize, *v.* —*v.t.* produce, create, realize, give SUBSTANCE; conjure,

call *or* whip up, summon, produce [out of thin air]. See PRODUCTION.
—*v.i.* appear, enter, show. See APPEARANCE.

MATERIALS

Nouns—**1,** materials, raw material, substances, stuff; stock, staples; FUEL; grist; stores, provisions, MEANS; baggage, personal property.

2, metal, stone, clay, brick, bricks and mortar, crockery, composition; putty; concrete, cement; wood, lumber, timber; ore; iron, copper, *etc.*; steel; paper; goods, fabric, cloth, material, textiles.

3, plastic(s); synthetic resin; nitrocellulose, cellulose nitrate, Celluloid; acetate cellulose, ethyl cellulose, Cellophane; vinyl, Vinylite, polyvinyl acetate; polystyrene, styrene; phenol-formaldehyde, Bakelite; hard rubber, Neolite, Velon, Nylon, Orlon, Dacron; synthetic rubber, butyl, Butadiene; rayon, fiber, viscose, Celanese; urea, casein, lignite, lignin, wood flour; teflon.

4, resin, rosin, gum, lac; bitumen, pitch, tar, asphalt, gilsonite.

---

maternal, *adj.* motherly, motherlike. See ANCESTRY.

mathematics, *n.* computation, calculation, reckoning, arithmetic. See NUMERATION.

matriarch, *n.* materfamilias, matron, dowager. *Colloq.,* queen bee. See FEMALE.

matrimony, *n.* MARRIAGE, espousal; nuptials. See RITE.

matron, *n.* married woman, wife, mother, widow; housekeeper, DIRECTOR. See MARRIAGE.

matter, *n. & v.i.* —*n.* substance, material; subject, TOPIC; BUSINESS; affair; cause, ground; predicament, DIFFICULTY. See SUBSTANCE. —*v.i.* signify, import; count. See IMPORTANCE.

matter-of-fact, *adj.* practical, prosaic, unimaginative, formal. See SIMPLENESS.

mattress, *n.* bedding; tick, bolster, pallet; featherbed. See SUPPORT.

mature, *adj. & v.i.* —*adj.* ripe, developed, full-grown, adult. *Ant.,* see YOUTH. —*v.i.* ripen, develop, grow up. See YOUTH, PREPARATION.

maturity, *n.* ripeness, completeness, adulthood. See PREPARATION, OLDNESS. *Ant.,* see YOUTH.

maudlin, *adj.* weepy, teary, sobby; sentimental; drunk. See LAMENTATION.

maul, *v.t.* MANHANDLE, punch, pummel, batter. *Slang,* beat up. See IMPULSE.

mausoleum, *n.* tomb, sepulcher, vault; pyramid, mastaba. See INTERMENT.

maverick, *n.* loner, lone wolf, nonconformist, dissenter. See UNCONFORMITY.

mawkish, *adj.* nauseous, offensive; effusive, maudlin. See REPULSION, FEELING.

MAXIM

Nouns—**1,** maxim, aphorism, apo(ph)thegm, dictum, saying, adage, saw, proverb; sentence, *mot,* motto, word, moral, byword, household word; axiom, theorum, scholium, truism, TRUTH, formula, principle, law, conclusion, reflection, proposition, protasis; precept, RULE, golden rule; epigram, slogan, device; epitaph. See MEANING.

2, commonplace, bromide, cliché; platitude, twice-told tale, text; wise, trite *or* hackneyed saying. *Colloq.,* old song, old story. *Slang,* chestnut. See DULLNESS.

Verbs—aphorize, epigrammatize.

Adjectives—aphoristic, proverbial, axiomatic, epigrammatic; sententious, bromidic, platitudinous.

Adverbs—aphoristically, proverbially, as the saying goes, as they say, to coin a phrase.

Antonym, see ABSURDITY.

maximum, *adj. & n.* —*adj.* supreme, utmost; greatest, highest. —*n.* most, utmost; greatest possible (number, degree, *etc.*). See SUPERIORITY. *Ant.*, see LITTLENESS.

may, *v.* can; might; be allowed, permitted, *etc.* See PERMISSION.

maybe, *adv.* perhaps, mayhap, perchance; possibly, conceivably, feasibly. See DOUBT.

mayhem, *n.* injury, mutilation, damage, harm, DESTRUCTION, VIOLENCE. See PAIN.

mayor, *n.* administrator, president; burgomaster, magistrate, major domo; city manager. See AUTHORITY.

maze, *n.* labyrinth, network; bewilderment, perplexity. See DISORDER.

meadow, *n.* mead, lea, pasture, mowing. See VEGETABLE, PLAIN.

meager, *adj.* spare, scanty, sparse, poor; lean, gaunt. See INSUFFICIENCY, NARROWNESS. *Ant.*, see SUFFICIENCY.

meal, *n.* repast, refection; breakfast, dinner, lunch, *etc.* *Slang,* feed, eats. See FOOD.

mean, *adj.* humble; ignoble; insignificant; sordid, niggardly. See PARSIMONY, SERVILITY.

MEAN

Nouns—mean, medium; average, normal, rule, balance; mediocrity, generality; golden mean, middle course, middle compromise, neutrality, MODERATION, middle of the road. *Colloq.*, fence-sitting. See MIDDLE.
Verbs—split the difference, reduce to a mean, strike a balance, pair off; average, divide; take a middle course.
Adjectives—mean, intermediate, middle, medial, medium, average, mediocre, middle-class, commonplace, normal; median.
Adverbs—on the average, in the long run, taking all things together, in round numbers.

---

meander, *v.i.* wind, drift, twist, turn; go with the wind, the tide *or* the current; float *or* move aimlessly; wander, roam, ramble. See DEVIATION.

MEANING

Nouns—1, meaning, significance, signification; sense, expression; import, purport, implication, drift, tenor, spirit, bearing; scope, purpose, aim, intent, INTENTION, object; allusion, suggestion, synonym, INTERPRETATION, connotation.
2, matter, subject, subject matter, argument, text, sum and substance, gist.
Verbs—mean, signify, express, import, purpose, convey, imply, connote, infer, indicate, tell of, speak of; touch on; point to, allude to, drive at, have in mind, intend, aim at, declare; understand by, interpret.
Adjectives—meaning, meaningful, expressive, suggestive, allusive, significant, eloquent, pithy, full of meaning, pregnant with meaning; declaratory, intelligible, literal; synonymous, tantamount, equivalent; implied, explicit, express, implicit.
Adverbs—meaningly, significantly, *etc.*; to that effect, that is to say, to all intents and purposes.

Antonym, see ABSURDITY.

---

meaningless, *adj.* senseless, pointless; trivial, insignificant; nonsensical. See ABSURDITY. *Ant.*, see MEANING.

MEANS

Nouns—means, resources, POWER, SUPPORT, wherewithal, MONEY, MATERIALS, WEALTH, ways and means, capital, backing, stock in trade, PROVISION, STORE, appliances, conveniences, cards to play, expedients, measures, two strings to one's bow, AID, INFLUENCE, medium, INSTRUMENT, INSTRUMENTALITY. *Colloq.*, ace in the hole; enough rope.

Verbs—have means, have the power; enable, empower; back, finance, underwrite.

Adverbs—by means of, with, by all means; wherewith, herewith, therewith, wherewithal, how, in what manner, through, by the instrumentality of, with the aid of, by the agency of, with the help of.

Antonym, see IMPOTENCE.

mean–spirited, *adj.* abject, groveling; contemptible, petty.

measure, *n.* QUANTITY, extent; gauge; standard; amount, allotment; legislative bill; step, course. See MEASUREMENT, APPORTIONMENT.

measureless, *adj.* without measure, immensurable, immeasurable; infinite, endless, fathomless; vast, astronomical. See GREATNESS, INFINITY.

MEASUREMENT

Nouns—**1,** measurement, measure, admeasurement, mensuration, survey, valuation, appraisement, appraisal, metage, assessment, assize, estimate, estimation; dead reckoning, reckoning, gauging; extent, SIZE, LENGTH, DISTANCE, quantity, amount.

2, measure, standard, rule, foot-rule, yardstick, balance, sextant, quadrant, compass, calipers, gauge, meter, gas meter, line, rod, check; level, plumb line, lead, log, tape, square, T square, index, scale, Beaufort scale (wind velocity measure), engineer's chain, Gunter's chain (surveyor's), graduated scale, vernier, anemometer, dynamometer, THERMOMETER, barometer, bathometer, galvanometer, goniometer, speedometer, micrometer, hydrometer, tachometer, altimeter, hygrometer, ammeter, voltimeter; pedometer; radiometer, potentiometer, sphygmomanometer, *etc.*

3, coördinates, ordinate and *abscissa*, polar coördinates, latitude and longitude, declination and right ascension, altitude and azimuth.

4, geometry, *etc.*; stereometry, chronometry, barometry, thermometry, hypometry; surveying, geodesy, geodetics, orthometry, topography, micrometry, altimetry, anthropometry, electrometry, craniometry.

5, measurer, surveyor, geometer, geodetist, topographer.

Verbs—measure, meter, value, assess, rate, appraise, estimate, set a value on, appreciate, size up, span, pace, step; gauge, plumb, weigh, probe, sound, fathom; heave the lead; survey, graduate, calibrate.

Adjectives—measuring, metric, metrical, measurable; geodetic(al); barometric(al); latitudinal, *etc.*

meat, *n.* pith, essence, SUBSTANCE, core. See FOOD.

mechanic, *n.* mechanician, repairman, serviceman. See RESTORATION.

mechanical, *adj.* machinelike, automatic, powerdriven, powered; involuntary, unreasoning. See POWER, COMPULSION.

mechanism, *n.* apparatus, contraption (see MACHINE).

medal, *n.* medallion, medalet; badge, decoration, ORDER, prize, award, ribbon.

medallion, *n.* medal, plaque, relief, coin. See FORM, REPRESENTATION.

meddle, *v.i.* tamper; interfere, intrude. See ACTIVITY, BETWEEN.

meddlesome, *adj.* officious, obtrusive, interfering. See ACTIVITY, BETWEEN.

meddlesomeness, *n.* officiousness; interference, intrusion. See ACTIVITY, BETWEEN.

media, *n.pl.* mediums; magazines, newspapers, journals, house organs; radio, television; billboards, posters, *etc.* See PUBLICATION, COMMUNICATION.

mediation, *n.* intermediation, intercession, intervention; interference; parley, negotiation, arbitration; intercession; COMPROMISE. See PACIFICATION.

medicine, *n.* REMEDY, drugs; therapy, physic; medical profession.

medieval, *adj.* feudal, knightly, courtly; antiquated, old-fashioned, outdated, quaint. See OLDNESS.

MEDIOCRITY

Nouns—mediocrity, MIDDLE course, moderate degree, medial standard, moderate *or* average circumstances; normality, average, golden mean; MODERATION, temperance, respectability; middle classes, *bourgeoisie.* See INFERIORITY.

Verbs—be mediocre, be moderate, jog on; go *or* get on tolerably, fairly *or* quietly; get along, get by, pass [in the dark], muddle through.

Adjectives—mediocre, ordinary, commonplace, everyday; moderate, middling, normal, average, mean, medium, medial; indifferent, passable, tolerable, *comme ci comme ça*, presentable, respectable, fair, second-rate, run of the mill *or* mine, of poor quality; middle-class, *bourgeois.* *Colloq.*, no great shakes, nothing to write home about, just so-so, namby-pamby. *Slang*, no ball of fire.

meditate, *v.* muse, ponder, cogitate; contemplate, purpose. See THOUGHT.

medium, *n.* MEAN; surrounding; go-between, agent; AGENCY, instrumentality, means. See BETWEEN, COMPROMISE.

medley, *n.* jumble, miscellany, variety, MIXTURE. See DISORDER.

meek, *adj.* subdued, humble, patient, submissive. See MODESTY.

meet, *v.* encounter; intersect; oppose; greet, welcome; satisfy; refute; assemble, gather; contend. See ARRIVAL, AGREEMENT, OPPOSITION, ASSEMBLAGE.

meeting, *n.* encounter; assembly; JUNCTION; duel; tangency. See ARRIVAL, ASSEMBLAGE.

melancholy, *adj.* dejected, dispirited, sad, depressed. *Colloq.*, blue. See DARKNESS, DEJECTION.

mêlée, *n.* CONTENTION, combat, brawl, ruckus (see FIGHT); DISORDER, turmoil.

mellow, *adj.* soft, rich, ripe; mellifluous; subdued, delicate. See SOFTNESS, SOUND, PREPARATION. *Ant.*, see HARDNESS.

melodious, *adj.* melodic, melic, melopoeic; musical, euphonious, tuneful, lilting, lyric(al), singable; *bel canto.* See MUSIC, CONCORD.

melodrama, *n.* tragicomedy, seriocomedy; penny-dreadful, thriller, shocker; sentimentality, bathos; bravado, derring-do. *Slang*, horse opera, tearjerker. See DRAMA, EXCITEMENT.

melody, *n.* tune, theme, song, aria. See MUSIC.

melon, *n.* fruit, cantaloupe, honeydew, Persian melon, watermelon, *etc.* *Slang*, pot, boodle, graft. See VEGETABLE, MONEY.

melt, *v.* thaw, dissolve, disappear, vanish; fuse, thaw, dissolve, soften. See PITY, TRANSIENTNESS.

member, *n.* unit, constituent, element, PART; fellow, adherent, partner, *etc.* See MANKIND, SOCIALITY.

membership, *n.* members, body, WHOLE, entirety; affiliation, participation, INCLUSION, admission.

membrane, *n.* film, lamina, sheet, sheath, layer. See NARROWNESS.

memento, *n.* keepsake, souvenir, relic, token, memorial. See RECORD, MEMORY.

memoir, *n.* RECORD; reminiscence, autobiography. See DESCRIPTION.

memorable, *adj.* noteworthy, signal, outstanding; unforgettable. See IMPORTANCE, MEMORY.

memorandum, *n.* RECORD, note, reminder. *Colloq.*, memo. See COMMUNICATION.

memorial, *adj. & n.* —*adj.* commemorative. See MEMORY. —*n.* monument, shrine, tablet; anniversary. See RECORD.

MEMORY

Nouns—**1,** memory, remembrance, retention, retentiveness, tenacity, reminiscence, recognition, recurrence, recollection, retrospect, retrospection, afterthought.

2, reminder, suggestion, prompting, hint, cue; token, memento, souvenir,

keepsake, relic, memorandum, memo, memoir; memorial, commemoration, Memorial or Decoration Day, monument; memorabilia; flashback.
3, art of memory; artificial memory, mnemonics, mnemotechnics, mnemotechyn, Mnemosyne; retentive or photographic memory; rote, repetition; prompter. *Colloq.*, a string around a finger.
Verbs—**1**, remember, remind, retain the memory of; keep in view, bear in mind, hold in memory, remain in one's memory, mind or head.
2, recur to the mind, flash across the memory; haunt, run in the head.
3, recognize, recollect, bethink oneself, recall, call up, retrace, look back, think back upon, review, call to mind, carry one's thoughts back, reminisce.
4, suggest, prompt, put or keep in mind, remind, call or summon up; renew; tax, jog, refresh or awaken the memory.
5, memorize; have, learn, know or say by heart or rote; repeat, have at the tip of one's tongue; commit to memory; con, fix, make a note of.
6, keep the memory alive, keep in memory, commemorate, memorialize, honor the memory of.
Adjectives—remembering, remembered, mindful, reminiscent, retentive, retained in the memory, fresh, alive, green, unforgotten, within one's memory, indelible; uppermost in one's thoughts; memorable, memorial, commemorative.
Adverbs—by heart or rote, without prompting, word for word; in memory of, in memoriam.

Antonym, see OBLIVION.

---

menace, *n. & v.* —*n.* threat, danger, hazard, peril. —*v.t.* threaten, intimidate, bully; impend, loom. See WARNING. *Ant.*, see SAFETY.
mend, *v.t.* repair, restore, correct, improve. See IMPROVEMENT, RESTORATION.
mendacity, *n.* untruthfulness, UNTRUTH, FALSENESS, DECEPTION, duplicity.
mendicancy, *n.* beggary, mendicity. *Colloq.*, panhandling. See POVERTY.
menial, *n. & adj.* —*n.* SERVANT, slave, flunky. —*adj.* humble; servile; degrading, mean. *Ant.*, see AUTHORITY.
menopause, *n.* change of life, climacteric; middle age. See CHANGE, OLDNESS.
mental, *adj.* intellectual, cognitive, rational, psychologic. See INTELLECT.
mentality, *n.* INTELLECT, intelligence, mind, understanding.
mention, *v.t.* communicate, designate, let fall; cite, speak of. See INFORMATION.
mentor, *n.* teacher (see TEACHING).
menu, *n.* bill of fare, fare, diet, LIST, carte. See FOOD.
mercenary, *adj.* calculating, selfish, sordid, venal, grasping. See PARSIMONY.
merchandise, *n. & v.* —*n.* wares, commodities; effects; goods, articles; stock, stock in trade; produce; supplies, stores, cargo. —*v.* buy, sell; market, vend; trade, barter, traffic, deal; retail, wholesale; peddle, hawk; distribute. See SALE, BUSINESS.
merchant, *n.* trader, dealer, tradesman, merchandiser; shopkeeper, storekeeper; businessman; retailer, wholesaler, middleman, jobber; salesman, -woman or -person, seller, vendor, vender, monger, huckster, hawker, peddler; sutler, costermonger, fishmonger; canvasser, agent, door-to-door salesman. See SALE, BUSINESS.
merciless, *adj.* cruel, hardhearted, pitiless, relentless. See SEVERITY. *Ant.*, see PITY.
mercy, *n.* PITY, LENIENCY, forbearance, compassion. *Ant.*, see SEVERITY.
mere, *adj.* nothing but, plain, bare, simple. See LITTLENESS.
merely, *adv.* barely, simply, only, purely. See LITTLENESS.
merge, *v.t.* unite, blend, coalesce, absorb. See MIXTURE, JUNCTION.
meridian, *n.* longitude; HEIGHT, culmination, zenith, apex, apogee, summit.

merit, *n.* desert(s), reward, due; worth, excellence; VIRTUE. See GOODNESS.

merry, *adj.* jovial, gay, blithe, vivacious. See CHEERFULNESS. *Ant.,* see DEJECTION.

mesh, *n.* meshwork; network, web, net; lacework; tangle, snarl; lattice, trellis, grille, grate, gridiron, sieve. See CROSSING, RETENTION, INTERVAL.

mesmerize, *v.t.* hypnotize; fascinate, captivate. See SORCERY, ATTRACTION.

mess, *n.* DIFFICULTY; predicament; DISORDER, litter, jumble; botch. See UNSKILLFULNESS.

message, *n.* COMMUNICATION, dispatch; note. See INFORMATION.

messenger, *n.* emissary, envoy, apostle, missionary; courier, carrier, bearer, errand boy, runner. See COMMUNICATION.

metal, *n.* MINERAL, MATERIAL, element, alloy, ore.

metaphorical, *adj.* allegorical, FIGURATIVE.

metaphysical, *adj.* abstruse, speculative, esoteric, transcendental.

meteoric, *adj.* sudden, rapid, fast, shooting. See LIGHT, VELOCITY.

meter, *n.* rhythm, cadence, lilt; gauge, measuring device. See POETRY, MEASUREMENT.

METHOD

Nouns—method, way, manner, wise, gait, form, mode, MEANS, style, FASHION, design, tone, behavior, guise; *modus operandi, modus vivendi,* procedure, process, practice, regimen, technique, methodology, strategy, tactics, routine, line of CONDUCT; system, PLAN, scheme, formula, RULE.

Verbs—methodize, systematize, arrange, regularize, organize.

Adjectives—methodic(al), systematic, schematic, stylistic, modal, procedural, planned, arranged, orderly, routine.

Adverbs—how; in what way, manner *or* mode; so, thus, in this way, after this fashion; one way or another, anyhow, by any means, somehow or other, however; by way of, via, on the high road to.

Antonym, see DISORDER.

---

metropolitan, *adj.* civil, urban, oppidan, city-wide, cosmopolitan, urbane, sophisticated, worldly. See ABODE, INHABITANT.

mettle, *n.* spirit, COURAGE, disposition.

mettlesome, *adj.* high-strung, courageous, plucky. See COURAGE, EXCITEMENT.

microbe, *n.* bacterium, germ. See LITTLENESS.

microphone, *n.* pickup, lavaliere. *Colloq.,* mike. see SOUND, COMMUNICATION.

microscopic, *adj.* minute, tiny, infinitesimal. See LITTLENESS.

MIDDLE

Nouns—**1,** middle, midst, MEAN, medium, middle term; center, core, hub, kernel; umbilicus; halfway house; nave, navel, nucleus; heart, axis, bull's-eye; marrow, pith; equidistance, bisection, half distance, equator; diaphragm, midriff; interjacence.

2, focus, focal point, convergence, concentration, centralization, corradiation.

Verbs—center on, focus, concentrate, meet, unite, converge.

Adjectives—middle, medial, median, mean, mid; midmost, intermediate, equidistant, central, focal, axial, equatorial, concentric, convergent.

Adverbs—in the middle, midway, halfway *or* midships, *in medias res.*

Antonym, see EXTERIOR.

---

middle–aged, *adj.* mature, in (one's) prime. See AGE.

middle-class, *adj.* common, ordinary (see MEDIOCRITY); bourgeois, conservative, conventional. See POPULACE, INSIPIDITY.

middleman, *n.* go-between, intermediary, AGENT. See COMPROMISE.

midget, *n.* dwarf, pygmy, homunculus. *Slang,* shrimp. See LITTLENESS.

midmost, *adj.* central; MIDDLE, mean.

midway, *adj.* halfway, MIDDLE.

mien, *n.* APPEARANCE, AIR, demeanor, bearing. See CONDUCT.

might, *n.* POWER, force, STRENGTH. *Ant.*, IMPOTENCE.

migrate, *v.i.* journey, TRAVEL; emigrate, immigrate.

mild, *adj.* gentle, easy, bland, soft, harmless; lenient, tolerant, merciful, humane, generous, forbearing; weak, neutral; placid, tranquil, temperate, moderate; comfortable, clement (of weather, temperature); meek, submissive, conciliatory. See MODERATION.

mildew, *n.* mold, decay, rot, must. See DETERIORATION.

milestone, *n.* LANDMARK; giant step, progress, advance. See PROGRESSION.

militant, *adj.* aggressive, warlike, pugnacious, bellicose. See CONTENTION.

military, *adj.* martial, soldierly. See WARFARE. *Ant.*, see PACIFICATION.

militia, *n.* standing army, reserves, minutemen, soldiery. See COMBATANT.

milk, *v.* extract; extort, bleed; get the most out of, exploit; interrogate, question. *Colloq.*, play for what it's worth. See EXTRACTION, STEALING, INQUIRY.

milky, *adj.* lacteal; white, pale, chalky; spiritless, timorous. See COLOR.

mill, *n.* grinder, millstone, millrace; factory, plant, works, shop, (*pl.*) industry. See BUSINESS.

mimic, *v.t.* imitate, impersonate; ape, copy; mock. See IMITATION.

mind, *n. & v.t.* —*n.* consciousness, understanding; INTELLECT; purpose, intention, opinion. See INTELLIGENCE, REASONING. —*v.t.* heed, obey; notice, tend; object to. See ATTENTION, CARE.

mindful, *adj.* heedful, cautious, careful; watchful, alert. See CAUTION.

mindless, *adj.* heedless, careless, negligent, absent(minded); senseless, insane. *Colloq.*, blind, deaf, dumb. See IGNORANCE, INATTENTION.

mine, *n.* lode, vein, deposit; pit, open pit, burrow, excavation; explosive, bomb; source, treasure trove. See RECEPTACLE.

MINERAL

Nouns—**1,** mineral, mineral world *or* kingdom, inorganic matter, unorganized *or* inanimate matter, inorganization; lithification, petrification, petrifaction; stone, metal (see MATERIALS).

2, mineralogy, geology, geognosy, geoscopy, metallurgy, lithology, petrology.

Verbs—mineralize, petrify, lithify; turn to dust.

Adjectives—mineral, inorganic, inorganized, inanimate, azoic.

---

mingle, *v.t.* blend, mix, merge, intermingle, conjoin. See MIXTURE.

miniature, *adj. & n.* —*adj.* diminutive, minuscule, minute, petite, minikin; dwarf, pygmy, Lilliputian. —*n.* scale model, reduction. See LITTLENESS.

minimize, *v.* reduce, lessen; belittle, gloss over, run down, deprecate, detract from. See DETRACTION, LITTLENESS, UNDERESTIMATION.

minimum, *n.* modicum; least amount, least quantity. See LITTLENESS.

minister, *n.* legate, envoy, ambassador; cabinet officer, clergyman, pastor, *etc.* See DEPUTY, CLERGY.

ministry, *n.* state officers (*Brit.*); diplomatic service; priesthood, CLERGY.

minor, *adj.* lesser, inferior, secondary. See INFERIORITY. *Ant.*, see SUPERIORITY.

minority, *n.* few, handful; smaller group; nonage, childhood. See RARITY, YOUTH. *Ant.*, see MULTITUDE, SUPERIORITY.

minstrel, *n.* poet, troubadour, bard. See POETRY, MUSICIAN.

minus, *adj.* less, lacking; negative. See LOSS, ABSENCE. *Ant.*, see ADDITION.

minuteness, *n.* LITTLENESS, meticulousness, precision, exactitude. See ATTENTION, UNIMPORTANCE. *Ant.*, see SIZE, IMPORTANCE.

minutiae, *n.pl.* details, trivia. See UNIMPORTANCE.

miracle, *n.* WONDER, marvel, prodigy; IMPOSSIBILITY, fluke, phenomenon; divine intervention, *deus ex machina.* See SUPERNATURALISM.

miraculous, *adj.* preternatural, supernatural, prodigious, wondrous. See WONDER.

mirage, *n.* See HALLUCINATION.

mire, *n.* mud, muck, dirt; quagmire, MARSH. See UNCLEANNESS.

mirror, *n.* looking glass, glass, reflector; cheval *or* pier glass, *etc.* See DESCRIPTION, SMOOTHNESS.

mirth, *n.* hilarity, jollity, merriment, glee. See CHEERFULNESS. *Ant.,* see DEJECTION, MODERATION.

misanthrope, *n.* man-hater, antisocial person, cynic, egotist; woman-hater, misogynist. See MALEVOLENCE. *Ant.,* see BENEVOLENCE.

misapprehend, *v.t.* misunderstand, mistake, misinterpret. *Ant.,* see KNOWLEDGE.

misbegotten, *adj.* illegitimate, bastard; illicit, illegal. See ILLEGALITY.

misbehavior, *n.* misconduct, mischief, DISOBEDIENCE, BADNESS.

miscalculate, *v.t.* misjudge, err, misreckon. See MISJUDGMENT.

miscarry, *v.i.* fail, go wrong, fall through; abort. See FAILURE. *Ant.,* see SUCCESS.

miscellaneous, *adj.* heterogeneous, indiscriminate, mixed, many-sided. See MIXTURE.

miscellany, *n.* anthology, analecta; medley, MIXTURE. See BOOK.

mischief, *n.* harm, injury; prank. See BADNESS, MALEVOLENCE.

misconception, *n.* delusion, mistake, misunderstanding. See ERROR.

misconduct, *n.* impropriety, misdemeanor, misbehavior, mismanagement. *Colloq.,* monkey business. See BADNESS.

misdeed, *n.* offense, WRONG, malefaction. See GUILT.

misdemeanor, *n.* crime, infraction, malfeasance. See ILLEGALITY, STEALING.

miser, *n.* hoarder, niggard, moneygrubber, skinflint. *Slang,* penny pincher, tightwad. See PARSIMONY.

miserable, *adj.* wretched, forlorn, doleful; mean, paltry. See PAIN, UNIMPORTANCE. *Ant.,* see PLEASURE.

misery, *n.* wretchedness, privation; distress, anguish. See PAIN. *Ant.,* see PLEASURE.

misfire, *v.* fail, abort; fizzle, sputter; backfire. See ERROR, FAILURE.

misfit, *n.* mismatch, poor fit; neurotic; rejectee, odd man, FAILURE. *Slang,* schlemiel, oddball, schnook, jerk, queer. See UNCONFORMITY.

misfortune, *n.* bad luck; mishap, disaster, calamity, catastrophe; ADVERSITY. *Ant.,* see CHANCE, WEALTH.

misgiving, *n.* DOUBT, apprehension, premonition, anxiety; qualm. See FEAR.

mishap, *n.* accident, mischance, misfortune. See ADVERSITY, CHANCE.

misinformation, *n.* misintelligence; misteaching, misguidance, misdirection; misinstruction, misleading, perversion; sophistry. See FALSEHOOD. *Ant.,* see TRUTH, INFORMATION.

misinterpretation, *n.* misapprehension, misunderstanding, misconstruction, misapplication; misconception, mistake; misrepresentation, perversion, EXAGGERATION, false construction, falsification. See DISTORTION, FALSEHOOD. *Ant.,* see TRUTH, INTERPRETATION.

MISJUDGMENT

Nouns—**1,** misjudgment, miscalculation, misconception, miscomputation, ERROR, hasty conclusion, misinterpretation.

2, prejudgment, prejudication, foregone conclusion, preconception, predilection, presumption, presentiment, preconceived idea, *idée fixe.*

3, partisanship; clannishness, provincialism; bias, warp, twist, prejudice; hobby, fad, quirk, crotchet; partiality, infatuation, blind side *or* spot, mote in the eye; onesided views, narrow conception, superficial ideas, narrowmindedness, bigotry, pedantry, hypercriticalness.

Verbs—**1,** misjudge, misestimate, misconceive, misreckon, miscompute, miscalculate, overestimate, underestimate.

2, forejudge, prejudge, presuppose, prejudicate, dogmatize; have a bias, have only one idea, jump *or* rush to conclusions, view with a jaundiced eye, not see beyond one's nose; bias, warp, twist, prejudice.

Adjectives—misjudging, wrongheaded, prejudiced, jaundiced, short-sighted, purblind, one-sided, superficial, narrowminded, illiberal, intolerant, hyper-critical, besotted, infatuated, fanatical, dogmatic, opinionated, self-opinionated, bigoted, crotchety, impracticable, unreasoning.

Antonym, see JUSTICE, INTERPRETATION.

mislay, *v.t.* misplace, lose. See LOSS.

mislead, *v.t.* deceive, delude, lead astray. See ERROR, DECEPTION.

mismanage, *v.t.* botch, mishandle; misconduct, maladminister. See UN-SKILLFULNESS.

misnomer, *n.* misnaming; malapropism; nickname, so(u)briquet, pet name, assumed name, alias; pen name, *nom de plume,* stage name, pseudonym. See NOMENCLATURE.

misplace, *v.t.* derange; mislocate, displace, mislay. See LOSS.

mispronounce, *v.t.* misspeak, missay; garble. See SPEECH.

misquote, *v.t.* miscite, misrepresent; twist, garble, distort. See UN-TRUTH, ERROR.

misrepresentation, *n.* misstatement, DISTORTION, EXAGGERATION, perversion, falsification; bad likeness; caricature, burlesque, travesty; mimicry, mockery, parody, takeoff, IMITATION. *Ant.,* see REPRESENTATION, TRUTH.

misrule, *n.* mismanagement, misgovernment; confusion, tumult, DIS-ORDER. See UNSKILLFULNESS.

miss, *v.* fail; omit, skip, overlook; avoid; escape; lose. See FAILURE, NEGLECT.

misshapen, *adj.* deformed, malformed, distorted, grotesque. See DISTOR-TION. *Ant.,* see FORM, BEAUTY.

missile, *n.* projectile, trajectile; guided missile. See ARMS.

missing, *adj.* omitted; gone, absent; lacking. See ABSENCE.

mission, *n.* errand, task, assignment; calling; deputation. See BUSINESS, COMMISSION.

missionary, *n.* evangelist, proselytizer, emissary. See CLERGY, RELIGION.

misstatement, *n.* ERROR, mistake; MISREPRESENTATION, perversion, FALSE-HOOD.

mist, *n.* fog, haze, vapor, drizzle. See CLOUDINESS.

mistake, *v.t. & n.* —*v.t.* misunderstand, err, misidentify. See MISJUDG-MENT. —*n.* ERROR, blunder, misunderstanding, slip.

mistreat, *v.t.* maltreat; mishandle, abuse, NEGLECT; treat shabbily, oppress, victimize, overburden. See PUNISHMENT, SEVERITY, MALEVOLENCE.

mistress, *n.* possessor, employer; matron, head, TEACHER; paramour, sweetheart. See LIBERTINE.

misunderstanding, *n.* misapprehension; quarrel, disagreement, falling-out. See CONTENTION, ERROR.

misuse, *n. & v.* —*n.* misusage, misemployment; misapplication; misappropriation; abuse, profanation, perversion, prostitution, ill-use; desecration; WASTE. —*v.t.* misemploy, misapply, misappropriate; ill-use. *Ant.,* see USE.

mite, *n.* louse, insect, chigoe, chigger, *etc.*; coin, penny, sou. See LITTLE-NESS.

mitigate, *v.t.* lessen, moderate, ameliorate, palliate, allay, relieve. See RELIEF, MODERATION.

MIXTURE

Nouns—**1,** mixture, admixture, commixture, intermixture, alloyage; matrimony, JUNCTION, COMBINATION, union, amalgamation; permeation, imbuement, impregnation, fusion, infusion, suffusion, transfusion, infiltration; seasoning, sprinkling, interlarding, interpolation, adulteration; assortment, variety; miscegenation, interbreeding, intermarriage, mixed marriage; hybridization, crossing, crossbreeding.

2, tinge, tincture, TOUCH, dash, smack, sprinkling, spice, seasoning, infusion, soupçon.

3, alloy, amalgam, compound, blend, mixture, mélange, miscellany, medley, olio, mess, hodgepodge, patchwork, odds and ends, jumble; salad, sauce; hash, mash; gallimaufry, salmagundi, potpourri, mosaic; crazy quilt, mishmash; pi.

4, half-breed, half-caste, half-blood, mulatto; quadroon, octoroon; cross, hybrid, mongrel; ladino, mestizo; Eurasian; mestee, *métis, métisse.*

5, mixer, blender, eggbeater; social, John Paul Jones.

Verbs—mix, join, combine, commix, intermix, mix up with, mingle, commingle, intermingle, stir up, knead, brew, impregnate with, interlard, intertwine, interweave, associate with; instil(l), imbue, transfuse, infuse, suffuse, infiltrate, tinge, tincture, season, sprinkle, blend, cross, allow, amalgamate, compound, adulterate, contaminate, infect.

Adjectives—mixed, composite, half-and-half; hybrid, mongrel; combined, united; amalgamated, alloyed; impregnated (with), ingrained; heterogeneous, motley, variegated, miscellaneous, promiscuous, indiscriminate, miscible.

Prepositions—among, amongst, amid, amidst, with, in the midst of.

---

mix-up, *n.* confusion, imbroglio, muddle, contretemps; MIXTURE, hodgepodge; DISAGREEMENT, CONTENTION, quarrel, brawl. *Slang,* hassle, rhubarb.

moan, *v.* wail, sigh, groan, bewail, lament. See LAMENTATION.

mob, *n.* rabble, riffraff; *hoi polloi;* common herd, *canaille;* crowd, POPULACE. See ASSEMBLAGE.

mobile, *adj.* movable, loose, free, animate. See MOTION. *Ant.,* stationary, fixed.

mobilize, *v.* motorize, activate, set in action; summon, muster, rally; arm, equip. See MOTION, ASSEMBLAGE, WARFARE, PREPARATION.

mock, *v.t. & adj.* —*v.t.* RIDICULE, mimic, tantalize, jeer at; disappoint. See IMITATION. —*adj.* false, IMITATION, sham, pseudo. See DECEPTION. *Ant.,* see TRUTH.

mode, *n.* STATE, manner, method, custom; FASHION, style.

model, *n.* PROTOTYPE, pattern, mock-up; COPY, miniature, replica; style, type; mannequin, lay figure; exemplar, paragon. See REPRESENTATION, GOODNESS.

MODERATION

Nouns—**1,** moderation, moderateness, temperance, temperateness, gentleness, SOBRIETY; quiet; tranquillity, inexcitability, relaxation, abatement, remission, mitigation, tranquilization, assuagement, pacification; *juste milieu,* golden mean (see MIDDLE).

2, SEDATIVE, palliative, lenitive, balm, opiate, anodyne; lullaby; moderator, temperer.

3, LENIENCY, lenity, tolerance, toleration, clemency, PITY.

4, abstainer, nondrinker, teetotaler, dry, prohibitionist; W.C.T.U. (Women's Christian Temperance Union), Anti-Saloon League, Alcoholics Anonymous.

Verbs—**1,** be moderate, keep within bounds, sober up, settle down, keep the peace, relent; abstain, be temperate, take the pledge, swear off.

2, moderate, soften, mitigate, temper, mollify, dull, blunt, subdue, chasten, tone down, lessen, check, palliate; tranquilize, assuage, appease, lull, soothe, still, calm, cool, quiet, hush, quell, sober, pacify, tame, allay, slacken, smooth, alleviate, deaden, smother; cool off, tone down, taper off.

3, tolerate, bear with; indulge, spare the rod; spare; give quarter; PITY. *Slang,* pull one's punches; let one down easy.

Adjectives—moderate, lenient, gentle, mild, soft, tolerant, easy-going, forbearing; SOBER, temperate; reasonable, tempered; tame, lulling, hypnotic, sedative, palliative. *Colloq.*, on the (water) wagon.
Adverbs—moderately, gingerly, within bounds *or* reason.
Antonym, see VIOLENCE.

modern, *n.* contemporary; late, recent; up-to-date. See NEWNESS.
modernism, *n.* modernity, height of fashion; surrealism, *etc.*; liberalism. See NEWNESS, FASHION, PAINTING. *Ant.*, see OLDNESS.

MODESTY

Nouns—modesty; HUMILITY; diffidence, timidity, bashfulness; shyness, unobtrusiveness; shame; reserve, constraint; demureness.
Verbs—**1,** be modest, retire, give way to, draw in one's horns, retire into one's shell, keep in the background, keep one's distance, hide one's light under a bushel.
2, be humble; deign, condescend; demean oneself, stop, submit; hide one's face, hang one's head, eat humble pie; blush, redden, change color; feel small. *Colloq.*, eat crow, draw in one's horns.
Adjectives—modest, diffident, humble, timid, timorous, bashful, shy, nervous; coy; sheepish, shamefaced, blushing; overmodest, unpretentious, unobtrusive, unassuming, unaspiring, reserved, demure. *Colloq.*, decent.
Adverbs—modestly, humbly, meekly; quietly, privately; without ceremony; with downcast eyes, on bended knee.
Antonym, see VANITY.

modicum, *n.* little, pittance, bit. See LITTLENESS, APPORTIONMENT.
modification, *n.* CHANGE, alteration, mutation; limitation, QUALIFICATION; modulation. See SOUND.
modify, *v.t.* CHANGE, vary, alter; limit, reduce; temper, soften.
modish, *adj.* chic, stylish, fashionable, à la mode, smart. See FASHION.
modulation, *n.* regulation, abatement, inflection, modification. See CHANGE, SOUND.
mogul, *n.* autocrat, ruler; capitalist, entrepreneur, financier, tycoon. *Slang*, bigwig, bigshot. See IMPORTANCE, DIRECTOR.
Mohammedan, *n. & adj.* —*n.* Mussulman, Moslem, Islamite. —*adj.* Moslem, Islamic. See RELIGION.

MOISTURE

Nouns—moisture, moistness, humidity, dampness, damp, dew, fog, mist, marsh; hygrometry; dankness, clamminess; wet, wetness. See WATER.
Verbs—moisten, wet, sponge, sprinkle, damp, dampen, bedew, saturate, soak, drench, water.
Adjectives—moist, damp, watery, humid, wet; dank, muggy, dewy, juicy; wringing wet, wet through, wet to the skin, saturated; soggy, reeking, dripping, soaking, soft, sodden, sloppy, muddy, swampy, marshy.
Antonym, see DRYNESS.

mold, *n. & v.t.* —*n.* matrix, die; FORM, shape, figure; stamp, cast. —*v.t.* frame, shape, model, cast; knead, work. See SCULPTURE.
molding, *n.* necking, surbase, baseboard, platband; cornice, fillet, tringle, chaplet, *etc.*; edging, border, ornamentation. See ORNAMENT.
moldy, *adj.* musty, mildewed, fusty; stale, antiquated. See UNCLEANNESS, OLDNESS.
molecule, *n.* particle, atom, mite, micron. See LITTLENESS.
molest, *v.t.* disturb, annoy, vex, pester, harass. See PAIN.
mollify, *v.t.* placate, pacify, soothe, appease, calm. See RELIEF.
mollycoddle, *n. & v.t.* —*n.* milksop, sissy. *Slang*, pantywaist. —*v.t.* pamper, coddle, spoil. See SOFTNESS, IMPOTENCE.
molt, *v.t.* shed; cast *or* slough off. See DIVESTMENT.
molten, *adj.* melted, fused, liquefied. See HEAT.

moment, *n.* IMPORTANCE, consequence, significance; momentum, IM-PULSE; instant, trice, flash. See INSTANTANEITY.

momentous, *adj.* important, consequential, great, notable, signal; serious, solemn, memorable; influential. See IMPORTANCE.

momentum, *n.* impetus, moment. See IMPULSE.

monarch, *n.* sovereign, ruler, potentate, king. See AUTHORITY.

monastery, *n.* cloister, lamasery, abbey, convent, priory. See TEMPLE.

monasticism, *n.* monkhood, monachism, friarhood. See CLERGY, RE-LIGION.

MONEY

Nouns—**1,** money, finance, funds, treasure, capital, assets; ways and means, wherewithal, almighty dollar; money matters, resources, backing.

2, sum, amount; balance, balance sheet; proceeds, accounts, lump sum, round sum.

3, gold, silver, copper, nickel; bullion, ingot, nugget, gold brick; currency, circulating medium, specie, coin, cash, hard cash, dollar, sterling; money in hand, ready money; lucre, pelf. *Slang,* dough, jack, brass, spondulix, boodle, gelt, folding money, lettuce, cabbage, kale, mazuma, moolah, long green, skekels, simoleons, beans, chips, berries, bucks; the needful; pony, quid, bob, tenner, grand, century, sawbuck, two bits; bill, yard, G note, C note; red cent.

4, WEALTH, opulence, affluence, riches, fortune; competence, solvency; prosperity; substance; property; mint, gold mine, Golconda, El Dorado, purse of Fortunatus.

5, petty cash, pocket money, pin money, mad money, change, small coin, stiver, mite, farthing, sou, penny, shilling, groat, guinea; wampum; paper money, money order, note, bank note, promissory note, i.o.u.; bond, bill, bill of exchange; draft, check, cheque, traveler's check; order, warrant, coupon, debenture, assignat, greenback. *Slang,* blue chips.

6, counterfeit, false *or* bad money, stage money; base coin, flash note. *Colloq.,* slug.

7, DEARNESS, costliness (see DEAR); overcharge, extravagance, exorbitance, pretty penny; inflation. *Slang,* highway robbery. See EXPENDITURE.

8, rich man, capitalist, financier, millionaire, multimillionaire, billionaire; nabob, Croesus, Dives, Maecenas, Midas, Barmecide; plutocrat, tycoon; heir, heiress. *Slang,* moneybags.

9, numismatics, science of coins, coin-collecting.

Verbs—**1,** monetize, issue, utter; circulate; coin, mint, enrich; counterfeit, forge; amount to, come to, total.

2, have money, roll in money, wallow in wealth, make a fortune, feather one's nest, strike it rich. *Colloq.,* have money to burn, hit the jackpot, make a killing.

Adjectives—**1,** monetary, pecuniary, fiscal, financial, numismatical.

2, wealthy, rich, affluent, opulent, well-to-do, well off. *Colloq.,* flush. *Slang,* in the chips; filthy rich; loaded.

3, DEAR, expensive, costly; precious, extravagant, at a premium.

Antonym, see POVERTY.

---

mongrel, *n. & adj.* —*n.* crossbreed, hybrid, half-caste; cur, mutt, stray. —*adj.* crossed, mixed, hybrid; impure. See MIXTURE, IMPURITY.

monitor, *n. & v.* —*n.* monitress; overseer, disciplinarian, censor; MASTER, controller; watchdog, troubleshooter. —*v.* keep order, watch, oversee, supervise; check, regulate, sample; listen in (on). See DIRECTION, DEFENSE.

monk, *n.* friar, brother, cleric; pilgrim, palmer, mendicant; ascetic, hermit, anchorite, cenobite, eremite, recluse, solitary; abbot, prior, father, abbé. See RELIGION.

monkey, *n.* simian, primate, ape; imitator, mimic. See ANIMAL, IMITATION.

monocle, *n.* eyeglass, eyepiece, lens, *lorgnon.* See VISION.

monologue, *n.* recitation, monodrama; soliloquy, apostrophe; SPEECH; reverie, stream of consciousness. See DRAMA.

monopolize, *v.t.* engross, absorb, appropriate, corner. See ANIMAL, IMITATION.

monopoly, *n.* trust, cartel, syndicate, pool; corner. See PARTY, RESTRAINT.

monotonous, *adj.* wearisome, humdrum, tedious; unvaried, repetitious. See REPETITION. *Ant.,* see CHANGE.

monster, *n.* monstrosity, freak; prodigy; giant; DEMON, brute. See UNCONFORMITY, SIZE, UGLINESS.

monstrous, *adj.* huge, enormous; hideous, terrifying, revolting; fiendish, heinous; abnormal, freakish. See SIZE, UGLINESS, EVIL, UNCONFORMITY.

monument, *n.* memorial, cenotaph, tombstone; outstanding work. See INTERMENT, RECORD.

mooch, *v., slang,* sponge, cadge, bum, borrow; lift, snitch. See REQUEST, STEALING.

mood, *n.* temper, humor, disposition, inclination. See TENDENCY.

moody, *adj.* capricious, variable; gloomy, pensive, sad; peevish, testy; sullen, glum. See TENDENCY.

moon, *n.* satellite; month; lunation. See UNIVERSE.

moonshine, *n.* ABSURDITY, nonsense, idle talk. *Colloq.,* home brew, bootleg. *Slang,* booze, hooch, white lightning, mountain dew. See DRUNKENNESS.

moor, *n.* heath, moorland, down, brae.

mop, *n. & v.* swob, wipe; floor mop, dry mop; brush, broom; tuft. See CLEANNESS.

mope, *v.i.* brood, fret, sulk, pout. See DEJECTION, IRASCIBILITY.

moral, *adj.* ethical; righteous, just, virtuous; logical, probable. See PROBITY, VIRTUE. *Ant.,* see EVIL, IMPROBITY.

morale, *n.* spirit, cheer, nerve, COURAGE, faith, hope; *esprit de corps;* gumption, RESOLUTION, determination.

morality, *n.* VIRTUE, righteousness, uprightness, rectitude, ethics, morals. See DUTY. *Ant.,* immorality; see EVIL, IMPROBITY.

morbid, *adj.* unhealthy, diseased; gloomy, unwholesome. See DISEASE, DEJECTION.

more, *adj. & adv.* additional, in addition, added, beside, besides, to boot, over and above, further. See ADDITION.

morgue, *n.* mortuary, death *or* charnel house, deadhouse; files, records, dead records file. See DEATH, RECORD.

moribund, *adj.* dying, mortally ill *or* wounded, on one's last legs, with one foot in the grave; as good as dead, done for. See DEATH, DISEASE.

morning, *n.* morn, morningtide, forenoon, ante meridian, a.m., A.M., dawn, crack of dawn, daybreak, break of day; aurora; sunrise, sunup, cockcrow. See TIME. *Ant.,* see EVENING.

moron, *n.* simpleton, halfwit, imbecile. See IGNORANCE.

morose, *adj.* sulky, sullen, gloomy, crabbed, glum, dour. See IRASCIBILITY. *Ant.,* see CHEERFULNESS.

morsel, *n.* mouthful, bite, crumb, scrap, bit. See LITTLENESS, FOOD.

mortal, *adj.* human, ephemeral; fatal, deadly; dire; implacable. See MANKIND, TRANSIENTNESS, KILLING.

mortar, *n.* cannon, howitzer; cement, bond; vessel, cup; grinder, crucible. See ARMS, COHERENCE, RECEPTACLE.

mortgage, *n. & v.* —*n.* pledge, SECURITY, encumbrance, loan, bond, debenture; PROMISE; hypothec. —*v.* borrow, pledge, hypothecate. See DEBT.

mortician, *n.* undertaker, funeral director, embalmer. See INTERMENT.

mortification, *n.* humiliation, vexation, embarrassment, chagrin. See PAIN.

mortuary, *n. & adj.* —*n.* morgue, funeral home. —*adj.* funerary, funereal. See INTERMENT.

mosaic, *n. & adj.* —*n.* rilework, inlay, (in)tarsia; jigsaw puzzle; tesserae, tessellation; MIXTURE, montage, kaleidoscope. —*adj.* mosaical, motley; tessellated; pieced, joined. See ORNAMENT, VARIEGATION, REPRESENTATION.

most, *adj.* greatest, most numerous; the majority of, nearly *or* almost all. See NUMERATION.

motel, *n.* motor court *or* hotel; stopover, inn; cabins. See ABODE.

moth-eaten, *adj.* worn, shabby, tattered, ragged. See OLDNESS, DETERIORATION.

mother, *n.* parent, mamma; abbess, prioress; matron, matriarch. See ANCESTRY, CLERGY.

motif, *n.* musical theme; subject, TOPIC, concept. See MUSIC.

MOTION

Nouns—**1,** motion, movement, move, mobility, moveableness; APPROACH; motive power; mobilization; evolution, CHANGEABLENESS, restlessness, unrest; kinematics, kinetics.

2, progress, locomotion; journey, voyage, transit, TRAVEL; speed, VELOCITY, rate, clip.

3, stream, flow, flux, run, course, flight, drift, DIRECTION.

4, step, pace, tread, stride, gait, footfall, carriage.

Verbs—**1,** be in motion, move, go; hie; budge, stir; pass, flit, hover round; shift, slide, glide; roll on, flow, stream, run, drift, sweep along; wander, walk; dodge; keep moving, pull up stakes.

2, put *or* set in motion, move, impel, propel, mobilize, motivate.

3, motion, signal, gesture, direct, guide.

Adjectives—moving, in motion, transitional, motory, motive, shifting, movable, mobile; mercurial, restless, changeable, nomadic, erratic; kinetic; impending, imminent.

Adverbs—under way, on the move, on the wing, on the march.

Antonyms, see INACTIVITY, REPOSE.

---

motionless, *adj.* still, immobile, stationary, inert, fixed. See REPOSE, INACTIVITY.

motivate, *v.* induce, move; draw on, give an impulse to, inspire, prompt, stimulate, inspirit, rouse, arouse, animate, incite, provoke, instigate, INFLUENCE, bias, sway; tempt, seduce; bribe, suborn; enforce, impel, propel, whip, lash, goad. See IMPULSE, ACTIVITY. *Ant.*, see INACTIVITY.

motive, *n.* motivation, reason, ground, CAUSE; OCCASION; principle, mainspring, keystone; intention; inducement, consideration, ATTRACTION; temptation, enticement; bewitchment, spell, fascination; INFLUENCE, IMPULSE, incitement, instigation; inspiration, encouragement, ADVICE, incentive, stimulus, spur, goad, bribe, bait; sop.

motley, *adj.* colorful, many-colored, variegated; assorted, jumbled, heterogeneous, diverse, kaleidoscopic, crazy-quilt, incongruous. See MIXTURE.

motor, *n.* engine; see POWER.

motorboat, *n.* speedboat, launch, cruiser; runabout, hydroplane. See SHIP.

motorist, *n.* automobilist; driver, chauffeur; speeder. *Colloq.*, Sunday driver, roadhog. See TRAVEL.

mottled, *adj.* spotted, blotched, dappled; motley. See COLOR.

motto, *n.* MAXIM, adage, precept, device.

mound, *n.* heap, hillock, knoll, hill, tumulus. See HEIGHT.

mount, *v.t.* ascend, rise, soar, go up, climb; set, place. See ASCENT, ELEVATION.

mountain, *n.* hill, peak, elevation, alp, mount. See HEIGHT.

mountaineer, *n.* highlander, mountain climber. *Slang*, hillbilly. See HEIGHT.

mountainous, *adj.* hilly, craggy, peaked; towering, sheer, lofty, precipitous; rugged, massive; Alpine, cordilleran. See HEIGHT, SIZE.

mountebank, *n.* charlatan, quack, swindler, impostor, poseur. *Colloq.*, fake(r). *Slang*, phony. See DECEPTION, FALSENESS.

mourn, *v.* lament, sorrow, grieve; bewail, bemoan, deplore. See LAMENTATION.

mourner, *n.* lamenter, griever; mute, pallbearer. See INTERMENT, LAMENTATION.

mouth, *n.* oral cavity, lips; muzzle; entrance, exit, INLET. *Slang*, kisser, trap. See OPENING.

mouthpiece, *n.* reed, embouchure, lip, bit, pipe stem, *etc. Slang*, spokesman, parrot, speaker; lawyer. See MUSICAL INSTRUMENTS, SPEECH, LAWSUIT.

movable, *adj.* portable, mobile; changeable. See CHANGEABLENESS.

move, *v.* transport, impel, actuate, incite, arouse, influence, propose; stir, act; remove. See IMPULSE, ACTION.

movement, *n.* MOTION, gesture; maneuver; progress; crusade, drive. See ACTION.

movie, *n.* motion picture, moving picture, movies, pictures, film, cinema; photoplay, show, the screen, screenplay, silver screen. *Colloq.*, talkie, flicker. *Slang*, the flicks. See DRAMA.

moving, *adj.* motile; stirring; touching, affecting; impressive, exciting. See MOTION, FEELING.

mow, *v.t.* cut, clip, reap, scythe. See DECREASE.

much, *n. & adj.* —*n.* abundance, ample, plenty, a lot, a great deal, a volume; wealth, SUFFICIENCY. —*adj.* many; abundant, ample, copious, plentiful, profuse. *Ant.*, see INSUFFICIENCY.

muck, *n.* dirt, foulness, filth, slime, mud; pornography, smut. See UNCLEANNESS, IMPURITY.

muckraker, *n.* reformer, scandal- *or* gossipmonger. See DETRACTION.

mud, *n.* mire, muck, ooze, gumbo. See FLUIDITY, UNCLEANNESS.

muddle, *n.* confusion, mess, DISORDER, befuddlement.

mudslinger, *n.* slanderer, muckraker; character assassin. See DETRACTION.

muffle, *v.t.* deaden, stifle, mute, dampen; wrap up, swathe, envelop. See SILENCE, CLOTHING.

muffled, *adj.* muted, dampened; enwrapped, swathed. See SILENCE.

muffler, *n.* scarf, comforter; silencer, deadener. See CLOTHING, SILENCE.

mug, *n. & v.* —*n.* cup, stein, tankard. *Slang*, face, puss, kisser; fool, dolt, clod; gangster, mobster, thug. See RECEPTACLE, FRONT, FOLLY, DECEPTION, EVIL. —*v.*, *slang*, pose, posture, ham [it up], make faces; assault, assail, ATTACK, stick up, hold up. See DRAMA, FEELING, STEALING.

muggy, *adj.* humid, dank; oppressive; sultry, sticky. See MOISTURE.

mule, *n.* hinny, crossbreed; intransigent, pighead. See ANIMAL, OBSTINACY.

mull, *v.i.* think, reflect, consider, ruminate, ponder. See THOUGHT.

multiformity, *n.* variety, diversity; multifariousness, diversification. See NUMBER.

multiplication, *n.* procreation, reproduction; INCREASE, productiveness. See PRODUCTION, NUMERATION.

MULTITUDE

Nouns—**1,** multitude, numerousness, multiplicity, profusion.
2, legion, host, crowd, great numbers, numbers, array, army, sea, galaxy, scores, peck, bushel, swarm, bevy, cloud, flock, herd, drove, flight, covey, hive, brood, litter, farrow. *Colloq.*, lots, stacks, heaps, scads, oodles, barrels, rafts, piles, millions.
3, greater number, majority; multiplication.

Verbs—be numerous, swarm, teem, crowd; outnumber, multiply, swarm like locusts.

Adjectives—many, several, sundry, divers, various, not a few; ever so many, numerous, endless, countless, numberless, myriad, legion, profuse,

manifold, multiplied, multitudinous, multiple, teeming, swarming, pullulating, populous, crowded, thick, studded; a world of, no end of, thick as fleas, infinite. *Slang*, lousy with.
Adverbs—galore; countlessly, numberlessly, infinitely, *etc.*
Antonym, see RARITY.

mumble, *v.t.* mutter, murmur, mouth. See SPEECH.
munch, *v.* chew, masticate, crunch, nibble, eat. See FOOD.
mundane, *adj.* worldly, earthly; temporal, carnal. See IRRELIGION. *Ant.*, see DEITY, HEAVEN.
municipal, *adj.* civic, civil, city; local; governmental. See AUTHORITY.
munificent, *adj.* generous, liberal, lavish, bounteous, bountiful, freehanded, openhanded; benevolent, philanthropic, charitable, altruistic; unsparing, princely, profuse. See BENEVOLENCE.
munitions, *n.pl.* see ARMS.
mural, *n.* wall painting, fresco; mosaic, marouflage; shoji. See ART.
murder, *n.* homicide, manslaughter. See KILLING.
murderer, *n.* assassin, manslayer, cutthroat; killer, butcher. See KILLING.
murderous, *adj.* bloodthirsty, sanguinary, deadly, brutal. See KILLING.
murk, *n.* gloom, dusk, dark, blackness, obscurity. See DIMNESS.
murmur, *v.i.* mumble, mutter, grumble; rustle, purl, ripple; whisper, breathe. See LAMENTATION.
muscle, *n.* thew, tendon, sinew; musculature, build, physique, huskiness, beef, weight, burliness; STRENGTH, brawn, POWER; armed might, ARMS, firepower.
muscular, *adj.* strong, brawny, sinewy, vigorous. See POWER. *Ant.*, see IMPOTENCE.
muse, *v.i.* ponder, meditate, dream, ruminate. See THOUGHT.
museum, *n.* gallery, repository, archives, exhibition. See STORE.
Muses, *n.* the Nine; inspiration. See MUSICIAN.
mush, *n.* porridge, pottage, oatmeal, cereal; SOFTNESS, pap, sop. *Colloq.*, sentimentality, emotionalism, corn, romance, LOVE; slop. See FOOD.
mushroom, *v.i.* boom, INCREASE, expand, spread like wildfire, snowball, swell, puff up. See EXPANSION.

MUSIC

Nouns—**1,** music, melody, strain, tune, air, sonata; rondo, rondeau, pastorale, concerto, concert, musicale, overture, symphony, cadenza; cadence; fugue, toccata, round, canon; serenade; opera, light *or* comic opera, operetta; oratorio, composition, opus, arrangement, movement; full score; minstrelsy, band, concert piece; score; musical score (screen music).
2, vocal music, chant; psalm, psalmody, Gregorian chant, plain song, hymn, anthem, song, canticle, cantata, lay, ballad, ditty, carol, pastoral, recitative, aria; sea chantey, work song, folk song, popular song, ballade, jingle.
3, slow music, adagio, minuet; lullaby; dirge, pibroch; martial music, march; instrumental music, band music, symphonic music, concert music, light music, dinner music, *etc.*
4, dance music, syncopation, ragtime, jazz; bolero, fandango, tango, mazurka, gavotte, minuet, polka, waltz, two-step, fox trot, reel, jig, hornpipe, conga, rumba, samba, cha-cha; rock [and roll], acid, hard *or* soft rock, soul [music]. *Slang*, swing, jive; blues, progressive jazz, bop, bebop, stomp, yodeling, hillbilly *or* country music, crooning.
5, solo, duet, duo, trio, quartet, part song, descant, glee, madrigal, catch, round, chorus, antiphony, accompaniment, second; bass, basso profundo, alto, contralto, tenor, soprano, mezzo-soprano, baritone, barytone; coloratura, dramatic *or* lyric soprano, *etc.*
6, staff, key, bar, space, clef, signature, note, tone, rest, slur, pitch.
Verbs—compose, arrange, adapt, transpose, melodize, harmonize, orchestrate; perform, play, sing.

Adjectives—musical, instrumental, vocal, choral, singing, lyric, operatic; harmonious, melodious, tuneful, symphonic, orchestral.

Adverbs—*adagio, largo, andante, a cappella*; *moderato, allegro, spiritoso, vivace*; *presto, sforzando, scherzo, rallentando, staccato, crescendo, diminuendo, obbligato, pizzicato*; *forte, fortissimo, piano, pianissimo, etc.*

MUSICAL INSTRUMENTS

Nouns—**1,** musical instruments; band; orchestra; trio, quartet, quintet, *etc.*

2, harp, lyre, lute, dulcimer, mandolin, guitar, gittern, cithern, rebec, cither, zither, ukulele, banjo; violin, fiddle, cello, viol, viola, viola da gamba; Cremona, Stradivarius, Amati, Guarnerius; violoncello, bass; bass viol, theorbo, psaltery, recorder.

3, piano, pianoforte, grand piano, grand, baby grand, harpsichord, clavichord, spinet, virginal, hurdy-gurdy, (A)eolian harp, calliope.

4, organ, pipe organ, harmonium, barrel organ; sirene; pipe, pitchpipe, flute, fife, piccolo, flageolet, clarinet, cornet; oboe, hautboy, bassoon, serpent, horn, bugle, French horn, saxhorn, sackbut, trumpet, trombone, saxophone; accordion, concertina; bagpipes; whistle; ocarina; althorn, tuba; harmonica, mouth organ, kazoo. *Slang,* squawk box (harmonium), squeeze box (accordion), sax(e) (saxophone), 88s *or* eighty-eights (piano), licorice stick (clarinet), *etc.*

5, cymbal, bell, gong, tambour, tambourine, tympanum, snare *or* trap drum, drum, bass drum, bongo, tomtom; kettledrum; timbal, timbrel; castanets; musical glasses, sounding board, rattle, bones, steel drums.

6, tuning fork *or* bar; triangle, Jews' harp; xylophone, marimba, vibraphone *or* -harp; glockenspiel, celeste; harmonium.

7, baton, wand, stick; drumsticks; music stand; metronome.

8, strings, brass, winds, drums, percussion, woodwinds, reeds, horns.

MUSICIAN

Nouns—**1,** musician, artist(e), performer, player, minstrel; bard, instrumentalist, organist, pianist, violinist, flutist, flautist, harper, harpist, cellist, fiddler, bugler, fifer, trumpeter, piper, oboist, drummer, saxophonist, trombonist, clarinetist, accordionist, *etc.*

2, band, orchestra, string orchestra, brass band, jazz *or* rock band, combo, ensemble; choir, chorus.

3, vocalist, melodist, singer, warbler, *minnesinger,* chanter, chantress, songstress, caroler, chorister; crooner, blues singer, folk singer, yodeler, calypso singer, scat singer, patter singer.

4, songbird, nightingale, philomel, thrush, mockingbird.

5, Orpheus, Apollo, the Muses, Euterpe, Terpsichore; siren, Lorelei.

6, conductor, lead, bandmaster, choirmaster, concertmaster; composer, arranger; first violin.

7, performance, execution, TOUCH, expression, solmization, fingering.

Verbs—**1,** play, pipe, strike up, fiddle, beat the drum; blow *or* sound the horn; twang, plunk, pluck, pick, thrum, strum.

2, execute, perform; accompany; compose, set to music, arrange.

3, sing, chant, hum, warble, carol, chirp, chirrup, trill, twitter, whistle, intone, lilt.

musket, *n.* GUN, firearm; flintlock, blunderbuss; brown Bess. See ARMS.

muss, *n.* DISORDER, tangle, confusion, mix-up, mess, muddle.

must, *v.* ought, should, have [got] to, need, needs must, have no choice [but to]; be required, obliged, bound, compelled, doomed, destined, *etc.* See NECESSITY.

mustache, *n.* hairline, toothbrush, Charlie Chaplin, Hitler, Kaiser Wilhelm, waxed, handlebar *or* walrus mustache. *Slang,* soup-strainer, tickler, cookie duster. See ROUGHNESS.

muster, *v.t.* assemble, collect, gather, mobilize; poll. See ASSEMBLAGE.

mutation, *n.* CHANGE, variation, DEVIATION; mutant, freak, aberrancy, monster.

mute, *v. & adj.* —*v.* SILENCE; speak softly, whisper; still, muzzle, muffle, suppress, smother, gag, strike dumb. *Colloq.*, squelch. —*adj.* dumb, mum, tongue-tied, tongueless, voiceless, speechless; aphonic; tacit; silent, gagged, muzzled; inarticulate. *Ant.*, see SOUND.

mutilate, *v.t.* maim, destroy, cripple; disfigure, deface, mar. See DISTORTION, DETERIORATION.

mutiny, *n.* rebellion, revolt, uprising, insurrection, insurgence. See DISOBEDIENCE, REVOLUTION.

mutter, *v.* murmur, grumble, mumble, growl. See SPEECH, LAMENTATION.

mutual, *adj.* reciprocal, common, joint, correlative. See INTERCHANGE.

muzzle, *v.t.* restrain, bridle, gag, silence, throttle. See RESTRAINT, SILENCE.

myriad, *adj.* innumerable, numberless, multitudinous, teeming. See MULTITUDE.

mystery, *n.* SECRET, enigma, puzzle, cabala; RITE, sacrament. See CONCEALMENT.

mystic, *adj.* hidden, secret; mysterious; esoteric, occult. See SECRET, CONCEALMENT.

mystify, *v.t.* puzzle, perplex, bewilder, obscure, confound, baffle. See CONCEALMENT. *Ant.*, see MEANING.

myth, *n.* legend, tradition; phantasy, fiction. See IMAGINATION, FALSEHOOD, MYTHICAL DEITIES.

mythical, *adj.* unreal; fabulous, fictitious, mythological. See IMAGINATION, FALSEHOOD.

MYTHICAL DIETIES

Nouns—**1,** mythical deities, heathen gods and goddesses; god, goddess, deity, divinity, demigod; pantheon, mythology, folklore.
2, *Greek:* Zeus, Apollo, Ares, Hephaestus, Hermes, Poseidon, Hades, Eros, Dionysus; Hera, Athena, Artemis, Aphrodite; Titans: Uranus, Gaea, Cronos, Oceanus, Coeus, Crius, Hyperion, Rhea, Mnemosyne, Themis, Phoebe, Dione, Cyclops.
3, *Roman:* Jupiter, Jove, Apollo, Mars, Vulcan, Mercury, Neptune, Pluto, Cupid, Bacchus; Juno, Minerva, Diana, Venus.
4, *Norse:* Woden, Odin, Thor, Balder, Loki, Bragi; Freya; Sigurd, Brynhild, Gudrun, Fafnir, the Valkyries.
5, *Hindu:* Vishnu; Siva, Shiva, Brahma, Indra, Buddha.
6, *Egyptian:* Ra, Osiris, Horus, Set, Anubis, Thoth; Isis.
7, *Babylonian & Semitic:* Baal, Bel, Astarte, Ashtoreth, Ishtar, Ashur.
8, nymph, dryad, hamadryad, naiad, nereid, oread; sylph; salamander, undine; Pan, faun, satyr; mermaid, merman.
9, fairy, fay, sprite, elf, brownie, pixie, pixy, Puck, Robin Goodfellow, dwarf, gnome, troll, kobold, peri, hobgoblin, leprechaun.
10, familiar spirit, familiar, genius, genie, jinni; demon, incubus, succubus, vampire, harpy, werewolf; ogre, ogress.
Adjectives—mythical, mythological, legendary; fairylike, nymphlike, elfin.

N

nab, *v.t., colloq.*, grab, catch, seize; collar, latch on to; corner, tree, ensnare; make a pinch, take prisoner. See TAKING, RETENTION, RESTRAINT.

nag, *n. & v.* —*n.* horse; nagging person. —*v.* pester, badger, scold; fret, complain; irritate, annoy, plague. See CONTENTION, PAIN.

nail, *n. & v.t.* —*n.* fingernail, toenail, ungula; talon, claw; tack, brad, spoke; hobnail, clout; pin, peg. —*v.t.* pin, fix. *Colloq.*, capture, catch. See RESTRAIN, JUNCTION.

naïve, *adj.* ingenuous, unsophisticated, unworldly, artless. See SIMPLE-NESS.

naked, *adj.* uncovered, bare, stripped; nude, unclothed, unclad, unappareled. See DIVESTMENT. *Ant.*, see CLOTHING.

name, *n. & v.t.* —*n.* nomen, praenomen, cognomen, surname; NOMEN-CLATURE, appellation; TITLE, term, denomination; alias, nickname, pen name, pseudonym; sobriquet, epithet; designation; reputation, fame, RE-PUTE. —*v.t.* TITLE, call, designate, christen, entitle; appoint, call, nominate; style; mention. See COMMISSION.

nameless, *adj.* anonymous, unnamed; obscure, unknown, unchristened, untitled; inglorious, unnamable, abominable, indescribable. See DIS-REPUTE. *Ant.*, see REPUTE, NOMENCLATURE.

namely, *conj. & adv.* to wit, as follows, specifically, viz., *videlicet*, that is, *i.e.* See SPECIALITY, INTERPRETATION.

nap, *n.* sleep; pile, surface, TEXTURE.

nape, *n.* scruff, scuff, nuque, scrag. See REAR.

napkin, *n.* linen, serviette; towel, diaper, handkerchief; sanitary napkin, maxi- *or* minipad. *Slang*, wipe. See CLEANNESS.

narcotic, *n. & adj.* —*n.* soporific, anesthetic; opiate, anodyne; dope, drug; sedative, tranquillizer. See REMEDY. —*adj.* stupefying, narcotizing, tranquillizing.

narrate, *v.t.* describe, tell, relate; recount, recite; inform, rehearse; RECORD, state, report, retail. See DESCRIPTION.

narrative, *n.* tale, statement, account, RECORD, story, report, recital, history; recitation. See DESCRIPTION.

narrator, *n.* raconteur, chronicler, storyteller; RECORDER. See DESCRIP-TION.

NARROWNESS

Nouns—1, narrowness, closeness, exiguity, LITTLENESS; THINNESS, tenuity, emaciation; narrowing; tapering, CONTRACTION; hair's-breadth, finger's-breadth, line; strip, streak, vein.

2, shaving, chip, filament, thread, hair; skeleton, shadow, spindleshanks, lantern jaws, skin and bone; neck, waist, isthmus, hourglass; pass; ravine, narrows, gap.

Verbs—be narrow, narrow, taper; slice, shave, pare, trim, thin, thin down *or* out, slim, reduce, attenuate.

Adjectives—1, narrow, close; slender, thin, fine; threadlike, finespun, slim; wasp-waisted; scant, scanty; spare, delicate; contracted, unexpanded.

2, emaciated, lean, meager, gaunt, rawboned, lanky, weedy, skinny; starved, attenuated, shriveled, worn to a shadow.

3, confined, limited; cramped, pinched, close, tight, constricted, prejudiced, illiberal, insular, provincial, circumscribed, small. *Colloq.*, stiff-necked.

Antonym, see BREADTH.

---

nasty, *adj.* foul, filthy; distasteful, disgusting, horrid; dirty; nauseating, loathsome; obscene; ill-tempered, disagreeable, dangerous. See IM-PURITY, PAIN. *Ant.*, see PURITY, PLEASURE.

nation, *n.* country, state, realm; republic, kingdom, empire; sovereignty, AUTHORITY, polity, body politic; commonwealth, community; tribe, people.

national, *adj. & n.* —*adj.* federal, countrywide, nationwide; national-istic, patriotic. See AUTHORITY, POPULACE. —*n.* citizen, subject. See INHABITANT.

nationalism, *n.* patriotism, civism, paternalism; CHAUVINISM; socialism, totalitarianism. *Colloq.*, spread-eagleism. See AUTHORITY.

native, *n. & adj.* —*n.* INHABITANT, aborigine, countryman. —*adj.* indigenous; innate, inherent; aboriginal; endemic, natal, natural.

natty, *adj.,* smart, chic, stylish, modish, dapper. *Colloq.,* snappy. See CLOTHING, BEAUTY.

natural, *adj.* unaffected, spontaneous, artless, unstudied; unsophisticated, naïve, ingenuous; normal, ordinary, regular; unadorned, unadulterated; inherent, innate, inborn. See SIMPLENESS, TRUTH. *Ant.,* see AFFECTATION, DECEPTION.

naturalist, *n.* zoölogist, herpetologist, botanist, horticulturist, ichthyologist, geologist, arborist, arboriculturist.

nature, *n.* character, type, sort, kind; essence, basis, essential; constitution, quality; disposition, structure; temperament, bent, CLASS, FORM; heart; creation, universe.

naughty, *adj.* disobedient, wayward, mischievous, troublesome, perverse. See DISOBEDIENCE.

nausea, *n.* qualm, seasickness, queasiness; disgust, aversion, loathing; illness, sickness. See DISEASE. *Ant.,* see HEALTH.

nauseate, *v.t.* sicken, disgust, revolt. See PAIN, HATRED.

nauseous, *adj.* sick, queasy, qualmish; emetic; offensive, loathsome, repulsive, sickening. See PAIN, DISEASE.

nautical, *adj.* marine, oceangoing; (jack-)tarrish. See NAVIGATION, SHIP.

NAVIGATION

Nouns—**1,** navigation; boating, yachting, yacht-racing, seafaring, sailing, cruising, voyaging; oarsmanship, rowing, sculling, canoeing, paddling; racing.

2, voyage, sail, cruise, race, boat *or* yacht race; PASSAGE; circumnavigation; headway, sternway, leeway; sideslip; seaway; dead reckoning.

3, oar, paddle, scull, screw, sail, gaff, canvas, fish's tail; paddle wheel, side wheel, stern wheel; rudder, leeboards, rigging, sail, sheet, line, rope, mainsheet; mast, boom, pole; beam; keep; bow, stern.

4, navigator, sailor, mariner, seaman, seafarer, tar, jack, old salt, able seaman, A.B.; bluejacket, marine, naval cadet, midshipman, middy; captain, skipper, mate; ferryman, bargeman, longshoreman, bargee, gondolier; rower, sculler, canoeist, paddler, oarsman; boatswain, coxswain, bosun, steersman, leadsman, helmsman, pilot, crew; watch.

Verbs—**1,** navigate, sail, set sail, put to sea, take ship, weigh anchor, get under way, spread sail, have sail; plow the deep, buffet the waves, ride the storm; warp, luff, scud, float, drift, cruise, coast, stream, hug the shore, circumnavigate.

2, row, paddle, pull, scull, punt, raft, float.

Adjectives—sailing, seafaring, nautical, maritime, naval, seagoing, coasting, afloat, navigable.

Adverbs—under way, under sail, under canvas, under steam.

navy, *n.* fleet; ships, warships. See COMBATANT.

Nazi, *n. & adj.* fascist, Hitlerite, racist; National Socialist, NSDAP; reactionary, economic royalist; brownshirt, blackshirt; authoritarian, totalitarian. See AUTHORITY, RIGHT.

NEARNESS

Nouns—**1,** nearness, closeness, proximity, propinquity, approximation, vicinity, neighborhood, adjacency, contiguity; APPROACH, convergence; likeness, SIMILARITY.

2, short distance, step, *or* way; shortcut; earshot; close quarters, close range, stone's throw, hair's-breadth, span.

3, purlieus, neighborhood, vicinage, environs, suburbs, confines, borderland.

4, bystander, neighbor; abutter, tangent (see CONTIGUITY).

Verbs—**1,** adjoin, abut, hang about, touch on, border on, verge upon;

stand by, approximate, tread on the heels of, cling to, clasp, hug; hover over.

2, near, draw near, come near, APPROACH, converge, crowd, press.

Adjectives—near, nigh, close at hand, near at hand; close, neighboring; adjacent, adjoining, proximate; impending, imminent, at hand, handy; near the mark, intimate.

Adverbs—**1,** near, nigh; hard, close *or* fast by; close to, at the point of; next door to, within reach, within call, within earshot, within an ace of, but a step, not far from, at no great distance; on the verge *or* brink of; on the outskirts, in the neighborhood of, in the offing, around the corner, at one's fingertips, on the tip of one's tongue, under one's nose; within a stone's throw, in sight of, at close quarters; cheek by jowl; beside, alongside, side by side, tête-à-tête; in juxtaposition, at the threshold, bordering upon, in the way.

2, nearly, almost, about, thereabouts; roughly, in round numbers; approximately, as good as, well nigh.

Antonym, see DISTANCE.

---

nearsighted, *adj.* shortsighted, myopic. See VISION.

neat, *adj.* tidy, orderly; compact, trim, shapely; pure, unmixed; deft, skillful, adroit; pat, felicitous. See AGREEMENT, CLEANNESS, SIMPLENESS, SKILL. *Ant.,* see DISAGREEMENT, UNCLEANNESS, UNSKILLFULNESS.

nebulous, *adj.* nebular; cloudy, hazy, misty; amorphous, indistinct, unclear, confused, vague, turbid. See CLOUDINESS, DIMNESS, OBSCURITY.

NECESSITY

Nouns—**1,** necessity, necessitation, obligation, COMPULSION, subjection; dire necessity, inexorable fate; what must be.

2, requirement, need, want, requisite, demand; needfulness, essentiality, indispensability; urgency, exigency; *sine qua non*, matter of life and death; stress, pinch.

3, DENSITY, fatality, fate, kismet, doom, foredoom, predestination, foreordination, lot, fortune, inevitableness, fatalism.

4, Fates, Parcae, three Sisters, book of fate; God's will, will of heaven, will of Allah; wheel of fortune; Hobson's choice; last shift, last resort.

Verbs—**1,** lie under a necessity; be doomed, be destined, be in for, be under the necessity of, have no choice, have no alternative, have one's back to the wall, be driven into a corner.

2, necessitate, demand, REQUIRE; destine, doom, foredoom, predestine, preordain; compel, force, oblige, constrain.

Adjectives—**1,** necessary, needful, required, requisite, essential, imperative, indispensable; compulsory, uncontrollable, inevitable, unavoidable, irresistible, irrevocable, inexorable, ineluctable; urgent, exigent, pressing, crying; instant.

2, fated, destined, preordained, fateful, doomed.

3, involuntary, instinctive, automatic, blind, mechanical, unconscious, unwitting, unthinking, impulsive.

Adverbs—necessarily, of necessity, of course, needs must, perforce, willing or unwilling, willy-nilly, compulsorily; like it or not.

Antonym, see WILL.

---

neck, *n. & v.* —*n.* channel, isthmus, strait, pass; cervix; constriction, narrowing; scruff, nape. See NARROWNESS. *Ant.,* see BREADTH. —*v.i., slang,* make LOVE, smooch, pet, make out. See ENDEARMENT.

necklace, *n.* beads, chain, string, pearls; pendant, lavaliere; collar, choker. See ORNAMENT.

necktie, *n.* tie, cravat, scarf; string, bow, four-in-hand, Ascot, Windsor, half-Windsor, black, white, *etc.* (tie). See CLOTHING.

necrology, *n.* obituary. See DEATH.

necromancy, *n.* SORCERY, enchantment, magic.

nectar, *n.* honey, honeydew; delicious beverage. See SWEETNESS.

need, *n. & v.t.* —*n.* NECESSITY, REQUIREMENT; DESIRE, want, privation, lack, POVERTY, destitution; USE. —*v.t.* require, crave, claim, demand, yearn; lack, want.

needle, *v.t., colloq.*, rib, josh, tease, RIDICULE, heckle, prick, goad; harass, torment, ride. See AGITATION, RESENTMENT.

needless, *adj.* unnecessary, pointless, purposeless, superfluous, repetitious. See REPETITION.

needlework, *n.* darning, stitching, sewing; embroidery, lace(work), needlepoint; tatting, appliqué, sampler, brocade. See PRODUCTION, ORNAMENT.

needy, *adj.* in want, destitute, indigent, moneyless, impecunious, penniless, poverty-stricken; poor as a churchmouse. See POVERTY.

ne'er-do-well, *n.* wastrel, loafer, idler, do-nothing, fainéant, good-for-nothing, FAILURE. *Slang*, bum, deadbeat, no-good. See INACTION.

nefarious, *adj.* EVIL, unlawful; detestable, base, shameful; wicked, illegal.

NEGATION

Nouns—negation, negativeness, abnegation, denial, disavowal, disclaimer, abjuration, contradiction, contravention, protest, QUALIFICATION, repudiation, retraction, refutation, rebuttal, disproof, confutation, REFUSAL, prohibition.

Verbs—negate, deny, contradict, contravene, controvert, gainsay, disown, disaffirm, disclaim, disavow, recant, revoke, abrogate, veto; dispute, impugn, traverse, call in question, doubt, give the lie to; repudiate, set aside, ignore, confute, rebut, refute, qualify, refuse.

Adjectives—negative, denying, denied, contradictory, contrary, recusant, dissenting.

Adverbs—no, nay, not, nowise, not a bit, not at all, not in the least, no such thing, nothing of the kind, quite the contrary, far from it, on no consideration, on no account, in no respect, by no means, for the life of me; negatively, never, not ever. *Dial.*, nohow. *Slang*, like fun; in a pig's eye; not on your life.

Antonym, see AFFIRMATION.

NEGLECT

Nouns—**1,** neglect, negligence, carelessness, heedlessness, thoughtlessness, DERELICTION; omission, oversight, laches, default, supineness; RASHNESS, imprudence, recklessness; procrastination; inexactness, inaccuracy (see ERROR).

2, LAXITY, laxness, slackness, looseness, slovenliness; unpreparedness, improvidence, unreadiness; disregard, nonobservance, evasion, nonperformance, FAILURE.

3, INATTENTION, absence of mind, preoccupation, woolgathering.

4, neglector, trifler, procrastinator, waster, wastrel, drifter, slacker; Micawber.

Verbs—**1,** be negligent, neglect, let slip, let go, lay aside, lose sight of, overlook, disregard, ignore; pass over, up *or* by; let pass, wink at, connive at, gloss over, leave out in the cold; leave in the lurch.

2, be lax, loose, remiss, slack, unprepared, *etc.*; relax; ignore, *laisser faire*; hold a loose rein, give enough *or* too much rope, tolerate.

3, scamp, do by halves, cut, slight, skimp, trifle with, slur *or* skip over, skim the surface; miss, skip, omit, postpone, procrastinate, put off, defer, shelve, pigeonhole, table, shut one's eyes to, turn a deaf ear to, forget, be caught napping, let the grass grow under one's feet.

Adjectives—**1,** neglectful, unmindful, negligent, LAX, slack, heedless, careless, thoughtless, forgetful, perfunctory, remiss, inconsiderate; unprepared, unready, off one's guard, unwary, unguarded, unwatchful; offhand, cursory; supine, asleep, indolent; inattentive, unobservant, unmindful, unheeding, thoughtless, inadvertent; indifferent, imprudent, slovenly, inexact, inaccurate, improvident, asleep at the switch.

2, neglected, unheeded, uncared for, unnoticed, unattended to, unmissed,

shunted, shelved, abandoned, unweighed, unexplored, hid under a bushel, out in the cold.
Adverbs—neglectfully, negligently, anyhow, in an unguarded moment.
Antonym, see CARE.

---

negligee, *n.* deshabille; morning dress; peignoir, kimono, *robe de chambre,* nightgown. See CLOTHING.

negotiable, *adj.* conveyable, assignable, transferable. *Colloq.,* spendable. See TRANSFER, POSSIBILITY.

negotiate, *v.* accomplish, arrange; bargain, dicker, contract, overcome, achieve, EFFECT. See AGREEMENT.

Negro, *n.* African, Ethiopian, Sudanese; black, Afro-American.

neighborhood, *n.* community, vicinity, district, REGION, environs, presence, venue. See NEARNESS.

neology, *n.* See SPEECH.

neophyte, *n.* beginner, tyro, novice, apprentice; initiate, debutant. *Colloq.,* greenhorn, greeny. *Slang,* rookie. See LEARNING, BEGINNING.

nepotism, *n.* favoritism, patronage; partiality, favor. See INJUSTICE.

nerve, *n. & v.t.* —*n.* COURAGE, STRENGTH, vigor, vitality; grit, determination, RESOLUTION. —*v.t.* embolden, steel, strengthen, invigorate.

nervous, *adj.* jumpy, jittery, fidgety, uneasy; tense, fearful; sensitive, neurotic. See EXCITEMENT, AGITATION.

nest, *n.* aerie, hammock lair, den; hotbed, coterie; nursery, cradle; resort, haunt, retreat. See ASSEMBLAGE, CAUSE, ABODE.

nest egg, *n.* reserve [fund], savings; rainy-day fund, hope chest; MONEY.

nestle, *v.i.* lodge, snuggle, lie, cuddle. See ENDEARMENT.

net, *n.* seine, web, snare, mesh; trap, catch. See DECEPTION.

nettle, *v.* trouble, irritate; prickle; ruffle, annoy, provoke; vex, offend. See PAIN. *Ant.,* see PLEASURE.

network, *n.* reticulation; net, netting, mesh, interlacing, openwork; hookup, web, interconnection. See CROSSING.

neurosis, *n.* nervous *or* mental disorders, illness, sickness *or* DISEASE; psychoneurosis, melancholia, nervous breakdown; phobia, mania, obsession, compulsion, hypochondria; psychosis, INSANITY. See FEAR, EXCITABILITY.

neutral, *adj.* nonpartisan; indifferent, disinterested, unconcerned; undecided, irresolute, indeterminate; inert, inactive; impartial; neuter, asexual, sexless; barren, unfruitful, sterile. See MEAN.

neutrality, *n.* indifference, nonpartisanship, aloofness, noninterference, unconcern, impartiality, indecision, indetermination. See COMPENSATION, RETALIATION. *Ant.,* see SIDE.

neutralize, *v.t.* nullify, cancel; offset, negate, counterbalance; destroy, defeat, overpower. See COMPENSATION, RETALIATION.

never, *adv.* ne'er, nevermore, not ever. See TIME.

nevertheless, *adv.* nonetheless, anyhow, anyway, still, yet, just the same, for all that, notwithstanding; in any event, however that may be, all things considered, regardless. See QUALIFICATION, COMPENSATION.

newcomer, *n.* immigrant, alien, foreigner; initiate. *Colloq.,* Johnny-come-lately. See ARRIVAL, NEWNESS.

NEWNESS

Nouns—**1,** newness, recentness, freshness, greenness, novelty, immaturity, YOUTH; innovation, renovation.
2, modernism, modernity, latest fashion, latest thing, upstart, mushroom, *nouveau riche,* upstart, parvenu.
Verbs—renew, restore, modernize, renovate.
Adjectives—**1,** new, novel, recent, fresh, green, young, evergreen, raw, immature, virgin, untried, not dry behind the ears; untrodden, unbeaten.
2, late, modern, neoteric, new-fashioned, newfangled, just out, up to the minute, brand new, vernal, renovated, fresh as a daisy, up-to-date, abreast of the times; jet- *or* space-age; hot off the press; a-go-go.

Adverbs—newly, freshly, afresh, anew, lately, just now, only yesterday, latterly, of late, not long ago, a short time ago.
Antonym, see OLDNESS.

NEWS

Nouns—1, news, INFORMATION, INTELLIGENCE, tidings, word, ADVICE; KNOWLEDGE, enlightenment, revelation, cognizance; message, COMMUNICATION, account, dispatch, bulletin, communiqué; broadcast, telecast, newscast; telegram, cable(gram), letter; news flash, news channel, radio, television; report, rumor, hearsay, CRY, buzz, bruit, fame, talk, gossip, table talk, town talk, scandal, uttle-tattle, canard, whisper; good news, glad tidings, gospel, evangel. *Colloq.*, story, copy; grapevine, pipeline, earful, hot line. *Slang*, scoop, beat. See PUBLICATION.
2, narrator, announcer, reporter, newsman, broadcaster, newscaster, anchorman, commentator, news analyst; newsmonger, scandalmonger, informer, talebearer, telltale, tattletale, gossip, tattler, blabber, chatterer.
Verbs—report, disseminate, publish, notify, broadcast, televise; rumor, gossip, chatter, tattle, prate; make news, make the headlines. *Slang*, scoop.
Adjectives—reported, rumored, circulated, in circulation; rife, current, floating, going around, all over the town, the talk of the town, in every mouth, at second hand; newsworthy, fit to print. *Colloq.*, newsy.
Adverbs—as the story goes *or* runs, as they say, it is said.

---

newspaper, *n.* paper; daily, journal, weekly, gazette, sheet, tabloid. See PUBLICATION, RECORD.

New Testament, see SACRED WRITINGS.

next, *adv.* beside, nearest; adjacent, adjoining, bordering, contiguous; following, ensuing, succeeding, successive; after, later. See NEARNESS, SEQUENCE.

nibble, *v. & n.* —*v.* browse, gnaw, graze; nip, peck, pick at; snack, nosch. —*n.* nip, chew, bite, morsel, bit, snack. See FOOD, ESSAY.

nice, *adj.* pleasing, agreeable, attractive, enjoyable; tasteful, proper, genteel; precise, accurate, exact, meticulous; delicate, fine, sensitive; appealing; overrefined, critical, squeamish. See PLEASURE, TRUTH.

niche, *n.* hollow, recess; corner, nook. See ANGULARITY.

nick, *n. & v.t.* —*n.* NOTCH, chip, gouge, dent, jag, indentation. —*v.t.* cut, chip, dent, jag, gouge.

nickname, *n.* pet name, diminutive, sobriquet; appellation. See NOMENCLATURE.

niggardly, *adj.* cheap, stingy, miserly, close, parsimonious, ungenerous; grudging; tight; mean. See CHEAPNESS, PARSIMONY.

night, *n.* DARKNESS, evening, nightfall, midnight, nighttime, eventide. *Ant.*, see LIGHT.

nightclothes, *n.pl.* nightgown *or* -shirt, pajamas, *robe de nuit*. *Colloq.*, nightie, P.J.'s. See CLOTHING.

nightclub, *n.* cabaret, cafe, supper club; discotheque. *Colloq.*, nightspot. *Slang*, speakeasy, joint, nightery. See FOOD, AMUSEMENT, DRUNKENNESS.

nightmare, *n.* bad dream, hallucination; *cauchemar*; incubus, succubus, DEMON, night hag; terror, fright, daymare. See FEAR, PAIN.

nimble, *adj.* spry, active, sprightly, supple, agile, lively, brisk, alert, quick. See VELOCITY, ACTIVITY. *Ant.*, see GRAVITY.

nine, *n.* See NUMERATION.

nip, *v.t.* nibble, bite; cut, snip, pinch, chip, shorten. See DISJUNCTION.

nipple, *n.* dug, mammilla, pap(illa), teat; tit; rubber nipple. See CONVEXITY.

nirvana, *n.* bliss, ecstasy, HEAVEN, paradise; nibbana; FREEDOM.

nitwit, *n.*, *slang*, dimwit, bonehead, jughead, fool. See IGNORANCE, FOLLY.

no, *adv.* none, not; NEGATION. *Ant.*, see AFFIRMATION.

NOBILITY

Nouns—**1,** nobility, aristocracy, quality, gentility, rank, condition, distinction, blood, blue blood, birth, high birth, high degree; pedigree, lineage.
2, the nobility, aristocracy, peerage, upper classes, *haut monde*, élite, *noblesse*, gentry, fashionable world, *beau monde*, high society.
3, noble, nobleman, lord, peer, grandee, magnifico, hidalgo, don, aristocrat, gentleman, patrician. *Slang*, swell, nob, toff.
4, king, emperor, prince, crown prince, duke, marquis, marquess, earl, viscount, baron, baronet, knight, chevalier, squire, count, laird, thane, seignior, esquire, Kaiser, czar, margrave; emir, sheik, raja(h), maharajah, sultan.
5, queen, empress princess, begum, rani, ranee, maharani, sultana, czarina; duchess, marchioness, countess; lady, dame.
6, personage, *crême de la crême*, notable, celebrity, bigwig, magnate. *Slang*, big shot, upper crust, four hundred.
Adjectives—noble, exalted, princely, titled, patrician, aristocratic, wellborn, highborn, of gentle blood, of family, genteel, blue-blooded.
Antonym, see POPULACE.

---

nobody, *n.* nonentity, cipher, upstart, jackanapes. *Slang*, jerk, twirp. See UNIMPORTANCE. *Ant.,* see IMPORTANCE.

nocturnal, *adj.* nightlike, nightly; nighttime; noctivagant, noctambulant; dark, black as night. See LATENESS, DARKNESS.

nocturne, *n.* night piece *or* music, evensong, *Nachtmusik;* serenade. See MUSIC.

nod, *n. & v.* —*n.* salute, greeting, recognition; sign, signal; permission, agreement. —*v.t.* dip, incline, bob. —*v.i.* greet, signal, sign; sleep, nap, doze. See COURTESY, INACTIVITY, INDICATION.

node, *n.* DIFFICULTY, nodus, Gordian knot; protuberance, CONVEXITY, lump, bump, knurl, gnarl; nodosity, nodule, tumescence. See DISEASE.

noise, *n.* uproar, hubbub, din, racket, clamor, pandemonium; crash, rattle, clatter. See LOUDNESS. *Ant.,* see SILENCE.

noiseless, *adj.* soundless, quiet, silenced, muted, hushed, still. See SILENCE. *Ant.,* see SOUND.

noisome, *adj.* destructive, harmful, baneful, EVIL; fetid, malodorous, rank, foul(-smelling); disgusting, loathsome. See BADNESS, MALODOROUSNESS.

nomad, *n.* wanderer, gypsy, rover. See TRAVEL.

NOMENCLATURE

Nouns—**1,** nomenclature; naming, nomination, terminology, glossology, baptism, christening.
2, name, appellation, appellative, designation, TITLE, head, heading, nomination, byname, epithet; proper name, Christian name, first name, cognomen, patronymic, surname, nickname, alias, synonym, antonym; honorific, title; pseudonym, pen name, *nom de plume* (see MISNOMER). *Slang,* moniker, handle.
3, term, expression, noun, WORD, byword, technical term, cant.
Verbs—name, call, term, denominate, designate, style, entitle, dub, christen, baptize, characterize, specify, label; misname, nickname.
Adjectives—named, called, so-called, hight, yclept; known as, alias, cognominal, titular, nominal; pseudonymous, *soi-disant,* so-called, selfstyled; nameless, anonymous.
Antonym, see MISNOMER.

---

nominal, *adj.* titular, (so-)called, known as; in name only, token; slight, little; moderate, reasonable. See NOMENCLATURE, LITTLENESS, CHEAPNESS.

nominate, *v.t.* propose, name; suggest, propound; appoint. See BEGINNING.

nominee, *n.* appointee, designee, candidate, aspirant; grantee. See INDICATION.

nonalcoholic, *adj.* abstemious, teetotal; nonintoxicating; unfermented. See MODERATION. *Ant.,* see DRUNKENNESS.

nonbeliever, *n.* atheist, heathen; agnostic, skeptic. See DOUBT, IRRELIGION.

nonchalance, *n.* INDIFFERENCE, insouciance, unconcern; casualness, carelessness.

non-Christian, *adj.* pagan, heretic, heathen, infidel; antichrist. See IRRELIGION.

noncommittal, *adj.* neutral, nonpartisan; ambiguous, vague; careful, cautious, circumspect, close-mouthed, politic. See CAUTION, CONCEALMENT.

nonconformity, *n.* HETERODOXY, individuality, rebellion; originality. See UNCONFORMITY. *Ant.,* see CONFORMITY.

nondescript, *adj.* indefinable, unclassifiable, indescribable, random; odd; casual, undistinguished. See UNCONFORMITY. *Ant.,* see CONFORMITY.

nonentity, *n.* nothing, negation; nobody; nullity. See NONEXISTENCE. *Ant.,* see EXISTENCE.

nonessential, *adj.* unimportant, irrelevant, unnecessary, incidental, accidental. See UNIMPORTANCE. *Ant.,* see IMPORTANCE.

nonesuch, *n.* rarity, unicum, WONDER; paragon, exemplar; nonpareil(le), one in a thousand *or* million. See PERFECTION, UNCONFORMITY.

NONEXISTENCE

Nouns—1, nonexistence, inexistence, nonentity, nonsubsistence, negativeness, nullity, nihility, blank, nothingness, ABSENCE, no such thing, void, vacuum, OBLIVION.

2, annihilation, extinction, obliteration, nullification, destruction.

Verbs—1, not exist, be null and void, cease to exist, pass away, perish, become extinct, die out, disappear, melt away, dissolve, leave no trace, go, be no more, die.

2, annihilate, render null, nullify, abrogate, destroy, obliterate, extinguish, remove. See DESTRUCTION, KILLING.

Adjectives—1, nonexistent, null and void, negative, blank, missing, omitted, absent.

2, unreal, baseless, unsubstantial, imaginary, visionary, ideal, fabulous, legendary, chimerical, supposititious, vain.

3, unborn, uncreated, unbegotten, unconceived, unproduced, unmade.

4, annihilated, extinct, exhausted, perished, gone, lost, departed, defunct, dead.

Antonym, see EXISTENCE.

nonfiction, *n.* reality; history, (auto)biography, ARTICLE, DISSERTATION; journalism, exposé. See WRITING, BOOK, REPORT.

nonpareil, *adj. & n.* —*adj.* nonpareille; unequaled, matchless, incomparable, in a class by itself. See PERFECTION, SUPERIORITY. —*n.* See NONESUCH.

nonpartisan, *adj. & n.* —*adj.* neutral, uncommitted, disinterested; impartial, unbiased, broad-minded. —*n.* independent, neutral, freethinker, sideliner; judge, arbiter, umpire. See DISINTERESTEDNESS.

NONPAYMENT

Nouns—1, nonpayment, default; protest, repudiation, evasion, whitewashing, reneging; unprofitableness; bad debt; cancellation, write-off, moratorium; insolvency, bankruptcy, FAILURE, INSUFFICIENCY, a run on the bank; free admission, free seats, [free] pass, Annie Oakley. *Slang,* welshing. See DEBT, POVERTY.

2, bankrupt, insolvent, debtor; absconder, defaulter, *etc.*; tax dodger. *Slang,* deadbeat, deadhead, welsher, lame duck.

Verbs—not pay, fail, stop payment; run up bills, go into debt *or* the red; become insolvent, go bankrupt, crash, fail, go under, fold (up);

protest, dishonor, repudiate, nullify; default; write off, wipe the slate clear, declare a moratorium, cancel. *Slang*, go broke, skip out, shoot the moon, fly kites, welsh.
Adjectives—insolvent, bankrupt, defaulting, in DEBT, in arrears; unpaid, unrequited.

Antonym, see PAYMENT.

nonplus, *v.t.* perplex, confound, baffle; bring up short *or* to a standstill, stop dead [in one's tracks]. *Colloq.*, squelch, throw [for a loop]. See UNCERTAINTY, DIFFICULTY.
nonsense, *n.* absurdity, senselessness, silliness, trash, foolishness. See ABSURDITY.
nook, *n.* retreat, corner, cover, niche, recess. See ANGULARITY.
noon, *n.* noontime, midday, noonday, lunchtime. See MORNING.
noose, *n.* hitch, catch; loop, halter, ring, lariat, lasso. See CONNECTION.
norm, *n.* normalcy, CONFORMITY; norma, model, standard, par, criterion, yardstick, rule of thumb; precept, canon, FASHION. See ORDER, RULE, MEASUREMENT.
normal, *adj.* ordinary, regular, average, usual, typical. See CONFORMITY. *Ant.*, see UNCONFORMITY.
north, *adj. & n.* northerly, northern, northward; arctic, polar.
nose, *n.* proboscis, snout, muzzle, beak; nasal organ, olfactory organ; nostrils. See ANIMAL.
nosedive, *n.* plunge, DESCENT, fall; FAILURE, crash, DESTRUCTION. See AVIATION.
nosegay, *n.* posy, bouquet, corsage. See FRAGRANCE.
nostalgia, *n.* homesickness; pathos, REGRET, wistfulness; nostomania.
nosy, *adj.*, *colloq.*, inquisitive, meddlesome, prying, snoopy. See CURIOSITY.
notability, *n.* worthiness, achievement, position; celebrity, lion, dignitary. See NOBILITY.
notable, *adj.* celebrated, noteworthy, distinguished, renowned, famous, remarkable. See REPUTE.
notarize, *v.t.* certify, attest, witness, stamp, validate. See AUTHORITY.
notch, *n. & v.* —*n.* nick, cut, gash, score; groove, rut, pit, pock; cleft, dent, dint, indentation; dimple; defile, pass, gap, OPENING; hole, belt hole; saw, serra, tooth; crenel, scallop; embrasure, battlement, machicolation, castellation; tally, mark, degree, calibration, step, peg. —*v.t.* nick, cut, gash, score, dent, indent, jag; scarify; crimp, scallop; crenelate; tally, calibrate, mark (in degrees), peg.
note, *n. & v.t.* —*n.* letter, epistle, missive; acknowledgment, comment, reminder; observation, memo(randum), excerpt, notation; explanation, remark, annotation, abstract; distinction, fame; tone, sound, pitch. See ATTENTION, WRITING, INDICATION, INTERPRETATION, MUSIC, RECORD, REPUTE. —*v.t.* observe, notice, remark, attend, need, jot. See INTELLECT, MEMORY, WRITING.
noted, *adj.* famous, notable, eminent, distinguished, celebrated. See REPUTE. *Ant.*, see DISREPUTE.
noteworthy, *adj.* extraordinary, notable, remarkable, considerable, exceptional. See GREATNESS. *Ant.*, see LITTLENESS.
nothing, *n.* zero, cipher, nought, blank; nothingness; nonentity, bagatelle, trifle. *Slang*, zilch. See UNIMPORTANCE, INSUBSTANTIALITY. *Ant.*, see IMPORTANCE, SUBSTANCE.
notice, *n. & v.t.* —*n.* ATTENTION, observation, recognition, perception; circular, poster, bulletin; placard, announcement; warning, sign; consideration. See PUBLICATION, INFORMATION, RESPECT. —*v.t.* see, observe, perceive, regard, heed, detect, recognize, note. See ATTENTION, CARE.
noticeable, *adj.* striking, conspicuous, perceptible, prominent, observable. See GREATNESS. *Ant.*, see LITTLENESS.

notify, *v.* inform, warn, apprise, advise, tell, acquaint. See ADVICE, INFORMATION.

notion, *n.* IDEA, THOUGHT, opinion; fancy, caprice, inclination; BELIEF, conception.

notoriety, *n.* flagrancy, blatancy, notoriousness, DISREPUTE.

notwithstanding, *adv. & prep.* —*adv.* nevertheless, although, however, yet. See COMPENSATION. —*prep.* despite, even.

nourish, *v.t.* nurture, sustain, feed, foster, support. See AID, FOOD.

novel, *n. & adj.* story, book, romance, epic. See DESCRIPTION. —*adj.* new, unusual, different, remarkable, surprising, unique, unexpected. See NEWNESS.

novelist, *n.* storyteller, writer, author, romancer, fictionist. See WRITING.

novelty, *n.* NEWNESS, originality, singularity, innovation, new departure, CHANGE, REVOLUTION; fad, FASHION, *le dernier cri,* craze; marvel, freak, CURIOSITY, neology, neoterism. See DIFFERENCE.

novice, *n.* beginner, LEARNER, student, amateur, probationer, neophyte, apprentice; tyro, greenhorn. See BEGINNING, IGNORANCE. *Ant.,* see END, KNOWLEDGE.

now, *adv.* immediately, here, presently, today, yet. See PRESENT [TIME].

nowhere, *adv.* [in] no place, neither here nor there, absent. See ABSENCE.

noxious, *adj.* noisome, harmful, poisonous, injurious, deleterious, pernicious. See BADNESS. *Ant.,* see GOODNESS.

nozzle, *n.* spout, outlet, vent, valve, faucet, nose, OPENING.

nuance, *n.* variation, modulation, shade, subtlety, nicety, fine point, distinction; suggestion, innuendo, hint. See DISCLOSURE, MEANING, DIFFERENCE.

nubile, *adj.* marriageable; pubescent, ripe, developed. See MARRIAGE, OLDNESS.

nucleus, *n.* center, heart, core, kernel; basis, foundation. See MIDDLE.

nude, *adj.* naked, stripped, bare, unclad, unclothed, exposed. *Colloq.,* raw. See DIVESTMENT. *Ant.,* see CLOTHING.

nudge, *n. & v.t.* —*n.* push, TOUCH, jolt, poke, contact. —*v.t.* poke, push, TOUCH, jog, remind. See INDICATION.

nugatory, *adj.* useless, ineffectual, worthless, futile; helpless. See IMPOTENCE, UNIMPORTANCE. *Ant.,* see POWER, IMPORTANCE.

nuisance, *n.* pest, annoyance, irritation, bore, bother. See PAIN. *Ant.,* see PLEASURE.

NULLIFICATION

Nouns—nullification, abrogation, annulment, cancellation, revocation, repeal, rescission, defeasance, renege; dismissal, deposal, deposition, dethronement, disestablishment, disendowment, deconsecration; abolition, abolishment, dissolution; counterorder, countermand, denial, repudiation, recantation, retroaction; *nolle prosequi*; thumbs down, veto.

Verbs—1, abrogate, annul, cancel, destroy, abolish, revoke, repeal, reverse, retract, recall, overrule, override, set aside, dissolve, quash, nullify, invalidate, nol-pros, declare null and void, disestablish, disendow, deconsecrate.

2, disclaim, deny, ignore, repudiate, record, break off.

3, countermand, counterorder, do away with, throw overboard, throw to the dogs, scatter to the winds.

4, dismiss, discharge, discard, cast off, out, aside, away *or* adrift; get rid of. *Slang,* fire, sack, bounce; send packing; give the gate *or* the boot *or* one's walking papers; give the pink slip.

5, depose, divest of office, cashier, displace, break, oust, unseat, unsaddle, dethrone, unfrock, ungown, disbar, disbench.

Antonym, see AFFIRMATION.

nullity, *n.* NEGATION, invalidation, annihilation, obliteration, blankness, nothingness. *Ant.,* see AFFIRMATION.

numb, *adj. & v.* —*adj.* unfeeling; deadened; frozen, benumbed; dazed, shocked; an(a)esthetized, narcotized, drugged, paralyzed; dull, torpid, insensitive; desensitized; lifeless. —*v.t.* deaden, benumb, freeze; narcotize, drug, desensitize; stupefy, paralyze. See INSENSIBILITY, COLD. *Ant.,* see SENSIBILITY, FEELING.

NUMBER

Nouns—**1,** number, symbol, numeral, figure, cipher, digit, integer, counter, round number, formula, function, series.

2, total, amount, quantity, sum, DIFFERENCE, product, multiplier, multiplicand, coefficient, dividend, divisor, factor, quotient, subtrahend, FRACTION, mixed number, numerator, denominator, decimal, reciprocal; Arabic *or* Roman numbers *or* numerals.

3, ratio, proportion, PROGRESSION; arithmetical *or* geometrical progression, percentage.

4, power, root, exponent, index, logarithm, differential, integral.

Verbs—number, numerate, count. See NUMERATION.

Adjectives—numeral, numerable, divisible, reciprocal, whole, prime, fractional, decimal, proportional; Arabic, Roman; exponential, algebraic, logarithmic, differential, integral, positive, negative; rational, irrational; radical, real, imaginary, impossible; approximate, round; exact; perfect.

NUMERATION

Nouns—**1,** numeration, numbering, counting, tally, enumeration, pagination, summation, reckoning, computation, calculation, cybernetics, MEASUREMENT; statistics, poll, census, roll call, recapitulation.

2, mathematics; arithmetic, algebra, trigonometry, (differential, integral) calculus; addition, subtraction, multiplication, division; equation; (square, cube) root; exponent, prime; reduction, approximation, differentiation, integration.

3, abacus, logometer, slide rule, table, Napier's rods, logarithm, log, antilogarithm; calculator, calculating machine, adder, adding machine, cash register; computer, electronic computer *or* brain, punch-card machine, IBM machine, Univac (*T.N.*). *Slang,* magic brain.

5, mathematician, arithmetician, calculator, abacist, algebraist, statistician.

6, UNITY; duality, dualism, biformity; triality, trinity; quaternity.

7, duplication, duplicate; triplication, triplicate; trebleness, trine; quadruplication, quadruplicate, *etc.*

8, bisection, bipartition, halving; trisection, tripartition; quadrisection, quadripartition, quartering, quarter; quinquesection; decimation.

9, one, single, unity, ace; two, deuce, couple, brace, pair, binomial, square; three, trey, triad, triplet, trio, trinomial, third power, cube; four, tetrad, quartet, quaternion; five, quintet; six, sextet, half-a-dozen; seven, septet; eight, octet; nine, ennead; ten, decade, decad; twelve, dozen; twenty, score; hundred, century, centenary; thousand, million, billion, trillion. See ZERO.

Verbs—**1,** number, count, tell, tally, enumerate, muster, poll, count noses, recapitulate; score, cipher, compute, calculate, sum up, total, add, subtract, multiply, divide.

2, check, prove, demonstrate, balance, audit, take stock.

3, double, couple, pair, yoke; triple, treble, triplicate, cube; quadruplicate.

4, bisect, halve, trisect, quarter, decimate.

Adjectives—**1,** numeral, numerical, arithmetical, analytic, algebraic, statistical, numerable, computable.

2, one, first, annual, single, unique; two, second, double, duplicate, twain, dual, biannual, biennial, binary, binomial, twin, duplex; three, third, triple, treble, triform, trinary, trinal, trinomial, tertiary, trine, triplicate, threefold; four, fourth, quadruple, quadruplicate, quarter, quaternary, quaternal, quadratic; five, fifth, quintuple, quinary; sixth, sextuple; eight, octuple; tenth, decimal, tenfold; twelfth, dozenth, duodenary; hundredth, centennial, centenary, centuplicate; thousandth, millennial.

3, bisected, bipartite, bifid; trisected, tripartite, trifid; quartered, quadripartite; quinquepartite, quinquefid; octifid; tenth, decimal, tithe; twelfth, duodecimal; sixtieth, sexagesimal; sexagenary; hundredth, centesimal; thousandth, millesimal.

Adverbs—twice, doubly; thrice, trebly, triply, thirdly; fourthly.
Prepositions—plus, minus, times.

numerous, *adj.* many, myriad, multitudinous, plentiful, numberless, various, thick. See MULTITUDE. *Ant.*, see RARITY.
numskull, *n.* numbskull, *Dummkopf.* Slang, meathead, bonehead. See IGNORANCE.
nun, *n.* sister, ecclesiastic, *religieuse.* See CLERGY.
nunnery, *n.* convent, cloister, cenacle, sisterhood, order. See CLERGY.
nuptial, *adj. & n.* —*adj.* connubial, bridal. —*n.pl.* MARRIAGE, wedding.
nurse, *n. & v.t.* —*n.* attendant, nursemaid. *Colloq.*, nanny. —*v.t.* foster, tend, serve, cherish; suckle; entertain, manage. See REMEDY.
nursery, *n.* nursery school, *crèche* (see SCHOOL); the cradle, infancy, babyhood; conservatory, green- *or* hothouse; hatchery, incubator; spawning ground. See RECEPTACLE, AGRICULTURE.
nurture, *v.t.* sustain, support, feed, nourish; foster, cherish; educate, train, rear. See AID, PREPARATION.
nut, *n.* kernel, stone, nutmeat; seed, core. See FOOD. *Slang,* eccentric, crank, crackpot, kook. See UNCONFORMITY, INSANITY.
nutritious, *adj.* nutritive, wholesome, digestible, nourishing. See FOOD, HEALTH.
nutshell, *n.* husk, hull, COVERING; synopsis, digest, minimum. See SMALLNESS.
nutty, *adj.* nutlike, meaty, rich, tasty. *Slang,* crazy, insane, cracked; kooky, off one's nut, nuts. See INSANITY, UNCONFORMITY, TASTE.
nuzzle, *v.* nose, muzzle; burrow, snuff, root, pry; suckle; cuddle, nestle, press, snuggle. See TOUCH, INQUIRY, ENDEARMENT.
nymph, *n.* dryad, naiad, houri, undine. See MYTHICAL DEITIES.

O

oaf, *n.* FOOL, dullard, dunce, blockhead, idiot. *Slang,* dope, jerk.
oar, *n. & v.* —*n.* paddle, blade, sweep, scull, pole. See MEANS, SHIP. —*v.* row, paddle, propel, stroke; scull. See NAVIGATION.
oarsman, *n.* rower, paddler, *etc.*; crewman, bowman, helmsman; gondolier; thalamite, zygite, thranite. See NAVIGATION.
oasis, *n.* waterhole, wallow, VEGETATION; refuge, shelter. See WATER, RELIEF.
oath, *n.* curse, epithet, expletive, imprecation, profanity; pledge, bond. See AFFIRMATION, IMPRECATION.
obdurate, *adj.* flinty, adamant, unyielding, inflexible; stubborn, adamantine, hardened, unshakable, unfeeling; firm. See HARDNESS, RESOLUTION. *Ant.*, see SOFTNESS.

OBEDIENCE

Nouns—**1,** obedience, compliance; SUBMISSION, submissiveness, SUBJECTION; nonresistance; passiveness, passivity, resignation, malleability, tractability, ductility; acquiescence, obsequiousness, SERVILITY.
2, allegiance, loyalty, fealty, homage, deference, devotion.

Verbs—obey, comply, SUBMIT; observe, respect, abide by, meet, fulfill, carry out; perform, satisfy, discharge; kneel *or* bow to, kowtow, salaam, make an obeisance; resign oneself, grin and bear it, make a virtue of necessity; be at the beck and call of, do one's bidding, do what one is told, serve (see SERVANT).

Adjectives—obedient, observant, acquiescent, complying, compliant; loyal, faithful, devoted; at one's call, at one's command, at one's orders, at one's beck and call; tame, tamed, under control; restrainable; resigned, passive; tractable, docile, submissive; henpecked; pliant, unresisting.

Adverbs—obediently, *etc.*; in compliance with, in obedience to; as you please, if you please.

Antonym, see DISOBEDIENCE.

---

obeisance, *n.* homage, deference, obedience; bow, salaam, kowtow, curts(e)y, genuflection; prostration. See COURTESY, OBEDIENCE.

obelisk, *n.* column, monolith, needle, tower, pillar, shaft; memorial; dagger, obelus. See HEIGHT, RECORD, INDICATION.

obese, *n.* fat, overweight, stout, plump, fleshy, bulky; corpulent, ponderous, adipose, HEAVY.

obituary, *n.* obit; necrology; obsequies, exequy; elegy, eulogy. See DEATH.

object, *n. & v.i.* —*n.* thing, item; goal, aim, purpose, objective. —*v.i.* disapprove, demur, challenge, protest, resist, kick. *Slang*, beef, gripe. See OPPOSITION.

objection, *n.* remonstrance, protest; drawback, criticism; barrier, obstacle; exception, protestation. See DISAPPROBATION, HINDRANCE. *Ant.*, see APPROBATION, AID.

objectionable, *adj.* censurable, culpable; unpleasant, undesirable, obnoxious, offensive, harmful. See DISAPPROBATION.

objective, *adj. & n.* —*adj.* not subjective; unemotional, unprejudiced, unbiased, impersonal. See INDIFFERENCE. —*n.* object, goal, aim, ambition. See DESIRE.

oblation, *n.* offering, sacrifice, corban; WORSHIP; expiation. See RITE.

obligation, *n.* DUTY, PROMISE; debt; AGREEMENT, bond, incumbency, responsibility, liability, indebtedness; contract, mortgage.

oblige, *v.* compel, force, constrain, bind, impel; accommodate, favor, assist, gratify, please. See AID, COMPULSION.

obliging, *adj.* accommodating, helpful, considerate, serviceable, kind, gracious. See COURTESY. *Ant.*, see DISCOURTESY.

OBLIQUITY

Nouns—**1,** obliquity, obliqueness, DEVIATION, divergence; inclination, slope, slant; crookedness; leaning; bevel, tilt; bias, list, twist, swag, cant, DISTORTION; bend (see CURVATURE); ANGULARITY; tower of Pisa; indirectness.

2, acclivity, rise, ascent, gradient, upgrade, rising ground, hill, bank; steepness, diagonality; cliff, precipice (see VERTICAL); escarpment, scarp; declivity, downhill, dip, fall, ascent, descent.

3, clinometer; sine, cosine, angle, hypotenuse; diagonal; zigzag; talus.

Verbs—**1,** be oblique, diverge, deviate; slope, slant, lean, incline, shelve, stoop; decline, descend; bend, heel, careen, sag, slough, cant, sidle.

2, render oblique; sway, bias; slope, slant; incline, bend, crook; cant, tilt; distort (see DISTORTION).

Adjectives—**1,** oblique, inclined; sloping, tilted, recumbent, clinal, askew, aslant, indirect, wry, awry, crooked; knockkneed, distorted (see DISTORTION); beveled, out of the perpendicular; diagonal; transverse, CROSSING, athwart, antiparallel; curved (see CURVATURE).

2, uphill, rising, ascending, acclivitous; downhill, falling, descending; declining, anticlinal; steep, sheer, abrupt, precipitous, breakneck; not straight, not true.

Adverbs—obliquely, diagonally; on one side; askew, askant, askance, edgewise; out of plumb; at an angle; sidelong, sideways; slopewise, slantwise; by a side wind; out of kilter.

Antonym, see PARALLEL, STRAIGHT, DIRECTION.

---

obliterate, *v.t.* efface, erase, expunge, cancel; blot out, take out, rub, sponge *or* scratch out; dele, delete, strike out, wipe out, wash out; wipe w.iy; deface, render illegible; leave no trace. See DESTRUCTION, OBLIVION, ABSENCE. *Ant.*, see RECORD, PRESENCE.

OBLIVION

Nouns—oblivion, obliviousness, forgetfulness, obliteration (of the past); INSENSIBILITY; amnesia, failure *or* lapse of memory; waters of Lethe, waters of oblivion, nepenthe; limbo.

Verbs—forget, be forgetful, fall, sink *or* fade into oblivion; have on the tip of one's tongue; come in at one ear and go out the other; misremember; unlearn, efface, obliterate; think no more of; put behind one; let the dead bury the dead; let bygones be bygones (see FORGIVENESS); slip *or* escape the memory; fade; lose, lose sight of. *Colloq.*, file and forget, kiss *or* laugh off.

Adjectives—oblivious, forgetful, mindless, nepenthean, Lethean; forgotten, unremembered, past recollection, bygone, buried *or* sunk in oblivion; clean forgotten; gone out of one's head.

Adverbs—in limbo; out of sight, out of mind.

Antonym, see MEMORY.

---

oblong, *adj.* elongate, rectangular; elliptical, oval, lozenge-shaped. See LENGTH, FORM.

obloquy, *n.* traduction, slander, calumny, denunciation, DETRACTION; odium, shame, opprobrium, humiliation, DISREPUTE, ignominy. See HUMILITY.

obnoxious, *adj.* repulsive, loathsome, hateful, offensive, odious. See HATE. *Ant.*, see PLEASURE.

oboe, *n.* reed, English horn; hautboy; chalumeau, shawm, schalmei. See MUSICAL INSTRUMENTS.

obscene, *adj.* foul, lewd, dirty, indecent, coarse, smutty. See IMPURITY. *Ant.*, see PURITY.

OBSCURITY

Nouns—**1,** obscurity, dimness, DARKNESS, obscuration, obfuscation, OPACITY; shade, cloud, gloom, CLOUDINESS, duskiness, *etc.* See CONCEALMENT.

2, unclearness, indefiniteness, vagueness, UNINTELLIGIBILITY, INCOHERENCE, ambiguity, intricacy, confusion, involution; abstruseness, mystery.

3, humbleness, HUMILITY, lowliness, inconspicuousness; SECLUSION, privacy, retirement, remoteness.

Verbs—obscure, shade, cloud, darken, conceal, hide; dim, bedim, becloud, befog; confuse, bewilder, befuddle, fluster, mystify, perplex, obfuscate.

Adjectives—**1,** obscure, dim, unlighted, unilluminated, rayless, dusky, dark, darksome; shadowy, murky, hazy, foggy, shaded, clouded; gloomy, somber, opaque, indistinct, bleary.

2, unclear, indefinite, vague, unintelligible, incomprehensible, incoherent, ambiguous, enigmatical, equivocal, indefinable, doubtful, difficult; involved, confused, complex, intricate, abstruse, transcendental; indeterminate, inexact, inaccurate; mystic(al), mysterious, cabalistic, cryptic, recondite, hidden, concealed, blind. See KNOWLEDGE.

3, humble, lowly, ignoble, nameless, unknown, unnoticed, unnoted, inconspicuous; undistinguished, uncelebrated, unhonored, renownless, inglorious; secluded, retired, remote, private.

Antonym, see LIGHT, COHERENCE.

obsequies, *n.pl.* funeral, burial. See INTERMENT.

obsequious, *adj.* abject, fawning, sycophantic, cringing, subservient, truckling, compliant. See SERVILITY. *Ant.,* see INSOLENCE.

observance, *n.* performance, compliance; OBEDIENCE; fulfillment, satisfaction, discharge; acquittance, acquittal; adhesion; acknowledgment; fidelity; orthodoxy, ceremony, RITE, punctilio, protocol. See CELEBRATION, CARE. *Ant.,* see NEGLECT, IRRELIGION.

observation, *n.* notice, perception, regard; comment, consideration, remark. See AFFIRMATION, ATTENTION. *Ant.,* see NEGATION, NEGLECT.

observe, *v.* see (see VISION); comply with, RESPECT, acknowledge, abide by; obey, cling to, adhere to, be faithful to, meet, fulfil(l); carry out, carry into execution; execute, perform, keep, satisfy, discharge, do one's duty; perform, fulfil(l) *or* discharge an obligation; acquit oneself; perform an office; keep one's word *or* promise; keep faith with; officiate. See CELEBRATION, CARE. *Ant.,* see NEGLECT.

obsess, *v.t.* haunt, beset, besiege. See FEAR.

obsession, *n.* preoccupation, fixation, mania, phobia, COMPULSION, *idée fixe. Colloq.,* one-track mind. *Slang,* hang-up. See ATTENTION, INSANITY, FEAR.

obsolescence, *n.* disuse, disappearance; antiquity. See OLDNESS. *Ant.,* see NEWNESS.

obsolete, *adj.* past, extinct, outworn, disused, discarded, antiquated, dead. See OLDNESS. *Ant.,* see NEWNESS.

obstacle, *n.* HINDRANCE, DIFFICULTY, OPPOSITION, barrier, obstruction, snag, impediment; barrage; baffle. *Ant.,* see AID, FACILITY, COÖPERATION.

OBSTINACY

Nouns—**1,** obstinacy, stubbornness, TENACITY, doggedness; obduracy, obduration, insistence, RESOLUTION; intransigency, immovability, inflexibility, HARDNESS, will power; self-will, will of iron, will *or* mind of one's own; contumacy, pigheadedness, perversity, contrariness, recalcitrance, indocility. *Colloq.,* cussedness. See CERTAINTY, UNWILLINGNESS.

2, bigotry, intolerance, dogmatism, narrow-mindedness (see NARROWNESS).

3, opinionist, pighead, stickler, diehard, intransigent; enthusiast, fanatic, bigot, zealot. *Colloq.,* mule, bitter-ended, stand-patter.

Verbs—be obstinate, stickle, insist, persist, persevere; fly in the face of facts, be wedded to an opinion, hug a belief; have one's own way *or* will; have the last word, die hard, fight to the last ditch, not yield an inch, stand firm. *Colloq.,* stand pat, fight city hall.

Adjectives—**1,** obstinate, stubborn, tenacious, persevering, pertinacious, persistent, dogged; obdurate, indurate, insistent, resolute, firm, sturdy, immovable, inflexible, unmoving, unyielding, unbending, not to be moved; rigid, set, settled, fixed, hard; unfeeling, unchangeable, intransigent, inexorable, determined; bullheaded, pigheaded, headstrong, *entêté,* mulish, stubborn as a mule. *Colloq.,* tough, bitter-end, diehard.

2, self-willed, wil(l)ful, perverse, heady, headstrong, refractory, unruly, intractable, incorrigible, contumacious, difficult, balky, contrary, froward, cantankerous, recalcitrant; stiff-necked *or* -backed, hidebound; deaf to advice, impervious to reason. *Colloq.,* cussed.

3, bigoted, intolerant, prejudiced, prepossessed, illiberal, narrow-minded; dogmatic, opinionated, fanatic.

Antonym, see UNCERTAINTY, CHANGEABLENESS.

obstreperous, *adj.* noisy, troublesome, clamorous, recalcitrant, riotous, vociferous. See VIOLENCE. *Ant.,* see MODERATION.

obstruct, *v.t.* block, stop, impede, choke, retard, clog; occlude, shut; dam, foul; barricade, blockade; check, hedge; overgrow; encumber. See HINDRANCE. *Ant.,* see AID.

obtain, *v.t.* acquire, get, procure, gain, secure, attain. See ACQUISITION, SECURITY. *Ant.,* see LOSS.

obtainable, *adj.* attainable, procurable, accessible. See CHANCE, ACQUISITION.

obtrude, *v.* intrude, thrust, interfere. See HINDRANCE.

obvious, *adj.* manifest, patent, clear, evident, plain; undisguised, unconcealed. See EVIDENCE. *Ant.,* see CONCEALMENT.

OCCASION

Nouns—occasion, opportunity, OPENING, room; CIRCUMSTANCE, EVENT; opportuneness; crisis, turn, juncture, psychological moment, conjuncture; turning point; given time; nick of time; chance of a lifetime; golden opportunity; clear field; spare time; LEISURE.

Verbs—seize an opportunity; suit the occasion; strike while the iron is hot; make hay while the sun shines, take time by the forelock; take the bull by the horns. *Slang,* get the jump on, jump the gun.

Adjectives—opportune, timely, well-timed, seasonable; providential, lucky, fortunate, happy, favorable, propitious, auspicious, critical; apropos, suitable (see AGREEMENT).

Adverbs—opportunely, *etc.*; in proper time, in due time, course *or* season; for the nonce; in the nick of time, in the fullness of time; just in time, at the eleventh hour; now or never; by the way, by the by; *en passant, à propos*; parenthetically, while on the subject; *ex tempore*; on the spur of the moment; on the spot (see EARLINESS); when the coast is clear.

Antonym, see LATENESS.

occult, *adj.* mystic, mysterious, supernatural, SECRET, hidden.

occupant, *n.* possessor, tenant, lodger, transient, occupier, INHABITANT, roomer, holder.

occupation, *n.* tenure, occupancy, holding, tenancy; habitation; work, trade, BUSINESS, employment, calling, profession, pursuit. See POSSESSION.

occupy, *v.t.* hold, inhabit, keep, fill, tenant, have; take, beset, garrison; interest, engage, engross, busy; employ. See BUSINESS.

OCCURRENCE

Nouns—**1,** occurrence, eventuality, event, incident, happening, affair, episode, situation, milestone, transaction, proceeding, BUSINESS, concern, CIRCUMSTANCE, advent, opportunity, particular; fact, matter of fact, phenomenon; adventure, happening; accident (see CHANCE), casualty, crisis, pass, PASSAGE, emergency, contingency. *Colloq.,* happenstance, goings-on.

2, the world, life, things, doings, affairs; things in general, affairs in general, the times, state of affairs, order of the day; course, tide, stream, current, run *or* march of events; ups and downs of life.

Verbs—**1,** occur, happen, take place, be, take effect; concur, accompany, coincide; come, become of, come off, come about, come into EXISTENCE, come into view, come to mind, come forth, come to pass, come on, pass; appear (see APPEARANCE), offer, present itself, be met with, be found, meet the eye; fall, fall out, turn out; run, be afoot; fall in, befall, betide, bechance; prove, supervene, eventuate, transpire, hap; draw on, turn up, crop up, spring up; issue, ensue, result (see EFFECT); arrive, arise, rise, start, hold, take its course; pass on *or* off (see PAST). *Colloq.,* come off, go.

2, meet with, experience; fall to the lot of; be one's chance, fortune *or* lot; find, encounter, undergo; pass through, go through; suffer, endure (see FEELING).

Adjectives—occurring, happening, going on, under way, current, prevailing; in the wind, afloat, on foot, at issue, in question; incidental, eventful, episodic, stirring, bustling, full of incident.

Adverbs—eventually, in the event of, in case; in the [natural] course of things; as things go, as times go, as the world goes, as the tail wags; as the tree falls, as the cat jumps; as it may turn out, as it may happen.

---

ocean, *n.* sea, great sea, high seas; salt water, deep water, blue water; the [bounding] main, the [briny] deep; the Seven Seas; the big pond, the ditch; the big sea water; the South Seas, the frozen seas; the billow, wave, tide *or* flood; the deep blue sea, wine-dark sea; Father Neptune, Poseidon; the watery waste. See WATER. *Ant.*, see LAND.

ocular, *adj.* optic, visual; retinal, conjunctival; perceptible, visible. See VISION.

odd, *adj.* strange, unusual, unnatural; curious, quaint, queer, bizarre, droll; singular, single; unmatched, unpaired, lone; extra, left. See REMAINDER, ABSURDITY.

oddity, *n.* curiosity, freak; singularity, strangeness, peculiarity; quaintness, eccentricity, oddness; crank, eccentric. See INSANITY, UNCONFORMITY. *Ant.*, see SANITY, CONFORMITY.

odds, *n.* DIFFERENCE, PROBABILITY, advantage; disparity. See CHANCE.

ode, *n.* poem, lyric; psalm, canticle, hymn; monody. See POETRY.

odious, *adj.* disgusting, repulsive, detestable, offensive, loathsome, hateful. See PAIN. *Ant.*, see PLEASURE.

ODOR

Nouns—odor, odorousness, smell, scent, effluvium; emanation, exhalation; fume, essence, trail, redolence; pungency, FRAGRANCE; sense of smell, olfaction; act of smelling. See MALODOROUSNESS.

Verbs—1, have an odor, smell of, smell, exhale; give out a smell; scent, reek, stink.

2, smell, scent; snuff, snuff up; sniff; nose, inhale; get wind of.

Adjectives—odorous, odoriferous; smelling, strong-smelling; strong-scented; redolent, aromatic, fragrant, pungent; reeking; olfactory.

---

odyssey, *n.* wandering, TRAVEL, journey; quest, pilgrimage, search.

offal, *n.* garbage, rubbish; WASTE; ordure, filth, excrement. See REMAINDER, EXCRETION.

offbeat, *adj.*, *colloq.*, strange, unfamiliar, unconventional, unorthodox, weird, queer. *Slang*, dizzy, crazy, wacky, kooky. See UNCONFORMITY.

off-color, *adj.* improper, indelicate; risqué, racy, dirty. See IMPURITY.

offend, *v.* break the law, err, WRONG, sin, trespass; give offense, displease, upset, vex, provoke, hurt; disgust; affront, spite, insult, hurt one's feelings. *Colloq.*, aggravate, rub the wrong way. See ILLEGALITY, PAIN, RESENTMENT.

offense, *n.* insult, affront, DISCOURTESY; aggression, ATTACK; transgression, fault, crime, sin, WRONG, EVIL.

OFFER

Nouns—1, offer, proffer, presentation, tender, bid, overture, advance; ultimatum, last word, final offer; proposal, proposition, MOTION, invitation; asking price; candidature, candidacy; offering (see GIVING). See WILL.

2, attempt, endeavor, ESSAY, trial, try, venture.

3, bidder; by-bidder, Peter Funk. *Slang*, come-on man, capper.

Verbs—1, offer, proffer, present, tender, bid, make an offer; suggest, propose, prefer, move, make a motion; advance, make advances; start, invite, hold out, submit, exhibit, put forward; place in one's way, place at one's disposal, lay at one's feet; offer for sale, hawk about (see SALE); press, urge upon (see REQUEST); furnish, propound, show, give.

2, offer *or* present oneself; volunteer, come forward, be a candidate, throw one's hat in the ring; stand for, seek; be at one's service; bribe.

3, endeavor, attempt, try, ESSAY, venture, undertake.

Adjectives—offering, offered; on the market, for sale, to let, for hire.
Antonym, see REQUEST.

---

offhand, *adv. & adj.* —*adv.* casually, impromptu, extemporaneously;
abruptly, carelessly. —*adj.* casual, abrupt, extemporaneous, careless;
unpremeditated, unplanned. See IMPULSE.

office, *n.* headquarters, department, bureau, room, branch; position,
status, rank, function; post, job, duty, service. See AGENCY, BUSINESS.

officer, *n.* policeman; functionary, official, bureaucrat; president, vice-
president, secretary, treasurer; registrar; mayor, governor. See AU-
THORITY, BUSINESS.

official, *n. & adj.* —*n.* officer, functionary, dignitary. *Ant.,* see SERVANT.
—*adj.* authoritative, functional, authentic, authorized. See AUTHORITY.

officiate, *v.* preside, serve, supervise, direct, function. See BUSINESS,
RITE.

officious, *adj.* interfering, meddlesome, obtrusive, pushing, presumptuous;
bossy. See ACTIVITY. *Ant.,* see INACTIVITY.

offset, *v.t.* neutralize, balance, counteract, cancel, counterbalance, counterpoise. See COMPENSATION, OPPOSITION.

offshoot, *n.* ramification, incidental, result; branch, shoot, sprout; scion.
See ADDITION.

offspring, *n.* child, children, young, sons, daughters, progeny, descendants. See POSTERITY. *Ant.,* see ANCESTRY.

often, *adv.* ofttime(s), oftentimes, frequently, repeatedly, recurrently,
oft. See FREQUENCY. *Ant.,* see RARITY.

ogre, *n.* giant(ess), maneater, cannibal; monster, beast, DEMON, fiend;
cyclops; ogress, orgillon; bog(e)y, bugbear, golliwog(g).

OIL

Nouns—**1,** oil, fat, lipid, grease, wax; mineral, animal *or* vegetable oil,
ethereal, volatile *or* essential oil; lubricant, lubricator; ointment, demulcent, liniment, lotion, embrocation, vaseline, glycerine, pomade,
brilliantine, unguent, emollient; suntan lotion *or* oil, face *or* cold
cream, *etc.*; lard, tallow, beeswax, lanolin, spermaceti, paraffin; petroleum, gasoline, naphtha, benzine, kerosene, vaseline, toluene. *Colloq.,*
gas.
2, lubrication, oiling, oiliness; unction, unctuosity, lubricity; lubri-
terium, grease rack *or* pit. *Slang,* grease *or* lube job.
3, unctuousness, FLATTERY, blandishment, SMOOTHNESS; fervor, fervency; SERVILITY, compliance, sycophancy; bribery. *Slang,* soft soap,
banana oil.
Verbs—oil, lubricate, grease; anoint, lather, soap, wax, slick (up), smear,
smooth, butter, lard, make slippery. *Colloq.,* bribe, tip, grease the
palm; flatter, butter up, softsoap. See DRUNKENNESS.
Adjectives—**1,** oily, greasy, slippery, lubricous, slick, smooth, lubricant,
emollient; fat(ty), adipose, gummy, mucous, slimy, soapy, oleose,
sebaceous.
2, unctuous, ingratiating, bland, suave, glib, plausible, gushing, fervid;
fawning, flattering, sycophantic, parasitic, obsequious, subservient, servile, compliant.

---

ointment, *n.* unguent, balm, pomade, salve, cream. See REMEDY.
old-fashioned, *adj.* See OLDNESS, STABILITY.

OLDNESS

Nouns—**1,** oldness, AGE, antiquity; maturity; decline, decay, senility;
seniority, eldership; primogeniture.
2, archaism; relic (of the past); antiquities, fossils, prehistoric animal;
antiquarianism; antiquary (see PAST).
3, tradition, prescription, custom, immemorial usage, common law.

Verbs—be old; have had *or* seen its day; whiten; turn gray *or* white; become old, AGE, fade, obsolesce, senesce.

Adjectives—**1,** old, older, oldest, eldest, ancient, antique; of long standing, time-honored, venerable, hoary; senior, elder, eldest; first-born.

2, prime; primitive, primeval, primordial, primordinate; aboriginal (see BEGINNING); diluvian, antediluvian; prehistoric, patriarchal, preadamite; fossil, paleozoic, preglacial, antemundane.

3, archaic, classic, medieval, pre-Raphaelite; immemorial, traditional, prescriptive, customary; inveterate, rooted; antiquated, obsolete, of other times, of the old school, out of date, out of fashion; stale, old-fashioned, dated, superannuated, behind the times; exploded; gone out, gone by; passé, run out; senile (see AGE); timeworn; crumbling (see DETERIORATION); extinct; secondhand; old as the hills, old as Methuselah, old as history. *Colloq.*, back-number, has-been; old-fangled, rinky-dink.

Antonym, see NEWNESS.

Old Testament, see SACRED WRITINGS.

old-timer, *n., colloq.,* veteran, old hand *or* soldier, war horse, oldster, duffer. See INHABITANT, OLDNESS.

oligarchy, *n.* clique, junta, PARTY; aristocracy, autocracy. See AUTHORITY.

omen, *n.* WARNING, foreboding; sign, significance, portent; PREDICTION, straw in the wind; INDICATION, harbinger, token, foretoken; prognostication, soothsaying, augury, prophecy, foreshadowing; presage; evil omen, good omen.

ominous, *adj.* forboding, inauspicious; prophetic; significant, bodeful, doomful, fateful; unlucky, ill-omened, ill-fated; WARNING, prognosticating; unpropitious, unfavorable. See PREDICTION, NECESSITY. *Ant.,* see HOPE.

omission, *n.* EXCLUSION, exception, elimination, cut; FAILURE, NEGLECT, DERELICTION; apostrophe, ellipsis; deficit, shortage; evasion. *Ant.,* see COMPLETION.

omit, *v.t.* NEGLECT, skip, spare, overlook; delete, remove, reject; evade, except, exclude, miss, drop; pass, forget. *Ant.,* see CARE.

omnibus, *n. & adj.* —*n.* BUS; collection, compilation; reader, portable. See BOOK, ASSEMBLAGE. —*adj.* large, commodious, inclusive, catchall, comprehensive, all-embracing, extensive. See COMPLETENESS, INCLUSION.

omnipotence, *n.* almightiness, infinite power. See DEITY, POWER.

omniscient, *adj.* all-seeing, all-knowing. See KNOWLEDGE.

omnivorous, *adj.* devouring, all-consuming, gluttonous, eating everything. See FOOD.

on, *adv. & prep.* —*adv.* forward, onward, ahead. See PROGRESSION. —*prep.* upon, at.

once, *adv.* formerly, previously, latterly. See TIME.

once-over, *n., slang,* glance, look, JUDGMENT, scrutiny, survey; runthrough, skimming, the eye, ogle, sizing-up, double-O.

oncoming, *adj.* impending, menacing (see APPROACH, NEARNESS).

one, *adj.* individual, sole, only, solitary, single. See NUMERATION.

onerous, *adj.* difficult, troublesome, burdensome, wearing, oppressive; discouraging. See EXERTION, DIFFICULTY, GRAVITY.

onesided, *adj.* unfair, biased, partial; prejudiced; unbalanced, lopsided, asymmetric, awry; unilateral. See DISTORTION, MISJUDGMENT, SIDE.

onlooker, *n.* SPECTATOR, observer, watcher, viewer, witness, bystander; nonparticipant.

only, *adv. & adj.* —*adv.* solely, singly, exclusively, merely, but. —*adj.* sole, solitary, apart, alone, unique. See NUMERATION.

onset, *n.* aggression, assault, ONSLAUGHT; OPENING, BEGINNING, outbreak.

onslaught, *n.* onset, ATTACK, charge, assault, offensive, thrust, drive; blame, censure, ACCUSATION, DETRACTION. See DISAPPROBATION.

ooze, *v.* seep, leak, filter; drip, percolate. See EGRESS.

opacity, *n.* opaqueness, nontransparency, DIMNESS, filminess, CLOUDINESS. See DARKNESS. *Ant.*, see TRANSPARENT, VISION.
opaque, *adj.* nontransparent, adiaphanous, dim; filmy, cloudy; obscure, unintelligible, obtuse. See DIMNESS, CLOUDINESS. *Ant.*, TRANSPARENT.

OPENING

Nouns—**1,** opening, hole, foramen; aperture, hiatus, yawning, oscitancy, dehiscence, pandiculation; chasm (see INTERVAL).
2, puncture, perforation, interstice, terebration; pinhole, keyhole, loophole, porthole, peephole, pigeonhole; eye, eyelet, slot, oriel; porousness, porosity.
3, outlet, inlet; vent, vomitory; embouchure; crater, orifice, mouth, sucker, muzzle, throat, gullet; pore; nozzle.
4, door, doorway, entrance, entry, portal, porch, gate, astiary, postern, wicket, trapdoor, hatch; arcade; gateway, hatchway, gangway; embrasure, window, casement, LIGHT; skylight, fanlight; lattice.
5, way, path, thoroughfare; CHANNEL, PASSAGE, tube, pipe; vessel, tubule, canal, gutter, fistula; chimney, flue, tap, funnel, gully, tunnel, main; mine, pit, adit, shaft; gallery, alley, aisle, glade, vista, bay window, bow window; dormer, lantern; bore, caliber.
6, sieve, screen, colander; honeycomb; NOTCH, cleft, embrasure.
7, opener, key, skeleton key, passkey, master key; passe-partout; latch; passport, password, pass; can opener; punch.
Verbs—**1,** open, gape, gap, yawn, bilge; fly open; ope (*Poet.*).
2, perforate, pierce, tap, bore, drill; mine; tunnel; transfix; enfilade, impale, spike, spear, gore, spit, stab, pink, puncture, lance, stick, prick, riddle, punch; stave in; cut a passage through, make way for, make room for, open up *or* out; cut, expose, lay open, break open, breach, broach.
Adjectives—open; perforate(d), wide open, ajar; unclosed, unstopped; ope (*Poet.*), oscitant, gaping, yawning; patent; tubular, cannular, fistulous; pervious, permeable; foraminous; vesticular, vascular porous, follicular, honeycombed; notched, nicked, crenate; infundibular, riddled; tubulous, tubulated; opening; aperient.
Antonym, see CLOSURE.

open-minded, *adj.* broad-minded; impartial, unbiased; candid, receptive, tolerant, understanding, worldly. See JUSTICE, LIBERALITY.
opera, *n.* grand opera, comic opera; music drama, operetta, light opera, music theater; libretto. See MUSIC, DRAMA.
operate, *v.* CONDUCT, manage, direct, go, run, work, function, act. See ACTION, AGENCY.
operative, *adj.* effective; operating, acting, working, functioning, effectual. See AGENCY.
opiate, *n.* narcotic, palliative, drug, sedative, tranquillizer, analgesic. See MODERATION, REMEDY.
opinion, *n.* IDEA, THOUGHT, BELIEF, conviction; theory, JUDGMENT, view; MOTION, mind, tenet, dogma; verdict; speculation, apprehension; public opinion, poll, survey.
opinionated, *adj.* convinced; unconvincible, bigoted, dogmatic, prejudiced, hidebound, positive. See RESOLUTION, MISJUDGMENT. *Ant.*, see FREEDOM.
opium, *n.* opiate, NARCOTIC, sedative, soporific. *Slang,* poppy, hops, mud, the pipe. See REMEDY, HABIT.
opponent, *n.* antagonist, adversary; OPPOSITION; enemy, foe, assailant, oppositionist, disputant, rival, competitor. *Ant.*, see AID.
opportune, *adj.* fortuitous, timely, seasonable, felicitous, suitable, apt, apropos. See OCCASION. *Ant.*, see EARLINESS, LATENESS.
opportunity, *n.* OPENING; OCCURRENCE; CHANCE, OCCASION; SPACE, SCOPE, PLACE; leisure.

oppose, *v.t.* contrast, confront; combat, counter, resist, hinder; contradict, refute, cross; repel, withstand; obstruct; contravene. See OPPOSITION. *Ant.,* see AID.

OPPOSITION

Nouns—**1,** opposition, antagonism, antipathy; ENMITY, dislike, HATE; oppugnancy, oppugnation; impugnation; contravention, contradiction; counteraction; counterplot; crossfire, undercurrent, riptide, undertow, headwind; race; RESISTANCE, RESTRAINT, HINDRANCE, CONTRARINESS.
2, opposition, contraposition, polarity; INVERSION; opposite side, reverse, inverse; counterpart; antipodes; opposite poles; north and south; heads or tails; anode and cathode.
3, insurrection, rebellion, riot; strike, lockout, walkout; boycott.
Verbs—**1,** oppose, counteract, run counter to, withstand, resist, counter, restrain (see RESTRAINT); hinder (see HINDRANCE); antagonize, oppugn, fly in the face of, kick against, fall foul of; set against, pit against; DEFY, face, confront, cope with; make a stand, make a stand against; protest against, vote against, raise one's voice against; disfavor, turn one's back upon; set at naught, slap in the face, slam the door in one's face; freeze out; be at cross purposes, play at cross purposes; thwart.
2, breast, encounter; stem *or* breast the tide, current *or* flood; beat up against; grapple with; contend (see CONTENTION); do battle (see WARFARE); contradict, contravene; belie; run against, beat against; militate against; come in conflict with; emulate, compete, rival, vie with.
3, be opposite, oppose, juxtapose, contrapose; subtend.
Adjectives—**1,** opposing, opposed; adverse, antagonistic; contrary; at variance (see DISAGREEMENT); at issue, at war with; unfavorable, unfriendly; hostile, inimical, cross, unpropitious; up in arms; resistant; competitive, emulous.
2, opposite; reverse, inverse; antipodal, fronting, facing, diametrically opposite.
Adverbs—contrarily, conversely; *vice versa*; at cross purposes; against the grain; against the current, stream, wind *or* tide; with a head wind, in spite, in despite, in defiance; in the way of, in the teeth of, in the face of; across; athwart.
Prepositions—over, against; over *or* up against; face to face, *vis-à-vis*; counter to, in conflict with; *versus, contra*.
Antonym, see COÖPERATION, SIDE.

---

oppress, *v.t.* persecute, burden, crush, afflict, grieve, load, depress; overbear, compress, overtax, overburden; tyrannize. See GRAVITY, MALEVOLENCE.
oppressive, *adj.* tyrannical, cruel, burdensome, onerous, hard, grinding, grievous. See GRAVITY, SEVERITY. *Ant.,* see LIGHT.
oppressor, *n.* persecutor, bully, boss, slave driver, Simon Legree, MASTER; tyrant, martinet, dictator. See SEVERITY, AUTHORITY.
opprobrious, *adj.* abusive, insulting, offensive, slanderous, derogatory, contemptuous, malicious. See DETRACTION, ATTACK, DISCOURTESY.
opt, *v.i.* decide, incline (toward), approve (of); opt for, vote for, elect, choose, select, pick, favor. See CHOICE, APPROBATION.

OPTICAL INSTRUMENTS

Nouns—**1,** optical instruments, lens; spectacles, glasses, bifocals, pince-nez, eyeglass, monocle, lorgnette, goggles; Polaroid lenses, contact lenses; sunglasses; spyglass, magnifying glass; opera glass, fieldglass, binoculars; glass eye; telescope, periscope, spectroscope, microscope; optics, optometry. *Slang,* specs, cheaters.
2, mirror, looking glass, pierglass, cheval glass; reflection.
3, camera, camera lucida, camera obscura; motion-picture camera; kinescope, television camera; stereoscope, stereopticon, viewer, magic lantern, kaleidoscope; projector.

4, optometrist; lens grinder; oculist, optician; microscopist, *etc.*
5, electric eye, photoelectric cell.

optimism, *n.* hopefulness, HOPE, CHEERFULNESS, encouragement, brightness, enthusiasm; confidence, assurance. *Ant.,* PESSIMISM.

option, *n.* CHOICE, preference, discretion, alternative; privilege, RIGHT; first call, choice *or* say; put, call. See BUSINESS, PLEASURE, DESIRE, WILL.

optional, *adj.* discretionary, voluntary, elective, nonobligatory. See CHOICE.

oracle, *n.* prophet, seer, soothsayer, augur, fortune-teller, witch; sibyl; Delphic oracle; Sphinx, Cassandra, sorcerer, interpreter. See PREDICTION.

oral, *adj.* verbal, vocal, spoken, unwritten. See SPEECH.

orange, *n. & adj.* See COLOR.

oration, *n.* SPEECH, declamation, oration, discourse, address.

oratory, *n.* SPEECH, elocution, declamation, eloquence, expression.

orbit, *n.* path, track, circuit, REVOLUTION, COURSE; REGION, range, sphere, realm, scope; province; sphere of INFLUENCE. See CIRCUITY, ASTRONAUTICS.

orchard, *n.* fruit-garden, grove, vineyard, plantation. See AGRICULTURE.

orchestra, *n.* See MUSICAL INSTRUMENTS.

ordain, *v.* install, appoint, invest; decree, predestine, destine; frock. See CLERGY, COMMISSION. *Ant.,* see MANKIND.

ordeal, *n.* trial, strain, cross, tribulation, test.

ORDER

Nouns—**1,** order, orderliness, REGULARITY, uniformity, SYMMETRY, harmony, precision; METHOD, system, disposition, ARRANGEMENT; regimentation, composition, coördination, adoption, subordination; management, discipline, ECONOMY; PLAN, FORM, array; COURSE, routine, even tenor.

2, gradation, graduation, PROGRESSION; series, SEQUENCE; classification, ordering; rank, place, step, DEGREE; CLASS, kind, sort, set; category, division.

3, COMMAND, charge, DIRECTION, injunction, enjoinment, dictate, demand, directive, COMMISSION; regulation, RULE; ban, interdiction, RESTRAINT.

4, requisition, application, booking, reservation, REQUEST; amount purchased, consignment, shipment, supply, carload, QUANTITY.

5, fraternity, society, brotherhood, community (see ASSEMBLAGE).

Verbs—**1,** be in order; form, fall in, draw up; arrange, range *or* place itself; fall into place *or* rank, take one's place, rally round.

2, (put in) order, make *or* restore order; organize, regulate, regularize; classify, alphabetize; arrange, range, array, align, trim, dispose, place; LIST, file, put away.

3, COMMAND, direct, instruct, give an order; dictate, decree, charge, REQUEST; RULE, govern; prohibit, interdict, ban.

4, buy, reserve, engage, book, bespeak, retain; write for, send for, arrange for, secure, stipulate; requisition, COMMISSION.

Adjectives—orderly, regular; in order, in good form, in trim, in its proper place, fixed; neat, tidy, trim, spruce; methodical, classified, symmetrical, shipshape; businesslike, systematic, schematic. *Colloq.,* in apple-pie order.

Adverbs—orderly, in order; methodically, in turn, in its turn; step by step, by regular steps, stages, intervals *or* gradations (see INTERVAL); *seriatim*, systematically, by *or* like clockwork.

Antonym, see DISORDER.

ordinance, *n.* law, regulation, ORDER, decree; appointment, DESTINY; rule, enactment. See COMMAND.

ordinary, *adj.* usual, medium, average, unremarkable, commonplace, regular, common; inferior, low; middling, second-rate; undistinguished. See CONFORMITY. *Ant.*, see UNCONFORMITY.

ordnance, *n.* guns, cannon, artillery. See ARMS.

organ, *n.* hand organ, hurdygurdy, barrel organ; organette, regal, organophone, harmonium; calliope; medium, AGENCY, MEANS; component, PART, member; PUBLICATION, journal; gland, heart, *etc.* See MUSICAL INSTRUMENTS.

ORGANIZATION

Nouns—**1,** organization, organic matter, organized nature *or* world, animated *or* living nature, living beings; flora, fauna, biota; organic remains, fossils, petrified organisms.

2, organism, plankton; cell, plasma; DNA, RNA; egg *or* sperm cell, semen, seed; spore; cell division, mitosis.

3, biology, natural history; organic chemistry, anatomy, zoology, BOTANY, *etc.*; cytology, chromosomology, genetics; biologist, zoologist, *etc.*

Adjectives—organic, vital, biotic, biological; protoplasmic, plasmic, plasmatic, cellular, structural, anatomic(al).

orgy, *n.* debauch, carouse, dissipation; rite; revelry, carousal. See DRUNKENNESS.

orient, *v.t.* orientate; find one's bearings, locate; acquaint, familiarize, adapt, adjust; indoctrinate, educate, train. See DIRECTION, TEACHING.

orifice, *n.* See OPENING.

origin, *n.* BEGINNING, CAUSE, commencement; descent, source, fountainhead, derivation, rise.

original, *adj.* novel, unique; primary, initial; creative; earliest, primal, aboriginal; inventive. See BEGINNING, IMAGINATION, UNCONFORMITY. *Ant.*, see END, CONFORMITY.

originate, *v.* start, invent, begin, inaugurate, initiate, CAUSE, proceed, spring. See BEGINNING, DESCENT, IMAGINATION.

ORNAMENT

Nouns—**1,** ornament, ornamentation, ornateness; adornment, decoration, embellishment.

2, garnish, polish, varnish, gilding, lacquer, enamel; cosmetics; ormolu.

3, pattern, diaper, powdering, paneling, lining, graining; detail, texture, richness; tracery, moulding, filet, flourish, fleur-de-lis, arabesque, fret, astragal, zigzag, acanthus, pilaster.

4, pargeting, embroidery; brocade, trocatelle, lace, fringe, trapping, border, edging, trimming; hanging, tapestry, arras.

5, wreath, festoon, garland, chaplet, flower, nosegay, bouquet, posy, lei; tassel, shoulderknot, epaulet, aiguillette, frog; star, rosette, bow; feather, plume, plumage, panache, aigrette, fine feathers.

6, jewelry, bijoutry; bijou, trinket, locket, necklace, bracelet, anklet, earring, carcanet, chain, chatelaine, brooch, pin, torque; slave bracelet, costume jewelry; gem, precious stone; diamond, brilliant, beryl, emerald, chalcedony, agate, heliotrope; girasol(e); onyx, sardonyx; garnet, lapislazuli, opal, peridot, chrysolite, sapphire, ruby; spinel, topaz; turquoise; zircon, jacinth, hyacinth, carbuncle, rhinestone, amethyst; pearl, coral.

7, finery, frippery, gewgaw, gimcrack, tinsel, spangle, clinquant, brummagem, pinchbeck, paste; gaudiness, VULGARITY.

8, illustration, illumination, vignette; headpiece, tailpiece, scroll, flowers, rhetoric, work of art.

Verbs—**1,** ornament, embellish, decorate, adorn, beautify, smarten; furbish, polish; gild, varnish, whitewash, enamel, japan, lacquer, paint, grain, enrich, silver, chrome.

2, garnish, trim, dizen, bedizen, prink, prank; trip out; deck, bedeck, dight, bedight, array; dress up, spangle, bespangle, powder, embroider, work; chase, emboss, fret; emblazon, illuminate; illustrate.

Adjectives—**1,** ornamented, beautified (see BEAUTY); ornate, rich, gilt, gilded; tasselated, festooned, ornamental, decorative, becoming, smart, gay, flowery, glittering; spangled.
2, pranked out, bedight, well-groomed, fresh as a daisy; in full dress *or* fashion, *en grande toilette*; in best bib and tucker, in Sunday best, showy, flashy; gaudy, garnish; gorgeous. *Slang*, sporty, sharp; snazzy, Sunday-go-to-meeting; in glad rags, dressed to kill, all dressed up like a Christmas tree.

Antonym, see SIMPLENESS.

ornate, *adj.* See ORNAMENT.
orphan, *n.* waif, stray, gamin(e), urchin; foundling. See YOUTH, LOSS.
orphanage, *n.* home, foundlings' home, shelter, refuge. See ABODE.
orthodoxy, *n.* See RELIGION.

OSCILLATION

Nouns—oscillation; vibration, libration, pendulation, motion of a pendulum, nutation, undulation; pulsation, pulse; fluctuation; vacillation, wavering; irresolution, indecision, UNCERTAINTY; wave, swing, beat, shake, wag, see-saw, dance; alternation; reciprocation; coming and going; ebb and flow, flux and reflux, ups and downs; CHANGEABLENESS.
Verbs—oscillate; vibrate, librate, reciprocate, alternate, undulate, wave; rock, swing; pulsate, beat; wag; tick; play; fluctuate, dance, curvet, reel, quake; quiver, quaver; shake, flicker; wriggle; roll, toss, pitch; flounder, stagger, totter; move up and down, bob up and down; pass and repass, ebb and flow, come and go; waver, teeter, seesaw, vacillate; hesitate, shilly-shally, hem and haw, blow hot and cold.
Adjectives—oscillating, ascillatory, undulatory, pulsatory, libratory; vibratory, pendulous; wavering, fluctuating, IRRESOLUTE.
Adverbs—to and fro, up and down, backward and forward, seesaw, zigzag, in and out, from side to side.

Antonym, see INACTIVITY, REPOSE.

ostensible, *adj.* apparent, outward; professed, pretended. See APPEARANCE.

OSTENTATION

Nouns—**1,** ostentation, ostentatiousness, display, show, flourish, parade; pomp, array, STATE, solemnity, flourish; dash, splash, glitter, strut, bombast, pomposity; tinsel, tawdriness; pretense, pretension, pretentiousness; airs, showing off; veneer, façade, gloss; magnificence, splendor; AFFECTATION, VANITY, ORNAMENT, VULGARITY. *Colloq.*, dog, swank. *Slang*, side, front, ritz, ritziness.
2, pageant, pageantry, DEMONSTRATION, exhibition, flying colors, tomfoolery; flourish *or* fanfare of trumpets; spectacle, procession; fête, gala, field day, review, march, promenade. *Colloq.*, turnout.
3, dress; court dress, full dress, evening dress *or* gown, ball dress, fancy dress; full regalia, tailoring; millinery, frippery; foppery, equipage. *Slang*, glad rags, Sunday best.
4, ceremony, ceremonial; ritual; form, formality; etiquette; punctilio, punctiliousness; stateliness, RITE; protocol.
5, attitudinarian; fop, dude; posturer, poser, poseur, pretender, hypocrite (see DECEIVER). *Colloq.*, show-off. *Slang*, grandstander.
Verbs—be ostentatious; put oneself forward; court attention; star; figure; make a show *or* display; glitter; show off, parade; display, exhibit, put forward; sport, brandish, blazon forth; dangle, flaunt, emblazon, prink, primp; set off, mount, have framed; put a good face upon. *Colloq.*, cut a figure, cut a dash, cut a wide swath, make a splash, splurge, play to the gallery, trot out, put on the dog, show off. *Slang*, grandstand, put on a front, strut one's stuff.
Adjectives—ostentatious, showy, dashing, pretentious; jaunty; grand, pom-

pous, palatial; high-sounding; turgid, garish; gaudy, gaudy as a peacock; conspicuous, flaunting, flashing, flaming, glittering; gay, splendid, magnificent, sumptuous; theatrical, dramatic, spectacular; ceremonial, ritual; solemn, stately, majestic, formal, stiff, ceremonious, punctilious, starched; in best bib and tucker, in Sunday best, on parade.

Adverbs—ostentatiously, pompously, *etc.*; with a flourish of trumpets, with flying colors.

Antonym, see PLAINNESS.

---

ostracize, *v.t.* exclude, banish, bar, blackball; outcast. See EXCLUSION, EJECTION.

other, *adj.* different, separate, distinct; else, another, additional. See ADDITION, DIFFERENCE.

otherwise, *adv.* else, if not, besides; contrarily, contrariwise; conversely, vice versa; quite the contrary; alias. See DISSIMILARITY, DIFFERENCE.

otherworldly, *adj.* unworldly, religious, spiritual, supernatural, extramundane, unearthly; idealistic, unreal. *Slang,* out of this world. See INSUBSTANTIALITY, RELIGION, SUPERNATURALISM, IMAGINATION.

oust, *v.t.* depose, evict, remove, dismiss, dislodge. See EJECTION.

out, *adv.* without, outside; outdoors. See EXTERIOR. *Ant.,* see INTERIOR.

outbreak, *n.* outburst, eruption; rebellion, uprising; revolt, insurrection; outburst, disturbance. See DISOBEDIENCE, VIOLENCE. *Ant.,* see OBEDIENCE.

outburst, *n.* eruption, explosion, blowup; outpouring, flood, breakthrough; paroxysm, spasm, upheaval; uproar. See VIOLENCE, EJECTION, EXCITEMENT.

outcast, *n.* pariah, derelict, exile; castaway, outsider, outlaw; leper. See UNCONFORMITY. *Ant.,* see CONFORMITY.

outcome, *n.* issue, END, termination, result, consequence, outgrowth, sequel, upshot. See EFFECT. *Ant.,* see CAUSE.

outcry, *n.* clamor, tumult, exclamation, shout, uproar, bellow. See CRY.

outdo, *v.t.* excel, exceed, overdo, surpass, outstrip, beat. See SUPERIORITY. *Ant.,* see INFERIORITY.

outdoor, *adj.* open-air; out-of-door(s), alfresco; drive-in. See EXTERIOR.

outer, *adj.* outside, outward, external, EXTERIOR. *Ant.,* see INTERIOR.

outfit, *n.* ensemble, garments, suit; group, unit; equipment, gear. See CLOTHING. *Ant.,* see DIVESTMENT.

outflow, *n.* effluence, efflux, outpouring, issue, effusion; ESCAPE. See EGRESS.

outgrowth, *n.* development, result, outcome, offshoot; excrescence. See EFFECT. *Ant.,* see CAUSE.

outing, *n.* excursion, junket, field day, picnic. See SOCIALITY.

outlandish, *adj.* bizarre, *outré,* eccentric, strange, odd, foreign, barbarous, grotesque, queer. See ABSURDITY.

outlast, *v.* outlive, survive, outwear. See DURABILITY.

outlaw, *n.* criminal, bandit, fugitive, outcast; desperado. See EVILDOER.

outlet, *n.* loophole, port; sluice, floodgate; faucet, tap, spout, conduit; exit, vent, opening. See EGRESS, ESCAPE.

outline, *n. & v.* —*n.* profile, silhouette, contour; lines, features, lineaments; tracing, tracery; bounds, boundary; EDGE, circumference, perimeter; sketch, plan, blueprint, schematic, scheme, drawing, draft, rough sketch; synopsis, summary, résumé; diagram, skeleton, broad outline; chart, map. —*v.t.* sketch; diagram; silhouette, delineate; model, block in, plan; boil down, summarize, trace, draw, depict, delimit, design, picture, demonstrate. See APPEARANCE, DESCRIPTION, SHORTNESS.

outlive, *v.t.* survive, outlast. See DURABILITY. *Ant.,* see CHANGE.

outlook, *n.* APPEARANCE, prospect, probabilities, forecast; scene, view, vista. See FUTURITY.

outlying, *adj.* distant, suburban, remote; frontier. See EXTERIOR.

outmoded, *adj.* outdated, out-of-date; antiquated, out-of-style, out-worn; old-style, behind the times, passé, obsolete, archaic; timeworn, stale; superseded. *Slang,* old hat, square. See OLDNESS, DISUSE.

out-of-date, *adj.* See OUTMODED.

out-of-the-way, *adj.* off the beaten track, secluded, isolated; bizarre, out of the ordinary, outlandish. See DISTANCE, SECLUSION, UNCON-FORMITY.

outpost, *n.* sentry, scout; picket; vanguard; border, march, frontier; out-station, fort. See COMBATANT, DEFENSE, EDGE.

output, *n.* produce, yield, harvest, product, PRODUCTION.

outrage, *n.* VIOLENCE, WRONG, affront, harm, damage, injury, abuse; transgression, infraction, violation. See EVIL.

outright, *adj.* complete, unqualified, unmitigated, consummate, out-and-out. See COMPLETION.

outrun, *v.t.* overtake, defeat, outdistance, outstrip. See SUPERIORITY.

outset, *n.* BEGINNING, start, commencement, departure. *Ant.,* see END.

outshine, *v.t.* outdo, eclipse, excel, overshadow, outstrip. See DISREPUTE.

outside, *adj.* EXTERIOR, outer, external, outward. *Ant.,* see INTERIOR.

outsider, *n.* alien, stranger, foreigner; layman; onlooker, passerby, intruder, pariah, rebel, *etc.* See EXCLUSION, UNCONFORMITY.

outskirts, *n.pl.* suburbs, environs, surroundings; border, EDGE; purlieus. See NEARNESS. *Ant.,* see CENTRALITY.

outspoken, *adj.* frank, bluff, unreserved, blunt, loud, plain-spoken. See SIMPLENESS. *Ant.,* see DECEPTION, CONCEALMENT.

outstanding, *adj.* prominent, exceptional, superior, conspicuous, remarkable, noticeable, eminent; unpaid, uncollected, owed, due, unsettled. See IMPORTANCE, DEBT. *Ant.,* see UNIMPORTANCE.

outstretched, *adj.* extended, reaching; proffered, offered; expanded, outspread. See BREADTH.

outstrip, *v.t.* outspace, outrun, excel, exceed, outdo, outdistance; eclipse, surpass. See SUPERIORITY. *Ant.,* see INFERIORITY.

outward, *adj.* EXTERIOR, outer, outside, out. *Ant.,* see INTERIOR.

outweigh, *v.t.* overweigh, outbalance, overbalance, exceed. See SUPERIORITY. *Ant.,* see INFERIORITY.

outwit, *v.t.* frustrate, circumvent, outsmart. See DECEPTION.

oval, *adj.* elliptical, ovoid, ovate. See CIRCULARITY.

ovation, *n.* APPLAUSE, kudos, tribute; acclamation, cheers, APPROBATION.

oven, *n.* stove, range, roaster, broiler; hearth; furnace, kiln; rotisserie, rotary oven, Dutch oven, hibachi. See HEAT, FOOD.

over, *adv. & prep.* —*adv.* past, across, by; again; beyond; extra, above, more, remaining, left. —*prep.* on, above. See END, OPPOSITION, REPETITION, SUPERIORITY.

overawe, *v.t.* frighten, intimidate, daunt, abash, cow; impress. See FEAR.

overbalance, *v.t.* surpass, overweigh, outweigh, nubalance. See SUPERIORITY. *Ant.,* see INFERIORITY.

overbearing, *adj.* domineering; bullying; lordly, arrogant, dictatorial; overwhelming. See INSOLENCE. *Ant.,* see SERVILITY.

overcast, *adj.* cloudy, murky, shadowy, gloomy, dark, leaden. See CLOUDINESS.

overcautious, *adj.* timorous, fearful, overcareful, unenterprising. See CARE. *Ant.,* see RASHNESS.

overcharge, *v.* rook, fleece, do, cheat, extort. *Colloq.,* scalp, gyp. See PAYMENT. *Ant.,* see CHEAPNESS.

overcoat, *n.* greatcoat, duster, topcoat, ulster, raglan. See CLOTHING.

overcome, *v. & adj.* —*v.* conquer, subdue, defeat, overthrow, surmount. See SUCCESS. *Ant.,* see FAILURE. —*adj.* subdued, conquered, defeated, broken, crushed, downcast.

overconfident, *adj.* reckless, cocksure, cocky, complacent, brash, incautious, conceited. *Colloq.,* brassy, cheeky, nervy. See CERTAINTY, RASHNESS, VANITY.

overestimation, *n.* EXAGGERATION; overvaluation, VANITY; megalomania; eulogy; optimism, pessimism, overenthusiasm; much ado about nothing; storm in a teacup, tempest in a teapot; overstatement. See MISJUDGMENT. *Ant.,* see MODERATION, UNDERESTIMATION.

overflow, *v. & n.* —*v.* inundate, flood; brim *or* well over; boil over, run over. See FLUIDITY, QUANTITY. —*n.* inundation, flooding, deluge, alluvion; spate, profusion, excess. See REDUNDANCE, QUANTITY, WATER.

overgrown, *adj.* overrun, weedy; swollen, bloated, oversize, outsize. See SIZE.

overhaul, *v.t.* examine, check, inspect; repair, renovate. See RESTORATION.

overhead, *n.* costs, EXPENDITURE, outlay, capital, investment.

overlap, *v.* imbricate, shingle; overhang, overlie; superimpose. See COVERING.

overlook, *v.* look out on, command; oversee, manage, direct, supervise; pass over *or* by, ignore, omit, disregard, skip; forgive, indulge, excuse, condone, wink at. See VISION, DIRECTION, NEGLECT, LENIENCY.

override, *v.t.* annul, nullify (see OVERRULE).

overrule, *v.t.* override, annul, reverse, set aside, contravene, rescind, veto, cancel, countermand. See NULLIFICATION, REJECTION, SUPERIORITY.

overrunning, *n.* overstepping; trespass; inroad, encroachment, infringement; infraction; extravagation, transcendence; redundance, EXAGGERATION.

overseas, *adj. & adv.* —*adj.* transoceanic, ultramarine, foreign, colonial; —*adv.* beyond the sea, abroad, away. *Colloq.,* over there. See DISTANCE.

oversee, *v.t.* manage, superintend, direct, supervise, COMMAND; overlook. See DIRECTION.

overseer, *n.* superintendent, bailiff, MASTER, foreman. See AUTHORITY.

overshoe, *n.* boot, arctic, galosh, rubber. See CLOTHING.

oversight, *n.* omission, ERROR, blunder, slip; management, directorship, supervision. See DIRECTION. *Ant.,* see COMMISSION.

overstate, *v.t.* exaggerate, overclaim, overdo, overdraw, overembellish. See EXAGGERATION. *Ant.,* see DETRACTION.

overstep, *v.i.* transgress, trespass, cross, encroach, exceed; intrude, infringe.

overtake, *v.t.* catch, pass, reach, overhaul. See ARRIVAL.

overthrow, *v.t.* overcome, defeat, upset, abolish, confute; overturn, demolish, ruin. See DEPRESSION, DESTRUCTION, SUCCESS.

overtone, *n.* suggestion, hint, implication, intimation, innuendo, insinuation, inference. See MEANING, FEELING.

overture, *n.* advance, approach, proposal, bid; prelude, preliminary, introduction. See OPENING.

overturn, *v.t.* invert, upset, reverse; overthrow, destroy. See REVOLUTION.

overwhelm, *v.t.* overpower, crush, submerge, defeat, conquer, overcome. See DESTRUCTION.

overwork, *v.* overdo, tire, weary, exhaust, overtax, overburden, overtask. See WEARINESS, WASTE.

overwrought, *adj.* elaborate, pretentious, ornate; overworked, tired; distraught, hysterical, nervous, frenetic, high-strung. See EXCITABILITY.

ovum, *n.* cell, egg, seed. See CIRCULARITY.

owe, *v.i.* See DEBT. *Ant.,* see CREDIT.

own, *v.* admit, confess, concede, acknowledge; possess, have, hold. See DISCLOSURE, POSSESSION.

owner, *n.* holder, master, bearer, proprietor, proprietress, occupant. See POSSESSION.

ownership, *n.* proprietorship, PROPERTY, possessorship, dominion, title; holding. See POSSESSION.

P

pace, *n. & v.* —*n.* rate, speed, VELOCITY; step, measuring step; stride; gait, amble, rack, single-foot. —*v.* walk, step, stride; walk to-and-fro; measure; lead, set the pace. See MOTION.

pachyderm, *n.* thick-skinned animal; elephant, rhinoceros; insensitive person. See ANIMAL, INSENSIBILITY.

PACIFICATION

Nouns—**1,** pacification, conciliation; reconciliation, reconcilement; propitiation, appeasement, mollification, mediation; shaking of hands, accommodation, ARRANGEMENT, adjustment; terms, COMPROMISE; amnesty; deed of release; fraternization.

2, peace offering; peace treaty; olive branch; truce, armistice; suspension of hostilities; breathing spell; convention; flag of truce, white flag.

3, pacifier, PEACEMAKER, conciliator.

Verbs—**1,** pacify, tranquilize, compose; allay (see MODERATION); reconcile, unite, reunite, propitiate, placate, conciliate, meet halfway, hold out the olive branch, accomodate, heal the breach, make peace, restore harmony, bring to terms, pour oil on troubled waters, handle with kid gloves.

2, settle differences, arrange matters; set straight; make up a quarrel, come to an understanding, come to terms; bridge over, hush up; make it up; make matters up; shake hands. *Colloq.*, bury the hatchet, smoke the peace-pipe.

3, raise a siege; sheathe the sword; lay down one's arms; beat swords into plowshares; come around.

Adjectives—pacific, peaceful, calm; peaceable, unwarlike, peace-loving, peace-making; pacifying, soothing, mollifying; appeasing; pacificatory, propitiatory, conciliatory; pacified.

Antonyms, see CONTENTION, WARFARE.

---

pack, *n. & v.* —*n.* stow, bale, package, packet; load, burden, bundle; knapsack; crowd, mob, MULTITUDE; herd, flock, bevy, covey. See ASSEMBLAGE. —*v.* stow, bale, package; cram, tamp; cake, solidify; add to; stuff; load, burden.

package, *n.* parcel, package, pack, carton. See ASSEMBLAGE, RECEPTACLE.

packet, *n.* PACKAGE; packet boat, *paquebot*; mail boat, steamer, coaster. See SHIP.

packing, *n.* contents, filler, stuffing, wadding; CLOSURE, stopper, bung, plug; pad, cushioning, buffer; lute, seal, gasket. See SOFTNESS.

pact, *n.* compact, covenant, treaty; bargain, AGREEMENT.

pad, *n. & v.* —*n.* cushion, mat, buffer; writing tablet. —*v.* walk softly; cushion, stuff, wad; enlarge, overstate, inflate. See INCREASE.

padding, *n.* pads, cushion, wadding (see PACKING); fill-ins, additions; excess, extras, surplus; REPETITION, tautology; featherbedding. *Colloq.*, falsies.

paddle, *n. & v.* —*n.* oar, scull, sweep, flipper, pole. —*v.* canoe, row, ply the oar; backwater, feather, steer; beat, thrash, spank, drub; toddle, pad, waddle. See NAVIGATION, PUNISHMENT, TRAVEL.

pagan, *adj. & n.* —*adj.* heathen, ungodly; idolatrous. —*n.* heathen, idolater. See IRRELIGION, RELIGION.

page, *n. & v.* —*n.* servant; attendant; call boy, pageboy, bellboy; folio, leaf. —*v.* summon, call; number pages. See NUMBER, SERVANT.

pageant, *n.* exhibition, show, parade, display. See OSTENTATION.

pail, *n.* bucket, can, canister, pot, pan, kettle. See RECEPTACLE.

PAIN

Nouns—**1,** pain, suffering, sufferance; ache; aching, smart; twinge, twitch, gripe, headache; hurt, cut; sore, soreness, painfulness; discomfort, malaise; spasm, cramp, nightmare; crick, stitch, thrill, twinge, convulsion, throe; throb, throbbing, pang; sharp, piercing, throbbing, shooting, gnawing *or* burning pain; anguish, agony; excruciation, torment, torture; rack; crucifixion; martyrdom; vivisection.

2, mental suffering, pang, anguish, agony, torture, torment, purgatory (see HELL).

3, ADVERSITY; trial, ordeal, shock, blow, burden, load; concern, grief, sorrow, distress, affliction, woe, bitterness; lovesickness; heartache; unhappiness, infelicity, misery, tribulation, wretchedness, desolation; despair; extremity, prostration, depth of misery; hell on earth; reign of terror; slough of despond (see ADVERSITY); peck *or* sea of troubles; dog's life.

4, embarrassment, shame, DISCONTENT; DEJECTION; DISEASE.

Verbs—**1,** feel, experience, suffer, endure *or* undergo pain; suffer, ache, smart, bleed; tingle, shoot; twinge, twitch, writhe, wince; make a wry face. *Colloq.*, see stars.

2, grieve; mourn, lament (see LAMENTATION); yearn, repine, pine, droop, languish, sink; despair; break one's heart; eat one's heart out.

3, give, cause *or* inflict pain; pain, hurt, wound, chafe, sting, bite, gnaw, gripe; pinch, tweak, grate, gall, fret, prick, pierce, wring, convulse; embarrass, shame; torment, torture; rack, agonize; crucify; excruciate; break on the wheel, put on the rack; spank, beat, thrash, flog (see PUNISHMENT).

4, sicken, disgust, revolt, nauseate, disenchant; repel, offend, shock, stink in the nostrils; turn the stomach; make one sick, set the teeth on edge; go against the grain, grate on the ear, stick in one's throat *or* craw; rankle, gnaw, corrode; horrify, appall, chill the blood; make the flesh creep, make the hair stand on end; make the blood curdle *or* run cold; make one shudder; raise one's hackles.

Adjectives—**1,** in pain, suffering, pained, afflicted, worried, displeased, aching, griped, sore; on the rack, in limbo; in hell; heavy-laden, stricken, crushed, victimized, ill-used; unfortunate, hapless; unhappy, heartbroken; lovesick, lovelorn, brokenhearted; in despair; agonized, tortured, crucified, racked, broken on the wheel.

2, causing pain, hurting, hurtful, painful; dolorous; cutting, corroding, consuming, racking, excruciating, searching, grinding, grating, agonizing; envenomed.

3, distressing, afflicting, afflictive; grievous, piteous; woeful, rueful, mournful, deplorable, pitiable, lamentable; sad, affecting, touching, pathetic; ruinous, disastrous, calamitous, tragical.

4, intolerable, insufferable, insupportable, unbearable, unendurable; more than flesh and blood can bear; enough to drive one mad.

Antonym, see PLEASURE.

---

painkiller, *n.* alleviative, lenitive, anodyne, analgesic, [local] anaesthetic, NARCOTIC, morphine, paregoric, novocaine, codeine, sleeping pills. See REMEDY.

painless, *adj.* bearable, sufferable, easy [to take]. See FACILITY, RELIEF.

pains, *n.pl.* EXERTION, labor, effort; ATTENTION, seriousness. See PERFECTION.

painstaking, *adj.* careful, particular, meticulous, scrupulous; diligent. See EXERTION, CARE.

PAINTING

Nouns—**1,** painting; depicting; drawing; design; chiaroscuro; composition; treatment, perspective, balance, technique; portrait, miniature, landscape, seascape, mural, still life, scene; prospect; panorama; cartoon.

2, school, style; the grand style, fine art, high art, commercial art, genre, portraiture; classicism, romanticism, impressionism, realism, pointillism, Dadaism, modernism, surrealism, cubism.

3, palette; easel; brush, paintbrush, pencil, charcoal, crayons, chalk, pastel; paint, water color, oils, oil paint; varnish, gouache, tempera, distemper, fresco, enamel; encaustic painting.

4, painting, picture, piece, tableau, canvas; oil painting; fresco, cartoon; drawing, pencil drawing, watercolor drawing; sketch, outline; study, scene, view; illustration.

5, picture gallery, art gallery, studio, atelier, museum, exhibition, show.

6, painter, ARTIST, portrait *or* landscape painter, *etc.*; realist, surrealist, impressionist, cubist, pointillist, postimpressionist, *etc.*; house painter, *etc.*

Verbs—paint, design, limn, draw, sketch, pencil, scratch, shade, stipple, hatch, crosshatch, hachure, dash off, block out, chalk out, square up; color, tint, dead-color, wash, varnish; paint in oils; stencil; depict, represent.

Adjectives—pictorial, graphic, picturesque; painted; classic, romantic, realistic, impressionistic, *etc.*; pencil, oil, pastel, tempera, water-color, *etc.*

---

pair, *n. & v.* —*n.* couple, duo, brace; mates; two of a kind. —*v.* match, mate, couple, suit, unite. See NUMERATION, SIMILARITY.

pajamas, *n.* See NIGHTCLOTHES.

pal, *n., colloq.*, [bosom *or* boon] companion, crony, comrade, mate; sidekick, buddy, chum. See FRIEND.

palace, *n.* alcazar, CASTLE, tower, chateau, mansion, great house, *palazzo, palais*; ARENA, pleasure dome, Crystal Palace. See ABODE, AMUSEMENT.

palatable, *adj.* tasty, savory; toothsome, appetizing; pleasant, agreeable; easy to take. See TASTE, PLEASURE.

palaver, *n. & v.* —*n.* colloquy, conference, parley, CONVERSATION; babble, chatter; FLATTERY, nonsense, ABSURDITY. *Colloq.*, soft soap. —*v.i.* converse, confer; dicker, bargain; gossip, drivel, babble, chatter. See COUNCIL, SPEECH.

pale, *adj., v.i. & n.* —*adj.* wan, waxen, ashy, ashen, colorless, bloodless; blond; faint, dim, vague; sickly. See COLORLESSNESS, DIMNESS, LIGHT. *Ant.*, see COLOR. —*v.i.* whiten, blanch, blench; fade, dim. —*n.* fence; border, boundary, LIMIT. See CIRCUMSCRIPTION.

pall, *v.i. & n.* —*v.i.* jade, weary; cloy, sicken, satiate. See SUFFICIENCY. —*n.* murk, smoke, smog, fog; gloomy atmosphere. See CLOUDINESS.

palliate, *v.t.* extenuate, excuse; mitigate, soften; relieve, ameliorate. See FORGIVENESS, VINDICATION, SOFTNESS, MODERATION.

pallor, *n.* paleness, bloodlessness, wanness, sallowness, whiteness, COLORLESSNESS. *Ant.*, see COLOR.

palm, *n. & v.* —*n.* palmetto, palmyra; honor, prize, reward, trophy, guerdon, laurel(s). —*v.* handle, TOUCH; conceal, hide, cover; steal, pilfer; palm off, impose *or* foist (on), get ride of, deceive. See TAKING, STEALING, DECEPTION.

palpable, *adj.* evident, PLAIN, clear, manifest, obvious, apparent, unmistakable, definite, unquestionable, distinct. See EVIDENCE.

palpitate, *v.i.* beat, pulse, throb; vibrate; quake, shake. See AGITATION.

paltry, *adj.* trifling, trivial, inconsequential; mean, petty, worthless; contemptible, sorry, pitiable; insignificant. See UNIMPORTANCE, POVERTY, PITY.

pamper, *v.t.* humor, indulge, spoil, pet, coddle, gratify, overindulge. See PLEASURE. *Ant.*, see SEVERITY.

pamphlet, *n.* booklet, folder, brochure, leaflet; monograph, manual. See BOOK.

pamphleteer, *n.* tract writer, essayist, propagandist. See WRITING.

pan, *n.* pot, kettle, saucepan; skillet, spider, grill; dishpan; utensil, vessel. See RECEPTACLE.

panacea, *n.* universal remedy, REMEDY, cure-all, cure.

pancake, *n.* hotcake, flapjack, battercake, buckwheat cake, flannel cake, silver dollar, griddle cake; crêpe suzette; fritter, *crêpe.* See FOOD.

pandemonium, *n.* HELL, inferno; noise, racket, din; EXCITEMENT, DISORDER, convulsion, frenzy, bedlam, Babel, DISCORD. *Colloq.,* all hell breaking loose. See LOUDNESS, VIOLENCE.

pander, *v. & n.* —*v.* cater to; encourage (in bad habits); pimp. —*n.* pimp; go-between. See EVIL, EVILDOER.

pane, *n.* WINDOW, windowpane, light, skylight; sheet glass, plate glass; SIDE, face, section, surface. See TRANSPARENCY.

panegyric, *n.* praise; encomium, eulogy; APPROBATION, laudation.

panel, *n.* jury, board of judges; board, table. See LIST.

pang, *n.* PAIN, twinge, shoot, throe, ache.

panhandle, *v., slang,* beg, solicit, bum; make a touch. See REQUEST.

panic, *n. & v.* —*n.* terror, fright, FEAR, consternation, wild alarm; stampede; business disaster, widespread depression. See FAILURE. —*v.* alarm, frighten; stampede. *Colloq.,* bring down the house, wow (the audience).

panoply, *n.* full armour, regalia, armor, ARMS, arsenal, DEFENSE, protection, shield; pageantry, pomp, OSTENTATION; array, spread, ASSEMBLAGE.

panorama, *n.* vista, view, scene, perspective; REPRESENTATION, cyclorama, diorama.

pant, *v.* gasp, breathe heavily, puff, blow; crave, yearn for, long for. See WEARINESS, DESIRE.

pantomime, *n.* mime, mimicry, chironomy; dumbshow, tableau, charades, silent film; gestures, gesticulation, hand talk, puppet show.

pantry, *n.* STORE, cupboard, larder, kitchen, scullery; galley, cuddy; buttery, butlery; ewery, china closet. See FOOD.

pants, *n.pl.* trousers, breeches; slacks, flannels, jeans, Levis, dungarees; pantaloons, knickerbockers, knickers, plus-fours; shorts, pedal-pushers, chinos, jodpurs; bloomers, briefs, panties. See CLOTHING.

papacy, *n.* papal system *or* office; the Vatican. See CLERGY.

paper, *n.* writing paper; wallpaper; newsprint; rag paper, pulp paper, foolscap, *etc.*; free tickets; paper money, bill, banknote; certificate, deed, document; newspaper, journal; monograph, article, composition. *Colloq.,* folding money. See COVERING, WRITING, MONEY, PUBLICATION, RECORD.

paperback, *n. & adj.* See BOOK.

par, *n.* EQUALITY, equal footing; par *or* face value; level; expert golf score.

parable, *n.* allegory, analogy; fable, moral tale; comparison, similitude. See FIGURATIVE, DESCRIPTION.

parachute, *n. & v.* —*n.* chute, drogue; airdrop, free fall. *Colloq.,* the silk. —*v.* bail out, drop, jump, LEAP. *Colloq.,* hit the silk. See AVIATION.

parade, *n. & v.* —*n.* show, display, pageant, pageantry; march, procession; OSTENTATION, pretension. See CONTINUITY. —*v.* show, display; march; air, vent; flaunt, show off.

paradise, *n.* Eden, HEAVEN, Promised Land, Canaan, land of milk and honey; Utopia, Arcadia; never-never land; bliss, happiness; Elysian fields, Elysium; Shangri-La. *Ant.,* see HELL.

paradox, *n.* inconsistency; illogical truth; ABSURDITY.

paragon, *n.* ideal, model, perfect example, pattern; nonesuch, nonpareil. See PERFECTION. *Ant.,* see IMPERFECTION.

parallel, *n. & adj.* —*n.* parallelism; coextension, parallel lines; analogy, comparison. —*adj.* coextensive, side by side. See SIMILARITY.

paralysis, *n.* stroke, disablement, complete halt (of activity); paraplegia, hemiplegia, malfunction. See DISEASE, IMPOTENCE.

paralyze, v. cripple; demoralize; disable; deaden; bring to a full stop. See IMPOTENCE.

paramount, adj. chief, first, supreme, all-important. See SUPERIORITY.

paramour, n. mistress, ladylove; lover. See LOVE.

paranoid, adj. & n. —adj. paranoiac; fearful, suspicious, distrustful; deranged, obsessed, compulsive; psychotic, maniac(al), lunatic, sick, insane. —n. psychotic, schizophrenic; alarmist, pessimist. See INSANITY, FEAR.

parapet, n. wall, rampart, breastwork, embankment, DEFENSE; railing.

paraphernalia, n.pl. apparatus, gear, equipment; belongings; PROPERTY.

paraphrase, n. & v. —n. free translation, restatement. Colloq., switch. —v. restate, alter, express differently, reword. See INTERPRETATION.

parasite, n. sycophant, flatterer, fawner, hanger-on; leech, bloodsucker; (Biol.) inquiline, commensal; symbion(t), symbiotic (inhabitant of host's body). Colloq., free loader. See SERVILITY.

paratrooper, n. paramarine, paramedic. Colloq., chutist. See AVIATION, COMBATANT.

parboil, v.t. brew, simmer, seethe, coddle, HEAT.

parcel, n. package, bundle, pack, packet; PART, portion, piece; LAND, lot, division, section. See ASSEMBLAGE.

parch, v. dry, dry up; roast, scorch; become thirsty. See DRYNESS.

parchment, n. vellum; sheepskin; pell, scroll; document, diploma; bond paper, ragpaper. See MATERIALS, WRITING.

pardon, v.t. & n. —v.t. forgive, excuse; release (from penalty); overlook; tolerate. See FORGIVENESS. —n. excuse, release, FORGIVENESS; indulgence; remission; toleration.

pare, v.t. peel, trim, cut, shave, slice; reduce, shorten. See LAYER, DECREASE, CONTRACTION.

parent, n. begetter, procreator, progenitor; forebear, ancestor, father, mother; foster parent; fount, source. See CAUSE, PRODUCTION, AGENCY.

parental, adj. motherly, fatherly, maternal, paternal; protective, loving, tender. See ANCESTRY.

parenthetical, adj. in parentheses; inserted, interpolated; incidental; disconnected, irrelevant. See INSERTION, IRRELATION, BETWEEN.

pariah, n. outcast, untouchable, outcaste. See DISREPUTE.

parish, n. fold, church; LAITY, congregation, flock; parsonage, vicarage, manse; territory, REGION, area. See RELIGION.

parity, n. EQUALITY, equal basis; SIMILARITY, equivalence; par. Ant., see INEQUALITY.

park, v. & n. —v. leave standing (as a car); leave, deposit, place. See LOCATION, CIRCUMSCRIPTION. —n. parkway; playground; public gardens, botanical gardens, zoo; woodland, pleasance; grove; picnic grounds; village or bowling green, common; parking lot or space; amusement park, fair grounds, fun fair. See AMUSEMENT, LOCATION.

parley, n. & v.i. —n. conference, talk, discussion, CONVERSATION, COUNCIL; palaver. —v. talk, confer, palaver, converse.

parliament, n. assembly, COUNCIL, convocation; ASSEMBLAGE, house.

parlor, n. living room, front room, drawing room. See RECEPTACLE.

parochial, adj. provincial, local; narrow, illiberal; of the parish; church-controlled (as schools, etc.). See REGION, MISJUDGMENT, SCHOOL.

parody, n. takeoff; IMITATION; travesty, burlesque. See COPY.

parole, n. & v. —n. pledge, PROMISE; custody, release, FREEDOM, probation. —v.t. free, liberate, let go, release, put on probation.

paroxysm, n. fit, seizure, spasm; convulsion, ATTACK; outburst, frenzy. See AGITATION, EXCITEMENT, VIOLENCE, PAIN.

parrot, n. & v. —n. polly, par(r)akeet; prater, chatterbox, magpie, jay; imitator, mimic, ape. Colloq., copycat; blabbermouth. —v.t. imitate, echo, mime, repeat, say by rote, prate. See COPY, IMITATION, LOQUACITY.

parry, v. fend or ward off, avert, turn aside; evade; fence; deflect. See AVOIDANCE, NEGATION.

PARSIMONY

Nouns—**1,** parsimony, parsimoniousness, stinginess, miserliness; stint; illiberality, avarice, greed, avidity, rapacity, extortion, venality, cupidity; SELFISHNESS. See also ECONOMY.

2, miser, niggard, churl, skinflint, scrimp, lickpenny, curmudgeon, harpy; extortioner, usurer; scrooge. *Slang,* tightwad, pennypincher.

Verbs—be parsimonious, grudge, begrudge, stint, pinch, gripe, dole out, hold back, withhold, starve, famish, live on nothing; drive a hard bargain; cheapen, beat down; have an itching palm, grasp, grab.

Adjectives—parsimonious, penurious, stingy, miserly, mean, shabby, piddling, scrubby, pennywise, near, niggardly, close; close-fisted, grasping, tight-fisted; tight, sparing, chary; grudging, griping; illiberal, ungenerous, hidebound, sordid, mercenary, venal, covetous, usurious, avaricious, greedy, extortionate, rapacious. *Colloq.,* skimping.

Antonym, see GIVING.

parson, *n.* clergyman; pastor, minister, preacher, rector. See CLERGY.
parsonage, *n.* parson's house; manse, rectory. See TEMPLE.

PART

Nouns—**1,** part, portion, sector, segment, fragment, fraction, item, particular, dose; aught, any; division, subdivision, section, ward, parcel, compartment, department, detachment, CLASS; county, REGION, place; partition, instal(l)ment, interest (see APPORTIONMENT); chapter, verse, article, clause, paragraph; PASSAGE, excerpt, serial (see BOOK). See INCOMPLETENESS, IMPERFECTION.

2, component *or* integral part, part and parcel, contents; crux, kernel (see IMPORTANCE); element, factor, constituent, ingredient, complement, material, specification, leaven; feature, principle, radicle. *Colloq.,* makings, fixings. See COMPOSITION.

3, piece, lump, bit, chip, slab, dollop, slice, cut, cutting; shard, cob, crumb, flake, tatter; scale, lamina, LAYER; small part, morsel, soupçon (see LITTLENESS); shred, snip, paring, shaving, scrap, remnant, sliver, splinter. *Colloq.,* hunk, chunk, smithereen.

4, member, limb, organ, lobe, lobule, arm, wing, flipper; joint, link, offshoot, ramification, appurtenance; scion, branch, bough, twig, bush, spray, leaf(let), stump.

5, debris, odds and ends, oddments, flinders, detritus, matchwood.

6, role, character, impersonation, personification (see DRAMA); voice, instrument (see MUSIC).

7, side, PARTY, faction, cause; concern, interest, PARTICIPATION, business, work; office, function, duty, charge.

Verbs—part, divide, subdivide, break, disjoin (see DISJUNCTION); partition, share, allot, dole out, mete, apportion; split, tear, rend, cleave, cut, open, rupture, sunder, tear asunder; sever, dissever, distribute, disunite, hold apart; break up, disrupt, dismember, disconnect, disassociate, detach, terminate; chip, splinter, snip, snap, shred, tatter, flake; part company, separate.

Adjectives—**1,** part, partial, fractional, fragmentary, sectional, aliquot, incomplete; divided, cleft, multifid, separated, individual, in compartments, bipartite, tripartite, *etc.*, multipartite; broken, splintered, severed, disrupt(ed), scrappy; branch(y), branching, subsidiary.

2, component, constituent, intrinsic, integral; essential, inherent, innate; inclusive, comprehensive (see INCLUSION).

Adverbs—partly, in part, partially, piecemeal, part by part; by instal(l)ments, by snatches, by inches, by driblets; in detail; bit by bit, inch by inch, foot by foot, drop by drop; in detail, in lots; somewhat.

Antonym, see WHOLE.

partake, *v.* share, share in; take (food *or* drink); receive (part of). See COÖPERATION.

partial, *adj.* incomplete, fractional, unfinished, PART; biased, partisan, onesided, prejudiced; favoring. See MISJUDGMENT, SIDE.

partiality, *n.* preference, favoring; bias, prejudice, one-sidedness, liking, taste (for), penchant, predilection. See MISJUDGMENT, DESIRE. *Ant.,* see EQUALITY.

participate, *v.i.* partake; share, share in; come in for a share; prorate; go shares, go halves; share and share alike; have *or* own in common, possess *or* use jointly; join in; go in with, have a hand in; coöperate. *Colloq.,* go Dutch. *Slang,* kick in, feed the kitty. See SOCIALITY. *Ant.,* see SECLUSION.

participation, *n.* sharing, COÖPERATION, partaking; gregariousness, mixing, SOCIALITY; mutuality, common use of; joint stock, common stock, partnership; collectivism, communism, socialism; communion; community; mutual benefit, action *or* enjoyment; joint endeavor *or* enterprise. *Slang,* cahoots.

particle, *n.* speck, iota, jot, whit, bit; atom, molecule; (*Gram.*) suffix, prefix; conjunction, preposition, interjection. See LITTLENESS, GRAMMAR.

particular, *adj. & n.* —*adj.* demanding, painstaking, meticulous; definite, specific; fussy, finicky, per(s)nickety, overnice; special, outstanding; personal; precise, exact. See TASTE, IMPORTANCE. —*n.* fact, specification, datum, detail.

particularize, *v.* specify, itemize, mention particularly, detail. See DESCRIPTION.

parting, *n.* leavetaking, DEPARTURE; farewell, severance, separation; partition, division. See DISJUNCTION.

partisan, *adj. & n.* —*adj.* partial, one-sided, pro, favoring, interested. —*n.* supporter, ally, follower, adherent; aide; champion; guerrilla, underground fighter. See AID.

partisanship, *n.* party spirit, loyalty (to party); unfairness, bias, prejudice; clannishness, closeness (of relations); provincialism. See PARTY, INJUSTICE.

partition, *n.* wall, screen, diaphragm, barrier; separation, severance, cutting-off; section, portion; division. See DISJUNCTION, BETWEEN.

partly, *adv.* in part, not wholly; incompletely, partially, in a way, not quite.

partner, *n.* sharer, associate, co-owner; spouse, mate. *Colloq.,* sidekick, pal, pard, pardner. See ACCOMPANIMENT, MARRIAGE.

partnership, *n.* co-ownership, business association; coöperation, alliance. See ACCOMPANIMENT.

PARTY

Nouns—**1,** party, faction, side; denomination, communion; community, body, fellowship, fraternity; confraternity; brotherhood, sisterhood; sodality; family, clan (see ANCESTRY).

2, gang, crew, band, horde, posse, phalanx; clique, ring, set, circle, coterie, club. *Colloq.,* crowd, mob, bunch.

3, corporation, corporate body, company; guild; establishment, partnership, copartnership; firm, house; joint concern, joint stock company; syndicate, trust; joint account.

4, society, association; institute, institution; union, trade union; league, alliance, *Verein, Bund, Zollverein*; combination, trust, syndicate; coalition, federation; confederation, confederacy; junta, cabal; freemasonry. See COÖPERATION.

5, party, entertainment, affair; tea party, dinner party, birthday party, *etc.* See SOCIALITY.

Adjectives—in league, in partnership, in alliance; partisan, denominational; bonded together, banded together, linked together; confederated, federative; joint, mutual.

Antonym, see AGREEMENT, SECLUSION.

parvenu, *n.* pretender, newcomer, upstart, social climber, snob; *nouveau riche. Colloq.,* Johnny-come-lately, pusher. See PROSPERITY, NEWNESS.

pass, *n. & v.* —*n.* gap, gorge; way, OPENING, NOTCH, defile, PASSAGE; free ticket; crisis, predicament, condition, CIRCUMSTANCE. —*v.* go through *or* by, bypass; get a passing mark, make the grade, do (pass muster); cross; hand over; admit, allow, tolerate; while away *or* spend (the time); authorize, O.K., sanction; permit (see PERMISSION).

passable, *adj.* allowable, acceptable, tolerable; passing, fair, good enough. See IMPERFECTION.

PASSAGE

Nouns—**1,** passage, transmission; permeation; penetration; interpenetration; transudation, infiltration; osmosis, endosmosis, exosmosis; intercurrence; access, ingress, egress; road, highway, thoroughfare, boulevard, avenue, street; byway, lane, pike, alley, trail; high road, the King's highway; roadway; turnpike, thruway, expressway, interstate [highway], freeway, parkway, super-highway, limited-access highway.

2, CHANNEL, gate, OPENING; progress, flow, current, stream, flight; duration, COURSE.

3, transference, transportation, transit; conveyance, VEHICLE; portage, cartage, freight, shipment; shifting, transposition, transplantation, translation.

Verbs—**1,** pass, pass through; perforate, penetrate, permeate, thread, enfilade; go through, go across; go over, pass by, bypass, pass over; cut across; ford, cross; work *or* make one's way through; thread *or* worm one's way through; force one's way; find a way; transmit, make way; clear the course *or* track; traverse, go over ground.

2, TRANSFER, transport, convey, bear; conduct, convoy; ship, shift, send, dispatch, consign, post, mail, deliver, transfuse, draw, decant.

Adjectives—passing, elapsing, progressive; intercurrent; transient, portable, assignable, movable.

Adverbs—in passing, *en passant,* in transit, under way.

Antonym, see INERTNESS.

---

passenger, *n.* rider, commuter, fare; hitchhiker, pickup, stowaway. See TRAVEL.

passerby, *n.* onlooker, witness, looker-on; man on the scene, man in the street, pedestrian, bystander. *Slang,* sidewalk superintendent. See TRAVEL, VISION.

passion, *n.* LOVE; fervor, ardor; intensity, fever; infatuation, DESIRE; emotion; rage, anger, fury; EXCITEMENT. *Colloq.,* predilection, preference.

passive, *adj.* nonresistant; inactive, inert, quiet; unemotional, untouched, unstirred, indifferent. See INACTIVITY. *Ant.,* see ACTION, ACTIVITY, FEELING.

passiveness, *n.* inaction, INACTIVITY, inertness; nonresistance, passivity, QUIESCENCE; INDIFFERENCE; neutrality; sluggishness, SUBMISSION.

passport, *n.* official permit; pass; safe-conduct. See PERMISSION.

password, *n.* countersign, shibboleth, watchword. See INDICATION.

PAST

Nouns—**1,** past, past tense, preterition; PRIORITY; the past, yesterday; days of yore *or* of old; times past *or* gone by; bygone days; olden times, the good old days, yesteryear; auld lang syne; eld.

2, antiquity, antiqueness; time immemorial; remote past; archaism, antiquarianism, medievalism, pre-Raphaelitism; retrospection; looking back; MEMORY; ANCESTRY. *Colloq.,* ancient history.

3, paleontology, paleography, paleology, arch(a)eology.

4, antiquary, antiquarian; paleologist, archaeologist, medievalist.

Verbs—be past, have expired, have run its course, have had its day; pass; pass by, go by, go away, pass away, pass off; lapse, blow over; look back, trace back; exhume.

Adjectives—past, gone, bygone, foregone; elapsed, lapsed, expired, no more, run out, blown over, that has been, extinct, never to return, exploded, forgotten, irrecoverable; obsolete (see OLDNESS); once, former, pristine, quondam, *ci-devant*, late; ancestral; foregoing; last, latter; recent, overnight; past, perfect, preterite, past perfect, pluperfect; looking back; retrospective, retroactive; arch(a)eological, *etc.* Colloq., ex-.

Adverbs—formerly; of old, of yore; erst, erstwhile, whilom, erewhile, time was, ago; over; in the olden time; anciently, long ago, long since; a long time ago; yesterday; last year, season *or* month; *ultimo*; lately, retrospectively; before now; hitherto, heretofore; no longer; once, once upon a time; from time immemorial, in the memory of man; time out of mind; already, yet, up to this time; *ex post facto*.

Antonym, see TIME, FUTURITY.

---

paste, *n. & v.* —*n.* cement, bond, binder, glue, adhesive, mucilage; rhinestones, glass; gaudery, trinkery, frippery. See COHERENCE, ORNAMENT. —*v.t.* paste up, cement, stick, glue. See COHERENCE, CONNECTION. *Slang*, lambaste, sock, clout, wallop, punch, slug, larrup. See IMPULSE.

pasteboard, *n. & adj.* —*n.* card-, paper-, pulp-, *or* chipboard, Bristol board. See MATERIALS. —*adj.* fake, phony, stagy, theatrical, simulated, lifeless. See IMITATION.

pastel, *adj.* pale, LIGHT, soft, delicate; tinted, hued, shaded. See COLOR.

pastime, *n.* AMUSEMENT, recreation, entertainment, play, diversion.

pastor, *n.* clergyman, minister, *etc.* See CLERGY.

pastry, *n.* cake, crust, shell; pie, tart, strudel. See FOOD.

pasture, *n.* field, meadow, grassland; paddock, pasturage, range. See LAND.

pasty, *adj.* doughy, soft; pallid, pale; gluey; viscid, glutinous. See COLORLESSNESS.

pat, *n. & adj.* —*n.* caress, stroke; rap, tap; strike, beat, smack. —*adj.* apt, suitable, ready, appropriate, fitting; timely, fortuitous. See AGREEMENT.

patch, *n. & v.t.* —*n.* piece, segment, spot; repair, mend; field, lot —*v.t.* repair, reconstruct, rebuild, revamp, adjust. See COMPROMISE, RESTORATION.

patent, *adj.* obvious, plain, clear, evident, apparent; noticeable; open. See EVIDENCE.

paternal, *adj.* fatherly, patriarchal; ancestral, parental; indulgent, benign, benevolent; paternalistic, protective, autocratic; socialistic. See AUTHORITY.

paternity, *n.* fatherhood, fathership, parentage. See ANCESTRY.

path, *n.* trail, lane, road, footpath, route, way, course; lead, example. See DIRECTION.

pathetic, *adj.* piteous, pitiable, saddening, touching; distressing, heart-rending, sad; pitiful. See PAIN, PITY, FEELING. *Ant.*, see PLEASURE.

pathos, *n.* passion, warmth; sentiment, FEELING.

pathfinder, *n.* trail blazer, explorer, pioneer, frontiersman, SCOUT, FORERUNNER.

patience, *adj.* LENIENCY, tolerance; PERSEVERANCE, persistence; forbearance, long-suffering, SUBMISSION, endurance. *Ant.*, see EXCITEMENT, DISCONTENT.

patio, *n.* courtyard, INCLOSURE, court, atrium; yard; terrace, piazza, veranda.

patriarch, *n.* forefather, forebear, elder, graybeard; leader, headman, chief, MASTER; priest, primate, ecclesiarch, hierarch. See ANCESTRY, CLERGY.

patrician, *adj.* noble, well-born, aristocratic. See NOBILITY. *Ant.,* see POPULACE.

patriotism, *n.* civic *or* national PRIDE; loyalty, allegiance; love of country, civism, nationalism; chauvinism, jingoism, fascism; isolationism, provincialism, xenophobia. See AFFECTIONS, BOASTING.

patrol, *n. & v.* —*n.* patrolman, guard, warden, ranger; lookout, sentinel, sentry; guardsman, picket; watchman, watch; coast guard; vigilante, POLICEMAN. See COMBATANT, AGENT. —*v.* guard, stand watch *or* guard, watch over, keep watch and ward; scout; walk the beat. See DEFENSE.

patron, *n.* customer; benefactor, supporter; saint, DEITY; defender, backer. See AID.

patronage, *n.* condescension, favor; custom, interest, SUPPORT, assistance; auspices. See AID.

patronize, *v.t.* SUPPORT, endorse, AID; deal *or* do business with; buy from, frequent, go to, shop at; look down upon, show contempt *or* condescension, condescend toward. See PURCHASE, AFFECTATION, VANITY.

patter, *v.i. & n.* —*v.i.* chatter, mumble, ramble, babble, jabber, mutter; tap, pitter-patter. —*n.* dialect, cant, chatter, babble. See LOQUACITY, SPEECH.

pattern, *n.* FORM, original; mold, example; PLAN, last; model, ideal. See PERFECTION. *Ant.,* see IMPERFECTION.

paunch, *n.* stomach, abdomen (see BELLY); fat.

pauper, *n.* beggar, bankrupt, mendicant. See POVERTY. *Ant.,* see MONEY.

pause, *n. & v.i.* —*n.* CESSATION, REST, hesitation, INACTION; lull, stop, discontinuance, suspension. —*v.i.* desist, halt, stop, cease, break. *Ant.,* see CONTINUITY.

pave, *v.t.* coat, cover, floor, cobble, surface; tar, macadamize, concrete, asphalt; prepare, pave the way for. See COVERING, SMOOTHNESS, PREPARATION.

pavement, *n.* paving; road, street, sidewalk; macadam, asphalt, cement, tar, concrete, tile, bricks, stone, flagging, cobbles; pavestone, paving blocks, flagstone. See BASE, COVERING.

pavilion, *n.* tent, canopy, canvas; kiosk; summerhouse. See ABODE, COVERING.

paw, *n. & v.* —*n.* forepaw; pad, mitt. —*v.* handle, TOUCH, finger; mishandle, rough up, maul; stamp, kick; feel, caress, stroke. See RETENTION.

pawn, *v.t.* pledge. *Slang,* hock. See DEBT, SECURITY.

pawnshop, *n.* pawnbrokery, *mont-de-piété. Slang,* hockshop, spout. See LENDING.

PAYMENT

Nouns—**1,** payment, defrayment; discharge; acquittance, quittance; settlement, clearance, liquidation, satisfaction, reckoning, arrangement, repayment, reimbursement; retribution. *Colloq.,* a pound of flesh; an arm and a leg. See MONEY.

2, COMPENSATION, recompense, remuneration, REWARD, indemnity, EXPENDITURE; alimony, [child] support; welfare.

3, salary, stipend, wages, pay, emolument, allowance; bonus, premium, fee, honorarium, tip, scot; tribute, hire; bribe, blackmail, hush money.

4, PRICE, charge, expense; dues, duty, tariff, toll; tax; sales, excise, income, poll, head tax; assessment, tithe, exaction; ransom, salvage, brokerage, *etc.*

Verbs—**1,** pay, defray, make payment; pay down, pay in advance; redeem; pay in kind; discharge, settle, quit, acquit oneself of; account with, reckon with, settle with, be even with, be quits with; strike a balance; settle *or* square accounts with; wipe off old scores; satisfy; pay in full; clear, liquidate; pay up.

2, pay one's way, pay the piper, pay the costs, do the needful; ante up; expend; lay down. *Colloq.*, foot the bill, chip in. *Slang*, tickle *or* grease the palm, cough up, kick in, fork over, shell out.

3, disgorge, make repayment; expend, disburse; repay, refund, reimburse, retribute; REWARD, make compensation. *Slang*, pay through the nose, pay cash on the barrel-head *or* on the line; pay cold cash.

Adjectives—paying, paid, owing nothing, out of debt, quits, square.

Adverbs—to the tune of; on the nail; money down.

Antonym, see NONPAYMENT.

---

peace, *n.* amity, friendship, harmony, concord; tranquility, REPOSE, quiescence; truce, PACIFICATION; neutrality. *Ant.*, see CONTENTION, WARFARE.

peacemaker, *n.* pacifier; mediator, intermediary, intercessor. See COMPROMISE, PACIFICATION. *Ant.*, see WARFARE, CONTENTION.

peak, *n.* SUMMIT, top, apex, pinnacle; point, crag; crest, HEIGHT; climax. See SHARPNESS. *Ant.*, see LOWNESS.

peaked, *adj.* wan, worn, pale, haggard, tired, weary, fatigued; ailing, unwell, unhealthy, ill, poorly, sickly; thin, gaunt, frail. See WEARINESS.

peal, *n. & v.i.* —*n.* reverberation, blast, ring, outburst, boom. —*v.i.* ring, toll, reverberate, SOUND. See LOUDNESS.

pearl, *n.* margarite, nacre, mother-of-pearl; artificial *or* cultured pearl; gem, treasure, jewel; pearl beyond price. See ORNAMENT, GOOD, PERFECTION.

pearly, *adj.* nacreous, silvery, grayish, whitish. See COLOR.

peasant, *n.* countryman; peon, *paisano*, coolie, boor, muzhik, fellah; farmer, laborer, worker; rustic. See POPULACE, AGRICULTURE.

pebble, *n.* pebblestone, gravel, nugget, stone. See LAND, LITTLENESS.

peck, *v.i.* nip, bite, pick, snip; tap, rap. See IMPULSE.

peculiar, *adj.* individual, indigenous, idiosyncratic; idiomatic; strange, odd, unusual, queer; particular, especial. See UNCONFORMITY. *Ant.*, see CONFORMITY.

pedagogic, *adj.* academic, educational, teacherly, professional, scholastic. See TEACHING.

pedal, *n.* treadle, lever; soft pedal, mute. See MEANS, IMPULSE.

pedant, *n.* SCHOLAR, theorist, academician, doctrinaire; prig, bluestocking. See AFFECTATION.

pedantic, *adj.* precise, formal, narrow; bookish, stilted; affected, sophomoric. See SCHOLAR, AFFECTATION.

peddle, *v.t.* sell; canvass, hawk, retail. See SALE.

peddler, pedlar, *n.* hawker, huckster, colporteur, sutler, vendor, trader, dealer. See SALE.

pedestrian, *n.* walker, ambler, stroller, peregrinator, hiker, itinerant. See TRAVEL.

pedigree, *n.* genealogy, lineage, ANCESTRY, DESCENT, family; background.

peek, *v.i.* peep, glance, look, watch; pry. See VISION.

peel, *v.t.* strip, divest, bare, uncover, skin, shell, husk, pare. See DIVESTMENT.

peep, *n. & v.i.* —*n.* chirp, cheep, chirrup; sly look. —*v.i.* peer, peek, look; spy, pry. See SOUND, VISION.

peer, *n. & v.i.* —*n.* equal; nobleman, lord; match. —*v.i.* squint, stare, peep, pry; gaze; scrutinize. See NOBILITY, EQUALITY, VISION. *Ant.*, see POPULACE.

peerage, *n.* aristocracy, NOBILITY, noblemen, the upper classes.

peerless, *adj.* unequaled, matchless, unbeatable, supreme, unrivaled; imdomitable. See SUPERIORITY. *Ant.*, see INFERIORITY.

peevish, *adj.* irascible, fretful, complaining, cranky, cross, irritable, touchy. See IRASCIBILITY. *Ant.*, see CHEERFULNESS.

pellet, *n.* pill, tablet, capsule; missile, pebble, hailstone, bullet. See ARMS.

pellmell, *adv.* madly, frantically; helter-skelter, hurry-scurry, breakneck, headlong. *Colloq.,* every which way. *Slang,* lickety-split. See HASTE.

pelt, *n. & v.* —*n.* fur, hide, skin, peltry. —*v.* bombard, pepper, stone, strike; drive, beat; hurl, throw, pitch, fling. See IMPULSE, PROPULSION.

pen, *n. & v.t.* —*n.* stockade, INCLOSURE, fold, stall, coop, cage, pound, corral, paddock; stylus, quill. —*v.t.* confine, jail, impound, enclose, restrain, cage, coop; write, indite, inscribe. See RESTRAINT, WRITING.

penalize, *v.t.* punish; fine; imprison, chastise; handicap. See PUNISHMENT.

penalty, *n.* retribution, PUNISHMENT; PAIN, penance, ATONEMENT; the devil to pay; penalization; handicap, fine, amercement; forfeit, forfeiture, damages, confiscation.

penance, *n.* ATONEMENT, discipline, punishment; flagellation, fasting; PRICE, suffering, repayment. See RITE.

penchant, *n.* aptitude, leaning, inclination, flair, TENDENCY; predisposition, propensity, TASTE; DESIRE, longing, yearning. *Slang,* yen. See CHOICE, LOVE.

pencil, *n.* crayon, stylus, pastel, chalk. See WRITING, INSTRUMENTALITY.

PENDENCY

Nouns—**1,** pendency, dependency, dependence, pendulousness, pendulosity, pensility; droop, sag, sagging, drooping; suspension, hanging, overhang.

2, pendant, drop, earring, eardrop, lavaliere, necklace; pedicel, pedicle, peduncle; hanging, lobe, wattle, tail, train, flag, tag, bob, skirt, tassel, swag; pigtail, queue; bell rope; pendulum, chandelier; appendage, appendix, ADDITION; suspender, belt, garter, fastening, button, SUPPORT; peg, knob, hook, hanger, nail, stud, ring, staple, pothook, tenterhook, spar; clothesline, clothespin; gallows.

Verbs—**1,** be pendant, hang, depend, swing, dangle, droop, sag, draggle; flap, trail, flow, overhang, project, jut; impend, hang fire.

2, suspend, pend, hang, sling, hook up, hitch, fasten to, append.

Adjectives—pendent, pendulous, pensile; hanging, pending, drooping, cernuous, flowing, loose; suspended, dependent; overhanging, projecting, jutting; pedunculate, tailed, caudate.

Antonym, see SUPPORT.

pendulum, *n.* oscillator, swing, bob, pendant. See PENDENCY, OSCILLATION.

penetrate, *v.t.* bore, burrow, pierce, enter, perforate, permeate; invade; cut; discern, perceive, understand; uncover. See INGRESS, INTELLIGENCE, PASSAGE.

penetrative, *adj.* astute, discerning, piercing; sharp, subtle, acute, penetrating. See FEELING, INTELLIGENCE.

peninsula, *n.* projection, chersonese, neck, tongue of land. See PART, LAND.

PENTIENCE

Nouns—**1,** penitence, contrition, compunction, repentance, remorse, REGRET.

2, self-reproach, self-reproof, self-accusation, self-condemnation, self-humiliation; pangs, qualms, prickings, twinge, *or* voice of conscience; awakened conscience.

3, acknowledgment, confession (see DISCLOSURE); apology, penance, ATONEMENT; recantation.

4, penitent, Magdalene, prodigal son, a sadder and a wiser man.

Verbs—**1,** repent, be penitent, be sorry for; rue; REGRET, think better of; recant; plead guilty; sing *miserere,* sing *de profundis;* confess oneself in the wrong; acknowledge, confess (see DISCLOSURE); humble oneself; beg pardon, apologize, do penance (see ATONEMENT).

Adjectives—penitent, regretful, regretting, sorry, contrite; regrettable, lamentable.

Antonym, see IMPENITENCE.

penitentiary, *n.* PRISON, jail, reformatory.
penmanship, *n.* chirography, handwriting. See WRITING.
pennant, *n.* banner, flag, streamer, pennon. See INDICATION.
penniless, *adj.* indigent, needy, bankrupt, inpecunious, poor. *Slang,* broke. See POVERTY. *Ant.,* see MONEY.
pension, *n.* allowance, annuity, allotment, settlement.
pensive, *adj.* thoughtful, reflective, meditative, musing; melancholy, sad, dejected. See THOUGHT, DEJECTION. *Ant.,* see CHEERFULNESS.
pent-up, *adj.* held in, suppressed, repressed. See RESTRAINT, FEELING.
penurious, *adj.* stingy, mean, miserly, parsimonious. See PARSIMONY.
penury, *n.* POVERTY, lack, indigence, destitution, pauperism. *Ant.,* see MONEY.
people, *n.* See MANKIND, POPULACE.
pep, *n., slang,* peppiness; ENERGY, vitality, VIGOR, vim, dash, zest; liveliness, PUNGENCY, SHARPNESS, gusto, go, pepper, zing. See CHEERFULNESS.
per, *prep. & adv.* —*prep.* by, as, by means *or* way of, through, via. See MEANS. —*adv., slang,* apiece, each, a head, per unit. See UNITY, APPORTIONMENT.
perceive, *v.t.* apprehend, appreciate, discern; observe, notice, see; comprehend, know. See FEELING, KNOWLEDGE.
percentage, *n.* COMPENSATION, COMMISSION, discount; fee; allowance.
perceptible, *adj.* appreciable, discernible, visible; tangible, observable, sensible; cognizable. See KNOWLEDGE.
perceptive, *adj.* knowledgeable, observant, understanding; aware, sympathetic; knowing, cognitive. See KNOWLEDGE.
perch, *n. & v.i.* —*n.* rest, roost, nest, seat. —*v.i.* poise, PLACE, roost, settle, alight, sit.
percolate, *v.i.* drip, trickle, permeate; ooze, filter.
perdition, *n.* DESTRUCTION, downfall, ruin, LOSS, fall. See FAILURE.
peremptory, *adj.* commanding, arbitrary, tyrannical, dogmatic; compulsory, binding; absolute, decisive, conclusive. See AUTHORITY, COMPULSION, SEVERITY.
perennial, *adj.* enduring, lasting, endless, persistent; successive, consecutive. See CONTINUITY. *Ant.,* see DISJUNCTION, END.

PERFECTION

Nouns—**1,** perfection, perfectness, indefectibility; impeccancy, impeccability, faultlessness, excellence.
2, paragon; pink of perfection, acme of perfection; *ne plus ultra,* SUMMIT, model, standard, pattern, mirror; masterpiece; transcendence, transcendency, SUPERIORITY, quintessence.
3, see COMPLETION.
Verbs—be perfect, transcend; bring to perfection, perfect, ripen, mature, consummate, COMPLETE.
Adjectives—perfect, faultless; indefective, indeficient, indefectible; immaculate, spotless, impeccable; unblemished, sound, scatheless, intact; right as rain; consummate, finished, best, model, standard; inimitable, unparalleled, nonpareil; superhuman, divine; *sans peur et sans reproche.*
Adverbs—to perfection, to a fare-thee-well; perfectly, *etc.*

Antonym, see IMPERFECTION.

perfidous, *adj.* TREACHEROUS, crooked, shifty, double-dealing; perjurious, lying, truthless, untrue; deceitful, insidious, snakelike. *Colloq.,* twotiming, double-crossing, phony, like a snake in the grass. See DECEPTION, UNTRUTH, IMPROBITY.

perforate, *v.t.* bore, drill, pierce, puncture, penetrate, prick; punch, riddle; tunnel. See OPENING.

perforator, *n.* piercer, borer, augur, gimlet, stylet, drill, awl, bradawl; corkscrew; dibble; trocar, trepan, probe; bodkin, needle, stiletto; reamer; can opener; warder; lancet; punch, gouge; spear. See OPENING.

perforce, *adv.* compulsorily, by *or* of necessity; against one's will, in spite of oneself. See NECESSITY, COMPULSION.

perform, *v.t.* enact, play, execute; fulfill, achieve, discharge; act, do; operate, work, CONDUCT. See ACTION, AGENCY, COMPLETION, DRAMA, MUSIC, SUPPORT. *Ant.,* see INACTIVITY.

performance, *n.* ACTION, REPRESENTATION, achievement; rendition, execution, TOUCH. See EFFECT, DRAMA.

perfume, *n.* FRAGRANCE, aroma; cologne, scent; sachet, attar, perfumery.

perfunctory, *adj.* formal, indifferent, careless; mechanical, crude. *Ant.,* see COMPLETION.

perhaps, *adv.* MAYBE, possibly, perchance, mayhap, conceivably.

peril, *n.* DANGER, hazard, risk, CHANCE, exposure. *Ant.,* see SAFETY.

perimeter, *n.* periphery, circumference, CIRCUMSCRIPTION, outline, contour; outside, border, boundary; LIMIT; EDGE, rim, hem, margin, fringe.

period, *n.* second, minute, hour; day, week, month; quarter, year, decade; lifetime, generation, TIME; century, age, milennium, era, epoch; stop, full stop (see WRITING).

periodic, *adj.* recurrent, cyclic, intermittent, epochal; periodical, seasonal.

periodical, *n.* magazine, journal, quarterly, weekly, monthly. See BOOK.

periodicity, *n.* REGULARITY, reoccurrence, cycle. *Ant.,* see IRREGULARITY.

peripheral, *adj.* outer, EXTERIOR, neighboring; subsidiary, AUXILIARY, secondary, lesser; marginal. See INFERIORITY, IRRELATION.

perish, *v.i.* expire, die, crumble. See DEATH, DESTRUCTION, NONEXISTENCE. *Ant.,* see LIFE.

perishable, *adj.* impermanent, destructible; temporal, mortal; unenduring. See TRANSIENTNESS. *Ant.,* see DURABILITY.

perjury, *n.* false swearing, FALSEHOOD, perversion, forswearing, fraud. *Ant.,* see TRUTH.

perk, *v.* perk up, cheer (up), brighten, animate, liven, show signs of life. *Colloq.,* bubble, percolate. See CHEERFULNESS.

PERMANENCE

Nouns—1, permanence, STABILITY, immutability, fixity; persistence, endurance, CONTINUITY; DURABILITY, duration; constancy, PERPETUITY; *status quo.*

2, preservation, maintenance, QUIESCENCE, OBSTINACY, conservation, conservatism, MODERATION, establishment; law of the Medes and the Persians; conservative, reactionary, right-winger, nonprogressive, Tory, Hunker, fixture. *Colloq.,* stick-in-the-mud, diehard, holdout, fogy, standpatter. *Slang,* mossback, fuddy-duddy.

Verbs—1, be permanent, persist, remain, stay; hold [out], hold on; last, endure, (a)bide, maintain, keep; stand [fast]; subsist, survive.

2, be conservative, oppose change, hold one's ground, hold good.

Adjectives—1, permanent, stable, fixed, standing, immovable, immutable, established, settled, steadfast; constant, eternal, lifelong, lasting, durable, persistent, unending, perpetual, monotonous; unfading, unfailing, *etc.*; invariable, indelible, indestructible, inextinguishable, intact, inviolate; conservative, reactionary, stationary.

Adverbs—*in statu quo*, as usual; at a standstill, permanently, finally, for good, forever.

Antonym, see CHANGE, CHANGEABLENESS.

---

permeate, *v.t.* pervade, saturate, overspread, infiltrate, penetrate. See PASSAGE, PRESENCE.

PERMISSION

Nouns—**1,** permission, leave; allowance, sufferance; tolerance, toleration; FREEDOM, liberty, law, license, concession, grace; indulgence, lenity; favor, ASSENT, dispensation, EXEMPTION, release; connivance; vouchsafement; open door.

2, authorization, warranty, accordance, admission, permit, warrant, brevet, precept, sanction, authority, firman; free hand, pass, passport; furlough, license, *carte blanche*, ticket of leave; grant, charter, patent. *Colloq.,* green light, go-ahead signal, okay, O.K.

Verbs—**1,** permit; give permission, give power; let, allow, admit; suffer, bear with, tolerate, recognize; accord, vouchsafe, favor, humor, indulge, stretch a point; wink at, connive at; shut one's eyes to; gratify, give *carte blanche*; leave alone, leave to one's own devices, leave the door open; open the door to, open the floodgates; give the reins *or* free rein to.

2, grant, empower, character, enfranchise, confer a privilege, license, authorize, warrant; sanction; entrust, COMMISSION; sanctify, ordain, prescribe. *Colloq.,* okay, O.K., write one's own ticket.

Adjectives—permitting, permissive, indulgent; permitted, permissible, allowable, lawful (see LEGALITY); unconditional.

Adverbs—permissibly, by leave, with leave, on leave; under favor of; *ad libitum,* freely; with no holds barred.

Antonym, see RESTRAINT.

---

permutation, *n.* See CHANGE.
pernicious, *adj.* malign, ruinous, poisonous, detrimental, injurious, harmful; wicked. See BADNESS. *Ant.,* see GOODNESS.
perpendicular, *adj.* erect, upright; sheer, precipitous; VERTICAL, plumb.
perpetrate, *v.t.* commit, inflict; perform, do, practice. See ACTION.

PERPETUITY

Nouns—perpetuity; everlastingness, unceasingness, *etc.*; eternity, infinity, aye, TIME without end, perennity, sempiternity; deathlessness, immortality, athanasia; incessance, CONTINUITY, DURABILITY, perpetuation, preservation.

Verbs—be perpetual, last *or* endure forever, have no end, never end *or* die; perpetuate, eternalize, eternize, immortalize, continue, preserve.

Adjectives—perpetual, everlasting, unceasing, endless, unending, having no end; eternal, co-eternal, everliving, everflowing, sempiternal, continual, ceaseless, incessant, uninterrupted, interminable, infinite; never-ending, *etc.*; unfailing, evergreen, amaranthine; deathless, immortal, undying, imperishable, perdurable; permanent, lasting, enduring; perennial, long-lived, dateless, illimitable, continued, constant.

Adverbs—perpetually, in perpetuity, always, ever, evermore, aye; forever, for evermore, for aye, for ever and a day, for ever and ever; in all ages, from age to age, without end, world without end, time without end; to the end of time, to the crack of doom, till death [do us part], till doomsday; constantly. *Colloq.,* for keeps, for good, till hell freezes over, till the cows come home.

Antonym, see TRANSIENTNESS.

---

perplex, *v.* puzzle, bewilder, confuse, mystify, confound, nonplus; distract, disconcert. See DOUBT. *Ant.,* see CERTAINTY.
perplexity, *n.* UNCERTAINTY, bewilderment, confusion, quandary, puzzlement, embarrassment, predicament, hesitation. See DIFFICULTY. *Ant.,* see CERTAINTY.
perquisite, *n.* REWARD, bonus, gratuity, tip; bribe; due.
per se, *adv.* by itself, intrinsically, essentially; virtually, in the main; by nature, as a thing apart. See INTRINSIC, IDENTITY, SPECIALITY.

persecute, *v.t.* molest, oppress, maltreat, pursue, beset; abuse, injure; hound, annoy, trouble. See MALEVOLENCE, PAIN.

perseverance, *n.* continuance, PERMANENCE; firmness, STABILITY; constancy, steadiness; tenacity *or* singleness of purpose; persistence, plodding, patience; industry; pertinacity; gameness, pluck, stamina, backbone; indefatigability; bulldog courage, sand, grit; patience, determination. *Colloq.,* stick-to-itiveness. See RESOLUTION. *Ant.,* see CHANGEABLENESS, DOUBT.

persist, *v.i.* persevere, continue, remain, endure, stand, abide, plod. See CONTINUITY, DURABILITY. *Ant.,* see END.

persistent, *adj.* durable, permanent, persevering, constant, steadfast, unfailing; enduring, unchanging. See PERMANENCE. *Ant.,* see END.

person, *n.* individual, body, somebody, anybody; man, woman, child; human, humanity. See MANKIND.

personable, *adj.* presentable; charming, (con)genial. See BEAUTY, SOCIALITY.

personage, *n.* dignitary, official, celebrity, notable, figure, somebody, bigwig. *Colloq.,* VIP, big wheel. See IMPORTANCE. *Ant.,* see UNIMPORTANCE.

personal, *adj.* private, individual, intimate, own, special, particular. See SPECIALITY.

personality, *n.* character, individuality, self, ego; celebrity, notable. See MANKIND, REPUTE.

personify, *v.t.* embody, typify, symbolize, exemplify; represent, personate. See REPRESENTATION.

personnel, *n.* employees, workers, help; faculty, hands, squad, crew, gang, staff, team, rank and file; staffers. *Slang,* stable. See AGENCY, SERVANT.

perspective, *n.* view, angle, aspect, position; field of view *or* vision, vista, prospect, scene, vantage [point]; outlook, viewpoint; scope; grasp, appreciation, comprehension; point of view, JUDGMENT; remove, DISTANCE; context, orientation, insight. *Colloq.,* slant. See RELATION.

perspicacity, *n.* discernment, DISCRIMINATION, acuteness, keenness; shrewdness; penetration, insight, acumen. See INTELLIGENCE.

perspicuity, *n.* INTELLIGIBILITY; manifestation; definiteness, definition; exactness.

perspire, *v.i.* exude, sweat, exhale, excrete, swelter. See EXCRETION, HEAT.

persuade, *v.t.* induce, prevail upon, win; convince, satisfy, assure. See BELIEF, CAUSE.

persuasible, *adj.* docile, tractable, convincible; amenable, unresistant; persuadable. See ASSENT. *Ant.,* see REFUSAL.

persuasion, *n.* argument, PLEA, exhortation; conviction; INFLUENCE, insistence. See BELIEF, CAUSE.

persuasive, *adj.* inducive; cogent, convincing, logical; winning. See CAUSE.

pert, *adj.* impudent, saucy, flippant; forward, bold; perky. *Slang,* fresh, flip, sassy. See DISCOURTESY, INSOLENCE. *Ant.,* see COURTESY, SERVILITY, MODESTY.

pertain, *v.i.* apply, refer; belong, relate; appertain, concern; affect. See RELATION.

pertinacious, *adj.* persevering, persistent; obstinate, unyielding, constant, resolute, firm. See RESOLUTION.

pertinent, *adj.* relevant, apposite, applicable; apt. See RELATION.

perturbation, *n.* disturbance; disquiet, uneasiness, discomposure, apprehension, worry; trepidation, restlessness. See AGITATION, EXCITEMENT, FEAR.

peruse, *v.t.* read, con, study; examine.

pervade, *v.t.* fill, permeate, penetrate, imbue, overspread, impregnate, saturate; infiltrate. See PRESENCE.

perverse, *adj.* contrary, stubborn, obstinate; reactionary, ungovernable, wayward; cross, petulant. See RESOLUTION, SULLENNESS.

perversion, *n.* DISTORTION, misuse, UNCONFORMITY, misrepresentation, misconstruction; corruption, debasement. See EVIL. *Ant.*, see CONFORMITY, VIRTUE.

perversity, *n.* OBSTINACY, obduracy, perverseness; waywardness, UNCONFORMITY, contumacy, wickedness; OBLIQUITY. *Slang,* mulishness, cussedness. See EVIL. *Ant.*, see VIRTUE, CONFORMITY.

pervert, *v.t.* apostasize, distort, twist, garble, debase, misrepresent, corrupt, mislead, misinterpret, misstate; equivocate. See DISTORTION, EVIL.

pessimism, *n.* despondency; gloom, depression, despair, DEJECTION, cynicism, morbidity. *Ant.*, see CHEERFULNESS, HOPE.

pest, *n.* plague, pestilence, epidemic; parasite, infestation; nuisance, trouble; BANE, SCOURGE, curse. *Ant.*, see REMEDY.

pester, *v.t.* plague, annoy, trouble, vex, irritate, displease. See PAIN.

pestilence, *n.* DISEASE, plague, epidemic. *Ant.*, see HEALTH.

pet, *n. & v.t.* —*n.* FAVORITE, beloved, LOVE, dearest, darling. —*v.t.* cherish, fondle, caress, embrace, stroke, cuddle. See ENDEARMENT, LOVE.

petal, *n.* seoak, perianth; corolla, calyx, corona. See BOTANY, VEGETABLE.

petite, *adj.* small, mignon, diminutive, trim, tiny, miniature. See LITTLENESS.

petition, *n. & v.t.* —*n.* PLEA, REQUEST, entreaty, supplication, prayer; asking, address. —*v.t.* ask, beg, entreat, REQUEST, plead, appeal, implore.

petrify, *v.t.* calcify, turn to stone, lapidify, fossilize; stun, astonish; stupefy, shock; stiffen, harden, paralyze. See DENSITY, HARDNESS, MINERAL, WONDER.

petroleum, *n.* petrol, OIL; black gold.

petticoat, *n.* slip, chemise, underskirt, crinoline, camisole, balmoral, half-slip. See CLOTHING.

petty, *adj.* trivial, unimportant, small, mean, trifling; contemptible, spiteful; beggarly. See DISREPUTE, UNIMPORTANCE. *Ant.*, see IMPORTANCE, BENEVOLENCE.

petulant, *adj.* fretful, irritable, complaining, peevish, cross. See IRASCIBILITY.

phantom, *n.* unreality, VISION; spector, illusion, apparition, ghost, spirit, SHADE, shadow. See APPEARANCE. *Ant.*, see SUBSTANCE.

pharmacist, *n.* chemist, apothecary, druggist. See REMEDY.

phase, *n.* APPEARANCE, STATE, condition, situation, aspect; shape, FORM, angle. See CIRCUMSTANCE, SIDE.

phenomenon, *n.* PRODIGY; marvel, WONDER; happening, OCCURRENCE; event.

philanderer, *n.* dallier, trifler, lecher, Romeo, Casanova, lover, rake, roué, libertine. *Colloq.,* playboy. *Slang,* sugar daddy; wolf. See IMPURITY, LOVE.

philanthropy, *n.* altruism, humanity, humanitarianism; BENEVOLENCE, good will to men, public welfare; generosity, openheartedness, openhandedness. See UNSELFISHNESS. *Ant.*, see MALEVOLENCE, SELFISHNESS.

philistine, *n.* vandal; bigot, uncultured person: yahoo, barbarian; mediocrity. See NARROWNESS.

philosophical, *adj.* contemplative, deliberative, thoughtful, speculative; imperturbable, calm; wise, rational; stoical, Platonic, Socratic. See REASONING, THOUGHT.

phlegmatic, *adj.* stolid, dull, apathetic; calm, imperturbable, languid, unemotional, inert, COLD. See INSENSIBILITY. *Ant.*, see SENSIBILITY.

phobia, *n.* FEAR, dread, aversion, revulsion, REPULSION, dislike, antipathy; acrophobia, claustrophobia, *etc.* See INSANITY.

phonetic, *adj.* phonic, phonal, phonetical, sonant; vocal, voiced, lingual, tonic, oral, spoken. See SOUND, SPEECH.

phonograph, *n.* gramophone, Graphophone, panatrope, Victrola, record player; pickup, playback, turntable; dictating machine. See RECORD.

phony, *adj. & n., slang.* —*adj.* spurious, fraudulent, IMITATION, fake, sham, mock, put on, trumped-up, forged; gimcrack, pasteboard; deceitful, false-hearted, lying; glib, canting, superficial. —*n.* fake, counterfeit, fraud; faker, charlatan, quack, impostor, mountebank. See FALSENESS, UNTRUTH, DECEPTION.

photograph, *n.* picture; photo, film, snapshot, reproduction; portrait. See REPRESENTATION.

phrase, *n. & v.* —*n.* expression; sentence, paragraph, clause; figure of speech, euphemism; idiom; locution; motto, maxim. —*v.t.* express, word, term, couch; voice. See FIGURATIVE, WRITING, INTERPRETATION.

physic, *v.t.* —*n.* laxative, cathartic, purgative; drug, medicine; pill, dose. —*v.t.* purge, drench; treat, doctor. See REMEDY.

physical, *adj.* bodily, anatomical; material, substantial. See SUBSTANCE. *Ant.,* see INSUBSTANTIALITY, INTELLECT.

physician, *n.* doctor, medic, medico, surgeon, specialist; [general] practitioner, G.P.; consultant, adviser, healer. See ADVICE, REMEDY.

physique, *n.* frame, body, FORM; APPEARANCE, SIZE; build, musculature. See MUSCULARITY.

piano, *n.* pianoforte, fortepiano, spinet, pianette, upright; clavier, (clavi)cembalo. *Slang,* eighty-eight. See MUSICAL INSTRUMENTS.

piazza, *n.* square, PLACE, street; porch, veranda, portico.

picaresque, *adj.* roguish, swaggering, adventurous. See WRITING, DESCRIPTION.

pick, *n. & v.t.* —*n.* best, cream, flower, élite, CHOICE; selection. —*v.t.* select, choose; pluck, garner, gather; cull. See ACQUISITION, GOODNESS. *Ant.,* see REFUSAL.

picket, *n. & v.t.* —*n.* post, pale, fence; sentry, guard, sentinel, patrol. See SHARPNESS, WARNING. —*v.t.* enclose, bar, fence; tether, restrain. See CIRCUMSCRIPTION, RESTRAINT, WARNING.

pickle, *v.t.* preserve, salt, corn, brine, marinate. See PRESERVATION.

pickpocket, *n.* THIEF, robber, cutpurse. *Slang,* dip. See STEALING.

picnic, *n.* excursion, junket, outing, festivity; cookout, barbecue, fishfry, *etc.* See AMUSEMENT, FOOD.

pictorial, *adj.* delineatory, graphic, depicting; illustrated. See PAINTING.

picture, *n.* image, likeness, counterpart; portrayal, REPRESENTATION, view, scene, tableau, setting; drawing, PAINTING, photograph, sketch, etching, canvas. See APPEARANCE, PAINTING.

picturesque, *adj.* artistic, graphic, attractive; vivid; quaint. See BEAUTY. *Ant.,* see UGLINESS.

pie, *n.* pastry, pasty, patisserie, tart; mud pie; dessert. See FOOD.

piece, *n. & v.t.* —*n.* scrap, morsel, bit; section, fragment, PART. —*v.t.* unite, combine, patch, repair. See RESTORATION, JUNCTION. *Ant.,* see WHOLE.

piecemeal, *adv.* one at a time, one by one; little by little, bit by bit, step by step, in drops; by stages *or* degrees, by dribs and drabs. See PART, LITTLENESS, SLOWNESS.

pied, *adj.* mottled, brindled, piebald, dappled; colorful. See VARIEGATION.

pier, *n.* wharf, quay, mole, dock, breakwater; pillar, shaft, SUPPORT.

pierce, *v.t.* puncture, penetrate, perforate, bore, drill; stab, wound; affect; nip, chill. See SHARPNESS, OPENING, COLD.

piercing, *adj.* sharp, penetrating, keen, acute; discerning; cutting, biting; painful, affecting, chilling; high, shrill. See COLD, FEELING, SHARPNESS.

PIETY

Nouns—**1,** piety, piousness, devoutness; RELIGION, theism, faith, BELIEF; religiousness, holiness, saintliness; reverence, worship, veneration, devotion; grace, unction, edification; sanctity, sanctitude; consecration; theopathy.

2, beatification, canonization; sanctification; adoption, regeneration, palingenesis, conversion, justification, salvation, redemption; inspiration; bread of life; body and blood of Christ.

3, believer, convert, theist, Christian, devotee, pietist; the good, the righteous, the just, the believing, the elect; saint, Madonna; the children of God, the Kingdom *or* light; born-again Christian. *Slang*, Jesus freak.

Verbs—**1,** be pious, have faith, believe, venerate, revere; be converted.

2, sanctify, beatify, canonize, inspire, consecrate, enshrine, keep holy; convert, edify, redeem, save, regenerate.

Adjectives—pious, religious, devout, devoted, reverent, godly, humble, pure, holy, spiritual, pietistic; saintly, saintlike; seraphic, sacred, solemn; believing, faithful, Christian, Catholic; elected, adopted, justified, sanctified, beatified, canonized, regenerated, inspired, consecrated, converted, unearthly.

Antonym, see IMPIETY.

---

pig, *n.* hog, sow, boar, swine; glutton; sloven, slob. See ANIMAL, GLUTTONY, UNCLEANNESS.

pigeon, *n.* dove, homer, squab, pouter, turbit, tumbler, roller, fantail, nun. *Slang*, sucker, dupe, easy mark, pushover, chump; clay pigeon, sitting duck, gull. See DECEPTION, CREDULITY, ANIMAL.

pigeonhole, *n. & v.* —*n.* cubbyhole; niche, compartment. See RECEPTACLE. —*v.t.* file away, file and forget; postpone, put off, delay. See LATENESS, NEGLECT.

pigheaded, *adj.* piggish; stubborn, tenacious, obstinate, *entêté*. See OBSTINACY.

pigment, *n.* COLOR, stain, dye, tint, paint, SHADE. *Ant.*, see COLORLESSNESS.

pike, *n.* tip, point, spike; pikestaff, spear, lance, halberd, javelin. See ARMS.

piker, *n., slang*, pennypincher, tightwad, cheapskate, miser. See PARSIMONY.

pile, *n. & v.* —*n.* structure, building, edifice; heap, mass; quantity. See ASSEMBLAGE. —*v.t.* accumulate, load, amass, furnish.

pilfer, *v.* filch, rob, steal plunder, thieve; shoplift. See STEALING.

pilgrim, *n.* wayfarer, traveler, migrant; settler, pioneer, newcomer; palmer, devotee. See PASSAGE.

pilgrimage, *n.* JOURNEY, crusade, mission, quest, expedition; LIFE, lifetime.

pill, *n.* bolus, tablet, capsule. *Slang*, goofball. See REMEDY, CIRCULARITY.

pillage, *n. & v.t.* —*n.* spoliation, plunder, vandalism, theft, depredation. —*v.t.* plunder, rape, thieve, rob, steal. See STEALING.

pillar, *n.* column, pedestal, SUPPORT, post, obelisk.

pillow, *n.* cushion, bolster, headrest, pad. See REPOSE.

pilot, *n.* helmsman, steersman, guide; counselor; aviator, airman. See AVIATION, DIRECTION, INFORMATION, NAVIGATION.

pimp, *n.* procurer, solicitor, panderer, tout; white slaver; whoremonger; *maquereau. Colloq.*, hustler. *Slang*, cadet. See IMPURITY, AGENT.

pimple, *n.* pustule, boil, gathering, papule, pock, blemish. See DISEASE.

pinpoint, *v.* locate, localize, place. *Colloq.*, pin down, nail. See LOCATION, CERTAINTY.

pin, *n. & v.t.* —*n.* peg, spoke, dowel; fastener, bolt, toggle; needle, bodkin, skewer, style; brooch, scarfpin, fraternity pin, tiepin; badge. —*v.t.* fasten, hold, bind, rivet, attach, secure. See ORNAMENT, JUNCTION.

pinch, *n. & v.* —*n.* stress, strain, pressure, emergency, DIFFICULTY, plight, predicament; pinching, nip. See CIRCUMSTANCE, PAIN. —*v.* nip, compress, tighten, squeeze; chill, bite, hurt. See CONTRACTION, PAIN.

pine, *v.i.* languish, long, crave; wither, droop. See DEJECTION, DESIRE.

pinnacle, *n.* SUMMIT, peak, top, acme, crown.

pioneer, *n.* forerunner, settler; originator; leader. See PRECEDENCE.

pious, *adj.* devout, religious, holy, dedicated. See PIETY. *Ant.,* see IMPIETY.

pipe, *n.* PASSAGE, tube, main; briar, corncob, meerschaum; flute, fife, bagpipe, flageolet. See MUSICAL INSTRUMENTS, OPENING, RECEPTACLE.

piquant, *adj.* pungent, flavorful, strong, sharp; tart; keen, stimulating. See FEELING, SHARPNESS.

pique, *v.t.* sting, cut, nettle, irritate, vex, offend; prick, jab; intrigue, stimulate, arouse interest. See EXCITEMENT, PAIN, ATTENTION.

pirate, *n. & v.t.* —*n.* buccaneer, marauder, corsair, freebooter, searobber, privateer. —*v.t.* plagiarize, steal; rob, plunder, picaroon, appropriate. See STEALING.

pistol, *n.* automatic, firearm, gun, derringer, revolver. *Colloq.,* shooting iron. *Slang,* gat, heater. See ARMS.

pit, *n.* hole, hollow, indentation, crater, excavation; abyss, HELL, Hades; mine, chasm; trap, snare. See CONCAVITY.

pitch, *n. & v.* —*n.* note, modulation, tone; ROLL, plunge, toss, dip, reel, lurch; slant, slope, drop; ascent, rise, grade, HEIGHT, range; resin, tar. —*v.t.* throw, toss; build, erect, set, establish; cast, heave. —*v.i.* ROLL, reel, plunge, toss; slope.

pitcher, *n.* carafe, jug, jar, bottle, vessel, ewer, cruet, decanter; hurler, tosser, chucker; lefty, southpaw, portsider; righthander, righty; spitballer; relief *or* starting pitcher. *Slang,* arm. See RECEPTACLE, PROPULSION.

piteous, *adj.* grievous, sorrowful; pitiable, pathetic; wretched, miserable, deplorable. See PAIN, PITY.

pitfall, *n.* trap, snare, gin, pit; rocks, reefs, coral reef, sunken rocks, snags; sands, quicksands, slippery ground; breakers, shoals, shallows; precipice. See DANGER. *Ant.,* see SAFETY.

pith, *n.* pulp, core, heart; essence, kernel, substance, gist. See MEANING, CONTRACTION.

pithy, *adj.* concise; vigorous, forceful, powerful; meaningful; terse, brief, laconic. See CONTRACTION, MEANING. *Ant.,* see LOQUACITY.

pitiable, *adj.* miserable, paltry, wretched, deplorable; insignificant, woeful, pathetic. See BADNESS, PAIN, PITY.

pitiful, *adj.* compassionate (see PITY); deplorable, disreputable, pitiable, wretched; lamentable, piteous. See BADNESS, CONTEMPT, DISREPUTE.

pitilessness, *n.* inclemency; severity; MALEVOLENCE; mercilessness, cruelty, unfeelingness, ruthlessness. *Ant.,* see FEELING, PITY.

pittance, *n.* bit, mite, driblet; dole; pension, alms, allowance. See INSUFFICIENCY.

pitted, *adj.* blemished, variolate; honeycombed, favose, pocked, dented; cratered. See CONCAVITY. *Ant.,* see SMOOTHNESS.

PITY

Nouns—pity, compassion, commiseration; lamentation, condolence; empathy, fellow-feeling, tenderness, yearning, forbearance, humanity, mercy, clemency; LENIENCY, lenity, charity, ruth, quarter, grace.

Verbs—1, pity; have, give, show *or* take pity; commiserate, condole, sympathize; feel for, be sorry for; weep, melt, thaw, forbear, relax, relent, give quarter; give the *coup de grâce*, put out of one's misery; have mercy; be charitable; be lenient.

2, excite pity, touch, affect, soften; melt, melt the heart; propitiate, disarm; deprecate, deplore.

Adjectives—pitying, piteous, pitiful; compassionate, sympathetic, affected, touched; merciful, clement, ruthful; humane; humanitarian, philanthropic, tenderhearted, softhearted, lenient, forbearing; melting, weak.

Antonym, see SEVERITY.

---

pivot, *n. & v.i.* —*n.* axis, turning point; gudgeon; joint, axle, hinge; focus; jewel. —*v.i.* swivel, turn, whirl; ROLL. See CAUSE, JUNCTION, ROTATION.

placard, *n.* notice, poster, billboard, advertisement, bill. See PUBLICATION.

placate, *v.* soothe, quiet; satisfy, give satisfaction, make it up. *Colloq.,* butter up, rub the right way. See PACIFICATION.

place, *n.* lieu spot, point; niche, nook, hole; pigeonhole, RECEPTACLE, compartment; premises, precinct, station; locality; somewhere, someplace, anyplace; situation.

placement, *n.* LOCATION, installation, situation, disposition, ARRANGEMENT, assignment, employment, engagement.

placid, *adj.* serene, unruffled; calm, cool, collected; gentle, peaceful, quiet, undisturbed. See INACTIVITY. *Ant.,* see EXCITEMENT, AGITATION.

plagiarize, *v.t.* pirate, infringe on, COPY, transcribe; imitate, simulate, ape; forge, counterfeit. *Colloq.,* crib, lift, sneak; pick one's brains. *Slang,* swipe, snitch, pinch. See STEALING, FALSENESS.

plague, *n. & v.* —*n.* affliction, woe, visitation; nuisance, pest; bane, scourge, curse; pestilence, DISEASE, epidemic; bubonic plague, white *or* black death; cholera, tuberculosis, smallpox, typhoid. —*v.t.* annoy, tease, pester, molest, bother. *Colloq.,* be on one's back, get on one's nerves. See ATTACK, PAIN.

plaid, *n.* plaidie, tartan; check, pattern, design; kilt, shawl. See VARIEGATION, CLOTHING.

plain, *adj.* simple; unornamented, unadorned, unvarnished; homely, homespun; neat; severe, chaste, pure; Anglo-Saxon; dry, unvaried, monotonous, earthy, down-to-earth; outspoken, blunt, direct, forthright, straight from the shoulder, down to brass tacks; in plain words, in plain English See SIMPLENESS. *Ant.,* see ORNAMENT.

plain, *n.* prairie, tableland, steppe, savanna, tundra, heath, desert, pampas, mesa, llana; meadow, pasture, field. See LAND. *Ant.,* see HEIGHT.

plaintive, *adj.* mournful, wistful, sad, melancholy, sorrowful. See LAMENTATION. *Ant.,* see REJOICING.

PLAN

Nouns—**1,** plan, scheme, design, project, undertaking, aim, INTENTION; proposal, proposition, suggestion; RESOLUTION, resolve, MOTION, precaution, PROVISION, PREPARATION, calculation, meditation; operation, METHOD, way, process, setup, custom, *modus operandi.*

2, sketch, skeleton, outline, draft, diagram, blueprint, layout, schematic; delineation, pattern, representation, specifications, tabulation; chart, MAP, graph.

3, program, prospectus, syllabus, forecast, card, bill; protocol, order of the day, agenda; procedure, line, COURSE, plank, platform; strategy, regime, line of CONDUCT.

4, contrivance, invention, idea, conception, expedient, recipe, formula, nostrum; artifice, device, stratagem; trick (see CUNNING, DECEPTION); alternative, loophole, makeshift; last resort. *Colloq.,* dodge. *Slang,* gadget, gimmick.

5, plot, intrigue, cabal, counterplot, countermine, conspiracy, machination, collusion. *Slang,* racket.

6, schemer, strategist, machinator, tactician; planner, architect, promoter, organizer, designer; conspirator, plotter, conniver, dreamer, Machiavelli.

Verbs—plan, scheme, design, frame, diagram, sketch, map, delineate, figure, represent; contrive, project, schedule, forecast, aim, propose, suggest, premeditate, spring a project; devise, invent, concoct; blueprint, chalk out, cut out, lay out, block out, map out, lay down a plan; shape, mark *or* set a course; (pre)concert, pre-establish, prepare; study, calculate, envision, contemplate, digest, mature, resolve, intend, destine, provide, take steps, take measures; (re)cast, systematize, organize, arrange; hatch [a plot], plot, counterplot, intrigue; machinate, incubate, rig, conspire. *Colloq.*, cook up.

Adjectives—planned, arranged, *etc.*; on the table, on the agenda, laid out, under consideration; planning, strategic(al), systematic, schematic; premeditated, deliberate, purposed, meant, intended, intentional; conspiratorial, scheming, designing. *Colloq.*, in the works, put-up.

Antonym, see CHANCE.

plane, *n. & v.t.* —*n.* level, stratum, grade, surface. —*v.t.* smooth, mill, even, traverse, shave, level. See SMOOTHNESS.

planet, *n.* heavenly body; planetoid, asteroid; satellite, moon. See UNIVERSE.

plank, *n.* board, timber; flooring, deck; gangplank *or* -board; platform, slate, ticket, campaign plank, policy, PLAN, PROMISE.

plant, *n. & v.* —*n.* VEGETABLE, herb, organism, flower, seedling, shrub, sprout, shoot; machinery, factory, equipment. *Slang,* hoax, trick, frameup. See INSTRUMENT, DECEPTION. —*v.* implant, deposit, settle; colonize; sow, seed; engender. See AGRICULTURE, LOCATION.

plantation, *n.* outpost, colony, settlement; farm(stead), ranch, spread; nursery, orchard, grove, vineyard, stand. See AGRICULTURE, ABODE.

plaque, *n.* tablet, sign, nameplate. *Colloq.*, shingle. See ORNAMENT, INDICATION.

plaster, *n. & v.* —*n.* plaster of Paris, mortar, parget, stucco, gesso; paste, lime; clay, adobe, mud; fresco, plaster painting, mural art; poultice, dressing, bandage. See MATERIALS, ART, REMEDY. —*v.t.* coat, cover, conceal, smear; caulk, repair, mend; stick up, paste. See COVERING, COHERENCE.

plastic, *adj.* moldable, malleable, ductile, formable, pliant, impressionable, formative. See FORM, SOFTNESS. *Ant.,* see HARDNESS.

plate, *n. & v.t.* —*n.* platter, dish, utensil, tray; slab, sheet, planch; coating, veneer, coat. See LAYER, RECEPTACLE. —*v.t.* overlay, laminate; gild, silver, platinize; veneer; electroplate. See COVERING.

plateau, *n.* PLAIN, mesa; platform; highland, tableland.

platform, *n.* stand, dais, rostrum, pulpit, stage; foundation, base, basis; policy, PLAN. See SCHOOL, SUPPORT.

platform, *n.* stand, dais, rostrum, pulpit, stage; foundation, base, basis; policy, PLAN. See SCHOOL, SUPPORT.

platitude, *n.* commonplace, cliché, truism, axiom, banality, proverb, triteness. See MAXIM, TRUTH.

platonic, *adj.* idealistic, abstract, spiritual, intellectual; unsexual, uncarnal, chaste; pure, perfect. See THOUGHT, PURITY, FRIENDSHIP.

platter, *n.* trencher, tray, waiter, dish, plate. See RECEPTACLE.

plaudit, *n.* acclaim, praise, applause, compliment, encomium, clapping. See APPROBATION. *Ant.,* see DISAPPROBATION.

plausible, *adj.* suave, smooth, bland, credible, reasonable, believable; specious, colored; justifiable, defensible. See CHANCE, INDICATION.

play, *n. & v.* —*n.* sport, frolic, fun, AMUSEMENT, game, recreation; DRAMA, comedy, tragedy; scope, latitude, sweep, range. —*v.* operate, wield, ply; act, perform; compete; pluck, bow, strike, beat; move, caper, gambol, gad, idle, disport. See FREEDOM.

playboy, *n., colloq.,* idler, do-nothing, loafer; voluptuary, sensualist, pleasure seeker, sybarite, epicurean, hedonist. See AMUSEMENT.

player, *n.* performer, actor, MUSICIAN, instrumentalist; participant, competitor. See DRAMA.

playful, *adj.* frolicsome, mischievous, sportive, frisky; roguish, prankish; jolly, rollicking. See AMUSEMENT, CHEERFULNESS.

plaything, *n.* toy, doll, bauble; puzzle, kite, ball, top; bagatelle, trifle, trinket. See AMUSEMENT, UNIMPORTANCE.

playwright, *n.* playwriter, dramaturgist; scenario writer, scenarist, librettist; farceur. See DRAMA.

plaza, *n.* piazza; forum, marketplace. See PASSAGE.

plea, *n.* REQUEST; petition; assertion, allegation, advocation, advocacy; pretext; excuse, VINDICATION; pretense, subterfuge, feint; blind.

plead, *v.* allege, assert, state; use as a plea; take one's stand upon; beg, petition, urge, REQUEST. See VINDICATION.

pleasant, *adj.* See PLEASURE.

pleasantry, *n.* WIT, jest, banter, chaff, chit chat, persiflage.

please, *adv. & v.* —*adv.* if you please, pray, *s'il vous plât, bitte, por favor;* kindly, do. See REQUEST, COURTESY. —*v.* gratify, satisfy, delight. See PLEASURE, APPROBATION. *Ant.,* see DISAPPROBATION.

PLEASURE

Nouns—**1,** pleasure, enjoyment, gratification; voluptuousness, sensuality; luxuriousness; GLUTTONY; titillation, appetite, gusto; creature comforts, comfort, ease, luxury, lap of luxury; purple and fine linen; bed of down, bed of roses, life of Riley; velvet, clover; treat; refreshment, feast; AMUSEMENT; fleshpots, epicureanism, sybaritism, hedonism.

2, delectation; relish, zest; satisfaction, contentment, complacency; well-being; good, snugness, comfort, cushion, *sans souci*, peace of mind.

3, joy, gladness, delight, glee, cheer, sunshine; CHEERFULNESS; happiness, felicity, bliss; beatitude, beatification; enchantment, transport, rapture, ravishment, ecstasy; *summum bonum*; HEAVEN; unalloyed happiness. *Slang,* bang, thrills, kicks, charge.

4, honeymoon, palmy days, halcyon days; golden age, golden time; Arcadia, Eden, Utopia, happy valley, time of one's life; prime, heyday.

5, pleasurableness, pleasantness, agreeableness, delectability; attractiveness, charm, fascination, enchantment, glamour, liveliness, BEAUTY; sunny side, bright side.

Verbs—**1,** feel pleasure, be pleased, take pleasure in; revel in, delight in, rejoice in, like, LOVE; take to, take a fancy to; enjoy, relish, luxuriate in, riot in, bask in, swim in, wallow in; thrive on, feast on; gloat over, smack the lips; be in clover, live on the fat of the land, walk on air, live in comfort, bask in the sunshine. *Colloq.,* live high off the hog; take the gravy train. *Slang,* have a ball; dig, get off (on), get a kick (from).

2, cause, give *or* afford pleasure, please, charm, delight; gladden, take, captivate, enamor, fascinate; enchant, entrance, enrapture, transport, bewitch; ravish, enravish; bless, beatify; satisfy, gratify; slake, satiate, quench; indulge, humor, flatter, tickle, tickle the palate, regale, refresh; enliven; treat; amuse; strike *or* tickle one's fancy; tickle one pink; warm the cockles of the heart; do one's heart good; attract, allure, stimulate, interest; thrill. *Colloq.,* hit the spot. *Slang,* send; give a kick, bang *or* charge.

Adjectives—**1,** pleased, glad, gladsome; pleased as Punch; happy, blissful; happy as a king, as a lark *or* as the day is long; thrice blest; in clover, in paradise, in raptures, on top of the world; ecstatic; overjoyed, entranced, *etc.*; ecstatic, beatific; unalloyed, cloudless.

2, causing pleasure; pleasing, pleasant, pleasurable; agreeable; grateful, gratifying, welcome, welcome as the flowers in May; to one's taste *or* liking, after one's own heart; cordial, genial; sweet, delectable, nice, dainty; delicate, delicious, dulcet, luscious, palatable; cozy, snug; sumptuous, luxurious, voluptuous; attractive, inviting, prepossessing, engaging; winning, winsome, taking, fascinating, captivating; seductive, alluring, enticing; appetizing, *etc.*; empyrean, elysian, heavenly; palmy, halcyon. *Slang,* scrumptious, hunky-dory.

Antonym, see PAIN.

---

pleat, *n. & v.* —*n.* plait, corrugation, wrinkle; FOLD, plicature, ply; doubling. —*v.t.* crease, gather, flounce, ruffle; fold over, play, pucker, corrugate.

plebeian, *adj.* unrefined, ill-bred, common, vulgar; lowborn, obscure, proletarian. See POPULACE. *Ant.,* see NOBILITY.

plebiscite, *n.* referendum, election, ballot, vote. See CHOICE.

pledge, *n. & v.t.* —*n.* PROMISE, SECURITY, gage, pawn, collateral, hostage, deposit; WORD, troth, vow, guarantee; bond, oath. —*v.t.* deposit, wage, pawn, hypothecate, mortgage; vow, undertake, engage, honor; toast. *Slang,* hock. See PASSAGE, REPUTE, DEBT.

plenty, *n.* SUFFICIENCY, abundance, profusion, amplitude, copiousness; wealth, luxury. *Ant.,* see INSUFFICIENCY.

pleonasm, *n.* REDUNDANCE, verbosity, diffuseness, tautology, superfluity, circumlocution, wordiness.

pliable, *adj.* plastic, ductile, malleable; flexible, supple, limber, yielding; docile, tractable, obedient, compliant, submissive. See SOFTNESS, OBEDIENCE.

pliant, *adj.* pliable, malleable, flexible, compliant, yielding. See SOFTNESS. *Ant.,* see HARDNESS.

pliers, *n.pl.* pincers, pinchers; grippers, nippers, tongs, grip, clamp, forceps; wire cutter, tooth extractor. See RETENTION, EXTRACTION.

plight, *n.* quandary, predicament, dilemma; trouble, DIFFICULTY, scrape, crisis; situation, condition; betrothal, engagement. See CIRCUMSTANCE.

plod, *v.i.* persevere, persist; trudge, walk; labor, drudge, toil, work. See ACTIVITY, RESOLUTION, SLOWNESS.

plot, *n. & v.* —*n.* diagram, PLAN, outline; field, enclosure, paddock, lot; scheme, conspiracy, intrigue, collusion. See REGION, LAND. —*v.* conspire, machinate, scheme, intrigue; chart, PLAN, lay out.

plow, plough, *v.t.* cultivate, dig, till, turn, break, FURROW. See AGRICULTURE.

pluck, *n. & v.t.* —*n.* COURAGE, bravery, valor, stamina, endurance, grip, determination, WILL. See RESOLUTION. *Ant.,* see COWARDICE. —*v.t.* pull, jerk; pick, gather, garner. See ACQUISITION.

plug, *n.* stopper, cork, dowel, plunger, tampon; quid, wad; wadding, padding, stopple, spigot. See CLOSURE.

plum, *n.* prune, sloe; prize, haul, windfall, trophy; REWARD, patronage. See FRUIT.

plumage, *n.* feathers, down, feathering. See COVERING, ORNAMENT.

plumb, *adj. & v.* —*adj.* perpendicular, VERTICAL, erect; straight, true. *Colloq.,* downright; utterly. See DIRECTION. —*v.t.* sound (depths), fathom; do plumbing. See DEPTH.

plume, *n.* quill, feather, egret, panache, plumage. See COVERING, ORNAMENT.

plummet, *n. & v.* —*n.* weight, plumb, bob, lead. See GRAVITY. —*v.i.* fall, droop, plunge. See DESCENT.

plump, *adj., adv. & v.* —*adj.* corpulent, fat, chubby, stout, fleshy, buxom, pudgy, rotund; blunt, direct, unqualified. —*adv.* suddenly, directly. —*v.* fatten, fill, distend; blurt; fall. *Colloq.,* plop (down); SUPPORT, root (for). See SIZE, IMPULSE.

plumpness, *n.* rotundity, obesity, corpulence, chubbiness, fatness. See SIZE.

plunder, *n. & v.* —*n.* pillage, loot, sack, spoil, booty; advantage, gain; spoliation, rapine. —*v.* devastate, harry, despoil, strip, rifle, loot, forage, pillage, ransack, maraud, rob, depredate. See STEALING.

plunge, *v. & n.* —*v.* dip, submerge; dive; sink, fall, drop; douse, go *or* put under water; gamble, bet heavily; fling, jump. *Colloq.,* go off the deep end. —*n.* dive, swim, dip; submersion. *Colloq.,* venture, a bold action. See DESCENT, CHANCE.

plural, *adj.* not singular; more than one; at least two. See NUMBER.

plus, *adj., adv. & prep.* and; additional, extra, added (to). See ADDITION.

plush, *n. & adj.* —*n.* pile, nap, hair; plushette; velvet, fluff. See MATERIALS. —*adj.* plushy, nappy, velvety, piled, woolly; see SOFTNESS, ROUGHNESS. *Slang,* rich, luxurious, posh, swank(y), elegant, hightoned. See ELEGANCE.

ply, *v.t.* exert, urge, ATTACK, apply; play, work; USE, exercise, manipulate, wield. See EXERTION.

poach, *v.* steal, thieve, filch, pilfer; encroach, infringe, trespass; boil, parboil, coddle. See STEALING, HEAT.

pocket, *n. & v.* —*n.* pouch, bin, purse; hollow, placket. See CONCAVITY, RECEPTACLE. —*v.t.* appropriate, take, steal. See STEALING.

pocketbook, *n.* purse, wallet; bag, handbag; pouch, sporran. *Slang,* leather, kick. See RECEPTACLE.

pod, *n.* hull, husk, jacket, skin, shuck, shell, peapod; pouch. See COVERING.

podium, *n.* stand, dais, rostrum, platform. See SUPPORT.

POETRY

Nouns—**1,** poetry, *ars poetica,* poesy; Muse, Calliope, Erato; versification, rhyming, prosody, orthometry; poem, ode, epode, idyl, lyric, blank verse, free verse, *vers libre;* eclogue, pastoral, bucolic, dithyramb, anacreontic; sonnet, ode, roundelay, rondeau, rondo, roundel, ballade, villanelle, triolet, pantoum, madrigal, canzonet, cento, monody, elegy; dramatic poetry, lyric poetry; opera, libretto; light verse, comic verse, *vers de société.*

2, song, ballad, lay; lullaby (see MUSIC); nursery rhymes; popular song.

3, doggerel, jingle, limerick, purple patches, macaronics.

4, canto, stanza, stich, verse, line; couplet, heroic couplets, triplet, quatrain; strophe, antistrophe.

5, rhyme, rime, assonance; meter, measure, foot, numbers, strain, rhythm; accentuation, stress, ictus; iamb(ic), dactyl, spondee, trochee, anapest; hexameter, pentameter, *etc.*

6, poet, poet laureate; bard, lyrist, skald, troubadour, trouvère, minstrel, minnesinger, meistersinger; versifier, poetaster.

Verbs—poetize, sing, versify, make verses; rhyme; scan.

Adjectives—poetic, lyric; epic, heroic, bucolic, *etc.*; lofty, sublime, eloquent.

pogrom, *n.* raid, ATTACK; KILLING, massacre, carnage, butchery, slaughter, genocide, hecatomb, mass murder; persecution.

poignant, *adj.* painful, pungent, intense, piercing, sharp, keen, biting. See PAIN, SHARPNESS.

point, *n.* object, MEANING, significance, intent, aim; speck, dot, spot; PLACE, LOCATION; pin, needle, prick, spike, prong, tip, END; PERIOD, LIMIT; goal, site. See IMPORTANCE, SHARPNESS, LITTLENESS.

point-blank, *adj.* close, straight, direct, undeviating; blunt, frank, candid, open, honest, truthful. See TRUTH.

pointed, *adj.* direct, concise, terse, pithy, brief; sharp, barbed, spiked. See CONTRACTION, SHARPNESS. *Ant.,* see LOQUACITY.

poise, *n.* equilibrium, balance, steadiness; self-possession, dignity, composure, imperturbability, coolness, nonchalance. See ORDER. *Ant.,* see AGITATION, EXCITEMENT.

poison, *n. & v.* —*n.* venom, toxicity, virus, bane. —*v.t.* corrupt, defile; intoxicate; drug, envenom; kill, murder. See DETERIORATION, KILLING.

poisonous, *adj.* venomous, toxic, deadly, virulent, noxious. See BADNESS.

poke, *v.* prod, nudge, stick, push; jab, punch. See IMPULSE.

poker, *n.* fire iron, rod, branding iron, ramrod, salamander; see IMPULSE.

poker-faced, *adj., colloq.,* deadpan, frozen-faced, wooden, unrevealing, unreadable, secretive. See CONCEALMENT, SECRET.

polar, *adj.* extreme, ultimate, furthest, outermost; magnetic, attracting; polarized; COLD, frigid, icy, frozen. See ATTRACTION.

polarize, *v.* orient, align, concentrate, gather; split, separate, dichotomize, oppose. See ARRANGEMENT, OPPOSITION.

pole, *v. & n.* —*v.t.* push, jab, prod, thrust, punch, nudge. See IMPULSE. —*n.* shaft, staff, stick, post, beam, mast; terminal, axis, hub, pivot; extremity, North *or* South Pole. See CENTRALITY, OPPOSITION.

polemic, *adj. & n.* —*adj.* controversial, disputatious, eristic(al), dialectical; quarrelsome, contentious. —*n.* polemics, debate, discussion, CONTENTION, dialectics, disputation; debater, disputant, polemicist, dialectician.

polestar, *n.* lodestar, Polaris; guide; magnet, cynosure. See ATTRACTION, DIRECTION, UNIVERSE.

policeman, *n.* patrolman, officer; peace officer, traffic cop, motorcycle cop; constable, sheriff, deputy, state trooper; detective, plainclothesman; gendarme, bobby. *Slang,* cop, copper, flatfoot, bull, flic, Smokey [the Bear], fuzz, pig, the Man, nark. See SAFETY.

policy, *n.* CONDUCT, administration, management; EXPEDIENCE, tactics, strategy; art, WISDOM; platform, PLAN.

polish, *n. & v.t.* —*n.* sheen, luster, shine, glaze, gloss; refinement, culture; COURTESY, tact, suavity, diplomacy; discernment, DISCRIMINATION. —*v.t.* shine, buff, burnish; scrub, scour, brighten; refine, perfect. See PERFECTION, SMOOTHNESS. *Ant.,* see DISCOURTESY, ROUGHNESS.

polite, *adj.* mannerly, civil, courteous, gracious; gallant, courtly, polished, refined. See COURTESY. *Ant.,* see DISCOURTESY.

politic, *adj.* discreet, expedient, artful, strategic; prudent, wise, judicious; wary, calculating. See CARE, KNOWLEDGE. *Ant.,* see RASHNESS.

politician, *n.* office-holder *or* -seeker; legislator, senator, *etc.*; diplomat, machinator, Machiavellian, strategist, wirepuller. See EXPEDIENCE, CUNNING.

poll, *n. & v.t.* —*n.* election, ballot; register; pate, head, skull. See CHOICE. —*v.t.* cut, crop, top; survey, canvass, tabulate.

pollute, *v.t.* contaminate; foul, desecrate; taint, soil, defile; corrupt, demoralize. See DETERIORATION, UNCLEANNESS. *Ant.,* see CLEANNESS.

poltroon, *n.* cad; dastard, craven, coward. See COWARDICE. *Ant.,* see COURAGE.

polygamy, *n.* bigamy, trigamy; Mormonism; polyandry, polygyny. See MARRIAGE.

pommel, pummel, *v.t.* pound, beat, punch, maul, trounce, drub, flail, flog; sandbag, blackjack. See PUNISHMENT.

pomp, *n.* glory, grandeur, show, OSTENTATION, magnificence, display, STYLE, splendor. *Ant.,* see SIMPLENESS.

pompous, *adj.* boastful, self-important, ostentatious; high-flown, bombastic, stilted; haughty, vain, grandiose, puffed-up, arrogant. *Colloq.,* stuffy, snooty, stuffed-shirt. See OSTENTATION. *Ant.,* see SIMPLENESS.

pond, *n.* LAKE, pool, fishpond, millpond, tarn.

ponder, *v.* think, muse, cogitate; reflect, meditate, weigh, deliberate, consider. See THOUGHT.

ponderous, *adj.* heavy, weighty, bulky, massive. See GRAVITY.

pontificate, *v.i.* declaim, state; preach, orate, lecture. See AUTHORITY, OSTENTATION, SPEECH.

pontoon, *n.* float, raft; boat, bladder, floater, buoy. See NAVIGATION, PASSAGE.

pony, *n.* scrub horse; cob, cow pony, cayuse; glass, half-jigger, dram. See HORSE, RECEPTACLE. *Slang,* translation; crib, trot, horse. See INTERPRETATION.

pool, *n. & v.t.* —*n.* association, amalgamation, fund; pond, puddle; reservoir, lake; swimming pool, natatorium. —*v.t.* combine, coöperate, share, contribute. See COÖPERATION.

poor, *adj.* indigent, penniless, impoverished, needy, beggarly, impecunious, insolvent, moneyless; inferior, faulty, unsatisfactory, imperfect, defective; humble; weak, flimsy. See BADNESS, INSUFFICIENCY, POVERTY. *Ant.,* see GOODNESS, SUFFICIENCY, MONEY.

POPULACE

Nouns—**1,** populace; the people, multitude, crowd, masses; bourgeoisie; commonalty; democracy; common people, lower classes, hoi polloi, rank and file, the ruck, proletariat, great unwashed, silent majority.

2, mob, rabble, rout; horde, canaille; dregs; scum of society *or* the earth; riffraff, ragtag and bobtail; small fry.

3, commoner, man in the street, the average man, the little man, one of the people, democrat, plebeian, proletarian, republican, bourgeois; Mrs. Grundy, Philistine, Babbitt. *Slang*, Joe Blow, John Q. Public.

4, peasant, countryman, boor, churl, villein; serf; dockwalloper, longshoreman, navvy; swain, clown, clod, clodhopper; hobnail, yokel, bumpkin; plowman, rustic, tiller of the soil; white-collar man, girl *or* worker; hewers of wood and drawers of water. *Slang*, hick, jay, hayseed, rube; goon.

5, beggar, mudlark, *sans culotte*, raff, tatterdemalion, hobbledehoy, caitiff, ragmuffin, pariah; guttersnipe, urchin, street urchin *or* arab; tramp, hobo, knight of the road, vagabond, vagrant, bum, weary Willie. *Slang*, bindlestiff.

Adjectives—plebeian, proletarian, common, democratic; homely, homespun; vulgar, lowborn, baseborn; unknown to fame, obscure, untitled; rustic, loutish, boorish, clownish, churlish; barbarous, barbarian, barbaric.

Antonym, see NOBILITY.

---

popular, *adj.* common, public, plebeian; acceptable, cheap; approved, like, praised; elect, chosen; desirable; admired, famous, celebrated, noted. See APPROBATION, CHOICE, DESIRE, REPUTE. *Ant.,* see DISAPPROBATION, REFUSAL, DISREPUTE.

population, *n.* inhabitants, people, race; residents; nation. See INHABITANT.

porch, *n.* veranda, portico, piazza; entrance, portal; stoa. See OPENING, RECEPTACLE.

pore, *n. & v.* —*n.* breathing hole, skin hole, orifice; stoma, ostiole, porus; OPENING. —*v.i.* read, peruse, scan, scrutinize, examine closely; mull over, consider. See THOUGHT, INQUIRY, VISION.

pornography, *n.* ribaldry, bawdiness, lewdness; erotica; prurience, sexuality; impudicity, obscenity, indecency, IMPURITY; vulgarity, dirt, smut, UNCLEANNESS, filth. *Slang*, porn.

porous, *adj.* open; absorbent; perforated, honeycombed; sandy; permeable, loose, pervious. See OPENING. *Ant.,* see SMOOTHNESS.

porridge, *n.* pottage, stew, soup; gruel, mush, cereal, samp, pap, burgoo; stirabout, hasty pudding, pease porridge. See FOOD.

port, *n.* REFUGE, harbor, shelter, haven; OPENING, embrasure, porthole; APPEARANCE, bearing, deportment, demeanor; LEFT, larboard (*Naut.*).

portable, *adj.* transportable, movable, carriable.

portal, *n.* entrance, door, entry, doorway, gateway, portcullis. See OPENING.

portend, *v.t.* signify, presage, augur, forebode, foreshadow, omen, foretoken, mean. See PREDICTION, INDICATION.

portent, *n.* WONDER, marvel, phenomenon; sign, foreshadowing, foreboding, token; importance, MEANING. See INDICATION.

porter, *n.* doorman, *concierge*, gatekeeper, guard, sentinel, warder; bearer. *Colloq.*, redcap. See CARRIER.

portfolio, *n.* briefcase, bag, portmanteau, attaché case; LIST (of stocks, *etc.*), catalog. See RECEPTACLE.

portico, *n.* colonnade, stoa, veranda, porch. See RECEPTACLE.

portion, *n. & v.t.* —*n.* share, allotment, due, ration; PART, serving, morsel, fragment; fate, lot, DESTINY; dividend; section. —*v.t.* dower, apportion, divide, endow. See APPORTIONMENT. *Ant.,* see WHOLE.

portly, *adj.* dignified, imposing, stately; fat, fleshy, stout, corpulent; bulky. See SIZE.

portmanteau, *n.* trunk, suitcase, valise; PORTFOLIO; combined word. See RECEPTACLE.

portrait, *n.* picture, likeness; depiction, DESCRIPTION; photograph, sketch. See PAINTING, REPRESENTATION.

pose, *n. & v.i.* —*n.* attitude; AFFECTATION; position, posture; aspect, figure. —*v.i.* attitudinize, affect; propound; question, puzzle, quiz, inquire, nonplus. See AFFIRMATION, DOUBT.

position, *n.* SITUATION, placement, point, spot, PLACE, LOCATION, site; billet, berth, post, station office, rank, status; caste; LOCATION, site; incumbency; dignity, honor. See BUSINESS, CIRCUMSTANCE, REPUTE.

positive, *adj.* certain, decided, emphatic, unqualified, absolute; inescapable, peremptory, firm. See AFFIRMATION, CERTAINTY. *Ant.,* see DOUBT, NEGATION.

posse, *n.* deputation, deputies, vigilantes; riot squad. See DEFENSE, MASTER.

POSSESSION

Nouns—**1,** possession, ownership (see PROPERTY); occupancy, occupation; hold, holding; tenure, tenancy, feudality, dependency; monopoly, corner, retention; heritage, inheritance, heirship, reversion; fee, seigniority; bird in hand; nine points of the law; vested interests.

2, possessor, holder; occupant, occupier; tenant; renter, lodger, lessee; owner; proprietor, proprietress; master, mistress, lord; landholder, landowner, landlord, landlady; lord of the manor, laird; legatee, devisee; heir, heiress, inheritress, inheritrix.

Verbs—**1,** possess, have, hold, occupy, enjoy; be possessed of, own, command; inherit, come to, come in for; acquire (see ACQUISITION); RETAIN.

2, belong to, appertain to, pertain to; be in one's possession; vest in.

Adjectives—**1,** possessing, having; worth; possessed of, seized of, master of, in possession of; in fee simple; outright; endowed with, blest with, fraught with; possessed; on hand, by one; in hand, in store, in stock; in one's hands, at one's command, to one's name, at one's disposal; one's own.

2, retentive, retaining, tenacious; reserved, entailed.
Antonym, see POVERTY, DEBT.

POSSIBILITY

Nouns—possibility, potentiality, likelihood, LIABILITY; what may be, what is possible; compatibility (see AGREEMENT); reasonability, reasonableness (see REASONING); practicability, EXPEDIENCE, feasibility, potency, workability, workableness, accessibility, attainability; contingency, LATENCY, PROBABILITY, CHANCE, hazard, outlook. *Colloq.,* toss-up, show, outside chance.

Verbs—be possible, stand a chance; admit of, bear; put in the way of.

Adjectives—possible, potential, in *or* on the cards *or* dice, within the bounds of possibility, *in posse*; conceivable, imaginable, credible, thinkable, reasonable, plausible, presumable; compatible (see AGREEMENT); practicable, feasible, workable, performable, achievable, accessible, superable, surmountable, attainable, obtainable, expedient, within reach; contingent (see DOUBT); probable, likely. *Colloq.,* liable.

Adverbs—possibly, by possibility; perhaps, perchance, peradventure; it may be, maybe, haply, mayhap; if [humanly] possible, [wind and] weather permitting, everything being equal, as luck may have it, God willing, *Deo volente,* D.V. *Colloq.,* on the off chance, could be.
Antonym, see IMPOSSIBILITY.

post, *n. & v.* —*n.* station, position; incumbency, PLACE, office, mail; stake, picket, newel, pillar, pier. —*v.* mail; inform, publish, RECORD, enter, transfer; speed, hurry. See BUSINESS, LOCATION, VELOCITY.

poster, *n.* PUBLICATION, billboard, advertisement, placard, bill.

posterior, *adj. & n.* —*adj.* subsequent, later, succeeding, ensuing; postern, REAR, hindmost. See SEQUENCE. —*n.* See BUTTOCKS.

POSTERITY

Nouns—**1,** posterity, progeny, issue, fruit, seed, offspring; brood, litter, farrow, spawn, spat, clutch, seed, product; family, children, grandchildren, heirs; younger, rising *or* succeeding generation.
2, child, son, daughter, grandchild, bantling, bairn, baby, infant; bastard, illegitimate *or* natural child; scion, shoot, sprout, sprit, [olive] branch, offshoot, offset, ramification; descendant, heir(ess); heir apparent *or* presumptive; chip off the old block; foster child; stepchild, stepson, stepdaughter.
3, straight descent, sonship, line, lineage, succession, filiation, primogeniture, heredity, origin, extraction. See ANCESTRY.
4, race, breed, strain, stock, stirps, root, generation; tribe, clan, sept, nationality (see MANKIND).
Adjectives—filial, sonly, daughterly, family; lineal, hereditary; tribal, national.

Antonym, see ANCESTRY.

---

posthaste, *adv.* speedily, hastily, at top speed, apace, expeditiously, swiftly. See RASHNESS, VELOCITY.

posthumous, *adj.* post-obit, post-mortem; late; postponed, delayed. See LATENESS, DEATH.

postman, *n.* mail carrier, mailman, courier, mail clerk. See CORRESPONDENCE, COMMUNICATION.

post-mortem, *adj. & n.* —*adj.* See POSTHUMOUS. —*n.* autopsy, pathology, necropsy, necrotomy; investigation, examination, INQUIRY, study, recapitulation. See DEATH.

postpone, *v.t.* procrastinate, delay, defer; shelve, adjourn, table. See LATENESS, NEGLECT.

postscript, *n.* ADDITION, appendix, afterthought; P.S., P.P.S.

postulate, *n. & v.* —*n.* proposition, axiom, SUPPOSITION; hypothesis, premise; fact, datum, TRUTH. —*v.* suppose, surmise, theorize, hypothesize. See THOUGHT.

posture, *n.* pose, attitude; bearing, position, carriage; mood, condition. See FORM.

pot, *n.* crock, jug, tankard; kettle, pan, vessel; mug. See RECEPTACLE.

potboiler, *n.* trash, dime novel. *Colloq.,* junk. *Slang,* tripe. See WRITING.

potent, *adj.* powerful, strong, mighty; intense, influential; effectual, effective, forceful; capable, able. See POWER. *Ant.,* see IMPOTENCE.

potentate, *n.* king, sovereign, ruler, monarch. See AUTHORITY.

potential, *adj.* dynamic, magnetic, charged; dormant, latent; unfulfilled, promising. See POWER.

potion, *n.* potation; philter, elixir, brew, libation. See REMEDY, FOOD.

potpourri, *n.* blend, medley, hodgepodge, miscellany, mélange; salmagundi, gallimaufry, pastiche. See MIXTURE.

pottery, *n.* earthenware, china, porcelain, CERAMICS; dishes, utensils.

pouch, *n.* bag, sack; purse, reticule, wallet; pocket, sac. See RECEPTACLE.

poultry, *n.* chickens, ducks, geese, turkeys; fowl(s), hens, broilers, fryers, roosters; pigeons, squab. See ANIMAL.

pounce, *v.i.* spring, leap, jump; snatch, grasp, seize; ambush. See SURPRISE.

pound, *v.t.* beat, thump, drum, bruise, tenderize; pulverize. See POWDERINESS, IMPULSE.

pour, *v.* flow, emerge; decant, fill; issue; rain, flood, shower. See EGRESS, WATER.

pout, *v.i.* sulk, grimace, moue. See DEJECTION.

POVERTY

Nouns—1, poverty, inpecuniousness, indigence, penury, pauperism, destitution, want; need, neediness; lack, necessity, privation, distress, difficulties; bad, poor *or* needy circumstances; reduced *or* straitened circumstances; slender means, straits; hand-to-mouth existence; beggary; mendicancy, loss of fortune, bankruptcy, insolvency (see DEBT).

2, poor man, pauper, mendicant, beggar, starveling.

Verbs—1, be poor, want, lack, starve, live from hand to mouth, have seen better days, go down in the world, go to the dogs, go to wreck and ruin; not have a penny to one's name; beg one's bread; tighten one's belt. *Slang*, go broke.

2, render poor, impoverish, reduce to poverty; pauperize, fleece, ruin, strip.

Adjectives—poor, indigent; poverty-stricken; poor as a church mouse; poor as Job's turkey; penniless, impecunious; hard up; out at elbows *or* heels; seedy, shabby; beggarly, beggared; destitute, bereft, in want, needy, necessitous, distressed, pinched, straitened; unable to keep the wolf from the door, unable to make both ends meet; embarrassed, involved; insolvent, bankrupt, on one's uppers, on the rocks, on the beach. *Colloq.*, in the hole, broke, stony, looking for a handout.

Antonym, see MONEY.

POWDERINESS

Nouns—1, powderiness; grittiness, sandiness; efflorescence; friability.

2, powder, dust, sand, sawdust; grit; meal, bran, flour, farina; crumb, seed, grain; particle (see LITTLENESS); filings, débris, detritus, floc.

3, pulverization, grinding, comminution, attenuation, granulation, disintegration, subaction, trituration, levigation, abrasion, detrition, crystalization, limation; filing; erosion, corrosion (see DETERIORATION).

4, mill, grater, rasp, file, mortar and pestle, teeth, grinder, grindstone, quern; chopper.

Verbs—pulverize, comminute, crystallize, granulate, triturate, levigate; scrape, file, abrade, rub down, grind, grate, rasp, pound, contuse, beat, crush, crunch, crumble; rust, shatter, disintegrate.

Adverbs—powdery, pulverulent, granular, mealy, floury, farinaceous, branny, furfuraceous, flocculent, dusty, sandy; arenose, arenarious, arenaceous; gritty; efflorescent; friable, crumbly, shivery; attrite; in pieces, shards, flinders, *etc.*

Antonym, see COHERENCE.

POWER

Nouns—1, power, potence, potency, potentiality; puissance, might, force; ENERGY; dint; right hand, right arm; ascendancy, ascendency, sway, control; prepotency; almightiness, omnipotence; AUTHORITY, STRENGTH. *Slang*, steam.

2, ability ableness; competency; efficiency, efficacy; validity, cogency; enablement; vantage ground; INFLUENCE; MEANS, capability, capacity; faculty, quality, attribute, endowment, virtue, gift, property, qualification, susceptibility. *Slang*, the stuff, something on the ball, what it takes.

3, pressure, elasticity; gravity, electricity, magnetism, electromagnetism; ATTRACTION; force of inertia, dead force, living force; ENERGY, hydroelectric power, waterpower; atomic power, horsepower; FRICTION, suction; torque, thrust.

4, engine, motor, dynamo, generator; pump, mill, windmill; power plant; Diesel, gas, gasoline, internal combustion *or* steam engine; reciprocating, rotary, Wankel, jet *or* rocket engine; turbine.

Verbs—1, be powerful; be able; can; sway, control; compel (see COMPULSION).

2, strengthen, fortify, harden; empower, enable, invest, endue, arm, reinforce.

3, invigorate, energize, stimulate, kindle, refresh, restore.

Adjectives—**1,** powerful, puissant; potent, potential; capable, able; equal to, up to; cogent, valid; effective, effectual; efficient, efficacious, adequate; competent; STRONG, omnipotent; all-powerful, almighty; electric, magnetic; attractive; energetic, forcible, forceful, incisive, trenchant, electrifying; influential (see IMPORTANCE);· productive (see PRODUCTION).

2, resistless, irresistible; invincible, indomitable, invulnerable, impregnable, unconquerable; overpowering, overwhelming.

Adverbs—powerfully, strongly, irresistibly, *etc.*

Antonym, see IMPOTENCE.

---

powerlessness, *n.* IMPOTENCE; paralysis, incapacity, weakness, inability, disablement. *Ant.,* see POWER.

powwow, *n.* conjurer, medicine man; CONVERSATION, discussion. See SORCERY.

pox, *n.* smallpox, chicken pox, cow pox, variola, varicella, vaccinia; popules, maculas, vesicles, pustules; acne, eruption, breaking out; pocks, pockmarks; CURSE. See DISEASE.

practicable, *adj.* possible, feasible; useful, practical; workable, achievable. See POSSIBILITY.

practical, *adj.* pragmatical, useful, operative; effective. See AGENCY, UTILITY. *Ant.,* see USELESSNESS.

practice, *n. & v.* —*n.* training, drill, exercise; custom, HABIT; manner, METHOD, procedure. —*v.* exercise, apply; perform, act, do; drill, rehearse. See ACTION, TEACHING, USE, CONDUCT.

pragmatic, *adj.* practical, empirical; active, businesslike; materialistic, prosaic, pedantic, pedestrian. See ACTIVITY, OBSTINACY, DULLNESS.

prairie, *n.* PLAIN, grassland, mesa, steppe, llano, savanna.

praise, *n. & v.t:* —*n.* commendation, acclaim, approval, applause; eulogy; homage; benediction, thanksgiving, grace. —*v.t.* acclaim, approve, commend, extol, eulogize, applaud; glorify, laud. See APPROBATION. *Ant.,* see DISAPPROBATION.

praiseworthy, *adj.* commendable, good, laudable, meritorious, admirable. See APPROBATION. *Ant.,* see DISAPPROBATION.

prance, *v.t.* CAPER, cavort, spring, dance, slip. See LEAP.

prank, *n.* CAPRICE, frolic, caper, trick, jest, escapade.

prankster, *n.* joker, jokester, trickster, practical joker. See LEVITY, CAPRICE.

prattle, *n. & v.i.* —*n.* chitchat, babbling, chatter. —*v.i.* murmur, chatter, babble, jabber. See LOQUACITY, SPEECH.

pray, *v.i.* implore, ask, beg, REQUEST, solicit, petition, entreat; WORSHIP.

prayer, *n.* worship; invocation, supplication; intercession; orison, matin; beseeching, petition, entreaty, REQUEST; collect; litany, liturgy; Lord's prayer, paternoster; hallelujah, hosanna, praise to the Lord; Mass; communication with God; devotion(s), praise, thanksgiving; Hail Mary, Ave Maria; the rosary; Psalm; (*Jewish:*) Shema, Kol Nidre, Kaddish; (*Moslem:*) Allahu akbar, Fatihah, shahada, rak'ah; (*Hindu:*) Ram, Ram, Siva, Siva. See RELIGION.

preach, *v.* exhort, evangelize, lecture, sermonize, moralize. See RITE, TEACHING.

preamble, *n.* prologue, introduction, preface, prelude. See BEGINNING.

precarious, *adj.* dangerous, risky; critical; doubtful, uncertain, unsafe, insecure, unstable. See TRANSIENTNESS, DOUBT. *Ant.,* see SAFETY.

precaution, *n.* CARE, CAUTION, WARNING; safeguard, PROVISION, protection; anticipation, forethought. See PREPARATION, SAFETY. *Ant.,* see NEGLECT, RASHNESS.

PRECEDENCE

Nouns—**1,** precedence, coming before; SUPERIORITY, supremacy, preëminence, IMPORTANCE, preference, advantage; PRIORITY, preexistence, antecedence, precedency, antecedency, anteposition, anteriority. See ANCESTRY, BEGINNING, PAST.

2, precession, leading, heading, forerunning, going before; going *or* being first; the lead, the van (see FRONT).

3, precursor, forerunner, antecedent, precedent, predecessor, forebears; pioneer, scout, picket, vanguard, outrider, leader, bellwether, herald, harbinger, announcer; dawn; HABIT, standard, model; PROTOTYPE; custom, practice, usage; prefigurement, PREDICTION, omen, foretaste, foresight. See LAWSUIT.

4, foreword, prelude, preamble, preface, prologue, prolusion, proem, prolepsis, prefix, introduction, heading, frontispiece, groundwork, PREPARATION (see OPENING); overture, voluntary, symphony; premises.

Verbs—**1,** precede; come before, come first, antecede; introduce, usher in; set the fashion (see INFLUENCE); take *or* have precedence; outrank, rank; place before, prefix, premise, prelude, preface.

2, forerun; go before, go ahead, go in the van, go in advance; pioneer, herald, head, take the lead; lead [the way], get *or* have the start; steal a march; get before, get ahead, get in front of, outstrip. *Colloq.,* get in on the ground floor.

3, foresee, forecast, anticipate, predict (see EARLINESS, FUTURITY).

Adjectives—preceding, precedent, antecedent; anterior; prior, before; *avant-garde;* former, foregoing; above- *or* aforementioned, aforesaid, said; precursory, precursive, preliminary, prefatory, introductory; prodromal, premonitory (see WARNING); prelusive, prelusory, preludious; proemial, preparatory; forerunning, inaugural.

Adverbs—in advance, before, ahead, in front; in the van, forefront *or* vanguard; foremost, headmost.

Antonym, see SEQUENCE.

---

precept, *n.* instruction, charge; prescript, prescription; recipe, receipt; golden rule; MAXIM, rule, canon, law, code, act, statute, rubric, regulation; FORM, formula, formulary, order, COMMAND. See TEACHING.

precession, *n.* precedence, PRIORITY, forerunning, antecedence, going before; FRONT, van, lead; going *or* being first. *Ant.,* see SEQUENCE.

precinct, *n.* neighborhood, district, area; enclosure, boundary, LIMIT; environs. See REGION.

precious, *adj.* priceless, costly; precise, overnice; beloved, dear. See PAYMENT, LOVE. *Ant.,* see CHEAPNESS.

precipice, *n.* cliff, drop, bluff, declivity. See HEIGHT, DESCENT.

precipitate, *adj. & v.* —*adj.* rash, hasty, hurried, headlong, impetuous. See RASHNESS, HASTE. *Ant.,* see CARE, LEISURE. —*v.* CAUSE, foment; hasten, speed, expedite; separate (as a chemical solution); fall (as rain, snow, *etc.*).

precipitation, *n.* HASTE, impetuosity, rush; RASHNESS; deposit, silt; rain, snow, dew, hail; condensation. *Ant.,* see SLOWNESS.

precipitous, *adj.* steep, abrupt, clifflike, sheer. See OBLIQUITY.

precise, *adj.* exact, accurate, definite, punctilious; fastidious; unbending, rigid; prim, precious. See FORM, TRUTH. *Ant.,* see ERROR.

preclude, *v.t.* prevent, stop, prohibit, obviate, check; forestall. See HINDRANCE.

precocious, *adj.* advanced, overforward, premature. See EARLINESS. *Ant.,* see LATENESS.

preconception, *n.* anticipation, prejudgment; prejudice. See MISJUDGMENT.

precursor, *n.* See FORERUNNER.

predacious, *adj.* rapacious, predatory, raptorial, plundering, pillaging, ravening. See STEALING.

predatory, *adj.* robbing, ravening, predacious, plundering. See STEAL-ING.

predecessor, *n.* FORERUNNER, precursor, harbinger, herald; ancestor, antecedent, progenitor. See ANCESTRY. *Ant.,* see SEQUENCE.

predestine, *v.* foredoom, predestinate, preordain, foreordain. See PRE-DICTION.

predetermine, *v.t.* premeditate, predestine, preresolve; preconcert; pre-arrange; foreordain, doom; plan. *Colloq.,* stack the cards. See NECES-SITY, PREDICTION. *Ant.,* see IMPULSE, CHANCE.

predicament, *n.* condition, quandary, fix, corner, dilemma, mess, scrape, crisis, emergency. *Colloq.,* spot. See CIRCUMSTANCE, DIFFICULTY.

PREDICTION

Nouns—**1,** prediction, announcement; premonition, WARNING; intuition, prophecy, prognosis, prognostication, premonstration; augury, augura-tion; foreboding, presentiment, premonition; ominousness; auspices, forecast; OMEN, horoscope, soothsaying; fortune-telling; divination; necromancy (see SORCERY); spiritualism, clairvoyance; extrasensory per-ception, ESP, psi; sixth sense; astrology, horoscopy; prefiguration, pre-figurement; prototype, type.

2, FORESIGHT, precognition, prescience, prevision.

3, prophet, oracle, fortune-teller, soothsayer, crystal-gazer; Cassandra.

4, crystal ball, tea leaves, divining rod, *etc.*; Ouija board.

Verbs—**1,** predict, prognosticate, prophesy, divine, foretell, soothsay, augur, tell fortunes; cast a horoscope; advise, PROMISE; forewarn (see WARNING); presage, bode, forebode, foretoken, portend, foreshadow; typify, protypify; herald, announce; loom, impend.

2, bid fair; promise; lead one to expect; be the precursor *or* fore-runner.

3, foresee, anticipate, foreknow, presurmise, expect.

Adjectives—**1,** predicting, predictive, prophetic, oracular, sibylline; omi-nous, portentous; auspicious; prescient; minatory, monitory, premoni-tory.

2, premeditated, predesigned, predetermined; psychokinetic.

Antonym, see CHANCE.

---

predilection, *n.* partiality, preference, prejudice, bias. See TENDENCY, MISJUDGMENT. *Ant.,* see HATE.

predisposed, *adj.* inclined, prone, partial; prepared, ready, willing. See TENDENCY, WILLINGNESS.

predominant, *adj.* prevalent, controlling, ascendant, ruling, supreme. See POWER. *Ant.,* see IMPOTENCE, INFERIORITY.

preëminent, *adj.* outstanding, conspicuous, notable, distinguished, re-nowned; foremost, paramount, superior, supreme. See REPUTE, SU-PERIORITY. *Ant.,* see INFERIORITY.

preempt, *v.t.* commandeer, usurp, occupy, arrogate. See TAKING, AC-QUISITION.

preen, *v.t.* groom, primp, prettify; strut. *Slang,* doll up. See CLEAN-NESS, VANITY.

prefabricated, *adj.* ready-built *or* -made. *Colloq.,* prefab. See PRO-DUCTION.

preface, *n. & v.* —*n.* foreword, prologue, preamble, introduction, pre-lude, preliminary. —*v.t.* introduce, open, premise, precede. See PRIORITY.

prefer, *v.t.* select, fancy, choose, adopt; OFFER; promote, advance. See CHOICE, IMPROVEMENT.

preference, *n.* CHOICE, pick, DESIRE, TASTE, liking. *Colloq.,* druthers.

pregnant, *adj.* significant, weighty, potential; gravid, parturient; impreg-nated, big (with child), *enceinte.* See IMPORTANCE, PRODUCTION. *Ant.,* see UNIMPORTANCE.

prehistoric, *adj.* early, pristine, original; primeval, primal, primitive; archaic, lost to history, from before time; unrecorded, unwritten. See OLDNESS.

prejudge, *v.t.* presuppose, assume, presume. See MISJUDGMENT.

prejudice, *n. & v.* —*n.* partiality, bias, opinion; predilection, prepossession; detriment; injury; intolerance. —*v.t.* bias, INFLUENCE, color, jaundice. See MISJUDGMENT.

prelate, *n.* ecclesiastic, churchman; primate, bishop, cardinal. See CLERGY.

preliminary, *adj.* introductory, preparatory, prefatory. See BEGINNING, PREPARATION.

prelude, *n.* preface, foreword, prologue, introduction, precursor. See MUSIC, PRIORITY.

premature, *adj.* untimely, underripe, immature, precocious, unprepared, incomplete; forward. See EARLINESS.

premeditate, *v.t.* calculate, PLAN, predesign, resolve, prearrange.

premiere, *n.* opening, debut, first night, inauguration, bow. See DRAMA.

premises, *n.pl.* building, LAND, house, apartment, office, *etc.*; bases, data, testimony, facts. See EVIDENCE, PLACE, REASONING.

premium, *n.* REWARD, prize, PAYMENT, recompense, gift, bounty, fee, bonus. See RECEIVING.

premonition, *n.* foreboding, presentiment, portent, forewarning. See WARNING.

preoccupation, *n.* inattentiveness, prepossession, distraction, absorption, engrossment. *Colloq.,* brown study. *Ant.,* see ATTENTION.

PREPARATION

Nouns—**1,** preparation, preparing; providing; provision, providence, prearrangement, anticipation, FORESIGHT; precaution, predisposition; forecast, PLAN; rehearsal; training, education (see TEACHING); inurement, HABIT; novitiate.

2, ARRANGEMENT, clearance; adjustment (see AGREEMENT); tuning, equipment, outfit.

3, groundwork, keystone, cradle, steppingstone; foundation.

4, preparation of food, cuisine, cooking, cookery; culinary art; preparation of the soil, tilling, plowing, sowing, semination, cultivation; manufacture, PRODUCTION.

5, preparedness, readiness, ripeness, mellowness; maturity.

6, preparer, trainer, TEACHER; pioneer, pathfinder, trailblazer; FORERUNNER.

Verbs—**1,** prepare; get ready, make ready; make preparations, settle preliminaries, get up, predispose; set *or* put in order (see ARRANGEMENT); forecast, PLAN; lay the foundations, basis *or* groundwork; roughhew; nurture (see AID); hatch, cook, brew.

2, equip, arm, man; fit out, fit up; furnish, rig, dress; ready, set, prime, attune; adjust, put in working order, put in tune; pack; prepare for, train, teach, rehearse; make provision for; take steps, measures *or* precautions; provide, provide against, set one's house in order; clear the decks for action.

3, prepare oneself; serve an apprenticeship; get into harness, gird up one's loins, buckle on one's armor; shoulder arms, get up steam; save for a rainy day; keep one's powder dry.

Adjectives—**1,** preparing, in preparation, in embryo, in hand; brewing, hatching, brooding; in store for, in reserve; precautionary, provident; preparative, preparatory; provisional; under revision; preliminary (see PRECEDENCE).

2, prepared, in readiness, ready, handy; planned, strategic, schematic; in working order; in practice; practised, skilled; in battle array, in war paint; armed to the teeth, sword in hand; booted and spurred; on the

alert, vigilant, *semper paratus*. *Colloq.*, on the mark, all set, on tap, ready to roll, all systems go.
Adverbs—in preparation, in anticipation of; against, for; under construction, afoot, afloat, under consideration, on foot. *Colloq.*, in the works, on the fire.
Antonym, see NEGLECT.

---

preponderance, *n.* prevalence, control, predominance, supremacy, ascendancy. See INFLUENCE, SUPERIORITY.
prepossessing, *adj.* appealing, attractive; charming, winning, winsome, engaging. See ATTRACTION, PLEASURE. *Ant.*, see UGLINESS.
preposterous, *adj.* ridiculous, absurd, nonsensical, idiotic; foolish, extravagant; improper, unsuitable. See ABSURDITY.
prerequisite, *n.* requirement, essential, NECESSITY, proviso; stipulation, QUALIFICATION. *Colloq.*, must.
prerogative, *n.* franchise, RIGHT, privilege; birthright; liberty, advantage.
presage, *n.* portent, prophecy, augury, forecast, OMEN; PREDICTION, precursor, harbinger, FORERUNNER; inkling, PROMISE.
prescribe, *v.t.* urge, suggest, advise; order, advocate, decree; appoint, institute; ordain. See ADVICE, COMMAND.
prescription, *n.* medicine; formula, recipe; mandate, decree, edict. See REMEDY, COMMAND.

PRESENCE

Nouns—**1**, presence, attendance; ASSEMBLAGE; occupancy, occupation, habitation, inhabitancy, residence, ABODE; permeation, pervasion; diffusion, dissemination; occurrence; ubiety, ubiquity, omnipresence, EXISTENCE.
2, SPECTATOR, bystander, attender, patron, audience; beholder, observer, witness.
Verbs—**1**, be present; exist; look on, witness, watch; attend, remain; find oneself, present oneself; show one's face; occur; lie, stand. *Colloq.*, show up.
2, occupy, people, inhabit, dwell, reside, stay, sojourn, live, abide, lodge, nestle, roost, perch; take up one's abode (see LOCATION); frequent, haunt; tenant. *Slang*, hang out.
3, fill, pervade, permeate; be diffused, be disseminated; overspread, overrun; run across.
Adjectives—present; occupying, inhabiting; moored (see LOCATION); resident, residential; domiciled, domiciliary; ubiquitous, omnipresent; peopled, populated, inhabited.
Adverbs—here, there, where, everywhere, aboard, on board, at home, afield; on the spot; here, there and everywhere (see SPACE); in the presence of, before, in person; under the eyes of, under the nose of; in the face of. *Colloq.*, in the flesh; live (*Radio & T.V.*).
Antonym, see ABSENCE.

PRESENT [TIME]

Nouns—present time, day, moment, juncture *or* occasion; the present, the times, the time being, the nonce; this day and age, existing times, nowadays; epoch, day, hour, age, time of life; now, the here and now, twentieth century; present tense, the historic(al) present (see GRAMMAR). See NEWNESS.
Adjectives—present, actual, instant, current, existing, living, immediate; up-to-date, latter-day, present-day, modern, contemporary, topical.
Adverbs—**1**, at this time, at this moment, immediately (see INSTANTANEITY); at the present time, at present, now; at this time of day, today, nowadays; already, even now, but now, just now, as of now; on the present occasion; for the time being, for the nonce; on the spot; on the spur of the moment *or* occasion; until now, to this day,

to the present day; in this day and age, in our time; forthwith, presently, soon, shortly, eventually.

2, to date, up to now, as yet, thus far, so far, hereunto.

Antonym, see PRIORITY, SEQUENCE, FUTURITY, PAST.

---

present, *n. & v.* —*n.* gift, favor, gratuity, offering, bonus, donation. See GIVING. *Ant.*, see RECEIVING. —*v.t.* award, endow, give, assign, deliver, proffer, tender, pass, bestow; introduce. See GIVING.

presentable, *adj.* attractive, personable, engaging; decent; passable, tolerable, up to snuff *or* par.

presentiment, *n.* PREDICTION, foreboding, anticipation, premonition, apprehension; foretaste, prescience; OMEN.

presently, *adv.* soon, shortly, immediately, eventually. See EARLINESS. *Ant.*, see LATENESS.

PRESERVATION

Nouns—**1,** preservation; conservation; safekeeping (see STORE); maintenance, SUPPORT; conservation, ECONOMY; salvation, deliverance.

2, preserver, conserver, preservative; embalming; curing, pickling, salting, smoking, canning; dehydration; tanning; refrigeration, freezing, quick-freezing.

Verbs—**1,** preserve, maintain, keep, sustain, support; keep up, keep alive; bank up, nurse; save, rescue; make safe (see SAFETY); take care of, guard, defend (see DEFENSE).

2, conserve, dry, cure, salt, pickle, corn, smoke; dehydrate, quick-freeze; bottle, pot, tin can; tan; husband; embalm, mummify; immortalize.

Adjectives—preserving, preservative; hygienic; preserved, unimpaired, unsinged, unmarred, safe and sound; intact, unscathed, with a whole skin.

Antonyms, see WASTE, DETERIORATION.

---

preside, *v.i.* supervise, superintend, control, rule, direct, manage. See AUTHORITY.

president, *n.* head, chairman, dean, principal, chief, ruler. See AUTHORITY.

press, *n. & v.* —*n.* crush, throng, crowd; pressure, urgency; closet, wardrobe, repository; printing machinery; ASSEMBLAGE; newspapers. See IMPORTANCE, PRINTING, PUBLICATION, RECEPTACLE. —*v.* crush, push, force; iron, smooth; compel, force, urge, beg, persuade; hug, embrace; squeeze, wring; solicit, entreat, importune. See COMPULSION, ENDEARMENT, GRAVITY, SMOOTHNESS.

pressing, *adj.* critical, important, urgent; exacting, demanding; persistent. See IMPORTANCE, COMPULSION.

pressure, *n.* strain, COMPULSION, NECESSITY, urgency, stress; persuasion, coercion, persuasiveness; affliction, trouble; distress; heaviness, compression. See ADVERSITY, GRAVITY, IMPORTANCE, CONTRACTION.

prestige, *n.* REPUTE, reputation, dignity, fame, note, importance.

presume, *v.i.* impose, venture; deduce, assume, infer, presuppose; infringe, take liberties. See FREEDOM, SUPPOSITION.

presumption, *n.* audacity, assurance, arrogance, haughtiness; impetuosity; deduction, conclusion, inference, guess, hypothesis. See INSOLENCE, RASHNESS.

presuppose, *v.t.* assume, presume, imply. See SUPPOSITION.

pretend, *v.i.* sham, feign, dissemble, simulate; counterfeit, lie, fake; claim, aver. See FALSEHOOD. *Ant.*, see TRUTH.

pretender, *n.* claimant; impostor; fraud, humbug, hypocrite; deceiver. See DECEPTION.

pretense, *n.* show, pretension, AFFECTATION, sham, IMITATION, OSTENTATION; UNTRUTH, makeshift, simulation, excuse, pretext, evasion.

pretentious, *adj.* showy, gaudy; overdone, exaggerated; affected, un-

natural; garish, ostentatious; conceited, vain. See AFFECTATION, OSTEN-
TATION, VANITY. *Ant.*, see MODESTY, SIMPLENESS.

pretext, *n.* subterfuge, pretense, excuse, justification, VINDICATION;
cover, cloak, blind, sham, evasion. See DECEPTION.

pretty, *adj. & adv. adj.* attractive, comely, good-looking; delicate, precise. See BEAUTY. *Ant.*, see UGLINESS. —*adv.*, *colloq.*, rather; moderately.

prevail, *v.i.* preponderate, predominate, rule, obtain; exist, be; overcome; succeed, induce, persuade. See EXISTENCE, HABIT, SUCCESS,
CAUSE. *Ant.*, see FAILURE.

prevalence, *n.* dominance, prominence; ubiquitousness, commonness,
universality, currency; reign, power, sway. See SUPERIORITY.

prevalent, *adj.* customary, current; predominant, prominent, prevailing,
preponderant; general, rife, current. See HABIT.

prevaricate, *v.i.* quibble, cavil, equivocate, palter. See FALSEHOOD.
Ant., see TRUTH.

prevent, *v.t.* preclude, hinder, stop, check, impede, forestall, avert, restrain, prohibit. See HINDRANCE, RESTRAINT. *Ant.*, see AID.

previous, *adj.* antecedent, anterior; preceding, foregoing, former, prior.
See PRIORITY.

prey, *n. & v.i.* —*n.* victim, quarry, game, kill; loot, prize, spoil. See
KILLING. —*v.i.* plunder, pillage, ravage; haunt, wear. See STEALING.

PRICE

Nouns—**1**, price, amount, cost, expense, prime cost, charge, figure, demand; fare, hire, bill, rental; rent charge or seck, rackrent, quitrent;
expenditure, outlay (see PAYMENT). *Slang*, damage, score, bad news,
the tab, nick, ante, setback, shakedown, tune.

2, dues, duty, toll, tax, cess, levy, impost; custom, excise, assessment,
tithe, tenths, exaction, ransom, salvage, tariff; brokerage, wharfage,
freightage, carriage.

3, worth, rate, value, valuation, appraisement, appraisal, estimate,
evaluation, costliness; money's worth, pennyworth; current or market
price, quotation, going rate, what it will fetch; pegged or fixed price,
prix fixe, flat rate, package price. See DEARNESS.

4, recompense, pay, compensation, wages, remuneration, prize, guerdon,
requital, return.

5, price index, [price] ceiling or floor, floor or ceiling price; price controls, guidelines or supports; price fixing; escalator clause.

Verbs—**1**, price; set, quote, fix or peg a price; value, appraise, assess,
estimate, rate, evaluate; charge, demand, ask, require, exact tax, levy,
impose, apportion; distrain, liquidate; have one's price.

2, amount to, come to, mount up to, fetch, sell for, cost, bring in,
yield, afford. *Colloq.*, stand one, stick for, set one back.

Adjectives—priced, appraised; taxable, dutiable; mercenary, venal.

Adverbs—to the tune of, at a price, for a consideration.

---

priceless, *adj.* invaluable, precious; expensive, costly. See DEARNESS.

prick, *v.t.* puncture, pierce, stick; sting, wound; prod, urge, incite, goad,
spur. See SHARPNESS, PAIN.

prickly, *adj.* thorny, barbed, bristly, spiny, thistly, burry; stinging, tingling. See ROUGHNESS, SHARPNESS. *Ant.*, see SMOOTHNESS.

PRIDE

Nouns—**1**, pride, hauteur; dignity, decorum, GRAVITY, self-respect, self-
esteem, self-sufficiency, *noblesse oblige*, reserve.

2, arrogance, INSOLENCE; OSTENTATION, pomposity, VANITY, vainglory,
crest, airs, high notions; purse-pride; BOASTING, conceit, self-compla-
cency, self-exaltation, self-glorification, self-satisfaction, self-importance,
self-admiration, self-love, *amour-propre*, ego(t)ism; pretention, presumption, swagger, patronizing air. *Slang*, swank, side.

3, proud man, ego(t)ist, boaster, high flier, peacock; fine gentleman, fine lady; boast, pride and joy. *Slang*, swellhead.

Verbs—**1,** be proud, look one in the face, lift *or* hold up one's head, hold one's head high, perk oneself up; pride oneself on, glory in, take pride in, stand upon, be proud of.

2, be conceited; plume, preen, *or* hug oneself; put a good face on, carry with a high hand; boast, swagger, strut, presume, look big; set one's back up, bridle, toss the head, give oneself airs; condescend, talk down to, patronize, stoop, lower oneself. *Colloq.*, get on one's high horse. *Slang*, put on side *or* airs, put on the dog, put on the ritz.

3, fill with pride, puff up, swell, inflate, turn one's head, give a big head.

Adjectives—**1,** proud, exalted, lordly, noble (see NOBILITY); mettlesome, (high-)spirited; imposing, magnificent, splendid, majestic, grand.

2, arrogant (see INSOLENCE); vain, conceited, unblushing (see VANITY); haughty, puffed up, swollen, flushed, blown, vainglorious; supercilious, disdainful, contemptuous, presumptuous, condescending, cavalier; boastful, overweening, high and mighty; purse-proud; self-satisfied, self-confident, *etc.*; ego(t)istical; proud as a peacock *or* as Lucifer, bloated with pride, puffed up. *Colloq.*, uppish, uppity. *Slang*, high-hat.

3, stiff, formal, stiff-necked, starchy, prim, straitlaced; aristocratic (see NOBILITY); affected. *Colloq.*, stuck-up.

Adverbs—proudly, haughtily; with dignity, with head erect, with nose in the air. *Colloq.*, on one's high horse.

Antonym, see HUMILITY, MODESTY.

---

priest, *n.* father, clergyman, *etc.* See CLERGY.

priggish, *adj.* pedantic, affected; fastidious, prim, precious; conceited, egotistic. See AFFECTATION.

prim, *adj.* precise, demure, formal, priggish; fussy, prudish. See AFFECTATION.

primary, *adj.* chief, original, initial, first, elementary; immediate; primitive, prime, principal. See BEGINNING, CAUSE, IMPORTANCE. *Ant.*, see END, EFFECT, UNIMPORTANCE.

primate, *n.* chief, leader, head, MASTER; bishop, archbishop, metropolitan, diocesan, suffragan, patriarch. See CLERGY.

prime, *adj.* original, first, initial; primitive, primeval; chief, leading, main; CHOICE, finest. See BEGINNING, IMPORTANCE, OLDNESS. *Ant.*, see END, UNIMPORTANCE, NEWNESS.

primitive, *adj.* aboriginal, primeval, crude, unpolished, unrefined; primal, primary; prime; old, original, antiquated. See OLDNESS. *Ant.*, see NEWNESS.

primness, *n.* prudery, prudishness, priggishness; formality; preciousness, stiffness. See AFFECTATION.

primp, *v.* prink, preen, groom, bedizen, prettify, freshen up. *Colloq.*, deck out, put one's face up. *Slang*, doll up. See ORNAMENT, CLOTHING.

prince, *n.* monarch, ruler, sovereign; nobleman; chief. *Slang*, swell guy. See NOBILITY, AUTHORITY, SUPERIORITY.

princely, *adj.* regal, royal, titled, noble; magnanimous, generous, munificent. See NOBILITY. *Ant.*, see POPULACE, PARSIMONY.

principal, *n. & adj.* —*n.* chief, leader, head; constituent, client; buyer, seller; capital, *corpus*. See MONEY. —*adj.* foremost, chief, prime, greatest, main, leading. See IMPORTANCE. *Ant.*, see UNIMPORTANCE.

principality, *n.* principate, dominion, domain, sovereignty, RULE; princedom, satrapy, country, province, REGION; duchy, palatinate, margraviate; shiekdom, imamate, emirate, caliphate, sultanate.

principle, *n.* tenet, code, doctrine, conviction; theory, premise; postulate; RULE, law, precept; equity, integrity, PROBITY, nature, origin, source, CAUSE. See BELIEF. *Ant.*, see IMPROBITY.

PRINTING

Nouns—**1**, printing; typography, stereotype, electrotype; block printing; lithography, planography, collotype; offset, letterpress, gravure, rotogravure; instant printing, Xerox; photoprinting, photoengraving, Itek; intaglio; ENGRAVING; PUBLICATION; composition, typesetting, phototypesetting; Linotype, Monotype, Intertype, cold *or* hot type; imposition; mat, matrix; reproduction; graphic arts. See COPY.

2, type, case, lower case, upper case, capital; font; typeface, roman, italic, lightface, boldface; stick, stone; shank, serif; Gothic, oldstyle *or* modern type, *etc.*; print.

3, impression, proof, galley, galley proof, page proof, repro(duction) proof, revise, run, rerun; plate, replate.

4, printing press, press, proof press; job press, flatbed press, cylinder press, rotary press.

5, printer, compositor, typographer, pressman, makeup man, proofreader, copyholder; stone hand; printer's devil, proof boy.

Verbs—print, imprint; Xerox, offset; compose, impose, set, make up; proofread, revise; makeready; go to press.

Adjectives—printed; in type; typographical; graphic; in black and white.

PRIORITY

Nouns—priority, antecedence, anteriority, precedence, primogeniture; preexistence; precession; precursor, forerunner; PAST; premises.

Verbs—**1**, be prior, precede, come *or* go before; lead; pre-exist; dawn; presage (see PREDICTION).

2, be beforehand, be early (see EARLINESS); steal a march upon, anticipate, forestall; have *or* gain a start; steal one's thunder, anticipate. *Slang*, beat out, scoop; jump the gun.

Adjectives—prior, previous; preceding, precedent; anterior, antecedent; forehanded; pre-existing, pre-existent; former, foregoing; afore-mentioned, above-mentioned; aforesaid; said; introductory, precursory; preliminary, prefatory; preparatory.

Adverbs—before, formerly, prior to; earlier; previously, ere, heretofore, erstwhile, already, yet, beforehand; in advance, ahead; in the van *or* forefront; in front, foremost; on the eve of; *ante bellum*; before Christ; B.C.; antediluvian, before the fact.

Antonym, see SEQUENCE.

---

prismatic, *adj.* prismal; sparkling, coruscant, colorful, chromatic; kaleidoscopic; spectral, rainbowlike. See VARIEGATION, COLOR.

PRISON

Nouns—**1**, prison, penitentiary; jail, lockup, gaol, cage, coop, den, cell; cell block; stronghold, fortress, keep, dungeon, Bastille, oubliette; Sing Sing, Dartmoor, Alcatraz; Bridewell, house of correction, debtors' prison, prison farm, workhouse; guardroom, guardhouse; alimony jail; brig, hold; roundhouse, station house, station, police station; house of correction, reformatory, reform school, protectory; house of detention; pen, fold, corral, pound; INCLOSURE; penal colony *or* settlement; stocks, stone walls. *Slang*, jug, can, calaboose, calabozo, hoosegow, pen, big house, stir, clink, cooler, school, quad. See RESTRAINT.

2, prisoner, captive, felon; convict, inmate, détenu; trusty, parolee; prisoner of war, P.O.W.; ticket-of-leave man. *Colloq.*, jailbird. *Slang*, lag, con.

3, warden, KEEPER, jailer, gaoler, turnkey, guard, warder. *Slang*, screw.

Verbs, *Adjectives*—see RESTRAINT.

Antonym, see FREEDOM.

---

prissy, *adj.*, *colloq.*, priggish, prim; sissified, effeminate. See SOFTNESS.
pristine, *adj.* prime, first, dawnlike, primordial; fresh, dewy, pure, virginal. See PRIORITY, CLEANNESS, NEWNESS.

private, *adj.* personal; secluded; intimate; sequestered; privy, confidential, unofficial; individual, special. See SECLUSION. *Ant.,* see SOCIALITY.

privation, *n.* want, LOSS, POVERTY, indigence; deprivation, bereavement, dispossession. *Ant.,* see MONEY, SUFFICIENCY.

privilege, *n.* option, franchise; prerogative, RIGHT; favor, EXEMPTION, exception, immunity, liberty. See FREEDOM. *Ant.,* see RESTRAINT.

privy, *adj.* personal, SECRET; privy to, apprised of, informed of. *Colloq.,* posted on, in on, on to, wise to. See CONCEALMENT, SPECIALITY.

prize, *n. & v.t.* —*n.* TROPHY, medal, award, decoration, laurel; premium, bonus, REWARD; advantage, privilege; pick, élite. —*v.t.* cherish, treasure, esteem, value. See APPROBATION, LOVE. *Ant.,* see DISAPPROBATION.

probable, *adj.* likely; hopeful; to be expected; in a fair way; plausible, ostensible, well-founded, reasonable, credible, believable, presumable, presumptive, apparent, *prima facie*; in the cards. See CHANCE.

probation, *n.* trial, test, examination. See ESSAY.

probe, *v.t.* prod, pierce, stab; sound, fathom; search, investigate, sift, explore; verify. See INQUIRY, MEASUREMENT.

PROBITY

Nouns—**1,** probity, integrity, rectitude; uprightness; honesty, faith; honor; good faith, *bona fides*; clean hands, PURITY; dignity, respectability; right, JUSTICE; INNOCENCE, VIRTUE.
2, constancy; faithfulness, fidelity, loyalty; incorruption, incorruptibility; allegiance, devotion; trustworthiness, TRUTH, candor, veracity, sincerity.
3, punctilio, delicacy, nicety, conscientiousness; scrupulosity, scrupulousness, scruple, point of honor; punctuality, honor system.
4, loftiness of purpose; unselfishness, disinterestedness, sublimity, chivalry.
5, gentleman, man of honor, honest man, man of his word, *fidus Achates*; truepenny. *Colloq.,* square-shooter, brick. *Slang,* trump, regular fellow, good egg, right guy.
Verbs—be honorable; deal honorably, squarely, impartially *or* fairly; speak *or* tell the truth; do one's duty; keep one's promise *or* word; be as good as one's word; keep faith with; his word is his bond. *Colloq.,* be on the level; be on the up and up; level.
Adjectives—**1,** upright; honest; veracious, truthful; virtuous, honorable, law-abiding; fair, right, just, equitable, impartial, square; open and above-board; straightforward, frank, candid, openhearted. *Slang,* on the level, on the up and up, straight, square-shooting, legit, kosher.
2, constant, faithful, loyal, staunch; true, true-blue, true to the core; trusty, trustworthy; as good as one's word, reliable, dependable, to be depended on, steadfast, incorruptible, above suspicion.
3, conscientious; DISINTERESTED, right-minded; high-principled, high-minded; scrupulous, religious, strict; nice, punctilious, correct, punctual; respectable, reputable, gentlemanly.
4, inviolable, inviolate; innocent, pure; stainless, unstained, untarnished, unsullied, untainted; uncorrupt, incorruptible; chivalrous, *sans peur et sans reproche.*
Adverbs—honorably, bone fide; on one's honor, on the square, in good faith, honor bright, with clean hands.
Antonym, see IMPROBITY.

---

problem, *n.* question, proposition, exercise; perplexity, poser, puzzle, enigma, riddle; issue; query. See INQUIRY, SECRET. *Ant.,* see ANSWER.

problematical, *adj.* questionable, unsettled, perplexing; uncertain, enigmatic. See DOUBT. *Ant.,* see CERTAINTY.

proboscis, *n.* trunk, snout, nose. See CONVEXITY.

procedure, *n.* process, METHOD, tactics, proceeding, way, course; practice, CONDUCT; policy, FORM. See AGENCY.

proceed, *v.i.* continue, progress, advance; move, arise; emanate, result, issue. See PROGRESSION, CONTINUITY. *Ant.*, see REGRESSION, DISJUNCTION, END.

proceeding, *n.* ACTION, progress, move, measure, step, procedure. *Ant.*, see INACTIVITY.

proceeds, *n.pl.* balance, profit, gain, yield, earnings, receipts, issue, outcome, results; income. See ACQUISITION, MONEY.

process, *n.* CONDUCT, METHOD, procedure, COURSE, practice; outgrowth, protuberance, appendage, projection. See CONVEXITY.

procession, *n.* cavalcade, parade, train, column, file; PROGRESSION, sequence, succession. See CONTINUITY, TRAVEL.

proclaim, *v.t.* announce, declare, broadcast, circulate, publish, herald. See PUBLICATION.

proclivity, *n.* inclination, TENDENCY, propensity, proneness. See IMPULSE.

procrastination, *n.* postponement, delay, dilatoriness; negligence, omission. See LATENESS, NEGLECT. *Ant.*, see EARLINESS, CARE.

procreate, *v.* breed, reproduce, generate, beget, give birth. See REPRODUCTION.

proctor, *n.* monitor, overseer, housemaster; agent, steward. See MASTER, AGENCY.

procure, *v.t.* acquire, purchase, get, obtain; buy, hire; effect. See ACQUISITION, CAUSE. *Ant.*, see LOSS, SALE.

procurer, *n.* pander, bawd, pimp, procuress; obtainer. See EVILDOER.

prod, *v.t.* shove, goad, prick, spur, poke, jab; motivate, impel, instigate, incite. See IMPULSE, ACTIVITY, HASTE.

prodigality, *n.* profligacy, unthriftness, WASTE; profusion, profuseness; extravagance; squandering; excess, lavishness; liberality. *Ant.*, see PARSIMONY.

prodigious, *adj.* immense, enormous, vast, gargantuan, huge; remarkable, wonderful; monstrous; astonishing. See GREATNESS, WONDER. *Ant.*, see LITTLENESS.

prodigy, *n.* phenomenon; wonder, marvel, miracle; monster; curiosity, sight, spectacle; precocious child, child prodigy. *Slang,* boy wonder. See UNCONFORMITY.

produce, *n. & v.* —*n.* goods, yield, harvest; fruit, vegetables; stock, commodity, product. See ACQUISITION, SALE. —*v.t.* show, exhibit; create, originate, bear, breed, hatch; make, FASHION, manufacture. See PRODUCTION.

product, *n.* yield, output, produce; outcome, result. See ACQUISITION, EFFECT, PRODUCTION.

PRODUCTION

Nouns—**1,** production, creation, construction, formation, fabrication, manufacture; building, architecture, erection, edification; coinage; organization; putting together, establishment; workmanship, performance, operation; achievement, COMPLETION.

2, bringing forth, parturition, birth, childbirth, delivery, confinement, travail, labor, midwifery, obstetrics; gestation, evolution, development, growth; genesis, generation, procreation, progeneration, propagation; fecundation, impregnation; spontaneous generation; biogenesis, abiogenesis, parthenogenesis; authorship, PUBLICATION, works.

3, product; edifice, building, structure, fabric, erection; invention, composition; WRITING, BOOK, PAINTING, MUSIC; flower, fruit, work, handiwork.

4, productiveness, fecundity, fertility, luxuriance; pregnancy, pullulation, fructification, multiplication; fertilization.

5, producer, creator, originator, inventor, author, founder, generator, mover, architect, maker.

6, manufacture, manufacturing, fabrication; mass production, assembly line; automation.

Verbs—**1**, produce, perform, operate, do, make, form, construct, fabricate, frame, contrive; mass produce, manufacture; weave, forge, coin, carve, chisel; build, raise, rear, erect, put together; set up, run up, establish, constitute, compose, organize, institute; achieve, accomplish, complete, perfect.

2, produce, flower, bear fruit, fructify; teem, ean, yean, farrow, drop, whelp, pup, kitten; bear, lay, bring forth, give birth to, lie in, be delivered of; evolve, pullulate, usher into the world.

3, make productive, create; beget, get, generate, fecundate, impregnate; reproduce, proliferate, procreate, progenerate, propagate; fertilize, spermatize, conceive; bud, bloom, blossom, burgeon; engender; bring into being, call into being, bring into existence; breed, hatch, develop, bring up; induce, superinduce; suscitate, CAUSE, acquire (see ACQUISITION).

Adjectives—produced, producing, productive, prolific, fertile, fecund, creative, procreative; formative; genetic, genital; pregnant; *enceinte*, big with; fraught with; teeming, parturient, puerperal. *Colloq.*, expectant, in the family way.

Antonym, see DESTRUCTION.

---

profane, *adj. & v.* —*adj.* vulgar; sacrilegious, impious, unhallowed. —*v.t.* debase, desecrate, defile, pollute; abuse. See IMPIETY.

profess, *n.* pretend, feign; teach, instruct; affirm, declare, avow; own, admit. See AFFIRMATION, TEACHING. *Ant.,* see NEGATION.

profession, *n.* vocation, calling, occupation; sham, evasion, pretense; AFFECTATION, pretension; relief; acknowledgment, declaration, avowal. See AFFIRMATION, TEACHING. *Ant.,* see NEGATION.

professor, *n.* academician, teacher, instructor, scholar, don, MASTER. *Colloq.,* prof. *Slang,* doc. See TEACHING.

proficient, *adj.* expert, dext(e)rous, adept, adroit; well-versed, practiced; masterly, skillful. See SKILL. *Ant.,* see UNSKILLFULNESS.

profile, *n.* OUTLINE, side, shape, contour.

profit, *n. & v.* —*adj.* advantage, benefit, interest; gain, earnings, return. See ACQUISITION, INCREASE. *Ant.,* see LOSS, DECREASE.

profitable, *adj.* remunerative, lucrative, paying, gainful; advantageous, productive; serviceable, useful. See ACQUISITION, RECEIVING, USE. *Ant.,* see LOSS, DECREASE.

profiteer, *n. & v.* —*n.* extortionist, leech. *Colloq.,* highway robber. —*v.i.* overcharge, fleece, extort. *Colloq.,* hold up, skin, bleed. *Slang,* stick, sting. See TAKING, PARSIMONY, STEALING.

profligate, *adj. & n.* —*adj.* wanton, reckless, wild, intemperate; extravagant, wasteful. See WASTE. —*n.* roue, rake(hell), LIBERTINE, lecher, reprobate; wastrel, spendthrift, quanderer. *Colloq.,* playboy. See PLEASURE, WASTE, IMPURITY.

profound, *adj.* erudite, learned, abstruse; heavy, weighty, deep; heartfelt, intense; complete, thorough. See FEELING, GREATNESS, KNOWLEDGE. *Ant.,* see LITTLENESS, IGNORANCE.

profusion, *n.* abundance, multiplicity; excess, waste, superfluity, extravagance; plenty. See MULTITUDE, SUFFICIENCY. *Ant.,* see RARITY, INSUFFICIENCY.

progeny, *n.* children, offspring, descendants, family. See POSTERITY. *Ant.,* see ANCESTRY.

prognosticate, *v.t.* prophesy, foretell, augur, predict. See PREDICTION.

program, *n.* playbill, prospectus, syllabus; agenda; forecast, draft, outline. See LIST, PLAN.

PROGRESSION

Nouns—progression, progress, progressiveness; MOTION; advance, advancing, advancement; ongoing; flood-tide, headway; march (see TRAVEL); rise; IMPROVEMENT.

Verbs—progress, advance, proceed; get on, get along, get underway; gain ground; go with the stream, current *or* tide; hold *or* keep one's course; go, move, pass on, push *or* press on, forward *or* ahead; make one's way, work one's way; make progress *or* headway; make rapid strides; gain leeway. *Slang*, go great guns, get rolling, get cracking.

Adjectives—advancing, progressing, progressive, advanced.

Adverbs—progressively; forward, onward; forth, on, ahead; under way, enroute, on one's way, on the road, on the high road; in progress.

Antonym, see REGRESSION.

---

progressive, *adj.* enterprising, advanced, moving; improving, advancing; successive, continuing, continuous. See CONTINUITY, IMPROVEMENT, PROGRESSION. *Ant.*, see DISJUNCTION, REGRESSION.

PROHIBITION

Nouns—prohibition, inhibition, forbiddance, disallowance, restriction (see RESTRAINT), ILLEGALITY; veto, injunction, interdict(ion), proscription; embargo, ban, taboo, no-no, forbidden fruit; prevention, stoppage, HINDRANCE; temperance, act, Volstead Act, Eighteenth Amendment, dry law (see TEMPERANCE).

Verbs—1, prohibit, inhibit, forbid, disallow; veto, kill, ban, interdict; put *or* place under an interdiction *or* ban; taboo, proscribe, enjoin, deny, (de)bar, forfend; preclude, prevent, hinder; set *or* put one's foot down.

2, keep in, keep within bounds, restrain; limit, cohabit, withhold, block, check, circumscribe, clip the wings of, restrict; exclude, shut out, padlock; draw the color line, discriminate; shut *or* bolt the door; warn off; forbid the banns; disbar, unfrock.

Adjectives—1, prohibitive, prohibitory, prohibiting, forbidding, *etc.*

2, prohibited, forbidden, *verboten*, not permitted; unauthorized, unlicensed, illegal; banned, contraband, taboo; out of bounds, off limits.

Adverbs—on no account (see NEGATION).

Interjections—Heaven forbid! hands off! keep off! keep out! hold! stop! avast! no thoroughfare! no trespassing!

Antonym, see PERMISSION.

---

project, *n. & v.t.* —*n.* PLAN, purpose, enterprise; endeavor. —*v.t.* protrude, bulge, jut; throw, hurl, pitch; devise, PLAN, scheme, intend. See CONVEXITY, PROPULSION.

projectile, *n.* ball, pellet, bullet, missile, shell. See ARMS.

projection, *n.* extension, shelf; protuberance, protrusion; prominence, spur, eminence; transference, visualization. See CONVEXITY.

proletariat, *n.* working class, laborers, wage earners, labor force, POPULACE.

prolific, *adj.* fruitful, fecund, productive, fertile; lavish. See PRODUCTION.

prolix, *adj.* lengthy, wordy, long-winded, discursive, verbose, diffuse; tedious. See LOQUACITY, WEARINESS. *Ant.*, see CONTRACTION.

prologue, *n.* preface, introduction, proem, preamble, prelude. See BEGINNING.

prolong, *v.t.* extend, protract, hold; sustain, perpetuate, continue; lengthen. See CONTINUITY, LENGTH. *Ant.*, see END, SHORTNESS.

promenade, *n. & v.* —*n.* mall, alameda, boulevard, esplanade, boardwalk; promenade deck; stroll, outing, march. —*v.* walk, stroll, saunter. See TRAVEL.

prominent, *adj.* notable, important, salient, memorable; convex, raised, protuberant, projecting; influential, distinguished, eminent; conspicuous, noticeable. See CONVEXITY, IMPORTANCE, REPUTE. *Ant.*, see UNIMPORTANCE, DISREPUTE.

promiscuous, *adj.* indiscriminate, mixed, miscellaneous, confused. See MIXTURE. *Ant.*, see TASTE.

PROMISE

Nouns—promise, UNDERTAKING, word, troth, pledge, parole, word of honor, vow, avowal; oath (see AFFIDAVIT); profession, assurance, warranty, guarantee, insurance, obligation; covenant, contract, COMPACT; affidavit; engagement, affiance; betrothal, betrothment, troth, engagement, *etc.*

Verbs—**1,** promise; give *or* make a promise; undertake, engage; make *or* enter into an engagement; bind, pledge, *or* commit oneself; take upon oneself; vow; dedicate, swear (see AFFIRMATION); give, pledge *or* plight one's word; plight one's troth; betroth, plight faith; assure, warrant, guarantee; covenant (see COMPACT); attest (see EVIDENCE); contract an obligation; become bound to, become sponsor for; answer for, be answerable for; secure; give security; underwrite.

2, extract a promise, adjure, administer an oath, put to one's oath, swear a witness, swear in.

Adjectives—promising, promissory; votive; under hand and seal, upon oath, under oath; promised, affianced, pledged, bound; committed, compromised; in for it.

---

promontory, *n.* spit, headland, cape. See HEIGHT.

promote, *v.t.* advance, further; AID; improve, dignify, elevate, raise; back, SUPPORT, encourage. See IMPROVEMENT. *Ant.*, see DETERIORATION.

promoter, *n.* founder, organizer, planner; backer, supporter, encourager. See PLAN.

prompt, *v.t. & adj.* —*v.t.* incite, induce, motivate; actuate; remind, suggest, mention. See INFORMATION, MEMORY, CAUSE. —*adj.* immediate, ready, punctual, unretarded; alert, quick, active; instant, instantaneous; reasonable, early. See ACTIVITY, EARLINESS. *Ant.*, see LATENESS.

prompter, *n.* reminder; note, tickler, teleprompter; promptbook. See MEMORY, AID.

promulgate, *v.t.* publish, disseminate, proclaim, sponsor, advocate. See PUBLICATION.

prone, *adj.* inclined, disposed, likely, predisposed; recumbent, flat, prostrate, HORIZONTAL. *Ant.*, see VERTICAL.

prong, *n.* tine, point, pincer, spike, tooth, fang; extension. See SHARPNESS.

pronounce, *v.t.* speak, say, utter, enunciate, articulate; deliver, JUDGE, conclude; affirm, assert. See AFFIRMATION, SPEECH, VOICE.

pronunciation, *n.* utterance, saying, voicing, articulation, enunciation, orthoëpy. See VOICE.

proof, *n.* EVIDENCE, substantiation, verification, confirmation; conclusiveness; corroboration, ratification; trial, test; sample, impression. *Ant.*, see NEGATION.

prop, *n. & v.t.* —*n.* SUPPORT, brace, stay, pillar, underpin, shore, column, block, base; foundation; mainstay, assistant, helper, staff; fulcrum; truss. —*v.t.* SUPPORT, uphold, brace, encourage, back; truss; shore, underpin, underset.

propaganda, *n.* publicity; persuasion, proselytization, movement. See TEACHING.

propagate, *v.t.* breed, generate, produce, disseminate; spread, broadcast, publish, increase; multiply. See PRODUCTION, PUBLICATION.

propel, *v.t.* push, force, impel, thrust, shove, activate, move, drive. See PROPULSION.

propeller, *n.* propellant; propulsor, impeller; rotor, blade, airfoil, screw. *Colloq.*, prop. See PROPULSION.

propensity, *n.* TENDENCY, aptitude, inclination, talent, bent, proclivity, disposition.

proper, *adj.* correct, fastidious; suitable, becoming; decorous, demure, chaste, delicate; individual, special, limited, own, appropriate, pertinent, apropos, meet; seemly, befitting; equitable, fair, RIGHT, just.

PROPERTY

Nouns—**1,** property, POSSESSION, ownership, proprietorship, lordship; seigniory; empire, dominion (see AUTHORITY); interest, stake, estate, RIGHT, title, claim, demand, holding; tenure; vested, contingent, beneficial, *or* equitable interest; USE, trust, benefit; fee simple, fee tail.

2, dower, dowry, dot; jointure, appanage; inheritance, heritage; patrimony; alimony; legacy (see GIVING).

3, assets, belongings, MEANS, resources, circumstances; wealth, MONEY; credit; patent, copyright; landed property, real property, real estate, realty, land, lands; tenements; hereditaments; territory, state, kingdom, principality, realm, empire; dependence; protectorate, sphere of influence; manor, domain, demesne; farm, plantation, hacienda; freehold, leasehold; fixtures, plant; easement. See ABODE.

4, personal property *or* effects; personalty, chattels, goods, effects, movables; stock in trade; things, traps, gear, paraphernalia; equipage; parcels, appurtenances; impedimenta; luggage, dunnage, baggage; bag and baggage; pelf; cargo, lading, freight.

Verbs—possess (see POSSESSION); own; belong to, pertain to.

Adjectives—one's own; landed, manorial, allodial; freehold, leasehold; feudal.

Antonym, see POVERTY.

---

prophecy, *n.* PREDICTION, prognosis, forecast, prognostication, presage, augury, divination.

prophet, *n.* oracle, soothsayer, prognosticator, sibyl; predictor, seer, diviner. See PREDICTION.

prophylactic, *adj.* preventive; precautionary; preservative, protective. See HEALTH. *Ant.*, see DISEASE.

propinquity, *n.* NEARNESS; vicinity, proximity; adjacence; RELATION; juxtaposition. *Ant.*, see DISTANCE.

propitiate, *v.t.* pacify, conciliate, reconcile; intercede, calm, mediate; atone. See ATONEMENT, COMPROMISE, PACIFICATION. *Ant.*, see HATE, OPPOSITION.

propitious, *adj.* encouraging, auspicious; gracious; fortunate, prosperous, favorable; timely, opportune; thriving. See HOPE, PROSPERITY. *Ant.*, see FEAR, ADVERSITY.

proponent, *n.* advocate, supporter; defender, champion, backer. See SUPPORT.

proportion, *n.* dimension, ratio, extent; share, PART, quota, distribution, allotment; adjustment, UNIFORMITY; magnitude. See APPORTIONMENT, RELATION, SIZE, FORM. *Ant.*, see LITTLENESS, DISTORTION.

proportional, *adj.* commensurable, measurable, proportionate. See NUMBER.

proportionate, *adj.* commensurate, proportionable, proportional, according. See AGREEMENT, EQUALITY, RELATION.

proposal, *n.* OFFER, statement, recommendation, proposition, MOTION, suggestion; REQUEST; overture, advance.

propose, *v.t.* propound, advance, present, state; recommend; suggest; court, WOO; intend; proffer, nominate. See ENDEARMENT, MOTION, SUPPOSITION.

proposition, *n.* OFFER, PLAN, project, proposal, undertaking; axiom, hypothesis, theorem, postulate, problem, thesis, predication. See REASONING.

propound, *v.t.* propose, state, suggest. See SUPPOSITION.

proprietor, *n.* manager, owner; MASTER, lord. See POSSESSION.

propriety, *n.* decorum, conventionality, suitability; aptness, fitness; fastidiousness, becomingness, delicacy, seemliness; prudery. See AGREEMENT. *Ant.*, see DISAGREEMENT.

PROPULSION

Nouns—**1,** propulsion, projection; push (see IMPULSE); ejaculation; EJECTION; throw, fling, toss, shot; see ARMS.

2, propeller, driver, turbine (see POWER); shooter, archer, bowman, rifleman, marksman, pitcher; good shot, crackshot; sharpshooter.

Verbs—propel, project, throw, fling, cast, pitch, chuck, toss, jerk, heave, shy, hurl; pitch; dart, lance, tilt; jet, squirt, spurt, ejaculate; fulminate, bolt, drive, sling, pitchfork; send; send off, let off, fire off; discharge, shoot; launch, catapult, send forth; let fly; dash; put *or* set in motion; set going, start; give a start, give an impulse to; impel, expel, put to flight, send flying.

Adjectives—propelled, propelling, propulsive, projectile.

Antonym, see HINDRANCE.

---

prosaic, *adj.* unimaginative, dull, uninteresting, commonplace, prosy, plain, sober. See DULLNESS. *Ant.,* see WIT, ORNAMENT.

proscribe, *v.t.* outlaw, forbid, interdict, prohibit, condemn, excommunicate, exile, curse. See RESTRAINT. *Ant.,* see PERMISSION.

prose, *n.* WRITING, SPEECH, style; fiction, nonfiction, prose poem, ESSAY, DISSERTATION; journalese, hack work. *Colloq.,* deathless prose. See BOOK, DULLNESS.

prosecute, *v.t.* urge, pursue, follow, continue, press; arraign, sue, indict, charge. See LAWSUIT, PURSUIT.

proselyte, *n.* convert, follower, neophyte. See CHANGE.

prosody, *n.* metrics, poetics, versecraft; rhyme, rhythm, meter. See POETRY.

prospect, *n.* view, outlook, scene, landscape, vista, sight; PROMISE, probability, HOPE, EXPECTATION, foresight. See APPEARANCE, FUTURITY.

prospective, *adj.* probable, foreseen, expected; coming; imminent. See EXPECTATION, FUTURITY.

prospector, *n.* miner, gold panner, placer miner. *Colloq.,* desert rat, sourdough, forty-niner. See WEALTH, MINERAL.

prospectus, *n.* presentation, brochure; description, sketch; design, scheme. See LIST, PLAN.

PROSPERITY

Nouns—prosperity, welfare, well-being; affluence, WEALTH, SUCCESS; thrift; good fortune, blessings, luck; sunshine; fair weather, fair wind; fat years, palmy days, halcyon days; golden time, golden age; bed of roses; fat of the land, milk and honey, good times; godsend, windfall, manna from heaven. *Colloq.,* land-office business; lucky break, streak *or* run of luck, Lady Luck; boom; heyday.

Verbs—**1,** prosper, grow, multiply, thrive, flourish; be prosperous; go well, smoothly *or* swimmingly; flower, blow, burgeon, blossom, bloom, fructify, bear fruit; fatten, batten.

2, rise, rise in the world, get on in the world; climb the ladder of success; make one's way *or* fortune; feather one's nest; bear a charmed life; bask in the sunshine; have a run of luck; have good fortune; take a favorable turn; live on the fat of the land, live in clover; win out, make a strike. *Slang,* make one's pile, make a hit, strike it rich.

Adjectives—prosperous; thriving, rich, wealthy; fortunate, lucky, in luck; auspicious, propitious, providential; palmy, halcyon.

Phrases—every dog has his day; sitting on top of the world, born with a silver spoon in one's mouth, be fruitful and multiply; have money to burn.

Antonym, see ADVERSITY.

---

prostitute, *n. & v.* —*n.* whore, harlot, strumpet, courtesan, slut, tart, bawd; trollop, trull, doxy, jade; *putain,* streetwalker, lady of the evening, daughter of joy, fallen woman, kept woman, concubine, demimondaine, camp follower. *Slang*, chippy, floozy, hustler, pro, pickup, hooker, callgirl, B-girl, V-girl. —*v.t.* sell, debase, corrupt, lower, demean (oneself); pander, cater. See IMPURITY.

prostrate, *adj. & v.t.* —*adj.* recumbent, prone, flat, supine; debased, abased, humbled; helpless, powerless, resigned. —*v.t.* debase, abase, flatten; bow, submit. See IMPOTENCE, OBEDIENCE.

prosy, *adj.* prosaic, DULL, stupid, commonplace; unpoetic, uninspired, pedestrian; jejune, tedious. See WEARINESS. *Ant.*, see WIT, AMUSEMENT.

protect, *v.t.* defend, guard, shelter, shield, screen; preserve, save, champion, secure. See SAFETY. *Ant.*, see ATTACK.

protection, *n.* safeguard, DEFENSE, shelter, screen; AID, SUPPORT, PRESERVATION; championship, custody, care, guard; foil. See INFLUENCE, RESTRAINT, SECURITY. *Ant.*, see ATTACK, FREEDOM.

protégé, *n.* protégée; ward, charge; pupil, trainee. See FRIEND, AID.

protest, *n. & v.t.* —*n.* objection, complaint, remonstrance, contradiction, disapproval, expostulation, protestation. See DISSENT, DISAPPROBATION. *Ant.*, see APPROBATION, ASSENT. —*v.t.* object, remonstrate, complain, contradict, repudiate, default. See DEBT.

prototype, *n.* original; model, pattern; precedent; standard, type; archetype; module, exemplary, example, paradigm; test, copy, design; keynote, die, mold; matrix, last.

protract, *v.t.* extend, lengthen; prolong, continue; postpone, defer, delay. See CONTINUITY, LATENESS, LENGTH. *Ant.*, see END, SHORTNESS.

protrude, *v.* jut, bulge, extend, project. See CONVEXITY. *Ant.*, see CONCAVITY.

protuberance, *n.* projection, bulge, jut, protuberancy, prominence, excrescence, lump, swelling. See CONVEXITY. *Ant.*, see SMOOTHNESS.

proud, *adj.* See PRIDE.

prove, *v.t.* confirm, verify, substantiate, show, demonstrate, document, check, try, test. See EVIDENCE. *Ant.*, see NEGATION.

proverb, *n.* MAXIM, axiom, adage, precept, saying.

provided, *adv.* if, supposing, though. See CIRCUMSTANCE.

providential, *adj.* fortunate, lucky, fortuitous, timely, opportune, reasonable, auspicious. See PROSPERITY, OCCASION. *Ant.*, see ADVERSITY.

province, *n.* function, sphere; field, department, division, bailiwick, district; control; domain, jurisdiction. See BUSINESS, REGION.

provincial, *adj.* intolerant, illiberal; insular, narrow; local, rural, countrified; rustic. See NARROWNESS, MISJUDGMENT.

PROVISION

Nouns—**1,** provision, purveyance, replenishment, reinforcement, subsidy, grant (see AID); stock, STORE, fund, supply, supplies, hoard, reserve, resources (see MEANS); equipment, furnishings, accoutrements, appurtenances, outfit, apparatus, gear, trappings; rig, tackle; matériel, ARMS; grist [to the mill], FOOD, feed, fare, victuals, eatables, viands, nourishment, nutrition, provender.

2, PREPARATION, preparedness, planning, ARRANGEMENT, precaution, provident care.

3, provider, caterer, purveyor, supplier, commissary, commissariat, quartermaster, feeder, batman, victualer, grocer, merchant, steward, mancible, purser, restaurateur, sutler; breadwinner.

4, see QUALIFICATION.

Verbs—**1,** provide, furnish, supply, equip, gear, accouter; arm; provision, victual, provender, cater, purvey, forage, feed, recruit, find; stock, lay in; make good, replenish, fill (up).

2, make provision for, take measures for, prepare *or* plan for; STORE, have in store, have in reserve; keep [handy *or* at hand]; have to fall back on, save for a rainy day (see ECONOMY).

3, provide for, make *or* earn a living, support; manage.

Adjectives—provided, prepared; well-stocked, -equipped, *etc. Slang,* (well-)heeled.

Antonym, see WASTE.

---

proviso, *n.* CONDITION(s), stipulation, clause, AGREEMENT; reservation, covenant.

provisory, *adj.* provisional, conditional, dependent, subject. See CONDITION.

provocation, *n.* AGGRAVATION, irritation, vexation, annoyance, indignity, affront. See RESENTMENT. *Ant.,* see PACIFICATION.

provoke, *v.t.* annoy, irritate, exasperate, nettle; excite, anger, incite, evoke, elicit; vex. See AGGRAVATION, CAUSE, EXCITEMENT, RESENTMENT. *Ant.,* see PACIFICATION.

prow, *n.* bow, FRONT, beak, nose, stem.

prowess, *n.* COURAGE, bravery, heroism; SKILL, competence. *Ant.,* see COWARDICE, UNSKILLFULNESS.

prowl, *v.i.* ramble, wander, roam; lurk, slink, sneak; rove. See CONCEALMENT, MOTION.

proximity, *n.* NEARNESS, vicinity, propinquity, neighborhood. See PRESENCE. *Ant.,* see DISTANCE, ABSENCE.

proxy, *n.* SUBSTITUTE, AGENT, delegate, representative; AGENCY; procurator. See COMMISSION.

prude, *n.* formalist, puritan, prig. See AFFECTATION, MODESTY. *Ant.,* see IMPURITY.

prudence, *n.* discretion, carefulness, caution, circumspection, tact; policy, foresight; CARE; thoughtfulness, judiciousness. See KNOWLEDGE, REASONING. *Ant.,* see RASHNESS.

prudent, *adj.* discreet, wary, circumspect, prudential, careful, heedful, chary, cautious; wise, politic. See CARE, KNOWLEDGE. *Ant.,* see RASHNESS.

prudery, *n.* propriety; prudishness, stiffness, coyness, primness, preciousness. See AFFECTATION, MODESTY. *Ant.,* see IMPURITY.

prudish, *adj.* prim, demure, precious, affected, precise. See AFFECTATION, MODESTY.

prune, *v.t.* trim, stop, abbreviate, thin, lop. See DECREASE, AGRICULTURE.

pry, *v.* examine, search, seek, peer, ransack, peek, reconnoiter; raise, force, prize, lever. See CURIOSITY, INQUIRY, VISION.

pseudo, *adj.* spurious, counterfeit, simulated, false, fake, mock. See IMITATION, SIMILARITY.

pseudonym, *n.* sobriquet, alias, pen name, *nom de plume,* byname, nickname, epithet; disguise, incognito, John Doe, Richard Roe. See CONCEALMENT, NOMENCLATURE.

psyche, *n.* soul, pneuma, anima; self-personality, spirit, inner being, essence, essential nature, id, ego and superego; INTELLECT. See INSUBSTANTIALITY.

psychiatrist, *n.* mental doctor, (psycho)analyst *or* -therapist, alienist, psychiater. *Slang,* crazy *or* bug doctor, headshrinker, shrink. See REMEDY.

psychic, *adj. & n.* —*adj.* clairvoyant, prophetic, extrasensory, parapsychological, spiritualistic, telepathic. —*n.* teleporter, mind reader, fortuneteller, seer, spiritualist, mentalist, clairvoyant, medium. See SUPERNATURALISM, PREDICTION.

psychopath, *n.* neurotic, psychotic, madman. *Slang,* psycho. See INSANITY.

psychosis, *n.* neuropsychosis, schizophrenia, dementia praecox. See INSANITY.

psychotherapy, *n.* psychotherapeutics, psychiatry. See SANITY.

psychotic, *adj.* psychopathic, demented, deranged, lunatic, insane; paranoid, autistic, manic, phobic, hallucinatory, catatonic, hebephrenic. See INSANITY.

puberty, *n.* pubescence, adolescence, nubility, maturity. See REPRO-DUCTION.

public, *adj.* popular, common, general; civic, political, national; notorious, known, published; communal, free. See POPULACE, PUBLICATION. *Ant.,* see SECLUSION.

PUBLICATION

Nouns—**1,** publication; announcement; NEWS, intelligence, INFORMATION; promulgation, propagation, proclamation; circulation; bulletin, edition; hue and cry; banns; notification; divulgation, DISCLOSURE; publicity, notoriety, currency; *vox populi*; report; newscast, broadcast, telecast, simulcast, radio. *Colloq.,* spotlight, blurb; white glare of publicity. *Slang,* plug, write-up.

2, the press; newspaper, journal, gazette, paper; daily, weekly; BOOK, volume; magazine, review, periodical; monthly, bimonthly, *etc.*

3, advertisement; press *or* publicity release; placard, bill, broadside; poster; billboard, hoarding; circular, brochure, circular letter, [bulk] mailing; manifesto; public notice, skywriting. *Colloq.,* ad, want ad, classified ad; commercial; spot announcement; hitchhiker, cowcatcher.

4, publisher, publicist, journalist, columnist, press agent; announcer, broadcaster, newscaster, commentator, analyst.

Verbs—**1,** publish; make public, make known, publicize, advertise, circularize; AIR; voice, broach, utter; circulate, promulgate; spread abroad; disseminate; edit, get out; issue; bandy about; bruit abroad; drag into the open; raise a hue and cry; spread the word *or* the Gospel; put on the wire; wash one's dirty linen in public; make a scene; wear one's heart on one's sleeve.

2, report; proclaim, herald, blazon; trumpet forth; announce; beat the drum; shout from the housetops; advertise, post; rumor, gossip, chatter, tattle.

Adjectives—published, public, current, newsy, new, in circulation; notorious; flagrant, arrant; open; encyclical, promulgatory; broadcast.

Adverbs—publicly; in print; in the air; on the air.

Antonym, see SILENCE, CONCEALMENT.

---

publicity, *n.* notoriety, limelight; utterance, outlet, vent. See AIR, PUBLICATION.

pucker, *n. & v.* —*n.* wrinkle, crease, crinkle, ruffle, shirring. —*v.* contract; corrugate, crinkle, wrinkle, shirr, ruffle. See FOLD.

pudding, *n.* dessert, custard, junket. See FOOD.

puddle, *n.* pool, pond; mud puddle, wet spot. See WATER.

pudgy, *adj.* thickset, stocky, squat; plump, chubby, roly-poly. See FAT.

puerile, *adj.* trivial, foolish, trifling, weak, nonsensical; childish, immature, boyish, juvenile. See YOUTH, UNIMPORTANCE. *Ant.,* see AGE, IMPORTANCE.

puff, *n. & v.* —*n.* swelling; blow, breath, cloud, wind, breeze; gesture, praise. —*v.* brag, boast, praise, commend; blow, pant, gasp; inflate. See APPROBATION, BOASTING, INCREASE, VANITY.

pugilism, *n.* boxing, fisticuffs. See CONTENTION.

pugnacious, *adj.* combative, quarrelsome, militant, belligerent, contentious, bellicose. See CONTENTION, IRASCIBILITY. *Ant.,* see PACIFICATION.

pull, *n. & v.* —*n.* POWER, sway; jerk, wrench, tug; magnetism, GRAVITY, ATTRACTION, influence. —*v.* tug, wrench, haul, drag, draw; extract; row, paddle; tow. See EXTRACTION.

pulpiness, *n.* pulp; paste, dough; curd; pap; jam, pudding; poultice; SOFTNESS; mush, mushiness, squashiness, fleshiness, pastiness.

pulpit, *n.* platform, rostrum, desk; priesthood, ministry. See CLERGY, TEMPLE.

pulse, *v.i.* throb, beat, quiver, palpitate; thump; shudder, tremble; pulsate, vibrate. See OSCILLATION, AGITATION.

pulverizable, *adj.* friable, crushable, powderable, crumbly, pulverable. See POWDERINESS. *Ant.*, see HARDNESS.

pump, *v.t.* interrogate, question, catechize; inflate, puff up. See INQUIRY, WIND. *Ant.*, see CONTRACTION.

pun, *n.* wordplay, paronamasia, pundigrion, *calembour*, equivoque; quip, joke, *double entendre*; paragram. See WIT.

punch, *v.t.* strike, hit, poke, beat, knock; puncture, perforate, pierce. See IMPULSE.

punctilious, *adj.* conscientious, scrupulous; exact, precise; formal, ceremonious; severe, strict. See OSTENTATION, TRUTH. *Ant.*, see DISCOURTESY.

punctual, *adj.* prompt, regular, precise, punctilious; periodical; early; timely. See EARLINESS. *Ant.*, see LATENESS.

punctuate, *v.t.* point, interpoint, interpunctuate; accentuate; interrupt. See END, IMPORTANCE.

puncture, *n. & v.t.* —*n.* perforation, hole, pinprick, OPENING. —*v.t.* pierce, jab, perforate, prick.

pundit, *n.* wise man, sage, savant. *Slang*, know-it-all, wise guy. See SAGACITY.

PUNGENCY

Nouns—**1,** pungency, piquancy, poignancy, tang, raciness, *haut goût*, strong TASTE; SHARPNESS, keenness, acrimony, acritude, acridity, astringency, acerbity; SOURNESS, ROUGHNESS, gaminess; tartness, spiciness, HEAT, penetration, acidity, causticity. *Colloq.*, zip, nip, punch, ginger.

2, mustard, cayenne, pepper, salt, brine, mace, onion, garlic, pickle, ginger, caviar; seasoning, spice, relish, CONDIMENT, catsup, curry, vinegar, *sauce piquante*; ammonia, smelling salts, niter; nicotine, tobacco, snuff, quid, CIGARETTE, CIGAR

Verbs—be pungent, bite the tongue, sting; render pungent, flavor, season, (be)spice, salt, pepper, pickle, curry, brine, devil; smoke chew, take snuff.

Adjectives—pungent, piquant, poignant, tangy racy, sharp, keen, acrid, acerb, acrimonious, astringent, bitter; sour, rough, unsavory (see TASTE); gamy, high, strong, high-flavored, full-flavored, high-tasted; biting, stinging, mordant, caustic, pyrotic, burning, acid; odiferous (see ODOR); piercing, pricking, penetrating, stimulating, appetizing; tart, spicy, spiced, seasoned, peppery, hot [as pepper]; salt(y), saline, brackish, briny; nutty, zesty. *Colloq.*, zippy, snappy.

Antonym, see INSIPIDITY, FLATNESS.

PUNISHMENT

Nouns—**1,** punishment; chastisement, chastening; correction, castigation; discipline, infliction, trial; judgment, PENALTY; retribution; thunderbolt, Nemesis; requital, RETALIATION; penology.

2, capital punishment, execution, electrocution, hanging, gassing, firing squad, decapitation, crucifixion, lynching, stoning; imprisonment (see PRISON and RESTRAINT); torture, rack, thumbscrew, question; transportation, banishment, expulsion, exile; ostracism; Coventry; stocks, pillory; penal servitude, hard labor; solitary confinement; galleys; beating, hiding, rawhiding, flagellation, the lash, gauntlet, whipping post; rap on the knuckles, spanking, thrashing, box on the ear; blow (see IMPULSE); walking the plank, keelhauling; picket, picketing; martyrdom, *auto-da-fé*: hara kiri, tarring and feathering, riding on a rail. *Colloq.*, the chair. *Slang*, hot seat, rope necktie, necktie party, kangaroo court, Judge Lynch, Jack Ketch.

3, SCOURGE, whip, lash, *etc.*; drop, gallows, gibbet, scaffold, rope, noose, halter; block, ax; stake, cross; guillotine, electric chair, gas chamber.

Verbs—**1,** punish, chastise, chasten; castigate, correct, inflict punishment; retaliate, administer correction, deal out justice; visit upon; pay; make short work of, give short shrift, give a lesson to, serve one right, make an example of. *Colloq.*, give one his come-uppance; paddle; settle one's hash. *Slang*, give what for, give hell, make it hot for.

2, strike, hit, *etc.* (see IMPULSE).

3, execute, electrocute; behead, decapitate, guillotine; hang, gibbet, bowstring; shoot; decimate; burn at the stake; boil in oil; break on the wheel; crucify; impale flay; lynch; torture, put on the rack, picket. *Colloq.*, string up. *Slang*, burn, fry.

4, banish, exile, transport, expel, ostracize; rusticate; drum out; dismiss, disbar, disbench; strike off the roll, unfrock; post.

5, suffer punishment; take one's medicine; pay the piper *or* the price. *Slang*, take it.

Adjectives—punishing, penal, punitory, punitive; castigatory.

Antonym, see REWARD.

---

punk, *n.*, *slang*, hood, mug; henchman; kid, delinquent, snotnose (kid). See YOUTH.

puny, *adj.* small, underdeveloped, undersized, tiny; stunted. See LITTLENESS, IMPOTENCE.

pupil, *n.* student, schoolchild, schoolgirl, schoolboy; learner, tyro, SCHOLAR. *Ant.*, see TEACHING.

puppet, *n.* marionette; manikin, doll; figure, tool, cats'-paw, hireling, henchman, vassal. See AID, REPRESENTATION. *Ant.*, see AUTHORITY.

puppy, *n.* pup, whelp, cub, youngling; child, tad, *etc.* See YOUTH.

purblind, *adj.* obtuse, dull, stupid; mole-eyed. See FOLLY, DIMNESS. *Ant.*, see INTELLIGENCE, VISION.

PURCHASE

Nouns—**1,** purchase, buying, emption; purchasing power; bargain (see CHEAPNESS); instal(l)ment buying *or* plan, time purchase plan, buying on time, deferred payment, layaway plan, revolving charge plan, hire-purchase (*Brit.*); ACQUISITION, acquirement, procurement, expenditure, PAYMENT; bribery, bribe, dealing. *Colloq.*, buy. See OFFER.

2, purchaser, buyer, *emptor*, vendee; shopper, marketer, patron, employer; client, customer, consumer; trafficker; clientry, clientele, patronage. See BUSINESS.

Verbs—purchase, buy, invest in, procure, acquire; shop, market, go shopping, bargain for; rent, hire (see BORROWING); repurchase, buy in, redeem; pay (for), spend; make *or* complete a purchase; buy over *or* under the counter; be in the market for; keep in one's pay, bribe, buy off, suborn.

Adjectives—purchased; purchasable, buyable, available, obtainable; bribable, venal, commercial.

Phrase—caveat emptor.

Antonym, see SALE.

---

purgative, *n.* & *adj.* —*n.* cathartic, emetic, laxative, physic, aperient. —*adj.* purifying, cleansing; abstergent, evacuant, cathartic, expulsive, emetic, aperient, physic, laxative; restorative. See CLEANNESS, RESTORATION.

purgatory, *n.* limbo, netherworld, underworld; ATONEMENT. See HELL, PUNISHMENT.

purge, *v.t.* cleanse, clarify, purify; flush, wash, clear; atone; pardon, absolve, acquit; expiate; evacuate, remove; liquidate, kill. See ATONEMENT, CLEANNESS. *Ant.*, see UNCLEANNESS, KILLING.

puritanical, *adj.* strict, prudish, prim, severe, rigid. See AFFECTATION, SEVERITY.

PURITY

Nouns—**1,** purity; pureness, clearness, *etc.* (see *Adjectives*); CLEANNESS, SIMPLENESS, homogeneity, excellence; VIRTUE, INNOCENCE, simplicity;

honesty, integrity, TRUTH; PIETY, sanctity, idealism; MODESTY, chastity, continence, pudicity, virginity; decency, decorum, delicacy, shame.

2, refinement, purification, clarification, cleansing; defecation, depilation; filtering, filtration; sublimation, distillation; percolation, leaching, lixiviation; elutriation; strain, sieve (see SECLUSION).

3, refinery; cleanser, clarifier, defecator, *etc.*; filter, sieve, colander, strainer, screen.

4, innocent, virgin, vestal, prude; thoroughbred.

Verbs—purify, make pure, free from impurity, decrassify; clear, clarify, clean, wash, cleanse; rectify; refine, purge, defecate, depurate, expurgate, sublimate; strain, percolate, liviviate, leach; elutriate; filter, filtrate; sift, sieve, screen.

Adjectives—pure, unadulterated, unalloyed, unmixed, unpolluted, undefiled, untainted, uncorrupted; refined; genuine, real, true, simple, perfect, clear; thoroughbred; clean, immaculate, unsullied, unstained, stainless, spotless, unspoiled, unblemished, untarnished, unviolated, wholesome; innocent, guiltless, guileless, blameless, sinless, unerring; honest, incorrupt, incorruptible, upright, virtuous; modest, chaste, continent, virgin(al), vestal, lily; recent, decorous, delicate; Platonic.

Antonym, see IMPURITY, IMPROBITY.

---

purlieus, *n.pl.* neighborhood, environs, surroundings, outskirts, limits, bounds, confines. See NEARNESS. *Ant.,* see DISTANCE.

purple, *adj.* See COLOR.

purport, *n.* MEANING, significance, import, sense. *Ant.,* see ABSURDITY.

purpose, *n.* INTENTION, determination, RESOLUTION, resolve; END, aim, view. See WILL. *Ant.,* see CHANCE.

purse, *n.* handbag, reticule, pocketbook, wallet, moneybag; money, exchequer, funds. See MONEY.

PURSUIT

Nouns—**1,** pursuit; pursuing, prosecution; pursuance; enterprise, UNDERTAKING, BUSINESS; adventure, quest, INQUIRY; hue and cry; game, hobby.

2, chase, hunt, steeplechase, coursing; venery; foxhunt.

3, pursuer, hunter, huntsman, sportsman, Nimrod; hound, bloodhound.

Verbs—**1,** pursue, prosecute, follow; run, take, make *or* chase after; gun for; carry on, engage in, undertake, set about; endeavor, court, REQUEST; seek, aim at, fish for; press on.

2, chase, give chase, course, dog, hunt, hound; track down; tread *or* follow on the heels of; run down; trail, shadow, dog. *Slang,* tail.

Adjectives—pursuing, in quest of, in pursuit, in full cry, in hot pursuit; on the trail *or* scent.

Adverbs—in pursuance of; after. *Colloq.,* on the prowl.

Antonym, see AVOIDANCE.

---

purvey, *v.t.* deliver, yield, hand, give; provide, furnish, cater, PROVISION.

pus, *n.* matter, suppuration, purulence. See UNCLEANNESS.

push, *n. & v.* —*n.* nudge, thrust, shove; pressure, exigency; crisis, pinch; endeavor, effort, drive, determination, perseverance, persistence, aggressiveness. —*v.t.* drive, urge, force; propel, advance, impel; shove, encourage, hearten; prosecute. See IMPULSE, PROPULSION, PURSUIT, DIFFICULTY, EXERTION.

pushover, *n., slang,* CINCH, duck soup, setup, easy mark, sucker. See FACILITY, FOLLY.

put, *v.t.* PLACE, locate, set, deposit, plant, fix, lay; cast, throw; thrust; impose, rest, stick. See LOCATION, PROPULSION.

putative, *adj.* THOUGHT, alleged, considered, reputed, presumed. See BELIEF.

putrefy, *v.i.* rot, decay, decompose. See DECOMPOSITION.

putrid, *adj.* decomposed, decayed, rank, foul, rotten, corrupt. See UN-CLEANNESS. *Ant.,* see CLEANNESS.

putter, *v.i.* dabble, dawdle, idle, loaf, tinker. *Colloq.,* fiddle, monkey. See AMUSEMENT, ACTIVITY.

puzzle, *n. & v.t.* —*n.* riddle, conundrum, poser, enigma; mystification, perplexity, complication; dilemma, bewilderment, confusion. See SECRET, DOUBT. *Ant.,* see CERTAINTY, ANSWER. —*v.t.* confound, perplex, bewilder, confuse, mystify.

pygmy, pigmy, *n.* dwarf, midget, atomy; Lilliputian. See LITTLENESS. *Ant.,* see SIZE.

pyramid, *n.* monument, tomb; pyramidion, polyhedron; PROGRESSION, pile, accumulation, snowball. See INTERMENT, FORM.

Q

quack, *n.* charlatan, quacksalver, mountebank. See DECEPTION.

quackery, *n.* charlatanism, charlatanry. See FALSEHOOD.

quadrangle, *n.* rectangle, square, quadrilateral; yard, compound, court-(yard), INCLOSURE. *Colloq.,* quad. See ANGULARITY.

quaff, *v.t.* drink; swill, guzzle. See FOOD.

quagmire, *n.* quag, quicksand, marshland, mire, fen, morass, bog, slough; dilemma, problem, DIFFICULTY. *Colloq.,* fix, pickle. See LAND, MOISTURE.

quail, *v.i.* shrink, cower, recoil, flinch. See AVOIDANCE, FEAR.

quaint, *adj.* pleasingly odd, old-fashioned, picturesque. See UNCONFORMITY.

quake, *v.i.* tremble, quiver, shake, shudder. See AGITATION, EXCITEMENT.

QUALIFICATION

Nouns—**1,** qualification, limitation, modification, restriction, coloring, leavening; allowance, consideration, extenuating circumstances; condition, proviso, PROVISION, exception; prerequisite, EXEMPTION; stipulation, specification, saving clause.
2, see ABILITY, REPUTE, SKILL.

Verbs—qualify, LIMIT, modify, leaven, allow for, make allowance for, discount.

Adjectives—qualifying, conditional, provisional; restrictive, contingent.

Adverbs—conditionally, admitting, admittedly, provided, if, unless, but, yet; according as; supposing; with the understanding, even, although, though, for all that, after all, at all events; with a grain of salt; wind and weather permitting; if possible; subject to; with this proviso.

quality, *n.* attribute, property; excellence; trait, characteristic; status, brand, grade; NOBILITY, gentility.

qualm, *n.* twinge, pang, throe; misgiving, uneasiness; remorse. See PAIN, FEAR, PENITENCE.

quandary, *n.* dilemma, plight, perplexity, bewilderment. See DOUBT.

QUANTITY

Nouns—**1,** quantity, magnitude, SIZE, amplitude, extent, DEGREE, volume, GREATNESS; numbers, STRENGTH; amount, CONTENT, mass, bulk, weight, sum, SUBSTANCE, aggregate; measure, MEASUREMENT, dimensions, LENGTH, duration, extension; number, quantifier; MULTITUDE, mathematics.
2, portion, share, quota, quantum, proportion; handful, armful,

pocketful, mouthful, spoonful, *etc.*; batch, lot, dose, dole, stock, supply, STORE; some(what), aught, any.

Verbs—quantify, measure (see MEASUREMENT).

Adjectives—quantitative, quantitive, numerical, metrical; counted, weighed, figured, calculated, estimated; measurable, weighable, estimable; in bulk, mass *or* quantity; some, any, more, less.

---

quantum, *n.* QUANTITY, amount; SUBSTANCE, mass; particle, photon, phonon, magneton, light quantum, ENERGY. See PHYSICS.

quarantine, *n. & v.* —*n.* detention, detainment, RESTRAINT, confinement, SECLUSION, segregation, sequestration, isolation; *cordon sanitaire.* —*v.t.* detain, segregate, separate, isolate, sequester. See PROHIBITION, INQUIRY.

quarrel, *n. & v.i.* —*n.* altercation, wrangle, squabble; dispute, controversy, feud. *Colloq.,* spat. See DISCORD, ARMS. —*v.i.* dispute, disagree, wrangle, squabble; find fault.

quarrelsome, *adj.* contentious, disputatious, pugnacious, combative. See IRASCIBILITY, CONTENTION.

quarry, *n.* prey, game; catch, bag, take; target, PURSUIT; stonepit, lode, bed, mine, pit; STORE, source. See MINERAL, LAND.

quarter, *n. & v.i.* —*n.* one-fourth; three-month period; 25 cents; district, REGION, DIRECTION; lodging, billet; mercy. *Colloq.,* two bits. See NUMERATION, SIDE, PITY. —*v.t.* quadrisect; divide, cut up; billet, station. See LOCATION.

quarters, *n.* ABODE, lodgings, residence; billet, barracks.

quash, *v.t.* suppress, subdue, crush; set aside, nullify, annul, void. See NULLIFICATION.

quasi, *adj. & adv.* —*adj.* apparent, seeming, so-called, pseudo, IMITATION, near, approximate. —*adv.* almost, in a sense, nearly, not quite; as though, as if, as it were, so to speak. See APPEARANCE, FALSENESS.

quaver, *v.i.* quiver, shake, tremble; tremolo, warble, trill. See OSCILLATION, MUSIC.

quay, *n.* wharf, dock, pier, mole, levee. See EDGE.

queasy, *adj.* nauseous; squeamish, uneasy; timid, fearful, apprehensive; finicky, skittish; risky, precarious. *Slang,* jittery. See DISEASE, FEAR, DANGER.

queen, *n.* woman ruler, mistress; king's wife, king's widow; belle. See AUTHORITY, NOBILITY.

queer, *adj.* odd, singular, strange; giddy, faint. *Colloq.,* deranged. *Slang,* shady, counterfeit. See UNCONFORMITY.

quell, *v.t.* subdue, suppress, crush; quiet, allay. See REPOSE, SUBJECTION.

quench, *v.t.* put out, snuff out, extinguish; damp, chill; slake, sate, satisfy. See DESTRUCTION.

querulous, *adj.* whining, complaining, fretful, petulant, peevish; finicky. See LAMENTATION.

query, *n.* INQUIRY, question, DOUBT.

quest, *n.* search, PURSUIT; probe, investigation, INQUIRY; adventure, mission, expedition; aim, goal, objective, DESIRE.

question, *n. & v.t.* —*n.* problem, subject; query, interrogation; DOUBT, dispute. See INQUIRY. —*v.t.* interrogate, examine, cross-examine, quiz, dispute, challenge, DOUBT.

questionnaire, *n.* FORM, examination, interrogation, INQUIRY, survey, canvass, poll.

queue, *n. & v.* —*n.* cue, pigtail; line(up), file, rank. See ROUGHNESS, SEQUENCE. —*v.i.* line *or* queue up, form a line, fall in, wait. See ASSEMBLAGE.

quibble, *n.* evasion, EQUIVOCATION, sophism, cavil.

quick, *adj.* rapid, swift, fleet; brief; prompt, alert; ready, unhesitating; hasty, irascible; sensitive, keen; alive, living, sentient. See VELOCITY, ACTIVITY, FEELING, IRASCIBILITY. *Ant.,* see SLOWNESS, INACTIVITY.

quicken, *v.t.* revive, refresh, arouse, animate; hasten, speed, accelerate. See VELOCITY, RESTORATION. *Ant.,* see SLOWNESS.

quicksand, *n.* quagmire, mire, morass, bog, slough. See LAND, MOISTURE.

quick-tempered, *adj.* impetuous, hotheaded, irascible, hot, peppery. See EXCITEMENT, IRASCIBILITY.

quiddity, *n.* essence, quintessence, SUBSTANCE, kernel, pith; EQUIVOCATION, quibble, hairsplitting. See INTRINSIC.

quiescent, *adj.* still; motionless, moveless; fixed; stationary; stagnant; becalmed, quiet; tranquil, unmoved, undisturbed, unruffled; calm, restful; sleeping, silent. See INACTIVITY. *Ant.,* see MOTION, ACTIVITY, AGITATION.

quiet, *adj. & n.* —*adj.* peaceful, tranquil, serene; hushed, silent; modest, restrained; gentle, calm; unostentatious. See MODERATION, SILENCE, REPOSE. —*n.* peacefulness, calm; SILENCE, hush. *Ant.,* see AGITATION, LOUDNESS.

quill, *n.* feather; plume; pen; spine, bristle, seta, barb, spike, needle. See ROUGHNESS, SHARPNESS.

quilt, *n.* bedspread, counterpane, coverlet, patchquilt, comforter, goosedown, quilting. See COVERING.

quip, *n.* joke, witticism, retort, repartee. *Slang,* (wise)crack. See WIT, LEVITY.

quirk, *n.* flourish; quip, taunt, jibe; quibble, evasion; peculiarity, trick, eccentricity. See WIT, INSANITY.

quit, *v.* satisfy, requite; resign, abandon, relinquish; leave; cease, stop, desist. See PAYMENT, RELINQUISHMENT, END.

quite, *adv.* entirely, utterly, wholly; really, actually. *Colloq.,* rather, somewhat, very. See COMPLETION.

quittance, *n.* ACQUITTAL, FREEDOM; quitclaim, RELINQUISHMENT; RETALIATION, VINDICATION, ATONEMENT, PAYMENT.

quitter, *n.* shirker, evader, avoider. *Slang,* slacker, welsher. See AVOIDANCE.

quiver, *v.i.* tremble, shudder, shiver, flutter, vibrate, shake, quaver. See AGITATION.

quixotic, *adj.* visionary, unrealistic, whimsical; foolish, crazy. See ABSURDITY, RASHNESS, FOLLY.

quiz, *v.t.* interrogate, question, examine; tease, banter. See INQUIRY.

quorum, *n.* plenum, showing, SUFFICIENCY, majority; minyan; ASSEMBLAGE.

quota, *n.* allotment, share, proportion, percentage. See APPORTIONMENT.

quotation, *n.* citation, excerpt, REPETITION; PRICE. See EVIDENCE.

quote, *v.t.* repeat, cite, instance, refer to, abstract. See EVIDENCE.

R

rabbi, *n.* MASTER, teacher; rabbin, rabbinist. See CLERGY.

rabble, *n.* crowd, proletariat, POPULACE, common herd, *hoi polloi*; mob, *canaille,* riffraff, scum.

rabid, *adj.* mad, furious; fanatical, overzealous. See FEELING, EXCITEMENT.

rabies, *n.* hydrophobia, lyssa; foaming at the mouth. See DISEASE, INSANITY.

race, *n. & v.* —*n.* onrush, advance; competition; sprint, dash, speed contest; STREAM; channel, millrace, tide, RIVER; career; family, clan, tribe; people, ethnic group. See RELATION, VELOCITY. —*v.* run swiftly, career; hasten; compete; speed, drive fast. See VELOCITY.

racial, *adj.* tribal, family; hereditary, ancestral. See RELATION, ANCESTRY.

racism, *n.* prejudice, bigotry; segregation, color line, apartheid; white *or* black supremacy, black nationalism; genocide. *Colloq.,* Jim Crow.

rack, *v.t.* strain, exert; torture, distress, torment, agonize. See THOUGHT, PAIN.

racket, *n.* uproar, din, clatter, hubbub; frolic, carouse, rumpus. *Slang,* pursuit, activity, criminal activity. See LOUDNESS, DISORDER, BADNESS, EVIL.

racketeer, *n.* mobster, gangster, hoodlum. *Colloq.,* crook. See ILLEGALITY, EVIL.

racy, *adj.* spirited, lively; piquant; risqué, suggestive. See VIGOR, PUNGENCY, FEELING. *Ant.,* see PURITY.

radiant, *adj.* shining, sparkling, glowing; splendid, resplendent, glorious. See LIGHT, BEAUTY.

radiate, *v.* emit, scatter, diffuse, spread, dispense, shine, glare, beam, glow. See LIGHT, DISPERSION, DIFFUSION.

radiation, *n.* DISPERSION, DIFFUSION, emission, emanation; radiance, illumination. See LIGHT.

radical, *adj. & n.* —*adj.* fundamental, INTRINSIC; extreme, drastic, thorough; sweeping, revolutionary. —*n.* liberal, leftist, left-winger (see LEFT); reformer, rebel, revolutionary; anarchist, nihilist, Communist, Bolshevik. *Colloq.,* red, pink, parlor pink, fellow-traveler. *Slang,* Commie, pinko. See COMPLETION, REVOLUTION.

radio, *n.* wireless, radio telegraphy, radio telephony; radiogram. See COMMUNICATION.

radius, *n.* half-diameter; spoke; range, scope, sphere, LENGTH. See CIRCULARITY.

raffle, *n.* drawing, door prize, lottery, sweepstake(s). See CHANCE.

raft, *n.* flatboat, barge, float, pontoon. See SHIP.

rafter, *n.* beam, timber, crosspiece, joist. See SUPPORT.

rag, *n. & v.* —*n.* shred, tatter, scrap, remnant; (*pl.*) castoffs, hand-me-downs. See OLDNESS, MATERIALS, CLOTHING. —*v.,* slang, tease, rib, kid, RIDICULE.

rage, *n. & v.i.* —*n.* fury, frenzy, wrath, violence; fashion, fad, craze. See INSANITY. —*v.i.* storm, rave, bluster. See EXCITEMENT.

ragged, *adj.* tattered, frayed, shabby, seedy, worn; in shreds; in patches; patched, torn, rough; tatterdemalion, ragamuffin; dogeared. See DETERIORATION. *Ant.,* see TASTE.

raid, *n. & v.t.* —*n.* ATTACK, invasion, onset, incursion; foray. See STEALING. —*v.t.* ATTACK, invade; pounce upon.

rail, *v.* rant, scold, chide; inveigh, carry on, harangue. See DISAPPROBATION.

railing, *n.* fence, barrier, balustrade. See INCLOSURE.

raillery, *n.* banter, badinage, persiflage, quizzing. *Slang,* kidding, ribbing. See RIDICULE.

railroad, *n. & v.* —*n.* railway; main *or* trunk line, spur; model railroad; tramline, tramway, trolley *or* streetcar line, street railway, subway. —*v.,* colloq., rush *or* push through, expedite. *Slang,* frame, jail. See INJUSTICE.

raiment, *n.* CLOTHING, apparel, attire, vesture, garb.

rain, *n. & v.* —*n.* shower, precipitation, rainstorm, downpour. —*v.* shower, pour, drizzle; bestow, lavish, shower upon. See GIVING, WATER.

raincoat, *n.* slicker, oilskin, poncho, mackintosh, trenchcoat, rainproof, plastic raincoat. See CLOTHING, COVERING.

raise, *v.t.* lift, elevate; rouse, arouse, stir up, incite; resurrect; erect, build, exalt, honor; INCREASE; cultivate, breed. See ELEVATION, DOMESTICATION, AGRICULTURE, EXCITEMENT, IMPROVEMENT.

rake, *v.t. & n.* —*v.t.* gather, collect; comb, ransack, search, rummage; enfilade, spray with bullets. See ASSEMBLAGE, INQUIRY. —*n.* LIBERTINE, roué, rakehell.

rakeoff, *n.,* slang, rebate, refund, PAYMENT, return, kickback, payoff; payola, share, cut, percentage; bribe; extortion.

rally, *v.t.* muster, marshal; call together; revive, restore, rouse, encourage; banter, chaff. See ARRANGEMENT, COURAGE.

ram, *v.t.* butt, batter, bump; pound, drive, tamp; cram, stuff. See INSERTION.

ramble, *v.i.* stroll, saunter, stray, wander; digress, maunder. See TRAVEL, LOQUACITY, DEVIATION.

rambunctious, *adj., colloq.,* boisterous, pugnacious, quarrelsome. See VIOLENCE.

ramification, *n.* divergence, division, branching; PART, offshoot, spur. See DISJUNCTION.

ramp, *n.* incline, slant, slope, OBLIQUITY, inclined way; runway, PASSAGE.

rampage, *v. & n.* —*v.i.* ramp, rage, go berserk, run amuck, go crazy. —*n.* tantrum, VIOLENCE, disturbance, frenzy, turmoil. See IRASCIBILITY.

rampant, *adj.* rife, widespread, raging, epidemic; luxurious, lush; wild, unrestrained, unchecked; turbulent, tempestuous. See GENERALITY, VIOLENCE.

rampart, *n.* parapet, fortification, wall, bulwark, embankment. See DEFENSE.

ramrod, *n.* rammer, ram, stick, rod, poker, iron. See HARDNESS.

ramshackle, *adj.* dilapidated, tumbledown, rickety. See DETERIORATION.

ranch, *n.* range, farm, grange. See LAND, ABODE.

rancid, *adj.* rank, stale, putrid, malodorous, frowzy. See DETERIORATION. *Ant.,* see SWEETNESS, NEWNESS.

rancor, *n.* spite, malice, bitterness, vengefulness, vindictiveness, MALEVOLENCE, HATE, hatred. See IRASCIBILITY, RETALIATION.

random, *adj.* haphazard, casual, CHANCE, fortuitous, aimless.

range, *n.* row, series, chain; scope, extent; habitat; LIMIT, span, latitude; compass, register; DISTANCE; STOVE. See CONTINUITY, SPACE.

rank, *adj. & n.* —*adj.* lush, luxuriant, vigorous; coarse; malodorous, fetid, rancid, offensive; arrant, extreme, gross. —*n.* row, line; position, caste, quality; status, grade, standing, footing. See REPUTE.

rankle, *v.i.* fester, irritate, gall, pain. See PAIN.

ransack, *v.t.* rummage, scour, search diligently; rifle, loot, pillage. See INQUIRY, STEALING.

ransom, *v. & n.* —*v.t.* redeem, liberate, rescue. —*n.* redemption, release, liberation, rescue. See FREEDOM. *Ant.,* kidnap, TAKE.

rant, *v.i.* rage, rave, scold, nag; harangue. See IRASCIBILITY.

rap, *v.t.* tap, knock, blow, cuff, box, clout. *Slang,* swat, sock, criticize. See IMPULSE, DISAPPROBATION.

rapacity, *n.* greed, cupidity, extortion, ravenousness, voracity. See DESIRE, GLUTTONY.

rape, *v.t.* seize, plunder; seduce, debauch, ravish. See IMPURITY.

rapid, *adj. & n.* —*adj.* swift, speedy, fleet, prompt, quick. See VELOCITY. *Ant.,* see SLOWNESS. —*n.pl.* white water, chute, shoot. See WATER.

rapport, *n.* TOUCH, sympathy, understanding, COMMUNICATION; affinity, empathy, compatibility, seeing eye to eye, being in tune (with). See AGREEMENT.

rapt, *adj.* ecstatic, enraptured, transported; absorbed, engrossed. See PLEASURE, ATTENTION, THOUGHT.

rapture, *n.* ecstasy, transport, bliss, joy, delight. See PLEASURE.

rare, *adj.* scarce, unusual; tenuous (see RARITY); underdone, half-done, half-cooked, raw.

RARITY

Nouns—**1,** rarity, tenuity, subtlety, thinness, lightness, compressibility; rarefaction, attenuation, dilatation, inflation.

2, rareness, scarcity, uncommonness, INFREQUENCY; collector's item.

Verbs—rarefy, expand, dilate, attenuate, thin out.

Adjectives—**1,** rare, subtle, thin, fine, tenuous, compressible, slight, light, ethereal; rarefied, unsubstantial.

2, scarce, unusual, infrequent, uncommon, few; odd, curious, singular.

Adverbs—rarely, infrequently, *etc.*; seldom, once in a great while, once in a blue moon, by the skin of one's teeth.

Antonym, see DENSITY, FREQUENCY, MULTITUDE.

rascal, *n.* scoundrel, knave, rogue, reprobate, blackguard; imp, scamp. See EVILDOER. *Ant.*, see GOODNESS.

rascality, *n.* knavery, villainy, roguery, blackguardism. See IMPROBITY. *Ant.*, see PROBITY.

RASHNESS

Nouns—**1,** rashness, temerity, incautiousness, imprudence, indiscretion, recklessness, overconfidence, audacity, precipitancy, precipitation, impetuosity, foolhardiness, heedlessness, thoughtlessness, desperation, Quixotism; gaming, gambling, blind bargain, leap in the dark, fool's paradise.

2, desperado, hotspur, madcap, daredevil, fire-eater, bully, bravo, scapegrace, Don Quixote, adventurer; gambler, gamester; stunter, stuntman; speeder. *Slang*, speed demon.

Verbs—be rash, stick at nothing, play a desperate game, play with fire, walk on thin ice, go out of one's depth, take a leap in the dark, buy a pig in a poke, tempt Providence, clutch at straws, lean on a broken reed; run the ga(u)ntlet; dare, risk, hazard, gamble. *Slang*, take a flyer.

Adjectives—rash, daring, incautious, indiscreet, imprudent, improvident, temerarious, heedless, careless, reckless, giddy, wild; madcap, desperate, devil-may-care, hot-blooded, hotheaded, headlong, headstrong, breakneck; foolhardy, harebrained, precipitate, overconfident, adventurous, venturesome, Quixotic, free-and-easy; risky, hazardous.

Adverbs—rashly, recklessly, *etc.*; hotfoot, headlong, posthaste, head-over-heels, headforemost.

Antonym, see CARE, CAUTION, SAFETY.

rasp, *v. & n.* —*v.* scrape, file, grate; chafe, nag, worry, abrade. See FRICTION. —*n.* file, scraper, rasper, abrasive; hoarseness, huskiness. See ROUGHNESS.

rat, *n. & v.* —*n.*, *colloq.*, sneak, polecat, skunk; traitor, turncoat, renegade; welsher, liar, informer, nark. See IMPROBITY, EVIL. —*v.i.*, *slang*, betray, squeal, inform, spill the beans; desert, bolt, sell out. See IMPROBITY.

rate, *n.* ratio, percent; DEGREE; proportion, rank, class; PRICE, value; VELOCITY.

rather, *adv.* somewhat, passably, preferably, more correctly, sooner. See LITTLENESS, CHOICE.

ratification, *n.* confirmation, validation, approval, sanction; indorsement, authentication, corroboration. See EVIDENCE, ASSENT. *Ant.*, see DISAPPROBATION.

ratify, *v.t.* approve, confirm, validate; indorse, verify. *Slang*, O.K. See EVIDENCE, ASSENT. *Ant.*, see DISAPPROBATION.

ratio, *n.* proportion, rate, percentage, relative value. See RELATION.

ration, *v.t.* apportion, allocate, allot, dole out; limit, restrict, withhold. See APPORTIONMENT.

rational, *adj.* sound, sane, logical, sensible, reasonable. See REASONING, INTELLIGENCE.

rationale, *n.* theory, explanation, *raison d'être*, justification, VINDICATION; REASONING, INTENTION; METHOD, philosophy, principle.

rattle, *v.* clatter, chatter, clack; babble, prattle, gabble, jabber; fluster, befuddle, upset. See ABSURDITY.

raucous, *adj.* harsh, grating, rasping, hoarse, strident. See LOUDNESS.

ravage, *v.t.* lay waste, pillage, plunder, sack, devastate, destroy. See DESTRUCTION.

rave, *v.i.* bluster, storm, rant, tear; ramble, wander. See EXCITEMENT, INSANITY.

ravel, *v.* entangle, involve; unravel, untangle, disentangle, separate. See ARRANGEMENT, ORDER.

ravenous, *adj.* rapacious, hungry, greedy, voracious, gluttonous. See DESIRE, GLUTTONY.

ravine, *n.* gorge, gulf, canyon, cañon, gully, gap, notch.

ravish, *v.t.* CHARM, captivate, fascinate, enchant, enthrall; deflower, rape, violate. See VIOLENCE.

raw, *adj.* crude; unprepared, uncooked; undisciplined, unexperienced; skinned, scraped, abraded; bleak, piercing; unpolished, boorish. See COLD, UNSKILLFULNESS, VULGARITY.

ray, *n.* skate; beam, gleam, radiation. See ANIMAL, LIGHT.

raze, *v.t.* demolish, level, tear down, obliterate. See DESTRUCTION.

razz, *v.,* slang, RIDICULE, heckle, scoff (at), jeer (at).

reach, *v. & n.* —*v.* TOUCH, attain, gain, get to, arrive at, pass, INFLUENCE; stretch, extend. See EQUALITY, DISTANCE, TRANSPORTATION. —*n.* stretch, span, range, expanse, scope. See DISTANCE, FREEDOM.

reaction, *n.* response, revulsion, reflex, RECOIL. See OPPOSITION.

reactionary, *n.* conservative, recalcitrant, Tory, [John] Bircher, standpatter, diehard; fogy. See STABILITY.

read, *v.* peruse, con; interpret, decipher, predict; pronounce; study; teach, admonish. See INTERPRETATION.

reader, *n.* peruser; critic; elocutionist; proofreader; lecturer, prelector; textbook. See PRINTING, TEACHING, SPEECH, BOOK.

ready, *adj.* prepared, available, handy; prompt, quick; apt, ingenious; alert; ripe. See UTILITY, PREPARATION, ACTIVITY, SKILL.

readymade, *adj.* ready-to-wear; prefabricated, ready-built; oven-ready, instant, precooked; unoriginal, cut and dried, derivative. See PREPARATION, IMITATION.

real, *adj.* actual, veritable, true, genuine; certain, sure, authentic; fixed. See EXISTENCE, TRUTH. *Ant.,* see FALSEHOOD, IMAGINATION.

realism, *n.* actuality, naturalism, genre, verity. See TRUTH, PAINTING. *Ant.,* see FALSEHOOD.

realistic, *adj.* lifelike, faithful, graphic. See DESCRIPTION.

reality, *n.* TRUTH, actuality, verity, factuality, fact. See EXISTENCE.

realize, *v.t.* comprehend, appreciate, understand; objectify, imagine; gain, net; produce, bring in; fulfill, attain. See KNOWLEDGE, COMPLETION, ACQUISITION, SALE.

really, *adv.* surely, indeed, truly, honestly, certainly, positively, absolutely; very, emphatically; genuinely, actually. See AFFIRMATION.

realm, *n.* kingdom, empire, domain; sphere, bailiwick, province; LAND, REGION.

realty, *n.* real estate, landed property. See PROPERTY.

reap, *v.t.* mow, cut, gather, harvest; acquire. See AGRICULTURE, ACQUISITION.

reappearance, *n.* reincarnation, revival; rebirth, resurgence, return, comeback; rerun, reprint. See APPEARANCE.

rear, *v.* erect, construct, establish; raise, elevate; foster, nurture, bring up; breed. See ELEVATION, DOMESTICATION, TEACHING.

REAR

Nouns—**1,** rear, back, posteriority; rear guard; background, hinterland, back door; postern; rumble seat; reverse; END. *Slang,* backdoor.

2, nape, chine, heels, tail, tail end, rump, croup, buttocks, posterior, backside; breech, loin, dorsal region, lumbar region, hindquarters; bottom, *derrière.*

3, stern, poop, afterpart, heelpiece, crupper, tail; wake, train; straggler.

Verbs—be behind, fall astern, bend backwards, straggle, bring up the rear; follow, need; END, tail off; back, back up, reverse.

Adjectives—back, rear, hind, hindmost, hindermost, postern, dorsal, after, caudal, lumbar, posterior, aftermost, aft.

Adverbs—behind, in the rear, in the background, behind one's back, back to back, backward, rearward; after, aft, abaft, astern, aback.

Antonym, see FRONT.

---

reason, *n.* SANITY, INTELLECT, common sense, JUDGMENT, explanation; ground, CAUSE. See INTELLIGENCE. *Ant.*, see INSANITY.

reasonable, *adj.* sound, sensible; fair, moderate; rational, logical. See REASONING, INTELLIGENCE, KNOWLEDGE, CHEAPNESS. *Ant.*, see INSANITY.

REASONING

Nouns—**1,** reasoning, ratiocination, rationalism, deduction, dialectics, induction, generalization, logic, synthesis, analysis, rationalization.

2, debate, polemics, CONTENTION; discussion, INQUIRY; dissertation, exposition, explanation.

3, argument, case, proposition, terms, premise, postulate, data, principle, inference, syllogism, hypothesis; induction, deduction.

4, reasoner, logician, dialectician, disputant, controversialist, wrangler, arguer, debater, polemicist, polemist, casuist, rationalist, rationalizer.

Verbs—reason, deduce, induce, infer; argue, discuss, debate, dispute, wrangle; philosophize, consider.

Adjectives—**1,** reasoning, thinking, sapient; rationalistic; argumentative, controversial, dialectic, polemical, discursive; disputatious.

2, logical, relevant, rational; inductive, deductive, syllogistic; *a priori, a posteriori.*

Adverbs—for, because, hence, seeing that, since, so, inasmuch as, whereas, in consideration of; therefore, consequently, ergo, accordingly, *a fortiori*; Q.E.D., *reductio ad absurdum.*

Antonym, see INTUITION.

---

reassure, *v.* comfort, placate, set at rest, CONTENT; encourage. See COURAGE.

rebate, *n.* DISCOUNT, refund, repayment, DEDUCTION.

rebel, *v.i.* revolt, resist, mutiny, rise up. See DISOBEDIENCE.

rebellion, *n.* revolt, uprising, insurrection, insurgence, mutiny, sedition, revolution. See DISOBEDIENCE.

rebirth, *n.* resurrection, reincarnation, renascence, renaissance, revival; resurgence, upsurge; SALVATION, redemption; new life. See LIFE, ACTIVITY.

rebound, *v.i.* bounce, ricochet, react, bound back, RECOIL.

rebuff, *n. & v.* —*n.* snub, slight, cut; repulse, rout, check. See CONTEMPT, FAILURE. —*v.t.* repel, repulse; snub, cut, slight. *Slang,* high-hat, cold-shoulder.

rebuild, *v.t.* recreate, refashion, reform, restore. See RESTORATION.

rebuke, *n. & v.* —*n.* reproof, reprimand, admonition. See DISAPPROBATION. —*v.t.* reprove, reprimand, chide, admonish, upbraid. See DISAPPROBATION.

rebus, *n.* picture puzzle, hieroglyphic, pictograph *or* -gram; charade. See SECRET.

rebut, *v.t.* ANSWER, contradict, oppose, refute. See NEGATION.

rebuttal, *n.* refutation, rejoinder, retort, ANSWER, DEFENSE; counterstatement, NEGATION, disclaimer. *Colloq.,* clincher, crusher, the perfect squelch.

recalcitrant, *adj.* refractory, stubborn, difficult, intractable; balky, mulish. *Colloq.,* cussed, cantankerous. See DISOBEDIENCE, OBSTINACY, RESISTANCE.

recall, *v.t.* recollect, remember; revoke, annul, withdraw; retract; revive, restore. See MEMORY, NULLIFICATION, CHANGEABLENESS.

recant, *v.t.* withdraw, take back, renounce, retract, disavow, repudiate. See CHANGEABLENESS, NULLIFICATION.

recapitulate, *v.t.* summarize, restate, review, rehearse. *Colloq.*, recap. See REPETITION, DESCRIPTION.

recast, *v.t.* recompose, reconstruct, refashion; remold; recompute. See REVOLUTION.

recede, *v.i.* retrograde, retrogress, retrocede; go, retire, withdraw; shrink, ebb, wane; move away, drift away, move off, sheer off, fall back, depart, retreat, run away. See REGRESSION. *Ant.*, see PROGRESSION.

receipt, *n.* recipiency, reception, RECEIVING; share, receipts; income, revenue; proceeds, return, net profits, earnings; rent; remuneration, wages, stipend, salary, emolument, pay, fee, commission; pension, annuity, alimony, allowance; allotment. *Slang*, split, take, gate. See PAYMENT, ACQUISITION. *Ant.*, see GIVING.

RECEIVING

Nouns—**1,** receiving, reception, receipt, recipiency, acquisition, acceptance, admission; absorbency, absorption.

2, receiver, recipient, assignee, devisee, heir, legatee, grantee, donee, lessee, beneficiary, pensioner.

3, receipts, income, revenue, intake, proceeds, return, yield, earnings, dividends; box office; salary, remuneration (see PAYMENT); rent; pension; alimony, allowance. *Slang*, split, take, gate.

Verbs—**1,** receive, take, get, acquire, obtain, take in, catch, pocket, put into one's pocket; accept, admit, take off one's hands; absorb, inspire, suck.

2, be received, come in, come to hand, go into one's pocket, fall to one's lot, accrue; yield, pay, return, bear.

Adjectives—receiving, recipient, receptive, pensionary; absorbent.

Antonym, see GIVING.

---

recent, *adj.* late, new, fresh, modern. See NEWNESS. *Ant.*, see OLDNESS.

RECEPTACLE

Nouns—**1,** receptacle, recipient, receiver; compartment, cell, follicle, hole, corner, niche, recess, nook, crypt, booth, stall, pigeonhole, cubbyhole, cove.

2, capsule, vesicle, cyst, pod, calyx, utricle, arc.

3, stomach, paunch, ventricle, crop, craw, maw, gizzard, mouth, gullet.

4, pocket, pouch, fob, sheath, scabbard, socket, bag, sack, purse, wallet, scrip, poke, knapsack, haversack, briefcase, valise, suitcase, handbag, portmanteau, satchel, etui, reticule, quiver. *Slang*, kick.

5, chest, box, coffer, caddy, case, casket, caisson, trunk, bandbox, cage, manger, rack.

6, vessel, bushel, barrel, canister, basket, pannier, hopper, creel, crate, cradle, bassinet, hamper, tray, hod, scuttle, utensil, CARRIER.

7, vat, ca(u)ldron, tank, cistern; cask, puncheon, keg, tun, butt; firkin; carboy, amphora; bottle, jar, decanter, ewer, cruse, vase, carafe, crock, flagon, magnum, demijohn, flask, stoup, jigger, noggin; vial, phial, flacon; cruet; urn, tub, bucket, pail; pot, pan, tankard, jug, pitcher, mug; retort, alembic, test tube; tin, can, kettle, bowl, basin, punchbowl, cup, goblet, chalice, tumbler, glass; saucepan, skillet, tureen; vacuum bottle *or* jug.

8, plate, platter, dish, trencher, porringer, saucer, crucible.

9, shovel, trowel, spoon, spatula, ladle, dipper, scoop.

10, closet, commode, cupboard, cellaret, locker, chiffonier, bin, bunker, buffet, press, safe, sideboard, desk, bureau, secretary, till, bookcase, cabinet.

11, chamber, apartment, room, cabin, office, court, hall; suite, flat, salon, parlor; dining, living, waiting, sitting, *or* drawing room; antechamber; stateroom; gallery, pew, box; boudoir, sanctum, bedroom, dormitory,

refectory, playroom, nursery, schoolroom, library, study, studio; bathroom, lavatory, smoking room, den, lounge; rumpus room.
12, attic, loft, garret; cellar, basement, vault, hold, cockpit; kitchen, pantry, scullery; storeroom; dairy; laundry, bathroom, lavatory, outhouse; penthouse; lean-to, garage, hangar, shed, toolhouse, roundhouse.
13, portico, porch, veranda, lobby, court, hall, vestibule, foyer, corridor, PASSAGE.
14, conservatory, greenhouse, summerhouse, hothouse, alcove, grotto, hermitage.

reception, *n.* admission, admittance, entrée, entrance; importation; introduction, taking; party, affair. See RECEIVING. *Ant.,* see EJECTION, EXCLUSION.
recess, *n.* alcove, niche, nook, bay; intermission, pause, interim, rest, break, breathing spell, coffee *or* lunch break. See END, RESTORATION, RECEPTACLE, CONCAVITY.

RECESSION

Nouns—recession, retirement, withdrawal, retrocession, retrogression, retrogradation, retroaction, DEPARTURE, retreat, flight; REGRESSION, regress, RECOIL; DEPRESSION, temporary setback, hard times, decline, shakeout; bear market. *Colloq.,* slump. See ADVERSITY.
Verbs—recede, retrocede, retrogress, retrograde, retroact, regress, retire, withdraw; go, go back; move back, away, from *or* off, sheer off, avoid; shrink, ebb, wane; drift *or* fade away, stand aside; fall back, RECOIL, depart, retreat, run away, flee; decline. *Colloq.,* slump.
Adjectives—recessive, receding, recedent, regressive, retrogressive.
Antonym, see APPROACH, PROGRESSION.

recherché, *adj.* uncommon, out of the ordinary, rare; esoteric, obscure; elegant, CHOICE, refined. See UNCONFORMITY, RARITY, ELEGANCE.
recipe, *n.* receipt, formula, instructions, directions, method, prescription, ingredients. See FOOD.
recipient, *n.* receiver, donee, beneficiary, devisee, legatee, heir, pensioner. See RECEIVING.
reciprocal, *adj.* mutual, complementary, interchangeable, alternative, correlative. See RELATION, OSCILLATION, INTERCHANGE.
reciprocation, *n.* repayment, INTERCHANGE, exchange, reciprocity, alternation. See RELATION, OSCILLATION.
recital, *n.* telling, narration, rehearsal; account, recapitulation; concert, musicale. See REPETITION, SPEECH, MUSIC.
recitation, *n.* declamation, elocution, recital, lesson. See SPEECH, TEACHING.
recite, *v.* rehearse, relate, repeat, declaim, detail, recapitulate. See NUMERATION, SPEECH, DESCRIPTION.
reckless, *adj.* careless, foolhardy, incautious, heedless, rash, devil-may-care. See RASHNESS, NEGLECT. *Ant.,* see CARE.
reckon, *v.* calculate, count, compute, estimate; esteem, consider, believe; think, suppose. *Colloq.,* guess. See ADDITION, REASONING, BELIEF.
reckoning, *n.* calculation, computation, count; accounting, settlement; bill, tally, score. See ADDITION, NUMBER, PAYMENT.
reclaim, *v.t.* redeem, restore, reform, recover, retrieve. See PENITENCE, RESTORATION.
recline, *v.i.* lie, rest, couch, repose, loll. See REPOSE.
recluse, *n.* hermit, anchorite, ascetic, eremite. See SECLUSION.
recognition, *n.* identification, perception, cognizance; acknowledgment, commendation, appreciation. See KNOWLEDGE, MEMORY, COURTESY.
recognize, *v.t.* acknowledge, concede, remember; perceive, realize, know, distinguish; salute, greet, appreciate. See VISION, DISCLOSURE, KNOWLEDGE.

RECOIL

Nouns—recoil, reaction, retroaction, revulsion, rebound, ricochet, bounce, boomerang, kick, backlash, repercussion, reflex, return, repulse, reverberation, echo; reactionary, reactionist.

Verbs—1, recoil, react, rebound, reverberate, echo, spring back, fly back, kick, ricochet, reflect, boomerang, carom, bounce, shy.

2, cringe, cower, wince, flinch, quail, shrink; retreat, fall back, retire; falter, fail.

Adjectives—recoiling, refluent, repercussive, recalcitrant, reactionary; flinching, cowering, *etc.*

---

recollection, *n.* remembrance, reminiscence, MEMORY, retrospection, reflection.

recommend, *v.t.* commend, advise, suggest; commit, entrust; urge, advocate. See ADVICE, APPROBATION.

recompense, *n. & v.t.* —*n.* REWARD, COMPENSATION, PAYMENT, requital. —*v.t.* requite, REWARD, repay, remunerate, indemnify, atone. See COMPENSATION, ATONEMENT.

reconcile, *v.t.* conciliate, propitiate, placate, appease; harmonize, accord; settle. See CONFORMITY, PACIFICATION.

recondite, *adj.* mysterious, obscure, SECRET, abstruse, profound, esoteric, cryptic. See CONCEALMENT.

recondition, *v.t.* repair, renew, overhaul, renovate, restore, regenerate, rejuvenate. See RESTORATION.

reconnaissance, *n.* survey, surveillance, espionage, OBSERVATION, inspection, INQUIRY; aerial reconnaissance. See VISION.

reconnoiter, *v.* investigate, survey, spy out, scout. *Slang,* case. See VISION.

reconsider, *v.* reexamine, review, think over, have second thoughts, think again, change one's mind, tergiversate. See THOUGHT, CHANGE.

reconstruct, *v.t.* rebuild; make over, redo, restore, renovate, recondition; overhaul; piece together, project. See REPRODUCTION, RESTORATION, MEMORY.

RECORD

Nouns—1, record, note, minute; register, roll, diptych, entry, memorandum, COPY, duplicate, docket; muniment, deed; document; testimony, deposition, affidavit, certificate; notebook, statistic; registry, registration, enrollment; tabulation, transcript, transcription, entry, booking, signature.

2, gazette, newspaper, magazine; almanac, calendar; diary, log, journal, daybook, ledger; archive, scroll, chronicle, annals; legend, history, biography.

3, monument, hatchment, slab, tablet, trophy, obelisk, pillar, column, monolith; memorial; memento, testimonial, medal; commemoration.

4, trace, vestige, relic, remains, scar, footstep, footprint, track, mark, wake, trail, spoor, scent.

5, phonograph record, 45 L.P.; recording, tape recording, transcription. *Colloq.,* disk, disc, waxing, platter.

6, recorder, registrar, register, notary, prothonotary, clerk, amanuensis, secretary, stenographer, scribe, bookkeeper; editor, author, journalist; annalist, historian, chronicler, biographer, antiquary, antiquarian, archivist.

7, recording instrument, recorder, ticker, ticker tape; tracer; timer, dater, stopwatch, speedometer (see MEASUREMENT), log, turnstile; seismograph; phonograph, record player, turntable; tape *or* wire recorder, dictating machine, Dictaphone; adding machine, cash register.

Verbs—record, put on record, chronicle, hand down to posterity, commemorate, write, put in writing; jot down, note, make a note; enter, book; post, make an entry of, enroll, register; mark, sign, attest, file; wax, tape, transcribe.

Antonyms, see OBLIVION, OBLITERATE.

recount, *v.t.* tell, recite, repeat, rehearse, relate, narrate, enumerate; recapitulate. See NUMERATION, DESCRIPTION.

recoup, *v.t.* regain, retrieve, indemnify, reimburse. See RESTORATION.

recourse, *n.* appeal, resort, resource, expedient; AID. See EXPEDIENCE, MEANS.

recover, *v.* regain, get back, redeem, retrieve, reclaim, salvage; get well, recuperate. See RESTORATION, ACQUISITION.

recreant, *adj.* cowardly, craven, dastardly, disloyal, false, treacherous; apostate, renegade. See COWARDICE, CHANGEABLENESS.

recreation, *n.* diversion, sport, pastime, REFRESHMENT. See AMUSEMENT.

recrimination, *n.* countercharge, RETALIATION, *tu quoque*, rejoinder, reply in kind; name calling, bickering. See ACCUSATION.

recruit, *v.t. & n.* —*v.t.* enlist, raise, furnish, supply, replenish; restore, renew. See STORE, RESTORATION. —*n.* conscript, draftee; newcomer, novice, tyro. *Slang*, rookie, boot. See COMBATANT, LEARNER. *Ant.*, see VETERAN.

rectangular, *adj.* orthogonal, oblong, foursquare, square. See LENGTH, ANGULARITY.

rectify, *v.t.* correct, improve, repair, purify, redress, amend. See IMPROVEMENT, RIGHT.

rectitude, *n.* uprightness, integrity, righteousness, goodness, VIRTUE, honesty. See PROBITY. *Ant.*, see IMPROBITY.

rector, *n.* rectress; pastor, parson; DIRECTOR, monitor, prefect. See CLERGY.

rectory, *n.* manse, parsonage, vicarage, parish house, deanery, presbytery; benefice. See CLERGY, ABODE.

recumbent, *adj.* lying, reclining, leaning. See OBLIQUITY.

recuperation, *n.* recovery, IMPROVEMENT, convalescence. See RESTORATION.

recur, *v.* return, come back, reoccur, repeat, intermit, revert. See REPETITION.

recusant, *n. & adj.* —*n.* nonconformist, dissenter, schismatic, sectarian, Protestant; separatist, apostate. —*adj.* rebellious, dissenting, apostate, disobedient. See DISSENT, UNCONFORMITY, SECTARIANISM.

recycle, *v.t.* reuse; restart, rebegin. See BEGINNING, UTILITY.

redden, *v.* encrimson, incarmine; blush, flush, glow; bloody. See COLOR.

redecorate, *v.* renovate, refurbish, restore, remodel, do over. *Colloq.*, fix up. See REPRODUCTION, RESTORATION.

redeem, *v.t.* ransom, recover, rescue, restore, liberate, deliver, convert, fulfill, perform. See RESTORATION, PENITENCE.

redeemer, *n.* savio(u)r, Messiah, Christ, the Lord, *etc.*; emancipator. See PRESERVATION, FREEDOM.

redolent, *adj.* fragrant, odorous, aromatic, perfumed; heady, musky; reminiscent, remindful, having an aura (of). See ODOR, MEMORY, INDICATION.

redound, *v.* bounce back, rebound; do credit (to). See REDUNDANCE, REPUTE.

redress, *v.t. & n.* —*v.t.* RIGHT, correct, repair, reform, relieve, remedy. See RESTORATION, ATONEMENT. —*n.* amends, restitution, reparation, requital.

red tape, bureaucracy, officialdom; paperwork; delay, HINDRANCE.

reduce, *v.t.* diminish, lessen, curtail, lower; allay, alleviate; set (a fracture); demote, abase, subjugate, subdue; diet, slenderize. See DECREASE, CONTRACTION, NARROWNESS. *Ant.*, see INCREASE.

redundance, *n.* redundancy; repetition, tautology; superabundance, superfluity, superfluence; profuseness, profusion, repletion, plethora; surfeit, surplus, surplusage; coals to Newcastle. See SUFFICIENCY. *Ant.*, see INSUFFICIENCY.

reed, *n.* stem, stalk, straw, rush; pastoral pipe. See MUSICAL INSTRUMENTS.

reef, *n.* sandbar, shoal, bank, ledge. See LAND, DANGER.

reek, *n. & v.* —*n.* VAPOR, fumes, ODOR; STENCH, stink, malodor, fetor, miasma. —*v.* stink, smell; give off, exude; sweat, perspire.

reel, *v.i.* sway, stagger, waver, spin, wheel. See AGITATION.

reëstablish, *v.t.* restore, renew, revive, refound. See RESTORATION.

refashion, *v.t.* make over, remake, remodel, revolutionize. See REVOLUTION.

refer, *v.* submit, commit, send, direct, assign, ascribe, attribute. See CAUSE, EVIDENCE, ADVICE. —*v.i.* allude, advert, apply, concern, appeal. See RELATION.

referee, *n.* arbiter, arbitrator, umpire, mediator, moderator, JUDGE.

reference, *n.* citation, allusion; testimonial, credentials; bearing, concern, applicability. See RELATION, EVIDENCE.

reference book, encyclopedia, dictionary, yearbook, atlas, almanac, catalog(ue), concordance, thesaurus. See BOOK.

referendum, *n.* vote, plebiscite, initiative, *vox populi.* See CHOICE.

refine, *v.t.* purify, cleanse, educate, improve, cultivate, elaborate. See CLEANNESS, IMPROVEMENT.

refined, *adj.* well-bred, cultivated, polished; subtle. See ELEGANCE, COURTESY.

refinement, *n.* elegance, finish, culture, polish; delicacy, propriety, TASTE, DISCRIMINATION. See IMPROVEMENT, TRUTH, COURTESY.

reflect, *v.* throw back, cast back, mirror, COPY, imitate, reproduce, echo, meditate, ponder, muse, ruminate. See THOUGHT, IMITATION, SOUND.

reflection, *n.* refraction, image, echo, duplication, counterpart, COPY; meditation, rumination, retrospection; insinuation, innuendo. See LIGHT, SOUND, THOUGHT, DISAPPROBATION.

reflex, *n. & adj.* —*n.* reaction, instinct, repercussion, RECOIL, rebound; —*adj.* reflective; involuntary, reactive, automatic, conditioned. See COMPULSION.

reflux, *n.* ebb, refluence, subsidence, backwater. See DECREASE, REGRESSION. *Ant.*, see INGRESS.

reform, *v. & n.* —*v.t.* better, reclaim, restore, improve, redeem, regenerate, convert. See CHANGE, PENITENCE. —*n.* IMPROVEMENT, amendment, regeneration, reformation; crusade.

reformation, *n.* reform, improvement, betterment, correction; regeneration. See IMPROVEMENT, PIETY. *Ant.*, see DETERIORATION.

reformer, *n.* altruist, crusader, zealot, missionary. See IMPROVEMENT.

refraction, *n.* bending, deflection, DISTORTION; distorted image. See DEVIATION, LIGHT, VISION.

refractory, *adj.* unruly, unmanageable, obstinate, stubborn, intractable. See RESOLUTION. *Ant.*, see OBEDIENCE.

refrain, *v. & n.* —*v.i.* abstain, cease, desist, forbear. —*n.* chorus, burden, repetend. See REPETITION. *Ant.*, see CONTINUITY.

REFRESHMENT

Nouns—refreshment, invigoration, recuperation, RESTORATION, revival, repair, renewal, renovation, stimulation, RELIEF; ventilation; relaxation, recreation, diversion, regalement, repast, FOOD, nourishment, bait. *Colloq.*, pick-me-up.

Verbs—**1**, refresh, brace, strengthen, invigorate, exhilarate, stimulate; brisken, freshen (up), recruit, enliven; repair, retouch, restore, renew, renovate, revive, revivify, recreate, (re)animate; regale, cheer, cool, fan, ventilate, AIR, slake. *Colloq.*, give a new lease on life, buck up. **2**, breathe, respire, take a long breath; recuperate, recover, get better, revive, regain one's strength, come to oneself, raise one's head, perk (up).

Adjectives—refreshing, *etc.*; brisk, cool, restorative, recuperative, restful, pleasant, comfortable; refreshed, fresh, untired, unwearied.
Antonym, see WEAKNESS, WEARINESS.

---

refrigerate, *v.* cool, ice, freeze, congeal, infrigidate; benumb, chill, chill to the marrow; quickfreeze. See COLD. *Ant.*, see HEAT.

refrigerator, *n.* See COLD.

refuge, *n.* asylum, sanctuary; hideout, hideaway; safe harbor; any port in a storm; last resort; SUPPORT, SECLUSION; anchor, anchorage; home, hospital; retreat, den, lair. See SAFETY. *Ant.*, see DANGER.

refugee, *n.* fugitive, displaced person, evacuee, escapee, runaway. See ESCAPE.

refund, *v.t.* return, give back, payback, repay, reimburse. See PAYMENT, RESTORATION.

refurbish, *v.* See REDECORATE.

REFUSAL

Nouns—**1,** refusal; nonacceptance, denial, declining, declination; rejection, repudiation, exclusion; resistance; repulse, rebuff; disapproval; recusancy, abnegation, protest, disclaimer; DISSENT, revocation, renunciation.

2, UNWILLINGNESS, indisposition, disinclination, reluctance, aversion.

Verbs—refuse, REJECT, deny, decline; negate; grudge, begrudge, be deaf to; turn a deaf ear to; discountenance, not hear of, turn down, wash one's hands of, stand aloof. See RESISTANCE.

Adjectives—**1,** refusing, recusant; uncomplying, unaccommodating, unconsenting, deaf to; UNWILLING.

2, refused, rejected, ungranted, out of the question, not to be thought of, impossible.

Adverbs—no, on no account, not for the world; no, thank you; never. *Colloq.*, not a chance, not on your life.
Antonym, see OFFER.

---

refuse, *n.* trash, truck, rubbish, waste, leavings, garbage. See USELESSNESS.

refute, *v.t.* confute, controvert, disprove, deny, dispute. See NEGATION.

regain, *v.t.* recover, retrieve, get back, get back to. See ACQUISITION.

regal, *adj.* royal, splendid, stately, majestic; kingly, autocratic. See AUTHORITY, NOBILITY.

regale, *v.t.* entertain, feast, wine and dine, treat; give PLEASURE. See FOOD.

regalia, *n.pl.* emblems, decorations, insignia. See INDICATION.

regard, *v.t. & n.* —*v.t.* consider, deem, observe, mark, note, RESPECT, esteem, concern. See INTELLECT. —*n.* reference, concern, gaze, ATTENTION, deference, esteem. See CARE, REPUTE.

regardless, *adj.* heedless, careless, indifferent, negligent. See NEGLECT. *Ant.*, see CARE, ATTENTION.

regenerate, *adj. & v.t.* —*adj.* reformed, reborn, converted. See PIETY. —*v.t.* produce anew, make over; revivify; reform, convert. See RESTORATION, PIETY.

regent, *n.* viceroy, deputy, ruler, trustee. See AUTHORITY, COMMISSION.

regime, *n.* RULE, reign, sovereignty; rulers, incumbents; policy, program, PLAN. See AUTHORITY, DIRECTION.

regimen, *n.* COURSE, METHOD, prescription, program, procedure, schedule; drill, training; diet(etics). See FOOD, REMEDY.

regiment, *n. & v.* —*n.* corps, troop(s), army, company; MULTITUDE, ASSEMBLAGE. See COMBATANT. —*v.t.* muster, enlist; organize, systematize, train, drill, discipline; LIMIT, harness, enslave. See RESTRAINT, CONFORMITY.

REGION

Nouns—**1,** region, sphere, ground soil, area, hemisphere, latitude, meridian, zone, clime, climate; quarter, district, beat, orb, circuit, circle; vicinity, neighborhood, precinct, pale, department, domain, bailiwick, dominion, section, tract, territory. See PLACE, LOCATION, SPACE.

2, country, canton, county, shire, province, arrondissement, parish, township, hundred, riding, principality, duchy, realm, kingdom, empire.

3, arena, march; patch, plot, enclosure, enclave, field, court.

Adjectives—regional, sectional, territorial, local, parochial, vicinal, provincial, topographical.

---

register, *n. & v.t.* —*n.* RECORD, ROLL, LIST; registration, enrollment. —*v.* enroll, LIST; mark, RECORD; express, indicate. See INDICATION, DRAMA.

REGRESSION

Nouns—**1,** regression, retrocession, retrogression, retrogradation, retroaction, retreat, withdrawal, retirement, return, REVERSION; RELAPSE, RECESSION, recess; recidivism, backsliding, fall, DETERIORATION.

2, reflux, refluence, backwater, regurgitation, ebb, resilience, reflection, RECOIL.

Verbs—regress, recede, return, revert, retreat, retire, retrograde; lapse, relapse; back down *or* out, withdraw, rebound; recoil, turn back, fall back, put back; lose ground, fall astern, back water, put about, wheel, countermarch; ebb, regurgitate, balk, jib, shrink, shy; turn, turn tail, about-face, turn around, turn one's back upon; retrace one's steps, beat a retreat, go home; backslide. *Slang,* pull in one's horns.

Adjectives—**1,** regressive, receding; retrograde; retrogressive, refluent, reflex, recidivous, crablike, reactionary, recessive, receding.

2, relapsing, backsliding, recrudescent; reversionary, atavistic.

Adverbs—back, backward(s), reflexively, in retreat.

Antonym, see PROGRESSION.

REGRET

Nouns—regret, remorse, qualms, compunction, contrition, attrition, repentance, PENITENCE; LAMENTATION, mourning, heartache, sorrow, grief, bitterness, DISAPPOINTMENT, DISCONTENT; repining, homesickness, nostalgia, *mal du pays.*

Verbs—regret, deplore, feel sorry *or* contrite; sorrow, grieve, repent, repine, rue [the day]; weigh *or* prey on the mind, leave an aching void.

Adjectives—**1,** regretting, regretful, sorry, contrite, remorseful, rueful, mournful, penitent, ashamed; repining, homesick, nostalgic.

2, regretted, regrettable, deplorable, unfortunate, lamentable; culpable, blameworthy, opprobrious.

Interjections—what a pity! what a shame! too bad! *Slang,* tough luck!

Antonym, see CONTENT, REJOICING.

REGULARITY

Nouns—**1,** regularity, periodicity; evenness, steadiness, STABILITY, constancy, consistency, invariability, punctuality; intermittence, alternation, OSCILLATION, beat, pulse, pulsation, cadence, swing, rhythm (see MUSIC).

2, round, bout, turn, REVOLUTION, ROTATION, period, circuit (see CIRCUITRY), CYCLE, ROUTINE.

3, ORDER, RULE, METHOD, system, even tenor; SYMMETRY, balance, harmony, UNIFORMITY, CONFORMITY, CORRESPONDENCE, congruity, compliance, proportion.

4, anniversary, jubilee; centennial, biennial, *etc.*; feast, festival, celebration, fast day, birthday, saint's day, holy day, holiday.

Verbs—recur, return, reappear, come again, come (a)round, come in
its turn, revolve, circle; beat, pulsate, throb, alternate, intermit, oscillate;
come and go.
Adjectives—regular, steady, constant, uniform, even, balanced, symmetrical, consistent, punctual, systematic, methodical, orderly, unvarying, congruous; periodic(al), serial, recurrent, cyclical, seasonal, rhyth-
mic(al), intermittent, remittent, alternate, every other; fixed, established, settled, continued, permanent; normal, natural, customary,
habitual, usual, conventional, ordinary, typical, correct; hourly, diurnal,
daily, quotidian, tertian, weekly, biweekly, fortnightly, monthly, yearly;
annual, biennial, triennial, centennial; secular, paschal, lenten, menstrual, catamenial.
Adverbs—regularly, normally, periodically, constantly, punctually; at
regular intervals, like clockwork, at fixed periods, at stated times, from
day to day, day by day; by turns, in turn, in rotation, alternately,
every other day, off and on, round and round, year after year.
　　　　　Antonym, see IRREGULARITY.

---

regulate, *v.t.* ORDER, manage, legislate, rule, direct; adjust, rectify, fix,
organize, systematize, tranquilize, moderate. See ARRANGEMENT.
regulation, *n.* adjustment (see REGULATE); LAW, rule, order, ordinance.
rehabilitate, *v.t.* restore, reinstate, reëstablish. See RESTORATION.
rehash, *v.t.* review, repeat, restate; summarize, recapitulate, sum up.
Colloq., chew one's cud; post-mortem, recap. See REPETITION, IN-
QUIRY.
rehearse, *v.t.* repeat, recite, enumerate; drill, practice, prepare. See
REPETITION, PREPARATION.
reign, *v.i.* rule, govern, command, hold sway. See AUTHORITY.
reimburse, *v.t.* repay, compensate, indemnify. See PAYMENT, RESTORA-
TION.
reincarnation, *n.* See REBIRTH.
reinforce, *v.t.* strengthen, support, buttress, replenish. See POWER,
RESTORATION.
reinforcements, *n.pl.* replenishment, AID, recruits, auxiliaries. See STORE.
reins, *n.pl.* lines, RESTRAINT, guidance.
reinstate, *v.t.* restore, put back, reinstall, rehabilitate. See RESTORATION.

REJECTION

Nouns—rejection, repudiation, EXCLUSION, REPULSION, rebuff; REFUSAL,
declination, disallowance, disavowal, disclaimer, denial, renunciation,
refutation, DISAPPROBATION, veto; disbelief, DOUBT; ostracism, relegation,
dismissal, discard (see DISUSE); DIVORCE. *Slang*, the brush-off, cold
shoulder.
Verbs—**1,** reject, repudiate, abandon, renounce, exclude, except, repulse,
repel, rebuff, spurn, slight; set *or* lay aside, pass over, give up, cast off,
discard, cast behind one, cast to the winds, set at naught, throw to
the dogs, toss overboard, throw away, wash one's hands of, have done
with; scrap, dismiss, cashier, deport, eject, relegate, resist; jilt, DIVORCE.
Colloq., brush off.
2, resuse, disallow, disapprove, disclaim, overrule, refute, abnegate,
abjure; decline, deny, veto, be deaf to.
Adjectives—rejected, repudiated, refused, not chosen, not granted, out
of the question, impossible; unaccepted, unloved, unwelcome, discarded, castaway, excluded, jilted; rejective, repudiative; declinatory.
　　　　Antonym, see APPROBATION, CHOICE.

REJOICING

Nouns—**1,** rejoicing, exultation, triumph, jubilation, joy, revelry, reveling,
merrymaking, jubilee, CELEBRATION, paean, thanksgiving, congratulation.
2, smile, simper, smirk, gloat, grin; laughter, giggle, titter, snigger,

snicker, crow, chuckle, horse laugh, guffaw; fit, shout, roar *or* peal of laughter; risibility.

3, cheer, hurrah, hooray, shout, yell, hallelujah.

Verbs—1, rejoice, thank one's stars, congratulate oneself, clap one's hands, fling up one's cap; dance, skip; sing, chirrup, hurrah; cry for joy, leap with joy, exult, glory, triumph, celebrate; be tickled.

2, make merry, smile, simper, smirk, grin, laugh, giggle, titter, snigger, crow, snicker, chortle, chuckle, cackle; cheer, hurrah, yell, shout, roar, split one's sides.

3, enjoy, revel in, delight in, be glad.

Adjectives—rejoicing, jubilant, exultant, triumphant, flushed, glad, gladsome, elated, laughing, risible, bursting with laughter, convulsed with laughter; laughable.

Interjections—hurrah! three cheers! hail! Heaven be praised! *Slang,* swell! great! oh, boy!

Antonym, see LAMENTATION.

---

rejoin, *v.t.* reply, retort, respond; reunite, reassemble, join again. See ANSWER, ASSEMBLAGE.

rejoinder, *n.* ANSWER, reply, retort, response.

rejuvenation, *n.* rejuvenescence, reinvigoration. See YOUTH.

relapse, *n. & v.* —*n.* recurrence (of illness *or* behavior); DETERIORATION, backsliding, REGRESSION. —*v.i.* lapse, fall back, backslide, fall ill again.

relate, *v.t.* TELL, recount, report, narrate. See INFORMATION, DESCRIPTION.

RELATION

Nouns—relation, relationship, bearing, reference, CONNECTION, concern, dependence, cognation; CORRELATION, analogy, SIMILARITY, affinity, reference; alliance, homogeneity, association, approximation, affiliation, kinship, CONSANGUINITY, interest, relevancy; COMPARISON, ratio, proportion, link, tie, bond of union.

Verbs—1, be related, relate to, refer to, bear upon, regard, concern, touch, affect, have to do with; pertain to, belong to, interest; correspond.

2, relate, bring into relation with, bring to bear upon, connect, associate, draw a parallel, link, COMPARE; correlate, interrelate, reciprocate, alternate.

Adjectives—1, relative, correlative, cognate, relating, referable; belonging, appurtenant.

2, related, connected, implicated, associated, affiliated, allied to; akin, like, similar, relevant; reciprocal, mutual, common, correspondent, interchangeable, alternate.

3, approximating, proportionate, proportional, allusive, comparable.

Adverbs—relatively, pertinently, comparatively; *en rapport*, in touch with.

Prepositions—as to, as for, as regards, regarding, about, concerning, anent, relating to, with relation to, with reference to, with regard to, apropos of, on the score of; under the head of, in the matter of, in re, re.

Antonym, see DIFFERENCE.

---

relative, *n.* relation, kinsman; comparative, dependent. See RELATION.

relax, *v.t.* rest, relent, slacken, loosen, abate, relieve, ease, mitigate. See SOFTNESS, INACTIVITY, PITY. *Ant.*, see HARDNESS, EXCITEMENT.

relaxation, *n.* ease, REPOSE, diversion, recreation; abatement, loosening. See AMUSEMENT, MODERATION.

relaxed, *adj.* loose, slack; not tense, at ease. See REPOSE. *Ant.*, see ACTIVITY, AGITATION.

relay, *n. & v.* —*n.* replacement, substitute, shift; intermediary, medium, go-between, agent, AGENCY. —*v.* forward, advance, transmit. See TRANSFERENCE, CHANGE.

release, *v.t.* free, liberate, give out, relinquish. See RELINQUISHMENT.

relegate, *v.t.* consign, commit, assign, refer, banish. See EJECTION, GIVING.

relent, *v.i.* soften, yield, submit, PITY. See SOFTNESS.

relentless, *adj.* pitiless, merciless, implacable, remorseless; inexorable, indefatigable. See RESOLUTION, RETALIATION, SEVERITY. *Ant.,* see PITY.

relevant, *adj.* pertinent, fitting, apposite, apropos, germane, appropriate. See RELATION.

reliable, *adj.* trustworthy, dependable, trusty, responsible. See CERTAINTY, PROBITY. *Ant.,* see DOUBT, IMPROBITY.

reliance, *n.* dependence, trust, confidence, faith, credence. See BELIEF.

relic, *n.* memento, souvenir, keepsake, token, antique, remains. See MEMORY, RECORD.

RELIEF

Nouns—1, relief, deliverance, amelioration, easement, softening, alleviation, mitigation, MODERATION, palliation, soothing, assuagement, slaking. 2, solace, consolation, comfort, encouragement.
3, lenitive, restorative, palliative, alleviative, cushion, anodyne, tranquilizer, painkiller, analgesic. See LENIENCY.

Verbs—1, relieve, ease, alleviate, mitigate, palliate, soothe, salve, soften, mollify, poultice; replace, take over, spell, substitute for; assuage, allay, disburden, lighten; quench, slake.
2, cheer, comfort, console, encourage, bear up, pat on the back, set at ease; remedy, cure, refresh.
3, be relieved, breathe more freely, take comfort, breathe a sigh [of relief].

Adjectives—relieving, consolatory, comforting, soothing, assuaging, assuasive, balmy, lenitive, palliative, remedial, curative.

Antonym, see AGGRAVATION, INCREASE.

RELIGION

Nouns—1, religion, faith; theology, divinity, deism, theism, monotheism, polytheism; hagiology; truth, belief, creed, doctrine, dogma, canonicity; declaration, profession *or* confession of faith; articles of faith; conformity, orthodoxy, strictness. See PIETY.
2, Christianity, Catholicism, Protestantism (Presbyterianism, Methodism, Lutheranism, Quakerism, Mormonism, Christian Science, *etc.*); Judaism; Mohammedanism, Moslemism, Islam; Buddhism, Shintoism, Confucianism, Hinduism, Brahmanism, Sikhism, Lamaism, *etc.*
3, the Church, Holy Church, Established Church; temple of the Holy Ghost, Universal Church, Apostolic Church, Roman Catholic Church, Greek Orthodox Church, Church of Christ, Scientist; Church of the New Jerusalem; Presbyterian, *etc.* Church; Society of Friends; Church of Jesus Christ of Latter-Day Saints; Church of Christ.
4, true believer, Christendom, Christians; Islam; Jewry; Christian, Catholic, Protestant (Presbyterian, Christian Scientist, Swedenborgian, Moravian, *etc.*), Quaker, Friend, Mormon; Jew; Moslem; Buddhist; Brahman, Hindu, *etc.*
5, scriptures, canons, SACRED WRITINGS; catechism; Apostles Creed, Nicene Creed, Athanasian Creed; Articles of Religion.
6, WORSHIP; PRAYER; HYMN, hymnody, psalmody; sacrifice, oblation, incense, libation, offering, offertory; disciple, fasting, asceticism; RITE, divine service, office, duty, Mass, matins, evensong, vespers.
7, CLERGY, clergyman; theologian, theist, monotheist; congregation, flock, worshiper, communicant, celebrant; presbyter, elder, vestryman, usher.

Verbs—WORSHIP, adore, revere; pray, invoke, supplicate, say one's prayers, tell one's beads; return thanks, say grace; praise, glorify, magnify; bless, give benediction; attend services, attend Mass, go to church; communicate, take communion.

Adjectives—religious, pious, devout; Godfearing; reverential (see RE-SPECT); orthodox, sound, strict, canonical, authentic, faithful, catholic; theological; doctrinal, dogmatic, denominational, sectarian; Christian, Catholic, Protestant, Lutheran, Calvinistic, *etc.*; evangelical, scriptural; divine, true; Jewish, Judaic, Hebrew, Hindu, Mohammedan, *etc.*

Antonym, see IRRELIGION.

RELINQUISHMENT

Nouns—**1,** relinquishment, abandonment, renunciation, abjuration, abrogation, expropriation, dereliction; cession, surrender, dispensation; resignation, abdication, withdrawal, retirement; riddance.

2, desertion, defection, secession, withdrawal; discontinuance, DISUSE, desuetude.

3, derelict, foundling, outcast, castaway.

Verbs—**1,** relinquish, give up, surrender, yield, cede, let go, spare, drop, RESIGN, forgo, renounce, abandon, expropriate, give away, dispose of, part with, lay aside, lay on the shelf, discard, cast off, dismiss, get rid of, eject, divest oneself of, wash one's hands of, throw overboard, throw to the winds; sweep away, jettison, maroon.

2, desert, forsake, leave in the lurch, depart from, secede from, renege, withdraw from, back out of, leave, quit, vacate. *Slang*, ditch, give the gate.

3, break off, leave off, desist, stop, cease, give over, shut up shop, throw in the sponge, give up the argument, drop out.

Adjectives—**1,** relinquished, abandoned, cast off, derelict, unowned, unappropriated, left; dropped.

2, renunciatory, abjuratory, abdicant; relinquishing, *etc.*

Antonym, see POSSESSION.

---

relish, *n.* zest, gusto, flavor, spice, CONDIMENT, appetizer; liking, fondness. See PLEASURE, DESIRE.

reluctance, *n.* unwillingness, hesitation, aversion, disinclination. *Ant.,* see ASSENT.

rely, *v.i.* trust, depend, count. See BELIEF.

REMAINDER

Nouns—**1,** remainder, residue, result, remains, remnant, vestige, rest, relic, leavings, heeltap, odds and ends, cheese parings, orts, residuum, dregs, lees, grounds, silt, sediment, slag, refuse, stubble, fag end, ruins, wreck, butt, skeleton, stump, alluvium; dross, cinder, ash, clinker.

2, surplus, overplus, excess, balance, superfluity, survival.

Verbs—remain, be left, be left over, exceed, survive.

Adjectives—remaining, left; left over, left behind, residual, residuary, over, odd, unconsumed, sedimentary, surviving; net, exceeding, over and above; superfluous.

---

remand, *v.* send *or* order back, recommit, recall, return to custody. See COMMAND.

remark, *v.t. & n.* —*v.t.* note, observe, animadvert, comment on, mention. See ATTENTION. —*n.* observation, statement, comment. See SPEECH.

remarkable, *adj.* noteworthy, notable, extraordinary, striking, unusual, singular, uncommon. See UNCONFORMITY, WONDER. *Ant.,* see CONFORMITY.

REMEDY

Nouns—**1,** remedy, help, redress, RESTORATION; antidote, counterpoison, counterirritant, counteragent, antitoxin, antibody, prophylactic, antiseptic, corrective, restorative, sedative, palliative, febrifuge; germicide, specific, emetic, carminative, antibiotic (see ANTIBIOSIS).

2, physic, medicine, simples, drug, potion, draught, draft, dose, pill, tincture, medicament.

3, nostrum, receipt, recipe, prescription; panacea, sovereign remedy, cure, cure-all, elixir, *elixir vitae*, philosopher's stone, balm, balsam, cordial, ptisan, tisane, patent medicine.

4, salve, ointment, oil, lenitive, lotion, cosmetic, embrocation, liniment, depilatory; compress, bandage, poultice, plaster.

5, treatment, therapy, regimen; dietetics; bloodletting, bleeding, venesection, phlebotomy, cupping, leeches; surgery, operation, section.

6, pharmacy, pharmacology, pharmaceutics; chemotherapy; shock treatment, therapeutics, pathology, neurology, homeopathy, allopathy, hydrotherapy, surgery, orthopedics, osteopathy, chiropractic, dentistry, midwifery, obstetrics, psychiatry.

7, hospital, infirmary, pesthouse, lazaretto, dispensary, clinic, sanatorium, spa, halfway house; Red Cross.

8, doctor, physician; dentist; surgeon, general practitioner, neurologist, pathologist, psychiatrist, oculist, *etc.*; resident, interne; anesthetist; attendant; apothecary, pharmacist, druggist; leech, *accoucheur, accoucheuse*, midwife, oculist, dentist, aurist, nurse, sister.

Verbs—remedy, doctor, dose, physic, nurse, operate, minister to, treat, attend; dress the wounds, plaster; prevent, relieve, cure, palliate, restore; bleed; respond to treatment.

Adjectives—remedial, restorative, corrective, curative, palliative, healing, sanatory, sanative; antitoxic, antiseptic, prophylactic, medical, medicinal, surgical, therapeutic, tonic, analeptic, balsamic, anodyne, hypnotic, neurotic, narcotic, sedative, lenitive, demulcent, emollient, detergent; disinfectant, febrifugal, laxative, dietetic, alimentary, nutritious, nutritive, peptic; curable.

Antonym, see DISEASE.

---

remember, *v.t.* keep *or* bear in mind, call to mind, recall, recollect. See MEMORY. *Ant., see* OBLIVION.

remind, *v.t.* prompt, hint, suggest, jog. See MEMORY.

reminiscent, *adj.* retrospective, suggestive, reminding. See MEMORY.

remiss, *adj.* lax, slack, careless, neglectful, dilatory, sluggish. See NEGLECT.

remission, *n.* annulment, cancellation; pardon, forgiveness; suspension, respite. See FORGIVENESS, NULLIFICATION, END.

remit, *v.t.* forgive, pardon, excuse, exempt, relax, slacken; pay, send. See FORGIVENESS, RESTORATION, PAYMENT.

remnant, *n.* REMAINDER, residue, fragment, scrap, vestige.

remodel, *v.t.* rearrange, rebuild, modernize; renovate, rehabilitate, refurbish. See NEWNESS, RESTORATION.

remonstrance, *n.* protest, objection; reproof, expostulation. See DISSENT.

remorse, *n.* self-reproach, regret, compunction, contrition, PENITENCE.

remorseless, *adj.* impenitent, hardened, callous, obdurate; hard, cold, ruthless. See RETALIATION, IMPENITENCE.

remote, *adj.* distant, secluded, alien, irrelevant, slight. See DISTANCE, SECLUSION. *Ant., see* NEARNESS.

remove, *v.* depart, go away, move; displace, shift, eliminate, take off, discharge, evict. See DESTRUCTION, EJECTION, DEPARTURE.

remunerate, *v.t.* pay, reimburse, recompense, requite, REWARD.

remunerative, *adj.* profitable, paying, rewarding, compensatory, gainful, lucrative; worthwhile. See ACQUISITION, COMPENSATION, UTILITY.

renaissance, *n.* new birth, revival. See RESTORATION.

rend, *v.t.* tear, shred, rip, rive, split; harrow; cut, cleave. See DISJUNCTION.

render, *v.t.* give, pay, deliver, furnish, supply, yield, produce, perform; express, translate, interpret. See GIVING, INTERPRETATION.

rendezvous, *n.* tryst, appointment, date, meeting, assignation; ASSEMBLAGE.

rendition, *n.* rendering; execution, performance, REPRESENTATION; view, version, INTERPRETATION, reading, paraphrase.

renegade, *n. & adj.* —*n.* traitor, turncoat, apostate, defector; mutineer. —*adj.* treacherous, disloyal; rebellious, mutinous. See CHANGEABLENESS, IMPROBITY.

renege, *v., colloq.,* break one's word *or* promise, disavow, disclaim, take back, go back (on), cancel, back out. See NULLIFICATION, NEGATION.

renew, *v.t.* revive, restore, renovate; resume, continue; replace, renovate, replenish. See RESTORATION.

renounce, *v.t.* abjure, disclaim, disown, repudiate, reject, give up, abandon, surrender. See NEGATION, REJECTION, RELINQUISHMENT.

renovate, *v.t.* renew, restore, repair, freshen, purify. See RESTORATION.

renown, *n.* REPUTE, fame, reputation, glory, distinction, kudos.

rent, *n.* tear, slit, fissure; split, division, rupture, schism; payment, return, rental. *Colloq.,* tenement. See INTERVAL, RECORD.

reorganize, *v.t.* resystematize, remodel, reform, rehabilitate, reëstablish. See CHANGE, RESTORATION.

repair, *v. & n.* —*v.i.* betake oneself, go. See TRAVEL. —*v.t.* mend, renovate, restore; amend, remedy. *Ant.,* see DETERIORATION. —*n.* RESTORATION, renovation, mending, redress.

reparation, *n.* amends, redress, RESTITUTION, indemnity. See PAYMENT, ATONEMENT.

reparative, *adj.* mending, restorative, remedial, corrective, compensatory. See COMPENSATION, RESTORATION.

repartee, *n.* witty retort, clever rejoinder, sally, persiflage, banter. *Slang,* snappy comeback, wisecrack. See ANSWER, WIT.

repast, *n.* meal, feast, banquet, collation, snack, spread. See FOOD.

repay, *v.t.* reimburse, indemnify, refund; recompense, requite. See PAYMENT.

repeal, *v.t.* revoke, annul, nullify, vacate, abrogate. See NULLIFICATION.

repeat, *v.t.* iterate, quote, recite; redo, duplicate. See REPETITION.

repel, *v.t.* repulse, resist, reject, scatter, drive apart; disgust, revolt. See REFUSAL, PAIN. *Ant.,* see ATTRACTION.

repellent, *adj.* repulsive, resistant, forbidding, distasteful. See RESISTANCE, PAIN. *Ant.,* see ATTRACTION.

repent, *v.* rue, regret; be contrite, be penitent. See PENITENCE.

repercussion, *n.* rebound, RECOIL, impact, reverberation, kick; result, EFFECT.

repertory, *n.* repertoire; LIST, catalogue, collection, STORE; acts, routines. *Colloq.,* bag of tricks, one's paces. See DRAMA.

REPETITION

Nouns—**1,** repetition, reiteration, harping; recurrence, renewal, reappearance; résumé, recapitulation, succession, run; tautology, monotony, rhythm, periodicity, redundance, alliteration; diffuseness (see LOQUACITY).

2, echo, burden of a song, refrain, repetend, encore, rehearsal; reverberation, drumming, chimes; twice-told tale, old story, second edition; old wine in new bottles. *Slang,* chestnut.

Verbs—**1,** repeat, iterate, reiterate, reproduce, duplicate, renew, echo, reecho, drum, harp upon, hammer, redouble.

2, recur, revert, return, reappear; redound, resume, rehearse, retell, go over the same ground, return to, capitulate, reword; chew one's cabbage twice.

3, reproduction, DUPLICATION, reduplication; COPY; SIMILARITY.

Adjectives—repeated, repetitive, repetitious, recurrent, recurring, frequent, incessant; monotonous, harping, iterative, chiming, retold, aforesaid, above-mentioned, habitual.

Adverbs—repeatedly, often, again, anew, over again, afresh, once more, ditto, encore, over and over, time after time, frequently.

Antonym, see END.

repine, *v.i.* fret, complain, mope, grieve, despond. See DISCONTENT, DEJECTION.

replace, *v.t.* put back; supplant, succeed, supersede; substitute; restore, return; move. See SUBSTITUTION, RESTORATION.

replenish, *v.t.* refill, restock, renew; stock up. See RESTORATION.

repletion, *n.* surfeit, SATIETY, overfullness, glut, engorgement. See SUFFICIENCY.

replica, *n.* image, double, twin, likeness; facsimile, COPY, reproduction, IMITATION, duplicate, model; photostat, print, transfer, impression.

reply, *n.* ANSWER, response, retort, rejoinder; countermove.

report, *v. & n.* —*v.t.* state, review; rehearse, give tidings, announce, give notice of, proclaim. See INFORMATION, PUBLICATION. —*n.* RECORD, account, statement; news; rumor; hearsay; fame, REPUTE; bang, blast, detonation. See INFORMATION.

reporter, *n.* news gatherer, journalist, newspaperman. *Slang,* leg man, newshound, newshawk. See BOOK, NEWS.

REPOSE

Nouns—**1,** repose, rest, INACTIVITY, relaxation, breathing time *or* spell, halt, pause, respite; sleep, slumber.

2, LEISURE, spare time, idleness, ease.

3, quiescence, quiet, stillness, tranquillity, calm, peace, composure; stagnation, stagnancy, immobility.

4, day of rest, Sabbath, Sunday, Lord's day, holiday, vacation, recess; pause, lull.

Verbs—**1,** repose, rest, take one's ease, recline, lie down, go to bed, go to sleep, slumber.

2, relax, unbend, slacken, take breath, rest upon one's oars, pause; loaf, idle, while away the time, take a holiday, shut up shop. *Colloq.,* take it easy, take a breather, take time out, kill time.

Adjectives—reposing, reposed, reposeful, calm, quiet, restful, relaxed, unstrained; QUIESCENT, quiet; leisurely, slow, unhurried, calm; ASLEEP.

Adverbs—at rest, at ease, calmly, peacefully; at a standstill; at leisure, unhurriedly.

Antonyms, see EXERTION, ACTIVITY.

---

repose, *v.t.* lay, place, entrust, deposit, put. See SUPPORT.

repository, *n.* vault, warehouse, museum, burial vault. See STORE, RECEPTACLE.

reprehensible, *adj.* blameworthy, hateful, censurable. See DISAPPROBATION.

REPRESENTATION

Nouns—**1,** representation, IMITATION, illustration, delineation, depiction, depictment, imagery, portraiture, design, designing, art, fine arts, PAINTING, drawing, SCULPTURE, ENGRAVING, photography.

2, personation, personification, impersonation; drama, motion picture, movie, *etc.*

3, picture, drawing, sketch, draft, tracing, COPY, photograph, daguerreotype; image, likeness, icon, portrait, effigy, facsimile.

4, figure, puppet, marionette, doll, figurine, manikin, model, waxwork, bust, statue, statuette, figurehead.

5, map, plan, chart, ground plan, blueprint, projection, elevation; diagram, cartography, atlas, outline, view.

6, ARTIST, designer, sculptor, draftsman, delineator.

Verbs—**1,** represent, delineate, depict, portray; photograph, figure, picture, describe, draw, sketch, trace, copy, mould, illustrate, symbolize, paint, carve, engrave.

2, personate, personify, impersonate, pose as, act, play, mimic, imitate.

Adjectives—representative, representing, depictive, illustrative, imitative, figurative, like, graphic, descriptive.

representative, *adj. & n.* —*adj.* typical, characteristic, illustrative, descriptive, exemplary; (of government) democratic, legislative, popular, republican. —*n.* delegate, nominee, agent, DEPUTY; Congressman, Assemblyman, legislator, Member of Congress *or* Parliament, M.P. See AGENCY, REPRESENTATION.

repress, *v.t.* suppress, restrain, check, curb, control, quell, stifle, smother. See RESTRAINT. *Ant.,* see FREEDOM.

reprieve, *n.* delay, stay, respite, suspension; pardon. See LATENESS, FORGIVENESS.

reprimand, *n.* reproof, rebuke, censure, admonition, reprehension. See DISAPPROBATION.

reprint, *n.* reissue, new edition, revision; COPY, replica. See BOOK.

reprisal, *n.* RETALIATION, REVENGE, requital, indemnity.

reproach, *v. & n.* —*v.t.* blame, rebuke, upbraid, censure; stigmatize. See DISAPPROBATION, ACCUSATION. *Ant.,* see APPROBATION. —*n.* reproof, blame, disgrace, discredit, dishonor. See DISAPPROBATION, DISREPUTE, ACCUSATION.

reprobate, *n.* sinner, scoundrel; rogue, blackguard. See EVILDOER.

REPRODUCTION

Nouns—1, reproduction, renovation, RESTORATION, renewal; revival, revivification, palingenesis, apotheosis, resuscitation, reanimation, recreation, resurrection, resurgence, reappearance; (re)generation, PRODUCTION, propagation, multiplication, reenactment, REPETITION, immutation; procreation, fructification, breeding, begetting.

2, COPY, duplicate, reprint; transcript(ion), reconstruction, REPRESENTATION, facsimile, IMITATION, replica, offprint, illustration.

Verbs—1, reproduce, renovate, restore, renew, refashion, reconstruct; regenerate, revive, resuscitate, reanimate; multiply, propagate, procreate, revivify, impregnate, breed, populate, crop up.

2, COPY, portray, duplicate, repeat, reprint, transcribe.

Adjectives—reproductive, reproduced, recreative, procreative, creative, generative, renascent, resurgent, reappearing.

---

reprove, *v.t.* admonish, censure, rebuke, chide, criticize. See DISAPPROBATION. *Ant.,* see APPROBATION.

reptile, *n.* saurian, crocodilian, serpent, lizard, *etc.*; toady, bootlicker. See ANIMAL, SERVILITY.

republic, *n.* democracy, free state, commonwealth, *res publica*; self-government, *vox populi*; people's republic, soviet, COUNTRY. See MANKIND, AUTHORITY.

repudiate, *v.t.* renounce, disavow, disclaim, disown, divorce, deny; disclaim. See DISSENT, REFUSAL.

repugnance, *n.* DISLIKE, aversion, antipathy, disgust; inconsistency, contradictoriness; OPPOSITION. *Ant.,* see ATTRACTION.

repugnant, *adj.* distasteful, repulsive, incompatible, contrary, antagonistic. See DISAGREEMENT, HATE.

REPULSION

Nouns—1, repulsion, repulse, repellency (see PROPULSION); abduction; REJECTION, rebuff, spurning; diamagnetism; RESISTANCE.

2, abhorrence, aversion, hostility, antagonism, antipathy; repugnance, DISLIKE, disgust, loathing, detestation; distaste, displeasure.

Verbs—1, repulse, repel, drive from, beat back; push *or* send away; send, ward, beat, fight *or* drive off; fling *or* throw back; chase, dispel, abduce, scatter, rout, disperse.

2, rebuff, reject, refuse, discard, snub, spurn, kick aside; keep at arm's length, turn one's back upon, give the cold shoulder to. *Colloq.,* cold-shoulder. *Slang,* freeze.

Adjectives—repulsive, repelling, repellent, abducent, abductive; abhorrent, repugnant, loathsome, odious, offensive, nauseating, revolting; diamagnetic.

Antonym, see ATTRACTION.

REPUTE

Nouns—**1,** repute, reputation, distinction, mark, name, figure; note, notability, vogue, celebrity, fame, famousness, renown, popularity, credit, prestige, glory, honor; luster, illustriousness, account, regard, RESPECT, reputableness, respectability, good name, fair name.

2, dignity, stateliness, solemnity, grandeur, splendor, NOBILITY, majesty, sublimity; greatness, IMPORTANCE, eminence, pre-eminence.

3, rank, standing, station, place, status, precedence, position, place in society, degree, caste, condition.

4, elevation, ascent, exaltation, dignification, aggrandizement; dedication, consecration, enthronement, canonization, CELEBRATION, enshrinement, glorification.

5, hero, man of mark, celebrity; lion, notability, somebody, pillar of the church; chief, first fiddle, flower, pink, pearl, paragon, star. *Slang*, VIP, big wheel.

6, ornament, honor, feather in one's cap, halo, aureole, nimbus, blaze of glory, laurels.

7, memory, posthumous *or* lasting fame, immortality, immortal name.

Verbs—**1,** be distinguished, shine, shine forth, figure, cut a figure, splash; make a splash, live, flourish, glitter, gain honor, play first fiddle, take precedence, win laurels, win spurs, leave one's mark, star, come into vogue.

2, rival, surpass, outshine, outrival, outvie, emulate, eclipse, cast into the shade, overshadow.

3, enthrone, immortalize, deify, exalt; consecrate, dedicate, enshrine, lionize, crown with laurel; honor, confer honor, do honor to, accredit, dignify, glorify, look up to, aggrandize, elevate. *Slang*, build up.

Adjectives—**1,** reputable, creditable, honorable, respectable, in good order, in high favor.

2, distinguished, *distingué*, noted, of note, honored, popular; fashionable; remarkable, notable, celebrated, renowned, talked of, famous, famed, conspicuous, foremost, in the ascendant; illustrious, glorious, splendid, brilliant, radiant, bright.

3, eminent, prominent; peerless, superior, pre-eminent; great, dignified, proud, noble, worshipful, lordly, grand, stately, august, princely, imposing, solemn, transcendent, majestic, sacred, sublime, heroic.

4, imperishable, deathless, immortal, neverfading, time-honored, sacrosanct.

Antonym, see DISREPUTE.

REQUEST

Nouns—**1,** request, requisition, petition, PLEA, suit, prayer; motion, overture, application, proposition, proposal, offer, canvass, address, appeal, apostrophe, orison, incantation.

2, mendancy; asking, begging, postulation, solicitation, invitation, entreaty, importunity, beseechment, supplication, imploration, obtestation, invocation, interpellation; charity case.

3, requester, petitioner, beggar, solicitor, canvasser, door-to-door salesman; applicant, suppliant, suitor, demander, importuner, bidder, asker. *Slang*, moocher, cadger, sponge, free-loader, panhandler.

Verbs—**1,** request, ask, beg, crave; sue, pray, petition, solicit; invite, beg, beg leave, crave *or* ask a boon; apply to, call upon, call for, commandeer, enlist, requisition, ask a favor.

2, entreat, beseech, plead, supplicate, implore, adjure, cry to, kneel to, appeal to; invoke, ply, press, urge, beset, importune, dun, cry for help; hound. *Colloq.*, buttonhole.

3, beg from door to door, go a-begging, cadge, pass the hat. *Slang,* sponge, mooch, panhandle, free-load.

Adjectives—**1,** requesting, precatory, suppliant, supplicant, supplicatory. **2,** importunate, clamorous, urgent, cap in hand, on bended knee.

Adverbs—prithee, do, please, pray, be so good as, be good enough, if you please.

Antonym, see DISOBEDIENCE.

requirement, *n.* want; NECESSITY; the necessary *or* requisite; requisition, demand; needfulness, essentiality, indispensability; urgency, exigency, *sine qua non*, matter of life and death. See COMPULSION. *Ant.*, see FREEDOM, CHANCE.

requisite, *adj.* necessary, required; imperative, essential, indispensable, urgent, pressing. See NECESSITY, COMPULSION.

requisition, *n.* demand, ORDER, claim, exaction, REQUEST. See COMMAND.

requital, *n.* retribution, RETALIATION; compensation, REWARD.

requite, *v.t.* retaliate, avenge; repay, indemnify, make amends, REWARD.

rescind, *v.t.* revoke, repeal, recall, annul. See NULLIFICATION.

rescue, *v.t.* liberate, set free, deliver, save; recover, reclaim. See FREEDOM.

research, *n.* INQUIRY, investigation, study, exploration.

resemblance, *n.* SIMILARITY, likeness, similitude; IMITATION, COPY.

RESENTMENT

Nouns—**1,** resentment, displeasure, animosity, anger, wrath, indignation, exasperation; pique, umbrage, huff, miff, soreness, dudgeon, acerbity, virulence, bitterness, acrimony, asperity, spleen, gall, rankling; ill-humor, bad humor, temper, irascibility, hate, irritation, bile, choler, ire, fume, dander, ferment, ebullition, pet, dudgeon, tiff, passion, fit, tantrums. See IRASCIBILITY, MALEVOLENCE.

2, sullenness, moroseness, sulks, black looks, scowl.

Verbs—**1,** resent, take amiss, take to heart, take offense, take in bad part, fly into a rage, bridle, bristle, flare up; sulk, pout, frown, scowl, lower, glower, snarl, growl, gnarl, gnash, snap, look daggers, grind one's teeth; chafe, fume, kindle, seethe, boil, boil with indignation, rage, storm, foam, vent one's spleen, lose one's temper, quiver with rage; burst with anger. *Colloq.*, take hard, blow one's top, fly off the handle.

2, anger, affront, offend, give umbrage, hurt the feelings, insult, fret, ruffle, nettle, pique, irritate, sting to the quick, rile, provoke, chafe, wound, incense, inflame, enrage, aggravate, envenom, embitter, exasperate, infuriate, rankle, put out of humor, raise one's dander, make one's blood boil, drive one mad.

Adjectives—**1,** resentful, offended, SULLEN; wrought up, worked up, indignant, hurt. *Colloq.*, sore.

2, angry, irate; wrathful, wroth, cross, sulky, bitter, virulent; acrimonious, warm, burning; boiling, fuming, raging; foaming at the mouth; convulsed with rage; in a stew, fierce, wild, rageful, furious, mad with rage, fiery, rabid, savage; flushed with anger, in a huff, in a passion, up in arms, in high dudgeon. *Colloq.*, hot under the collar, steamed up.

Adverbs—resentfully, angrily, *etc.*; in the heat of passion, in the heat of the moment.

Antonym, see GRATITUDE.

---

reserve, *n.* restriction, QUALIFICATION; RESTRAINT, CAUTION, reticence, dignity; STORE, stock. See SILENCE, MODESTY.

reserved, *adj.* undemonstrative, diffident, distant, reticent; set aside. See MODESTY, SILENCE.

reservoir, *n.* cistern, reserve, source, supply. See WATER, STORE.

reside, *v.i.* live, dwell, abide, sojourn, lodge. See PRESENCE.

residence, *n.* ABODE, home, dwelling, habitation; sojourn. See PRESENCE.

residual, *adj.* left over, extra, surplus; future, continuing. See RE-
MAINDER.

residue, *n.* REMAINDER, rest, remnant, leavings.

RESIGNATION

Nouns—**1,** resignation, demission, retirement, abdication, renunciation,
disclaimer, withdrawal, surrender, quitting; RELINQUISHMENT, abjuration.

2, resignedness, patience, forbearance, long-suffering, sufferance, acquiescence (see LENIENCY), passiveness, meekness, stoicism.

Verbs—**1,** resign, withdraw, demit, yield, surrender, submit, desert, retire, tender one's resignation, lie down, give up, throw in the towel
or sponge, quit.

2, forgo, disclaim, relinquish, abandon, abjure, renounce, forsake,
leave, waive, retract, deny, abrogate, abdicate, vacate; get rid of,
throw up, lay down, wash one's hands of.

Adjectives—**1,** resigning, renunciatory, abjuratory, abdicant; retired, in
retirement. *Colloq.,* out to pasture.

2, resigned, submissive, patient, long-suffering, acquiescent, unresisting,
complying, yielding, uncomplaining, reconciled, philosophical, stoical.

resilient, *adj.* elastic, pliable, rubbery; tensile, ductile, malleable; recuperative, tough, rugged; irrepressible, indestructible; resistant, renitent; buoyant, youthful. See ELASTICITY, DURABILITY.

resin, *n.* rosin; gum; lac; sealing wax; amber; bitumen, pitch, tar, asphalt, asphaltum; varnish, copal, mastic, megilp, lacquer, japan. See
COHERENCE.

RESISTANCE

Nouns—**1,** resistance, OPPOSITION, oppugnance, renitence, stand, FRONT;
reluctance, recalcitrance, OBSTINACY, impeding, kicking, parrying, imperviousness, endurance, fastness, immunity, immovability, DEFIANCE,
repulse, REPULSION, rebuff, snub, REFUSAL; impedance; FRICTION.

2, insurrection, rebellion, revolt, REVOLUTION, insurgence, mutiny; RE-
TALIATION; riot, uprising, DISORDER, sabotage; strike, turnout, lockout,
walkout, tieup, slowdown, boycott; sit-down strike, passive resistance,
[civil] DISOBEDIENCE.

Verbs—**1,** resist, withstand, stand [firm], stand one's ground, hold one's
own, stick to own's guns, hold out, make a stand, take one's stand,
show a bold front. *Colloq.,* stick it out.

2, oppose, defy, face, confront, stand up against, strive against, bear
up against; kick (against), grapple with, keep at bay; obstruct, impede. See HINDRANCE.

3, fight, struggle, put up a fight, attack, defend, persevere, die hard,
sell one's life dearly, fight to the last ditch. See TENACITY.

4, strike, walk out, turn out, boycott, picket, remonstrate, disobey,
sabotage; riot, rebel, revolt.

Adjectives—resisting, resistant, renitent, resistive, refractory, recalcitrant,
disobedient; repellent, repulsive, proof against, up in arms; unconquerable, irresistible, resistless, indomitable, unyielding, invincible; stubborn,
obstinate, obdurate, dogged, firm, uncompromising.

Antonym, see OBEDIENCE, SUBMISSION.

resistless, *adj.* powerless, unresisting; irresistible, ineluctable. See NECES-
SITY, ATTRACTION.

RESOLUTION

Nouns—**1,** resolution, resoluteness, determination, WILL, decision, strength
of mind, resolve, firmness, steadfastness, ENERGY, manliness, VIGOR,
pluck, backbone, COURAGE, devotion, devotedness.

2, mastery over self, self-control, self-command, self-possession, self-reliance, self-restraint, self-denial, moral courage, PERSEVERANCE, tenacity, OBSTINACY, doggedness.

Verbs—**1,** resolve, determine, have determination, be resolved, make up one's mind, will, decide, form a resolve; conclude; devote oneself to, set one's teeth, put one's foot down, take one's stand; stand firm, steel oneself, stand no nonsense; put one's heart into, take the bull by the horns, go in for, insist upon, make a point of, set one's heart upon; stick at nothing, go the limit. *Colloq.,* go all out, go the whole hog.

2, PERSEVERE, persist; stick it out, die hard, fight, insist.

Adjectives—resolute, resolved, determined, strong-willed, self-possessed, decided, definitive, peremptory, unhesitating, unflinching, firm, indomitable, game, inexorable, relentless, unshakable, inflexible, OBSTINATE, steady, persevering. *Colloq.,* together.

Adverbs—resolutely, in earnest, seriously, earnestly, heart and soul, at any risk, at any price, cost what it may, all or nothing, rain or shine, sink or swim.

Antonym, see DOUBT.

---

resonance, *n.* vibration; reverberation, resounding, rebound; reflection, echo; ringing, tintinnabulation; ring, boom, rumble; deep note, bass note. See LOUDNESS.

resort, *v.i. & n.* —*v.i.* gather, flock, frequent; turn to; have recourse to. See TRAVEL, PRESENCE, USE. —*n.* haunt, meeting place; REFUGE, resource. See ABODE.

resound, *v.i.* echo, reëcho, ring, reverberate, peal. See LOUDNESS, SOUND.

resourceful, *adj.* ingenious, inventive, imaginative, versatile, skillful; adaptable, resilient, prepared; devious, CUNNING. See INTELLIGENCE, SKILL.

resources, *n.* assets, WEALTH, prosperity; ingenuity, expedients. See MONEY, MEANS.

RESPECT

Nouns—**1,** respect, regard, consideration, COURTESY, ATTENTION, deference, reverence, honor, esteem, estimation, veneration, admiration; approbation, devotion, homage. See WORSHIP.

2, homage, fealty, obeisance, genuflection, genuflexion, kneeling, prostration, obsequiousness, salaam, kowtow, bow, salute.

3, respects, regards, duty, devoirs.

Verbs—**1,** respect, regard, revere, reverence, hold in reverence, honor, venerate, esteem, think much of, look up to, defer to, pay attention to, do honor, hail, salute, pay tribute to, kneel to, bow to, bend the knee to, prostrate oneself, WORSHIP.

2, command *or* inspire respect; awe, overawe; dazzle; impress.

Adjectives—**1,** respectful, deferential, decorous; reverent, reverential, worshipful (see RELIGION); obsequious, ceremonious.

2, respected, estimable, in high esteem, time-honored, venerable, emeritus.

Adverbs—deferentially, *etc.*; with due respect, in honor (of), in homage (to).

Antonym, see DISRESPECT.

---

respectable, *adj.* worthy, reputable, estimable; moderate, fairly good. See REPUTE.

respective, *adj.* particular, individual, several. See SPECIALITY.

respectively, *adv.* severally, one by one, each to each; in order. See APPORTIONMENT, SEQUENCE.

respire, *v.i.* breathe. See WIND.

respite, *n.* postponement, intermission, pause, reprieve, cessation, intermission. See LATENESS, REPOSE.

resplendent, *adj.* shining, lustrous, radiant, gleaming, gorgeous. See LIGHT, BEAUTY.

response, *n.* ANSWER, reply, rejoinder; responsory. See MUSIC.

responsible, *adj.* trustworthy, dependable; answerable, accountable, liable, chargeable; solvent. See ANSWER, DUTY, MONEY.

responsive, *adj.* sympathetic, sensitive, receptive, adaptable; antiphonal. See SOFTNESS, ANSWER.

rest, *n.* REMAINDER, remains, balance, residuum; REPOSE.

restaurant, *n.* café, eating house, coffee house, cafeteria, diner, automat, canteen. See ABODE.

restful, *adj.* soothing, quiet, reposeful, tranquil. See REPOSE.

restitution, *n.* RESTORATION, reparation, amends, *amende honorable*; ATONEMENT; remuneration; recovery, repossession; redemption; return, compensation; making good; rehabilitation; indemnification; retrieval; repair. *Ant.,* see ACQUISITION.

restive, *adj.* nervous, skittish, balky; refractory, disobedient, unruly; RESTLESS. See AGITATION, DISOBEDIENCE, REVOLUTION.

restless, *adj.* nervous, restive, impatient; fidgety, skittish, jumpy, unquiet, disturbed. See AGITATION, EXCITEMENT.

restlessness, *n.* AGITATION, disquiet, fidgets, jitters; wanderlust. See CHANGEABLENESS. *Ant.,* see STABILITY.

RESTORATION

Nouns—**1,** restoration, reinstatement, replacement, rehabilitation, re-establishment, reconstruction, REPRODUCTION, renovation, renewal, revival, REFRESHMENT, resuscitation, reanimation, revivification, reorganization.

2, renaissance, renascence, second youth, rejuvenescence, resurrection, resurgence, rebirth, recrudescence, new birth; regeneration, regeneracy, reconversion.

3, recovery, convalescence, recuperation, cure, repair, reparation, reclamation, redress, retrieval, relief, healing, rectification, cicatrization.

4, restitution, return, rendition, redemption, reinvestment, atonement; redress, replevin, REVERSION; *status quo ante*.

5, see REMEDY.

Verbs—**1,** restore, put back, reinstate, rehabilitate, re-establish, reinstall; reconstruct, rebuild, reorganize, reconstitute, reconvert; renew, renovate, regenerate; make *or* do over.

2, recover, rally, revive, come to, come around, pull through, be oneself again, get well, rise from the grave, survive, live again.

3, redeem, reclaim, recover, retrieve, rescue.

4, redress, cure, heal, REMEDY, doctor, physic, medicate; bring round, set on one's legs; resuscitate, reanimate, revivify, reinvigorate, refresh, make whole, recoup, make good, make all square, rectify, put to rights, set straight, correct, put in order, refit, recruit, reinforce.

5, repair, mend, fix, retouch, vamp, tinker, patch up, darn, stop a gap, staunch, caulk, splice, bind up wounds.

6, return, give back, bring back, render up, give up, let go, disgorge, reimburse, remit; get back, revert. *Slang,* cough up, kick back.

Adjectives—**1,** restored, renewed, convalescent, none the worse; refreshed.

2, restoring, restorative, recuperative, sanative, curative, remedial, sanatory, salubrious (see HEALTH); refreshing, bracing.

3, restorable, recoverable, retrievable, curable.

Antonym, see DESTRUCTION.

RESTRAINT

Nouns—**1,** restraint, HINDRANCE, coercion, constraint, COMPULSION, inhibition, deterrence, DISSUASION, repression, discipline, control, check, curb; limitation, restriction; PROHIBITION; monopoly.

2, confinement, durance, duress; imprisonment, incarceration, solitary confinement; isolation ward; entombment; limbo; captivity; blockade, siege, besiegement, beleaguerment.

3, arrest, custody, keep, CARE, charge, ward, protection. See KEEPER.
4, bond(s), irons, chains, pinions, gyves, fetters, shackles, manacles, handcuffs (*slang*, bracelets); straitjacket; muzzle, gag, yoke, collar, halter, harness; bit, brake, curb, snaffle, bridle, seine; martingale, lead; tether, hobble, picket, band, leash; bolt, bar, lock, latch; bars, PRISON.
Verbs—**1,** restrain, check, put under restraint, enthrall, enslave, restrict, debar, hinder, constrain, enjoin; coerce, curb, control, hold back, hold in, hold in check, hold in leash; withhold, keep under, repress, suppress, smother, pull in, rein in; prohibit, inhibit, DISSUADE. *Colloq.*, hold one's horses.
2, enchain, fasten, fetter, shackle, trammel; bridle, gag, pinion, manacle, handcuff, hobble, bind, pin down, tether, picket, tie up, tie down, secure; moor, anchor, belay. *Colloq.*, hogtie.
3, confine; shut up, lock up, box, bottle up, cork up, seal up, hem in, bolt in, wall in, rail in; impound, pen, coop, enclose, cage.
4, imprison, immure, incarcerate, entomb, put in irons; arrest, take into custody, capture, take prisoner, lead into captivity; send to prison; commit; give in custody, subjugate.
Adjectives—**1,** restrained, constrained, imprisoned, pent up, jammed in, wedged in, under lock and key, on parole; in custody, laid by the heels; bound; icebound, snowbound.
3, prohibitive, prohibitory; proscriptive, restrictive; taboo, prohibited, forbidden, banned, illegal, not allowed, unauthorized; out of bounds, off limits.
4, stiff, restringent, straitlaced, hidebound, reserved, binding.
Interjections—hands off! keep out! no trespassing; no thoroughfare.
Antonym, see FREEDOM.

---

restrict, *v.t.* check, LIMIT, confine, restrain, circumscribe, hinder, impede. See CIRCUMSCRIPTION, HINDRANCE, RESTRAINT.
result, *n.* consequence, conclusion, outcome, upshot, fruit, EFFECT, product. See PRODUCTION.
resume, *v.t.* recommence, reoccupy, retake, reassume; continue. See REPETITION, ACQUISITION, CONTINUITY.
résumé, *n.* abstract, summary, COMPENDIUM, condensation, digest, brief, precis, outline, review, synopsis; job summary.
resurgence, *n.* reappearance, renewal, revival (see REBIRTH); recovery, refreshment, RESTORATION; IMPROVEMENT, growth, INCREASE, rise, surge.
resurrect, *v.t.* restore, revive, rebuild, reëstablish, renew, rehabilitate. See RESTORATION.
resuscitate, *v.t.* revive, restore, reanimate; refresh, revivify. See RESTORATION, IMPROVEMENT.
retail, *v.t.* sell, dispense, vend, peddle, spread (gossip). See SALE, COMMUNICATION.
retain, *v.t.* See RETENTION.
retainer, *n.* emolument, remuneration, PAYMENT; adherent, SERVANT; hireling, henchman; guardian, bodyguard; (*pl.*) household, retinue. See ACCOMPANIMENT.
retake, *v.t.* resume; recover, recapture, retrieve; refilm. See ACQUISITION.

RETALIATION

Nouns—**1,** retaliation, reprisal, requital, counterstroke, retribution, COMPENSATION, reciprocation, reciprocity, retort, recrimination, ACCUSATION, tit for tat, give and take, blow for blow, *quid pro quo*, measure for measure, the biter bit.
2, revenge, vengeance, avengement; vendetta, feud; an eye for an eye.
3, vengefulness, vindictiveness, implacability, rancor, MALEVOLENCE, ruthlessness.
4, avenger, vindicator, Nemesis, Eumenides.

Verbs—**1,** retaliate, retort, requite, repay, turn upon, pay back, return in kind, pay in the same coin, cap, reciprocate, turn the tables upon, return the compliment, give as good as one gets, give and take, be quits, be even with, pay off old scores; make it quits.
2, revenge, avenge, take one's revenge, wreak vengeance, have a bone to pick, harbor a grudge, bear malice, rankle in the breast.
Adjectives—**1,** retaliative, retaliatory, recriminatory, retributive.
2, revengeful, vengeful, vindictive, rancorous, ruthless, unforgiving, implacable, relentless.
Antonym, see FORGIVENESS.

---

retard, *v.t.* delay, slow down, check, hinder, impede, postpone, hold up. See SLOWNESS, HINDRANCE.
retarded, *adj.* delayed; mentally deficient *or* handicapped, brain-damaged, moronic; backward, slow. *Colloq.,* mental. See IGNORANCE.

RETENTION

Nouns—**1,** retention, retraining, holding, keeping, custody, detention, maintenance, reservation, reserve, RESTRAINT, TENACITY; hold, grasp, gripe, grip, clutch(es); snare, trap. See POSSESSION.
2, retentiveness, retentivity, MEMORY, remembrance, recollection, reminiscence.
3, fangs, teeth, claws, talons, nails, hooks, tentacles, nipper, pincer, tusk; paw, hand, finger, digit, fist, wrist; jaws; tongs, forceps, tweezers, pincers, nippers, pliers, clasp, dog, wrench, cramp, clamp, chuck, vise, Visegrip; grapnel, grappling iron *or* hook.
Verbs—**1,** retain, hold, keep, detain, maintain, restrain, hold fast *or* tight, hold one's own; clinch, clench, grasp, clutch, grip, gripe, hug; save, preserve, secure, husband, reserve, STORE, withhold, hold *or* keep back, keep close, have a firm hold on, have in stock; entail, tie up, settle.
2, remember, recall, recollect, bear in mind.
Adjectives—retentive, detentive, retaining, keeping, holding, prehensile; unforfeited, undeprived, undisposed, incommunicable, uncommunicated, inalienable; unforgetting, dependable, tenacious, of good memory.
Antonym, see RELINQUISHMENT.

---

reticence, *n.* reserve, TACITURNITY, secretiveness, muteness. See CONCEALMENT. *Ant.,* see LOQUACITY, DISCLOSURE.
retinue, *n.* train, following, suite, cortège, attendants, retainers. See ACCOMPANIMENT.
retire, *v.* withdraw, retreat, leave, resign, rusticate, lie low, keep aloof; put out. *Colloq.,* go to bed. See DEPARTURE.
retirement, *n.* withdrawal, departure, SECLUSION, privacy, isolation, retreat, RESIGNATION.
retiring, *adj.* modest, unassuming, self-effacing, bashful, withdrawn. See MODESTY.
retort, *n.* reply, rejoinder, witticism, sally; alembic. *Slang,* comeback. See ANSWER, WIT, HEAT.
retract, *v.t.* withdraw, recall, take back, recant, disavow, repudiate, revoke. See CHANGEABLENESS, NULLIFICATION.
retreat, *n. & v.i.* —*n.* withdrawal, retirement, SECLUSION; shelter, asylum; REFUGE, resort. See ABODE, REGRESSION. —*v.i.* withdraw, retire, fall back.
retrench, *v.* cut (down), reduce, DECREASE, curtail; cut back. See ECONOMY.
retribution, *n.* compensation, redress, separation, reprisal, reciprocation; nemesis; amends. See RETALIATION, PAYMENT.
retrieve, *v.t.* recover, regain, reclaim, repair, restore, make amends, fetch. See ACQUISITION.
retroactive, *adj.* retrospective, regressive, *ex post facto.* See PAST.

retrograde, *adj.* retreating, retrogressive, reversed, deteriorating, degenerate, decadent. See REGRESSION, DETERIORATION.

retrospect, *n.* reminiscence, remembrance, retrospection, review. See MEMORY.

retrospective, *adj.* looking backward, reminiscent; retroactive. See PAST.

return, *v. & n.* —*v.* restore, put back, bring back, echo, yield, render, reply, reciprocate; nominate, elect; come back, recur, reappear, revert. —*n.* ARRIVAL, homecoming, REVERSION, recurrence, reappearance, rebound, ANSWER, reply, recovery, RETALIATION, RESTITUTION, COMPENSATION. See REPETITION.

reunion, *n.* gathering, ASSEMBLAGE, assembling, convention; reconciliation. See SOCIALITY, RESTORATION.

revamp, *v.t.* do *or* make over; recast, rework, rewrite; rehash, remodel, redesign, modernize, improve. See NEWNESS, RESTORATION, IMPROVEMENT.

reveal, *v.t.* disclose, show, divulge, announce, display, exhibit, expose, bare. See OPENING, DISCLOSURE.

revel, *v.i. & n.* —*v.i.* disport, gambol, romp, carouse; delight in, enjoy. See PLEASURE. —*n.* lark, spree, carouse. See AMUSEMENT.

revelation, *n.* disclosure, manifestation, exposition, revealment; Bible. See APPEARANCE, SACRED WRITINGS.

revelry, *n.* merrymaking, festivity, conviviality, jollification. See AMUSEMENT.

revenge, *n. & v.* —*n.* retaliation, reprisal; vengeance, vindictiveness, vengefulness; spite, rancor; feud, vendetta, grudge fight; requital; nemesis; tit-for-tat; retribution. —*v.* avenge, strike back, retaliate, requite, pay back, take an eye for an eye *or* a pound of flesh; spite; feud with; satisfy a grudge. See RETALIATION, MALEVOLENCE. *Ant.,* see FORGIVENESS, PITY.

revenue, *n.* income, receipts; earnings, profits, net, yield, dividends; taxes, tariff, customs, duties. See RECEIVING.

reverberate, *v.i.* reëcho, respond, be reflected. See SOUND.

reverberation, *n.* echo, repercussion, reflection, rebound. See SOUND.

revere, *v.t.* venerate, honor, RESPECT, esteem, admire; WORSHIP. See LOVE.

reverie, *n.* daydream, musing, fancy, brown study, wool-gathering. See IMAGINATION.

reversal, *n.* setback; turnabout, tit-for-tat; inversion; repeal; change of decision; upset; abrogation. See CHANGE, DETERIORATION. *Ant.,* see STABILITY.

reverse, *n. & v.t.* —*n.* antithesis, converse, opposite; misfortune, setback, comedown, defeat; tail, back (of coin), about-face, rightabout. See OPPOSITION, ACTIVITY, CHANGEABLENESS. —*v.t.* transpose, invert, evert, turn around; back; revoke, annul, set aside. See NULLIFICATION.

REVERSION

Nouns—**1,** reversion, reverse, reversal, return(ing); reconversion; atavism, reversion to type; turning point, turn of the tide; REGRESSION, relapse, recurrence; RESTORATION; INVERSION; RECOIL, alternation, reaction, backlash.

2, throwback, revenant, atavist; repeater, recidivist, backslider; escheat, lapse, succession; reversionist.

Verbs—revert, return, reverse; turn, hark *or* go back; recur, recidivate, recrudesce, relapse; restore; retreat, RECOIL; turn the tide *or* scale(s); regress, retrogress, backslide; escheat, lapse.

Adjectives—reversionary, reversive, reversional, regressive, retrogressive, recidivist; reactionary; atavistic; reversionable.

Antonym, see REGRESSION.

review, *v.t. & n.* —*v.t.* reëxamine, reconsider, revise, recall, rehearse, criticize, inspect. See INQUIRY, MEMORY. —*n.* retrospection, recollection; critique; criticism; inspection, parade; résumé, recapitulation, summary. See THOUGHT, DESCRIPTION.

revile, *v.t.* abuse, vilify, malign, asperse, calumniate, deride. See IMPRECATION, CONTEMPT.

revise, *v.t.* alter, correct, reconsider, edit, rewrite. See IMPROVEMENT.

revision, *n.* redaction; CHANGE, emendation, IMPROVEMENT; new version, remake, rewrite, new edition; old wine in new bottles; innovation, enlargement.

revival, *n.* resuscitation, revivification, reanimation; WORSHIP, camp meeting; reëstablishment, reintroduction. See RESTORATION.

revivalist, *n.* evangelist, gospel shouter, jubilee singer; religionist, missionary, salvationist. *Slang,* holy Joe, holy roller, Jesus freak, born-again Christian. See PIETY, RELIGION.

revive, *v.t.* reanimate, revivify; refresh; bring back, reëstablish; rally, perk up. See MEMORY, RESTORATION.

revoke, *v.t.* recall, repeal, annul, rescind, withdraw, abrogate; recant, repudiate, disavow. See NULLIFICATION, CHANGEABLENESS.

revolt, *n.* uprising, rebellion, insurgence, insurrection, mutiny, sedition. See DISOBEDIENCE.

revolting, *adj.* disgusting, repellent, loathsome, repulsive. See UNCLEANNESS.

REVOLUTION

Nouns—**1,** revolution, radical *or* sweeping change, clean sweep, *coup d'état,* uprising, counterrevolution, rebellion, breakup, upset, overthrow, reversal, débacle, cataclysm, convulsion.
2, ROTATION, turning, spinning, gyration, revolving; cycle.

Verbs—**1,** revolutionize, change radically, rebel, revolt, remodel, recast, reform, change the face of, break with the past.
2, revolve, rotate, turn, spin, whirl, twirl, gyrate, wheel go (a)round.

Adjectives—**1,** revolutionary, rebellious, insurgent, radical, revulsionary, cataclysmic.
2, rotating, turning, revolving, spinning, *etc.* See ROTATION.

Antonym, see INACTIVITY.

---

revolve, *v.* rotate, roll, circle, spin, recur. See ROTATION.

revolver, *n.* handgun, PISTOL, repeater. *Colloq.,* six-shooter, sixgun. See ARMS.

revulsion, *n.* DISLIKE, distaste, aversion, repugnance, disgust, REPULSION.

reward, *n. & v.* —*n.* recompense, remuneration, meed, prize, guerdon; indemnity, indemnification; quittance; COMPENSATION, reparation, redress, requital, amends, return, *quid pro quo*; salvage; perquisite; spoils; salary, pay, PAYMENT, emolument; tribute, bonus, tip, premium, fee, honorarium. *Slang,* jackpot, payoff. —*v.* recompense, repay, requite, remunerate, compensate; enrich, indemnify, satisfy; pay off. *Ant.,* see PUNISHMENT.

rhapsody, *n.* ecstasy, exaltation, transport, rapture; FEELING, EXCITEMENT; effusion, tribute, eulogy, panegyric, lyricism. See APPROBATION, POETRY, MUSIC.

rhetoric, *n.* oratory, eloquence, elocution, declamation, floridity. See SPEECH, ORNAMENT.

rheumatism, *n.* inflammation, ache, PAIN; rheumatoid arthritis, sciatica, gout, bursitis, lumbago, backache; neuritis, rheumatic fever. *Colloq.,* rheumatics, the rheumatiz, the misery. See DISEASE.

rhyme, *n.* alliteration, assonance; verse, poesy, doggerel; AGREEMENT, harmony, CONCORD, SIMILARITY. See POETRY.

rhythm, *n.* meter, cadence, lilt, pulsation. See POETRY, MUSIC.

rhythmic, *adj.* metrical, pulsating, periodic, recurrent. See REGULARITY.

ribald, *adj.* coarse, low, broad, vulgar; profane, blasphemous. See IMPURITY.

rich, *adj.* wealthy, affluent, opulent; fruitful, fertile, luxuriant; abundant, bountiful; sumptuous; gorgeous; sonorous, mellow. See MONEY, PRODUCTION. *Ant.,* see POVERTY, INSUFFICIENCY.

riches, *n.pl.* wealth, possessions, fortune, affluence, opulence.

rich man, Croesus, Midas, Dives, millionaire, capitalist, moneybags. See MONEY. *Ant.,* see POVERTY.

rickety, *adj.* shaky, infirm, weak, ramshackle; rachitic. See IMPOTENCE. *Ant.,* see POWER, STABILITY.

ricochet, *n. & v.* —*n.* bounce, rebound, carrom, RECOIL. —*v.i.* bounce off, cannon, glance off, deflect, reflect, skip, skim.

rid, *v.t.* eliminate, abolish, clear, eject; free, disburden, disencumber; get rid of. See EJECTION.

riddance, *n.* ridding, EJECTION, disposition, retirement, discharge; disencumberment, *etc.* (see RID); freedom, deliverance, release.

riddle, *n.* conundrum, enigma, puzzle; problem, poser. See SECRET.

ride, *v.i.* drive, tour, journey, travel; jog, gallop, trot, *etc.*; cycle, pedal. —*v.t.* be borne (on, in, by); sit (a horse); mount, straddle. See PASSAGE.

rider, *n.* postscript, codicil, appended clause, ADDITION; horseman, cyclist, passenger. See TRAVEL.

ridge, *n.* fold, welt, wrinkle, flange; arete, spine, esker. See CONNECTION, HEIGHT.

RIDICULE

Nouns—**1,** ridicule, derision, scoffing, mockery, quiz, banter, irony, persiflage, raillery, chaff, badinage; sarcasm; squib, lampoon, satire, skit, quip, grin, leer.

2, parody, burlesque, travesty, farce, caricature; comedy, buffoonery, practical joke.

3, ridiculousness, *etc.*; ABSURDITY, anticlimax, laughingstock, FOOL, object of ridicule, fair game, April fool, jest, joke, queer fish, odd fish, mockery, monkey, buffoon.

Verbs—**1,** ridicule, deride, jeer; laugh, grin *or* smile at; snigger, snicker, scoff, banter, rally, chaff, joke, twit, poke fun at, play tricks upon, fool, show up; satirize, parody, caricature, lampoon, burlesque, travesty, make fun of, make game of, make a fool of.

2, be ridiculous, play the fool, make a fool of oneself, commit an absurdity, raise a laugh.

Adjectives—derisive, derisory, mock; sarcastic, ironical, quizzical, burlesque, satirical, scurrilous. See ABSURDITY.

Antonym, see RESPECT.

riding, *n.* horsemanship, motoring; district, bailiwick (*Eng.*). See TRAVEL, REGION.

rife, *adj.* prevalent, widespread, epidemic; abundant, plentiful, profuse, teeming. See MULTITUDE. *Ant.,* see INSUFFICIENCY.

riffraff, *n.* rabble, *canaille,* dregs of society. See POPULACE.

rifle, *n.* GUN, firearm; piece, carbine, automatic rifle; (sub)machine gun; *chassepot,* culverin, needle gun; flintlock, wheellock, matchlock. See ARMS.

rift, *n.* crack, cleft, crevice, fissure; schism, breach. See CONTENTION.

rig, *v. & n.* —*v.* equip, furnish, fit out; improvise, jury-rig; scheme, manipulate, maneuver. *Colloq.,* fix; clothe, outfit. *Slang,* frame. —*n.* rigging, ropes, ropework, cordage, ratlines, shrouds, stays, wires; equipment, outfit, fittings, furnishings; VEHICLE; apparatus, machinery, pump, derrick, well, CONNECTION. See FILAMENT, SHIP, MEANS, ARRANGEMENT.

right, *n. & adj.* —*n.* dextrality; dexter; starboard; off side; reactionism, conservatism, Toryism. —*adj.* dextral, dexter; off (side), starboard, recto; rightist, conservative, Tory, antileftist; reactionary. See SIDE. *Ant.*, LEFT.

RIGHT, RIGHTNESS

Nouns—**1**, rightness, right, what ought to be, what should be, fitness, propriety; JUSTICE, morality, PROBITY, honor, virtue, lawfulness.

2, privilege, prerogative, title, claim, grant, POWER, franchise, license.

3, rightness, correctness, accuracy, precision; exactness; TRUTH.

Verbs—**1**, be right, be just, stand to reason.

2, right, make right, correct, remedy, see justice done, play fair, do justice to, recompense, hold the scales even, give every one his due.

Adjectives—**1**, right, upright, good, just (see JUSTICE); reasonable, suitable, becoming.

2, right, correct, proper, precise, exact, accurate, true. *Slang*, right on.

Adverbs—rightly, justly, fairly, correctly; in justice, in equity, in reason, without distinction of persons, on even terms.

Antonym, see WRONG.

---

righteous, *adj.* godly, upright, just, moral, good; puritanical. See VIRTUE, PIETY. *Ant.*, see IMPIETY.

rightful, *adj.* lawful, legal, equitable, just, true, fit, legitimate, entitled. See JUSTICE.

rigid, *adj.* stiff, inflexible, unyielding; set, firm, obdurate, strict; rigorous, cleancut. See HARDNESS, TRUTH, SEVERITY. *Ant.*, flexible, lax.

rigor, *n.* harshness, hardness, austerity, SEVERITY, stringency, rigorousness, strictness, rigidity, inflexibility, sternness. *Ant.*, see SOFTNESS.

rim, *n.* EDGE, border, margin, curb, brink.

rime, *n.* ice, frost, hoarfrost. See COLD.

rind, *n.* skin, peel, epicarp, integument. See COVERING.

ring, *v. & n.* —*v.* encircle, girdle, environ, encompass, hem in; toll, chime, clang; peal, toll, chime, tinkle; resound, reverberate. See SOUND. —*n.* circlet, circle, annulet, hoop, signet, girdle; machine, gang; ARENA; ringing, peal, chime. See CIRCULARITY.

ringer, *n., slang,* dead ringer, double, look-alike; substitute; pretender, fraud, poseur. See SIMILARITY, DECEPTION, SUBSTITUTION.

rink, *n.* course, drome, skating palace; icedrome, rollerdrome. See ARENA.

rinse, *v. & n.* —*v.* rewash, dip, splash; tint, COLOR, touch up. —*n.* shampoo, hairdressing, hair rinse. See CLEANNESS.

riot, *n.* brawl, meeting, uprising; DISORDER, row, fracas, uproar, tumult. See DISOBEDIENCE.

riotous, *adj.* seditious, insurgent; boisterous, unruly, clamorous. See DISOBEDIENCE, VIOLENCE.

rip, *v.t.* TEAR, split, rend, slit, sever, part. See DISJUNCTION.

ripe, *adj.* matured, perfected, complete, mellow, consummate. See PREPARATION, COMPLETION.

ripen, *v.t.* mature, prepare, perfect, mellow, season, temper. See PERFECTION, PREPARATION.

riposte, *n.* thrust, counterthrust *or* -stroke, parry, stroke; ANSWER; repartee, witticism, mot. *Slang*, (wise)crack. See WIT.

ripple, *v.i. & n.* —*v.i.* gurgle, babble, purl. See RIVER. —*n.* riffle, wavelet.

rise, *v.i. & n.* —*v.i.* arise, ascend, soar, slope upward; loom, appear; increase, augment; originate, spring from; get up; prosper; revolt. See ASCENT, OBLIQUITY, BEGINNING. *Ant.*, see DESCENT. —*n.* ASCENT; acclivity, slope; origin, source; appreciation, INCREASE; promotion, advancement; revolt. See CAUSE, IMPROVEMENT.

rising, *adj.* mounting, growing, advancing, ascending. See ASCENT.

risk, *v.t.* CHANCE, venture, hazard, gamble, jeopardize; invest. See DANGER.

risqué, *adj.* suggestive, indelicate, off-color, racy, spicy, sexy, daring. See IMPURITY.

RITE

Nouns—**1,** rite, ceremony, ceremonial, ordinance, observance, duty, form, function, solemnity, sacrament; service. See RELIGION.

2, ministration, preaching, sermon, homily, lecture, discourse, preachment.

3, seven sacraments; baptism, christening, immersion; confirmation, laying-on of hands; Eucharist, Lord's supper, communion, consecration, transubstantiation, consubstantiation, Mass; penance, ATONEMENT, repentance, confession; extreme unction, last rites; holy orders, ordination; matrimony.

4, canonization, transfiguration, telling of beads, processional, purification, incense, holy water, aspersion, offertory, burial, excommunication.

5, relics, rosary, beads, reliquary, host, cross, crucifix, pax, pyx, *agnus Dei*, censer, rood.

6, ritual, rubric, canon, ordinal, liturgy, prayer book, Book of Common Prayer, litany, lectionary, missal, breviary, Mass book; psalter, hymn book, hymnal, psalmody.

7, ritualism, ceremonialism, Sabbatarianism; ritualist, Sabbatarian.

8, holyday, feast, fast, Sabbath, Passover, Pentecost, Advent, Christmas, Epiphany, Lent, Holy Week, Easter, Whitsuntide, Michaelmas.

Verbs—perform service, minister, officiate, baptize, confirm, lay hands on, administer *or* receive the sacrament; administer *or* receive extreme unction, anoint, anele; preach, sermonize, lecture.

Adjectives—ritual, ritualistic, ceremonial, liturgical, baptismal, eucharistical, sacramental.

---

ritzy, *adj., slang,* classy, swell, swank(y), plush, posh. See OSTENTATION.

rival, *n. & v.t.* —*n.* competitor, contender, antagonist, emulator, OPPONENT. —*v.t.* vie with, cope with; exceed, excel. See CONTENTION, SUPERIORITY.

rivalry, *n.* CONTENTION, competition, OPPOSITION; emulation.

river, *n.* waterway, stream, creek, brook, watercourse, spring, fount, fountain, rill, rivulet, streamlet, runnel, tributary; torrent, rapids, flood, freshet; current, tide, race; waterfall, cascade; cataract; jet, spurt, squirt, spout, sluice; shower, downpour. See WATER.

rivulet, *n.* runnel, runlet, streamlet, rill, brooklet, rillet; freshet, trickle, riverlet, beck, burn. See WATER.

road, *n.* way, path, track, PASSAGE, highway, roadway, thoroughfare, trail.

roam, *v.i.* wander, range, ramble, rove, stray, stroll. See DEVIATION.

roar, *v.i. & n.* —*v.i.* shout, bellow, howl, bawl; resound, ROLL, rumble, thunder; guffaw. See LAMENTATION. —*n.* uproar, vociferation; ROLL, rumble, boom, rote; guffaw. See LOUDNESS.

roast, *v.t.* grill, barbecue, broil; bake; toast, parch. See HEAT. *Slang,* RIDICULE.

rob, *v.t.* plunder, rifle, pillage, steal, purloin, burglarize; defraud. See STEALING.

robe, *n.* cloak, mantle, gown, vestment, robe of state; purple. See CLOTHING.

robot, *n.* automaton, golem, mechanical man, cybernaut; slave, drudge, worker; pawn, catspaw, puppet, dummy. *Colloq.,* stooge. See MEANS, SUBMISSION.

robust, *adj.* vigorous, healthy, lusty, strong, sturdy, stalwart. See POWER, HEALTH.

rock, *v.i. & n.* —*v.i.* swing, sway, oscillate, teeter. See OSCILLATION. —*n.* crag, boulder, cliff; REFUGE, haven, SUPPORT, DEFENSE. *Colloq.,* stone. See LAND.

rocket, *n.* projectile, missile; propulsor; rocket ship, space ship; sky-rocket, firework. See ASTRONAUTICS, ARMS, VEHICLE.

rocky, *adj.* rugged, stony, hard; unfeeling. See ROUGHNESS, HARDNESS. *Slang,* dizzy, shaky.

rod, *n.* wand, pole, staff, switch, SCEPTER, caduceus. See SUPPORT. *Slang,* pistol, gat.

rogue, *n.* vagabond, scoundrel, cheat, scamp; imp, skeesicks.

roguish, *adj.* dishonest; mischievous, prankish, waggish. See AMUSEMENT.

roister, *v.i.* rollick, frolic, make merry, riot; rejoice, celebrate. *Colloq.,* paint the town [red], carry on, raise hell. See REJOICING, CELEBRATION.

role, *n.* PART, character, career, function, BUSINESS, CONDUCT, DRAMA.

roll, *n. & v.* —*n.* drumming, rumble, rattle, clatter, patter, toll; reverberation, echoing, thunder; tattoo, rat-a-tat, rub-a-dub, pitter-patter, dingdong, ticktock, charivari, quaver, peal of bells. —*v.* drum, rumble, thunder, rattle, clatter, patter, hum, trill, chime, peal, toll, tick, beat; reverberate, re-echo, resound. See RECORD, MUSIC.

roller, *n.* cylinder, wheel, roll, rouleau, platen, mill. See ROTATION, MEANS.

romance, *n.* novel, love story; exaggeration, fiction, tall story; love affair, gest, fantasy. See FALSEHOOD, DESCRIPTION.

romantic, *adj.* sentimental, heroic, picturesque, idealistic; dreamy, poetic, fantastic, visionary, quixotic. See IMAGINATION, SENSIBILITY.

romp, *v.i.* frolic, caper, cavort, gambol, frisk. See AMUSEMENT.

roof, *n.* COVERING, housetop, rooftop, shelter, ceiling; home, rooftree; top, summit. See ABODE, HEIGHT.

rookie, *n., slang,* beginner, novice, greenhorn, tenderfoot. See BEGINNING.

room, *n.* chamber, hall, apartment; SPACE, capacity, elbow-room; lodging. See RECEPTACLE.

roomer, *n.* tenant, lodger, occupant, boarder, INHABITANT.

roommate, *n.* berth *or* bunk mate. *Colloq.,* bunkie. *Slang,* roomie. See FRIEND.

roomy, *adj.* spacious, commodious, capacious, ample. See SPACE.

roost, *n. & v.* —*n.* perch, foothold, limb, branch; nest, rookery; ABODE, residence; refuge, place, berth, bunk, niche. —*v.i.* alight, land, perch on; stay, remain, settle, nestle, bed down; ledge, inhabit. See ABODE, LOCATION.

root, *n. & v.* —*n.* rootlet, radicle, radicel, taproot; radical; base, origin, essence, source; etymon. See NUMBER, CAUSE, WORD. —*v.* plant, implant; eradicate, extirpate; take root; acclaim, cheer. See LOCATION, APPROBATION, EJECTION.

rope, *n.* cord, line; hawser, painter, lanyard; lasso, riata; hangman's noose, execution; string, twist. See FILAMENT.

roseate, *adj.* rosy, blooming; optimistic, promising, propitious. See COLOR, HOPE. *Ant.,* see DEJECTION.

roster, *n.* LIST, register, roll call, muster; membership; census, count, tally, RECORD, catalog, slate.

rostrum, *n.* platform, dais, podium, stand, floor, pulpit, lectern. See SUPPORT.

rosy, *adj.* blushing, blooming, bright, promising, hopeful. See COLOR, HOPE.

rot, *v. & n.* —*v.i.* decay, decompose, putrefy; degenerate, waste. See DETERIORATION. —*n.* decay, decomposition, putrefaction. *Slang,* nonsense, piffle, twaddle, baloney.

ROTATION

Nouns—**1,** rotation, REVOLUTION, gyration, turning, circulation, roll; circumrotation, circumvolution, circumgyration, turbination, convolution. **2,** whir, whirl, turn, wheel, pirouette, eddy, vortex, whirlpool, cyclone, tornado; vertigo; maelstrom.

3, wheel, screw, whirligig, windmill, propeller, top, roller, flywheel; caster; axis, axle, spindle, pivot, pin, hinge, pole, swivel, bobbin, mandrel, reel.

Verbs—rotate, roll, revolve, spin, turn, turnaround, circulate, gyrate, wheel, whirl, twirl, eddy, trundle, bowl, roll up, furl, spin like a top; whirl like a dervish.

Adjectives—rotary, rotating, rotatory, rotational, rotative, whirling, circumrotatory, trochilic, dizzying, vertiginous, gyratory, vortical; centrifugal, centripetal.

Antonym, see DIRECTION, INACTIVITY.

---

rotten, *adj.* decomposed, putrefied, putrid; unsound, treacherous; corrupt, dishonest; offensive, disgusting. See UNCLEANNESS, DETERIORATION.

ROTUNDITY

Nouns—**1,** rotundity, roundness, cylindricity, sphericity, spheroidicity, orbicularity, globosity, globularity. See CIRCULARITY, CURVATURE.

2, cylinder, cylindroid, barrel, drum, roll, rouleau, roller, column, rundle; sphere, globe, ball, spheroid, ellipsoid, drop, spherule, globule, vesicle, bulb, bullet, pellet, bead, pill, BB, shot, marble, pea, knob, pommel; cone, conoid; funnel, cornet; pear-, egg- *or* bell-shape.

3, corpulence, obesity, fatness, *embonpoint*, stoutness, plumpness, weight. See CONVEXITY, SIZE.

4, resonance, sonority, grandiloquence, magniloquence (see SOUND).

Verbs—make rotund, round, round out, fill out, sphere, form into a sphere, ball, roll into a ball; snowball, bead.

Adjectives—**1,** rotund(ate), round, circular; cylindric(al) columnar; conic(al), funnel-shaped, infundibular; spherical, orbicular, globular, global, globous, gibbous; beadlike, moniliform; pear-shaped, pyriform; egg-shaped, oval, ovoid, oviform, elliptical; bulbous, fungilliform; bell-shaped, campanulate, campaniform.

2, corpulent, obese, fat, stout, plump, chubby, pudgy, buxom, full, full-fleshed, well-padded, roly-poly.

3, resonant, sonorous, rounded, grandiloquent, magniloquent.

Antonym, see ANGULARITY, STRAIGHTNESS.

ROUGHNESS

Nouns—**1,** roughness, unevenness, ruggedness, asperity, rugosity, corrugation, nodosity, nodulation, hairiness, arborescence, tooth, grain, texture, ripple. See TEXTURE.

2, brush, hair, beard, shag, mane, whiskers, mustache, imperial, toupée, goatee, tress, lock, curl, ringlet; plumage, plumosity, bristle, plume, crest, feather, tuft, fringe.

3, plush, corduroy, nap, pile, floss, fur, down, moss, bur.

Verbs—rough, roughen, ruffle, crisp, crumple, corrugate, make one's hackles stand up; rub the wrong way; rumple; go against the grain.

Adjectives—**1,** rough, uneven, scabrous, knotted, rugged, angular, irregular, crisp, gnarled, unpolished, unsmooth, roughhewn, craggy, cragged, scraggy; prickly, bristling, sharp; lumpy, bumpy, knobbed, ribbed, corduroy.

2, feathery, plumose, tufted, hairy, ciliated, filamentous, hirsute; bushy, leafy, whiskery, bearded, pilous, pilose, filar, shaggy, shagged, fringed, setaceous, bristly.

Antonym, see SMOOTHNESS.

---

round, *adj. & n.* —*adj.* circular, annular, spherical, globular, cylindrical; approximate. See CIRCULARITY, NUMBER. —*n.* REVOLUTION, cycle; CIRCUIT, ambit, course, itinerary, beat; series, catch, rondeau; routine, rut.

roundabout, *adj.* circuitous, indirect (see CIRCUITY). See DEVIATION, DECEPTION.

rouse, *v.* waken, arouse, animate, stir, stimulate, excite, incite, inflame. See POWER, VIOLENCE.

roustabout, *n.* longshoreman, stevedore, navvy, loader, lader, docker, dockman, dockwalloper; circus hand, ranch hand, odd-job man. See EXERTION.

rout, *v.t.* stampede, panic; discomfit, defeat, repulse. See SUCCESS.

route, *n.* path, road, way, course, PASSAGE, track, itinerary.

routine, *n.* practice, procedure, system, HABIT, round, rut.

rove, *v.i.* wander, ramble, meander. See DEVIATION, TRAVEL.

roving, *adj.* vagrant, restless, inconsistent, vacillating. See CHANGEABLENESS.

row, *v. & n.* —*v.t.* paddle, scull. See NAVIGATION. —*n.* rank, file, tier, range. See CONTINUITY, ARRANGEMENT.

row, *n.* quarrel, brawl, rumpus, melee. See DISORDER, CONTENTION.

rowboat, *n.* skiff, dinghy, dory, longboat, whaleboat, shell, punt, gig. See SHIP.

rowdy, *n.* ruffian, tough, hoodlum, bully, thug. See EVILDOER.

rowdyism, *n.* hoodlumism, ruffianism, delinquency. See VULGARITY.

rower, *n.* oarsman, oar, sculler, galley slave, waterman, gondolier. See NAVIGATION.

royal, *adj.* regal, imperial, princely, magnificent. See AUTHORITY, NOBILITY.

rub, *v.t.* buff, abrade, scour, polish; chafe, massage, stroke; graze. See FRICTION, NEARNESS, SMOOTHNESS.

rubber, *n.* eraser, eradicator; latex, gum arabic, caoutchouc; vulcanite; overshoe, galosh, arctic, boot, wader, hipboot; rubber band; session, game, series. See MATERIALS, CLOTHING.

rubbish, *n.* trash, waste, debris, litter, junk. See USELESSNESS.

rubble, *n.* rubbish, litter, trash, refuse, WASTE; ruins, debris, remains, detritus, wreckage, shards, pieces. See DESTRUCTION, REMAINDER.

rude, *adj.* barbarous, crude, primitive, rustic; harsh, rugged; coarse, uncouth; discourteous, uncivil, insolent. See VULGARITY, NEGLECT, DISCOURTESY. *Ant.,* see COURTESY, COMPLETION.

rudiment, *n.* element, germ, embryo, root. See CAUSE.

rudimentary, *adj.* elementary, abecedarian; embryonic, undeveloped, imperfect, vestigial. See BEGINNING.

rudiments, *n.* elements, beginnings, principia. See BEGINNING.

rueful, *adj.* sorrowful, regretful, doleful; pitiable, deplorable, pathetic. See DEJECTION, PAIN. *Ant.,* see CHEERFULNESS.

ruffian, *n.* rowdy, bully, tough, thug. See EVILDOER.

ruffle, *v.t.* gather, shir(r), crinkle, corrugate, plait; agitate, ripple, tousle, rumple, disarrange; vex, irritate. See AGITATION, EXCITEMENT.

rug, *n.* mat, carpet; lap robe. See COVERING.

rugged, *adj.* craggy, shaggy, rough, unkempt; harsh, stern, austere; robust, hale. See ROUGHNESS, POWER. *Ant.,* see SMOOTHNESS, IMPOTENCE.

ruin, *n. & v.* —*n.* DESTRUCTION, downfall, perdition; wreck, remains, relic. See FAILURE, REMAINDER. —*v.t.* wreck, raze, demolish, impoverish, seduce. See POVERTY, IMPURITY.

ruinous, *adj.* dilapidated, rundown; disastrous, calamitous, desolating, tragic. See DETERIORATION, PAIN.

RULE

Nouns—**1,** rule, law, ordinance, regulation, canon, code, act, measure, statute, decision, ruling (see JUDGMENT); commandment, COMMAND, ORDER; DIRECTION, guide, gospel, INFLUENCE, formula, FORM, standard, model, precept; MAXIM, aphorism, axiom; natural *or* normal state, normality, average (see MIDDLE), order of things, standing order, Procrustean law, law of the Medes and the Persians, hard and fast rule.

2, REGULARITY, UNIFORMITY, constancy, consistency, CONFORMITY, punctuality, exactness; routine, custom, HABIT, system, METHOD, ORDER.

3, sovereignty, supremacy, dominion, domination, predominance, control, sway; AUTHORITY, JURISDICTION, government, governance, administration, ministration, management, prerogative, POWER; lordship, mastership, mastery, majesty, regency, regnancy, regime, reign, empire.
4, ruler, governor, chief, lord, overlord; sovereign, potentate, monarch, regent, KING, EMPEROR; manager, director, minister, head, president; ruling class. See MASTER.
5, ruler, rule, straightedge, folding rule; guide; slide rule. See MEASUREMENT.
Verbs—**1,** rule, govern, reign, control, regulate, administer, minister, conduct, direct, lead; ORDER, COMMAND, dictate; predominate, domineer, MASTER, advise, persuade, prevail (on), guide, restrain, curb, bridle.
2, settle, fix, establish, determine, decide, adjudicate, judge (see JUDGMENT).
Adjectives—**1,** regular, uniform, symmetrical, constant, steady, systematic, methodical, according to rule; customary, conformable, natural, habitual, normal.
2, ruling, controlling, governing, commanding, leading, reigning, regnant, regent, chief; predominant, prevailing, prevalent.
3, conventional, formalistic, rigid, legalistic, ceremonious.
Adverbs—by the rule, as a rule.
                     Antonym, see DISOBEDIENCE.

---

rumble, *n.* roll, hollow roar, reverberation; back seat (of car). See SUPPORT.

rumor, *n.* report, hearsay, gossip, common talk. See INFORMATION.

rump, *n.* croup, buttocks; REMAINDER, fag, end; steak. See REAR, FOOD.

rumple, *v.t.* muss, dishevel, tousle, wrinkle, crumple. See ROUGHNESS.

run, *v. & n.* —*v.* scurry, hasten, travel, ply, flow, liquefy, act, function, extend, complete, pass into, continue, elapse; operate, thrust, compete, smuggle. *Colloq.,* streak. See TIME, MOTION, VELOCITY, DIRECTION, STEALING. —*n.* swift pace; race; trip, flow; SEQUENCE; demand; yard; brook.

runaway, *n. & adj.* —*n.* ESCAPE; fugitive, escapee, truant, renegade; refugee, turntail, fly-by-night, hit and run; landslide, no contest. *Colloq.,* walkover, whitewash. *Slang,* lam(mi)ster. See COWARDICE, SUCCESS. —*adj.* fugitive, uncontrollable, wild, speeding. See VIOLENCE, IMPULSE, SUCCESS.

run-down, *adj.* dilapidated, broken-down, tumbledown; weakened, weary, debilitated. *Colloq.,* done up, used up, in a bad way. See WEAKNESS.

rung, *n.* rundle, round, spoke; step, degree. See SUPPORT.

runner, *n.* race horse, racer, sprinter; MESSENGER, courier, solicitor; blade, skid; rotor; rug, mat, scarf; operator; sarmentum; tackle.

runt, *n. & adj.* —*n.* dwarf; pigmy. —*adj.* stunted, underdeveloped, tiny, wee. See LITTLENESS.

rupture, *n.* DISCORD, schism, split, falling-out; break, rift, breach; hernia. See DISEASE.

rural, *adj.* rustic, provincial, countrified, bucolic, pastoral, arcadian, agrarian. See ABODE.

ruse, *n.* trick, stratagem, artifice, wile, subterfuge. See DECEPTION.

rush, *v. & n.* —*v.* hurry, scurry, dash, speed, gush, surge; hasten, hurry, expedite, precipitate, urge, drive; assault, attack; advance. See HASTE. —*n.* HASTE, dash, precipitation; surge, gush, onrush; stampede. See VELOCITY.

rust, *v.* corrode, oxidize; deteriorate. See DETERIORATION.

rustic, *adj. & n.* —*adj.* rural, countrified, bucolic; artless, unsophisticated; unpolished, rude, backwoods. —*n.* peasant, farmer, bumpkin, boor. See POPULACE.

rustle, *v.i.* crackle, swish, whisk, whisper. *Colloq.,* steal (cattle).

rusty, *adj.* reddish-brown; timeworn, frowsy, antiquated; out of practice. See OLDNESS, INACTIVITY, DETERIORATION.

rut, *n.* groove, beaten path, track, FURROW; HABIT, routine.

ruthless, *adj.* relentless, merciless, inexorable, cruel. See SEVERITY.

S

Sabbath, *n.* day of rest, Lord's Day; Sunday, Saturday; First Day. See RITE.

saber, *n.* sabre; sword, scimitar, broadsword, cutlass. See ARMS.

sabotage, *n. & v.* —*n.* DESTRUCTION, vandalism; subversion. —*v.t.* destroy, cripple, disable, undermine, scuttle. *Colloq.,* throw a monkey wrench in the works. See HINDRANCE.

sac, *n.* pouch, pocket, cyst; vesicle; sound, bladder. See RECEPTACLE.

saccharine, *adj.* sweet, sickening, cloying, sugary. See SWEETNESS.

sack, *n. & v.t.* —*n.* bag; DESTRUCTION, pillage; wine. —*v.t.* ravage, plunder, pillage, despoil.

sacrament, *n.* RITE, ceremony; host, consecrated bread *or* wine.

sacred, *adj.* hallowed, sanctified, sacrosanct, holy; consecrated, dedicated, inviolable. See DEITY, PIETY.

sacred cow, *n.* idol, god; tradition; taboo, superstition. See IDOLATRY, BELIEF.

SACRED WRITINGS

Nouns—**1,** Scripture, the Scriptures, the Bible, the Book, the Good Book, Holy Writ, Holy Scriptures; inspired writings, Gospel; revelation, inspiration; text; King James Bible, Douay Bible, Vulgate; Talmud, Masorah, Torah; Haggadah, Halakah; exegesis.

2, Old Testament, Septuagint, Pentateuch; Octateuch; the Law, Jewish Law, the Prophets; major Prophets, minor Prophets; Hagiographa, Hagiology; Hierographa, Apocrypha.

3, New Testament; Gospels, Evangelists, Acts, Epistles, Apocalypse, Revelation.

4, Koran, Alcoran; the Eddas; Zend-Avesta; Veda, Upanishad, Bhagavad-Gita; Book of Mormon.

5, prophet (see ORACLE); evangelist, apostle, disciple, saint; the Apostolic Fathers; Holy Man.

6, Gautama Buddha; Zoroaster; Lao-tse; Mohammed; Confucius; Joseph Smith.

Adjectives—scriptural, biblical, sacred, prophetic; evangelical, evangelistic, apostolic, inspired, apocalyptic, ecclesiastical, canonical, textuary; exegetic, Masoretic, Talmudic; apocryphal.

Antonym, see IMPIETY.

sacrifice, *n. & v.* —*n.* oblation, offering, hecatomb, holocaust; immolation, self-denial. See RELIGION, WORSHIP. —*v.t.* renounce, give up; immolate. See GIVING.

sacrilege, *n.* desecration, profanation, blasphemy, IMPIETY, irreverence, DISRESPECT, IRRELIGION; defilement; sin, trespass, transgression; vandalism.

sacrosanct, *adj.* hallowed, only (see SACRED); saintly, snowwhite; inviolable, inviolate; sanctimonious. *Slang,* lily-white. See PURITY, RIGHT, DEITY.

sad, *adj.* sorrowful, downcast, dejected, unhappy, woeful, woebegone, depressed, disconsolate; melancholy, gloomy, cheerless, somber, dismal; heavy, heavy-hearted; regrettable, shameful. *Colloq.,* blue. See DEJECTION, PAIN, BADNESS. *Ant.,* see PLEASURE, CHEERFULNESS.

saddle, *n. & v.* —*n.* seat, pad; packsaddle, panel, pillion; back, joint, ridge, hump, crest. *Slang,* rig, hull, smacker. See SUPPORT. —*v.t.*

harness; load, encumber, embarrass; blame, accuse. See GRAVITY, ATTRIBUTION, ACCUSATION.

sadistic, *adj.* perverted, twisted; cruel, brutal, fiendish; malicious, pernicious, EVIL. See MALEVOLENCE.

safari, *n.* journey, expedition, excursion, trek; caravan. See TRAVEL, PURSUIT.

safeguard, *n.* DEFENSE, protection, safety device, shield, (a)egis; passport, safe-conduct, convoy. See SAFETY, PERMISSION.

safekeeping, *n.* CARE, custody, guardianship, protection. See SAFETY.

SAFETY

Nouns—**1,** safety, safeness, security, surety, impregnability; invulnerability, invulnerableness; ESCAPE, means of escape, safety valve; safeguard, passport, safe conduct; confidence (see HOPE).

2, guardianship, wardship, wardenship; tutelage, custody, safekeeping; preservation, protection, auspices, aegis.

3, protector, guardian; KEEPER, warden, warder; preserver, custodian; duenna, chaperone; escort, convoy; guard, shield (see DEFENSE); guardian angel, tutelary saint; watchman, policeman; sentinel, sentry, scout (see WARNING); garrison; watchdog; Cerberus, doorman, doorkeeper.

4, REFUGE, asylum; precaution (see PREPARATION); quarantine, *cordon sanitaire.*

Verbs—**1,** be safe; save one's bacon; ride out *or* weather the storm; land upon one's feet; bear a charmed life; ESCAPE.

2, safeguard; protect; take care of (see CARE); preserve, cover, screen, shelter, shroud, flank, ward; guard (see DEFENSE); escort, convoy; garrison; watch, mount guard, patrol; take precautions (see PREPARATION); take shelter *or* REFUGE.

Adjectives—**1,** safe, secure; in safety, in security; on the safe side; under the shield *or* aegis of; under the wing of; under cover, under lock and key; out of danger, out of harm's way; on sure ground, at anchor, high and dry, above water; unthreatened, unmolested; protected.

2, snug, seaworthy; weatherproof, waterproof, fireproof, bulletproof, bombproof; defensible, tenable, proof against, invulnerable; unassailable, unattackable, impregnable, inexpugnable.

3, safe and sound; harmless; scatheless, unscathed; not dangerous; protecting, guardian, tutelary; preservative; trustworthy.

Adverbs—safely, with safety, with impunity, without risk; out of danger; in the clear.

Antonym, see DANGER.

---

sag, *v.* droop, buckle, warp, curve; slouch, slump; weaken, wilt; decline, languish; lapse, fall off. See DEPRESSION, PENDENCY, DETERIORATION.

sagacious, *adj.* penetrating, shrewd, astute, hardheaded. See SAGE.

sage, *n. & adj.* —*n.* wise man, magus, savant, philosopher, wise counselor, Nestor, Solon, pundit. —*adj.* wise, intelligent, sapient, astute, discerning; grave, serious; prudent, judicious; thoughtful. See KNOWLEDGE. *Ant.,* see IGNORANCE.

sail, *v.* cruise, voyage; navigate, traverse. See NAVIGATION.

sailor, *n.* seaman, mariner, seafarer, sea dog, salt, tar, bluejacket. *Slang,* windjammer, gob. See NAVIGATION.

saint, *n.* hallow, pietist, apostle; votary; saintess, patroness; martyr; pir; saintling, saint-errant. *Colloq.,* angel, paragon. See PIETY.

sake, *n.* purpose, MOTIVE, reason, CAUSE; behalf, regard, GOOD. See AID.

salad, *n.* greens, herb, VEGETABLE, lettuce; tossed salad, cole slaw, aspic, vinaigrette. See FOOD.

salary, *n.* stipend, pay, remuneration, wage(s), hire, COMPENSATION, PAYMENT.

SALE

Nouns—**1,** sale, selling, disposal; auction, market, custom, BARTER; BUSINESS; salesmanship; vendibility, vendibleness, salability.

2, seller, vendor, vender; MERCHANT; auctioneer, pedler, peddler, huckster, pitchman; salesman, saleswoman, salesperson, *etc.*

3, clearance sale, end-of-month sale; bargain basement *or* counter; fire sale; black market, gray market; garage *or* tag sale.

4, MERCHANDISE, stock, produce, *etc.*

Verbs—sell, vend, dispose of, effect a sale; trade, merchandise, market, offer, barter, distribute, dispense, wholesale, retail; deal in; traffic (in); liquidate, turn into money, realize, auction (off); bring under the hammer; put up [at auction *or* for sale]; hawk, peddle, bring to market; undersell; make *or* drive a bargain.

Adjectives—salable, marketable, vendible; unsalable, unpurchased, unbought; cutrate, bargain-counter.

Adverbs—for sale, on the market, over the counter, under the counter; marked up, marked down, under the hammer, on the auction block; in *or* on the market.

Antonym, see PURCHASE.

---

salesman, *n.* MERCHANT, shopman, storekeeper, seller; solicitor, peddler, hawker, pitchman, huckster, drummer, traveling salesman; clerk, salesclerk, saleswoman (-girl, -lady, *etc.*), salesperson.

salient, *adj.* outstanding, prominent, striking, conspicuous; notable, momentous, signal. See IMPORTANCE.

saliva, *n.* spit, spittle, sputum. See EXCRETION.

salivate, *v.i.* spit, expectorate; drool, slaver. See EJECTION.

sallow, *adj.* yellow, muddy, sickly, pallid, wan, jaundiced. See COLOR, COLORLESSNESS.

sally, *n.* sortie, raid, foray, ATTACK; excursion, expedition, trip; outburst, outbreak; banter, riposte, repartee. See TRAVEL, WIT.

salmon, *n.* kipper, lox; alevin, parr, smolt, samlet, *etc.* See FISH, FOOD.

salon, *n.* drawing room, parlor, ballroom; gathering, reception, exhibition; gallery, studio, atelier, WORKSHOP, showroom. See ASSEMBLAGE, SOCIALITY.

saloon, *n.* hall, dining room, main cabin; sedan, four-door; bar, tavern, taproom, bistro. *Slang*, oasis. See DRUNKENNESS, RECEPTACLE.

salt, *v.t.* salinize; season; pickle, brine, drysalt, preserve, souse. See PRESERVATION. *Colloq.*, salt away, invest, bank, save. See STORE.

salty, *adj.* briny, brackish, saline; corned, salted, racy, pungent. See TASTE.

salubrity, *n.* healthfulness, wholesomeness. See HEALTH. *Ant.*, see DISEASE.

salutary, *adj.* healthful, salubrious, wholesome; healing, medicinal, sanatory; tonic; beneficial, GOOD. See HEALTH, IMPROVEMENT.

salutation, *n.* salute, address, greeting, welcome; RECEPTION, respects, salvo; salaam, bow, curtsy. See COURTEOUS, RESPECT.

salute, *v.* welcome, greet, hail; uncover, how, curtsy, present arms, dip colors. See INDICATION, SPEECH, COURTESY.

salvage, *n. & v.* —*n.* salvation, rescue, retrieval, recovery, reclamation; flotsam, jetsam, lagan. —*v.t.* rescue, save, recover, retrieve, redeem, reclaim, rehabilitate; snatch from the jaws of death. See RESTORATION, SAFETY.

salvation, *n.* redemption, deliverance, reclamation, salvage. See RESTORATION, PRESERVATION.

salve, *n.* ointment, balm, unguent; REMEDY, lenitive, emollient; FLATTERY.

salvo, *n.* volley, gunfire, burst; discharge, broadside, fusillade, rafale; strafing, shellfire; peppering, riddling; fanfare, salute; proviso, QUALIFICATION. See ARMS, PROPULSION, CELEBRATION, EXPEDIENCE.

same, *adj.*   identical, selfsame, interchangeable, alike, equal, equivalent; monotonous. See IDENTITY. *Ant.,* see DIFFERENCE.

sample, *n.*   specimen, example, exemplar, pattern; prototype, archetype; trial, portion, taste, teaser. See CONFORMITY.

sanatorium, sanitarium, *n.*   health resort, retreat, hospital, rest home. See REMEDY, INSANITY.

sanctify, *v.t.*   consecrate, bless, hallow, purify, beatify; sanction, authorize. See DEITY, PIETY, PERMISSION.

sanctimonious, *adj.*   pietistic, sacrosanct; self-righteous, holier-than-thou; hypocritical. *Colloq.,* goody-goody. See IMPIETY, AFFECTATION.

sanction, *n.*   PERMISSION, confirmation, ratification, approval, APPROBATION; interdiction, penalty, PUNISHMENT. See DISAPPROBATION.

sanctuary, *n.*   sacred place, chancel; REFUGE, asylum, immunity.

sand, *n. & v.*   —*n.* grit, granules; particle, grain, speck; beach, strand, desert, dune; abrasive; silica, otolith. *Slang,* COURAGE, pluck, spunk. See LAND, POWDERINESS.   —*v.* sprinkle, dust, powder; smooth, polish, abrade, sandpaper. See POWDERINESS, SMOOTHNESS.

sanguinary, *adj.*   sanguineous, gory, bloody, bloodthirsty, murderous; savage, cruel. See KILLING.

sanitarium, *n.*   See SANATORIUM.

sanitary, *adj.*   hygienic, clean, sterilized, germfree, safe, aseptic, antiseptic. See CLEANNESS, HEALTH. *Ant.,* see UNCLEANNESS, DISEASE.

SANITY

Nouns—sanity, saneness, soundness, reason; rationality, normality, sobriety; lucidity; senses, sound mind, *mens sana.*

Verbs—be sane, keep one's senses *or* reason; come to one's senses, sober up; bring to one's senses.

Adjectives—sane, rational, reasonable, *compos mentis*, of sound mind; self-possessed; sober, in one's right mind; in possession of one's faculties.

Adverbs—sanely, reasonably, *etc.*; in reason, within reason.

Antonym, see INSANITY.

---

sap, *n. & v.*   —*n.* plant juice, lifeblood; vigor, vitality; trench, FURROW. —*v.t.* undermine; tunnel; enfeeble, debilitate, devitalize. See CONCAVITY, IMPOTENCE. *Ant.,* see IMPROVEMENT.

sapid, *adj.*   See SAVORY.

sapling, *n.*   seedling, treelet, treeling; stripling, youngster. See YOUTH.

sarcastic, *adj.*   scornful, contemptuous, withering, cynical, satiric, ironical, sardonic. See RIDICULE, CONTEMPT.

sardonic, *adj.*   scornful, derisive; caustic, malicious, twisted. See CONTEMPT.

sash, *n.*   casement, casing; waistband, cummerbund, scarf; obi, baldric. See CLOTHING, SUPPORT.

Satan, *n.*   the Devil, Lucifer, Mephistopheles, Belial; Beelzebub, Asmodeus, Apollyon; the tempter, EVIL, the evil one, the evil spirit, the Prince of Darkness, the cloven hoof; Pluto, god of the underworld; the foul fiend, the archfiend; the devil incarnate; the serpent, 666 (*Rev. or Apoc.* 13:18); DEMON. *Slang,* the deuce, the dickens, old Nick, old Scratch, old Harry. *Ant.,* see ANGEL.

satanic, *adj.*   diabolic, demonic, demoniac, devilish; infernal, hell-born, hellish, fiendish, Plutonic; Mephistophelian. See DEMON. *Ant.,* see ANGEL.

satchel, *n.*   bag, carpetbag; schoolbag. See CARRIER, RECEPTACLE.

satellite, *n.*   hireling, dummy, puppet; moon; artificial satellite, space station; slave state. See SUBJECTION, ASTRONAUTICS, UNIVERSE.

satiate, *v.*   sate, satisfy; cloy, jade, make blasé; quench, slake; pall; glut, gorge, surfeit; bore; spoil; have enough of, have one's fill, have too much of. See SUFFICIENCY. *Ant.,* see INSUFFICIENCY.

satire, *n.* RIDICULE, sarcasm, irony, mockery, travesty, burlesque. See CONTEMPT.

satirical, *adj.* cutting, bitter, sarcastic, wry, ironic, sardonic, lampooning, cynical. See CONTEMPT, DISAPPROBATION.

satisfaction, *n.* COMPENSATION, gratification, enjoyment, contentment; ATONEMENT, reparation, redress, amends; fulfillment. See PLEASURE, RESTORATION. *Ant.,* see DISCONTENT.

satisfy, *v.t.* CONTENT, set at ease; gratify, sate, appease; convince, assure; pay, liquidate, discharge; fulfill, meet; suffice, do, answer. See PLEASURE, BELIEF, PAYMENT, SUFFICIENCY. *Ant.,* see DISCONTENT, DOUBT, INSUFFICIENCY.

saturate, *v.t.* soak, fill, drench, impregnate, imbue. See MIXTURE, COMPLETION, WATER.

saturnalia, *n.* festival, carnival; revel(ry), REJOICING, CELEBRATION.

satyr, *n.* faun, goat-man, panisc, demigod, godling; sensualist, lecher, rake, roué, wanton. See MYTHICAL DEITIES, IMPURITY.

sauce, *n.* dressing, dip, gravy; fillip, flavor, zest, TASTE. See FOOD, CONDIMENT.

saucy, *adj.* pert, impertinent, impudent, bold; smart, chic, piquant. See INSOLENCE.

saunter, *v.i.* stroll, loiter, amble, meander, ramble. See TRAVEL.

sausage, *n.* frankfurter, *Wurst,* kielbasy, salami, pepperoni; liverwurst, bratwurst, *etc. Colloq.,* hot dog, wienie. *Slang,* frank. See FOOD.

savage, *adj.* wild, untamed, uncivilized, uncultivated, barbarous, ferocious; fierce, feral, cruel, rude; angry, enraged. See VIOLENCE, MALEVOLENCE. *Ant.,* see BENEVOLENCE.

save, *v. & prep.* —*v.t.* rescue, deliver, preserve, salvage, safeguard; STORE, lay up, keep, hoard; redeem, convert; spare, avoid; economize, conserve. See PRESERVATION, PIETY. —*prep.* saving, except, excepting, barring, but, excluding.

savings, *n.pl.* backlog, reserves, nest egg, bank account. See STORE.

Saviour, Savior, *n.* Christ, Jesus [of Nazareth], Messiah, the [Lord's] Anointed; Redeemer, Son of God, [our] Lord. See DEITY.

savoriness, *n.* savor, palatability; relish, zest, gusto; tastiness, TASTE; delicacy, appetizingness; nidor. *Ant.,* see UNSAVORINESS.

savory, *adj.* zestful, to one's taste, good, palatable; nice, dainty, delectable; toothsome, gustful, appetizing, delicate, delicious, exquisite, rich, luscious, ambrosial; mouth-watering. *Colloq.,* tasty. *Slang,* scrumptious. See TASTE.

saw, *n. & v.* —*n.* SAYING; tool, blade, handsaw, hacksaw, ripsaw, *etc.*; serration. See MEANS, SHARPNESS. —*v.t.* cut, kerf; scratch, scrape, rasp, grate. See DISJUNCTION.

say, *v.t.* speak, tell, declare, state, aver, affirm, mention, allege, recite. See SPEECH, AFFIRMATION.

saying, *n.* saw, MAXIM, proverb, adage, byword, epigram, precept, apo(ph)thegm; dictum, *ipse dixit.* See AFFIRMATION.

scab, *n.* crust, cicatrice, eschar, incrustation; nonunion worker, strikebreaker. *Slang,* fink. See COVERING, DETERIORATION.

scaffold, *n.* framework, scaffolding, platform; gallows, gibbet. See SUPPORT.

scald, *v.* (par)boil, steam, broil, stew, cook; burn, scorch, scathe, sear, seethe, simmer. See HEAT.

scale, *n. & v.* —*n.* balance, steelyard; lamina, flake, incrustation, horny plate, squama, lamella, eschar; DEGREE, graduation, table, ratio, proportion; gamut. See MEASUREMENT, LAYER, COVERING, MUSIC. —*v.* weigh; peel, husk, exfoliate, flake; climb, surmount. See DIVESTMENT, ASCENT.

scalp, *n. & v.* —*n.* hair, epicranium. —*v.t.* strip, flay; fleece, gouge, overcharge (see CHEAT).

scamp, *n. & v.* —*n.* good-for-nothing, rogue, rascal, scalawag. See EVILDOER. —*v.t.* skimp, scrimp; slight, botch, work carelessly. See NEGLECT.

scamper, *v.* run; scurry, scuttle, skitter, scoot; flit, dash, dart. *Colloq.,* skip, hotfoot. *Slang,* skiddoo. See HASTE, DEPARTURE.

scan, *v.* examine, study, scrutinize; lookover, peruse, survey; contemplate. *Slang,* take a gander at, give the once-over. See VISION, INQUIRY, POETRY.

scandal, *n.* disgrace, infamy, shame, humiliation, stigma; defamation, slander, backbiting, calumny. See DISPUTE.

scandalize, *v.* insult, defame, calumniate, stigmatize; horrify, shock, appall, outrage. See DETRACTION, DISREPUTE, REPULSION.

scant, *adj.* limited, meager, inadequate, sparse; barely sufficient. See INSUFFICIENCY. *Ant.,* see SUFFICIENCY.

scapegoat, *n.* goat, whipping boy; butt, tool, victim; dupe. See SUBSTITUTION, ACCUSATION. *Slang,* see SUCKER.

scar, *n. & v.* —*n.* BLEMISH, flaw, cicatrice, pock; scab, crust, precipice, rock, crag, cliff. See ELEVATION. —*v.* cicatrize, mark, pit, scarify, BLEMISH, disfigure, deface, mutilate; mar, damage, dent, scratch. See DETERIORATION.

scarce, *adj.* rare, uncommon, deficient, scanty, few. See INSUFFICIENCY. *Ant.,* plentiful; see SUFFICIENCY.

scare, *v. & n.* frighten (see FEAR).

scarf, *n.* muffler, neckerchief, shawl; boa; sash, cornet, fichu, choker, veil, stole; snood, wimple, babushka; prayer shawl, talith. See CLOTHING.

scathe, *v.t.* injure, harm, hurt, scorch; castigate, denounce. *Colloq.,* tear apart, lash into. *Slang,* lambaste. See PUNISHMENT, DISAPPROBATION.

scatter, *v.t.* strew, DISPERSE, disseminate, dispel, dissipate. *Ant.,* see ASSEMBLAGE.

scatterbrained, *adj.* absent-minded, flighty, harebrained, daft. *Colloq.,* dizzy, daffy. *Slang,* barmy (*Brit.*). See INATTENTION, FOLLY.

scavenge, *v.* look (for), comb, pick, sift, hunt, cull, ransack, glean; dig, grub, root, scratch. *Slang,* scrounge. See INQUIRY.

scenario, *n.* plot, script, text, BOOK, libretto; summary, skeleton; screenplay, photoplay; typescript. See DRAMA.

scene, *n.* view, vista, landscape, panorama; site, LOCATION, setting; episode, event; outburst, tantrum; picture, tableau, pageant. See APPEARANCE, RESENTMENT.

scenery, *n.* prospect, landscape, view, scene; *mise en scène,* setting, backdrop, wings, borders, *etc.* See APPEARANCE, DRAMA.

scent, *v. & n.* —*v.t.* smell, detect; perfume. —*n.* ODOR, FRAGRANCE, aroma; sachet, perfume; track, trail, spoor.

scepter, sceptre, *n.* staff, mace, rod, baton, wand; rod of empire; insignia of authority. See INDICATION, AUTHORITY.

schedule, *n. & v.* —*n.* LIST, catalogue, inventory, RECORD, docket; agenda, outline, register; timetable, calendar, time sheet. —*v.t.* PLAN, ORDER, program, slate, book, TIME, docket, designate, appoint.

scheme, *n.* PLAN, plot, project, design, intrigue; system, method.

schism, *n.* DISJUNCTION, division, DISSENT, separation, split; heterodoxy; factionalism, faction, sect, subdivision. See HETERODOXY.

scholar, *n.* savant, pundit, pandit, sage; professor; graduate, academician, academist; master, doctor; fellow, don; licentiate; philosopher; magus; mathematician, scientist; littérateur, intellectual; intelligentsia; bookworm; learned *or* literary man; man of learning, letters *or* education; pedant, pedagogue; student. See KNOWLEDGE, SCHOOL. *Ant.,* see IGNORANCE.

scholarship, *n.* learning, erudition, KNOWLEDGE; scholastic *or* financial aid, fellowship. See REPUTE.

SCHOOL

Nouns—**1,** school, academy, university, alma mater, college, seminary, lyceum; institute, institution, institution of learning; gymnasium; class, semester.

2, day, boarding, primary, elementary, grammar, grade, secondary, high, junior high, summer, [college] preparatory *or* graduate school; parochial, denominational, public *or* private school; kindergarten, nursery school; crêche; reformatory; law *or* medical school; teachers' college, dental college; normal school; correspondence school; vocational, trade, business, secretarial, finishing *or* music school; conservatory; art, dramatic *or* dancing school; military school *or* academy. *Colloq.*, prep school; reform school.

3, curriculum, course; tuition; catalog; class, form, grade, seminar; classroom, lecture room; desk, blackboard; textbook, schoolbook; slate, chalk, eraser; three R's, ABC's.

4, learner, student, scholar, schoolboy, pupil; novice, neophyte, probationer; matriculation, graduation; undergraduate, freshman, sophomore, junior, senior, plebe, yearling, collegian, upperclassman; graduate, alumnus, alumna; faculty, professorship; chair, fellowship; master, proctor, teacher, instructor, lecturer, professor; provost, dean, bursar. See TEACHING.

Verbs—go to school, attend; matriculate, enroll, register; graduate, be graduated; TEACH, LEARN.

Adjectives—scholastic, academic, collegiate; educational, curricular, extracurricular.

---

science, *n.* KNOWLEDGE, SKILL, efficiency, technology.

scientific, *adj.* systematic, accurate, exact, sound. See TRUTH.

scintillate, *v.* glisten, twinkle, sparkle, glitter, coruscate, shine; be charming *or* witty, effervesce. *Slang,* turn on the charm. See LIGHT, SOCIALITY, WIT.

scion, *n.* sprout, shoot, twig, cutting, graft; heir, descendant. See DESCENT.

scissors, *n.* shears, trimmer, cutter, clipper, secateur. See SHARPNESS.

scoff, *v.i.* jeer, be contemptuous *or* derisive, flout, laugh. See CONTEMPT.

scold, *v.* reprove, rebuke, rate, chide, berate, tongue-lash. *Slang,* bawl out. See DISAPPROBATION.

scoop, *n. & v.* —*n.* scooper, ladle, dipper, spoon. *Colloq.*, profit, gain. *Slang,* NEWS, dope, story; beat, lead, exclusive. See CONCAVITY. —*v.* dig out, lade, hollow, rout, gouge, excavate. *Slang,* beat out. See CONCAVITY, PRECEDENCE.

scoot, *v.i.*, *colloq.*, dash, run, dart, scurry, scamper; leave, depart, go, decamp, exit. *Slang,* beat it, scram, vamoose, get lost. See VELOCITY, HASTE.

scope, *n.* extent, range, compass, capacity, SPACE, sphere, field. See BUSINESS.

scorch, *v.t.* char, singe, brown, blacken, toast, roast, parch, shrivel, wither; denounce, upbraid. See DRYNESS, HEAT. *Colloq.*, speed, burn up the road.

score, *n.* account, reckoning, tally, RECORD, reason; twenty; music, orchestration, arrangement. *Slang,* chart. See ACCOUNTING, MUSIC.

scorn, *n. & v.t.* —*n.* CONTEMPT, disdain, superciliousness; derision, ridicule. —*v.t.* despise, disdain, contemn, spurn. *Ant.*, see APPROBATION.

scoundrel, *n.* knave, villain, rascal, rogue, blackguard. See EVILDOER.

scour, *v.t.* scrub, abrade, polish, cleanse. See FRICTION.

scourge, *n. & v.* —*n.* whip, strap, belt, lash, horsewhip; PUNISHMENT, curse, affliction, bane, nuisance, plague. —*v.t.* whip, lash, flay, beat; punish, afflict, plague.

scout, *n.* spy, observer, spotter, outrider, reconnoiterer, FORERUNNER. See CONCEALMENT.

scowl, *v.i.* frown; lower, glower. See IRASCIBILITY.

scramble, *v.i.* clamber, swarm, struggle, scrabble, tussle, scuffle. See ASCENT, CONTENTION.

scrap, *n.* bit, crumb, morsel; splinter, chip; whit, tittle, jot, speck; fight, bout, tussle. See LITTLENESS, CONTENTION.

scrape, *v. & n.* —*v.* graze, brush; scratch, rasp, abrade, grind, grate; rasp, grate; curtsy, bow. See NEARNESS, FRICTION. —*n.* abrasion, scratch; DIFFICULTY, plight, PREDICAMENT.

scratch, *v.* score, gash, scrape, rasp, wound, lacerate, deface; erase, withdraw, reject; scribble, scrawl; irritate, scrape; rasp, sputter; scribble. See DETERIORATION, FRICTION.

scrawl, *v.t.* scribble, scratch. See WRITING.

scrawny, *adj.* underweight, puny, rawboned, bon(e)y (see SKINNY).

scream, *v.i.* shriek, screech, shrill, yell, CRY. See LOUDNESS.

screen, *n. & v.* —*n.* partition, curtain, shield, mask, protection, shelter; netting, mesh; sieve, sifter, bolter; cinema, movies, silver screen. See COVERING, DARKNESS. —*v.t.* shelter, shield, protect, hide, conceal, veil, shroud; sift, sort. See DEFENSE, CONCEALMENT.

screw, *n.* spiral, helix, volute; twist; propeller, prop, jack; pressure, coercion; extortionist, niggard, skinflint. *Slang,* jailer, turnkey. See CONVOLUTION, ROTATION, PARSIMONY.

scribble, *v. & n.* —*v.t.* scrawl, scratch, write carelessly. —*n.* scrawl, hen tracks. See WRITING.

scribe, *n.* scrivener, secretary, amanuensis, clerk, copyist; writer, author. See WRITING, BOOK.

scrimmage, *n.* free-for-all, fracas, scuffle, tussle, brawl. See CONTENTION.

scrimp, *v.* curtail, LIMIT, pinch, tighten, reduce; economize, skimp, stint, save, niggardize. See CONTRACTION, ECONOMY, PARSIMONY.

script, *n.* handwriting, penmanship, calligraphy; cursive, round hand; scenario, libretto, BOOK, screenplay, dialogue. See WRITING, DRAMA.

scriptural, *adj.* biblical, sacred; prophetic, evangelical, evangelistic, apostolic, inspired, apocalyptic, ecclessiastical. See SACRED WRITINGS.

Scriptures, *n.pl.* See SACRED WRITINGS.

scroll, *n.* ROLL, rolled manuscript, LIST, memorial; volute, flourish. See WRITING, ORNAMENT.

scrub, *v.t.* rub, scour, holystone, swab, mop. See FRICTION, CLEANNESS.

scruple, *n.* DOUBT, perplexity, misgiving, reluctance, unwillingness, qualm, conscience. See PROBITY.

scrupulous, *adj.* exact, careful; FASTIDIOUS, meticulous, punctilious; conscientious. See PROBITY. *Ant.,* see IMPROBITY.

scrutiny, *n.* examination, inspection, investigation, INQUIRY. See VISION.

scuff, *v.* scratch, abrade, scrape; disfigure. See FRICTION.

scuffle, *n.* strife, tussle, struggle, contest, CONTENTION, fray, fracas, brawl.

SCULPTURE

Nouns—**1,** sculpture, sculpting; carving; statuary, statue, statuette, bust, head (see REPRESENTATION); cast (see COPY); relief, relievo; high relief, low relief, bas relief; intaglio, cameo; anaglyph; medal, medallion.

2, marble, bronze, terra cotta, clay, alabaster; ceramics, ceramic ware, pottery, porcelain, china, earthenware.

3, sculptor, sculptress, carver, chiseler, modeler. See ARTIST, ENGRAVING.

Verbs—sculpture, carve, grave, cut, chisel, model, mould; cast.

Adjectives—sculptured; carven, graven; in relief; ceramic, marble, anaglyptic.

---

scum, *n.* froth, foam; slag, dross; mother (in fermentation); riffraff. See REMAINDER, POPULACE.

scurfy, *adj.* flaky, scabby, squamous, flocculent, furfuraceous. See LAYER, POWDERINESS.

scurrilous, *adj.* abusive, foul-mouthed, vituperative, insulting, coarse, vulgar, opprobrious. See IMPURITY.

scurry, *v.i.* hasten, dash, scuttle, scoot (see SCAMPER).

scurvy, *n. & adj.* —*n.* scorbutus, scurf, Werlhof's *or* Barlow's DISEASE. —*adj.* scorbutic, scurfy; villainous, mean, low, nasty, vile. See EVIL, DISREPUTE.

scuttle, *n. & v.* —*n.* hod, RECEPTACLE, pail, bucket; scoop, shovel; hatch(way), hole, OPENING. —*v.i.* flee, ESCAPE, run, scurry (see SCAMPER). —*v.t.* sink, scupper, swamp, destroy, sabotage; demolish, overthrow, suppress; see DESTRUCTION.

sea, *n.* OCEAN, main, lake; wave, billow, swell; vast amount, profusion, MULTITUDE. See WATER, GREATNESS.

seacoast, *n.* seashore, seaside, seaboard. See LAND.

seal, *n. & v.* —*n.* die, stamp, signet; embossment, wafer, stamp; guarantee, confirmation; safeguard, stopper. See PROTOTYPE, ASSENT. —*v.t.* stamp, ratify, confirm; fasten, secure, occlude. See COMPLETION, ASSENT, CLOSURE.

seam, *n.* ridge, JUNCTION; scar, wrinkle, furrow; stratum, bed, LAYER.

seaman, *n.* mariner, sailor, salt, tar, seadog, seafarer. *Slang,* gob. See NAVIGATION.

seamstress, *n.* sewer, stitcher; dressmaker, tailor(ess). See CLOTHING, PRODUCTION.

séance, *n.* ASSEMBLAGE, session, gathering, sitting, COUNCIL; spiritualism, spirit-rapping. See SUPERNATURALISM.

seaplane, *n.* flying boat; hydroplane, amphibian, water plane, aeroboat, supermarine. See AVIATION.

sear, *adj. & n.* —*adj.* dry, arid, desiccated; waterless, dry-as-dust; barren, sterile, effete; yellow, pale, colorless. See DRYNESS, USELESSNESS, COLORLESSNESS —*v.* dry, dehydrate, desiccate; singe, burn, scorch; brand, cauterize; wither, blast· fade, yellow. See HEAT, DRYNESS, INDICATION, DETERIORATION.

search, *v. & n.* —*v.t.* hunt, seek, look for; explore, examine; probe; test. See INQUIRY. —*n.* quest, PURSUIT; INQUIRY, examination, scrutiny, exploration.

searching, *adj.* penetrating, keen, sharp; rigorous, unsparing. See SEVERITY.

seasickness, *n. mal de mer,* naupathia; nausea, queasiness, qualm. See DISEASE.

seashore, *n.* seaside, shore, strand, beach; (sea)coast, littoral, coastline, waterfront. See EDGE, LAND.

season, *n. & v.* —*n.* period, TIME, spell, interval. —*v.t.* harden, acclimate, habituate, accustom; prepare, AGE, cure, ripen, dry out; spice, flavor. See HABIT, PREPARATION, PUNGENCY.

seat, *n.* chair, bench, *etc.* (see SUPPORT); site, LOCATION, ABODE; villa, estate; membership. *Colloq.,* buttocks, rump.

seaweed, *n.* algae, fucus, kelp, conferva. See VEGETABLE.

secede, *v.i.* withdraw, separate, bolt. See RELINQUISHMENT.

SECLUSION

Nouns—**1,** seclusion, privacy; retirement; reclusion, recess; snugness; delitescence; rustication, *rus in urbe*; solitude; solitariness, isolation; loneness, withdrawal, hermitism, eremitism, anchoritism, voluntary exile, aloofness; inhospitality, inhospitableness; unsociability; domesticity.

2, cell, hermitage; cloister, convent; holy of holies, Most Holy Place, *sanctum sanctorum*; depopulation, desertion, desolation; desert, wilderness.

3, recluse, hermit, cenobite, eremite, anchoret, anchorite; St. Anthony; Simeon Stylites; Timon of Athens; solitaire, ruralist, cynic, Diogenes. *Colloq.,* lone wolf, loner.

Verbs—be secluded, keep aloof, stand in the background; shut oneself up, creep into a corner, rusticate; retire; take the veil, take orders; abandon (see RELINQUISHMENT).

Adjectives—secluded, sequestered, retired, delitescent, private; conventual, cloistered, out of the world; out of the way; snug, domestic, stay-at-home; unsociable, unsocial, antisocial; inhospitable, cynical, solitary; lonely, lonesome; isolated, single; unfrequented, uinhabited, uninhabitable; tenantless; abandoned.

Antonym, see SOCIALITY.

---

second, *n.* moment, instant, trice, twinkling; interval, lower part, lower voice; backer, supporter, assistant. See INSTANTANEITY, MUSIC, AID.

secondary, *adj.* subordinate, minor, inferior, second-rate; resultant, consequent. See INFERIORITY. *Ant.*, primary; see IMPORTANCE.

secondhand, *adj.* used, hand-me-down; indirect, hearsay, unoriginal. See OLDNESS. *Ant.*, new, original; see NEWNESS.

second-rate, *adj.* inferior, lesser, secondary, next best; mediocre, second-class. *Colloq.*, also-ran. See INFERIORITY, MEDIOCRITY.

SECRET

Nouns—secret; dead secret, profound secret; mystery; sealed book; skeleton in the closet; confidence; problem, enigma, riddle, puzzle, crossword puzzle, acrostic, double acrostic, jigsaw puzzle, nut to crack, conundrum, charade, rebus, logograph (see DIFFICULTY); anagram; Sphinx, riddle of the Sphinx; labyrinth; unintelligibility; *terra incognita; arcanum,* esotery, esotericism, occult, occultism. See CONCEALMENT.

Verbs—secrete, hide, conceal, disguise; classify; keep to oneself, keep under one's hat.

Adjectives—**1,** secret, concealed, patent, enigmatical, puzzling, labyrinthine, veiled, hidden, problematical, paradoxical, inscrutable, unintelligible; esoteric, occult, mystic.

2, classified; restricted, confidential, secret, top secret, most secret.

Antonyms, see DISCLOSURE, INFORMATION.

---

secretary, *n.* amanuensis, clerk; minister, administrator; desk, escritoire. See WRITING, AGENCY, RECEPTACLE.

secrete, *v.t.* hide, conceal, mask; separate, prepare, excrete. See CONCEALMENT, EJECTION, EXCRETION.

sect, *n.* denomination, faction, following, school, fellowship. See RELIGION.

sectarian, *adj.* denominational; nonconformist, unorthodox, heterodox, heretical; dissident, schismatic, recusant, iconoclastic. See DISSENT, IRRELIGION, SECTARIANISM.

section, *n. & v.* —*n.* separation, DISJUNCTION, division; segment, PART, portion, cross section; BOOK, chapter; LAND, subdivision, sector, REGION; subdivision, subgenus, group, CLASS. —*v.t.* disjoin, divide, separate, bisect, slice, dismember, partition, distribute. See DISJUNCTION, ARRANGEMENT.

secular, *adj.* LAY, temporal, profane, mundane, earthly. See IRRELIGION.

SECURITY

Nouns—**1,** security, guaranty, guarantee; gage, warranty, bond, tie, pledge, plight, mortgage, debenture, hypothecation, bill of sale, lien, pawn; stake, deposit, earnest, collateral.

2, promissory note; bill, bill of exchange; I.O.U.; covenant, acceptance, indorsement, signature; execution, stamp, seal; sponsor, sponsorship; surety, bail; hostage; recognizance; indemnity; authentication, verification, warrant, certificate, voucher, RECORD; probate, attested copy; receipt, acquittance; discharge, release.

3, title deed, instrument; deed, deed poll; assurance, indenture; charter,

COMPACT; charter-poll; paper, parchment, settlement, will, testament, last will and testament; codicil.

4, see SAFETY, JUSTICE.

Verbs—give security, give bail, go bail; put up, deposit, pawn, mortgage, hypothecate; guarantee, warrant, assure; accept, indorse, underwrite, insure; execute, stamp; sign, seal.

Antonym, see DANGER.

---

sedan, *n.* VEHICLE, automobile, limousine, landau(let), closed *or* touring car; litter, palanquin, palkee. See SUPPORT.

sedate, *adj.* staid, calm, INEXCITABLE, serious, dignified, serene, demure, decorous. *Ant.,* frivolous, gay; see EXCITEMENT.

sedation, *n.* PACIFICATION, alleviation; narcosis, hypnosis; sedative. See REMEDY.

sedative, *n.* sedation; tranquilizer, bromide, calmant; sleeping pill; drug, narcotic, opiate, morphine; hypnotic; painkiller, barbiturate, analgesic; Demerol, Nembutal. *Slang,* goof ball. See PACIFICATION, REMEDY.

sedentary, *adj.* stationary, seated; inactive, sluggish, passive; non-migratory, white-collar, desk, office. *Colloq.,* stay-at-home. See QUIESCENCE, INACTION.

sediment, *n.* alluvium, silt, settlings, precipitate, lees, dregs, heel taps. See REMAINDER.

sedition, *n.* AGITATION, incitement, insurgence, disloyalty. See DISOBEDIENCE.

seduce, *v.t.* lead astray, lure, entice, corrupt, inveigle; debauch, betray. See IMPURITY.

sedulous, *adj.* diligent, industrious, assiduous, persevering, persistent. See ACTIVITY. *Ant.,* see NEGLECT, INACTIVITY.

see, *v.* view, descry, behold; discern, perceive, comprehend; observe, note; know, experience; ascertain, make sure; meet; escort. See VISION, KNOWLEDGE.

seed, *n.* germ, ovule, semen, milt; CAUSE, origin; offspring, children, descendants; grain. See BEGINNING, DESCENT.

seedy, *adj.* gone to seed *or* to pot; shabby, rundown, shoddy; broken-down, ramshackle; poor, indigent. *Colloq.,* grubby, grimy. See DETERIORATION, POVERTY.

seek, *v.t.* search for, hunt, pursue; request, solicit; try, attempt. See INQUIRY, PURSUIT.

seem, *v.i.* appear, look. See APPEARANCE.

seemly, *adj.* decorous, proper, becoming, decent, fitting. See OCCASION.

seep, *v.* leak, ooze, drain, drip, exude; trickle. See EGRESS, STREAM, WATER.

seer, *n.* prophet, crystal gazer, clairvoyant; soothsayer, ORACLE.

seesaw, *v.i.* teeter, teeter-totter; waver, vacillate, dilly-dally; crossruff. See OSCILLATION.

seethe, *v.* boil, stew, simmer; steep, soak; fume, chafe. See HEAT, RESENTMENT.

segment, *n.* slice, portion (see SECTION); component, member, branch, PART.

segregate, *v.t.* separate, set *or* keep apart, single out, discriminate, be prejudiced *or* biased; quarantine, isolate; exclude. See REMOVAL, EXCLUSION.

seize, *v.t.* grasp, clutch; capture, arrest, appropriate, confiscate; comprehend, understand. See ACQUISITION, INTELLIGENCE.

seizure, *n.* confiscation, appropriation, arrest, capture; attack, fit, spell, stroke. See ACQUISITION, RESTRAINT, DISEASE.

seldom, *adv.* rarely, not often, infrequently. See RARITY.

select, *v.t.* choose, pick, prefer, elect, opt, specify, designate. See CHOICE.

self, *n.* ego, I; being, essence; personality, IDENTITY, individuality, persona; mind, soul, spirit, self-esteem; inner self or being, inner man.

self-confident, *adj.* self-reliant *or* -assured, sure of oneself, poised, cocky, cocksure, smug. See CERTAINTY.

self-conscious, *adj.* self-aware, introspective; shy, embarrassed; unsure, hesitant; unnatural, stylized, theatrical. See THOUGHT, MODESTY, AFFECTATION.

self-control, *n.* self-discipline, -possession *or* -RESTRAINT; poise, composure; reserve.

self-denial, *n.* self-sacrifice, abnegation, renunciation, ASCETICISM.

self-esteem, *n.* PRIDE, self-respect; egotism, conceit, VANITY. *Ant.,* see MODESTY.

self-governing, *adj.* autonomous, independent, sovereign. See FREEDOM.

self-indulgent, *adj.* unrestrained, selfish, sensual, voluptuous, unbridled, sybaritic. See SELFISHNESS. *Ant.,* see MODERATION, RESTRAINT.

SELFISHNESS

Nouns—**1,** selfishness, self-indulgence, self-interest; egotism, egoism; VANITY; nepotism; worldliness; egomania, megalomania; illiberality; meanness, PARSIMONY.
2, selfish person, self-seeker, fortune-hunter, worldling; egotist, egoist, monopolist, nepotist; dog in the manger; spoiled child *or* brat.
Verbs—be selfish; indulge oneself; look after one's own interests; feather one's nest; take care of number one; have an eye to the main chance; know on which side one's bread is buttered; give an inch and take an ell.
Adjectives—selfish, self-seeking, self-indulgent, self-interested, self-centered; egotistic, egotistical; mean, mercenary, venal; earthly, mundane; worldly, materialistic, worldly-wise.
Adverbs—selfishly, ungenerously.
Antonym, see GIVING.

---

self-made, *adj.* autogenous, spontaneous; self-educated, self-taught, autodidactic; raised up by one's own bootstraps. See IMPROVEMENT, SUCCESS.

self-righteous, *adj.* smug, priggish; supercilious; sacrosanct, sanctimonious; hypocritical, holier than thou. See VANITY, AFFECTATION.

sell, *v.* See SALE.

sellout, *n., colloq.,* DECEPTION, betrayal, treachery, double-dealing; depletion, exhaustion; clearance, liquidation, closeout, fire sale; SUCCESS, hit, smash, full house, standing room only, S.R.O. See SALE.

semblance, *n.* likeness, resemblance, aspect; counterfeit, COPY, IMITATION; APPEARANCE, seeming, similitude, show, PRETEXT. See SIMILARITY. *Ant.,* see DIFFERENCE.

semiliquidity, *n.* stickiness, viscidity, viscosity; glutinosity; adhesiveness; inspissation, incrassation; thickening, gelatinousness; muddiness, miriness, slushiness. See COHERENCE.

seminal, *adj.* germinal; rudimentary, fundamental; productive, creative, catalytic, far-reaching. See PRODUCTION, ACTIVITY, LIFE.

seminary, *n.* SCHOOL, academy; theological school; seminar.

senator, *n.* legislator, congressman; solon, lawgiver, statesman. See COUNCIL.

send, *v.t.* dispatch, forward, transmit, broadcast; impel, drive. See PASSAGE, PROPULSION. *Slang,* excite, move.

send-off, *n., colloq.,* farewell, GOOD-BYE; outset, BEGINNING. See CELEBRATION.

senility, *n.* dotage, second childhood, superannuation, old age, degeneration, decrepitude. See AGE, OLDNESS, INSANITY.

senior, *adj.* elder, older; superior, top ranking. See AGE. *Ant.,* see YOUTH.

sensation, *n.* FEELING, perception, consciousness, impression; furor. See SENSIBILITY.

sensational, *adj.* melodramatic, thrilling, startling; lurid, yellow. See EXCITEMENT.

sense, *n.* MEANING, import; perception, FEELING; JUDGMENT, appreciation; opinion, consensus. See SENSIBILITY, WISDOM.

senseless, *adj.* unconscious; foolish, stupid, dull; meaningless, unreasonable, absurd. See INSENSIBILITY, ABSURDITY. *Ant.*, sensible, wise; see MEANING.

SENSIBILITY

Nouns—**1,** sensibility, sensitivity, sensitiveness; FEELING, perceptivity, esthetics; sensation, impression; consciousness (see KNOWLEDGE).
2, sensibleness, impressionableness, affectibility; susceptibleness, susceptibility, susceptivity; mobility; tenderness, SOFTNESS; sentimentality, sentimentalism.
3, sensation, tickle, tickling, titillation, itch, itchiness, itching; formication; aura; tingling, prickling; pins and needles.
Verbs—**1,** sensible of; feel, perceive; render sensible, sharpen, cultivate, tutor; cause sensation, impress; excite *or* produce an impression.
2, be sensitive, have a tender, warm *or* sensitive heart; take to, treasure; shrink; touch to the quick, touch the heart.
3, itch, tingle, creep, thrill, sting; prick, prickle, formicate; tickle, titillate.
Adjectives—sensible, sensitive, sensuous; esthetic, perceptive, sentient; conscious; acute, sharp, keen, vivid, lively, impressive, thin-skinned; impressionable; susceptive, susceptible; alive to; gushing; warmhearted, tenderhearted, softhearted; tender, soft, sentimental, romantic; enthusiastic, high-flying, spirited, mettlesome, vivacious, lively, expressive, mobile, excitable; oversensitive, thin-skinned; fastidious; alert, aware.
Antonym, see INSENSIBILITY.

---

sensitive, *adj.* perceptive, conscious, impressionable, tender, susceptible, sentient; alert, aware; sentimental. See SENSIBILITY, FEELING.

sensual, *adj.* voluptuous, carnal; salacious, lewd; sybaritic, epicurean. See IMPURITY.

sensualist, *n.* voluptuary; epicure; LIBERTINE. *Ant.*, see ASCETICISM.

sensuous, *adj.* sensitive, aesthetic, hedonistic; emotional, pleasurable. See SENSIBILITY, PLEASURE.

sentence, *n.* statement, expression; JUDGMENT, decision, penalty. See SPEECH.

sententious, *adj.* terse, laconic, pithy, succinct, curt. See CONTRACTION. *Ant.*, see LOQUACITY.

sentient, *adj.* perceptive, sensitive, feeling, responsive, alive. See SENSIBILITY, FEELING.

sentiment, *n.* opinion, FEELING; sensitivity, delicacy, sympathy; motto, toast. See SENSIBILITY.

sentimental, *adj.* emotional, romantic, simpering, maudlin, mawkish. See SENSIBILITY. *Ant.*, see HARDNESS.

sentinel, *n.* watchman, sentry, guard, lookout, picket. See DEFENSE.

separate, *v. & adj.* —*v.t.* divide, disunite, disconnect, part, detach, sever, keep apart, isolate, segregate, sift, screen. —*adj.* disconnected, distinct, alone, isolate, unconnected, individual. See DISJUNCTION. *Ant.*, see JUNCTION.

sepulcher, *n.* tomb, vault, crypt, mausoleum, sarcophagus. See INTERMENT.

sepulchral, *adj.* funer(e)al; gloomy, solemn, lugubrious; sonorous, resonant, deep-toned. See INTERMENT, DEATH, LAMENTATION, SOUND.

sequel, *n.* upshot, outcome, following event; continuation; consequence; appendix, postscript; second part; epilogue, afterword. See SEQUENCE, ACCOMPANIMENT, REAR.

SEQUENCE

Nouns—**1,** sequence, coming after; going after, following, consecutiveness, succession, extension, continuation, order of succession, successiveness; CONTINUITY.

2, successor, SEQUEL, continuance; FUTURITY, posteriority.

Verbs—**1,** succeed; come after, come on, come next; follow, ensue, step into the shoes of; alternate; place after, suffix, append.

2, follow, pursue, go after, fly after; attend, beset, dance attendance on, dog; hang on the skirts of; tread on the heels of; lag, get behind.

Adjectives—**1,** succeeding, successive; sequent, subsequent, consequent; ensuing, proximate, next; consecutive, alternate; latter, POSTERIOR.

2, following, attendant, trailing.

Adverbs—after, subsequently; behind, in the rear of, in the wake of; successively; sequentially, consequentially, consequently.

Antonym, see PRIORITY.

---

sequester, *v.* seclude, isolate, SEPARATE; cloister, shut up *or* away, immure, confine; confiscate, commandeer, expropriate. See SECLUSION, TAKING.

serenade, *n. & v.* —*n.* evening song, serenata, cassation, nocturne, shivaree. —*v.* sing to, entertain, perform for; court, WOO. See MUSIC.

serene, *adj.* calm, placid, tranquil, unperturbed; INEXCITABLE; clear, unclouded.

serf, *n.* bondman, esne, villein, vassal; peasant. See SERVANT.

sergeant, *n.* noncommissioned officer, N.C.O.; staff sergeant, sergeant, major, *etc. Colloq.,* top sergeant, top. *Slang,* [top] kick, gunny. See MASTER, COMBATANT.

serial, *adj.* seriatim; sequential, continuous, ordered, ranked, episodic; consecutive; to be continued. See SEQUENCE, CONTINUITY.

series, *n.* sequence, set, succession, chain, progression, cycle. See CONTINUITY.

serious, *adj.* grave, momentous, solemn; earnest, resolute; important, weighty; alarming, critical. See IMPORTANCE, RESOLUTION.

sermon, *n.* homily, lecture, discourse, DISSERTATION, exhortation. See SPEECH.

serpentine, *adj.* snaky, reptilian, herpetic; sinuous, slithery; winding, tortuous, snaking; CUNNING, wily, venomous, cold-blooded. See ANIMAL, CONVOLUTION, EVIL.

serrate, *adj.* serrated, saw-edged *or* -toothed, dentate; jagged; crenulate, scalloped. See SHARPNESS, NOTCH.

serum, *n.* antitoxin, vaccine; antigen, agglutinin; plasma; whey, WATER. See REMEDY.

SERVANT

Nouns—**1,** servant, servitor, domestic, menial, help; retainer, follower, henchman, subject, liegeman; retinue, suite, cortège, staff, court; major domo, chamberlain.

2, attendant, squire, usher, page; waiter, butler, steward; livery servant, lackey, footman, flunky, bellboy, valet, *valet de chambre*; man; equerry, groom; jockey, hostler; orderly, messenger.

3, employee, staff, personnel, secretary; clerk; subsidiary; AGENT.

4, maid, maidservant; handmaid(en); lady's maid, nurse, *bonne,* ayah, wet nurse, nursemaid, housemaid, parlor maid, waitingmaid, chambermaid, kitchen maid, scullery maid; *femme de chambre, fille de chambre; chef de cuisine,* cook, scullion; maid of all work, hired hand, laundress, charwoman.

5, serf, vassal, slave, bondsman, bondswoman; bondslave; villein; pensioner, dependent; hanger-on, satellite; parasite (see SERVILITY); protégé, ward; hireling, underling, mercenary, puppet, creature, henchman, cat's-paw, myrmidon, errand boy, office boy; batman, dog robber.

Verbs—serve, work for, tend; wait on, attend (upon), squire.

Adjectives—serving, ministering, tending; in the train of, in one's pay, in one's employ, on the payroll; at one's call (see OBEDIENCE); in bondage.

Antonym, see AUTHORITY.

service, *n.* AID, help, duty; servitude, ministration, employment; public utility; worship, ritual, armed forces; wear, usefulness, USE; set, equipment, serving, helping. See BUSINESS, UTILITY, RITE, FOOD.

SERVILITY

Nouns—**1,** servility, obsequiousness, subserviency; abasement; prostration, genuflection, WORSHIP; fawning, ingratiation; tuft-hunting, time-serving, flunkyism; sycophancy, FLATTERY; humility. *Slang,* apple-polishing.

2, sycophant, parasite; toady; tuft-hunter; snob, flunky, slavey, lapdog; hanger-on, leech, sponger; time-server, fortune-hunter; flatterer, lickspittle; henchman, hireling, tool, cat's-paw; courtier. *Slang,* yesman, handshaker, baby-kisser, back-slapper. See SERVANT.

Verbs—**1,** cringe, bow, stoop, kneel, bend the knee; sneak, crawl, crouch, cover; truckle to, curry favor with; grovel, fawn, lick the feet of, kiss the hem of one's garment.

2, pay court to; dance attendance on, hang on the sleeve of, fetch and carry, do the dirty work of.

3, flatter, adulate; wheedle, cajole; overpraise; humor, puff. *Colloq.,* soft-soap, butter up, lay it on thick. *Slang,* brown-nose.

Adjectives—servile, obsequious, abject; soapy, oily, unctuous; flattering, adulatory, mealy-mouthed, fulsome; pliant, cringing, fawning, slavish, groveling, sniveling, mealy-mouthed; beggarly, sycophantic, parasitical; base, mean, sneaking, skulking.

Adverbs—servilely, abjectly, *etc.;* with hat in hand; abased.

Antonym, see INSOLENCE.

session, *n.* sitting, meeting; period, term, semester; conference, hearing, convocation. See ASSEMBLAGE.

set, *v. & n.* —*v.* place, put, station; arrange, prepare; adjust, regulate; fix, assign, appoint; plant, set out; overthrow, unsettle; sink, go down, solidify, jell, harden; start out; tend; fit. See LOCATION, COMMAND, DESCENT, DENSITY. —*n.* clique, coterie, group; collection, series, outfit; TENDENCY, trend, drift; carriage, posture; agglutination, solidification. See COHERENCE, DIRECTION, PARTY.

setback, *n.* backslide; relapse, reverse, REVERSION, REGRESSION; defeat, LOSS, upset, check, discouragement. See ADVERSITY, DETERIORATION, DIFFICULTY.

settee, *n.* seat; settle, bench, form; sofa, lounge (see COUCH).

setting, *n.* background, backdrop; LOCATION, place(ment), site, locale, scene, ENVIRONMENT, milieu, REGION; mounting, BASE, frame, monture, collet, chape.

settle, *v.* define, fix, confirm, appoint; agree upon; resolve, determine, decide, conclude; tranquilize, calm; reconcile, adjust, compose; discharge, square, pay, set at rest; place, establish; colonize; defeat, outwit; locate, settle down, take residence; sink, subside, sag, solidify; precipitate; alight; arrange, agree. See LOCATION, STABILITY, RESOLUTION, AGREEMENT, PAYMENT.

settlement, *n.* ARRANGEMENT; disposition, reconciliation, AGREEMENT, JUDGMENT; colony, base, outpost, LOCATION; bestowal, PAYMENT, discharge, award.

settler, *n.* colonist, pioneer, emigrant, homesteader. See INHABITANT.

setup, *n.* ARRANGEMENT, situation, facilities, plant, layout; make-up, PLAN, COMPOSITION, rig. *Slang,* frameup, fix; gull, fall guy.

sever, *v.t.* cut off, cleave, separate, sunder, part; disjoin, dissolve. See DISJUNCTION. *Ant.,* see JUNCTION.

several, *adj.* individual, distinct, separate, particular; different, various; few, sundry. See MULTITUDE.

SEVERITY

Nouns—**1,** severity; strictness, harshness, rigor, stringency, austerity; inclemency; pitilessness, arrogance.

2, arbitrary power, absolutism, despotism; dictatorship, autocracy, tyranny, domineering, oppression; inquisition, reign of terror, martial law; iron heel *or* hand; brute force *or* strength; coercion, COMPULSION; strong hand.

3, tyrant, dictator, disciplinarian, martinet, stickler, despot, taskmaster, hard master, Draco, oppressor, inquisitor, extortioner, harpy, vulture, Simon Legree, slavedriver, drillmaster.

Verbs—be severe, give no quarter, domineer, bully, tyrannize; rack, put the screws on, be hard on; come down on; ill-treat; rule with a rod of iron; oppress, override; trample (under foot); tread upon; crush under an iron heel, ride roughshod over; keep a tight rein; work in a sweatshop.

Adjectives—severe, strict, hard, harsh, dour, rigid, stiff, stern, rigorous, uncompromising, exacting, exigent, inexorable, inflexible, obdurate, austere, relentless, Draconian, Spartan, stringent, straitlaced, searching, unsparing, ironhanded, peremptory, absolute, positive, imperative; coercive, tyrannical, extortionate, grinding, withering, oppressive, inquisitorial; inclement, ruthless, cruel; haughty, arrogant.

Adverbs—severely, *etc.*; with a high hand, with a heavy hand; at sword's point.

Antonym, see MODERATION.

sew, *v.t.* stitch, mend, baste, seam. See JUNCTION.

sewage, *n.* refuse, garbage, rubbish, WASTE, offal; drainage. See UNCLEANNESS.

sewer, *n.* seamstress; drain, cloaca, culvert, conduit, PASSAGE, sluice.

sex, *n.* gender; sexuality; MALE, FEMALE, masculine, feminine.

sexless, *adj.* neuter, asexual; gelded, castrated, emasculated, spayed, altered; impotent; cold, frigid, passionless. *Colloq.,* fixed. See IMPOTENCE.

sexton, *n.* sacristan, verger; vestryman, beadle. See CLERGY.

sexy, *adj.* voluptuous, seductive; lewd, lascivious; wanton, sensational, bold; pornographic, X-rated. See IMPURITY.

shabby, *adj.* dilapidated, seedy, rundown, threadbare; mean, sorry, pitiful, contemptible. See DETERIORATION, UNIMPORTANCE.

shack, *n.* hut, shanty, shed, hovel. See ABODE.

shackle, *n. & v.* —*n.* fetter, manacle, gyve, handcuff, bond; check, curb. See PRISON, RESTRAINT. —*v.t.* bind, restrain; handcuff, manacle, chain.

shade, *n. & v.* —*n.* shadiness, shadow, umbrage, gloom, gloaming, DIMNESS, DARKNESS; obscurity; duskiness; shading, tone; curtain, veil, film, haziness, haze, mist, mistiness, CLOUDINESS; COLOR, hue, tint; nuance; DEGREE, slight difference; blind, curtain, shutter, Venetian blind; spirit, ghost, phantom, specter, apparition, haunt. —*v.t.* hide, conceal; darken, shadow; cover, veil; COLOR, tinge, tint; obscure, overshadow. *Colloq.,* beat, outdo. *Ant.,* see LIGHT.

shadow, *n. & v.* —*n.* umbra, silhouette, SHADE; inseparable companion, sleuth; reflection; shelter, protection; trace, suggestion; ghost. —*v.t.* overcast, darken, shade; foreshadow, adumbrate; trail, tail, dog. See DARKNESS, CLOUDINESS, SEQUENCE, PREDICTION.

shaft, *n.* arrow, spear; beam, ray; handle; bar, axle; thill; column, pillar; well, pit. See ARMS, DEPTH, HEIGHT, SUPPORT.

shaggy, *adj.* nappy, fuzzy, wooly; unkempt, scragg(1)y, stubbly, bearded, hirsute; matted, tangled; rough(hewn), crude. See ROUGHNESS.

shake, *v.* vibrate, agitate, shiver, brandish, flourish, rock, sway, wave, rattle, jolt, worry, jar; unsettle, disillusion, impair, unnerve; tremble, quiver, quaver, quake, shudder, flutter, vibrate. See AGITATION, EXCITE-MENT.

shakeup, *n.* AGITATION, disturbance; reorganization, overhaul, REVOLU-TION, CHANGE, reformation, rearrangement, reconstruction.

SHALLOWNESS

Nouns—**1,** shallowness, shoalness, FLATNESS, emptiness, vacuity, super-ficiality; flightiness, CHANGEABLENESS, inanity, FOLLY; banality, in-sipidity, DULLNESS, vapidity, SIMPLENESS, IGNORANCE; triviality, frivol-ity, UNIMPORTANCE.

2, shallow, shoal, flat, shelf, sandbank, bar, [coral] reef, ford; façade, gloss, veneer, front; scratch, pinprick; surface or flesh wound; trivia.

Verbs—scratch, the surface, skim over, touch upon.

Adjectives—shallow, shoal(y), depthless, flat; empty, superficial, cursory; skin-, angle- *or* knee-deep; flighty, silly, slight, unintelligent, simple, foolish, ignorant; banal, fatuous, inane, insipid, puerile, jejune, vapid; trivial, frivolous, trifling, flimsy, trashy, meretricious, tawdry; obvious, dull, bland, gentle, mild, moderate, soothing.

Antonym, see DEPTH.

---

sham, *n. & adj.* —*n.* counterfeit, imitation, fake; pretense, dissimulation; humbug. —*adj.* make-believe, spurious, bogus, fake. See DECEPTION, FALSEHOOD.

shambles, *n.pl.* slaughterhouse, abattoir (see KILLING); wreck, chaos, MESS.

shame, *n. & v.* —*n.* humiliation, mortification, abashment; ignominy, re-proach, disgrace, dishonor. —*v.t.* humiliate, mortify, abash, disgrace. See DISREPUTE.

shameless, *adj.* brazen, barefaced, unblushing, graceless, wanton, im-modest. See INSOLENCE, IMPURITY.

shanghai, *v.t., slang,* abduct, kidnap, impress, commandeer. See COM-PULSION.

shank, *n.* leg, shin; shaft, stem; handle. *Colloq.,* END, REMAINDER. See SUPPORT.

shanty, *n.* shack, shed; hovel, tumbledown; hutch, bungalow. See ABODE.

shape, *n.* FORM, figure, contour; pattern, mold; STATE, condition.

shapeless, *adj.* amorphous, vague, ill-defined; disorganized; misshapen, distorted; unshapely, blobby. See FORMLESSNESS, DISTORTION, IN-ELEGANCE.

shapely, *adj.* well-built, -proportioned *or* -developed; handsome, beau-tiful, gainly, svelte, lissom(e), lithe; buxom, voluptuous. *Colloq.,* curvaceous, chesty, busty. *Slang,* stacked. See BEAUTY.

shard, *n.* potsherd; fragment, piece, splinter. See PART, LITTLENESS.

share, *n. & v.* —*n.* portion, PART, allotment, quota, dole. *Slang,* cut. —*v.t.* apportion, allot, assign, mete; participate. See APPORTIONMENT, COÖPERATION.

shark, *n.* dogfish, hammerhead, *etc.*; sharper, swindler. *Slang,* expert. See ANIMAL, THIEF.

sharper, *n.* cardsharp, slicker, cheat(er), swindler, crook. *Colloq.,* chiseler, crook. *Slang,* con man, gyp; shark, mechanic. See IM-PROBITY, DECEPTION.

SHARPNESS

Nouns—**1,** sharpness, acuity, acumination; spinosity; PUNGENCY, acerbity.

2, point, spike, spine, spiculum; needle, pin; prick, prickle; spur, rowel; barb, barbwire; spit, cusp; horn, antler; snag, thorn, briar, bramble, thistle; bristle; nib, tooth, tusk, fang; spoke, cog, ratchet.

3, crag, crest, *arête*, cone, peak, sugarloaf, pike; spire, pyramid, steeple.

4, wedge, KNIFE, cutting edge, blade, razor; scalpel, probe, lancet; plowshare; hatchet, ax(e), pickax(e), mattock, pick, adz(e), bill; billhook, cleaver, slicer, cutter; scythe, sickle, scissors, shears; sword (see ARMS); bodkin, PERFORATOR.

5, sharpener, hone, strop; grindstone, whetstone, steel; ABRASIVE.

Verbs—be sharp, have a point; bristle with; sharpen, point, aculeate, whet, barb, spiculate, set, strop, grind; cut (see DISJUNCTION).

Adjectives—**1**, sharp, keen; acute, acicular, aciform; aculeated, acuminated; pointed; tapering; conical, pyramidal; spiked, spiky, ensiform, peaked, salient; cusped, cuspidate cornute; prickly, spiny, spinous; thorny; bristling; studded; thistly, briary; craggy, rough, snaggy; digitated, two-edged, fusiform; dentiform; toothed, odontoid; starlike, stellate; arrow-headed; arrowy, barbed, spurred; cutting; sharp-edged, knife-edged; sharpened.

2, PUNGENT, stinging, acrid, caustic, spicy, strong. See TASTE.
Antonym, see BLUNT.

---

sharpshooter, *n.* marksman *or* -woman, crackshot; sniper. See COMBATANT, SKILL.

shatter, *v.* splinter, shiver, smash, disintegrate; destroy; madden, craze; crash, shatter. See BRITTLENESS, DISJUNCTION, INSANITY.

shave, *v.t.* pare, plane, crop; skim, graze; cheapen, mark down, trim. See DECREASE, CHEAPNESS.

shawl, *n.* scarf, stole, mantle, serape, mantilla, wrap; tallith. See CLOTHING.

sheaf, *n. & v.* —*n.* bundle, fag(g)ot; cluster, batch, bunch; quiver; fascicle, packet, bale. —*v.t.* sheave; bundle, tie, bind; gather. See ASSEMBLAGE.

shear, *v.* clip, scissor; cut, lop, snip, trim, prune; shave, mow, fleece; despoil, rob of, strip, denude. See DEDUCTION, DIVESTMENT.

sheath, *n.* scabbard, case, envelope, casing; involucre, capsule, fascia, lorica. See COVERING.

shed, *n. & v.* —*n.* shelter, lean-to; shack, shanty, hangar, trainshed. See ABODE. —*v.t.* spill, pour out; drop, cast off; mo(u)lt, slough off; spread, diffuse, scatter. See DIVESTMENT, EJECTION.

sheen, *n.* LIGHT, gleam, luster, shine, glow, shimmer, splendor. See SMOOTHNESS.

sheep, *n.* ram, ewe, lamb; bighorn, karakul; mutton; congregation, parish; follower. See ANIMAL, MANKIND.

sheepish, *adj.* shamefaced, blushing, downcast, coy. See MODESTY.

sheer, *adj.* utter, absolute; mere, simple; thin, diaphanous; perpendicular, precipitate, VERTICAL, steep. See COMPLETION.

sheet, *n.* bedsheet; shroud, winding sheet, cerement; page, leaf, folio; plane, surface, plate, lamina, LAYER, membrane; rope, mainsheet. See COVERING, FLATNESS, SHIP, INTERMENT.

shelf, *n.* ledge, mantel, mantelpiece; sandbank, reef. See SUPPORT, HEIGHT.

shell, *v. & n.* —*v.t.* bomb, bombard, cannonade, strafe, pepper; shuck, strip, pod, hull. See ATTACK, DIVESTMENT. —*n.* case; carapace; husk, seashell; bomb, grenade, explosive, shrapnel, torpedo; boat, cockleshell, racing boat. See COVERING, ARMS.

shell shock, combat fatigue; psychosis, neurosis; amnesia. See INSANITY, FEAR.

shelter, *n.* REFUGE, retreat, sanctuary, asylum; cover, security, protection, SAFETY. See COVERING.

shepherd, *n.* herder, sheepherder, herdsman; pastor, clergyman; Good Shepherd. See DOMESTICATION, CLERGY, DEITY.

sherbet, *n.* ice, slush, sorbet, granita. See FOOD.

shield, *n.* armor, safeguard, screen; protection, protector, aegis, egis; ARMS, escutcheon. See DEFENSE, COVERING, INDICATION.

shift, *v. & n.* —*v.* veer, vary, CHANGE; equivocate; contrive, get along; transfer; substitute. —*n.* CHANGE, SUBSTITUTION, DISLOCATION; expedient, subterfuge, trick; period *or* spell of work. See DEVIATION.

shiftless, *adj.* lazy, indolent, improvident, thriftless, negligent, happy-go-lucky. See NEGLECT, INACTIVITY. *Ant.*, see ACTIVITY, PREPARATION.

shifty, *adj.* unreliable, tricky; CUNNING; evasive, slippery; alert, resourceful.

shimmer, *n.* flicker, glimmer, gleam, sheen, glint, twinkle. See LIGHT.

shin, *n. & v.* —*n.* shinbone, tibia, shank, leg. —*v.* climb, creep up, clamber, scale; kick. *Colloq.*, shinny. See SUPPORT, ASCENT.

shindig, *n., colloq.*, shindy; party, gala, affair, CELEBRATION, spree.

shine, *v.* glow, gleam, scintillate; excel; polish, wax, burnish. See LIGHT, FRICTION, SKILL.

shingle, *n.* roof slate, wall slate; signboard; beach gravel; bob, short haircut. See COVERING.

SHIP

Nouns—1, ship, vessel, sail; craft, bottom; airship (see AVIATION).

2, navy, marine, fleet, flotilla; shipping, merchant marine.

3, warship, man-of-war, battleship, cruiser, destroyer, submarine (aircraft) carrier, flattop; transport, tender, storeshop; freighter, merchant ship, merchantman; packet; whaler, slaver, collier, coaster, lighter; fishing *or* pilot boat; dragger, trawler; hulk; yacht; liner; tanker, oiler.

4, bark, barque, brig, brigantine, barkantine; schooner; sloop, cutter, corvette, clipper, yawl, ketch, smack, lugger; barge, scow; cat, sailer, sailing vessel; steamer, steamboat, steamship paddle steamer; tug; tugboat.

5, boat, pinnacle, launch; lifeboat, longboat, jollyboat, bumboat, flyboat, cockboat, canalboat, ferryboat; shallop, gig, skiff, dinghy, scow, cockleshell, wherry, punt, outrigger; float, raft, rubber raft, pontoon; fireboat, motorboat; cabin cruiser, houseboat; class boat.

6, catamaran, coracle, gondola, carvel, caravel; felucca, caique; dugout; canoe; bireme, trireme; galley, hooker, argosy, carrack; galliass, galleon, galliot; junk, praam, proa, prahu, saic, sampan, xebec, dhow; dahabeah.

Verbs—sail, cruise, steam, drift, navigate. See NAVIGATION.

Adverbs—afloat, aboard, on board, aboardship, on shipboard, amidship(s).

---

shipment, *n.* delivery, conveyance, carriage, truckage; load, cargo, freight, lading; order, consignment. See TRANSPORTATION.

shipshape, *adj.* trim, tidy, neat, orderly, spruce; prepared, set; methodical; taut, seaworthy; tiptop, in the pink, perfect. See ORDER, PREPARATION.

shipwreck, *n. & v.* —*n.* derelict, castaway, wreckage, flotsam, hulk; ruin, bankruptcy, *etc.* —*v.* wreck, ruin, scuttle, sink, capsize, run ashore; ground; shatter, destroy, fail. See ADVERSITY, DESTRUCTION, FAILURE.

shirk, *v.* evade, shun, NEGLECT; slack, soldier, malinger. *Slang*, goldbrick. See AVOIDANCE.

shirt, *n.* blouse, chemise(tte), camisole, shift, plastron. See CLOTHING.

shiver, *v.i.* tremble, shudder, quiver, shake; shatter, splinter, burst. See AGITATION, BRITTLENESS.

shoal, *n.* SCHOOL, MULTITUDE, host, horde; shallow, sandbar. See ASSEMBLAGE, LOWNESS.

shock, *v. & n.* —*v.t.* shake, jar, jolt; startle, surprise, horrify, scandalize, disgust; paralyze, stun; galvanize, electrify. See SURPRISE, PAIN. —*n.* concussion, jar, impact; brunt, onset, assault; earthquake, temblor; prostration, stroke, paralysis, shellshock, apoplexy; ordeal, calamity; stack, stook; crop, thatch, mop (of hair). See VIOLENCE, AGITATION, DISEASE, ASSEMBLAGE, ROUGHNESS.

shocking, *adj.* distressing, horrible, abominable, odious, opprobrious, ghastly, indecent; dire, frightful, fearful, appalling, horrendous. See BADNESS, FEAR, DISREPUTE.

shoddy, *adj.* inferior, low-grade, shabby; tawdry, gimcrack; sham, IMITATION; vulgar, common; low, mean, ignoble. See VULGARITY, IMPROBITY, MALEVOLENCE.

shoe, *n.* footwear; footgear; sandal, boot, loafer, casual, sneaker; runner, (tire) casing; brake lining. See CLOTHING.

shoemaker, *n.* cobbler, bootmaker, cordwainer. See CLOTHING.

shoo, *v. & interj.* —*v.t.* chase, disperse, scatter, dispel. —*interj.* scat! get away! get out! go away! *Slang,* scram; beat it! blow! See DISPERSION.

shoot, *v.* rush, dart; sprout, burgeon, grow; fire, discharge; detonate, explode; kill, wound, hit; propel, drive, emit. See VELOCITY, VIOLENCE, INCREASE, KILLING, PROPULSION.

shop, *n.* mart, MARKET, store, bazaar, emporium; office, workshop, works, factory, mill. See BUSINESS.

shopkeeper, *n.* tradesman, MERCHANT, dealer, retailer. See SALE.

shore, *n.* coast, beach, coastline; bank, strand, shingle, seaside. See LAND.

shortcoming, *n.* failing, foible, weakness, fault; deficiency, defect, default; delinquency, FAILURE, NEGLECT, remissness; inadequacy, INSUFFICIENCY, shortage, lack. See IMPERFECTION, ERROR. *Ant.,* see SUFFICIENCY, PERFECTION.

shortening, *n.* fat, lard, butter, suet, (oleo)margarine, OIL.

shorthand, *n.* stenography, phonography, stenotypy, stenology; Pitman, Gregg, Speedwriting. See WRITING.

shorthanded, *adj.* understaffed, short (of help). See INSUFFICIENCY.

short-lived, *adj.* transitory, impermanent, mortal, perishable, ephemeral, fugitive, evanescent; doomed. See SHORTNESS, TRANSIENTNESS, FAILURE.

SHORTNESS

Nouns—shortness, brevity, briefness; LITTLENESS; shortening, abbreviation, abridgement, retrenchment, curtailment; compression, digest, condensation, reduction, CONTRACTION; epitome, synopsis, compendium; conciseness.

Verbs—be short, shorten, curtail, abridge, boil down, abstract, condense, digest, abbreviate, take in, reduce; compress, contract; epitomize; retrench, cut short, scrimp, cut, chop up, hack, hew; cut down; clip, dock, lop, prune; shear, shave; mow, reap, crop; snub; truncate, stunt, nip in the bud, check the growth of; foreshorten; come to the point.

Adjectives—short, brief, curt, succinct, epitomized, compendious, compact, concise, summary, stubby, shorn, stubbed; stumpy, thickset, pug; squat, dumpy; dwarfed, dwarfish, little; oblate.

Adverbs—shortly, in short; concisely in brief, in fine, in a nutshell, in a word, in a few words; to come to the point, to make a long story short, to be brief; abruptly.

Antonym, see LENGTH.

---

shortsighted, *adj.* myopic, nearsighted (see DIMSIGHTED); improvident, unimaginative, lacking foresight. See VISION.

short-winded, *adj.* dyspn(o)eic, broken-winded, asthmatic, wheezy. See WEARINESS.

shot, *adj. & n.* —*adj.* propelled, struck (see SHOOT); interspersed, interwoven. See MIXTURE. —*n.* bullet, ball, pellet; discharge, stroke, attempt; injection, inoculation, hypodermic, hypo. See ARMS, REMEDY.

shoulder, *n. & v.* *n.* scapula; projection, abutment. See ANGULARITY. —*v.* assume, bear, carry; sustain, maintain, SUPPORT; jostle, poke (see SHOVE).

shout, *v. & n.* scream, call, bawl, bellow, yell; whoop, cheer, bawl, roar. See CRY, REJOICING.

shove, *v.* push, hustle; urge, thrust, force; crowd, cram, wedge; shoulder, jostle, jog, jar, elbow, nudge. See IMPULSE.

shovel, *n. & v.* —*n.* spade, digger; scoop(er), excavator, trowel, scuttle. —*v.* dig, excavate, unearth; ladle, dip. See EXTRACTION, CONCAVITY.

show, *v. & n.* —*v.t.* exhibit, display; explain, teach; demonstrate, prove, guide, escort. See INDICATION, TEACHING, EVIDENCE, DISCLOSURE. *Ant.* see CONCEALMENT. —*n.* display, exhibition, play, entertainment, pageant, spectacle; pomp, OSTENTATION; semblance, APPEARANCE, PRETEXT. See DRAMA.

showcase, *n.* display case *or* window; vitrine, *étalage*; exhibition; repository, reliquary; étagère, whatnot, mantelpiece. See RECEPTACLE, DEMONSTRATION.

showdown, *n.*, *colloq.*, confrontation; climax, denouement; settling of accounts, putting one's cards on the table, show of hands. See TRUTH.

shower, *n.* rain, sprinkle, drizzle; spate; volley; fall; gift party. See WATER, ASSEMBLAGE, GIVING.

showman, *n.* exhibitor, impresario, producer, DIRECTOR. See DRAMA, AMUSEMENT.

showmanship, *n.* SKILL, stagecraft; dramaturgy, histrionics; OSTENTATION, style, garishness, exhibitionism, fanfare, pageantry, display, theatricality.

show-off, *n.* display, OSTENTATION. *Colloq.*, exhibitionist, peacock, hot shot, ham.

showy, *adj.* conspicuous, colorful; ornate, florid, flashy, gaudy, pretentious, ostentatious. See COLOR, VULGARITY, OSTENTATION.

shred, *n. & v.* —*n.* strip, tatter, remnant, snippet, scrap; modicum, bit, particle, speck; trace, vestige. See PART, FILAMENT, REMAINDER, LITTLENESS. —*v.* grate; macerate, mangle, lacerate; tear, rip. See DISJUNCTION.

shrew, *n.* termagant, scold, virago, vixen, fishwife, henpecker, beldame. See IRASCIBILITY.

shrewd, *adj.* clever, keen, farsighted, astute; CUNNING, wily, artful; sharp, acute, piercing. See SKILL. *Ant.*, DULL, fumbling.

shriek, *v.i.* scream, screech, shrill, squeal. See LOUDNESS.

shrill, *adj.* sharp, piercing, STRIDENT, high-pitched, piping, penetrating, poignant. see LOUDNESS.

shrine, *n.* altar, TEMPLE; receptacle (for sacred objects); reliquary; tomb.

shrink, *v.* contract, shrivel, diminish, wizen; flinch, draw back, RECOIL, wince, quail, cower; compress, reduce, DECREASE. See CONTRACTION. *Ant.*, INCREASE, EXPANSION.

shrivel, *v.* shrink, wrinkle, wizen, pucker; wither, sear. See CONTRACTION, DETERIORATION, DRYNESS.

shroud, *n.* winding sheet, graveclothes; pall; screen, cloak, veil; CONCEALMENT. See INTERMENT, COVERING.

shrub, *n.* shrubbery; scrub, bush, arbuscle, hedge, treelet. See VEGETABLE.

shudder, *v.i.* tremble, quake, quiver, shiver, vibrate. See COLD, FEAR.

shuffle, *v.* rearrange, switch, shift, mix, intermingle, jumble; scuff, drag; fidget, shift; rearrange, mix; scuffle, shamble, slouch; equivocate, quibble, evade. See INTERCHANGE, MIXTURE, SLOWNESS, CHANGEABLENESS.

shun, *v.t.* avoid, elude, evade, eschew; cut, ignore; steer clear of. See AVOIDANCE, CONTEMPT. *Ant.*, see ACCOMPANIMENT, SOCIALITY.

shut, *v.t.* close, fold; imprison, confine; silence; cease operations, terminate; bar, exclude blockade. See CLOSURE. *Ant.*, see OPENING.

shutdown, *n.* stoppage, cessation, END, termination, halt; layoff, sitdown strike, closing, foreclosure; lockout, walkout; CLOSURE.

shutter, *n.* blind(s), louver, persiennes; screen, grille. See CLOSURE.

shy, *adj.* bashful, reserved, retiring, demure; cautious, suspicious, wary; timid, skittish, fearful. See MODESTY, COWARDICE. *Slang,* short, lacking. *Ant.*, see INSOLENCE, COURAGE.

sibilant, *adj. & n.* hissing; whispering; whistling. See SOUND.

sick, *adj.* ill, ailing, diseased; nauseated; disgusted; bored. *Slang,* fed-up. See DISEASE, WEARINESS. *Ant.*, see HEALTH.

sicken, *v.* ail, become ill; languish; droop, waste away; be nauseated; feel disgust; cloy, weary; make ill, afflict; nauseate, revolt. See DISEASE, PAIN, DISLIKE. *Ant.*, see REMEDY.

sickly, *adj.* invalid, ailing, unwell; debilitated, languid, peaked; wan, pale, washed out, faint; mawkish, nauseating. See DISEASE, COLORLESSNESS.

SIDE

Nouns—**1,** side, flank, quarter, lee, leeward, weather, windward; skirt, EDGE, margin, border; hand; cheek, jowl; wing; profile; temple; loin, haunch, hip; laterality; gable, gable-end; broadside; outside, inside (see EXTERIOR, INTERIOR); east, west (see DIRECTION); orientation.

2, see RIGHT (side), LEFT (side), PARTY (partisanship).

Verbs—be on one side, flank, outflank; sidle; skirt, border.

Adjectives—side, lateral, sidelong; collateral; parietal, flanking, skirting; flanked; sidelong, bordering.

2, many-sided, multilateral; bilateral, trilateral, quadrilateral.

Adverbs—sideways, sidewise, sidelong; laterally; broadside on; on one side, abreast, alongside, beside, aside; by, by the side of; side by side; cheek by jowl; to windward, to leeward; right and left.

Antonym, see MIDDLE.

---

sidestep, *v.* avoid, circumvent; jockey, parry; equivocate. See AVOIDANCE.

sidewalk, *n.* walk, footwalk, crosswalk, pavement; footpath, footway, banquette; boardwalk, *trottoir,* promenade, mall. See PASSAGE.

siding, *n.* sidetrack, [track] spur; paneling, boarding. See COVERING.

sidle, *v.* EDGE, crab; sidestep, skirt, flank; slither. See DEVIATION, OBLIQUITY.

siege, *n.* investment, encirclement; besiegement, blockade, beleaguerment; PERIOD, long spell. See ATTACK.

siesta, *n.* nap, snooze, doze, rest. See INACTIVITY, REPOSE.

sieve, *n.* riddle, colander, sifter, screen, strainer, bolter. See OPENING.

sift, *v.t.* separate, bolt, screen, sort; examine, scrutinize, segregate, eliminate. See ARRANGEMENT, CHOICE.

sigh, *v.i.* breathe heavily, sadly *or* wearily; suspire, sough, moan; long, yearn, grieve (with *for*). See WIND, DESIRE.

sight, *n.* VISION, eyesight; view, vista, scene; APPEARANCE, aspect, look; spectacle, display; visibility; aim, observation; eyesore (see UGLINESS). *Colloq.,* abundance, quantity. *Ant.*, see BLINDNESS.

sightseeing, *n.* tour(ing), tourism; excursion, expedition; globetrotting, vacationing. *Slang,* rubbernecking. See CURIOSITY, TRAVEL.

sightless, *adj.* blind, eyeless, unseeing; amaurotic; invisible, imperceptible. See BLINDNESS, INVISIBILITY.

sign, *n.* OMEN, portent; INDICATION, symptom, token, mark; symbol, emblem; gesture, signal; trace, vestige; signboard, shingle; guidepost. See RECORD.

signal, *n., adj. & v.* —*n.* sign, watchword, cue; alarm, WARNING, DIRECTION, order; traffic light, beacon, foghorn, wigwag; CAUSE; broadcast radio impulse. —*adj.* memorable, conspicuous, momentous. See IMPORTANCE. —*v.t.* signalize, speak, hail, call, beckon, gesticulate; semaphore, wigwag; radio, broadcast, beam. See NAVIGATION, INDICATION.

signatory, *n.* signer, signator; witness, testifier; subscriber, party, underwriter, endorser, cosigner, comaker. See ASSENT, AGREEMENT.

signature, *n.* autograph, hand, sign-manual; subscription; mark, endorsement; identifying theme, music, letters, *etc.*; identification; attestation. *Slang,* fist, John Hancock. See INDICATION, NOMENCLATURE.

signify, *v.t.* show; declare, portend; mean, denote, express, connote, indicate. See MEANING, IMPORTANCE, INDICATION.

SILENCE

Nouns—1, silence; stillness, quiet, peace, hush, lull; inaudibility.
2, muteness, dumbness, aphony, voicelessness; taciturnity, reticence; deadness, dullness.
3, silencer, muffler, damper, MUTE; gag, nuzzle.
Verbs—be silent, hold one's tongue, silence, render silent, strike dumb, quiet, still, hush; stifle, muffle, stop, cut one short, cut off; smother, muzzle, mute, gag, put to silence. *Colloq.*, shush.
Adjectives—1, silent; still, stilly; quiet, noiseless, soundless; hushed, soft, solemn, awful, tomblike, deathlike, silent as the tomb *or* grave; inaudible, FAINT; tacit.
2, MUTE, dumb, mum, tongue-tied, voiceless, speechless, muffled, gagged; TACITURN, reticent, uncommunicative, inarticulate.
Adverbs—silently, mutely, *etc.*; with bated breath, *sotto voce, tacet.*
Interjections—hush! silence! shut up! cat got your tongue?
Antonym, see SOUND.

---

silhouette, *n.* shadow, shadow figure, shadowgram, skiagraph *or* -gram; outline, profile, cutout, cameo. See REPRESENTATION.
silky, *adj.* silken, sericeous; satiny, lustrous; flossy, sleek, smooth, luxurious; suave, mellifluous. See MATERIALS, SMOOTHNESS, ELEGANCE.
sill, *n.* windowsill, ledge, shelf; threshold, BASE, SUPPORT; frame, beam.
silly, *adj.* witless, foolish, stupid, childish; fatuous, inane; senseless, absurd, ridiculous. See ABSURDITY.
silo, *n.* grainery, granary, grain elevator; crib, bin; storehouse (see STORE).
silt, *n.* sediment, deposit, alluvium, loess, clay. See UNCLEANNESS, REMAINDER.
silver, *n. & adj.* —*n.* argentum, sterling, silver plate; [small *or* loose] change, cash; pin *or* hard money; silverware. —*adj.* argent(al); silvery, silver-gray; eloquent, silver-tongued, mellisonant. See MINERAL, COLOR, VOICE.

SIMILARITY

Nouns—1, similarity, resemblance, likeness, similitude, semblance; affinity, approximation, parallelism; AGREEMENT; analogy; family likeness; alliteration, rhyme, pun.
2, REPETITION; sameness, IDENTITY, uniformity, EQUALITY; parallel; simile; image, REPRESENTATION; etc.; striking, speaking *or* faithful likeness; double, twin, picture. *Slang*, ringer, spittin' image.
Verbs—1, be similar, look like, look alike, resemble; bear resemblance; smack of; approximate; parallel, match; take after; imitate; assimilate.
2, COMPARE, identify, parallel, relate.
Adjectives—similar; resembling, like, alike; twin, analogous, analogical; parallel, of a piece; so; much the same; near, close, something like; comparable; mock, pseudo, simulating, representing; exact, lifelike, faithful; true to nature, true to life, the very image, the very picture of; like two peas in a pod, cast in the same mold.
Adverbs—similarly, as if, so to speak, as it were, quasi, just as.
Antonym, see DIFFERENCE.

---

simmer, *v.* boil, cook, bubble, parboil; effervesce, fizz; fume, chafe, brood, fret, ferment. See HEAT, AGITATION, RESENTMENT.
simper, *v.i.* smile, smirk; strut, prance. See LEVITY, AFFECTATION.

SIMPLENESS

Nouns—1, simpleness, purity, homogeneity; CLEANNESS.
2, simplicity, ARTLESSNESS; plainness, homeliness; undress; chastity, SEVERITY.
Verbs—simplify; clear, purify, clean; disentangle (see DISJUNCTION).
Adjectives—1, simple, homogeneous, single, pure, clear, sheer, neat; un-

mixed, uncomplex; elementary; unadulterated, unsophisticated, unalloyed; pure and simple; free from, exempt from; exclusive.
2, PLAIN, homely, homespun; ordinary; bald, flat; dull, ARTLESS, ingenuous, unaffected, free from affectation *or* ornament; chaste, severe; unadorned, unornamented, ungarnished, unvarnished, unarranged, untrimmed.
Adverbs—simply, purely; solely, only; unadornedly; in plain terms, words, English, *etc.*; bluntly, pointblank.
Antonyms, see MIXTURE, ORNAMENT.

---

simpleton, *n.* dunce, blockhead, moron, ninny, nincompoop, innocent, FOOL. *Slang*, nitwit, dope, jerk.

simulate, *v.t.* imitate, resemble, mimic; feign, counterfeit, pretend. See FALSEHOOD, AFFECTATION, IMITATION.

simultaneous, *adj.* coincident, concurrent, contemporaneous, in concert, in unison, synchronous. See TIME, INSTANTANEITY.

sin, *n. & v.* —*n.* IMPIETY, sacrilege, transgression, wickedness, IMPURITY, iniquity, VICE; offense, crime, fault, ERROR, peccadillo. —*v.i.* transgress, err, offend. See GUILT. *Ant.,* see VIRTUE.

since, *adv. & conj.* —*adv.* ago, later, subsequently, afterwards. See SEQUENCE. —*conj.* because, inasmuch as, after. See CAUSE.

sincere, *adj.* honest, genuine; ingenuous, forthright, unreserved, candid; cordial, hearty, earnest. See TRUTH. *Ant.,* see FALSEHOOD.

sinecure, *n.* easy job. *Slang*, snap, pipe, cinch, gravy. See FACILITY.

sinewy, *adj.* fibrous, wiry; strong, well-knit. See STRENGTH, TEXTURE.

sing, *v.* troll; chant, carol, intone, warble; laud, praise; vocalize; yodel; versify; hum, whistle. See MUSICIAN, POETRY.

singe, *v.t.* scorch, sear, burn slightly. See HEAT.

singer, *n.* vocalist, songster, cantor, precentor, troubadour, minstrel; *chanteur, chanteuse*; nightingale, thrush, crooner; chantyman, chanter; bard, poet. See MUSICIAN.

single, *adj.* one, separate, solitary, individual; unmarried; unique, sole; sincere, honest, unequivocal. See NUMBER, CELIBACY.

single-handed, *adj.* alone, solo; by oneself, independent, unassisted, oneman; with one hand tied behind one's back. See UNITY.

singleminded, *adj.* one-track, narrow(-minded); resolute, stubborn, determined; obsessive, monomaniacal. See SIMPLENESS, NARROWNESS, RESOLUTION.

singular, *adj.* unique, individual; peculiar, unusual, odd, eccentric; exceptional, rare; extraordinary. See UNCONFORMITY, NUMBER, SPECIALITY.

sinister, *adj.* ominous, unlucky, portentous; LEFT; EVIL, bad; unpropitious, baleful, injurious; ill-starred. See BADNESS, ADVERSITY. *Ant.,* see GOODNESS, RIGHT.

sink, *v.* founder, drown, go down; ebb, wane, decline, lapse, settle, subside, precipitate; retrograde, go downhill; languish, droop, flag; despond; fail, deepen, dig, lower; debase, abase, bring low; submerge, immerse, bury; discourage, dampen; invest, risk, venture. See DEPTH, DESCENT, DEPRESSION, DETERIORATION, DEJECTION.

sinless, *adj.* impeccable, virtuous, innocent, immaculate; absolved, shriven, purified, forgiven; unfallen, prelapsarian. See PURITY, INNOCENCE, PROBITY.

sinuous, *adj.* twisting, winding, serpentine, meandering, crooked, devious, tortuous. See CONVOLUTION. *Ant.,* see DIRECTION.

sip, *v. & n.* —*v.* drink, imbibe, taste; siphon, suck. —*n.* TASTE, soupçon, sampling; drink, draft; modicum. See FOOD, DRUNKENNESS.

siren, *n.* water nymph; temptress, Circe, Lorelei, Delilah, Jezebel; alarm, WARNING, signal. *Slang*, vamp, vampire, gold digger.

sissy, *n., colloq.*, weakling, milksop, milquetoast, mama's boy, mollycoddle; effeminate, transvestite. *Slang*, chicken, scaredy-cat. See WEAKNESS.

sister, *n.* kinswoman; nun, sister of mercy, *religieuse*; woman associate, *soror*, sorority member, fellow member; nurse; counterpart. See RELATION, CLERGY, SIMILARITY.

sit, *v.i.* sit down, perch; pose; hold session, convene; fit, suit; brood; be situated. See DEPRESSION, DOMESTICATION, LOCATION.

site, *n.* See LOCATION.

situate, *v.* place, locate; set, station, put; lie, be situated. See LOCATION.

situation, *n.* place, LOCATION; position, site; STATE, predicament, plight, case, circumstances; job, office, post, station, employment. See BUSINESS.

SIZE

Nouns—**1,** size, magnitude, dimension, bulk, volume; largeness; GREATNESS, expanse, SPACE; extent, scope; amplitude; mass; proportions, MEASUREMENT; capacity, LIMIT, tonnage; caliber; corpulence, obesity; plumpness, fatness, *embonpoint*, avoirdupois, girth, corporation; hugeness, enormousness, immensity, monstrosity.

2, giant, titan, Brobdingnagian, Antaeus, Goliath, Anak, Gog and Magog, Gargantua, Cyclops; monster, mammoth, whale, porpoise, behemoth, leviathan, elephant, hippopotamus; colossus. *Colloq.,* whopper, bumper.

Verbs—be *or* become large, expand, enlarge; grade, assort, graduate.

Adjectives—**1,** large, big, great; considerable, bulky, voluminous, ample, massive, massy; capacious, comprehensive; spacious, mighty, towering, magnificent; huge, immense, enormous, mighty; vast, stupendous; monstrous, titanic, gigantic; giant, stupendous, colossal; Cyclopean, Brobdingnagian, Gargantuan.

2, corpulent, stout, fat, plump, full, lusty, strapping, bouncing; portly, burly, well-fed, full-grown; stalwart, brawny, fleshy; goodly; lumbering, unwieldy; whopping, thumping, thundering, hulking; overgrown, bloated; big as a house.

Antonym, see LITTLENESS.

---

sizzle, *v.* crepitate, fizz, crackle, sp(l)utter; scorch, broil, fry, sear; burn, swelter. See SOUND, AGITATION, HEAT.

skeleton, *n.* frame, framework; OUTLINE, diagram; bones, bony structure. See SUPPORT.

skeptic, *n.* doubter, agnostic, freethinker, doubting Thomas, questioner; infidel; unbeliever. See IRRELIGION, DOUBT. *Ant.,* see BELIEF.

sketch, *v.t.* draw, outline, block out, rough in; state briefly; draft, chart, map. See REPRESENTATION, PREPARATION.

skid, *n. & v.* —*n.* sideslip; incline; runner, check, curb, brake; skidway, travois. *Slang, pl.,* skid row, downfall, bankruptcy. —*v.* slide, (side)slip, spin; grind, grip, brake, lock. See DEVIATION, FRICTION, HINDRANCE.

SKILL

Nouns—**1,** skill, skillfulness, address; dexterity, dexterousness; adroitness, expertise, proficiency, adequacy, competence, craft, finesse, facility, knack; mastery, mastership; excellence, ambidexterity, versatility; artistry, wizardry.

2, accomplishment, acquirement, attainment; art, science; technicality, technology; KNOWLEDGE, experience, SAGACITY; discretion, diplomacy; craftiness, cunning; management.

3, cleverness, talent, ability, ingenuity, capacity, parts, faculty, endowment, forte, turn, gift, genius; INTELLIGENCE, sharpness, readiness, IMAGINATION; aptness, aptitude; capability, qualification. *Slang,* the goods, what it takes, know-how.

4, masterpiece, master stroke, *coup de maître, chef d'oeuvre, tour de force.*

5, EXPERT, master, virtuoso; strategist, diplomat; adept.

Verbs—be skillful, excel in, be master of; have a turn for, play one's cards well; hit the nail on the head; have all one's wits about one; have one's hand in. *Slang*, know one's stuff; have been around.

Adjectives—1, skillful, dext(e)rous; adroit, expert, apt, handy, quick, deft, ready, smart, proficient, good at, up to, at home in, master of, a good hand at; masterly, crack, accomplished, versed in, conversant (see KNOWLEDGE); experienced, practiced, skilled, up in, well up in; in practice; competent, efficient, qualified, capable, fitted, fitted for, up to the mark, trained, initiated, prepared, primed, finished.

2, clever, able, ingenious, felicitous, gifted, talented, endowed; inventive, shrewd, sharp, intelligent; ambidextrous, sure-footed; artistic, workmanlike, businesslike, statesmanlike.

Adverbs—skillfully, well, artistically; with skill.

Antonym, see UNSKILLFULNESS.

---

skillet, *n.* frying pan, frypan, spider; saucepan, casserole. See RECEPTACLE, HEAT.

skim, *v.* scum; strain, cream, separate; scan, thumb through; glide, skip, skid, graze, brush, TOUCH. See VELOCITY, PURITY, INQUIRY.

skimp, *v., colloq.,* scrimp, stinge, stint; economize; LIMIT. See PARSIMONY.

skin, *v. & n.* —*v.t.* flay, peel, decorticate. *Slang*, fleece, cheat. See DIVESTMENT. —*n.* integument, cuticle, dermis, epidermis; pelt, hide; rind; veneer, plating, lamina; parchment. See COVERING.

skinflint, *n.* niggard, scrimp, hoarder (see MISER).

skinny, *adj.* thin, lean, slim, slender (see THIN).

skip, *v.* caper, spring, LEAP, hop, trip, frisk, gambol, frolic; omit, pass over, stay away; ricochet. *Slang*, decamp, play truant. See NEGLECT, DEPARTURE.

skipper, *n.* captain, MASTER, pilot; commodore, commander. See NAVIGATION.

skirmish, *n.* clash, brush, tilt, encounter, engagement. See CONTENTION.

skirt, *n.* overskirt, kilt, petticoat, coattail; purlieu, borderland, EDGE, margin, outskirts. See CLOTHING. *Slang*, woman, girl.

skit, *n.* burlesque, satire, parody, lampoon, pasquinade; sketch, playlet, vignette, tableau. See RIDICULE, DRAMA.

skittish, *adj.* lively, frisky, spirited; excitable, restive, nervous; timorous, fearful; coy, bashful; capricious, fickle. *Slang*, jittery. See AGITATION, FEAR.

skulk, *v.i.* lurk, sneak, slink, steal, hide; cower. See CONCEALMENT, COWARDICE.

sky, *n.* firmament, heavens, HEAVEN, welkin.

skyscraper, *n.* high-rise, tower. See PRODUCTION.

slab, *n.* slice, wedge, section, piece, cut; plate, board, plank, shingle; tablet, gravestone. *Colloq.,* hunk, chunk. See PART, INTERMENT, FLATNESS.

slack, *adj.* careless, lax, negligent, remiss; loose, limp, flaccid, relaxed; sluggish, stagnant; dull, slow, not busy. See NEGLECT, INACTIVITY, SOFTNESS, INSUFFICIENCY. *Ant.,* see ACTIVITY, SEVERITY, HARDNESS.

slacken, *v.* retard, diminish, lessen; loosen, relax; abate; languish, decline; ease up, dwindle. See MODERATION, REPOSE, SLOWNESS.

slacker, *n.* shirker, quitter, evader. See AVOIDANCE.

slake, *v.t.* quench, satisfy, appease, allay, abate, sate. See SUFFICIENCY, MODERATION.

slam, *v. & n.* —*v.* shut, close; swat, pound, batter. *Colloq.,* bash, slug. See CLOSURE, IMPULSE. —*n.* impact, closing, crash, clang; buffet.

slander, *n.* scandal, aspersion, defamation, calumny, disparagement. See DETRACTION.

slang, *n.* argot, jargon, cant, lingo, patois, vernacular; dialect; colloquialism, neologism, vulgarism. See SPEECH.

slant, *n.* OBLIQUITY, slope, inclination, declination, tilt, pitch; bias, leaning.

slap, *v.t. & n.* hit, smack, swat, cuff; insult. See IMPULSE, DISCOURTESY, PUNISHMENT.

slapdash, *adj.* precipitate, hasty, careless, hit *or* miss; superficial, sketchy, rough, hack, sloppy. See HASTE, UNSKILLFULNESS, DISORDER.

slash, *v.* hack, cut, gash, cleave, sever, sunder, slice, carve; whip, scourge; mark down, reduce, lower. See DISJUNCTION, DEDUCTION.

slate, *n.* LIST, ballot, ticket; blackboard; slab, rock, roof. See LAYER.

slattern, *n.* sloven; slut, trollop. See FEMALE, IMPURITY.

slaughter, *n.* butchering; butchery, massacre, carnage, murder. See KILLING.

slave, *n. & v.* —*n.* bondsman, bond servant, thrall, serf; drudge, peon, vassal, menial; addict, victim. See SERVANT. *Ant.,* see FREEDOM. —*v.i.* toil, drudge; overwork.

slavery, *n.* bondage; forced labor; servitude, chains, captivity; drudgery, toil; addiction, submission. See SUBJECTION.

slay, *v.i.* kill, slaughter, dispatch; murder, assassinate. See KILLING.

sleazy, *adj.* flimsy, gauzy; shabby; shoddy, cheap. See CHEAPNESS, INFERIORITY.

sled, *n.* sledge, sleigh; bobsled; dogsled; skid, cutter, pung. See VEHICLE.

sleek, *adj.* slick, oily, smooth, glossy; well-groomed; chic, soigné, elegant, suave, urbane, skillful, adroit. See ELEGANCE, SKILL, SMOOTHNESS.

sleep, *n. & v.* —*n.* slumber, somnolence, nap, doze, drowse, rest, REPOSE; coma; hypnosis. —*v.i.* slumber, repose, doze, nap; be dead *or* dormant. See INACTIVITY. *Ant.,* see ACTIVITY.

sleeping pill, barbiturate, opiate; tranquil(l)izer, sedative. *Slang,* goof ball.

sleepless, *adj.* wakeful, insomniac, restless; alert, vigilant. See ACTIVITY, CARE. *Ant.,* see REPOSE, INACTIVITY.

sleepwalker, *n.* somnambulist, noctambulist, nightwalker.

sleeve, *n.* COVERING, envelope, pipe; mandrel, quill, bushing, coupling, union. See CONNECTION.

slender, *adj.* slim, thin, skinny, attenuated; tenuous, slight, meager. See NARROWNESS, INSUFFICIENCY. *Ant.,* see BREADTH.

sleuth, *n.* bloodhound; detective, Hawkshaw, gumshoe; plainclothesman; shadow, operative, (private) investigator. *Slang,* dick, private eye, shamus, op. See CONCEALMENT.

slice, *v.t.* cut, slash, carve, shave, skive. See DISJUNCTION, LAYER.

slick, *adj.* glossy, shiny, polished; oily, slippery, greasy; unctuous, obsequious; sophisticated, urbane. *Colloq.,* crooked, cheap, glib; CUNNING, tricky. See SMOOTHNESS, DECEPTION, SHALLOWNESS.

slicker, *n.* raincoat, waterproof, poncho, oilcoat, oilskin. See CLOTHING.

slide, *v.i.* glide, slip, coast, skim; steal, pass. See MOTION.

slight, *adj., v. & n.* —*adj.* slender, slim, frail, delicate; trivial; meager, scant. See NARROWNESS, UNIMPORTANCE. —*v.t.* ignore, cut, snob, rebuff; scamp, neglect. —*n.* snub, rebuff, cut. See CONTEMPT.

slim, *adj.* slender, thin, slight; frail, weak, meager. See NARROWNESS, INSUFFICIENCY. *Ant.,* see BREADTH, SIZE.

slime, *n.* ooze, mire, sludge, mud, muck; primordial slime; filth. See COHERENCE, UNCLEANNESS.

sling, *v. & n.* —*v.t.* propel, fling, catapult, shoot, pitch; hang, fasten up, suspend. *Colloq.,* chuck, peg. See PROPULSION, PENDENCY. —*n.* slingshot, catapult, perrier, ballista; bandage, strap, suspensory, SUPPORT.

slink, *v.i.* sneak, steal, skulk, slither; creep, snoop. See CONCEALMENT.

slip, *v. & n.* —*v.* glide, slide; misstep; steal; ESCAPE, elapse; blunder, err; don (with *on*). See FAILURE, ERROR. —*n.* misstep, slide; blunder, ERROR; scion, graft; *faux pas,* indiscretion; ESCAPE; undergarment; pillowcase; dock; strip, sheet; chit, girl; ceramic cement.

slippery, *adj.* slimy, greasy, slick, glassy, glare; shifty, elusive, unreliable. See SMOOTHNESS. *Ant.,* see ROUGHNESS.

shipshod, *adj.* negligent, slovenly, careless (see SHODDY, SLAPDASH).

slit, *v. & n.* cut, gash, slash, slice. See OPENING, DISJUNCTION.

slither, *v.* slink, sinuate, worm; crawl, creep. See SMOOTHNESS, CONCEALMENT.

sliver, *n.* splinter, shive; slice, chip, shaving; shard, fragment. See PART.

slob, *n., colloq.,* sloven, slattern; pig, slovenly Peter. See UNCLEANNESS.

slobber, *v.i.* slaver, drivel, dribble, drool, be sentimental. See EJECTION.

slogan, *n.* watchword, shibboleth, password, byword, motto, MAXIM.

slop, *n. & v.* —*n.* spillage, muck, slush, slime; spillings, refuse, garbage, swill, WASTE, SEWAGE. *Slang,* chow, FOOD; gush, sloppiness, schmaltz. —*v.* spill, overflow, splash. See FLUIDITY, UNCLEANNESS.

slope, *n.* slant, tilt, pitch, inclination; incline, grade, gradient, ramp, ascent, rise. See OBLIQUITY.

slosh, *v.* See SLOP.

slot, *n.* aperture, slit, OPENING; groove, NOTCH, nick, channel, PASSAGE.

sloth, *n.* laziness, idleness, INACTIVITY, inertia; SLOWNESS, sluggishness. *Ant.,* see ACTIVITY.

slouch, *v.* droop, flag, slump, sag, bend; shamble, shuffle, lounge, loll. See SLOWNESS, INACTION, PENDENCY.

slovenly, *adj.* slatternly, sluttish; untidy, unkempt, disorderly; slipshod, lax. *Colloq.,* sloppy, tacky. See DISORDER, UNCLEANNESS, INATTENTION.

SLOWNESS

Nouns—**1,** slowness, languor, INACTIVITY; leisureliness; retardation; slackening; delay, LATENESS; walk, stroll, saunter, snail's pace, jog-trot, dog-trot; slow motion. *Colloq.,* slowdown, slowup.

2, DULLNESS, flatness, monotony; boredom.

3, laggard, lingerer, loiterer, sluggard, tortoise, plodder; snail; dawdler. *Colloq.,* slowpoke.

Verbs—**1,** move slowly, creep, crawl, lag, linger, loiter, stroll, saunter, walk, plod, trudge, stump along, lumber; trail, drag; dawdle, worm one's way, steal along; toddle, waddle, slouch, shuffle, halt, hobble, limp, shamble; flag, falter, totter, stagger; take one's time; hang fire (see LATENESS). *Colloq.,* take one's own sweet time. *Slang,* get no place fast, mosey along.

2, slow, retard, relax; slacken, check, moderate, rein in, curb; reef; strike sail, shorten sail, take in sail; put on the drag, brake, apply the brake; clip the wings; reduce the speed; slacken speed, slacken one's pace; lose ground; slack off *or* down.

Adjectives—slow, slack; tardy; dilatory, inactive, gentle, easy, leisurely; deliberate, gradual; dull, uninteresting; languid, sluggish, slow-paced; snail-like; creeping. *Colloq.,* slow as molasses.

Adverbs—slowly, leisurely; at half speed, under easy sail; at a snail's pace; in slow time; in slow motion; gradually, by degrees *or* inches, step by step, drop by drop, inch by inch, bit by bit, little by little.

Antonym, see VELOCITY.

---

sludge, *n.* mud, mire, filth; ooze, slime, slush; slag; sewage. See MOISTURE, WASTE, UNCLEANNESS.

slug, *v., colloq.,* hit, swat, belt; bash, smash, whale. See IMPULSE.

sluggish, *adj.* inactive, stagnant, torpid, slow; lazy, slothful, dull, indolent; languid, apathetic, lethargic. See INACTIVITY. *Ant.,* see ACTIVITY.

slum, *n.* tenements, skidrow, wrong side of the tracks; ghetto. See ABODE, POVERTY.

slumber, *n.* sleep, nap, doze, quiescence. See INACTIVITY, REPOSE.

slump, *v. & n.* —*v.i.* fall, settle, sink, drop; slouch, lounge, sprawl; sag, droop; decline, diminish, wane, languish; fail, collapse. —*n.* decline; setback, DEPRESSION, recession, REGRESSION, REVERSION, comedown, collapse, FAILURE. *Colloq.,* slowdown, slack season.

slur, *v.t.* slight, disparage, calumniate, traduce, asperse; skim, skip, gloss over; elide. See DETRACTION, NEGLECT. *Ant.,* see VINDICATION.

slush, *n.* slosh, sludge, slop; gush, effusiveness, sentimentality. See COHERENCE, LOQUACITY.

slut, *n.* sloven, slattern, slob; PROSTITUTE. *Slang,* doxy, chippy. See FEMALE, IMPURITY.

sly, *adj.* CUNNING, furtive, wily; crafty, deceitful, stealthy, underhand; roguish, mischievous. See CONCEALMENT.

smack, *n. & v.* —*n.* clap, whack, slap; kiss, buss; savor, tastiness, flavor, gusto, relish, TASTE. See IMPULSE, ENDEARMENT. —*v.* slap, strike, smite, whack; TASTE, savor; smack of, recall, call to mind. See ATTRIBUTION, SIMILARITY.

small, *adj.* little, tiny, short, wee; dwarfish, undersized, stunted; minute, infinitesimal; dainty, petite; trivial, unimportant, petty; puny, slight, weak; mean, paltry, unworthy; pygmy, Lilliputian, minikin. See LITTLENESS. *Ant.,* see SIZE, GREATNESS.

small-time, *adj., slang,* minor, unimportant, trivial, petty; one-horse, jerkwater, tinhorn, minor-league. See INFERIORITY, UNIMPORTANT.

smart, *adj. & v.* —*adj.* chic, stylish, jaunty, dapper; severe, sharp, keen; witty, pert, sparkling; brisk, energetic, fresh; shrewd, clever. See SKILL, FASHION, FEELING, WIT. —*v.i.* sting, PAIN, rankle.

smash, *v.t.* shatter, crush; hit, strike; ruin, destroy, disintegrate. See DESTRUCTION.

smashup, *n.* crash, collision, wreck, crackup, pileup; accident; calamity, catastrophe, disaster. See IMPULSE, DESTRUCTION, ADVERSITY, DIVORCE.

smattering, *n.* superficiality, slight knowledge, sciolism. See IGNORANCE.

smear, *v.t.* daub, bedaub, besmirch, smudge; grease, anoint, defame; slander. See UNCLEANNESS, DISREPUTE.

smell, *v.* scent; stink; sniff, snuff, inhale; detect, nose out. See ODOR, MALODOROUSNESS, DISCLOSURE.

smile, *v.i.* grin, simper, smirk; beam, look with favor; sneer, RIDICULE. See REJOICING.

smirk, *n.* simper, grin, leer; smug look, grimace. See AFFECTATION, PLEASURE.

smite, *v.* strike, hit, cuff, pummel; captivate, enamor, entrance. See IMPULSE.

smith, *n.* blacksmith, tinsmith, tinker. See PRODUCTION.

smock, *n.* blouse, housecoat, house dress; coverall, apron. See CLOTHING.

smog, *n.* smoky fog; inversion. See CLOUDINESS.

smoke, *v.* reek, fume, smo(u)lder; steam; puff, inhale; smoke-dry, cure; fumigate; begrime, pollute. See DRYNESS, UNCLEANNESS, HEAT.

smolder, smoulder, *v.i.* reek, fume, smoke; hang fire, be latent, lurk. See HEAT, CLOUDINESS.

SMOOTHNESS

Nouns—**1,** smoothness, polish, gloss, glaze; slickness, slipperiness; suavity; blandness; evenness. See TEXTURE.

2, smooth surface, level, plane; velvet, silk, satin; glass, ice; FLATNESS.

3, lubrication, greasing, oiling; oiliness, unctuousness; lubricant, grease, oil, fat, soap, emollient, ointment; Teflon, graphite.

4, plane, roller, steamroller; sandpaper, ABRASIVE, buffer, burnisher, polisher; wax, varnish; iron, mangle.

Verbs—smooth, plane; file; mow, shave; level, roll; pave; polish, rub, shine, buff, burnish, calender, glaze; varnish, wax; iron, press; LUBRICATE.

Adjectives—**1,** smooth; polished, even; level; plane, flat, HORIZONTAL;

sleek, glossy; silken, silky; downy, velvety; slippery, glassy; greasy, oily; soft, unwrinkled; smooth as glass, silk, ice *or* velvet; slippery as an eel; bald, bald as an egg *or* billiard ball.

2, slippery, greasy, oily, slick, unctuous, lubricating.

Antonym, see ROUGHNESS.

---

smother, *v.t.* suffocate, stifle; suppress, repress; extinguish, deaden. See KILLING, RESTRAINT.

smudge, *n. & v.* —*n.* soot, grime, dirt, blotch, smear; smolder. See HEAT, UNCLEANNESS. —*v.* soil, smear, mark, daub, dirty.

smug, *adj.* sleek, trim, neat; self-satisfied, complacent; priggish, conceited. See AFFECTION.

smuggler, *n.* contrabandist, bootlegger, runner. See STEALING.

smut, *n. & v.* —*n.* soot, smudge, spot, BLEMISH; dirt, filth, pornography; fungus, rot, mildew. See IMPURITY. —*v.* blacken, sully, smudge. See UNCLEANNESS.

snack, *n.* repast, collation, refreshment, coffee break. See FOOD.

snag, *n. & v.* —*n.* catch, detent, snaggletooth; HINDRANCE, DIFFICULTY. See RETENTION. —*v.t.* catch, fix, entangle; snarl, impede, hamper, hinder.

snake, *n.* serpent, reptile, ophidian; snake in the grass, deceiver, double-dealer. See ANIMAL, DECEPTION.

snap, *n. & v.* —*n.* snap, crackle, rapping; pop, crack; report; clap, smack; vigor; pep, verve, dash, élan; smartness, spruceness, crispness. *Colloq.,* sinecure, cinch, soft job; spell (of weather). —*v.* break, crack, crackle; knock, rap, tap; snarl, bark, scold; bite, nip. See DISJUNCTION, IMPULSE, IRASCIBILITY.

snare, *n.* trap, springe, gin; artifice, pitfall, ambush. See DECEPTION.

snarl, *v.i.* growl, gnarl; speak savagely, be surly; grumble. See DISCOURTESY.

snatch, *v.t.* grab, seize, grasp, clutch, jerk, twitch, pluck, wrench; steal. *Slang,* kidnap. See STEALING.

sneak, *v. & n.* —*v.i.* slink, skulk, crawl, steal. —*n.* skulker, sneak thief; coward. See COWARDICE; STEALING.

sneer, *v.* smile, jeer, taunt, scoff; flout, deride. See CONTEMPT.

snicker, *v.i.* snigger, titter, laugh, giggle, chuckle; RIDICULE.

snide, *adj., slang,* spiteful, malicious, sarcastic, cynical, derogatory. See DETRACTION, MALEVOLENCE.

sniff, *v.* sniffle; smell, scent; breathe, inhale, detect. See ODOR, WIND.

snip, *v.* cut, slice, shear, scissor; prune, trim, lop. See DISJUNCTION, DEDUCTION.

sniper, *n.* marksman, sharpshooter; critic. See ATTACK, DISAPPROBATION.

snitch, *v., slang,* swipe, pinch, filch (see STEALING).

snivel, *v.i.* snuffle, sniff, blubber; whimper, CRY, weep; cower, grovel, crawl, cringe. See LAMENTATION, SERVILITY.

snob, *n.* sycophant, toady, fawner, bounder, upstart; parvenu, social climber. See SERVILITY, VULGARITY, AFFECTATION.

snoop, *v. & n.* —*v.i.* pry; investigate, probe; meddle; play detective. —*n.* snooper, pry, meddler, busybody. See ACTIVITY.

snooze, *n.* nap, doze, sleep, forty winks. See INACTIVITY.

snore, *n.* stertor; wheeze; rhoncus, rale; zzz. See SOUND, REPOSE.

snort, *v. & n.* —*v.* grunt, snortle, guffaw. See CRY. —*n.* grunt, laugh; drink, draft, dram, jigger. *Colloq.,* shot. See FOOD.

snout, *n.* nose, nostrils, muzzle, beak, bill, trunk. See FRONT, ODOR.

snow, *n. & v.* —*n.* snowfall, snowflake, flurry; snowstorm, blizzard; snowslide, drift, avalanche; hail, sleet. —*v.* snow in *or* under; swamp, flood, inundate. *Slang,* impress, flatter, do a snow job on. See COLD, REDUNDANCE, FLATTERY, ATTRACTION.

snowball, *v.i.* accelerate, gain momentum, pick up speed. See INCREASE.

snub, *v., n. & adj.* —*v.t.* cut, ignore, slight, rebuff, cold-shoulder; check,

curb, halt. —*n.* rebuff, slight, cut. —*adj.* turned-up, blunt, retroussé.
See DISCOURTESY, HINDRANCE.

snuff, *v.t.* extinguish, put out; quench; sniff, inhale; smell, scent; snuffle,
sniffle. See END, WIND, ODOR.

snug, *adj.* cozy, comfortable; sheltered, trim, compact, neat. See
PLEASURE, CLOSURE.

snuggle, *v.i.* nestle, cuddle, lie snug. See ENDEARMENT.

soak, *v.t.* wet, drench, saturate, steep; absorb; permeate. *Slang,* strike,
drink. See WATER. *Ant.,* see DRYNESS.

soap, *n.* cleanser, cleansing agent; lather; detergent; shampoo. *Slang,*
softsoap; corniness, sentimentality. See CLEANNESS.

soar, *v.i.* fly, fly high; tower; glide. See AVIATION, HEIGHT.

sob, *v.i.* weep, cry; sigh; cough, moan. See LAMENTATION.

sober, *adj.* grave, quiet, sedate, staid, serious; abstemious, not drunk;
drab, plain, severe, unadorned; calm, moderate; thoughtful; subdued;
inconspicuous; demure; earnest; solemn, somber. See MODERATION.
Ant., see DRUNKENNESS, LOUDNESS, OSTENTATION.

sob story, *slang,* tear jerker, mush, schmaltz, melodrama, human interest; tale of woe, hard-luck story. See FEELING, ADVERSITY.

social, *adj. & n.* See SOCIALITY.

socialism, *n.* public ownership, communism, collectivism; communalism.
See AUTHORITY, COÖPERATION.

SOCIALITY

Nouns—**1,** sociality, sociability, sociableness, FRIENDSHIP; social intercourse, community; fellowship, companionship, camaraderie; familiarity,
intimacy; brotherhood; gregariousness; congeniality, compatibility.

2, conviviality, good fellowship, joviality, jollity, *savoir vivre,* festivity,
festive board, merrymaking. See REJOICING.

3, welcome, greeting; hearty *or* warm welcome *or* reception; urbanity
(see COURTESY); familiarity; hospitality, heartiness, cheer.

4, social circle, sewing circle, family circle; coterie, society; club; social
gathering, assembly (see ASSEMBLAGE); PARTY, entertainment, reception, levee, at home, *conversazione, soirée;* garden party; housewarming;
reunion; debut, visit, visiting; call. *Colloq.,* get-together, hen party,
stag party, coming-out party, mixer.

5, sociable person, good company, companion, crony. *Colloq.,* joiner;
good mixer, back-slapper, hand-shaker, hail-fellow-well-met.

Verbs—**1,** be sociable, know; be acquainted, associate with, keep company with, club together, consort, bear one company, join; make
acquaintance with; make advances, fraternize, hobnob, mix with,
mingle with; embrace; be, feel *or* make oneself at home with; make free
with; be hospitable.

2, visit, pay a visit; call upon, drop in, look in; look one up; entertain,
give a party, be at home, keep open house, do the honors; receive with
open arms, welcome, bid one welcome, give a warm reception to; kill
the fatted calf; see one's friends.

Adjectives—sociable, companionable, friendly; conversable, cozy, chatty,
conversational; social, neighborly, gregarious, affable; convivial, festive,
festal; jovial, jolly, hospitable; welcome; free and easy. *Colloq.,* clubby,
chummy.

Adverbs—socially, companionably, intimately, *etc.*

Antonym, see SECLUSION.

---

society, *n.* MANKIND, humanity, folk; culture, civilization, group; companionship, fellowship; *bon ton,* élite, aristocracy; sodality, solidarity,
association, league, union, alliance; parish, congregation. See SOCIALITY,
PARTY. *Ant.,* see SECLUSION.

sock, *n. & v.* —*n.* [half] hose, anklet, stocking. *Slang,* slug, punch,
clout, wallop, jab. See CLOTHING, IMPULSE. —*v.t., slang,* strike, slug,
etc.

socket, *n.* holder, cup, RECEPTACLE, CONCAVITY, hole, pit. See OPENING.

sod, *n.* turf, sward, glebe; clod, divot. See VEGETABLE, LAND.

soda, *n.* carbonated water, [soda] pop, seltzer, fizz, mineral WATER.

sodden, *adj.* soaked, saturated, soggy, doughy, dull; drunken, befuddled. See MOISTURE, DRUNKENNESS.

sofa, *n.* couch, seat, lounge, divan, settee, love seat. See SUPPORT.

SOFTNESS

Nouns—**1,** softness, pliableness, pliancy, pliability, flexibility; malleability; ductility, tractility; extendability, extensibility; plasticity; flaccidity, flabbiness, laxity; sensitivity, responsiveness, susceptibility.
2, clay, wax, butter, dough, pudding; cushion, pillow, featherbed, down, padding, wadding; foam rubber.
3, softening, modification; mellowness, relaxation; MODERATION.

Verbs—soften, mollify, mellow, relax, temper; mash, knead, squash; melt, liquefy; bend, yield, relent, relax, give.

Adjectives—soft, tender, supple, pliant, pliable; flexible, flexile; sensitive, responsive, susceptible; lithe, lithesome, lissom, limber, plastic; ductile; tractile, tractable; malleable, extensile; yielding, flabby, limp, flimsy; flaccid, flocculent, downy, feathery, fleecy, spongy, doughy; mellow, velvety, silky, satiny.

Adverbs—soft as butter, soft as down, soft as silk; yielding as wax.
Antonym, see HARDNESS.

---

soft-soap, *v.t., colloq.,* flatter, snow, feed a line to. See DECEPTION, FLATTERY.

soft-spoken, *adj.* unassertive, quiet, gentle, kindly. See MODERATION, COURTESY.

soggy, *adj.* saturated, soppy, soaked; sodden, doughy. See MOISTURE.

soil, *n.* & *v.* —*n.* loam, earth, sod, topsoil, dirt, mold, ground; stain, blotch, smudge, smear, filth. —*v.t.* besmear, dirty, daub, stain; defile, sully. See LAND, UNCLEANNESS.

sojourn, *v.i.* tarry, abide, stay, lodge, stop over, visit. See PRESENCE.

solace, *n.* & *v.* —*n.* comfort, consolation, RELIEF. —*v.t.* soothe, calm, comfort; cheer, console; assuage, mitigate. See PITY.

solder, *v.* spelter, fuse, braze, weld; bond, cement, mend. See JUNCTION.

soldier, *n.* warrior, fighting man. See COMBATANT.

soldierly, *adj.* military, martial; brave, courageous; gallant; snappy, spruce; erect. See WARFARE.

sole, *adj.* only, one, single, unique, exclusive, individual. See NUMBER, SIMPLENESS.

solecism, *n.* ERROR, lapse, slip, blunder; grammatical error; barbarism, *faux pas,* social error, impropriety; incongruity, mistake. See GRAMMAR, MISJUDGMENT.

solemn, *adj.* awesome, impressive; grave, serious, dignified; formal, ceremonious; reverent, ritualistic. See IMPORTANCE, DEJECTION, PIETY. *Ant.,* see CHEERFULNESS, UNIMPORTANCE.

solicit, *v.t.* REQUEST, invite, ask, entreat, importune, beg, canvass.

solicitous, *adj.* considerate; anxious, concerned; eager, careful. See CARE.

solicitude, *n.* CARE, concern, anxiety; consideration; uneasiness. See FEAR.

solid, *adj.* dense, compact, hard, firm, rigid; substantial; unbroken, undivided, whole, intact; sound, valid; stable, solvent; genuine, real. See DENSITY, STABILITY, SUBSTANCE, CERTAINTY, ASSENT, TRUTH. *Ant.,* FLUID, liquid; see INSUBSTANTIALITY.

soliloquy, *n.* monologue; apostrophe. *Colloq.,* aside. See SPEECH.

solitary, *adj.* alone, lonesome; single, individual, lone; deserted, remote, unfrequented; unsocial, retiring. See ASCETICISM, SECLUSION. *Ant.,* see SOCIALITY.

solitude, *n.* SECLUSION, privacy, isolation; remoteness; loneliness; wilderness. *Ant.*, see SOCIALITY.

solo, *n. & adj.* —*n.* single; aria, arietta; recital, solo flight. —*adj.* lone, single, singlehanded; one-man; unaided. See UNITY.

solution, *n.* ANSWER, explanation, INTERPRETATION, key, clue; disintegration, dissolution; lixivium, decoction; LIQUEFACTION.

solve, *v.t.* explain, interpret; ANSWER; resolve, clear up; decipher, decode.

solvent, *adj. & n.* —*adj.* financially sound, moneyed; responsible, reliable; soluble, separative, dissolvent, diluent. —*n.* dissolvent, dissolver, liquefier. See WATER.

somber, *adj.* gloomy, dark, overcast; sad, dismal, leaden, depressing, funeral. See DARKNESS, CLOUDINESS, DEJECTION. *Ant.*, see LIGHT, CHEERFULNESS.

some, *adj., pron. & adv.* —*adj.* several, [a] few, a number of; one, any; certain, divers, various, sundry. *Colloq.*, what a, quite a. —*pron.* any, a few, one or more, someone, somebody. —*adv.* about, around, approximately, nearly, almost, in a way; to a degree. See GENERALITY, PART, NEARNESS.

somebody, *n.* one, someone; person, individual; bigwig, person of importance, personage. See PARTY, IMPORTANCE. *Ant.*, see UNIMPORTANCE.

somehow, *adv.* some way, by some means. See CAUSE.

something, *n.* thing, object, anything; matter, part; affair, event. See SUBSTANCE.

sometimes, *adv.* occasionally, now and then. See OCCASION.

somewhere, *adv.* someplace; anywhere, somewhere about; approximately. See LOCATION.

somnolent, *adj.* sleepy, drowsy, slumb(e)rous; dozing; lethargic. See REPOSE, INACTIVITY. *Ant.*, see ACTIVITY.

son, *n.* male child, boy, offspring; descendant, inheritor. See RELATION.

song, *n.* lyric, ballad, popular song; aria; carol, lilt, madrigal, glee, ditty; minstrelsy, poem, chanty, lay, birdsong, folksong, spiritual, *etc.* See MUSIC, POETRY.

sonorous, *adj.* resonant, deep-toned, rich, majestic; grandiloquent, high-flown. See LOUDNESS, ORNAMENT.

soon, *adv.* anon, presently; promptly, quickly; readily, willingly. See EARLINESS. *Ant.*, see LATENESS.

soot, *n.* smoke, carbon dust, smut, grit, coal dust; lampblack; smog, smaze. See UNCLEANNESS.

soothe, *v.t.* calm, quiet, tranquilize; relieve, assuage, mitigate, console, comfort. See MODERATION, RELIEF. *Ant.*, see AGITATION.

sop, *n. & v.* —*n.* morsel, pacifier; bribe, inducement, COMPENSATION, propitiation, token; milksop. —*v.* steep, dunk; wet, moisten. See MOISTURE.

sophisticate, *n.* worldling; blasé person; cosmopolitan, man-about-town, man of the world. See KNOWLEDGE. *Ant.*, see SIMPLENESS.

sophistication, *n.* pretentious wisdom; affectation; worldliness; worldly-wise attitude; blasé airs; superficial polish *or* culture; cosmopolitan veneer. See KNOWLEDGE, SKILL. *Ant.*, see SIMPLENESS.

sophistry, *n.* sophism; false *or* specious reasoning; casuistry; fallaciousness, paralogism; shift, subterfuge, equivocation; ABSURDITY, inconsistency; hair-splitting. See FALSEHOOD. *Ant.*, see REASONING, TRUTH.

sophomoric, *adj.* immature, callow; inane, foolish. See YOUTH, IGNORANCE.

soporific, *adj.* sedative, narcose, soothing; lethargic, torpid, dull, slow, sluggish; tedious, wearisome. See DULLNESS, REPOSE, PACIFICATION.

SORCERY

Nouns—**1,** sorcery; the occult; magic, the black art, necromancy, theurgy, thaumaturgy; demonology, diablerie, bedevilment; voodoo, obeah, witchcraft, witchery; white magic, black magic; black Mass; fetishism, vampirism; conjuration; bewitchery, enchantment, mysticism, second sight, mesmerism, animal magnetism; od force, odylic force; clairvoyance; spiritualism, spirit-rapping, table-turning; divination (see PREDICTION); sortilege, hocus-pocus (see DECEPTION). See SECRET.

2, spell, charms, incantation, cabala, runes, abracadabra, open sesame, mumbo-jumbo, evil eye.

3, exorcism; countercharm; bell, book and candle; talisman, amulet, periapt, phylactery, philter; fetish, agnus Dei.

4, wand, caduceus, rod, divining rod, magic lamp *or* ring, wishing cap, Fortunatus' cap.

5, sorcerer, magician; thaumaturgist, theurgist; conjuror, voodooist, necromancer, seer, wizard, witch; lamia, hag, warlock, charmer; medicine-man; shaman, medium, clairvoyant, mesmerist; *deus ex machina*; soothsayer, ORACLE; Cagliostro, Mesmer; Circe, siren, weird sisters. See also DEMON.

Verbs—practice sorcery, conjure, charm, enchant; bewitch, bedevil; entrance, mesmerize, magnetize; fascinate; taboo; wave a wand; rub the ring *or* lamp; cast a spell; hold a seance, call up spirits, raise spirits from the dead. *Slang,* hoodoo, jinx.

Adjectives—magic, magical; occult; SECRET, mystic, weird, cabalistic, talismanic, phylacteric, incantatory; charmed, bewitched; spellbound, haunted.

Antonym, see RELIGION.

---

sordid, *adj.* mean, base, ignoble; covetous, niggardly; mercenary, self-seeking; dirty, foul. See PARSIMONY.

sore, *adj. & n.* —*adj.* painful, tender; grieved, distressed; harsh, severe, intense, dire. *Slang,* aggrieved, resentful, disgruntled. See PAIN, DISCONTENT. —*n.* wound, abrasion, ulcer, sore spot. See DISEASE.

sorrow, *n.* grief, sadness, distress; contrition, remorse, PENITENCE; affliction, woe. See DEJECTION, ADVERSITY. *Ant.,* see PLEASURE, REJOICING.

sorry, *adj.* rueful, regretful, penitent; sympathetic, sorrowful; pitiful, shabby, paltry, wretched, mean. See PENITENCE, UNIMPORTANCE. *Ant.,* see REJOICING, PLEASURE.

sort, *n. & v.* —*n.* CLASS, kind, variety, group, category, DESCRIPTION. —*v.t.* segregate, separate, isolate; size, grade, group, match; assort, arrange, classify; sift, screen. See SIZE, ARRANGEMENT.

so-so, *adj.* passable, FAIR; *comme ci, comme ça.* See MEDIOCRITY.

soubrette, *n.* actress, ingenue, comedienne; coquette, flirt. See DRAMA, FEMALE.

soul, *n.* psyche, spirit, mind; vital principle; essence; person, mortal, individual; ego; heart, fire, élan; genius. See MANKIND, INTELLIGENCE.

sound, *adj., n. & v.* —*adj.* whole, undamaged; healthy, robust; logical, true, valid, reliable, trustworthy; solvent; strong, firm; thorough; unbroken. See PERFECTION, HEALTH, STABILITY, CERTAINTY, MONEY. —*n.* channel, bay, GULF. —*v.* fathom, plumb, measure; probe; investigate, examine. See DEPTH, INQUIRY.

SOUND

Nouns—**1,** sound, noise, strain; accent, twang, intonation, tone; cadence; sonorousness, audibility (see HEARING); resonance, voice, LOUDNESS.

2, sound, tone, tonality, intonation, inflection, modulation; pitch, key, timbre, tone color.

3, acoustics, phonics, phonetics, phonology, phonography; diacoustics, diaphonics, telephonics, radiophony.

4, vociferation, roar, cry, utterance, voice; snap, crash, bang, boom, roll, clatter, detonation, explosion.

Verbs—**1,** sound, make a noise; give out *or* emit sound.

2, speak (see SPEECH), snap, roll, reverberate, detonate, *etc.* See LOUDNESS.

Adjectives—sounding; soniferous, sonorous, resonant, audible, distinct; sonant, sonic, stertorous; phonetic, audible; acoustic, phonic.

Antonym, see SILENCE.

---

soundproof, *adj.* insulate, sound-absorbing; muted, muffled, noiseproof; noiseless, quiet, silent. See SILENCE.

soup, *n.* stock, broth, bouillon; potage, purée, bisque, chowder. See FOOD.

SOURNESS

Nouns—**1,** sourness, acid(ity), acerbity, acridity, astringency, tartness, SHARPNESS, rancidness, unsavoriness. See TASTE, PUNGENCY, DISCORD.

2, moroseness, sullenness, *etc.*; DISCONTENT; acrimony, asperity, harshness, petulance, IRASCIBILITY, ill-humor.

3, vinegar, acetum, verjuice, acetic acid, alum; lemon, lime, crab, pickle, sauerkraut; sour milk, sour cream, buttermilk, *crème fraiche*, yogurt; sour grapes.

Verbs—**1,** sour, be *or* turn sour, ferment, set the teeth on edge; acidify, acidulate, curdle, clabber, turn.

2, exasperate, exacerbate, irritate.

Adjectives—**1,** sour, acid, subacid, acidulous; acetic, acerbic, astringent, acrid, acetous, acetose; tart, crabbed, vinegary; sourish, sour as vinegar, sour as a pickle *or* lemon; green, unripe; styptic, hard, rough, caustic, bitter; soured, rancid, curdled, coagulated, turned, spoiled, musty, bad.

2, morose, sullen, surly, churlish, currish, crusty, crabbed, peevish, pettish, cross; acrimonious, ill-humored, -natured *or* -tempered, fretful, petulant, testy, snarling, irascible; glum, gloomy, dismal, sad, austere.

Antonym, see SWEETNESS.

---

source, *n.* CAUSE, origin, fountainhead, fount, derivation. See BEGINNING.

southern, *adj.* southerly, austral. See DIRECTION.

souvenir, *n.* memento, keepsake, relic. See MEMORY.

sovereign, *n.* monarch, ruler; potentate; king, queen, emperor. See AUTHORITY

sow, *v.t.* strew, scatter, disseminate, broadcast; plant, seed. See AGRICULTURE, DISCLOSURE.

spa, *n.* mineral spring, watering place, thermal spring, mud baths, balneum, hydro, *Bad*, waters; health club; resort. See WATER, REMEDY.

SPACE

Nouns—**1,** space, extension, extent, superficial extent, area, expanse; sphere, range, latitude, field, way, expansion, compass, sweep, play, swing, spread, capacity, stretch; open space, free space; void, emptiness, ABSENCE of space; waste, wild, wilderness; moor, prairie, campagna; abyss, unlimited space, INFINITY, universe, creation; heavens, sky; interplanetary space; world; length and breadth of the land. See ASTRONAUTICS.

2, room, scope, spare room, elbow room; margin; leeway, headway. *Slang,* room to swing a cat.

3, proportions, dimensions, acreage, acres, breadth, width; square inches, feet, yards, *etc.* See MEASUREMENT.

Adjectives—spacious, roomy, extensive, expansive, capacious, ample; widespread, vast, worldwide, uncircumscribed; unlimited, endless; infinite, universal; boundless, shoreless, trackless, pathless, bottomless.

Adverbs—extensively, wherever; everywhere; far and near, far and wide, right and left, all over, all the world over; throughout the world; under the sun, in every quarter, in all quarters, in all lands; here, there and everywhere; from pole to pole, from end to end; on the face of the earth, in the wide world, from all points of the compass; to the four winds, to the uttermost parts of the earth; infinitely, *ad infinitum*.

Antonym, see CIRCUMSCRIPTION.

---

space-age, *adj.* twentieth-century, modern, contemporary. See NEW-NESS.

spacecraft, *n.* rocket, transport (see ASTRONAUTICS, VEHICLE).

spade, *n. & v.* —*n.* shovel, spud; card suit (*pl.*). —*v.* dig, delve, shovel, excavate. See CONCAVITY.

span, *v. & n.* —*v.t.* measure; encircle; stretch over, bridge. —*n.* bridge; extent; period; lifetime; nine-inch spread; team, yoke. See MEASURE-MENT, JUNCTION, AGE.

spangle, *n. & v.* —*n.* sequin, paillette, ORNAMENT, bead, gem, stud, bauble, trinket, sparkler. —*v.t.* bespangle, jewel, stud, ORNAMENT, decorate. —*v.i.* sparkle, glitter, glisten, scintillate, coruscate. See LIGHT.

spank, *v.t.* slap, paddle, wallop; punish, chastise. See PUNISHMENT.

spanking, *adj. & n.* —*adj.* brisk, lively, fresh; moving swiftly. See VE-LOCITY. —*n.* PUNISHMENT, hiding, thrashing.

spar, *v. & n.* —*v.i.* box; stall; bandy words, argue, bicker. See CON-TENTION. —*n.* mast, pole, gaff, boom, sprit, yard; varnish. See HEIGHT, COVERING.

spare, *v. & adj.* —*v.t.* be lenient; save; refrain, abstain, forbear, with-hold; exempt; give up, surrender, forego, relinquish. See PRESERVATION, INACTIVITY, RELINQUISHMENT. —*adj.* lean, gaunt, bony; extra, reserve; frugal. See NARROWNESS, STORE. *Ant.* see WASTE.

spark, *n.* flash; inspiration; iota, jot; beau, swain, gallant. See HEAT, LOVE.

sparkle, *v.i.* glisten, spark, twinkle, flash, glitter, scintillate; effervesce, bubble; be vivacious. See LIGHT.

sparse, *adj.* scattered, sporadic; thin, few, meager, scanty. See RARITY.

spasm, *n.* throe, paroxysm, convulsion, seizure; fit, furor, momentary enthusiasm. See DISEASE, AGITATION.

spatter, *v.t.* splash, sprinkle; besprinkle, bedraggle, bespatter; sully, soil. See WATER, UNCLEANNESS.

spawn, *v. & n.* —*v.* deposit, lay; propagate, breed, beget; produce, bring forth, give birth to, engender. —*n.* eggs, roe, ova; products, handiwork; offspring, scions, progeny, brood. See PRODUCTION, POS-TERITY, PRODUCTION.

speak, *v.* talk, converse; lecture, discourse, orate; say, utter, pronounce; express, communicate. See SPEECH.

speaker, *n.* presiding officer, chairman, orator, spokesman; loudspeaker. See SPEECH, AUTHORITY.

spear, *n.* lance, pike, javelin, blade. See ARMS.

SPECIALITY

Nouns—**1,** speciality, individuality, originality, particularity, peculiarity, distinction; state, trait, feature, mark, stamp, property, attribute, IDEN-TITY, character (see INTRINSIC); personality, characteristic, TENDENCY, mannerism, trick, idiosyncrasy, the nature of the beast; technicality, singularity (see UNCONFORMITY).

2, specialty, specialization; hobby, métier. *Colloq.*, keynote.

3, particulars, details, items, counts, circumstances (see CIRCUMSTANCE).

4, I, self, I myself, me, ego, psyche. See UNITY.

Verbs—specialize, specify, be specific, particularize, individualize, realize; designate, indicate, determine, define, name, detail, earmark, show clearly, clarify; give particulars, go into detail, come to the point. *Colloq.*, get down to cases *or* brass tacks.

Adjectives—special, particular, individual, specific, specifical, singular, exceptional, extraordinary, original, unique, uncommon, unlike, picked, marked, distinct, distinctive, *sui generis* (see UNCONFORMITY); proper, own, personal, private, privy, partial, PARTY; respective, certain, definite, express, determinate, detailed, diagnostic; especial, esoteric, endemic, idiomatic, idiosyncratic, characteristic, in character, true to form, appropriate, typical, exclusive, several.

Adverbs—specially, in particular, for my part, personally, *ad hominem*; each, apiece, one by one, severally, individually, respectively, each to each; seriatim, in detail, bit by bit; namely, that is to say, *videlicet*, viz., to wit.

Antonym, see GENERALITY.

---

species, *n.* variety, sort, CLASS, category.

specific, *adj. & n.* —*adj.* special, distinct (see SPECIALITY); limited, exact, precise, absolute, unequivocal, RIGHT. See LIMIT, CERTAINTY. —*n.* REMEDY, medicine, medicament, cure, treatment.

specify, *v.* name, mention, identify, enumerate, indicate, stipulate, define, state, itemize, detail; order, REQUEST. See SPECIALITY, INDICATION, PERMISSION.

specimen, *n.* sample, example, representative, instance, pattern, taster. See CONFORMITY.

specious, *adj.* plausible, ostensible, apparent, casuistic, insincere. See DECEPTION, APPEARANCE. *Ant.,* genuine, sincere.

speck, *n.* BLEMISH, speckle, spot, macula; particle, iota, mite, mote, dot. See LITTLENESS.

spectacle, *n.* sight; phenomenon; pageant, parade, show; exhibition, scene, display. See APPEARANCE, OSTENTATION, RIDICULE.

spectacles, *n.pl.* eyeglasses, glasses, goggles; contact lenses; lorgnette. *Slang,* specs, cheaters. See OPTICAL INSTRUMENTS.

spectator, *n.* beholder, observer, looker-on, onlooker, watcher, viewer, witness, eyewitness, bystander, passerby; sightseer, rubberneck, sidewalk superintendent; inspector; audience, house; the gallery, grandstand *or* bleachers.

specter, spectre, *n.* ghost, spirit, apparition, vision, shadow, shade; wraith, phantom, phantasm, haunt, spook; aura, emanation, materialization, reincarnation, illusion, delusion, hallucination. See INSUBSTANTIALITY.

speculate, *v.i.* ponder, contemplate, meditate, conjecture, surmise; gamble, play the market. See THOUGHT, CHANCE, BUSINESS.

SPEECH

Nouns—**1,** speech, talk, faculty of speech; locution, parlance, vernacular, oral communication, word of mouth, parole, palaver, prattle; effusion, discourse; SOLILOQUY; interlocution, CONVERSATION, LOQUACITY. *Colloq.,* gab, confab, powwow, corroboree.

2, formal speech, speechifying, oration, recitation, delivery, peroration, valedictory; oratory, elocution, eloquence; rhetoric, declamation; bombast, grandiloquence; burst of eloquence; fecundity; flow *or* command of language; power of speech, gift of gab, blarney. *Slang,* spiel, line, earful, pep talk.

3, allocution, exhortation, appeal, harangue, lecture, sermon, tirade, diatribe, invocation.

4, LANGUAGE, linguistics, grammar, lexicography, etymology; semantics, general semantics, meaning, denotation, connotation; WRITING, literature, philology, classics, letters, *belles lettres*, humanities, Muses.

5, WORD, phone, phoneme, syllable, stem, root; PHRASE, sentence; syntax, idiom; utterance, remark, statement, pronouncement, observation, comment; question, INQUIRY; answer, reply; aside, apostrophe, rhetorical question.

6, vocalization, enunciation, articulation, delivery; vociferation, exclamation, ejaculation; clearness, distinctness; whisper, stage whisper.

7, speaker, spokesman; prolocutor, interlocutor; mouthpiece, orator;

Demosthenes, Cicero; rhetorician; stump *or* platform orator; speech-maker, patterer, improvisator, monologist; gossip.

8, linguist, philologist, grammarian; semanticist, etymologist, lexicographer.

9, accent, accentuation; emphasis, stress; brogue, burr; pronunciation, euphony.

Verbs—**1,** speak, talk, speak of; say, utter, pronounce, deliver, comment, remark, recite, VOICE, give utterance to; breathe, let fall, come out with; rap out, blurt out; chatter, open one's mouth; lift *or* raise one's voice; speak one's mind; state, assert, declare. *Colloq.*, gab, shoot one's mouth off, shoot the breeze, talk a blue streak.

2, hold forth; make *or* deliver a speech, speechify, orate, declaim, stump, flourish, spout, rant, recite, discourse, have *or* say one's say; expatiate, be eloquent, have the gift of gab.

3, soliloquize, apostrophize, talk to oneself; tell, impart, inform (see INFORMATION); converse, speak to, talk together; communicate; divulge (see DISCLOSURE); express, phrase, put into words; translate, interpret.

4, allocute, exhort, appeal, harangue, lecture, preach, invoke, sermonize.

5, enunciate, pronounce, articulate; accentuate, aspirate; exclaim, ejaculate, cry; shout, yell, mouth.

Adjectives—**1,** speaking, spoken; vocal, oral, lingual, phonetic, outspoken; eloquent, elocutionary; oratorical, rhetorical; declamatory, bombastic, grandiloquent; talkative (see LOQUACITY).

2, lingual, linguistic; idiomatic, colloquial, dialectic, vernacular, provincial; polyglot; literary.

3, conversational, discursive, interlocutory; chatty, sociable.

Adverbs—orally; vocally; by word of mouth, *viva voce*, from the lips of; loudly, out loud, aloud; softly, *sotto voce*.

Antonym, see SILENCE.

---

speechless, *adj.* See SILENCE, MUTENESS, TACITURNITY.

speed, *v.* & *n.* —*v.i.* HASTE, hasten, hurry, accelerate. —*n.* VELOCITY, dispatch, expedition, swiftness. *Ant.*, see SLOWNESS.

speedway, *n.* expressway, superhighway; racecourse, track, dragstrip. See PASSAGE.

spell, *n.* charm, trance; talisman; incantation, sorcery, magic; witchery, allure, glamour; enchantment; spellbinding. See SORCERY, RELIEF, LETTER.

spell, *n.* term, period, interval; TIME; turn, stretch; breathing spell, respite.

spend, *v.t.* disburse, pay out, expend; consume, exhaust; pass. See PAYMENT, BUSINESS.

spendthrift, *n.* wastrel, prodigal, profligate, squanderer. See WASTE. *Ant.*, see PARSIMONY.

spent, *adj.* used up, exhausted, fatigued, dead-tired, fagged; effete, worn-out, impotent. See WEARINESS, DETERIORATION.

sperm, *n.* semen, seed, germ. See CAUSE.

spew, *v.* vomit, regurgitate, retch, throw up; gush, shoot, spout, eject, emit, expel; spit; discharge. See EJECTION.

sphere, *n.* orb, globe, ball; environment, province, status, field, range. See CIRCULARITY, CLASS.

spice, *v.t.* season, flavor; make piquant. See TASTE.

spigot, *n.* See FAUCET.

spike, *n.* & *v.* —*n.* cleat, skewer, spindle; projection; goad, prod. See SHARPNESS. —*v.* pierce, gore; nail, rivet, impale, transpierce. See CONNECTION, OPENING. *Slang,* lace (with), needle. See DRUNKENNESS.

spill, *v.* overturn, upset; splash; brim over, slop, pour out. See EJECTION, DEPRESSION. *Slang,* tell, let slip. See DISCLOSURE.

spin, *v.* twirl, whirl, rotate; protract, draw out; gyrate, swirl, reel, eddy. See ROTATION, LOQUACITY.

spindle, *n.* axis, axle, shaft; stick, spike, mandrel, arbor; stalk, stem. See SUPPORT, ROTATION.

spine, *n.* backbone; ridge, *arête*; thorn, prickle, spike, spiculum, quill, barb. See REAR, HEIGHT, SHARPNESS.

spineless, *adj.* invertebrate, boneless; pliant, limp, flabby; irresolute, cowardly, craven. *Slang,* gutless, yellow. See COWARDICE, WEAKNESS.

spinster, *n.* maid, maiden, old maid; spinner. See CELIBACY.

spiral, *adj.* coiled, winding, helical, turbinate, cochlear. See CONVOLUTION.

spire, *n.* steeple, minaret; flèche; point, pinnacle, peak; pyramid, obelisk; epi, finial, aiguille. See HEIGHT, SHARPNESS.

spirit, *n.* vitalness, essence; soul; ghost, fairy, ANGEL, DEMON; disposition, temper, mood, humor; ENERGY, vivacity, élan, verve, intrepidity, enthusiasm, dash, gallantry, intent. See MEANING, ACTIVITY.

spirited, *adj.* animated, lively, mettlesome, bold, ardent; blithe, debonair, jaunty; sparkling, racy. See ACTIVITY, CHEERFULNESS.

spiritual, *adj.* immaterial, incorporeal, insubstantial, fleshless; divine, exalted, celestial, holy, sacred; religious; inspired, supernatural, virtuous, platonic; occult. See INSUBSTANTIALITY, PIETY, VIRTUE, SUPERNATURALISM.

spit, *v.* impale, transfix, pierce, stab; sprinkle, drizzle, discharge (bullets); sputter, utter explosively; expectorate, hiss. See OPENING, EJECTION.

spite, *n.* malice, ill-will, grudge, malignity, MALEVOLENCE. *Ant.,* see BENEVOLENCE.

spitfire, *n.* firebrand, hothead, tigress, hellcat. See IRASCIBILITY.

splash, *v.* spatter, bespatter; dash, plop, spill; slop, splash, dabble, paddle. See EJECTION, WATER, UNCLEANNESS.

spleen, *n.* IRASCIBILITY, RESENTMENT, wrath, choler; spite, MALEVOLENCE.

splendid, *adj.* gorgeous, magnificent; heroic, glorious; resplendent. See BEAUTY, REPUTE, ELEGANCE. *Colloq.,* excellent. *Ant.,* see UGLINESS.

splice, *v.t.* join, unite, interweave. *Slang,* marry. See JUNCTION.

splint, *n.* splinter; slat, strip; SUPPORT, cast, brace, bracket.

splinter, *n. & v.* —*n.* splint; shard, sliver, shaving, shive; fragment, particle, toothpick, matchwood. See PART, LITTLENESS. —*v.* sliver, rend, smash, fragmentize, fracture. See DISJUNCTION.

split, *v.t.* rive, rend, cleave, splinter; divide, separate, divorce; apportion. See DISJUNCTION. *Ant.,* see JUNCTION.

splurge, *n. & v., colloq.* —*n.* extravagance, WASTE, expense. —*v.* indulge (oneself), extravagate, lavish. *Slang,* shoot the works; go [the] whole hog.

spoil, *v. & n.* —*v.* damage, ruin, impair; overindulge, humor; despoil, plunder, sack, pillage, rob; decay, putrefy, rot, mold, ferment. See DETERIORATION. —*n.* plunder, loot, booty, spoliation. See ACQUISITION.

spoken, *adj.* oral, vocal; verbal. See SPEECH. *Ant.,* see WRITING.

spokesman, *n.* VOICE, mouthpiece; front, figurehead; representative, go-between, proxy, AGENT, delegate, advocate. See SPEECH, REPRESENTATION.

sponge, *n. & v.* —*n.* swab, blotter, dryer. *Colloq.,* hanger-on, parasite, leech, dependent. *Slang,* moocher, scrounge, freeloader. See CLEANNESS, SERVILITY. —*v.* sop, soak up, mop, swab, blot, absorb, dry, suck in, drink up. *Colloq.,* touch, live off. *Slang,* scrounge, mooch, freeload.

sponsor, *n.* patron, backer; surety, guarantor; godparent; advertiser. See AID.

spontaneous, *adj.* instinctive, automatic, involuntary; extemporaneous, uninhibited, unforced, natural. See IMPULSE, WILL.

spoof, *n. & v., slang.* —*n.* jest, joke, banter, hoax; satire, burlesque, parody, take-off, caricature, lampoon. —*v.* deceive, hoodwink, fool; needle, josh, kid; lampoon, parody, satirize, RIDICULE. See DECEPTION, WIT, LEVITY.

spool, *n.* spindle, bobbin, reel. See ROTATION.

sport, *n.* recreation, athletics, pastime, angling, hunting, chase; jesting, merriment; mockery, RIDICULE; freak, mutant; gamester, gambler. *Slang*, spender, flashy dresser. See AMUSEMENT.

sportsman, *n.* Nimrod, hunter, angler; athlete, ballplayer, golfer, *etc.*; honorable competitor. See PURSUIT, AMUSEMENT.

spot, *n.* place, locality, site; blotch, dapple, speckle, macula; smear, spatter, daub, blot; BLEMISH, flaw, stain, stigma. See LOCATION, UNCLEANNESS.

spotless, *adj.* clean, unsullied, immaculate; pure, unblemished, impeccable. See PERFECTION, CLEANNESS. *Ant.*, see UNCLEANNESS.

spotlight, *n.* & *v.* —*n.* limelight, spot(lamp), searchlight, beacon, headlamp; notoriety, ATTENTION. —*v.t.* feature, star, play up. See PUBLICATION, DRAMA.

spouse, *n.* mate, husband, wife, consort. See MARRIAGE.

spout, *n.* tube, pipe, trough, nozzle, rainspout, gargoyle; jet, spurt, geyser, waterspout. See PASSAGE.

sprain, *v.t.* wrench, strain, twist. See DETERIORATION.

sprawl, *v.* spread, extend, slump, slouch, lounge, loll. See LENGTH, REPOSE.

spray, *n.* & *v.* —*n.* spindrift, spume, scud; fusillade, barrage; sprinkler, atomizer; slender branch, sprig. —*v.t.* sprinkle, atomize; pepper, riddle (with bullets). See VAPOR, WATER, ATTACK.

spread, *v.* & *n.* —*v.* scatter, strew; disseminate, diffuse, circulate; cover; unfold, stretch; part, separate; show, display; expand, disperse, deploy. —*n.* diffusion, expansion; extent, expanse; bedspread, coverlet; meal, banquet, collation; layout; ranch. See SIZE, COVERING, FOOD, INCREASE, PUBLICATION, OPENING.

spree, *n.* frolic, lark, escapade, fling, revel; carousal, saturnalia. *Slang*, souse, jag, toot, binge, bat, bust. See PLEASURE, DRUNKENNESS, INTEMPERANCE.

sprightly, *adj.* gay, brisk, vivacious, animated; scintillating, smart. See CHEERFULNESS, WIT. *Ant.*, DULL.

spring, *v.* & *n.* —*n.* LEAP, bound, dart, start; bounce, RECOIL, rebound; arise, rise; result from, derive from; release; detonate; reveal, disclose; bend, twist. *Slang*, release; bail. —*n.* LEAP, bound; elasticity, RECOIL; well, fount, origin, source; coil. See BEGINNING.

sprinkle, *v.* scatter, spread, sow; spray, wet; speckle, mottle, powder; drizzle, shower. See DISCLOSURE, WATER.

sprinkler, *n.* spray, sprayer, atomizer, nozzle, watering can, watering cart; fire-extinguishing system. See WATER.

sprint, *n.* run, dash; speed, rush; bolt, dart, tear. *Colloq.*, hotfoot. See VELOCITY.

sprout, *v.i.* germinate, shoot, bud, burgeon. See INCREASE.

spruce, *adj.* trim, neat, tidy, shipshape; smart, dapper, chic. See ARRANGEMENT. *Ant.*, see DISORDER.

spry, *adj.* lively, alert, athletic, nimble, agile. See ACTIVITY, STRENGTH.

spunky, *adj.*, *colloq.*, plucky, mettlesome, brave, intrepid. See COURAGE.

spur, *n.* spine; rowel; incentive, goad, stimulus; projection, headland, siding. See SHARPNESS, CAUSE.

spurious, *adj.* false, counterfeit, sham, specious; bastard, illegitimate. See DECEPTION, ILLEGALITY. *Ant.*, see LEGALITY, TRUTH.

spurn, *v.t.* flout, scout, reject, repudiate, repel, contemn, scorn, disdain. See REFUSAL, CONTEMPT. *Ant.*, see RECEIVING.

spurt, *v.* & *n.* —*v.i.* gush, squirt, spray, gush; burst. See WATER, VELOCITY.

sputter, *v.* spit, spew, splutter, spatter, eject, splash; blurt, babble, jabber, stammer; misfire, fizzle. See MOISTURE, EJECTION, SPEECH, FAILURE.

spy, *n.* secret agent, scout, undercover man, informer, stool pigeon. See INFORMATION, CONCEALMENT.

squabble, *v. & n.* —*v.* quarrel, bicker, altercate, fall out. —*n.* falling out, quarrel, dispute, wrangle, spat, argument. See CONTENTION, DISCORD.

squad, *n.* band, patrol; squadron, wing, unit; crew, team. See ASSEMBLAGE.

squalid, *adj.* filthy, dirty, foul, sordid, repulsive, wretched. See UNCLEANNESS. *Ant.,* see CLEANNESS.

squall, *n. & v.* —*n.* gust, blow, blast; turmoil; scream, CRY. See WIND, DISORDER. —*v.i.* blow, bluster; scream, bawl, wail.

squalor, *n.* dirt, filth, decay, UNCLEANNESS, misery, POVERTY. See IMPURITY.

squander, *v.t.* WASTE, lavish, dissipate. *Ant.,* see PARSIMONY.

square, *n. & v.* —*n.* tetragon, quadrilateral, equilateral rectangle; block; quadrangle; plaza, court; T square. See NUMERATION, ABODE, MEASUREMENT. *Slang,* meal; misfit, booby. —*v.t.* quadrate; balance, settle, reconcile; set, adjust. See AGREEMENT.

squash, *v.t.* crush, mash, squeeze, flatten; squelch. See DESTRUCTION.

squat, *adj.* dumpy, stocky, pudgy. See SHORTNESS. *Ant.,* see HEIGHT.

squawk, *v. & n.* —*v.* CRY, call, scream, screech. *Slang,* complain, kick, gripe, grouse. —*n.* outcry, squeak, croak, caw, screech. See LAMENTATION.

squeak, *v.* creak, CRY. *Colloq.,* squeak by, just make it, pull through. See ESCAPE, NARROWNESS.

squeal, *v.* yell, CRY, yelp, shriek, screech. *Slang,* confess, inform, blab, stool, tattle, tell (on), spill [the beans], sing. See DISCLOSURE.

squeamish, *adj.* queasy, qualmish, nauseous; reluctant, fearful, skittish, nervous; fastidious, picky; hypercritical. See CARE, FEAR, AFFECTATION.

squeeze, *v.t.* press, compress; express, extract; stuff, cram; exact, extort, blackmail. See CONTRACTION, COMPULSION. *Ant.,* see INCREASE.

squelch, *v.t.* disconcert, discomfit, rout, crush; SILENCE, stifle, muffle. See DESTRUCTION.

squint, *n.* cross-eye, strabismus; peek, peering, glance. See VISION.

squirm, *v.i.* twist, turn, thrash (about); wriggle, writhe. See CONVOLUTION.

squirt, *v. & n.* —*v.* spray, jet, douche, hose, spatter. See FLUIDITY, EJECTION. —*n.* spurt, jet, stream(let); syringe, spray(er), atomizer. *Colloq.,* upstart, runt, shrimp, imp. *Slang,* half pint, snotnose. See UNIMPORTANCE, YOUTH.

stab, *v.t.* pierce, puncture, perforate, stick, prick, pink; distress, hurt. See SHARPNESS, PAIN.

STABILITY

Nouns—1, stability; immutability, unchangeableness, constancy, firmness, equilibrium, immobility, soundness, vitality, stiffness, solidity, aplomb; establishment, fixture; permanence; obstinacy, RESOLUTION; inflexibility (see HARDNESS).

2, rock, pillar, tower, foundation, leopard's spots; rock of Gibraltar.

Verbs—1, be stable, be *or* stand firm; stick fast; weather the storm; settle down, take root; entrench oneself.

2, establish, settle, ascertain, fix, set, retain, keep *or* take hold; make good, make sure; perpetuate.

Adjectives—1, stable, fixed, steadfast, firm, fast, steady, balanced; confirmed, valid, immovable, irremovable, riveted, rooted; settled, established, vested; incontrovertible; tethered, anchored, moored; firm as a rock; firmly seated *or* established; deep-rooted, ineradicable; inveterate; obstinate; stuck fast, aground, high and dry, stranded.

2, unchangeable, immutable; unaltered, unalterable; constant, PERMANENT; invariable, undeviating; durable, perennial; indefeasible, irrevocable, irreversible, inextinguishable, irreducible; indissoluble; indestructible, undying, deathless, immortal, imperishable, indelible, indeciduous.

3, conservative, Tory, reactionary, diehard.

Adverbs—in statu quo; at a standstill.
Antonym, see CHANGEABLENESS.

---

stable, *n.* barn, stall, mews. See DOMESTICATION.
stack, *n. & v.* —*n.* pile, heap, mound; rick, sheaf, faggot; chimney, flue. *Colloq.*, piles, heaps, lots. See ASSEMBLAGE, MULTITUDE —*v.* pile, heap, bundle. *Colloq.*, doctor, rig, prearrange; fix, load. See DECEPTION.
stadium, *n.* See ARENA.
staff, *n.* walking stick, cane, cudgel; scepter, wand, baton, truncheon, crosier; flagpole; assistants, crew, aides, associates, personnel, force. See SUPPORT, SERVANT.
stage, *n.* platform, rostrum, scaffold; DRAMA, theater; ARENA, field, scene; DEGREE, step, phase; PERIOD, stretch, interval, span; stagecoach, diligence, omnibus. See SUPPORT, VEHICLE.
stagger, *v.* reel, sway, totter, lurch; waver, hesitate; surprise, stun, jar, shock, startle, take aback; alternate. See AGITATION, OSCILLATION.
stagnant, *adj.* static, inert; foul; sluggish, dull, torpid. See INACTIVITY. *Ant.*, flowing; see ACTIVITY.
staid, *adj.* demure, serious, sedate, settled, INEXCITABLE.
stain, *n.* COLOR, dye, dyestuff; discoloration; blotch, blot, smear, smudge; BLEMISH, tarnish; stigma, taint, brand. See UNCLEANNESS, DISREPUTE.
stairway, *n.* stairs, steps, staircase, Escalator; companionway, ladder. See ASCENT, DESCENT.
stake, *n.* post, peg, pile; palisade; burning, execution; wager, bet, ante, pot; SECURITY, earnest, deposit; interest, claim, holding; prize, REWARD. See CHANCE, PROPERTY.
stale, *adj.* passé; rancid, dried up, tasteless, INSIPID, flat, vapid; trite, DULL, banal; overtrained. *Slang*, corny. See DETERIORATION.
stalemate, *n.* draw, deadlock, standoff, tie; stall; RESISTANCE, OPPOSITION; impasse, standstill; check, HINDRANCE, bottleneck, jam. See END.
stalk, *n.* stem, pedicle, petiole. See SUPPORT.
stall, *n. & v.* —*n.* stable, manger; INCLOSURE, chamber; booth, concession, kiosk; alcove, niche. See RECEPTACLE. *Colloq.*, pretext, evasion. See AVOIDANCE. —*v.* stick, stand still, bog down; fail, go dead. *Colloq.*, delay, dodge, play for time, put *or* hold off, stave off. See LATENESS.
stalwart, *adj.* strong, brawny, husky; dauntless, steadfast. See POWER. *Ant.*, WEAK, timid.
stamina, *n.* staying power, hardiness, force, VIGOR; vitality, STRENGTH; grit, pluck, backbone; endurance, DURABILITY, resilience.

STAMMERING

Nouns—stammering, stuttering, *etc.*; hesitancy, broken voice; speech, impediment; lisp, drawl; mispronunciation, slip of the tongue, *lapsus linguae.*
Verbs—stammer, stutter, falter, sputter, splutter, stumble, halt, hesitate, pause, balbutiate, hem and haw, trip over one's tongue, be unable to put two words together; mumble, mutter, dither; lisp, speak thickly, swallow one's words, mispronounce, missay.
Adjectives—inarticulate, indistinct, hesitant, halting; guttural, nasal, husky, throaty, tremulous, tongue-tied.
Antonym, see SPEECH.

---

stamp, *n.* impression, symbol, device, SEAL, trademark, brand; authorization, certification, approval, ASSENT; postage; die, rubber stamp; certificate, wafer, label; kind, sort, quality. See INDICATION.
stampede, *n. & v.* —*n.* flight, charge, rampage, onrush. —*v.t.* panic, rout, scare, alarm, incite, inflame. See FEAR, DISORDER.

stance, *n.* foothold, placement, post, station; posture, carriage, bearing; pose, FORM, APPEARANCE; standpoint, view(point). *Colloq.,* slant. See SUPPORT.

stanch, staunch, *adj.* loyal, reliable, faithful, constant, steadfast; seaworthy, strong. See PROBITY.

stand, *v.* abide, tolerate, endure, SUPPORT; last, persist; remain upright; pause, halt, stop; be, remain; stagnate; be valid; put, place; bear, undergo; stand for, represent, mean. See DURABILITY, MEANING, INDICATION.

standard, *n.* emblem, ensign; criterion, measure, grade, exemplar, norm, canon, prototype, ethics. See INDICATION, MEASUREMENT.

stand-by, *n.* FRIEND, mainstay, ally, supporter; staple; alternate, replacement, substitute (see SUBSTITUTION).

standing, *n.* station, rank, REPUTE; duration, continuance; status, rating. See DURABILITY.

standpoint, *n.* vantage [point]; viewpoint, point of view. See RELATION.

standstill, *n.* full *or* dead stop, halt, suspension, impasse. See INACTION.

stanza, *n.* verse, stave, strophe. See POETRY.

staple, *adj.* chief, principal; stable, established, regular; marketable, popular. See STABILITY, SALE.

star, *n.* sun, celestial body; pentagram; asterisk; prima donna, leading man, chief performer; DESTINY; planet. See INDICATION, DRAMA.

stare, *v.i.* gaze, gape, gawk; stand out, be conspicuous. See VISION, CURIOSITY.

starry, *adj.* spangled, stellar, stellate, star-studded; starlit; shiny, glittering. See LIGHT.

start, *v.* begin, commence, set out; jerk, jump, shy; loosen, crack; originate; set going; loosen, crack; startle, rouse. See BEGINNING, PROPULSION, IMPULSE, SURPRISE.

startle, *v.t.* start, alarm, frighten, shock, surprise, amaze. See SURPRISE.

starve, *v.* hunger, famish, fast; pine; pinch, scrimp, deny. See ASCETICISM, PARSIMONY, POVERTY. *Ant.,* see SUFFICIENCY.

state, *n. & v.* —*n.* condition; category; estate; lot; case, mood, disposition, temper; pickle, contretemps, quandary, dilemma, plight; aspect, APPEARANCE; constitution, habitude, frame; pomp, great dignity, formality, CIRCUMSTANCE; mode, modality; FORM, tone, tenor, turn; FASHION, style, character, rank, situation, position, status; nation, country, government; commonwealth. *Colloq.,* make-up; kilter; shape. —*v.* allege, say, assert, declare, avow, aver, express, make a statement. See CIRCUMSTANCE, SPEECH.

stately, *adj.* impressive, imposing, grand; dignified, noble, lofty. See OSTENTATION, IMPORTANCE. *Ant.,* see PLAINNESS, UNIMPORTANCE.

statement, *n.* assertion, declaration, AFFIRMATION; report; bill, account. See ACCOUNTING.

statesman, *n.* legislator, diplomat, solon, Draco; politician. See DIRECTION.

static, *adj. & n.* —*adj.* immobile, motionless, inert, passive, inactive; unchanging, the same, conservative. See INACTION, STABILITY. —*n.* interference, noise; crackling, snow, ghosts, jamming. See ENERGY.

station, *n. & v.* —*n.* place, position; office, situation; rank, standing; depot, terminal; headquarters, stopping place, post. —*v.t.* set, place, assign, post. See LOCATION, REPUTE.

stationary, *adj.* fixed, rooted, planted, immovable; constant, unchanging, static. See PERMANENCE, STABILITY.

statistics, *n.* data, charts, graphs, computations. See NUMERATION.

statue, *n.* SCULPTURE, effigy, image.

statuesque, *adj.* monumental, marmoreal; dignified, majestic, tall, well-proportioned. See SCULPTURE, BEAUTY.

stature, *n.* SIZE, HEIGHT, FORM; standing, rank, status, IMPORTANCE, REPUTE.

status, *n.* position, rank, standing; state, condition. See CIRCUMSTANCE.

statute, *n.* law, ordinance, enactment; rule. See LEGALITY.

stave, *n. & v.* —*n.* slat, strip. See PART. —*v.t.* break (up), penetrate, puncture, pierce; stave off, fend off, hold off *or* back. See DESTRUCTION.

stay, *v.* check, stop; detain, delay; defer; SUPPORT, brace; appease; outlast; linger, tarry, remain; endure, last; dwell, sojourn; stick, stay put; continue. See HINDRANCE, END, DURABILITY, PRESENCE.

steadfast, *adj.* firm, unswerving, constant, sta(u)nch. See RESOLUTION, PROBITY. *Ant.*, capricious, unreliable; see DOUBT.

steady, *adj.* firm, secure, stable; constant, unvarying, uniform; regular, habitual; trustworthy. See STABILITY.

STEALING

Nouns—**1,** stealing, theft, thievery, robbery; abduction, kidnaping; abstraction, appropriation; plagiarism; rape, depredation, poaching, raid; spoliation, plunder, pillage, sack, rapine, brigandage, foray; extortion, blackmail; graft; piracy, privateering, buccaneering; burglary; housebreaking; peculation, pilfering, embezzlement; fraud, swindle (see DECEPTION); kleptomania; larceny, grand larceny, petty larceny; pickpocketing, shoplifting, highway robbery; holdup, stickup, mugging; hijacking. *Slang,* make, heist, snatch; haul, score; rip-off.

2, THIEF, robber, burglar, sneak thief, housebreaker.

Verbs—**1,** steal, thieve; rob, purloin, pilfer, filch, swipe, crib, palm; abstract, appropriate, plagiarize; abduct, kidnap; make, walk *or* run off *or* away with; seize, TAKE; spirit away; plunder, pillage, rifle, sack, loot, ransack; spoil, spoliate, despoil, strip, sweep, gut, forage; blackmail, pirate, maraud, poach, smuggle, run; hold up, stick up, hijack, skyjack. *Slang,* heist; snatch; rip off.

2, swindle, peculate, embezzle; sponge, mulct, rook, bilk, milk, pluck, fleece, defraud; obtain under false pretenses; live by one's wits; rob Peter to pay Paul; set a thief to catch a thief. *Colloq.,* rook, shake down. *Slang,* wrangle.

Adjectives—stealing, thieving, thievish, light-fingered, furtive; piratical, predaceous, predacious, predatory; stolen. *Slang,* hot.

Antonym, see PROBITY.

---

stealth, *n.* furtiveness, secrecy, slinking action, skulking, stalking. See CONCEALMENT.

steam, *n. & v.* —*n.* VAPOR, water vapor, mist, fog, gas, evaporation. —*v.* cook, boil, simmer; soften, moisten; clean, renovate; progress, speed, travel (propelled by steam). See HEAT, WATER, VELOCITY.

steamer, *n.* river boat, steamboat, steamship, launch, liner, packet boat, side wheeler, stern-wheeler, paddle-wheeler. See SHIP.

steed, *n.* horse, mount, charger. See CARRIER.

steel, *v.t.* plate, armor, coat; temper, anneal, case harden; harden, inure, strengthen, toughen; brace, gird, fortify. See HARDNESS, STRENGTH, PREPARATION.

steep, *v. & adj.* —*v.t.* soak, macerate. See WATER. —*adj.* precipitous, abrupt, sheer, declivitous; VERTICAL. *Colloq.,* expensive, costly. See DIRECTION, DESCENT. *Ant.*, see LOWNESS, SMOOTHNESS, CHEAPNESS.

steeple, *n.* spire, finial, flèche, belfry, campanile. See HEIGHT, TEMPLE.

steer, *v.t.* guide, pilot, control; manage, direct; follow (a course). See NAVIGATION, DIRECTION.

stellar, *adj.* starry, astral, celestial; radiant, glorious; feature(d), top, star(ring). See UNIVERSE, LIGHT, SUPERIORITY, IMPORTANCE.

stem, *n.* tree trunk, stalk, petiole, pedicle; tube, shaft; cutwater, prow; lineage, extraction, derivation. See SUPPORT, OPENING, ANCESTRY.

stench, *n.* fetor, stink, mephitis, fetidness, malodor, (strong) smell. See MALODOROUSNESS. *Ant.*, see FRAGRANCE.

stenography, *n.* See SHORTHAND.

step, *n.* pace, stride, football; footprint; gait, tread; stair, rung; short distance; interval, gradation; measures, ACTION. See TRAVEL, INDICATION.

stereotype, n. & v. —n. type cast, COPY, REPRODUCTION (see PRINTING); pattern, type, CONFORMITY, IMITATION, REPETITION; cliché, convention; preconception. —v.t. reproduce, print, COPY; stylize, type, conventionalize, conform.

sterile, adj. barren, UNPRODUCTIVE, unfruitful, unfertile; aseptic, germ-free.

sterling, adj. genuine, unalloyed, pure; noble, excellent, exemplary; silver. See TRUTH, VIRTUE, MONEY.

stern, adj. & n. —adj. rigorous, austere; forbidding, grim; strict, harsh, uncompromising. See TRUTH, RESOLUTION, SEVERITY. Ant., see SOFTNESS. —n. poop, counter, REAR. Ant., see FRONT.

stew, v. & n. —v. simmer, seethe, (pressure-)cook, steam. Colloq., worry, fret, fume; stew in one's own juice. —n. pepperpot, ragout, goulash, fricassee. Colloq., AGITATION, dither, sweat. Slang, tizzy. See FOOD, RESENTMENT.

steward, n. AGENT, manager, trustee; provider, caterer; SERVANT, waiter. See DIRECTION, SERVICE.

stick, v. & n. —v.t. stab, puncture, prick; put, place, thrust; glue; transfix, impale. See OPENING, COHERENCE. Slang, puzzle, stump. —v.i. adhere, cling; stay, remain, tarry; stall, freeze, be immobile. See COHERENCE, HINDRANCE. —n. piece, branch; cane, staff, cudgel, rod, baton. See SUPPORT.

stickler, n. purist, pedant, quibbler; puritan, prig; perfectionist; poser, puzzle, enigma, baffler. See OBSTINACY, SEVERITY.

sticky, adj. adhesive, mucilaginous, glutinous, viscous, tenacious. Colloq., humid, muggy; sweaty; tacky. See COHERENCE.

stiff, adj. rigid, inflexible, firm, nonfluid; strong, brisk; difficult, hard; severe, excessive; formal, unreserved; awkward, stilted. See HARDNESS, SEVERITY, AFFECTATION. Ant., see SOFTNESS.

stifle, v.t. smother, suffocate; extinguish, put down, suppress; repress, check. See KILLING, CONCEALMENT, RESTRAINT.

stigma, n. BLEMISH, birthmark; brand, blot, stain, reproach. See DISREPUTE, IMPERFECTION. Ant., see REPUTE, PERFECTION.

stigmatize, v.t. denounce, reproach, brand, vilify. See DISREPUTE. Ant., see VINDICATION.

still, adj. silent, quiet, hushed; calm, peaceful, tranquil; motionless, at rest, stationary. See SILENCE, MODERATION, REPOSE.

stilted, adj. formal, stiff; unnatural, affected, mannered, prim; inflated, florid, flowery, pedantic. Colloq., stuffy. See AFFECTATION, INELEGANCE.

stimulant, n. excitant, stimulus, bracer, tonic, spur; liquor. See ENERGY, REMEDY.

stimulate, v.t. excite, rouse, animate, stir, spur, invigorate, exhilarate. See EXCITEMENT.

sting, v. & n. —v. smart, tingle; irritate, trouble, PAIN; wound; nettle, gall. See RESENTMENT. —n. wound, prickle, smart, irritation; stimulus, goad; stinger, prickle, nettle. See PAIN, BANE. Ant., see MODERATION.

stingy, adj. penurious, miserly, niggardly; scanty, meager. Colloq., near, tight, close. See PARSIMONY. Ant., generous, LIBERAL.

stink, n. & v. See MALODOROUSNESS.

stint, v. & n. —v. restrain, LIMIT; scrimp, skimp, economize. See PARSIMONY. —n. RESTRAINT, LIMIT; turn, shift, bout; task, chore, job. See EXERTION.

stipend, n. compensation, wage, pay, salary. See COMPENSATION.

stipple, v. mottle, speckle, pepper; splatter, dapple. See VARIEGATION, COLOR.

stipulate, v.t. specify, demand, insist upon, negotiate. See AGREEMENT.

stir, v.t. move, budge; agitate, incite, arouse; animate, stimulate, provoke. See AGITATION, MOTION, EXCITEMENT. Ant., see REPOSE.

stitch, *n. & v.* —*n.* seam, suture. —*v.t.* sew, knit, crochet, tack, smock, overcast; darn, mend. See CONNECTION, PRODUCTION.

stock, *n.* stem, bole, trunk; race, family; livestock, cattle; gun butt; capital; MERCHANDISE, goods; MATERIALS, raw materials; repertory. *Colloq.,* BELIEF. See ANCESTRY, ANIMAL, STORE, DRAMA.

stockade, *n.* palisade, estacade, palings, INCLOSURE; wall, barrier, barricade, fort, fortification; pen, compound, PRISON. See DEFENSE.

stocking, *n.* sock, hose, anklet, bobby sox; hosiery. See CLOTHING.

stockpile, *n.* reserve, STORE; hoard, cache; MATERIALS, surplus. See SUFFICIENCY.

stocky, *adj.* thickset, sturdy, chunky, squat. See SHORTNESS.

stodgy, *adj.* short, thickset (see STOCKY); sluggish, slow, obstinate, stolid; tedious, dull, unimaginative; backward, old-fashioned. See DULLNESS, CONFORMITY.

stoic, *adj.* stoical; self-controlled, impassive, unfeeling; long-suffering, ascetic. See RESTRAINT, INSENSIBILITY, REASONING, ASCETISM.

stoke, *v.* tend, poke, prod, stir; FUEL, fire, feed. See HEAT, IMPULSE.

stole, *n.* scarf, cape, mantle, fur piece; surplice. See CLOTHING.

stolid, *adj.* inexcitable, impassive, dull, lethargic, sluggish. See MODERATION.

stomach, *n.* appetite, hunger; DESIRE, craving, inclination; maw, craw. *Colloq.,* belly, paunch, corporation. See RECEPTACLE.

stone, *n.* cobblestone, pebble; mineral; gem, jewel; gravestone, tombstone, millstone, whetstone, hearthstone, flagstone, *etc.*; pit, endocarp, pyrene; concretion, calculus. See LAND, INTERMENT.

stooge, *n., colloq.,* dupe, butt, tool; straight man; SERVANT, henchman, lackey. *Slang,* fall guy, patsy, sucker; yes man, sidekick. See SERVILITY.

stool, *n.* cricket, hassock; seat; footrest, footstool; prie-dieu, kneeling stool; piano stool, milking stool, cuckoing stool. See SUPPORT.

stool pigeon, *n., slang,* decoy, informer, betrayer. See DISCLOSURE.

stoop, *v.i.* bend, bow, crouch; condescend, deign; submit. See DEPRESSION, SERVILITY. *Ant.,* see ASCENT.

stop, *v., n. & interj.* —*v.* close; obstruct; sta(u)nch; arrest, halt, impede; inhibit; delay, hold up, detain; discontinue, suspend; END, terminate, conclude; cease, desist. —*n.* halt, standstill, pause; discontinuance, stoppage; stay, sojourn; stopping place, station; period, punctuation mark; brake, catch, skid, detent, curb. —*interj.* halt! belay! avast! stay! cease! See END, CLOSURE, LATENESS.

stopgap, *n.* expedient, makeshift; temporary. See SUBSTITUTION, EXPEDIENCE.

stopper, *n.* plug, seal, valve, cork, bung, stopcock, stopple, tamp, spike, ramrod, wad, wadding, stuffing, pad, padding; barrier, tourniquet. See CLOSURE. *Ant.,* see OPENING.

STORE

Nouns—**1,** store, accumulation, hoard; mine, vein, lode, quarry; spring, wellspring; treasure, reserve, savings, nest-egg; stock, stock in trade, merchandise; supply, heap (see ASSEMBLAGE); crop, harvest, vintage; supplies, provisions. See PROPERTY.

2, storage, conservation; storehouse, storeroom, depository; depot, warehouse, cache, repository, magazine, arsenal, armory; buttery, larder, granary; bank, vault, safe-deposit box, treasury; museum, gallery, conservatory; menagerie, zoo; reservoir, tank, cistern, pond, millpond.

3, store, department store, shop, mart, market, emporium, commissary, bazaar, fair.

4, storekeeper, clerk, salesclerk, man behind the counter; MERCHANT, purveyor, supplier, caterer, commissary, peddler, sutler; grocer, druggist, *etc.*; quartermaster, batman, steward, purser, supercargo.

Verbs—store; put by, lay by, lay away, set by; stow away; store, lay, heap, put *or* save up, accumulate, amass, hoard, garner, save; reserve;

keep back, hold back; husband, husband one's resources; salt away; deposit; stow, stack, load; harvest; heap, collect, stock up, lay in store, keep file; lay in, provide; preserve. *Slang*, stash.

Adjectives—stored, in store, in reserve; spare, supernumerary; extra.

Antonyms, see WASTE, POVERTY.

---

storehouse, *n.* warehouse, depository, magazine, elevator, granary, arsenal. See STORE.

storm, *n. & v.* —*n.* hurricane, tempest, tornado; spate, flood; cloudburst, blizzard; outburst, commotion; assault, onslaught, ATTACK. —*v.* assault, assail, ATTACK; rage, rant; bluster; blow violently, pour, rain, snow. See RESENTMENT, WIND, WATER, VIOLENCE.

story, *n.* tale, narrative, yarn; report, account, news article; plot; floor, stage, level. See DESCRIPTION, NEWS, RECEPTACLE.

stout, *adj.* stalwart, robust, brawny; doughty, bold, dauntless, resolute; determined, stubborn; stocky, thickset, portly. See POWER, COURAGE, SIZE.

stove, *n.* oven, range, rangette, cookstove, cooker; heater, furnace; kiln, etna, hot plate, rotisserie. See HEAT.

stow, *v.t.* put away, conceal, stash, STORE; fill, cram, pack. *Slang*, stop, leave off; chuck, can, junk. See LOCATION, CONCEALMENT, END, CONTENTS.

straddle, *v.t.* bestride, bestraddle; equivocate; be neutral, sit on the fence. See MIDDLE.

strafe, *v.* ATTACK, fusillade, pepper, riddle (see SHOOT); castigate, assail, chasten, chastise. See PUNISHMENT.

straggle, *v.* drag, dawdle, bring up the rear, trail, drag one's feet; disperse, meander; wander, rove, stray. See SLOWNESS, DISPERSION, DEVIATION.

STRAIGHTNESS

Nouns—**1,** straightness, directness (see *Adjectives*); rectilinearity, alignment, truing; straight, direct *or* right line, beeline, short cut; inflexibility, stiffness (see HARDNESS); verticality, perpendicularity (see VERTICAL).

2, honesty, fairness, reliability, dependability, PROBITY.

Verbs—be straight; not turn, not bend, *etc.*; go straight, steer for, aim for (see DIRECTION); straighten, rectify, set straight; line, align, true, level; unbend, uncurl, unravel, unfold, unwrap.

Adjectives—**1,** straight, rectilinear, rectilineal; direct, even, RIGHT, true, near, short; linear, in a line, straight as an arrow *or* a die, point-blank; unbent, invariable, inflexible, unbroken; VERTICAL, perpendicular.

2, honest, fair, square, reliable, conscientious, trustworthy, truthful, straightforward, aboveboard, honorable, upright, equitable, just.

Adverbs—straight(way), directly, immediately, forthwith, at once, speedily, suddenly, without delay; continuously, through; correctly, rightly, bluntly, point-blank; upright; honestly, honorably, openly, straightforwardly.

Ant., see CURVATURE.

---

strain, *v.t.* stretch, make taut; strive, exert; sprain; overtax, overstretch; filter, percolate. See EXERTION, CLEARNESS.

strainer, *n.* sieve, sifter, colander, screen, filter, percolator; cheesecloth, tamis, riddle. See PURITY, MEANS.

straitlaced, *adj.* severe, stern, dour, stiff; proper, formal, self-righteous; prim, prudish, fastidious. *Colloq.*, bluenosed. See SEVERITY, PROBITY.

strand, *n.* thread, string, fiber, rope, FILAMENT. See LAND.

stranded, *adj.* aground, stuck, left high and dry, grounded; embarrassed, penniless. See STABILITY, DIFFICULTY.

strange, *adj.* unusual, odd, unfamiliar; queer, fantastic; alien, foreign,

EXTRANEOUS, outlandish, exotic; eccentric, mysterious. See UNCON-
FORMITY.

strangle, *v.t.* choke, garrotte, stifle, suffocate; suppress, repress; squeeze,
constrict. See KILLING, IMPOTENCE.

strap, *n. & v.* —*n.* band, bond, strip, tape, tether; strop, thong, rope;
rein; cinch, girdle. —*v.t.* secure, tether, fasten, tie, SUPPORT, lash;
thrash, flagellate; strop, hone. See FILAMENT, CONNECTION, PUNISH-
MENT.

stratagem, *n.* trick, subterfuge, artifice, ruse, guile, wile. See DECEPTION.

strategy, *n.* generalship, maneuvering, CONDUCT, warcraft, artifice. See
WARFARE.

stray, *v.i.* wander, straggle, roam, rove, ramble; digress; deviate, err.
See DEVIATION, ERROR, TRAVEL.

streak, *n.* band, stripe, smear; vein, LAYER; trait, idiosyncrasy. See IN-
DICATION, COLOR.

stream, *n. & v.* —*n.* RIVER, rivulet; rill; gush; trickle; creek, brook,
runnel, runlet; current, flow, flux, course, flood, tide, race; shower, outpouring, downpouring. —*v.i.* issue; pour out, forth *or* down; flow, run,
rush; shed; blow, extend, run across *or* along; drift, tend; jet, spurt,
gush. See WATER, MOTION, WIND, LIGHT.

streamlined, *adj.* efficient, simplified; smooth, fast, speedy; trim, tapering; up-to-date, modernized. See NEWNESS, SIMPLENESS, VELOCITY.

street, *n.* thoroughfare, avenue, boulevard, alley; roadway. See PASSAGE.

streetcar, *n.* tram(car), tramway, trolley, street railway. See CARRIER,
VEHICLE.

streetwalker, *n.* See PROSTITUTE.

STRENGTH

Nouns—**1,** strength, POWER, ENERGY, VIGOR; might, main [force], physical
or brute force, manpower, horsepower; spring, ELASTICITY, tone,
tonicity, tension; mettle, stamina; brawn, nerve, muscle, muscularity,
sinew, gristle, thews and sinews, pith(iness); physique; HEALTH, virility,
vitality, masculinity, manhood. *Slang,* beef, grit.
2, strong man, tower of strength, powerhouse; athlete, gymnast, acrobat, equilibrist; Atlas, Hercules, Antaeus, Samson, Cyclops, Goliath;
amazon; horse, ox; oak, rock; iron, steel, nails; iron grip, grit, bone,
horn; feats of strength, athletics, athleticism, gymnastics, calisthenics.
3, see COURAGE, RESOLUTION, TENACITY, HARDNESS, STABILITY, SUPPORT.
Verbs—strengthen, SUPPORT, fortify, buttress, bulwark, sustain, inure,
harden, case harden, steel, toughen, indurate, roborate, brace, nerve,
gird, drill, train; set on one's legs, gird up one's loins; recruit, refresh,
freshen; build (up), reinforce, restore; confirm, corroborate, foster,
clinch, fix, establish, justify; invigorate, vitalize, stimulate, enliven,
energize, animate, encourage, lift, reman; enhance, heighten, brighten,
intensify; regain strength, rally, thrive, bloom, prosper, flourish; grow,
wax, INCREASE. *Slang,* give a shot in the arm, pep up.
Adjectives—**1,** strong, powerful; lusty, robust, stout, stalwart, strapping,
hardy, burly, husky, leathery, brawny, thewy, sturdy, sinewy, muscular,
wiry, limber, hale, hearty, healthy, vibrant; athletic, gymnastic, able-
bodied, broad-shouldered, well-built, knot *or* developed, strong as a
lion, horse *or* ox; titanic, gigantic, Herculean; manly, manlike, manful, masculine, male, virile; mettlesome in fine feather *or* fettle.
2, strengthening, refreshing, bracing, tonic, roborant.
3, irresistible, invincible, impregnable, unconquerable, indomitable,
more than a match for; proof, resistant, tight.
4, strong-smelling, pungent, piquant, *etc.* (see ODOR).
5, intense, concentrated, BRILLIANT, bright, vivid, dazzling.
6, alcoholic, spirituous, hard, bodied, heady, proof (see DRUNKEN-
NESS).

Adverbs—by [main] force, by main strength.
Antonym, see IMPOTENCE, WEAKNESS.

strenuous, *adj.* vigorous, energetic, dynamic; arduous, exhausting, straining, laborious. See EXERTION.

stress, *n.* pressure, COMPULSION; emphasis, urgency, IMPORTANCE; accent.

stretch, *v. & n.* —*v.* extend, lengthen, spread, expand, INCREASE; stretch out, sprawl; exaggerate, strain, force. —*n.* EXPANSION, reach, range; LENGTH, field, expanse; ELASTICITY; long run, DISTANCE, homeor backstretch; overstatement, EXAGGERATION. *Slang,* sentence, hitch.

stretcher, *n.* litter, CARRIER; frame, brace. See SUPPORT.

strew, *v.* scatter, disperse, disseminate, scatter; throw to the winds. See DISPERSION.

stricken, *adj.* hurt, ill, disabled; knocked out, afflicted, beset. See PAIN, DISEASE, DETERIORATION.

strict, *adj.* exact, precise; rigid; accurate, meticulous; scrupulous, punctilious; conscientious, nice; stringent, exacting; strait-laced, puritanical. See TRUTH, SEVERITY, PROBITY.

stricture, *n.* censure, criticism, blame, reprehension, RESTRAINT; compression, constriction, CONTRACTION. See DISAPPROBATION, HINDRANCE.

stride, *n. & v.* —*n.* step, pace; (*pl.*) progress, IMPROVEMENT. —*v.* walk, march, step; straddle. See TRAVEL.

stridency, *n.* stridulation; shrillness, harshness; discord, dissonance, LOUDNESS, ROUGHNESS, SHARPNESS; noise, noisiness, raucousness, cacophony; clangor, clamor. See LOUDNESS, SOUND. *Ant.,* see LOWNESS, SILENCE.

strife, *n.* CONTENTION, emulation, rivalry; altercation; dissension, discord, dispute, quarrel; war, WARFARE; struggle, conflict.

strike, *v.* hit, smite, beat, thump; give, deliver, deal; affect, TOUCH, impress, occur to; blast; lower, take down; collide, bump; conclude, agree upon; attack, smite; hit, collide; walk out, quit, rebel. See IMPULSE, OPPOSITION, EXCITEMENT.

string, *n.* twine, thread, cord; catgut; series, row, line, chain; set, stud; stringed instrument. See FILAMENT, CONTINUITY, MUSICAL INSTRUMENT.

stringent, *adj.* severe, stern (see STRICT).

strip, *v. & n.* —*v.* divest, denude, decorticate, peel, pull off; dismantle; plunder, fleece; dispossess, deprive; disrobe, undress; cut in strips. *Slang,* skin. See STEALING, DIVESTMENT. —*n.* hue, stripe, bend, fillet, shred; lath, ribbon. See LENGTH, FILAMENT. *Slang,* comic strip.

stripe, *n.* line, band, streak, belt; CLASS, ilk. *Slang,* hash mark.

stripling, *n.* lad, boy, teenager, YOUTH. *Colloq.,* shaver, kid, nipper.

strive, *v.i.* endeavor, strain, ESSAY; struggle, contend; quarrel. See CONTENTION. *Ant.,* see INACTIVITY.

stroke, *n.* blow, impact; beat, throb, pulsation; bolt, blast; seizure, apoplexy, shock, feat, exploit, coup; mark, flourish. See IMPULSE, DISEASE, ACTION.

stroll, *n.* ramble, saunter, promenade, walk. *Colloq.,* constitutional. See TRAVEL.

strong, *adj.* See STRENGTH.

stronghold, *n.* REFUGE; fort, fortress, citadel; blockhouse; fastness, bulwark. See DEFENSE.

structure, *n.* building, edifice, construction, fabrication; framework, makeup, ARRANGEMENT, composition, anatomy, constitution. See FORM.

struggle, *v. & n.* —*v.i.* strive, strain, endeavor, contend, labor; flounder, writhe, squirm; fight, battle. —*n.* endeavor, effort, CONTENTION, ESSAY; fight, conflict, WARFARE. See EXERTION.

strut, *v.* swagger; stalk, peacock. See VANITY, OSTENTATION.

stub, *n. & v.* —*n.* stump, END, stubble; receipt, RECORD; butt. —*v.t.* bump, bunk, hit, strike. See IMPULSE.

stubble, *n.* stumps, stalks, stubs, remnants; beard, bristles. See ROUGH-NESS.

stubborn, *adj.* perverse, obstinate; dogged, persistent; intractable, un-yielding. See RESOLUTION, OBSTINACY. *Ant.,* see ASSENT.

stuck-up, *adj., colloq.,* vain, conceited, aloof, snooty. See VANITY, SUPERIORITY.

stud, *n. & v.* —*n.* boss, knop, projection, jewel; timber, SUPPORT; studhorse, breeder. —*v.t.* bestud, ornament, bejewel, spangle; dot, scatter. See ORNAMENT, CONVEXITY, DISPERSION.

student, *n.* learner; pupil; apprentice; schoolboy, schoolgirl; scholar, schoolman, pedant. See SCHOOL.

studio, *n.* atelier, salon, WORKSHOP; study; station.

studious, *adj.* scholarly, thoughtful, speculative, contemplative, bookish. See KNOWLEDGE, THOUGHT. *Ant.,* see IGNORANCE.

study, *n. & v.* —*n.* meditation, research, examination, investigation; library, atelier, den; sketch, cartoon; étude. —*v.* investigate, weigh, consider, examine; scrutinize; con; memorize; ponder. *Colloq.,* grind. See THOUGHT, INQUIRY.

stuff, *v. & n.* —*v.* cram, pack, jam, fill; pad, wad; plug, block; cast illegal votes; gormandize, gorge, overeat. See COMPLETION, GLUTTONY. —*n.* fabric, cloth, material; nonsense; substance. *Slang,* the goods, the ability.

stuffing, *n.* dressing, filling, forcemeat, farce; CONTENTS. See SOFT-NESS.

stuffy, *adj.* ill-ventilated, close, stifling, airless; sultry, oppressive, musty. *Colloq.,* dull, stiff, stodgy. See DENSITY, HEAT, DULLNESS.

stumble, *v.i.* trip, stub one's toe; hobble, stagger, lumber; blunder, flounder, stammer; err, slip, backslide. See DESCENT, AGITATION, ERROR.

stump, *n. & v.* —*n.* stub, butt, snag, remnant, fag end; rostrum, pulpit; hobble, heavy tread. See REMAINDER, SUPPORT. —*v.t., colloq.,* con-found, puzzle.

stun, *v.t.* benumb, deaden, daze, stupefy; dizzy; dum(b)found, astound, astonish, bewilder. See INSENSIBILITY, SURPRISE.

stunning, *adj., colloq.,* striking, lovely. *Slang,* knockout. See BEAUTY.

stunt, *v. & n.* —*v.* dwarf; cramp, retard, check; perform feats, do tricks, grandstand. See SHORTNESS, CONTRACTION, SKILLFULNESS. —*n.* trick, feat, daredevil(t)ry, tour de force.

stupefy, *v.t.* deaden, dull, numb, narcotize; stun, astound, daze, dum(b)-found. See INSENSIBILITY, SURPRISE.

stupendous, *adj.* prodigious, enormous, astounding, amazing, wonderful, immense, vast, colossal, overwhelming. See GREATNESS, WONDER.

stupid, *adj.* slow-witted, dull, obtuse; benumbed, bemused; absurd, inane; banal, tiresome, tedious, DULL. See IGNORANCE, DESTINY. *Ant.,* see IN-TELLIGENCE, WIT, KNOWLEDGE.

stupor, *n.* lethargy, torpor, apathy, coma, daze. See INSENSIBILITY.

sturdy, *adj.* stalwart, hardy, husky, robust; durable, long-wearing; firm, stubborn, unyielding. See POWER. *Ant.,* WEAK.

stutter, *v.i.* See STAMMERING.

sty, *n.* pigpen, pigsty; pen; hovel, shed; stable. See INCLOSURE, UN-CLEANNESS.

style, *n.* FORM, manner, method, way; FASHION; smartness, vogue, mode, chic; craze, fad, rage, last word; practice, habit, (characteristic) be-havior, air; diction, phraseology, wording, rhetoric; distinction, elegance. See SPEECH.

stymie, *v.* hinder, obstruct, impede; thwart, frustrate, puzzle, perplex, put at a loss, baffle. *Colloq.,* throw, floor. See DIFFICULTY, HINDRANCE.

suave, *n.* urbane, bland, courteous, gracious; oily, smooth, ingratiating. See COURTESY, SMOOTHNESS. *Ant.,* see ROUGHNESS, DISCOURTESY.

subconscious, *adj. & n.* —*adj.* subliminal, nonconscious, unconscious, automatic. See INTELLECT. —*n.* subliminal self, id, unconscious [men-tal life *or* functioning].

subdue, *v.t.* tame, overcome, master; vanquish, conquer; repress, restrain; soften, tone down. See SUBJECTION, MODERATION.

subject, *n. & v.* —*n.* topic, theme; matter; liege, vassal; citizen. See SERVANT, INHABITANT. *Ant.,* see AUTHORITY. —*v.t.* reduce, control, restrain, tame. See SUBJECTION, RESTRAINT.

SUBJECTION

Nouns—subjection; dependence, dependency; subordination; thrall, thraldom, enthralment, subjugation, oppression, bondage, serfdom; feudalism, vassalage, villenage; slavery, enslavement, servitude; constraint, yoke, RESTRAINT; OBEDIENCE.

Verbs—1, be subject, be at the mercy of; depend, lean *or* hang upon; fall a prey to, fall under, not dare to call one's soul one's own; drag a chain; serve (see SERVANT); obey, comply, submit.

2, subject, subjugate, break in, tame; master; tread down, tread under foot; enthrall, enslave, take captive; take into custody; rule (see AUTHORITY); drive into a corner, hold at sword's point; keep under; hold in bondage; tie to one's apron strings.

Adjectives—subject, dependent, subordinate; feudal, feudatory, in harness; subjected, enslaved, constrained, downtrodden, under the lash, led by the nose; henpecked; the puppet or plaything of; under orders *or* command; under one's thumb; a slave to; in the toils; at the mercy of, in the power, hands *or* clutches of; at the feet of; at one's beck and call (see OBEDIENCE).

Antonym, see FREEDOM.

subjective, *adj.* nonobjective; personal, individual, selfish; introspective, introverted. See THOUGHT.

subjugate, *v.t.* conquer, vanquish, master, subdue; overthrow; enslave. See SUBJECTION.

sublime, *adj.* inspiring, impressive; noble, lofty, exalted, elevated; superb, magnificent, glorious. See HEIGHT, REPUTE, BEAUTY.

submarine, *adj. & n.* —*adj.* suboceanic, undersea *or* -water. See WATER. —*n.* torpedo boat; U-boat, submersible. *Colloq.,* sub. *Slang,* pigboat. See SHIP.

submerge, *v.* drown, sink, plunge, dive, submerge, immerse, engulf, inundate; be overshadowed, subordinate to, play second fiddle to. See NAVIGATION, UNIMPORTANCE, WATER.

SUBMISSION

Nouns—1, submission, submissiveness, OBEDIENCE, resignation, patience, HUMILITY, self-abasement, compliance, pliancy, docility, passivity, WEAKNESS, acquiescence, sufferance, CONFORMITY, SUBJECTION; capitulation, surrender, cession, yielding, RELINQUISHMENT.

2, obeisance, homage, kneeling, curtsy, kowtow, salaam; white flag.

Verbs—1, submit, succumb, yield, comply, acquiesce, accede, resign, bend, stoop, obey, defer to, be subject, be submissive.

2, capitulate, surrender, cede, come to terms, retreat, lay down *or* deliver up one's arms, lower, haul down *or* strike one's flag *or* colors; show the white flag; give up *or* in, give way, give ground, cave in, bend before the storm; knuckle down *or* under. *Slang,* throw in the towel *or* sponge, say uncle.

3, be submissive, eat dirt, humble pie or crow; bite *or* lick the dust; throw oneself at the feet of, be *or* fall at one's feet, swallow the pill, kiss the rod, turn the other cheek; crouch before, kneel to, bow to, pay homage to, cringe to; truckle to, bend the neck *or* knee; kneel, fall on one's knees, curtsy, kowtow, salaam, make an obeisance, bow submission.

4, endure, tolerate, put up with, bear with, be reconciled to, swallow the insult, pocket the affront, grin and bear it, submit with a good grace.

5, offer, proffer, advance, propose, present, suggest, affirm, propound, send in (manuscripts, *etc.*).

Adjectives—submissive, subdued, yielding, unresisting, tractable, compliant, dutiful, long-suffering, patient, passive, acquiescent, unassertive, manageable, governable, docile, agreeable; obsequious, slavish, servile, fawning, deferential, defeatist, self-abasing, lowly; prostrate, crouching, downtrodden, on bended knee, down on one's knees.

Antonym, see DEFIANCE, RESISTANCE.

---

subordinate, *adj.* lower, inferior, secondary; dependent, subservient. See INFERIORITY, UNIMPORTANCE, SUBJECTION. *Ant.*, see SUPERIORITY, IMPORTANCE.

subpoena, *n.* summons, writ, order, monition, citation. See COMMAND.

subscribe, *v.* sign, endorse, contribute; ASSENT, AID, abet, back, patronize; undertake, contract. *Ant.*, see DISAPPROBATION, REFUSAL.

subsequent, *adj.* succeeding, following, sequent, later, ensuing, consequent. See SEQUENCE.

subservient, *adj.* servile, submissive, obsequious, cringing, abject; subordinate, contributory, instrumental, subsidiary. See AID, SERVILITY. *Ant.*, see AUTHORITY, SUPERIORITY, IMPORTANCE.

subside, *v.i.* sink, fall, ebb, lower; abate, lessen; settle, precipitate. See DESCENT, DECREASE, GRAVITY. *Ant.*, see ASCENT, INCREASE.

subsidiary, *adj.* branch, incidental; helpful; supplementary. See PART, AID.

subsidize, *v.t.* AID, SUPPORT, promote; patronize, finance, underwrite, back, pay for, subscribe to; endow, invest in; encourage. See PAYMENT.

subsist, *v.i.* exist, live, be, continue, survive, abide; eke out a living. See EXISTENCE.

subsistence, *n.* EXISTENCE, being, continuance; maintenance, livelihood, sustenance. See AID.

SUBSTANCE

Nouns—**1,** substance, matter; *corpus*, frame, protoplasm, principle; person, thing, object, article; something, a being, an existence; creature, body, stuff.

2, substantiality, materiality, materialness, reality, corporeality; tangibility; flesh and blood.

3, physics, physical science; somatology, somatics; materialism; materialist, physicist.

Verbs—embody, incorporate, incarnate, actualize, materialize, subsist, be.

Adjectives—substantive, substantial; sound, solid, personal; bodily, tangible, corporeal, real, MATERIAL.

Adverbs—substantially, bodily, essentially, *etc.*. on solid ground; in the flesh.

Antonym, see INSUBSTANTIALITY.

---

substantiate, *v.t.* embody (see SUBSTANCE); EVIDENCE, corroborate, verify, bear out, demonstrate, confirm, SUPPORT. See DEMONSTRATION, TRUTH, VINDICATION.

substitute, *n., v. & adj.* —*n.* understudy, replacement, delegate, deputy, agent, factor; scapegoat, whipping boy; proxy; lieutenant, henchman; supplanter; representative; alternate; vicar; stopgap, expedient; SUBSTITUTION; shift, makeshift, apology for. *Colloq.*, sub, stand-in, dummy, ringer, pinchhitter. —*v.* replace, replace with *or* for; exchange, INTERCHANGE; understudy; depute, delegate, act for, play for; supersede; shift, exchange, supplant, alternate, take the place of. *Colloq.*, palm off, ring in, stand in (for), pinch hit (for), go to bat for, take the rap (for). —*adj.* artificial, ersatz; makeshift; imitation, counterfeit, pseudo, tentative, replacing, impermanent; resembling. *Colloq.*, near.

SUBSTITUTION

Nouns—1, substitution, commutation; supplanting, supersession, replacement; metonymy (see FIGURATIVE); INTERCHANGE; TRANSFER.

2, SUBSTITUTE, proxy, makeshift, shift, *pis aller*, stopgap, jury-mast, *locum tenens*; dummy, scapegoat; double; changeling; *quid pro quo*, alternative; representative, surrogate, alternate, DEPUTY; viceroy, vicegerent, viceregent; palimpsest; PRICE, purchase money, consideration, equivalent. *Colloq.*, stand-in, pinch-hitter, ghostwriter. *Slang*, ringer, fall guy, goat, patsy.

Verbs—1, substitute, put in the place of, change for; deputize, accredit, appoint; make way for, give place to.

2, substitute *or* be deputy for; represent; stand for, appear *or* answer for; fill, step into *or* stand in the shoes of; take the place of, supplant, supersede, replace, cut out; rob Peter to pay Paul. *Slang*, cover up for; be the goat; ghostwrite.

Adjectives—substitutive, substituted, vicarious, temporary, deputy, acting; vice, viceregal.

Adverbs—instead; in the place of, on behalf of, in lieu of, in the stead of; *faute de mieux*, by proxy; for want of something better.

Antonym, see IDENTITY.

---

subterfuge, *n.* ruse, shift, pretext, artifice, device, stratagem, CUNNING.

subterranean, *adj.* underground; infernal, Stygian, nether. See DEPTH, HELL.

subtle, *adj.* sly, artful, crafty, wily, CUNNING; discerning, acute, penetrating; elusive, unobvious, abstruse, delicate; dainty, fragile, rarefied, ethereal, unsubstantial. See INTELLIGENCE, NARROWNESS.

subtract, *v.* deduct, take away; remove, reduce, detract. See DEDUCTION.

suburban, *adj.* out-of-town, rural, nearby, provincial. See LOCATION, DULLNESS.

suburbs, *n.* outskirts, environs, purlieus. See NEARNESS.

subversion, *n.* overthrow, defeat, disruption, DISORDER, mutiny, rebellion, REVOLUTION; disloyalty, treason; sedition, sabotage, DECEPTION.

subvert, *v.i.* overthrow, overturn, upset; ruin, fell, raze. See DESTRUCTION, DEPRESSION.

subway, *n.* underground, subrailway, *Métropolitain*; underpass. *Colloq.*, tube, *Métro.* See VEHICLE, PASSAGE.

succeed, *v.* follow, come after; displace, supplant; thrive (see SUCCESS). See SEQUENCE.

SUCCESS

Nouns—1, success, successfulness; speed; advance; progress; good fortune, luck, run of luck; PROSPERITY; proficiency (see SKILL); profit, ACQUISITION; accomplishment (see COMPLETION).

2, great success, hit, stroke; (lucky) strike; master stroke; *coup de maître*; checkmate; half the battle, prize; trump card. *Colloq.*, smash, smash hit; sleeper; dark horse.

3, victory, triumph, advantage; upper hand, whip hand; ascendance, ascendancy, advantage, SUPERIORITY; mastery (see AUTHORITY); expugnation, conquest, subjugation, SUBJECTION.

4, winner, conqueror, victor; master of the situation, king of the mountain.

Verbs—1, succeed; be successful, gain one's end *or* ends; crown with success; gain, carry *or* win a point; manage to, contrive to; accomplish, effect (see COMPLETION); do *or* work wonders; score a success. *Colloq.*, pan out.

2, speed, make progress, advance; win, make *or* find one's way; prosper (see PROSPERITY); make profit (see ACQUISITION); reap the fruits *or* benefit of; reap *or* gather the harvest; make one's fortune, turn to good account. *Colloq.*, do a land-office business. *Slang*, sell like hotcakes; wow them, knock them dead.

3, win, prevail, triumph, be triumphant; gain *or* obtain a victory *or* advantage; master; get *or* have the best *or* better of; get *or* have the upper hand, ascendancy *or* whip hand; distance, surpass (see SUPERIORITY); come off well, come off with flying colors; make short work of; take *or* carry by storm; win one's spurs; win the battle; win the day, carry the day, win *or* gain the prize *or* palm; have the best of it, have it all one's own way, call the turn, set the pace, have the world at one's feet; carry all before one, remain in possession of the field. *Slang*, win in a walk; romp home; score standing up.

4, defeat, conquer, vanquish, discomfit; overcome, overthrow, overpower, overmaster, overmatch, overset, override, overreach; outwit, outdo, outflank, outmaneuver, outgeneral, outvote; take the wind out of one's sails; beat, beat hollow; rout, lick, drub, floor, best, worst; put down, put to flight, put to rout.

5, surmount *or* overcome a difficulty *or* obstacle; make headway against; stem the torrent, tide *or* current; weather the storm; turn a corner, keep one's head above water, tide over.

6, silence, quell, checkmate, upset, confound, nonplus, stalemate, trump; baffle (see HINDRANCE); circumvent, elude; trip up, drive into a corner, drive to the wall; run hard, put one's nose out of joint.

7, settle, do for; break the back of; capsize, sink, shipwreck, drown, swamp; subdue, subjugate, subject; victimize, roll in the dust, trample under foot.

8, answer, answer the purpose; avail, take effect, do, turn out well, work well, take, tell, bear fruit; hit the mark, hit the nail on the head; turn up trumps, make a hit; find one's account in.

Adjectives—succeeding, successful, fortunate; prosperous (see PROSPERITY); triumphant; flushed *or* crowned with success; victorious; set up, in the ascendant; unbeaten; felicitous, effective.

Adverbs—successfully, with flying colors, in triumph, swimmingly.

Antonym, see FAILURE.

---

succession, *n.* series; SEQUENCE, progression; heirship, inheritance, heritage, primogeniture, reversion; lineage, family. See DESCENT.

succinct, *adj.* terse, concise, crisp, laconic, meaty, pithy, sententious. See CONTRACTION, SHORTNESS. *Ant.*, see LOQUACITY.

succor, *v.t.* help, AID, assist, serve, comfort.

succulent, *adj.* juicy, succulous, fleshy, tender; savory, tasty, toothsome; wet, watery, moist; interesting, spicy, piquant. See TASTE, MOISTURE.

succumb, *v.* give in, yield, submit, surrender, ASSENT; die, expire, give up the ghost. See WEAKNESS, SUBMISSION, FAILURE, DEATH.

such, *adj. & adv.* —*adj.* like, suchlike, similar, of the same kind; such and such, aforementioned; such a, some, one who. —*adv., colloq.*, so, thus, that; very; such as, like, resembling. See INDICATION, SIMILARITY.

suck, *v.* draw, extract, absorb, pull in, sponge up; pump; nurse, suckle; drain, leech, bleed, extort; suck in, seduce, lure. See EXTRACTION, FOOD.

sucker, *n., colloq.*, lollipop, all-day sucker, sourball. *Slang*, dupe, gull, pushover, [easy] mark, soft touch. See CREDULITY, SWEETNESS.

suckle, *v.* give suck, nurse, nurture; wet-nurse, breast-feed. See FOOD.

suction, *n.* inhalation, EXTRACTION; absorption, siphonage, capillarity.

sudden, *adj.* abrupt, unexpected; hasty, quick, unpremeditated; instantaneous; precipitate; hot-tempered, rash. See SURPRISE, INSTANTANEITY.

suds, *n.* lather, foam, bubbles, froth, spume. See CLOUDINESS.

sue, *v.* prosecute, bring suit, petition; beg, solicit, REQUEST; court, woo. See LAWSUIT, ENDEARMENT.

suffer, *v.* —*v.t.* endure, encounter, undergo, experience, sustain; allow, permit, tolerate. See FEELING, PERMISSION. —*v.i.* endure pain, be troubled, ache; ail, be ill. See PAIN, DISEASE. *Ant.*, see PLEASURE, HEALTH.

SUFFICIENCY

Nouns—**1,** sufficiency, adequacy, enough, satisfaction, competence; MEDIOCRITY; fill, fullness, completeness; plenitude, plenty; abundance, copiousness; amplitude, profusion, prodigality; full measure; luxuriance, affluence, WEALTH; fat of the land; cornucopia, horn of plenty; mine (see STORE); outpouring; flood. *Colloq.*, lots. *Slang*, scads, oodles, rafts, loads.

2, satiety, satiation, saturation, repletion, glut, excess, surfeit, superfluity; too much of a good thing, a drug on the market. See REPETITION.

Verbs—be sufficient, suffice, do, just do, satisfy, pass muster; sate, be satiated, have enough, eat, drink *or* have one's fill; roll in, swim in; wallow in; abound, exuberate, teem, flow, stream, rain, shower down; pour, pour in; swarm, bristle with, replenish.

Adjectives—**1,** sufficient, enough, adequate, up to the mark, commensurate, competent, satisfactory, valid, tangible; measured, moderate, temperate, full, COMPLETE; ample; plenty, plentiful, plenteous; copious, abundant, abounding, replete, enough and to spare, flush; chock-full, well-stocked, well-provided; liberal; unstinted, unstinting, stintless; without stint; unsparing, unmeasured, lavish, wholesale; rich; luxuriant; affluent, WEALTHY; big with, pregnant; unexhausted, unwasted; exhaustless, inexhaustible.

2, satiated, sated, gorged; blasé, jaded; sick (of), fed up.

Adverbs—sufficiently, amply, full, in abundance, in full measure; to one's heart's content; *ad libitum*, without stint.

Antonym, see INSUFFICIENCY.

suffix, *n.* affix, addition, ending. See ADDITION.

suffocate, *v.* smother, stifle, asphyxiate; choke; extinguish; strangle. See KILLING.

suffrage, *n.* franchise, right to vote; vote, ballot. See CHOICE.

suffuse, *v.* spread (out), overspread, pervade; permeate, imbue; wash, dye, tinge. See DIFFUSION, COLOR.

sugar, *n.* sweetening, sucrose, lactose, glucose, dextrose, maltose, fructose, *etc.* See SWEETNESS.

suggest, *v.t.* intimate, hint, insinuate; propose, submit; imply, connote; recommend, advise, advocate. See INFORMATION, MEANING, ADVICE.

suggestive, *adj.* indicative, expressive; thought-provoking, stimulating; remindful, mnemonic; risqué, indecent. See MEANING, SUPPOSITION, MEMORY.

suicide, *n.* self-destruction, self-ruin; *felo-de-se,* hara-kiri. See KILLING.

suit, *n. & v.* —*n.* petition, appeal, prayer; courtship, wooing; suite, retinue, train; outfit, set, group, SEQUENCE; LAWSUIT, action, litigation. See REQUEST, ENDEARMENT, ACCOMPANIMENT. —*v.t.* satisfy, please; become, befit; fit, adapt. See AGREEMENT, BEAUTY.

suitable, *adj.* fitting, appropriate, proper, convenient, apropos, becoming, fit, fitted, compatible. See AGREEMENT. *Ant.*, see UNCOMFORMITY, DISAGREEMENT.

suitcase, *n.* bag, valise, grip; (*pl.*) luggage, baggage. See CARRIER, RECEPTACLE.

suite, *n.* company, train, retinue, following, escort; set, series, group; apartment. See ACCOMPANIMENT, CONTINUITY, RECEPTACLE, MUSIC.

suitor, *n.* lover, wooer. *Colloq.*, beau, swain, admirer, boy friend. See LOVE, ENDEARMENT.

sulk, *v.i.* be sullen, pout, mope; grumble, gripe, grouch. See IRASCIBILITY. *Ant.*, see CHEERFULNESS.

sullen, *adj.* sulky; ill-tempered, ill-humored; out of sorts, temper *or* humor; crusty, crabbed; sour, surly, discourteous; moody; spleenish,

splenetic; resentful; cross, cross-grained; perverse, wayward, froward; dogged, stubborn; grumpy, glum, grim, morose; scowling, glowering, growling; peevish, irascible. See IRASCIBILITY, DISCOURTESY. *Ant.*, see CHEERFULNESS, COURTESY.

sully, *v.* soil, stain, tarnish, smear; defile, dishonor, blemish, stigmatize. See UNCLEANNESS, DISREPUTE.

sultry, *adj.* hot, oppressive, sweltering, humid, muggy, stifling, close; voluptuous, sensual, sexy. See HEAT.

sum, *n.* QUANTITY, amount; total, aggregate, sum total; substance, gist; problem; summary. See WHOLE, MONEY. *Ant.*, part; see DISJUNCTION.

summary, *n. & adj.* —*n.* compendium, abridgment, abstract, brief, epitome, résumé, digest. —*adj.* prompt, expeditious, speedy, fast, immediate; brief, concise, compact, condensed. See EARLINESS, CONTRACTION. *Ant.*, see WHOLE.

summer, *n.* summertime, summertide; high point, zenith, acme, *etc.* See TIME.

summit, *n.* top, vertex, apex, zenith, pinnacle, acme, peak, culmination; meridian; utmost height; *ne plus ultra*; maximum; climax; culminating, high, crowning *or* turning point; tiptop; crown, point, crest, cap; extremity; mountain top; housetop, rooftop. See HEIGHT. *Ant.*, see LOWNESS, BASE.

summon, *v.t.* call, send for; cite, arraign, subp(o)ena; convoke; rouse, invoke, evoke. See COMMAND, LAWSUIT.

sumptuous, *adj.* lavish, luxurious, splendid, imposing, costly. See OSTENTATION. *Ant.*, see SIMPLENESS, POVERTY.

sun, *n.* daystar, Sol; sunshine, sunlight; prosperity, happiness; star. See UNIVERSE.

Sunday, *n.* day of rest, Lord's Day, holy day, sabbath; day off, holiday.

sunder, *v.t.* break, separate, sever, dissever, divide. See DISJUNCTION.

sundial, *n.* sun-clock, solarium, dial; gnomon, style. See TIME, MEASUREMENT.

sundry, *adj.* various, divers; several, numerous. See MULTITUDE.

sunny, *adj.* warm, bright, sunshiny; cheerful, cheery, blithe; prosperous, palmy, halcyon. See HEAT, CHEERFULNESS, PROSPERITY.

sunrise, *n.* dawn, prime, daybreak, dayspring, aurora, cockcrow, sunup. See MORNING, TIME.

sunset, *n.* twilight, sundown, dusk, nightfall, curfew, eventide. See EVENING, TIME.

sunstroke, *n.* insolation, heatstroke; siriasis, heliosis. See DISEASE.

superb, *adj.* magnificent, impressive, stately; admirable, excellent; costly, rich, gorgeous, sumptuous. See GOODNESS, BEAUTY.

supercilious, *adj.* disdainful, contemptuous, scornful; arrogant, cavalier. See INSOLENCE.

superficial, *adj.* SHALLOW, cursory, dilettante, slight, slender, trivial, inane; surface, skin-deep. See UNIMPORTANCE. *Ant.*, see DEPTH, GRAVITY.

superfluous, *adj.* unnecessary, needless; excessive, overmuch. See REPETITION.

superhuman, *adj.* sublime, divine; Olympian, Jovian; herculean, preterhuman, phenomenal, extraordinary. See STRENGTH, WONDER.

superimpose, *v.* superpose, stratify, overlay, cover. See COVERING, ADDITION.

superintend, *v.t.* oversee, direct, control; boss. See DIRECTION, AUTHORITY.

SUPERIORITY

Nouns—**1,** superiority; greatness, excellence (see GOODNESS); majority, plurality; advantage; preponderance, preponderation; vantage point *or* ground, prevalence, partiality; lead, gain; NOBILITY.

2, supremacy, primacy, preëminence, precedence; victory, triumph;

championship; maximum; climax; culmination, SUMMIT, transcendence, transcendency, prepotence, *ne plus ultra*; lion's share, excess, surplus; PERFECTION, sovereignty (see AUTHORITY).

Verbs—be superior, exceed, excel, transcend; outdo, outbalance, outweigh, outrival; pass, surpass, get ahead of; overtop, override, overpass, overbalance, overweigh, overmatch; top, cap, beat, cut out; beat hollow; outstrip, eclipse, throw into the shade, put one's nose out of joint; have the upper hand, have the whip hand, have the advantage; turn the scale, play first fiddle (see IMPORTANCE); preponderate, predominate, prevail; precede, take precedence, come first; come to a head, culminate; beat all others, bear the palm, break the record; become larger, INCREASE, expand. *Colloq.*, run circles around, get the drop on, have it all over (someone).

Adjectives—superior, greater, major, higher; exceeding; great, distinguished, ultra; vaulting; more than a match for; supreme, greatest, utmost, paramount, preëminent, foremost, crowning; first-rate, important, excellent, unrivaled, peerless, matchless; champion, second to none, nonpareil; unparalleled, unequaled, unapproached, unsurpassed; superlative, inimitable, incomparable, sovereign, without parallel, *ne plus ultra*; beyond compare, beyond comparison; culminating, topmost; transcendent, transcendental; increased, enlarged. *Slang*, tops.

Adverbs—beyond, more, over; over the mark, above the mark; above par, at the top of the scale, at its height; eminently, preëminently, surpassing, prominently, superlatively, supremely, above all, *par excellence*, principally, especially, particularly, peculiarly, even, yea, still more.

Antonym, see INFERIORITY.

---

superlative, *adj.* See SUPERIORITY.

supernatural, *adj.* miraculous, preternatural; abnormal, unearthly, superhuman, occult. See UNCONFORMITY, PREDICTION.

supernumerary, *n.* bit, subordinate, walk-on, bit player, stand-in, extra. *Colloq.*, super. See DRAMA, UNIMPORTANCE.

supersede, *v.t.* replace, displace, supplant, succeed. See SUBSTITUTION.

superstition, *n.* irrationality, CREDULITY; FEAR, phobia; paganism, witchcraft, animism; old wives' tale, fairy tale, folklore. See BELIEF, SORCERY.

supervision, *n.* oversight, surveillance, superintendence. See DIRECTION.

supine, *adj.* recumbent, reclining, prostrate; apathetic, sluggish, torpid; indifferent, passive. See DIRECTION, INACTIVITY, INSENSIBILITY. *Ant.*, prone, erect.

supper, *n.* meal, repast, refection; banquet, feast, entertainment. See FOOD.

supplant, *v.* supersede, succeed, replace (see SUBSTITUTION, DISPLACEMENT).

supple, *adj.* limber, lithe, pliant, flexible; yielding, compliant, adaptable; fawning, servile. See SOFTNESS. *Ant.*, see HARDNESS.

supplement, *n.* adjunct, ADDITION, addendum, appendix, complement, conclusion. See COMPLETION.

supplicate, *v.t.* entreat, petition, pray, beg, beseech. See REQUEST.

supply, *v.t.* PROVIDE, furnish, give, afford, present, contribute, substitute.

SUPPORT

Nouns—**1,** support, maintenance, upkeep, sustenance.

2, ground, foundation, groundwork, substratum, BASE, basis; *terra firma*; purchase, grip, footing, hold, foothold, toehold, handhold; landing, landing stage, landing place; stage, platform; block; rest, resting place; basement, supporter, AID, prop, stand; anvil, bearing; fulcrum, rowlock, oarlock; stay, shore, skid, rib, lap; bar, rod, boom, sprit, outrigger.

3, staff, stick, crutch, alpenstock, baton, walking stick.

4, post, pillar, shaft, column, pilaster, atlas, atlantes (*pl.*), caryatid;

pediment, pedicle; pedestal; plinth, shank, leg; buttress, jamb, mullion, abutment; baluster, banister, stanchion; balustrade, railing.

5, frame, framework; scaffold, skeleton, beam, rafter, girder, lintel, joist, travis, trave, cornerstone, summer, transom; rung, round, step, sill, tholepin.

6, backbone; keystone; axle, axletree; axis; arch, mainstay.

7, board, ledge, shelf, hob, bracket, trevet, trivet, arbor, rack; mantel, mantelpiece, mantelshelf; slab, console; counter, dresser; flange, corbel; table, trestle; shoulder; perch; stand, sawhorse, horse; easel, desk.

8, seat, throne, dais; divan; chair, bench, form, stool, sofa, settee, stall, armchair, easy chair, rocking chair, Morris chair; love seat, couch, *fauteuil*, ottoman, settle, bench; saddle; pillion; saddle; pommel.

9, bed, berth, bunk, pallet, tester, crib, cot, hammock, shakedown, cradle, litter, stretcher, bedstead; bedding, mattress, paillasse, box spring, spring, pillow, bolster; mat, rug, carpet, linoleum, cushion, four-poster, truckle bed; chair bed, sofa bed, convertible.

10, footstool, hassock; tabo(u)ret; tripod.

11, Atlas, Persides, Hercules.

Verbs—**1,** be supported; lie, sit, recline, lean, loll, rest, stand, step, repose, about, bear *or* be based on; have at one's back; bestride, straddle, bestraddle.

2, support, bear, carry, hold, sustain, shoulder; hold, back, bolster, shore up; uphold; bear; shore up, prop; underpin; bandage, tape, brace.

3, give *or* support foundations; found, base, ground, imbed, embed.

4, maintain, keep on foot; AID.

Adjectives—supporting, supported, braced, propped, bolstered; founded, based, basic, grounded, built on; fundamental, bottom, undermost.

Adverbs—astride, astraddle.

Antonym, see PENDENCY.

SUPPOSITION

Nouns—supposition, assumption, postulation, condition, presupposition, hypothesis, postulate, theory, data; proposition, position; thesis, theorem; proposal; conceit; conjecture; guess, guesswork; rough guess, shot; surmise, suspicion, inkling, suggestion, association of ideas, hint; presumption (see BELIEF); divination, speculation. *Colloq.,* hunch.

Verbs—**1,** suppose, conjecture, surmise, suspect, guess, divine; theorize; presume, presuppose; assume, fancy, take it; give a guess, speculate, believe, dare say, take it into one's head, take for granted.

2, put forth; propound, propose; start, put *or* give a case, move, make a motion; hazard a suggestion *or* conjecture; put forward a suggestion; submit; allude to, suggest, hint, put it into one's head.

Adjectives—supposing, supposed, given, postulatory; assumed, suppositive, supposititious; gratuitous, speculative, conjectural, hypothetical, theoretical, supposable, presumptive, putative, academic; suggestive, allusive.

Adverbs—supposedly, theoretically, seemingly, if, if so be; on the supposition of, in case of, in the event of; quasi, as if, provided; perhaps; for all one knows; for the sake of argument.

Antonym, see KNOWLEDGE.

---

suppress, *v.t.* put down, quell, subdue; repress, restrain; conceal; quash; withhold; abolish, ban; stanch, check. See RESTRAINT, CONCEALMENT. *Ant.,* see FREEDOM.

suppurate, *v.* run, fester, putrefy, rankle; pustulate, ulcerate. See DISEASE.

supremacy, *n.* mastery, SUPERIORITY, ascendancy, domination, AUTHORITY.

supreme, *adj.* highest, utmost, paramount, prime, chief, dominant. See SUPERIORITY.

sure, *adj.* certain, positive; dependable, trustworthy; safe, secure; confident, convinced; unfailing, infallible. See CERTAINTY, SAFETY, PROBITY. *Ant.,* see DOUBT, DANGER.

surf, *n.* sea, waves, breakers, rollers, whitecaps, white horses, billows, surge, spume, sea-foam, froth, spindrift, spray. See WATER.

surface, *n.* outside, EXTERIOR, superficies; outward aspect. *Ant.,* see INTERIOR.

surfeit, *n.* excess, glut, superfluity, superabundance, plethora; SATIETY, repletion, engorgement. See SUFFICIENCY. *Ant.,* see INSUFFICIENCY.

surge, *v.i.* rise, swell, billow, seethe, swirl; sweep, rush, stream, gush. See WATER, ASSEMBLAGE.

surgeon, *n.* doctor, PHYSICIAN. *Slang,* sawbones, medic, knife man. See REMEDY.

surly, *adj.* sullen, morose, churlish, gruff, uncivil. See DISCOURTESY, IRASCIBILITY. *Ant.,* urbane, affable; see COURTESY.

surmise, *v.t.* guess, conjecture, suppose, suspect, presume. See BELIEF, SUPPOSITION.

surmount, *v.t.* overtop, rise above; master, surpass, transcend; crown, cap, top; scale, climb over; overcome, conquer. See HEIGHT, ASCENT, SUCCESS. *Ant.,* see FAILURE.

surpass, *v.t.* exceed, excel, overtop, outshine, outdo, outclass, eclipse, outstrip. See SUPERIORITY.

surplus, *n.* surplusage; excess, oversupply, glut; REMAINDER, overage; profit, balance. See SUFFICIENCY, REPETITION. *Ant.,* see INSUFFICIENCY.

SURPRISE

Nouns—nonexpectation, unexpectedness, the unforeseen, unforeseen contingency, miscalculation, astonishment, wonder, surprise, thunderclap, blow, shock, bolt out of the blue.

Verbs—1, not expect, be taken by surprise, miscalculate, not bargain for. **2,** be unexpected, come unawares, turn up, pop up, drop from the clouds, burst, steal, creep upon one, take by surprise, take unawares, catch napping. *Slang,* come from left field. **3,** surprise, astonish, amaze, astound; dumfound, startle, dazzle; strike with wonder *or* awe; electrify; stun, stagger, strike dumb, stupefy, petrify, confound, bewilder, flabbergast, fascinate, turn the head, take away one's breath; make one's hair stand on end, make one's eyes pop, take by surprise. *Colloq.,* bowl over, knock for a loop.

Adjectives—1, surprised, nonexpectant, unsuspecting, unwarned, off one's guard, inattentive. See WONDER. **2,** surprising, unexpected, unlooked for, unforeseen, unhoped for, beyond expectation, unheard of, startling, sudden.

Adverbs—surprisingly, unexpectedly, abruptly, plump, pop, unawares, without warning, like a bolt from the blue, suddenly. *Colloq.,* smack. *Antonym,* see EXPECTATION.

---

surrender, *n. & v.* —*n.* capitulation, cession; RELINQUISHMENT, abandonment, SUBMISSION. —*v.* capitulate, yield, give up; cede, renounce, relinquish. *Ant.,* see OPPOSITION.

surround, *v.t.* encompass, enclose, hem in, encircle; ring; circumscribe; environ; invest, besiege; embrace. See NEARNESS, RESTRAINT, ATTACK.

surveillance, *n.* watch, observation, scrutiny, vigilance, CARE, ATTENTION; oversight, supervision, superintendence; lookout, patrol, guardianship; espionage, reconnaissance, watch and ward. *Colloq.,* keeping tabs on. *Slang,* stakeout. See VISION, INQUIRY.

survey, *v.t.* view, examine, inspect, appraise; measure, lay out, plot. See VISION, MEASUREMENT.

survive, *v.* outlive, outlast; live; escape (with one's life); continue, persist, remain, endure, abide, last. See DURABILITY, LIFE. *Ant.,* see DEATH, END.

susceptibility, *n.* liability; allergy; propensity; vulnerability; impressionableness, sensitivity, SENSIBILITY. See TENDENCY. *Ant.*, see HARDNESS, RESOLUTION.

suspect, *v.t.* surmise, infer, conjecture, imagine, suppose, believe; mistrust, DOUBT. See SUPPOSITION. *Ant.*, see BELIEF.

suspend, *v.t.* hang, dangle; defer, postpone, stave off; adjourn, recess, intermit, prorogue, interrupt; debar, exclude. See SUPPORT, LATENESS, END.

suspenders, *n.pl.* braces, garters, elastics. *Colloq.*, galluses. See CLOTHING.

suspense, *n.* anxiety, apprehension; uncertainty, indecision, hesitation; discontinuance, interruption, pause, cessation; inaction, abeyance. See EXPECTATION, DOUBT.

suspicion, *n.* mistrust, distrust, apprehension; DOUBT, misgiving, jealousy; SUPPOSITION, inkling, intimation, hint; trace, touch, shade, modicum. See LITTLENESS. *Ant.*, see BELIEF.

sustain, *v.t.* bear up, SUPPORT; maintain, prolong, protract; nourish, provide for; suffer, undergo, experience; uphold, encourage, comfort; corroborate, confirm, ratify, substantiate. See AID, CONTINUITY, FOOD.

sustenance, *n.* FOOD, nourishment; SUPPORT, maintenance, subsistence; AID.

svelte, *adj.* slim, narrow-waisted (see LITHE).

swab, *n. & v.* —*n.* mop; swab stick, applicator, Q-tip; sponge. —*v.* mop, scrub, cleanse; wipe, dab, daub. See CLEANNESS.

swagger, *v. & n.* —*v.i.* strut, stalk, BLUSTER, boast, bully. —*n.* arrogance, braggadocio, pomposity. *Colloq.*, swank, side. See VANITY, OSTENTATION. *Ant.*, see MODESTY, SIMPLENESS.

swallow, *v.t.* ingest, gulp, devour, consume; absorb, engulf, assimilate, envelop; retract; bear, endure, submit to; believe, accept. See FOOD, SUBJECTION, CREDULITY.

swamp, *n. & v.* —*n.* swampland, marsh, bog, wetland, moor, slough, fen, morass, quagmire. —*v.t.* submerge, sink, flood, inundate, immerse, drench, deluge; overwhelm, snow under. See LAND, MOISTURE, REDUNDANCE.

swanky, *adj., slang,* showy, ostentatious, smart, elegant, fancy; swell, ritzy, classy, posh, plush. See ELEGANCE.

swap, *n. & v., colloq.* See BARTER.

swarm, *n.* group, crowd, MULTITUDE, horde, colony, hive. See ASSEMBLAGE.

swarthy, *adj.* dark, swart, dusky; dark-complexioned. See COLOR, DARKNESS. *Ant.*, see COLORLESSNESS.

sway, *v. & n.* —*v.* swing, rock; influence, direct, control, rule, bias, prejudice, warp; lurch, rock, roll, reel, dangle, swing. —*n.* domination, rule; influence; OSCILLATION. See CAUSE, AUTHORITY, AGITATION.

swear, *v.i.* affirm, depose, depone, vow; testify, witness; blaspheme, curse. See AFFIRMATION, EVIDENCE, IMPRECATION.

sweat, *v. & n.* —*v.* perspire, sudate; run, exude, secrete, ooze, drip; bead, dew, wet. *Colloq.*, drudge, overwork; suffer, extract; force out; exploit. —*n.* perspiration, sudor, exudation. *Colloq.*, EXERTION, toil, sweat of one's brow; AGITATION, stew, EXCITEMENT. See MOISTURE.

sweater, *n.* knitwear, jersey, guernsey, pullover, cardigan. See CLOTHING.

sweep, *v.* brush, clean, vacuum; push, drive, blow, impel; scan; strum; bend, curve; stream, glide, skim. See CLEANNESS, CURVATURE, MOTION.

sweepstakes, *n.* lottery, draw, raffle, CHANCE; winner-take-all; contest.

sweetheart, *n.* lover, love, suitor, beloved, truelove, ladylove. *Colloq.*, beau, swain, boy friend, girl, best girl. *Slang*, gal, sweetie, flame, steady. See LOVE, ENDEARMENT.

SWEETNESS

Nouns—**1,** sweetness, sugariness, saccharinity; sweetening, sugar, molasses, honey, sirup, syrup; saccharine; nectar.

2, sweets, confection, confectionery, confectionary; conserve, preserve, confiture, jam, julep; sugarplum; licorice, marmalade, caramel, candy, candy bar, lollipop, lemon drops, chewing gum, bonbon, jujube, comfit, sweetmeat; taffy, butterscotch, peppermint, chocolate, fudge, *etc.*; manna, nectar, mead, liqueur, cordial, sweet wine, punch; soda, soda water *or* pop, lemonade, carbonated drink; pastry, pie, tart, cream puff, pudding; ice cream, custard; dessert.

3, amiability, gentleness, kindness, good disposition *or* humor, COURTESY; dearness, lovableness; sentimentality, stickiness.

Verbs—be sweet; sweeten; sugar-coat; candy; mull.

Adjectives—**1,** sweet, saccharine; dulcet, candied, honeyed; luscious, lush; sweetened; sweet as sugar, honey *or* candy; sugar-coated, sirupy.

2, amiable, gentle, courteous, *etc.*; dear, lovable, affectionate.

Antonym, see SOUR, DISCOURTESY.

---

swell, *v. & n.*   —*v.i.* expand, dilate, bulge, protrude; billow; INCREASE, grow, surge.   —*n.* swelling, INCREASE; billow, wave, groundswell, sea, roller; rise, slope, knoll. See CONVEXITY. *Slang,* aristocrat, toff. *Ant.,* see DECREASE, CONTRACTION.

swelter, *v.i.* perspire, sweat; be hot. See HEAT.

swerve, *v.i.* turn aside, deviate, shift, sheer, veer, yaw; dodge. See DEVIATION, AVOIDANCE.

swift, *adj.* quick, rapid, fast, fleet, speedy; expeditious. See VELOCITY. *Ant.,* see SLOWNESS.

swig, *v.t., colloq.,* guzzle, toss off *or* down. *Slang,* chug-a-lug. See DRUNKENNESS.

swill, *v. & n.*   —*v.* flood, drench, swamp, soak, slosh; wash, rinse; guzzle, swizzle, swallow. *Colloq.,* swig.   —*n.* garbage, refuse, WASTE, slop(s), mess, filth; eyewash, hogwash. See GLUTTONY, DRUNKENNESS.

swim, *v.* paddle, crawl, stroke, float, kick, tread water; feel dizzy, faint, swoon, reel, whirl; soak, be saturated, steep. See SUPPORT, MOISTURE, WEAKNESS.

swindle, *v.t.* defraud, hoax, cheat, fleece, victimize, trick. *Slang,* gyp. See STEALING, DECEPTION.

swine, *n.* pig, hog, porker, sow, boar; scoundrel; sloven, wretch. See ANIMAL, POPULACE.

swing, *v. & n.*   —*v.i.* oscillate, sway, wag; depend, dangle; pivot, turn. See OSCILLATION, SUPPORT.   —*n.* sweep, sway; rhythm, lilt, scope, range, latitude, FREEDOM; REGULARITY.

swipe, *v., colloq.,* strike, hit, thwack. See IMPULSE. *Slang,* steal, grab, snitch, snatch, pilfer, lift, filch, cop, borrow. See STEALING.

switch, *n. & v.*   —*n.* twig, sprig, spray; rod, cane, birch; shunt. *Slang,* paraphrase; CHANGE, new version.   —*v.t.* cane, whip, lash; shunt, deflect, turn, shift; paraphrase, modify, change; transpose. See PUNISHMENT, DEVIATION.

swivel, *v.* turn, pivot, rotate, wheel, veer, swing. See ROTATION.

swoop, *v.t.* sweep up, catch up, clutch, carry off.   —*v.i.* pounce, hawk, souse, fly, fall on, descend, sweep down, dive. See DESCENT, ATTACK.

sword, *n.* blade, broadsword, falchion, glaive; repier, foil, épée, saber, cutlass, *etc.*; war, vengeance, destruction. See ARMS, WARFARE.

sycophant, *n.* parasite, toady, bootlicker, lickspittle, flatterer, fawner, truckler. See SERVILITY.

syllable, *n.* sonant, phone; (*pl.*) tone, accent, inflection. See SPEECH.

syllabus, *n.* outline, schedule, PLAN, calendar; prospectus (see SUMMARY).

sylvan, *adj.* forest, wooded, wood(s)y, arboreous; rural, bucolic. See VEGETATION.

symbol, *n.* token, emblem, mark, badge, device, character, letter. See INDICATION, WRITING.

symbolize, *v.t.* represent, indicate, signify, typify, mean, betoken, express, imply. See MEANING, INDICATION.

SYMMETRY

Nouns—symmetry, proportion, balance, parallelism; UNIFORMITY, COR-RESPONDENCE, CONFORMITY, congruity, CENTRALITY, REGULARITY, regular ARRANGEMENT; ORDER, harmony, eurhythmy; shapeliness, FORM, BEAUTY, eur(h)ythmics.

Verbs—symmetrize, make symmetrical, balance, proportion, regularize, harmonize, coördinate, equalize.

Adjectives—symmetric(al), proportional, balanced, parallel, coextensive; corresponding, congruent, consistent, coördinate, equal (see EQUALITY); even, regular, uniform, orderly, harmonious, eur(h)ythmic; shapely, well-set, well-formed, finished, beautiful, classic, chaste, severe.

Antonym, see DISTORTION.

sympathize, *v.i.* feel for, sorrow for; condole; understand; feel sorry for, commiserate. See FEELING.

sympathizer, *n.* upholder, supporter, advocate, champion, well-wisher; commiserator, condoler, FRIEND. See AID. *Ant.*, ENEMY.

sympathy, *n.* AGREEMENT, understanding, accord; compassion, PITY, condolence, commiseration, fellow-feeling; empathy. See FRIEND, ASSENT.

symphony, *n.* consonance, harmony, concert, CONCORD; sinfonia, sinfonietta; symphony orchestra, philharmonic. See MUSIC.

symposium, *n.* banquet, collation, feast; panel [discussion], colloquium, colloquy, round table, forum; gathering, social. See ASSEMBLAGE, SOCIALITY.

symptom, *n.* sign, INDICATION, token, mark.

SYNCHRONISM

Nouns—synchronism, synchronization, coexistence, coincidence, CON-CURRENCE; simultaneity, coinstantaneity, concomitance, unity of TIME, isochronism. See AGREEMENT.

Verbs—synchronize, agree in time, be simultaneous; coexist; coincide, agree, concur, fit, match, correspond, harmonize, mesh, dovetail, work together, accompany, go hand in hand, keep pace with; coöperate, coördinate, intermesh, interlock, interact; syncromesh, synthesize, synthetize, syncretize, contemporize. *Colloq.*, gee, sync, jibe, fit to a T.

Adjectives—synchronous, synchronal, synchronical, synchronistical; simultaneous, coinstantaneous, coexistent, coexisting, coincident, concomitant, concurrent; coeval, contemporary, contemporaneous, coetaneous; coeternal; isochronous.

Adverbs—at the same time, simultaneously, contemporaneously, during the same time, in concert, together, in the same breath; at the very moment.

syncopation, *n.* syncope; jazz, blues, ragtime; IRREGULARITY. See MUSIC.

syndicate, *n.* cartel, combine, pool, monopoly, trust; directorate. See PARTY.

synod, *n.* council, convocation, congregation, conclave. See ASSEM-BLAGE, CLERGY.

synonym, *n.* equivalent, word (see MEANING, WORD). *Ant.*, antonym.

synonymous, *adj.* similar, equivalent, analogous. See MEANING.

synopsis, *n.* condensation, abridgment, digest (see SUMMARY).

synthesis, *n.* COMBINATION, composite, amalgamation, UNITY; construct, fabrication; blend, marriage; syncretism.

syringe, *n.* sprinkler, atomizer, spray(er); enema, clysma, clyster, douche; needle, hypodermic; syringium. See WATER, CLEANNESS.

syrup, *n.* concentrate, extract, elixir; glucose, sugar water; sorghum, molasses, treacle. See SWEETNESS, LIQUIDITY.

system, *n.* coördination, organization, routine, ARRANGEMENT, METHOD, PLAN; classification; complex. *Ant.*, see DISORDER.

tab 498

T

tab, *n. & v.* —*n.* flap, tag, strip, lug; label; earmark, ticket. *Colloq.*, tabulation, bill, check, charge, reckoning. —*v.t., colloq.*, appoint, select, designate, nominate, choose, pick [out]. *Slang*, finger. See INDICATION.

tabernacle, *n.* See TEMPLE.

table, *n.* board; slab; desk, counter; FOOD, diet, fare; cuisine, menu; index, compendium, catalog(ue); chart, tabulation, LIST, schedule; tableland, plateau, mesa. See SMOOTHNESS.

tableau, *n.* group; picture, scene, backdrop, set, diorama. See DRAMA, PAINTING.

tablet, *n.* slab, stone, memorial; slate, plaque, signboard; pad, booklet; pill, lozenge, pastille, wafer. See FLATNESS, BOOK, INDICATION, REMEDY.

tabloid, *n.* yellow journal, scandal sheet. *Slang*, rag, blat. See NEWS.

taboo, tabu, *n., v. & adj.* —*n.* prohibition, interdiction, forbiddance. —*v.t.* forbid, prohibit, keep inviolate. —*adj.* forbidden; untouchable, unprofanable, inviolate. See RESTRAINT.

tabulate, *v.t.* chart, graph; LIST, catalogue; calculate, figure, enumerate, tally; enroll, RECORD. See ARRANGEMENT, ADDITION.

tacit, *adj.* unspoken, unexpressed; silent, mute; implied, understood. See SILENCE. *Ant.*, see INFORMATION.

TACITURNITY

Nouns—taciturnity, uncommunicativeness, reticence, reserve, closeness, curtness; SILENCE, MUTENESS, pauciloquy, laconicism; secrecy, CONCEALMENT, SECRET; man of few words. *Colloq.*, clam. See SECLUSION.

Verbs—be taciturn *or* silent, keep SILENCE, not speak, say nothing; hold *or* put a bridle on one's tongue, hold one's peace, seal the lips, close the mouth, keep one's tongue between one's teeth, lay a finger on the lips, not let a word escape one, make no sign, keep a secret, not have a word to say.

Adjectives—taciturn, uncommunicative, reticent, reserved, close, close-mouthed *or* -tongued, tight-lipped, unconversable, unsociable, short, curt, laconic, sparing of words; silent, still, mute; pauciloquent, concise, terse, sententious; secretive.

Antonym, see LOQUACITY.

---

tack, *n. & v.* —*n.* thumbtack, carpet tack, *etc.*; nail; change of course, yaw, veer; route, course, path. —*v.* change course *or* direction; yaw; zigzag (while sailing). See DEVIATION.

tackle, *n. & v.* —*n.* pulley; gear, equipment, apparatus, instruments; luggage. —*v.t.* grapple with; seize; address, attack; attempt, try, undertake. See UNDERTAKING.

tacky, *adj., colloq.,* shabby, shoddy, seedy; cheap, tawdry, sleazy; in poor taste. *Slang*, cheesy. See UNCLEANNESS.

tact, *n.* diplomacy; finesse; discretion, consideration. See SKILL, COURTESY. *Ant.*, see DISCOURTESY.

tactics, *n.pl.* strategy, generalship; CONDUCT; maneuvering; policy, diplomacy; mode, METHOD.

tactless, *adj.* thoughtless, insensitive, inconsiderate; callous, unfeeling, blunt, direct. See DISCOURTESY, INSENSIBILITY.

tag, *n.* stub, tab, flap; tail, tassel, pendant; slogan, phrase, name, catchword; tatter, shred, rag. See ADDITION, END, INDICATION.

tail, *n.* appendage, END; cauda; tip, extremity; REAR, rudder, queue, pigtail, train. *Slang*, shadow. *Ant.*, see FRONT.

tailor, *n. & v.* —*n.* sartor, clothier, costumier, couturier, dressmaker, seamstress. —*v.* fit, design, make, cut, trim, alter; sew, stitch, style, FASHION, shape, drape, hand-tailor, finish. See CLOTHING, PRODUCTION.

taint, *v. & n.* —*v.* corrupt, spoil, poison; be corrupted; tarnish, stain, sully; pollute, infect, contaminate. —*n.* corruption; spoilage; stigma, dishonor, defilement; fault, flaw, blemish. See IMPROBITY, DISEASE, DISREPUTE, IMPERFECTION. *Ant.*, see PROBITY, HEALTH, PERFECTION.

take, *v. & n.* —*v.* catch, nab, bag, pocket; capture, seize; take away, deduct; receive; accept; reap, crop, gather; get, draw; acquire, appropriate, assume, confiscate, take possession of; lay hands on; commandeer, help oneself to; snatch, grab; pre-empt, usurp; expropriate; deprive of; take *or* carry off, abstract; plagiarize, shoplift, pirate; steal, filch; take by storm; snap up, pick up; do; work; be effective; snap a picture. *Slang*, latch onto, hook, snag. —*n.* taking. *Colloq.*, receipts, gate, haul, swag; shooting of a scene (*Photography*). See ACQUISITION, STEALING. *Ant.*, see GIVING, RELINQUISHMENT, LOSS.

take-off, *n.*, *colloq.*, IMITATION, parody, satire, burlesque, skit. See RIDICULE.

taking, *n. & adj.* —*n.* reception; RECEIVING; appropriation, expropriation, confiscation; apprehension; seizure; abduction; subtraction, deduction; abstraction; extortion, theft, STEALING, kidnap(p)ing; dispossession; deprivation, bereavement, DIVESTMENT; distraint, distress; commandeering; haul, catch. —*adj.* fetching, winning, endearing. See ACQUISITION.

tale, *n.* story, account, recital; count, counting, tally; report; fable, yarn, legend. See DESCRIPTION, NUMERATION, FALSEHOOD.

talent, *n.* gift, faculty, ability, POWER; turn, knack, aptitude; genius. See SKILL. *Ant.*, see UNSKILLFULNESS.

talisman, *n.* lucky piece; charm, amulet, fetish. See SORCERY.

talk, *n. & v.* —*n.* CONVERSATION; chatter, chat, gossip; SPEECH; lecture, discourse; rumor, hearsay. —*v.* say, speak, chat, converse. See INFORMATION, LOQUACITY, COMMUNICATION.

talkative, *adj.* talky, verbose (see LOQUACITY).

tall, *adj.* high, lofty, towering; long, long-limbed; exaggerated. See HEIGHT. *Ant.*, see LOWNESS.

tally, *n. & v.* —*n.* count, tale, counting; score, check; match, matching; roll call. —*v.* count, tell; suit, correspond, agree, harmonize; check. See LIST, NUMERATION, INDICATION, AGREEMENT.

tame, *adj. & v.* —*adj.* tamed, domestic, domesticated; broken, subdued; meek, gentle; flat; spiritless, feeble. —*v.t.* subdue, cow, break; harness; domesticate. See DOMESTICATION, SUBJECTION. *Ant.*, see VIOLENCE.

tamper, *v.i.* meddle, intermeddle, interfere; bribe, seduce, corrupt, taint; CHANGE, alter. *Colloq.*, doctor, monkey (with). See ACTIVITY, DETERIORATION.

tang, *n.* savor, flavor, TASTE, zest; sharpness, PUNGENCY, tanginess; bite, nip, snappiness.

tangible, *adj.* material, real; touchable, palpable; concrete, perceptible. See FEELING, SUBSTANCE. *Ant.*, see INSUBSTANTIALITY.

tangle, *n. & v.* —*n.* snarl, mixup, jumble, mattedness; complication, involvement. —*v.* mat, snarl; knot, mix inextricably; snare, trap, enmesh; embroil, complicate. See MIXTURE, DISORDER, DIFFICULTY. *Ant.*, see ARRANGEMENT.

tank, *n.* reservoir, cistern; boiler; (*pl.*) armor; panzer; pond, swimming pool. See WATER, RECEPTACLE, STORE, ARMS.

tantalize, *v.* tease, tempt, excite, provoke; balk. See DESIRE.

tantrum, *n.* fit, outburst; display (of ill temper); rage, passion, frenzy, paroxysm. See RESENTMENT, IRASCIBILITY. *Ant.*, MODERATION.

tap, *n. & v.* —*n.* spigot, faucet, valve; plug, bung, stopper; knock, rap; tapping, tap dance, soft shoe; shoe tap; taproom, bar, saloon. —*v.* knock, rap, strike, TOUCH; tapdance; broach, draw off (liquor, *etc.*); wiretap; draw upon, nominate. See IMPULSE, OPENING.

tape, *n. & v.* —*n.* band, strip, ribbon; cellophane, Scotch, masking, electrical *or* friction tape; tapeline. —*v.* bind, bandage, swaddle, mummify. *Colloq.*, tape-record, COPY. See FILAMENT, COHERENCE, MEASUREMENT.

taper, *v. & n.* —*v.* narrow; come to a point; lessen, slacken, slack off. —*n.* candle, LIGHT; pyramidal *or* cone shape. See NARROWNESS.

tar, *n. & v.* —*n.* asphalt, pitch, resin, bitumen; goo, sludge. —*v.* besmirch, stain, blacken, defame; tar and feather. See UNCLEANNESS, DETRACTION.

tardy, *adj.* overdue, late, behindtime; slow, slack, dilatory. See LATE-NESS. *Ant.*, see EARLINESS.

target, *n.* aim, mark; goal; bull's-eye; quarry, object; butt. See PURSUIT.

tariff, *n.* duty, customs, impost. *Colloq.*, price, cost. See TAX.

tarnish, *v.* smirch, taint; dishonor; stain, sully, besmirch; defame; dull, smudge, dim, spot, blemish. See IMPERFECTION, DISREPUTE, UNCLEAN-NESS. *Ant.*, see REPUTE, CLEANNESS.

tarpaulin, *n.* tarp; canvas, oilcloth; tent; poncho, slicker. See COVERING.

tarry, *v.i.* linger, stay, wait; idle, dawdle; visit (with); bide a while, sojourn; delay, dally. See LATENESS, CONTINUITY. *Ant.*, see TRAN-SIENTNESS.

tart, *adj. & n.* —*adj.* acid, sour; sarcastic, acerbic; snappy, sharp; as-tringent. —*n.*, *slang,* strumpet. See SOURNESS, DISCOURTESY.

tartan, *n.* plaid, check; kilt, trews, filibeg. See VARIEGATION, INDICATION.

task, *n. & v.* —*n.* work, stint, job, labor; lesson, assignment, charge, DUTY, chore; drudgery, burden. —*v.t.* strain, tax, overburden, over-work; impose, assign, charge. See BUSINESS, USE, WEARINESS.

taskmaster, *n.* overseer, martinet; slavedriver. See DIRECTION, SEVERITY.

TASTE

Nouns—**1,** taste, tastefulness; good taste, cultivated taste; delicacy, refine-ment, tact, finesse; nicety, DISCRIMINATION; polish, ELEGANCE; grace; virtu; connoisseurship, dilettantism; fine art; culture, cultivation, fas-tidiousness; aesthetics.

2, taste, flavor, gusto, savor; sapor, sapidity, aftertaste, tang; sample; tinge, bit, trace, scrap, soupçon; tasting, gustation, degustation; palate, tongue, tooth, stomach.

3, savoriness, tastiness, palatability; unsavoriness, unpalatability, aus-terity; sweetness, sourness, acidity, acerbity; PUNGENCY.

4, seasoning, CONDIMENT; spice, relish; tidbit, dainty, delicacy, morsel, appetizer, *hors d'œuvres*; antipasto, delicatessen; ambrosia; nectar; rue, hemlock, myrrh, aloes, gall and wormwood.

5, man of taste, connoisseur; epicure, gourmet; judge, critic, virtuoso; amateur, dilettante.

Verbs—**1,** have good taste, appreciate; judge, criticize, discriminate, dis-tinguish, particularize; single out, draw the line, sift, estimate, weigh, consider, diagnose; pick and choose, split hairs, know which is which.

2, savor, taste, sample; relish, like, enjoy, smack the lips; tickle the palate; turn the stomach, disgust; pall, stale, spoil; sour, curdle, ferment, turn.

Adjectives—**1,** in good taste; tasteful, unaffected, pure, chaste, classical, cultivated, refined; dainty, nice, delicate, aesthetic, artistic; elegant; euphemistic; fastidious, discriminating, discriminative, discerning, per-ceptive; to one's taste, after one's fancy; *comme il faut.*

2, tasty, flavorful, sapid, saporific; palatable, gustable, gustatory, tast-able; PUNGENT, strong; flavored, spicy, hot; sweet, sour, salt, bitter; SAVORY, UNSAVORY.

Adverbs—tastefully, elegantly; purely, aesthetically, *etc.*

Antonym, see VULGARITY.

---

tasteless, *adj.* insipid, flat; inelegant; inept, clumsy, vulgar, savorless, un-appetizing. See INSIPIDITY, VULGARITY, TASTE.

tatters, *n.pl.* rags, odds and ends, fragments; POVERTY. See PART.

tattle, *v.* prattle, prate; chat, chatter; jabber, talk; reveal (a secret), inform. *Colloq.*, peach, tell on, tell tales. *Slang*, blab; spill the beans. See LOQUACITY, DISCLOSURE. *Ant.*, see SECRET.

taunt, *v.* RIDICULE, scoff, jeer, twit; mock, flout, deride. See ACCUSATION.

taut, *adj.* tight, stretched, tense, strained; keyed up, on edge; snug, tidy, shipshape. See HARDNESS, ARRANGEMENT. *Ant.*, see SOFTNESS, DISORDER.

tautology, *n.* REPETITION, reiteration; redundance; verbosity.

tavern, *n.* inn, hostel, restaurant, cafe; saloon, bar, rathskeller, cocktail lounge, bistro, bar and grill, barroom, taproom, alehouse, public house, ordinary. *Slang*, pub, barrelhouse. See ABODE, DRUNKENNESS.

tawdry, *adj.* cheap, showy, flashy; loud, garish; tinsel, gimcrack. See VULGARITY, OSTENTATION. *Ant.*, see ELEGANCE.

tax, *n. & v.* —*n.* assessment, levy, duty, tariff, excise, toll, tithe; impost, custom; rate, income tax, internal revenue. *Slang*, charge. —*v.* assess, rate, COMMAND; charge, accuse; take to task; strain, overwork, burden, fatigue. See ACCUSATION, PAYMENT, EXERTION.

taxicab, *n.* taximeter cab, taxi, cab; hack(ney), jitney; taxiplane; fiacre, droshky, (jin)rickshaw, pedicab. See VEHICLE.

tea, *n.* pekoe, souchong, oolong, *etc.* tea; beef tea, broth, bouillon; collation, afternoon *or* five-o'clock tea, high tea, snack. See FOOD, SOCIALITY.

TEACHING

Nouns—**1,** teaching, instruction, edification, education, tuition; tutorship, tutelage; direction, guidance; preparation, training, schooling; discipline; exercise, drill, practice; indoctrination, inculcation, inoculation; explanation, INTERPRETATION. See SCHOOL.

2, lesson, lecture, sermon; apologue, parable; discourse, prelection, preachment; exercise, task.

3, teacher, educator, trainer, instructor, master, tutor, director, coach, disciplinarian; professor, lecturer, reader, prelector, prolocutor; preacher, pastor (see CLERGY); schoolmaster, dominie, pedagogue, abecedarian; schoolmistress, governess; monitor; expositor, interpreter; preceptor, guide, mentor, adviser (see ADVICE); pioneer, apostle, missionary, propagandist.

Verbs—**1,** teach, instruct, edify, school, tutor; cram, prime, coach; enlighten, inform; inculcate, indoctrinate, inoculate, infuse, instil, infiltrate; imbue, impregnate, implant; graft, sow the seeds of, disseminate; give an idea of; put up to, set right, sharpen the wits, broaden one's horizon, open the eyes, bring forward, improve; direct, guide; direct attention to, impress upon the mind *or* memory; beat into, beat into the head; convince (see BELIEF).

2, expound, interpret, lecture, hold forth, preach; sermonize, moralize.

3, train, discipline; bring up, educate, form, ground, prepare, qualify, drill, exercise, practice; nurture, breed, rear, take in hand; break, break in; tame; preinstruct; initiate, inure, habituate. *Colloq.*, show the ropes.

Adjectives—teaching, taught, educational; scholastic, academic, doctrinal; disciplinal, disciplinary; instructive, didactic, homiletic; professorial, pedagogic.

Antonym, see LEARNING.

team, *n.* crew, side, aggregation; nine, five, eleven (baseball, basketball *and* football teams); rig, span (of horses); combat team, group; brace, pair, foursome, *etc.* See ASSEMBLAGE, COÖPERATION.

teamster, *n.* wagonmaster, muleteer; carter, drayman, wagoner; truck driver, truckman, trucker, CARRIER, vanman. See TRAVEL.

tear, *v. & n.* —*v.* rip, rend, tatter, shred; split, burst, break, part, separate; give; snatch, race, speed, dash, fly. —*n.* break, rent, split; wound;

crack, fissure, gap; teardrop (see TEARS). *Slang,* binge, toot, spree, bender, jag. See DISJUNCTION. *Ant.,* mend; see JUNCTION, RESTORATION.

tears, *n.* teardrops; weeping, crying, LAMENTATION.

tease, *v.* plague, annoy, vex, harass; taunt, mock; beg; tantalize; titillate, excite. See PAIN, REQUEST, EXPECTATION.

technicality, *n.* fine point, minutiae (*pl.*); nuance, detail, subtlety, formality; law, RULE, rubric; loophole, letter of the law; precedure, problem.

technique, *n.* technic, execution, style, METHOD. See SKILL.

technology, *n.* technics; KNOWLEDGE, INFORMATION, craft, science, engineering, mechanics; SKILL, practise; automation, mechanization. *Colloq.,* know-how.

tedious, *adj.* wearisome, wearing, dry, dry-as-dust, boring, tiresome; irksome; DULL, monotonous, prosy, uninteresting. See WEARINESS, DRYNESS. *Ant.,* see AMUSEMENT.

teem, *v.i.* swarm, abound; multiply, pullulate; rain heavily, pour; bear, generate, produce. See PRODUCTION, SUFFICIENCY.

teeming, *adj.* swarming, abounding, abundant, plentiful; crowded, chockfull, jam-packed; replete, fraught, full, pullulating; raining. See MULTITUDE, SUFFICIENCY. *Ant.,* see RARITY.

teenager, *n.* YOUTH, adolescent. *Colloq.,* bobbysoxer, teen.

teeter, *v.i.* seesaw, rock, sway, totter, tremble; hesitate, vacillate. See OSCILLATION, DOUBT.

teetotal, *adj. Colloq.,* all, entire, WHOLE; abstinent; dry, prohibitionist. *Ant.,* see DRUNKENNESS.

telegram, *n.* message; wire, cable. See COMMUNICATION.

telegraph, *n. & v.* —*n.* telegram; wireless, Morse, wire, cable, semaphore, heliograph, pantelegraph, phototelegraph. —*v.t.* signal, wire, radio, cable. *Colloq.,* betray, disclose, reveal. See COMMUNICATION, INDICATION.

telepathy, *n.* psychic communication, thought transference, extrasensory perception; psi.

telephone, *v.* call [up], phone, dial, get through to. See COMMUNICATION.

telescope, *n. & v.* —*n.* glass, spyglass, fieldglass. —*v.* collapse, fold; foreshorten, condense, abridge. See OPTICAL INSTRUMENTS.

television, *n.* video, TV; telefilm, kinescope, tape; station, studio, channel, network; closed-circuit *or* pay television; telecast. See COMMUNICATION.

tell, *v.* recount, relate, narrate; inform, apprise, acquaint; explain; weigh, matter, influence; reveal, disclose, own, confess, acknowledge, discern, distinguish, make out, see; count, number, reckon, tally; speak, state, declare. See INFORMATION, DESCRIPTION, IMPORTANCE, SPEECH, NUMBER.

teller, *n.* bank clerk, cashier. See AGENT.

temerity, *n.* RASHNESS, boldness, audacity, recklessness, daring. *Slang,* nerve, gall, brass, cheek. *Ant.,* CAUTION, COWARDICE.

temper, *n. & v.* —*n.* temperament, nature, disposition; mood, humor, tone; tantrum, passion, rage; mettle, quality; calmness, composure, equanimity. See IRASCIBILITY, WILL. —*v.t.* moderate, soften; harden, anneal, toughen. See HARDNESS, SOFTNESS.

temperament, *n.* constitution; disposition; nature; humor. See WILL.

temperance, *n.* MODERATION; forbearance; abnegation, renunciation, self-denial, self-restraint, self-control, continence, asceticism; vegetarianism, abstinence; sobriety, soberness, teetotalism, abstemiousness; prohibitionism, dryness. *Ant.,* see DRUNKENNESS.

temperate, *adj.* moderate; ascetic; cautious; mild; SOBER, abstemious, abstinent; continent; Pythagorean; vegetarian. See MODERATION.

tempest, *n.* storm, gale, hurricane, squall, blizzard; EXCITEMENT, tumult, disturbance; maelstrom. See AGITATION, WIND.

tempestuous, *adj.* stormy, raging, furious; gusty, blowy, squally; violent, tumultuous, turbulent. See ROUGHNESS, WIND, AGITATION. *Ant.,* see SMOOTHNESS, INACTIVITY.

TEMPLE

Nouns—**1,** temple, place of worship; house of God, house of prayer; cathedral, minister, church, kirk, chapel, meetinghouse, tabernacle, basilica, holy place, chantry, oratory; synagogue; mosque; marabout; pantheon; pagoda.

2, altar, shrine, sanctuary, Holy of Holies, *sanctum sanctorum,* communion table; pyx; baptistery, font; sedilia; reredos; rood-loft, roodscreen; chancel, nave, aisle, transept, vestry, sacristy, crypt, cloisters, churchyard, golgotha, calvary; stall pew; pulpit, ambo, lectern, readingdesk, confessional; apse, oriel, belfry.

3, parsonage, rectory, vicarage, manse, deanery, presbytery, Vatican, bishop's palace.

4, monastery, priory, abbey, friary, convent, nunnery, cloister; sanctuary. *Adjectives*—churchly, claustral, cloistral, cloistered; monastic, conventual.

---

tempo, *n.* TIME, beat, rate; pace; rhythm. See MUSIC.

temporal, *adj.* worldly, mundane, secular; civil, political, profane, unsacred; temporary, ephemeral, impermanent. See IRRELIGION, TRANSIENTNESS.

temporary, *adj.* impermanent, irregular, seasonal, provisional, momentary, brief, fleeting, transitory; stopgap, makeshift, ersatz. See TRANSIENTNESS.

temporize, *v.i.* adapt oneself, maneuver; vacillate, procrastinate, stall, hedge. *Colloq.,* blow hot and cold, play for time. See LATENESS, IRRESOLUTION.

tempt, *v.t.* entice, cajole, fascinate, lure, decoy, seduce; provoke, incite, instigate, appeal, attract. See DESIRE.

temptation, *n.* ATTRACTION, enticement, allurement; bait; siren song; provocativeness. See DESIRE.

TENACITY

Nouns—tenacity, cohesion, COHERENCE, adhesion, holding, STRENGTH; viscidity, viscosity; pertinacity, perseverance, persistence, patience; OBSTINACY, intransigence, resistance, insistence, RESOLUTION, constancy, STABILITY, pluck, COURAGE, RETENTION. *Colloq.,* stick-to-itiveness.

Verbs—adhere (to), stick (to), cling (to); persevere, persist, hold on *or* out, never say die, fight to the last ditch, be in at the death, stick to one's guns; keep on, hold one's course *or* ground, bear *or* keep up, continue, plod, follow through *or* up. *Colloq.,* stick it out, muddle through, see it through, hang on for dear life, keep a stiff upper lip, keep one's chin up.

Adjectives—tenacious, cohesive, adhesive, clinging, holding, fast, resisting, tough, strong; sticky, gummy, tacky, waxy, glutinous, viscous, viscid; pertinacious, persistent, persevering, dogged, determined, unyielding, uncompromising, unwavering, unfaltering; obstinate, stubborn, intransigent, insistent, opinionated, positive, single-minded; steady, steadfast, firm, resolute, constant, purposeful, relentless, grim; retentive, unforgetful, unforgetting. *Colloq.,* pigheaded, never-say-die. *Antonym,* see WEAKNESS.

---

tenant, *n.* occupant, occupier, resident, INHABITANT, renter; inmate.

tend, *v.* mind, watch, care for, guard, keep; attend, serve, wait on, incline, bend, bear toward, lean, gravitate. See AID, SERVANT, TENDENCY.

TENDENCY

Nouns—tendency; aptness, aptitude; proneness, proclivity, predilection, bent, turn, tone, bias, set, leaning to, penchant, predisposition, inclination, propensity, susceptibility; likelihood, LIABILITY; quality, nature, temperament; idiosyncrasy; cast, vein, grain; humor, mood; trend, drift; conduciveness, conducement; applicability.

Verbs—tend, contribute, conduce, lead, dispose, incline, verge, bend to, trend, affect, carry, redound to, bid fair to, gravitate toward; be liable; promote, AID.

Adjectives—tending, conducive, working toward, in a fair way to, calculated to; liable; subservient; useful, subsidiary.

Antonym, see OPPOSITION.

tender, *v., adj. & n.* —*v.t.* present, OFFER, proffer, hold out; propose, suggest; volunteer. —*adj.* gentle, kind; loving, amorous; sympathetic, soft; humane, merciful; young; fragile, delicate; pathetic, touching; painful, sore. See BENEVOLENCE, LOVE, SOFTNESS, YOUTH, PAIN. *Ant.*, see ROUGHNESS, HARDNESS, SEVERITY. —*n.* MONEY; supply ship; supply car, coal car. See SHIP, VEHICLE.

tenderfoot, *n.* newcomer, recruit, novice. *Colloq.*, greenhorn. See NEWNESS.

tenement, *n.* apartment house; flat, dwelling, ABODE; slum.

tenet, *n.* dogma, BELIEF, opinion, creed, doctrine.

tenor, *n.* drift, TENDENCY, import, MEANING, significance; gist, sense; course, manner, mood, nature; DIRECTION. See MUSICIAN, MUSICAL INSTRUMENTS.

tense, *adj. & n.* —*adj.* taut, rigid; intent; excited; high-strung, nervous, strained. See EXCITEMENT, HARDNESS. *Ant.*, see SOFTNESS, MODERATION. —*n.* time, verb, form, inflection. See GRAMMAR.

tensile, *adj.* stretchable, ductile, flexile; resilient, pliable. See ELASTICITY.

tension, *n.* strain; tensity; tenseness; stretching; anxiety, nervousness. See HARDNESS, EXCITEMENT.

tent, *n.* canvas; wigwam, tepee; pavilion; shelter. See COVERING, ABODE.

tentacle, *n.* process, feeler, palp; (*pl.*) POWER, grasp. See RETENTION.

tentative, *adj.* experimental, provisional, conditional, temporary, makeshift. See DOUBT.

tenuous, *adj.* unsubstantial, flimsy; thin, slender; rarefied. See NARROWNESS, RARITY. *Ant.*, see BREADTH, DENSITY.

tenure, *n.* holding; tenancy, occupancy; occupation; habitation, POSSESSION.

tepid, *adj.* lukewarm, mild; indifferent. See HEAT.

term, *n.* word, expression, locution; LIMIT, bound; period, TIME, tenure, duration; semester.

termination, *n.* END, ending, conclusion; LIMIT, bound; result, outcome, consequence, COMPLETION; suffix. *Ant.*, see BEGINNING.

terminology, *n.* See NOMENCLATURE.

terms, *n.* provisions, limitations, stipulations, conditions; AGREEMENT; relationship, footing.

terrace, *n.* level, plateau, plane; parterre, esplanade, promenade; porch, patio, embankment. See FLATNESS, PASSAGE, ELEVATION.

terrestrial, *adj.* earthly; worldly, mundane, secular, temporal. See LAND.

terrible, *adj.* terrifying, dreadful; awesome, appalling, frightful, horrible, shocking, fearful, alarming. *Colloq.*, excessive. See FEAR. *Ant.*, see CHEERFULNESS.

terrific, *adj.* TERRIBLE. *Colloq.*, sensational, wonderful, fabulous, stupendous. *Slang*, out of this world. See GREATNESS, GOOD.

terrify, *v.t.* terrorize, frighten, alarm; appall, dismay; cow, intimidate; panic, stampede. See FEAR. *Ant.*, see COURAGE.

territory, *n.* REGION, district; POSSESSION; kingdom, state, realm, province. See PROPERTY, LAND.

terror, *n.* FEAR, dread; fright, alarm; dismay, horror; panic. *Ant.*, see COURAGE.

terrorism, *n.* oppression, tyranny, anarchy, REVOLUTION, bolshevism, nihilism; VIOLENCE, DESTRUCTION, sabotage, intimidation, AGITATION. See FEAR.

terse, *adj.* concise, brief, curt; pithy, laconic, succinct; short, compact. See CONTRACTION. *Ant.,* see LOQUACITY.

test, *n.* examination; trial, ESSAY; criterion; EXPERIMENT.

testify, *v.* affirm, declare, state, depose, swear, avow, witness. See EVIDENCE.

testimony, *n.* declaration, affirmation; profession; attestation, witness, EVIDENCE; Scriptures. See SACRED WRITINGS.

testy, *adj.* irritable, irascible, petulant, cross. *Colloq.,* ornery. See IRASCIBILITY.

tether, *v.t.* picket, stake, tie, fasten. See RESTRAINT. *Ant.,* see FREEDOM.

text, *n.* COMPOSITION; matter; textbook; topic, subject, theme. See BOOK, WRITING.

TEXTURE

Nouns—**1,** texture, structure, make(-up), architecture, frame(work), mold; construction, COMPOSITION, constitution, anatomy; organization, ARRANGEMENT, disposition, stratification, FORM; character, quality, surface, fiber, nap, tooth, tissue, weave, warp and woof, weft, grain, fineness *or* coarseness of grain; SMOOTHNESS, ROUGHNESS.

2, SUBSTANCE, stuff, staple (see MATERIALS); mat, web(bing), braid, plait, trellis, mesh, lattice(work), tissue.

Verbs—texture; braid, plait, *etc.*; coarsen, grain.

Adjectives—textured, textural, textile, woven; structural, anatomic(al), organic; coarse, grainy, coarse-grained, homespun; shaggy, nappy; fine, fine-grained, delicate, subtle, filmy, downy, gossamery, smooth.

---

thankful, *adj.* grateful, appreciative; much obliged. See GRATITUDE. *Ant.,* see INGRATITUDE.

thankless, *adj.* ungrateful, unthankful, unappreciative, ingrate; ungracious; unrewarding; unpleasant. See INGRATITUDE.

thanks, *n.* GRATITUDE; acknowledgment, appreciation; thank you; grace. *Ant.,* see INGRATITUDE.

thanksgiving, *n.* grace, PRAYER, praise. See GRATITUDE. *Ant.,* see INGRATITUDE.

thaw, *v.* melt, dissolve, liquefy; soften, unbend. See HEAT, SOFTNESS. *Ant.,* freeze; see COLD, HARDNESS.

theater, theatre, *n.* stage; ARENA; field [of action]; playhouse; DRAMA; motion-picture house; studio.

theatrical, *adj.* dramatic, melodramatic; histrionic; scenic; showy, stagy, affected; vivid, moving. See AFFECTATION, DRAMA, OSTENTATION.

theft, *n.* See STEALING.

theme, *n.* subject, TOPIC, text; essay, thesis, treatise, dissertation; composition; melody, motif. See MUSIC, WRITING.

then, *adv.* soon, next, immediately; consequently, therefore, evidently; again; afterwards. See TIME, REASONING.

theology, *n.* RELIGION; creed, BELIEF; doctrine, dogma.

theoretical, *adj.* speculative, hypothetical, conjectural; unapplied; pure, abstract. See NONEXISTENCE, SUPPOSITION. *Ant.,* see SUBSTANCE, EXISTENCE.

theory, *n.* speculation, surmise, conjecture; contemplation; principle, philosophy, doctrine; hypothesis; guess, idea, plan. See SUPPOSITION. *Ant.,* see EXISTENCE.

therapy, *n.* therapeutics, REMEDY, healing, cure; rehabilitation, RESTORATION; physical therapy, psychotherapy, *etc.* See IMPROVEMENT.

thereafter, *adv.* after(wards), after that; subsequently, (t)henceforth, from that moment; after which; later, in the future. See POSTERIORITY.

therefore, *adv.* consequently, hence, wherefore, so, accordingly. See REASONING.

thermometer, *n.* thermostat, pyrometer, calorimeter; clinical thermometer. *Colloq.,* mercury, glass. See MEASUREMENT.

thesis, *n.* proposition, TOPIC, argument; AFFIRMATION; postulate; statement; composition, treatise, dissertation. See WRITING, REASONING.

thick, *adj.* broad, wide, massive, thickset, stout, fat; dense, solid; populous, crowded; heavy, viscous, creamy; foggy, smoky, hazy; hoarse, guttural, throaty; slow(-witted), witless. *Slang,* gooey. See SIZE, BREADTH, DENSITY, MULTITUDE.

thicket, *n.* brush, underbrush; grove, coppice, covert. See VEGETABLE.

thief, *n.* robber, crook; sneak thief; pilferer; swindler, confidence man; shoplifter, kleptomaniac; stealer, pirate, purloiner, filcher; burglar, second-story man, *etc.* See STEALING, IMPROBITY.

thin, *adj.* slender, lean, narrow, slim, skinny, underweight, slight, frail; puny; scrawny, bony; lank, lanky; thinned out; watery, weak, diluted; attenuated; faint, dim, threadlike; fine, delicate; gaunt, haggard, drawn, emaciated; spare, meager, spindly, spindling; poor, lame (as an excuse); flimsy, sheer, filmy. See RARITY, NARROWNESS. *Ant.,* see BREADTH, SIZE.

thing, *n.* affair, matter, CIRCUMSTANCE; deed, act, occurrence; entity, person; POSSESSION, belonging, chattel; item, object, detail, article. See SUBSTANCE. *Ant.,* see NONEXISTENCE.

think, *v.* See THOUGHT.

thirst, *n.* dryness; craving, DESIRE; dipsomania, thirstiness, parchedness.

thirsty, *adj.* dry, parched, unslaked, unquenched; arid, craving water; greedy, avid. See DESIRE.

thorn, *n.* spine, briar, bramble; annoyance, irritation. See SHARPNESS.

thorough, *adj.* thoroughgoing; painstaking, exact, careful; complete, absolute, unqualified, arrant, out-and-out; exhaustive, deep, sweeping. See COMPLETION, WHOLE. *Ant.,* see NEGLECT.

thoroughbred, *adj.* purebred, full-blooded, pedigreed; blueblooded, noble, aristocratic; to the manor born; well-bred *or* -mannered. See PURITY, NOBILITY.

thoroughfare, *n.* avenue, highway, street; PASSAGE, way; thruway, stop street, boulevard, turnpike.

thousand, *n.* fifty score, M. *Slang,* thou, yard, grand, G. See NUMERATION.

THOUGHT

Nouns—**1,** thought, thoughtfulness; reflection, cogitation, consideration, meditation, study, lucubration, speculation, deliberation, pondering; headwork, brainwork; cerebration; deep reflection, rumination, close study, application, ATTENTION; abstract thought, abstraction; contemplation, musing, preoccupation, brown study, reverie, Platonism; self-counsel, self-communing, self-consultation; association of ideas, succession of ideas, flow of ideas; train *or* current of thought.

2, afterthought, mature thought, reconsideration, second thought; retrospection, hindsight; MEMORY; excogitation; examination (see INQUIRY); invention (see IMAGINATION).

3, IDEA; topic, subject of thought, material for thought; food for thought; subject, subject matter; matter, theme, thesis, text, business, affair, matter in hand, argument; motion, resolution; head, chapter; case, point; proposition, theorem; field of inquiry; moot point, problem.

Verbs—**1,** think, reflect, cogitate, cerebrate, excogitate, consider, deliberate, lucubrate; rationalize, speculate, contemplate, meditate, ponder, muse, dream, ruminate; brood upon; animadvert, study; bend *or* apply the mind; digest, discuss, weigh; realize, appreciate; fancy.

2, take into consideration; take counsel, commune with oneself, bethink oneself; collect one's thoughts; revolve, turn over *or* run over in the mind; sleep on; rack one's brains; set one's wits to work; puzzle over; take into one's head; bear in mind; reconsider. *Colloq.,* sweat over, chew the cud, mull over. *Slang,* kick around.

3, occur, present itself, suggest itself; come into one's head; strike one, cross the mind, occupy the mind; have on one's mind; make an impression; sink in, penetrate the mind; engross the thoughts.

Adjectives—thinking, thoughtful, pensive, meditative, reflective, musing, wistful, contemplative, speculative, deliberative, studious, sedate, introspective, Platonic, philosophical; rational; lost in thought, engrossed, absorbed, rapt, preoccupied; in the mind, under consideration.

Adverbs—thoughtfully, reflectively; all things considered.

Antonyms, see RASHNESS.

---

thoughtful, *adj.* considerate, kind, tactful; meditative. See THOUGHT, BENEVOLENCE.

thoughtless, *adj.* rash, reckless, heedless; casual; inconsiderate, unthinking, mindless; unreasoning; careless, indifferent. See RASHNESS. *Ant.,* see CARE.

thrash, *v.t.* beat, spank, whip; flog; strike; defeat, overcome, conquer. See PUNISHMENT, SUCCESS.

thread, *n.* FILAMENT, fiber, hair; string; yarn; linen, cotton, silk, lisle, nylon, *etc.*; course, drift, train (of thought). See DIRECTION, MEANING.

threadbare, *adj.* frayed, tattered, worn(out); jaded, weary. See OLDNESS.

THREAT

Nouns—**1,** threat, menace, intimidation, commination, minacity; empty threat; denunciation, fulmination, admonition, abuse, DEFIANCE; yellow menace *or* peril; blackmail, extortion. See OPPOSITION, FUTURITY, FEAR. **2,** thunder(bolt), gathering clouds, red sky in the morning; foreboding, imminence, omen, WARNING, notice (see PREDICTION); peril, jeopardy, DANGER.

Verbs—**1,** threaten, menace, intimidate, comminate, fulminate; terrorize, frighten, alarm, hector, cow, bully, browbeat; snarl, growl, mutter, bark, thunder, bluster, brandish; defy, caution, warn; jeopardize, imperil, endanger; blackmail, extort; talk big, look daggers, shake the fist at.

2, portend, presage, augur, omen, (fore)bode, foreshadow; impend, be imminent, overhang, lower, lour, loom; prophesy, forecast (see PREDICTION).

Adjectives—threatening, menacing, intimidative, denunciatory, abusive, fulminatory, defiant, bullying; WARNING, cautionary, dangerous, perilous, jeopardous; ominous, foreboding, lowering, looming, *etc.*; baleful, baneful, thundery, dire(ful); awful, sinister, dark, black.

Antonym, see SAFETY.

---

threshold, *n.* sill, doorsill, entrance; outset, BEGINNING; limen, threshold of pain, *etc.* See EDGE. *Ant.,* see END.

thrift, *n.* thriftiness, ECONOMY, frugality, saving; providence, husbandry; vigor, growth, thriving. *Ant.,* see WASTE.

thrifty, *adj.* frugal, saving; sparing; economical; foresighted; provident. See ECONOMY. *Ant.,* see WASTE.

thrill, *n. & v.* —*n.* EXCITEMENT; tremor, vibration; sensation; tingle. *Slang,* kick, charge. —*v.* throb, tingle, shiver; stir, excite, move deeply; vibrate, tremble. See FEELING.

thriller, *n.* chiller, shocker; pulp story, dime novel, cloak-and-dagger *or* spy story; swashbuckler. *Slang,* whodunit. See BOOK, EXCITEMENT.

thrive, *v.i.* prosper; batten; succeed; grow, flourish, bloom, flower. See PROSPERITY. *Ant.,* see ADVERSITY, POVERTY.

throat, *n.* neck; gullet; gorge, maw; windpipe, throttle. See OPENING.

throb, *v.i.* beat, pulsate, vibrate, palpitate; quiver, shudder, tremble; ache, hurt. See AGITATION, PAIN.

throne, *n.* royal seat; chair; sovereignty, scepter. See AUTHORITY.

throng, *n.* MULTITUDE, crowd, mob, horde; army, host. See ASSEMBLAGE. *Ant.,* see RARITY.

throttle, *v.* choke, strangle, suffocate; silence, stifle; close. See CLOSURE, KILLING.

through, *prep. & adv.* among, via, by way of; during, throughout; by; with. See PASSAGE, TIME.

throw, *v.* pitch, toss, cast, fling, hurl, sling; propel, project, unhorse, unseat. *Slang,* stop; disconcert; confound. See PROPULSION.

thrust, *v. & n.* —*v.* push, drive, shove, propel; lunge, plunge, ram; stab, pierce; interpose, interject. —*n.* blow, jab, poke; ATTACK, sortie; dig; repartee; POWER. See IMPULSE. *Ant.,* see DEFENSE, RECOIL.

thug, *n.* cutthroat, assassin, killer; ruffian, hooligan, tough. *Colloq.,* hoodlum. *Slang,* mugger, hood, goon, yegg, torpedo, gorilla. See EVILDOER.

thunder, *v.* shout, bellow; resound, peal, boom, roar, roll, crash. See LOUDNESS.

thus, *adv.* so; consequently, hence. See CIRCUMSTANCE.

thwart, *v.t.* oppose, baffle, foil, frustrate, defeat, block, contravene. See HINDRANCE. *Ant.,* see AID.

ticket, *n.* notice, memorandum, RECORD; label; list, slate, ballot; admission ticket. *Slang,* ducat. See INDICATION.

tickle, *v.t.* excite; gladden, delight, overjoy; please; titillate; amuse, divert. See PLEASURE.

ticklish, *adj.* tickly, excitable; sensitive; unstable, touchy; delicate; critical; risky, dangerous. See EXCITEMENT, DANGER, SENSIBILITY.

tidbit, *n.* morsel, bite, snack; goody, treat, bonbon; gem, pearl, jewel; NEWS, INFORMATION, juicy bit. See FOOD, PERFECTION.

tide, *n.* flow, current, flood. See WATER.

tidings, *n.pl.* news, message, intelligence, INFORMATION. See COMMUNICATION.

tidy, *adj. & v.* —*adj.* neat, orderly, trim; prim. *Colloq.,* sizable, considerable. —*v.* arrange, put in order, straighten. See CLEANNESS, ARRANGEMENT. *Ant.,* see UNCLEANNESS, DISORDER.

tie, *n. & v.* —*n.* bond, obligation; shoelace; necktie, cravat, four-in-hand *or* bow tie; fastening, ligature; draw, tied score, dead heat; beam, post; sleeper. —*v.t.* fasten, attach, join; bind, restrict, confine; knot; equal. See CLOTHING, DUTY, JUNCTION, CONNECTION, EQUALITY. *Ant.,* see DISJUNCTION.

tier, *n.* rank, row, level, LAYER, gallery, boxes, balcony. See SUPPORT.

tie-up, *n.* halt, stoppage, blockade, impediment, snarl, [traffic] jam, impasse. See HINDRANCE. *Colloq.,* association, CONNECTION, tie-in, liaison.

tiff, *n.* temper, fit, tantrum; squabble, spat. *Colloq.,* miff. See CONTENTION.

tight, *adj.* close, compact, hermetic, impervious; snug, close-fitting; hemmed-in; strict, stringent; scarce, in short supply. See CLOSURE, NARROWNESS. *Colloq.,* stingy, parsimonious (see PARSIMONY). *Slang,* intoxicated, inebriated, loaded. See DRUNKENNESS.

tightfisted, *adj.* stingy, frugal, parsimonious, grudging, niggard(ly), miserly, moneygrubbing, avaricious. *Colloq.,* tight, cheap. See PARSIMONY.

till, *prep. & v.* —*prep.* until, up to, down to. See TIME. —*v.* cultivate, plow, farm. See AGRICULTURE.

tilt, *v. & n.* —*v.* tip, slant, incline, slope; joust. —*n.* joust, tournament; altercation, dispute; speed; slant, slope. See CONTENTION, VELOCITY, OBLIQUITY.

timber, *n.* wood, lumber; log; beam; forest, woodland, stand of timber, timberland. See MATERIALS.

timbre, *n.* resonance; tonal quality; SOUND; tone color; ring, clang. See MUSIC.

TIME

Nouns—**1**, time, duration; period, term, stage, space, span, spell, season, fourth dimension; the whole time; era, epoch, AGE; time of life; moment, instant; INSTANTANEITY, SYNCHRONISM; course, progress, flow, march, stream *or* lapse of time; Time, Father Time, ravages of time.

2, intermediate time, while, interim, interval, pendency; intervention, intermission, intermittence, interregnum, interlude; LEISURE, spare time; respite.

3, REGULARITY, periodicity, recurrence; anniversary, jubilee; diamond, golden, silver, wooden, paper, *etc.* anniversary; holiday, Christmas, Easter, Thanksgiving, New Year's Day, Independence Day, Memorial Day, Labor Day, Dominion Day, Bastille Day, Boxing Day, *etc.*

4, CHRONOMETRY; calendar, date, millennium, century, decade, year, month (January, February, *etc.*), week, fortnight; day (Sunday, Monday, *etc.*); timepiece, clock, watch; second, minute, hour; MORNING, EVENING, noon, midday, afternoon, twilight, night, midnight; season, spring, summer, fall, autumn, winter; term, semester, trimester, quarter.

Verbs—**1**, continue, last, endure, go on, remain, persist; intervene, elapse, lapse, pass, flow, advance, roll on, go by, go on; flit, fly, slip, slide *or* glide by; take time, take up time, fill time, occupy time; pass, spend, waste, while away *or* consume time; talk against time; tide over; seize an opportunity, take time by the forelock.

2, synchronize, coexist, coincide, keep pace with, concur.

3, recur, return; alternate, intermit.

Adjectives—**1**, continuing; permanent, perpetual, eternal; REGULAR, steady, periodic, intermittent; synchronous, simultaneous, coeval, contemporary, contemporaneous, coincident(al), concomitant, concurrent; elapsing, passing, aoristic; timely, untimely, punctual, fast, slow, leisurely, unhurried, early, late. See EARLINESS, LATENESS, SLOWNESS.

2, hourly, diurnal, daily, weekly, fortnightly, monthly, menstrual, yearly, annual, biennial, centennial; morning, matutinal, antemeridian; evening, vesper, crepuscular; nocturnal, nightly; vernal, estival, autumnal, wintry, brumal.

Adverbs—**1**, during, pending; during the time, during the interval; in the course of time; for the time being, day by day; in the time of; when; since times immemorial; meantime, meanwhile; in the meantime, in the interim, from day to day, from hour to hour; hourly, always; for a time, for a season; till, until, up to, yet; the whole time, all the time; all along; throughout, for good; hereupon, thereupon, whereupon; then; *anno Domini*, A.D., before Christ, B.C., once upon a time; in time, in due time, in season, in the fullness of time, some fine day.

2, regularly, periodically, punctually, synchronously, *etc.*; off and on, now and then *or* again; semi-, bi-(weekly, annual *or* annually, *etc.*); at dawn, daybreak, sunrise, sun-up, twilight, sunset, *etc.*; together, at the same time, just as, as soon as.

---

timeless, *adj.* endless, perpetual, everlasting, deathless, immortal; dateless, ageless, immemorial, prehistoric, legendary. See PERPETUITY, OLDNESS.

timely, *adj.* well-timed, seasonable, opportune; auspicious, RIGHT. See TIME.

timepiece, *n.* clock, watch, chronometer (see CHRONOMETRY).

timid, *adj.* fearful, cowardly, afraid, fainthearted, timorous; shrinking, bashful, shy, retiring, diffident; irresolute, hesitant; weak. See FEAR, MODESTY. *Ant.,* see COURAGE, RESOLUTION.

tincture, *n.* trace, vestige, touch, dash; tinge, tint, shade; soupçon. See COLOR, MIXTURE.

tine, *n.* prong, branch, point, tip; skewer, spike, bodkin, barb. See SHARPNESS.

tinge, *n.* tint, shade, COLOR, dye, stain; flavor, cast. See MIXTURE.

tingle, *v.i.* sting, prickle; thrill. See PAIN, EXCITEMENT.

tinker, *n. & v.* —*n.* handyman, jack-of-all-trades; blunderer, bungler. *Colloq.,* Mr. Fixit. —*v.* mend, repair; botch; tamper, putter. *Colloq.,* doctor; fiddle, fuss, play *or* monkey with. See RESTORATION, UNSKILL-FULNESS.

tinsel, *n.* tawdriness, gaudiness, frippery, show; baubles, gewgaws. See ORNAMENT.

tint, *n.* COLOR, tinge, hue, dye, shade; tone, cast, nuance.

tiny, *adj.* minute, miniature, small, diminutive, wee; microscopic. *Slang,* halfpint. See LITTLENESS. *Ant.,* see SIZE, GREATNESS.

tip, *v. & n.* —*v.* overturn, capsize, upset; incline, slant, tilt; reward. See INVERSION, PAYMENT. —*n.* point, END; apex, summit; clue, hint, WARN-ING, pointer; gratuity, gift, fee, perquisite, *pourboire.* See HEIGHT, GIV-ING, INFORMATION. *Ant.,* BASE; see DIRECTION.

tiptoe, *v.i.* steal, sneak, walk on tiptoes; creep, sidle. See CAUTION, SILENCE.

tirade, *n.* harangue, screed, diatribe, jeremiad; SPEECH, sermon; out-pouring, flood, spate. See LOQUACITY, DISAPPROBATION.

tire, *v.* weary, FATIGUE, bore, exhaust, jade, fag. See WEARINESS. *Ant.,* see RESTORATION.

tireless, *adj.* See UNTIRING.

tiresome, *adj.* See TEDIOUS.

tissue, *n.* gauze, fabric; web, net, mesh; membrane, cartilage, muscle; tissue paper; structure. See LAYER, FORM.

title, *n. & v.* —*n.* name; form of address (sir, madam, Doctor, *etc.*); subheading, subtitle; appellation, designation, caption; legend; epithet; honorific, title of nobility, peerage; status, degree; cognomen, surname. *Colloq.,* handle. —*v.* name, call. See NOMENCLATURE, BOOK, NOBILITY.

toady, *n.* fawner, sycophant, truckler. *Colloq.,* bootlicker. See SER-VILITY.

toast, *v.t. & n.* —*v.t.* brown; heat, warm; drink to, pledge, honor. —*n.* toasted bread, zwieback, rusk; health, pledge. See HEAT, CELEBRATION.

tobacco, *n.* smoking; leaf, Burley, latakia, Turkish, Havana, Virginia; cigar, cigarette; snuff, plug, chew. *Colloq.,* weed, Lady Nicotine.

to-do, *n., colloq.,* ado, turmoil, bother, bustle, commotion. See EX-CITEMENT.

together, *adv.* mutually, reciprocally, unitedly; coincidentally, concur-rently, simultaneously. See ACCOMPANIMENT, TIME. *Ant.,* see DISJUNC-TION.

toil, *n. & v.* —*n.* labor, drudgery; task, work; effort, exhaustion. —*v.* work, drudge, moil, labor; strive. See EXERTION. *Ant.,* see REPOSE, INACTIVITY.

toilet, *n.* toilette, prinking, makeup; powder room, washroom, bath-room, lavatory, restroom, comfort station, watercloset, W.C., cabinet; outhouse, latrine, privy; chamberpot, bidet, slop pail. *Slang,* john, head, can. See CLEANNESS.

toils, *n.pl.* snare, net, trap, mesh, web; grip, clutches. See RESTRAINT.

token, *n.* sign, symbol, emblem; feature, trait; souvenir, memento, keep-sake; badge, EVIDENCE; slug, substitute coin; earnest, INDICATION.

tolerance, *n.* toleration, allowance; MODERATION, temperance, endurance, forbearance, sufferance, laxity; clemency, leniency. See PERMISSION, FORGIVENESS. *Ant.,* see SEVERITY.

toll, *n.* TAX, impost, charge, fee. See PAYMENT.

tomb, *n.* grave, sepulcher, mausoleum, vault, catacombs. See INTER-MENT.

tomorrow, *adv.* on the morrow, the next day, henceforth, *mañana.* See FUTURITY.

tone, *n.* SOUND; quality; accent, pitch, inflection, modulation, intonation; strain, key, spirit; elasticity, resilience; tension, firmness, tonus; condi-tion; frame of mind, mood; tint, shade, hue. See COLOR.

tongs, *n.pl.* pincers, nippers, pliers, forceps. See RETENTION.

tongue, *n.* communication, SPEECH, LANGUAGE, dialect; pole; flap, projection. See SUPPORT.

tongue-tied, *adj.* silent, mute, inarticulate, STAMMERING; bashful, shy.

tonic, *adj.* & *n.* —*adj.* invigorating, bracing, refreshing; voiced, sonant; stressed, accented. See HEALTH, SOUND. —*n.* medicine, stimulant; key, keynote. See MUSIC, REMEDY.

too, *adv.* also, likewise; over; additionally, excessively. See ADDITION, REPETITION.

tool, *n.* INSTRUMENT, implement, utensil, device, machine; cat's-paw, dupe; henchman; intermediary. See AID.

tooth, *n.* fang, tusk; canine, incisor, molar, cuspid, bicuspid; eyetooth; tine; cog; TASTE, fondness. *Colloq.*, grinder, chopper. See SHARPNESS.

toothsome, *adj.* toothy, palatable, appetizing; delicious, luscious, dainty, delectable. See TASTE.

top, *n.* & *v.* —*n.* crown, head; acme, summit, pinnacle; pick, élite; lid, cover. —*v.* crown, cap; prune, excel, dominate. See HEIGHT, SUPERIORITY, CLOSURE, COVERING. *Ant.*, see SUPPORT, LOWNESS, INFERIORITY.

topic, *n.* subject, theme, text, thesis, subject-matter; item, question; BUSINESS, point, point of argument; proposition, statement. See INQUIRY.

topple, *v.* —*v.i.* fall over *or* down, tumble, somersault, pitch, plunge; fail, collapse, go bankrupt. *Slang,* fold. —*v.t.* push, trip, knock over *or* down; overturn, upset; overthrow, subvert, defeat, smash. See DESCENT, DESTRUCTION, FAILURE.

torch, *n.* LIGHT, torchlight, brand; flambeau; flashlight. *Slang,* firebug, arsonist. See HEAT, LIGHT.

torment, *n.* & *v.* —*n.* languish, distress; torture, agony, PAIN. —*v.t.* torture, distress, agonize, rack, afflict. *Ant.,* see PLEASURE.

tornado, *n.* WIND, windstorm, twister, cyclone, typhoon. See VIOLENCE.

torpid, *adj.* dormant, sleepy; numb; inert, unmoving, still, stagnant; dull, stupid, apathetic, slothful, sluggish, lethargic; listless. See INACTIVITY. *Ant.,* see ACTIVITY, EXERTION.

torrent, *n.* cascade, deluge, downpour; current, rapids; outburst, outbreak, spurt, spate, surge, flood, Niagara. See WATER, VIOLENCE, VELOCITY.

torrid, *adj.* hot, burning, arid, parched, sizzling, scorching; equatorial, tropical. See HEAT. *Ant.,* see COLD.

tortuous, *adj.* spiral, snaky, sinuous, serpentine. See CIRCUITY, CONVOLUTION.

torture, *n.* & *v.* —*n.* PAIN, excruciation, agony, torment; martyrdom, crucifixion; anguish; cruelty. —*v.t.* punish; torment, rack, agonize, martyr; garble, distort, twist, misrepresent. See PUNISHMENT, DISTORTION.

toss, *v.* fling, buffet; agitate, stir; throw, cast; tumble, sway; pitch, roll. See AGITATION, PROPULSION, MOTION.

total, *adj., n. & v.* —*adj.* complete, entire, utter, absolute, WHOLE. —*n.* sum, amount, aggregate, quantity, WHOLE. —*v.t.* add, reckon, tot up; amount to; constitute. See NUMBER, ADDITION.

totter, *v.* shake, tremble, rock, reel, waver; falter, stumble, stagger. See OSCILLATION.

TOUCH

Nouns—**1,** touch, tact(us), contact, impact, taction; tactility, palpability, tangibility, tangency; FEELING, sensation, perception; manipulation, massage; stroke, tap, nudge, feel, brush, graze, glance, tickle, caress, kiss, osculation, lick, pat, rap, hit, handclasp. *Slang,* soft touch.

2, hand, finger, palm, paw, toe; tongue; feeler, antenna, flipper, vibrissa, palp(us), barbel.

3, see TASTE, COMMUNICATION, CORRESPONDENCE, SKILL, SENSIBILITY.

Verbs—**1,** touch, feel, contact, handle, finger, thumb, palm, paw, toe; caress, kiss, lick, lap, pat, tap; fumble, grope, twiddle; brush, graze, glance, skim; palpate, manipulate, wield, massage, rub, knead; hit, strike, smite, jab (see IMPULSE).

2, border on, be contiguous to, impinge, meet, reach, come to, abut, adjoin, neighbor, juxtapose. See NEARNESS.

3, concern, regard, relate to, pertain to, affect, bear upon; touch upon, allude to, refer to, speak of, deal with, make reference to. See RELATION.

4, touch up, delineate lightly, refine, improve, correct (see IMPROVEMENT).

5, move, stir, melt, soften, mollify, arouse PITY. See SENSIBILITY.

Adjectives—touching, FEELING, tactual, tactile; tangible, touchable, palpable; lambent, licking; adjacent, bordering, tangent, abutting, neighboring, contiguous; affecting, moving, melting, distressing, heartrending, pitiable, tender, pathetic, impressive.

---

tough, *adj.* strong, firm; stiff, resilient; vigorous, robust, hardy; stubborn, intractable. *Colloq.*, vicious, rowdy, unruly; difficult, troublesome. See HARDNESS.

tour, *n.* trip, journey, expedition, excursion, junket, jaunt; turn, shift (tour of duty). See TRAVEL.

tourist, *n.* traveler, voyager, sightseer; ugly American. See TRAVEL.

tournament, *n.* tourney, jousting, contest; match. See CONTENTION.

tousled, *adj.* disheveled, untidy, unkempt, tangled, snarly. See DISORDER.

tow, *v.t.* draw, pull, drag, haul; take in tow. See ATTRACTION.

tower, *n. & v.* —*n.* fortress, castle; skyscraper; campanile, belfry, spire. —*v.i.* rise, soar; loom, transcend. See DEFENSE, ASCENT, HEIGHT. *Ant.*, see LOWNESS.

town, *n.* hamlet, burgh, village, city. See ABODE.

toxic, *adj.* poisonous, venomous, virulent, noxious. See DANGER, DISEASE.

toy, *n. & v.* —*n.* plaything, trinket, trifle; doll, puppet. —*v.* trifle *or* play (with); fiddle, dally. See AMUSEMENT, UNIMPORTANCE.

trace, *v. & n.* —*v.* draw, sketch, delineate, copy; track, trail, follow, scent, detect; deduce. See INQUIRY, REPRESENTATION. —*n.* course, path; track, footprint, trail; hint, shade, vestige. See INDICATION, RECORD, LITTLENESS.

track, *v. & n.* —*v.t.* trail, follow, scent; traverse. —*n.* trace, trail, wake; vestige; footprints, spoor, scent; path, course; succession; rails; race track, course, turf, cinders; footracing. See INDICATION, CONTENTION.

tract, *n.* expanse, area, REGION; composition, dissertation, treatise. See WRITING.

tractable, *adj.* docile, well-behaved, manageable, adaptable, yielding; malleable, plastic. See FACILITY, SOFTNESS. *Ant.*, see DIFFICULTY, HARDNESS.

TRACTION

Nouns—traction; drawing, dragging, *etc.* (see *Verbs*); draft, draw, drag, pull, haul, tow, tug, jerk, twitch; suction, grip, FRICTION; CONTRACTION, tension, ATTRACTION; tractor.

Verbs—draw, drag, draggle, haul, pull, tow, trail, lug, tug, take in tow; jerk, twitch, heave, wrench, yank.

Adjectives—tractional, tractive; tractile; attractive.

Antonym, see PROPULSION, REPULSION.

---

trade, *n. & v.* —*n.* BUSINESS; profession, occupation; livelihood; craft; merchandising; commerce, traffic, barter; clientele; purchase and sale, deal. —*v.t.* barter, buy and sell, bargain. See SALE.

trademark, *n.* brand [name], cachet; logo(type), colophon, label. See IDENTITY.

tradition, *n.* belief, practice, usage, custom, culture, folklore. See OLDNESS.

traduce, *v.* slander, calumniate, vilify, defame, asperse, malign, disparage. See DETRACTION.

traffic, *n. & v.* —*n.* trade, barter, commerce, BUSINESS; vehicular movement, transportation; dealings, familiarity, intercourse, fraternization. —*v.* trade, deal, have dealings.

tragedy, *n.* DRAMA; disaster, calamity, catastrophe; crushing blow; DEATH.

tragic, *adj.* dramatic, melodramatic; fatal, dire, disastrous. See DRAMA, DEATH.

trail, *n. & v.* —*n.* track, spoor, footprints; tire, *etc.,* tracks; vestige, scent; path, wake; train. —*v.* TRACK, scent; hang; lag, dawdle, crawl, straggle. See INDICATION. *Ant.,* see PRIORITY.

train, *n. & v.* —*n.* retinue, suite, entourage, procession, cortège; order, SEQUENCE, sequel, succession; railroad cars. —*v.t.* instruct, discipline, drill; educate. See VEHICLE, TEACHING.

trait, *n.* quality, characteristic, peculiarity, idiosyncrasy; custom; feature. See INDICATION, UNCONFORMITY.

traitor, *n.* betrayer; turncoat, renegade; deserter, conspirator; informer; Judas, fifth columnist, quisling. See EVILDOER.

trajectory, *n.* orbit, curve, arc, parabola; circuit, CIRCUITY, COURSE; PASSAGE.

trammel, *n. & v.* —*n.* net; tether, manacle, chain, fetter; impediment, HINDRANCE: CONFINEMENT, RESTRAINT, LIMIT. —*v.t.* entangle, catch, trap; bind, hobble, tether, shackle, bridle, manacle, chain; restrain, imprison; impede, hinder.

tramp, *n. & v.* —*n.* traveler, vagabond, hobo, vagrant, bum, panhandler; jaunt, journey, hike, freighter; tread, walk, stroll. —*v.i.* walk, tread, step, plod, trudge, travel, hike; trample, stamp. See TRAVEL.

trample, *v.t.* crush, tread, grind, squash, stamp on. See DESTRUCTION.

trance, *n.* daze, stupor; abstraction, ecstasy; somnambulism, sleepwalking; coma, catalepsy; hypnosis. See INSENSIBILITY.

tranquil, *adj.* calm, quiet, undisturbed, composed, serene, placid, peaceful. See MODERATION, REPOSE. *Ant.,* see EXCITEMENT, AGITATION.

tranquilize, *v.* pacify, soothe, appease; calm, still. See PACIFICATION.

transact, *v.* negotiate, deal; CONDUCT, bring about; do; perform, execute.

transaction, *n.* deal, proceeding, ACTION, affair; CONDUCT, act, deed. See BUSINESS.

transcend, *v.* exceed, overpass, surpass, excel, outstrip, outdo. See SUPERIORITY. *Ant.,* see INFERIORITY.

transcribe, *v.* COPY, write, reproduce, engross; decode, decipher.

TRANSFER

Nouns—**1,** transfer, transference, transmission, transmittal, transmittance, transfusion, transformation, permutation, sublimation; DISPLACEMENT, dislodgment; metastasis; shift, CHANGE, removing, removal, remotion, relegation, deportation, extradition; convection, conduction; contagion, infection.

2, conveyance, assignment, assignation, alienation; enfeoffment, cession, grant, deed, quitclaim, limitation; conveyancing, bargain and sale, lease and release; exchange, INTERCHANGE, BARTER, SUBSTITUTION, delegation; succession, accession, REVERSION; demise, devise, bequest, legacy, gift.

Verbs—transfer, convey, assign, alienate; grant, cede, deed, confer (see GIVING), consign, enfeoff, sequester; sell, rent, let, lease, charter, (see SALE); make over, hand down, pass (on *or* down), transmit, negotiate, change hands; demise, devise, bequeath, will, leave, give; devolve, succeed, come into possession, acquire (see ACQUISITION); disinherit, dispossess; substitute (see SUBSTITUTION).

Adjectives—transferable, transmittible, assignable, conveyable; contagious, catching, infectious, communicable; metathetic(al), metastatic.

Antonym, see POSSESSION.

transformation, *n.* CHANGE, alteration, transmutation; conversion, transfiguration; metamorphosis; wig, switch.

transfuse, *v.t.* set into, insert, infuse, instill; pour, inject. See TRANSFER.

transgression, *n.* trespass, sin, DISOBEDIENCE, violation, fault, offense, crime, misdeed, slip, misdemeanor; infraction, infringement. See DEVIATION, IMPROBITY, ILLEGALITY. *Ant.,* see VIRTUE.

TRANSIENTNESS

Nouns—transientness, transience, evanescence, impermanence, fugacity, mortality, span; nine days' wonder, bubble, ephemerality; spurt; temporary arrangement, interregnum; brevity, SHORTNESS; VELOCITY, suddenness (see INSTANTANEITY); CHANGEABLENESS.

Verbs—be transient, flit, pass away, fly, gallop, vanish, evanesce, fade, evaporate; blow over.

Adjectives—transient, transitory, transitive; passing, evanescent, volatile, fleeting; flying; fugacious, fugitive; shifting, slippery; spasmodic; temporal, temporary; provisional, provisory; cursory, short-lived, meteoric, ephemeral, deciduous; perishable, mortal, precarious; impermanent; brief, quick, extemporaneous, summary; sudden, momentary, short and sweet.

Adverbs—temporarily, *pro tempore*; for the moment, for a time; awhile, *en passant*, briefly.

Antonym, see DURABILITY.

transit, *n.* PASSAGE; CHANGE, transition; conveyance, transportation.

transition, *n.* PASSAGE, passing; CHANGE, development, flux, modulation; break, graduation, rise, fall; metastasis, metabasis.

translate, *n.* transfer, decipher, decode, render; construe, (re)interpret; transform, transmute, CHANGE.

translucent, *adj.* lucid, clear, diaphanous, hyalescent, semiopaque, frosty. See TRANSPARENCY, LIGHT.

transmission, *n.* conveyance, transference, sending, communication, conductance; gearshift, gears, torque converter. See PASSAGE, COMMUNICATION.

transmit, *v.* send, TRANSFER, convey, forward, post, mail, wire, telegraph; impart, hand down; admit, conduct; broadcast, COMMUNICATE. See INFORMATION.

TRANSPARENCY

Nouns—**1,** transparency, translucency, transpicuity, diaphaneity, lucidity, pellucidity, limpidity, clearness, sheerness, thinness. See INVISIBILITY. **2,** glass, crystal, lucite, cellophane, pane, prism, water, lymph, gauze. **3,** see COHERENCE, SIMPLENESS.

Adjectives—transparent, translucent, transpicuous, diaphanous, lucid, pellucid, lucent, limpid; glassy, hyaline, hyaloid, vitreous, crystal(line), clear as crystal, crystal-clear; gauzy, flimsy, see-through, thin, sheer, gossamer; serene, unclouded.

Antonym, see OPACITY.

transpire, *v.* transude, exhale, pass through, ooze *or* leak out, sweat, perspire, come to light, issue, unfold, crop up; occur, happen, come to pass, take place. See PASSAGE, DISCLOSURE, OCCURRENCE.

transplant, *v.t.* replant, repot, graft; relocate, resettle; colonize. See TRANSPORTATION, DISPLACEMENT.

transport, *n. & v.* —*n.* transformation, conveyance; movement; *pl.* emotion, ecstasy, rapture; troopship; airplane, CARRIER. —*v.* convey, carry, move, ship; transfer; delight, overjoy. See TRANSPORTATION, PLEASURE.

TRANSPORTATION

Nouns—**1,** transportation, transport, transfer, transference, transmission, conveyance; movement, PASSAGE, transit, removal, delivery; carriage, portage, cartage, *etc.*, shipment, postage, express, messenger service; mass *or* public transportation. See TRAVEL, COMMUNICATION.

2, cart, wagon, carriage, coach, stage, stagecoach; automobile, motorcar, (omni)bus, taxicab, taxi, cab, truck, van; train, streetcar, subway, monorail; airplane, SHIP, ferry, troopship, transport. See VEHICLE.

3, shipment, traffic, freight, haul, cargo, lading, goods, baggage, luggage.

Verbs—transport, convey, transmit, transfer, remove, move; carry, bear, cart, haul, truck, drive, SHIP, transship, row, float, ferry; conduct, convoy, bring, take, pull, lug, pack, reach, run, smuggle; freight, express, railroad, forward, deliver, TRAVEL. See PASSAGE.

---

transpose, *v.* exchange, interchange, reverse, rearrange, invert; substitute, transliterate; CHANGE. See INVERSION, MUSIC.

transverse, *adj.* crossing, cross, athwart, oblique. See OBLIQUITY.

trap, *n. & v.* —*n.* pitfall, snare, net, deadfall; AMBUSH; carriage; trapdoor; (*pl.*) equipment, luggage. —*v.* catch, entrap, snare, net, enmesh, fool, AMBUSH. See DECEPTION, CONCEALMENT, VEHICLE.

trappings, *n.pl.* caparison, regalia, habiliments, outfit, rigging, panoply, vestments, decorations; indications, earmarks. See CLOTHING, INDICATION.

trash, *n.* rubbish, garbage, refuse, offal, litter, debris; junk, scrap, WASTE.

travail, *n.* labor, work, drudgery, toil; agony, PAIN. See EXERTION.

TRAVEL

Nouns—**1,** travel; traveling, wayfaring, itineracy, tourism; journey, excursion, expedition, tour, trip, crossing, cruise, grand tour, circuit; procession, caravan; discursion; pilgrimage; ambulation; sleepwalking, somnambulism. *Colloq.*, globe-trotting. See NAVIGATION, PASSAGE.

2, walk, promenade, stroll, saunter, tramp, ramble, jog-trot, turn, perambulation, pedestrianism; driving, riding, posting, motoring, touring; outing, ride, drive, airing, jaunt. *Colloq.*, constitutional, hike, spin. See VEHICLE.

3, roving, vagrancy, nomadism; vagabondism, vagabondage; gadding; flitting; migration, emigration, immigration, intermigration.

4, itinerary, course, route, road, path; bypass, detour, loop; handbook, road map; Baedeker, Michelin, guidebook.

5, traveler, wayfarer, voyager, itinerant, passenger, tourist, excursionist; explorer, adventurer, mountaineer, peregrinator, wanderer, rover, straggler, rambler; bird of passage; gadabout, vagrant, tramp, vagabond, nomad, Bohemian, gypsy, Arab, Wandering Jew, Hadji, pilgrim, palmer; peripatetic; somnambulist; emigrant, fugitive, refugee; runner, courier; pedestrian, walker, cyclist, passenger; rider, horseman, equestrian, jockey; driver, coachman, whip, charioteer, postilion, postboy; cabdriver; engineer; chauffeur.

Verbs—**1,** travel, journey, course; take a journey; take a walk, go for a walk, have a run; take the air; flit, take wing; migrate, emigrate, immigrate; rove, prowl, roam, range, patrol, pace up and down, traverse; perambulate, circumambulate; nomadize, wander, ramble, stroll, saunter, go one's rounds, gad, gad about.

2, walk, march, step, tread, pace, plod, wend; promenade, trudge, tramp; stalk, stride, strut, foot it, bowl along, toddle; paddle; tread a path; jog on, shuffle on; bend one's steps; make one's way, find one's way, wend one's way, pick *or* thread one's way, plow one's way; slide, glide, skim, skate; march in procession; go to, repair to, hie oneself to, betake oneself to. *Colloq.*, hike, hitchhike, thumb [a ride], hotfoot, stump. *Slang*, stir one's stumps.

3, ride, take horse, drive, trot, amble, canter, prance, gallop; ride, drive, fly; go by car, train, rail *or* air. *Colloq.*, joyride. *Slang*, burn up the road.

Adjectives—traveling, ambulatory, itinerant, peripatetic, roving, rambling, gadding, discursive, vagrant, migratory, nomadic; footloose; locomotive, automotive; wayfaring; travel-stained.

Adverbs—on foot, on horseback, on shanks' mare; abroad; en route.

Antonym, see STABILITY.

---

traverse, *v.* cross, ford, range, patrol. See TRAVEL.

travesty, *n.* caricature, burlesque, farce, parody, lampoon; fiasco, FAILURE; ABSURDITY. *Colloq.*, takeoff. *Slang*, spoof. See RIDICULE.

trawl, *n. & v.* —*n.* net, dragnet, seine. See RECEPTACLE. —*v.* beam *or* otter trawl, fish, net, haul, drag, seine. See PURSUIT.

tray, *n.* platter, salver, server, trencher; galley. See RECEPTACLE, CARRIER.

treachery, *n.* treason, perfidy, faithlessness, disloyalty, infidelity, falsity, falseness. See IMPROBITY. *Ant.*, see PROBITY.

tread, *v.* walk, step, pace; trample, crush; stamp, tramp; DANCE. See TRAVEL.

treason, *n.* betrayal, disloyalty, faithlessness, sedition, treachery. See IMPROBITY.

treasure, *n. & v.* —*n.* hoard, STORE; wealth, riches. —*v.* value, prize, cherish, appreciate; remember. See MONEY, MEMORY, LOVE. *Ant.*, see HATE.

treasurer, *n.* bursar, purser; financier, banker, cashier, teller; receiver; steward, trustee; paymaster.

treasury, *n.* bank, exchequer; depository, vault, safe, safe-deposit box; till, strongbox, cash register; coffer, chest; purse, wallet, handbag, pocketbook. See RECEPTACLE, STORE, MONEY.

treat, *v.* negotiate, bargain, deal, parley; entertain, pay for; deal with, discuss, teach; dose, attend, doctor. See AGREEMENT, REMEDY, PLEASURE.

treatise, *n.* BOOK, textbook; exposition, discussion, composition, commentary, tract, monograph, dissertation.

treaty, *n.* COMPACT, pact, covenant, concordat, entente, AGREEMENT.

tree, *n.* plant, sapling, scrub, shrub, bush; timber; whiffletree; stake; gibbet, gallows; family tree, pedigree, lineage. See VEGETABLE, PUNISHMENT, ANCESTRY.

trek, *v. & n.* —*v.i.* walk, hike, TRAVEL, tramp, trudge. —*n.* journey, hike, migration, expedition, PASSAGE.

trellis, *n.* lattice, grill(e); network, screen, espalier, grid; arbor, bower, pergola, gazebo. See CROSSING, SUPPORT, INCLOSURE.

tremble, *v.* shake, shiver; vibrate, totter, quake, quaver; shudder, pulsate. See FEAR, OSCILLATION. *Ant.*, see STABILITY.

tremendous, *adj.* stupendous, colossal, huge; extraordinary. See SIZE. *Ant.*, see LITTLENESS.

tremolo, *n.* tremolando; TRILL, twitter, warble, crack. See SOUND, OSCILLATION.

tremor, *n.* trembling, shivering, shaking, quivering, vibration. See FEAR, OSCILLATION, AGITATION.

trench, *n.* ditch, fosse, dugout; FURROW. See DEFENSE.

trenchant, *adj.* cutting, incisive, penetrating; clearcut, keen, sharp, biting, crisp; energetic. See POWER. *Ant.*, FEEBLE.

trend, *n.* DIRECTION, course, TENDENCY, inclination, drift, tide.

trepidation, *n.* quaking, trembling; alarm, FEAR, AGITATION, perturbation, dread, dismay. *Ant.*, see COURAGE.

trespass, *v.* sin, offend, transgress; encroach, infringe, intrude, invade. See IMPROBITY. *Ant.*, see VIRTUE.

tress, *n.* strand, curl, ringlet, lock, cowlick; (*pl.*) hair. See ROUGHNESS.

trial, *n.* test, EXPERIMENT; hearing, ordeal; cross, tribulation, affliction; effort, attempt. See ADVERSITY, INQUIRY, LAWSUIT.

triangle, *n.* trigon, delta, pyramid, triquetra; gore, gusset; triad, trio, threesome; the eternal triangle. See ANGULARITY, NUMERATION.

tribe, *n.* race, people, sect, group; clan, nation, society; lineage, family stock. See RELATION, ASSEMBLAGE.

tribulation, *n.* sorrow, woe; CARE, trouble, ordeal. See PAIN, PUNISHMENT.

tribunal, *n.* court; board, forum; bench, judicatory; court of justice *or* law; court of arbitration; inquisition; seat of judgment *or* justice; bar, bar of justice; drumhead, court-martial. *Slang,* kangaroo court. See JUDGE, JUSTICE.

tributary, *n. & adj.* —*n.* stream, source, affluent; prayer of tribute. —*adj.* subject, subordinate; contributory. See WATER, SUBJECTION.

tribute, *n.* PAYMENT, tax, contribution; gift, offering, service; praise, encomium, compliment. See GIVING.

trick, *n.* artifice, stratagem, craft; illusion, wile, ruse, subterfuge, fraud, imposture, DECEPTION; tour, shift, turn; trait, idiosyncrasy, peculiarity. See DECEPTION, SKILL, UNCONFORMITY.

trickle, *v.i.* drip, dribble, seep. See WATER.

tricky, *adj.* ticklish, intricate; deceitful, evasive, artful, shifty. See DECEPTION, DIFFICULTY. *Ant.,* see INNOCENCE, FACILITY.

trifle, *n. & v.* —*n.* bagatelle, nothing, triviality; gewgaw, trinket, knick-knack, gimcrack; particle, bit, morsel, trace. See LITTLENESS, UNIMPORTANCE. —*v.i.* toy, play, dally, fool. See NEGLECT.

trill, *n & v.* —*n.* vibration, tremor, quaver, tremolo, vibrato. —*v.* sing; quaver; warble. See MUSIC.

trim, *adj. & v.* —*adj.* neat, well-ordered, compact, tidy. —*v.* order, tidy, adjust, dress, arrange; decorate, ORNAMENT, adorn; defeat; cheat; balance, equalize; cut, lop, shear, prune, barber. See ARRANGEMENT, CLEANNESS, SHORTNESS.

trinket, *n.* TOY, plaything, bauble, gewgaw. See ORNAMENT.

trip, *n. & v.* —*n.* journey, excursion, voyage. —*v.* skip; stumble; offend, err; obstruct, halt. See ERROR, LEAP, HINDRANCE.

trite, *adj.* commonplace, ordinary; hackneyed, stale, old; boring, DULL; banal. *Slang,* corny, Mickey Mouse. See WEARINESS.

triumph, *n. & v.* —*n.* joy, exultation, celebration; victory, conquest; accomplishment. —*v.i.* win, conquer, succeed; celebrate, rejoice. See REJOICING, SUCCESS. *Ant.,* see LAMENTATION, FAILURE.

trivial, *adj.* insignificant, unimportant, trifling, picayune, paltry; mean, piddling, small, petty. See UNIMPORTANCE. *Ant.,* see IMPORTANCE.

trollop, *n.* harlot, whore (see PROSTITUTE); slut, hussy, baggage.

troop, *n. & v.* —*n.* group, number, party, company, crowd, ASSEMBLAGE. —*v.i.* march, tramp, go. See PROGRESSION.

trophy, *n.* medal, prize, award, cup, loving cup; statuette; palm, laurel, garland of bays; crown, wreath, insignia, feather in one's cap, honor, decoration, garland. *Colloq.,* Oscar, Emmy, Edgar, Obie, Tony, Grammy. See PAYMENT, REPUTE, APPROBATION.

tropical, *adj.* torrid, hot, fiery; equatorial. See HEAT.

trot, *v.i.* run, jog, lope; hasten. See MOTION.

troubadour, *n.* trouvere, poet, bard, minstrel, jongleur, meistersinger, minnesinger, balladeer, street singer; laureate; serenader. See MUSICIAN, POETRY.

trouble, *n. & v.* —*n.* affliction, distress, misfortune, ADVERSITY, calamity; disorder, unrest; DIFFICULTY; pains, exertion, effort; anxiety, perturbation, sorrow, worry. —*v.* disturb, disquiet, perturb; annoy, molest, harass, agitate; worry, distress, grieve; afflict, ail, plague; inconvenience. See AGITATION, PAIN.

troublesome, *adj.* disturbing, annoying, distressing; vexatious, burdensome, grievous, worrisome; DIFFICULT. See PAIN. *Ant.,* see PLEASURE, FACILITY.

trough, *n.* manger, hutch, bin; trench, ditch, FURROW. See RECEPTACLE.

trounce, *v.* thrash, beat, flog. See PUNISHMENT.

troupe, *n.* troop, band, group, party, company; *dramatis personae.* See DRAMA.

trousers, *n.* breeches, pantaloons, pants; jeans, slacks, Levis. See CLOTHING.

truant, *n.* shirker, absentee, deserter. See ABSENCE. *Ant.,* see PRESENCE.

truce, *n.* armistice, peace; respite; delay; cessation, lull. See PACIFICATION.

truck, *n.* VEHICLE; lorry, van, pick-up, dump, panel, rack; six-wheeler, half-track; cart, wagon, dray; barrow, dolly.

truculent, *adj.* fierce, savage, deadly; bestial; vitriolic, scathing, mean. *Colloq.,* with a chip on one's shoulder. See IRASCIBILITY, MALEVOLENCE.

trudge, *v.* march, slog, tramp, walk, plod. See SLOWNESS. *Ant.,* see VELOCITY.

true, *adj.* faithful, loyal, constant, sincere; certain, correct, accurate; truthful; actual, genuine; legitimate, rightful; real, straight, undeviating. See PROBITY, TRUTH. *Ant.,* see FALSEHOOD, DEVIATION, ERROR.

truism, *n.* See TRUTH, MAXIM.

trumpet, *n. & v.* —*n.* cornet, bugle, horn; ear trumpet. See MUSICAL INSTRUMENT. —*v.* bellow, roar; blow, toot, blare; proclaim. See PUBLICATION, LOUDNESS.

truncate, *v.* cut (off *or* down), clip, snip, lop, chop off; abridge, reduce, shorten, curtail, decrease. See SHORTNESS, DEDUCTION.

trundle, *v.* roll; wheel; revolve, rotate. See ROTATION.

trunk, *n.* stem, bole; body, torso; proboscis, snout; chest, box; circuit. See RECEPTACLE, SUPPORT.

truss, *v. & n.* —*v.t.* gird(le), belt; tie, bind *or* do up; lace, button, strap, buckle; skewer, sew, stitch; SUPPORT, strengthen bandage. —*n.* bundle, bale; holder, fastening; supporter, belt. See CLOSURE, SUPPORT.

trust, *n. & v.* —*n.* faith, reliance, confidence, credence, BELIEF; hope, expectation, anticipation; office, charge, task, duty, custody, keeping; CREDIT; cartel, monopoly, association. —*v.* rely, depend, count; commit, entrust, consign; believe, hope, expect; commission; give credit to. See SAFETY. *Ant.,* see DOUBT.

trustee, *n.* guardian, fiduciary, overseer, supervisor. See AGENCY.

trustworthy, *adj.* reliable, dependable, faithful, trusty, responsible, credible, believable; constant, true, loyal. See PROBITY, BELIEF. *Ant.,* see IMPROBITY, DISBELIEF.

TRUTH

Nouns—**1,** truth, fact, reality; verity, gospel, authenticity; plain, unvarnished, sober *or* naked truth; the Gospel truth; the truth, the whole truth and nothing but the truth. *Slang,* the [real] McCoy, the goods.
2, truthfulness, VERACITY; accuracy, exactitude; exactness, preciseness, precision.

Verbs—**1,** be true, be the case; stand the test; hold good, hold true, have the true ring; render true, prove true, substantiate (see EVIDENCE); get at the truth (see DISCOVERY). *Colloq.,* hold water.
3, be truthful; speak *or* tell the truth; not lie; speak one's mind; make a clean breast (see DISCLOSURE); cross one's heart.

Adjectives—**1,** true, factual, real, actual, existing; veritable, certain (see CERTAINTY); unimpeachable; unrefuted, unconfuted; genuine, authentic, legitimate; orthodox; pure, sound, sterling, unadulterated, unvarnished, uncolored; well-grounded, well-founded; solid, substantial, tangible, valid; undistorted, undisguised; unaffected, unexaggerated, unromantic, unflattering. *Colloq.,* all wool and a yard wide.
2, exact, accurate, definite, precise, well-defined, just, right, correct, strict; literal; undisguised; faithful, constant, unerring.
3, truthful, veracious; sincere, candid, frank, open, straightforward, aboveboard; honest, trustworthy, reliable, dependable; pure, guileless, bona fide, true blue; scrupulous, conscientious (see PROBITY).

Adverbs—**1,** truly, verily, indeed, really, in reality; with truth, certainly, actually; exactly, verbatim, word for word, literally, *sic,* to the letter, chapter and verse, to an inch; to a nicety, to a hair, to a turn, to a T;

neither more nor less; in every respect, in all respects; at any rate, at all events; strictly speaking.

2, truthfully, *etc.*; from the bottom of one's heart; honor bright.

Antonym, see ERROR, FALSEHOOD.

try, *v.* ESSAY, endeavor, attempt; test, examine, assay, EXPERIMENT; refine, purify; afflict, beset; strain, tax; judge, hear. See CLEANNESS, PAIN, LAWSUIT.

trying, *adj.* DULL, wearisome, boring; annoying, bothersome, galling, irritating. See WEARINESS.

tryout, *n.* trial; audition, hearing; test, dry run; EXPERIMENT.

tryst, *n.* assignation, meeting, appointment, rendezvous. See SOCIALITY.

tub, *n.* pot, vat, cauldron; washtub, bathtub. See RECEPTACLE. *Slang,* (old *or* slow) ship; tramp, freighter.

tube, *n.* pipe, hose, conduit; tunnel, subway. See PASSAGE.

tuck, *n.* FOLD, pleat, lap.

tuft, *n.* cluster, clump, wisp, bunch, brush; tussock; fetlock, topknot, crest. See ROUGHNESS.

tug, *v.* pull, strain, drag, haul; toil, labor, strive, drudge; tow. See EXERTION. *Ant.,* see PROPULSION.

tuition, *n.* tutelage, training, coaching, education; fees, cost, charge, bill. See TEACHING, LEARNING, PRICE.

tumble, *v.* fall, roll; LEAP, spring; throw, overturn, disarrange, dishevel, tousle. See DESCENT, PROPULSION, DISORDER.

tumbler, *n.* glass, vessel, goblet; acrobat, gymnast, juggler. See RECEPTACLE, DRAMA, SKILL.

tumid, *adj.* swollen, distended, enlarged; protuberant, bulging; bombastic, pompous, inflated; teeming, bursting. See INCREASE, CONVEXITY.

tumor, *n.* tumefaction, swelling, wen, cyst, tubercle, GROWTH; neoplasm, sarcoma, cancer, carcinoma. See EXPANSION, CONVEXITY, DISEASE.

tumult, *n.* commotion, AGITATION, turbulence, DISORDER. *Ant.,* see INACTIVITY.

tune, *n. & v.* —*n.* melody, air; harmony, concord. —*v.* modulate, adjust, attune; harmonize. See MUSIC.

tunnel, *n.* passageway; burrow; crosscut; subway, tube. See OPENING, PASSAGE.

turbid, *adj.* roiled, muddy, cloudy, clouded; muddled. See DISORDER, CLOUDINESS.

turbine, *n.* rotator, rotor, rotary wheel; propeller, turboprop *or* -jet. See PROPULSION, ROTATION, MEANS.

turbulence, *n.* DISORDER, VIOLENCE, unrest, disturbance, EXCITEMENT. *Ant.,* see INACTIVITY, MODERATION.

turf, *n.* sod, sward; peat; racetrack. See ARENA, LAND.

turgid, *adj.* distended, swollen, tumid, inflated, bloated; diffuse, pompous, ostentatious, high-flown, bombastic. See INCREASE, LOQUACITY, ORNAMENT.

turmoil, *n.* confusion, tumult, turbulence, disturbance, AGITATION, commotion; DISORDER. *Ant.,* see INACTIVITY.

turn, *n. & v.* —*n.* ROTATION, REVOLUTION; twirl, twist; deflection, diversion; coil, CONVOLUTION; CHANGE; crisis; aptitude, ability, SKILL; act, skit; spell, shift, tour, trick. —*v.* revolve, rotate, pivot; reel, rebel, retaliate; shape, round, finish; CHANGE, move; invert, reverse; upset, derange; deflect, divert, veer, shift; pervert, prejudice, repel; avert; curdle, ferment, SOUR. See INVERSION, ROTATION.

turncoat, *n.* renegade, deserter, traitor; apostate, recreant. See EVILDOER.

turnpike, *n.* tollroad, pike, throughway, thruway, skyway. See PASSAGE.

turpitude, *n.* depravity, baseness, wickedness, IMPROBITY. *Ant.,* see PROBITY.

turret, *n.* tower, gazebo, belvedere, cupola. See HEIGHT.

tutor, *n.* teacher, instructor, coach; guardian. See TEACHING.

tuxedo, *n.* dinner jacket, dress suit, smoking jacket. *Colloq.*, black tie. *Slang*, tux, tuck, monkey suit, soup-and-fish. See CLOTHING.

twaddle, *n.* gabble, nonsense, fustian. See ABSURDITY. *Ant.*, see MEANING.

twice, *adv.* doubly, twofold. See NUMBER.

twig, *n.* shoot, branch, tendril, slip, scion. See VEGETABLE.

twilight, *n.* dusk, gloaming, nightfall; shade, shadow. See TIME.

twin, *adj.* double, twofold; fraternal, identical; like. See SIMILARITY, RELATION.

twine, *n.* cord, string, line. See FILAMENT, CONNECTION.

twinge, *n.* pinch, throb (see SPASM); qualm, DOUBT.

twinkle, *v.* blink, wink; scintillate, sparkle, shine. See LIGHT.

twirl, *v.* twist, spin, rotate, turn, whirl. See CONVOLUTION, ROTATION.

twist, *v.* wind, wreathe, twine, interlace; coil; wrench, contort; wring, screw; pervert. See CONVOLUTION, DEVIATION, DISTORTION.

twitch, *v.i.* jerk, writhe, shake, pull; tug, vellicate. See AGITATION.

two-faced, *adj.* hypocritical, double-dealing; faithless, false. See DECEPTION.

tycoon, *n.* shogun. *Colloq.*, magnate, millionaire. See IMPORTANCE.

type, *n.* sign, emblem; kind, CLASS, sort, nature; standard, model, example, ideal; group; letter, figure, character. See INDICATION, PRINTING, SIMILARITY.

typhoon, *n.* hurricane, tornado, storm. See WIND.

typical, *adj.* emblematic, symbolic; characteristic, representative, model, ideal, conforming. See CONFORMITY, INDICATION. *Ant.*, see UNCONFORMITY.

typify, *v.* symbolize, exemplify, embody, represent; prefigure. See INDICATION, REPRESENTATION.

tyranny, *n.* despotism, autocracy, totalitarianism; SEVERITY, rigor, harshness, oppression. See AUTHORITY, ILLEGALITY. *Ant.*, see MODERATION, FREEDOM.

tyrant, *n.* despot, autocrat, oppressor. See AUTHORITY, SEVERITY.

tyro, *n.* beginner, novice, amateur, LEARNER.

U

UGLINESS

Nouns—**1,** ugliness, deformity, disfigurement, blemish; inelegance; want of symmetry, DISTORTION; squalor (see UNCLEANNESS); IMPERFECTION; homeliness, plainness, unloveliness; grotesqueness; unsightliness, gruesomeness, loathsomeness, hideousness; sordidness, squalor.

2, eyesore, sight, fright, specter, scarecrow, hag, harridan, satyr, witch, toad, baboon, monster; Quasimodo, Caliban; gargoyle.

Verbs—be ugly, look unprepossessing; make faces; render ugly, uglify; deface; disfigure; distort, BLEMISH; make sordid *or* squalid.

Adjectives—**1,** ugly, ugly as sin; plain, homely, ordinary, unornamental, inartistic; squalid, unsightly, unseemly, uncomely, unshapely, unlovely; not fit to be seen; unbeautiful; beautiless; foul, dingy.

2, gruesome, misshapen, repulsive, hideous, loathsome, disgusting, nauseating, misproportioned, deformed, disfigured, monstrous; gaunt, thin; dumpy, ill-made, ill-shaped, ill-favored, ill-proportioned; crooked, distorted, hard-featured; ill-looking, haggard, unprepossessing.

3, graceless, inelegant; ungraceful, ungainly, uncouth; stiff; rugged, rough, gross, rude, awkward, inept, clumsy, slouching, rickety; gawky; lumpish; lumbering; hulking, unwieldy; ludicrous.

4, grim, grim-faced, grim-visaged; grisly, ghastly; ghostlike, deathlike;

cadaverous, frightful, odious, uncanny, forbidding, repellent, grotesque, horrid, horrible; shocking.

Antonym, see BEAUTY.

---

ulcer, *n.* abscess, infection, sore, fistula. See DISEASE.

ulterior, *adj.* beyond, farther; further, remote; hidden, unavowed. See DISTANCE, FUTURITY. *Ant.,* see NEARNESS, DISCLOSURE.

ultimate, *adj.* farthest, most remote; extreme, last; maximum; terminal, final, conclusive; elemental; eventual. See DISTANCE, END, SIMPLENESS. *Ant.,* see BEGINNING.

ultimatum, *n.* demand, requirement, exaction. See COMMAND.

ultra, *adj.* radical, extreme. See SUPERIORITY. *Ant.,* see INFERIORITY.

ululate, *v.i.* howl, wail, CRY, hoot, bark, mewl, mew, meow, bellow, moo, roar, caterwaul.

umbrage, *n.* RESENTMENT, offense, dudgeon, pique, huff.

umbrella, *n.* shade, screen; parasol, sunshade, bumbershoot; canopy, COVERING.

umpire, *n.* referee, arbitrator; linesman. See JUDGE, MODERATION. *Ant.,* see VIOLENCE.

unabashed, *adj.* shameless, brazen, unblushing, unashamed. See INSOLENCE.

unabated, *adj.* tireless, relentless, ceaseless, constant. See FREEDOM, CONTINUITY.

unaccompanied, *adj.* alone, unattended, solitary, lone. *Ant.,* see ACCOMPANIMENT.

unaccountable, *adj.* inexplicable, mysterious, strange; not responsible, unanswerable. See WONDER, FREEDOM. *Ant.,* see MEANING, RESTRAINT.

unaccustomed, *adj.* unwonted, unused (to); a stranger (to); uncommon, unusual, rare, strange. See NEWNESS, UNSKILLFULNESS.

unacquainted, *adj.* ignorant, unknowing, uninformed; never introduced, strange. See IGNORANCE.

unadorned, *adj.* bare, severe, austere, unornamented, plain, simple; naked, blank; terse, trenchant. See SEVERITY, SIMPLENESS. *Ant.,* see ORNAMENT, EXAGGERATION.

unadulterated, *adj.* clear, simple; pure, undiluted; genuine, true. See PURITY, TRUTH. *Ant.,* see MIXTURE, EXAGGERATION.

unaffected, *adj.* natural, simple, plain; genuine, sincere; ingenuous, artless; untouched, uninfluenced, unmoved. See INSENSIBILITY. *Ant.,* see AFFECTATION, FEELING.

unaided, *adj.* unsupported (see AID); single, single-handed.

un-American, *adj.* anti-American, subversive, fascist, unpatriotic. See IMPROBITY.

unanimity, *n.* AGREEMENT, consent, accord. See ASSENT, COÖPERATION.

unanticipated, *adj.* unexpected, unforeseen; surprising, startling. See SURPRISE. *Ant.,* see EXPECTATION.

unappetizing, *adj.* unsavory, distasteful, repugnant; tasteless, insipid. See TASTE, REPULSION, INSIPIDITY.

unapproachable, *adj.* inaccessible; cold, cool, forbidding, distant. See INDIFFERENCE, PRIDE.

unarmed, *adj.* weaponless, unprepared, defenseless. See IMPOTENCE.

unasked, *adj.* voluntary, spontaneous; gratis, free; uninvited. See WILL.

unassuming, *adj.* modest, retiring, reserved. See MODESTY. *Ant.,* see VANITY.

unattached, *adj.* loose, independent, alone; unengaged, fancy-free. See DISJUNCTION.

unattractive, *adj.* ugly, homely, plain, unsightly. See UGLINESS, REPULSION.

unauthorized, *adj.* unwarranted, unsanctioned; illegal, illegitimate, unconstitutional. See ILLEGALITY, DISOBEDIENCE. *Ant.,* see PERMISSION.

unavailing, *adj.* useless, vain, futile; ineffectual, bootless. See USELESSNESS, IMPOTENCE.

unavoidable, *adj.* inevitable, certain, unpreventable, necessary. See CERTAINTY, NECESSITY.

unaware, *adj.* unwary, unwarned; oblivious, ignorant. See IGNORANCE.

unbalanced, *adj.* unpoised, lopsided, out of kilter; unhinged, deranged. *Slang*, off one's rocker. See INSANITY, IRREGULARITY, DERANGEMENT.

unbearable, *adj.* unendurable, intolerable, insufferable, odious. See PAIN.

unbecoming, *adj.* indecorous, unseemly, inappropriate (to), unfitting; ugly, unattractive, ill-suited, inharmonious. See UGLINESS.

unbelievable, *adj.* incredible; unthinkable, unimaginable, far-fetched, implausible, impossible. See DOUBT. *Ant.*, see BELIEF.

unbeliever, *n.* skeptic, doubter, infidel, agnostic, heretic. See DOUBT, IRRELIGION. *Ant.*, see CREDULITY, BELIEF.

unbiased, *adj.* impartial, unprejudiced, objective, dispassionate; fair, just, equitable. See JUSTICE. *Ant.*, see CERTAINTY.

unbounded, *adj.* boundless, limitless, unlimited, INFINITE. See SPACE, FREEDOM.

unbreakable, *adj.* indestructible; shatterproof, tough, durable. See DURABILITY. *Ant.*, see BRITTLENESS.

unbridled, *adj.* unrestrained; violent, licentious; unruly, intractable. See VIOLENCE. *Ant.*, see MODERATION.

unbroken, *adj.* intact, WHOLE; continuous, constant, uninterrupted, even; untamed, unsubdued. See CONTINUITY, WHOLE. *Ant.*, see DISJUNCTION.

uncalled-for, *adj.* undue, unnecessary, superfluous, gratuitous; ill-timed, untimely, inopportune. See REDUNDANCE, INSOLENCE.

uncanny, *adj.* mysterious, eery, ghostly, weird, unnatural. See DEMON.

unceasing, *adj.* continuous, uninterrupted; perpetual, eternal, endless. See CONTINUITY.

uncertainty, *n.* uncertainness, incertitude, DOUBT; hesitation; suspense; perplexity, embarrassment, dilemma, quandary, bewilderment; timidity; indecision, vacillation, irresolution, vagueness, obscurity; riskiness, precariousness, insecurity. *Ant.*, see STABILITY, CERTAINTY, RESOLUTION.

unchanged, *adj.* unaltered, *etc.* (see CHANGE); pristine, erstwhile, undiminished, good as new, the same, as of old; continuous, maintained.

unchaste, *adj.* lewd, incontinent, wanton, lascivious, lecherous, dissolute, immoral; unfaithful, adulterous. See IMPURITY. *Ant.*, see PURITY.

uncivilized, *adj.* primitive, simple; barbarous, savage, barbaric. See SIMPLENESS, UNCONFORMITY, VIOLENCE.

UNCLEANNESS

*Nouns—***1,** uncleanness, IMPURITY; filth, defilement, contamination, soilure; abomination; taint, tainture; MALODOROUSNESS; decay, putrescence, putrefaction; corruption, mold, must, mildew, dry rot; slovenliness, slovenry, squalor, sordidness.

2, offal, garbage, carrion; EXCRETION; feces, excrement, ordure, dung; slough; pus, matter, gangrene, suppuration; sewage, sewerage; muck, guano, manure, compost.

3, dregs, grounds, lees; sediment; dross, precipitate, scoria; ashes, cinders, clinkers, slag; scum, froth; swill, hogwash; ditchwater, dishwater, bilgewater; rinsings, parings, offscourings, sweepings; scurvy, scurviness, scurf, scurfness; dandruff, tartar.

4, dirt, filth, soil, slop; dust, cobweb, smoke, soot, smudge, smut, grime; muck, mud, mire, quagmire, alluvium, silt, sludge, slime, slush.

5, drab, slut, slattern, sloven, riffraff; vermin, louse, flea, cockroach.

6, dunghill, dungheap, midden, bog, sink, latrine, outhouse, head, privy, cesspool; sump, slough, dump, dumpheap, cloaca, scrapheap, junkyard, boneyard; drain, sewer; sty, pigsty, lair, den, Augean stables, sink of corruption; slum, rookery.

7, foul-mindedness, obscenity, foulmouthedness; evil-mindedness, dirtiness; foul, evil *or* dirty mind, filthiness; foul play. *Slang*, dirty fighting, dirty deal.

Verbs—**1,** be unclean, become unclean; rot, putrefy, fester, rankle, reek, stink (see MALODOROUSNESS); mold, go bad, spoil, become tainted.
2, render unclean, dirty, soil, smoke, tarnish, spot, smear, daub, blot, blur, smudge, smirch; drabble, draggle; spatter, besmear, bemire, beslime, begrime, befoul; splash, stain, sully, pollute, defile, debase, contaminate, taint, corrupt (see DETERIORATION).

Adjectives—**1,** unclean, dirty, filthy, grimy; soiled; dusty, smutty, sooty, smoky; thick, turbid, draggy; slimy; uncleanly, slovenly, untidy, slatternly, sluttish, draggletailed; uncombed, unkempt; unscoured, unswept, unwiped, unwashed, unpurified; squalid, nasty, coarse, foul, impure, offensive, abominable, piggish, beastly, reeky, sweaty, fetid, obscene; disgusting, nauseating, stomach-turning, revolting, sordid. *Slang*, grungy.
2, moldy, musty, mildewed, rusty, motheaten, rancid, bad, gone bad, fusty; scabrous, scrofulous, leprous; rotten, corrupt, tainted; gamy, high, flyblown, verminous, maggoty; putrid, putrescent, putrefied; purulent, carious, infected, infested, peccant, fecal, scurfy, impetiginous; gory, bloody; rotting, crapulous.

Antonym, see CLEANNESS.

---

uncomfortable, *adj.* uneasy; cramped; disturbed, restless; embarrassing, DIFFICULT; unpleasant, distressing. See PAIN.

uncommon, *adj.* unusual, rare, infrequent, sporadic; scarce; remarkable, extraordinary, strange; exceptional, original, unconventional. See RARITY, UNCONFORMITY. *Ant.*, see CONFORMITY.

uncompromising, *adj.* inflexible, unyielding; rigid, strict. See SEVERITY.

unconcerned, *adj.* indifferent, uninterested; disinterested; detached, aloof; unmoved, uncurious. See INSENSIBILITY. *Ant.*, see DESIRE, FEELING.

unconditional, *adj.* absolute, unreserved, unqualified; full, plenary; free. See COMPLETION, FREEDOM. *Ant.*, see LIMIT, RESTRAINT.

unconfined, *adj.* unrestrained, free, unhampered. See FREEDOM.

UNCONFORMITY

Nouns—**1,** unconformity, nonconformity, unconventionality, informality, abnormality; anomaly, anomalousness; exception, peculiarity, irregularity; infraction, breach, violation *or* infringement of law, custom *or* usage; recusance; eccentricity, oddity, DISAGREEMENT.
2, individuality, speciality, idiosyncrasy, originality, mannerism; unusualness, strangeness; aberration; variety, singularity; exemption; mannishness, eonism.
3, nonconformist, nondescript, original; nonesuch, monster, prodigy, wonder, miracle, curiosity, *rara avis*; mongrel, hybrid (see MIXTURE); hermaphrodite; transsexual; homosexual, bisexual, Lesbian; invert, pervert; monstrosity, rarity, freak; fish out of water; freak of nature; neither one thing nor another; neither fish, flesh nor fowl; one in a million; outcast, pariah, outlaw. *Colloq.*, character, card. *Slang*, crank, crackpot, screwball, fluke, queer fish, wack; homo, fairy, nance, pansy, fag, queer, ladylover, dike.
4, phoenix, chimera, hydra, sphinx, minotaur; griffin, centaur; hippogriff; cockatrice, roc, dragon, sea-serpent; mermaid; unicorn; Cyclops, Medusa, Hydra.

Verbs—be unconformable, leave the beaten track *or* path; baffle *or* beggar description. *Slang*, beat the Dutch.

Adjectives—**1,** unconformable, exceptional, abnormal, anomalous, out of place *or* keeping; irregular, arbitrary; lawless, aberrant, peculiar, unnatural, eccentric, uncommon, extraordinary, outside the pale.
2, unusual, uncommon; rare, singular, unique, curious, odd, extraor-

dinary, out of the ordinary, strange, monstrous; wonderful, unaccountable; outré, out of the way, remarkable, noteworthy; queer, quaint, *sui generis*; original, unconventional, unfashionable; unprecedented, unparalleled, unexampled, unheard of; fantastic, grotesque, bizarre; outlandish, exotic, weird, out of this world; preternatural; unsymmetric. *Colloq.*, offbeat, offtrail, wacky, kinky.
Adverbs—unconformably; except, unless, save, barring, beside, without, let alone; however, yet, but.
Antonym, see CONFORMITY.

---

unconquerable, *adj.* indomitable, invincible; irresistible; impregnable. See POWER. *Ant.*, see IMPOTENCE.

unconscionable, *adj.* unscrupulous, WRONG, unethical; extravagant, excessive; immoderate, inordinate, intolerable. See IMPROBITY, GREATNESS.

unconscious, *adj.* unaware, insensible; stupefied, asleep, out; uninformed, ignorant; submerged, subconscious, suppressed, repressed. *Colloq.*, blotto. See IGNORANCE, INSENSIBILITY.

unconstitutional, *adj.* illegal, illicit; unfair, unjust, against one's rights; un-American. See ILLEGALITY.

uncoöperative, *adj.* reluctant, resistant, recalcitrant, obstinate, stubborn, difficult, contrary. See OPPOSITION, SELFISHNESS, DIFFICULTY.

uncouth, *adj.* boorish, rude, crude, common, vulgar, UNCULTIVATED; awkward, gauche, ungraceful. See VULGARITY. *Ant.*, see TASTE.

uncover, *v.t.* open, unclose, unseal; disclose, discover; reveal, lay bare, expose; undress, denude, bare. See DISCLOSURE, OPENING, DIVESTMENT.

unction, *n.* anointing; unguent, ointment; unctuousness, gushing; fervor. See FEELING.

unctuous, *adj.* bland, fervid; ingratiating, gushing; glib; fatty, oily, greasy; oleaginous, adipose, sebaceous, saponaceous; slippery. See SERVILITY, SMOOTHNESS.

uncultivated, *adj.* unrefined, uncultured, UNCOUTH, rough; illiterate; wild, untilled, primeval. See WASTE, VULGARITY.

undaunted, *adj.* courageous, undismayed; bold, intrepid, dauntless, cool, reckless. See COURAGE. *Ant.*, see COWARDICE.

undeceive, *v.t.* disabuse, disillusion, correct. See INFORMATION.

undecided, *adj.* undetermined, unresolved, unsettled, problematical, uncertain, irresolute, doubtful, hesitant. See DOUBT. *Ant.*, see CERTAINTY.

undemonstrative, *adj.* restrained, reserved; impassive, inexpressive, stolid, apathetic, calm. See MODERATION. *Ant.*, see EXCITEMENT, ENDEARMENT.

undeniable, *adj.* indisputable, incontestable, unquestionable, incontrovertible, irrefutable. See CERTAINTY. *Ant.*, see DOUBT.

under, *prep. & adj.* below, beneath, underneath; subject to, controlled by; inferior, subordinate. See LOWNESS, SUBJECTION. *Ant.*, OVER.

underage, *adj.* immature, premature; minor, in one's minority. See YOUTH.

underbrush, *n.* bush, thicket, brake, bracken, scrub, shrubbery, boscage; furze, gorse, heather. See VEGETABLE.

underclothes, *n.* See UNDERWEAR.

undercover, *adj.* masked, in disguise, incognito; SECRET, top-secret, clandestine, *sub rosa*. See CONCEALMENT.

undercurrent, *n.* undertow; LATENCY; undertone, innuendo, FEELING. See SECRET.

underestimate, *v.* underrate, undervalue, underreckon; depreciate, disparage, detract from; not do justice to; misprize, disprize, RIDICULE; slight, NEGLECT; slur over; make light of, play down, underplay, understate, take no account of; minimize, belittle. See DETRACTION, MODESTY.

underestimation, *n.* understatement, depreciation, DETRACTION; pessimism, pessimist; underestimate, undervaluation, undervaluing; MODESTY, belittlement. *Ant.*, see EXAGGERATION, OVERESTIMATION.

undergo, *v.t.* suffer, experience, endure, sustain, bear, stand, withstand, put up with. See OCCASION, CIRCUMSTANCE, PAIN.

undergraduate, *n.* freshman, sophomore, junior; lowerclassman. *Colloq.,* undergrad; plebe, frosh, soph, coed. See LEARNING.

underground, *n.* & *adj.* —*n.* subway, tube, Metro; (the) resistance, partisans, guerrillas, Maquis. —*adj.* subterranean, buried, interred. See INTERMENT.

underhand, underhanded, *adj.* hidden, secret; deceitful, fraudulent, unfair, tricky; stealthy, sly, clandestine, furtive, devious. See DECEPTION.

underline, *v.t.* underscore; accent, emphasize, urge. See REQUEST.

underling, *n.* subordinate, assistant, inferior, AID, deputy, AUXILIARY, apprentice; SERVANT, menial, flunky, retainer. See INFERIORITY.

undermine, *v.t.* excavate, mine, sap; honeycomb; subvert, weaken, demoralize, thwart, frustrate. See CONCAVITY, HINDRANCE, IMPOTENCE.

underneath, *prep.* & *adv.* beneath, below, lower, nether. See LOWNESS.

underpass, *n.* underwalk, tunnel, tube, viaduct. See PASSAGE, LOWNESS.

underprivileged, *adj.* impoverished, deprived, depressed, downtrodden, unfortunate; un(der)developed. See ADVERSITY, POVERTY.

underrate, *v.t.* undervalue, UNDERESTIMATE, depreciate; disparage, belittle.

undersigned, *n.* signer, subscriber, endorser, petitioner. See WRITING.

understand, *v.t.* know, comprehend, grasp, catch; perceive, discern, realize, penetrate, apprehend; interpret, construe, fathom; gather, infer, assume. See MEANING, INTELLIGENCE.

understanding, *n.* discernment, comprehension, INTELLIGENCE, KNOWLEDGE, insight, perception; AGREEMENT. See INTELLECT.

understate, *v.* underestimate, undervalue, underrate; play *or* tone down, palliate, belittle, degrade, deprecate; whitewash. *Colloq.,* soft-pedal. *Slang,* pull one's punches. See DETRACTION.

understudy, *n.* alternate, substitute, standby, stand-in, second, double. See DRAMA, SUBSTITUTION.

undertaker, *n.* funeral director, mortician; sexton; embalmer. See INTERMENT.

UNDERTAKING

Nouns—undertaking; compact, engagement, promise; enterprise, emprise, project; endeavor, venture, pilgrimmage; matter in hand, BUSINESS; move, first move, beginning. *Colloq.,* tall order. *Slang,* caper.

Verbs—undertake; engage in, embark on; launch into, plunge into; volunteer; apprentice oneself to; engage, promise, contract, compact; take upon oneself, take on, devote oneself to, take up, take in hand; set about, go about; set to, fall to, fall to work; take the plunge, launch forth; set up shop; put in hand, put in execution; set forward; put one's hand to, turn one's hand to, throw oneself into; begin; broach, institute, originate; put one's hand to the plow, put one's shoulder to the wheel; have in hand, have many irons in the fire. *Colloq.,* tackle, bite off more than one can chew, go in for, go off the deep end, give it a whirl.

Adjectives—venturesome, adventurous.

Adverbs—on the fire. *Colloq.,* in the works.

Antonym, see REFUSAL.

undertow, *n.* riptide, undercurrent, backlash; eddy, vortex. See WATER.

underwear, *n.* underclothes, undergarments, lingerie, drawers, union suit, B.V.D.'s®, briefs, panties, pantyhose; foundation [garment], girdle, pantygirdle, brassiere, bra, corset. *Colloq.,* unmentionables. See CLOTHING.

underworld, *n.* netherworld, infernal regions, HELL, Hades; world of crime; criminals, gangsters. *Colloq.,* gangland. See EVIL.

underwrite, *v.t.* insure, guarantee, warrant; sanction, authorize; sponsor, finance, subscribe to, SUPPORT, back; defray, pay (for). *Colloq.,* stake, grubstake. *Slang,* bankroll. See ASSENT, APPROBATION, PAYMENT.

undesirable, *adj.* disagreeable, distasteful, objectionable, disliked; inadvisable, INEXPEDIENT. See DISLIKE.

undignified, *adj.* discreditable, inelegant, ludicrous, awkward, *gauche*; mean, degrading; indecorous, ill-bred. See VULGARITY.

undisciplined, *adj.* wild, chaotic; lawless, licentious; primitive, savage; spontaneous, capricious, erratic. See DISOBEDIENCE, FREEDOM, FEELING.

undisguised, *adj.* true, genuine; evident, obvious; candid, frank, open. See EVIDENCE.

undisputed, *adj.* unchallenged, indisputable; accepted, agreed. See BELIEF, CERTAINTY, TRUTH.

undivided, *adj.* concentrated, exclusive, WHOLE, intact, entire; single, united.

undo, *v.t.* loose, unlock, unfasten, untie, release; reverse, cancel, neutralize; destroy, ruin. See DISJUNCTION, DESTRUCTION.

undoing, *n.* downfall, defeat, ruin, reversal. See DESTRUCTION.

undone, *adj.* destroyed, lost, ruined; discovered. See FAILURE.

undoubted, *adj.* undisputed, *etc.* (see DOUBT); accepted, sure, assured, certain. See CERTAINTY.

undress, *v.* strip, disrobe, unclothe, dismantle, expose. *Slang,* peel. See DIVESTMENT.

undue, *adj.* unjust, inequitable; improper, inappropriate; extreme, excessive, immoderate, inordinate, exorbitant, unwarranted. See GREATNESS.

undulate, *v.* surge, fluctuate, ripple, pulsate, wave. See AGITATION.

unearth, *v.t.* exhume, disinter; expose, disclose, discover, uncover; eradicate, uproot. See EJECTION, DISCLOSURE. *Ant.,* see INTERMENT.

unearthly, *adj.* supernatural, uncanny, ghostly, spectral, eerie; appalling, hair-raising. *Colloq.,* exceptional, unusual. See WONDER.

uneasy, *adj.* restless, restive; disturbed, perturbed, disquieted, uncomfortable; anxious, apprehensive, fearful; fidgety, jittery, on edge, jumpy; uncertain, unstable, touch-and-go. See DISCONTENT, FEAR.

uneducated, *adj.* ignorant, untaught, untutored, illiterate. See IGNORANCE.

unemotional, *adj.* apathetic, calm, cool, impassive, unfeeling. See INSENSIBILITY.

unemployed, *adj.* idle, jobless, out of work; loafing, at leisure, at liberty, free, available; looking [around]. See INACTIVITY.

unequal, *adj.* disparate, disproportionate; inadequate; uneven, mismatched, one-sided; inequitable, UNFAIR. See DIFFERENCE. *Ant.,* see EQUALITY.

unequaled, *adj.* unparalleled, unrivaled, unique, matchless, inimitable, peerless, nonpareil, incomparable. See SUPERIORITY. *Ant.,* see EQUALITY, INFERIORITY.

unequivocal, *adj.* unmistakable, unqualified; clear, definite, yes or no, black and white. See SIMPLENESS, CERTAINTY.

unethical, *adj.* WRONG, immoral, reprobate; corrupt, criminal, venal, mercenary, deceitful, underhanded, sneaky. See IMPROBITY.

uneven, *adj.* variable; odd; UNEQUAL, disparate; rough, lumpy, broken, rugged. See DIFFERENCE, ROUGHNESS.

uneventful, *adj.* monotonous, humdrum, dull. See INACTION, DULLNESS.

unexpected, *adj.* unforeseen; sudden, SURPRISE, abrupt, accidental, coincidental, contingent, CHANCE; from nowhere, out of the blue.

unfair, *adj.* unjust, unreasonable, UNEQUAL, inequitable; unsporting; disingenuous; partial, biased, prejudiced, discriminatory. See BADNESS.

unfaithful, *adj.* disloyal, faithless; adulterous, philandering, cheating, untrue, fickle; inaccurate, untrustworthy. See IMPROBITY, FALSEHOOD. *Ant.,* see PROBITY.

unfamiliar, *adj.* unknown; uncommon, strange, novel, new; unacquainted. See UNCONFORMITY.

unfashionable, *adj.* dowdy, old-fashioned, out-of-date; passé, antiquated. *Slang,* corny, old hat. See OLDNESS. *Ant.,* see NEWNESS.

unfasten, *v.t.* loose, loosen; liberate; disconnect, unbind, unfix, unpin. See DISJUNCTION, FREEDOM. *Ant.,* see JUNCTION.

unfathomable, *adj.* fathomless, bottomless, unplumbed, unsounded; unintelligible, inexplicable, incomprehensible. See DEPTH, SECRET.

unfavorable, *adj.* adverse, disadvantageous, inauspicious, unpropitious, unlucky; unfriendly, antagonistic; negative, contrary; inclement; inopportune, untimely. See ADVERSITY.

unfeasible, *adj.* impracticable, impossible, unthinkable. See IMPOSSIBILITY.

unfeeling, *adj.* hard, hard-hearted, cold, cold-blooded, cruel; heartless, inhuman, callous, dispassionate; merciless, pitiless, unmerciful, relentless, adamant. See INSENSIBILITY. *Ant.,* see SENSIBILITY, PITY.

unfettered, *adj.* unchained, unrestrained, at liberty. See FREEDOM.

unfinished, *adj.* crude, raw, sketchy, rough; incomplete; amateurish, inept; unpainted, *etc.* See IMPERFECTION, UNSKILLFULNESS.

unfit, *adj.* incapable, unqualified, *etc.* (see SKILL); incapacitated, unhealthy, in poor condition; unsuitable, inappropriate, *etc.* (see RIGHTNESS).

unfold, *v.* open, unroll, smooth out (see FOLD); disclose, expose, announce; develop, progress. See INFORMATION.

unforgiving, *adj.* relentless, unrelenting, implacable, unappeasable, inexorable; merciless, pitiless; vengeful. See MALEVOLENCE. *Ant.,* see FORGIVENESS.

unfortunate, *adj.* unlucky, hapless, ill-fated, ill-starred, star-crossed, luckless; unsuccessful, abortive, disastrous, ruinous. *Slang,* out of luck, S.O.L., behind the eight-ball, jinxed, hexed. See ADVERSITY.

unfounded, *adj.* baseless, vain, groundless, ungrounded. See ERROR.

unfriendly, *adj.* hostile, inimical, antagonistic; unfavorable. See HATE.

unfrock, *v.t.* dismiss, discharge, oust, disgrace. See EJECTION, PUNISHMENT.

unfruitful, *adj.* barren, unproductive, infertile, sterile; fruitless. See FAILURE.

unfurl, *v.t.* unroll, open, spread out, fly, wave; display. See OPENING.

ungainly, *adj.* awkward, clumsy; gawky, ungraceful, lumbering; grotesque. See UGLINESS.

ungenerous, *adj.* illiberal; mean, harsh, exacting. See SELFISHNESS.

ungodly, *adj.* godless, pagan, freethinking; profane, unholy, impious; EVIL, satanic, diabolic. See IRRELIGION. *Colloq.,* bad, outrageous. See BADNESS.

ungovernable, *adj.* unbridled, irrepressible, unruly, headstrong, uncontrollable, unmanageable, incorrigible; licentious. See DISOBEDIENCE. *Ant.,* see OBEDIENCE.

ungrateful, *adj.* unthankful, ingrate, unappreciative, thankless, forgetful (of favors); unwanted, unpleasing, unwelcome. *Ant.,* see GRATITUDE.

unguarded, *adj.* inadvertent, thoughtless, incautious; with one's guard down; not guarded (see DEFENSE).

unhappy, *adj.* unlucky, UNFORTUNATE; sad, sorrowful, wretched, miserable, dolorous, despondent, disconsolate, inconsolable, gloomy, joyless; inappropriate, dismal; calamitous, disastrous, catastrophic. See DISCONTENT, DEJECTION, ADVERSITY.

unhealthy, *adj.* sickly, infirm, ailing, invalided; delicate, frail; undesirable, inauspicious, ominous. See DISEASE.

unheard-of, *adj.* UNPRECEDENTED, unexampled; unbelievable, inconceivable. See WONDER.

unhinge, *v.t.* unsettle, derange, unbalance. See INSANITY.

unholy, *adj.* unhallowed, unconsecrated, unsanctified; wicked, profane; ungodly, impious, irreligious. *Colloq.,* frightful. See IRRELIGION, IMPIETY.

uniform, *adj.* homogeneous, homologous; of a piece, consistent; monotonous, even, invariable, changeless; stable. See CONFORMITY, AGREEMENT. *Ant.,* see DIFFERENCE, DISAGREEMENT, UNCONFORMITY.

unify, *v.t.* consolidate, combine, amalgamate, join. See JUNCTION.

unimaginative, *adj.* uninventive, uncreative, uninspired; imitative, stereotyped, hack, pedestrian, prosaic. See DULLNESS, INSENSIBILITY, IGNORANCE.

unimpeachable, *adj.* irreproachable, above reproach; innocent, faultless; reliable, authoritative. See PROBITY, PERFECTION.

UNIMPORTANCE

Nouns—**1,** unimportance, insignificance, nothingness, immateriality, inconsequentiality, inconsequence; triviality, levity, frivolity; paltriness, LITTLENESS, USELESSNESS; matter of indifference; no object.

2, trivia, trifle, minutiae, details, minor details; drop in the ocean *or* bucket, pinprick, fleabite, molehill; nothing, nothing worth speaking of, nothing particular, nothing to boast of *or* speak of; bosh; small matter, no great matter, trifling matter; mere joke, mere nothing; hardly *or* scarcely anything; nonentity, cipher; no great shakes; child's play; small beer, small potatoes.

3, toy, plaything, gimcrack, gewgaw, bauble, trinket, bagatelle, kickshaw, knickknack, trifle; trumpery, trash, rubbish, stuff, frippery; chaff, froth, bubble, smoke, cobweb; weed; refuse, scum; joke, jest, snap of the fingers; fudge, fiddlesticks; pack of nonsense, straw, pin, fig, button, feather, two cents, halfpenny, penny, farthing, brass farthing; peppercorn, jot, rap, pinch of snuff, old song. *Colloq.,* red cent, row of pins, hill of beans.

4, nobody, nonentity, cipher, mediocrity, small fry, nine days' wonder, flash in the pan, dummy, straw man. *Colloq.,* lightweight, no great shakes.

Verbs—be unimportant, not matter; signify nothing; not matter a straw; make light of; dispense with; underestimate, belittle, set no store by, not care a straw about; catch at straws, overestimate. *Colloq.,* not give a damn, continental, rap *or* hang.

Adjectives—**1,** unimportant; of little, small *or* no account *or* importance; immaterial; unessential, nonessential; indifferent; subordinate, inferior, mediocre, average; passable, fair; respectable, tolerable, commonplace; uneventful, mere, common; ordinary, habitual, inconsiderable, so-so, insignificant.

2, trifling, trivial; slight, slender, light, flimsy, frothy, idle; puerile; airy, shallow; weak, powerless (see IMPOTENCE); frivolous, petty, niggling, picayune, piddling; inane, ridiculous, ludicrous, farcical; finical, namby-pamby, wishy-washy, milk and water; inappreciable.

3, poor, paltry, pitiful; contemptible, sorry, mean, meager, shabby, miserable, wretched, vile, scrubby, niggardly, scurvy, beggarly, worthless, cheap, trashy, gimcrack, trumpery; not worth the pains, not worth while, not worth mentioning, not worth speaking of, not worth a thought, damn *or* straw; beneath notice *or* consideration; futile, vain. *Slang,* measly, punk.

Adverbs—slightly, rather, somewhat, pretty well, tolerably.

Interjections—no matter! tut-tut! pshaw! pooh! pooh-pooh! bosh! humbug! fiddlesticks! fiddlededee! never mind! what of it! what's the odds! stuff and nonsense! *Slang,* nuts! baloney! bunk!

Antonym, see IMPORTANCE.

uninhabited, *adj.* unpopulated, unpeopled, unsettled, vacant. See ABSENCE.

uninhibited, *adj.* unhampered, free [and easy], natural, spontaneous. See LIBERTY.

UNINTELLIGIBILITY

Nouns—**1,** unintelligibility, incoherence; OBSCURITY, ambiguity; UNCERTAINTY, intricacy, perplexity; confusion, DISORDER; mystification (see CONCEALMENT).

2, paradox, enigma, mystery, riddle, [Chinese] puzzle (see SECRET); sealed book; cryptography, steganography, code; gibberish, jargon (see UNMEANINGNESS), Greek, Hebrew, Dutch, *etc.*

Verbs—**1,** be unintelligible *or* incomprehensible, pass comprehension; conceal, veil, obscure, obfuscate; confuse, perplex, mystify, speak in riddles.

2, not understand, lose [the clue], miss [the point]; not know what to make of, be able to make nothing of, give up; not be able to account for, not be able to make heads or tails of, be at sea; WONDER; see through a glass darkly, not understand one another, work at cross purposes.

Adjectives—**1,** unintelligible, unaccountable, incomprehensible, inapprehensible, unrecognizable, unfathomable, undiscoverable, inexplicable, inscrutable, impenetrable, unsolvable, meaningless; incoherent, irrational; illegible, undecipherable, unexplained, as Greek to one; enigmatic(al), paradoxical, puzzling, baffling, intricate.

2, obscure, dark, muddy, muzzy, shadowy, misty, seen through a mist; dim, nebulous, indefinite, indistinct, undiscernible, invisible; perplexed, confused, undetermined, crabbed, vague, loose, inexact, ambiguous, abstruse, abstract; hidden, latent, occult, recondite, transcendental; mystic, mysterious, shrouded in mystery; inconceivable, beyond comprehension, beyond one's depth, over one's head. *Colloq.*, clear as mud.

3, inexpressible, indescribable, undefinable, unspeakable, incommunicable; inarticulate, mumbled.

Phrases—I don't understand, it's Greek to me.

Antonym, see MEANING.

---

unintentional, *adj.* accidental, involuntary, inadvertent, unpremeditated, spontaneous. See CHANCE. *Ant.,* see WILL.

uninteresting, *adj.* dull, dreary, tedious, humdrum. See DULLNESS, WEARINESS.

union, *n.* UNITY, concord, uniting, joining, connection; COMBINATION, fusion, coalescence; marriage; confederation, association, alliance. See AGREEMENT, JUNCTION.

unique, *adj.* sole, single; singular, only, *sui generis;* UNEQUALED, matchless, unparalleled, unprecedented. See UNCONFORMITY. *Ant.,* see CONFORMITY.

unison, *n.* harmony, CONCORD; AGREEMENT; union; unanimity.

UNITY

Nouns—**1,** unity, oneness, individuality; indivisibility, inseparability, homogeneity, integrality; solitude, SECLUSION, isolation; IDENTITY, sameness, UNIFORMITY, consistency, COHERENCE; unification, amalgamation, consolidation, integration, coalescence, fusion, junction (see COMBINATION).

2, harmony, CONCURRENCE, AGREEMENT, CONSENT, accordance, accord, concord, consonance, concert, peace; unison, union, unanimity, solidarity.

3, unit, one, ace, solo, monad, module, integer, integrant, figure, number; individual, person, entity, none else, no other; detail, particular; item, object, thing, article, whole, ensemble.

Verbs—be one *or* alone, isolate; unite, unify, join, merge, mix, blend, fuse, weld, cement, consolidate, solidify; marry, wed; reconcile, harmonize, attune, fraternize.

Adjectives—**1,** one, single, sole, solo, solitary, monistic; individual, apart, alone, unaccompanied, unattended, unaided, unassisted; singular, odd, unique, azygous, unrepeated, first and last, three in one; isolated, insulated, insular; single-handed, singleminded.

2, inseparable, inseverable, indivisible, indissoluble, indiscerptible, irresolvable, integral, uniform, compact; unipartite, one-piece, unilateral, unilinear, unipolar, *etc.*; united, unified, joined, combined, connected, unseparated, undivided, homogeneous.

3, harmonious, concordant, unanimous. See AGREEMENT.

4, unifying, uniting, connective, conjunctive, combinative, coalescent.

Adverbs—singly, individually, independently, severally, separately; solely, simply, alone, each, apiece, by itself, only apart, *per se*; in the singular, in the abstract, one by one, one at a time, as an individual, as one man, in unison.

UNIVERSE

Nouns—**1,** universe, cosmos, celestial sphere, macrocosm; infinity, span, [all] creation, earth and heaven, [all the] world, ether.

2, HEAVEN, the heavens, sky, empyrean, firmament, vault *or* canopy of heaven, celestial spaces, ceiling.

3, heavenly bodies, luminaries, starry host; nebula, galaxy, Milky Way, constellation, Zodiac; Aries, Aquarius, Cancer, Capricornus, Gemini, Leo, Libra, Pisces, Sagittarius, Scorpius, Taurus, Virgo; Great Bear, Little Bear, Ursa Major, Ursa Minor, Big Dipper, Little Dipper; Andromeda, Auriga, Boötes, Canis Major, Canis Minor, Cassiopeia, Centaurus, Cepheus, Cygnus, Draco, Hercules, Lyra, Orion, Perseus, Pleiades; star, Achenar, Arcturus, Aldebaran, Altair, Antares, Betelgeuse, Canopus, Capella, Centauri, Pollux, Procyon, Rigel, Sirius, Vega; falling star, shooting star, nova, double star, cluster.

4, solar system, sun, orb; planet, Mercury, Venus, Earth, Mars, Jupiter, Saturn, Uranus, Neptune, Pluto; planetoid, asteroid, satellite, moon, Luna, man in the moon, new moon, half moon, crescent, first, *etc.*, quarter, comet, meteor, meteorite; Earth, Terra, [terrestrial] globe, sphere, oblate spheroid, WORLD; cosmic rays, sunspots, aurora borealis *or* australis, northern *or* southern lights; artificial satellite, bird, space station.

5, astronomy, astrometry, astrophysics, spectroscopy, cosmography, cosmogony, cosmology, geography, geodesy, geology, geognosy, geophysics; almagest, ephemeris, star atlas, star map, nautical almanac; observatory, planetarium.

Adjectives—**1,** universal, cosmic, empyrean, ethereal, celestial, heavenly; stellar, astral, sidereal, starry; solar, lunar, planetary, nebular; earthly, terrestrial, mundane.

2, astronomical, astrometrical, astrophysical, spectroscopic, *etc.*; geocentric, heliocentric, Copernican, Ptolemaic; 1st, 2nd, *etc.* magnitude.

3, general, common, natural; worldwide; widespread, broad, wide, catholic, entire, total, unlimited, encyclopedic, all-embracing, complete; prevalent, comprehensive.

---

university, *n.* college, SCHOOL, academy, seminary, institute, institution [of higher learning]; campus. *Colloq.,* U.

unjust, *adj.* unfair, inequitable, undue, biased. See WRONG.

unkempt, *adj.* uncombed, disordered, ill-kept; slovenly, untidy, bedraggled. See DISORDER. *Ant.,* see ARRANGEMENT, CLEANNESS.

unkind, *adj.* pitiless, merciless, hard-hearted, cruel, brutal, harsh, inhuman. See MALEVOLENCE. *Ant.,* see PITY, BENEVOLENCE.

unknown, *adj.* incognito; unrecognized; unperceived. See IGNORANCE.

unlawful, *adj.* See ILLEGALITY.

unleash, *v.t.* uncage, unshackle, (un)loose, release, set loose. See LIBERATION.

unless, *conj. & prep.* if [not], but, save, except(ing), other than, aside from, let alone, without, barring. See CIRCUMSTANCE, CONDITIONS.

unlike, *adj.* dissimilar, diverse, different, disparate; distinct, separate. See DIFFERENCE. *Ant.,* see SIMILARITY.

unlikely, *adj.* improbable, doubtful, dubious; farfetched, inconceivable; impracticable, implausible; inauspicious. See IMPROBABILITY.

unlimited, *adj.* undefined; indefinite; boundless, limitless, uncounted, infinite, full, absolute, unconfined, unconstricted, unrestrained. See FREEDOM, GREATNESS.

unload, *v.* empty, disgorge, discharge, unpack. See DIVESTMENT.

unlock, *v.* unfasten, unbolt, disengage, undo; open; release, uncover, solve (mystery, *etc.*). See OPENING, DISCLOSURE.

unlucky, *adj.* UNFORTUNATE, ill-starred, ill-omened, hopeless, disastrous.

unman, *v.t.* emasculate, devitalize, unnerve, enervate, weaken; effeminize. See IMPOTENCE.

unmanly, *adj.* cowardly; ignoble; effeminate. See COWARDICE.

unmannerly, *adj.* rude, uncivil, ill-mannered; caddish, discourteous. See DISCOURTESY.

unmarried, *adj.* single; bachelor, spinster, maiden, virgin; widowed, divorced; celibate; unwed. See CELIBACY. *Ant.*, see MARRIAGE.

UNMEANINGNESS

Nouns—**1,** unmeaningness, meaninglessness, senselessness, *etc.*; ABSURDITY, inanity; ambiguity (see UNINTELLIGIBILITY).

2, nonsense, verbiage, mere words, empty sound, dead letter; gibberish, jargon, jabber, babble, drivel, palaver, hocus-pocus, mumbo-jumbo, Jabberwocky; balderdash, rigmarole, flummery, twaddle, twattle, fudge, trash, rubbish, humbug, moonshine, fiddle-faddle, wish-wash, stuff [and nonsense]; fustian, rant, bombast, rodomontade; platitude, truism; scribble, scrabble, doodle. *Colloq.*, bosh, poppycock, flapdoodle, buncombe, double-talk. *Slang,* tommyrot, applesauce, baloney, gobbledygook, hogwash, hooey, bunk, blah, malarkey.

Verbs—be meaningless, mean nothing, not mean a thing; jabber, babble, twaddle (see *Nouns*); scrabble, scribble, scrawl, doodle; drivel, slaver, drool. *Slang,* bull, gas, talk through one's hat, run off at the mouth.

Adjectives—unmeaning, meaningless, senseless, reasonless, nonsensical, void of sense, without rhyme or reason; unintelligible, illegible, inexpressive, expressionless, vacant, blank, inane, vague, ambiguous; inexpressible, ineffable, undefinable, incommunicable; not significant, worthless, trashy, rubbishy; trivial, trumpery, twaddling, quibbling, fiddle-faddle. *Colloq.*, wishy-washy.

Antonym, see MEANING.

---

unmentionable, *adj.* ineffable, unutterable, unspeakable, nameless, despicable. See SECRET, EVIL, DISREPUTE.

unmerciful, *adj.* merciless, pitiless, inhuman, cruel; unfeeling, relentless, unrelenting; stern, hard-hearted, cold-blooded, callous. See SEVERITY, MALEVOLENCE.

unmistakable, *adj.* obvious, evident, MANIFEST, patent, clear, apparent, plain, open; downright, overt, certain. See EVIDENCE.

unmitigated, *adj.* unalleviated; downright, utter, sheer, out-and-out. See COMPLETION, PERFECTION.

unmoved, *adj.* unaffected, impassive, unsympathetic, *etc.* (see FEELING); unconvinced, firm, unwavering, unshaken, steadfast. See INSENSIBILITY, RESOLUTION, STABILITY.

unnatural, *adj.* artificial, factitious; affected, stagy, insincere; strange, abnormal, foreign; monstrous, freakish, misshapen; merciless, cold. See AFFECTATION, MALEVOLENCE, UNCONFORMITY.

unnecessary, *adj.* useless, needless, inessential, superfluous, dispensable. See USELESSNESS.

unnerve, *v.t.* unhinge, disconcert, frighten, perturb. *Colloq.*, rattle. *Slang,* give the jitters. See FEAR, AGITATION.

unobtrusive, *adj.* unassertive, unpretentious, shy, modest, retiring, timid. See MODESTY, RESTRAINT.

unoccupied, *adj.* empty, vacant, tenantless; unemployed. See ABSENCE, INACTIVITY.

unofficial, *adj.* unauthorized, unauthoritative; private. *Slang,* off the cuff, off the record, not for publication. See UNCERTAINTY.

unpack, *v.t.* unwrap, uncover, open; unload, put away. See OPENING.

unpaid, *adj.* owing, due, unsatisfied; unsalaried, volunteer. See DEBT, WILL.

unpalatable, *adj.* distasteful, unsavory, unappetizing; INSIPID; inedible, uneatable, tasteless. See TASTE.

unparalleled, *adj.* UNEQUALED, peerless, unmatched, inimitable.

unpleasant, *adj.* disagreeable, offensive, displeasing, bad, nasty, sickening; noisome; unattractive, unsatisfactory; surly, UNFRIENDLY.

unpopular, *adj.* disliked, unloved, distasteful; out of favor.

unprecedented, *adj.* new, novel, unheard-of, original. See NEWNESS.

unprejudiced, impartial, dispassionate, UNBIASED, uninfluenced.

unpremeditated, *adj.* extempore, impromptu, extemporary, impulsive, spontaneous. See IMPULSE.

UNPREPAREDNESS

Nouns—**1,** unpreparedness, unreadiness, improvidence, imprudence, inadvertence, INATTENTION; negligence, prodigality; improvisation, unpremeditation (see IMPULSE); IMPERFECTION, disqualification; immaturity, crudity, rawness, INCOMPLETENESS; abortion, prematurity. See EARLINESS, UNSKILLFULNESS.

2, [state of] nature, absence of art; virgin soil, fallow ground, unweeded garden; raw material, diamond in the rough; rough copy (see PLAN); embryo, germ (see CAUSE).

Verbs—be unprepared; lie fallow, live from hand to mouth, take no thought of tomorrow; extemporize, improvise. *Colloq.*, cook up, go off half-cocked.

Adjectives—**1,** unprepared, unready, untutored, undrilled, unexercised; untaught, uneducated, uncultured; unqualified, disqualified, unfit(ted), ill-fitted, unsuited, ineligible; unorganized, unarranged, unfurnished, unprovided, unequipped, untrimmed; out of gear, out of order, dismantled.

2, immature, unripe, raw, green; uncooked, unboiled, unconcocted, undigested, ill-digested, unmellowed, unseasoned, unleavened; crude, coarse, rough(cast), roughhewn, in the rough; unhewn, unformed, unfashioned, unwrought, unpolished.

3, rudimentary, rudimental, embryonic, *in ovo*, vestigial, inchoate, abortive, premature; undeveloped, unhatched, unfledged, unlicked, unnurtured; incomplete, imperfect.

4, fallow, unsown, untilled, uncultivated, unplowed, idle; natural, in a state of nature; undressed, in dishabille, *en déshabillé*.

5, shiftless, improvident, unthrifty, thriftless, empty-handed; negligent, unguarded, thoughtless, caught napping.

6, unpremeditated, improvised, improvisatory, improviso, extemporaneous, extempore, extemporary, impromptu, offhand; unintentional. *Colloq.*, off the cuff.

Adverbs—unpreparedly, extemporaneously, extempore, impromptu, offhand, without preparation, on the spur of the moment.

Antonym, see PREPARATION.

unprincipled, *adj.* unscrupulous, thievish, rascally; lawless, perfidious, dishonest, fraudulent; wicked, evil. See IMPROBITY.

unproductive, *adj.* inoperative; barren, unfertile, unprolific; arid, dry, sterile, unfruitful; fruitless, bootless; fallow; impotent, issueless; unprofitable, useless; null and void, of no effect. See USELESSNESS, IMPOTENCE. *Ant.,* see PRODUCTION, USE.

unprofitable, *adj.* profitless, unbeneficial, unproductive; useless, futile, bootless, fruitless; costly, expensive; unwise, inexpedient. See USELESSNESS.

unpromising, *adj.* discouraging, disappointing, hopeless. See HOPELESSNESS.

unqualified, *adj.* unfit, unsuited, ineligible; straight, thoroughgoing; certain, out-and-out, outright, unconditional, consummate, complete. See CERTAINTY, UNSKILLFULNESS.

unquenchable, *adj.* . quenchless, insatiate; thirsty, parched, arid. See DESIRE.

unquestionable, *adj.* indubitable, indisputable, certain, sure, undeniable, irrefutable, incontrovertible. See CERTAINTY.

unquiet, *adj.* disturbed, agitated; restless, unpeaceful. See AGITATION.

unravel, *v.t.* ravel, untwine, disentangle, untangle; develop, explain, unfold. See ARRANGEMENT, INTERPRETATION. *Ant.*, see MISINTERPRETATION.

unreal, *adj.* imaginary, illusionary, illusory, shadowy; imponderable, unsubstantial, fanciful, fictitious; ideal. See IMAGINATION, NONEXISTENCE.

unreasonable, *adj.* irrational, illogical, absurd, senseless, preposterous, ridiculous; immoderate, excessive, extravagant, exorbitant; stubborn, obstinate. See ABSURDITY, RESOLUTION, GREATNESS.

unrefined, *adj.* unpurified, crude, raw, natural, native; unfastidious, uncultivated, rude, coarse, inelegant, vulgar, common. See ROUGHNESS, VULGARITY.

unrelenting, *adj.* relentless, inexorable, unyielding, rigorous, obdurate, remorseless, stern. See MALEVOLENCE, VULGARITY. *Ant.*, see FORGIVENESS.

unreliable, *adj.* untrustworthy, irresponsible, unstable, treacherous, inconstant; unsure, uncertain, fallible. See IMPROBITY, DOUBT.

unremitting, *adj.* unrelieved, unceasing, unending; endless, relentless, perpetual, continuous, chronic. See CONTINUITY.

unrequited, *adj.* unrewarded, unanswered; ignored, scorned. See NEGLECT, NONPAYMENT.

unreserved, *adj.* frank, outspoken; demonstrative, cordial; unrestricted, absolute. See TRUTH, FREEDOM.

unresisting, *adj.* nonresistant, yielding, acquiescent, submissive, passive. See OBEDIENCE.

unrest, *n.* restlessness, disquiet, uneasiness; AGITATION, insurgence, rebellion. See CHANGEABLENESS.

unrestrained, *adj.* unbridled, unchecked, uncurbed, untrammeled, unbounded, free; inordinate, uninhibited, wanton, lax, loose, rampant. See FREEDOM. *Ant.*, see SUBJECTION, RESTRAINT.

unrestricted, *adj.* unlimited, unconfined, unqualified. See FREEDOM.

unripe, *adj.* premature, immature; precocious, crude. See YOUTH, ROUGHNESS.

unruffled, *adj.* serene, calm, placid, poised, undisturbed. See SMOOTHNESS, CHEERFULNESS.

unruly, *adj.* unmanageable, insubordinate, obstreperous, fractious, refractory, ungovernable, turbulent, boisterous. See DISOBEDIENCE, VIOLENCE.

unsafe, *adj.* insecure, precarious, dangerous, risky; perilous; untrustworthy. See DANGER.

unsavory, *adj.* unpalatable, ill-flavored; bitter, acrid, acerb; offensive, repulsive, nasty; sickening, nauseous, nauseating, loathsome; unpleasant, disagreeable; disreputable, unprepossessing. See TASTE, DISREPUTE.

unscientific, *adj.* instinctive, intuitive, subjective; trial-and-error, untrue, unsound, unproved. See UNTRUTH, IGNORANCE, INTUITION.

unscramble, *adj.* untangle, unmix; decode, decipher, disclose, solve. *Colloq.*, crack. *Slang,* dope out. See INTERPRETATION.

unscrupulous, *adj.* unprincipled, conscienceless, dishonest. See IMPROBITY.

unseemly, *adj.* unbecoming, unsuitable, unfitting, improper, indecent, indecorous, tasteless. See UNCONFORMITY, VULGARITY. *Ant.*, see TASTE.

unseen, *adj.* imperceptible, INVISIBLE. *Ant.*, see VISION.

unselfish, *adj.* selfless, benevolent, altruistic; charitable, liberal, generous, magnanimous; disinterested, objective; self-sacrificing. See BENEVOLENT.

unselfishness, *n.* selflessness, devotion (to others); self-abnegation, self-sacrifice, self-denial, forgetfulness (of self); Good Samaritanism, good works; renunciation; loftiness, altruism, BENEVOLENCE, philanthropy, charity; highmindedness, NOBILITY, generosity, helpfulness; liberality, bountifulness, magnanimousness, magnanimity; openhandedness, largeness, largeheartedness; impartiality, fairness, lack of prejudice; disinterestedness; considerateness, consideration, tactfulness, thoughtfulness. See AID, GIVING. *Ant.*, see SELFISHNESS.

unsettle, *v.t.* upset, disturb, disarrange, displace, DISORDER; unhinge, derange, unbalance. *Ant.*, see ARRANGEMENT.

unsettled, *adj.* outstanding, unpaid; disturbed, troubled; unfixed, indeterminate. See DEBT, DOUBT. *Ant.*, see ARRANGEMENT, PAYMENT.

unsightly, *adj.* See UGLINESS, REPULSION.

UNSKILLFULNESS

Nouns—**1,** unskillfulness, incompetence; inability, inexperience; unproficiency; quackery, maladroitness, ineptness, clumsiness, awkwardness, two left feet.

2, mismanagement, misconduct; maladministration; misrule, misgovernment, misapplication, misdirection misfeasance.

3, bungling, FAILURE; too many cooks, BLUNDER, mistake, ERROR; gaucherie, act of folly, botch, botchery; bad job; much ado about nothing, confusion, wild-goose chase, boy on a man's errand. *Slang,* snafu.

4, blunderer, bumbler, botcher, butcher, bungler, fumbler, duffer, klutz; bull in a china shop; butterfingers; greenhorn, palooka; Mrs. Malaprop.

Verbs—**1,** blunder, bungle, boggle, fumble, botch, flounder, stumble, trip, hobble; make a mess of, make a hash of; make a fool of oneself; play the fool; lose one's head. *Colloq.*, put one's foot in it; foul up. *Slang,* snafu.

2, err, make a mistake (see ERROR); mismanage, misconduct, misdirect, misapply; do things by halves; work at cross purposes; put the cart before the horse; not know what one is about; not know a hawk from a handsaw; kill the goose that lays the golden eggs; cut one's own throat, burn one's fingers; run one's head against a stone wall; fall into a trap, catch a Tartar, bring down the house about one's ears; too many irons in the fire.

Adjectives—**1,** unskillful, unskilled, inexpert, bungling, awkward, ungainly, clumsy, lubberly, gauche, maladroit; left-handed, heavy-handed; inapt, unapt, inept; neglectful; stupid, incompetent; unqualified, ill-qualified; unfit; quackish; raw, green, inexperienced. *Colloq.*, half-baked, all thumbs.

2, unaccustomed, rusty, out of practice, unused, untrained, uninitiated, unconversant, ignorant (see IGNORANCE); shiftless; unadvised, ill-advised, ill-contrived; misguided; foolish, wild; infelicitous; penny wise and pound foolish, inconsistent.

Antonym, see SKILL.

unsociable, *adj.* reserved, aloof, distant, shy, solitary, retiring. See SECLUSION.

unsolicited, *adj.* unsought (for), undue, unlooked for; voluntary. See WILL.

unsophisticated, *adj.* ingenuous, innocent, simple, guileless, ARTLESS, genuine. See INNOCENCE, SIMPLENESS.

unsound, *adj.* unhealthy, diseased, sickly; deranged, unbalanced, unsettled; untrue, incorrect, faulty, imperfect, illogical; decayed. See DISEASE, ERROR, IMPERFECTION.

unspeakable, *adj.* shocking, dreadful, horrible, execrable, enormous; unutterable, inexpressible, unimaginable. See EVIL, FEAR.

unspoiled, *adj.* perfect, intact, WHOLE, wholesome; untouched, pristine; ingenuous. See PURITY.

unspoken, *adj.* tacit, implied; unsaid. See SILENCE, MEANING.

unstable, *adj.* irregular, fluctuating, unsteady; inconstant, vacillating, fickle, changeable, variable. See CHANGEABLENESS.

unsteady, *adj.* fluctuating, waving, shifting, vacillating, irresolute, shaky, tottery, wobbly, infirm. See CHANGEABLENESS, DOUBT.

unstinting, *adj.* unsparing, generous, lavish; unbounded. See LIBERALITY.

unstrung, *adj.* unhinged, nervous, unnerved, agitated. *Slang,* jittery. See AGITATION, EXCITEMENT.

unsuccessful, *adj.* unprosperous, unfortunate, disastrous, unavailing, UNPRODUCTIVE. See FAILURE. *Ant.,* see SUCCESS, PRODUCTION.

unsullied, *adj.* immaculate, spotless, unspotted, pure, flawless, untarnished. See CLEANNESS, PURITY.

unsung, *adj.* forgotten, obscure, neglected, slighted, ignored. See UNCERTAINTY.

unsurpassed, *adj.* unrivaled, unequaled, unexcelled, incomparable, nonpareil, nonesuch, inimitable, preeminent, superlative. *Colloq.,* tops. See SUPERIORITY.

unsuspicious, *adj.* trusting, trustful, unsuspecting, credulous, unquestioning, ARTLESS. See BELIEF, CREDULITY. *Ant.,* see DOUBT.

untangle, *v.* disentangle, (un)ravel, disengage; free, extricate; comb, tease, card, straighten (out); clear up, interpret. Se ARRANGEMENT.

untaught, *adj.* illiterate, unlettered, uneducated. See IGNORANCE. *Ant.,* see KNOWLEDGE.

untenable, *adj.* indefensible, insupportable, inconsistent, illogical. See ERROR. *Ant.,* see REASONING, TRUTH.

unthinkable, *adj.* inconceivable, unimaginable, IMPOSSIBLE; repugnant, out of the question; beyond belief, UNBELIEVABLE.

untidy, *adj.* slovenly, careless, disorderly; messy, littered; dowdy, frumpy, slipshod; unkempt. See DISORDER, UNCLEANNESS.

untie, *v.t.* loosen, free, unbind, unknot. See FREEDOM. *Ant.,* see RESTRAINT.

until, *prep.* till, to, up to [the time of]. See TIME.

untimeliness, *n.* intempestivity; inopportuneness, inopportunity, unseasonableness; evil hour; contretemps; intrusion; inexpedience, earliness, lateness, anachronism. *Ant.,* see OCCASION.

untiring, *adj.* tireless, indefatigable, unwearied, unremitting, unrelaxing. See RESOLUTION.

untold, *adj.* unknown, unrevealed, undisclosed; countless, measureless, legion, innumerable. See CONCEALMENT, MULTITUDE.

untouchable, *adj. & n.* —*adj.* inaccessible, out of reach; immune, exempt, sacrosanct, taboo. —*n.* pariah, outcast(e). See DISTANCE, PROHIBITION.

untoward, *adj.* inconvenient, perverse; vexatious; ungraceful, awkward. See ADVERSITY.

untrained, *adj.* unbroken, untamed; raw, inexperienced, green. See UNSKILLFULNESS.

untrue, *adj.,* **untruth,** *n.* See DECEPTION, FALSEHOOD.

unusual, *adj.* uncommon, rare; out-of-the-way, curious, odd, queer, singular; abnormal, anomalous, exceptional, extraordinary; irregular, bizarre, peculiar; unwonted, unaccustomed. *Colloq.,* off-beat. See UNCONFORMITY, DIFFERENCE.

unutterable, *adj.* UNSPEAKABLE; unpronounceable, incommunicable, indescribable; ineffable. See WONDER.

unveil, *v.t.* disclose, reveal, uncover. See DISCLOSURE.

unwarranted, *adj.* unjustified, uncalled-for. See UNCERTAINTY, DOUBT.

unwary, *adj.* rash, unwise, indiscreet, imprudent, unguarded, injudicious. See NEGLECT. *Ant.,* see CARE.

unwell, *adj.* ailing, sick, indisposed, ill, invalid, diseased. See DISEASE.

unwieldy, *adj.* clumsy, awkward, cumbersome, ungainly, bulky, ponderous. *Colloq.,* hulking. See GRAVITY, SIZE.

UNWILLINGNESS

Nouns—unwillingness, indisposition, disinclination, aversion, DISLIKE; nolleity, nolition, renitence; reluctance, INDIFFERENCE; indocility, OBSTINACY, recalcitrance, noncompliance, recalcitrancy, DISSENT, REFUSAL; scrupulousness, fastidiousness, delicacy; scruple, qualm, demur, shrinking; hesitancy, irresolution, indecision, UNCERTAINTY.

Verbs—be unwilling, grudge, DISLIKE, not have the stomach to; scruple, stickle, stick at, boggle at, shy at, demur, hesitate, hang back, hang fire, lag, RECOIL, shrink; avoid (see AVOIDANCE); *oppose* (see OPPOSITION); DISSENT, refuse. *Slang*, duck.

Adjectives—unwilling, not in the mood *or* vein; loath, disinclined, indisposed, averse, renitent, reluctant, indifferent, restive, not content; recalcitrant, balky, demurring, objecting, unconsenting, refusing, grudging, dragging, adverse, opposed, laggard, backward, remiss, slack, slow (to); scrupulous, squeamish, fastidious; involuntary, forced; repugnant.

Adverbs—unwillingly, grudgingly, with bad grace, with an ill will; against one's will, *à contre-cœur*, against one's wishes, against the grain, with a heavy heart; *nolens volens*, willy-nilly; in spite of oneself, *malgré soi*; perforce, under protest, not for the world; no. *Colloq.*, not on your life. See NEGATION.

Antonym, see WILL.

---

unwind, *v.i.*, *colloq.*, relax, let down one's defenses, let one's hair down. See INACTIVITY.

unwise, *adj.* foolish, injudicious, imprudent, ill-advised; silly, fatuous, idiotic, senseless, impolitic, indiscreet. See IGNORANCE, ERROR.

unwitting, *adj.* unknowing, unaware, thoughtless, heedless; involuntary, inadvertent; blind, deaf. See INATTENTION, IGNORANCE.

unworkable, *adj.* inoperable, impractical; futile, no good. See IMPOSSIBILITY.

unworthy, *adj.* undeserving; worthless; unbecoming, disgraceful, shameful; despicable, discreditable, derogatory. See DISREPUTE.

unyielding, *adj.* immovable, unbending, rigid, inflexible, firm; grim, indomitable, obdurate, stubborn, obstinate, relentless, uncompromising; pertinacious, resolute; intractable, perverse. See HARDNESS, OPPOSITION, RESOLUTION, SEVERITY.

up, *adv.* upward, aloft. See ASCENT, HEIGHT. *Ant.*, down; see DESCENT.

upbraid, *v.t.* reprove, chide, admonish, rebuke, reprimand, scold; accuse, charge, revile. See DISAPPROBATION. *Ant.*, see APPROBATION.

upbringing, *n.* rearing, breeding, training, TEACHING, education; PREPARATION.

update, *v.t.* make current, modernize; revise, re-edit. See FASHION, IMPROVEMENT.

upgrade, *v.t.* improve, better; raise, INCREASE; dignify. See IMPROVEMENT.

upheaval, *n.* cataclysm, debacle; AGITATION, UNREST, revolution.

uphill, *adj.* ascending, rising; precipitous; laborious; difficult, strenuous. See EXERTION, OBLIQUITY.

uphold, *v.t.* maintain, support, sustain; champion; approve, encourage. See AID, DEFENSE, SUPPORT. *Ant.*, see OPPOSITION.

upkeep, *n.* CARE, maintenance; sustenance; overhead, expenses; pension.

uplift, *n.* elevation, IMPROVEMENT, refinement, inspiration.

upon, *prep.* on, on top of, above; by, by the act of, through; touching, against; about, regarding, concerning. See SUPERIORITY, TOUCH, SEQUENCE.

upper, *adj.* higher, superior. See HEIGHT. *Ant.*, see LOWNESS.

upper-class, *adj.* society, fashionable, elite; moneyed, propertied; exclusive. *Slang*, classy. See SUPERIORITY, WEALTH, NOBILITY.

upright, *adj.* vertical, perpendicular, erect; honorable, conscientious, upstanding, honest, righteous. *Colloq.*, straight. See DIRECTION, PROBITY. *Ant.*, horizontal; see OBLIQUITY, IMPROBITY.

uprising, *n.* revolt, REVOLUTION, rebellion, insurrection, [civil] war, coup.

uproar, *n.* tumult, hubbub, discord, pandemonium, bedlam, ado, bustle, din, clamor. *Colloq.*, hullabaloo. See DISORDER, LOUDNESS.

uproot, *v.t.* extirpate, eradicate, root out, abolish, destroy. See DESTRUCTION, EXTRACTION.

upset, *v. & n.* —*v.t.* overthrow, overturn, capsize; disturb, bother, discompose, disconcert; disarrange, unbalance; demoralize. —*n.* reversal, overturn, disorder. See DESTRUCTION, INVERSION, AGITATION.

upshot, *n.* outcome, conclusion, result, effect, meaning. See SEQUENCE.

upside-down, *adj.* reversed, inverted, head over heels, standing on one's head, bottom-side up; upended, capsized. See INVERSION, DISORDER.

upstage, *v., colloq.*, show up, overshadow. *Slang*, one-up. See INSOLENCE.

upstart, *n.* parvenu. *Colloq.*, pusher. See INSOLENCE.

upswing, *n.* IMPROVEMENT, upturn, uptrend, betterment, recovery. *Colloq.*, pickup.

up-to-date, *adj.* modern, new, fresh, current, timely; fashionable, modish, stylish; restored, renovated, revised, modernized. See NEWNESS, FASHION.

urban, *adj.* city, town, metropolitan, civic. See ABODE. *Ant.*, rural.

urbane, *adj.* suave, sophisticated, debonair; civil, polite, affable. See COURTESY.

urge, *v. & n.* —*v.* solicit, plead, importune, advocate, exhort, incite, instigate; press, push. —*n.* IMPULSE, desire, ambition. See HASTE, REQUEST.

urgent, *adj.* important, imperative, exigent, necessary, critical; importunate, pressing. See IMPORTANCE, REQUEST.

urn, *n.* vase, vessel, pot, amphora, jardiniere; samovar; cinerary urn, canopic urn. See RECEPTACLE, INTERMENT.

USE

Nouns—**1,** use, employ, employment; exercise, application, appliance; adhibition, disposal; consumption; usufruct; recourse, resort, avail; utilization, service, wear; usage, function, practice, method, HABIT; usefulness (see UTILITY); exploitation, sexism.

2, user, employer, applier, consumer, buyer, purchaser, enjoyer of.

Verbs—**1,** use, make use of, utilize, employ, put to use; put in action, operation *or* practice; set in motion, set to work; ply, work, wield, handle, maneuver, manipulate; play, play off; exert, exercise, practice, avail oneself of, profit by; resort to, have recourse to, betake oneself to; take advantage of, exploit; try.

2, render useful, turn to account, utilize; bring into play; press into service; bring to bear upon, devote, dedicate, consecrate; apply, adhibit, dispose of; make a cat's-paw of; fall back upon, make shift with; make the most of, make the best of.

3, use up, consume, absorb, dissipate; exhaust, drain; expend; tax, wear.

Adjectives—in use; used; well-worn, well-trodden; useful (see UTILITY).

Antonyms, see NEGLECT, WASTE.

USELESSNESS

Nouns—**1,** uselessness, inutility; inefficacy, futility; ineptitude, inaptitude; impracticableness, impracticality; inefficiency, incompetence, IMPOTENCE, UNSKILLFULNESS, worthlessness, vanity, inanity, nugacity; triviality, UNIMPORTANCE.

2, unproductiveness, unprofitableness; infertility, infecundity, barrenness, aridity; labor lost, wild-goose chase.

3, waste; desert, Sahara, wilderness, wild, tundra, marsh; litter, rubbish, odds and ends, cast-offs; shoddy, rags, orts, trash, refuse, sweepings, scourings, rubble, debris; stubble, leavings; dregs; weeds, tares; rubbish heap.

Verbs—1, be useless; be unproductive, come to nothing; fail; seek *or* strive after impossibilities; roll the stone of Sisyphus; bay at the moon, preach to the winds; lock the barn door after the horse is stolen; cast pearls before swine; carry coals to Newcastle. *Colloq.,* chase rainbows. 2, render useless; disable, hamper (see HINDRANCE); cripple, lame; spike guns, clip the wings; put out of gear; decommission, dismantle, disassemble, break up, tear down, raze, demolish. destroy; pull the fangs *or* teeth of, tie one's hands, put in a straitjacket.

Adjectives—1, useless, inutile, inefficacious, futile, unavailing, bootless; inoperative, unproductive, barren, infertile, sterile, fallow; unprofitable, null and void; inadequate, insufficient; inept, ineffectual, incompetent, unskillful (see UNSKILLFULNESS); superfluous, dispensable; thrown away, wasted; abortive.

2, worthless, valueless, unsaleable; not worth a straw; vain, empty, inane, gainless, profitless, fruitless; unserviceable, unprofitable; ill-spent; obsolete; good for nothing; of no earthly use; not worth having, unnecessary, unneeded.

Adverbs—uselessly, to little purpose, to no purpose, to little or no purpose.

Antonym, see UTILITY, USE.

---

usher, *v. & n.* —*v.t.* escort, introduce, announce, induct. —*n.* doorman; escort, groomsman, vestryman. See BEGINNING, RECEPTION.

usual, *adj.* customary, accustomed, habitual, ordinary, wonted, normal, regular, everyday; traditional. See HABIT. *Ant.,* see SURPRISE, UNCONFORMITY.

usurp, *v.t.* seize, expropriate, arrogate, appropriate; conquer, annex, snatch, grab. See ILLEGALITY.

UTILITY

Nouns—utility; usefulness, efficacy, efficiency, adequacy; service, stead, avail; help, AID; applicability, function, value; worth, GOODNESS; productiveness; utilization (see USE).

Verbs—be useful, avail, serve; subserve; conduce, tend; answer *or* serve a purpose; bear fruit, produce (see PRODUCTION); profit, remunerate, benefit, do good; perform *or* discharge a function; do *or* render a service; bestead, stand one in good stead; be the making of; help, AID.

Adjectives—useful, of use; serviceable, good for; instrumental, conducive, tending; subsidiary, helping, advantageous, beneficial, profitable, gainful, remunerative, worth one's salt; valuable; prolific, productive, practical, practicable; pragmatic; adequate; efficient, efficacious; effective, effectual; expedient, applicable, available, ready, handy, at hand, tangible; commodious, adaptable.

Adverbs—usefully, efficiently, *etc.*; pro bono publico.

Antonym, see USELESSNESS.

---

utmost, *adj.* most, greatest, farthest, furthest; last, final; total, unlimited, full, complete. See END, COMPLETION, WHOLE.

utopian, *adj. & n.* —*adj.* ideal(istic), optimistic, visionary, romantic; rosy; perfect; unrealistic, unworldly; Quixotic, Arcadian. —*n.* utopianist; dreamer, idealist, *etc.* (see *adj.*); Quixote. See IMAGINATION, HOPE, VISION.

utter, *adj. & v.* —*adj.* total, complete, entire; extreme, unusual; unqualified; stark, sheer, downright, absolute. —*v.t.* speak, voice; pronounce, express, enunciate, deliver. See COMPLETION, WHOLE, SOUND, SPEECH.

V

vacancy, *n.* emptiness, void, vacuum, SPACE; inanity, stupidity, idleness. See ABSENCE. *Ant.,* see PRESENCE, DENSITY.

vacant, *adj.* empty; open, free, untenanted, unoccupied, to let; blank, void, hollow; shallow, brainless, inane. See ABSENCE, OPENING. *Ant.,* see PRESENCE.

vacate, *v.* move out; leave, decamp; abandon, relinquish, surrender, quit; evacuate, leave empty; annul, cancel, invalidate, quash. See RELINQUISHMENT.

vacation, *n.* holiday, rest, time off, leave [of absence]; recess, respite; abandonment, DEPARTURE. See INACTIVITY.

vaccinate, *v.t.* jennerize, variolate; inoculate, inject; vastate, equinate, immunize; prick, scratch, scarify. *Colloq.,* give shots. See REMEDY.

vaccine, *n.* bacterin, serum, antitoxin, immunotoxin. See REMEDY.

vacillation, *n.* uncertainty; fluctuation; hesitation, faltering, shillyshallying. See DOUBT, OSCILLATION.

vacuum, *n.* void, vacancy, emptiness, nothingness; SPACE.

vagabond, *n.* hobo, tramp; vagrant, wanderer; idler; beggar. *Colloq.,* bum, knight of the road. See TRAVEL, POPULACE.

vagary, *n.* fancy, notion, CAPRICE, whim; quirk, foible. See UNCONFORMITY.

vagrant, *n. & adj.* —*n.* VAGABOND, *etc.* —*adj.* wandering, aimless, wayward, roving; erratic, capricious. See TRAVEL.

vague, *adj.* unclear, blurred, blurry; amorphous, shapeless; undefined, uncertain; indistinct; inexact, indefinite; obscure. See DIMNESS, DOUBT. *Ant.,* see CERTAINTY, VISION.

vain, *adj.* proud, conceited; futile, fruitless. See VANITY.

valediction, *n.* farewell speech, valedictory; farewell, good-by(e), adieu. See DEPARTURE, SPEECH.

valet, *n.* SERVANT; manservant, gentleman's gentleman, attendant.

valiant, *adj.* valorous, brave, courageous, gallant; daring, intrepid, dauntless, lionhearted. See COURAGE. *Ant.,* see COWARDICE.

valid, *adj.* sound, logical; legal, binding, well-grounded, just. See TRUTH, REASONING, LEGALITY. *Ant.,* see IMPOTENCE, ILLEGALITY.

valley, *n.* vale; river land; dale, dell, glen; canyon, hollow. See CONCAVITY.

valor, *n.* COURAGE, intrepidity, fearlessness; prowess, heroism, gallantry; daring, derring-do. *Ant.,* see COWARDICE.

valuable, *adj.* precious, costly; worthy, meritorious; estimable; useful. See IMPORTANCE, USE. *Ant.,* see USELESSNESS.

value, *n. & v.* —*n.* usefulness; worth; price, cost, rate, rating; estimation, valuation; merit; significance; SHADE, tone, emphasis. —*v.t.* esteem, prize, treasure, regard highly; appraise, evaluate, assess, rate. See IMPORTANCE. *Ant.,* see CHEAPNESS, UNIMPORTANCE.

valve, *n.* damper, cutoff, cock, butterfly, pallet, poppet; ventil, side valve; plug, piston, cusp. See CLOSURE, OPENING.

vamp, *n., slang,* flirt, coquette. See IMPURITY, FEMALE.

vampire, *n.* bloodsucker, bat; ghoul; parasite. *Slang,* siren, seducer, vamp, temptress. See EVILDOER, IMPURITY.

van, *n.* truck, lorry, moving van; forefront, vanguard; *avant garde*; FRONT, head. See VEHICLE. *Ant.,* see REAR.

vandalism, *n.* pillage, depredation, plundering; DESTRUCTION, mutilation, defacement; sabotage; desecration, profanation; barbarianism.

vane, *n.* girouette, anemometer; cone, sleeve, sock; arm, plate, fin, blade. See WIND, INDICATION.

vanguard, *n.* van; spearhead, front line, shock troops; Marines; *avant-*

garde; forerunner, leader; innovators, modernists. See COMBATANT, PRECEDENCE.

vanish, *v.i.* disappear, fade out; dissolve; become invisible. *Slang,* decamp, vamoose, beat it. See ABSENCE, DEPARTURE. *Ant.,* see APPEARANCE.

VANITY

Nouns—1, vanity, conceit, conceitedness; immodesty, self-esteem, self-love, self-praise; complacency, smugness, *amour propre*.

2, PRIDE, airs, pretensions, mannerism; egotism, egoism; priggishness; coxcombery, vainglory, pretense, OSTENTATION; assurance, INSOLENCE.

3, egotist, egoist, prig, pretender, fop, coxcomb, know-it-all.

4, vainness, futility, USELESSNESS.

Verbs—be vain; put oneself forward; fish for compliments; give oneself airs; BOAST; presume, swagger, strut; plume *or* preen oneself. *Colloq.,* get on one's high horse. *Slang,* put on side, the dog *or* the ritz.

Adjectives—vain, vain as a peacock, conceited, immodest, overweening, pert, forward; haughty, puffed-up (see PRIDE); prideful, vainglorious, high-flown, ostentatious; self-satisfied, smug, complacent, opinionated; imperious, arrogant, pretentious, priggish; egotistic; *soi-disant*; unabashed, unblushing. *Colloq.,* swell-headed.

Adverbs—vainly, priggishly, pridefully, proudly, haughtily, *etc.*

Antonym, see MODESTY.

vanquish, *v.t.* conquer, subdue, subjugate, overcome; quell, silence; worst, rout; MASTER. See SUCCESS. *Ant.,* see FAILURE.

vapid, *adj.* flat, tasteless, INSIPID; tame, spiritless, lifeless, DULL.

VAPOR

Nouns—1, vapor, vaporousness, vaporization, volatilization; gaseousness, gaseity; evaporation; distillation, aëration, sublimation, exhalation; volatility.

2, gas, elastic fluid; oxygen, ozone, hydrogen, nitrogen, argon, helium, fluorine, neon; natural gas, coal gas, illuminating gas; sewer gas, poison gas; damp, chokedamp; AIR, vapor, ether, steam, fume, reek, effluvium, miasma, flatus; cloud (see CLOUDINESS).

3, vaporizer, atomizer, still, retort; fumigation, steaming; spray, spray gun, airbrush, sprayer.

4, pneumatics, pneumostatics; aerostatics, aerodynamics.

Verbs—vaporize, volatize, render gaseous, distill, sublime; evaporate, exhale, smoke, transpire, emit vapor, fume, reek, steam, fumigate.

Adjectives—vaporous, volatile, volatilized, gaseous, gassy, reeking; aëriform, evaporable, vaporizable.

Antonym, see DENSITY.

variance, *n.* CHANGE, alteration; difference, DISAGREEMENT, DISCORD; jarring; dissension; variation, UNCONFORMITY.

variation, *n.* variance, alteration, CHANGE, modification; diversification; DIVERGENCE, DEVIATION, aberration; innovation. *Ant.,* see IDENTITY, STABILITY.

VARIEGATION

Nouns—1, variegation, diversification, diversity, diversion, heterogeneity; spottiness, maculation, striation, streakiness, marbling, elaboration, discoloration; parti- *or* party-color, dichroism, dichromatism, polychrome; iridescence, iridization, opalescence, play of colors. See COLOR.

2, stripes, bands, streaks, striae; vein, thread, line; check, plaid, tartan, motley, tricolor; marquetry, parquetry, mosaic, tessellation, tesserae; chessboard, checkers; confetti, patchwork, crazy quilt, harlequin, Joseph's coat [of many colors]; spectrum, rainbow, iris, tulip; peacock, chameleon, butterfly, zebra, leopard, piebald; tortoiseshell, mother-of-pearl, nacre, opal, marble, mackerel sky; kaleidoscope; color organ.

Verbs—variegate, vary, variate, varify, diversify; stripe, striate, streak, line, checker, counterchange; (be)spot, dot, mottle, dapple, brindle, pie, (be)speckle, freckle, (be)sprinkle, stipple, maculate, fleck, pepper, powder; inlay, tessellate, tattoo, damascene; vein, marble(ize), water; embroider, figure, braid, quilt, fret, lace, interlace.

Adjectives—variegated, varied, various, diverse, diversified; many-colored or -hued, multi- or varicolored, parti- or party-colored, divers-colored; bicolor, tricolor, versicolor, polychromatic, dichromatic, kaleidoscopic(al); chameleonic; iridescent, opalescent, opaline, prismatic, rainbow-hued, rainbowlike, nacreous, nacre, pearly, chatoyant, cymophanous, tortoise-shell, shot; pied, paint, pinto, piebald; mottled, motley, harlequin, marbled, dappled, clouded, paned, pepper-and-salt; spotted, spotty, dotted, speckled, freckled, studded, flecked, peppered, powdered, punctuated; striped, listed, streaked, streaky, banded, barred, cross-barred, striated, veined, lined, watered, brindle(d), tabby, tiger-striped, grizzled; mosaic, tessellated, plaid, tartan, checkered, checked, embroidered, daedal.

Antonym, see UNIFORMITY.

---

variety, *n.* variation, diversity, DIFFERENCE; assortment; kind, CLASS; brand; multifariousness; VAUDEVILLE.

various, *adj.* diversified, multiform, diverse; different; many, several; manifold, numerous, sundry; changeable, unfixed. See DIFFERENCE, MULTITUDE. *Ant.*, see SIMILARITY.

varnish, *n. & v.* —*n.* shellac, lac, lacquer; spar; gloss, mitigation, whitewash, excuse. —*v.t.* paint with shellac, *etc.*; palliate, gloze, gloss, excuse, whitewash; finish.

vary, *v.* CHANGE, alter; fluctuate; differ, disagree. See DIFFERENCE. *Ant.*, see UNIFORMITY.

vase, *n.* urn, cup, chalice, jug, amphora, ampulla. See RECEPTACLE.

vassal, *n.* liege, liegeman, (feudal) tenant; serf; thrall, bondman; subject. See SERVANT.

vast, *adj.* huge, immense; infinite, boundless; immeasurable; tremendous, enormous. See SIZE, SPACE. *Ant.*, see LITTLENESS.

vat, *n.* vessel, cistern, tank, drum, ca(u)ldron; tub, tun, puncheon, bac(k), barrel, cask, hogshead, keg, butt. See RECEPTACLE, COLOR.

vaudeville, *n.* turns, acts, variety; burlesque, music hall. See DRAMA.

vault, *n. & v.* —*n.* arch, dome, cupola; bank vault, safe; tomb, sepulcher, catacomb; dungeon, cell, cellar; LEAP, jump, pole-vault. —*v.* arch; leap over, jump; pole-vault. See CONVEXITY, INTERMENT.

vaunt, *v.* boast, brag, vapor, talk big. See BOASTING. *Ant.*, see MODESTY.

veer, *v.i.* swerve, shift; jibe, come about, yaw, deviate. See CHANGE, DEVIATION. *Ant.*, see DIRECTION.

VEGETABLE

Nouns—**1,** vegetable kingdom, vegetation, vegetable life; plants, flora, verdure.

2, vegetable, plant; tree, shrub, bush; vine, creeper; herb, herbage; grass; annual, perennial, biennial, triennial.

3, timber, timberland, forest; wood, woodlands; park, chase, greenwood, brake, grove, copse, coppice, thicket, spinney; underbrush, brushwood; tree, shade tree, *etc.*

4, brush, jungle, prairie; heath, heather; fern, bracken; furze, gorse, grass, sod, turf; pasture, pasturage; sedge, rush, weed; fungus, mushroom, toadstool; lichen, moss; growth.

5, foliage, foliation, branch, bough, ramage, leaf; flower, bloom, blossom, bine; pulse, legume, bean, root, bulb.

6, BOTANY, AGRICULTURE, agronomy, horticulture; silviculture; botanist, plant physiologist, horticulturist, *etc.*; botanical gardens, herbarium, arboretum.

Adjectives—vegetable, herbaceous, botanic; sylvan, arboreous, arborescent, dendritic, woody, grassy, verdant, verdurous; floral; mossy; lignous, ligneous; wooden; woodsy, leguminous; endogenous, exogenous.

vegetarian, *n. & adj.* —*n.* cerealist, herbivore, granivore, nutarian, lactovegetarian; phytophagan; food faddist. *Colloq.*, health nut. —*adj.* VEGETABLE; Lenten, meatless; herbivorous, vegetivorous, plantivorous; grain-eating, granivorous; uncarnivorous. See FOOD, ASCETICISM.

vegetation, *n.* vegetable life; flora, verdure, greenery. See VEGETABLE, INACTIVITY.

vehemence, *n.* VIOLENCE, VIGOR; impetuosity; force; ardor, fervor, warmth, zeal. See EXERTION. *Ant.*, see MODERATION.

vehement, *adj.* violent, furious, hot; forcible; impetuous, excited, passionate; fervent. See EXCITEMENT.

VEHICLE

Nouns—**1,** vehicle, conveyance, equipage, turnout, cart, rig, car, wagon, railroad train. See PASSAGE, TRAVEL.

2, carriage, coach, chariot, chaise, phaeton, landau, barouche, victoria, brougham, sulky; two-wheeler, dogcart, trap, buggy.

3, stage, stagecoach, diligence, mailcoach; hackney; omnibus, bus, cab, taxi, taxicab, hansom. *Colloq.*, jitney, hack.

4, sled, sledge, sleigh, bobsled, toboggan, travois, Alpine slide.

5, handcart, pushcart, barrow, wheelbarrow, handbarrow; sedan chair; gocart, baby carriage, perambulator, stroller; wheelchair, litter, stretcher. *Colloq.*, pram.

6, cycle, bicycle, wheel, two-wheeler, tricycle, velocipede, three-wheeler; motorcycle, motor scooter, scooter. *Slang*, bike, trike, motorbike.

7, automobile, car, motorcar; sedan, coupé, limousine, cabriolet, phaeton, convertible, roadster, touring car; stock car; trailer, caravan; racing car; patrol car, squad *or* police car, patrol wagon, Black Maria; ambulance, hearse; station wagon, beach wagon, suburban; dune buggy; Jeep; truck, lorry, tractor, van, moving van, semitrailer; wrecker. *Colloq.*, auto. *Slang*, bus, flivver, hotrod, rod; heap, jalopy; prowl car.

8, train, locomotive, passenger train, streamliner; express, local, limited, freight train; subway, subway train, underground, tube, Metro; trolley, streetcar, cable car, interurban, tram, trackless trolley; freight car, boxcar, Pullman, sleeper, refrigerator car, tender, tank car, caboose, dining car, smoking car, day coach.

veil, *n. & v.* —*n.* net, mesh; curtain, screen, cloak, cover; film, haze, CLOUDINESS. —*v.t.* conceal; becloud; disguise; shield, cover, shroud. See CONCEALMENT, COVERING, CLOTHING. *Ant.*, see DISCLOSURE.

vein, *n.* blood vessel; streak, stripe, marbling; rib (of a leaf); [ore] deposit, lode, seam, ledge, leader; thread; bent, humor, disposition, temper. See PASSAGE, COLOR.

vellum, *n.* parchment, skin, sheepskin; papyrus; manuscript, document. See WRITING, MATERIALS.

VELOCITY

Nouns—**1,** velocity, speed, celerity, swiftness, rapidity, expedition (see ACTIVITY); acceleration; HASTE; hurry, spurt, rush, dash; smart, lively, swift *or* spanking pace; flying, flight; gallop, canter, trot, run, scamper; race, horserace, steeplechase; sweepstakes, Derby; handicap; foot race, marathon, relay race.

2, lightning, light, electricity, wind; cannonball, rocket, arrow, dart, quicksilver; telegraph, express train; torrent; hustler; eagle, antelope, courser, racehorse, gazelle, cheetah, greyhound, hare, deer, doe, jackrabbit, squirrel.

Verbs—**1,** speed, hasten, post, scuttle; scud, scour, scamper; run, fly, race, cut away, shoot, tear, whisk, sweep, whiz, skim, brush; bowl along; rush, dash, bolt; trot, gallop, bound, flit, spring, charge, dart; march in double time; ride hard, cover the ground. *Colloq.*, cut along, step along, step lively, zip, cut and run, make it snappy. *Slang*, go all out, go hell-bent for election, go like a bat out of hell; skedaddle; go hell-for-leather, burn up the road; make tracks.
2, hurry, hasten (see HASTE); accelerate, quicken; wing one's way; spur on; crowd on sail; gain ground; show a clean pair of heels; overtake, overhaul, outstrip. *Slang*, stir one's stumps, step on the gas, give her the gun, boot home.

Adjectives—fast, speedy, swift, rapid, quick, fleet; nimble, agile, expeditious, express; flying, galloping, light-footed, nimble-footed; winged, mercurial, electric, telegraphic; light of heel; swift as an arrow; quick as lightning, quick as thought.

Adverbs—swiftly, apace; at a great rate, at full speed, full tilt, posthaste; all sails crowding, heeling over, full steam ahead; trippingly; instantaneously; in seven league boots; with whip and spur; as fast as one's legs will carry one; at top speed; by leaps and bounds. *Colloq.*, on the double, at a fast clip, like mad, like sixty, like all possessed, like greased lightning, like a streak, like a blue streak. *Slang*, P.D.Q., likety-split, like a bat out of hell; jet-propelled.
Antonym, see SLOWNESS.

---

velvet, *n. & adj.* —*n.* silk, plush, velour, velveteen; mossiness; SMOOTHNESS, SOFTNESS. *Slang*, surplus, winnings, profit; gravy, graft. —*adj.* velvety, mossy; smooth, soft, mild, soothing, bland; light, caressing.

venal, *adj.* money-loving, mercenary, sordid; corrupt, bribable; purchasable (of persons). See IMPROBITY, PARSIMONY. *Ant.*, see PROBITY.

vend, *v.* sell (see SALE); publish, issue. See PUBLICATION.

vendetta, *n.* feud, grudge fight, vengeance. See CONTENTION.

veneer, *n.* facing; overlay; coating; shell; superficial polish. See LAYER, COVERING, AFFECTATION.

venerable, *adj.* aged, hoary; respected, revered; patriarchal. See AGE.

veneration, *n.* esteem, RESPECT; admiration, WORSHIP; awe. *Ant.*, see DISRESPECT.

venereal, *adj.* sexual, genital, coital; syphilitic, luetic; gonorrheal, chancrous; aphrodisiac, cantharidian. See DESIRE, DISEASE.

vengeance, *n.* RETALIATION, revenge; vengefulness; reprisal, retribution, nemesis. *Ant.*, see FORGIVENESS.

venial, *adj.* excusable, pardonable, slight, trivial. See MODERATION.

venomous, *adj.* poisonous; spiteful, malicious, malignant; envenomed, noxious, toxic; virulent, deadly. See MALEVOLENCE, DISEASE.

vent, *v. & n.* —*v.t.* utter, express; let out, let off, emit, expel. —*n.* ventilator, OPENING, airhole, air pipe, outlet, funnel; emission; blowhole; utterance, expression. See SPEECH, WIND, AIR.

ventilate, *v.t.* AIR; freshen; disclose, publish. See PUBLICATION.

venture, *v. & n.* —*v.* dare, risk; speculate; undertake; presume, hazard, take a chance. —*n.* enterprise, UNDERTAKING; adventure; speculation, hazard, risk. See RASHNESS, CHANCE.

veracity, *n.* veraciousness, truthfulness, frankness, TRUTH; sincerity, candor, honesty, fidelity; plain dealing, *bona fides*; PROBITY; ingenuousness. *Ant.*, see FALSEHOOD, IMPROBITY.

verbal, *adj.* spoken, oral; unwritten; literal, verbatim, word-for-word. See SPEECH. *Ant.*, see WRITING.

verbatim, *adj. & adv.* —*adj.* word-for-word, literal, verbal, letter-perfect; unchanged, unedited. —*adv. sic, literatim.* See TRUTH, WORD.

verbose, *adj.* wordy, prolix, repetitive, talkative. See LOQUACITY.

verdant, *adj.* green, grassy; fresh, springlike; inexperienced, naïve, artless.

verdict, *n.* JUDGMENT, ruling, finding, decision, opinion, decree; determination, conclusion; award, sentence. See JUSTICE, LAWSUIT, CHOICE.

verdure, *n.* grass, growth, greenness, greenery. See VEGETABLE.

verge, *n. & v.* —*n.* EDGE, brink, marge. margin; point, eve; LIMIT. —*v.i.* be on the point (of); border, skirt, approach, touch; tend, incline. See TENDENCY, NEARNESS.

verify, *v.t.* corroborate, substantiate; confirm, prove, make certain; establish; identify. See EVIDENCE, SUPPORT. *Ant.,* see NEGATION.

veritable, *adj.* real, genuine, authentic; proven, valid; virtual. See TRUTH.

vermin, *n.* pests, insects, rats, mice; scum, riffraff. See ANIMAL, POPULACE.

vernacular, *n.* tongue, dialect; argot, SLANG. See SPEECH.

versatile, *adj.* many-sided; adaptable; skilled. See SKILL.

verse, *n.* versification; POETRY, prosody, poesy; line; stanza; meter, measure; poem, doggerel; (scriptural) passage.

versed, *adj.* skilled, skillful; knowledgeable; accomplished, trained, conversant. See SKILL, KNOWLEDGE. *Ant.,* see UNSKILLFULNESS, IGNORANCE.

version, *n.* rendition; account; translation. See INTERPRETATION.

vertex, *n.* top, apex, head, cap, crown, pinnacle, HEIGHT; acme, zenith.

VERTICAL

Nouns—**1,** vertical, perpendicular, upright; verticality, plumbness, aplomb, perpendicularity, orthogonality, ELEVATION, erection; right angle, normal, azimuth circle; square, plumb, plumbline, plummet. **2,** wall, precipice, cliff, steep, bluff, crag, escarpment, palisade. See ASCENT.

Verbs—be vertical, stand up, on end, erect *or* upright; stick *or* cock up; erect, rear, raise; set, stick, cock *or* raise up; upraise, upend, raise on its legs; true, plumb, square.

Adjectives—vertical, upright, erect, perpendicular, plumb, true, straight, bolt upright, up-and-down; sheer, steep; rampant, standing up; normal, rectangular, orthogonal, longitudinal.

Adverbs—vertically, uprightly, erectly, up, on end, right on end, *à plomb,* endways, endwise; on one's legs *or* feet; at right angles, square.

Antonym, see HORIZONTAL, CURVATURE.

vertigo, *n.* dizziness, giddiness, vertiginousness. See INSANITY.

verve, *n.* gusto, vivacity, dash, fervor, elan, VIGOR. See ENERGY, POWER, ACTIVITY.

very, *adv.* exceedingly, highly; emphatically, decidedly, notably; unusually, remarkably, uncommonly; extremely, surpassingly. See GREATNESS. *Ant.,* see MODERATION.

vessel, *n.* container; vase, urn, jug; boat, SHIP. See RECEPTACLE.

vest, *v. & n.* —*v.t.* furnish, endow, invest; clothe; give the power *or* right, enfranchise; authorize. —*n.* waistcoat; bodice. *Colloq.,* weskit. See LEGALITY, CLOTHING, PROVISION.

vestibule, *n.* foyer, lobby, hall(way), reception hall; PASSAGE, entry-(way); anteroom *or* -chamber, alcove; narthex; porch, portico. See INGRESS, APPROACH.

vestige, *n.* trace, REMAINDER, EVIDENCE, relic.

vestments, *n.* canonicals; cloth; habit; robe, gown, frock, surplice, cassock, scapular, scapulary, cope, scarf, amice, chasuble, alb, stole; fanon; tonsure, cowl, coif, hood; calotte; bands; pontificals, pall; mitre, miter, tiara, triple crown; cardinal's hat, red hat, biretta; crozier, pastoral staff; thurible. See CLOTHING.

vestry, *n.* vestiary, sacristy; chapel. See RECEPTACLE, PREPARATION, WORSHIP.

veteran, *n.* old man, elder, patriarch, graybeard; grandfather, grandmother; old campaigner, seasoned *or* old soldier, ex-soldier; octogenarian, nonagenarian, centenarian. *Colloq.*, oldster, old-timer, codger, gaffer. See COMBATANT, AGE. *Ant.*, see YOUTH.

veterinarian, *n.* veterinary, animal *or* horse doctor. *Colloq.*, vet. See REMEDY.

veto, *n. & v.* —*n.* NULLIFICATION; "no," nyet; pocket veto; disapproval, prohibition. —*v.t.* turn thumbs down; forbid; disallow, prevent, disapprove, prohibit, negate; kill, quash. See DISAPPROBATION, NEGATION, REFUSAL.

vex, *v.* tease, plague, harass, torment; roil, pique; fret, chafe, irritate, annoy, provoke, nettle. *Colloq.*, peeve, rile, upset. See RESENTMENT.

via, *prep.* through, along, on by way of, by means of, per. See DIRECTION.

viable, *adj.* fertile, capable; possible, workable, potential; alive, living, vibrant. See LIFE, POSSIBILITY.

viaduct, *n.* trestle, bridge, span, arch. See PASSAGE, CONNECTION.

vial, *n.* phial; flask, *flacon*, vessel, ampoule; test tube. See RECEPTACLE.

vibrant, *adj.* pulsing, athrob, seismic; resonant, sonorous; robust, healthy, dynamic, energetic, vital. See OSCILLATION, RESONANCE, VIGOR.

vibration, *n.* vibrating; shaking, shimmying; thrill, quiver, throb, pulsation; AGITATION, trembling; rattling. See OSCILLATION.

vicarious, *adj.* substitutive; once removed, secondhand, indirect; proxy, deputy; imaginary, fictive, fictional. See SUBSTITUTION, IMAGINATION.

vice, *n.* viciousness, evildoing, wrongdoing, wickedness, iniquity, sin, sinfulness; crime, criminality; immorality, IMPURITY, looseness of morals; demoralization, turpitude, moral turpitude, depravity, degradation; weakness, weakness of the flesh, fault, frailty, ERROR; besetting sin; delinquency; sink of iniquity. See EVIL, IMPROBITY. *Ant.*, see GOOD, VIRTUE, PROBITY.

vice versa, oppositely, contrariwise, conversely, turnabout. See OPPOSITION.

vicinity, *n.* neighborhood, locality, vicinage; NEARNESS, proximity; environs, ENVIRONMENT.

vicious, *adj.* sinful, wicked, iniquitous, immoral, WRONG; criminal, disorderly; vile, felonious, nefarious, infamous, heinous; demoralized, corrupt, depraved, perverted; evil-minded, shameless; abandoned, debauched, degenerate, dissolute; reprobate, beyond redemption. See EVIL, IMPROBITY.

vicissitude, *n.* CHANGE; change of fortunes; fluctuation.

victim, *n.* prey; sufferer; DUPE, gull, cat's-paw; sacrifice, martyr. See PAIN.

victimize, *v.t.* cheat, dupe, swindle; hoax, fool, gull; deceive, hoodwink. *Colloq.*, sell, bamboozle. See DECEPTION.

victor, *n.* champion, winner; conqueror, vanquisher. See SUCCESS. *Ant.*, see FAILURE.

victory, *n.* conquest, triumph, SUCCESS; winning, mastery; the palm, laurel, wreath, award, trophy, prize, pennant. *Ant.*, see FAILURE.

victuals, *n.pl.* See FOOD.

vie, *v.i.* rival, emulate; contend, strive, compete. See CONTENTION.

view, *n. & v.* —*n.* sight; panorama, vista, prospect, scene; viewpoint, angle; opinion, BELIEF, notion; APPEARANCE, aspect. —*v.t.* see; survey, scan; watch, witness; consider, regard, study. See VISION, THOUGHT.

vigilant, *adj.* alert, wary, watchful; wakeful, unsleeping; careful, cautious, circumspect; on the lookout, on the *qui vive*. See CARE. *Ant.*, see NEGLECT.

vignette, *n.* decoration, ornament; picture, illustration, depiction, sketch, squib, piece, DESCRIPTION. See ORNAMENTATION, WRITING.

VIGOR

Nouns—1, vigor, force, might, POWER, STRENGTH, ENERGY, potency, efficacy, ACTIVITY, vitality, virility; HEALTH, stamina; spirit, verve, warmth, glow, sap, pith, bloom, tone, mettle, elasticity. *Colloq.*, vim, zip. *Slang*, pep, punch.

2, ardor, fire, enthusiasm, piquancy, pungency, intensity, trenchancy; vehemence, point, cogency.

*Adjectives—***1,** vigorous, strong, mighty, powerful, potent, energetic, mettlesome, active, virile; healthy, hardy, hearty, hale, robust, SOUND, sturdy, stalwart, muscular, lusty, strenuous, well, buxom, brisk, alert, glowing, sparkling, in good health; thrifty, fresh, flourishing. *Slang*, peppy.

2, spirited, lively, racy, bold, sensational, nervous, trenchant, piquant, pungent, biting, slashing, sharp, severe; incisive, forcible, forceful, effective, cogent, pithy, pointed, full of point; picturesque, vivid, poetic.

Adverbs—vigorously, powerfully, *etc.*; emphatically, in glowing terms.

Antonym, see IMPOTENCE.

---

vile, *adj.* base, debased, low, lowly, mean; repulsive, odious; foul, nasty; EVIL, corrupt, wicked, depraved. See BADNESS, IMPURITY. *Ant.*, see GOODNESS, VIRTUE.

vilify, *v.t.* revile, calumniate; traduce, slander, libel; defame; decry, belittle, slur. See DETRACTION. *Ant.*, see APPROBATION.

village, *n.* town, hamlet, small town. See ABODE.

villain, *n.* blackguard, scoundrel; knave, rascal, rogue; badman; EVIL-DOER. *Slang*, heavy (see DRAMA). See EVIL. *Ant.*, see GOODNESS.

villainy, *n.* roguery, rascality; criminality, depravity, wickedness, wrongdoing. See EVIL. *Ant.*, see GOODNESS.

vim, *n.* zest, ENERGY, VIGOR. *Colloq.*, pep, zip, ginger.

VINDICATION

*Nouns—***1,** vindication, justification, warrant; exoneration, exculpation; ACQUITTAL; whitewashing; extenuation; palliation; softening, mitigation.

2, reply, DEFENSE, objection, demurrer, exception; apology, plea, pleading; excuse, extenuating circumstances; allowance, argument. *Colloq.*, alibi.

3, vindicator, apologist, justifier, defender, defendant (see ACCUSATION).

*Verbs—***1,** vindicate, justify, warrant; exculpate, ACQUIT; clear, set right, exonerate, whitewash; extenuate, palliate, excuse, soften; apologize, put a good face upon; mince; gloss over, bolster up. *Colloq.*, whitewash, give a clean bill of health.

2, defend; advocate; stand, stick *or* speak up for; bear out, support; plead, say in defense; propugn, put in a good word for. *Slang*, go to bat for.

3, make allowance for, take the will for the deed, do justice to; give one his due, give the devil his due; make good; prove one's case.

Adjectives—vindicated, vindicating, vindicatory, vindicative; palliative; exculpatory; apologetic, vindicable; excusable, defensible, pardonable; venial, specious, plausible, justifiable.

Antonym, see ACCUSATION, GUILT.

---

vindictive, *adj.* vengeful, spiteful; resentful; implacable, rancorous; bearing a grudge. See RETALIATION, RESENTMENT. *Ant.*, see FORGIVENESS.

vine, *n.* climber, creeper, runner, twiner, tendril, vinelet; liana, bine, stem, shoot; grapevine, ivy, wisteria, *etc.* See VEGETABLE.

vinegar, *n.* acetum, pickle; condiment, preservative; SOURNESS.

vintage, *n.* crop, produce, harvest; viticulture, viniculture; [vintage] wine, *vin du pays*; TIME, age, style, period. See FASHION, DRUNKENNESS, FOOD.

violate, *v.* break, breach; outrage, profane, desecrate; disrespect; transgress, infringe; usurp, encroach; rape, ravish. See ILLEGALITY, IMPURITY, IMPIETY. *Ant.*, see OBEDIENCE, RESPECT.

VIOLENCE

Nouns—**1,** violence, vehemence, intensity, might, impetuosity; boisterousness; effervescence, ebullition, ebullience; turbulence, bluster; uproar, riot, row, rumpus, devil to pay, the fat in the fire; turmoil, DISORDER; ferment, AGITATION; storm, tempest, rough weather; squall, earthquake, volcano, thunderstorm, cyclone, tornado, hurricane; maelstrom, whirlpool.

2, SEVERITY, ferocity, ferociousness, fierceness, rage, fury; exacerbation, exasperation, malignity; fit, frenzy, paroxysm, orgasm; force, brute force; outrage, strain, shock, spasm, convulsion, throe; hysterics, passion, EXCITEMENT.

3, outbreak, outburst; burst, discharge, volley, explosion, blast, detonation, rush, eruption, displosion, implosion; torrent; storm center.

4, fury, fiend, dragon, demon, tiger; wild beast; fire-eater, hellion, hellcat, virago, termagant, beldame; madcap; rabble rouser, lynch mob, terrorist, agitator, *agent provocateur*; thug, tough, strongarm man, gunman.

Verbs—**1,** be violent, run high; ferment, effervesce; rampage; run wild, run riot; break the peace; rush, tear; rush headlong, run amuck, raise a riot; lash out, make the fur fly; bluster, rage, roar, riot, storm; seethe, boil, boil over; fume, foam, come in like a lion, wreak, wreck, spread havoc, ride roughshod, out-Herod Herod; spread like wildfire. *Colloq.,* make *or* kick up a row, raise the devil, raise Cain, raise the roof; roughhouse; fly off the handle; blow one's top, let off steam.

2, break out, fly out, burst out; explode, implode, go off, displode, fly, detonate, thunder, blow up, flash, flare, burst; shock, strain.

3, render violent, stir up, excite, incite, urge, lash, stimulate; irritate, inflame, kindle, foment, touch off; aggravate, exasperate, exacerbate, convulse, infuriate, madden, lash into *or* goad to fury; fan the flames, add fuel to the flames.

Adjectives—**1,** violent, vehement; ungentle, boisterous, wild; impetuous; rampant.

2, turbulent; disorderly, blustering, raging, troublous, riotous, tumultuous, obstreperous, uproarious; extravagant, unmitigated; ravening, frenzied, desperate (see RASHNESS); infuriated, furious, outrageous, frantic, hysterical; fiery, flaming, scorching, hot, red-hot; seething; savage, fierce, ferocious, barbarous; headstrong, ungovernable, uncontrollable; convulsive, explosive; volcanic, meteoric; stormy.

Adverbs—violently, *etc.*; amain; by storm, by force, by main force; with might and main; tooth and nail; with a vengeance; headlong.

Antonym, see MODERATION.

---

violin, *n.* fiddle; string; Amati, Stradivarius, Strad, Guarnerius; violinist (see MUSICIAN); (*pl.*) string section. See MUSICAL INSTRUMENTS.

viper, *n.* snake, serpent; traitor, turncoat, Judas [Iscariot], Iago, doubledealer; viperess. *Slang,* rat. See EVIL.

virago, *n.* termagant, vixen, shrew, mænad, hellcat. See FEMALE, IRASCIBILITY.

virgin, *n. & adj.* —*n.* maiden; celibate; vestal; spinster. —*adj.* chaste, untouched; maidenly, fresh, virginal, pure; new, uncut, unexplored, primeval. See CELIBACY, NEWNESS, PURITY. *Ant.,* see MARRIAGE.

virile, *adj.* manly, MALE, masculine; vigorous, potent; fully-sexed. *Ant.,* see IMPOTENCE.

virtual, *adj.* practical; implied, implicit; substantial; true, veritable; potential. See SUBSTANCE, NEARNESS.

VIRTUE

Nouns—virtue; virtuousness, GOODNESS; morality; moral rectitude; integrity, PROBITY; nobleness (see REPUTE); prudence; morals, ethics,

DUTY; cardinal virtues; merit, worth, excellence, CREDIT; self-control (see RESOLUTION); fortitude, self-denial (see MODERATION); JUSTICE, PURITY; good deeds, good behavior; discharge, fulfillment *or* performance of duty; INNOCENCE.

Verbs—be virtuous, practice virtue; do, fulfill, perform *or* discharge one's duty; redeem one's pledge; behave; command *or* master one's passions; keep on the straight and narrow path; set an example, be on one's good *or* best behavior.

Adjectives—virtuous, good, innocent; meritorious, deserving, worthy, correct; dutiful, duteous, moral, right, righteous, right-minded; well-intentioned, creditable, laudable, commendable, praiseworthy; above *or* beyond praise; excellent, admirable; sterling, pure, noble, exemplary, matchless, peerless; saintly, saintlike; heaven-born, angelic, seraphic.

Adverbs—virtuously, *etc.*

Antonym, see EVIL, IMPROBITY.

virtuosity, *n.* dilettantism, dabbling; SKILL, mastery, proficiency, technique, know-how, expertise; finesse, flair, dexterity. *Slang*, chops. See SUPERIORITY.

virulent, *adj.* poisonous, venomous; deadly; toxic, noxious; malignant, malevolent; caustic, acrimonious. See BADNESS, DISEASE, RESENTMENT.

virus, *n.* venom, poison, contagium, germ, microorganism. See DISEASE.

visage, *n.* face, countenance, physiognomy; semblance, look, aspect, guise. *Slang*, puss, phiz, map. See APPEARANCE, FRONT.

vis-à-vis, *adv. & prep.* —*adv.* face-to-face, *tête-à-tête*, facing. —*prep.* opposite, contra, versus, against; contrasted to, as opposed to. See OPPOSITION.

viscous, *adj.* viscid, ropy, glutinous, slimy; mucid; sticky, mucilaginous; oleaginous, greasy. See COHERENCE.

vise, *n.* clamp, gripper, clinch. See RETENTION.

VISIBILITY

Nouns—visibility, perceptibility, apparency; conspicuity, precision; APPEARANCE, manifestation, VISION, exposure [to view]; ocular proof, evidence *or* demonstration: field of view, range; high *or* low visibility, visibility zero; view, prospect, horizon.

Verbs—1, appear, show, gleam, glimmer, glitter, glare, meet *or* catch the eye; present, show, manifest, produce, discover, reveal, expose *or* betray itself; stand out *or* forth, peep *or* peer out, crop out; start, spring, show, turn *or* crop up; float before the eyes, be conspicuous, be prominent, attract the attention, speak for itself. *Colloq.*, stand out like a sore thumb.

2, render visible, expose to view; show, display, reveal, expose, disclose, produce, present, discover; make conspicuous, signalize.

Adjectives—visible, visual, perceptible, perceivable, noticeable, observable, discernible, seeable, to be seen; in [full] view, in sight, in the open, exposed to view; apparent, manifest, evident, obvious, unhidden, unclouded, conspicuous, prominent, palpable, glaring, staring, standing out; before one, before one's eyes, under one's nose. *Colloq.*, plain as the nose on one's face.

Adverbs—visibly, perceptibly, *etc.*; in sight of, before one's eyes, *à vue d'œil*, as large as life.

Antonym, see INVISIBILITY.

VISION

Nouns—1, vision, sight, optics, eyesight, seeing; view, look, espial, glance, ken; glimpse, peep; gaze, stare, leer; perception, contemplation; regard, survey; observance, observation, examination; inspection, introspection; reconnaissance, watch, espionage, autopsy; ocular inspection; sightseeing; perspicacity, discernment. *Slang*, looksee; once over; eyeful.

2, 20-20 vision, *etc.*; farsightedness, eagle eye; nearsightedness, myopia; myosis, astigmatism, presbyopia; double vision, colorblindness, Daltonism, night blindness, nyctalopia, hemeralopia; strabismus, cross-eyes, cock-eyes; squint, cast, cataract, ophthalamania; goggle eyes, wall-eyes.

3, point of view, viewpoint; vantage point; observatory; gazebo, loophole, crow's nest; belvedere, watchtower; peephole, lookout post; field of view; theater, amphitheater, arena, vista, horizon; visibility; prospect, perspective; commanding view, bird's-eye view; periscope.

4, visual organ, organ of vision; eye; eyeball; naked eye; retina, pupil, iris, cornea, white. *Colloq.*, optics, orbs, peeper, peeled *or* weather eye.

5, refraction, distortion; illusion, optical illusion, mirage, phantasm, specter, apparition; reflection, mirror, image.

Verbs—**1,** see, behold, discern, perceive, have in sight, descry, sight, make out, discover, distinguish, recognize, spy, espy, get *or* catch a glimpse of; command a view of; watch, witness, look on; cast the eyes on; see at a glance. *Colloq.*, spot.

2, look, view, eye; lift up the eyes, open one's eyes, look around, survey, scan, inspect; run the eye over, reconnoiter, glance around, direct the eyes to, observe, peep, peer, pry, take a peep; stare (down); strain one's eyes; fix *or* rivet the eyes on; gaze; pore over; leer, ogle, glare; goggle, stare, gape, gawk, gawp; cock the eye. *Slang,* get a load of, give the eye, take a gander at, give the once-over.

3, dazzle, blind; wink, blink, squint; screw up the eyes; have a mote in the eye; see through a glass darkly.

Adjectives—visual, ocular, seeing; optic, optical; ophthalmic; clear-sighted; eagle-eyed, hawk-eyed, lynx-eyed, keen-eyed, Argus-eyed; visible; misty, dim. See DIMSIGHTED.

Adverbs—visibly; in sight of, with one's eyes open; at sight, at first sight, at a glance; at first blush; *prima facie.*

Antonyms, see BLIND, DIMSIGHTED.

---

visionary, *adj. & n.* —*adj.* idealistic, unpractical, quixotic, utopian; imaginary, delusory, chimerical. —*n.* dreamer, idealist, theorist. See IMAGINATION. *Ant.*, realist; see EXISTENCE.

visit, *n. & v.* —*n.* call; interview, appointment; stopover, sojourn. —*v.* call on, drop in; stop, stay, tarry; sojourn. See ARRIVAL, SOCIALITY.

visitation, *n.* visit; calamity, misfortune; seizure, stroke, blow; disaster; bad luck, hardship. See ADVERSITY, DISEASE. *Ant.*, see PROSPERITY.

visor, *n.* beaver, umbrere, vizard, mask, disguise, domino, (eye)shield, eyeshade, sunshade, peak, brim. See DEFENSE, COVERING.

vista, *n.* view, prospect, scene; landscape, panorama. See APPEARANCE, VISION.

visualize, *v.t.* picture, envision; imagine, project. See IMAGINATION.

vital, *adj.* essential, indispensable, necessary; life-supporting; vivifying, invigorating; alive, live, vibrant, animate. See NECESSITY, LIFE. *Ant.*, see USELESSNESS.

vitality, *n.* LIFE; vigor, virility; viability. *Ant.*, see DEATH.

vitiate, *v.t.* adulterate, weaken; impair, spoil; destroy, void, invalidate; corrupt, pollute; deteriorate. See DESTRUCTION, DETERIORATION. *Ant.*, see IMPROVEMENT.

vitreous, *adj.* glassy, crystalline, vitriform; brittle, hard; transparent, translucent. See TRANSPARENCY, BRITTLENESS.

vituperate, *v.t.* vilify, abuse, revile; reproach, inveigh (against), rebuke, scold, upbraid; objurgate, tongue-lash. See DETRACTION. *Ant.*, see APPROBATION.

vituperation, *n.* scurrility, invective, abuse; censure, reproach, blame; scolding. See DISAPPROBATION, DETRACTION. *Ant.*, see APPROBATION.

vivacious, *adj.* lively, animated, sprightly; gay, breezy, spirited; frolicsome, sportive, cheerful. See VIGOR, LIFE, CHEERFULNESS. *Ant.*, see DEJECTION.

vivid, *adj.* striking; telling; picturesque; lifelike, realistic; lively, vital; vibrant, glowing; fresh, intense, unfaded, brilliant. See MEANING, COLOR, LIFE, LIGHT. *Ant.,* DULL.

vixen, *n.* female fox; harridan, shrew, witch, scold, virago, harpy. See FEMALE, EVILDOER.

vocabulary, *n.* words, glossary, word-list; dictionary, lexicon; LANGUAGE.

vocal, *adj.* articulate; spoken, [to be] sung; choral, lyric; VERBAL, oral. See SPEECH, MUSIC.

vocalist, *n.* singer; tenor, alto, *etc. Slang,* crooner, warbler, songstress, thrush, nightingale. See MUSICIAN.

vocation, *n.* profession; work, trade; calling, occupation. See BUSINESS, PURSUIT.

vociferous, *adj.* loud, noisy, clamorous; blatant, obstreperous; loud-mouthed. See LOUDNESS. *Ant.,* see SILENCE.

vogue, *n.* mode, STYLE, FASHION; practice, custom, usage; favor; HABIT.

voice, *n. & v.* —*n.* vocality; speaking *or* singing voice; inflection, intonation; tone of voice; ventriloquism, ventriloquy; lung power; vocal cords, vocalization; CRY, expression, utterance, vociferation, enunciation, articulation; articulate sound, SPEECH; accent, accentuation; emphasis, stress; singer; tenor, baritone, barytone, bass, basso, soprano, contralto, alto, *etc.*; representation, vote, participation. —*v.t.* speak, utter; give voice, utterance *or* tongue to; shout, cry, exclaim, ejaculate; express; vocalize, articulate, enunciate, pronounce, enounce, announce; accentuate; deliver, mouth. *Ant.,* see SILENCE.

void, *adj., v. & n.* —*adj.* empty, vacuous, blank; unoccupied, untenanted; devoid, lacking, unfilled; null, invalid; not binding; vain, unreal, unsubstantial. —*v.t.* vacate; abrogate, nullify, negate; evacuate, eject, cast off. —*n.* emptiness, SPACE, nothingness; vacuum; abyss, chasm. See ABSENCE, NULLIFICATION, INSUBSTANTIALITY. *Ant.,* see SUBSTANCE, LEGALITY.

volatile, *adj.* gaseous, vaporizable; fickle, changeable, mercurial; light, giddy; lively; capricious; buoyant, airy. See VAPOR, CHANGEABLENESS.

volition, *n.* WILL, CHOICE, voluntariness; option, preference, willingness. *Ant.,* see COMPULSION, NECESSITY.

volley, *n.* broadside, salvo, fusillade, raking, round; burst. See PROPULSION.

voluble, *adj.* talkative, verbose; fluent, glib. See LOQUACITY.

volume, *n.* BOOK, tome; contents, capacity; bulk, mass, dimensions, SIZE, quantity. See GREATNESS, MEASUREMENT.

voluminous, *adj.* capacious, big, bulky, copious; ample. See SIZE, GREATNESS. *Ant.,* see LITTLENESS.

voluntary, *adj.* fresh, free-will; volunteered; willing; spontaneous; willed; unasked; deliberate, intentional; unforced. See WILL. *Ant.,* see COMPULSION.

volunteer, *n. & v.* —*n.* enlister; offerer. —*v.* enlist; offer, proffer; give, donate. See WILL.

voluptuous, *adj.* sensual, carnal, fleshy, meretricious; epicurean, worldly. *Slang,* sexy. See PLEASURE, DESIRE. *Ant.,* see MODERATION.

vomit, *v.* throw up, disgorge, puke; belch, spew, eject. See EJECTION.

voodoo, *n.* wanga, obeah, fetishism, witchcraft, black magic; witch doctor, shamanist, medicine [man], sorcerer. See SORCERY.

voracious, *adj.* ravenous, omnivorous; rapacious; starving, famished, hungry; gluttonous, edacious. See GLUTTONY. *Ant.,* see MODERATION.

vortex, *n.* eddy, whirlpool; maelstrom; whirl; storm center. See ROTATION, WIND, WATER.

votary, *n. & adj.* —*n.* votarist, devotee, disciple, follower, enthusiast, adherent, zealot. *Colloq.,* fan. —*adj.* votive, dedicated; consecrated; pledged; devoted. See DESIRE, AFFIRMATION, PIETY.

vote, *n. & v.* —*n.* poll, ballot; franchise, suffrage; CHOICE, voice, option, election; referendum, plebiscite. —*v.* cast a ballot; choose, select, elect, establish, enact, ratify, veto, nullify. See AFFIRMATION, REFUSAL.

vouch, *v.t.* guarantee, warrant; affirm, declare; answer for, attest; certify; SUPPORT, back, bear witness. See AFFIRMATION, EVIDENCE. *Ant.,* see NEGATION.

voucher, *n.* receipt, stub; warrant, testimonium, EVIDENCE, RECORD, SUPPORT.

vow, *v. & n.* —*v.* swear, take oath; vouch, affirm; pledge, promise; dedicate, devote; take vows. —*n.* dedication, devotion; oath, swearing; pledge, promise; consecration. See AFFIRMATION.

voyage, *n.* cruise, sea trip, crossing, sail, excursion. See TRAVEL.

voyeur, *n.* Peeping Tom; lecher, pervert, psychopath. See IMPURITY, INSANITY.

VULGARITY

Nouns—**1,** vulgarity, vulgarism; barbarism; bad taste; inelegance, indelicacy; gaucherie, ill-breeding, DISCOURTESY; incivility; coarseness, indecorum, boorishness; rowdyism, blackguardism; ribaldry, obscenity. *Slang,* risqué story, double entendre.

2, gaudiness, tawdriness, finery, frippery, brummagem, tinsel, gewgaws, knickknacks, OSTENTATION.

3, vulgarian, rough diamond; tomboy, hoyden, cub, unlicked cub; lout, churl, knave, clown; barbarian; snob, parvenu, frump, slattern, slut. *Colloq.,* cad, bounder, roughneck.

Verbs—be vulgar, offend, misbehave, roughhouse.

Adjectives—**1,** vulgar, in bad taste, unrefined, coarse, indecorous, ribald, gross; unseemly, unpresentable; common, boisterous, loud; tasteless, obnoxious.

2, dowdy, slovenly, shabby, low, plebeian, uncourtly; uncivil, discourteous, ill-bred, bad-mannered, ill-mannered; ungentlemanly, unladylike, unfeminine; unkempt, uncombed, unpolished, uncouth, rude, awkward; homespun, provincial, countrified, rustic; boorish, clownish; savage, blackguard, rowdy, snobbish; barbarous, barbaric; low, vile, ignoble, monstrous, shocking; obscene.

3, bizarre, outré, outlandish; affected, meretricious, ostentatious, extravagant; gaudy, tawdry, flashy; cheap; obtrusive.

Antonym, see TASTE.

---

vulnerable, *adj.* open (to attack); weak, defenseless; assailable; susceptible. See DANGER, IMPOTENCE. *Ant.,* see SAFETY, POWER.

vulpine, *adj.* foxlike; foxy, crafty, wily, CUNNING.

vulture, *n.* predator, scavenger; condor, buzzard, griffon; extortionist, bloodsucker, vampire, parasite, jackal, harpy. See TAKING, EVIL.

W

wad, *n.* lump, plug; stuffing, filling, batting. See CLOSURE.

waddle, *v. & n.* toddle, shamble; lurch, waggle, sway, duck walk. See SLOWNESS.

wade, *v.* walk through; traverse, ford; wallow, slog, slosh; stand up to one's ankles (in). *Colloq.,* wade into, ATTACK, undertake. See DIFFICULTY, TRAVEL.

wafer, *n.* biscuit, cracker, cookie; lozenge, tablet, troche. See FOOD.

waft, *v.* float, buoy; convey, transport, carry; roll, wave; see WIND, TRANSPORTATION.

wag, *v. & n.* —*v.* wave, shake, sway, jerk, waggle; wigwag; nod. See OSCILLATION, AGITATION. —*n.* WIT, humorist.

wage, *v.t.* wager; conduct, make, carry on, undertake (as war). See UNDERTAKING, WARFARE.

wager, *n. & v.* bet, stake, gamble, risk, hazard; gage. See CHANCE.

wages, *n.pl.* pay, PAYMENT, hire, COMPENSATION, remuneration; earnings, salary; income.

wagon, *n.* cart, dray, wain; truck, lorry, car; van. See VEHICLE.

waif, *n.* stray, foundling; [street] Arab; homeless child. See LOSS.

wail, *v. & n.* lament, CRY, moan, bewail; howl, ululate, caterwaul; complain. See LAMENTATION.

waist, *n.* girth, MIDDLE, midriff, loin, waistline; bodice, blouse, shirt, tunic. See CLOTHING.

wait, *v.* stay, linger, tarry, abide, remain, bide [one's time]; dally, procrastinate, delay; serve, attend; await, expect, look for. *Slang,* sit tight; cool one's heels; sweat it out. See EXPECTATION.

waiter, *n.* SERVANT, garçon, attendant, steward, servitor, waitress, carhop; tray, salver (see RECEPTACLE).

waive, *v.* relinquish, renounce, give up, forgo, disclaim, surrender (a right *or* claim). See RELINQUISHMENT.

wake, *n. & v.* —*n.* path, track, trail, swath; vigil, watch. See REAR, SEQUENCE, INTERMENT. —*v.* rouse, arouse, awake, awaken; stir, excite, animate. See ACTIVITY, CARE. *Ant.,* see REPOSE.

wakeful, *adj.* alert, watchful, on guard, on the *qui vive,* vigilant; restless, sleepless, insomniac. See ACTIVITY, CARE. *Ant.,* see INACTIVITY, REPOSE.

walk, *n. & v.* ramble, stroll, promenade, saunter, TRAVEL (on foot), march, parade, tramp, hike; tread, pace, step. *Colloq.* (*n.*) constitutional.

walk, *n.* calling, occupation; sphere, province, department; BUSINESS.

wall, *n.* SIDE, partition, bulkhead, flange, splashboard; rampart, DEFENSE; barrier; fence; cliff, precipice; levee, dike, seawall; (*pl.*) PRISON. See INCLOSURE, HINDRANCE.

wallet, *n.* purse, pocketbook, billfold; bag, pouch, sack, moneybag; pack, knapsack. See RECEPTACLE, MONEY.

wallop, *v.* thrash, beat, strike, punch, hit, clout. See IMPULSE.

wallow, *v.i.* tumble, grovel, ROLL, flounder, welter, toss; revel, delight in, luxuriate in. See LOWNESS, PLEASURE.

wan, *adj.* pale, pallid, waxen, waxy, ashen, ashy, bloodless. See COLORLESSNESS. *Ant.,* see COLOR, HEALTH.

wand, *n.* rod, caduceus, mace, SCEPTER; staff, stick, baton; divining rod, dowsing stick; withe. See SORCERY.

wander, *v.i.* rove, ramble, stroll, walk, range; digress, swerve, deviate, stray; rave, maunder, be delirious; moon; straggle, forage. See TRAVEL, DEVIATION, INSANITY. *Ant.,* see STABILITY.

wane, *v. & n.* —*v.i.* DECREASE, lessen, ebb, fade, diminish, peter out, dwindle; abate, subside; decline, sink, fail, slacken. —*n.* FAILURE, ebb, decline, decay, DECREASE. *Ant.,* see INCREASE.

wangle, *v.,* *colloq.,* wheedle, inveigle, coax; con; extort, wring, wrench; contrive; get by hook or crook, rustle up. See ACQUISITION, STEALING.

want, *n. & v.* —*n.* need; POVERTY, indigence; lack, dearth, deficiency, ABSENCE; shortage, inadequacy, scarcity; NECESSITY, requirement. —*v.* lack, need; DESIRE, wish, crave; fall short of, be deficient, miss, omit, NEGLECT, fail. See FAILURE, INSUFFICIENCY. *Ant.,* see SUFFICIENCY, WEALTH, INDIFFERENCE.

wanton, *adj. & n.* —*adj.* lewd, licentious, lustful, loose, dissolute, immoral; frolicsome; abandoned; capricious, willful; heedless, reckless; wayward, perverse; luxuriant, rampant, exuberant. See DESIRE, IMPURITY. —*n.* LIBERTINE; flirt, baggage, hussy, trollop. See EVILDOER.

warble, *v.* trill, sing. See MUSIC.

ward, *v. & n.* —*v.t.* watch, guard, defend, protect; fend, parry, stave (off). —*n.* watch, guard, DEFENSE, protector; CARE, charge, custody; protégé(e), dependent, minor; precinct, district; hospital room. See REGION.

warden, *n.* KEEPER; game warden, church warden; custodian, curator; ranger; jailer, turnkey; superintendent. See SAFETY, CLERGY.

warder, *n.* KEEPER; gatekeeper; warden; guard; mace, staff.

wardrobe, *n.* CLOTHING, outfit, togs, duds; apparel, attire; livery, uniforms, finery; clothes closet, cloakroom, vestry. See RECEPTACLE.

wares, *n.pl.* merchandise, goods, commodities; products, stock in trade, provisions, MATERIALS, STORE; kitchenware, tableware, *etc.*

warehouse, *n.* STORE, depot, supply dump; storehouse. See RECEPTACLE.

WARFARE

Nouns—**1,** warfare, state of war, fighting, hostilities; war, combat, ARMS, force of arms, the sword; appeal to arms; baptism of fire, ordeal of battle; war to the death, open war, internecine war, civil war; world war, global war; war to end war; revolutionary war, revolution, religious war, crusade; underground warfare; guerrilla warfare; chemical, germ *or* bacteriological warfare; trench warfare, war of position, war of attrition; aerial, naval *or* atomic warfare; Mars, Ares, Odin, Bellona; cold war, hot war.

2, campaign, campaigning, crusade, expedition, invasion; investment, siege.

3, battlefield, battleground, field; theater, front; camp, encampment, bivouac, billet; flank, center, salient, line.

4, art of war, tactics, strategy, generalship, soldiership; ballistics, ordnance, gunnery; chivalry; weapons (see ARMS); logistics.

5, battle, fighting (see CONTENTION); service, active service. See COMBATANT.

6, call to arms, mobilization; trumpet, clarion, bugle, pibroch; slogan; war cry, warwhoop; Rebel yell, battle cry; beat of drum; tom-tom; password, watchword; muster, rally.

7, warlikeness, belligerence, bellicosity, combativeness, contentiousness; militarism; chauvinism, jingoism.

Verbs—**1,** go to war, declare war, carry *or* wage war, let slip the dogs of war; cry havoc; take the field, give battle, join battle; set to, fall to, engage, measure swords with, cross swords; come to blows, come to close quarters; fight, combat; contend (see CONTENTION); battle with; fight it out, fight hand to hand; sell one's life dearly. *Colloq.,* flex one's muscles.

2, arm; raise troops, mobilize; enroll, enlist, sign up; draft, conscript, call to the colors, recruit; serve, be on active service; campaign; wield the sword, bear arms; live by the sword, die by the sword; shoulder a musket, smell powder, be under fire; spill blood. *Colloq.,* join up.

Adjectives—**1,** warring, battling, contending, contentious; armed, armed to the teeth, sword in hand; in arms, under arms, up in arms; at war with; in battle array, in open arms, in the field; embattled, beleaguered, besieged; at swords' points.

2, warlike, belligerent, combative, bellicose, martial; military, militant; soldierlike, soldierly; chivalrous; strategic, tactical.

Adverbs—at war, in the thick of the fray, in the cannon's mouth; at sword's point; on the warpath.

Antonyms, see PACIFICATION, PEACE.

---

warhorse, *n.* charger, courser, destrier (*archaic*). *Colloq.,* veteran, vet, war dog, oldtimer; chestnut, standby, old reliable. See OLDNESS, USE.

warm, *adj.* hot; tepid, lukewarm; sunny, mild, summery; close, muggy; ardent, fervid, fervent; passionate; responsive; glowing, enthusiastic, hearty, affectionate, cordial; lively, excitable; feverish; hasty, quick; alive, living. See HEAT, FEELING, EXCITEMENT. *Ant.,* see COLD.

warmonger, *n.* [war] hawk, war dog; war lord, militarist, mercenary; drumbeater, flagwaver, saber-rattler, firebrand, instigator; jingo(ist), xenophobe, rabblerouser. See BOASTING, CONTENTION, WARFARE.

WARNING

Nouns—**1**, warning, forewarning, caution, *caveat*; notice (see INFORMATION); premonition, foreboding, PREDICTION; lesson, dehortation; admonition, monition; ALARM; THREAT.

2, warning sign, handwriting on the wall; *mene, mene, tekel, upharsin*; red flag; foghorn; monitor, warning voice, Cassandra, signs of the times, Mother Carey's chickens, stormy petrel, bird of ill omen; gathering clouds, clouds on the horizon; symptom; watchtower, beacon, lighthouse; a cloud no bigger than a man's hand.

3, sentinel, sentry, lookout; watch, watchman; patrol, picket, scout, spy, advance guard, rear guard; watchdog, housedog; Cerberus.

Verbs—**1**, warn, caution; forewarn, prewarn; admonish, premonish; forebode; give notice, give warning; dehort; menace, threaten; put on one's guard; sound the alarm; ring the tocsin.

2, beware, take warning, take heed; keep watch; stop, look and listen.

Adjectives—warning, premonitory, monitory, cautionary; admonitory, admonitive; symptomatic; ominous, foreboding; warned, on one's guard, careful, cautious.

Interjections—beware! take care! look out! watch out!

Antonym, see RASHNESS.

---

warp, *v. & n.* —*v.* twist, bend, swerve, distort; bias, prejudice; pervert; deviate; incline. —*n.* bias, DISTORTION; deflection, TENDENCY; torsion, twist, malformation. See CHANGE, CAUSE.

warrant, *n. & v.* —*n.* warranty, guaranty; pledge, security, surety; authority; summons, writ, permit, pass. —*v.t.* guarantee; vouch for, answer for, certify, secure; affirm; state, maintain; assure, SUPPORT, sanction, authorize, justify. See COMMAND, PERMISSION, AUTHORITY, VINDICATION.

warren, *n.* hutch, rabbitry; slum(s), tenement, shantytown. See ABODE.

warrior, *n.* See COMBATANT.

warship, *n.* See COMBATANT, SHIP, ARMS.

wart, *n.* growth, BLEMISH, excrescence, callous, protuberance. See HARDNESS.

wary, *adj.* guarded, watchful; alert, cautious; suspicious; discreet, prudent; chary; scrupulous. See CARE. *Ant.*, see RASHNESS, NEGLECT.

wash, *v.* clean, cleanse, deterge, bathe, lave; wet, soak, rinse, drench; purify; irrigate, inundate, flood; scrub, swab; launder; paint, tint, COLOR; lap, lick; brim over, overflow. See CLEANNESS, PAINTING, WATER.

washout, *n., slang,* FAILURE, flop, turkey, dud, fiasco, fizzle.

washroom, *n.* lavatory, wash-up, bathroom, restroom (see TOILET).

washstand, *n.* sink, washbowl, washbasin, lavabo, lavatory, commode, washpot, water butt. See CLEANNESS, RECEPTACLE.

WASTE

Nouns—**1**, waste, wastage; exhaustion, depletion, dissipation; dispersion; ebb; leakage, LOSS; wear and tear; extravagance, wastefulness, PRODIGALITY; MISUSE; wasting, DETERIORATION.

2, waster, wastrel, spendthrift, spender, prodigal, squanderer, profligate. *Colloq.*, sport.

Verbs—waste, spend, misspend, expend, use, misuse, use up, consume, swallow up, overtax, exhaust; impoverish; spill, drain, empty; disperse; cast, throw, fling *or* fritter away; burn the candle at both ends; go through, squander; waste powder and shot, labor in vain; pour water into a sieve; leak, run out; ebb, melt away, run dry, dry up; deteriorate; throw to the winds.

Adjectives—wasted, thrown away; wasteful, penny-wise and pound-foolish; prodigal, improvident, thriftless, unthrifty, extravagant, lavish.

Antonym, see STORE, PARSIMONY.

watch, *v. & n.* —*v.* look (at), scrutinize, examine; view, stare, ogle; regard, follow, survey; be alert, guard; chaperone, tend, babysit; oversee, superintend; patrol. —*n.* vigil, surveillance, sentry duty; guardianship, CARE; guard, watchman, sentinel, lookout; timepiece, pocket watch, wristwatch. See SAFETY, VISION, CHRONOMETRY. *Ant.,* see REPOSE, NEGLECT.

watchdog, *n.* bandog, bloodhound, mastiff; police dog; censor, monitor, policeman; guard(ian), (see WATCHMAN). See DEFENSE, DIRECTION.

watchman, *n.* guard(ian), keeper, patrol(man), sentry, picket, night watch(man); caretaker; watchdog. See SAFETY, CARE, DEFENSE.

watchtower, *n.* beacon, lighthouse; lookout *or* observation post. See VISION.

watchword, *n.* countersign, shibboleth; password, catchword; slogan. See INDICATION.

WATER

Nouns—1, water, moisture, wetness; drinking water, spring water, mineral water; sea water, salt water, fresh water; serum, serosity; lymph; rheum; diluent; dilution, maceration, lotion; washing, immersion, infiltration, infusion, irrigation; douche, bath; baptism, RAIN, deluge, spate, flood, high water, flood tide. See FLUIDITY.

2, RIVER, waterway, stream; GULF, bay, cove, harbor; OCEAN, sea, LAKE, pond; MARSH, swamp.

3, wave, billow, surge, swell, ripple, rollers, surf, breakers, heavy sea; undercurrent, eddy, vortex, whirlpool, maelstrom; waterspout; jet, spurt, squirt, spout; splash, plash; rush, gush, sluice.

4, waterfall, cascade, linn, cataract, Niagara.

5, hydraulics, hydrodynamics, hydrokinetics, hydrostatics, hydroponics.

Verbs—1, be watery; be awash *or* afloat; swim, swim in, brim.

2, water, wet; moisten; dilute; dip, immerse, submerge, plunge, souse, duck, drown; drench, soak, steep, macerate, pickle; wash, sprinkle, lave, bathe, splash; slop; irrigate, inundate, deluge; syringe, douche, inject, gargle.

3, flow, run; issue, gush, pour, spout, roll, stream; drop, drip, dribble, drain, trickle, percolate; bubble, gurgle, spurt, ooze; spill, overflow.

Adjectives—1, watery, liquid, aqueous, aquatic, lymphatic; balneal, diluent; brimming, drenching, diluted; weak; wet, moist, soppy, sopping, soaked, wet to the skin.

2, oceanic, marina, maritime, briny; tidal, fluent, flowing, streaming, meandering; riparian, alluvial; lacustrine; marshy, swampy, boggy, paludal, miry, sloppy; showery, rainy, pluvial.

Adverbs—awash, afloat, adrift, asea, under water.

Antonyms, see LAND, DRYNESS.

---

watercourse, *n.* RIVER, stream, channel, canal; riverbed, wadi, arroyo; waterway.

waterfall, *n.* casade, falls, drop, rapids; cataract, Niagara. See WATER.

waterproof, *adj.* water-repellent *or* -resistant, watertight; leakproof, impermeable; seaworthy; hermetic, sealed. See DRYNESS, SAFETY.

watershed, *n.* runoff, catchment basin; basin, reservoir; crisis, crux, crossroad(s), milestone. See SUMMIT, HEIGHT.

watertight, *adj.* water-repellent, WATERPROOF; airtight, safe, binding, legal, ironclad, unbreakable. See CERTAINTY, LEGALITY.

wave, *v. & n.* —*v.* wag, shake, sway, flutter, stream (in the wind); signal, motion, gesture, INDICATION; ROLL, undulate; ripple, swell, billow, flood, surge; flaunt, flourish. —*n.* sea, tide, WATER, ripple, billow, *etc.*, wavelet, undulation; signal, gesture, flourish; CONVOLUTION, curl; marcel, permanent, finger wave.

waver, *v.i.* vacillate, fluctuate, hesitate; sway, tremble, totter; undulate; teeter. See DOUBT. *Ant.,* see RESOLUTION.

wax, *v. & n.* —*v.* cere; grease, coat; smooth; polish; grow, INCREASE, strengthen. See SMOOTHNESS. —*n.* tallow, paraffin(e), beeswax.

way, *n.* PASSAGE, road, route, path, roadway, highway, channel, street, avenue; journey, PROGRESSION, transit; trend, TENDENCY; approach, access, gateway; METHOD, manner, mode, style, fashion; SPACE, interval, stretch, DISTANCE; usage, custom, HABIT, practice, wont; course, routine; PLAN; CONDUCT, FORM; behavior; scheme, device; knack; charm, winsomeness.

wayfarer, *n.* traveler; walker, hiker, rambler, wanderer, pilgrim, journeyer. See TRAVEL.

waylay, *v.t.* accost, buttonhole, detain; ATTACK, SURPRISE (see AMBUSH). See APPROACH.

wayward, *adj.* perverse, willful, forward; capricious; delinquent; changeable; wanton. See OPPOSITION, DISOBEDIENCE.

weak-minded, *adj.* moronic, idiotic, imbecilic, feebleminded; brainless, foolish, witless, empty-headed, vacuous; vacillating; irresolute; fickle. See INSANITY, DOUBT, CHANGEABLENESS. *Ant.,* see RESOLUTION, SANITY.

WEAKNESS

Nouns—**1,** weakness, feebleness, debility, debilitation, infirmity, decrepitude, inanition; relaxation, WEARINESS, enervation, IMPOTENCE, strain, sprain; paleness, COLORLESSNESS; disability, attenuation, senility, superannuation, malnutrition, atony, asthenia, adynamia, cachexia, hyposthenia, an(a)emia; invalidity, delicacy, frailty, fragility, flaccidity, vapidity; effeminacy, feminality, femininity; invalidation, adulteration, dilution; vulnerability, perishability, accessibility; Achilles' heel.

2, reed, thread, rope of sand, house of cards, house built on sand; child, baby, kitten, cat, chicken; water, milk and water, gruel; weakling, softling, poor specimen; invalid, asthenic, hypochondriac; deficient, defective, dunce, imbecile, lackwit, wreck, runt; faintheart, jellyfish, effeminate; weathercock. *Colloq.,* sissy, softy, betty, baby, crybaby, whiner; pantywaist, mollycoddle, milksop, namby-pamby, softhead, weak sister, nebbish. *Slang,* doormat, pushover.

3, see UNCERTAINTY, IMPERFECTION, BRITTLENESS, COWARDICE, DOUBT, CHANGEABLENESS.

Verbs—**1,** be weak, faint, drop, crumble, droop, sag, fade, fail, flag, pine, decline, languish, give way, give in; deteriorate, waste, falter, halt, limp; soften, relent, relax, yield, submit, succumb; totter, tremble, dodder, potter, shake, have one foot in the grave.

2, render weak, weaken, enfeeble, debilitate, devitalize; deplete, WASTE; bate, soften up, slacken, blunt, (see DULLNESS); disintensify; undermine, sap, impair, damage, cripple, lame, maim, disable, paralyze, cramp, wrench, strain, sprain, decimate; stagger, stun.

3, dilute, thin, cut, attenuate, adulterate, debase; reduce, depress, lower, lessen, impoverish, invalidate.

Adjectives—weak(ly), feeble, infirm, invalid, debile, senile, decrepit; sickly, poorly, unhealthy, unsound; weakened, enfeebled, *etc.*; strengthless, impotent; an(a)emic, asthenic, atonic, cachectic, hyposthenic, adynamic, bloodless, short-winded; faltering, drooping, *etc.*; unsteady, shaken, palsied, laid low, weak as a child, baby *or* kitten; vulnerable, assailable, indefensible; unsupported, unaided, unassisted. *Colloq.,* doddering, namby-pamby, wishy-washy. *Slang,* woozy.

Antonym, see STRENGTH, POWER, VIGOR, RESOLUTION.

wealth, *n.* riches, fortune, opulence, affluence; PROSPERITY; MEANS, resources, PROPERTY, MONEY; plenty, plenitude, luxuriance, excess, plethora, sufficiency. *Ant.,* see POVERTY, INSUFFICIENCY.

wealthy, *adj.* rich, affluent, opulent, moneyed; worth a fortune; well-to-do, well-off; rich as Croesus. *Colloq.,* made of money, rolling in money; flush, in funds. *Slang,* in the chips, in the money, loaded, filthy rich; in the big time; rolling high. See MONEY. *Ant.,* see POVERTY.

wean, *v.* separate, withdraw, deprive; estrange; grow up. See DISUSE.

weapon, *n.* See ARMS.

wear, *v. & n.* —*v.* last, endure; USE, show, display; tire, fatigue, weary; bear, don, put on; carry, have on; WASTE, consume, spend; rub, chafe, fray, abrade; jibe, tack, veer, yaw. —*n.* CLOTHING, garb; USE, usage, hard usage; impairment, wear and tear. See DURABILITY, DETERIORATION.

WEARINESS

Nouns—**1,** weariness, tiredness, exhaustion, lethargy, lassitude, FATIGUE; drowsiness, languor, languidness; WEAKNESS, faintness.

2, bore, proser, nuisance. *Colloq.,* wet blanket. *Slang,* drip, creep, pain in the neck.

3, wearisomeness, tedium, tediousness, dull work, boredom, ennui, sameness, monotony, twice-told tale; satiety; heavy hours, time on one's hands.

Verbs—**1,** weary; tire, fatigue; bore, weary *or* tire to death; send *or* put to sleep; pall, sicken, nauseate, disgust; harp on, dwell on. *Slang,* bore stiff.

2, be weary of, never hear the last of; be tired of; yawn.

Adjectives—**1,** wearying, wearing, fatiguing, tiring; wearisome, tiresome, irksome; uninteresting, stupid, bald, devoid of interest, dry, monotonous, dull, arid, tedious, trying, humdrum, flat; prosy, slow, soporific, somniferous; disgusting.

2, weary, tired, spent, fatigued; toilworn, footsore; winded, out of breath; drowsy, sleepy; uninterested, flagging; used up, worn out, blasé; dog-tired, ready to drop, more dead than alive, played out; exhausted, prostrate, on one's last legs, *hors de combat. Slang,* done up, pooped, bushed, fagged, beat.

Adverbs—wearily, boringly, tiresomely, *etc.*

weasel, *n. & v.* —*n.* musteline, suck-egg; sneak, skulker, trickster; hedger. See ANIMAL. —*v. colloq.,* equivocate, bandy words, hem and haw, hedge, renege. *Slang,* pussyfoot, welsh. See AVOIDANCE, QUALIFICATION.

weather, *n.* atmospheric conditions; clime, climate. See AIR.

weatherbeaten, *adj.* weathered, seasoned; inured, acclimatized, case-hardened. See DETERIORATION, HARDNESS.

weathercock, *n.* girouette, weathervane; opportunist. See UNCERTAINTY.

weave, *v.* interlace, intertwine, twine, entwine; loom, spin, fabricate; plait, pleat, pleach, braid, mat. See COMPOSITION.

web, *n.* cobweb, spiderweb; weaving, woven material, TEXTURE, mesh, net; network, hookup; trap, snare, scheme, PLAN; tissue, gossamer.

wed, *v.* marry, espouse; couple, blend, join. See MARRIAGE.

wedge, *n.* tapering block; triangular slab; quoin, chock, sprag, block, shim. See FORM, DISJUNCTION.

wee, *adj.* tiny, little, minute, small; infinitesimal, microscopic; diminutive, petite. *Colloq.,* teenyweeny. See LITTLENESS. *Ant.,* see GREATNESS, SIZE.

weed, *v. & n.* —*v.t.* root out, extirpate, clear (of weeds); cull; remove, eliminate. See EJECTION. —*n.* unwanted plant; pest, nuisance. *Colloq.,* tobacco, smoking. See VEGETABLE.

weeds, *n.pl.* mourning, black, widow's weeds. See CLOTHING, LAMENTATION.

week, *n.* seven-night; see TIME.

weep, *v.* shed tears, CRY, lament, wail, sob, blubber; mourn, grieve; rain, flow, drip. See LAMENTATION.

weigh, *v.* measure (weight); lift, heft; balance, scale, counterbalance; examine, ponder, consider, mull over, estimate; tell, count; weigh down, be heavy, drag, load, press; oppress, burden, depress; overbalance, bear down. See GRAVITY, IMPORTANCE, MEASUREMENT.

weight, *n. & v.* —*n.* heaviness; heft; overweight, avoirdupois, tonnage, poundage; GRAVITY; ballast; MEASUREMENT; IMPORTANCE, INFLUENCE; significance; pressure, load, burden. —*v.* ballast, load, burden; favor; adjust, compensate.

weightless, *adj.* light, feathery; disembodied, immaterial, incorporeal, intangible; floating, drifting, lighter than air. See LEVITY, INSUBSTANTIALITY.

weird, *adj.* uncanny, eldritch, eerie; ghostly, spectral, unearthly; SUPERNATURAL. *Colloq.*, spooky. See UNCONFORMITY.

welcome, *n., v. & adj.* —*n.* greeting, salutation, cordial reception. *Slang*, glad hand. —*v.t.* greet, salute; embrace, receive (gladly), hail. —*adj.* pleasing, agreeable, acceptable, wanted, gratifying. See COURTESY, RECEIVING, SOCIALITY. *Ant.*, see DISCOURTESY, REFUSAL.

weld, *v.t.* fuse, unite, join, fasten; blend. See JUNCTION.

welfare, *n.* well-being; PROSPERITY, advancement, profit, sake, benefit; social work; happiness, SUCCESS. *Ant.*, see ADVERSITY.

well, *n. & v.* —*n.* fount, font, wellspring; wellhead; reservoir; spring; source, origin; hole, pit, shaft. —*v.i.* issue, gush, brim, flow, jet, rise. See BEGINNING, WATER.

well, *adj. & adv.* —*adj.* healthy, robust, strong, hale, hearty, in good health. —*adv.* rightly, properly; thoroughly, skillfully, accurately; amply, sufficiently, fully, adequately; favorably, worthily; very much; quite, considerably; easily, handily. See HEALTH, SKILL, SUFFICIENCY. *Ant.*, see DISEASE, UNSKILLFULNESS, INSUFFICIENCY.

well-being, *n.* GOOD, PROSPERITY; euphoria, good HEALTH, sanity, robustness, CONTENT, PLEASURE, contentment.

well-bred, *n.* well-behaved *or* brought up; noble, well-born, gentle; courteous, polished, suave, polite. See COURTESY, NOBILITY. *Ant.*, see DISCOURTESY, POPULACE.

well-known, *adj.* familiar, recognized, famous, renowned; notorious. See REPUTE, KNOWLEDGE. *Ant.*, see NEGLECT, DISREPUTE.

well-meaning, *adj.* well-intentioned, with the best intentions, kind(ly), well-disposed, sympathetic, innocent, blameless. See BENEVOLENCE, INNOCENCE.

well-read, *adj.* learned, erudite, scholarly, bookish. See INFORMATION, LEARNING.

wellspring, *n.* fountainhead, wellhead, *fons et origo*, source. See BEGINNING.

well-to-do, *adj.* comfortable, well off; prosperous, affluent; wealthy, rich. See MONEY, PROSPERITY. *Ant.*, see POVERTY.

welsh, *v., slang,* welch; default on, fail, hedge, renege; leave high and dry, leave holding the bag. See AVOIDANCE, NONPAYMENT, DECEPTION.

welt, *n.* wale, weal; edging, rim; binding; cord, ridge, rib. See PAIN.

welter, *n. & v.* —*n.* confusion, turmoil; jumble, hodgepodge, mishmash; ruck, masses. —*v.i.* WALLOW. See AGITATION, POPULACE, DISORDER.

wench, *n.* girl, maiden, lass, lassie, servant; maid; slut, slattern, tart, trollop, harlot (see PROSTITUTE). *Slang*, broad, piece. See FEMALE.

werewolf, *n.* wolf-man, lycanthrope, *loup-garou*; changeling. See SORCERY.

west, *n.* Occident; Europe; wild west. See DIRECTION.

wet, *adj., v. & n.* —*adj.* damp, moist, dewy; clammy, dank, humid, dripping; rainy, showery, foggy, misty; soaked, drenched, saturated; watery, waterlogged. —*v.t.* soak, moisten, dampen, drench, saturate; immerse, dip, sprinkle; rain upon. —*n.* wetness, WATER; rain, fog, dew, mist; dampness, MOISTURE, clamminess, *etc.*; antiprohibition. *Ant.*, see DRYNESS.

wet blanket, *n., colloq.,* spoilsport, killjoy; Cassandra, pessimist, alarmist; prophet of gloom *or* doom, crepehanger. *Slang*, party pooper. See DEJECTION.

whale, *n.* cetacean; finback; blue, humpback, killer, sperm, sulphurbottom *or* right whale; orca, rorqual, narwhal, blackfish, dolphin, porpoise, grampus; Moby Dick. *Colloq.,* whopper. See GREATNESS, SIZE.

wharf, *n.* dock, pier, quay, landing; waterfront. See EDGE.

what, *pron.* that which; sort of, kind of; which; how; how great, many, *or* remarkable; whatever, whatsoever, whichever.

whatnot, *n.* thing, something, what have you, whatever; cabinet, étagère, china closet. *Colloq.,* contraption, doodad. *Slang,* thingumabob, blankety-blank; doohickey, dingbat, gismo. See NOMENCLATURE, RECEPTACLE.

wheedle, *v.t.* coax, cajole, persuade; court, humor, flatter. See SERVILITY.

wheel, *n. & v.* —*n.* disk, circle, roller; roulette *or* fortune's wheel; bike, bicycle. *Slang,* VIP, big wheel, bigwig. See CIRCULARITY, VEHICLE. —*v.* roll; trundle, cycle; rotate, revolve, spin, twirl; pivot, about-face, turn, gyrate, whirl, wind.

wheeze, *v. & n.* —*v.* breathe hard, gasp, puff, choke. —*n,* *slang,* old joke, gag, chestnut. See WIND, WIT.

when, *adv.* at what time? at the same time; whereupon, just then, whenever. See TIME.

where, *adv.* in what place; whereabouts, whither; in what direction, from what source, place, *etc.* See TIME, PLACE.

whereas, *conj.* inasmuch as, since, while, as, in view of, forasmuch as, inconsideration of, considering that, seeing that. See ATTRIBUTION.

wherewithal, *n.* MEANS, resources; MONEY, funds, cash, capital, assets; POWER, ability, competence. *Colloq.,* the stuff, the goods, what it takes. See SUFFICIENCY.

whet, *v.t.* sharpen, hone, whetstone, grind; excite, stimulate, provoke, stir up, kindle, quicken, inspire. See SHARPNESS, EXCITEMENT.

whether, *conj.* if, in case; if it is so; in either case. See SUPPOSITION.

while, *conj. & v.* —*conj.* during, as long as, whilst, whereas; although. —*v.* pass the time, kill time. See TIME.

whim, *n.* caprice, fancy, DESIRE, vagary; notion, quirk, crotchet, whimsy; freak; IMPULSE. See CHANGEABLENESS.

whimper, *v. & n.* CRY, whine.

whimsical, *adj.* curious, odd, peculiar, freakish; humorous, waggish, droll; crotchety, capricious, queer, quaint. See CHANGEABLENESS, WIT.

whine, *v.i.* CRY, whimper, complain, moan, snivel. *Slang,* gripe, bellyache. See LAMENTATION.

whip, *n. & v.* —*n.* lash, SCOURGE; quick motion, SNAP. —*v.t.* lash, beat, flog; thrash; conquer, subdue; defeat. See PUNISHMENT, SUCCESS.

whirl, *n. & v.* —*n.* spin, spinning, gyration, turn; flutter, tizzy, confusion; pirouette. —*v.* spin, twirl, turn, rotate, revolve, gyre, gyrate; dance, pirouette. See ROTATION.

whirlpool, *n.* addy, swirl; vortex, malestrom. See WATER, ROTATION.

whirlwind, *n. & adj.* —*n.* tornado, twister, cyclone, typhoon, hurricane, windstorm. See WIND. —*adj.* fast, speedy, headlong, breakneck, dizzying. See VELOCITY.

whiskers, *n.pl.* beard, hair, stubble; hirsuteness; mustache, sideburns, goatee, Vandyke, muttonchops, *etc.*; bristles; feelers, antennae. See ROUGHNESS.

whiskey, whisky, *n.* [hard] liquor, spirits; bourbon, rye, corn; firewater. *Colloq.,* booze, moonshine, bootleg. *Slang,* hooch, white mule, rotgut, redeye. See FOOD, DRUNKENNESS.

whisper, *n. & v.* —*n.* murmur, whispering, sigh, breath; hint, intimation, rumor; aside, stage whisper. —*v.* murmur, breathe, divulge, reveal, hint, intimate. See DISCLOSURE, WIND. *Ant.,* see LOUDNESS.

whistle, *n. & v.* pipe, piping, flute. See SOUND.

white, *adj.* snow-white, snowy, milky, chalky; albino; pale, bloodless, colorless; whitewashed, kalsomined, bleached; silver, gray, hoar, frosty; cleansed, purified; Caucasian, Caucasoid. See COLOR, COLORLESSNESS.

white elephant, *n.* nuisance, embarrassment; dead weight, deadwood, drag, burden, impediment; plague, cross. *Slang*, lemon. See USELESS-NESS, HINDRANCE.

whiteness, *n.* whitish color, white, COLORLESSNESS, paleness; milkiness, chalkiness, snowiness; PURITY; hoariness, grayness (of age); lime, paper, milk, ivory, snow, sheet, alabaster; albinoism, blondness, fairness; pallor, ashiness, waxiness, bloodlessness; bleach, etiolation; silveriness; glare, LIGHT, lightness; INNOCENCE, stainlessness. *Ant.*, blackness (see COLOR), DARKNESS.

whitewash, *v.t.* calcimine, kalsomine; whiten; vindicate, exonerate. *Slang*, shut out, blank, skunk. See COVERING, VINDICATION.

whittle, *v.* shape, carve; pare, cut, slice, shave; deduct, curtail, dock, diminish; dwindle, eat away, erode. See SHARPNESS, DEDUCTION.

who, *pron.* which one, that. See IDENTITY.

WHOLE

Nouns—**1,** whole, totality, totalness, integrity; entirety, ensemble, collectiveness; UNITY, completeness, indivisibility, integration, embodiment; integer.

2, the whole, all, everything, total, aggregate, one and all, gross amount, sum, sum total, *tout ensemble*, length and breadth of, alpha and omega, be-all and end-all; bulk, mass, lump, tissue, staple, body, trunk, bole, hull, hulk, skeleton. *Slang*, whole kit and caboodle, whole show, whole shebang, whole shooting match; the works.

Verbs—form *or* constitute a whole; integrate, embody, amass; aggregate, assemble; amount to, come to, add up to.

Adjectives—**1,** whole, total, integral, entire, complete; one, individual, wholesale, sweeping.

2, unbroken, uncut, undivided, unsevered, unclipped, uncropped, unshorn; seamless; undiminished; undemolished, undissolved, undestroyed; indivisible, indissoluble, indissolvable.

Adverbs—wholly, altogether; totally, completely, entirely, all, all in all, wholesale, in a body, collectively, all put together; in the aggregate, in the mass, in the main, in the long run; *en masse*, on the whole, bodily, throughout, every inch, substantially, by and large.

Antonym, see PART.

---

wholesale, *adj.* bulk, job-lot, jobbing; at a discount, cheaper; mass, sweeping, general, widespread. See WHOLE, BUSINESS. *Ant.*, retail.

wholesome, *adj.* healthy, beneficial. See HEALTH, PURITY. *Ant.*, see DISEASE, IMPURITY.

whore, *n.* prostitute, harlot, baud, strumpet, streetwalker, call girl, B-girl, daughter of joy. See EVILDOER.

why, *adv.* wherefore, what for?, for what cause. *Slang*, how come. See CAUSE.

wicked, *adj.* EVIL, bad; criminal, depraved, iniquitous; cruel, heartless, sinful, vicious, immoral. See IMPROBITY, IMPURITY. *Ant.*, see GOODNESS, PURITY, VIRTUE.

wicker, *n.* twig, vimen, shoot, rod, osier, willow, withe, sallow; rattan, straw, buri, raffia; wickerware. See CROSSING, VEGETABLE, RECEPTACLE.

wide, *adj.* spacious, widespreading, comprehensive; generous, ample, all-embracing; broad, large, roomy, extensive; general. See BREADTH, SPACE. *Ant.*, see NARROWNESS.

wide-awake, *adj.* alert, quick; keen, knowing; informed, astute, watchful, on guard, unsleeping, vigilant. See CARE, KNOWLEDGE. *Ant.*, see IGNORANCE, REPOSE.

widespread, *adj.* general, common, rife, universal, prevalent; ubiquitous; extensive, inclusive, all-embracing; global. See GENERALITY, INCLUSION.

widow, *n.* survivor (of a husband); relict, dowager; divorcée, grass widow. See CELIBACY, DIVORCE.

width, *n.* BREADTH, broadness; wideness, span, beam; extent, expanse.

wield, *v.t.* handle, manipulate, ply; brandish, flourish, wave, shake; employ, control, manage. See USE.

wife, *n.* married woman; mate, spouse; *Frau*; housewife, helpmeet, helpmate. *Slang,* the Mrs., madam, little woman, old lady, ball and chain, better half. See MARRIAGE. *Ant.,* see CELIBACY.

wig, *n.* toupée, toupet; peruke, periwig, switch, transformation; fall; headdress. *Slang,* doily, divot, rug. See ORNAMENT.

wiggle, *v.i.* squirm, shake, wriggle, wag, shimmy. See OSCILLATION.

wild, *adj.* savage, untamed; uncivilized; feral, bloodthirsty, fierce; uncontrolled; amuck, frenzied; inaccurate, intemperate, unwise, foolish; eager, impetuous, unrestrainable, desert, uninhibited; rank, thick, junglelike, luxuriant; untended, uncultivated; shy, skittish; daring, reckless, rash, breakneck; freak. See VIOLENCE, VULGARITY. *Ant.,* see DOMESTICATION.

wildcat, *n. & adj.* —*n.* lynx, puma, mountain lion, panther, ocelot. —*adj., colloq.,* risky, venturesome, shoestring; unauthorized, splinter, spontaneous.

wilderness, *n.* wasteland, waste(s), wilds, badlands; desert, sands, Sahara. See LAND. *Ant.,* see HEAVEN.

wild-goose chase, fool's errand, chasing rainbows; red herring, snipe hunt, chasing one's own tail, tilting at windmills. See USELESSNESS.

wile, *n.* stratagem, subterfuge; CUNNING; trick, dodge.

WILL

Nouns—will, free will, volition, conation, velleity; pleasure; FREEDOM, discretion; option, CHOICE; voluntariness, spontaneity, spontaneousness; originality; pleasure, wish, mind; frame of mind, inclination, WILLINGNESS; intention, predetermination; self-control, determination, RESOLUTION.

Verbs—will, see fit, think fit; determine, resolve, settle, choose, volunteer; have a will of one's own; have one's own way; exercise one's discretion; take responsibility; take upon oneself; do of one's own accord.

Adjectives—voluntary, volitional, wilful; WILLING; free, optional; discretionary, minded; prepense; intended; autocratic; unbidden, spontaneous; original (see CAUSE).

Adverbs—voluntarily, at will, at pleasure; *ad libitum,* as one thinks proper, according to one's lights; of one's own accord *or* free will; by choice, purposely, intentionally, deliberately.

Antonym, see NECESSITY.

---

willful, wilful, *adj.* self-willed, arbitrary; headstrong, wayward, obstinate, stubborn, unruly; intentional, deliberate, premeditated. See WILL. *Ant.,* see OBEDIENCE.

willing, *adj.* minded, disposed, inclined, favorable; favorably inclined *or* disposed to; nothing loath; in the mood *or* humor; ready, forward, earnest, eager; bent upon, desirous, predisposed; docile, agreeable, easygoing, tractable, pliant; cordial, hearty; content, assenting, voluntary, gratuitous, spontaneous, unasked, unforced. See WILL, ASSENT. *Ant.,* see REFUSAL.

willingness, *n.* voluntariness; readiness; willing mind *or* heart; disposition, inclination, tendency, leaning; bent, turn of mind, propensity, predisposition, proclivity, penchant, DESIRE; docility, pliability; good will; alacrity, eagerness (see WILLING); ASSENT, compliance, CONSENT; PLEASURE. See WILL. *Ant.,* see REFUSAL, UNWILLINGNESS.

willy-nilly, *adv.* will I, nill I; *nolens volens*; like it or not, whether or not; perforce, inescapably. See COMPULSION, NECESSITY, IRRESOLUTION.

wilt, *v.i.* droop, sag; weaken, languish; wither; collapse. See SOFTNESS.

wily, *adj.* designing, tricky, crafty, foxy; deceitful, crooked, Machiavellian; clever, subtle, CUNNING. *Ant.,* see INNOCENCE, SIMPLENESS.

win, *v.* beat, conquer, MASTER; gain, obtain; get; achieve, accomplish, reach; persuade, sway, convince, influence; succeed, triumph, surpass. See ACQUISITION, SUCCESS, BELIEF.

wince, *v.i.* flinch, RECOIL; shy, quail, shrink. See FEAR, PAIN.

winch, *n.* See WINDLASS.

wind, *v.* twist, twine, entwine; coil, curl, spiral; bandage, loop; enfold, infold; wreathe, roll; crank, reel; sinuate, meander, wander. See CONVOLUTION, DEVIATION. *Ant.,* see DIRECTION.

WIND

Nouns—**1,** wind, windiness, draught, draft, flatus, afflatus, AIR; breath, breath of air; puff, whiff, blow, drift; aura; stream, current, undercurrent; sufflation, insufflation, inflation; blowing, fanning, ventilation. **2,** gust, blast, breeze, zephyr, squall, gale, half a gale, storm, tempest, hurricane, whirlwind, tornado, samiel, cyclone, twister, typhoon; simoom; harmattan, khamsin, chinook, monsoon, trade wind, sirocco, mistral, bise, tramontane, foehn, levanter; capful of wind; fresh breeze, stiff breeze; blizzard; rough, foul *or* dirty weather; dirty sky, mare's tail. **3,** anemography, aerodynamics; wind gauge, anemometer, pneumatics; weathercock, weathervane; Beaufort scale. **4,** breathing, respiration, sneezing, sternutation; hiccough, hiccup; catching of the breath. **5,** Aeolus, Boreas, Eurus, Zephyr, Notus, cave of the winds. **6,** airpump, lungs, bellows, blowpipe, fan, ventilator, vacuum cleaner, wind tunnel; air pipe; funnel.

Verbs—**1,** blow, waft; stream, issue; freshen, gather; blow up, bluster; sigh, moan, scream, howl, whistle; breeze. **2,** breathe, respire, inhale, exhale, puff; whiffle, gasp, wheeze; snuff, snuffle, sniff, sniffle; sneeze, cough. **3,** fan, ventilate; inflate; blow up, pump up.

Adjectives—windy, blowing, breezy, gusty, squally; stormy, tempestuous, blustering; boisterous; pulmonic, pulmonary, pneumatic.

Antonym, see CALM.

---

windbag, *n., colloq.,* bag of wind; braggart, blusterer; gossip, chatterer. *Slang,* gasbag, gasser, big mouth, blabbermouth. See LOQUACITY, BOASTING.

windfall, *n.* bonus, prize, blessing, boon; treasure trove, find; pennies or manna [from heaven], godsend, DISCOVERY. See ACQUISITION, CHANCE.

windlass, *n.* hoist, lifter; moulinet, reel, capstan, pinion, winch, crank. See ROTATION, ELEVATION.

window, *n.* casement, dormer, OPENING; pane; bay window, oriel; port, porthole; skylight; embrasure, loophole.

windpipe, *n.* airpipe, trachea; throat, throttle; weasand.

windup, *n.* END, termination, conclusion, CLOSURE, settlement, climax, denouement, RESOLUTION, outcome, upshot; preliminaries, PREPARATION.

wine, *n.* the grape; drink, liquor; DRUNKENNESS, intoxication; stimulant, alcohol; nectar.

wing, *n.* & *v.* —*n.* pinion, (feathered) limb, pennon, ala; arm, sail; flank; ell, annex, extension; airfoil; flight, flying. —*v.* fly; disable, wound. See ADDITION, AVIATION, COMBATANT, DRAMA.

wink, *v.* blink, nictitate, nictate; squint; twinkle; overlook, ignore, condone. See VISION, FORGIVENESS, NEGLECT.

winning, *adj.* conquering, victorious, triumphant; winsome, captivating, charming, engaging, entrancing, prepossessing, comely, attractive; persuasive, convincing. See SUCCESS, ATTRACTION, CAUSE.

winnow, *v.t.* select, cull, sift, separate, glean, pick; ventilate, fan, remove chaff. See CHOICE.

winsome, *adj.* gay, merry, lively, sportive; charming, winning, captivating; lovable, adorable, pleasant, attractive. See CHEERFULNESS, LOVE.

winter, *n.* COLD; hibernation; AGE; ADVERSITY.

wipe, *v.t.* clean, rub, brush, dust, mop; dry, towel. See CLEANNESS, DRYNESS.

wire, *n.* (metal) thread, FILAMENT; flex, cord, line; telephone, telegraph, cable; cablegram, telegram. See JUNCTION, COMMUNICATION.

wireless, *n.* radio; radiogram, Marconigram. See COMMUNICATION.

wiry, *adj.* filamentous, filar, threadlike; STRONG, muscular, sinewy; tough; flexible. See FILAMENT. *Ant.,* see SOFTNESS.

wise, *adj.* SAGE, sagacious; learned, profound, deep; judicious, well-advised. See KNOWLEDGE.

wisecrack, *n., slang,* crack, quip, witticism, comeback, answer. See WIT.

wish, *n. & v.* —*n.* DESIRE, WILL; PLEASURE; craving, yearning, want, hankering; INTENTION. —*v.* want, long for, dream of, hope for, ask (for), yearn, crave, hanker. See HOPE, EXPECTATION.

wishy-washy, *adj.* washed-out, anemic, colorless; weak-kneed *or* -willed, spineless, irresolute. See INSIPIDITY, MEDIOCRITY, UNCERTAINTY.

wistful, *adj.* musing, pensive, thoughtful; desirous, wishful, hopeful; eager; craving, yearning. See DESIRE, HOPE, EXPECTATION.

WIT

Nouns—**1,** wit, wittiness; Atticism; salt; esprit, point, fancy, whim, humor, drollery, pleasantry; jocularity; jocosity, jocoseness; levity, facetiousness; waggery, waggishness; comicality.

2, farce, buffoonery, clowning, fooling, tomfoolery; harlequinade; broad farce, broad humor; fun; slapstick; smartness, banter, badinage, retort, repartee, riposte; RIDICULE; horseplay.

3, witticism, jest, joke, conceit, quip, quirk, quiddity, pleasantry; sally; flash of wit, scintillation; *mot, bon mot,* smart saying, epigram; dry wit, cream of the jest. *Slang,* comeback, gag, wisecrack, gag, running gag.

4, wordplay, play upon words, pun, punning, double entendre, EQUIVOCATION; quibble; conundrum, riddle (see SECRET); trifling. *Slang,* chestnut.

5, wit, wag, joker, jester, comedian, comic, HUMORIST, punster.

Verbs—be witty, joke, jest; crack a joke; pun; make fun of, make sport of; retort; banter. *Slang,* wisecrack, come back at.

Adjectives—witty, Attic, quick-witted, nimble-witted; smart, jocular, jocose, droll, waggish, facetious, whimsical, humorous; playful, merry, pleasant, sprightly, sparkling, epigrammatic, pointed, comic.

Adverbs—jokingly, jestingly, *etc.*; in jest, in sport, in play; in fun; not seriously.

Antonym, see DULL.

---

witch, *n.* hag, beldam(e), crone; shrew, scold, dragon; sorceress, enchantress; charmer. See UGLINESS, BEAUTY, SORCERY.

witch hunt, vigilantism, persecution, baiting; purge, investigation, McCarthyism, redbaiting, superpatriotism. See INQUIRY, FEAR.

with, *prep.* by, by means of, through; accompanying, alongside, among(st), amid(st), beside, plus; upon, at, thereupon, *etc.* See ACCOMPANIMENT, MIXTURE, ADDITION. *Ant.,* without; see ABSENCE.

withdraw, *v.* remove, separate, subduct; retire, retreat, disengage, draw off; abstract, subtract; recall, rescind, recant; resign, relinquish; abdicate, decamp, depart; shrink, RECOIL, drop out, back out. See DISJUNCTION, DEPARTURE, NULLIFICATION.

wither, *v.* waste, decline, droop, wilt, fade; decay; contract, shrivel, pine, decline, languish; blast, destroy, burn, scorch; cut, scathe. See DETERIORATION, DESTRUCTION, DRYNESS, DISAPPROBATION, CONTEMPT.

withhold, *v.t.* keep back, restrain, detain; check, hold back; hinder; suppress; repress; reserve. See CONCEALMENT, RESTRAINT.

within, *adj. & prep.* in, inside; inward(s), indoor(s). See INTERIOR.

without, *adv. & prep.* outside, outdoor(s), outward, beyond; minus. See EXTERIOR, ABSENCE.

withstand, *v.t.* face, confront; fight off, oppose, defy. See OPPOSITION.

witless, *adj.* senseless, brainless; silly, foolish, pointless, idiotic, moronic, imbecilic; half-witted, DULL, thick, stupid, scatterbrained, muddle-headed. *Slang,* dumb, dopy. See DENSITY, INSANITY. *Ant.,* see WIT, INTELLIGENCE.

witness, *n. & v.* —*n.* testimony, proof, EVIDENCE, corroboration; deponent, eyewitness; testifier, attestor; beholder, observer. —*v.t.* see, observe; attest, sign, subscribe to, bear witness to. See EVIDENCE.

wizard, *n.* wonder-worker, conjuror; Merlin; magician, sorcerer. *Colloq.,* master, expert. See SORCERY, SKILL.

wobble, *v.* roll, rock, stagger, reel, lurch, yaw, sway; teeter, totter, flounder; hesitate, waver, quaver. See INSTABILITY, OSCILLATION.

woe, *n.* trouble, tribulation; sorrow, grief; unhappiness, misery. See PAIN. *Ant.,* see PLEASURE, CHEERFULNESS.

wolf, *n. & v.* —*n.* canid, wolfkin, cub, whelp; hyena; werewolf, wolfman; see ANIMAL. *Slang,* philanderer, rake, roué, womanchaser, ladykiller. See LOVE, IMPURITY. —*v.t.* raven, gulp, bolt, gobble. See FOOD.

woman, *n.* see FEMALE, MANKIND. *Ant.,* see MALE.

womanish, *adj.* effeminate, emasculated; unmanly, cowardly (of men); shrill, vixenish; soft, weak. See FEMALE. *Ant.,* see MALE, COURAGE.

WONDER

Nouns—wonder, wonderment, marvel, miracle, miraculousness, astonishment, amazement, bewilderment; amazedness, admiration, awe; stupor, stupefaction; fascination; sensation; SURPRISE.

Verbs—**1,** wonder, marvel, admire; be surprised, start; stare, open *or* rub one's eyes; gape, hold one's breath; look aghast, stand aghast; not believe one's eyes, ears *or* senses.

3, be wonderful, beggar *or* baffle description; stagger belief.

2, SURPRISE, astonish, startle, shock, take aback, electrify, stun, stagger.

Adjectives—**1,** wonderful, wondrous; miraculous; surprising, unexpected, unheard of; mysterious, indescribable, inexpressible, ineffable; unutterable, unspeakable; monstrous, prodigious, stupendous, marvelous, inconceivable, incredible; unimaginable, strange, uncommon, passing strange, striking, overwhelming. *Slang,* out of sight.

2, surprised, aghast, agog, breathless, agape; open-mouthed; awestruck, thunderstruck; spellbound; lost in amazement, wonder *or* astonishment; unable to believe one's senses.

Adverbs—wonderfully, fearfully; for a wonder; strange to say, *mirabile dictu,* to one's great surprise; with wonder.

Interjections—lo! lo and behold! O! what! wonder of wonders! will wonders never cease!

Antonym, see EXPECTATION.

---

wonderful, *adj.* miraculous, marvelous, amazing, astounding. *Colloq.,* great, swell, dandy; colossal, terrific. See WONDER.

wont, *n.* custom, USE, HABIT, routine, practice, usage.

woo, *v.* court, make love to; seek, pursue, solicit; importune. See LOVE, PURSUIT, ENDEARMENT.

wood, *n.* forest, grove, timber, copse, coppice, thicket, spinny, bosque, *bois*; woods, woodland; board, plank, log, lumber. See TREE, MATERIALS.

woodcut, *n.* wood block, woodprint; xylograph, lignograph, pyrograph, wood engraving. See REPRESENTATION.

wooden, *adj.* wood, woody, ligneous, xyloid; oaken, mahogany, ash, pine, teak, walnut, *etc.*; frame, clapboard, shingle(d); stiff, rigid, expressionless; lifeless. See MATERIALS. *Ant.,* see ANIMATE.

woodsman, *n.* woodcutter, lumberman; lumberjack, logger, timberjack; conservationist, forester, ranger; frontiersman, backwoodsman. See AGRICULTURE.

woodwork, *n.* molding, paneling, baseboard, didoes, frames, jambs, sashes; doors. See ORNAMENT.

wool, *n. & adj.* —*n.* fleece; down, hair, worsted, yarn. —*adj.* woolen; knitted; wooly, hairy, fleecy, downy. See SOFTNESS, ROUGHNESS.

woolly, wooly, *adj.* fleecy, fluffy, flocculent, downy. See SOFTNESS, FILAMENT. *Ant.,* see ROUGHNESS.

word, *n.* expression, utterance; syllable, phone, ideophone, phoneme; stem, root, derivative, inflected form; inflection, declension, conjugation; name, noun, pronoun, adjective, adverb, verb, preposition, postposition, conjunction, interjection; particle, article; prefix, suffix, combining form, element; compound, phrase (see SPEECH); neologism, coinage, nonce word; barbarism, corruption; PROMISE; password, watchword; news, INFORMATION.

word game, *n.* acrostic, palindrome, anagram, crossword puzzle, ghosts, riddles, word square, double acrostic; spelling bee; rebus, charades; Scrabble (*T.N.*), Jotto (*T.N.*); Guggenheim, categories, wordplay.

wordy, *adj.* verbose, talkative, loquacious, prolix, garrulous; rambling, circumlocutory, windy, longwinded. See LOQUACITY. *Ant.,* see SHORTNESS.

work, *n. & v.* —*n.* job, occupation, calling, trade, profession; task, stint, employment; drudgery, toil, moil, grind, routine; function; craftsmanship, workmanship; arts and crafts, craft, handicraft; opus, PRODUCTION, WRITING, BOOK, PUBLICATION; office; management; manufacture. —*v.* toil, moil, labor, plod, plug, drudge; run, act, operate, function; leaven, ferment, yeast; USE, employ; succeed, perform, do; effect, exert, strain; embroider, embellish, decorate. *Colloq.,* use elbow grease. See ACTION, SUCCESS, EXERTION. *Ant.,* see INACTIVITY, FAILURE.

workaday, *adj.* everyday, quotidian, common(place), matter-of-fact, homespun, humdrum; routine, orderly. See SIMPLENESS, CONFORMITY.

workman, *n.* worker, laborer; artisan, craftsman; operator, doer, performer; journeyman, yeoman; Trojan; drudge; mechanic; toiler, moiler. See ACTIVITY, EXERTION. *Ant.,* see INACTIVITY.

workmanship, *n.* craftsmanship, handiwork, SKILL, technique, expertness, competence; performance, execution, construction; finish, polish, art.

workout, *n.* trial, ESSAY; practise, rehearsal, run-through. See EXERTION.

works, *n.pl.* factory, plant, mill, workshop, shop; mechanism, machine; fort, rampart, breastworks, earthworks, barricade. *Slang,* everything; abuse. See AGENCY, DEFENSE.

workshop, *n.* workhouse, sweatshop; laboratory, factory, manufactory, mill, rolling mill, sawmill; works, steelworks, ironworks, foundry, furnace; mint; forge, loom; cabinet, atelier, studio, bureau, office, STORE, shop, plant. See BUSINESS.

world, *n.* creation, nature, universe; earth, globe, wide world; cosmos; macrocosm, megacosm; microcosm; sphere, hemisphere; heavens, sky, firmament (see HEAVEN); celestial space, outer space, interstellar space; the void; heavenly bodies, stars, nebulae; galaxy, Milky Way, solar system; constellation, planet, planetoid, satellite, comet, meteor; sun, moon.

worldly, *adj.* experienced, sophisticated; earthly, mundane; terrestrial; profane, secular, carnal; sordid, mercenary; proud, selfish, material, materialistic, unspiritual, irreligious. See SELFISHNESS, IRRELIGION.

worldwide, *adj.* universal, widespread; general, all-embracing, unlimited. See GREATNESS.

worm, *n. & v.* —*n.* earthworm, angleworm; maggot, larva, grub, caterpillar; insect; crawler, nightcrawler; flatworm, platyhelminth, tapeworm, cestode, nematode, roundworm, ascarid, pinworm, annelid; wretch; screw, spiral. See COWARDICE. —*v.* crawl, creep, belly; insinuate (oneself); bore; writhe, wriggle. See PROGRESSION, INSERTION.

worn, *adj.* used, secondhand; frayed, shabby, threadbare; shopworn. See DETERIORATION.

worry, *n. & v.* —*n.* CARE, anxiety, mental anguish, uneasiness, FEAR, apprehension; concern, misgiving. —*v.t.* tease, plague, vex; disturb, fret, upset; torment, torture, trouble, bait, badger; maul, chew, mangle. See PAIN, DISCONTENT.

WORSHIP

Nouns—**1,** worship, adoration, devotion, aspiration, homage, service; religious rites *or* observance; RESPECT, reverence, veneration; deification, idolization.

2, prayer, orison, invocation, supplication, rogation, intercession, petition (see REQUEST); collect, litany, miserere, Lord's prayer, paternoster, Ave Maria, Hail Mary, rosary, prayer wheel, missal; thanksgiving, grace; praise, laudation, exaltation, glorification, benediction; Magnificat, doxology, hosanna, hallelujah, alleluia, Te Deum, Trisagion; paean, psalm, psalmody, hymn, plainsong, chant (see MUSIC).

3, divine service, office, DUTY; Mass, Eucharist, Communion, Lord's Supper; morning prayer, matins, evening prayer, evensong, vespers, vigils, compline, prime [song], undersong, tierce, lauds, sext, nones; prayer meeting, revival. See RITE.

4, worship(p)er, adorer, venerator, reverer, glorifier; religionist, churchman, churchgoer, devout person, congregation; communicant, celebrant, cotary, pietist; idolizer, devotee, deifier, deist; idolator, idolatress, fetishist, pagan. *Colloq.*, psalmsinger. See CLERGY, RELIGION, PIETY.

Verbs—**1,** worship, adore, reverence, revere, inspire, aspire, lift up the heart; pay homage, humble oneself, kneel, genuflect, bend *or* bow the knee, fall on one's knees, prostrate oneself, bow down and worship; be devout.

2, RESPECT, adulate, idolize, lionize; deify, enshrine, immortalize.

3, pray, invoke, supplicate; offer up prayers, tell one's beads; return *or* give thanks, say grace, bless; praise, laud, glorify, magnify, exalt, extol, sing praises; give benediction, lead the choir, intone; go to church, attend service, attend Mass, communicate.

Adjectives—worshipful, adoring, prayerful, devout, devotional, pious, reverent, religious, spiritual-minded, paying homage; pure, solemn, fervent, fervid, heartfelt; reverential, venerating, obeisant.

Interjections—hallelujah! alleluia! hosanna! praise the Lord! *Deo gratias!* glory be to God! pray God that, *sursum corda.*

Antonym, see IRRELIGION, DISRESPECT.

---

worst, *adj. & v.* —*adj.* ultimate, greatest, most extreme *or* utmost (in a bad sense). See BADNESS, EVIL, ADVERSITY. —*v.t.* best; defeat, conquer. See SUCCESS, SUPERIORITY. *Ant.,* see PROSPERITY, LOSS.

worth, *n.* merit; USE; value; price, cost, estimation; worthiness, IMPORTANCE, VIRTUE, CREDIT; character. See MONEY. *Ant.,* see USELESSNESS.

worthless, *adj.* useless, no good, good-for-nothing; base, vile; valueless; poor, miserable; trashy; unserviceable; trifling; characterless. *Colloq.,* no-account. *Slang,* lousy. See USELESSNESS, WASTE. *Ant.,* see VIRTUE, IMPORTANCE, USE.

worthwhile, *adj.* beneficial, salubrious, GOOD; gainful, profitable, lucrative; meritorious, worthy. See EXPEDIENCE, PAYMENT.

worthy, *adj.* deserving, meritorious; virtuous, good; estimable, honest, upright, reputable. See REPUTE, VIRTUE. *Ant.,* see DISREPUTE, IMPROBITY.

would-be, *adj. & n.* —*adj.* hopeful, aspiring; pretended, so-called, self-styled, *soi-disant;* fraudulent. —*n.* aspirant, hopeful, candidate, pretender, impostor. See DESIRE, FALSENESS.

wound, *n. & v.* —*n.* injury, hurt; PAIN, painfulness. —*v.t.* injure, hurt, lame, cripple; PAIN; shoot, stab, cut, lacerate, tear, wing; insult, offend, gall, mortify. *Ant.,* see REMEDY.

wrangle, *v.i.* quarrel, bicker, squabble, dispute, altercate, argue, brawl.

wrap, *n. & v.* —*n.* robe, shawl, serape, cloak, coat, cape, cover, wrapper, blanket. —*v.t.* swathe, swaddle, clothe, cover, envelop, inclose; hide, muffle, conceal; fold, lap, wind; pack, package. See CLOTHING, COVERING, CONCEALMENT. *Ant.*, see DISCLOSURE, DIVESTMENT.

wrath, *n.* choler, anger, ire, indignation; fury, rage. See RESENTMENT.

wreath, *n.* garland, lei, chaplet, festoon; laurel wreath, garland of bays; floral ring, decoration. See ORNAMENT.

wreck, *n. & v.* —*n.* DESTRUCTION, ruin, undoing; accident, collision, crack-up, smash-up, crash; shipwreck; derelict; ruined person; human wreckage; break-up; ruins, demolition, wreckage; junk. —*v.t.* smash, crash, crack up; ruin, tear down, demolish, raze, destroy; shipwreck, strand, cast away; shatter, blight, blast. *Slang,* bust up. See FAILURE, REMAINDER. *Ant.*, see SUCCESS, PROSPERITY.

wrench, *v. & n.* —*v.t.* twist, wring; yank, pull; extort, wrest, snatch; sprain, strain, dislocate. —*n.* monkey wrench, spanner; twist, yank, *etc.* See DISTORTION, EXTRACTION.

wrest, *v.t.* turn, pull, twist, tear away, snatch, grab. See TAKING.

wrestle, *v.* grapple; strive; struggle with; contend. See CONTENTION.

wretch, *n.* sufferer; beggar, outcast, pariah; knave, villain; rogue, rascal. See PAIN, EVILDOER.

wretched, *adj.* beggarly, worthless, miserable; paltry; mean; pitiful; unhappy, unfortunate; woebegone, tormented, afflicted; shabby, disreputable, deplorable. See BADNESS, DISCONTENT, PAIN, UNIMPORTANCE. *Ant.*, see GOODNESS, CHEERFULNESS, IMPORTANCE.

wriggle, *v.* wiggle; shake, squirm, writhe; shimmy. See OSCILLATION.

wring, *v.t.* wrench, twist; rack, PAIN; squeeze, compress. See DISTORTION.

wrinkle, *n. & v.* —*n.* FURROW, crease, pucker, corrugation, rumple; crinkle, crow's-foot. *Slang,* angle, development, gimmick. —*v.t.* crease, rumple, FOLD. *Ant.*, see SMOOTHNESS.

writ, *n.* process, summons, warrant. See LAWSUIT.

writhe, *v.i.* wriggle, squirm, twist, contort. See DISTORTION, PAIN.

WRITING

Nouns—**1,** writing, chirography, calligraphy, pencraft, penmanship, handwriting, uncial writing, cuneiform, rune, hieroglyph(ic), LETTER; alphabet; stroke of the pen, pen and ink; shorthand, stenography, typewriting; cryptography, code, steganography.

2, cacography, bad hand, illegible hand, scribble, scrawl. *Slang,* hen tracks.

3, WORD, syllable, PHRASE, sentence, paragraph; authorship, composition; prose, poetry. See SPEECH, BOOK, PUBLICATION.

4, manuscript, Ms., Mss., COPY, transcript, rescript, typescript, rough copy *or* draft; fair copy; autograph, monograph, holograph.

5, writer, scribe, amanuensis, scrivener, secretary, clerk, penman, copyist, transcriber; typewriter, typist; calligrapher; author, novelist, poet.

Verbs—write, pen, COPY, engross; write out, transcribe; scribble, scrawl, scratch; interline; write down, record, sign; compose, indite, draw up, dictate; inscribe, dash off, draft, formulate; take pen in hand; typewrite, type; write shorthand.

Adjectives—writing, written, holographic; manuscript; shorthand, stenographic; in writing, in black and white; uncial, runic, cuneiform, hieroglyphic, hieratic; handwritten, cursive, printed, lettered; legible; Spencerian, backhand.

Antonyms, see SPEECH, PRINTING.

WRONG

Nouns—**1,** wrong, wrongfulness, INJUSTICE, imposition, oppression, corruption, foul play; ILLEGALITY, miscarriage of justice. See FALSENESS, ERROR.

2, wrongdoing, wickedness, sinfulness, BADNESS, EVIL, sin, vice, iniquity, immorality, guilt, reprehensibility, miscreancy, IMPROBITY,

DECEPTION, blackguardism; transgression, trespass, misdeed, misbehavior, misdoing, indiscretion, crime, violation, offense, misdemeanor, tort, injury, grievance, outrage, malefaction, shame, blame.

3, wrongdoer, transgressor (see EVILDOER).

Verbs—**1**, wrong, harm, injure, damage, maltreat, mistreat, ill-treat, abuse, oppress, persecute, outrage, offend, dishonor, defraud, misserve, do wrong to, do injury to, do injustice to, treat unjustly, sin against.

2, do wrong, transgress, be unjust, be inequitable, show partiality, favor, lean toward, encroach, impose.

Adjectives—**1**, wrong(ful), bad, EVIL, immoral, sinful, wicked, vicious, grievous, iniquitous, scandalous, reprehensible, blameworthy, guilty, criminal; harmful, injurious, hurtful, detrimental, pernicious, perverse, perverted.

2, unjust, unfair, inequitable, unequal; partial, biased, one-sided; unreasonable, unallowable, impermissible; unjustified, unlawful, illegal; illegitimate.

3, improper, inappropriate, inapposite, inapt, incongruous, unsuitable, unfit.

4, out of order, out of gear, damaged, deranged, disordered, faulty, amiss, awry. *Slang*, snafu.

5, inaccurate, incorrect (see ERROR).

Adverbs—wrong(ly), falsely, in the wrong; improperly, faultily, amiss, awry, bad; mistakenly, erroneously, inaccurately, incorrectly, in error. *Antonym*, see RIGHT.

---

wry, *adj.* crooked, twisted; askew, awry; distorted, contorted; warped. See DISTORTION, OBLIQUITY. *Ant.*, see DIRECTION.

X

xanthic, *adj.* yellow, yellowish; fulvous, tawny. See COLOR.

xanthous, *adj.* blond(e), fair, light-skinned; fair-haired, yellow-haired, golden-haired; yellowish; Mongolian. See COLORLESSNESS.

x-ray, *n.* Roentgen ray; radiation; radiograph. See LIGHT.

xylograph, *n.* woodcut, wood engraving. See ENGRAVING.

xyloid, *adj.* wood, woody, ligneous. See VEGETABLE.

xylophone, *n.* marimba, gamelan(g), vibraphone, vibraharp, glockenspiel, orchestra bells, sticcado, gigelira, straw fiddle.

Y

yacht, *n.* sailboat, pleasure boat; houseboat; sloop, yawl, ketch; cruiser. See SHIP.

yammer, *v.*, *colloq.*, complain, wail, whine, pule; CRY, howl; DESIRE, crave, yearn. *Slang*, gripe, grouse. See LOQUACITY, SPEECH.

yank, *n. & v.*, *colloq.*, pull, jerk, twist. See TRACTION.

yard, *n.* INCLOSURE, court, courtyard, patio. See MEASUREMENT.

yardstick, *n.* ruler; standard, criterion, rule, test, measure. See MEASUREMENT, RELATION.

yarn, *n.* thread, worsted, spun wool; tale, fib, tall story. See FILAMENT, DESCRIPTION, EXAGGERATION.

yawn, *v.i.* gape, open wide; split, part. See OPENING.

yea, *adv.* yes; indeed, truly. See AFFIRMATION, ASSENT.

year, *n.* twelvemonth; fiscal year, calendar year. See TIME.

yearbook, *n.* annual, annuary, calendar, almanac; journal, diary, RECORD. See BOOK.

yearling, *n.* teg; youngling, colt, filly, whelp, cub. See YOUTH.

yearn, *v.i.* pine, long, hanker; grieve, mourn. See DESIRE.

yeast, *n.* leaven, ferment, barm; spume, froth, foam. See AGITATION.

yell, *v. & n.* shout, CRY, scream, shriek, bawl, call; yelp, bark; bellow, roar, hoot. *Colloq.,* squawk, holler. See LOUDNESS.

yellow, *adj. & n.* —*adj.* fair, blond(e), flaxen, light-haired; golden, gold, saffron, ivory, creamy, lemon, xanthic; xanthous; buttery, yolky, ocherous; Mongolian, Mongoloid; jaundiced; jealous, envious; cowardly, craven, fearful, lily- *or* white-livered, afraid, unmanly, pusillanimous; lurid, sensational, melodramatic, scandal-mongering. —*n.* gold, saffron, yellow color; yolk. See COLOR, COWARDICE.

yelp, *n. & v.* bark, squawk, CRY, yap, yip.

yen, *n., slang,* DESIRE, craving, longing, hankering, yearning; TASTE, hunger, relish; passion; TENDENCY, appetite.

yeoman, *n.* freeholder, commoner, farmer; guardsman, beefeater; attendant, retainer; petty officer. See POSSESSION, POPULACE, SERVANT.

yes, *adv. & n.* —*adv.* yea, aye; indeed, true, verily; agreed, surely, certainly, of course, that's right. —*n.* AFFIRMATION; ASSENT. *Ant.,* see NEGATION, DISSENT.

yesterday, *n.* day before; the past. See TIME.

yet, *conj. & adv.* —*conj.* nevertheless, notwithstanding, still, however. —*adv.* still, besides, thus far, hitherto, till now, up to now *or* this time.

yield, *n. & v.* —*n.* crop, harvest, product. —*v.* surrender, cede, abandon, give up; give in, succumb; produce, bear, bring; furnish, supply, afford; soften, relax, give (way); ASSENT, comply, obey. See PRODUCTION, RELINQUISHMENT, OBEDIENCE.

yielding, *adj.* soft, pliant, tractable, docile; submissive, compliant, acquiescent; supple, plastic, flexible; productive, fertile. See SOFTNESS, OBEDIENCE. *Ant.,* see HARDNESS, OPPOSITION.

yoke, *n. & v.* —*n.* union, bond, chain, link, tie; bondage, slavery, oppression, servitude, enslavement, thralldom, vassalage; couple, pair, team. —*v.t.* couple, join, pair, wed; bind, tie, link; bracket, connect, associate. See MARRIAGE, JUNCTION, SUBJECTION.

yokel, *n.* rustic, peasant, countryman. *Colloq.,* hick, hayseed, rube; bumpkin; yahoo. See POPULACE.

yonder, *adj. & adv.* —*adj.* yon, that. —*adv.* in that place, thither, there, beyond; in the distance, afar, far away. See DISTANCE.

yore, *n.* antiquity, old times, olden days, time immemorial; yesterday; bygone, history, the PAST. *Colloq.,* good old days. See OLDNESS.

young, *adj. & n.* —*adj.* youthful; puerile; ageless; green; adolescent, juvenile, teen-age; fresh, new; inexperienced, immature. See YOUTH. *Ant.,* see AGE, OLDNESS. —*n.* offspring, children.

YOUTH

Nouns—**1,** youth, juvenility, juvenescence, immaturity, juniority; childhood, boyhood, maidenhood, girlhood, youthhood; minority, nonage, teen-age, teens, tender age, bloom; prime of life, flower of life; heyday of youth; school days; ADOLESCENCE, puberty; greenness, callowness, inexperience, puerility.

2, babyhood, infancy, cradle, nursery, apron strings.

3, child, infant, boy, girl, lad; maid, youth, hobbledehoy, stripling, teenager, adolescent. *Colloq.,* kid; bobby soxer; juvenile.

Adjectives—young, youthful, juvenile, immature, green, callow, budding, sappy, unfledged, under age, teen-age, in one's teens; hebetic, adolescent, pubescent; immature; younger, junior; boyish, beardless; maidenly, girlish; infant, infantile, newborn, babyish, childish, puerile.

Antonym, see AGE.

Z

zany, *n.* clown, madcap, buffoon, comic, FOOL, comedian, jester, merry-andrew, Punch, pickle-herring; nitwit, dunce. See ABSURDITY.

zeal, *n.* earnestness, devotion, dedication; passion; soul, spirit, ardor, fervor, verve, enthusiasm, eagerness, warmth, energy; zealotry, fanaticism. See ACTIVITY, WILL. *Ant.*, indifference; see COLD.

zealot, *n.* fanatic; visionary, dreamer, enthusiast; bigot; devotee, partisan. *Colloq.*, addict, fan. See CERTAINTY, RESOLUTION.

zenith, *n.* summit, top, acme, apex, pinnacle, apogee; climax, culmination; prime, heyday. See HEIGHT. *Ant.*, nadir; see LOWNESS.

zephyr, *n.* breeze, gentle wind, west wind. See WIND.

zero, *n.* nothing; naught, nought; cipher, none; (in games) love, blank; nobody, not a soul. *Slang*, goose-egg. See ABSENCE, INSUBSTANTIALITY.

zest, *n.* relish, gusto, appetite, enthusiasm, enjoyment, thrill, titillation, exhilaration; tang, twang, pungency, piquance; savor, sauce; edge. *Colloq.*, kick, zip. See TASTE, FEELING.

zigzag, *adj.* back-and-forth, tacking, serrated, jagged; crooked, tortuous. See DEVIATION. *Ant.*, straight, direct; see DIRECTION.

zip, *n. & v.* —*n.*, *Colloq.*, pep, vigor, zest, ginger, ENERGY; whiz, ping, swish. —*v.* move speedily; flash; swish, whiz; close (a zipper). See SOUND, CLOSURE.

zipper, *n.* slide fastener. See CLOSURE.

zither, *n.* zitter, cittern, cithara; koto. See MUSICAL INSTRUMENTS.

zodiac, *n.* constellations; horoscope, circle, circuit. See UNIVERSE, SEQUENCE.

zombi, zombie, *n.* walking dead, living ghost; automaton; monster. *Slang*, stooge; eccentric, oddball, nut, weirdo. See SUPERNATURALISM, DULLNESS.

zone, *n.* region, clime, climate; district, ward, area; belt, girdle, band, girth, cincture. See CIRCULARITY, LOCATION.

zoo, *n.* zoölogical park *or* garden; menagerie; vivarium, vivary; aviary, birdhouse; snakery, serpentarium; bear pit; aquarium. See ASSEMBLAGE, ANIMAL.

ZOÖLOGY

Nouns—**1,** zoölogy, natural science *or* history; fauna, animalia; animal morphology, anatomy, zoötony, histology, cytology, embryology, paleontology; zoöphysics; zoöchemistry, *etc.*; environment, balance of nature, ecology, bionomics, ethology, teleology, zoögraphy, zoögeography. See ANIMAL.

2, zoölogist, zoögraphist, naturalist; biologist, bionomist, *etc.*

Adjectives—zoölogical, morphological, anthropological, *etc.* (see *nouns*).

FOREIGN PHRASES

Translated, with reference to the applicable English categories

ab initio, *Lat.*, from the beginning; see BEGINNING.

ad nauseam, *Lat.*, to the point of nausea; boringly; see WEARINESS.

affaire d'amour, *Fr.*, love affair; see LOVE.

agent provocateur, *Fr.*, professional agitator; see AGITATION, DEMONSTRATION.

Agnus Dei, *Lat.*, Lamb of God; see DEITY.

al fresco, *It.*, in the open air; outdoors; see AIR.

alter ego, *Lat.*, another I; intimate friend; see FRIEND.

amour-propre, *Fr.*, self-esteem; see VANITY.

ancien régime, *Fr.*, the old order; see OLDNESS.

ante bellum, *Lat.*, before the war; see OLDNESS.

au contraire, *Fr.*, on the contrary; see DISAGREEMENT, OPPOSITION.

au courant, *Fr.*, up-to-date; informed; see INFORMATION.

au fait, *Fr.*, well informed; see INFORMATION.

au naturel, *Fr.*, nude; see DIVESTMENT.

ave atque vale, *Lat.*, hail and FAREWELL; see DEPARTURE.

Ave Maria, *Lat.*, Hail Mary!; see PRAYER, RELIGION.

beau geste, *Fr.*, a fine deed; see COURAGE.

beau monde, *Fr.*, fashionable society; see FASHION.

belles-lettres, *Fr.*, fine LITERATURE.

bête noire, *Fr.*, object of dislike; see HATE.

billet-doux, *Fr.*, witty saying; see WIT.

bon vivant, *Fr.*, epicure; good companion; see SOCIALITY, GLUTTONY.

cantus firmus, *Lat.*, plain song; see MUSIC.

carpe diem, *Lat.*, make use of the day; see ACTIVITY.

carte blanche, *Fr.*, unlimited authority; see AUTHORITY, FREEDOM.

casus belli, *Lat.*, event provoking war; see CONTENTION.

caveat emptor, *Lat.*, let the buyer beware; see CARE, WARNING.

cave canem, *Lat.*, beware the dog; see WARNING.

chacun à son goût, *Fr.*, each to his own taste; see FREEDOM.

chef d'oeuvre, *Fr.*, masterpiece; see SKILL.

cherchez la femme, *Fr.*, look for the woman; see DISCLOSURE.

comme il faut, *Fr.*, as it should be; see TASTE.

corpus delicti, *Lat.*, the facts connected with a crime; see GUILT.

coup de grâce, *Fr.*, a merciful finishing blow; see KILLING, COMPLETION.

coup d'état, *Fr.*, a political stroke; see REVOLUTION.

coup d'oeil, *Fr.*, GLANCE; see VISION.

cum laude *and* **summa cum laude,** *Lat.*, with [the highest] praise; see SUPERIORITY, APPROBATION.

de facto, *Lat.*, in fact; actual; realistically; see TRUTH.

Dei gratia, *Lat.*, by the grace of God; see POWER, RIGHTNESS.

de jure, *Lat.*, by right, lawfully; see RIGHTNESS.

de novo, *Lat.*, from the beginning; see BEGINNING.

Deo gratias, *Lat.*, thank God!; see GRATITUDE.

de profundis, *Lat.*, out of the depths; see PENITENCE.

de rigueur, *Fr.*, obligatory; see TASTE.

dernier cri, *Fr.*, the last word; MODERN; see NEWNESS.

de trop, *Fr.*, too much; see SUFFICIENCY.

deus ex machina, *Lat.*, a contrived instrumentality; see AGENCY.

dolce far niente, *It.*, sweet idleness; see REPOSE.

en déshabillé, *Fr.*, not dressed for receiving company; see DIVESTMENT.

en famille, *Fr.*, at home; informally; see REPOSE, UNCONFORMITY.

enfant terrible, *Fr.*, an unruly child; see DISOBEDIENCE.

en masse, *Fr.*, all together; in a group; see ASSEMBLAGE.

en rapport, *Fr.*, in harmony; see AGREEMENT.

entre nous, *Fr.*, [just] between us; see DISCLOSURE.

ex cathedra, *Lat.*, from the seat of authority; see AUTHORITY.

exempli gratia, *Lat.*, for example; see INTERPRETATION, TEACHING.

ex officio, *Lat.*, by right of office; see AUTHORITY.

ex post facto, *Lat.*, after the deed [is done]; see COMPLETION.

fait accompli, *Fr.*, an accomplished fact; see COMPLETION.

faux pas, *Fr.*, a false step; ERROR.

fin de siècle, *Fr.*, end of the century; see TIME.

flagrante delicto, *Lat.*, during the commission of the crime; see GUILT.

haute couture, *Fr.*, high FASHION.

haut monde, *Fr.*, upper classes; see FASHION.

hic jacet, *Lat.*, here lies; see INTERMENT.

hors de combat, *Fr.*, out of the fight; see DESTRUCTION, KILLING.

ibidem, *Lat.*, in the same place; see IDENTITY.

idée fixe, *Fr.*, a fixed idea; obsession; see BELIEF.

in extremis, *Lat.*, near death; see DEATH.

infra dignitatem, *Lat.*, beneath one's dignity; see DISREPUTE.

in loco parentis, *Lat.*, in the place of a parent; see AGENCY, AUTHORITY.

in statu quo, *Lat.*, in the same condition; see STABILITY.

571

inter nos, *Lat.,* [just] between us; see DISCLOSURE.

in toto, *Lat.,* in full; wholly; see COMPLETION.

ipse dixit, *Lat.,* he himself has said it; see AUTHORITY.

ipso facto, *Lat.,* [by virtue of] the same fact; see MEANING.

je ne sais quoi, *Fr.,* I don't know what; see SKILL, ELEGANCY.

jeunesse dorée, *Fr.,* gilded youth; see MONEY, WASTE.

laissez faire, *Fr.,* noninterference; TOLERANCE.

lapsus linguae, *Lat.,* a slip of the tongue; see ERROR.

loco citato, *Lat.,* in the place cited; see RELATION.

locum tenens, *Lat.,* a substitute; see SUBSTITUTION.

magnum opus, *Lat.,* masterpiece; see SKILL.

mañana, *Sp.,* tomorrow; see LATENESS.

man sagt, *Ger.,* they say; see INFORMATION.

mirabile dictu, *Lat.,* marvelous to relate; see WONDER.

mise en scène, *Fr.,* stage setting; see DRAMA.

modus operandi, *Lat.,* method of working; see PRODUCTION.

modus vivendi, *Lat.,* way of living or getting along; see AGREEMENT, CO-OPERATION.

ne plus ultra, *Lat.,* that which is peerless; see COMPLETION.

n'est-ce pas?, *Fr.,* isn't it [true]? see DOUBT.

nicht wahr?, *Ger.,* [is it] not true?; see DOUBT.

nil desperandum, *Lat.,* despair of nothing; see COURAGE.

noblesse oblige, *Fr.,* nobility obligates; see DUTY.

nom de plume, *Fr.,* pen name; see NOMENCLATURE.

non compos mentis, *Lat.,* not of sound mind; see INSANITY.

non sequitur, *Lat.,* it does not follow; see ABSURDITY.

nouveau riche, *Fr.,* newly rich; SNOB.

obiter dictum, *Lat.,* a passing remark; COMMENT.

on dit, *Fr.,* they say; see INFORMATION.

par excellence, *Fr.,* above all others; see SUPERIORITY.

particeps criminis, *Lat.,* ACCOMPLICE.

passim, *Lat.,* here and there; see DISJUNCTION.

peccavi, *Lat.,* I have sinned; see PENITENCE.

per annum, *Lat.,* by the year; see TIME.

per capita, *Lat.,* by the head; EACH.

per diem, *Lat.,* by the day; see COMPENSATION.

per se, *Lat.,* by itself; INTRINSIC.

persona non grata, *Lat.,* an unacceptable person; see HATE.

pièce de résistance, *Fr.,* the main dish, event, etc.; see IMPORTANCE.

pied-à-terre, *Fr.,* lodging; see ABODE.

prima facie, *Lat.,* at first sight; see EVIDENCE.

prosit, *Ger.,* to your health; see CELEBRATION.

pro tempore, *Lat.,* for the time being; see TIME, SUBSTITUTION.

quid pro quo, *Lat.,* something in return; see COMPENSATION, RETALIATION, SUBSTITUTION.

quien sabe?, *Sp.,* who knows?; see DOUBT.

qui vive, *Fr.,* alertness; see CARE.

quod erat demonstrandum, *Lat.,* which was to be proved; see EVIDENCE.

rara avis, *Lat.,* rare bird; unusual thing; see RARITY, UNCOMFORMITY.

Realpolitik, *Ger.,* practical politics; see EXPERIENCE.

reductio ad absurdum, *Lat.,* reduction to an absurdity; see PROOF.

requiescat in pace, *Lat.,* rest in peace; see INTERMENT.

res gestae, *Lat.,* things done; see COMPLETION.

rigor mortis, *Lat.,* the stiffness of death; see DEATH.

sanctum sanctorum, *Lat.,* holy of holies; see TEMPLE.

sang-froid, *Fr.,* calmness; see INDIFFERENCE.

sans souci, *Fr.,* without care; see CHEERFULNESS.

savoir-faire, *Fr.,* knowledge of what to do; POISE.

semper fidelis, *Lat.,* always faithful; see PROBITY.

sholom aleichem, *Semitic,* peace be with you; see BENEVOLENCE.

s'il vous plaît, *Fr.,* PLEASE.

sine die, *Lat.,* without [setting] a day [to meet again]; see TIME.

sotto voce, *It.,* under the breath; see SPEECH.

status quo, *Lat.,* existing condition; see STABILITY.

sub rosa, *Lat.,* secretly; see CONCEALMENT.

sui generis, *Lat.,* of its own kind; unique; see UNCONFORMITY.

tempus fugit, *Lat.,* time flies; see TIME.

terra firma, *Lat.,* solid ground; LAND.

tour de force, *Fr.,* a feat of skill or strength; see SKILL.

tout à fait, *Fr.,* entirely; see COMPLETION.

tout de suite, *Fr.,* at once; immediately; see EARLINESS.

vade mecum, *Lat.,* go with me; summons; see LAWSUIT.

vae victis, *Lat.,* woe to the vanquished; see RETALIATION.

verbum sapienti, *Lat.,* a word to the wise; see ADVICE.

vis-à-vis, *Fr.,* face to face; see OPPOSITION.

viva voce, *Lat.,* aloud; orally; see SPEECH.

wie geht's?, *Ger.,* how goes it?; how are you?; see CARE.

SIGNET and MENTOR BOOKS for Your Reference Shelf

(0451)

- ☐ **SLANG AND EUPHEMISM by Richard A. Spears.** Abridged. From slang terminology describing various bodily functions and sexual acts to the centuries-old cant of thieves and prostitutes to the language of the modern drug culture, here are 13,500 entries and 30,000 definitions of all the words and expressions so carefully omitted from standard dictionaries and polite conversation.

- ☐ **THE LIVELY ART OF WRITING by Lucile Vaughan Payne.** An essential guide to one of today's most necessary skills. It illumines the uses—and misuses—of words, sentences, paragraphs, and themes, and provides expertly designed exercises to insure through understanding. (618963—$1.95)

- ☐ **HOW TO WRITE, SPEAK AND THINK MORE EFFECTIVELY by Rudolf Flesch.** This renowned authority on writing offers you a complete, step-by-step course for improving your thinking, writing, and speaking abilities. A complete course in the art of communication. (121686—$3.50)

- ☐ **A DICTIONARY OF DIFFICULT WORDS by Robert H. Hill.** The essential companion volume to every abridged dictionary complete with 15,000 entries on business, technology, culture, medicine, science, acronyms and foreign words. (118030—$3.95)

- ☐ **THE BASIC BOOK OF SYNONYMS AND ANTONYMS by Laurence Urdang.** Expand your vocabulary while adding variety to your writing with thousands of the most commonly used words in the English language. Alphabetically arranged for quick and easy use, this indispensable guide includes sample sentences for each word. (117166—$2.75)*

*Prices slightly higher in Canada
